All correspondence and inquiries should be directed to
Reference Division, Houghton Mifflin Company
One Beacon Street, Boston, MA 02108

Library of Congress Cataloging in Publication Data
Main entry under title:

The Medical & health sciences word book.

1. Medicine—Terminology. 2. Spellers. I. Roe-Hafer,
Ann, 1938–   . II. Title: Medical and health sciences
word book. [DNLM: 1. Nomenclature. W 15 R699m]
R123.M38   1982   610′.14   82-15645
ISBN 0-395-32941-8

THE M... & SCI... WO... BOO...

SECOND EDITION

Compiled by Ann Roe-Hafer

 Houghton Mifflin • Boston

CONTENTS

Staff

Director of Editorial Operations
Margery S. Berube

Editors
Kaethe Ellis
Anne D. Steinhardt

Traffic Coordinator
Diane J. Neely

Text and Cover Designer
Geoffrey Hodgkinson

Special Consultants

Harry N. Antoniades, Ph.D.
Professor of Biochemistry
Harvard University
Cambridge, Massachusetts

Raymond K. Bush, M.D.
Honorary Attending, Medical Division
Westchester County Medical Center
Valhalla, New York

Cesar Augusto Caceras, M.D.
Clinical Systems Associates, Inc.
Washington, District of Columbia

Norma M. Casale, C.M.T.
President
School of Medical Secretarial Sciences
Providence, Rhode Island

Mark Dembert, M.D.
Department of Epidemiology and Public Health
Yale University School of Medicine
New Haven, Connecticut

Ellen C. Fitzgerald, B.S., R.R.A.
Director of Medical Records
Children's Hospital Medical Center
Boston, Massachusetts

Nancy L. Hendrickson
Medical Insurance and Transcription
San Diego, California

J. C. Laidlaw, M.D.
Chairman, Department of Medicine
McMaster University
Hamilton, Ontario, Canada

Judy Nasse, R.R.A.
Director, Medical Records
Choate Memorial Hospital
Woburn, Massachusetts

June Wise Pryor, M.D.
Associate Physician
Massachusetts Institute of Technology
Cambridge, Massachusetts

Michael Selig Wiedman, M.D.
Associate Surgeon
Massachusetts Eye and Ear Infirmary
Boston, Massachusetts

Anna Willhite
Attorney at Law
Boston, Massachusetts

HOW TO USE THIS BOOK

The Medical and Health Sciences Word Book, Second Edition has been prepared in order to fill a long-standing need for a full, adequate speller of terms used in medicine, nursing, and the other health sciences. You will find, listed in alphabetical order and in the clearest and most useful possible way, 60,000 such terms; you will be provided with information on how to spell these words, how to divide the words into syllables, and which syllables are stressed when the words are pronounced.

The terms have been analyzed according to the same morphological and phonetic criteria applied in *The American Heritage Dictionary, Second College Edition,* a recognized authority on words, and in *The Word Book* (Houghton Mifflin Company, 1976), a speller similar to this book but presenting a list of the most commonly used words in the English language.

The sources of the list of technical terms in *The Medical and Health Sciences Word Book, Second Edition* were many: the latest and most comprehensive medical dictionaries and technical and professional journals, the *Index Medicus,* and additional items supplied by citation readers and medical and nursing consultants. This ensures that within the number of vocabulary items selected for inclusion the list is as comprehensive and up to date as possible.

Words in common usage have been omitted unless they have technical senses; obsolete terms have been eliminated. Proper nouns have been entered only when they form part of a phrase or other compound in the scientific lexicon.

Additional words that may be formed with such suffixes as *-ly* and *-ment* have as a general rule been omitted from the list unless the suffixed form is distinct in meaning from the base form.

The Medical and Health Sciences Word Book, Second Edition has a number of additional useful features, including a list of abbreviations; trade names of drugs; a table of elements; a table of Latin and Greek terms used in prescriptions; a list of medical signs and symbols; a table of weights and measures; tables for converting apothecary weights and measures into the metric system; a table of thermometric equivalents; and a section that includes the names of surgical incisions, instruments, and positions, as well as the names of dressings, suture materials, and prostheses. Also included are a guide to the formation of the plurals of Latin and Greek nouns commonly used in this technical vocabulary and a special table of sound-spelling correspondences to aid in locating in the list words whose pronunciation is known but whose spelling may present difficulties.

The following guide to the book will enable you to make the maximum use of its special features.

ORDER OF ENTRIES

The list of entries is presented in strict alphabetical order for quick and easy access.

Series of multiword phrases sharing a common first element are listed under the key word in the following style:

cal'ci·no'sis
——cu'tis cir'cum·scrip'ta
——cutis u'ni·ver·sa'lis

In such a series the dash functions as a ditto mark, indicating that the key word (in this case *calcinosis*) is repeated in each subsequent phrase: *calcinosis cutis circumscripta* and *calcinosis cutis universalis.*

If an element of an individual phrasal entry that is not part of a series has a variant spelling (see the section entitled "Variants"), the dash similarly indicates which element remains constant:

Ab'ri·kos'soff tumor also Abrikosov ——

This should be read as saying that *Abrikosov tumor* is a variant of *Abrikossoff tumor.*

DIVISION OF WORDS

The Medical and Health Sciences Word Book, Second Edition shows how words may correctly be divided into syllables. With the exception of a few foreign words not yet assimilated into the language, all words have been analyzed and segmented according to English phonetic criteria; Latin terms have been included in this system of division because they are a part of the technical lexicon of native speakers of English and are pronounced accordingly.

Divisions are shown by means of a centered dot, an accent mark, or a hyphen:

ab·dom·i·nal   mel'a·no·cyte'   a·ba'si·a-a·sta'si·a

Syllable boundaries have throughout been assigned on the basis of information that the pronunciation of the entry words warrants such divisions. Therefore at the end of a line of type a word may with justification be broken wherever a syllable division is indicated. However, hyphenation restrictions such as those presented in style manuals should be followed wherever adherence to standard printing practice is desired. The following two rules are typical:

1. A syllable consisting of a single letter should not be separated from the rest of the word, as in:

a·ba'sic   de·cid'u·a

2. A hyphenated word should be divided only at the hyphen.

STRESS

This book indicates which syllables are stressed when a word is pronounced. Two different stress marks are used. The first, a boldface stress, indicates the syllable that receives the primary stress in the word:

fol'li·cle   mal'a·dy

Normally only one syllable in a word receives primary stress. However, certain compound words may have more than one primary stress:

Fried'rich-Bau'er operation   third'-de·gree' burn

The second mark, a lighter stress, indicates syllables that are pronounced with less stress than those marked with a primary stress but with stronger stress than unmarked syllables:

ab'em·bry·on'ic   de'cu·ba'tion

At times syllable stress shifts as a word shifts in part of speech, for example:

com'pound' *n.*   com·pound' *v.*

Both forms are shown in such cases, and both are identified by part-of-speech labels; *n.* (noun) and *v.* (verb) are the only such labels used in this book.

Added stress or shifts in stress in plural forms are also shown:

ly'sis *pl.* -ses'
me'ninx *pl.* me·nin'ges'

INFLECTED FORMS

Irregular inflected forms have been included for every entry word exhibiting such irregularity. These forms include the plurals of nouns (labeled *pl.*), the singulars of nouns (labeled *sing.*) where the plural is the main-entry form, and the past tense, past participle, and present participle of verbs. Such forms have been shortened to save space unless a shift in stress pattern or pronunciation necessitates showing the full form:

ac'e·tab'u·lum *pl.* lums *or* -la   a·buse', a·bused', a·bus'ing
da'ta *sing.* -tum   bite, bit, bit'ten *or* bit, bit'ing
pal·mar'is *pl.* -mar'es'   freeze, froze, fro'zen, freez'ing

In these examples you will notice that verbs may have either two or three inflected forms. If only two forms are shown, the first is both the past tense and the past participle (e.g., *abused*). If three forms are shown, the first is the past tense and the second is the past participle (e.g., *froze*—past tense; *frozen*—past participle).

If there are alternate inflected forms, these are also shown (e.g., the alternate plurals *-lums* and *-la* for *acetabulum*; the alternate past participles *bitten* and *bit* for *bite*).

Note: In general *The Medical and Health Sciences Word Book, Second Edition* shows the most complicated form of a word chosen for inclusion in the book. Consequently such words as *carbolate* and *age* appear as verbs:

car'bo·late', -lat'ed, -lat'ing   age, aged, ag'ing

even though both *carbolate* and *age* are also nouns. In such cases the book includes only the part of speech that has irregular inflected forms unless the stress pattern or word division changes, or unless the part of speech with irregular inflected forms does not warrant entry because it has no technical senses or is so rare that it has no currency.

VARIANTS

In this book variants are considered to be differently spelled but identically pronounced forms of the same word. These forms are included whenever they are in common use in the technical vocabulary; with the exceptions specified below, they are entered separately, even if the primary form and the variant are directly adjacent in the alphabetical listing. Irregular inflected forms are shown as required:

> cae·sar'e·an *also* cesarean
> ce·sar'e·an *var. of* caesarean
> a·moe'bu·la *pl.* -las *or* -lae', *also* amebula
> a·me'bu·la *pl.* -las *or* -lae', *var. of* amoebula
> em·bed', -bed'ded, -bed'ding, *also* imbed
> im·bed', -bed'ded, -bed'ding, *var. of* embed

In the case of extremely long lists of spelling variants beginning with a very productive prefix or combining form (e.g., *haem-, haema-, haemat-, haemato-,* and *haemo-*), it has been decided not to enter the variants separately but to provide notes directing the user to the entries beginning with the primary form of the prefix or combining form:

> haem-. See words spelled *hem-*.

This has been done in order to conserve space so that more vocabulary items can be entered.

Similarly, compound words consisting of a variant spelling of a word plus another element will not be entered. Thus while both *meter* and *metre* are included, the entries for such words as *decameter* and *kilometer* do not show the variants *decametre* and *kilometre*.

Variants that differ slightly in phonetic structure but are used with equal frequency—and they are few—appear as follows:

$$\text{bi'o·log'ic } \textit{or } \text{bi'o·log'i·cal}$$

Words or terms in which the variation involves more than a spelling difference—that is, the pronunciations differ even though frequently the forms have some resemblance, or the words are entirely different in form—are simply entered, without cross-references. Hence such semantically related groups as *achroma, achromia,* and *achromasia* are entries but are considered alternate terms rather than variants, and their relationship is not specified.

WORDS LIKELY TO BE CONFUSED

In *The Medical and Health Sciences Word Book, Second Edition* glosses, or short identifying definitions, are given for pairs or sets of words that are likely to be confused. Cross-references to the other words are included.

Such words fall into two categories:

1. Homophones, or words that are pronounced precisely the same but are spelled differently:

il'e·ac' (*pertaining to the ileum*)
♦ *iliac*

il'i·ac' (*pertaining to the ilium*)
♦ *ileac*

2. Words that are likely to be confused because they are closely related in spelling or pronunciation:

ab·sorb′ (*to take in*)   ad·sorb′ (*to hold on a surface*)
♦ *adsorb*   ♦ *absorb*

The glosses provided are not to be regarded as full definitions; they merely serve to point out possible sources of confusion. A dictionary should be consulted for more detailed and precise definitions.

PREFIXATION

Many terms beginning with such prefixes as *anti-* (e.g., *antifungal*), *counter-* (e.g., *countertransference*), and the like, have been included in this book, but it is impossible to enter all such words. However, most prefixes follow regular rules when they are combined with words to form compounds. *The American Heritage Dictionary, Second College Edition* provides specific information on hyphenation at its entries for individual prefixes; that book should be consulted when there is any doubt.

The guiding principle is that hyphens should be used only when necessary for clarity, that is, as a means of avoiding ambiguity.

1. Always use a hyphen between a prefix and a word beginning with a capital letter (e.g., *anti-Semite*).
2. Use a hyphen when not doing so would create an awkward combination of letters, particularly of vowels (e.g., *contra-angles, pre-excitation, pseudo-oedema*).
3. Use a hyphen after a prefix when the unhyphenated form and the hyphenated form differ in meaning (e.g., *coop* and *co-op*).

The following is a brief guide to the most commonly used prefixes.

ante-	counter-	mid-	pre-	sub-
anti-	de-	non-	pro-	super-
bi-	inter-	out-	pseudo-	trans-
co-	intra-	over-	re-	tri-
contra-	micro-	post-	semi-	ultra-
				un-

Compounds with these prefixes are usually formed according to rules 1, 2, and 3 mentioned previously. Compounds with the prefixes *all-* and *self-* are always formed with a hyphen.

PLURALS

Regular plurals of nouns have not been included in this book. Irregular plurals have been provided where it is has been felt that the plural occurs with sufficient frequency to warrant inclusion or that a logical need for the plural exists. Rules for the formation of both regular and irregular plurals in the standard English vocabulary may be found in *The Word Book* (Houghton Mifflin Company, 1976).

The formation of the plurals of Latin and Greek nouns in the medical vocabulary cannot be reduced to a set of rules that if applied will automatically produce correct forms, because in both Greek and Latin nouns are classified according to gender and declension, both of which determine the proper endings. However, it is almost always acceptable to pluralize these forms just as English nouns are pluralized; in fact, in most cases the English and foreign plurals exist side by side and are used with about the same frequency.

The chart below provides a typical—but not exhaustive—list of plural endings for Latin and Greek words; while it can be used for guidance, it should be borne in mind that there are exceptions to the rules.

Singular	Plural		Singular	Plural	
-a	-ae	abscissa, abscissae	-os	-i	omphalos, omphali
-ax	-aces	thorax, thoraces	-u	-ua	cornu, cornua
-en	-ina	flumen, flumina	-um	-a	serum, sera
-er	-era	tuber, tubera	-ur	-ora	femur, femora
-ex	-ices	apex, apices	-us	-udes	incus, incudes
-is	-es	analysis, analyses		-era	genus, genera
	-ides	cnemis, cnemides		-i	alveolus, alveoli
-ix	-ices	appendix, appendices		-ora	corpus, corpora
-oma	-omata	adenoma, adenomata	-x	-ces	calx, calces
-on	-a	phenomenon, phenomena		-ges	meninx, meninges

A TO Z WORD LIST

This section includes terminology encountered in general medicine and in the medical and surgical specialties. Excepted are proper names of surgical instruments, incisions, positions, dressings, suture materials, prostheses, and the like, which are listed in the Surgical Appendix. For trade names of the most commonly used drugs, please refer to Trade Names of Drugs.

A

a′bac·te′ri·al
Ab′a·die′ sign
ab·ap′i·cal
ab′ap·tis′ton′
a·bar′og·no′sis *pl.* -ses′
ab′ar·tic′u·lar
ab′ar·tic′u·la′tion
a·ba′si·a
——— trep′i·dans′
a·ba′si·a-a·sta′si·a
a·ba′sic
a·bate′, a·bat′ed, a·bat′ing
a·bate′ment
a·bat′ic
ab·ax′i·al
Ab′be-Zeiss′ cell
Ab′bott method
Ab′der·hal′den
——— reaction
——— test
Ab′der·hal′den- Kauf′mann-
Lig′nac syndrome
ab′do·men *pl.* -mens *or*
  ab·dom′i·na
ab·dom′i·nal
ab·dom′i·no·an·te′ri·or
ab·dom′i·no·car′di·ac′
ab·dom′i·no·cen·te′sis *pl.*
  -ses′
ab·dom′i·no·hys′ter·ot′o·
  my
ab·dom′i·no·jug′u·lar
ab·dom′i·no·per′i·ne′al
ab·dom′i·no·pos·te′ri·or
ab·dom′i·nos′co·py

ab·dom′i·no·tho·rac′ic
ab·dom′i·nous
ab·dom′i·no·u′ter·ot′o·my
ab·dom′i·no·ves′i·cal
ab·du′cens
ab·du′cent
ab·duct′
ab·duc′tion
ab·duc′tor *(a muscle that
  draws a part away from the
  axis of the body or an extremity)*
◆adductor
ab′em·bry·on′ic
ab′en·ter′ic
Ab′er·crom′bie degener-
  ation
ab·er′rant
ab′er·ra′tion
a·be′ta·lip′o·pro′te·in·
  e′mi· a
a·bey′ance
ab′i·ent
A′bi·es′
——— bal·sam′e·a
a′bi·et′ic
a′bi·e·tin′ic
A bile
a′bi·o·gen′e·sis *pl.* -ses′
a′bi·o·ge·net′ic
a′bi·og′e·nous
a′bi·on′er·gy
a′bi·o′sis
a′bi·ot′ic
a′bi·o·troph′ic
a′bi·ot′ro·phy
ab·ir′ri·tant
ab·ir′ri·tate′, -tat′ed, -tat′ing

ab·ir′ri·ta′tion
ab′lac·ta′tion
a·blas′tin
ab·late′, -lat′ed, -lat′ing
ab·la′ti·o′
——— pla·cen′tae′
ab·la′tion
a′ble·phar′i·a
a·bleph′a·ron′
a·blep′si·a
ab′lu·ent
ab·lu′tion
ab·mor′tal
ab·ner′val
ab·neu′ral
ab·nor′mal
ab′nor·mal′i·ty
ABO blood group
ab′o·ma·si′tis
ab′o·ma′sum *pl.* -sa
ab·o′rad′
ab·o′ral
a·bort′
a·bor′ti·cide′
a·bor′tient
a·bor′ti·fa′cient
a·bor′tin
a·bor′tion
a·bor′tion·ist
a·bor′tive
a·bor′tus *pl.* -tus·es
a·bra′chi·a
a·bra′chi·o·ceph′a·lus
a·bra′chi·us
a·bra′dant
a·brade′, a·brad′ed,
  a·brad′ing
A′brams test

a·bra′sion
a·bra′sive
a·bra′sor
ab′re·ac′tion
Ab′ri·kos′soff tumor *also*
Abrikosov—
Ab′ri·kos′ov tumor *var. of*
Abrikossoff—
a·bro′si·a
ab·rup′ti·o′
—— pla·cen′tae′
ab′scess′
ab·sces′sus
—— flat′u·o′sus
—— per de·cu′bi·tum
ab·scis′sa *pl.* -sas *or* -sae′
ab·scis′sion
ab′scon′si·o′
ab′sco·pal
ab′sence
ab·sen′te′ fe′bre′
ab·sen′ti·a ep′i·lep′ti·ca
ab′sinthe
ab′so·lute′
ab·sorb′ *(to take in)*
♦adsorb
ab·sorb′a·ble
ab·sorb′ance
ab·sor′be·fa′cient
ab·sorb′en·cy
ab·sorb′ent
ab·sorb′er
ab·sorp′ti·om′e·ter
ab·sorp′tion
ab·sorp′tive
ab′sorp·tiv′i·ty
ab′sti·nence
ab·strac′tion
a·bu′li·a
a·bu′lic
a·bu′lo·ma′ni·a
a·buse′, a·bused′, a·bus′ing
a·but′ment
a·ca′cia
a·cal′ci·co′sis
a′cal·cu′li·a
a·cal′cu·lous
a·camp′si·a
a·can′tha
a·canth′am·oe·bi′a·sis *pl.* -ses′
a·can′thes·the′si·a
a·can′thi·on′
a·can′tho·am′e·lo·blas·
  to′ma *pl.* -mas *or* -ma·ta
A·can′tho·ceph′a·la
a·can′tho·ceph′a·li′a·sis
  pl. -ses′

A·can′tho·chei′lo·ne′ma
—— per′stans′
a·can′tho·chei′lo·ne·mi′a·
  sis *pl.* -ses′
a·can′tho·cyte′
a·can′tho·cy·to′sis *pl.* -ses′
a·can′thoid′
a·can′tho·ker′a·to′ma *pl.*
  -mas *or* -ma·ta
ac′an·thol′y·sis *pl.* -ses′
—— bul·lo′sa
a·can′tho·lyt′ic
ac′an·tho′ma *pl.* -mas *or*
  -ma·ta
—— ad′e·noi′des′ cys′ti·cum
a·can′tho·pel′vis
a·can′tho·pel′yx
a·can′thor·rhex′is
ac′an·tho′sis *pl.* -ses′
—— nig′ri·cans′
a′can·thot′ic
a·cap′ni·a
a·cap′ni·al
a·cap′nic
a·cap′su·lar
a·car′bi·a
a·car′di·a
a·car′di·ac′
a′car·di′a·cus
—— a·ceph′a·lus
—— a·mor′phus
—— an′ceps′
a·car′di·o·he′mi·a
a·car′di·o·ner′vi·a
a·car′di·us
a·car′i·an
ac′a·ri′a·sis *pl.* -ses′
a·car′i·cide′
ac′a·rid
Ac′a·ri′na
ac′a·ri·no′sis *pl.* -ses′
ac′a·ro·der′ma·ti′tis
—— ur′ti·car′i·oi′des′
ac′a·roid′
ac′a·ro·pho′bi·a
ac′a·ro·tox′ic
ac′a·rus *pl.* -ri′
Ac′a·rus
—— fol·lic′u·lo′rum
—— scab′ie·i′
a·car′y·ote′
a·cat′a·la′si·a
a·cat′a·lep′si·a
a·cat′a·lep′tic
a·cat′a·ma·the′si·a
a·cat′a·pha′si·a
ac′a·tas·ta′si·a

ac′a·tas·tat′ic
ac′a·thex′i·a
ac′a·thex′is
ac′a·this′i·a *var. of* akathisia
a·cau′dal
a·cau′date′
ac·cel′er·ant
ac·cel′er·ate′, -at′ed, -at′ing
ac·cel′er·a′tion
ac·cel′er·a′tor
ac·cel′er·in
ac·cel′er·om′e·ter
ac·cep′tor
ac·ces′sion
ac′ces·so′ri·us
—— ad flex·o′rem dig′i·
  to′rum pro·fun′dum
ac·ces′so·ry
ac′ci·dent
ac′ci·den′tal
ac′ci·dent-prone′
ac·cip′i·ter
ac′cli·mate′, -mat′ed, -mat′-
  ing
ac′cli·ma′tion
ac·cli′ma·ti·za′tion
ac·cli′ma·tize′, -tized′,
  -tiz′ing
ac·com′mo·da′tion
ac·com′mo·da′tive
ac·couche·ment′
—— for·cé′
ac·cou·cheur′
ac·cou·cheuse′
ac′cre·men·ti′tion
ac·crete′, -cret′ed, -cret′ing
ac·cre′ti·o′
ac·cre′tion
ac·cu′mu·la′tor
a·ce′di·a
a·cel′lu·lar
a′ce·nes·the′si·a
a′cen·o·cou′ma·rol′
a·cen′tric
a′ce·pha′li·a
a′ce·phal′ic
a·ceph′a·lism
a·ceph′a·lo·bra′chi·a
a·ceph′a·lo·bra′chi·us
a·ceph′a·lo·car′di·a
a·ceph′a·lo·car′di·us
a·ceph′a·lo·chi′ri·a
a·ceph′a·lo·chi′rus
a·ceph′a·lo·cyst′
a·ceph′a·lo·cys′tis rac′e·
  mo′sa
a·ceph′a·lo·gas′ter

a·ceph′a·lo·gas·te′ri·a
a·ceph′a·lo·po′di·a
a·ceph′a·lo·po′di·us
a·ceph′a·lo·lor·rha′chi·a
a·ceph′a·lo·sto′mi·a
a·ceph′a·los′to·mus
a·ceph′a·lo·tho·ra′ci·a
a·ceph′a·lo·tho′rax′
a·ceph′a·lus
—— a·car′di·us
—— a·tho′rus
—— di·bra′chi·us
—— di′pus
—— mon′o·bra′chi·us
—— mon′o·pus
—— pseu′do·a·cor′mus
—— sym′pus
—— tho′rus a′car·di′a·cus
a·ceph′a·ly
ac′er·ate′
a·cer′bi·ty
a·cer′vu·line′
a·cer′vu·lus
a·ces′cence
a·ces′cent
a·ces′o·dyne′
ac′es·to′ma
ac′e·tab′u·lar
ac′e·tab′u·lec′to·my
ac′e·tab′u·lo·plas′ty
ac′e·tab′u·lum pl. -lums or
  -la
ac′e·tal′
ac′et·al′de·hyde′
a·cet′a·mide′
ac′et·a·mi′no·phen
ac′et·an′i·lid
ac′et·ar′sone′
ac′e·tate′
a·cet′a·zol′a·mide′
a·ce′tic
a·ce′ti·fi·ca′tion
a·ce′ti·fy′, -fied′, -fy′ing
ac′e·tin
ac′e·to·a·ce′tic
A·ce′to·bac′ter
ac′e·to·hex′a·mide′
a·ce′to·me·naph′thone′
a·ce′to·mor′phine′
ac′e·tone′
ac′e·to·ne′mi·a
ac′e·to·ne′mic
ac′e·to·nu′ri·a
ac′e·to·phen′a·zine′
a·ce′to·phe·net′i·din
a·cet′o·sal′
a·ce′tous

a·cet′phe·nol·i′sa·tin
ac′e·tri·zo′ate′
a·cet′ri·zo′ic
ac′e·tu′rate′
ac′e·tu′ric
a·ce′tyl
—— coenzyme A
ac′e·tyl·a·ce′tic
ac′e·tyl·a·den′y·late′
a·cet′y·lase′
a·cet′y·la′tion
ac′e·tyl-be′ta-meth′yl·
  cho′line′
ac′e·tyl·car·bro′mal
ac′e·tyl·cho′line′
ac′e·tyl·cho′lin·es′ter·ase′
ac′e·tyl·cys′te·ine′
ac′e·tyl·dig′i·tox′in
a·cet′y·lene′
a·cet′y·lide′
a·ce′tyl·sal′i·cyl′ic
a·ce′tyl·stro·phan′thi·din
a·ce′tyl·sul′fa·di′a·zine′
a·ce′tyl·sul′fa·gua′ni·dine′
a·ce′tyl·sul′fa·thi′a·zole′
ac′e·tyl·sul·fon′a·mide′
a·ce′tyl·trans′fer·ase′
ach′a·la′si·a
A·chard′-Cas·taigne′
—— method
—— test
A·chard′-Thiers′ syn-
  drome
ache, ached, ach′ing
a·chei′li·a
a·chei′lous
a·chei′lus
a·chei′ri·a also achiria
a·chei′rus also achirus
A·chil′les
—— bursa
—— jerk
—— reflex
—— tendon
a·chil′lo·bur·si′tis
a·chil′lo·dyn′i·a
ach′il·lor′rha·phy
a·chil′lo·te·not′o·my
a·chi′ri·a var. of acheiria
a·chi′rus var. of acheirus
a′chlor·hy′dri·a
a′chlor·op′si·a
a·cho′li·a
a·chol′ic
ach′o·lu′ri·a
ach′o·lu′ric
a·chon′dro·pla′si·a

a·chon′dro·plas′tic
a′chor′
a·chor′dal
A·cho′ri·on′
A′chor-Smith′ syndrome
a·chre′o·cy·the′mi·a
a·chres′tic
a·chro′a·cyte′
a·chro′a·cy·to′sis pl. -ses′
a·chroi′o·cy·the′mi·a
a·chro′ma
a·chro′ma·cyte′
ach′ro·ma′si·a
a′chro·mat′
a′chro·mat′ic
a·chro′ma·tin
a·chro′ma·tin′ic
a·chro′ma·tism
a′chro·mat′o·cyte′
a·chro′ma·tol′y·sis pl. -ses′
a·chro′ma·to·phil′
a·chro′ma·to·phil′i·a
a·chro′ma·top′si·a
a·chro′ma·to·sis pl. -ses′
a·chro′ma·tous
a·chro′ma·tu′ri·a
a·chro′mi·a
—— cu′tis
—— par′a·sit′i·ca
a·chro′mic
A·chro′mo·bac′te·ra′ce·ae′
a·chro′mo·der′ma
a·chro′mo·trich′i·a
a·chron′dro·gen′e·sis pl.
  -ses′
ach′ro·o·am′y·loid′
ach′ro·o·cy·to′sis pl. -ses′
ach′ro·o·dex′trin
A′chu·cár′ro stain
a·chy′la·ne′mi·a
a·chy′li·a
—— gas′tri·ca
—— pan′cre·at′i·ca
a·chy′lic
a·chy′lous
a·chy′mi·a
a·cic′u·lar
ac′id
ac′id·am′i·nu′ri·a
ac′i·de′mi·a
ac′id-fast′
a·cid′ic
a·cid′i·fi′a·ble
a·cid′i·fi·ca′tion
a·cid′i·fi′er
a·cid′i·fy′, -fied′, -fy′ing
ac′i·dim′e·ter

ac′i·dim′e·try
ac′id·ism
a·cid′i·ty
a·cid′o·cyte′
ac′i·do·cy′to·pe′ni·a
ac′i·do·cy·to′sis pl. -ses′
ac′i·do·gen′ic
a·cid′o·phil′
ac′i·do·phil′ic
ac′i·doph′i·lism
ac′i·doph′i·lous
ac′i·do′sis pl. -ses′
ac′i·dos′te·o·phyte′
ac′i·dot′ic
ac′id-re·sis′tant
a·cid′u·lant
a·cid′u·late′, -lat′ed, -lat′ing
a·cid′u·lous
ac′i·du′ri·a
ac′i·du′ric
ac′id·yl
a·cid′y·lat′ed
ac′i·nar
ac′i·ne′si·a
ac′i·no·tu′bu·lar
ac′i·nous
a-c interval
ac′i·nus pl. -ni′
a·clad′i·o′sis pl. -ses′
ac′la·sis pl. -ses′
a·clas′tic
a·cleis′to·car′di·a
ac′me
ac′mic
ac′ne
—— ag′mi·na′ta
—— al′bi·da
—— ar′ti·fi′ci·a′lis
—— a·troph′i·ca
—— ca·chec′ti·co′rum
—— co·ag′mi·na′ta
—— con′glo·ba′ta
—— cys′ti·ca
—— de·cal′vans′
—— in′du·ra′ta
—— ker′a·to′sa
—— me·chan′i·ca
—— med′i·ca·men·to′sa
—— mil′i·ar′is
—— ne·crot′i·ca
—— ne·o′na·to′rum
—— pan′cre·at′i·ca
—— pap′u·lo′sa
—— pus′tu·lo′sa
—— ro·sa′ce·a
—— scrof′u·lo·so′rum
—— tar′si′

—— trop′i·ca
—— ur′ti·ca′ta
—— var′i·o′li·for′mis
—— vul·gar′is
ac′ne·form′ var. of acnei-
 form
ac′ne·gen
ac′ne·gen′ic
ac·ne′i·form′ also acneform
ac·ne′mi·a
ac·ni′tis
ac′o·can′ther·in
a·coe′li·a
ac′o·la′si·a
ac′o·las′tic
a·co′lous
a·con′a·tive
ac′o·nine′
a·con′i·tase′
ac′o·nit′ic
a·con′i·tin
a·con′i·tine′
a·con′u·re′sis
a′cop·ro′sis pl. -ses′
a·cop′rous
a′cor′
ac′o·re′a (absence of the pupil)
♦acoria
a·co′ri·a (absence of the
 feeling of satiety), also ako-
 ria
♦acorea
a·cor′mus
A·cos′ta disease
a·cou′es·the′si·a also acues-
 thesia
a·cou′me·ter
ac′ou·met′ric
a·cou′o·pho′ni·a
a·cous′ma pl. -mas or -ma·ta
a·cous′ma·tag·no′sis
a·cous′ma·tam·ne′si·a
a·cous′tic
a·cous′ti·co·fa′cial
a·cous′ti·co·mo′tor
a·cous′ti·co·pal′pe·bral
a·cous′ti·co·pho′bi·a
a·cous′tics
a·cous′ti·gram′
ac·quired′
ac′ral
a·cra′ni·a
a·cra′ni·al
a·cra′ni·us
a·cra′si·a (intemperance)
♦acratia

a·cra′ti·a (impotence)
♦acrasia
a·crat′u·re′sis
Ac′ree-Ro′sen·heim′ test
ac′re·mo′ni·o′sis pl. -ses′
ac′rid
ac′ri·dine′
ac′ri·fla′vine′
ac′ri·mo′ny
ac′ri·sor′cin
a·crit′i·cal
ac′ri·to·chro′ma·cy
ac′ro·ag·no′sis
ac′ro·an′es·the′si·a
ac′ro·ar·thri′tis
ac′ro·a·tax′i·a
ac′ro·blast′
ac′ro·brach′y·ceph′a·ly
ac′ro·bys·ti′tis
ac′ro·cen′tric
ac′ro·ce·pha′li·a
ac′ro·ce·phal′ic
ac′ro·ceph′a·lo·pol′y·syn·
 dac′ty·ly
ac′ro·ceph′a·lo·syn′dac·
 tyl′i·a
ac′ro·ceph′a·lo·syn·dac′ty·
 lism
ac′ro·ceph′a·lo·syn·dac′ty·
 ly
ac′ro·ceph′a·ly
ac′ro·chor·do′ma pl. -mas
 or -ma·ta
ac′ro·chor′don′
ac′ro·ci·ne′sis
ac′ro·con·trac′ture
ac′ro·cy′a·no′sis pl. -ses′
ac′ro·der′ma·ti′tis
—— chron′i·ca a·troph′i·
 cans′
—— con·tin′u·a
—— en′ter·o·path′i·ca
—— hi′e·ma′lis
—— pus′tu·lo′sa per′stans′
ac′ro·dol′i·cho·me′li·a
ac′ro·dyn′i·a
ac′ro·es·the′si·a
ac′ro·ger′i·a
ac′rog·no′sis
ac′ro·hy′per·hi·dro′sis
ac′ro·hy′po·ther′my
ac′ro·ker′a·to′sis pl. -ses′
—— ver·ru′ci·for′mis
ac′ro·ki·ne′sis
a·cro′le·in
ac′ro·mac′ri·a
ac′ro·ma′ni·a

ac'ro·mas·ti'tis
ac'ro·me·ga'li·a
ac'ro·me·gal'ic
ac'ro·meg'a·loid'
ac'ro·meg'a·loid·ism
ac'ro·meg'a·ly
ac'ro·me·lal'gi·a
ac'ro·mere'
ac'ro·met'a·gen'e·sis *pl.*
  -ses'
a·cro'mi·al
ac'ro·mic'ri·a
a·cro'mi·o·cla·vic'u·lar
a·cro'mi·o·cor'a·coid'
a·cro'mi·o·hu'mer·al
a·cro'mi·on'
a·cro'mi·o·nec'to·my
a·cro'mi·o·scap'u·lar
a·cro'mi·o·tho·rac'ic
a·crom'pha·lus
ac'ro·my'o·to'ni·a
ac'ro·my·ot'o·nus
ac'ro·nar·cot'ic
ac'ro·neu·rop'a·thy
ac'ro·neu·ro'sis *pl.* -ses'
ac'ro·nine'
a·cron'y·chous
ac'ro·nyx'
ac'ro·os'te·ol'y·sis
ac'ro·pach'y
ac'ro·pach'y·der'ma
ac'ro·pa·ral'y·sis *pl.* -ses'
ac'ro·par'es·the'si·a
ac'ro·pa·thol'o·gy
a·crop'a·thy
a·crop'e·tal
ac'ro·pho'bi·a
ac'ro·pig'men·ta'tion
ac'ro·pig'men·ta'ti·o' re·
  tic'u·lar'is
ac'ro·pos·thi'tis
ac'ro·pur'pu·ra
ac'ro·scle'ro·der'ma
ac'ro·scle·ro'sis *pl.* -ses'
ac'ro·so'mal
ac'ro·some'
ac'ro·sphe'no·syn'dac·
  tyl'i·a
ac'ros·te·al'gi·a
ac'ro·te'ri·a
ac'ro·ter'ic
a·crot'ic
ac'ro·tism
ac'ro·tro'pho·neu·ro'sis
ac'ryl·al'de·hyde'
a·cryl'ic
ac'ry·lo·ni'trile'

ac'tin
ac'tin'ic
ac·tin'i·form'
ac'ti·nism
ac·tin'i·um
ac'ti·no·bac'il·lo'sis *pl.* -ses'
Ac'ti·no·ba·cil'lus
—— lig'ni·er·es'i·i'
—— mal'le·i'
ac'ti·no·chem'is·try
ac'ti·no·der'ma·ti'tis
ac·tin'o·gen
ac'ti·no·gen'e·sis *pl.* -ses'
ac'ti·no·gen'ic
ac'ti·no·gen'ics
ac·tin'o·graph'
ac·tin'o·lite' *var. of* actino-
  lyte
ac·tin'o·lyte' *also* actinolite
ac'ti·nom'e·ter
ac'ti·nom'e·try
ac'ti·no·my·ce'li·al
Ac'ti·no·my'ces'
—— as'ter·oi'des'
—— bau·de'ti·i'
—— bo'vis
—— is'ra·e'li·i'
—— ma·du'rae'
—— my'ce·to'ma
—— so·ma'li·en'sis
Ac'ti·no·my'ce·ta'ce·ae'
Ac'ti·no·my'ce·ta'les'
ac'ti·no·my'cete'
ac'ti·no·my·ce'tic
ac'ti·no·my·ce'tin
ac'ti·no·my'cin
ac'ti·no·my·co'ma *pl.* -mas
  or -ma·ta
ac'ti·no·my·co'sis *pl.* -ses'
ac'ti·no·my·cot'ic
ac'ti·no·my'co·tin
ac'ti·non'
ac'ti·no·neu·ri'tis
ac'ti·no·phy·to'sis *pl.* -ses'
ac'ti·no·rho'dine'
ac'ti·no·ru'bin
ac'ti·no·spec'to·cin
ac'ti·no·ther'a·py
ac'ti·vate', -vat'ed, -vat'ing
ac'ti·va'tion
ac'ti·va'tor
ac'tive
ac·tiv'i·ty
ac'to·my'o·sin
a·cu'es·the'si·a *var. of*
  acouesthesia
a·cu'i·ty

a·cu'le·ate'
a·cu'me·ter
a·cu'mi·nate'
ac'u·pres'sure
ac'u·punc'ture
a'cus
ac'u·sec'tion
ac'u·sec'tor
a·cus'ti·cus
a·cute'
a·cu'ti·cos'tal
a·cy'a·no·blep'si·a
a·cy'a·nop'si·a
a·cy'a·not'ic
a·cy'cli·a
a·cy'clic
ac'y·e'sis
ac'y·et'ic
ac'yl
ac'yl·a'tion
a·cys'ti·a
a·cys'ti·nu'ri·a
a·dac'ry·a
a·dac'tyl
a'dac·tyl'i·a
a·dac'ty·lism
a·dac'ty·lous *(lacking fin-
  gers or toes)*
♦adactylus
a·dac'ty·lus *(individual with
  congenital absence of fin-
  gers or toes)*
♦adactylous
A·dair' Digh'ton syn-
  drome
ad'a·man'tine'
ad'a·man'ti·no·car'ci·
  no'ma *pl.* -mas *or* -ma·ta
ad'a·man'ti·no'ma *pl.* -mas
  or -ma·ta
ad'a·man'ti·no'ma·toid'
ad'a·man'to·blast'
ad'a·man'to·blas'to·ma *pl.*
  -mas *or* -ma·ta
ad'a·man'to·ma *pl.* -mas *or*
  -ma·ta
A·dam'kie·wicz
—— reaction
—— test
Ad'am's ap'ple
ad'ams·ite'
Ad'ams-Stokes' syndrome
Ad'an·so'ni·a
—— dig'i·ta'ta
a·dapt'
a·dapt'a·ble
ad'ap·ta'tion

a·dapt'er *also* adaptor
a·dap'tive
ad'ap·tom'e·ter
a·dap'tor *var. of* adapter
ad'at'om
ad·ax'i·al
ad'de
ad'de·pha'gi·a
ad'dict
ad'di·ment
ad'di·men'ta·ry
Ad'dis
—— count
—— and Shev'sky test
—— test
Ad'di·son
—— anemia
—— disease
—— keloid
—— syndrome
ad'di·so'ni·an
ad'di·son·ism
ad·du'cent
ad·duct'
ad·duc'tion
ad·duc'tor *(a muscle that draws a part toward the axis of the body or an extremity)*
♦abductor
a·de'lo·mor'phic
a·de'lo·mor'phous
a·del'pho·tax'is
a·del'pho·tax'y
ad'e·nal'gi·a
ad'e·nase'
ad'en·as·the'ni·a
a·den'dric
a·den·drit'ic
ad'e·nec'to·my
ad'en·ec·to'pi·a
a·de'ni·a
a·de'nic
a·den'i·form'
ad'e·nine'
ad'e·ni'tis
ad'e·no·ac'an·tho'ma *pl.* -mas *or* -ma·ta
ad'e·no·a·mel'o·blas'to·ma *pl.* -mas *or* -ma·ta
ad'e·no·an'gi·o·sar·co'ma *pl.* -mas *or* -ma·ta
ad'e·no·blast'
ad'e·no·can'croid'
ad'e·no·car'ci·no'ma *pl.* -mas *or* -ma·ta
ad'e·no·cele'

ad'e·no·cel'lu·li'tis
ad'e·no·chon·dro'ma *pl.* -mas *or* -ma·ta
ad'e·no·cys'tic
ad'e·no·cys·to'ma *pl.* -mas *or* -ma·ta
—— lym'pho·ma·to'sum
ad'e·no·cys'to·sar·co'ma *pl.* -mas *or* -ma·ta
ad'e·no·dyn'i·a
ad'e·no·ep'i·the'li·o'ma
ad'e·no·fi·bro'ma *pl.* -mas *or* -ma·ta
ad'e·no·fi·bro'sis *pl.* -ses'
ad'e·no·gen'e·sis *pl.* -ses'
ad'e·no·gen'ic
ad'e·nog'e·nous
ad'e·no·hy·poph'y·se'al
ad'e·no·hy·poph'y·sis *pl.* -ses'
ad'e·noid'
ad'e·noid·ec'to·my
ad'e·noid·ism
ad'e·noid·i'tis
ad'e·no·lei'o·my'o·fi· bro'ma *pl.* -mas *or* -ma·ta
ad'e·no·lei'o·my·o'ma *pl.* -mas *or* -ma·ta
ad'e·no·li·po'ma *pl.* -mas *or* -ma·ta
ad'e·no·log'a·di'tis
ad'e·no·lym·phi'tis
ad'e·no·lym'pho·cele'
ad'e·no·lym·pho'ma *pl.* -mas *or* -ma·ta
ad'e·no'ma *pl.* -mas *or* -ma·ta
—— des'tru·ens
—— ma'lig'num
—— pseu'do·sar·co'ma· to'des'
—— se·ba'ce·um
—— sub·stan'ti·ae' cor'ti· ca'lis su'pra·re·na'lis
—— su'do·rip'a·rum
ad'e·no·ma·la'ci·a
ad'e·nom'a·toid'
ad'e·no·ma·to'sis *pl.* -ses'
ad'e·nom'a·tous
ad'e·no·meg'a·ly
ad'e·no·mere'
ad'e·no·my'o·hy'per· pla'si·a
ad'e·no·my·o'ma *pl.* -mas *or* -ma·ta
ad'e·no·my'o·me·tri'tis
ad'e·no·my'o·sal'pin·gi'tis

ad'e·no·my'o·sar·co'ma *pl.* -mas *or* -ma·ta
ad'e·no·my'o·sis *pl.* -ses'
ad'e·no·myx'o·chon'dro· sar·co'ma *pl.* -mas *or* -ma·ta
ad'e·no·myx·o'ma *pl.* -mas *or* -ma·ta
ad'e·no·myx'o·sar·co'ma *pl.* -mas *or* -ma·ta
ad'e·non'cus
ad'e·nop'a·thy
ad'e·no·phar'yn·gi'tis
ad'e·no·phleg'mon'
ad'en·oph·thal'mi·a
ad'e·no·sal'pin·gi'tis
ad'e·no·sar·co'ma *pl.* -mas *or* -ma·ta
ad'e·no·sar'co·rhab'do·my· o'ma *pl.* -mas *or* -ma·ta
ad'e·no·scle·ro'sis *pl.* -ses'
ad'e·nose'
a·den'o·sine'
—— 3'-phos'pha·tase'
—— 5'-phos'pha·tase'
—— di·phos'pha·tase'
—— di·phos'phate'
—— mon'o·phos'pha·tase'
—— mon'o·phos'phate'
—— py'ro·phos'phate'
—— tri·phos'pha·tase'
—— tri·phos'phate'
ad'e·no'sis *pl.* -ses'
ad'e·no·tome'
ad'e·not'o·my
ad'e·no·vi'rus
ad'e·nyl
—— cy'clase'
ad'e·nyl'ic
ad'e·nyl·py'ro·phos'pha· tase'
ad'e·nyl·py'ro·phos'phate'
ad'e·nyl·py'ro·phos·pho'ric
ad'e·pha'gi·a
ad'eps *pl.* ad'i·pes'
—— an'ser·i'nus
—— ben'zo·i·na'tus
—— la'nae'
—— lanae hy·dro'sus
—— praep'a·ra'tus
—— su·il'lus
a·der'mi·a
a·der'mo·gen'e·sis *pl.* -ses'
ad·here', -hered', -her'ing
ad·her'ence
ad·her'ent

ad·he'si·o' pl. -he'si·o'nes'
—— in'ter·tha·lam'i·ca
ad·he'sion
ad·he'si·ot'o·my
ad·he'sive
ad·he'sive·ness
a'di·ac·tin'ic
a'di·ad'o·cho'ki·ne'sis
a·di'a·pho·re'sis
a·di'a·pho·ret'ic
a'di·as'to·le
a'di·a·ther'mance
a'di·a·ther'man·cy
a'di·a·ther'mic
a'di·a·the'sic
a'di·a·thet'ic
a·dic'i·ty
A'die
—— pupil
—— syndrome
ad'i·ent
ad'i·pec'to·my
ad'i·phen'ine'
a·dip'ic
ad'i·po·cele'
ad'i·po·cel'lu·lar
ad'i·po·cer'a·tous
ad'i·po·cere'
ad'i·po·fi·bro'ma pl. -mas or
  -ma·ta
ad'i·po·gen'e·sis pl. -ses'
ad'i·po·gen'ic
ad'i·poid'
ad'i·po·ki·ne'sis pl. -ses'
ad'i·po·ki·net'ic
ad'i·po·ki'nin
ad'i·po·ly'y·sis
ad'i·po·lyt'ic
ad'i·po'ma pl. -mas or -ma·ta
ad'i·po·ne·cro'sis
—— ne'o·na·to'rum
—— sub'cu·ta'ne·a ne'o·na·
  to'rum
ad'i·po·pec'tic
ad'i·po·pex'i·a
ad'i·po·pex'ic
ad'i·po·pex'is
ad'i·po'sa dys·tro'phi·a
  gen'i·ta'lis
ad'i·pose'
ad'i·po'sis pl. -ses'
—— cer'e·bra'lis
—— do'lo·ro'sa
—— he·pat'i·ca
—— or·cha'lis
—— tu'be·ro'sa sim'plex'
ad'i·po'si·tas cer'e·bra'lis

ad'i·po·si'tis
ad'i·pos'i·ty
ad'i·po·su'ri·a
a·dip'si·a
a·dip'sy
ad'i·tus pl. ad'i·tus or -tus·es
—— ad an'trum
—— ad antrum mas·toi'de·
um
—— ad aq'uae·duc'tum
cer'e·bri'
—— glot'ti·dis inferior
—— glottidis superior
—— la·ryn'gis
—— or'bi·tae'
ad'junct'
ad·junc'tive
ad'ju·vant
ad lib'i·tum
ad·max'il·lar'y
ad·me'di·al
ad·me'di·an
ad'mi·nic'u·lum pl. -la
—— lin'e·ae' al'bae'
ad·mix'ture
ad·na'sal
ad nau'se·am
ad·nex'a
—— oc·u·li'
—— u'ter·i'
ad·nex'al
ad'nex·i'tis
ad·nex'o·gen'e·sis pl. -ses'
ad'o·les'cence
ad'o·les'cent
a·don'in
ad·o'ral
ad·or'bit·al
a·dre'nal
a·dre'na·lec'to·my
a·dren'a·line'
a·dren'a·li·ne'mi·a
a·dren'a·li·nu'ri·a
a·dre'nal·ism
a·dre'nal·i'tis
a·dre'na·lop'a·thy
ad're·ner'gic
a·dre'nic
a·dre'nin
ad're·ni'tis
a·dre'no·cep'tor
a·dre'no·chrome'
a·dre'no·cor'ti·cal
a·dre'no·cor'ti·cism
a·dre'no·cor'ti·coid'
a·dre'no·cor'ti·co·mi·
met'ic

a·dre'no·cor'ti·co·tro'phic
a·dre'no·cor'ti·co·tro'phin
a·dre'no·cor'ti·co·tro'pic
a·dre'no·cor'ti·co·tro'pin
a·dre'no·gen'i·tal
a·dre'no·lyt'ic
a·dre'no·med'ul·lar'y
a·dre'no·meg'a·ly
a·dre'no·pause'
a·dre'no·re·cep'tor
a·dre'no·ste·rone'
a·dre'no·sym'pa·thet'ic
a·dre'no·tox'in
a·dre'no·trope'
a·dre'no·tro'phic
a·dre'no·tro'phin
a·dre'no·tro'pic
a·dre'no·tro'pin
ad're·not'ro·pism
A'dri·an-Bronk' law
a·dro'mi·a
ad·sorb' (to hold on a surface)
♦absorb
ad·sor'bate'
ad·sor'bent
ad·sorp'tion
ad·sorp'tive
ad·ster'nal
ad·ter'mi·nal
ad·tor'sion
a·dul'ter·ant
a·dul'ter·ate', -at'ed, -at'ing
a·dul'ter·a'tion
ad'ven·ti'ti·a
ad'ven·ti'tial
ad'ven·ti'tious
ad·ver'sive
a'dy·nam'i·a
—— ep'i·sod'i·ca he·red'i·
  tar'i·a
a'dy·nam'ic
a·dy'na·my
A·ë'des
—— ae·gyp'ti'
ae'lu·rop'sis
ae'quum
aer'ate', -at'ed, -at'ing
aer·a'tion
aer'a'tor
aer·e'mi·a
aer·en'ter·ec·ta'si·a
aer'i·al
aer·if'er·ous
aer'i·form'
Aer'o·bac'ter
—— aer·og'e·nes'

aer'obe'
aer·o'bi·an
aer·o'bic
aer'o·bi·o'sis pl. -ses'
aer'o·bi·ot'ic
aer'o·cele'
aer'o·col'pos'
aer'o·cys'to·scope'
aer'o·cys·tos'co·py
aer'o·don·tal'gi·a
aer'o·duc'tor
aer'o·em'phy·se'ma
aer'o·gen
aer'o·gen'e·sis pl. -ses'
aer'o·gen'ic
aer·og'e·nous (forming gas)
♦erogenous
aer'o·gram'
aer'o·i'on·i·za'tion
aer'o·i'on·o·ther'a·py
aer'o·med'i·cine
aer·om'e·ter
aer'o·neu·ro'sis pl. -ses'
aer'o·o·ti'tis
aer·op'a·thy
aer'o·pause'
aer'o·per'i·to·ne'um
aer'o·per'i·to'ni·a
aer'o·pha'gi·a
aer·oph'a·gy
aer'o·phil'
aer'o·phil'ic
aer'o·pho'bi·a
aer'o·phore'
aer'o·phyte'
aer'o·pi·e·so'ther'a·py
aer'o·ple·thys'mo·
  graph'
aer'o·pleu'ra
aer'o·scope'
aer·os'co·py
aer'o·si'a·loph'a·gy
aer'o·si'nus·i'tis
aer·o'sis pl. -ses'
aer'o·sol'
aer'o·tax'is
aer'o·to·nom'e·ter
aer'o·to·nom'e·try
aer'o·trop'ic
aer·ot'ro·pism
aer'o·tym'pa·nal
aer'o·u·re'thro·scope'
aer'o·u·re·thros'co·py
a·feb'rile
a·fe'tal also afoetal
af'fect'
af·fect'a·bil'i·ty

af·fec'tion
af·fec'tive
af'fec·tiv'i·ty
af·fec'to·mo'tor
af'fer·ent (directed toward a
  central organ)
♦efferent
af·fin'i·ty
af'fir·ma'tion
af'flu·ence
af'flu·ent (copious; flowing
  freely)
♦effluent
af'flux'
af·flux'ion
af·fu'sion
a'fi·brin'o·ge·ne'mi·a
a·foe'tal var. of afetal
af'ter·birth'
af'ter·brain'
af'ter·care'
af'ter·cur'rent
af'ter·dis'charge
af'ter·ef·fect'
af'ter·hear'ing
af'ter·im'age
af'ter·im·pres'sion
af'ter·move'ment
af'ter·nys·tag'mus
af'ter·pains'
af'ter·per·cep'tion
af'ter·po·ten'tial
af'ter·pres'sure
af'ter·sen·sa'tion
af'ter·sound'
af'ter·taste'
af'ter·touch'
af'ter·treat'ment
af'ter·vi'sion
a·func'tion·al
a'ga·lac'ti·a
——— con·ta'gi·o'sa
a'ga·lac'tous
a'ga·lax'i·a
ag'a·lax'y
ag'a·lor·rhe'a also agalor-
  rhoea
ag'a·lor·rhoe'a var. of aga-
  lorrhea
a·gam'ete'
a'ga·met'ic
a·gam'ic
a·gam'ma·glob'u·li·ne'mi·a
a·gam'ma·glob'u·li·ne'mic
a·gam'o·cy·tog'o·ny
Ag'a·mo·fi·lar'i·a
a·gam'o·gen'e·sis

a·gam'o·ge·net'ic
ag'a·mog'o·ny
a·gam'o·sper'my
a·gam'o·spore'
ag'a·mous
a·gan'gli·on'ic
a·gan'gli·o·no'sis
a'gar'
a·gar'ic
A·gar'i·cus
a·gas'tri·a
a·gas'tric
A·ga've
——— a·mer'i·ca'na
age, aged, ag'ing
a'ge·ne'si·a
a·gen'e·sis pl. -ses'
a·ge'ni·o·ce·pha'li·a
a·ge'ni·o·ceph'a·lus
a·ge'ni·o·ceph'a·ly
a·gen'i·tal·ism
a·gen'o·so'mi·a
a'gent
ag'e·ra'si·a
a·geu'si·a
a·geu'sic
a·geu'sti·a
ag'ger
——— na'si'
ag·glom'er·ate
ag·glom'er·a'tion
ag·glu'ti·na·ble
ag·glu'ti·nate', -nat·ed,
  -nat'ing
ag·glu'ti·na'tion
ag·glu'ti·na'tive
ag·glu'ti·nin
ag'glu·tin'o·gen
ag·glu'ti·no·gen'ic
ag·glu'ti·noid'
ag·glu'ti·no·phil'ic
ag·glu'ti·no·phore'
ag·glu·tin'o·scope'
ag'gre·gate
ag'gre·ga'tion
ag·gres'sin
ag·gres'sion
ag·gres'sive
ag'i·tate', -tat·ed, -tat'ing
ag'i·ta'tion
ag'i·to·graph'i·a
ag'i·to·la'li·a
ag'i·to·pha'si·a
Ag·kis'tro·don'
——— con·tor'trix
——— pis·civ'o·rus
a·glan'du·lar

a'glo·mer'u·lar
a·glos'si·a
a·glos'so·sto'mi·a
a·glu'cone'
ag'lu·ti'tion
a'gly·ce'mi·a
a'gly·ce'mic
a·gly'cone'
a·gly'co·su'ri·a
a·gly'co·su'ric
ag'ma·tine'
ag'mi·nat'ed
ag·na'thi·a
ag·na'tho·ce·pha'li·a
ag·na'tho·ceph'a·lus
ag·na'tho·ceph'a·ly
ag·na'thus
ag'na·thy
ag·ne'a *also* agnoea
ag·noe'a *var. of* agnea
ag'no·gen'ic
ag·no'si·a
ag·nos'tic
ag'om·phi'a·sis
a·gom'phi·ous
a'go·nad'al
a·go'nad·ism
Ag'os·ti'ni test
a'go·nad'al
ag'o·nal
ag'o·nist
ag'o·ny
ag'o·ra·pho'bi·a
a·graffe'
a·gram'ma·pha'si·a
a·gram'ma·tism
a·gran'u·lar
a·gran'u·lo·cyte'
a·gran'u·lo·cyt'ic
a·gran'u·lo·cy·the'mi·a
a·gran'u·lo·cy·to'sis *pl.*
  -ses'
a·gran'u·lo·plas'tic
a·gran'u·lo'sis *pl.* -ses'
a·graph'es·the'si·a
a·graph'i·a
a·graph'ic
ag'ri·mo'ny
ag'ri·us
Ag'ro·bac·te'ri·um
ag'ro·ma'ni·a
ag'ryp·net'ic
a·gryp'ni·a
a·gryp'ni·an·al·ge'si·a
a·gryp'node'
ag'ryp·not'ic
a'gua·miel'

a'gue
a·gy'ri·a
a·gy'ric
A·hu·ma'da-Del Cas·ti'llo
  syndrome
a·hyp'ni·a
a'hyp·no'sis
aich'mo·pho'bi·a
ail'ing
ail'ment
ai·lu'ro·phil'i·a
ai·lu'ro·pho'bi·a
ain'hum
air'-con'trast
air'-flu'id
air'sick'ness
air'way'
a·kan'thes·the'si·a
a·kar'y·o·cyte'
ak'a·this'i·a *also* acathisia
a·ker'a·to'sis *pl.* -ses'
ak'i·ne'si·a
—— al'ger·a
—— am·nes'ti·ca
—— i'ri·dis
ak'i·ne'sic
a·kin'es·the'si·a
ak'i·net'ic
a·ko'ri·a *var. of* acoria
A'ku·rey'ri disease
a'la *pl.* a'lae'
—— au'ris
—— cer'e·bel'li'
—— ci·ne're·a
—— cris'tae' gal'li'
—— eth'moi·da'lis
—— il'i·i'
—— lat'er·a'lis
—— lob'u·li' cen·tra'lis
—— mag'na
—— magna os'sis sphe'noi·
da'lis
—— major ossis sphenoidalis
—— minor ossis sphenoidalis
—— na'si'
—— os'sis il'i·i'
—— ossis il'i·um
—— par'va os'sis sphe'noi·
da'lis
—— tem'po·ra'lis
—— vo'mer·is
al'a·bam'ine'
a·la'li·a
al'a·nine'
—— a·mi'no·trans'fer·ase'

L-al'a·nine'
al'a·nyl
al'a·nyl·gly·cine'
a'lar
a'la·ryn'ge·al
a·las'trim
a'late'
a'la-tra'gus
a·la'tus
al'ba
Al'bar·ran'
—— gland
—— test
al·bas'pi·din
Al'bee-Del'bet' operation
Al'bers-Schön'berg' dis-
  ease
Al'bert
—— disease
—— stain
al·bes'cent
al'bi·cans'
al'bi·du'ri·a
al'bi·dus
al'bi·nism
al'bi·nis'mus
—— cir'cum·scrip'tus
—— to·ta'lis
—— u'ni·ver·sa'lis
al·bi'no' *pl.* -nos'
al'bi·not'ic
al'bi·nu'ri·a
al'bo·ci·ne're·ous
Al'bright'-Mc·
  Cune'-Stern'berg' syn-
  drome
Al'bright' syndrome
al'bu·gin'e·a
—— oc'u·li'
—— o·var'i·i'
—— pe'nis
—— tes'tis
al'bu·gin'e·ot'o·my
al'bu·gin'e·ous
al'bu·gi·ni'tis
al'bu'go
al·bu'men *(a nutritive substance)*
♦albumin
al·bu'min *(a water-soluble
  protein)*
♦albumen
al·bu'mi·nate'
al·bu'mi·na·tu'ri·a
al·bu'mi·ne'mi·a
al·bu'min-glob'u·lin
al·bu'mi·nif'er·ous

al·bu'mi·nim'e·ter
al·bu'mi·nim'e·try
al·bu'mi·no·cy'to·log'ic
al·bu'mi·noid'
al·bu'mi·nol'y·sin
al·bu'mi·nol'y·sis *pl.* -ses'
al·bu'mi·nom'e·ter
al·bu'mi·no'sis *pl.* -ses'
al·bu'mi·nous
al·bu'min·u·ret'ic
al·bu'min·u'ri·a
—— ac'e·ton'i·ca
—— par'cel·laire'
al·bu'mi·nu'ric
al·bu'mo·scope'
al'bu·mose'
al·bu'mo·se'mi·a
al·bu'mo·su'ri·a
al·bu'te·rol
al·bu'to·in
Al'ca·lig'e·nes' fe·ca'lis
al·cap'ton *var. of* alkapton
al·cap'ton·u'ri·a *var. of* al-
  kaptonuria
Al'cock' canal
al'co·hol'
al'co·hol·ase'
al'co·hol'ic
al'co·hol·ism
al'co·hol·ize', -ized', -iz'ing
al'co·hol·om'e·ter
al'co·hol·o·phil'i·a
al'co·hol·u'ri·a
al'co·hol'y·sis *pl.* -ses'
al'cu·ro'ni·um
al'de·hyde'
Al'der
—— anomaly
—— phenomenon
al'do·hex'ose'
al'dol'
al'dol·ase'
al·don'ic
al'do·pen'tose'
Al'dor' test
al'dose'
al'do·side'
al'do·ste·rone'
al'do·ster'o·nism
al'do·ster'o·no'ma *pl.* -mas
  or -ma·ta
al'do·ster'o·nu'ri·a
al·dox'ime
Al'drich syndrome
a·lec'i·thal
A·lep'po boil
a·let'a·mine'

a'leu·ke'mi·a
a'leu·ke'mic
a·leu'ki·a hem'or·rha'gi·ca
a·leu'ko·cyt'ic
a·leu'ko·cy·to'sis *pl.* -ses'
al'eu·rone'
A·leu'tian disease
Al'ex·an'der
—— disease
—— operation
a·lex'i·a
a·lex'ic
a·lex'i·dine'
a·lex'in
a·lex'i·phar'mac'
a·ley'dig·ism
Al'ez·zan·dri'ni syndrome
al'ga *pl.* -gae' *or* -gas
al'gal
alg·an'aes·the'si·a
alg·an'es·the'si·a
al'ge·don'ic
al'ge·os'co·py
al·ge'si·a
al·ge'sic
al'ge·sim'e·ter
al'ge·sim'e·try
al'ges·the'si·a
al·ges'tone'
al·get'ic
al'gi·cide'
al'gid
al'gin
al'gi·nate'
al·gin'ic
al'gi·o·mo'tor
al'gi·o·mus'cu·lar
al'go·ge·ne'si·a
al'go·gen'e·sis *pl.* -ses'
al'go·gen'ic
al'go·lag'ni·a
al·gom'e·ter
al'go·pho'bi·a
al'gor'
—— mor'tis
al'go·spasm
al'go·spas'tic
al'i·ble
Al'ice in Won'der·land'
  syndrome
a'li·ces'
al'i·cy'clic
al'ien·a'tion
al'ien·ism
al'i·form'
al'i·ment
al'i·men'ta·ry

al'i·men·ta'tion
al'i·men'to·ther'a·py
al'i·na'sal
al'i·phat'ic
al'i·quot'
al'i·sphe'noid'
a·liz'a·rin
al'ka·le'mi·a
al'ka·les'cence
al'ka·les'cent
al'ka·li' *pl.* -lis' *or* -lies'
al'ka·lim'e·ter
al'ka·lim'e·try
al'ka·line'
al'ka·lin'i·ty
al'ka·lin·i·za'tion
al'ka·lin·ize', -ized', -iz'ing
al'ka·li·nu'ri·a
al'ka·li·ther'a·py
al'ka·li·za'tion
al'ka·lize', -lized', -liz'ing
al'ka·loid'
al'ka·loi'dal
al'ka·lo'sis *pl.* -ses'
al'ka·mine'
al'kane'
al'ka·nol'
al'ka·nol'a·mine'
al·kap'ton *also* alcapton
al·kap'ton·u'ri·a *also* alcap-
  tonuria
alk·ox'ide'
alk·ox'y
alk·ox'yl
al'kyl
al'kyl·a·mine'
al'kyl·ate', -at'ed, -at'ing
al'kyl·a'tion
al'kyl·o·gen
al'la·ches·the'si·a
al·lan'to·cho'ri·on'
al·lan'to·gen'e·sis *pl.* -ses'
al·lan'to·ic
al·lan·to'i·case'
al·lan'toid'
al·lan·toi'de·an
al·lan·toi'do·an'gi·op'a·
  gous
al·lan'to·in
al·lan'to·in·ase'
al·lan'to·is *pl.* al'lan·to'i·des'
al·las'so·ther'a·py
al·lax'is
al·lele'
al·le'lic
al·lel'o·ca·tal'y·sis *pl.* -ses'
al·lel'o·cat'a·lyt'ic

al·le′lo·morph′
al·le′lo·mor′phic
al·le′lo·mor′phism
al·lel′o·tax′is
al·lel′o·tax′y
Al′len
—— fossa
—— test
—— tract
—— treatment
al′lene′
al·len′the·sis pl. -ses′
al′ler·gen
al′ler·gen′ic
al·ler′gic
al′ler·gid
al′ler·gist
al′ler·gi·za′tion
al′ler·go′sis pl. -ses′
al′ler·gy
Al′les·che′ri·a
—— boyd′i·i′
al′les·the′si·a
al′le·thrin
al′li·cin
al′li·ga′tion
Al′ling·ham operation
Al′lis sign
al·lit′er·a′tion
Al′li·um
al′lo·al·bu′mi·ne′mi·a
al′lo·bar′bi·tal′
al′lo·chei′ri·a
al′lo·ches·the′si·a
al′lo·che′zi·a
al′lo·chro·ma′si·a
al′lo·ci·ne′si·a
al′lo·cor′tex′
al′lo·dip′loid′
al′loe·o′sis pl. -ses′
al′lo·e·rot′i·cism
al′lo·er′o·tism
al′lo·ge·ne′ic
al′lo·gen′ic
al′lo·graft′
al′lo·i′so·leu′cine′
al′lo·ker′a·to·plas′ty
al′lo·ki·ne′sis pl. -ses′
al′lo·la′li·a
al·lom′e·try
al′lo·mor′phic
al′lo·mor′phism
al′lo·mor′pho·sis pl. -ses′
al′lo·mor′phous
al′lo·path′
al′lo·path′ic
al·lop′a·thist

al·lop′a·thy
al·loph′a·sis pl. -ses′
al′lo·plasm
al′lo·plast′
al′lo·plas′ty
al′lo·pol′y·ploid′
al′lo·pol′y·ploi′dy
al′lo·psy′chic
al′lo·pu′ri·nol′
al′lo·rhyth′mi·a
al′lo·rhyth′mic
all′-or-none′ law
al′lose′
al′lo·some′
al′lo·ste′ric
al′lo·sy·nap′sis pl. -ses′
al′lo·syn′de·sis pl. -ses′
al′lo·therm′
al·lot′ri·o·don′ti·a
al·lot′ri·o·geu′si·a
al′lo·tri′o·lith′
al·lot′ri·u′ri·a
al′lo·trope′
al′lo·troph′ic (rendered non-
    nutritious by digestion)
✦allotropic
al′lo·trop′ic (exhibiting al-
    lotropy)
✦allotrophic
al·lot′ro·pism
al·lot′ro·py
al·lo·tryl′ic
al′lo·type′
al′lox·an′
al·lox′a·zine′
al·lox′ur
al′lox·u·re′mic
al′lox·u′ri·a
al′lox·u′ric
al′loy′
al′lyl
al′lyl·ene′
al′ma·drate′
Al′men reagent
a·lo′chi·a
al′oe
Al′o·e
al′oe-em′o·din
al′o·et′ic
al′o·e′tin
a·lo′gi·a
al′o·in
al′o·pe′ci·a
—— ad·na′ta
—— ar′e·a′ta
—— cic′a·tri·sa′ta
—— cir′cum·scrip′ta

—— con·gen′i·ta′lis
—— mu′ci·no′sa
—— pre′ma·tu′ra
—— se·ni′lis
—— syph′i·lit′i·ca
—— to·ta′lis
—— u′ni·ver·sa′lis
al′o·pe′cic
Al′per disease
al′pha
—— globulin
—— streptococci
al′pha-ad′re·ner′gic
al′pha-a·mi′no·a·dip′ic
    acid
al′pha-a·mi′no·ca·pro′ic
    acid
al′pha-a·mi′no·glu·tar′ic
    acid
al′pha-a·mi′no·hy′dro·cin·
    nam′ic acid
al′pha-a·mi′no·i′so·ca·
    pro′ic acid
al′pha-a·mi′no·i′so·va·
    ler′ic acid
al′pha-a·mi′no-n-va·ler′ic
    acid
al′pha-a·mi′no·pro′pi·on′ic
    acid
al′pha-a·mi′no-3-in′dole·
    pro′pi·on′ic acid
al′pha-a·mi′no·va·ler′ic
    acid
al′pha-fe′to·pro′te·in
al′pha-hy·poph′a·mine′
al′pha-i′o·dine′
al′pha-lo′be·line′
al′pha·my′col′ic acid
al′pha·naph′thol′
al′pha·pro′dine′
Al′pha·vi′rus
al′phos′
al·pho′sis pl. -ses′
al′pho·zone′
al′phus
al′pine′ papilla
Al′port′ syndrome
al·pren′o·lol′
al′ser·ox′y·lon′
al′ter·ant
al′ter e′go
al′ter·nans′
Al′ter·nar′i·a
al′ter·nar′ic
al′ter·na′tion
al′ter·na′tor
al′ter·no·bar′ic

Alt'hau'sen test
al·the'a
al·thi'a·zide'
Alt'mann-Gersh' method
Alt'mann granules
al'tri·gen'der·ism
al'trose'
al'um
a·lu'mi·na
al'u·min'i·um
a·lu'mi·num
a·lu'si·a
al've·at'ed
al·ve'o·lar
al·ve'o·late'
al·ve·o·lec'to·my
al·ve'o·li'
—— den·ta'les' man·dib'u·lae'
—— dentales max·il'lae'
—— pul·mo'nis
—— pul·mo'num
al've·o·lin'gual
al've·o·li'tis
al·ve'o·lo·ba'sal
al·ve'o·lo·bas'i·lar
al·ve'o·lo·cla'si·a
al·ve'o·lo·con·dyl'e·an
al·ve'o·lo·den'tal
al·ve'o·lo·la'bi·al
al·ve'o·lo·lin'gual
al·ve'o·lon'
al·ve'o·lo·na'sal
al·ve'o·lo·plas'ty
al've·o·lot'o·my
al·ve'o·lus pl. -li'
al've·o·sub·na'sal
al'ver·ine'
al've·us pl. -ve·i'
—— hip'po·cam'pi'
al'vus pl. -vi'
a·lym'phi·a
a·lym'pho·cy·to'sis pl. -ses'
a·lym'pho·pla'si·a
a·lys'mus
al'y·so'sis
Alz'hei'mer
—— cell
—— disease
—— plaque
—— stain
a'ma
a'maas'
am'a·cri'nal
am'a·crine
a·mal'gam

a·mal'ga·mate', -mat'ed, -mat'ing
a·mal'ga·ma'tion
a·man'din
Am'a·ni'ta
—— mus·car'i·a
—— phal·loi'des'
a·man'ta·dine'
a·ma'ra
am'a·ranth'
am'a·roid'
am'a·se'sis
a·mas'ti·a
am'a·tho·pho'bi·a
am'a·tive
am'a·to'ry
am'au·ro'sis pl. -ses'
—— fu'gax'
—— par'ti·a'lis fu'gax'
am'au·rot'ic
a·max'o·pho'bi·a
a·ma'zi·a
am·be·no'ni·um
am'bi·dex'ter
am·bi·dex·tral'i·ty
am'bi·dex'trism
am'bi·dex'trous
am'bi·ent
am·big'u·ous
am'bi·lat'er·al
am'bi·le'vous
am·bi·oc'u·lar'i·ty
am'bi·o'pi·a
am'bi·sex'u·al
am'bi·sex'u·al'i·ty
am'bi·sin'is·ter
am·biv'a·lence
am·biv'a·len·cy
am·biv'a·lent
am'bi·ver'sion
am'bi·vert'
am'bly·a·cou'si·a
am'bly·chro·ma'si·a
am'bly·chro·mat'ic
Am'bly·om'ma
am'bly·ope'
am'bly·o'pi·a
—— al'bi·nis'mus
—— ex a·nop'si·a
am'bly·op'ic
am'bly·o·scope'
am·bo·cep'tor
am'bo·my'cin
am'bon'
Am·boy'na button
Am·bro'si·a
am'bu·lance

am'bu·la·to'ry
am·bu'phyl·line'
am'bu·side'
am·bus'tion
am·cin'o·nide'
a·me'ba pl. -bas or -bae', var. of amoeba
am'e·bi'a·sis var. of amoebiasis
a·me'bic var. of amoebic
a·me'bi·ci'dal var. of amoebicidal
a·me'bi·cide' var. of amoebicide
a·me'bi·form' var. of amoebiform
a·me'bo·cyte' var. of amoebocyte
a·me'boid' var. of amoeboid
am'e·bo'ma var. of amoeboma
a·me'bu·la pl. -las or -lae', var. of amoebula
am'e·bu'ri·a var. of amoeburia
am'ei·o'sis pl. -ses'
a·mel'a·not'ic
a·mel'ei·a (apathy)
♦amelia
a·mel'i·a (congenital absence of the extremities)
♦ameleia
a·mel'i·fi·ca'tion
am'e·lo·blast'
am'e·lo·blas'tic
am'e·lo·blas·to'ma pl. -mas or -ma·ta
am'e·lo·blas'to·sar·co'ma pl. -mas or -ma·ta
am'e·lo·gen'e·sis
—— im'per·fec'ta
am'e·lus pl. -li'
a·me'ni·a
a·men'or·rhe'a
a·men'or·rhe'al
a'ment
a·men'ti·a
am'er·i'ci·um
am'er·ism
am'er·is'tic
a·met'a·bol'ic
am'e·tab'o·lon' pl. -la
am'e·tab'o·lous
a·meth'o·caine'
a·me'tri·a
a·me'tro·he'mi·a

am′e·trope′
am′e·tro′pi·a
am′e·tro′pic
a·me′trous
am′fo·nel′ic
am′i·an′thine′
am′i·an′thi·nop′sy
am′i·an′thoid′
am′i·an·tho′sis pl. -ses′
am′i·ce′tin
a′mi·cro′bic
a·mi′cron′
a·mic′u·lum pl. -lums or -la
am′i·dase′
am′ide′
am′i·deph′rine′
am′i·din (soluble starch)
  ♦amidine
am′i·dine′ (compound containing the univalent radical
  −C(NH₂):NH)
  ♦amidin
a·mi′do·ben′zene′
a·mi′do·ben′zol′
am′i·done′
a·mi′do·py′rine′
a·mil′o·ride′
a·mim′i·a
a·mi′na·crine′
a·mine′
a·mi′no
a·mi′no·a·ce′tic
a·mi′no·ac′i·de′mi·a
a′mi·no·ac′i·dop′a·thy
a·mi′no·ac′id·u′ri·a
a·mi′no·ac′ri·dine′
α-a·mi′no·a·dip′ic acid
a·mi′no·ben′zene′
a·mi′no·ben′zo·ate′
a·mi′no·ben·zo′ic
a·mi′no·ca·pro′ic
a·mi′no·eth·ane·sul·fon′ic
a·mi′no·eth·a′nol′
a·mi′no·fo′lic acid
a·mi′no·glu′cose′
a·mi′no·glu·tar′ic
a·mi′no·glu·teth′i·mide′
a·mi′no·gly′co·side′
a·mi′no·hep′tane′
a·mi′no·hex′a·no′ic
a·mi′no·hip·pu′ric
a·mi′no·hy′dro·cin·nam′ic
a·mi′no·hy·drox′y·bu′ta·
  no′ic
a·mi′no·hy·drox′y·pro′pa·
  no′ic

a·mi′no-in′dole·pro′pi·
  on′ic
a·mi′no·i′so·ca·pro′ic
a·mi′no·i′so·va·ler′ic
a·mi′no·lip′id
a·mi′no-mer·cap′to·pro′pa·
  no′ic
a·mi′no-meth′yl·bu′ta·
  no′ic
a·mi′no·met′ra·dine′
a·mi′no·pen′ta·mide′
a·mi′no·pep′ti·dase′
a·mi′no·phen′a·zone′
am′i·noph′er·ase′
a·mi′no·phyl′line′
a·mi′no·pol′y·pep′ti·dase′
a·mi′no·pro′pi·on′ic
a·mi′no·pu′rine′
a·mi′no·py′rine′
a·mi′no·sa·lic′y·late′
a·mi′no·sal′i·cyl′ic
a·mi′no·su′ri·a
a·mi′no·tol′u·ene′
a·mi′no·trans′fer·ase′
a·mi′no·va·ler′ic
am′i·nu′ri·a
am′i·phen′a·zole′
am′i·quin′sin
am′i·so·met′ra·dine′
am′i·thi′o·zone′
am′i·to′sis pl. -ses′
am′i·tot′ic
am′i·trip′ty·line′
am′me′ter
am′mo·nate′
Am′mon horn
am·mo′ni·a
am·mo′ni·ac′
am′mo·ni′a·cal
am·mo′ni·at′ed
am·mo′ni·e′mi·a
am·mon′i·fi·ca′tion
am·mo′ni·um
am·mo′ni·u′ri·a
am′mo·nol′y·sis pl. -ses′
am·ne′si·a
am·ne′si·ac′
am·ne′sic
am·nes′tic
am′ni·o·car′di·ac′
am′ni·o·cen·te′sis pl. -ses′
am′ni·o·cho′ri·al
am′ni·o·gen′e·sis
am′ni·og′ra·phy
am′ni·on′ pl. -ons′ or -ni·a
am′ni·on′ic
am′ni·o·ni′tis

am′ni·or·rhe′a
am′ni·or·rhex′is pl. -es′
am′ni·os′
Am′ni·o′ta
am′ni·ote′
am′ni·ot′ic
am′ni·o·ti′tis
am′ni·o·tome′
am′ni·ot′o·my
am′o·bar′bi·tal′
am′o·di′a·quine′
a·moe′ba pl. -bas or -bae′,
  also ameba
A·moe′ba
am′oe·bi′a·sis pl. -ses′, also
  amebiasis
—— cu′tis
a·moe′bic also amebic
a·moe′bi·ci′dal also amebi-
  cidal
a·moe′bi·cide′ also amebi-
  cide
A·moe′bi·dae′
a·moe′bi·form′ also
  amebiform
a·moe′bo·cyte′ also amebo-
  cyte
a·moe′boid′ also ameboid
am′oe·bo′ma also ameboma
a·moe′bu·la pl. -las or -lae′,
  also amebula
am′oe·bu′ri·a also ameburia
a·mo′la·none′
am′or′
—— in·sa′nus
—— les′bi·cus
—— su′i′
am′o·ra′li·a
a′morph′
a·mor′phi·a
a·mor′phic
a·mor′phin·ism
a·mor′phism
a·mor′phous (formless)
  ♦amorphus
a·mor′phus (anideus)
  ♦amorphous
—— glob′u·lus
a·mo′ti·o′ ret′i·nae′
a·mox′a·pine′
a·mox′i·cil′lin
am′per·age
am′pere′
am′pere·me′ter
am′phe·chlo′ral
am·phet′a·mine′
am′phi·ar·thro′sis pl. -ses′

am'phi·ar·throt'ic
am'phi·as'ter
am·phib'i·a
Am·phib'i·a
am·phib'i·ous
am'phi·blas'tic
am'phi·blas'tu·la pl. -las or -lae'
am'phi·bles·tri'tis
am'phi·bol'ic
am·phib'o·lous
am'phi·ce'lous
am'phi·cra'ni·a
am'phi·cre·at'i·nine'
am'phi·cyte'
am'phi·des'mic
am'phi·des'mous
am'phi·gas'tru·la pl. -las or -lae'
am'phi·gen'e·sis pl. -ses'
am'phi·gen'ic
am·phig'e·nous
am·phig'o·ny
am'phi·kar'y·on'
am'phi·mix'is
am'phi·mor'u·la pl. -lae'
am'phi·phile'
am'phi·tene'
am'phi·the'a·ter
am'pho·cyte'
am'pho·di·pol'pi·a
am'pho·lyte'
am'pho·phil'
am'pho·phil'ic
am·pho'ric
am'pho·ter'ic
am'pho·ter'i·cin B
am'pho·ter'ism
am·phot'er·o·di·plo'pi·a
am'pi·cil'lin
am'pli·fi·ca'tion
am'pli·fi'er
am'pli·fy', -fied', -fy'ing
am'pli·tude'
am'pro·tro'pine'
am'pule'
am·pul'la pl. -lae'
—— can'a·lic'u·li' lac'ri·ma'lis
—— duc'tus def'e·ren'tis
—— ductus lac'ri·ma'lis
—— hep'a·to·pan'cre·at'i·ca
—— lac·tif'er·a
—— mem'bra·na'ce·a anterior
—— membranacea lat'er·a'lis

—— membranacea posterior
—— membranacea superior
—— of Va'ter
—— os'se·a anterior
—— ossea lat'er·a'lis
—— ossea posterior
—— ossea superior
—— phren'i·ca
—— rec'ti'
—— tu'bae' u'ter·i'nae'
am·pul'lae'
—— mem'bra·na'ce·ae'
—— os'se·ae'
am·pul'lar
am'pul·lar'y
am'pul·late'
am·pul'lu·la pl. -lae'
am'pu·tate', -tat'ed, -tat'ing
am'pu·ta'tion
am'pu·tee'
am'py·zine'
am·quin'ate'
am'ri·none'
a·muck'
a·mu'si·a
am'y·cho·pho'bi·a
am'y·dri'a·sis pl. -ses'
a·my'e·len·ce·pha'li·a
a·my'e·len·ce·phal'ic
a·my'e·len·ceph'a·lus
am'y·e'li·a
am'y·el'ic
a·my'e·li·nat'ed
a·my'e·lin'ic
a·my'e·lon'ic
a·my'e·lus
a·myg'da·la pl. -lae'
a·myg'da·lase'
a·myg·dal'ic
a·myg'da·lin
a·myg'da·loid'
a·myg'da·loi·dec'to·my
a·myg'da·lo·lith'
a·myg'da·lot'o·my
am'yl
am'y·la'ceous
am'y·lase'
am'y·lene'
am'y·lo·bar'bi·tone'
am'y·lo·clast'
am'y·lo·clas'tic
am'y·lo·dex'trin
am'y·lo·dys·pep'si·a
am'y·loid'
am'y·loi·do'sis pl. -ses'
—— cu'tis
am'y·lol'y·sis pl. -ses'

am'y·lo·lyt'ic
am'y·lo·mal'tase'
am'y·lo·pec'tin
am'y·lo·pec'ti·no'sis pl. -ses'
am'y·lo·phos·pho'ry·lase'
am'y·lo·plast'
am'y·lop'sin
am'y·lor·rhe'a
am'y·lose'
am'y·lo·su'crase'
am'y·lum
am'y·lu'ri·a
a·my'o·es·the'si·a
a·my'o·pla'si·a
—— con·gen'i·ta
a·my'o·plas'tic
a·my'o·sta'si·a
a·my'o·stat'ic
a·my'os·the'ni·a
a·my'os·then'ic
a·my'o·tax'i·a
a·my'o·tax'ic
a·my'o·tax'y
a·my'o·to'ni·a
—— con·gen'i·ta
a·my'o·tro'phi·a
—— spi·na'lis pro'gres·si'va
a·my'o·troph'ic
am'y·ot'ro·phy
a·myx'i·a
a·myx'or·rhe'a
an'a
a·nab'a·sine'
an'a·bi·o'sis pl. -ses'
an'a·bi·ot'ic
an'a·bol'er·gy
an'a·bol'ic
a·nab'o·lin
a·nab'o·lism
an'a·camp'tic
an'a·ce'li·a·del'phous
an'a·cho·re'sis
an'a·cho·ret'ic
an'a·cid'i·ty
a·nac'la·sis (refraction of light or sound), pl. -ses'
♦anaclisis
an'a·clas'tic
a·nac'li·sis (the act of reclining), pl. -ses'
♦anaclasis
an'a·clit'ic
an·ac'me·sis pl. -ses'
an'a·crot'ic
a·nac'ro·tism
an'a·cu'si·a

an'a·cu'sis
an'a·de'ni·a
an'a·did'y·mus
an'a·dip'si·a
an·aer'obe'
an·aer'o·bi'ase'
an'aer·o'bic
an'aer·o·bi·o'sis pl. -ses'
an'aer·o·bi·ot'ic
an'aer·o·gen'ic
an'a·gen'e·sis pl. -ses'
an'a·ges'tone'
an'a·go'ge
an'a·gog'ic
an'a·kat'a·did'y·mus
an'a·ku'sis
a'nal
an'al·bu'mi·ne'mi·a
an'a·lep'tic
an'al·ge'si·a
—— al'ger·a
—— do'lo·ro'sa
an'al·ge'sic
an'al·ge'sist
an'al·get'ic
an'al·gize', -gized', -giz'ing
an'al·ler'gic
an'a·log' var. of analogue
a·nal'o·gous
an'a·logue' also analog
a·nal'o·gy
a·nal'y·sand'
a·nal'y·sis pl. -ses'
an'a·lyst
an'a·lyt'ic or an'a·lyt'i·cal
an'a·lyz'er
an·am·ne'sis pl. -ses'
an·am·nes'tic
An·am'ni·o'ta
an·am'ni·ot'ic
an'a·mor'pho·sis pl. -ses'
an·an·a·phy·lax'is
an·an·a·sta'si·a
an'an·cas'ti·a
an'an·cas'tic
an·an'gi·o·pla'si·a
an·an'gi·o·plas'tic
an'a·pau'sis pl. -ses'
an'a·pei·rat'ic
an'a·phase'
an·a'phi·a
an'a·pho·re'sis
an'a·pho·ret'ic
an'a·pho'ri·a
an·aph'ro·dis'i·a
an·aph'ro·dis'i·ac'
an·aph'ro·dite'

an'a·phy·lac'tic
an'a·phy·lac'tin
an'a·phy·lac'to·gen
an'a·phy·lac'to·gen'ic
an'a·phy·lac'toid'
an'a·phyl'a·tox'in
an'a·phyl'ax'is pl. -es'
an'a·phyl'o·tox'in
an'a·pla'si·a
An'a·plas'ma
an'a·plas·mo'sis pl. -ses'
an'a·plas'tic
an'a·plas'ty
an'a·ple·ro'sis pl. -ses'
an'a·poph'y·sis pl. -ses'
an·ap'tic
an'a·rith'mi·a
an·ar'thri·a
—— cen·tra'lis
—— lit'er·a'lis
an·ar'thric
an'a·sar'ca
—— hys·ter'i·cum
an'a·sar'cous
an'a·schis'tic
an'a·stal'sis pl. -ses'
an'a·stal'tic
a·nas'ta·sis pl. -ses'
an'a·state'
an'a·stat'ic
an'as·tig·mat'ic
a·nas'to·le'
a·nas'to·mose', -mosed',
-mos'ing
a·nas'to·mo'sis pl. -ses'
—— ar·te'ri·o·ve·no'sa
a·nas'to·mot'ic
an·as'tral
an'a·ther'a·peu'sis pl. -ses'
an'a·tom'ic or an'a·tom'i·cal
a·nat'o·mist
anatomist's snuff'box'
a·nat'o·my
an'a·tox'ic
an'a·tox'in
an'a·tri·crot'ic
an'a·tri'cro·tism
an'a·troph'ic
an'a·tro'pi·a
an'a·trop'ic
an·au'di·a
an'a·ven'in
an·az'o·tu'ri·a
an'chor
an'chor·age
an'co·nad'
an·co'nal or an·co'ne·al

an·co'ne·us pl. -ne·i'
—— in·ter'nus
an'co·noid'
An'cy·los'to·ma
—— a·mer'i·ca'num
—— bra·zil'i·en'se'
—— ca·ni'num
—— du'o·de·na'le'
An'cy·lo·sto'mat'i·dae'
an'cy·lo·sto·mi'a·sis pl.
-ses'
An'der·nach' ossicles
An'dersch ganglion
An'ders disease
An'der·sen
—— disease
—— syndrome
An'der·son-Fab'ry disease
an'dra·nat'o·my
an'drei·o'ma pl. -mas or
-ma·ta
An'dré test
An·dré' Thom'as sign
An'drews operation
an'dri·at'rics
an·dri'a·try
an'dro·blas·to'ma pl. -mas
or -ma·ta
an'dro·cyte'
an'dro·ga·lac'to·ze'mi·a
an'dro·gam'one'
an'dro·gen
an'dro·gen'e·sis
an'dro·gen'ic
an'dro·ge·nic'i·ty
an·drog'e·nous (of male off-
spring)
◆androgynous
an'dro·gyne'
an·drog'y·nous (hermaphro-
ditic)
◆androgenous
an'dro·gy·ne'i·ty
an·drog'y·nic
an·drog'y·nism
an·drog'y·noid'
an·drog'y·nus
an·drog'y·ny
an'droid'
an·drom'e·do·tox'in
an'dro·mi·met'ic
an'dro·mor'phous
an'drop'a·thy
an'dro·phile'
an·droph'i·lous
an'dro·pho'bi·a
an'dro·stane'

androstenediol **16**

an′dro·stene′di′ol
an′dro·stene′di′one
an·dros′ter·one′
a·ne′de·ous
an′e·lec·trot′o·nus
a·ne·mi·a
—— pseu′do·leu·ke′mi·ca
—— pseudoleukemica in·
fan′tum
a·ne′mic
an′e·mom′e·ter
A·nem′o·ne
a·nem′o·nin
an′e·mo·pho′bi·a
an′e·mot′ro·phy
an·en·ce·pha′li·a
an·en·ce·phal′ic
an′en·ceph′a·lus
an′en·ceph′a·ly
an·en′ter·ous
a·neph′ro·gen′e·sis *pl.* -ses′
an·ep′i·a
an·ep′i·plo′ic
an′er·ga′si·a
an′er·gas′tic
an·er′gic
an′er·gy
an′er·oid′
an′e·ryth′ro·blep′si·a
an′e·ryth′ro·cyte′
an′e·ryth′ro·pla′si·a
an′e·ryth′ro·plas′tic
an′e·ryth·rop′si·a
a·nes′the·ki·ne′si·a
a·nes′the·ki·ne′sis *pl.* -ses′
an′es·the′si·a
—— do′lo·ro′sa
a·nes′the·sim′e·ter
an′es·the·si·ol′o·gist
an′es·the·si·ol′o·gy
an′es·thet′ic
a·nes′the·tist
a·nes′the·ti·za′tion
a·nes′the·tize′, -tized′,
 -ti·z′ing
a·nes′the·tom′e·ter
an·es′trum
an·es′trus
an′e·thole′
a·ne′thum
an′e·to·der′ma
an′eu·ploid′
an′eu·ploi′dy
a·neu′ri·a *(deficiency of
 nervous energy)*
 ♦anuria

a·neu′ric *(pertaining to
 aneuria)*
 ♦anuric
an′eu·rin
an′eu·rysm
an′eu·rys′mal
an′eu·rys·mat′ic
an′eu·rys·mec′to·my
an′eu·rys·mo·plas′ty
an′eu·rys·mor′rha·phy
an′eu·rys·mot′o·my
an′eu·rys′mus
an·frac′tu·os′i·ty
an·frac′tu·ous
an·gel′i·ca
an′gi·as·the′ni·a
an′gi·ec·ta′si·a
an′gi·ec′ta·sis *pl.* -ses′
an′gi·ec·tat′ic
an′gi·ec′to·my
an′gi·ec·to′pi·a
an′gi·ec·top′ic
an′gi·i′tis
an·gi′na
—— ab·dom′i·nis
—— cor′dis
—— cru′ris
—— de·cu′bi·tus
—— fol·lic′u·lar′is
—— hy′per·cy′a·not′i·ca
—— in·ver′sa
—— lu′di·vig′i·i′
—— no′tha
—— pa·rot′i·de′a
—— pec′to·ris
—— pectoris va′so·mo·
to′ri·a
—— ton′sil·lar′es′
an′gi·nal
an′gi·noid′
an′gi·no·pho′bi·a
an′gi·nose′
an′gi·o′a·tax′i·a
an′gi·o·blast′
an′gi·o·blas′tic
an′gi·o·blas·to′ma *pl.* -mas
 or -ma·ta
an′gi·o·car′di·o·gram′
an′gi·o·car′di·o·graph′ic
an′gi·o·car′di·og′ra·phy
an′gi·o·car′di·o′ki·net′ic
an′gi·o·car′di·op′a·thy
an′gi·o′car·di′tis
an′gi·o·cav′ern·ous
an′gi·o·chei′lo·scope′
an′gi·o·cho·li′tis

an′gi·o·chon·dro′ma *pl.*
 -mas *or* -ma·ta
an′gi·o·crine′
an′gi·o·der′ma·ti′tis
an′gi·o·dys′tro′phi·a
an′gi·o·dys′tro·phy
an′gi·o·ec·ta′si·a
an′gi·o·e·de′ma
an′gi·o·el′e·phan·ti′a·sis
an′gi·o·en′do·the′li·o·ma
 pl. -mas *or* -ma·ta
an′gi·o·fi′bro·blas·to′ma *pl.*
 -mas *or* -ma·ta
an′gi·o·fi·bro′ma *pl.* -mas *or*
 -ma·ta
an′gi·o·gen′e·sis *pl.* -ses′
an′gi·o·gen′ic
an′gi·o·gli·o′ma *pl.* -mas *or*
 -ma·ta
an′gi·o·gli·o′ma·to′sis
an′gi·o·gram′
an′gi·og′ra·phy
an′gi·o·he′mo·phil′i·a
an′gi·o·hy′per·to′ni·a *(vaso-
 constriction)*
 ♦angiohypotonia
an′gi·o·hy′po·to′ni·a *(vaso-
 dilatation)*
 ♦angiohypertonia
an′gi·oid′
an′gi·o·ker′a·to′ma *pl.* -mas
 or -ma·ta
—— cor′po·ris dif·fu′sum
—— corporis diffusum
u′ni·ver·sa′le′
—— For′dyce
—— Mi·bel′li
an′gi·o′ki·net′ic
an′gi·o′leu·ki′tis
an′gi·o·li·po′ma *pl.* -mas *or*
 -ma·ta
an′gi·o·lith′
an′gi·o·lith′ic
an′gi·ol′o·gy
an′gi·o·lu′poid′
—— of Brocq and Pau′tri·er
an′gi·ol′y·sis *pl.* -ses′
an′gi·o′ma *pl.* -mas *or*
 -ma·ta
—— ar·te′ri·a′le′ rac′e·
mo′sum
—— in·fec′ti·o′sum
—— pig′men·to′sum
a·troph′i·cum
—— se·ni′le′
—— ser′pig·i·no′sum
an′gi·o·ma·la′ci·a

an'gi·o·ma·to'sis *pl.* -ses'
—— ret'i·nae'
an'gi·om'a·tous
an'gi·o·meg'a·ly
an'gi·om'e·ter
an'gi·o·my'o·li·po'ma *pl.*
-mas *or* -ma·ta
an'gi·o·my·o'ma *pl.* -mas *or*
-ma·ta
an'gi·o·my·op'a·thy
an'gi·o·my'o·sar·co'ma *pl.*
-mas *or* -ma·ta
an'gi·o·myx·o'ma *pl.* -mas
or -ma·ta
an'gi·o·neu·rec'to·my
an'gi·o·neu·ro'ma *pl.* -mas
or -ma·ta
an'gi·o·neu'ro·my·o'ma *pl.*
-mas *or* -ma·ta
an'gi·o·neu·ro'sis *pl.* -ses'
an'gi·o·neu·rot'ic
an'gi·o'neu·rot'o·my
an'gi·o·no'ma
an'gi·o·pa·ral'y·sis *pl.* -ses'
an'gi·o·par'a·lyt'ic
an'gi·o·pa·re'sis *pl.* -ses'
an'gi·o'pa·thol'o·gy
an'gi·op'a·thy
an'gi·o·pha·co'ma·to'sis *pl.*
-ses'
—— ret'i·nae' et cer'e·bel'li'
an'gi·o·plas'ty
an'gi·o·poi·e'sis *pl.* -ses'
an'gi·o·poi·et'ic
an'gi·o·pres'sure
an'gi·o·re·tic'u·lo'ma *pl.*
-mas *or* -ma·ta
an'gi·o·ret'i·nog'ra·phy
an'gi·or'rha·phy
an'gi·or·rhex'is *pl.* -es'
an'gi·o·sar·co'ma *pl.* -mas
or -ma·ta
an'gi·o·scle·ro'sis *pl.* -ses'
an'gi·o·scle·rot'ic
an'gi·o·scope'
an'gi·o·sco·to'ma
an'gi·o'sis *pl.* -ses'
an'gi·o·spasm
an'gi·o·spas'tic
an'gi·o·sperm'
an'gi·o·stax'is
an'gi·o·ste·no'sis
an'gi·os'te·o'sis
an'gi·os'to·my
an'gi·o·stron'gy·li'a·sis
an'gi·os'tro·phe
an'gi·o·tel'ec·ta'si·a

an'gi·o·te·lec'ta·sis *pl.* -ses'
an'gi·o·tel'ec·tat'ic
an'gi·o·ten'ic
an'gi·o·ten'sin
an'gi·o·ti'tis
an'gi·o·tome'
an'gi·ot'o·my
an'gi·o·ton'ic
an'gi·o·to'nin
an'gi·o·tribe'
an'gi·o·troph'ic
an·gi'tis
an'gle
—— of Lou'is
—— of Lud'wig
—— of Qua'tre·fages'
—— of Ro·lan'do'
—— of Syl'vi·us
An'gle classification
an'gle-clo'sure
an'gle-re·ces'sion
an'go·phra'si·a
an'gor'
—— an'i·mi'
—— noc·tur'nus
—— oc'u·lar'is
—— pec'to·ris
ang'strom *or* ang'ström
An·guil'lu·la
an'gu·lar
an'gu·la'tion
an'gu·lus *pl.* -li'
—— a·cro'mi·a'lis
—— cos'tae'
—— du'do·vi'ci
—— inferior scap'u·lae'
—— in'tra·ster·na'lis
—— i'ri·dis
—— i'ri·do·cor'ne·a'lis
—— lat'er·a'lis scap'u·lae'
—— man·dib'u·lae'
—— mas·toi'de·us os'sis
pa·ri'e·ta'lis
—— oc·cip'i·ta'lis os'sis
pa·ri'e·ta'lis
—— oc'u·li' lat'er·a'lis
—— oculi me'di·a'lis
—— o'ris
—— pa·ri'e·ta'lis a'lae'
mag'nae'
—— posterior py·ram'i·dis
—— pu'bis
—— sphe'noi·da'lis os'sis
pa·ri'e·ta'lis
—— ster'ni'
—— sub·pu'bi·cus
—— superior py·ram'i·dis

—— superior pyramidis os'-
sis tem'po·ra'lis
—— superior scap'u·lae'
an'ha·lo'nine'
an'he·do'ni·a
an·hem'a·to·poi·e'sis
an·he'ma·to'sis
an·he'mo·lyt'ic
an·he'mo·poi·e'sis
an'hi·dro'sis *pl.* -ses'
an'hi·drot'ic
an·hy'drase'
an'hy·dra'tion
an·hy'dre·mi·a
an·hy'dride'
an·hy'dro·hy·drox'y·pro·
ges'ter·one'
an·hy'dro·sug'ar
an·hy'drous
an'hyp·no'sis
a·ni'a·ci·no'sis *pl.* -ses'
an'i·an'thi·nop'sy
an'ic·ter'ic
a·nid'e·us
a·nid'i·an
an'i·ler'i·dine'
an'i·lide'
an'i·line'
a'ni·lin'gus
an'il·ism
a·nil'i·ty
an'i·ma
an'i·mal'cule'
an'i·mal'cu·lum *pl.* -la
an'i·ma mun'di'
an'i·ma'tion
an'i·ma·tism
an'i·mus *(feeling of hatred)*
♦anomous
an'i'on
an'i·on'ic
an'i·rid'i·a
an'i·sa·ki'a·sis *pl.* -ses'
an'ise
an'is·ei·kom'e·ter
an'is·ei·ko'ni·a
an'is·ei·kon'ic
an·i'so·chro·ma'si·a
an·i'so·chro·mat'ic
an·i'so·chro'mi·a
an·i'so·chro'mic
an·i'so·co'ri·a
an·i'so·cy·to'sis *pl.* -ses'
an·i'so·dac'ty·lous
an·i'so·dont'
an·i'so·g'a·mous
an·i'so·g'a·my

an′i•sog′na•thous
an′i•so•gyn′e•co•mas′ti•a
an•i′so•kar′y•o′sis *pl.* -ses′
an•i′so•mas′ti•a
an•i′so•me′li•a
an•i′so•mer′ic
an•i′so•met′rope′
an•i′so•me•tro′pi•a
an•i′so•me•trop′ic
an•i′so•mor′phic
an•i′so•mor′phous
an•i′so•my′cin
an•i′so•nu′cle•o′sis *pl.* -ses′
an•i′so•pho′ri•a
an′i•so′pi•a
an•i′so•poi•kil′o•cy•to′sis
   pl. -ses′
an•i′so•sphyg′mi•a
an•i′so•sthen′ic
an•i′so•ton′ic
an•i′so•trop′ic
an•i′so•tro′pine′ meth′yl•
   bro′mide′
an′i•sot′ro•py
an′i•su′ri•a
a′ni•trog′e•nous
A•nitsch′kow′ cell
an′kle
an′ky•lo•bleph′a•ron′
an′ky•lo•chei′li•a *also* anky-
   lochilia
an′ky•lo•chi′li•a *var. of* an-
   kylocheilia
an′ky•lo•col′pos′
an′ky•lo•dac•tyl′i•a
an′ky•lo•dac′ty•ly
an′ky•lo•glos′si•a
an′ky•lose′, -losed, -los′ing
an′ky•lo′sis *pl.* -ses′
an′ky•lo•sto•mi′a•sis *pl.*
   -ses′
an′ky•lo′ti•a
an′ky•lot′ic
an′ky•lot′o•my
an′la′ge *pl.* -la′gen *or* -la′ges
An•nam′ ulcer
an•neal′
an•nec′tent
   —— gy′ri′
an′ne•lid
An•nel′i•da
an′ne•lism
an•nex′a
an′nex•i′tis
an′nu•lar
an′nu•late′
an′nu•lose′

an′nu•lo•spi′ral
an′nu•lot′o•my
an′nu•lus *pl.* -li′
   —— ab•dom′i•na′lis
   —— cil′i•ar′is
   —— cru•ra′lis
   —— fem′o•ris
   —— fi′bro•car′ti•la•gin′e•us
mem•bra′nae′ tym′pa•ni′
   —— fi•bro′sus
   —— fibrosus fi′bro•car′ti•
lag′i•nis in′ter•ver′te•bra′lis
   —— in′gui•na′lis ab•dom′i•
na′lis
   —— inguinalis sub′cu•ta′ne•
us
   —— i′ri•dis major
   —— iridis minor
   —— mi′grans′
   —— of Zinn
   —— o•va′lis
   —— ten•din′e•us com•mu′nis
   —— tym•pan′i•cus
   —— um•bil′i•ca′lis
   —— u′re•thra′lis
an′o•chro•ma′si•a
a•no′ci•as•so′ci•a′tion
a•no′ci•the′si•a
a′no•coc•cyg′e•al
a′no•cu•ta′ne•ous
an•o′dal
an′ode′
an′o•der′mous
an•od′ic
an•od′i•nous
an•od′mi•a
an′o•don′ti•a
an′o•dyne′
an′o•dyn′i•a
an•o′e′si•a
an•o•et′ic
a′no•gen′i•tal
a•noi′a
a•nom′a•lo•scope′
a•nom′a•lous
a•nom′a•ly
an′o•mer
a•no′mi•a
a•nom′ic
an′o•mous *(without shoul-*
   ders)
♦animus
an′o•nych′i•a
an′o•op′si•a
a′no•pel′vic
a′no•per′i•ne′al
A•noph′e•les′

   —— al′bi•man′us
   —— ar′gy•ri•tar′sis
   —— cru′ci•ans′
   —— cul′li•ci•fa′ci•es′
   —— dar•lin′gi′
   —— gam′bi•ae′
   —— hyr•ca′nus
   —— mac′u•li•pen′nis
   —— quad′ri•mac′u•la′tus
a•noph′e•li•cide′
a•noph′e•li•fuge′
A•noph′e•li′ni′
an′o•pho′ri•a
an′oph•thal′mi•a
an′oph•thal′mic
an′oph•thal′mos′
an•o′pi•a
a′no•plas′ty
An′o•plu′ra
an•op′si•a
an•or′chi•a
an•or′chism
an•or′chous *(without testes)*
♦anorchus
an•or′chus *(an individual*
   without testes)
♦anorchous
a′no•rec′tal
an′o•rec′tic
a′no•rec′to•plas′ty
an′o•rec′tous
a′no•rec′tum
an′o•rex′i•a
   —— ner•vo′sa
an′o•rex′i•ant
an′o•rex′ic
an′o•rex′i•gen′ic
an•or•gas′mi•a
an•or′gas′my
an•or•thog′ra•phy
an•or•tho′pi•a
a′no•scope′
a•nos′co•py
an•os′mi•a
an•os′mic
a′no•sog•no′si•a
a′no•spi′nal
an•os•te•o•pla′sia
an•os•to′sis *pl.* -ses′
an•o′ti•a
an′o•tro′pi•a
an•o′tus
a′no•vag′i•nal
a′no•ves′i•cal
an•o′vu•lar
an•o′vu•la•to′ry
an′ox•e′mic

an·ox′i·a
a·nox′ic
An′rep′ effect
an′sa pl. -sae′
—— cer′vi·ca′lis
—— hy′po·glos′si′
—— len·tic′u·lar′is
—— len′ti·for′mis
—— ner′vi′ hy′po·glos′si′
—— of Vieus′sens
—— pe·dun′cu·lar′is
—— sa·cra′lis
—— sub·cla′vi·a
—— vit′el·li′na
an′sae′
—— ner′vi′ spi·na′lis
—— ner·vo′rum spi·na′li·um
an′sate′
an′si·form′
ant·ac′id
an·tag′o·nism
an·tag′o·nist
an·tag′o·nis′tic
ant·al′ka·line′
ant·aph′ro·dis′i·ac′
ant′ar·thrit′ic
ant′asth·mat′ic
an·taz′o·line′
an′te·bra′chi·al
an′te·bra′chi·um pl. -chi·a
an′te ci′bum
an′te·cu′bi·tal
an′te·cur′va·ture
an′te·flect′
an′te·flex′ion
an′te·hy·poph′y·sis pl. -ses′
an′te mor′tem
an′te·na′tal
an·ten′na pl. -nae′ or -nas
an′te·par′tum
an·te′ri·ad′
an·te′ri·or
an′ter·o·col′lis
an′ter·o·dor′sal
an′ter·o·ex·ter′nal
an′ter·o·grade′
an′ter·o·in·fe′ri·or
an′ter·o·in·te′ri·or
an′ter·o·in·ter′nal
an′ter·o·lat′er·al
an′ter·o·me′di·al
an′ter·o·me′di·an
an′ter·o·pa·ri′e·tal
an′ter·o·pi·tu′i·tar′y
an′ter·o·pos·te′ri·or
an′ter·o·su·pe′ri·or
an′ter·o·trans·verse′

an′te·vert′
an′te·vert′ed
an′te·ver′sion
ant·he′lix
ant′hel·min′tic
an′thel·my′cin
an′the·lone′
an·the′ma pl. -mas or -ma·ta
an′ther
an′tho·cy′a·nin
an′tho·cy′a·ni·nu′ri·a
An′tho·my′ia
An′tho·ny stain
an′thra·ce′mi·a
an′thra·cene′
an′thra·ci′dal
an′thra·coid′
an′thra·co·ne·cro′sis pl. -ses′
an′thra·co·sil′i·co′sis pl. -ses′
an′thra·co′sis pl. -ses′
an′thra·cot′ic
an′thra·lin
an′thra·nil′ic
an′thra·nol′
an′thra·qui·none′
an′thra·ro′bin
an′thrax′ pl. -thra·ces′
an′thro·poid′
An′thro·poi′de·a
an′thro·pol′o·gy
an′thro·po·met′ric
an′thro·po·mor′phic
an′thro·po·mor′phism
an′thro·poph′a·gy
an′thro·po·phil′ic
an′thro·po·pho′bi·a
an′ti·a·bor′ti·fa′cient
an′ti·ad′re·ner′gic
an′ti·ag·glu′ti·nat′ing
an′ti·ag·glu′ti·nin
an′ti·ag·gres′sin
an′ti·al′bu·mate′
an′ti·al·bu′min
an′ti·al·bu′mi·nate′
an′ti·a·lex′in
an′ti·am′bo·cep′tor
an′ti·a·me′bic var. of anti-
    amoebic
an′ti·a·moe′bic also anti-
    amebic
an′ti·am′y·lase′
an′ti·an′a·phy·lac′tin
an′ti·an′a·phy·lax′is pl.
    -lax′es′
an′ti·an′dro·gen

an′ti·a·ne′mic
an′ti·an′ti·bod′y
an′ti·an′ti·dote′
an′ti·an′ti·tox′in
an′ti·ar·ach·nol′y·sin
an′ti·a·rin
an′ti·a′ris
an′ti·ar·rhyth′mic
an′ti·ar·thrit′ic
an′ti·asth·mat′ic
an′ti·bac·te′ri·al
an′ti·bi·o′sis pl. -ses′
an′ti·bi·ot′ic
an′ti·blas′tic
an′ti·blen′nor·rhag′ic
an′ti·bod′y
an′ti·car·cin′o·gen
an′ti·car′i·o·gen′ic
an′ti·cat′a·lyst
an′ti·cat′a·lyz′er
an′ti·ca·thex′is
an′ti·ceph′a·lin
an′ti·chei·rot′o·nus
an′ti·cho·les′ter·e′mic
an′ti·cho′lin·er′gic
an′ti·cho′lin·es′ter·ase′
an′ti·clin′al
an′ti·co·ag′u·lant
an′ti·co·ag′u·la·tive
an′ti·co·ag′u·lin
an′ti·co′don′
an′ti·col′la·gen·ase′
an′ti·com′ple·ment
an′ti·com′ple·men′ta·ry
an′ti·con·cep′tive
an′ti·con·vul′sant
an′ti·con·vul′sive
an·ti·cus
an′ti·cu′tin
an′ti·cy′to·tox′in
an′ti·de·pres′sant
an′ti·di·a′bet′ic
an′ti·di′ar·rhe′al
an′ti·di·u′re′sis pl. -ses′
an′ti·di·u·ret′ic
an′ti·di·u·ret′in
an′ti·dot′al
an′ti·dote′
an′ti·drom′ic
an′ti·dys′en·ter′ic
an′ti·ec′ze·mat′ic
an′ti·e·dem′a·tous
an′ti·e·met′ic
an′ti·en′zyme′
an′ti·ep′i·lep′tic
an′ti·es′tro·gen
an′ti·fe′brile

an'ti·fer'ment
an'ti·fer·men'ta·tive
an'ti·fi·bril'la·to'ry
an'ti·fi'bri·nol'y·sin
an'ti·fi'bri·no·lyt'ic
an'ti·fi·lar'i·al
an'ti·flat'u·lent
an'ti·flux'
an'ti·fun'gal
an'ti·ga·lac'tic
an'ti·gen
an'ti·gen'ic
an'ti·ge·nic'i·ty
an'ti·glob'u·lin
an'ti·go·nad'o·trop'ic
an'ti·gon'or·rhe'ic
an'ti·hal·lu'ci·na·to'ry
an'ti·he'lix
an'ti·he·mol'y·sin
an'ti·he'mo·lyt'ic
an'ti·he'mo·phil'ic
an'ti·hem'or·rhag'ic
an'ti·hem'or·rhoi'dal
an'ti·hi·drot'ic
an'ti·his'ta·mine'
an'ti·his'ta·min'ic
an'ti·hor'mone'
an'ti·hy'a·lu·ron'i·dase'
an'ti·hy·drop'ic
an'ti·hy'per·cho·les'ter·ol·
  e'mic
an'ti·hy'per·gly·ce'mic
an'ti·hy'per·ten'sive
an'ti·hyp·not'ic
an'ti-ic·ter'ic
an'ti-im·mune'
an'ti-in·fec'tious
an'ti-in·fec'tive
an'ti-in·flam'ma·to'ry
an'ti-i'so·ly'sin
an'ti·ken'o·tox'in
an'ti·ke'to·gen
an'ti·ke'to·gen'e·sis pl. -ses'
an'ti·ke'to·gen'ic
an'ti·lac'tase'
an'ti·le·thar'gic
an'ti·leu·ke'mic
an'ti·leu'ko·ci'din
an'ti·leu'ko·cyt'ic
an'ti·lew'is·ite'
an'ti·li'pase'
an'ti·li·pe'mic
an'ti·lip·fan'o·gen
an'ti·lip'o·tro'pic
an'ti·lu·et'ic
an'ti·lym'pho·cyt'ic
an'ti·ly'sin

an'ti·ly'sis pl. -ses'
an'ti·lyt'ic
an'ti·ma·lar'i·al
an'ti·mel'lin
an'ti·me·nin'go·coc'cic
an'ti·men'or·rha'gic
an'ti·mere'
an'ti·mes'en·ter'ic
an'ti·me·tab'o·lite'
an'ti·me·tro'pi·a
an'ti·mi·cro'bi·al
an'ti·mo'nic
an'ti·mo'nous
an'ti·mo'ny
an'ti·mo'nyl
an'ti·mu'ta·gen
an'ti·my'cin
an'ti·my·cot'ic
an'ti·nar·cot'ic
an'ti·nau'se·ant
an'ti·ne'o·plas'tic
an'ti·ne·phrit'ic
an'ti·neu·ral'gic
an'ti·neu·rit'ic
an·tin'i·ad'
an·tin'i·al
an·tin'i·on'
an'ti·no'ci·cep'tive
an'ti·nu'cle·ar
an'ti·o'don·tal'gic
an'ti·on·cot'ic
an'ti·oph·thal'mic
an'ti·op'so·nin
an'ti·o'vu·la·to'ry
an'ti·oph·thal'mic
an'ti·ox'i·dant
an'ti·par'a·lyt'ic
an'ti·par'a·sit'ic
an'ti·par'kin·so'ni·an
an'ti·pep'sin
an'ti·pep'tone'
an'ti·pe·ri'od·ic
an'ti·per'i·stal'sis pl. -ses'
an'ti·per'i·stal'tic
an'ti·phag'o·cyt'ic
an'ti·phlo·gis'tic
an'ti·phone'
an'ti·phthi'ri·ac'
an'ti·plas'min
an'ti·plas'tic
an'ti·pneu'mo·coc'cic
an·tip'o·dal
an'ti·pode' pl. an·tip'o·des'
an'ti·pros'tate'
an'ti·pros'ta·ti'tis
an'ti·pro·throm'bin
an'ti·pro'to·zo'al

an'ti·pro'to·zo'an
an'ti·pru·rit'ic
an'ti·pso·ri'at'ic
an'ti·psy·chot'ic
an'ti·py'o·gen'ic
an'ti·py·re'sis
an'ti·py·ret'ic
an'ti·py'rine
an'ti·rab'ic
an'ti·ra·chit'ic
an'ti·ren'nin
an'ti·re·tic'u·lar
an'ti·rheu·mat'ic
an'ti·sca·be'tic
an'ti·schis'to·so'mal
an'ti·scor·bu'tic
an'ti·seb'or·rhe'ic
an'ti·se'cre·to'ry
an'ti·sep'sis pl. -ses'
an'ti·sep'tic
an'ti·se'ro·to'nin
an'ti·se'rum pl. -rums or -ra
an'ti·si·al'a·gogue'
an'ti·si·al'ic
an'ti·so'cial
an'ti·spas·mod'ic
an'ti·spas'tic
an'ti·spi'ro·che'tic
an'ti·staph'y·lol'y·sin
an'ti·ste·ril'i·ty
an'ti·ster'num
an'ti·strep'to·coc'cic
an'ti·strep'to·dor'nase'
an'ti·strep'to·he·mol'y·sin
an'ti·strep'to·ki'nase'
an'ti·strep·tol'y·sin
an'ti·su'do·ral
an'ti·su'do·rif'ic
an'ti·syph'i·lit'ic
an'ti·te·tan'ic
an'ti·the'nar
an'ti·ther'mic
an'ti·throm'bin
an'ti·throm'bo·plas'tin
an'ti·tox'ic
an'ti·tox'i·gen
an'ti·tox'in
an'ti·trag'ic
an'ti·tra'gus
an'ti·trich'o·mo'nal
an'ti·tris'mus
an'ti·trope'
an'ti·try·pan'o·so'mal
an'ti·tryp'sin
an'ti·tryp'tase'
an'ti·tus'sive
an'ti·ty'phoid'

an'ti·u're·ase'
an'ti·ven'ene'
an'ti·ve·ne're·al
an'ti·ven'in
an'ti·ven'om
an'ti·vi'ral
an'ti·vi·rot'ic
an'ti·vir'u·lin
an'ti·vi'rus
an'ti·vi'ta·min
an'ti·xen'ic
an'ti·xe'roph·thal'mic
an'ti·xe·rot'ic
an'ti·zy·mot'ic
ant'lo·pho'bi·a
An'ton' syndrome
an'tra·cele' var. of antrocele
an'tral
an·trec'to·my
an·tri'tis
an'tro·at'ti·cot'o·my
an'tro·cele' also antracele
an'tro·na'sal
an'tro·phose'
an'tro·scope'
an·tros'co·py
an·tros'to·my
an·trot'o·my
an'tro·tym·pan'ic
an'trum pl. -trums or -tra
—— car·di'a·cum
—— mas·toi'de·um
—— of High'more'
—— py·lo'ri·cum
—— tym·pan'i·cum
a·nu'cle·ar
a'nu·cle'o·lar
an'u·li'
—— fi·bro'si' cor'dis
an'u·lus pl. -li'
—— con'junc·ti'vae'
—— fem'o·ra'lis
—— fi'bro·car'ti·la·gin'e·us
mem·bra'nae' tym'pa·ni'
—— fi·bro'sus dis'ci' in'ter·
ver'te·bra'lis
—— in'gui·na'lis pro·fun'dus
—— inguinalis su'per·fi'ci·
a'lis
—— i'ri·dis major
—— iridis minor
—— ten·din'e·us com·mu'nis
—— tym·pan'i·cus
—— um'bil·i·ca'lis
an'u·re'sis pl. -ses'
an'u·ret'ic

an·u'ri·a (failure of urinary
function)
♦aneuria
an·u'ric (pertaining to an-
uria)
♦aneuric
an·u'rous
an'u·ry
a'nus pl. a'nus·es or a'ni'
—— vag'i·na'lis
—— ves'i·ca'lis
—— vul'vo·vag'i·na'lis
an'vil
anx·i'e·tas'
—— pre'se·ni'lus
—— tib'i·ar'um
a·or'ta pl. -tas or -tae'
—— ab·dom'i·na'lis
—— as·cen'dens
—— de·scen'dens
—— of Val·sal'va
—— tho'ra·ca'lis
—— tho·rac'i·ca
a·or'tal
a'or·tal'gi·a
a·or'tic
a·or'ti·co·pul'mo·nar'y
a·or'ti·co·pul·mon'ic
a·or'ti·co·re'nal
a'or·ti'tis
a·or'to·gram'
a·or'to·graph'ic
a'or·tog'ra·phy
a·or'to·il'i·ac'
a'or·tot'o·my
a·pan'cre·a
a·pan'cre·at'ic
ap·an'dri·a
ap'an·thro'pi·a
a·par'a·lyt'ic
ap'ar·thro'sis pl. -ses'
a·pas'ti·a
a·pas'tic
ap'a·thet'ic
a·path'ic
ap'a·thism
ap'a·thy
ap'a·tite' (phosphate)
♦appetite
ap·at'ro·pine'
ap'a·zone'
ap'ei·do'sis pl. -ses'
a·pel'lous
Ap'elt test
a·pe'ri·ent
a·pe'ri·od'ic
a·per'i·os'te·al

a·per'i·stal'sis pl. -ses'
a·per'i·tive
Ap'ert syndrome
ap'er·tu'ra pl. -rae'
—— aq'ue·duc'tus coch'le·
ae'
—— ex·ter'na aq'uae·
duc'tus ves·tib'u·li'
—— externa aq'ue·duc'tus
ves·tib'u·li'
—— externa can'a·lic'u·li'
coch'le·ae'
—— inferior can'a·lic'u·li'
tym·pan'i·ci'
—— lat'er·a'lis ven·tric'u·li'
quar'ti'
—— me'di·a'lis ven·tric'u·li'
quar'ti'
—— me'di·a'na ven·tric'u·li'
quar'ti'
—— pel'vis inferior
—— pelvis superior
—— pir'i·for'mis
—— si'nus fron·ta'lis
—— sinus sphe'noi·da'lis
—— superior can'a·lic'u·li'
tym·pan'i·ci'
—— tho·ra'cis inferior
—— thoracis superior
—— tym·pan'i·ca can'a·lic'u·
li' chor'dae'
—— tympanica canaliculi
chordae tym'pa·ni'
ap'er·ture
a'pex' pl. a'pex'es or a'pi·ces'
—— au·ric'u·lae'
—— auriculae Dar'win·i'
—— cap'i·tis fib'u·lae'
—— ca·pit'u·lae' fib'u·lae'
—— car'ti·lag'i·nis ar'y·tae·
noi'de·ae'
—— cartilaginis ar'y·te·
noi'de·ae'
—— co·lum'nae' pos'te·ri·
o'ris
—— cor'dis
—— cor'nus pos·te'ri·o'ris
me·dul'lae' spi·na'lis
—— cus'pi·dis
—— lin'guae'
—— na'si'
—— os'sis sa'cri'
—— par'tis pe·tro'sae' os'sis
tem'po·ra'lis
—— pa·tel'lae'
—— pros'ta·tae'
—— pul·mo'nis

—— py·ram'i·dis os'sis
tem·po·ra'lis
—— rad'i·cis den'tis
su·pra·re·na'lis
(glan'du·lae' dex'trae')
—— ve·si'cae' u'ri·nar'i·ae'
Ap'gar' score
a·pha'gi·a
—— al·ge'ra
a·pha'gic
a·pha'ki·a
a·pha'ki·al
a·pha'kic
aph'a·lan'gi·a
aph'a·lan·gi'a·sis
a·pha'si·a
a·pha'sic
aph'e·lot'ic
a·phelx'i·a
a·phe'mi·a
a·phe'mic
Aph'i·o·chae'ta
a·pho'ni·a
—— par'a·no'i·ca
a·phon'ic
a'phose'
a·phra'si·a
a·phra'sic
a·phre'ni·a
aph'ro·dis'i·a
aph'ro·dis'i·ac'
aph'tha pl. -thae'
—— ep'i·zo·ot'i·ca
—— ser'pens
aph'thae' trop'i·cae'
aph·thenx'i·a
aph'thoid'
aph·thon'gi·a
aph·tho'sis pl. -ses'
aph'thous
ap'i·cal
a'pi·cec'to·my
a'pi·ce·ot'o·my
ap'i·ci'tis
ap'i·co·ec'to·my
ap'i·col'y·sis pl. -ses'
ap'i·cot'o·my
ap'i·ec'to·my
a'pi·o·ther'a·py
A'pis
—— mel·lif'er·a
a'pi·tox'in
A'pi·um
—— grav'e·o'lens
a'pla·cen'tal
ap'la·na'si·a
ap'la·nat'ic

a·plan'a·tism
a·pla'si·a
—— ax'i·a'lis ex'tra·cor'ti·
ca'lis con·gen'i·ta
a·plas'tic
a·pleu'ri·a
ap'ne·a
—— va'gi'
—— ve'ra
ap·neu'ma·to'sis
ap·neu'mi·a
ap·neu'sis pl. -ses'
ap·neus'tic
ap'o·at'ro·pine'
ap'o·cam·no'sis
ap'o·ce·no'sis
ap'o·chro·mat'ic
ap'o·co'de·ine
a·poc'o·pe'
ap'o·cop'tic
ap'o·crine
ap'o·cy·nam'a·rin
a·poc'y·nin
a·poc'y·num
ap'o·dal
a·po'di·a
ap'o·dous
ap'o·en'zyme'
ap'o·fer'ri·tin
ap'o·gam'i·a
a·pog'a·my
ap'o·gee
ap'o·kam·no'sis pl. -ses'
a·po'lar
ap'o·mix'i·a
ap'o·mix'is pl. -mix'es'
ap'o·mor'phine'
ap'o·myt·to'sis pl. -ses'
ap'o·neu·rec'to·my
ap'o·neu·ror'rha·phy
ap'o·neu·ro'sis pl. -ses'
—— ep'i·cra'ni·a'lis
—— lin'guae'
—— mus'cu·li' bi·cip'i·tis
bra'chi·i'
—— pal·mar'is
—— plan·tar'is
ap'o·neu·ro·si'tis
ap'o·neu·rot'ic
ap'o·neu·ro·tome'
ap'o·neu·rot'o·my
a·pon'ic
a·poph'y·se'al
a·poph'y·sis pl. -ses'
a·poph'y·si'tis
ap'o·plec'tic
ap'o·plec'ti·form'

ap'o·plex'y
ap'o·qui'nine'
ap'or·rhip'sis
ap'o·sid'er·in
ap'o·si'ti·a
ap'o·sit'ic
ap'o·some'
a·pos'ta·sis pl. -ses'
a·pos'thi·a
ap'o·trip'sis pl. -ses'
ap'o·zy'mase'
ap'pa·ra'tus pl. ap'pa·ra'tus
—— di'ges·to'ri·us
—— lac'ri·ma'lis
—— re·spi'ra·to'ri·us
—— u'ro·gen'i·ta'lis
ap'pend'age
ap'pend'age cell
ap'pen·dec'to·my
ap'pen·dic'e·al
ap·pen'di·cec'to·my
ap·pen'di·ces'
—— ep'i·plo'i·cae
—— ep'o·oph'o·ri'
—— ve·sic'u·lo'si' ep'o·
oph'o·ri'
ap·pen'di·ci'tis
—— o·blit'er·ans'
ap·pen'di·co·coele'
ap·pen'di·co·en'ter·os'to·
my
ap·pen'di·co'li·thi'a·sis pl.
-ses'
ap'pen·dic'u·lar
ap'pen·dic'u·late
ap·pen'dix pl. -dix·es or -di·
ces'
—— au·ric'u·lar'is
—— ep'i·di·dym'i·dis
—— fi·bro'sa hep'a·tis
—— tes'tis
—— ven·tric'u·li' la·ryn'gis
—— ver'mi·for'mis
ap'per·cep'tion
ap'per·cep'tive
ap'per·son'i·fi·ca'tion
ap'pe·stat'
ap'pe·tite' (desire)
♦apatite
ap'pla·nate'
ap'pla·na'tion
ap'pla·nom'e·ter
ap·pose', -posed', -pos'ing
ap·po·si'tion
ap·prox'i·mal
ap·prox'i·mate', -mat'ed,
-mat'ing

ap·prox′i·ma′tion
a·prac′tic
a·prax′i·a
a·prax′ic
ap′ro·bar′bi·tal′
a·proc′ti·a
a·proc′tous
ap′ros·ex′i·a
—— na·sa′lis
a′pros·o′pi·a
a·pros′o·pus
a·pro′ti·nin
ap·sel′a·phe′si·a
ap′si·thy′ri·a
ap·sych′i·a
Apt test
ap·ty·a′li·a
ap·ty′a·lism
a′pus
a·py′e·tous
a·pyk′no·mor′phous
a·py′rene′
a′py·ret′ic
a′py·rex′i·a
a′py·rex′i·al
aq′ua pl. -uae′ or -uas
—— re′gi·a
aq′ua·pho′bi·a
aq′ue·duct′
—— of Fal·lo′pi·us
—— of Syl′vi·us
aq′ue·duc′tal
aq′ue·duc′tus
—— cer′e·bri′
—— coch′le·ae′
—— ves·tib′u·li′
aq′ue·ous
ar′a·bic
ar′a·chid′ic
a·ra′chis
a·rach′ne·pho′bi·a
a·rach′nid
A·rach′ni·da
a·rach′nid·ism
ar′ach·ni′tis
a·rach′no·dac′ty·ly
a·rach′no·gas′tri·a
a·rach′noid′
ar′ach·noi′dal
ar′ach·noi′de·a
—— en·ceph′a·li′
—— spi·na′lis
ar′ach·noi′de·an
a·rach′noid·ism
a·rach′noid·i′tis
—— os·sif′i·cans′

a·rach′noid′-u·re′ter·os′to·
my
a·rach′no·ly′sin
A′ra·ka′wa test
A·ra′li·a
—— rac′e·mo′sa
A·ran′-Du·chenne′
—— dystrophy
—— syndrome
a·ra′ne·ism
a·ra′ne·ous
ar′a·no′tin
A·ran′ti·us
—— ligament
—— ventricle
a·ra′phi·a
ar′a·ro′ba
Ar′a test
ar·bo′re·ous
ar′bo·res′cent
ar′bo·ri·za′tion
ar′bor·vi′tae′
—— cer′e·bel′i′
ar′bo·vi′rus
ar′bu·tin
arc
ar·cade′
ar·ca′num pl. -na
ar′ca·tu′ra
arc de cer′cle
arch
ar·cha′ic
ar′che·go′ni·um pl. -ni·a
arch′en·ce·phal′ic
arch′en·ceph·a·lon′ pl. -la
arch′en·ter′ic
arch·en′ter·on′ pl. -ter·a
ar′che·o·ki·net′ic
ar′che·py′on′
ar′che·type′
ar′chi·coele′
ar′chi·gas′tru·la pl. -las or
-lae′
ar′chi·neph′ric
ar′chi·neph′ron′
ar′chi·pal′li·um
ar′chi·stome′
ar′chi·tec·ton′ic
ar′cho·plasm
ar′cho·plas′ma
ar′cho·plas′mic
ar·chu′si·a
ar′ci·form′
arc·ta′tion
ar′cu·al
ar′cu·ate′
ar′cu·a′tion

ar′cus pl. ar′cus
—— al′ve·o·lar′is man·dib′u·
lae′
—— alveolaris max·il′lae′
—— anterior at·lan′tis
—— a·or′tae′
—— car′ti·lag′i·nis cri·coi′de·
ae′
—— cos·ta′lis
—— cos·tar′um
—— den·ta′lis inferior
—— dentalis superior
—— glos′so·pal′a·ti′nus
—— il′i·o·pec·tin′e·us
—— ju′ve·ni′lis
—— lum′bo·cos·ta′lis lat′er·
a′lis
—— lumbocostalis me′di·
a′lis
—— pal′a·ti′ni′
—— pal′a·to·glos′sus
—— pal′a·to·pha·ryn′ge·us
—— pal·mar′is pro·fun′dus
—— palmaris su′per·fi′ci·
a′lis
—— pal′pe·bra′lis inferior
—— palpebralis superior
—— pe′dis lon′gi·tu′di·na′lis
—— pedis trans′ver·sa′lis
—— pha·ryn′go·pal′a·ti′nus
—— plan·tar′is
—— posterior at·lan′tis
—— pu′bis
—— se·ni′lis
—— senilis len′tis
—— su′per·cil′i·ar′is
—— tar′se·us inferior
—— tarseus superior
—— ten·din′e·us
—— tendineus fas′ci·ae′
pel′vis
—— tendineus mus′cu·li′
lev′a·to′ris a′ni′
—— tendineus musculi
so′le·i′
—— ve·no′si′ dig′i·ta′lis
—— ve·no′sus dor·sa′lis pe′-
dis
—— venosus jug′u·li′
—— venosus pal·mar′is pro·
fun′dus
—— venosus palmaris
su′per·fi′ci·a′lis
—— venosus plan·tar′is
—— ver′te·brae′
—— vo·lar′is pro·fun′dus
—— volaris su′per·fi′ci·a′lis

—— volaris ve•no′sus pro•
fun′dus
—— volaris venosus su′per•
fi′ci•a′lis
—— zy′go•mat′i•cus
ar′dent pulse
ar′e•a *pl.* -as *or* -ae′
—— a•cu′sti•ca
—— Cel′si′
—— cen•tra′lis
—— cho•roi′de•a
—— coch′le•ae′
—— cri•bro′sa me′di•a
—— cribrosa pa•pil′lae′ re•
na′lis
—— cribrosa superior
—— em′bry•o•na′lis
—— ger′mi•na•ti′va
—— in′ter•con′dy•lar′is anterior tib′i•ae′
—— intercondylaris posteri-
or tibiae
—— ner′vi′ fa′ci•a′lis
—— nu′da
—— o•pa′ca
—— par′a•ter′mi•na′lis
—— par′ol•fac•to′ri•a (Bro′-
cae′)
—— pel•lu′ci•da
—— pos•tre′ma
—— sub′cal•lo′sa
—— vas′cu•lo′sa
—— ves•tib′u•lar′is
—— vestibularis inferior
—— vestibularis superior
—— vit′el•li′na
ar′e•ae′
—— gas′tri•cae′
ar′e•a′ta
ar′e•a′tus
a′re•flex′i•a
a′re•gen′er•a′tion
a′re•gen′er•a•tive
a′re•gen′er•a•to′ry
ar′e•na′ceous
ar′ene′
ar′e•no•vi′rus group
a•re′o•la *pl.* -lae′ *or* -las
—— mam′mae′
—— pap′il•lar′is
a•re′o•lar
ar•gam′bly•o′pi•a
Ar′gas
—— per′si•cus
Ar•gas′i•dae′
ar•gen′taf•fin
ar•gen′tic

ar•gen′tum
ar′gil•la′ceous
ar′gi•nase′
ar′gi•nine′
ar′gi•ni•no•suc•cin′ic
ar′gi•ni•no•suc•cin′ic•ac′id•
u′ri•a
ar′gon′
Ar′gyll′ Rob′ert•son
—— pupil
—— sign
ar•gyr′i•a
ar•gyr′ic
ar•gy′ro•phil′
ar•gy•ro′sis *pl.* -ses′
Ar′i•as-Stel′la cells
a•ri′bo•fla′vin•o′sis *pl.* -ses′
ar′i•cine′
a•ris′to•gen′ic
a•ris′to•gen′ics
A•ris′to•lo′chi•a
—— re•tic′u•la′ta
—— ser′pen•tar′i•a
Ar′i•zo′na bacteria
ar′ky•o•chrome′
Arlt trachoma
arm
ar′ma•men•tar′i•um *pl.* -i•a
or -ums
Ar•man′ni-Eb′stein′ ne-
phropathy
Ar•me′ni•an disease
arm′pit′
Ar′neth
—— count
—— classification
—— formula
—— index
—— method
ar′ni•ca
Ar′nold
—— neuralgia
—— sterilizer
Ar′nold-Chi•ar′i
—— malformation
—— syndrome
Ar•noux′ sign
ar′o•mat′ic
a•rous′al
ar•rec′tor *pl.* ar′rec•to′res′
ar′rec•to′res′ pi•lo′rum
ar•rhe′no•blas•to′ma *pl.*
-mas *or* -ma•ta
ar•rhe′no•to′ci•a
ar′rhin•en′ce•pha′li•a
ar•rhin′i•a
ar•rhin′ic

ar•rhyth′mi•a
ar•rhyth′mic
ar′se•nate′
ar′se•nic
ar′se•nide′
ar′se•nite′
ar′se•no•cho′line′
ar′se•nous
ar′sen•ox′ide′
ar′sine′
ar′sin′ic
ar′son•val′i•za′tion
ars•phen′a•mine′
ars′thi•nol′
ar′ter•ec′to•my
ar•te′re•nol′
ar•te′ri•a *pl.* -ae′
—— ac′e•tab′u•li′
—— al′ve•o•lar′is inferior
—— alveolaris superior posterior
—— an′gu•lar′is
—— a•non′y•ma
—— ap′pen•dic′u•lar′is
—— ar′cu•a′ta pe′dis
—— as•cen′dens il′e•o•col′i•
ca
—— au′di•ti′va in•ter′na
—— au•ric′u•lar′is posterior
—— auricularis pro•fun′da
—— ax′il•lar′is
—— bas′il•lar′is
—— bra′chi•a′lis
—— brachialis su′per•fi′ci•
a′lis
—— buc•ca′lis
—— buc′ci•na•to′ri•a
—— bul′bi′ pe′nis
—— bulbi u•re′thrae′
—— bulbi ves•tib′u•li′
—— ca•na′lis pter′y•goi′de•i′
—— ca•rot′is com•mu′nis
—— carotis ex•ter′na
—— carotis in•ter′na
—— cau′dae′ pan•cre′a•tis
—— ce•ca′lis anterior
—— cecalis posterior
—— cen•tra′lis ret′i•nae′
—— cer′e•bel′li′ inferior anterior
—— cerebelli inferior posterior
—— cerebelli superior
—— cer′e•bri′ anterior
—— cerebri me′di•a
—— cerebri posterior
—— cer′vi•ca′lis as•cen′dens

—— cervicalis pro·fun′da
—— cervicalis su′per·fi′ci·
a′lis
—— cho′ri·oi′de·a
—— cho·roi′de·a anterior
—— cir′cum·flex′a fem′o·ris
lat′er·a′lis
—— circumflexa femoris
me′di·a′lis
—— circumflexa hu′mer·i′
anterior
—— circumflexa humeri
posterior
—— circumflexa il′i·i′ pro·
fun′da
—— circumflexa ilii su′per·
fi′ci·a′lis
—— circumflexa scap′u·lae′
—— coe·li′a·ca
—— col′i·ca dex′tra
—— colica me′di·a
—— colica si·nis′tra
—— col′lat′er·a′lis me′di·a
—— collateralis ra′di·a′lis
—— collateralis ul·nar′is inferior
—— collateralis ulnaris superior
—— com′i·tans′ ner′vi′
is′chi·ad′i·ci′
—— com·mu′ni·cans′ anteri-
or cer′e·bri′
—— communicans posterior
cerebri
—— cor′o·nar′i·a dex′tra
—— coronaria si·nis′tra
—— crem′a·ster′i·ca
—— cys′ti·ca
—— def′e·ren′ti·a′lis
—— dor·sa′lis cli·to′ri·dis
—— dorsalis na′si′
—— dorsalis pe′dis
—— dorsalis pe′nis
—— duc′tus def′e·ren′tis
—— ep′i·gas′tri·ca inferior
—— epigastrica su′per·fi′ci·
a′lis
—— epigastrica superior
—— eth′moi·da′lis anterior
—— ethmoidalis posterior
—— fa′ci·a′lis
—— fem′o·ra′lis
—— fib′u·lar′is
—— fron·ta′lis
—— gas′tri·ca dex′tra
—— gastrica si·nis′tra
—— gas′tro·du′o·de·na′lis

—— gas′tro·ep′i·plo′i·ca
dex′tra
—— gastroepiploica si·
nis′tra
—— gen′u inferior lat′er·
a′lis
—— genu inferior me′di·a′lis
—— genu me′di·a
—— ge′nus de·scen′dens
—— genus inferior lat′er·
a′lis
—— genus inferior me′di·
a′lis
—— genus me′di·a
—— genus superior lat′er·
a′lis
—— genus superior me′di·
a′lis
—— gen′u superior lat′er·
a′lis
—— genu superior me′di·
a′lis
—— genu su′pre′ma
—— glu′tae·a inferior
—— glutaea superior
—— glu′te·a inferior
—— glutea superior
—— haem′or·rhoi·da′lis inferior
—— haemorrhoidalis
me′di·a
—— haemorrhoidalis superi-
or
—— he·pat′i·ca
—— hepatica com·mu′nis
—— hepatica pro′pri·a
—— hy′a·loi′de·a
—— hy′po·gas′tri·ca
—— il′e·o·col′i·ca
—— i·li′a·ca com·mu′nis
—— iliaca ex·ter′na
—— iliaca in·ter′na
—— il′i·o·lum·ba′lis
—— in′fra·or′bi·ta′lis
—— in′ter·cos·ta′lis su·
pre′ma
—— in′ter·os′se·a anterior
—— interossea com·mu′nis
—— interossea dor·sa′lis
—— interossea posterior
—— interossea re·cur′rens
—— interossea vo′lar′is
—— la′bi·a′lis inferior
—— labialis superior
—— lab′y·rin′thi′
—— lac′ri·ma′lis
—— la·ryn′ge·a inferior

—— laryngea superior
—— li′e·na′lis
—— lig′a·men′ti′ te·re′tis
u′ter·i′
—— lin·gua′lis
—— lo′bi′ cau·da′ti′
—— lum·ba′lis i′ma
—— mal′le·o·lar′is anterior
lat′er·a′lis
—— malleolaris anterior
me′de·a′lis
—— malleolaris posterior
lat′er·a′lis
—— malleolaris posterior
me′di·a′lis
—— mam·mar′i·a in′ter′na
—— mas′se·ter′i·ca
—— max′il·lar′is
—— maxillaris ex·ter′na
—— maxillaris in·ter′na
—— me′di·a′na
—— me·nin′ge·a anterior
—— meningea me′di·a
—— meningea posterior
—— men·ta′lis
—— mes′en·ter′i·ca inferior
—— mesenterica superior
—— mus′cu·lo·phren′i·ca
—— nu·tri′ci·a fem′or·is inferior
—— nutricia femoris superi-
or
—— nutricia fib′u·lae′
—— nutricia hu′mer·i′
—— nutricia tib′i·ae′
—— ob′tu·ra·to′ri·a
—— obturatoria ac′ces·
so′ri· a
—— oc·cip′i·ta′lis
—— oph·thal′mi·ca
—— o·var′i·ca
—— pal′a·ti′na a·scen′dens
—— palatina de·scen′dens
—— palatina major
—— pan′cre·at′i·ca dor·sa′lis
—— pancreatica inferior
—— pancreatica mag′na
—— pan′cre·at′i·co·du′o·de·
na′lis inferior
—— pancreaticoduodenalis
superior
—— pe′nis
—— per′fo·rans′ pri′ma
—— perforans se·cun′da
—— perforans ter′ti·a
—— per′i·car·di′a·co·phren′i·
ca

—— per'i·ne·a'lis
—— per'i·ne'i'
—— per·o·ne'a
—— pha·ryn'ge·a a·scen'dens
—— phren'i·ca inferior
—— plan·tar'is lat'er·a'lis
—— plantaris me'di·a'lis
—— pop·lit'e·a
—— prin'ceps' pol'li·cis
—— pro·fun'da bra·chi·i'
—— profunda cli·to'ri·dis
—— profunda fem'o·ris
—— profunda lin'guae'
—— profunda pe'nis
—— pu·den'da in·ter'na
—— pul'mo·na'lis
—— pulmonalis dex'tra
—— pulmonalis si·nis'tra
—— ra'di·a'lis
—— radialis in'di·cis
—— rec·ta'lis inferior
—— rectalis me'di·a
—— rectalis superior
—— re·cur'rens ra'di·a'lis
—— recurrens tib'i·a'lis anterior
—— recurrens tibialis posterior
—— recurrens ul·nar'is
—— re·na'lis
—— sa·cra'lis lat'er·a'lis
—— sacralis me'di·a
—— sacralis me'di·a'na
—— scap'u·lar'is de·scen'dens
—— scapularis dor·sa'lis
—— seg·men'ti' an·te'ri·o'ris
—— segmenti anterioris in·fe'ri·o'ris
—— segmenti anterioris su·pe'ri·o'ris
—— segmenti in·fe'ri·o'ris
—— segmenti lat'er·a'lis
—— segmenti me'di·a'lis
—— segmenti pos·te'ri·o'ris
—— segmenti su·pe'ri·o'ris
—— sper·mat'i·ca ex·ter'na
—— spermatica in·ter'na
—— sphe'no·pal'a·ti'na
—— spi·na'lis anterior
—— spinalis posterior
—— ster'no·clei'do·mas·toi'de·a
—— sty'lo·mas·toi'de·a
—— sub·cla'vi·a
—— sub'cos·ta'lis

—— sub'lin·gua'lis
—— sub'men·ta'lis
—— sub·scap'u·lar'is
—— su'pra·or'bi·ta'lis
—— su'pra·re·na'lis inferior
—— suprarenalis me'di·a
—— suprarenalis superior
—— su'pra·scap'u·lar'is
—— su'pra·troch'le·ar'is
—— tar'se·a lat'er·a'lis
—— tem'po·ra'lis me'di·a
—— temporalis pro·fun'da anterior
—— temporalis profunda posterior
—— temporalis su'per·fi'ci·a'lis
—— tes·tic'u·lar'is
—— tho'ra·ca'lis lat'er·a'lis
—— thoracalis su·pre'ma
—— tho·rac'i·ca in·ter'na
—— thoracica lat'er·a'lis
—— thoracica su·pre'ma
—— tho'ra·co·a·cro'mi·a'lis
—— tho'ra·co·dor·sa'lis
—— thy're·oi'de·a i'ma
—— thyreoidea inferior
—— thyreoidea superior
—— thy·roi'de·a i'ma
—— thyroidea inferior
—— thyroidea superior
—— tib'i·a'lis anterior
—— tibialis posterior
—— trans·ver'sa col'li'
—— transversa fa'ci·e'i'
—— transversa scap'u·lae'
—— tym·pan'i·ca anterior
—— tympanica inferior
—— tympanica posterior
—— tympanica superior
—— ul·nar'is
—— um·bil'i·ca'lis
—— u're·thra'lis
—— u·ter·i'na
—— vag'i·na'lis
—— ver'te·bra'lis
—— ves'i·ca'lis inferior
—— vesicalis superior
—— vo·lar'is in'di·cis ra'di·a'lis
—— zy'go·mat'i·co·or'bi·ta'lis

ar·te'ri·ae'
—— al've·o·lar'es' su·pe'ri·o'res' an·te'ri·o'res'
—— ar'ci·for'mes'
—— ar·cu·a'tae' re'nis

—— bron'chi·a'les'
—— cer'e·bri'
—— cil'i·ar'es' an·te'ri·o'res'
—— ciliares pos·te'ri·o'res' brev'es'
—— ciliares posteriores lon'gae'
—— con·junc'ti·va'les' an·te'ri·o'res'
—— conjunctivales pos·te'ri·o'res'
—— dig'i·ta'les' dor·sa'les ma'nus
—— digitales dorsales pe'dis
—— digitales pal·mar'es' com·mu'nes'
—— digitales palmares pro'pri·ae'
—— digitales plan·tar'es' com·mu'nes'
—— digitales plantares pro'pri·ae'
—— digitales vo·lar'es' com·mu'nes'
—— digitales volares pro'pri·ae'
—— ep'i·scle·ra'les'
—— gas'tri·cae' brev'es'
—— hel'i·ci'nae' pe'nis
—— il'e·ae'
—— il'e·i'
—— in'ter·cos·ta'les' pos·te·ri·o'res' I et II
—— intercostales posteriores III–XI
—— in'ter·lo·bar'es' re'nis
—— in'ter·lob'u·lar'es' hep'a·tis
—— interlobulares re'nis
—— in·tes'ti·na'les'
—— je'ju·na'les'
—— la'bi·a'les' an·te'ri·o'res' pu·den'di' mu'li·e'bris
—— labiales pos·te'ri·o'res' pu·den'di' mu'li·e'bris
—— lum·ba'les'
—— me'di·as'ti·na'les' an·te'ri·o'res'
—— met'a·car'pe·ae' dor·sa'les'
—— metacarpeae pal·mar'es'
—— metacarpeae vo·lar'es'
—— met'a·tar'se·ae' dor·sa'les'
—— metatarseae plan·tar'es'

—— na·sa'les' pos·te'ri·
o'res', lat'er·a'les', et sep'ti'
—— nu·tri'ci·ae' hu'mer·i'
—— nutriciae pel'vis re·
na'lis
—— oe'so·pha'ge·ae'
—— pal'a·ti'nae' mi·no'res'
—— pal'pe·bra'les' lat'er·
a'les'
—— palpebrales me'di·a'les'
—— pan'cre·at'i·co·du'o·de·
na'les' in·fe'ri·o'res'
—— per'fo·ran'tes'
—— phren'i·cae' in·fe'ri·
o'res'
—— phrenicae su·pe'ri·o'res'
—— rec'ur·ren'tes' ul·nar'es'
—— re'nis
—— ret'ro·du'o·de·na'les'
—— sa·cra'les' lat'er·a'les'
—— scro·ta'les' an·te'ri·
o'res'
—— scrotales pos·te'ri·o'res'
—— sig·moi'de·ae'
—— su'pra·du'o·de·na'les'
su·pe'ri·o'res'
—— su·ra'les'
—— tar'se·ae' me'di·a'les'
—— tem'po·ra'les' pro·
fun'dae'
—— thy'mi·cae'
—— ves'i·ca'les' in·fe'ri·
o'res'
—— vesicales su·pe'ri·o'res'
ar·te'ri·al
—— arc of Ri'o·lan'
ar·te'ri·al·i·za'tion
ar'te·ri·a'sis pl. -ses'
ar·te'ri·ec'ta·sis pl. -ses'
ar·te'ri·ec'to·my
ar·te'ri·ec·to'pi·a
ar·te'ri·o·cap'il·lar'y
ar·te'ri·o·fi·bro'sis pl. -ses'
ar·te'ri·o·gram'
ar·te'ri·o·graph'
ar·te'ri·og'ra·phy
ar·te'ri·o'la pl. -lae'
—— mac'u·lar'is inferior
—— macularis superior
—— me'di·a'lis ret'i·nae'
—— na·sa'lis ret'i·nae' inferior
—— nasalis retinae superior
—— rec'ta
—— tem'po·ra'lis ret'i·nae'
inferior

—— temporalis retinae su-
perior
ar·te'ri·o'lae' rec'tae' re'-
nis
ar·te'ri·o'lar
ar·te'ri·ole'
ar·te'ri·o·lith'
ar·te'ri·o·lith'ic
ar·te'ri·o·li'tis
ar·te'ri·o·lo·ne·cro'sis pl.
-ses'
ar·te'ri·o·lo·ne·crot'ic
ar·te'ri·o·lo·scle·ro'sis pl.
-ses'
ar·te'ri·o·lo·scle·rot'ic
ar·te'ri·o·ma·la'ci·a
ar·te'ri·o·mes'en·ter'ic
ar·te'ri·o·ne·cro'sis pl. -ses'
ar·te'ri·op'a·thy
ar·te'ri·o·plas'tic
ar·te'ri·o·plas'ty
ar·te'ri·o·pres'sor
ar·te'ri·o·punc'ture
ar·te'ri·o·re'nal
ar·te'ri·or'rha·phy
ar·te'ri·or·rhex'is pl.
-rhex'es'
ar·te'ri·o·scle·ro'sis pl. -ses'
—— o·blit'er·ans'
ar·te'ri·o·scle·rot'ic
ar·te'ri·o·spasm
ar·te'ri·o·spas'tic
ar·te'ri·o·ste·no'sis pl. -ses'
ar·te'ri·os·to'sis pl. -ses'
ar·te'ri·o·strep'sis pl. -ses'
ar·te'ri·o·tome'
ar·te'ri·ot'o·my
ar·te'ri·o·ve'nous
ar·te'ri·o·ver'sion
ar·te'ri'tis
—— de·for'mans'
—— o·blit'er·ans'
ar'ter·y
ar·thral'gi·a
—— hys·ter'i·ca
—— sat'ur·ni'na
ar·thral'gic
ar·threc'to·my
ar'thres·the'si·a
ar'thri·flu'ent
ar·thrit'ic
ar·thri'tis
—— de·for'mans'
—— deformans ju've·ni'lis
—— fun·go'sa
—— u're·thrit'i·ca
ar'thro·cele'

ar'thro·cen·te'sis pl. -ses'
ar'thro·chon·dri'tis
ar'thro·cla'si·a
ar'thro·cla'sis pl. -ses'
ar'thro·de'si·a
ar'thro·de'sis pl. -ses'
ar·thro'di·a pl. -ae'
ar·thro'di·al
ar'thro·dyn'i·a
ar'thro·dyn'ic
ar'thro·dys·pla'si·a
ar'thro·em·py'e·sis pl. -ses'
ar'thro·en·dos'co·py
ar'thro·e·rei'sis
ar'thro·gram'
ar·throg'ra·phy
ar'thro·gry·po'sis pl. -ses'
—— mul'ti·plex' con·gen'i·ta
ar'thro·ka·tad'y·sis pl. -ses'
ar'thro·lith'
ar'thro·li·thi'a·sis pl. -ses'
ar·throl'o·gy
ar·throl'y·sis pl. -ses'
ar·throm'e·ter
ar·throm'e·try
ar·thron'cus
ar'thro·neu·ral'gi·a
ar'thro·on'y·cho·dys·
pla'si·a
ar'thro·os'te·o·on'y·cho·
dys·pla'si·a
ar'thro·path'ic
ar·throp'a·thy
ar'thro·phyte'
ar'thro·plas'tic
ar'thro·plas'ty
ar'thro·scle·ro'sis pl. -ses'
ar'thro·scope'
ar·thros'co·py
ar·thro'sis pl. -ses'
ar'thro·spore'
ar·thros'to·my
ar'thro·tome'
ar·throt'o·my
ar'thro·trop'ic
ar'throus
Ar'thur performance
scale
Ar'thus phenomenon
ar·tic'u·lar
ar·tic'u·lar'e'
ar·tic'u·lar'is gen'us
ar·tic'u·late', -lat'ed, -lat'ing
ar·tic'u·la'ti·o' pl. -la'ti·
o'nes'
—— a·cro'mi·o·cla·vic'u·
lar'is

—— at·lan'to·ax'i·a'lis lat'er·a'lis

—— atlantoaxialis me'di·a'na

—— at·lan'to·ep'i·stroph'i·ca

—— at·lan'to·oc·cip'i·ta'lis

—— cal·ca'ne·o·cu·boi'de·a

—— cap'i·tis cos'tae'

—— ca·pit'u·li'

—— car'po·met'a·car'pe·a pol'li·cis

—— coch'le·ar'is

—— com·pos'i·ta

—— con'dy·lar'is

—— cos'to·trans'ver·sar'i·a

—— co·tyl'i·ca

—— cox'ae'

—— cri'co·ar'y·tae·noi'de·a

—— cri'co·ar'y·te·noi'de·a

—— cri'co·thy're·oi'de·a

—— cri'co·thy·roi'de·a

—— cu'bi·ti'

—— cu'ne·o·na·vic'u·lar'is

—— el'lip·soi'de·a

—— gen'u

—— ge'nus

—— hu'mer·i'

—— hu'mer·o·ra'di·a'lis

—— hu'mer·o·ul·nar'is

—— in·cu'do·mal'le·ar'is

—— in·cu'do·mal'le·o·lar'is

—— in·cu'do·sta·pe'di·a

—— man·dib'u·lar'is

—— ma'nus

—— me'di·o·car'pe·a

—— os'sis pi'si·for'mis

—— pe'dis

—— pla'na

—— ra'di·o·car'pe·a

—— ra'di·o·ul·nar'is dis·ta'lis

—— radioulnaris prox'i·ma'lis

—— sac'ro·i·li·a'ca

—— sel·lar'is

—— sim'plex'

—— sphae·roi'de·a

—— sphe·roi'de·a

—— ster'no·cla·vic'u·lar'is

—— sub'ta·lar'is

—— ta'li' trans·ver'sa

—— ta'lo·cal·ca'ne·a

—— ta'lo·cal·ca'ne·o·na·vic'u·lar'is

—— ta'lo·cru·ra'lis

—— ta'lo·na·vic'u·lar'is

—— tar'si' trans·ver'sa

—— tem'po·ro·man·dib'u·lar'is

– —— tib'i·o·fib'u·lar'is

—— tro·choi'de·a

ar·tic'u·la'tion

ar·tic'u·la'ti·o'nes'

—— ca·pit'u·lo'rum cos·tar'um

—— car'po·met'a·car'pe·ae'

—— cos'to·chon·dra'les'

—— cos'to·ver'te·bra'les'

—— dig'i·to'rum ma'nus

—— digitorum pe'dis

—— in'ter·car'pe·ae'

—— in'ter·chon·dra'les'

—— interchondrales cos·tar'um

—— in'ter·met'a·car'pe·ae'

—— in'ter·met'a·tar'se·ae'

—— in'ter·pha·lan'ge·ae' ma'nus

—— interphalangeae pe'dis

—— in'ter·tar'se·ae'

—— ma'nus

—— met'a·car'po·pha·lan'ge·ae'

—— met'a·tar'so·pha·lan'ge·ae'

—— os'sic'u·lo'rum au·di'tus

—— pe'dis

—— ster'no·cos·ta'les'

—— tar'so·met'a·tar'se·ae'

ar·tic'u·la'tor

ar·tic'u·la·to'ry

ar·tic'u·lus pl. -li'

ar'ti·fact'

ar'ti·fi'cial

ar'y·ep'i·glot'tic

ar'y·ep'i·glot'ti·cus

ar'yl·ar'so·nate'

ar'yl·ene'

ar'y·te·no·ep'i·glot'tic

ar'y·te'noid'

ar'y·te·noi·dec'to·my

ar'y·te·noi·di'tis

ar'y·te·noi·do·pex'y

as·a·fet'i·da

a·sa'phi·a

as'bes·to'sis pl. -ses'

as'ca·ri'a·sis pl. -ses'

as·car'i·cide'

as·ca·rid pl. -rids or as·car'i·des'

as·car'i·dole'

As'ca·ris

—— e·quo'rum

—— lum'bri·coi'des'

—— meg'a·lo·ceph'a·la

—— mys'tax'

—— su'um

Asch'heim-Zon'dek

—— reaction

—— test

Asch'ner phenomenon

Asch'off'

—— bodies

—— cell

—— nodules

Asch operation

as·ci'tes' pl. as·ci'tes'

—— ad'i·po'sus

—— chy·lo'sus

—— sac·ca'tus

—— vag'i·na'lis

—— vul·ga'ti·or'

as·cit'ic

as'co·carp'

as'co·go·nid'i·um pl. -i·a

As·co'li

—— test

—— treatment

As'co·my·ce'tes'

as'co·my·ce'tous

a·scor'bate'

a·scor'bic

as'co·spore'

as'cus pl. -ci'

A·sel'li glands

as'e·ma'si·a

a·se'mi·a

a·sep'sis pl. -ses'

a·sep'tic

a·sex'u·al

Ash'er·man syndrome

Ash'man phenomenon

a'si·a·li·a

A'sian influenza virus

a·si·at'i·co'side'

a·sid·er·o'sis pl. -ses'

a·sid·er·ot'ic

As'ken·stedt' method

a·so'ma

a·so'mous

a·so'ni·a

as·pal'a·so'ma

as·par'a·gin·ase'

as·par'a·gine'

as·par'a·gin'ic

as'par·a·gi·nyl

as'par·a·mide'

as·par'tase'

as·par'tate' a·mi'no·trans'fer·ase'

as·par'tic

as·par'to·cin
as·par'tyl
a·spas'tic
a'spe·cif'ic
as'pect'
as'per·gil'lic
as'per·gil'lin
as'per·gil·lo'sis *pl.* -ses'
As'per·gil'lus
as'per·lin
a'sper·mat'ic
a·sper'ma·tism
a·sper'ma·to·gen'e·sis
a·sper'mi·a
a·sper'mous
as·phyx'i·a
—— liv'i·da
—— ne'o·na·to'rum
—— pal'li·da
as·phyx'i·al
as·phyx'i·ant
as·phyx'i·ate', -at'ed, -at'ing
as'pi·do·sper'ma
as'pi·do·sper'mine'
as'pi·rate', -rat'ed, -rat'ing
as'pi·ra'tion
as'pi·ra'tor
as'pi·rin
As'pis
—— cor·nu'tus
a·sple'ni·a
a·sple'nic
a·spo'ro·gen'ic
as'po·rog'e·nous
a·spo'rous
a·spor'u·late'
As·sam' fever
as'say'
as'si·dent
as·sim'i·la·ble
as·sim'i·la'tion
Ass'mann focus
as·so'ci·a·tive
as'so·nance
a·sta'si·a
a·sta'si·a-a·ba'si·a
a·stat'ic
as'ta·tine'
as'ta·xan'thin
a·ste'a·to'sis *pl.* -ses'
as'ter
a·ste're·o·cog'no·sy
a·ste're·og·no'sis *pl.* -ses'
as·ter'ic
as·te'ri·on' *pl.* -ri·a
as'ter·ix'is
a·ster'nal

a·ster'ni·a
as'ter·oid'
as·the'ni·a
—— cru'rum par·es·thet'i·ca
—— pig'men·to'sa
—— u'ni·ver·sa'lis con·gen'i·ta
as·then'ic
as'the·no·bi·o'sis
as'the·no·co'ri·a
as'the·nom'e·ter
as'the·nope'
as'the·no·pho'bi·a
as'the·no'pi·a
as'the·nop'ic
as'the·no·sper'mi·a
as'the·nox'i·a
asth'ma
asth·mat'ic
a·stig'ma·graph'
as·tig'mat'ic
a·stig'ma·tism
a·stig'ma·tom'e·ter
as'tig·mat'o·scope'
a·stig'mi·a
as·tig'mic
as'tig·mom'e·ter
as'tig·mom'e·try
a·stig'mo·scope'
as'tig·mos'co·py
a·stom'a·tous
a·sto'mi·a
a·strag'a·lar
a·strag'a·lec'to·my
a·strag'a·lus *pl.* -li'
a·strin'gen·cy
a·strin'gent
as'tro·blast'
as'tro·blas·to'ma *pl.* -mas *or* -ma·ta
as'tro·cyte'
as'tro·cyt'ic
as'tro·cy·to'ma *pl.* -mas *or* -ma·ta
—— gi·gan'to·cel'lu·lar'e'
as'tro·cy·to'sis *pl.* -ses'
as·trog'li·a
as·trog'li·o'ma *pl.* -mas *or* -ma·ta
as'troid'
as·tro'ma *pl.* -mas *or* -ma·ta
a'syl·la'bi·a
a'sym·bo'li·a
a'sym·met'ric *or* a'sym·met'ri·cal
a·sym'me·try
a·sym'phy·tous

a·symp'to·mat'ic
as'ymp·tot'ic
a·syn'chro·nism
a·syn'cli·tism
a·syn'de·sis *pl.* -ses'
a'syn·det'ic
a'sy·nech'i·a
a'sy·ner'gi·a
a'sy·ner'gic
a·syn'er·gy
a'sy·no'di·a
a'syn·tax'i·a
a'sys·tem'ic
a·sys'to·le
a'sys·to'li·a
a'sys·tol'ic
a·tac'tic
a·tac'ti·form'
at'a·rac'tic
at'a·ral·ge'si·a
at'a·rax'i·a
at'a·rax'ic
at'a·rax'y
at'a·vism
at'a·vis'tic
a·tax'i·a
—— cor'dis
a·tax'i·a·graph'
a·tax'i·am'e·ter
a·tax'i·a·pha'si·a
a·tax'ic
a·tax'i·o·phe'mi·a
a·tax'i·o·pho'bi·a
a·tax'o·phe'mi·a
at'e·lec'ta·sis *pl.* -ses'
at'e·lec·tat'ic
a·tel'ei·o'sis *pl.* -ses'
a·tel'ei·ot'ic
at'el·en·ce·pha'li·a
at'el·en·ceph'a·ly
a·te'li·a
a·te'lic
a·tel'i·o'sis *pl.* -ses'
a·tel'i·ot'ic
at'e·lo·car'di·a
at'e·lo·ceph'a·lous
at'e·lo·chei'li·a
at'e·lo·chei'ri·a
at'e·lo·en'ce·pha'li·a
at'e·lo·glos'si·a
at'e·log·na'thi·a
at'e·lo·ki·ne'si·a
at'e·lo·po'di·a
at'e·lo·pro·so'pi·a
at'e·lo·ra·chid'i·a
at'e·lo·sto'mi·a
a·ten'o·lol'

a·the'li·a
ath'er·o·gen'e·sis *pl.* -ses'
ath'er·o·gen'ic
ath'er·o'ma *pl.* -mas *or*
  -ma·ta
ath'er·o·ma·to'sis *pl.* -ses'
ath'er·om'a·tous
ath'er·o·ne·cro'sis *pl.* -ses'
ath'er·o·scler'o·gen'ic
ath'er·o·scle·ro'sis *pl.* -ses'
—— o·blit'er·ans'
ath'er·o·scle·rot'ic
ath'e·toid'
ath'e·to'sis *pl.* -ses'
ath'e·tot'ic
a·thi'a·min·o'sis *pl.* -ses'
a·threp'si·a
a·threp'tic
a·thy'mi·a
a·thy'mic
a·thy're·a
a·thy're·o'sis *pl.* -ses'
a·thy're·ot'ic
a·thy'roid·ism
a'thy·ro'sis *pl.* -ses'
a'thy·rot'ic
at·lan'tal
at·lan'to·ax'i·al
at·lan'to·bas'i·lar'is in·
  ter'nus
at·lan'to·ep'i·stroph'ic
at·lan'to·oc·cip'i·tal
at'las
at'lo·ax'oid'
at·mol'y·sis *pl.* -ses'
at·mom'e·ter
a·to'ci·a
at'om·i·za'tion
at'om·ize', -ized', -iz'ing
at'om·iz'er
a·to'ni·a
a·ton'ic
a'to·nic'i·ty
at'o·ny
at'o·pen
a·top'ic
a·top'og·no'si·a
a·top'og·no'sis
at'o·py
a·tox'ic
a'tra·che'li·a
a·trach'e·lo·ceph'a·lus
a·trach'e·lous
a·tre'mi·a
a·tre'si·a
—— a'ni' vag'i·na'lis
—— fol·lic'u·li'

—— of i'ter
—— vul'vae'
a·tre'sic
a·tret'ic
a·tre'to·ceph'a·lus
a·tre'to·cor'mus
a·tre'to·cys'ti·a
a·tre'to·gas'tri·a
a·tre'to·le'mi·a
a·tre'to·me'tri·a
at're·top'si·a
a·tre'tor·rhin'i·a
a·tre'to·sto'mi·a
a·tret'u·re'thri·a
a'tri·al
a·trich'i·a
at'ri·chous
a'tri·o·meg'a·ly
a'tri·o·sep'to·pex'y
a'tri·o·sep'to·plas'ty
a'tri·ot'o·my
a'tri·o·ven·tric'u·lar
a'tri·o·ven·tric'u·lar'is
  com·mu'nis
a'tri·um *pl.* a'tri·a
—— cor'dis
—— cordis dex'trum
—— cordis si·nis'trum
—— dex'trum
—— me·a'tus me'di·i'
—— of infection
—— si·nis'trum
—— va·gi'nae'
at'ro·lac'ta·mide'
a·tro'phi·a
—— bul'bi'
—— cer'e·bri·se·ni'lis sim'-
  plex'
—— cho·roi'de·ae' et ret'i·
  nae'
—— cu'tis
—— do·lo·ro'sa
—— mac'u·lo'sa cu'tis
—— mus'cu·lo'rum lip'o·
  mas·to'sa
—— pi·lo'rum pro'pri·a
—— se·nil'is
—— stri·a'ta et' mac'u·lo'sa
—— tes·tic'u·li'
—— un'gui·um
a·troph'ic
at'ro·phied
at'ro·pho·der'ma
—— of Pa·si'ni and Pi'er·i'ni
—— re·tic'u·la'tum
—— ver·mic'u·lar'is
at'ro·phy

at'ro·pine'
at'ro·pin'i·za'tion
at'ro·scine'
at·ten'u·ant
at·ten'u·ate', -at'ed, -at'ing
at·ten'u·a'tion
at'tic
at'tic·i'tis
at'ti·co·an·trot'o·my
at'ti·co·mas'toid'
at'ti·cot'o·my
at'ti·tude'
at·tol'lens au'rem
at'tra·hens' au'rem
at·tri'tion
a·typ'i·a
a·typ'i·cal
Aub'-Du Bois' standards
Au'ber'ger blood group
Au'bert phenomenon
Auch'mer·o·my'ia
—— lu·te'o·la
au'di·mut'ism
au'di·o' analgesia
au'di·o·ep'i·lep'tic
au'di·o·gen'ic
au'di·o·gram'
au'di·ol'o·gist
au'di·ol'o·gy
au'di·om'e·ter
au'di·om'e·trist
au'di·om'e·try
au'di·o·oc'u·lar
au'di·o·vis'u·al
au'di·phone'
au·di'tion
au'di·tive
au'di·tog·no'sis *pl.* -ses'
au'di·to·oc'u·lo·gy'ric reflex
au'di·to'ry
au'di·to·sen'so·ry
Au'en·brug'ger sign
Au'er·bach'
—— ganglions
—— plexus
Au'er bodies
aug'men·ta'tion
aug·na'thus
Augs'ber'ger rule
Au'jesz'ky disease
au'ra *pl.* -ras *or* -rae'
—— asth·mat'i·ca
—— cur·so'ri·a
—— hys·ter'i·ca
au'ral *(of the ear)*
♦oral

au'ran·ti'a·sis *pl.* -ses'
—— cu'tis
au·ran'ti·um
au'rate'
au'ric
au'ri·cle
au·ric'u·la *pl.* -lae'
—— a'tri·i'
—— cor'dis
—— dex'tra
—— si·nis'tra
au·ric'u·lar
au·ric'u·lar'e' *pl.* -lar'i·a
au·ric'u·lar'is *pl.* -lar'es'
au·ric'u·lo·breg·mat'ic
au·ric'u·lo·fron·ta'lis
au·ric'u·lo·pal'pe·bral
au·ric'u·lo·pres'sor
au·ric'u·lo·tem'po·ral
au·ric'u·lo·ven·tric'u·lar
au'ri·form'
au'ris *pl.* -res'
—— dex'tra
—— ex·ter'na
—— in·ter'na
—— me'di·a
—— si·nis'tra
au'rist
au'ro·pal'pe·bral
au'ro·ther'a·py
au'ro·thi'o·glu'cose'
au'ro·thi'o·gly'ca·nide'
au'rous
au'rum
aus·cult'
aus'cul·tate', -tat'ed,
  -tat'ing
aus'cul·ta'tion
aus·cul'ta·to'ry
Aus'tin and Van Slyke'
  method
Austin Flint murmur
Aus·tra'lia antigen
Aus'tra·lor'bis
au'ta·coid'
aut'ar·ce'sis
au'to·al·ler'gic
au·te'cic
au·te'cious
au·te·me'si·a
au'tism
au·tis'tic
au'to·ag·glu'ti·na'tion
au'to·ag·glu'ti·nin
au'to·al·ler'gic
au'to·am'pu·ta'tion
au'to·a·nal'y·sis *pl.* -ses'

au'to·an'am·ne'sis *pl.* -ses'
au'to·an'ti·bod'y
au'to·au'di·ble
au'to·ca·tal'y·sis *pl.* -ses'
au'to·cat'a·lyst
au'to·cat'a·lyt'ic
au'to·ca·thar'sis *pl.* -ses'
au'to·cho'le·cys'to·du'o·
  de·nos'to·my
au'to·cho'le·cys'to·
  trans'verse·co·los'to·my
au·toch'tho·nous
au'to·cla'si·a
au·toc'la·sis *pl.* -ses'
au'to·clave'
au'to·cy'to·tox'in
au'to·di·ges'tion
au'to·ech'o·la'li·a
au'to·ec·ze'ma·ti·za'tion
au'to·er'o·tism
au'to·flu'o·res'cence
au'to·flu'o·res'cent
au'to·fluor'o·scope'
au'to·fluor·os'co·py
au·tog'a·mous
au·tog'a·my
au'to·gen'e·sis *pl.* -ses'
au'to·ge·net'ic
au'to·gen'ic
au·tog'e·nous
au'to·graft'
au'to·he'mag·glu'ti·nin
au'to·hy·drol'y·sis
au'to·hyp·no'sis *pl.* -ses'
au'to·hyp·not'ic
au'to·hyp'no·tism
au'to·im·mune'
au'to·im·mu'ni·ty
au'to·im'mu·ni·za'tion
au'to·in·fec'tion
au'to·in·fu'sion
au'to·in·oc'u·la'tion
au'to·in·tox'i·cant
au'to·in·tox'i·ca'tion
au'to·i'so·ly'sin
au'to·ki·ne'sis
au'to·ki·net'ic
au·tol'o·gous
au·tol'y·sate'
au·tol'y·sin
au·tol'y·sis
au'to·lyt'ic
au'to·lyze', -lyzed', -lyz'ing
au·tom'a·tism
au·tom'a·ton *pl.* -tons *or* -ta
au'to·ne·phrec'to·my
au'to·no·ma'si·a

au'to·nom'ic
au·ton'o·mous
au'to·oph·thal'mo·scope'
au'to·oph'thal·mos'co·py
au'to·ox'i·da'tion
au'to·path'ic
au·top'a·thy
au'to·pha'gi·a
au'to·pha'gic
au·toph'a·gy
au'to·phil'i·a
au'to·pho'ni·a
au·toph'o·ny
aut'oph·thal·mo·scope'
aut'oph·thal·mos'co·py
au'to·plast'
au'to·plas'tic
au'to·plas'ty
au'to·pneu'mo·nec'to·my
au'to·pol'y·mer·iz'ing res-
  in
au'to·pol'y·ploi'dy
au'to·pro·throm'bin
au'to·pro·tol'y·sis *pl.* -ses'
au'top·sy
au'to·psy'che
au'to·psy'chic
au'to·psy·cho'sis *pl.* -ses'
au'to·ra'di·o·gram'
au'to·ra'di·o·graph'
au'to·ra'di·og'ra·phy
au'to·reg'u·la'tion
au'to·re'in·fu'sion
au'to·sen'si·ti·za'tion
au'to·site'
au'to·sit'ic
au'to·so'mal
au'to·some'
au'to·sple·nec'to·my
au'to·sug·gest'i·bil'i·ty
au'to·sug·ges'tion
au'to·syn'de·sis
au·tot'o·my
au'to·top'ag·no'si·a
au'to·tox'ic
au'to·tox'in
au'to·trans·fu'sion
au'to·trans'plant'
au'to·trans·plan·ta'tion
au'to·troph'
au'to·tro'phic
au'to·vac'ci·na'tion
au'to·vac'cine'
au·tox'i·da'tion
aux·an'o·gram'
aux'a·no·graph'ic
aux'a·nog'ra·phy

aux·e′sis *pl.* -ses′
aux·et′ic
aux′in
aux′o·chrome′
aux′o·cyte′
aux′o·drome′
aux·om′e·ter
aux′o·ton′ic
aux′o·troph′ic
av′a·lanche′
a·val′vu·lar
a·vas′cu·lar
a·vas′cu·lar·i·za′tion
a·vas′cu·lar·ize′, -ized′, -iz′-
ing
A·vel′lis
—— paralysis
—— syndrome
a·vir′u·lent
a·vi′ta·min·o′sis *pl.* -ses′
AV
—— nicking
—— node
A-V
—— patterns
—— syndromes
a·void′ance
av′oir·du·pois′
a·vul′sion
a wave
a′xan·thop′si·a
Ax′en·feld′
—— intrascleral nerve loop
—— syndrome
a·xen′ic
a′xe·roph′thol′
ax′i·al
ax′i·a′tion
ax·if′u·gal
ax·il′la *pl.* -lae′ *or* -las
ax′il·lar′y
ax′il·lo′bi·fem′o·ral
ax′il·lo·fem′o·ral
ax′i·o·buc′cal
ax′i·o·buc′co·cer′vi·cal
ax′i·o·buc′co·gin′gi·val
ax′i·o·buc′co·lin′gual
ax′i·o·cer′vi·cal
ax′i·o·dis′tal
ax′i·o·dis′to·cer′vi·cal
ax′i·o·dis′to·gin′gi·val
ax′i·o·dis′to·in·ci′sal
ax′i·o·dis′to-oc·clu′sal
ax′i·o·gin′gi·val
ax′i·o·in·ci′sal
ax′i·o·la′bi·al
ax′i·o·la′bi·o·gin′gi·val

ax′i·o·la′bi·o·lin′gual
ax′i·o·lin′gual
ax′i·o·lin′gu·o·cer′vi·cal
ax′i·o·lin′gu·o·gin′gi·val
ax′i·o·lin′gu·o′-oc·clu′sal
ax·ip′e·tal
ax′is *pl.* ax′es′
—— bul′bi′ ex·ter′nus
—— bulbi in·ter′nus
—— len′tis
—— oc′u·li′ ex·ter′na
—— oculi in·ter′na
—— op′ti·ca
—— op′ti·cus
—— pel′vis
—— u′ter·i′
ax′o·den·drit′ic
ax·og′e·nous *(originating in an axon)*
♦*exogenous*
ax′oid′
ax·oi′de·an
ax′o·lem′ma
ax′o·mat′ic
ax′o·me′si·al
ax′i·o·me′si·o·cer′vi·cal
ax′i·o·me′si·o·dis′tal
ax′i·o·me′si·o·gin′gi·val
ax′i·o·me′si·o·in·ci′sal
ax′i·o·me′si·o′-oc·clu′sal
ax·om′e·ter
ax′on′
ax′o·nal
ax′on·a·prax′is
ax′one′
ax′o·ne′ma
ax′o·neme′
ax′o·nom′e·ter
ax′on·ot·me′sis *pl.* -ses′
ax′o·plasm
a′ya·huas′co
Ay′a·la
—— index
—— quotient
—— test
A·yer′za
—— disease
—— syndrome
az′a·cy′clo·nol′
az′a·gua′nine′
az′a·per′one′
az·ap′e·tine′
az′a·ri′bine′
az′a·ser′ine′
az·at′a·dine′
az′a·thi′o·prine′
a·zed′a·rach′

az′e·la′ic
a′ze·o·trope′
a′ze·o·trop′ic
az′e·pin′a·mide′
az′e·te′pa
az′ide′
az′ine′
az′o·ben′zene′
az′o·car′mine G
az′o·lit′min
a·zo′o·sper′ma·tism
a·zo′o·sper′mi·a
az′o·pro′te·in
az′ote′
az′o·te′mi·a
az′o·tem′ic
a·zot′ic
a·zot′i·fi·ca′tion
Az′o·to·bac′ter
az′o·to·my′cin
az′o·tor·rhe′a
az′o·tu′ri·a
az′o·tu′ric
az′ul′
az′u·lene′
az′ure
az′u·res′in
a·zu′ro·phil′
az′u·ro·phil′i·a
az′u·ro·phil′ic
az′y·go·ag′na·thus
az′y·gos′ *(unpaired anatomic structure)*
♦*azygous*
az′y·gous *(unpaired)*
♦*azygos*
a·zy′mi·a
a·zy′mic

B

Baas′trup disease
Bab′cock′
—— operation
—— test
Bab′cock-Le′vy test
Ba·bés′-Ernst′ bodies
Ba·be′si·a
—— bi·gem′i·na
—— bo′vis
—— ca′nis
—— e′qui′
—— o′vis
bab·e·si′a·sis *pl.* -ses′
ba·be·si·o′sis *pl.* -ses′

Ba·bés' nodules
Ba·bin'ski
—— platysma sign
—— phenomenon
—— pronation phenomenon
—— reflex
—— sign
—— syndrome
—— tonus test
Ba·bin'ski-Froeh'lich disease
Ba·bin'ski-Na·geotte' syndrome
Ba·bin'ski-Va·quez' syndrome
bac'ci·form'
Ba·cel'li sign
Bach'mann bundle
Bach'man test
Bach'ti·a'row' sign
bac'il·lar
bac'il·lar'y
bac'il·le'mi·a
ba·cil'li·form'
ba·cil'lin
bac'il·lo'sis pl. -ses'
bac'il·lu'ri·a
ba·cil'lus pl. -li'
—— Cal·mette'-Gué·rin'
Ba·cil'lus
—— ac'i·doph'i·lus
—— aer·og'e·nes' cap'su·la'tus
—— aer'try·cke
—— ag'ni'
—— an'thra·cis
—— bi'fi·dus
—— bot'u·li'nus
—— bo'vi·sep'ti·cus
—— brev'is
—— co'li'
—— diph·the'ri·ae'
—— dys'en·ter'i·ae'
—— en'ter·it'i·dis
—— er'y·sip'e·la'tos-su'is
—— fe·ca'lis al'ca·lig'e·nes'
—— fu'si·for'mis
—— gas·troph'i·lus
—— hof·man'ni·i'
—— in'flu·en'zae'
—— lac'tis aer·og'e·nes'
—— lac'u·na'tus
—— lep'rae'
—— mal'le·i'
—— mes'en·ter'i·cus
—— mu·co'sus cap'su·la'tum

—— oe'de·ma'ti·ens
—— oe·de'ma·tis ma'lig'ni'
—— par'a·bot'u·li'nus
—— par'a·ty·pho'sus A
—— paratyphosus B
—— per·frin'gens
—— per·tus'sis
—— pes'tis
—— pol'y·myx'a
—— pro·dig'i·o'sus
—— pro'te·us
—— pu'mi·lus
—— py'o·cy·a'ne·us
—— sub'ti·lis
—— su'i·sep'ti·cus
—— tet'a·ni'
—— tuberculosis
—— whit·mo'ri'
—— xe·ro'sis
bac'i·tra'cin
back'ache'
back'bone'
back'scat'ter
bac'te·re'mi·a
bac'te·re'mic
bac·te'ri·a sing. -ri·um
Bac·te'ri·a'ce·ae'
bac·te'ri·al
bac·te'ri·ci'dal
bac·te'ri·cide'
bac·te'ri·ci'din
bac'ter·id
bac'ter·in
bac·te'ri·o·chlo'ro·phyll
bac·te'ri·oc'la·sis pl. -ses'
bac·te'ri·o·er'y·thrin
bac·te'ri·o·flu'o·res'ce·in
bac·te'ri·o·gen'ic
bac·te'ri·og'e·nous
bac·te'ri·o·he·mol'y·sin
bac·te'ri·oid'
bac·te'ri·o·log'ic or bac·te'ri·o·log'i·cal
bac·te'ri·ol'o·gist
bac·te'ri·ol'o·gy
bac·te'ri·o·ly'sin
bac·te'ri·ol'y·sis pl. -ses'
bac·te'ri·o·lyt'ic
bac·te'ri·o·op'so·nin
bac·te'ri·o·phage'
bac·te'ri·o·pha·gi·a
bac·te'ri·o·phag'ic
bac·te'ri·o·pro'te·in
bac·te'ri·op·son'ic
bac·te'ri·op'so·nin
bac·te'ri·o'sis pl. -ses'
bac·te'ri·os'ta·sis pl. -ses'

bac·te'ri·o·stat'
bac·te'ri·o·stat'ic
bac·te'ri·o·ther'a·py
bac·te'ri·o'tox·e'mi·a
bac·te'ri·o·tox'ic
bac·te'ri·o·tox'in
bac·te'ri·o·trop'ic
bac·te'ri·ot'ro·pin
Bac·te'ri·um
—— a·ce'ti'
—— ae·rog'e·nes'
—— al'ka·les'cens
—— am·big'u·um
—— a'vi·sep'ti·cum
—— bo'vi·sep'ti·cum
—— chol'e·rae'-su'is
—— co'li'
—— dis'par'
—— dys'en·ter'i·ae'
—— en'ter·it'i·dis
—— flex'ner·i'
—— fried·län'der·i'
—— fu'si·for'mis
—— lac'tis aer·og'e·nes'
—— mon'o·cy·tog'e·nes'
—— par'a·dys'en·ter'i·ae'
—— par'a·ty·pho'sum A
—— paratyphosum B
—— paratyphosum C
—— pneu·mo'ni·ae'
—— shi'gae'
—— son'ne·i'
—— su'i·pes'ti·fer
—— su'i·sep'ti·cum
—— tu'la·ren'se'
—— ty'phi·mu'ri·um
—— ty·pho'sum
bac·te'ri·u'ri·a
bac'ter·oid'
Bac'ter·oi·da'ce·ae'
Bac'ter·oi'des'
—— frag'i·lis
—— fun'di·li·for'mis
—— me·lan'i·no·gen'i·cus
—— pneu'mo·sin'tes'
bac'ter·u'ri·a
Baer treatment
ba·gasse'
bag'as·so'sis pl. -ses'
Bagh'dad'
—— boil
—— spring anemia
Ba·hi'a ulcer
Bail·lar·ger'
—— bands
—— principle
—— sign

Bain'bridge' reflex
Ba'ker cyst
bal'ance, -anced, -anc·ing
ba·lan'ic
bal'a·ni'tis
—— xe·rot'i·ca ob·lit'er·ans'
bal'a·no·plas'ty
bal'a·no·pos·thi'tis
bal'a·no·pre·pu'tial
bal'a·nor·rha'gi·a
bal'a·nor·rhe'a
bal'an·tid'i·al
bal'an·ti·di'a·sis pl. -ses'
Bal'an·tid'i·um
—— co'li'
bal'an·ti·do'sis pl. -ses'
bal'a·nus
Bal'bi·a'ni rings
Bal·duz'zi sign
Bald'win operation
Bal'dy-Web'ster operation
Bal'four operation
Ba'lint syndrome
Bal'lance
—— operation
—— sign
Bal·let' sign
Bal'lin·gall disease
bal·lis'mus
bal·lis'tic
bal·lis'to·car'di·o·gram'
bal·lis'to·car'di·o·graph'
bal·loon'ing
Ball operation
bal·lotte·ment'
balm
Ba'lo concentric sclerosis
Bal'ser fat necrosis
Bal'tha·zar Fos'ter mur-
mur
ba'meth'an
bam'i·fyl'line'
Ban'croft' filariasis
ban'dage, -aged, -ag·ing
bands of Pic'co·lo·mi'ni
Bang
—— ba·cil'lus
—— disease
—— method
—— test
ban'ting·ism
Ban'ti syndrome
bap'ti·tox'ine
Bá'rá·ny test
bar'ba
—— am'a·ril'la
Bar·be'ri·o test

Bar'ber method
bar'bi·tal'
bar·bi'tu·rate'
bar'bi·tu'ric
bar·bi'tu·rism
bar·bo'tage'
Bar·coo' rot
Bar'dach' test
Bar'de·le'ben operation
Bar'den·heu'er operation
Bar·det'-Bie'dl syndrome
Bard'-Pic' syndrome
Bard sign
Bär'en·sprung' disease
bar'es·the'si·a
bar'es·the'si·om'e·ter
Bar'foed
—— reagent
—— test
bar'i·at'ric
bar'i·to'sis pl. -ses'
bar'i·um
Bar'ker operation
Bar'low
—— disease
—— syndrome
Barns'dale' bacillus
bar'o·cep'tor
bar'o·don·tal'gi·a
bar'og·no'sis pl. -ses'
bar'o·ma·crom'e·ter
bar'o·o·ti'tis
bar'o·re·cep'tor
bar'o·re'flex'
bar'o·scope'
bar'o·si'nus·i'tis
ba·ros'min
bar'o·ti'tis
—— ex·ter'na
—— me'di·a
bar'o·trau'ma pl. -ma·ta
Bar·ra'quer
—— disease
—— operation
Bar·ra'quer-Si'mons dis-
ease
Barr body
bar'ren
Bar·ré'
—— sign
—— syndrome
Barr'-Ep'stein' virus
Bart hemoglobin
Barth hernia
Bar'tho·lin
—— cyst
—— duct

—— gland
bar'tho·lin·i'tis
Bar'ton·el'la
bar'ton·el·lo'sis pl. -ses'
Bar'ton operation
Bart'ter syndrome
bar'y·la'li·a
bar'y·pho'ni·a
ba·ry'ta
ba'sal
ba'sal-cell' carcinoma
ba·sal'i·o'ma pl. -mas or
-ma·ta
ba'sal·oid'
base
bas'e·doid'
Ba'se·dow' disease
Ba·sel'la
ba'se·o'sis pl. -ses'
base'plate'
bas-fond'
Bash'am mixture
ba'si·al
ba'si·al·ve'o·lar
ba'si·bran'chi·al
ba'si·breg·mat'ic
ba'sic
ba'si·chro'ma·tin
ba·sic'i·ty
ba'si·cra'ni·al
Ba·sid'i·ob'o·lus
ba·sid'i·o·my·cete'
ba·sid'i·o·spore'
ba·sid'i·um pl. -i·a
ba'si·fa'cial
ba'si·hy'oid'
bas'i·lad'
bas'i·lar
bas'i·lar'is
—— cran'i·i'
ba'si·lat'er·al
ba·sil'ic
bas'i·lo'ma pl. -mas or -ma·
ta
bas'i·lo·men'tal
bas'i·lo·pha·ryn'ge·al
bas'i·lo·sub·na'sal
ba'si·na'sal
ba'si·o·al·ve'o·lar
ba'si·o·breg·mat'ic
ba'si·oc·cip'i·tal
bas'i·o·glos'sus
ba'si·on'
ba·sip'e·tal
ba'si·pha·ryn'ge·al
ba'si·pho'bi·a
ba'si·pre·sphe'noid'

ba'si·rhi'nal
ba'sis *pl.* -ses'
—— car'ti·lag'i·nis ar'y·tae·
noi'de·ae'
—— cartilaginis ar'y·te·
noi'de·ae'
—— cer'e·bri'
—— coch'le·ae'
—— cor'dis
—— cra'ni·i' ex·ter'na
—— cranii in·ter'na
—— glan'du·lae' su'pra·re·
na'lis
—— lin'guae'
—— man·dib'u·lae'
—— mo·di'o·li'
—— na'si'
—— os'sis met'a·car·pa'lis
—— ossis met'a·tar·sa'lis
—— ossis sa'cri'
—— os'si·um met'a·car·pa'li·
um
—— ossium met'a·tar·sa'li·
um
—— pa·tel'lae'
—— pe·dun'cu·li' cer'e·bri'
—— pha·lan'gis dig'i·to'rum
ma'nus
—— phalangis digitorum
pe'dis
—— pros'ta·tae'
—— pul·mo'nis
—— py·ram'i·dis re·na'lis
—— sta'pe·dis
ba'si·sphe'noid'
ba'si·tem'po·ral
ba'si·ver'te·bral
Basle Nom'i·na An'a·
tom'i·ca
ba'so·cyte'
ba'so·cy'to·pe'ni·a
ba'so·cy·to'sis *pl.* -ses'
ba'so·phil'
ba'so·phil'i·a
ba'so·phil'ic
ba·soph'i·lism
ba'so·phil'o·cyt'ic
ba·soph'i·lous
ba'so·plasm
ba'so·squa'mous
Bas'sen-Korn'zweig' syn-
drome
Bas·set' operation
Bas·si'ni operation
bas'so·rin
Bas'ti·an-Bruns' law
bath

bath'mo·trop'ic
bath·mot'ro·pism
bath'o·chrome'
bath'o·chro'mic
bath'ro·ceph'a·ly
bath'y·car'di·a
bath'y·chrome'
bath'y·chro'mic
bath'y·es·the'si·a
bat'o·pho'bi·a
ba·tra'chi·an
bat'ra·cho·plas'ty
Bat'son plexus
bat'ta·rism
bat'ta·ris'mus
Bat'ten-May'ou disease
bat'ter
bat'ter·y
Bat'tey operation
Bat'tle sign
Bau'er test
Bau'hin valve
Bau·mes' sign
Baum'gar'ten syndrome
Ba'u·ru' ulcer
Bayle disease
Baz'ett formula
Ba·zin' disease
Bdel'lo·nys'sus
—— ba·co'ti
beam
Be·ance' tu·baire' vol·un·
taire'
Beard disease
beat
Beau lines
be·bee'rine'
be·bee'ru'
be·can'thone'
Beck
—— operation
—— paste
—— triad
Beck'er disease
bec'lo·meth'a·sone'
Bec·que·rel' ray
be·dew'ing
Bed'nar aphthae
Bed·so'ni·a
—— psit'ta·ci'
bed'sore'
Beer
—— dye test
—— law
Bee'vor sign
be·hav'ior
be·hav'ior·al

be·hav'ior·ism
be·hav'ior·is'tic
Beh'çet syndrome
be·hen'ic
Behre test
Bei'gel disease
bej'el
Bé'ké·sy audiometry
Bekh'te·rev
—— arthritis
—— deep reflex
—— fibers
—— nucleus
—— reaction
—— reflex
—— sign
Bekh'te·rev-Men'del re-
flex
bel
bel'ae fruc'tus
Bell
—— disease
—— law
—— mania
—— muscle
—— palsy
—— phenomenon
—— spasm
bel'la·don'na
belle in·dif·fé·rence'
Belle'vue'
—— bridge
—— scale
Bel'ling ac'e·to·car'mine
stain
Bell'-Ma·gen·die' law
bel'ly
bem'e·gride'
ben·ac'ty·zine'
Ben'a·cus
—— gris'cus
ben·a'zo·line'
Bence'-Jones'
—— cylinders
—— protein
Ben'da test
ben'da·zac'
Ben'der gestalt test
Ben'dien' test
ben'dro·flu'me·thi'a·zide'
be'ne'
Ben'e·dict
—— and Franke method
—— and Hitch'cock' re-
agent
—— and New'ton method
—— and Theis method

—— method
—— solution
—— test
—— uric acid reagent
Ben′e·dikt syndrome
be·nign′
be·nig′nant
Ben′nett
—— angle
—— cells
—— fracture
—— movement
Benn′hold′ test
be·nor′ter·one′
ben·ox′i·nate′
ben·per′i·dol′
ben′sa·lan′
ben′ton·ite′
benz·al′de·hyde′
benz′al·dox′ime′
benz′al·ko′ni·um
benz·an′thra·cene′
ben′za·thine′
benz·az′o·line
ben′zene′
ben·zes′trol′
ben′ze·tho′ni·um
ben·zet′i·mide′
benz·hex′ol′
ben′zi·dine′
ben′zi·lo′ni·um
benz′im·id′az·ole′
ben′zin
benz′in·do·py′rine′
ben′zine′
ben′zo·ate′
ben′zo·caine′
benz·oc′ta·mine′
ben′zo·dep′a
ben′zo·di·ox′an′
ben′zo·di·ox′ane′
ben·zo′ic
ben′zo·in
ben·zo′i·nat′ed
ben′zol′
ben′zole′
ben′zo′na·tate′
ben′zo·ni′trile
ben′zo·phe·none′
ben′zo·qui·none′
ben′zo·qui·no′ni·um
ben′zo·sul′fi·mide′
ben′zo·yl
ben′zo·yl·ec′go·nine′
ben′zo·yl·gly′cine′
ben′zo·yl·guai′a·col′

ben′zo·yl·meth′yl·ec′go·
  nine′
benz·phet′a·mine′
benz·py′rene′
benz′py·rin′i·um
benz·quin′a·mide′
benz·thi′a·zide′
benz·tro′pine′
ben·zyd′a·mine′
ben′zyl
ben·zyl′i·dene′
ber′ber·ine′
ber′ber·is
Ber′ga·ra-War′ten·berg′
  sign
Ber′gen·hem operation
Ber′ger
—— disease
—— operation
—— rhythm
—— sign
Bergh test
Berg′mann
—— astrocytes
—— cords
Berg′meis′ter papilla
Ber·go·nié′-Tri·bon·deau′
  law
ber′i·ber′i
Ber′ke·feld′ filter
berke′li·um
Ber·lin′ disease
ber′lock′
ber·loque′
Ber·nard′
—— canal
—— granular layer
—— puncture
—— syndrome
Ber·nard′-Hor′ner syn-
  drome
Bern′hardt′ paresthesia
Bern′hardt-Roth′ syn-
  drome
Bern′heim′
—— syndrome
—— therapy
Ber·noul′li principle
Bern′reu′ter personality
  inventory
Bern′stein′ theory
Ber′ti·el′la
—— mu′cro·na′ta
—— stu′de·ri′
Ber·til·lon′ system
be·ryl′li·o′sis pl. -ses′
be·ryl′li·um

Ber·ze′li·us test
Bes·nier′-Boeck′-
  Schau′mann′ disease
  disease
Best disease
bes′ti·al′i·ty
be′syl·ate′
be′ta
—— globulin
Be′ta
be′ta-D-al′lo·py′ra·nose′
be′ta·eu′caine′
be′ta-he′mo·lyt′ic
be′ta·his′tine′
be′ta-hy·poph′a·mine′
be′ta·ine′
be′ta-ke′to·hy·drox′y·bu·
  tyr′ic
be′ta·meth′a·sone′
be′ta·naph′thol′
be′ta·naph′thyl
be′ta·to′pic
be′ta·tron′
be′ta·zole′
be·thane′chol′
be·than′i·dine′
Bet′ten·dorff′ test
be·tween′brain′
Betz cell
Bev′an operation
bev′a·tron′
bev′el
be′zoar′
Be′zold′
—— abscess
—— reflex
—— sign
Be′zold-Brü′cke effect
Be′zold-Jar′isch reflex
Bi′al
—— reagent
—— test
bi′al·am′i·col′
Bi·an′chi syndrome
bi′ar·tic′u·lar
bi′ar·tic′u·late′
bi′a·stig′ma·tism
bi′au·ric′u·lar
bi·ax′i·al
bi·cam′er·al
bi·cap′i·tate′
bi·car′bon·ate′
bi·car′di·o·gram′
bi·ceph′a·lous
bi′ceps′ pl. -ceps′es
bi·chlo′ride′
bi·chro′mate′

bi·cip'i·tal
bi'con·cave'
bi'con·vex'
bi·cor'nu·ate'
bi·cor'nu·ous
bi·cou·dé'
bi·cus'pid
bi·dac'ty·ly
Bid'der ganglion
Bie'brich scarlet
Bie'dl-Bar·det' syndrome
Biel·schow'sky
—— disease
—— sign
—— strabismus
Biel·schow'sky-Jan'sky
disease
Bier
—— method
—— spots
—— suction
Bier'mer anemia
Bier·nack'i sign
Bi·ett' disease
bi'fas·cic'u·lar
bi'fid, pl. -fid·us
bi·fo'cal
bi·fron'tal
bi'fur·ca'ti·o' pl. -ca'ti·
o'nes'
bi'fur·ca'tion
Big'e·low method
bi·gem'i·nal
bi·gem'i·ny
bi·go'ni·al
bi·is'chi·al
Bik'e·le sign
bi'labe'
bi·lam'i·nar
bi·lat'er·al
bi·lat'er·al·ism
bile
Bil·har'zi·a
bil'har·zi'a·sis
pl. -ses'
bil'i·ar'y
bil'i·cy'a·nin
bil'i·fla'vin
bil'i·fus'cin
bi·lig'u·late'
bi·lig'u·la'tus
bil'i·hu'min
bil'i·leu'kan'
bil'i·neu'rine'
bil'ious
bil'ious·ness
bil'i·pra'sin

bil'i·pur'pu·rin
bil'i·ru'bin
bil'i·ru'bin·ate'
bil'i·ru'bi·ne'mi·a
bil'i·ru'bin·glo'bin
bil'i·ru·bin'ic
bil'i·ru'bi·nu'ri·a
bil'i·u'ri·a
bil'i·ver'din
Bill'roth' operation
bi·lo'bar
bi·lo'bate'
bi·lobed'
bi·loc'u·lar
bi·loc'u·late'
bi·man'u·al
bi·mas'toid'
bi·max'il·lar'y
bin'an'gle
bi'na·ry
bi·na'sal
bi·nau'ral
bin'au·ric'u·lar
bind, bound, bind'ing
Bi·net'
—— age
—— formula
Bi·net'-Si·mon' intelli-
gence scale
Bing'-Neel' syndrome
Bing sign
bi·noc'u·lar
bi·no'mi·al
bi·no'tic
bin·ox'ide'
Bins'wang'er disease
bi·nu'cle·ar
bi·nu'cle·ate'
bi·nu'cle·at'ed
bi'o·as'say'
bi'o·au'to·graph'ic
bi'o·au·tog'ra·phy
bi'o·a·vail'a·bil'i·ty
bi'ob·jec'tive
bi'o·cat'a·lyst
bi'oc·cip'i·tal
bi'o·chem'i·cal
bi'o·chem'is·try
bi'o·chem·or'phic
bi'o·chem'or·phol'o·gy
bi'o·chrome'
bi'o·ci'dal
bi'o·cy'tin
bi'o·dy·nam'ics
bi'o·e·lec'tric
bi'o·e'lec·tric'i·ty
bi'o·en'er·get'ics

bi'o·feed'back'
bi'o·fla'vo·noid'
bi'o·gen'e·sis pl. -ses'
bi'o·ge·net'ic
bi·og'e·nous
bi·og'e·ny
bi'o·haz'ard
bi'o·ki·net'ic
bi'o·ki·net'ics
bi'o·log'ic or bi'o·log'i·cal
bi·ol'o·gist
bi·ol'o·gy
bi'o·lu'mi·nes'cence
bi'o·lu'mi·nes'cent
bi'o·me·chan'ics
bi'o·med'i·cal
bi'o·med'i·cine
bi·om'e·ter
bi'o·met'rics
bi·om'e·try
bi'o·mi'cro·scope'
bi'o·mi'cro·scop'ic
bi'o·mi·cros'co·py
bi·on'ics
bi'o·pa·thol'o·gy
bi'o·phore'
bi'o·pho'ric
bi'o·pho·tom'e·ter
bi'o·phys'ics
bi'o·plasm'
bi'o·plas'mic
bi'o·plas'tic
bi'op·sy
bi'o·psy'chic
bi'o·psy·cho·log'i·cal
bi'o·psy·chol'o·gy
bi·op'ter·in
bi·or'bi·tal
bi'ose'
bi'o·sta·tis'tics
bi·os'ter·ol'
bi'o·syn'the·sis pl. -ses'
bi'o·syn·thet'ic
bi·o'ta
Bi·ot' breathing
bi·o'ta
bi·o·te·lem'e·try
bi'o·te'si·om'e·ter
bi'o·te'si·om'e·try
bi·ot'ic
bi'o·tin
bi'o·trans'for·ma'tion
bi'o·type'
bi'o·typ'ic
bi'o·ty·pol'o·gy
bi·o'vu·lar
bip'a·ra pl. -ras or -rae'

bi'pa·ri'e·tal
bip'a·rous
bi'par'tite'
bi'ped'
bi·ped'al
bi·ped'i·cled
bi·pen'ni·form'
bi·per'i·den
bi·phos'phate'
bi·po'lar
bi'po·lar'i·ty
bi·po·ten'ti·al'i·ty
Bird disease
bi're·frac'tive
bi're·frin'gence
bi're·frin'gent
Birk'haug' test
birth
birth'mark'
bis'a·co'dyl
Bisch'off' test
bi·sect'
bi·sec'tion
bi·sex'u·al
bi·sex'u·al'i·ty
bis·fer'i·ens
bis·fer'i·ous
bis'hy·drox'y·cou'ma·rin
Bis'kra button
bis'muth
bis·mu'thi·a
bis'muth·o'sis *pl.* -ses'
bis'muth·o·tar'trate'
bis'muth·yl
bis'o·brin
bis·ox'a·tin
bis'tou·ry
bi·sul'fide'
bi·sul'fite'
bi·tar'trate'
bite, bit, bit'ten *or* bit, bit'ing
bi·tem'po·ral
bi·thi'o·nol'
Bi'tis
—— ga·bon'i·ca
—— la·che'sis
—— na'si·cor'nis
Bi·tot' spots
bit'ter·ling
Bitt'ner milk factor
bi·tu'ber·al
bi·tu'men
bi·u'rate'
bi·u'ret'
bi·va'lence
bi·va'len·cy
bi·va'lent

bi·val'vu·lar
bi·ven'ter
bi·ven·tric'u·lar
bi·zy'go·mat'ic
Biz'zo·ze'ro
—— blood platelet
—— nodules
Bjer'rum
—— screen
—— sign
Black
—— classification
—— test
black'out'
blad'der
Bla'lock-Taus'sig operation
Blan'din glands
Bland'-White'-Gar'land syndrome
Blan·for'di·a
blast
blas·te'ma *pl.* -mas *or* -ma·ta
blas·tem'ic
blas'tin
blas'to·chyle'
blas'to·coele'
blas'to·cyst'
Blas'to·cys'tis hom'i·nis
blas'to·derm'
blas'to·der'mal
blas'to·der'mic
blas'to·disc'
blas'to·gen'e·sis *pl.* -ses'
blas'to·gen'ic
blas·tog'e·ny
blas'to·ki·ne'sis *pl.* -ses'
blas'to·ki'nin
blas·tol'y·sis *pl.* -ses'
blas·to'ma *pl.* -mas *or* -ma·ta
—— e·pen'dy·ma'le'
blas·tom'a·to·gen'ic
blas·tom'a·tous
blas'to·mere'
Blas'to·my'ces'
—— bra·sil'i·en'sis
—— der'ma·tit'i·dis
blas'to·my·cete'
Blas'to·my·ce'tes'
blas'to·my·ce'tic
blas'to·my'cin
blas'to·my·co'sis *pl.* -ses'
blas'to·neu'ro·pore'
blas'to·pore'
blas'to·po'ric

blas'to·sphere'
blas'to·spore'
blas'to·spo'ric
blas·tot'o·my
blas'tu·la *pl.* -las *or* -lae'
blas'tu·lar
blas'tu·la'tion
Bla·tel'la
—— ger·man'i·ca
Blaud pill
bleb
bleed, bled, bleed'ing
bleed'er
blen'noph·thal'mi·a
blen'nor·rha'gi·a
blen'nor·rhe'a
ble'o·my'cin
bleph'ar·ad'e·ni'tis
bleph'a·ral
bleph'a·rec'to·my
bleph'a·re·de'ma
bleph'a·re·lo'sis *pl.* -ses'
bleph'a·rism
bleph'a·ri'tis
—— an'gu·lar'is
—— cil'i·ar'is
—— gan'grae·no'sa
—— mar'gi·na'lis
—— par'a·sit'i·ca
—— sim'plex'
—— squa·mo'sa
—— ul'ce·ro'sa
bleph'a·ro·ad'e·ni'tis
bleph'a·ro·ad'e·no'ma *pl.* -mas *or* -ma·ta
bleph'a·ro·ath'er·o'ma *pl.* -mas *or* -ma·ta
bleph'ro·blen'nor·rhe'a
bleph'a·ro·chal'a·sis *pl.* -ses'
bleph'a·ro·chrom'hi·dro'sis
belph'a·roc'lo·nus
bleph'a·ro·con·junc'ti·vi'tis
bleph'a·ro·di·as·ta·sis *pl.* -ses'
bleph'a·ro·dys·chroi'a
bleph'a·ro·me·las'ma
bleph'a·ron' *pl.* -ra
bleph'a·ron'cus *pl.* -ci'
bleph'a·ro·pa·chyn'sis
bleph'a·ro·phi·mo'sis *pl.* -ses'
bleph'a·roph'ry·plas'tic
bleph'a·roph'ry·plas'ty

bleph'a·ro·phy'ma *pl.* -mas
  or -ma·ta
bleph'a·ro·plast'
bleph'a·ro·plas'tic
bleph'a·ro·plas'ty
bleph'a·rop·to'sis *pl.* -ses'
bleph'a·ro·py'or·rhe'a
bleph'a·ror'rha·phy
bleph'a·ro·spasm
bleph'a·ro·sphinc'ter·ec'to·
  my
bleph'a·ro·stat'
bleph'a·ro·ste·no'sis *pl.*
  -ses'
bleph'a·ro·sym'phy·sis *pl.*
  -ses'
bleph'a·ro·sy·nech'i·a *pl.*
  -i·ae'
bleph'a·rot'o·my
Bles'sig-I·van'ov cystoid
  degeneration
blind
blind'ness
blink
blis'ter
bloat
Bloch method
Bloch'-Sulz'ber'ger syn-
  drome
block
block·ade', -ad'ed, -ad'ing
Blocq disease
Blond·lot' rays
blood
Blood'good' operation
blood'stream'
Bloom syndrome
Blount'-Bar'ber syndrome
Blum'berg' sign
Blu'me·nau'
—— nucleus
—— test
Blu'mer shelf
Blyth test
Bo·a'ri operation
Bo'as
—— point
—— reagent
—— sign
—— test
Bo'as-Op'pler bacillus
Bob'roff' operation
Boch'da·lek'
—— foramen
—— ganglion
—— triangle

Bock'hart' impetigo
Bo·dan'sky
—— method
—— unit
Bo'di·an staining method
Boeck
—— sarcoid
—— scabies
Boer'haa've syndrome
Boer'ner-Lu'kens test
Boet'ti·ger method
Bo·gros' space
Böh'ler splint
Böh'mer hematoxylin
Bohr
—— effect
—— mag'ne·ton'
boil
Boi'vin antigen
bo·las'ter·one'
bol·de'none'
bol'e·nol'
Bo'len test
Bo'ley gauge
Bolles splint
Bol'lin·ger granules
bol·man'ta·late'
bo·lom'e·ter
Bol'ton
—— cranial base
—— nasion plane
—— point
Bolt'worth' skate
Boltz test
bo'lus *pl.* -lus·es
Bom·bay' blood
Bo·nan'no test
bon'duc'
Bon'dy operation
bone
Bon·jean' ergotin
Bonne·vie'-Ull'rich syn-
  drome
Bon·nier' syndrome
Bon'will triangle
bon'y
Bo·oph'i·lus
—— an'nu·la'tus
boost'er
bo·rac'ic
bo'rate'
bo'rax'
bor'bo·ryg'mus *pl.* -mi'
Bor·deaux' mixture
bor'der
bor'der·line'
Bor'de·tel'la

—— bron'chi·sep'ti·ca
—— par'a·per·tus'sis
—— per·tus'sis
Bor·det'-Gen·gou' bacillus
Bor·det' test
Bord'ley-Rich'ards meth-
  od
bo'ric
bor'ne·ol'
Born'holm' disease
bor'nyl
bo'ro·cit'ric
bo'ro·glyc'er·ide'
bo'ro·glyc'er·in
bo'ron'
bo'ro·sal'i·cyl'ic
Bor·rel'i·a
—— buc·ca'le'
—— dut·to'ni·i'
—— no'vy·i'
—— re'cur·ren'tis
—— re·frin'gens
—— vin·cen'ti·i'
bor·rel'i·din
bos'se·lat'ed
bos'se·la'tion
Bos'ton sign
Bo·tal'lo duct
bo·thrid'i·um *pl.* -i·a *or*
  -i· ums
Both'ri·o·ceph'a·lus
—— a·ne'mi·a
both'ri·oid'
both'ri·on'
both'ri·um *pl.* -ri·a *or* -ri·
  ums
bo·throp'ic
Bo'throps'
—— al'ter·na'ta
—— at'rox'
—— jar'a·ra'ca
—— neu·wie'di·i'
—— num'mi·fer
bo·tog'e·nin
bot'ry·oid'
Bo·try'tis
Bött'cher cells
bot'u·li·form'
bot'u·lin
bot'u·li'num
bot'u·lism
bou'ba
Bou·chard' nodes
Bou'gain·ville' rheuma-
  tism
bou·gie'
—— à boule

Bouil·laud' disease
Bouin fixative
Bou·len'ge·ri'na
Boul'ton solution
bound
bound'a·ry
Bour·get' test
Bourne method
Bourne·ville' disease
Bour'quin-Sher'man
unit
bou'stro·phe·don'ic
bou·ton'
—— de bis'kra
—— d'o'ri·ent
bou·ton·neuse'
bou·ton·niere'
bou·tons' ter·mi·naux'
Bou·ve·ret' syndrome
Bo·ve'ri test
bo'vine'
Bow'ditch'
—— effect
—— law
bow'el
Bo'wen disease
bow'ing reflex
bow'leg'
Bow'man
—— capsule
—— glands
—— membrane
box'i·dine'
Boy'den sphincter
Boyle law
Boz·zo'lo disease
brace
bra'chi·a cer'e·bel'li'
bra'chi·al
bra'chi·al'gi·a
—— stat'i·ca par'es·thet'i·ca
bra'chi·a'lis
bra'chi·form'
bra'chi·o·ce·phal'ic
bra'chi·o·cru'ral
bra'chi·o·cu'bi·tal
bra'chi·o·cyl·lo'sis pl. -ses'
bra'chi·o·fa'ci·o·lin'gual
bra'chi·o·ra'di·a'lis
bra'chi·ot'o·my
bra'chi·um pl. -chi·a
—— col·lic'u·li' in·fe'ri·o'ris
—— colliculi su·pe'ri·o'ris
—— con'junc·ti'vum
—— conjunctivum cer'e·
bel'li'
—— pon'tis

—— quad'ri·gem'i·num in·
fe'ri·us
—— quadrigeminum su·
pe'ri·us
Brach'mann-de Lange'
syndrome
Bracht'-Wäch'ter bodies
brach'y·car'di·a
brach'y·ce·pha'li·a
brach'y·ce·phal'ic
brach'y·ceph'a·lism
brach'y·ceph'a·lous
brach'y·ceph'a·ly
brach'y·chei'li·a
brach'y·chei'rous
bra·chych'i·ly
brach'y·cra'ni·al
brach'y·dac·tyl'i·a
brach'y·dac·tyl'ic
brach'y·dac'ty·lous
brach'y·dac'ty·ly
brach'y·fa'cial
brach'y·glos'sal
brach'y·glos'si·a
brach'y·gna'thi·a
brach'y·gnath'ous
brach'y·ker'kic
brach'y·mei·o'sis pl. -ses'
brach'y·met'a·po'dy
brach'y·mor'phic
brach'y·mor'phy
brach'y·pel'lic
brach'y·pel'vic
brach'y·pha·lan'gi·a
brach'y·pha·lan'gous
brach'y·pha·lan'gy
brach'y·po'dous
brach'y·pro·sop'ic
brach'y·rhin'i·a
brach'y·rhyn'chus
brach'y·skel'ic
brach'y·sta'sis pl. -ses'
brach'y·stat'ic
brach'y·u·ran'ic
Brack'ett operation
brad'y·a·cu'si·a
brad'y·ar·rhyth'mi·a
brad'y·ar'thri·a
brad'y·aux·e'sis pl. -ses'
brad'y·car'di·a
brad'y·car'di·ac'
brad'y·car'dic
brad'y·crot'ic
brad'y·di·as'to·le
brad'y·di·as'to·li·a
brad'y·glos'si·a
brad'y·ki·ne'si·a

brad'y·ki·ne'sis pl. -ses'
brad'y·ki·net'ic
brad'y·ki'nin
brad'y·ki·nin'o·gen
brad'y·la'li·a
brad'y·lex'i·a
brad'y·pha'si·a
brad'y·phre'ni·a
brad'y·pne'a
brad'y·pra'gi·a
brad'y·prax'i·a
brad'y·rhyth'mi·a
brad'y·sper'ma·tism
brad'y·sper'mi·a
brad'y·tach'y·car'di·a
brad'y·tel'e·o·ki·ne'si·a
brad'y·tel'e·o·ki·ne'sis pl.
-ses'
Brag'ard sign
braille
Brails'ford-Mor'qui·o syndrome
Brain reflex
brain'stem'
branch'er
bran'chi·a pl. -ae'
bran'chi·al
bran'chi·o·gen'ic
bran'chi·og'e·nous
bran'chi·o'ma pl. -mas or
-ma·ta
bran'chi·o·mere'
bran'chi·om'er·ism
bran'chi·o·mo'tor
Brandt syndrome
Bran'ham sign
brash
Bras'si·ca
Brat'ton and Mar'shall
method
Brau'er operation
Brau'ne ring
Braun test
brawn'y
Brax'ton Hicks
—— contraction
—— sign
—— version
bra·ye'ra
bra·zal'um
breast
breast'bone'
breast'-fed'
breath
breathe, breathed, breath'-
ing
Bre'da disease

breech
breg'ma pl. -ma·ta
breg·mat'ic
breg'ma·to·dym'i·a
breg'ma·to·lamb'doid'
Breh and Gae'bler meth-
od
brei
Brem'er test
bren'ner·o'ma pl. -mas or
-ma·ta
Bren'ner tumor
breph'o·plas'tic
bre·tyl'i·um tos'y·late'
Breu'er reflex
Breus mole
Breutsch disease
brev'i·col'lis
brev'i·flex'or'
brev'i·lin'e·al
brev'i·ra'di·ate
Brew'er
—— infarcts
—— kidney
bridge, bridged, bridg'ing
bridge'work'
Briggs
—— bag
—— law
Bright
—— disease
—— murmur
Brill disease
Brill'-Sym'mers disease
Brill'-Zins'ser disease
Brin'ton disease
Bri·quet'
—— ataxia
—— syndrome
Bris·saud'
—— disease
—— reflex
Bris·saud'-Ma·rie' syn-
drome
broach
Broad'bent'
—— apoplexy
—— law
—— sign
Bro'ca
—— angle
—— aphasia
—— area
—— band
—— center
—— plane
—— point

Brock
—— operation
—— syndrome
Brocq disease
bro·cre'sine'
Bro'der classification
Bro'die
—— abscess
—— serocystic disease
—— tumor
Brod'mann
—— areas
—— map
bro'mate'
bro'ma·to·ther'a·py
bro'ma·to·tox'in
bro'ma·to·tox'ism
bro·maz'e·pam'
bro'ma·zine'
brom·chlor'e·none'
brom·cre'sol'
brom·eth'ol'
brom·hex'ine'
brom'hi·dro'si·pho'bi·a
brom'hi·dro'sis pl. -ses'
bro'mic
bro'mide'
bro'mi·dro'sis pl. -ses'
bro'min·ate'
brom'in·di'one'
bro'mine'
bro'min'ism
bro'mism
brom'i·so·val'um
bro'mo·ac'et·an'i·lid
bro'mo·cam'phor
bro'mo·cre'sol'
bro'mo·crip'tine'
bro'mo·de·ox'y·u'ri·dine'
bro'mo·der'ma
bro'mo·di'phen·hy'dra·
mine'
bro'mo·form'
bro'mo·hy'per·hi·dro'sis pl.
-ses'
bro'mo·hy'per·i·dro'sis pl.
-ses'
bro'mo·i'o·dism
bro'mo·ma'ni·a
bro'mo·men'or·rhe'a
bro'mo·phe'nol'
bro'mop·ne'a
bro'mo·thy'mol'
bro'mo·u'ra·cil
brom'phen·ir'a·mine'
bronch·ad'e·ni'tis
bron'chi·al

bron'chi·ec·ta'si·a
bron'chi·ec'ta·sis pl. -ses'
bron'chi·ec·tat'ic
bron'chi' lo·bar'es' et
seg'men·ta'les'
bron'chi·o·gen'ic
bron·chi'o·lar
bron'chi·ole'
bron'chi·o·lec'ta·sis pl. -ses'
bron·chi'o·li' res'pi·ra·
to'ri·i'
bron'chi·o·li'tis
—— fi·bro'sa ob·lit'e·rans'
—— ob·lit'e·rans'
bron·chi'o·lus pl. -li'
bron'chi·o·spasm
bron·chit'ic
bron·chi'tis
—— con'vul·si'va
bron'chi·um pl. -chi·a
bron'cho·al·ve'o·lar
bron'cho·bil'i·ar'y
bron'cho·blas'to·my·co'sis
pl. -ses'
bron'cho·can'di·di'a·sis
pl. -ses'
bron'cho·cav'ern·ous
bron'cho·cele'
bron'cho·ceph'a·li'tis
bron'cho·co'lic
bron'cho·con·stric'tor
bron'cho·dil'a·ta'tion
bron'cho·di·la'tor
bron'cho·e·de'ma
bron'cho·e·soph'a·ge'al
bron'cho·e·soph'a·gol'o·gy
bron'cho·e·soph'a·gos'co·
py
bron'cho·gen'ic
bron·chog'e·nous
bron'cho·gram'
bron'cho·graph'ic
bron·chog'ra·phy
bron'cho·lith'
bron'cho·li·thi'a·sis pl. -ses'
bron·chol'o·gy
bron'cho·me'di·as·ti'nal
bron'cho·mon'i·li'a·sis pl.
-ses'
bron'cho·mo'tor
bron'cho·my·co'sis pl. -ses'
bron·chop'a·thy
bron·choph'o·ny
bron'cho·plas'ty
bron'cho·ple'gi·a
bron'cho·pleu'ral
bron'cho·pneu·mo'ni·a

bron′cho•pneu′mo•ni′tis
bron′cho•pul′mo•nar′y
bron•chor′rha•phy
bron′chor•rhe′a
bron′chor•rhe′al
bron′cho•scope′
bron′cho•scop′ic
bron•chos′co•py
bron′cho•spasm
bron′cho•spi′ro•che•to′sis
pl. -ses′
bron′cho•spi•rog′ra•phy
bron′cho•spi•rom′e•ter
bron′cho•spi•rom′e•try
bron′cho•stax′is
bron′cho•ste•no′sis *pl.* -ses′
bron•chos′to•my
bron•chot′o•my
bron′cho•ve•sic′u•lar
bron′chus *pl.* -chi′
—— lin′gu•lar′is inferior
—— lingularis superior
—— lo•bar′is inferior dex′ter
—— lobaris inferior si•nis′ter
—— lobaris me′di•us dex′ter
—— lobaris superior dex′ter
—— lobaris superior si•nis′ter
—— prin′ci•pa′lis dex′ter et si•nis′ter
—— seg′men•ta′lis anterior lo′bi′ su•pe′ri•o′ris dex′tri′
—— segmentalis anterior lobi superioris si•nis′tri′
—— segmentalis ap′i•ca′lis lo′bi′ in•fe′ri•o′ris dex′tri′
—— segmentalis apicalis lobi inferioris si•nis′tri′
—— segmentalis apicalis lobi su•pe′ri•o′ris dex′tri′
—— segmentalis ap′i•co•pos•te′ri•or lo′bi′ su•pe′ri•o′ris si•nis′tri′
—— segmentalis ba•sa′lis anterior lo′bi′ in•fe′ri•o′ris dex′tri′
—— segmentalis basalis anterior lobi inferioris si•nis′tri′
—— segmentalis basalis car•di′a•cus lo′bi in•fe′ri•o′ris dex′tri′
—— segmentalis basalis cardiacus lobi inferioris si•nis′tri′
—— segmentalis basalis

lat′er•a′lis lo′bi′ in•fe′ri•o′ris dex′tri′
—— segmentalis basalis lateralis lobi inferioris si•nis′tri′
—— segmentalis basalis me′di•a′lis lo′bi′ in•fe′ri•o′ris dex′tri′
—— segmentalis basalis medialis lobi inferioris si•nis′tri′
—— segmentalis basalis posterior lo′bi′ in•fe′ri•o′ris dex′tri′
—— segmentalis basalis posterior lobi inferioris si•nis′tri′
—— segmentalis lat′er•a′lis lo′bi′ mo′di•i′ dex′tri′
—— segmentalis me′di•a′lis lo′bi′ mo′di•i′ dex′tri′
—— segmentalis posterior lo′bi′ su•pe′ri•o′ris dex′tri′
—— segmentalis sub•ap′i•ca′lis lo′bi′ in•fe′ri•o′ris dex′-tri′
—— segmentalis subapicalis lobi inferioris si•nis′tri′
—— segmentalis sub′su•pe′ri•or lo′bi′ in•fe′ri•o′ris dex′tri′
—— segmentalis subsuperi-or lobi inferioris si•nis′tri′
—— segmentalis superior lo′bi′ in•fe′ri•o′ris dex′tri′
—— segmentalis superior lobi inferioris si•nis′tri′
Brön′sted
—— and Low′ry substance
—— theory
Brooke tumor
Bro′phy operation
brow
Brown
—— ataxia
—— sheath syndrome
—— test
Browne sign
Brown′i•an motion
Brown′-Pearce′ tumor
Brown′-Sé•quard′ syndrome
bru•cel′la *pl.* -lae′
Bru•cel′la
—— a•bor′tus
—— mel′i•ten′sis
—— su′is
—— tu′la•ren′sis
Bru′cel•la′ce•ae′

bru•cel′lar
bru′cel•li′a•sis *pl.* -ses′
bru′cel•lo′sis *pl.* -ses′
Bruch membrane
bru′cine′
Bruck disease
Brü′cke
—— line
—— muscle
—— tunic
Brud•zin′ski signs
Brug′i•a
—— ma•lay′i′
bru•gi′a•sis *pl.* -ses′
Brugsch syndrome
bruis′a•bil′i•ty
bruise, bruised,
bruis′ing
bruisse•ment′
bruit
—— d′ai•rain′
—— de ca•non′
—— de cuir neuf
—— de di•able′
—— de Ro•ger′
Brun•hil′de virus
Brun′ner glands
Bruns
—— ataxia
—— law
—— syndrome
Brun′schwig operation
Brun sign
Brun′ton rule
Brush′field′ spots
Brush′y Creek fever
Bru′ton agammaglobu-linemia
brux′ism
brux′o•ma′ni•a
Bry′ant
—— line
—— operation
—— sign
—— triangle
bryg′mus
bry•o′ni•a
bu′bas
—— bra•zil′i•en′sis
bu′bo
bu′bon•ad′e•ni′tis
bu′bon•al′gi•a
bu•bon′ic
bu•bon′o•cele′
bu•bon′u•lus *pl.* -lus•es *or* -li′
bu•car′di•a

buc'ca pl. -cae'
—— ca'vi' o'ris
buc'cal
buc'ci·na'tor
buc'co·ax'i·al
buc'co·cer'vi·cal
buc'co·dis'tal
buc'co·fa'cial
buc'co·gin'gi·val
buc'co·la'bi·al
buc'co·lin'gual
buc'co·me'si·al
buc'co·na'sal
buc'co·clu'sal
buc'co·pha·ryn'ge·al
buc'co·pha·ryn'ge·us
buc'co·pul'pal
buc'co·ver'sion
buc'cu·la pl. -lae'
bu'chu
Buck
—— extension
—— fascia
—— operation
Buck'y diaphragm
bu'cli·zine'
buc·ne'mi·a
Budd
—— cirrhosis
—— disease
Budd'-Chi·a'ri syndrome
Bü'din·ger-Lud'loff-Lä'wen disease
Bueng'ner bands
Buer'ger disease
Buer'gi hypothesis
buff'er
buff'y coat
bu·for'min
bu'fo·ten'i·dine'
bu'fo·ten'in
bu'fo·tox'in
bug
bug'ger·y
Bu'ie operation
Buist method
bulb
bul'bar
bul'bo·a'tri·al
bul'bo·cap'nine'
bul'bo·cav'er·no'sus pl. -si'
bul'bo·mem'bra·nous
bul'bo·nu'cle·ar
bul'bo·spi'nal
bul'bo·spon'gi·o'sus pl. -si'
bul'bo·u·re'thral
bul'bous

bul'bo·ven·tric'u·lar
bul'bus pl. -bi'
—— a·or'tae'
—— ar·te'ri·o'sus
—— cor'dis
—— cor'nu pos·te'ri·o'ris
—— cor'nus pos·te'ri·o'ris
—— oc'u·li'
—— ol'fac·to'ri·us
—— pe'nis
—— pi'li'
—— u·re'thrae'
—— ve'nae' jug'u·lar'is inferior
—— venae jugularis superior
—— ves·tib'u·li' va·gi'nae'
bu·le'sis
bu·lim'i·a
bu·lim'ic
Bu·li'nus
bul'la pl. -lae'
—— eth'moi·da'lis ca'vi' na'si'
—— ethmoidalis os'sis ethmoidalis
—— tym'pa·ni'
bul'late'
bul·la'tion
bul·lec'to·my
bul'lous
Bum'ke pupil
bu·nam'i·dine'
bun'dle
—— of His
—— of Kent
Bun'ga·rus
—— can'di·dus
—— fas'ci·a'tus
bung'-eye'
bun'ion
bun'ion·ec'to·my
bun'ion·ette'
Bun'nell test
bu'no·dont'
Bun'sen
—— absorption coefficient
—— solubility coefficient
Bun'sen-Ros'coe law
Bun'yam·ve'ra virus
bun'ya·vi'rus
buph·thal'mi·a
buph·thal'mos
bu·piv'a·caine'
bur also burr
bu'ra·mate'
bur'bot

Bur'chard test
Bur'dach' nucleus
Burd'wan fever
bu·ret' also burette
bu·rette' var. of buret
Bur'kitt lymphoma
burn
Bur·nett' syndrome
bur'nish·er
Bu'row' solution
burr var. of bur
bur'sa pl. -sas or -sae'
—— an'se·ri'na
—— bi·cip'i·to·gas'troc·ne'mi·a'lis
—— bi·cip'i·to·ra'di·a'lis
—— clo·a'ca
—— cu'bi·ta'lis in'ter·os'se·a
—— i·li'a·ca sub'ten·din'e·a
—— il'i·o·pec·tin'e·a
—— in'fra·hy·oi'de·a
—— in'fra·pat'el·lar'is pro·fun'da
—— is'chi·ad'i·ca mus'cu·li' glu'tae·i' max'i·mi'
—— ischiadica musculi glu'te·i' max'i·mi'
—— ischiadica musculi ob·tu'ra·to'ri·i' in·ter'ni'
—— mu·co'sa
—— mucosa sub'cu·ta'ne·a
—— mucosa sub·fas'ci·a'lis
—— mucosa sub·mus'cu·lar'is
—— mucosa sub'ten·din'e·a
—— mus'cu·li' co'ra·co·bra'chi·a'lis
—— musculi gas'troc·ne·mi·i' lat'er·a'lis
—— musculi gastrocnemii me'di·a'lis
—— musculi la·tis'si·mi' dor'si'
—— musculi ob·tu'ra·to'ri·i' in·ter'ni'
—— musculi pop·lit'e·i'
—— musculi sar·to'ri·i' pro'pri·a
—— musculi sem'i·mem'bra·no'si'
—— musculi ster'no·hy·oi'de·i'
—— musculi sub·scap'u·lar'is
—— of Fab·ri'ci·us
—— o'men·ta'lis
—— o·var'i·ca

—— pha·ryn'ge·a
—— prae·pat'el·lar'is sub'cu·ta'ne·a
—— praepatellaris sub·fas'ci·a'lis
—— praepatellaris sub'ten·din'e·a
—— sub'a·cro'mi·a'lis
—— sub'cu·ta'ne·a a·cro'mi·a'lis
—— subcutanea o'le·cra'ni'
—— subcutanea pre·pat'el·lar'is
—— subcutanea tro'chan·ter'i·ca
—— sub'del·toi'de·a
—— sub·fas'ci·a'lis pre·pat'el·lar'is
—— sub'ten·din'e·a i·li'a·ca
—— subtendinea mus'cu·li' gas'troc·ne'mi·i' lat'er·a'lis
—— subtendinea musculi gastrocnemii me'di·a'lis
—— subtendinea musculi la·tis'si·mi' dor'si'
—— subtendinea musculi ob·tu'ra·to'ri·i' in·ter'ni'
—— subtendinea musculi sub·scap'u·lar'is
—— subtendinea pre·pat'el·lar'is
—— sy·no'vi·a'lis
—— synovialis sub'cu·ta'ne·a
—— synovialis sub·fas'ci·a'lis
—— synovialis sub·mus'cu·lar'is
—— synovialis sub'ten·din'e·a
—— ten'di·nis A·chil'lis
—— tendinis cal·ca'ne·i'
—— tro'chan·ter'i·ca mus'cu·li' glu'tae·i' me'di·i' anterior
—— trochanterica musculi glutaei min'i·mi'
—— trochanterica musculi glu'te·i' max'i·mi'
—— trochanterica musculi glutei min'i·mi'
bur'sae'
—— sub'ten·din'e·ae' mus'cu·li' sar·to'ri·i'
—— tro'chan·ter'i·cae' mus'cu·li' glu'te·i' me'di·i'
bur'sal

bur·sec'to·my
Bur'ser·a'ce·ae'
bur·si'tis
bur'so·lith'
Bur'y disease
Busch'ke disease
Bus·quet' disease
Bus'se-Busch'ke disease
bu·sul'fan'
bu'ta·bar'bi·tal'
bu'ta·caine'
bu·tac'e·tin
bu·tal'bi·tal'
bu·tam'ben
bu'ta·no'ic
bu'ta·nol'
bu'ta·per'a·zine'
bu'tene'
bu'te·nyl
bu'te·thal'
bu·teth'a·mine'
bu·thi'a·zide'
Bu'thus
—— co'ci·ta'nus
—— i·tal'i·cus
—— mar·ten'si'
But'ler
—— and Tut'hill method
—— solution
bu'to·py'ro·nox'yl
bu·tor'pha·nol'
bu·tox'a·mine'
bu·trip'ty·line'
butt
but'tock
but'ton
but'ton·hole'
but'tress
bu'tyl
—— par'a·hy·drox'y·ben'zo·ate'
—— p-hy·drox'y·ben'zo·ate'
bu'tyl·ene'
bu'tyl'i·dene'
bu'ty·ra'ceous
bu'ty·rate'
bu·tyr'ic
bu'ty·rin
bu'ty·rin·ase'
bu'ty·roid'
bu'ty·ryl
bux'ine'
Buz'zard reflex
Bwam'ba
—— fever
—— virus
By'ler disease

bys'si·no'sis pl. -ses'
bys'soid'
bys'so·phthi'sis pl. -ses'
By'wa'ters syndrome

C

Cab'ot
—— rings
—— splint
cac·a'tion
cac'a·to'ry
cac'er·ga'si·a
cac'es·the'nic
cac'es·the'si·a
cac'es·the'sic
ca·chec'tic
ca·chet'
ca·chex'i·a
—— ex'oph·thal'mi·ca
—— hy'po·phys'i·o·pri'va
—— stru'mi·pri'va
—— thy'ro·pri'va
cach'in·na'tion
cac'o·de'mo·no·ma'ni·a
cac'o·gen'e·sis
cac'o·geu'si·a
ca·cos'mi·a
ca·dav'er
ca·dav'er·ic
ca·dav'er·ine'
ca·dav'er·ous
cad'mi·um
ca·du'ca
ca·du'ce·us
caec–. See words spelled cec–.
caeci–. See words spelled ceci–.
cae'ci·tas
caeco–. See words spelled ceco–.
cae'cus
cae·sar'e·an var. of cesarean
ca·fard'
caf·fe'ic
caf'feine'
caf'fein·ism
Caf'fey disease
Caille test
Ca·jal'
—— cell
—— gold'-sub'li·mate' method

—— interstitial nucleus
—— silver method
caj′e·put
Cal′a·bar′
—— bean
—— swellings
cal′a·mine′
cal′a·mus *pl.* -mi′
—— scrip·to′ri·us
cal·ca′ne·al
cal·ca′ne·an
cal·ca′ne·i′tis
cal·ca′ne·o′a·poph′y·si′tis
cal·ca′ne·o·as·trag′a·lar
cal·ca′ne·o·ca′vus
cal·ca′ne·o·cu′boid′
cal·ca′ne·o·dyn′i·a
cal·ca′ne·o·fib′u·lar
cal·ca′ne·o·na·vic′u·lar
cal·ca′ne·o·plan′tar
cal·ca′ne·o·scaph′oid′
cal·ca′ne·o·tib′i·al
cal·ca′ne·o·val′gus
cal·ca′ne·um *pl.* -ne·a
cal·ca′ne·us *pl.* -ne·i′
cal·ca′no·dyn′i·a
cal′car′ *pl.* cal·car′i·a
—— a′vis
—— fem′o·ra′le′
cal′ca·rate′
cal·car′e·a
cal·car′e·ous
cal·ca·rine
cal·car′i·u′ri·a
cal·ce′mi·a
cal′ci·bil′i·a
cal′cic
cal′ci·co′sis *pl.* -ses′
cal·cif′a·mes′
cal·cif′er·ol′
cal·cif′er·ous
cal·cif′ic
cal′ci·fi·ca′tion
cal′ci·fy′, -fied′, -fy′ing
cal·cig′er·ous
cal·cim′e·ter
cal′ci·na′tion
cal′cine′, -cined′, -cin′ing
cal′ci·no′sis *pl.* -ses′
—— cu′tis cir′cum·scrip′ta
—— cutis u′ni·ver·sa′lis
—— universalis
cal′ci·pe′ni·a
cal′ci·phy·lac′tic
cal′ci·phy·lax′is *pl.* -lax′es′
cal′cite′
cal′ci·to′nin

cal′ci·um
cal′ci·u′ri·a
cal′co·glob′u·lin
cal′co·sphe′rite′
cal′co·spher′ule′
cal′cu·lar′y
cal′cu·lo·gen′e·sis *pl.* -ses′
cal′cu·lo′sis *pl.* -ses′
cal′cu·lous *(pertaining to calculi)*
♦*calculus*
cal′cu·lus *(an abnormal concretion in the body), pl.* -li′ *or* -lus·es
♦*calculous*
—— fel′le·us
Cald′well-Luc′ operation
Cald′well projection
cal′e·fa′cient
cal′en·tu′ra
calf *pl.* calves
ca′li·ber *also* calibre
cal′i·brate′, -brat′ed, -brat′-ing
cal′i·bra′tion
cal′i·bra′tor
cal′i·bre *var. of* caliber
cal′i·ce′al *var. of* calyceal
ca′li·cec′ta·sis *pl.* -ses′, *var. of* calycectasis
ca′li·cec′to·my *var. of* calycectomy
ca·lic′i·form′ *var. of* calyciform
ca·lic′i·nal *var. of* calycinal
ca′li·cine′ *var. of* calycine
ca·lic′u·lus *pl.* -li′, *also* caly-culus
—— gus′ta·to′ri·us
—— oph·thal′mi·cus
cal′i·per
cal′is·then′ics
ca′lix *pl.* ca′li·ces′, *var. of* ca-lyx
Cal′kins method
Cal′lan·der amputation
Call′-Ex′ner bodies
cal′li·pe′di·a
Cal·liph′o·ra
—— vom′i·to′ri·a
Cal′li·phor′i·dae′
cal′lo·ma′ni·a
cal·lo′sal
cal·los′i·tas
cal·los′i·ty
cal·lo′so·mar′gi·nal
cal·lo′sum *pl.* -sa

cal′lous *(hard)*
♦*callus*
cal′lus *(a callosity)*
♦*callous*
calm′a·tive
Cal·mette′
—— test
—— vaccine
cal′or
ca·lo′ric
cal′o·rie
cal′o·rif′ic
ca·lo′ri·gen′ic
cal′o·rim′e·ter
cal′o·ri·met′ric
cal′o·rim′e·try
Ca·lot′ triangle
cal·var′i·a *pl.* -ae′
cal·var′i·al
cal·var′i·um
Cal·vé′
—— disease
—— ver′te·bra pla′na
cal·vi′ti·es′
calx *pl.* cal′ces′
cal′y·can′thine′
cal′y·ce′al *also* caliceal
ca·ly·cec′ta·sis *pl.* -ses′, *also* calicectasis
ca·ly·cec′to·my *also* calicectomy
ca·ly·ces′
—— re·na′les′
—— renales ma·jo′res′
—— renales mi·no′res′
ca·lyc′i·form′ *also* calici-form
ca·lyc′i·nal *also* calicinal
ca′ly·cine′ *also* calicine
ca·lyc′u·li′ gus′ta·to′ri·i′
ca·lyc′u·lus *pl.* -li′, *var. of* caliculus
cal′y·ec′ta·sis *or* cal′i·ec′ta·sis
Ca·lym′ma·to·bac·te′ri·um gran′u·lo′ma·tis
ca′lyx *pl.* -lyx·es *or* -ly·ces′, *also* calix
cam′bi·um *pl.* -bi·ums *or* -bi·a
cam′er·a *pl.* -ae
—— anterior bul′bi′
—— lu′ci·da
—— oc′u·li′ anterior
—— oculi posterior
—— posterior bul′bi′
—— sep′ti′ lu′ci·di′
—— vit′re·a bul′bi′

cam'i·sole'
Cam'midge test
Camp'bell operation
Cam'per
—— fascia
—— ligament
—— line
cam·pes'ter·ol'
cam'phor
cam'pho·ra'ceous
cam'phor·at'ed
cam·pho'ric
cam'phor·ism
cam·pim'e·ter
cam·pim'e·try
camp'to·cor'mi·a
camp'to·dac'ty·ly
Cam'py·lo·bac'ter
—— fe'tus
—— je·ju'ni'/co'li'
Cam·u·ra'ti-En'gel·mann disease
ca·nal'
—— of Cor'ti
—— of Nuck
—— of Schlemm
ca·na'les'
—— al've·o·lar'es' max·il'lae'
—— di·plo'i·ci'
—— lon'gi·tu'di·na'les' mo·di'o·li'
—— pal·a'ti·ni'
—— palatini mi·no'res'
—— sem'i·cir'cu·lar'es' os'se·i'
can·a·lic'u·lar
can·a·lic'u·la'tion
can·a·lic'u·li'
—— ca·rot'i·co·tym·pan'i·ci'
—— den·ta'les'
—— vas'cu·lo'si'
can·a·lic'u·li·za'tion
can·a·lic'u·lo·plas'ty
can·a·lic'u·lus pl. -li'
—— chor'dae' tym'pa·ni'
—— coch'le·ae'
—— lac'ri·ma'lis
—— mas·toi'de·us
—— tym·pan'i·cus
can·a·line'
ca·na'lis pl. -les'
—— ad'duc·to'ri·us
—— al'i·men·tar'i·us
—— a·na'lis
—— ba'si·pha·ryn'ge·us

—— ca·rot'i·cus
—— car'pi'
—— cen·tra'lis
—— cer'vi·cis u'ter·i'
—— con'dy·lar'is
—— con'dy·loi'de·us
—— fa'ci·a'lis
—— fem'o·ra'lis
—— hy·a'loi'de·us
—— hy'po·glos'si'
—— in'ci·si'vus
—— in'fra·or·bi·ta'lis
—— in'gui·na'lis
—— man·dib'u·lae'
—— mus'cu·lo·tu·bar'i·us
—— na'so·lac'ri·ma'lis
—— nu·tri'ci·us
—— ob'tu·ra·to'ri·us
—— op'ti·cus
—— pal·a'ti·nus major
—— pal·a'to·vag'i·na'lis
—— pha·ryn'ge·us
—— pter'y·goi'de·us
—— pter'y·go·pal'a·ti'nus
—— pu·den·da'lis
—— py'lo·ri'cus
—— rad'i·cis den'tis
—— sa·cra'lis
—— sem'i·cir'cu·lar'is anterior
—— semicircularis lat'er·a'lis
—— semicircularis posterior
—— semicircularis superior
—— spi·na'lis
—— spi·ra'lis coch'le·ae'
—— spiralis mo·di'o·li'
—— ven·tric'u·li'
—— ver'te·bra'lis
—— vom'er·o·vag'i·na'lis
ca·nal'i·za'tion
ca·nal'ize', -ized, -iz'ing
ca·nal'o·plas'ty
canals of Pe·tit'
Can'a·van disease
can'a·van'ine'
can'cel·late'
can'cel·lat'ed
can'cel·lous
can'cer
—— en cui·rasse'
—— oc·cul'tus
can'cer·i·ci'dal
can'cer·i·gen'ic
can'cer·o·gen
can'cer·o·gen'ic
can'cer·o·pho'bi·a

can'cer·ous
can'cer·pho'bi·a
can'croid'
can'crum
—— na'si'
—— o'ris
—— pu·den'di'
can'di·ci'din
Can'di·da
—— al'bi·cans'
can'di·dal
can'di·di'a·sis pl. -ses'
can'di·did
Can'i·dae'
ca'nine'
ca·ni'nus pl. -ni'
ca·ni'ti·es'
—— un'gui·um
can'ker
can'na·bi·di'ol'
can'na·bin
can·nab'i·nol'
can'na·bis
can'na·bism
Can'niz·za'ro reaction
Can'non
—— law of denervation
—— ring
can'nu·la pl. -las or -lae'
can'nu·lar
can'nu·late', -lat'ed, -lat'ing
can'nu·la'tion
can'nu·li·za'tion
can'nu·lize', -lized', -liz'ing
can're·none'
can'thal
can'tha·ri'a·sis pl. -ses'
can·thec'to·my
can·thi'tis
can·thol'y·sis pl. -ses'
can'tho·plas'ty
can·thor'rha·phy
can·thot'o·my
can'thus pl. -thi'
caou'tchouc'
cap
—— of Zinn
ca·pac'i·tance
Cap·gras' syndrome
cap'il·lar'ec·ta'si·a
Cap'il·lar'i·a
—— aer'o·phi'la
—— he·pat'i·ca
—— phil'ip·pi·nen'sis
cap'il·la·ri'a·sis pl. -ses'
cap'il·la·ri'tis
cap'il·lar'i·ty

cap'il·la·ros'co·py
cap'il·lar'y
cap'il·li'ti·um *pl.* -ti·a
cap'il·lo·ve'nous
ca·pil'lus *pl.* -li'
cap'i·stra'tion
cap'i·tate'
cap'i·ta'tum *pl.* -ta
cap'i·tel'lar
cap'i·tel'lum *pl.* -la
ca·pit'u·lar
ca·pit'u·lum *pl.* -la
—— cos'tae'
—— fib'u·lae'
—— hu'mer·i'
—— mal'le·i'
—— man·dib'u·lae'
—— os'si·um met'a·car·pa'li·
um
—— ossium met'a·tar·sa'li·
um
—— ra'di·i'
—— San'to·ri'ni·i'
—— sta'pe·dis
—— ul'nae'
Ca'pi·vac'ci·us ulcer
Cap'lan syndrome
Capps pleural reflex
cap'rate'
cap're·o·late'
cap'ric
ca·pril'o·quism
cap'ro·ate'
ca·pro'ic
cap'ro·in
cap'ry·late'
ca·pryl'ic
cap'sid
cap'so·mer'
cap'su·la *pl.* -lae'
—— ad'i·po'sa re'nis
—— ar·tic'u·lar'is
—— articularis a·cro'mi·o·
cla·vic'u·lar'is
—— articularis ar·tic'u·la'ti·
o'nis ra'di·o·car'pe·ae'
—— articularis articula-
tionis tar'si' trans'ver'sae'
—— articularis articula-
tionis tem'po·ro·man·dib'u·
lar'is
—— articularis ar·tic'u·la'ti·
o'num ver'te·brar'um
—— articularis at·lan'to·
ax'i·a'lis lat'er·a'lis
—— articularis atlantoaxialis me'di·a'na

—— articularis at·lan'to·oc·
cip'i·ta'lis
—— articularis cal·ca'ne·o·
cu·boi'de·ae'
—— articularis cap'i·tis
cos'tae'
—— articularis car'po·met'a·
car'pe·a pol'li·cis
—— articularis cos'to·
trans'ver·sar'i·ae'
—— articularis cox'ae'
—— articularis cri'co·ar'y·
tae·noi'de·a
—— articularis cri'co·ar'y·
te·noi'de·a
—— articularis cri'co·thy're·
oi'de·a
—— articularis cri'co·thy·
roi'de·a
—— articularis cu·bi·ti'
—— articularis ge'nus
—— articularis hu'mer·i'
—— articularis man·dib'u·
lae'
—— articularis ma'nus
—— articularis os'sis pi'si·
for'mis
—— articularis ra'di·o·ul·
nar'is dis·ta'lis
—— articularis ster'no·cla·
vic'u·lar'is
—— articularis ster'no·cos·
ta'lis
—— articularis sub'ta·lar'is
—— articularis ta'lo·cal·
ca'ne·a
—— articularis ta'lo·cru·
ra'lis
—— articularis ta'lo·na·
vic'u·lar'is
—— articularis tib'i·o·fib'u·
lar'is
—— ex·ter'na
—— fi·bro'sa glan'du·lae'
thy·roi'de·ae'
—— fibrosa (Glis·so'ni')
—— fibrosa per'i·vas'cu·
lar'is
—— fibrosa re'nis
—— glo·mer'u·li'
—— in·ter'na
—— len'tis
—— nu'cle·i' den·ta'ti'
cap'su·lae'
—— ar·tic'u·lar'es' at·lan'to·
ep'i·stroph'i·cae'

—— articulares ca·pit'u·li'
cos'tae'
—— articulares car'po·
met'a·car'pe·ae'
—— articulares dig'i·to'rum
ma'nus
—— articulares digitorum
pe'dis
—— articulares in'ter·met'a·
car'pe·ae'
—— articulares in'ter·met'a·
tar'se·ae'
—— articulares in'ter·pha·
lan'ge·ar'um ma'nus
—— articulares interphalangearum pe'dis
—— articulares met'a·
car'po·pha·lan'ge·ae'
—— articulares met'a·ter'so·
pha·lan'ge·ae'
—— articulares tar'so·met'a·
tar'se·ae'
cap'su·lar
cap'sule'
cap·su·lec'to·my
cap'su·li'tis
cap'su·lo·len·tic'u·lar
cap'su·lo'ma *pl.* -mas *or*
-ma·ta
cap'su·lo·plas'ty
cap'su·lor'rha·phy
cap'su·lo·tha·lam'ic
cap'su·lo·tome'
cap'su·lot'o·my
cap'ta·mine'
cap'ti·va'tion
cap'to·di·ame'
cap'to·pril
cap'u·ride'
cap'ut *pl.* cap'i·ta
—— an'gu·lar'e' mus'cu·li'
qua·dra'ti' la'bi·i' su·pe'ri·
o'ris
—— brev'e' mus'cu·li' bi·
cip'i·tis bra'chi·i'
—— breve musculi bicipitis
fem'o·ris
—— cos'tae'
—— de·for'ma'tum
—— ep'i·dym'i·dis
—— fem'o·ris
—— fib'u·lae'
—— gal'e·a'tum
—— hu'mer·a'le' mus'cu·li'
ex·ten'so·ris car'pi' ul·nar'is
—— humerale musculi flex·
o'ris car'pi' ul·nar'is

—— humerale musculi flex-
oris dig'i·to'rum sub·li'mis
—— humerale musculi
pro'na·to'ris te·re'tis
—— hu'mer·i'
—— hu'mer·o·ul·nar'e'
mus'cu·li' flex·o'ris dig'i·
to'rum su·per·fi'ci·a'lis
—— in'fra·or'bi·ta'le'
mus'cu·li' qua·dra'ti' la'bi·i'
—— lat'er·a'le' mus'cu·li'
gas'troc·ne'mi·i'
—— laterale musculi tri·
cip'i·tis bra'chi·i'
—— lon'gum mus'cu·li' bi·
cip'i·tis bra'chi·i'
—— longum musculi bicipi-
tis fem'o·ris
—— longum musculi tri·
cip'i·tis bra'chi·i'
—— mal'le·i'
—— man·dib'u·lae'
—— me'di·a'le' mus'cu·li'
gas'troc·ne'mi·i'
—— mediale musculi tri·
cip'i·tis bra'chi·i'
—— me·du'sae'
—— mus'cu·li'
—— nu'cle·i' cau·da'ti'
—— ob·li'quum mus'cu·li'
ad·duc·to'ris hal'lu·cis
—— obliquum musculi
adductoris pol'li·cis
—— ob'sti·pum
—— os'sis met'a·car·pa'lis
—— ossis met'a·tar·sa'lis
—— pan·cre'a·tis
—— pha·lan'gis ma'nus
—— phalangis pe'dis
—— pro·fun'dum mus'cu·li'
flex·o'ris pol'li·cis brev'is
—— qua·dra'tum
—— ra'di·a'le' mus'cu·li'
flex·o'ris dig'i·to'rum su·per·
fi'ci·a'lis
—— ra'di·i'
—— sta·pe'dis
—— suc'ce·da·ne'um
—— su'per·fi'ci·a'le' mus'cu·
li' flex·o'ris pol'li·cis brev'is
—— ta'li'
—— trans·ver'sum mus'cu·
li' ad·duc·to'ris hal'lu·cis
—— transversum musculi
adductoris pol'li·cis
—— ul'nae'

—— ul·nar'e' mus'cu·li'
ex'ten·so'ris car'pi'ul·nar'is
—— ulnare musculi flex·
o'ris car'pi' ul·nar'is
—— ulnare musculi pro'na·
to'ris te·re'tis
—— zy'go·mat'i·cum
mus'cu·li' qua·dra'ti' la'bi·i'
su·pe'ri·o'ris
Car'a·bel'li cusp
car·am'i·phen
car'a·pace'
car'ba·chol'
car'ba·cryl'a·mine'
car'ba·cryl'ic
car'ba·dox'
car'ba·mate'
car'bam·az'e·pine'
car·bam'ic
car·bam'ide'
car·bam'i·dine'
carb'a·mi'no
carb'a·mi'no·he'mo·glo'bin
car'bam'yl
carb·an'i·on'
car·bar'sone'
car·baz'o·chrome'
car'ba·zole'
car·ben'i·cil'lin
car·be'ta·pen'tane'
car'bi·nol'
car'bin·ox'a·mine'
car'bi·phene'
car'bo
car'bo·ben·zox'y
car'bo·clo'ral
car'bo·cy'clic
car'bo·hy'drase'
car'bo·hy'drate'
car'bo·hy'dra·tu'ri·a
car·bo·late', -lat'ed, -lat'ing
car'bol'ic
car'bo·li'gase'
car'bo·lism
car'bo·lu'ri·a
car'bo·mer
car'bo·my'cin
car'bon
car'bo·na'ceous
car·bon·ate', -at'ed, -at'ing
car·bon'ic
car·bo'ni·um
car'bon·i·za'tion
car'bon·ize', -ized', -iz'ing
car'bon·u'ri·a
car'bon·yl
car·box'y·he'mo·glo'bin

car·box'y·he'mo·glo'bi·
ne'mi·a
car·box'yl
car·box'yl·ase'
car'box·yl'ic
car·box'y·my'o·glo'bin
car·box'y·pep'ti·dase'
car·box'y·pol'y·pep'ti·dase'
car'bro·mal
car'bun'cle
car·bun'cu·lar
car·bun'cu·loid'
car·bun'cu·lo'sis pl. -ses'
car'byl·a·mine'
Car'cas·sonne' ligament
car'ci·nec'to·my
car'ci·ne'mi·a
car·cin'o·gen
car'ci·no·gen'e·sis
car'ci·no·ge·net'ic
car'ci·no·gen'ic
car'ci·no·ge·nic'i·ty
car'ci·noid'
car'ci·noi·do'sis pl. -ses'
car'ci·no'ma pl. -mas or
-ma·ta
—— bron'chi·o·lo'rum
—— in si'tu
—— mu'co·cel'lu·lar'e'
o·var'i·i'
—— oc·cul'ta
—— sim'plex'
—— sub·stan'ti·ae' cor'ti·
ca'lis su'pra·re·na'lis
car'ci·nom'a·toid'
car'ci·no'ma·toi'des' al've·
o·gen'i·ca mul'ti·cen'tri·
ca
car'ci·no'ma·to'sis pl. -ses'
car'ci·nom'a·tous
car'ci·no·pho'bi·a
car'ci·no·sar·co'ma pl. -mas
or -ma·ta
car'ci·no'sis pl. -ses'
Car'den amputation
car'di·a pl. -ae' or -as
—— ven·tric'u·li'
car'di·ac'
car·di'a·co ne'gro
car'di·al
car·di·al'gi·a
car'di·as·the'ni·a
car'di·asth'ma
car'di·cen·te'sis pl. -ses'
car'di·ec'ta·sis pl. -ses'
car'di·ec'to·my
car'di·o·ac·cel'er·a'tor

car'di·o·ac'tive
car'di·o·an'gi·ol'o·gy
car'di·o·a·or'tic
car'di·o·ar·te'ri·al
car'di·o·asth'ma
car'di·o·au'di·to'ry
car'di·o·cele'
car'di·o·cen·te'sis *pl.* -ses'
car'di·o·cha·la'si·a
car'di·o·cir·rho'sis *pl.* -ses'
car'di·o·cla'si·a
car'di·o·di·la'tor
car'di·o·di·o'sis *pl.* -ses'
car'di·o·dy·nam'ic
car'di·o·dy·nam'ics
car'di·o·dyn'i·a
car'di·o·e·soph'a·ge'al
car'di·o·fa'cial
car'di·o·gen'e·sis *pl.* -ses'
car'di·o·gen'ic
car'di·o·gram'
car'di·o·graph'
car'di·o·graph'ic
car'di·og'ra·phy
car'di·o·he·pat'ic
car'di·o·hep'a·to·meg'a·ly
car'di·oid'
car'di·o'in·hib'i·tor
car'di·o·in·hib'i·to'ry
car'di·o·ki·net'ic
car'di·o·ky·mog'ra·phy
car'di·o·lip'in
car'di·o·lith'
car'di·ol'o·gist
car'di·ol'o·gy
car'di·ol'y·sis *pl.* -ses'
car'di·o·ma·la'ci·a
car'di·o·me·ga'li·a gly'co·
  gen'i·ca dif·fu'sa
car'di·o·meg'a·ly
car'di·o·mel'a·no'sis
  pl. -ses'
car'di·o·men'su·ra'tor
car'di·o·men'to·pex'y
car'di·om'e·ter
car'di·om'e·try
car'di·o·mo·til'i·ty
car'di·o·my'o·li·po'sis
car'di·o·my·op'a·thy
car'di·o·my'o·pex'y
car'di·o·my·ot'o·my
car'di·o·ne·cro'sis *pl.* -ses'
car'di·o·nec'tor
car'di·o·neph'ric
car'di·o·neu'ral
car'di·o·pal'u·dism
car'di·o·path'

car'di·o·path'i·a
car'di·o·path'ic
car'di·o·pa·thol'o·gy
car'di·op'a·thy
car'di·o·per'i·car'di·o·pex'y
car'di·o·per'i·car·di'tis
car'di·o·pho'bi·a
car'di·o·plas'ty
car'di·o·ple'gi·a
car'di·o·pneu·mat'ic
car'di·o·pneu'mo·graph'
car'di·o·pneu·mog'ra·phy
car'di·op·to'si·a
car'di·op·to'sis *pl.* -ses'
car'di·o·pul'mo·nar'y
car'di·o·pul·mon'ic
car'di·o·punc'ture
car'di·o·py·lo'ric
car'di·o·re'nal
car'di·o·res'pi·ra·to'ry
car'di·or·rha·phy
car'di·or·rhex'is *pl.* -rhex'es'
car'di·o·spasm
car'di·o·ste·no'sis *pl.* -ses'
car'di·o·sym'phy·sis
  pl. -ses'
car'di·o·ta·chom'e·ter
car'di·o·ther'a·py
car'di·o·thy'ro·tox'i·co'sis
  pl. -ses'
car'di·ot'o·my
car'di·o·ton'ic
car'di·o·tox'ic
car'di·o·val'vu·lar
car'di·o·val'vu·li'tis
car'di·o·val'vu·lot'o·my
car'di·o·vas'cu·lar
car'di·o·ver'sion
car·di'tis
car'ies
—— sic'ca
ca·ri'na *pl.* -nas *or* -nae'
—— na'si'
—— tra'che·ae'
—— u're·thra'lis va·gi'nae'
ca·ri'nal
car'i·nate'
car'i·o·gen'ic
car'i·ous
car·i'so·pro'dol'
Carl Smith disease
Car'man meniscus sign
car·min'a·tive
car'mine
car'mus·tine'
car'ne·ous
car·ni·fi·ca'tion

car'ni·tine'
car·niv'o·rous
car'no·sine'
car'no·si·ne'mi·a
car'no·si·nu'ri·a
car'o *pl.* car'nes'
—— qua·dra'ta ma'nus
—— quadrata syl'vi·i'
car'o·tene'
car'o·te·ne'mi·a *also* caro-
  tinemia
ca·rot'e·noid'
car'o·te·no'sis *pl.* -ses', *also*
  carotinosis
ca·rot'ic
ca·rot'i·co·cli'noid'
ca·rot'i·co·tym·pan'ic
ca·rot'id
ca·rot'i·dyn'i·a
car'o·tin
car'o·ti·ne'mi·a *var. of* caro-
  tenemia
car'o·ti·no'sis *pl.* -ses', *var.*
  of carotenosis
ca·rot'o·dyn'i·a
car'pa·ine'
car'pal
car·pec'to·my
Car'pen·ter syndrome
car·phen'a·zine'
car·phol'o·gy
car'po·car'pal
car'po·met'a·car'pal
car'po·pe'dal
car'po·pha·lan'ge·al
car'pop·to'sis *pl.* -ses'
car'pus *pl.* -pi'
Car·rel'-Da'kin treatment
car'ri·er
Car·ri·ón' disease
Carr'-Price' test
Car'ter operation
car'ti·lage
—— of San'to·ri'ni
—— of Wris'berg'
car'ti·lag'i·nes'
—— a·lar'es' mi·no'res'
—— la·ryn'gis
—— na·sa'les' ac'ces·so'ri·
  ae'
—— na'si'
—— ses'a·moi'de·ae' na'si'
—— tra'che·a'les'
car'ti·la·gin'i·fi·ca'tion
car'ti·lag'i·nous
car'ti·la'go *pl.* -lag'i·nes'
—— a·lar'is major

—— ar·tic′u·lar′is
—— ar′y·tae·noi′de·a
—— ar′y·te·noi′de·a
—— au·ric′u·lae′
—— cor·nic′u·la′ta
—— cos·ta′lis
—— cri·coi′de·a
—— cu·ne′i·for′mis
—— ep′i·glot′ti·ca
—— ep′i·phys′i·a′lis
—— me·a′tus a·cu′sti·ci′
—— na′si′ lat′er·a′lis
—— sep′ti′ na′si′
—— ses′a·moi′de·a
—— thy′re·oi′de·a
—— thy·roi′de·a
—— tri·tic′e·a
—— tu′bae′ au′di·ti′vae′
—— vom′er·o·na·sa′lis
car′un′cle
ca·run′cu·la *pl.* -lae′
—— hy′me·na′les′
—— lac′ri·ma′lis
—— sub′lin·gua′lis
ca·run′cu·lar
ca·run′cu·late′
ca·run′cu·lat′ed
Car·val′lo sign
Car′y-Blair′ medium
Ca·sal′ collar
cas·an′thra·nol′
Ca·sa′res Gil stain
cas·cade′, -cad′ed, -cad′ing
cas·car′a
—— sa·gra′da
ca′se·ase′
ca′se·ate′, -at′ed, -at′ing
ca′se·a′tion
ca′se·i·form′
ca′sein′
ca′sein′ate′
ca′se·o·cal·cif′ic
ca′se·ous
Case pad sign
Cas′i·mi·ro′a
—— ed′u·lis
Ca′so′ni test
Cas′sel·ber′ry position
Cas′ser (Cas·se′ri·o) fontanel
Cas·taigne′ method
Cas′ta·ñe′da
—— rat′-lung′ method
—— vaccine
Cas′tel·la′ni
—— disease
—— paint

Cas′tel method
cas·trate′, -trat′ed, -trat′ing
cas·tra′tion
cas′tro·phre′ni·a
cas′u·is′tics
cat′a·ba′si·al
ca·tab′a·sis *pl.* -ses′
cat′a·bat′ic
cat′a·bi·o′sis *pl.* -ses′
cat′a·bi·ot′ic
cat′a·bol′ic
ca·tab′o·lism
ca·tab′o·lite′
ca·tab′o·lize′, -lized′, -liz′ing
cat′a·caus′tic
cat′a·clei′sis *pl.* -ses′
cat′a·clon′ic
cat′a·clo′nus
cat′a·crot′ic
ca·tac′ro·tism
cat′a·did′y·mus *var. of* katadidymus
cat′a·di·op′tric
cat′a·lase′
cat′a·lep′sis *pl.* -ses′
cat′a·lep′sy
cat′a·lep′tic
cat′a·lep′ti·form′
cat′a·lep′toid′
ca·tal′y·sis *pl.* -ses′
cat′a·lyst
cat′a·lyt′ic
cat′a·ly·za′tion
cat′a·lyze′, -lyzed′, -lyz′ing
cat′a·lyz′er
cat′a·me′ni·a
cat′a·me′ni·al
cat′am·ne′sis *pl.* -ses′
cat′am·nes′tic
cat′a·pha′si·a
cat′a·pha′sis *pl.* -ses′
ca·taph′o·ra *(lethargy with periods of imperfect consciousness)*
♦cataphoria
cat′a·pho·re′sis *pl.* -ses′
cat′a·pho·ret′ic
cat′a·pho·ri·a *(double hypophoria)*
♦cataphora
cat′a·pho′ric
cat′a·phy·lac′tic
cat′a·phy·lax′is
cat′a·pla′si·a *also* kataplasia
ca·tap′la·sis *pl.* -ses′
cat′a·plasm
cat′a·plec′tic

cat′a·plex′y
cat′a·ract′
cat′a·rac′ta
—— cen·tra′lis pul′ver·u·len′ta
—— co′ro·nar′i·a
—— neu′ro·der·mat′i·ca
cat′a·rac′tous
ca·tarrh′
ca·tarrh′al
cat′ar·rhine′
cat′a·state′
ca·tas′tro·phe
cat′a·stroph′ic
cat′a·to′ni·a
cat′a·ton′ic
cat′a·tro′pi·a
catch′ment area
cat′e·chol′
cat′e·chol′a·mine′
cat′e·nat′ing
cat′gut′
ca·thar′sis *pl.* -ses′
ca·thar′tic
ca·thect′
ca·thec′tic
ca·thep′sin
ca·ther′e·sis
cath′e·ret′ic
cath′e·ter
cath′e·ter·i·za′tion
cath′e·ter·ize′, -ized′, -iz′ing
cath′e·ter·o·stat′
ca·thex′is *pl.* -thex′es′
cath′i·so·pho′bi·a
cath′ode′
ca·thod′ic
cat′i′on
cat′i·on′ic
cat′lin
Cat·tell′ test
Cau·ca′sian
cau′da *pl.* -dae′
—— cer′e·bel′li′
—— ep′i·di·dym′i·dis
—— e·qui′na
—— hel′i·cis
—— nu′cle·i′ cau·da′ti′
—— pan·cre′a·tis
—— stri·a′ti′
cau′dad′
cau′dal
cau·da′lis
cau′date′
cau′da·tum *pl.* -ta
cau′do·ceph′al·ad′
caul

cau'mes·the'si·a
caus'al
cau·sal'gi·a
caus'a·tive
caus'tic
cau'ter·ant
cau'ter·i·za'tion
cau'ter·ize', -ized', -iz'ing
cau'ter·y
ca'va *pl.* -vae'
ca'val
cav'a·scope'
cave of Meck'el
ca·ver'na *pl.* -nae'
—— cor'po·ris spon'gi·o'si'
pe'nis
—— cor'po·rum cav'er·no·
so'rum pe'nis
cav'er·ni'tis
cav'er·no'ma *pl.* -mas *or*
-ma·ta
cav'er·nos'to·my
cav'er·no'sum *pl.* -sa
cav'ern·ous
cav'i·tar'y
cav'i·tas *pl.* cav'i·ta'tes'
—— glen'oi·da'lis
—— pul'pae'
cav'i·tate', -tat'ed, -tat'ing
cav'i·ta'tion
Ca·vi'te
ca·vi'tis
cav'i·ty
ca'vo·gram'
ca'vo·sur'face
ca'vo·val'gus
ca'vum *pl.* -va
—— ab·dom'i·nis
—— ar·tic'u·lar'e'
—— con'chae'
—— co'ro·na'le'
—— den'tis
—— ep'i·du·ra'le'
—— hy'a·loi'de·um
—— in'fra·glot'ti·cum
—— la·ryn'gis
—— me'di·as'ti·na'le' an·
te'ri·us
—— mediastinale pos·te'ri·
us
—— med'ul·lar'e'
—— Mon·ro'i·i'
—— na'si'
—— o'ris
—— oris pro'pri·um
—— pel'vis
—— per'i·car'di·i'

—— per'i·to·nae'i'
—— per'i·to·ne'i'
—— pha·ryn'gis
—— pleu'rae'
—— pleu'ro·per'i·car·di·a·co·
per'i·to·ne·a'le'
—— pleu'ro·per'i·car'di·a'le'
—— psal·te'ri·i'
—— sep'ti' pel·lu'ci·di'
—— sub'a·rach'noi·de·a'le'
—— sub'du·ra'le
—— tho·ra'cis
—— tri·gem'i·na'le'
—— tym'pa·ni'
—— u'ter·i'
—— ve'li' in'ter·pos'i·ti'
—— Ver'gae'
ca'vus
Ca·ze·nave' disease
ce·as'mic
ce'bo·ceph'a·lus
ce'cal
ce·cec'to·my
ce·ci'tis
ce'co·cele'
ce'co·co'lic
ce'co·co'lon
ce'co·co·los'to·my
ce'co·fix·a'tion
ce'co·il'e·os'to·my
ce'co·pex'y
ce'co·pli·ca'tion
ce·cor'rha·phy
ce'co·sig'moi·dos'to·my
ce·cos'to·my
ce·cot'o·my
ce'cum *pl.* -ca
—— cu'pu·lar'e'
—— ves·tib'u·lar'e'
cef'a·clor'
cef'a·drox'il
cef'a·man'dole'
cef·az'o·lin
cef·ox'i·tin
ce'li·ac'
ce'li·ec·ta'si·a
ce'li·ec'to·my
ce'li·o'cen·te'sis *pl.* -ses'
ce'li·o·col·pot'o·my
ce'li·o·en'ter·ot'o·my
ce'li·o·gas·trot'o·my
ce'li·o·hys'ter·ec'to·my
ce'li·o'ma *pl.* -mas *or* -ma·ta
ce'li·o·my'o·mec'to·my
ce'li·o·my'o·si'tis
ce'li·o·par'a·cen·te'sis *pl.*
-ses'

ce'li·or'rha·phy
ce'li·o·sal'pin·gec'to·my
ce'li·o·sal'pin·got'o·my
ce'li·o·scope'
ce'li·os'co·py
ce'li·ot'o·my
ce·li'tis
cell
—— of Betz
cel'la *(an enclosure),* *pl.* -lae
♦*sella*
cells
—— of Bött'cher
—— of Ca·jal'
—— of Clau'di·us
—— of Dei'ters
—— of Gia·nuz'zi
—— of Hen'sen
—— of Kult·schitz'sky
—— of Mey'nert
—— of Pan'eth
—— of Schwann
—— of van Ge·huch'ten
cel'lu·la *pl.* -lae'
cel'lu·lae'
—— an·te'ri·o'res'
—— eth'moi·da'les'
—— mas·toi'de·ae'
—— me'di·ae'
—— pneu·ma'ti·cae'
—— pneumaticae tu'bae'
au'di·ti'vae'
—— pneumaticae
tu·bar'i·ae'
—— pos·te'ri·o'res'
—— tym·pan'i·cae'
cel'lu·lar
cel'lu·lar'i·ty
cel'lu·lase'
cel'lule
—— claire
cel'lu·lic'i·dal
cel'lu·lif'u·gal
cel'lu·lip'e·tal
cel'lu·li'tis
cel'lu·lose'
ce'lo·so'ma *pl.* -mas *or*
-ma·ta
ce'lo·so'mus *pl.* -mi' *or*
-mus·es
ce'lo·the'li·o'ma *pl.* -mas *or*
-ma·ta
Cel'si·us
ce·ment'i·cle
ce·ment'i·fi·ca'tion
ce·men'tin
ce·men'to·blast'

ce·men'to·blas·to'ma *pl.*
  -mas *or* -ma·ta
ce·men'to·den'ti·nal
ce·men'to·gen'e·sis *pl.* -ses'
ce'men·to'ma *pl.* -mas *or*
  -ma·ta
ce·men'to·path'i·a
ce·men·to'sis *pl.* -ses'
ce·men'tum *pl.* -ta
ce'nes·the'si·a
ce'nes·thet'ic
ce'nes·thop'a·thy
ce'no·gen'e·sis
ce'no·ge·net'ic
ce'no·site'
cen'ter
cen·te'sis *pl.* -ses'
cen'ti·grade'
cen'ti·gram'
cen'ti·li'ter
cen'ti·me'ter
cen'ti·nor'mal
cen'ti·poise'
cen'trad'
cen'trage
cen'tral
cen'tren·ce·phal'ic
cen'tric
cen'tri·cip'i·tal
cen·tric'i·put
cen·trif'u·gal
cen·trif'u·ga'tion
cen'tri·fuge'
cen'tri·lob'u·lar
cen'tri·ole'
cen·trip'e·tal
cen'tro·don'tous
cen'tro·dor'sal
cen'tro·me'di·an
cen'tro·mere'
cen'tro·phose'
cen'tro·some'
cen'tro·the'ca
cen'trum *pl.* -trums *or* -tra
  —— me'di·a'num
  —— o·va'le'
  —— sem'i·o·va'le'
  —— ten·din'e·um
  —— tendineum per'i·ne'i'
ceph'a·lad'
ceph'a·lal'gi·a
ceph'a·lal'gic
ceph'a·lal'gy
ceph'a·le'a
  —— at·ton'i·ta
ceph'al·e·de'ma *pl.* -mas *or*
  -ma·ta

ceph'a·lex'in
ceph'al·he·mat'o·cele'
ceph'al·he'ma·to'ma
  pl. -mas *or* -ma·ta
ceph'al·hy'dro·cele'
ce·phal'ic
ceph'a·lin
ceph'a·li'tis
ceph'a·li·za'tion
ceph'a·lo·bra'chi·al
ceph'a·lo·cau'dad'
ceph'a·lo·cau'dal
ceph'a·lo·cele'
ceph'a·lo·cen·te'sis *pl.* -ses'
ceph'a·lo·chord'
ceph'a·lo·dyn'i·a
ceph'a·lo·gas'ter
ceph'a·lo·gen'e·sis *pl.* -ses'
ceph'a·lo·gly'cin
ceph'a·lo·gram'
ceph'a·log'ra·phy
ceph'a·lo·gy'ric
ceph'a·lo·hem'a·to·cele'
ceph'a·lo·he'ma·to'ma
  pl. -mas *or* -ma·ta
ceph'a·loid'
ceph'a·lo·me'ni·a
ceph'a·lo·men'in·gi'tis
ceph'a·lom'e·ter
ceph'a·lo·met'ric
ceph'a·lom'e·try
ceph'a·lo·mo'tor
ceph'a·lone'
ceph'a·lo'ni·a
ceph'a·lo·or'bi·tal
ceph'a·lop'a·gus
  —— oc·cip'i·ta'lis
  —— pa·ri'e·ta'lis
ceph'a·lop'a·thy
ceph'a·lo·pel'vic
ceph'a·lo·pha·ryn'ge·us
ceph'a·lo·ple'gi·a
ceph'a·lor'i·dine'
ceph'a·los'co·py
ceph'a·lo·spo'rin
ceph'a·lo·spo'ri·o'sis
  pl. -ses'
Ceph'a·lo·spo'ri·um
ceph'a·lo·thin
ceph'a·lo·tho·rac'ic
ceph'a·lo·tho'ra·cop'a·gus
  —— a·sym'me·tros'
  —— di·bra'chi·us
  —— di·sym'me·tros'
  —— mon'o·sym'me·tros'
ceph'a·lo·tome'
ceph'a·lot'o·my

ceph'a·lo·trac'tor
ceph'a·pir'in
ceph'ra·dine'
ce·ra'ceous
cer·am'ide'
cer'a·to·cri'coid'
cer'a·to·hy'al
cer'a·to·pha·ryn'ge·us
cer·car'i·a *pl.* -ae'
cer·car'i·al
cer·car'i·an
cer·clage'
Cer'co·mo'nas
  —— in·tes'ti·na'lis
ce're·a flex'i·bil'i·tas
cer'e·bel'lar
cer'e·bel·lif'u·gal
cer'e·bel·lip'e·tal
cer'e·bel·li'tis
cer'e·bel'lo·med'ul·lar'y
cer'e·bel'lo·pon'tine'
cer'e·bel'lo·ret'i·nal
cer'e·bel'lo·ru'bral
cer'e·bel'lo·ru'bro·spi'nal
cer'e·bel'lo·spi'nal
cer'e·bel'lo·tha·lam'ic
cer'e·bel'lo·ves·tib'u·lar
cer'e·bel'lum *pl.* -lums *or* -la
cer'e·bral
cer'e·bra'tion
cer'e·bric
ce·re'bri·form'
cer'e·brif'u·gal
cer'e·brin'ic
cer'e·brip'e·tal
cer'e·bri'tis
cer'e·bro·car'di·ac'
cer'e·bro·cen'tric
cer'e·bro·cer'e·bel'lar
cer'e·bro·cor'ti·cal
cer'e·bro·cu'pre·in
cer'e·broid'
cer'e·bro'ma *pl.* -mas *or*
  -ma·ta
cer'e·bro·mac'u·lar
cer'e·bro·ma·la'ci·a
cer'e·bro·med'ul·lar'y
cer'e·bro·me·nin'ge·al
cer'e·bro·men'in·gi'tis
cer'e·bron
cer'e·bron'ic
cer'e·bro·oc'u·lar
cer'e·bro·path'i·a psy'chi·
  ca tox·e'mi·ca
cer'e·brop'a·thy
cer'e·bro·pon'tile'
cer'e·bro·pon'tine'

cer′e·bro·ret′i·nal
cer′e·bro·scle·ro′sis pl. -ses′
cer′e·brose′
cer′e·bro·side′
cer′e·bro·spi′nal
cer′e·bro·ten′di·nous
cer′e·brot′o·my
cer′e·bro·vas′cu·lar
cer′e·brum pl. -brums or
  -bra
ce′roid′
ce·ro′ma (waxy tumor), pl.
  -mas or -ma·ta
  ♦seroma
cer′ti·fi′a·ble
ce·ru′lo·plas′min
ce·ru′men
ce·ru′mi·nal
ce·ru′mi·no′ma pl. -mas or
  -ma·ta
ce·ru′mi·no′sis pl. -ses′
ce·ru′mi·nous
cer′vi·cal
cer′vi·ca′lis as·cen′dens
cer′vi·cec′to·my
cer′vi·ci′tis
cer′vi·co·au′ral
cer′vi·co·au·ric′u·lar
cer′vi·co·ax′il·lar′y
cer′vi·co·bra′chi·al
cer′vi·co·bra′chi·al′gi·a
cer′vi·co·buc′cal
cer′vi·co·col·pi′tis
cer′vi·co·dor′sal
cer′vi·co·dyn′i·a
cer′vi·co·fa′cial
cer′vi·co·la′bi·al
cer′vi·co·lin′gual
cer′vi·co′-oc·cip′i·tal
cer′vi·co·plas′ty
cer′vi·co·pu′bic
cer′vi·co·rec′tal
cer′vi·co·scap′u·lar
cer′vi·co·tho·rac′ic
cer′vi·co·u′ter·ine
cer′vi·co·vag′i·nal
cer′vi·co·vag′i·ni′tis
cer′vi·co·ves′i·cal
cer′vix pl. -vi·ces′ or -vix·es
  —— co·lum′nae′ pos·te′ri·
  o′ris gris′e·ae′
  —— den′tis
  —— ob·sti′pa
  —— u′ter·i′
  —— ve·si′cae′
ce′ryl
ce·sar′e·an also caesarean

Ce·sar′is-De·mel′ bodies
Ces·tan′
  —— sign
  —— syndrome
Ces·tan′-Che·nais′ syn-
  drome
Ces·to′da
ces′tode′
ces·to·di′a·sis pl. -ses′
ces′toid′
ces′tus
ce·ta′ce·um
cet′al·ko′ni·um
ce′tic
ce·tin′ic
ce′to·phen′i·col′
ce′tri·mide′
ce′tyl
  —— ce′tyl·ate′
  —— pal′mi·tate′
ce′tyl·pyr′i·din′i·um
Chad′dock
  —— reflex
  —— sign
chafe, chafed, chaf′ing
Cha′gas-Cruz′ disease
Cha′gas disease
cha·go′ma
Cha′gres fever
cha·la′si·a (relaxation of a
  sphincter)
  ♦chalaza
cha·la′za (spiral band of al-
  bumen extending from the
  end of an egg yolk to the
  shell), pl. -zae′ or -zas
  ♦chalasia
cha·la′zi·on′ pl. -zi·a
cha·la′zo·der′mi·a
chal·ci′tis
chal·co′sis pl. -ses′
chal′i·co′sis pl. -ses′
chal′one′
Cham′ber·lain
  —— line
  —— projection
Cham′ber·lain-Towne′
  technique
cham′e·ce·phal′ic
cham′e·ceph′a·lous
cham′e·ceph′a·lus pl. -li′
cham′e·ceph′a·ly
cham′e·cra′ni·al
cham′e·pro·so′pic
chan′cre
  —— re′dux′
chan′croid′

chan·croi′dal
chan′nel
Cha′oul
  —— therapy
  —— tube
chap, chapped, chap′ping
Chap′man bag
Cha·put′ method
char′bon
Char·cot′
  —— arthritis
  —— arthropathy
  —— arthrosis
  —— cirrhosis
  —— disease
  —— intermittent fever
  —— joint
  —— laryngeal vertigo
  —— syndrome
  —— triad
  —— zone
Char·cot′-Ley′den crystals
Char·cot′-Ma·rie′-Tooth′
  disease
Char·cot′-Wil′brand′ syn-
  drome
Char′lin syndrome
Charl′ton blanching test
char′ta pl. -tae′
char·treu′sin
char′tu·la pl. -lae′
Chas·sai·gnac′ tubercle
Chas′tek′ paralysis
Chauf·fard′-Min·kow′ski
  syndrome
Chauf·fard′-Still′
  —— disease
  —— syndrome
Chea′dle disease
Ché′di·ak′-Hi·ga′shi
  anomaly
cheek
chees′y
chei·lal′gi·a
chei·lec′to·my
chei·lec·tro′pi·on′
chei·li′tis
  —— ac·tin′i·ca
  —— ex·fo′li·a·ti′va
  —— glan′du·lar′is
  —— glandularis a·pos′te·ma·
to′sa
  —— ven′e·na′ta
chei′lo·an′gi·os′co·py
chei′lo·car·ci·no′ma pl.
  -mas or -ma·ta

chei'lo·gnath'o·pal'a·
  tos'chi·sis *pl.* -ses'
chei'lo·gnath'o·pros'o·
  pos'chi·sis *pl.* -ses'
chei'lo·gnath'o·u'ra·
  nos'chi·sis *pl.* -ses'
chei'lo·plas'ty
chei·lor'rha·phy
chei·los'chi·sis *pl.* -ses'
chei·lo'sis *pl.* -ses'
chei'lo·sto'ma·to·plas'ty
chei·lot'o·my
chei·rag'ra
chei·ral'gi·a
—— par'es·thet'i·ca
cheir'ar·thri'tis
chei'ro·kin'es·the'si·a
chei'ro·kin'es·thet'ic
chei'ro·meg'a·ly
chei'ro·plas'ty
chei'ro·pom'pho·lyx
chei'ro·spasm
che'late'
che·la'tion
chel'e·ryth'rine'
chel'i·do·nine'
chem'i·cal
chem'i·co·cau'ter·y
chem'ist
chem'is·try
che'mo·bi·ot'ic
chem'o·cep'tor
chem'o·co·ag'u·la'tion
chem'o·dec·to'ma *pl.* -mas
  or -ma·ta
chem'o·dif'fer·en'ti·a'tion
che'mo·im'mu·nol'o·gy
chem'o·ki·ne'sis *pl.* -ses'
chem'o·ki·net'ic
chem'o·pal'li·dec'to·my
chem'o·pro'phy·lax'is
  pl. -lax'es'
chem'o·re·cep'tor
chem'o·re'flex'
che·mo'sis *pl.* -ses'
chem'o·sur'ger·y
chem'o·syn'the·sis *pl.* -ses'
chem'o·tac'tic
chem'o·tax'is *pl.* -tax'es'
chem'o·ther'a·peu'tic
chem'o·ther'a·py
che·mot'ic
Che·nais' syndrome
che'no·de·ox'y·cho'lic
Cher'ry and Cran'dall test
cher'ub·ism
Ches'el·den operation

Chev'a·lier' Jack'son op-
  eration
Chèv're·mont-Com·baire'
  method
Cheyne'-Stokes' respira-
  tion
Chi·a'ri
—— malformation
—— network
—— syndrome
Chi·a'ri-From'mel
—— disease
—— syndrome
chi'asm
chi·as'ma *pl.* -ma·ta *or* -mas
—— op'ti·cum
—— ten'di·num
chi·as'mal
chi'as·mat'ic
chick'en·pox'
chi·cle'ro ulcer
chig'ger
chig'oe
Chi'lai·di'ti syndrome
chil'blain'
child'bear'ing
child'birth'
Chil'e
—— ni'ter
—— salt·pe'ter
Chi'lo·mas'tix
—— mes·nil'i'
chi·me'ra
chi·mer'ism
chin
Chi·nese' res'tau·rant'
  syndrome
chi'on·a·blep'si·a
chi'o·na·blep'sy
chi·rap'si·a
chi'rap·sy
chi·rop'o·dist
chi·rop'o·dy
chi'ro·prac'tic
chi'ro·prac'tor
chi'tin
chi'tin·ous
chi'to·bi'ose'
chi·to'sa·mine'
Chi·tral' fever
Chla·myd'i·a *pl.* -ae
—— psit'ta·ci'
—— tra·cho'ma·tis
chlam'y·do·spore'
chlo·as'ma *pl.* -ma·ta
—— grav'i·dar'um
—— he·pat'i·cum

—— pe'ri·o·ra'le vir·gin'i·um
—— u'te·ri'num
chlo'phe·di'a·nol'
chlor·ac'ne
chlo'ral
chlo'ral·am'ide'
chlo'ral·form·am'ide'
chlo'ra·lose'
chlo'ral·u're·thane'
chlor·am'bu·cil
chlor'a·mine'
chlor'am·phen'i·col'
chlor'a·ne'mi·a
chlo'rate'
chlor·cy'cli·zine'
chlor'dane'
chlor·dan'to·in
chlor·di·az'ep·ox'ide'
chlo·rel'lin
chlor·e'mi·a
chlor·gua'nide'
chlor·hex'i·dine'
chlor·hy'dri·a
chlo'ric
chlo'ride'
chlo'ri·du'ri·a
chlo'ri·nat'ed
chlo'ri·na'tion
chlor·in'da·nol'
chlo'rine'
chlor'i·son'da·mine
chlo'rite'
chlor·mad'i·none'
chlor·mer'o·drin
chlor·mez'a·none'
chlo'ro·ac'e·to·phe'none'
chlo'ro·a·ne'mi·a
chlo'ro·az'o·din
chlo'ro·bu'ta·nol'
chlo'ro·cru'o·rin
chlo'ro·form'
chlo'ro·for'mic
chlo'ro·form'ism
chlo'ro·form'i·za'tion
chlo'ro·gua'nide'
chlo'ro·leu·ke'mi·a
chlo'ro·lym·pho'ma
  pl. -mas *or* -ma·ta
chlo·ro'ma *pl.* -mas *or*
  -ma·ta
chlo'ro·my'e·lo'ma *pl.* -mas
  or -ma·ta
chlo'ro·per'cha
chlo'ro·phe'nol'
chlo'ro·phen'o·thane'
chlo'ro·phyll
Chlo·rop'i·dae'

chlo'ro·plast'
chlo'ro·plas'tin
chlo'ro·pro'caine'
chlo·rop'si·a
chlo'ro·pu'rine'
chlo'ro·quine'
chlo·ro'sis pl. -ses'
—— ru'bra
chlo'ro·then
chlo'ro·thi'a·zide
chlo'ro·thy'mol'
chlo·rot'ic
chlo'ro·tri·an'i·sene'
chlo'rous
chlo'ro·vi'nyl·di·chlo'ro·
ar'sine'
chlo'ro·xy'le·nol'
chlor·phen'e·sin
chlor'phen·ir'a·mine'
chlor·phe'nol'
chlor·phen'ter·mine'
chlor·pic'rin
chlor·prom'a·zine'
chlor·pro'pa·mide'
chlor'pro·phen'py·rid'a·
mine'
chlor'pro·thix'ene'
chlor'quin·al'dol'
chlor·tet'ra·cy'cline'
chlor·thal'i·done'
chlor·thy'mol'
chlor·zox'a·zone'
cho·a'na pl. -nae'
cho·a'nal
choke, choked, chok'ing
cho'la·gog'ic
chol'a·gogue'
chol'a·mine'
cho'lane'
cho·lan'e·re'sis
cho·lan'gi·ec'ta·sis pl. -ses'
cho·lan'gi·o·ad'e·no'ma pl.
-mas or -ma·ta
cho·lan'gi·o·car'ci·no'ma
pl. -mas or -ma·ta
cho·lan'gi·o·en'ter·os'to·
my
cho·lan'gi·o·gas·tros'to·my
cho·lan'gi·o·gram'
cho·lan'gi·og'ra·phy
cho·lan'gi·o·hep'a·ti'tis pl.
-tis·es or -tit'i·des'
cho·lan'gi·o·hep'a·to'ma
pl. -mas or -ma·ta
cho·lan'gi·o·je'ju·nos'to·
my
cho·lan'gi·ole'

cho·lan'gi·o·lit'ic
cho·lan'gi·o·li'tis
cho·lan'gi·o'ma pl. -mas or
-ma·ta
cho·lan'gi·os'to·my
cho·lan'gi·ot'o·my
chol'an·git'ic
chol'an·gi'tis
cho·lan'o·poi·e'sis pl. -ses'
cho·lan'o·poi·et'ic
cho'late'
cho'le·bil'i·ru'bin
cho'le·cal·cif'er·ol'
cho'le·chro'me·re'sis
cho'le·chro'mo·poi·e'sis
cho'le·cy'a·nin
cho'le·cyst'
cho'le·cyst'a·gogue'
cho'le·cys·tal'gi·a
cho'le·cys·tec·ta'si·a
cho'le·cys·tec'to·my
cho'le·cys·ten·ter'ic
cho'le·cyst·en'ter·or'rha·
phy
cho'le·cyst·en'ter·os'to·my
cho'le·cys'tic
cho'le·cys'tis
cho'le·cys·ti'tis pl. -tit'i·des'
cho'le·cys'to·cho·lan'gi·o·
gram'
cho'le·cys'to·co·lon'ic
cho'le·cys'to·co·los'to·my
cho'le·cys'to·co·lot'o·my
cho'le·cys'to·cu·ta'ne·ous
cho'le·cys'to·du·o·de'nal
cho'le·cys'to·du·od'e·no·
co'lic
cho'le·cys'to·du·o·de·
nos'to·my
cho'le·cys'to·e·lec'tro·co·
ag'u·lec'to·my
cho'le·cys'to·en'ter·os'to·
my
cho'le·cys'to·gas'tric
cho'le·cys'to·gas·tros'to·
my
cho'le·cys'to·gram'
cho'le·cys'to·graph'ic
cho'le·cys'to·tog'ra·phy
cho'le·cys'to·il'e·os'to·my
cho'le·cys'to·je'ju·nos'to·
my
cho'le·cys'to·ki'nase'
cho'le·cys'to·ki·net'ic
cho'le·cys'to·ki'nin
cho'le·cys'to·li·thi'a·sis
cho'le·cys'to·li·thot'o·my

cho'le·cys'to·lith'o·trip'sy
cho'le·cys'to·ne·phros'to·
my
cho'le·cys'top'a·thy
cho'le·cys'to·pex'y
cho'le·cys'top·to'sis pl.
-ses'
cho'le·cys'tor'rha·phy
cho'le·cys'tos'to·my
cho'le·cys'tot'o·my
cho·led'o·chal
cho·led'o·chec·ta'si·a
cho·led'o·chec'to·my
cho·led'o·chi'tis
cho·led'o·cho·cele'
cho·led'o·cho'cu·ta'ne·ous
cho·led'o·cho'cys·tos'to·
my
cho·led'o·cho'do·chor'rha·
phy
cho·led'o·cho·du'o·de·
nos'to·my
cho·led'o·cho·en'ter·os'to·
my
cho·led'o·cho'gas·tros'to·
my
cho·led'o·cho·gram'
cho·led'o·cho·il'e·os'to·my
cho·led'o·cho·je'ju·nos'to·
my
cho·led'o·cho'li·thi'a·sis pl.
-ses'
cho·led'o·cho'li·thot'o·my
cho·led'o·cho·lith'o·trip'sy
cho·led'o·cho·plas'ty
cho·led'o·chor'rha·phy
cho·led'o·chos'to·my
cho·led'o·chot'o·my
cho·led'o·chus pl. -chi'
cho'le·glo'bin
cho'le·hem'a·tin
cho·le'ic
cho'le·lith'
cho'le·li·thi'a·sis pl. -ses'
cho'le·lith'ic
cho'le·li·thot'o·my
cho'le·lith'o·trip'sy
cho·lem'e·sis pl. -ses'
cho·le'mi·a
cho·le'mic
cho'le·poi·e'sis pl. -ses'
cho'le·poi·et'ic
cho'le·pra'sin
chol'er·a
—— mor'bus
—— nos'tras
—— sic'ca

—— sid'er‧ans'
—— vib'ri‧o'
chol'er‧a'ic
cho'le‧re'sis pl. -ses'
cho'le‧ret'ic
chol'er‧ic
chol'er‧i‧form'
chol'er‧oid'
chol'er‧o‧ma'ni‧a
cho'le‧scin‧tig'ra‧phy
cho'les‧tane'
cho‧les'ta‧nol'
cho'le‧sta'sis pl. -ses'
cho'le‧stat'ic
cho‧les'te‧a‧to'ma pl. -mas
   or -ma‧ta
cho‧les'te‧a‧tom'a‧tous
cho‧les'te‧a‧to'sis pl. -ses'
cho‧les'te‧nol'
cho‧les'ter‧ase'
cho‧les'ter‧e'mi‧a
cho‧les'ter‧in
cho‧les'ter‧i‧nu'ri‧a
cho‧les'ter‧ol'
cho‧les'ter‧o‧le'mi‧a
cho‧les'ter‧ol‧er'e‧sis
   pl. -ses'
cho‧les'ter‧ol'o‧poi‧e'sis
   pl. -ses'
cho‧les'ter‧ol‧o'sis pl. -ses'
cho‧les'ter‧o'sis pl. -ses'
cho‧les'ter‧yl
cho'le‧ver'din
cho'line'
cho'line‧a‧cet'yl‧ase'
cho'lin‧er'gic
cho'lin‧es'ter‧ase'
cho'li‧no‧gen'ic
cho'li‧no‧mi‧met'ic
chol'o‧chrome'
cho'lo‧lith'
cho'lo‧li‧thi'a‧sis pl. -ses'
cho'lo‧lith'ic
chol'or‧rhe'a
cho‧lu'ri‧a
Cho'man method
chon'do‧den'drine'
Chon'do‧den'dron'
chon'dral
chon‧drec'to‧my
chon'dric
chon'dri‧fi‧ca'tion
chon'dri‧fy', -fied', -fy'ing
chon'dri‧o‧ki‧ne'sis pl. -ses'
chon'dri‧o'ma pl. -mas or
   -ma‧ta
chon‧dri'tis

chon'dro‧ad'e‧no'ma pl.
   -mas or -ma‧ta
chon'dro‧al‧bu'mi‧noid'
chon'dro‧an'gi‧o'ma pl.
   -mas or -ma‧ta
chon'dro‧an'gi‧o‧path'i‧a
   cal‧car'e‧a seu punc‧ta'ta
chon'dro‧blast'
chon'dro‧blas‧to'ma
   pl. -mas or -ma‧ta
chon'dro‧cal'ci‧no'sis pl.
   -ses'
chon'dro‧cal'syn‧o'vi'tis
chon'dro‧cla'sis pl. -ses'
chon'dro‧clast'
chon'dro‧cos'tal
chon'dro‧cra'ni‧um pl. -ni‧a
chon'dro‧cyte'
chon'dro‧cyt'ic
chon'dro‧der'ma‧ti'tis
—— nod'u‧lar'is hel'i‧cis
chon'dro‧dyn'i‧a
chon'dro‧dys‧pla'si‧a
—— punc‧ta'ta
chon'dro‧dys'tro'phi‧a
—— cal‧cif'i‧cans' con‧gen'i‧
ta
—— fe‧ta'lis
—— fetalis cal‧car'e‧a
—— fetalis cal‧cif'i‧cans'
—— fetalis hy'po‧plas'ti‧ca
—— hy'per‧plas'ti‧ca
—— hy'po‧plas'ti‧ca
—— ma‧la'ci‧a
chon'dro‧dys‧tro'phic
chon'dro‧dys'tro‧phy
chon'dro‧ec'to‧der'mal
chon'dro‧en'do‧the'li‧o'ma
   pl. -mas or -ma‧ta
chon'dro‧ep'i‧troch'le‧ar'is
chon'dro‧fi‧bro'ma pl. -mas
   or -ma‧ta
chon'dro‧fi'bro‧sar‧co'ma
   pl. -mas or -ma‧ta
chon'dro‧gen
chon'dro‧gen'e‧sis pl. -ses'
chon'dro‧ge‧net'ic
chon'dro‧gen'ic
chon'dro‧drog'e‧nous
chon'dro‧glos'sus
chon'dro‧hu'mer‧a'lis
chon'droid'
chon'dro‧it'ic
chon'dro'i‧tin
chon'dro‧li‧po'ma pl. -mas
   or -ma‧ta

chon'dro‧lip'o‧sar‧co'ma
   pl. -mas or -ma‧ta
chon‧drol'y'sis pl. -ses'
chon'dro'ma pl. -mas or
   -ma‧ta
chon'dro‧ma‧la'ci‧a
chon'dro‧ma‧to'sis
chon‧drom'a‧tous
chon'dro‧mere'
chon'dro‧met'a‧pla'si‧a
chon'dro‧mu'cin
chon'dro‧mu'coid'
chon'dro‧my'o‧ma pl. -mas
   or -ma‧ta
chon'dro‧myx'oid'
chon'dro‧myx‧o'ma pl.
   -mas or -ma‧ta
chon'dro‧myx'o‧sar‧co'ma
   pl. -mas or -ma‧ta
chon'dro‧ne‧cro'sis pl. -ses'
chon'dro‧os'te‧o‧dys'tro‧
   phy
chon'dro‧os'te‧o'ma
   pl. -mas or -ma‧ta
chon'dro‧os'te‧o‧sar‧co'ma
   pl. -mas or -ma‧ta
chon‧drop'a‧thy
chon'dro‧pha‧ryn'ge‧us
chon'dro‧phyte'
chon'dro‧pla'si‧a
chon'dro‧plast'
chon'dro‧plas'ty
chon'dro‧po‧ro'sis pl. -ses'
chon'dro‧pro'te‧in
chon‧dro'sa‧mine'
chon'dro‧sar‧co'ma
   pl. -mas or -ma‧ta
—— myx'o‧ma‧to'des'
chon'dro‧sar‧co'ma‧tous
chon'dro‧sin
chon'dro'sis pl. -ses'
chon'dro‧ster'nal
chon'dro‧tome'
chon'drot'o‧my
cho'ne‧chon'dro‧ster'non'
Cho‧part'
—— amputation
—— joint
Cho'pra test
chor'da pl. -dae'
—— dor‧sa'lis
—— gu'ber‧nac'u‧lum
—— o‧bli'qua mem‧bra'nae'
in'ter‧os'se‧ae' an'te‧bra'‧
chi‧i'
—— sa‧li'va
—— tym'pa‧ni'

chor′dae′
— ten·din′e·ae′
— Wil·lis′i·i′
chor′dal (pertaining to noto-
chord)
♦cordal
chor′da·mes′o·blast′
chor′da·mes′o·derm′
chor·dee′
chor·de′ic
chord′en·ceph′a·lon′
chor·di′tis
— fi′bri·no′sa
— no·do′sa
— tu′be·ro′sa
chor′do·blas·to′ma pl. -mas
or -ma·ta
chor′do·car′ci·no′ma
pl. -mas or -ma·ta
chor′do·ep′i·the′li·o′ma pl.
-mas or -ma·ta
chor′doid′
chor·do′ma pl. -mas or
-ma·ta
chor·dot′o·my also cor-
dotomy
cho·re′a
— grav′i·dar′um
— in·sa′ni·ens
cho·re′al
cho′re·at′ic
cho·re′ic
— a·bra′si·a
cho·re′i·form′
cho′re·o·ath′e·toid′
cho′re·o·ath′e·to′sis pl.
-ses′
cho′ri·o·ad′e·no′ma
pl. -mas or -ma·ta
— des′tru·ens
cho′ri·o·al′lan·to′ic
cho′ri·o·al·lan′to·is
cho′ri·o·am′ni·on′ic
cho′ri·o·am′ni·o·ni′tis
cho′ri·o·an′gi·o′ma pl. -mas
or -ma·ta
cho′ri·o·blas·to′sis pl. -ses′
cho′ri·o·cap′il·lar′is
cho′ri·o·car′ci·no′ma
pl. -mas or -ma·ta
cho′ri·o·cele′
cho′ri·o·ep′i·the′li·o′ma pl.
-mas or -ma·ta
cho′ri·o·gen′e·sis pl. -ses′
cho′ri·oid′
cho′ri·oi′de·a

cho′ri·o′ma pl. -mas or
-ma·ta
cho′ri·o·men′in·gi′tis
cho′ri·on′
— al′lan·toi′de·um
— av′il·lo′sum
— fron·do′sum
— lae′ve′
— om′pha·loi′de·um
— vil·lo′sum
cho′ri·on·ep′i·the′li·o′ma
pl. -mas or -ma·ta
cho′ri·on′ic
cho′ri·o·ni′tis
cho′ri·o·ret′i·nal
cho′ri·o·ret′i·ni′tis
cho′ri·o·ret′i·nop′a·thy
chor′i·sis pl. -ses′
cho·ris′to·blas·to′ma
pl. -mas or -ma·ta
cho′ris·to′ma pl. -mas or
-ma·ta
cho′roid′
cho·roi′dal
cho·roi′de·a
cho·roi·dec′to·my
cho′roid·e·re′mi·a
cho′roid·i′tis
— gut·ta′ta
cho·roi′do·cy·cli′tis
cho·roi′do·i·ri′tis
cho·roi′do·ret′i·ni′tis
Chris·tel′ler method
Chris′ten·sen-Krab′be disease
Chris′tian disease
Chris′tian-Web′er disease
Christ′mas
— disease
— factor
chro′maf·fin
chro·maf′fi·no·blas·to′ma
pl. -mas or -ma·ta
chro·maf′fi·no′ma pl. -mas
or -ma·ta
chro·maf′fi·nop′a·thy
chro′ma·phil′
chro′ma·phobe′
chro·ma′si·a
chro′mate′
chro′ma·te·lop′si·a
chro·mat′ic
chro′ma·tid
chro′ma·tin
chro′ma·tism
chro′ma·to·der′ma·to′sis
pl. -ses′

chro′ma·to·dys·o′pi·a
chro′ma·tog′e·nous
chro·mat′o·gram′
chro·mat′o·graph′
chro·mat′o·graph′ic
chro′ma·tog′ra·phy
chro′ma·toid′
chro′ma·tol′o·gy
chro′ma·tol′y·sis pl. -ses′
chro·ma·to·lyt′ic
chro·ma·tom′e·ter
chro′ma·tom′e·try
chro′ma·to·phil′
chro·mat′o·phore′
chro′ma·to·pho′ric
chro′ma·to·phor·o′ma
pl. -mas or -ma·ta
chro′ma·to·pho′ro·troph′ic
chro′ma·to·pho′ro·trop′ic
chro′ma·toph′o·rous
chro·mat′o·plasm
chro·mat′o·plast′
chro′ma·top′si·a
chro′ma·top′sy
chro′mat·op·tom′e·ter
chro′mat·op·tom′e·try
chro′ma·to′sis pl. -ses′
chro′ma·tu′ri·a
chro′mes·the′si·a
chrom′hi′dro′sis pl. -ses′
chro·mi·cize′, -cized′, -ciz′-
ing
chro·mid′i·al
chro·mid′i·um pl. -i·a
chro′mi·dro′sis pl. -ses′
chro′mo·blast′
chro′mo·blas′to·my·co′sis
pl. -ses′
chro′mo·cen′ter
chro′mo·crin′i·a
chro′mo·cys·tos′co·py
chro′mo·cyte′
chro′mo·dac′ry·or·rhe′a
chro′mo·der′ma·to′sis pl.
-ses′
chro′mo·gen
chro′mo·gen′e·sis pl. -ses′
chro′mo·gen′ic
chro′mo·lip′oid′
chro′mo·mere′
chro′mo·my′co′sis pl. -ses′
chro′mo·nar′
chro′mo·ne′ma pl. -ma·ta
chro′mo·ne′mal
chro′mo·nu·cle′ic
chro′mo·nych′i·a
chro′mo·par′ic

chro'mo·pex'y
chro'mo·phane'
chro'mo·phil'
chro'mo·phile'
chro'mo·phil'ic
chro·moph'i·lous
chro'mo·phobe'
chro'mo·pho'bi·a
chro'mo·pho'bic
chro'mo·phore'
chro'mo·pho'ric
chro·moph'o·rous
chro'mo·phose'
chro'mo·phy'to·sis pl. -ses'
chro'mo·plasm
chro'mo·plast'
chro'mo·plas'tid
chro'mo·pro'te·in
chro·mop'si·a
chro·mos'co·py
chro'mo·so'mal
chro'mo·some'
chro'mo·trop'ic
chron'ic
chro·nic'i·ty
chron'o·log'ic or chron'o·
  log'i·cal
chron'o·trop'ic
chrys'a·ro'bin
chrys'a·zin
Chrys'o·my'ia
—— bez'zi·a'na
chrys'o·pho·re'sis pl. -ses'
Chry'sops'
chrys'o·ther'a·py
chthon'o·pha'gi·a
chtho·noph'a·gy
Church'ill-Cope' reflex
Chvos'tek' sign
chy·lan'gi·o'ma pl. -mas or
  -ma·ta
chyle
chy·le'mi·a
chy'lo·cele'
chy'lo·der'ma
chy'loid'
chy'lo·me'di·as·ti'num
chy'lo·mi'cro·ne'mi·a
chy'lor·rhe'a
chy'lo·sis pl. -ses'
chy'lo·tho'rax'
chy'lous (pertaining to
  chyle)
  ♦chylus
chy·lu'ri·a
chy'lus (chyle)
  ♦chylous

chyme
chy'mi·fi·ca'tion
chy'mo·sin
chy'mo·sin'o·gen
chy'mo·tryp'sin
chy'mo·tryp·sin'o·gen
chy'mous
chy'mus
Ciac'ci·o fixatives
ci·bis'o·tome'
cic'a·tri'cial
cic'a·tric'u·la pl. -lae'
cic'a·trix' pl. cic'a·tri'ces' or
  -trix'es
cic'a·tri'zant
cic'a·tri·za'tion
cic'a·trize', -trized', -triz'ing
cic'lo·pir'ox'
Cie·szyn'ski rule
cil'i·a sing. -i·um
cil'i·ar'y
Cil'i·a'ta
cil'i·ate'
cil'i·at'ed
cil'i·o·scle'ral
cil'i·o·spi'nal
cil'i·ot'o·my
cil'i·um in·ver'sum
cil·lo'sis
cil·lot'ic
ci·met'i·dine'
Ci'mex'
—— he·mip'ter·us
—— lec'tu·lar'i·us
—— ro'tun·da'tus
ci·nan'ser·in
cin·cham'i·dine'
cin·cho'na
cin·chon'a·mine'
cin·chon'ic
cin·chon'i·dine'
cin'cho·nine'
cin'cho·nism
cin·chon'i·za'tion
cin'chon·ize', -ized', -iz'ing
cin'cho·phen
cin'e
cin'e·an'gi·o·car'di·o·gram'
cin'e·an'gi·o·car'di·og'ra·
  phy
cin'e·an'gi·o·gram'
cin'e·e·soph'a·go·gram'
cin'e·flu'o·rog'ra·phy
cin'e·ra'di·og'ra·phy
ci·ne're·a
cin'e·roent'gen·og'ra·phy
cin·ges'tol'

cin'gu·late'
cin'gu·lec'to·my
cin'gu·lo·trac'to·my
cin'gu·lum pl. -la
—— ex·trem'i·ta'tis in·fe'ri·
  o'ris
—— extremitatis su·pe'ri·
  o'ris
—— mem'bri' in·fe'ri·o'ris
—— membri su·pe'ri·o'ris
cin'na·med'rine'
cin'na·mene'
cin·nam'ic
cin·nar'i·zine'
cin'per·ene'
cin'ta·zone'
cin·tri'a·mide'
cir·ca'di·an
cir'ci·nate'
cir'cle
—— of diffusion
—— of Hal'ler
—— of Wil'lis
—— of Zinn
cir'cuit
cir'cu·lar
cir'cu·late', -lat'ed, -lat'ing
cir'cu·la'tion
cir'cu·la·to'ry
cir'cu·lus pl. -li'
—— ar·te'ri·o'sus cer'e·bri'
—— arteriosus hal'ler·i'
—— arteriosus i'ri·dis major
—— arteriosus iridis minor
—— arteriosus (Wil·lis'i·i')
—— ar·tic'u·lar'is vas'cu·
  lo'sus
—— vas'cu·lo'sus ner'vi'
  op'ti·ci'
cir'cum·a'nal
cir'cum·ar·tic'u·lar
cir'cum·cise', -cised', -cis'-
  ing
cir'cum·ci'sion
cir'cum·cor'ne·al
cir'cum·duc'tion
cir'cum·fer·en'ti·a
—— ar·tic'u·lar'is ra'di·i'
—— articularis ul'nae'
cir'cum·fer·en'tial
cir'cum·flex'
cir'cum·in'su·lar
cir'cum·len'tal
cir'cum·lo·cu'tion
cir'cum·loc'u·to'ry
cir'cum·ne'vic
cir'cum·nu'cle·ar

cir'cum·o'ral
cir'cum·or'bi·tal
cir'cum·pen'nate'
cir'cum·po'lar·i·za'tion
cir'cum·pul'par
cir'cum·re'nal
cir'cum·scribed'
cir'cum·stan'ti·al'i·ty
cir'cum·su'ture
cir'cum·ton'sil·lar
cir'cum·val'late'
cir'cum·vas'cu·lar
ci·ro'le·my'cin
cir·rho'sis *pl.* -ses'
cir·rhot'ic
cir'rus *pl.* -ri'
cir·sec'to·my
cir·sod'e·sis
   pl. -ses'
cir'soid'
cis'sa
cis'tern
cis·ter'na *pl.* -nae'
—— am'bi·ens
—— cer'e·bel'lo·med'ul·lar'is
—— chi·as'ma·tis
—— chy'li'
—— cor'po·ris cal·lo'si'
—— fos'sae' lat'er·a'lis cer'e·
bri'
—— in'ter·pe·dun'cu·lar'is
—— lam'i·nae' ter'mi·na'lis
—— mag'na
—— per'i·lym·phat'i·ca
—— pon'tis
—— ve'nae' mag'nae' cer'e·
bri'
cis·ter'nae'
—— sub'a·rach'noi·da'les'
—— sub'a·rach'noi·de·a'les'
cis·ter'nal
ci·ten'a·mide'
cit'rate'
cit'ric
cit'ri·nin
ci·tro'vo·rum
ci·trul'lin
cit'rul·line'
cit'rul·li·ne'mi·a
ci·trul'li·nu'ri·a
cit·to'sis *pl.* -ses'
Ci·vatte' poikiloderma
Civ'i·ni'ni spine
Cla·do'ni·a
clam·ox'y·quin
clamp
Clar'a cell

Clark
—— rule
—— sign
—— test
Clarke
—— column
—— dorsal nucleus
Clarke'-Had'field' syn-
drome
clas·mat'o·cyte'
clas·mat'o·cyt'ic
clas·mo·cy·to'ma *pl.* -mas
   or -ma·ta
clas'tic
Clat'wor'thy sign
Claude syndrome
clau'di·cant'
clau'di·ca'tion
claus'tral
claus'tro·phil'i·a
claus'tro·pho'bi·a
claus'trum *pl.* -tra
clau·su'ra
cla'va *pl.* -vae'
cla'val
cla'vate'
clav'i·cle
clav'i·cot'o·my
cla·vic'u·la *pl.* -lae'
cla·vic'u·lar
cla·vic'u·late'
cla·vic'u·lec'to·my
clav'i·pec'to·ral
cla'vus *pl.* -vi'
Clay'brook' sign
clear'ance
clear'ing
cleav'age
cleft
clei'do·cos'tal
clei'do·cra'ni·al
clei'do·hu'mer·al
clei'do·hy'oid'
clei'do·mas'toid'
clei'do·oc·cip'i·tal
clei'do·scap'u·lar
clei'do·ster'nal
clei'dot'o·my
clem'as·tine'
clem'i·zole'
cle'oid'
Cle'ram·bault'-Kan·
din'sky complex
click
click'-mur'mur syndrome
cli·din'i·um
cli'mac·ter'ic

cli·mac'tic
cli'max'
clin'da·my'cin
clin'ic
clin'i·cal
cli·ni'cian
cli'no·ce·phal'ic
cli'no·ceph'a·lus *pl.* -li'
cli'no·ceph'a·ly
cli'no·dac'ty·lism
cli'no·dac'ty·lous
cli'no·dac'ty·ly
cli'noid'
cli'no·scope'
cli·ox'a·nide'
clip
clis'e·om'e·ter
clit'i·on'
clit'o·ral'gi·a
clit'o·rid'e·an
clit'o·ri·dec'to·my
clit'o·ri·di'tis
clit'o·ri·dot'o·my
clit'o·ris *pl.* -ris·es *or* cli·to'ri·
des'
clit'o·rism
clit'o·ri'tis
clit'o·ro·meg'a·ly
clit'o·rot'o·my
cli'vus *pl.* -vi'
—— mon·tic'u·li'
clo·a'ca *pl.* -cae'
clo·a'cal
clo'a·co·gen'ic
clo·cor'to·lone'
clo·faz'i·mine'
clo·fi'brate'
clo·ges'tone'
clo·ma·cran'
clo·me·ges'tone'
clo·meth'er·one'
clo·min'o·rex'
clo·mi·phene'
clo·mip'ra·mine'
clo'nal
clo·na'ze·pam'
clone, cloned, clon'ing
clo'nic
clo·nic'i·ty
clon'i·co·ton'ic
clo'nic-ton'ic
clo'ni·dine'
clon'ism
clo·ni'trate'
clo'nor·chi'a·sis *pl.* -ses'
Clo·nor'chis
—— si·nen'sis

clo'no·spasm
clo'nus
clo·pam'ide'
clo'pen·thix'ol'
clo·per'i·done'
Clo·quet'
—— canal
—— ganglion
—— node
clor·az'e·pate'
clor·eth'ate'
clor·ex'o·lone'
clor'o·phene'
clor·pren'a·line'
clor·ter'mine'
clos·trid'i·al
Clos·trid'i·um
—— bot'u·li'num
—— chau·vo'ei'
—— his'to·lyt'i·cum
—— no'vy·i'
—— par'a·bot'u·li'num e'qui'
—— per·frin'gens
—— sep'ti·cum
—— spo·rog'e·nes'
—— tet'a·ni'
—— wel'chi·i'
clo'sure
clot, clot'ted, clot'ting
clo·thi'a·pine'
clo·thix'a·mide'
clo·trim'a·zole'
clove'-hitch'
clown'ism
clox'a·cil'lin
clubbed
club'bing
club'foot'
club'hand'
clump'ing
clu'ne·al
clus'ter
Clute incision
clut'ter·ing
Clut'ton joints
clys'ter
cne'mic
cne'mis pl. cnem'i·des'
co'ad·ap·ta'tion
co·ag'u·la·bil'i·ty
co·ag'u·la·ble
co·ag'u·lant
co·ag'u·lase'
co·ag'u·late', -lat'ed, -lat'ing
co·ag'u·la'tion
co·ag'u·la'tive
co·ag'u·la'tor

co·ag'u·lop'a·thy
co·ag'u·lum pl. -la
Coak'ley operation
co'a·lesce', -lesced', -lesc'ing
co'a·les'cence
co'a·les'cent
co·apt'
co'ap·ta'tion
co·arc'tate'
co'arc·ta'tion
co'arc·tot'o·my
co'ar·tic'u·la'tion
Coats disease
co·bal'a·min
co'balt'
co·caine'
co·cain'ism
co'car·box'y·lase'
co'car·cin'o·gen
co'car·cin'o·gen'e·sis pl.
  -ses'
coc'cal
Coc·cid'i·a
coc·cid'i·al
coc·cid'i·oi'dal
Coc·cid'i·oi'des'
—— im·mi'tis
coc·cid'i·oi'din
coc·cid'i·oi'do·my·co'sis
  pl. -ses'
coc·cid'i·oi·do'sis pl. -ses'
coc·cid'i·o'sis pl. -ses'
coc·cid'i·o·stat'
coc·cid'i·o·stat'ic
coc·cid'i·um pl. -i·a
coc'ci·gen'ic
coc'co·bac'il·lar'y
coc'co·ba·cil'li·form'
coc'co·ba·cil'lus pl. -li'
coc'coid'
coc'cu·lin
coc'cu·lus
coc'cus pl. -ci'
Coc'cus
coc'cy·al'gi·a
coc'cy·ceph'a·lus pl. -li'
coc'cy·dyn'i·a
coc'cy·ge'al
coc'cy·gec'to·my
coc'cy·ge'us pl. -e·i'
coc'cy·go·dyn'i·a
coc'cyx pl. coc'cy·ges' or
  -cyx·es
coch'le·a pl. -ae' or -as
coch'le·ar
coch'le·ar'i·form'
coch'le·i'tis

coch'le·o·or·bic'u·lar
coch'le·o·pal'pe·bral
coch'le·o·ves·tib'u·lar
Coch'li·o·my'ia
—— a·mer'i·ca'na
—— hom'i·ni·vo'rax'
—— mac'e·lar'i·a
Cock'ayne' syndrome
coc'to·an'ti·gen
coc'to·im·mu'no·gen
coc'to·la'bile
coc'to·pre·cip'i·tin
coc'to·sta'bile
co'de·car·box'y·lase'
co'de·hy'dro·gen·ase'
co'deine'
Cod'man
—— triangle
—— tumor
co·dom'i·nance
co·dom'i·nant
co'don'
co·dox'ime'
co·ef·fi'cient
coeli-. See words spelled
  celi-.
coelio-. See words spelled
  celio-.
coe'lo·blas·to'ma pl. -mas
  or -ma·ta
coe'lom pl. -loms or coe·
  lo'ma·ta
coe·lom'ic
coe·los'chi·sis pl. -ses'
co·en'zyme'
coeur en sa·bot'
co'fac'tor
co·fer'ment
Cof'fey operation
Co'gan syndrome
cog'nate'
cog·ni'tion
cog'ni·tive
co·hab'i·ta'tion
co·here', -hered', -her'ing
co·her'ence
co·her'ent
co·he'sion
co·he'sive
Cohn'heim' theory
Cohn method
co'hort'
coil
co'i·tal
co·i'tion
co'i·to·pho'bi·a
co'i·tus

—— in'ter·rup'tus
—— res'er·va'tus
co·la'tion
col'a·to'ri·um *pl.* -ri·a
col'a·ture
col'chi·cine'
col'chi·cin·i·za'tion
co·lec'to·my
Cole'man-Shaf'fer diet
co'le·op·to'sis *pl.* -ses'
co'les'
—— fem'i·ni'nus
Co'ley toxin
co'li·bac'il·le'mi·a
co'li·bac'il·lo'sis *pl.* -ses'
co'li·bac'il·lu'ri·a
co'li·ba·cil'lus *pl.* -li'
col'ic
co'li·ca
col'i·cin
col'ick·y
col'i·form'
co'li·gran'u·lo'ma
co·lis'ti·meth'ate'
co·lis'tin
co·li'tis
—— cys'ti·ca pro·fun'da
—— cystica su'per·fi'ci·a'lis
—— pol'y·po'sa
—— ul'cer·a·ti'va
col'i·u'ri·a
col'la·gen
col'la·gen·ase'
col'la·gen'ic
col'la·gen·i·za'tion
col'la·gen·o'sis *pl.* -ses'
col·lag'e·nous
col·lapse', -lapsed', -laps'ing
col'lar·bone'
col'lar·ette'
col·lat'er·al
Col'les
—— fascia
—— fracture
—— law
—— ligament
Col·let' syndrome
col·lic'u·lec'to·my
col·lic'u·li'tis
col·lic'u·lus *pl.* -li'
—— ab'du·cen'tis
—— car'ti·lag'i·nis ar'y·
tae'noi'de·ae'
—— cartilaginis ar'y·te·
noi'de·ae'
—— fa'ci·a'lis
—— inferior

—— sem'i·na'lis
—— superior
—— u're·thra'lis
col'li·dine'
Col'lin·so'ni·a
Col'lip unit
col'li·qua'tion
col·liq'ua·tive
col·lo'di·on'
col'loid'
col·loi'dal
col·loi'do·cla'si·a
col·loi'do·cla'sis *pl.* -ses'
col·loi'do·clas'tic
col'loid·oph'a·gy
col'lum *pl.* -la
—— an'a·tom'i·cum
hu'mer·i'
—— chi·rur'gi·cum hu'mer·i'
—— cos'tae'
—— den'tis
—— dis·tor'tum
—— fem'o·ris
—— fol·lic'u·li' pi'li'
—— glan'dis
—— mal'le·i'
—— man·dib'u·lae'
—— ra'di·i'
—— scap'u·lae'
—— ta'li'
—— ve·si'cae' fel'le·ae'
col'lu·to'ry
col·lyr'i·um *pl.* -i·a *or* -ums
Col'o·bi'nae'
col'o·bine'
col'o·bo'ma *pl.* -ma·ta
—— au'ris
—— pal'pe·brae'
col'o·bo'ma·tous
co·lo·ce·cos'to·my
co·lo·cen·te'sis *pl.* -ses'
co·lo·co·los'to·my
co·lo·hep'a·to·pex'y
co'lon *pl.* -lons *or* -la
—— as·cen'dens
—— de·scen'dens
—— sig·moi'de·um
—— trans·ver'sum
co·lon'ic
co·lon'o·scope'
co'lo·nos'co·py
col'o·ny
col'o·pex'y
col'or
co'lo·rec'tal
col'or·im'e·ter
col'or·i·met'ric

col'or·im'e·try
co·lor'rha·phy
co'lo·sig'moid·os'to·my
co·los'to·my
co·los'tror·rhe'a
co·los'trous
co·los'trum
co·lot'o·my
co'lo·vag'i·nal
co'lo·ves'i·cal
col·pal'gi·a
col'pa·tre'si·a
col'pec·ta'si·a
col·pec'to·my
col'pe·de'ma
col·peu'ry·sis *pl.* -ses'
col·pi'tis
col'po·cele'
col'po·cys'to·plas'ty
col'po·cys·tos'to·my
col'po·hy'per·pla'si·a
cys'ti·ca
col'po·per'i·ne'o·plas'ty
col'po·per'i·ne·or'rha·phy
col'po·pex'y
col'po·plas'ty
col·por'rha·phy
col'por·rhex'is *pl.* -rhex'es'
col'po·scope'
col'po·scop'ic
col·pos'co·py
col·pot'o·my
Co·lum'bi·a-SK virus
col'u·mel'la *pl.* -lae'
col'umn
—— of Ber'tin
—— of Bur'dach'
—— of Goll
co·lum'na *pl.* -nae'
—— anterior me·dul'lae' spi·
na'lis
—— for'ni·cis
—— lat'er·a'lis me·dul'lae'
spi·na'lis
—— na'si'
—— posterior me·dul'lae'
spi·na'lis
—— ru·gar'um anterior
—— rugarum posterior
—— ver'te·bra'lis
co·lum'nae'
—— a·na'les'
—— car'ne·ae'
—— gris'e·ae'
—— rec·ta'les'
—— re·na'les'
—— ru·gar'um

co·lum'ni·za'tion
columns of Mor·ga'gni
co'ma
com'a·tose'
Com'by sign
com'e·do' *pl.* com'e·do'nes'
com'e·do·car'ci·no'ma
   pl. -mas *or* -ma·ta
co'mes' *pl.* com'i·tes'
com'mi·nute', -nut'ed,
  -nut'ing
com'mi·nu'tion
com'mis·su'ra *pl.* -rae'
—— al'ba me·dul'lae' spi·
na'lis
—— anterior alba medullae
spinalis
—— anterior cer'e·bri'
—— anterior gris'e·a me·
dul'lae' spi·na'lis
—— for'ni·cis
—— ha·ben'u·lar'um
—— hip'po·cam'pi'
—— inferior (Gud·den'i')
—— la'bi·o'rum anterior
—— labiorum o'ris
—— labiorum posterior
—— mol'lis
—— pal'pe·brar'um lat'er·
a'lis
—— palpebrarum me'di·a'lis
—— posterior cer'e·bri'
—— posterior me·dul'lae'
spi·na'lis
—— superior (Mey'ner·ti')
com'mis·su'rae' su'pra·
op'ti·cae'
com·mis'su·ral
com'mis·sure
—— of Fo·rel'
com·mis·su·ror'rha·phy
com·mis'sur·ot'o·my
com·mit'ment
com·mo'ti·o'
—— cer'e·bri'
—— ret'i·nae'
—— spi·na'lis
com·mu'ni·ca·ble
com·mu'ni·cans'
com·mu'ni·cate', -cat'ed,
  -cat'ing
com·mu'ni·ca'tion
com·mu'nis
com'mu·ta'tor
com·pac'ta
com·pac'tion
com·pat'i·bil'i·ty

com·pat'i·ble
com'pen·sate', -sat'ed,
  -sat'ing
com'pen·sa'tion
com·pen'sa·to'ry
com'pe·tence
com'ple·ment
com'ple·men'ta·ry
com'ple·men·ta'tion
com·plex'
com·plex'ion
com·plex'us
com·pli'ance
com'pli·cate', -cat'ed, -cat'-
  ing
com'pli·ca'tion
com·po'nent
com·pos'ite
com·po·si'tion
com'pos men'tis
com·pound' *n.*
com·pound' *v.*
com'press' *n.*
com·press' *v.*
com·pres'sion
com·pres'sor
—— bul'bi' pro'pri·us muscle
—— hem'i·sphe'ri·cum bul'-
bi muscle
—— la'bi·i' muscle
—— nar'is muscle
—— na'si'
—— rad'i·cis pe'nis
—— u·re'thrae'
—— va·gi'nae'
—— ve'nae' dor·sa'lis
Comp'ton
—— effect
—— electron
com·pul'sion
com·pul'sive
co·na'tion
con'a·tive
Con·ca'to disease
con'cave'
con·cav'i·ty
com·ca'vo-con'vex'
con·ceive', -ceived', -ceiv'ing
con'cen·tra'tion
con·cen'tric
con·cept'
con·cep'tion
con·cep'tion·al
con·cep'tive
con·cep'tu·al
con·cep'tus *pl.* -tus·es *or* -ti'

con'cha *pl.* -chae'
—— au·ric'u·lae'
—— na·sa'lis inferior
—— nasalis me'di·a
—— nasalis superior
—— nasalis su·pre'ma
—— nasalis suprema
(San'to·ri'ni)
—— sphe'noi·da'lis
con·chi'tis
con'cho·tome'
con·cli·na'tion
con·com'i·tant
con·cor'dance
con·cre·ment
con·cres'cence
con·cre'ti·o'
—— cor'dis
—— per'i·car'di·i'
con·cre'tion
con·cre·tiz'ing
con·cus'sion
con·di'tion
con·di'tion·al
con'dom
con·duc'tion
con·duc'tor
—— so·no'rus of Berg'mann
con·du'pli·ca'to cor'po·re'
con'dy·lar
con'dy·lar·thro'sis *pl.* -ses'
con'dyle'
con'dy·lec'to·my
con·dyl'i·on'
con'dy·loid'
con'dy·lo'ma *pl.* -mas *or*
  -ma·ta
—— a·cu'mi·na'tum
—— la'tum
con'dy·lo'ma·to'sis *pl.* -ses'
con'dy·lom'a·tous
con'dy·lot'o·my
con'dy·lus *pl.* -li'
—— hu'mer·i'
—— lat'er·a'lis fem'or·is
—— lateralis tib'i·ae'
—— me'di·a'lis fem'or·is
—— medialis tib'i·ae'
—— oc·cip'i·ta'lis
cone
con·fab'u·la'tion
con·fi·den'ti·al'i·ty
con·fig'u·ra'tion
con·fine'ment
con·flu'ence
con'flu·ens sin'u·um
con'flu·ent

con·fo′cal
con′for·ma′tion
con′for·ma′tion·al
con·fu′sion
con·fu′sion·al
con·ge·la′tion
con·gen′i·tal
con·gest′ed
con·ges′tion
con·ges′tive
con·glo′bate′
con·glom′er·ate′, -at′ed,
  -at′ing
con·glom′er·a′tion
con·glu′ti·nant
con·glu′ti·na′tion
con·glu′ti·nin
Con′go red test
con·gru′ence
con·gru′ent
con·hy′drine′
co′ni′
—— ep′i·di·dym′i·dis
—— tu′bu·lo′si′
con′i·cal
co′ni·o′sis pl. -ses′
co′ni·o·spo′ri·o′sis pl. -ses′
co′ni·ot′o·my
con′i·za′tion
con·joined′
con·joint′
con′ju·gal
con′ju·ga′ta pl. -tae′
—— ve′ra
con′ju·gate′, -gat′ed, -gat′-
  ing
con′ju·ga′tion
con′junc·ti′va pl. -vas or
  -vae′
con′junc·ti′val
con·junc′ti·vi′tis
—— cat′ar·rha′lis aes·ti′va
—— gran′u·lo′sa
—— med′i·ca·men·to′sa
—— no·do′sa
con′junc·ti′vo·plas′ty
con·nec′tive
con·nec′tor
Con′nell suture
con·nex′us
—— in′ter·ten·din′e·us
—— in′ter·tha·lam′i·cus
Conn syndrome
co′noid′
Con·ol′ly system
Con′rad′i disease
con·san·guin′i·ty

con′scious
con′scious·ness
con·sen′su·al
con·sent′
con·ser′va·tive
con·sis′tence
con·sis′ten·cy
con·sol′i·dant
con·sol′i·date′, -dat′ed,
  -dat′ing
con·sol′i·da′tion
con·sper′gent
con′stel·la′tion
con′sti·pa′tion
con′sti·tute′, -tut′ed, -tut′ing
con′sti·tu′tion
con′sti·tu′tion·al
con′sti·tu′tive
con·stric′tion
con·stric′tive
con·stric′tor
—— rad′i·cis pe′nis
—— va·gi′nae′
con·sult′
con·sul′tant
con′sul·ta′tion
con·sume′, -sumed′, -sum′-
  ing
con·sump′tion
con′tact′
con·tac′tant
con·ta′gion
con·ta′gious
con·tam′i·nant
con·tam′i·nate′, -nat′ed,
  -nat′ing
con·tam′i·na′tion
con·tem·pla′ti·o′
con·tem′pla·tive
con·ti·gu′i·ty
con·tig′u·ous
con′ti·nence
con′ti·nent
con·tor′tion
con′tour′
con′tra-an′gles
con′tra·cep′tion
con′tra·cep′tive
con·trac′tile
con·trac·til′i·ty
con·trac′tion
con·trac′ture
con′tra·fis′sure
con′tra·in′di·cant
con′tra·in′di·cate′, -cat′ed,
  -cat′ing
con′tra·in·di·ca′tion

con′tra·lat′er·al
con·trar′i·ness
con′trast′
con′tra·stim′u·lant
con′tre·coup′
con·trol′
con·tuse′, -tused′, -tus′ing
con·tu′sion
co′nus pl. -ni′
—— ar·te′ri·o′sus pul′mo·
  na′lis
—— e·las′ti·cus la·ryn′gis
—— med·ul·lar′is
—— ter′mi·na′lis
—— tu′bu·lo′si′
con′va·les′cence
con′va·les′cent
con′val·lar′i·a
con·vec′tion
con·ver′gence
con·ver′gent
con·ver′sion
con·ver′tin
con′vex′
con·vex′i·ty
con·vex′o-con′cave′
con·vex′o-con′vex′
con′vo·lut′ed
con′vo·lu′tion
con′vo·lu′tion·al
con·vul′sant
con·vul′sion
con·vul′si·o′ par·tic′u·lar′is
con·vul′sive
Con′way′
—— cell
—— method
Con′way-Byrne′ diffusion
  method
Cooke′-Pon′der method
Coo′ley
—— anemia
—— trait
Coo′lidge tube
Coombs
—— serum
—— test
Coons fluorescent anti-
  body method
Coo′per
—— disease
—— fascia
—— hernia
—— ligament
—— method
co·or′di·na′tion
cop′ing

cop'per·as
co'pre·cip'i·tate', -tat'ed,
  -tat'ing
co'pre·cip'i·ta'tion
cop·rem'e·sis
cop'ro·an'ti·bod'y
cop·roc'tic
cop'ro·lag'ni·a
cop'ro·la'li·a
cop'ro·lith'
cop·roph'a·gy
cop'ro·phil'i·a
cop·roph'i·lous
cop'ro·pho'bi·a
cop'ro·por'phy·rin
cop'ro·por'phy·rin·u'ri·a
co·pros'ta·nol'
co·pros'ter·ol'
cop'ro·zo'ic
cop'u·la *pl.* -las *or* -lae'
cop'u·late', -lat'ed, -lat'ing
cop·u·la'tion
cor
—— bi'au·ric'u·lar'e'
—— bi·loc'u·lar'e'
—— bi'ven·tric'u·lar'e'
—— bo·vi'num
—— pseu'do·tri·loc'u·lar'e'
—— tri·a'tri·a'tum
—— tri'au·ric'u·lar'e'
—— tri·loc'u·lar'e'
—— triloculare bi·a'tri·um
—— trioculare bi'ven·tric'u·
lar'e'
—— trioculare mon·a'tri·
a'tum
—— vil·lo'sum
cor'a·cid'i·um *pl.* -i·a
cor'a·co·a·cro'mi·al
cor'a·co·bra'chi·a'lis *pl.*
  -les'
—— brev'is
—— superior
cor'a·co·cla·vic'u·lar
cor'a·co·hu'mer·al
cor'a·coid'
cor'a·coi·di'tis
cor·al'li·form'
cord
cord'al *(pertaining to vocal
  cord)*
♦*chordal*
cor'date'
cor·dec'to·my
cor'di·form'
cor·di'tis

—— no·do'sa
cor'do·pex'y
cor·dot'o·my *var. of* chor-
  dotomy
Cor'dy·lo'bi·a
—— an'thro·poph'a·ga
core
cor'e·cli'sis *pl.* -ses'
cor·ec'ta·sis *pl.* -ses'
cor·ec'tome'
co·rec'to·my
cor'ec·to'pi·a
cor'e·di·al'y·sis *pl.* -ses'
co·rel'y·sis *pl.* -ses'
cor'e·om'e·ter
cor'e·o·plas'ty
co'-re·pres'sor
cor'e·ste·no'ma
Co'ri
—— cycle
—— ester
—— gly'co·ge·no'ses'
—— lim'it dex'tri·no'sis
co'ri·a'ceous
—— strep'i·tus
co'ri·um *pl.* -ri·a
cor'ne·a
—— gut·ta'ta
cor'ne·al
Cor·ne'li·a de Lange' syndrome
Cor'nell'
—— response
—— unit of riboflavin
Cor·nell'-Coxe' scale
cor'ne·o·bleph'a·ron'
cor'ne·o·man·dib'u·lar
cor'ne·o·oc'u·lo·gy'ric
cor'ne·o·pter'y·goid'
cor'ne·o·scle'ra
cor'ne·o·scle'ral
cor'ne·ous
cor'ne·um
cor·nic'u·late
cor·nic'u·lum *pl.* -la
—— la·ryn'gis
cor'ni·fi·ca'tion
cor'ni·fied'
cor'noid'
cor'nu *pl.* -nu·a
—— Am·mo'nis
—— an·te'ri·us me·dul'lae'
spi·na'lis
—— anterius ven·tric'u·li'
lat'er·a'lis
—— cer'vi'
—— coc·cyg'e·a

—— coc·cyg'e·um
—— cu·ta'ne·um
—— in·fe'ri·us car'ti·lag'i·nis
thy're·oi'de·ae'
—— inferius cartilaginis
thy·roi'de·ae'
—— inferius fos'sae' o·va'lis
—— inferius mar'gi·nis
fal'ci·for'mis
—— inferius ven·tric'u·li'
lat'er·a'lis
—— lat'er·a'le' me·dul'lae'
spi·na'lis
—— ma'jus os'sis hy·oi'de·i'
—— mi'nus os'sis hy·oi'de·i'
—— pos·te'ri·us me·dul'lae'
spi·na'lis
—— posterius ven·tric'u·li'
lat'er·a'lis
—— sa·cra'le'
—— su·pe'ri·us car'ti·lag'i·
nis thy're·oi'de·ae'
—— superius cartilaginis
thy·roi'de·ae'
—— superius fos'sae'
o·va'lis
—— superius mar'gi·nis
fal'ci·for'mis
cor'nu·al
cor'nu·com·mis'sur·al
cor'o·clei'sis *pl.* -ses', *var. of*
coroclisis
cor'o·cli'sis *pl.* -ses', *also*
corocleisis
co·rol'la
co·rom'e·ter
co·ro'na *pl.* -nae'
—— cap'i·tis
—— cil'i·ar'is
—— clin'i·ca
—— den'tis
—— glan'dis pe'nis
—— ra'di·a'ta
—— seb'or·rhe'i·ca
—— ven'er·is
co·ro'nal
cor'o·na·le'
cor'o·na·lis
cor'o·nar'y
cor'o·na·vi'rus
co·ro'ne'
cor'o·ner
co·ro'ni·on' *pl.* -ni·a
cor'o·noid'
co·ros'co·py
Cor'per and Cohn method
cor'po·ra

—— al'bi·can'tes'
—— am'y·la'ce·a
—— A·ran'ti·i'
—— ar·e·na'ce·a
—— bi·gem'i·na
—— cav'er·no'sa
—— hem'or·rhag'i·ca
—— par'a·a·or'ti·ca
—— quad'ri·gem'i·na
—— res'ti·for'mi·a
corpse
cor'pu·lence
cor'pu·lent
cor'pus *pl.* -po·ra
—— ad'i·po'sum buc'cae'
—— adiposum fos'sae'
is'chi·o·rec·ta'lis
—— adiposum in'fra·pat'el·lar'e'
—— adiposum or'bi·tae'
—— al'bi·cans'
—— a·myg'da·loi'de·um
—— a·tret'i·cum
—— cal·ca'ne·i'
—— cal·lo'sum
—— can'di·cans'
—— ca·ver·no'sum cli·to'ri·dis
—— cavernosum pe'nis
—— cavernosum u·re'thrae'
—— cer'e·bel'li'
—— cil'i·ar'e'
—— cli·to'ri·dis
—— coc·cyg'e·um
—— cos'tae'
—— de·lic'ti'
—— ep'i·di·dym'i·dis
—— fem'o·ris
—— fi·bro'sum
—— fib'u·lae'
—— for'ni·cis
—— ge·nic'u·la'tum
—— geniculatum lat'er·a'le'
—— geniculatum me'di·a'le'
—— glan'du·lae' bul'bo·u're·thra'lis
—— glandulae su'do·rif'er·ae'
—— glan'du·lar'e' pros'ta·tae'
—— hem'or·rhag'i·cum
—— hu'mer·i'
—— in·cu'dis
—— lin'guae'
—— lu'te·um
—— Lu·y'si·i'
—— mam'il·lar'e'

—— mam'mae'
—— man·dib'u·lae'
—— max·il'lae'
—— med'ul·lar'e' cer'e·bel'li'
—— nu'cle·i' cau·da'ti
—— os'sis hy·oi'de·i'
—— ossis il'i·i'
—— ossis il'i·um
—— ossis is'chi·i'
—— ossis met'a·car·pa'lis
—— ossis met'a·tar·sa'lis
—— ossis pu'bis
—— ossis sphe'noi·da'lis
—— os'si·um met'a·car·pa'li·um
—— ossium met'a·tar·sa'li·um
—— pan·cre'a·tis
—— pap'il·lar'e' co'ri·i'
—— pe'nis
—— pha·lan'gis dig'i·to'rum ma'nus
—— phalangis digitorum pe'dis
—— pin'e·a'le'
—— pon'to·bul·bar'e'
—— quad'ri·gem'i·na
—— ra'di·i'
—— res'ti·for'me'
—— re·tic'u·lar'e' co'ri·i'
—— spon'gi·o'sum pe'nis
—— spongiosum u·re'thrae' mu'li·e'bris
—— ster'ni'
—— stri·a'tum
—— ta'li'
—— tib'e·ae'
—— trap'e·zoi'de·um
—— ul'nae'
—— un'guis
—— u'ter·i'
—— ven·tric'u·li'
—— ver'te·brae'
—— ve·si'cae' fel'le·ae'
—— vesicae u'ri·nar'i·ae'
—— ve·sic'u·lae' sem'i·na'lis
—— vit're·um
—— Wolf'fi'
cor'pus·cle
—— of Gol'gi
cor·pus'cu·la
—— ar·tic'u·lar'i·a
—— bul·boi'de·a
—— gen'i·ta'li·a
—— lam'el·lo'sa
—— ner·vo'rum ar·tic'u·lar'i·a

—— nervorum gen'i·ta'li·a
—— nervorum ter'mi·na'li·a
—— ner·vo'sa ter'mi·na'li·a
—— re'nis
—— tac'tus
cor·pus'cu·lar
cor·pus'cu·lum *pl.* -la
—— ar·tic'u·lar'e' mo'bi·le'
cor·rec'tion
cor·rec'tive
cor're·late', -lat'ed, -lat'ing
cor're·la'tion
cor·rel'a·tive
Cor'ri·gan
—— pulse
—— respiration
cor·ro'sion
cor·ro'sive
cor'ru·ga'tor
—— cu'tis a'ni'
—— su'per·cil'i·i'
cor'tex *pl.* -ti·ces'
—— cer'e·bel'li'
—— cer'e·bri'
—— glan'du·lae' su'pra·re·na'lis
—— len'tis
—— no'di' lym·phat'i·ci'
—— re'nis
cor'ti·cal
cor'ti·cate'
cor'ti·cec'to·my
cor'ti·cif'u·gal
cor'ti·cin
cor'ti·cip'e·tal
cor'ti·co'a·dre'nal
cor'ti·co·af'fer·ent
cor'ti·co·au'to·nom'ic
cor'ti·co·bul'bar
cor'ti·co·cer'e·bral
cor'ti·co·col·lic'u·lar
cor'ti·co·ef'fer·ent
cor'ti·co·ge·nic'u·late'
cor'ti·co·hy'po·tha·lam'ic
cor'ti·coid'
cor'ti·co·ni'gral
cor'ti·co·nu'cle·ar
cor'ti·co·pal'li·dal
cor'ti·co'pleu·ri'tis
cor'ti·co·pon'tile'
cor'ti·co·pon'tine'
cor'ti·co·pon'to·cer'e·bel'lar
cor'ti·co·ru'bral
cor'ti·co·spi'nal
cor'ti·co·ste'roid'
cor'ti·cos'ter·one'

cor'ti·co·stri'ate'
cor'ti·co·stri'a·to·spi'nal
cor'ti·co·stri'o·ni'gral
cor'ti·co·tha·lam'ic
cor'ti·co·troph'ic
cor'ti·co·tro'pic
cor'ti·co·tro'pin
cor'tin
cor'ti·sol'
cor'ti·sone'
cor'to·dox'one'
cor'tol'
cor'to·lone'
cor·us·ca'tion
cor'vus
co·rym'bi·form'
Cor'y·ne·bac·te'ri·um
—— diph·the'ri·ae'
—— hof·man'ni·i'
—— pseu'do·diph'the·rit'i·
cum
—— xe·ro'sis
co·ry'za
cos·met'ic
cos'ta pl. -tae'
—— fluc'tu·an'tes'
—— spu'ri·ae'
—— ve'rae'
cos'tal
cos·tal'gi·a
cos·ta'lis
cos·tec'to·my
Cos'ten syndrome
cos'ti·car'ti·lage
cos'ti·form'
cos'tive
cos'to·ar·tic'u·lar
cos'to·car'ti·lage
cos'to·cer'vi·cal
cos'to·cer'vi·ca'lis
cos'to·chon'dral
cos'to·chon·dri'tis
cos'to·cla·vic'u·lar
cos'to·col'ic
cos'to·cor'a·coid'
cos'to·di'a·phrag·mat'ic
cos'to·gen'ic
cos'to·in·fe'ri·or
cos'to·lum'bar'
cos'to·me'di·as·ti'nal
cos'to·phren'ic
cos'to·pleu'ral
cos'to·scap'u·lar
cos'to·ster'nal
cos'to·su·pe'ri·or
cos'to·tome'
cos·tot'o·my

cos'to·trans·verse'
cos'to·trans'ver·sec'to·my
cos'to·ver'te·bral
cos'to·xiph'oid'
co'syn·tro'pin
co·tar'nine'
co·throm'bo·plas'tin
co'ti·nine' fu'ma·rate'
co'trans·am'i·nase'
cot'ton
Cot'ton fracture
cot'y·le'don
cot'y·loid'
couch'ing
cou·dé'
cough
cou'ma·rin
Coun'cil·man bodies
coun'ter·ex·ten'sion
coun'ter·fis'sure
coun'ter·im'mu·no'e·
lec'tro·pho·re'sis pl. -ses'
coun'ter·in·ci'sion
coun'ter·in·di·ca'tion
coun'ter·in·vest'ment
coun'ter·ir'ri·tant
coun'ter·ir'ri·tate', -tat'ed,
-tat'ing
coun'ter·ir'ri·ta'tion
coun'ter·o'pen·ing
coun'ter·pho'bi·a
coun'ter·pho'bic
coun'ter·poi'son
coun'ter·pres'sure
coun'ter·punc'ture
coun'ter·shock'
coun'ter·stain'
coun'ter·stroke'
coun'ter·trac'tion
coun'ter·trans'fer·ence
coup
—— de fouet'
—— de sabre'
—— de sang'
—— de so·leil'
—— sur coup'
Cour'voi·sier' law
cou·vade'
Cou've·laire' uterus
co·va'lence
Cow'dri·a ru'mi·nan'ti·um
Cow'en sign
Cow'ie test
Cow'ling rule
Cow'per
—— cyst
—— glands

—— ligament
cow'per·i'tis
Cox
—— vaccine
—— yolk-sac method
cox'a pl. -ae'
—— mag'na
—— pla'na
—— val'ga
—— var'a
cox'al
cox·al'gi·a
cox·al'gic
cox'ar·thri'tis
Cox'i·el'la
—— bur·net'i·i'
cox·i'tis pl. -it'i·des'
—— cot'y·loi'de·a
cox'o·dyn'i·a
cox'o·fem'o·ral
Cox·sack'ie
—— disease
—— virus
co·zy'mase'
Coz'zo·li'no zone
Crab'tree' effect
Crä'mer method
cramp
Cran'dall test
cra'ni·ad'
cra'ni·al
cra'ni·a'lis
cra'ni·ec'to·my
cra'ni·o'a·cro'mi·al
cra'ni·o·ba'sal
cra'ni·o·buc'cal
cra'ni·o·car'po·tar'sal
cra'ni·o·cele'
cra'ni·o·cer'vi·cal
cra'ni·oc'la·sis pl. -ses'
cra'ni·o·clast'
cra'ni·o·clas'ty
cra'ni·o·clei'do·dys'os·
to'sis pl. -ses'
cra'ni·o·did'y·mus pl. -mi'
cra'ni·o·fa'cial
cra'ni·o·fe·nes'tri·a
cra'ni·o·graph'
cra'ni·og'ra·phy
cra'ni·o·la·cu'ni·a
cra'ni·ol'o·gy
cra'ni·o·me·nin'go·cele'
cra'ni·om'e·ter
cra'ni·o·met'ric
cra'ni·om'e·try
cra'ni·op'a·gus pl. -gi'
—— fron·ta'lis

—— oc·cip'i·ta'lis
—— par'a·sit'i·cus
—— pa·ri'e·ta'lis
cra'ni·op'a·thy
cra'ni·o·pha·ryn'ge·al
cra'ni·o·pha·ryn'gi·o'ma
  pl. -mas *or* -ma·ta
cra'ni·o·plas'ty
cra'ni·o·ra·chis'chi·sis *pl.*
  -ses'
—— to·ta'lis
cra'ni·o·sa'cral
cra'ni·os'chi·sis *pl.* -ses'
cra'ni·o'scle·ro'sis *pl.* -ses'
cra'ni·o·spi'nal
cra'ni·o·ste·no'sis *pl.* -ses'
cra'ni·os·to'sis *pl.* -ses'
cra'ni·o·syn'os·to'sis
  pl. -ses'
cra'ni·o·ta'bes'
cra'ni·o·ta·bet'ic
cra'ni·o·tome'
cra'ni·ot'o·my
cra'ni·o·trac'tor
cra'ni·o·tym·pan'ic
cra'ni·o·ver'te·bral
cra'ni·um *pl.* -ni·ums *or* -ni·a
—— bif'i·dum
—— cer'e·bra'le'
—— vis'ce·ra'le'
crap'u·lent
craque·lé'
cra'ter
cra·ter'i·form'
cra'ter·i·za'tion
C'-re·ac'tive
cre·at'ic
cre·at'i·nase'
cre'a·tine'
cre'a·ti·ne'mi·a
cre'a·tine·phos·pho'ric
cre·at'i·nine'
cre'a·tin·u'ri·a
cre'a·tor·rhe'a
cre·mas'ter
crem'as·ter'ic
cre'na *pl.* -nae'
—— a'ni'
—— clu'ni·um
cre'nate'
cre'nat'ed
cre·na'tion
cre'o·sol'
cre'o·sote'
crep'i·tance
crep'i·tant
crep'i·tate', -tat'ed, -tat'ing

crep'i·ta'ti·o'
crep'i·ta'tion
crep'i·tus
cres'cent
—— of Gian·nuz'zi
cre'sol'
cre·sot'ic
cres'o·tin'ic
crest
cres'yl
cres'yl·ate'
cre·syl'ic
cre'tin
cre'tin·ism
Cré·tin' method
cre'tin·oid'
cre'tin·ous
Cré·tin'-Pou·yanne' meth-
  od
Creutz'feldt-Ja'kob dis-
  ease
crev'ice
cre·vic'u·lar
crib'rate'
crib'ri·form'
cri'brum *pl.* -bra
Crich'ton-Browne' sign
cri'co·ar'y·te'noid'
cri'co·e·soph'a·ge'al
cri'coid'
cri'coi·dec'to·my
cri'coi·dyn'i·a
cri'co·pha·ryn'ge·al
cri'co·pha·ryn'ge·us
cri'co·thy'roid'
cri'co·thy·rot'o·my
cri·cot'o·my
cri'co·tra'che·al
cri'co·tra'che·ot'o·my
cri'co·vo'cal
cri'-du-chat'
Crig'ler-Naj·jar' syndrome
Crile theory
cri'nis *pl.* -nes'
crin'o·gen'ic
cri·nos'i·ty
cri'nous
crise de dé·glo·bu·li·sa·
  tion'
cri'sis *pl.* -ses'
Crisp aneurysm
cris·pa'tion
cris'pa·tu'ra
—— ten'di·num
cris'ta *pl.* -tae'
—— a·cous'ti·ca
—— am'pul·lar'is

—— anterior fib'u·lae'
—— anterior tib'i·ae'
—— ar'cu·a'ta
—— bas'i·lar'is
—— buc'ci·na·to'ri·a
—— cap'i·tis cos'tae'
—— ca·pit'u·li' cos'tae'
—— col'li' cos'tae'
—— con·cha'lis max·il'lae'
—— conchalis os'sis pal'a·
ti'ni'
—— div'i·dens
—— eth'moi·da'lis max·
il'lae'
—— ethmoidalis os'sis pal'a·
ti'ni'
—— fal'ci·for'mis
—— fe·nes'trae' coch'le·ae'
—— fron·ta'lis
—— gal'li'
—— i·li'a·ca
—— in'fra·tem'po·ra'lis
—— in'ter·os'se·a fib'u·lae'
—— interossea ra'di·i'
—— interossea tib'i·ae'
—— interossea ul'nae'
—— in'ter·tro'chan·ter'i·ca
—— lac'ri·ma'lis anterior
—— lacrimalis posterior
—— lat'er·a'lis fib'u·lae'
—— mar'gi·na'lis den'tis
—— me'di·a'lis fib'u·lae'
—— mus'cu·li' su'pi·na·to'ris
—— na·sa'lis max·il'lae'
—— nasalis os'sis pal'a·ti'ni'
—— ob'tu·ra·to'ri·a
—— oc·cip'i·ta'lis ex·ter'na
—— occipitalis in·ter'na
—— pal'a·ti'na
—— pu'bi·ca
—— sa·cra'lis in'ter·me'di·a
—— sacralis lat'er·a'lis
—— sacralis me'di·a
—— sacralis me'di·a'na
—— sep'ti' mar'gi·na'lis
—— sphe'noi·da'lis
—— su'pra·ven·tric'u·lar'is
—— ter'mi·na'lis a'tri·i'
dex'tri'
—— trans·ver'sa
—— tu·ber'cu·li' ma·jo'ris
—— tuberculi mi·no'ris
—— u're·thra'lis u·re'thrae'
fem'i·ni'nae'
—— urethralis urethrae
mas'cu·li'nae'

—— urethralis urethrae mu'li·e'bris
—— urethralis urethrae vir'i·lis
—— ves·tib'u·li'
cris'tae'
—— cu'tis
—— ma'tri·cis un'guis
—— sa·cra'les' ar·tic'u·lar'es'
—— sacrales lat'er·a'les'
cris'tate'
crit
Cri·thid'i·a
cri·thid'i·al
crit'i·cal
Crock'er tumor
Crocq disease
cro'cus
Crohn disease
cro'mo·lyn
Crooke
—— cells
—— change
Crookes tube
cross'bite'
cross'-eye'
cross'-re·act'ing
crot'a·line'
cro·ta·lo·tox'in
cro·tam'i·ton'
cro·taph'i·on'
crotch
cro'ton·ism
cro·tox'in
croup
croup'ous
Crou·zon'-A'pert disease
Crou·zon' disease
Crowe sign
cru'ces'
—— pi·lo'rum
cru'cial
cru'ci·ate'
cru'ci·ble
cru'ci·form'
cru'fo·mate'
cru'ra
—— am'pul·lar'i·a
—— ant·hel'i·cis
—— mem'bra·na'ce·a
—— membranacea am'pul·lar'i·a duc'tus sem'i·cir'cu·lar'is
—— os'sea
—— ossea am'pul·lar'i·a
cru'ral

cru're·us
cru'ro·scro'tal
cru'ro·ves'i·cal
crus pl. cru'ra
—— an·te'ri·us cap'su·lae' in·ter'nae'
—— anterius sta·pe'dis
—— brev'e' in'cu·dis
—— cer'e·bri'
—— cli·to'ri·dis
—— com·mu'ne'
—— dex'trum di'a·phrag'ma·tis
—— fas·cic'u·li' a'tri·o·ven·tric'u·lar'is dex'trum et si·nis'trum
—— for'ni·cis
—— hel'i·cis
—— in·fe'ri·us an'nu·li' in'gui·na'lis sub'cu·ta'ne·i'
—— in·ter·me'di·um di'a·phrag'ma·tis
—— lat'er·a'le' an'u·li' in'gui·na'lis su'per·fi'ci·a'lis
—— laterale car'ti·lag'i·nis a·lar'is ma·jo'ris
—— laterale di'a·phrag'ma·tis
—— lon'gum in'cu·dis
—— me'di·a'le' an'u·li' in'gui·na'lis su'per·fi'ci·a'lis
—— mediale car'ti·lag'i·nis a·lar'is ma·jo'ris
—— mediale di'a·phrag'ma·tis
—— mem'bra·na'ce·um com·mu'ne'
—— membranaceum sim'·plex'
—— os'se·um com·mu'ne'
—— osseum sim'plex'
—— pe·dun'cu·li'
—— pe'nis
—— pos·te'ri·us cap'su·lae' in·ter'nae'
—— posterius sta·pe'dis
—— sim'plex'
—— si·nis'trum di'a·phrag'ma·tis
—— su·pe'ri·us an'nu·li' in'gui·na'lis sub'cu·ta'ne·i'
crus·ot'omy
crus'ta pl. -tae'
—— lac'te·a
crutch
Cru'veil·hier'
—— disease

—— sign
Cru'veil· hier'-Baum'-gar'ten syndrome
crux pl. cru'ces'
Cruz disease
cry'al·ge'si·a
cry'an·es·the'si·a
cry'es·the'si·a
cry'mo·dyn'i·a
cry'mo·phil'ic
cry'o·bi·ol'o·gy
cry'o·cau'ter·y
cry'o·chem'
cry'o·crit'
cry'o·ex·trac'tion
cry'o·ex·trac'tor
cry'o·gen
cry'o·gen'ic
cry'o·glob'u·lin
cry'o·glob'u·li·ne'mi·a
cry'o·hy·poph'y·sec'to·my
cry·om'e·ter
cry'o·phake'
cry'o·probe'
cry'o·pro'te·in
cry'o·scope'
cry'o·stat'
cry'o·sur'ger·y
cry'o·thal'a·mot'o·my
cry'o·ther'a·py
cry'o·tome'
crypt
cryp'ta pl. -tae'
cryp'tae'
—— ton'sil·lar'es' ton·sil'lae' pal'a·ti'nae'
—— tonsillares tonsillae pha·ryn'ge·ae'
crypt'am·ne'si·a
cryp·ten'a·mine'
cryp'tic
cryp·ti'tis
cryp'to·coc·co'sis pl. -ses'
Cryp'to·coc'cus
—— ne'o·for'mans'
cryp'to·gen'ic
cryp'to·lith'
cryp'to·men·or·rhe'a
cryp'to·mere'
cryp'to·mer'o·ra·chis'chi·sis pl. -ses'
cryp'tom·ne'si·a
cryp'toph·thal'mi·a
cryp'toph·thal'mos
cryp·tor'chid
cryp·tor·chi·dec'to·my

cryp·tor′chid·ism
cryp′tor·chid′o·pex′y
cryp·tor′chis
cryp·tor′chism
cryp′to·xan′thin
cryp′to·zo′ite′
cryp′to·zy′gous
crys′tal
crys′tal·bu′min
crys′tal·fi′brin
crys′tal·lin (a globulin of the crystalline lens)
♦crystalline
crys′tal·line (similar to a crystal)
♦crystallin
crys′tal·li·za′tion
crys′tal·lize′, -lized′, -liz′ing
crys′tal·loid′
crys′tal·lu′ri·a
Cten′o·ce·phal′i·des′
cu′bi·form′
cu′bi·tal
cu′bi·to·car′pal
cu′bi·to·ra′di·al
cu′bi·tus pl. -ti′
——— val′gus
——— var′us
cu′boid′
cu·boi′dal
cu·boi′de·o·na·vic′u·lar
cu·boi′do·dig′i·tal
cui·rass′
cul′-de-sac′
cul′do·cen·te′sis pl. -ses′
cul′do·plas′ty
cul′do·scope′
cul·dos′co·py
cul·dot′o·my
Cu′lex′
——— fat′i·gans′
——— pi′pi·ens
——— quin′que·fas′ci·a′tus
cu′li·cide′
cu·lic′i·fuge′
Cul′len sign
cul′men pl. -mens or -mi·na
cul′ti·vate′, -vat′ed, -vat′ing
cul′ti·va′tion
cul′tur·al
cul′ture, -tured, -tur·ing
cu′mic
cu′mu·la′tive
cu′mu·lus pl. -li′
——— o·oph′o·rus
——— o·vig′er·us
——— pro·lig′er·us

cu′ne·ate′
cu·ne′i·form′
cu′ne·o·cu′boid′
cu′ne·o·na·vic′u·lar
cu′ne·o·scaph′oid′
cu·ne·us pl. -ne·i′
cu·nic′u·lar
cu·nic′u·lus pl. -li′
cun′ni·lin′gus
cun′nus pl. -ni′
cu′o·rin
cup, cupped, cup′ping
cu′pram·mo′ni·a
cu′pre·a
cu′pre·ine′
cu′pric
cu′prous
cu′pu·la pl. -lae′
——— coch′le·ae′
——— cris′tae′ am′pul·lar′is
——— op′ti·ca
——— pleu′rae′
cu′rage
cu·ra′re
cu′ra·tive
curd
cure, cured, cur′ing
cu·ret′ var. of curette
cu′ret·tage′
cu·rette′ also curet
cu′rie
Cur′ling ulcer
Cur′rens formula
cur′rent
Cursch′mann spirals
cur·va′tor coc·cyg′e·us
cur′va·tu′ra pl. -rae′
——— ven·tric′u·li′ major
——— ventriculi minor
cur′va·ture
curve, curved, curv′ing
cur′vi·lin′e·ar
Cush′ing
——— incision
——— law
——— syndrome
cush′ing·oid′
cusp
cus′pate′
cus′pid
cus′pi·dal
cus′pi·date′
cus′pis pl. -pi·des′
——— anterior val′vae′ a′tri·o·ven·tric′u·lar′is dex′trae′
——— anterior valvae atrio-ventricularis si·nis′trae′

——— anterior val′vu·lae′ bi·cus′pi·da′lis
——— anterior valvulae tri·cus′pi·da′lis
——— co·ro′nae′ den′tis
——— me′di·a′lis val′vu·lae′ tri·cus′pi·da′lis
——— posterior val′vae′ a′tri·o·ven·tric′u·lar′is dex′trae′
——— posterior valvae atrio-ventricularis si·nis′trae′
——— posterior val′vu·lae′ bi·cus′pi·da′lis
——— posterior valvulae tri·cus′pi·da′lis
——— sep·ta′lis val′vae′ a′tri·o·ven·tric′u·lar′is dex′trae′
cut, cut, cut′ting
cu·ta′ne·o·gas′tro·in·tes′ti·nal
cu·ta′ne·o·in·tes′ti·nal
cu·ta′ne·o·mu·co′sal
cu·ta′ne·ous
cut′down′
cu′ti·cle
cu·tic′u·la pl. -lae′
——— den′tis
cu·tic′u·lar
cu′tin
cu′tin·i·za′tion
cu′ti·re·ac′tion
cu′tis pl. -tes′ or -tis·es
——— an′se·ri′na
——— hy′per·e·las′ti·ca
——— lax′a
——— mar′mo·ra′ta
——— pen′du·la
——— rhom′boi·da′lis nu′chae′
——— ve′ra
——— ver′ti·cis gy·ra′ta
cu′ti·za′tion
Cut′ler-Pow′er-Wil′der test
Cut′ting colloidal mastic test
cu·vette′
Cu·vier′
——— canals
——— ducts
cy·an′a·mide′
cy′a·nate′
cy′a·ne′mi·a
cy′an·hem′a·tin
cy′an·he′mo·glo′bin
cy′an·hi·dro′sis pl. -ses′

cy·an'ic
cy'a·nide'
cy·an·met·he'mo·glo'bin
cy'a·no·co·bal'a·min
cy'a·no·der'ma
cy·an'o·gen
cy'a·no·ge·net'ic
cy'a·nol'
cy·an'o·phil'
cy'a·no·phil'ic
cy·a·noph'i·lous
cy·an'o·phose'
cy·a·no'pi·a
cy'a·nop'si·a
cy'a·nop'sin
cy'a·nosed'
cy'a·no'sis pl. -ses'
cy'a·not'ic
cy·as'ma pl. -ma·ta
cy'ber·net'ic
cy'cla·cil'lin
cyc'la·mate'
cy·clam'ic
cy·clan'de·late'
cy'clase'
cy·claz'o·cine'
cy'cle
—— of Gol'gi
—— of Ross
cy·clec'to·my
cy'clen·ceph'a·lus pl. -li'
cy'clen·ceph'a·ly
cy'clic
cy·clir'a·mine'
cy·clit'ic
cy·cli'tis
cy'clize', -clized', -cliz'ing
cy'cli·zine'
cy'clo·bar'bi·tal'
cy'clo·ben'za·prine'
cy'clo·ceph'a·lus pl. -li'
cy'clo·ceph'a·ly
cy'clo·cu'ma·rol'
cy'clo·di·al'y·sis pl. -ses'
cy'clo·di'a·ther'my
cy·clog'e·ny
cy·clo·gua'nil
cy'clo·hex'ane'
cy'clo·hex'a·nol'
cy'clo·hex'i·mide'
cy'cloid'
cy'clo·mas·top'a·thy
cy'clo·meth'y·caine'
cy'clo·pen'ta·mine'
cy'clo·pen'tane'
cy'clo·pen·te'no·phe·
nan'threne'

cy'clo·pen·thi'a·zide'
cy'clo·pen'to·late'
cy'clo·phen'a·zine'
cy'clo·pho'rase'
cy'clo·pho'ri·a
cy'clo·phos'pha·mide'
cy·clo'pi·a
cy'clo·ple'gi·a
cy'clo·ple'gic
cy'clo·pro'pane'
cy'clops'
cy'clo·scope'
cy'clo·ser'ine'
cy·clo'sis pl. -ses'
cy'clo·thi'a·zide
cy'clo·thy'mi·a
cy'clo·thy'mi·ac'
cy'clo·thy'mic
cy'clo·tome'
cy·clot'o·my
cy'clo·tron'
cy'clo·tro'pi·a
cy'cri·mine'
cy·do'ni·um
cy·e'sis pl. -ses'
cyl'in·der
cy·lin'dric or cy·lin'dri·cal
cy·lin'dri·form'
cyl'in·droid'
cyl'in·dro'ma pl. -mas or
-ma·ta
cyl'in·dru'ri·a
cyl'lo·so'ma pl. -mas or
-ma·ta
cy·ma'rose'
cym'ba con'chae'
cym'bi·form'
cym'bo·ce·phal'ic
cym'bo·ceph'a·lous
cym'bo·ceph'a·ly
cy'me·nyl
cy'mol'
cy·nan'che
cyn·an·thro'pi·a
cyn·an'thro·py
cyn'ic
cyn·o'rex'i·a
cy·o'pho'ri·a
cy·ot'ro·phy
cy·pen'a·mine'
cy·praz'e·pam'
cy·pro·hep'ta·dine'
cy·pro'li·dol'
cy·pro·quin'ate'
cy·pro'ter·one'
cy·prox'i·mide'
cyr·to'graph'

cyr·tom'e·ter
cyr·tom'e·try
cyr·to'sis pl. -ses'
cyr·tu·ran'us
cyst
cyst·ad'e·no·car'ci·no'ma
pl. -mas or -ma·ta
cyst·ad'e·no·fi·bro'ma pl.
-mas or -ma·ta
cyst·ad·e·no'ma pl. -mas or
-ma·ta
—— ad'a·man'ti·num
—— cy·lin'dro·cel'lu·lar'e'
cel·loi'des' o·var'i·i'
—— pap'il·lif'er·um
cyst·ad'e·no·sar·co'ma
pl. -mas or -ma·ta
cys·tal'gi·a
cys'ta·thi'o·nine'
cys'ta·thi'o·nin·u'ri·a
cys'ta·tro'phi·a
cys'tec·ta'si·a
cys·tec'to·my
cys'te·ine'
cys'te·in'yl
cys'tic
cys'ti·cer·ci'a·sis pl. -ses'
cys'ti·cer'coid'
cys'ti·cer·co'sis pl. -ses'
cys'ti·cer'cus pl. -ci'
cys'ti·form'
cys'tine'
cys'ti·ne'mi·a
cys'ti·no'sis pl. -ses'
cys'ti·nu'ri·a
cys·ti'tis pl. -tit'i·des'
—— cys'ti·ca
—— em'phy·se'ma·to'sa
—— fol·lic'u·lar'is
—— glan'du·lar'is
cys'ti·tome'
cys'to·blast'
cys'to·car'ci·no'ma pl. -mas
or -ma·ta
cys'to·cele'
cys'to·co·los'to·my
cys'to·du·od'e·nos'to·my
cys'to·dyn'i·a
cys'to·en'ter·o·cele'
cys'to·ep'i·the'li·o'ma pl.
-mas or -ma·ta
cys'to·fi·bro'ma pl. -mas or
-ma·ta
—— pap'il·lar'e'
cys'to·gen'e·sis pl. -ses'
cys'to·gram'
cys'to·graph'ic

cys·tog'ra·phy
cys'toid'
cys'to·je'ju·nos'to·my
cys'to·lith'
cys'to·li·thec'to·my
cys'to·li·thi'a·sis *pl.* -ses'
cys'to·lith'ic
cys'to·li·thot'o·my
cys·to'ma *pl.* -mas *or* -ma·ta
—— o·var'i·i' pseu'do·mu'ci·
no'sum
cys·to'ma·tous
cys·tom'e·ter
cys'to·met'ro·gram'
cys·tom'e·try
cys·to·mor'phous
cys'to·pex'y
cys'to·plas'ty
cys'to·pros'ta·tec'to·my
cys'to·py'e·li'tis
cys'to·py'e·log'ra·phy
cys'to·py'e·lo·ne·phri'tis
cys'to·ra'di·og'ra·phy
cys'to·rec'to·cele'
cys·tor'rha·phy
cys'to·sar·co'ma *pl.* -mas *or*
-ma·ta
—— phyl·lo'des'
—— phyl·loi'des'
cys'to·scope'
cys'to·scop'ic
cys·tos'co·py
cys'to·ste'a·to'ma *pl.* -mas
or -ma·ta
cys·tos'to·my
cys'to·tome'
cys·tot'o·my
cys'to·u·re'ter·o·cele'
cys'to·u're·thri'tis
cys'to·u·re'thro·cele'
cys'to·u·re'thro·gram'
cys'to·u·re'thro·graph'ic
cys'to·u're·throg'ra·phy
cys'to·u·re'thro·scope'
cys'tyl
cyt'ar·a·bine'
cy'tase'
cy·tas'ter
cyth'e·mol'y·sis *pl.* -ses'
cyt'i·dine'
cyt'i·dyl'ic
cy'to·al'bu'mi·no·log'ic
cy'to·ar'chi·tec'ton'ic
cy'to·ar'chi·tec'ture
cy'to·bi·ol'o·gy
cy'to·blast'
cy'to·blas·te'ma

cy'to·cen'trum
cy'to·chem'ism
cy'to·chem'is·try
cy'to·chrome'
cy'to·chy·le'ma
cy'to·ci'dal
cy'to·cide'
cy·toc'la·sis *pl.* -ses'
cy'to·clas'tic
cy'to·crine'
cy'to·crin'i·a
cy'tode'
cy'to·den'drite'
cy'to·derm'
cy'to·di'ag·no'sis *pl.* -ses'
cy'to·di·er'e·sis *pl.* -ses'
cy'to·dis'tal
cy'to·gene'
cy'to·gen'e·sis *pl.* -ses'
cy'to·ge·net'ic
cy'to·ge·net'ics
cy'to·gen'ic
cy·tog'e·nous
cy·tog'e·ny
cy'to·glob'u·lin
cy'toid'
cy'to·ki·ne'sis
cy'to·ki·net'ic
cy'to·lip'o·chrome'
cy'to·log'ic *or* cy'to·log'i·cal
cy·tol'o·gist
cy·tol'o·gy *(the branch of
biology dealing with the
cells)*
⁜sitology
cy·tol'y·sin
cy·tol'y·sis *pl.* -ses'
cy'to·ly'so·some'
cy'to·lyt'ic
cy·to'ma *pl.* -mas *or* -ma·ta
cy'to·me·gal'ic
cy'to·meg'a·lo·vi'rus
cy·tom'e·ter
cy'to·met'ric
cy·tom'e·try
cy'to·mi'tome'
cy'to·mor·phol'o·gy
cy'to·mor·pho'sis *pl.* -ses'
cy'to·my·co'sis *pl.* -ses'
cy'ton'
cy'to·path'ic
cy'to·path'o·gen'ic
cy'to·pa·thol'o·gy
cy·top'a·thy
cy'to·pe'ni·a
cy·toph'a·gous

cy·toph'a·gy
cy'to·phil'
cy'to·phys'i·ol'o·gy
cy'to·plasm
cy'to·plas'mic
cy'to·plas'tin
cy'to·poi·e'sis *pl.* -ses'
cy'to·prox'i·mal
cy'to·re·tic'u·lum
cy'tor·rhyc'tes'
cy'to·scop'ic
cy·tos'co·py
cy'to·sid'er·in
cy'to·sine'
—— ar'a·bin'o·side'
cy'to·skel'e·ton
cy'to·some'
cy'tost'
cy'to·stat'ic
cy'to·stome'
cy'to·tac'tic
cy'to·tax'is
cy·toth'e·sis *pl.* -ses'
cy'to·tox'ic
cy'to·tox·ic'i·ty
cy'to·tox'i·co'sis *pl.* -ses'
cy'to·tox'in
cy'to·troph'o·blast'
cy'to·trop'ic
cy·tot'ro·pism
cy'to·zo'on' *pl.* -zo'a
cy'to·zyme'

D

Da Cos'ta syndrome
dac'ry·ag'o·ga·tre'si·a
dac'ry·a·gog'ic
dac'ry·a·gogue'
dac'ry·o·ad'e·nal'gi·a
dac'ry·o·ad'e·nec'to·my
dac'ry·o·ad'e·ni'tis
dac'ry·o·ag'o·ga·tre'si·a
dac'ry·o·blen'nor·rhe'a
dac'ry·o·cele'
dac'ry·o·cyst'
dac'ry·o·cys·tec'to·my
dac'ry·o·cys·ti'tis
dac'ry·o·cys'to·blen'nor·
rhe'a
dac'ry·o·cys'to·cele'
dac'ry·o·cys'to·gram'
dac'ry·o·cys'top·to'sis
dac'ry·o·cys'to·rhi·nos'to·
my

dac'ry·o·cys·tos'to·my
dac'ry·o·cys·tot'o·my
dac'ry·o·lin
dac'ry·o·lith'
dac'ry·o·li·thi'a·sis *pl.* -ses'
dac'ry·o'ma *pl.* -mas *or*
  -ma·ta
dac'ry·on' *pl.* -ry·a
dac'ry·ops'
dac'ry·op·to'sis
dac'ry·or·rhe'a
dac'ry·o·so'le·ni'tis
dac'ry·o·ste·no'sis *pl.* -ses'
dac'ry·o·syr'inx *pl.* -sy·
  rin'ges' *or* -syr'inx·es
dac'ti·no·my'cin
dac'tyl
dac'ty·lar
dac'ty·late'
dac'tyl·e·de'ma *pl.* -mas *or*
  -ma·ta
dac'ty·lif'er·ous
dac'ty·li'tis
—— syph'i·lit'i·ca
dac'ty·lol'y·sis *pl.* -ses'
—— spon·ta'ne·a
dac'ty·lo·meg'a·ly
dac'tyl·o·spasm
dac'ty·lus *pl.* -li'
Da·gni'ni ex·ten'sion-ad·
  duc'tion reflex
Da'kin solution
Dall'dorf' test
dal'ton·ism
Dal'ton law
D-a·mi'no acid oxidase
Da·moi·seau' curve
Da'na operation
Da'na-Put'nam syndrome
Dan'bolt-Closs' syndrome
Dance sign
dan'der
dan'druff
Dan'dy-Walk'er syndrome
Dan'iell cell
Dan'iels·sen-Boeck' dis-
  ease
Dan'los syndrome
dan'thron'
D'An'to·ni stain
dan'tro·lene'
Dan'ysz phenomenon
Dan'zer and Hook'er
  method
dap'sone'
Dar'i·er
—— abscess

—— disease
Dark·sche'witsch nucleus
Dar'ling disease
Dar'row solution
dar'tos'
dar'trous
Dar'win tubercle
da'ta *sing.* -tum
Da·tu'ra
dau'no·my'cin
dau'no·ru'bi·cin
Da·vai'ne·a
—— for'mo·sa'na
—— mad'a·gas·car'i·en'sis
Dav'en·port' method
Da'vid·sohn
—— differential test
—— presumptive test
Da'vis graft
Daw'son encephalitis
Day operation
daz'zle reflex of Pei'per
de·ac'ti·vate', -vat'ed, -vat'-
  ing
de·ac'ti·va'tion
de·af'fer·en·ta'tion
deaf
deaf'-mute'
deaf'ness
de·al'co·hol'i·za'tion
de·am'i·dase'
de·am'i·di·za'tion
de·am'i·nase'
de·am'i·nate', -nat'ed, -nat'-
  ing
de·am'i·na'tion
de·an'es·the'si·ant
dea'nol' ac'et·am'i·do·
  ben'zo·ate'
de·a'qua'tion
De·bar'y·o·my'ces' ne'o·
  for'lmans'
de Beur'mann-Gou·ge·rot'
  disease
de·bil'i·tant
de·bil'i·tate', -tat'ed, -tat'ing
de·bil'i·ty
De·bove' disease
de·branch'er
De·bré'-de To'ni-Fan·co'ni
  syndrome
De·bré'-Sé·mé·laigne' syndrome
de·bride', -brid'ed, -brid'ing
de·bride·ment'
de·bri'so·quin
dec'a·dence

de·cal'ci·fi·ca'tion
de·cal'ci·fy', -fied', -fy'ing
dec'a·li'ter
de·cal'vant
dec'a·me'ter
dec'a·me·tho'ni·um
de·can·cel·la'tion
dec'ane'
de·can'nu·la'tion
dec'a·nor'mal
de·cap'i·tate', -tat'ed, -tat'-
  ing
de·cap'i·ta'tion
de·cap'su·la'tion
de·car'bon·i·za'tion
de·car'bon·ize', -ized', -iz'-
  ing
de'car·box'yl·ase'
de'car·box'yl·ate', -at'ed,
  -at'ing
de'car·box'yl·a'tion
de·ca·thec'tion
dec'a·vi'ta·min
de·cay'
de·cen'tered
de'cen·tra'tion
de·cer'e·bel·la'tion
de·cer'e·brate', -brat'ed,
  -brat'ing
de·cer'e·bra'tion
de·cer'e·brize', -brized',
  -briz'ing
de·chlo'ri·da'tion
de·chlo'ri·na'tion
de·chlor'u·ra'tion
dec'i·bel'
de·cid'u·a *pl.* -ae'
—— ba·sa'lis
—— cap'su·lar'is
—— mar'gi·na'lis
—— men'stru·a'lis
—— pa·ri'e·ta'lis
—— re·flex'a
—— se·rot'i·na
—— sub·cho'ri·a'lis
—— ve'ra
de·cid'u·al
de·cid'u·ate
de·cid'u·a'tion
de·cid'u·i'tis
de·cid'u·o'ma
—— ma·lig'num
de·cid'u·o'sis
dec'i·gram'
dec'i·li'ter
dec'i·me'ter
dec'i·nor'mal

dec′li·na′tion
de·clive′
de′co·ag′u·lant
de·coc′tion
de′col·la′tion
de·col′la′tor
de′com·pen·sa′tion
de′com·pose′, -posed′, -pos′-
  ing
de·com′po·si′tion
de′com·pres′sion
de′con·di′tion
de′con·di′tion·ing
de′con·ges′tant
de′con·ges′tive
de′con·tam′i·nate′, -nat′ed,
  -nat′ing
de′con·tam′i·na′tion
de·cor′ti·cate′, -cat′ed, -cat′-
  ing
de·cor′ti·ca′tion
dec′re·ment
dec′re·men′tal
de′cre·scen′do
de·cres′cent
de′cu·ba′tion
de·cu′bi·tal
de·cu′bi·tus *pl.* -ti′
de·cus′sate′
de·cus·sa′ti·o′ *pl.* -sa′ti·
  o′nes′
  —— bra′chi·i′ con′junc·ti′vi′
  —— lem′nis·co′rum
  —— ner·vo′rum troch′le·
  ar′i·um
  —— pe·dun′cu·lo′rum cer′e·
  bel·lar′i·um su·pe′ri·o′rum
  —— py·ram′i·dum
de′cus·sa′tion
  —— of Fo·rel′
  —— of the bra′chi·a
  con′junc·ti′va
  —— of the lem·nis′ci′
de·cus·sa′ti·o′nes′
  —— teg·men′ti′
  —— teg′men·to′rum
de·dif′fer·en′ti·a′tion
de-ep′i·car′di·a·li·za′tion
Dees operation
Deet′jen bodies
def′e·cate′, -cat′ed, -cat′ing
def′e·ca′tion
de·fem′i·ni·za′tion
de·fem′i·nize′, -nized′, -niz′-
  ing
def′er·ens
def′er·ent

def′er·en′tial
def′er·en′ti·o·ves′i·cal
def′er·en·ti′tis
de′fer·ox′a·mine′
de′fer·ves′cence
de′fer·ves′cent
de·fib′ril·late′, -lat′ed, -lat′-
  ing
de·fib′ril·la′tion
de·fib′ril·la′tor
de·fi′bri·nate′, -nat′ed, -nat′-
  ing
de·fi′bri·na′tion
de·fi′cien·cy
de·fi′cient
def′i·cit
def′lo·ra′tion
de′flo·res′cence
de·flu′vi·um
  —— cap′il·lo′rum
  —— un′gui·um
de·flux′i·o′
de·form′
de·for′mi·ty
de·func′tion·al·i·za′tion
de·fu′sion
de·gan′gli·on·ate′, -at′ed,
  -at′ing
de·gen′er·a·cy
de·gen′er·ate′, -at′ed, -at′ing
de·gen′er·a′tion
de·gen′er·a·tive
de·germ′
de·glu′ti·ble
de′glu·ti′tion
de·glu′ti·tive
de·glu′ti·to′ry
De·gos′-De·lort′-Tri·cot′
  syndrome
De·gos′ disease
deg′ra·da′tion
de·grade′, -grad′ed, -grad′ing
de′gus·ta′tion
Di·hi′o test
de·his′cence
de·hu′man·i·za′tion
de·hy′drate′, -drat′ed,
  -drat′ing
de′hy·dra′tion
de·hy′dro·cho′late′
de·hy′dro·cho·les′ter·ol′
de·hy′dro·cho′lic
de·hy′dro·cor′ti·cos′ter·
  one′
de·hy′dro·ep′i·an·dros′ter·
  one′
de·hy′dro·gen·ase′

de·hy′dro·gen·ate′, -at′ed,
  -at′ing
de·hy′dro·gen·a′tion
de·hy′dro·gen·ize′, -ized′,
  -iz′ing
de·hy′dro·i′so·an·dros′ter·
  one′
de·i′on·ize′, -ized′, -iz′ing
Dei′ters
  —— cells
  —— nucleus
dé·jà′
  —— pen·sé′
  —— vu′
de·jec′ta
de·jec′tion
De·jer·ine′
  —— anterior bulbar syn-
  dromes
  —— cortical sensory syndrome
De·jer·ine′-Klump′ke syn-
  drome
De·jer·ine′-Sot′tas disease
De·jer·ine′-Thom′as atro-
  phy
de′lac·ta′tion
Del′a·field′ hematoxylin
de·lam′i·na′tion
de Lange′ syndrome
Del′a·so′a sore
Del Cas·ti′llo syndrome
del·e·te′ri·ous
de·le′tion
Delfft test
Del′hi boil
De Li′ma operation
de·lim′i·ta′tion
de·lim′it·ed
del·ip′i·da′tion
del′i·quesce′, -quesced′,
  -quesc′ing
del′i·ques′cence
del′i·ques′cent
de·liq′ui·um
  —— an′i·mi′
de·lir′i·ant
de·lir′i·fa′cient
de·lir′i·ous
de·lir′i·um
  —— cor′dis
  —— gran′di·o′sum
  —— mi′te′
  —— mus′si·tans′
  —— tre′mens
del′le *pl.* del′len
de·lo·mor′phous

de·louse', -loused', -lous'ing
Del·phin'i·um
del Ri'o Hor·te'ga silver
   method
del'ta
del'toid'
del'to·pec'to·ral
de·lu'sion
de·lu'sion·al
de·lu'sive
de·mar'cate', -cat'ed, -cat'-
   ing
de'mar·ca'tion
De·ma'ti·um
dem'e·car'i·um
dem'e·clo·cy'cline'
dem'e·cy'cline'
de·ment'
de·ment'ed
de·men'ti·a
   —— ag'i·ta'ta
   —— par'a·lyt'i·ca
   —— par'a·noi'des'
   —— prae'cox'
   —— pre'cox'
de·meth'yl·ate', -at'ed, -at'-
   ing
de·meth'yl·a'tion
de·meth'yl·chlor·tet'ra·
   cy'cline'
dem'i·fac'et
dem'i·lune'
   —— of Gian·nuz'zi'
   —— of Hei'den·hain'
dem'i·mon·stros'i·ty
de·min'er·al·i·za'tion
de·min'er·al·ize', -ized', -iz'-
   ing
dem'i·pen'ni·form'
dem'o·dec'tic
Dem'o·dex'
   —— fol·lic'u·lo'rum
de·mog'ra·phy
de'mon·o·ma'ni·a
de'mon·o·ma'ni·ac'
de'mon·op'a·thy
de'mon·o·pho'bi·a
de'mo·pho'bi·a
De Mor'gan spot
de·mor'phin·i·za'tion
de·mul'cent
de Mus·sy' point
de·my'e·lin·ate', -at'ed, -at'-
   ing
de·my'e·lin·a'tion
de·my'e·lin·ize', -ized', iz'-
   ing

de·nar'co·tize', -tized', -ti-
   z'ing
de·na'tur·a'tion
de·na'ture, -tured, -tur·ing
de·na'tur·i·za'tion
den'drite'
den·drit'ic
den'droid'
den'dron' *pl.* -drons' *or* -dra
den'dro·phag'o·cy·to'sis
den'dro·phil'i·a
de·ner'vate', -vat'ed, -vat'-
   ing
de'ner·va'tion
den'gue
den'i·da'tion
den'i·gra'tion
Den'is method
Den'nie-Mar'fan' syn-
   drome
Den'on·vil'liers fascia
dens *pl.* den'tes'
   —— ep'i·stro'phe·i'
   —— in den'te'
   —— se·rot'i·nus
den·sim'e·ter
den'si·met'ric
den'si·tom'e·ter
den·sog'ra·phy
den'tal
den'ta·ry
den'tate'
den'ta·tec'to·my
den·ta'tion
den·ta'to·re·tic'u·lar
den·ta'to·ru'bral
den·ta'to·tha·lam'ic
den·ta'to-thal'a·mo-cor'ti·
   cal
den·ta'tum
den'te·la'tion
den'tes'
   —— a·cu'sti·ci'
   —— ca·ni'ni'
   —— de·cid'u·i'
   —— in'ci·si'vi'
   —— mo'lar·es'
   —— per'ma·nen'tes'
   —— prae'mo·lar·es'
   —— pre'mo·lar·es'
den'tia
   —— prae'cox'
   —— pre'cox'
   —— tar'da
den'ti·cle
den·tic'u·late'
den'ti·fi·ca'tion

den'ti·form'
den'ti·frice
den·tig'er·ous
den'tin
den'ti·nal
den'tine'
den·tin'i·fi·ca'tion
den'ti·no·blas·to'ma
   pl. -mas *or* -ma·ta
den'ti·no·ce·men'tal
den'ti·no·e·nam'el
den'ti·no·gen'e·sis *pl.* -ses'
   —— im'per·fec'ta
den'ti·no·gen'ic
den'ti·noid'
den'ti·no'ma *pl.* -mas *or*
   -ma·ta
den'ti·nos'te·oid'
den·ti'num
den·tip'a·rous
den'ti·phone'
den'tist
den'tis·try
den·ti'tion
den'to·al·ve'o·lar
den'to·fa'cial
den'toid'
den'tu·lous
den'ture
de·nu'cle·at'ed
de'nu·da'tion
de·nude', -nud'ed, -nud'ing
de·or'sum·duc'tion
de·or'sum·ver'gence
de·os'si·fi·ca'tion
de·ox'y·a·den'o·sine'
de·ox'y·cho'late'
de·ox'y·cho'lic
de·ox'y·cor'ti·cos'ter·one'
de·ox'y·cor'tone'
de·ox'y·cos'tone'
de·ox'y·cy'ti·dine'
de·ox'y·e·phed'rine'
de·ox'y·gen·a'tion
de·ox'y·gua'nine'
de·ox'y·pen'tose'
de·ox'y·pen'tose·nu·cle'ic
de·ox'y·pyr'i·dox'ine'
de·ox'y·ri'bo·nu'cle·ase'
de·ox'y·ri'bo·nu·cle'ic
de·ox'y·ri'bo·nu'cle·o·tide'
de·ox'y·ri'bose'
de·ox'y·sug'ar
de·ox'y·u'ri·dine'
de·par'af·fin·ize', -ized', -iz'-
   ing
de·per'son·al·i·za'tion

de·pig′ment
de·pig′men·ta′tion
dep′i·late′, -lat′ed, -lat′ing
de·pil′a·to′ry
dep′i·lous
de·plete′, -plet′ed, -plet′ing
de·ple′tion
de·po·lar·i·za′tion
de·po·lym′er·i·za′tion
de·po·lym′er·ize′, -ized′,
   -iz′ing
de·pos′it
de·press′
de·pres′sant
de·pres′sion
de·pres′sive
de·pres′sor
—— a′lae′ na′si′
—— an′gu·li·o′ris
—— ep′i·glot′ti·dis
—— la′bi·i′ in·fe′ri·o′ris
—— sep′ti′ na′si′
—— su′per·cil′i·i′
dep′ri·va′tion
dep′side′
de Quer′vain disease
der′a·del′phus
de·range′ment
Der′cum disease
de·re′al·i·za′tion
de·re′ism
de′re·is′tic
der′en·ceph′a·lus
der′en·ceph′a·ly
de′re·pres′sion
der′i·va′tion
de·riv′a·tive
der′ma·bra′sion
Der′ma·cen′tor
—— an′der·so′ni′
—— var′i·a′bi·lis
Der′ma·cen·trox′e·nus
—— ak′a·ri′
—— pe·dic′u·li′
—— rick·ett′si′
—— rickettsi con·o′ri′
der′ma·he′mi·a
der′mal
der′ma·my·i′a·sis pl. -ses′
—— lin′e·ar′is mi′grans′ oes·
tro′sa
Der′ma·nys′sus
—— a′vi·um
—— gal·li′nae′
der′ma·tag′ra
der′ma·tal′gi·a
der′ma·ta·neu′ri·a

der′mat·he′mi·a
der′ma·therm′
der·mat′ic
der′ma·ti′tis pl. -tis·es or
   -tit′i·des′
—— ac·tin′i·ca
—— au′to·fac·ti′ti·a
—— ca·lor′i·ca
—— coc·cid′i·oi′des′
—— con′ge·la′ti·o′nis
—— con·ti·nu·ée′
—— con·tu′si·for′mis
—— dys·men′or·rhe′i·ca
—— es′cha·rot′i·ca
—— ex·fo′li·a·ti′va ne′o·na·
to′rum
—— ex·sic′cans′ pal·mar′is
—— fac·ti′ti·a
—— gan′gre·no′sa
—— gangrenosa in·fan′tum
—— her·pet′i·for′mis
—— hi′e·ma′lis
—— hy′po·stat′i·ca
—— med′i·ca·men·to′sa
—— nod′u·lar′is ne·crot′i·ca
—— pap′il·lar′is cap′il·li′ti·i′
—— pap′u·lo·squa·mo′sa
a·troph′i·cans′
—— re′pens
—— rhus
—— seb′or·rhe′i·ca
—— trau·mat′i·ca
—— veg′e·tans′
—— ven′e·na′ta
—— ver′ru·co′sa
Der′ma·to′bi·a
—— hom′i·nis
der′ma·to·bi′a·sis pl. -ses′
der′ma·to·cele′
der′ma·to·cel′lu·li′tis
der′ma·to·cha·la′sis
der′ma·to·co′ni·o′sis pl.
   -ses′
der′ma·to·cyst′
der′ma·to·dyn′i·a
der′ma·to′dys·pla′si·a
der′ma·to·fi·bro′ma
   pl. -mas or -ma·ta
der′ma·to·fi′bro·sar·co′ma
   pl. -mas or -ma·ta
—— pro·tu′ber·ans′
der′ma·to·graph′i·a
der′ma·tog′ra·phism
der′ma·tog′ra·phy
der′ma·to·het′er·o·plas′ty
der′ma·tol′

der′ma·to·log′ic or der′ma·
   to·log′i·cal
der′ma·tol′o·gist
der′ma·tol′o·gy
der′ma·tol′y·sis
der′ma·tome′
der′ma·to·meg′a·ly
der′ma·tom′ic
der′ma·to·my′ces′
der′ma·to·my′cete′
der′ma·to·my·co′sis pl.
   -ses′
der′ma·to·my·o′ma pl. -mas
   or -ma·ta
der′ma·to·my′o·si′tis
der′ma·to·neu·rol′o·gy
der′ma·to·neu·ro′sis pl.
   -ses′
der′ma·to·path′i·a
der′ma·to·path′ic
der′ma·to·pa·thol′o·gy
der′ma·to·path′o·pho′bi·a
der′ma·top′a·thy
der′ma·to·phi·li′a·sis pl.
   -ses′
der′ma·to·phi·lo′sis pl. -ses′
Der′ma·toph′i·lus pen′e·
   trans′
der′ma·to·phyte′
der′ma·to·phy′tid
der′ma·to·phy·to′sis pl.
   -ses′
der′ma·to·plas′tic
der′ma·to·plas′ty
der′ma·to·pol′y·neu·ri′tis
der′ma·tor·rha′gi·a
der′ma·tor·rhex′is
der′ma·to·scle·ro′sis pl.
   -ses′
der′ma·tos′co·py
der′ma·to·si·o·pho′bi·a
der′ma·to′sis pl. -ses′
—— pap′u·lo·sa ni′gra
der′ma·to·ther′a·py
der′ma·to·thla′si·a
der′ma·tot′o·my
der′ma·to·zo′on′ pl. -zo′a
der′ma·to·zo′o·no′sis pl.
   -ses′
der′ma·tro′phi·a
der′mic
der′mis
der′mo·blast′
der′mo·ep′i·der′mal
der′mo·graph′i·a
—— al′ba
—— ru′bra

der'mo·graph'ic
der·mog'ra·phism
der·mog'ra·phy
der'mo·he'mi·a
der'moid'
der'moi·dec'to·my
der'mo·la'bi·al
der'mo·li·po'ma
der·mom'e·ter
der·mom'e·try
der'mo·my·co'sis *pl.* -ses'
der·mop'a·thy
der'mo·phle·bi'tis
der'mo·skel'e·ton
der'mo·ste·no'sis *pl.* -ses'
der'mo·syn'o·vi'tis
der'mo·vas'cu·lar
des·am'i·dase'
de·sat'u·ra'tion
des'ce·me·ti'tis
Des'ce·met' membrane
des'ce·met'o·cele'
de·scen'dens
—— cer'vi·cis
—— hy'po·glos'si'
de·scen'sus *pl.* de·scen'sus
—— tes'tis
—— u'ter·i'
—— ven·tric'u·li'
des·cin'o·clone' a·cet'o·nide'
de·sen'si·ti·za'tion
de·sen'si·tize', -tized', -ti·z'ing
de·ser'pi·dine'
de·sex'u·al·i·za'tion
des'ic·cant
des'ic·cate', -cat'ed, -cat'ing
des'ic·ca'tion
des'ic·ca'tive
des'ic·ca'tor
de·sip'ra·mine'
Des'i·vac'
des·lan'o·side'
des·mal'gi·a
des·mi'tis
des'mo·cra'ni·um
des'mo·cyte'
des'moid'
des'mo·lase'
des'mo·pla'si·a
des'mo·plas'tic
des'mo·sis *pl.* -ses'
des'mo·some'
des·mos'ter·ol'
des·mot'o·my
Des'nos' pneumonia

des'o·mor'phine'
des'o·nide'
de·sorp'tion
des·ox'i·meth'a·sone'
des·ox'y·cor'ti·cos'ter·one'
des·ox'y·e·phed'rine
des·ox'y·pyr'i·dox'ine'
des·ox'y·ri'bose'
d'Es·pine' sign
des'qua·mate', -mat'ed, -mat'ing
des'qua·ma'ti·o'
—— in'sen·sib'i·lis
—— ne'o·na·to'rum
des'qua·ma'tion
des·quam'a·tive
de·stru'do
de·ter'mi·nant
de·ter'mi·na'tion
de To'ni-Fan·co'ni-De·bré' syndrome
de·tor'sion
de·tox'i·cant
de·tox'i·cate', -cat'ed, -cat'ing
de·tox'i·ca'tion
de·tox'i·fi·ca'tion
de·tox'i·fy', -fied', -fy'ing
Det're reaction
de·tri'tion
de·tri'tus *pl.* de·tri'tus
de·trun·ca'tion
de·tru'sion
de·tru'sor
—— u·ri'nae'
—— ve·si'cae'
de·tu·mes'cence
deu'ter·a·nom'a·ly
deu'ter·a·nope'
deu'ter·a·no'pi·a
deu'ter·a·nop'ic
deu'ter·a·nop'si·a
deu'ter·o·path'ic
deu'ter·op'a·thy
deu'ter·o·plasm
deu'ter·os'to·ma *pl.* -mas *or* -ma·ta
deu'ton'
Deutsch'län'der disease
de·vas'cu·lar·i·za'tion
de·vel'op·ment
de·vel'op·men'tal
de'vi·ant
de'vi·ate', -at'ed, -at'ing
de'vi·a'tion
Dev'ic disease
de'vi·om'e·ter

de·vi'tal·ize', -ized', -iz'ing
de·vi'tal·i·za'tion
dev'o·lu'tion
dex'a·meth'a·sone'
dex·brom'phen·ir'a·mine'
dex·chlor'phen·ir'a·mine'
dex·iv'a·caine'
dex·ox'a·drol'
dex·pan'the·nol'
dex'pro·pan'o·lol'
dex'ter
dex'trad'
dex'tral
dex·tral'i·ty
dex'tran'
dex·tran'o·mer
dex·trau'ral
dex'tri·fer'ron'
dex'trin
dex'tri·no'sis *pl.* -ses'
dex'tri·nu'ri·a
dex'tro·am·phet'a·mine'
dex'tro·car'di·a
dex'tro·car'di·o·gram'
dex'tro·cer'e·bral
dex'tro·con'dy·lism
dex·troc'u·lar
dex·troc'u·lar'i·ty
dex'tro·duc'tion
dex'tro·gram'
dex'tro·gy'rate'
dex'tro·man'u·al
dex'tro·meth·or'phan
dex'tro·mor·am'ide'
dex'tro·pe'dal
dex'tro·po·si'tion
dex'tro·ro'ta·to'ry
dex'tro·sco'li·o'sis *pl.* -ses'
dex'trose'
dex'tro·sin'is·tral
dex'tro·su'ri·a
dex'tro·thy·rox'ine'
dex'tro·tor'sion
dex'trous
dex'tro·ver'sion
D-fruc'tose'
D-ga·lac'to·meth'yl·ose'
D-glu'cose'
dho'bie
di'a·be'tes'
—— de·cip'i·ens
—— in·sip'i·dus
—— mel·li'tus
di'a·bet'ic
di'a·be·to·gen'ic
di'a·be·tog'e·nous
di'ac·e·te'mi·a

di·a·ce′tic
di·ac′e·tin
di·ac′e·tu′ri·a
di·ac′e·tyl·mor′phine′
di′a·cho·re′sis pl. -ses′
di′a·cla′si·a
di·ac′la·sis pl. -ses′
di′a·clast′
di′a·clas′tic
di·ac′ri·sis pl. -ses′
di′a·crit′ic or di′a·crit′i·cal
di′ac·tin′ic
di′a·derm′
di·ad′o·cho′ki·ne′si·a
di·ad′o·cho′ki·ne′sis
di′ag·nose′, -nosed′, -nos′ing
di′ag·no′sis pl. -ses′
di′ag·nos′tic
di′ag·nos·ti′cian
di′a·ki·ne′sis pl. -ses′
Di·ak′i·o·gi·an′nis sign
di′al·kyl′a·mine′
di·al′lyl·bar′bi·tu′ric
di·al′y·sance
di·al′y·sate′
di·al′y·sis pl. -ses′
di′a·lyze′, -lyzed′, -lyz′ing
di′a·lyz′er
di·am′e·ter
—— o·bli′qua pel′vis
—— trans·ver′sa pel′vis
di′a·met′ric or di′a·met′ri·cal
di′a·mine′
di′a·mi′no·di·phen′yl·sul′fone′
di′a·mi′no·pu′rine′
di′a·mi·nu′ri·a
Di′a·mond method
di′a·mor′phine′
di·am′tha·zole′
di·ap′a·mide′
di′a·pa′son
di′a·pe·de′sis pl. -ses′
di′a·pe·det′ic
di′a·phane′
di·aph′a·no·scope′
di·aph′a·nos′co·py
di·aph′e·met′ric
di·aph′o·rase′
di′a·pho·re′sis pl. -ses′
di′a·pho·ret′ic
di′a·phragm′
di′a·phrag′ma pl. -ma·ta
—— pel′vis
—— sel′lae′
—— u′ro·gen′i·ta′le′
di′a·phrag·mat′ic

di′a·phrag′ma·ti′tis
di′a·phrag′mat′o·cele′
di′a·phrag·mi′tis
di·aph′y·se′al
di·aph′y·sec′to·my
di·aph′y·sis pl. -ses′
di·ap′la·sis pl. -ses′
di′a·poph′y·sis pl. -ses′
di′ar·rhe′a
di′ar·rhe′al
di′ar·rhe′ic
di′ar·rhe′mi·a
di·ar′thric
di′ar·thro′di·al
di′ar·thro′sis pl. -ses′
di·ar·tic′u·lar
di·as′chi·sis pl. -ses′
di′a·schis′tic
di′a·scope′
di·as′co·py
di′a·stase′
di·as′ta·sis pl. -ses′
—— rec′ti′ ab·dom′i·nis
di′a·stat′ic
di′a·ste′ma pl. -ma·ta
di′a·ste′ma·to·my·e·li·a
di·as′ter
di·as′to·le
di·a′stol′ic
di′a·tax′i·a
di′a·ther′mal
di′a·ther′mic
di′a·ther′mo·co·ag′u·la′tion
di′a·ther′my
di·ath′e·sis pl. -ses′
di·a′thet′ic
di·az′e·pam′
di·a·zine′
di·az′o
di·az′o·re·sor′ci·nol′
di·az′ox·ide′
di·ben′ze·pin
di·bu′caine′
di·bu′to·line′
di·cal′ci·um
di·car′box·yl′ic
di·cen′tric
di′ce·pha′li·a
di·ceph′a·lism
di·ceph′a·lous *(having two heads)*
♦*dicephalus*
di·ceph′a·lus *(an individual with two heads),* pl. -li′
♦*dicephalous*
—— di·auch′e·nos′

—— mon·auch′e·nos′
—— mon′o·so′mus
—— par′a·sit′i·cus
—— tet′ra·bra′chi·us
—— tri·bra′chi·us
di·ceph′a·ly
di·chei′lus
di·chei′rus
di·chlor′a·mine′
di·chlo′ro·a·ce′tic
di·chlo′ro·i′so·pro·ter′e·nol′
di·chlo′ro·phen·ar′sine′
di·chlo′ro·phe′nol·in′do·phe′nol′
di·chlo′ro·phen·ox′y·a·ce′tic
di′chlor·phen′a·mide′
di·cho′ri·al
di·cho·ri·on′ic
di·chot′o·mize′, -mized′, -miz′ing
di·chot′o·my
di·chro′ic
di·chro′ine′
di′chro′ism
di·chro′ma·sy
di′chro·mat′
di·chro′mate′
di·chro·mat′ic
di·chro′ma·tism
di·chro′ma·top′si·a
di·chro′mic
di′chro′mism
di·chro′mo·phil′
di′chro·moph′i·lism
Dick
—— test
—— toxin
di·clox′a·cil′lin
di·co′ri·a
di·cou′ma·rin
di·cou′ma·rol′
Di′cro·coe′li·um
—— den·drit′i·cum
di·crot′ic
di′cro·tism
di′cro·tous
dic′ty·o·ki·ne′sis
dic′ty·o·some′
dic′ty·o·tene′
di·cy′clo·mine′
di·dac′ty·lism
di·del′phi·a
di·del′phic
Di′dot operation
did′y·mi′tis

did'y·mous
Di·e'go blood group
di·el'drin
di·em'bry·o·ny
di'en·ce·phal'ic
di'en·ceph'a·lon'
di'en·es'trol'
Di·ent'a·moe'ba
—— frag'i·lis
di·es'ter·ase'
di·es'trum
di·es'trus
di'et
di·e·tar'y
di·e·tet'ic
di·e·tet'ics
Die'thelm method
di·eth'yl
di·eth'yl·bar·bi'tu·rate'
di·eth'yl·bar'bi·tu'ric
di·eth'yl·car·bam'a·zine'
di·eth'yl·ene'
di·eth'yl·stil·bes'trol'
—— di·pro'pi·o·nate'
di·e·ti'cian var. of dietitian
di·e·ti'tian also dietician
Die'tl crisis
di'e·to·ther'a·py
Dieu·la·foy' disease
dif'fer·en'tial
dif'fer·en'ti·ate', -at'ed, -at'-
  ing
dif'fer·en'ti·a'tion
dif'flu·ence
dif·frac'tion
dif·fu'sate'
dif·fuse'
dif·fus'i·bil'i·ty
dif·fus'i·ble
dif·fu'si·om'e·ter
dif·fu'sion
di·flor'a·sone'
di·flu'a·nine'
di·flu'cor'to·lone'
di·flu'mi·done'
di·gas'tric
di·gen'ic
Di George' syndrome
di·gest'
di·ges'tant
di·gest'i·bil'i·ty
di·gest'i·ble
di·ges'tion
di·ges'tive
Digh'ton syndrome
dig'it
dig'i·tal

dig'i·tal'gi·a
—— par'es·thet'i·ca
dig'i·tal'in
dig'i·tal'is
dig'i·tal'i·za'tion
dig'i·tal'ose'
dig'i·tate'
dig'i·ta'tion
dig'i·ti'
—— ma'nus
—— pe'dis
dig'i·ti·form'
dig'i·to'nin
dig'i·to·plan'tar
dig'i·tox'in
dig'i·tox'ose'
dig'i·tox'o·side'
dig'i·tus pl. -ti'
—— I
—— II
—— III
—— IV
—— V
—— an'u·lar'is
—— me'di·us
—— min'i·mus
—— pri'mus
—— quar'tus
—— quin'tus
—— se·cun'dus
—— ter'ti·us
di·glyc'er·ide'
di·gox'in
di Gu·gliel'mo syndrome
di·hex'y·ver'ine'
di·hy'brid
di·hy'drate'
di·hy'dric
di·hy'dro·cho·les'ter·ol'
di·hy'dro·co·en'zyme'
di·hy'dro·er·got'a·mine'
di·hy'dro·mor'phi·none'
di·hy'dro·quin'ine'
di·hy'dro·ta·chys'ter·ol'
di·hy'dro·the'e·lin
di·hy·drox'y·a·ce'tic
di'hy·drox'y·ac'e·tone'
di'hy·drox'y·an'thra·nol'
di'hy·drox'y·ben'zene'
di'hy·drox'y·es'trin
di'hy·drox'y·phen'yl·al'a·
  nine'
di'i·o'do·hy·drox'y·quin
di'i·o'do·hy·drox'y·quin'o·
  line'
di·i'so·pro'pyl
—— flu'o·ro·phos'phate'

—— phos'pho·ro·fluor'i·
date'
dik'ty·o'ma pl. -mas or
  -ma·ta
di·lac'er·a'tion
di·lat'a·ble
di·la'tan·cy
dil'a·ta'tion
di·late', -lat'ed, -lat'ing
di·la'tion
di·la'tor
—— i'ri·dis
—— nar'is
—— pu·pil'lae'
—— tu'bae'
Dil'ling rule
dil'u·ent
di·lute', -lut'ed, -lut'ing
di·lu'tion
di·mef'a·dane'
di·me·fline'
di·men·hy'dri·nate'
di'mer
di·mer·cap'rol'
dim'er·ous
di·meth·in'dene'
di·meth·i'so·quin
di·meth·is'ter·one'
di·meth·ox'a·nate'
di·meth'yl
di·meth'yl·ni'tros·a·mine'
di·me'tri·a
Di·mi'tri disease
dim'pling
di·neu'ric
din'ic or din'i·cal
di·nu'cle·o·tide'
di·op'ter
di·op'tral
di·op·tom'e·ter
di·op·tom'e·try
di·op'tric
di·op'trics
di'ose'
di·ox'ide'
di·ox'y·line'
di·pep'ti·dase'
di·pep'tide'
di·per'o·don'
Di·pet'a·lo·ne'ma per'-
  stans'
di·pet'a·lo·ne·mi'a·sis pl.
  -ses'
di·phal'lic
di·phal'lus
di·pha'sic
di·phem'a·nil

di·phen'a·di'one'
di·phen'an'
di·phen·hy'dra·mine'
di·phen·ox'yl·ate'
di·phen·yl·hy·dan'to·in
di·pho'ni·a
diph·the'ri·a
diph·the'ri·al
diph·ther'ic
diph'the·rit'ic
diph'the·roid'
diph'the·ro·tox'in
diph·thon'gi·a
di·phyl'lo·both·ri'a·sis pl.
  -ses'
Di·phyl'lo·both'ri·um
—— er'i·na'ce'i'
—— la'tum
di·phy'o·dont'
dip·la·cu'sis pl. -ses'
—— bin'au·ra'lis
—— u'ni·au·ra'lis
di'plas·mat'ic
di·ple'gi·a
—— fa·ci·a'lis
di·ple'gic
dip'lo·al·bu'mi·nu'ri·a
dip'lo·ba·cil'lus pl. -li'
dip'lo·blas'tic
dip'lo·car'di·ac'
dip'lo·ce·pha'li·a
dip'lo·ceph'a·lus pl. -li'
dip'lo·ceph'a·ly
dip'lo·coc'coid'
dip'lo·coc'cus pl. -ci'
Dip'lo·coc'cus
—— gon'or·rhoe'ae'
—— in'tra·cel'lu·lar'is
men'in·git'i·dis
—— pneu·mo'ni·ae'
dip'lo·co'ri·a
dip'lo·ĕ'
dip'lo·et'ic
Dip'lo·go·nop'o·rus
—— gran'dis
di·plo'ic
dip'loid'
dip'lo·kar'y·on'
dip'lo·mate'
dip'lo·mel'li·tu'ri·a
dip'lo·my·e'li·a
dip'lo·ne'ma pl. -ma·ta or
  -mas
di·plop'a·gus pl. -gi'
di·plo'pi·a
di·plo'pi·om'e·ter
dip'lo·scope'

di·plo'sis pl. -ses'
dip'lo·so·ma'ti·a
dip'lo·tene'
di·po'lar
di'pole'
dip'ping
di·pro'so·pus
—— dir·rhi'nus
—— par'a·sit'i·cus
—— tet'roph·thal'mus
—— tetrophthalmus te·
tro'tus
di'pro·tri·zo'ate'
dip·se'sis
dip·set'ic
dip'si·a
dip'so·ma'ni·a
dip'so·ma'ni·ac'
dip'so·pho'bi·a
dip'so·ther'a·py
dip'stick'
dip'ter·ous
di'pus
di·py'gus
—— par'a·sit'i·cus
—— tet'ra·pus
—— tri'pus
dip'y·li·di'a·sis pl. -ses'
Di·py·lid'i·um
—— ca·ni'num
di'ro·fil'a·ri'a·sis pl. -ses'
di·sac'cha·ri·dase'
di·sac'cha·ride'
dis·ag'gre·ga'tion
dis·ar·tic'u·la'tion
dis·as·sim'i·la'tion
dis·as·so'ci·a'tion
disc var. of disk
dis·ci'form'
dis·ci' in'ter·ver'te·bra'les'
dis·cis'sion
dis·ci'tis
dis·co·blas'tu·la pl. -las or
  -lae'
dis·co·gas'tru·la pl. -las or
  -lae'
dis·cog'ra·phy
dis'coid'
dis·coi'dal
dis·col'or·a'tion
dis·cop'a·thy
dis·coph'o·rous
dis·co·pla·cen'ta
dis·cor'dance
dis·co'ri·a var. of dyscoria
dis·crete'

dis·crim'i·nate', -nat'ed,
  -nat'ing
dis·crim'i·na'tion
dis'cus pl. -ci'
—— ar·tic'u·lar'is
—— articularis ar·tic'u·la'ti·
o'nis a·cro'mi·o·cla·vic'u·
lar'is
—— articularis articula-
tionis man·dib'u·lar'is
—— articularis articula-
tionis ra'di·o·ul·nar'is dis·
ta'lis
—— articularis articula-
tionis ster'no·cla·vic'u·lar'is
—— articularis articula-
tionis tem'po·ro·man·dib'u·
lar'is
—— in'ter·pu'bi·cus
—— ner'vi' op'ti·ci'
—— pro·lig'er·us
dis·cu'tient
dis·ease'
dis·e'qui·lib'ri·um
dis'gre·gate', -gat'ed, -gat'-
  ing
dis'gre·ga'tion
dis·im·mune'
dis·im·mu'ni·ty
dis·in·fect'
dis·in·fec'tant
dis·in·fec'tion
dis·in·fes'ta·tion
dis·in·ser'tion
dis·in'te·grate', -grat'ed,
  -grat'ing
dis·in'te·gra'tion
dis·in'te·gra'tor
dis·in·vag'i·na'tion
dis·joint'
dis·junc'tion
dis·junc'tive
disk also disc
disk·ec'to·my
disk'i·form'
dis'ko·gram'
dis·lo·ca'tion
dis·mem'ber
dis·mem'ber·ment
dis·mu·ta'tion
dis'oc·clude', -clud'ed,
  -clud'ing
di·so'di·um
—— cro'mo·gly'cate'
—— e·dath'a·mil
—— ed'e·tate'
di·so'ma

di·so'mus pl. -mi' or -mus·es
di'so·pyr'a·mide'
dis·or'der
dis·or'ga·ni·za'tion
dis·o'ri·en·ta'tion
dis'par·ate
dis·par'i·ty
dis·pen'sa·ry
dis·pense', -pensed', -pens'-
  ing
di·sper'mine'
di'sper'my
dis·perse', -persed', -pers'ing
dis·per'sion
dis·per'sive
dis·per'soid'
dis·place'ment
dis'po·si'tion
dis'pro·por'tion
dis·rup'tive
dis·sect'
dis·sec'tion
dis·sec'tor
dis·sem'i·nate', -nat'ed,
  -nat'ing
dis·sem'i·na'tion
dis·sim'i·late', -lat'ed, -lat'-
  ing
dis·sim'u·la'tion
dis·so'ci·ant
dis·so'ci·ate', -at'ed, -at'ing
dis·so'ci·a'tion
dis·so'ci·a'tive
dis'so·lu'tion
dis·solve', -solved', -solv'ing
dis·sol'vent
dis'tad'
dis'tal
dis'tal·ly
dis·ten'si·bil'i·ty
dis·ten'si·ble
dis·ten'tion
dis'ti·chi·a'sis pl. -ses'
dis·till'
dis'til·land
dis'til·late'
dis'til·la'tion
dis'to·buc'cal
dis'to·buc·co·oc·clu'sal
dis'to·cer'vi·cal
dis'to·clu'sion
dis'to·gin'gi·val
dis'to·in·ci'sal
dis'to·la'bi·al
dis'to·lin'gual
dis'to·lin'guo·oc·clu'sal
Dis·to'ma

—— hae'ma·to'bi·um
—— he·pat'i·cum
di·sto'mi·a
dis'to·mi·a'sis pl. -ses'
dis'to·mo'lar
di·sto'mus
dis'to·oc·clu'sal
dis·tor'tion
dis'to·ver'sion
dis'tri·chi·a'sis pl. -ses'
dis'trix
di·sul'fate'
di·sul'fide'
di'thi·az'a·nine'
di·thy'mol' di·i'o·dide'
dit'o·kous
Ditt'rich stenosis
di'u·rese'
di'u·re'sis pl. -ses'
di'u·ret'ic
di·u'ri·a
di·ur'nal
di·ur'nule'
di'va·ga'tion
di·va'lent
di·var'i·ca'tion
di·ver'gence
di·ver'gent
di'ver·tic'u·la am·pul·lae'
  duc'tus def'er·en'tis
di·ver·tic'u·lar
di·ver·tic'u·lec'to·my
di'ver·tic'u·li'tis
di'ver·tic'u·lo'sis
di'ver·tic'u·lum pl. -la
—— il'e·i'
Div'ry-van Bo'gaert dis-
  ease
di·vulse', -vulsed', -vuls'ing
di·vul'sion
di·vul'sor
di'zy·got'ic
Do·bell' solution
do·bu'ta·mine'
Do'chez serum
doc'tor
Dö'der·lein' bacillus
Doeh'le bodies
Doer'fler-Stew'art test
Do'giel
—— cells
—— corpuscle
doigts en lor·gnette'
dol'i·cho·ce·phal'ic
dol'i·cho·ceph'a·lus pl. -li'
dol'i·cho·ceph'a·ly
dol'i·cho·cne'mic

dol'i·cho·co'lon
dol'i·cho·cra'ni·al
dol'i·cho·de'rus
dol'i·cho·fa'cial
dol'i·cho·hi·er'ic
dol'i·cho·ker'kic
dol'i·cho·kne'mic
dol'i·cho·mor'phic
dol'i·cho·pel'lic
dol'i·cho·pel'vic
dol'i·chor·rhine'
Dol'i·chos'
dol'i·cho·sten·o·me·li·a
dol'i·cho·u·ran'ic
Do'lin method
Dol'man test
do'lor
—— cap'i·tis
—— cox'ae
—— va'gus
do·lo·res'
—— prae·sa'gi·en'tes'
do·lo·rif'ic
do·lo·rim'e·ter
do·lo·ro·gen'ic
dom'i·nance
dom'i·nant
do'mi·phen'
dom·per'i·done'
Don'a·hue' syndrome
Do'nath-Land'stei'ner test
Don'der law
do·nee'
Don'nan equilibrium
Don·né' corpuscles
do'nor
Don'o·van
—— bodies
—— solution
Don·o·va'ni·a gran·u·
  lo'ma·tis
don·o·va·ni·a·sis pl. -ses'
do'pa
do'pa·mine'
do'pa·mi·ner'gic
do'pa-ox'i·dase'
do'pase'
Dopp'ler
—— effect
—— phenomenon
—— principle
Do·rel'lo canal
dor'mant
Dor'ner spore stain
Dor'rance operation
dor'sad'
dor'sal

dor·sal'gi·a
dor·sa'lis
—— pe'dis
Dor'set egg medium
dor'si·flex'ion
dor'si·flex'or
dor'si·spi'nal
dor'so·an·te'ri·or
dor'so·ceph'a·lad'
dor'so·cu·boi'dal
dor'so·in'ter·cos'tal
dor'so·lat'er·al
dor'so·lum'bar
dor'so·me'di·al
dor'so·me'di·an
dor'so·me'si·al
dor'so·na'sal
dor'so·nu'chal
dor'so·pos·te'ri·or
dor'so·ra'di·al
dor'so·sa'cral
dor'so·scap'u·lar
dor'so·ul'nar
dor'so·ven'trad'
dor'so·ven'tral
dor'so·ver'te·bral
dor'sum pl. -sa
—— lin'guae'
—— ma'nus
—— na'si'
—— pe'dis
—— pe'nis
—— sel'lae'
dos'age
dose
do·sim'e·ter
do'si·met'ric
do·sim'e·try
do'sis pl. -ses'
—— cu'ra·ti'va
—— ef'fi·cax'
—— re·frac'ta
—— tol'er·a'ta
dou'ble-blind' test
douche
Doug'las
—— bag
—— septum
Do'ver powder
dow'el
Dow'ney cells
Down syndrome
dox'a·pram'
dox'e·pin
dox'o·ru'bi·cin
dox'y·cy'cline'
dox·yl'a·mine'

Doyne choroiditis
drachm var. of dram
dra·cun'cu·li'a·sis
Dra·cun'cu·lus
—— med'i·nen'sis
draft also draught
dra·gée'
Drag'stedt
—— graft
—— operation
drain
drain'age
dram also drachm
dram'a·tism
drape, draped, drap'ing
draught var. of draft
drep'a·no·cyte'
drep'a·no·cy·the'mi·a
drep'a·no·cyt'ic
drep'a·no·cy·to'sis pl. -ses'
Dres'bach' syndrome
Dress'ler
—— beat
—— syndrome
Driesch law
Drink'er
—— method
—— respirator
Drink'er-Col'lins resuscitation
driv'el·ing
drom'o·graph'
dro·mo·trop'ic
drop'per
drop'si·cal
drop'sy
drug'-re·sis'tant
drunk·om'e·ter
dru'sen
Dry·op'ter·is
—— fil'ix-mas'
—— mar·gi·na'lis
D'-state'
du'al·ism
du'al·is'tic
Du·ane' retraction syndrome
Du·bi'ni chorea
Du'bin-John'son syndrome
Du'bin-Sprinz' syndrome
Du·bois' cyst
Du·boi'si·a
Du·bos'-Bra·chet' method
Du·boscq' colorimeter
Du'bo·witz' syndrome
Du·chenne'

—— attitude
—— disease
—— muscular dystrophy
—— paralysis
Du·chenne'-A·ran' disease
Du·chenne'-Erb' palsy
Du·chenne'-Grie'sin·ger disease
Du·crey' bacillus
duct
—— of A·ran'ti·us
—— of Bel·li'ni
—— of Cu·vier'
—— of San'to·ri'ni
—— of Ste'no
—— of Sten'sen
—— of Wir'sung
duc'tal (pertaining to a tube or channel)
♦ductile
duc'tile (capable of being reshaped without breaking)
♦ductal
duc'tion
duct'less
duc'tu·lar
duc'tule'
duc'tu·li'
—— ab'er·ran'tes'
—— al've·o·lar'es'
—— bi·lif'er·i'
—— ef'fe·ren'tes' tes'tis
—— ex'cre·to'ri·i' glan'du·lae' lac'ri·ma'lis
—— in'ter·lob'u·lar'es'
—— pro·stat'i·ci'
—— trans·ver'si' ep'o·oph'o·ri'
duc'tu·lus pl. -li'
—— a·ber'rans' superior
duc'tus pl. duc'tus
—— ar·te'ri·o'sus
—— arteriosus bi·lat'er·a'lis
—— bi·lif'er·i'
—— ca·rot'i·cus
—— cho·led'o·chus
—— coch'le·ar'is
—— cys'ti·cus
—— def'er·ens
—— e·jac'u·la·to'ri·us
—— en'do·lym·phat'i·cus
—— ep'i·di·dym'i·dis
—— ep'o·oph'o·ri' lon'gi·tu'di·na'lis
—— ex'cre·to'ri·us glan'du·lae' bul'bo·u're·thra'lis

—— excretorius ve·sic'u·lae' sem'i·na'lis
—— glan'du·lae' bul'bo·u're·thra'lis
—— he·pat'i·cus com·mu'nis
—— hepaticus dex'ter
—— hepaticus si·nis'ter
—— in·ci·si'vus
—— in'ter·lob'u·lar'es'
—— lac'ri·ma'les'
—— lac·tif'er·i'
—— lin·gua'lis
—— lo'bi' cau·da'ti' dex'ter
—— lobi caudati si·nis'ter
—— lym·phat'i·cus dex'ter
—— mes'o·neph'ri·cus
—— Muel'ler·i'
—— na'so·lac'ri·ma'lis
—— pan'cre·at'i·cus
—— pancreaticus ac'ces·so'ri·us
—— par'a·mes'o·neph'ri·cus
—— par'a·u're·thra'les'
—— par'o·ti·de'us
—— per'i·lym·phat'i·ci'
—— per'i·lym·phat'i·cus
—— pro·stat'i·ci'
—— re·u'ni·ens
—— sem'i·cir'cu·lar'es
—— sem'i·cir'cu·lar'is ante-rior
—— semicircularis lat'er·a'lis
—— semicircularis posterior
—— semicircularis superior
—— sub'lin·gua'les' mi·no'res'
—— sub'lin·gua'lis major
—— sub'man·dib'u·lar'is
—— sub·max'il·lar'is
—— su'do·rif'er·us
—— tho·rac'i·cus
—— thoracicus dex'ter
—— thy're·o·glos'sus
—— thy'ro·glos'sus
—— u·tric'u·lo·sac'cu·lar'is
—— ve·no'sus
—— Wolf'fi'
Duf'fy blood group
Du'gas test
Dug'be fever
Duhr'ing disease
Dukes
—— disease
—— test
dul'ca·ma'ra
dul'cin

Du·long' and Pe·tit' law
dump'ing
du'o·chrome'
du'o·crin'in
du'o·de'nal
du'o·de·nec'ta·sis pl. -ses'
du'o·de·nec'to·my
du'o·de·ni'tis
du'o·de'no·chol'an·gi'tis
du'o·de'no·chol'e·cys·tos'to·my
du'o·de'no·cho·led'o·chot'o·my
du'o·de'no·col'ic
du'o·de'no·cys·tos'to·my
du'o·de'no·en'ter·os'to·my
du'o·de'no·gram'
du'o·de'no·og'ra·phy
du'o·de'no·he·pat'ic
du'o·de'no·il'e·os'to·my
du'o·de'no·je·ju'nal
du'o·de'no·je'ju·nos'to·my
du'o·de'no·nol'y·sis
du'o·de'no·mes'o·col'ic
du'o·de'no·pan'cre·a·tec'to·my
du'o·de'no·plas'ty
du'o·de'no·py'lo·rec'to·my
du'o·de'no·nor'rha·phy
du'o·de'nos'co·py
du'o·de·nos'to·my
du'o·de·not'o·my
du'o·de'num pl. -na or -nums
Du·play' operation
du·plex'i·ty
du'pli·ca'ta cru·ci·a'ta
du'pli·ca'tion
du·pli·ca·ture
du·plic'i·tas
—— cru·ci·a'ta
du·plic'i·ty
Du·puys'-Du·temps' phe-nomenon
Du'puy·tren'
—— contracture
—— operation
du'ra
—— ma'ter
—— mater en·ceph'a·li'
—— mater spi·na'lis
du'ral
Du·rand' disease
Du·rand'-Ni·co·las'-Favre' disease
Du·ran'-Rey'nals factor

du'ra·plas'ty
Dürck nodes
Du·ret' hemorrhages
du·ri'tis
du'ro·ar'ach·ni'tis
du'ro·sar·co'ma pl. -mas or -ma·ta
Du'ro·ziez'
—— disease
—— murmur
Du·temps' sign
Dut'ton disease
Du·val' bacillus
Du'ven·hage'
dwarf
dwarf'ism
dy'ad'
dy·ad'ic
dy·clo'nine'
dy'dro·ges'ter·one'
dy·man'thine'
dy·nam'e·ter
dy'na·mo·gen'e·sis pl. -ses'
dy·nam'o·graph'
dy'na·mog'ra·phy
dy·nam'o·mter
dy·nam'o·neure'
dy'na·moph'a·ny
dy'na·mos'co·py
dy'na·therm'
dyne
dy·phyl'line'
dys'a·cou'si·a
dys'a·cou'sis pl. -ses'
dys'a·cous'ma
dys·ad'ap·ta'tion
dys·an'ag·no'si·a
dys·an'ti·graph'i·a
dys'a·phi·a
dys'ap·ta'tion
dys'ar·te'ri·ot'o·ny
dys·ar'thri·a
dys·ar'thric
dys'ar·thro'sis pl. -ses'
dys·au'to·no'mi·a
dys·ba'si·a
—— lor·dot'i·ca pro'gres·si'va
—— neu'ras·then'ic·a in'ter·mit'tens
dys·bu'li·a
dys'ce·pha'li·a man·dib'u·lo·oc'u·lo·fa'ci·a'lis
dys·chi'ri·a
dys·chon'dro·pla'si·a
dys'chro·a

dys·chroi′a
dys·chro′ma·to·der′mi·a
dys·chro′ma·tope′
dys·chro′ma·top′si·a
dys·chro′mi·a
dys·chro′mo·der′mi·a
dys′chro·na′tion
dys′chro·nous
dys·co′ri·a *also* discoria
dys·cra′si·a
dys·cra′sic
dys·crat′ic
dys′di·ad′o·cho′ki·ne′si·a
dys′e·coi′a
dys·em′bry·o′ma
dys·em′bry·o·pla′si·a
dys′e·me′si·a
dys·em′e·sis
dys·e′mi·a
dys·en′ce·pha′li·a
  splanch′no·cys′ti·ca
dys′en·te′ri·a
dys′en·ter′ic
dys′en·ter′y
dys′er·ga′si·a
dys′er·ga′sy
dys·er′gi·a
dys·es·the′si·a
dys·es·thet′ic
dys·func′tion
dys′ga·lac′ti·a
dys·gam′ma·glob′u·li·ne′mi·a
dys·gen′e·sis *pl.* -ses′
dys·gen′ic
dys·ger′mi·no′ma *pl.* -mas *or* -ma·ta
dys·geu′si·a
dys·glan′du·lar
dys·glob′u·li·ne′mi·a
dys·gnath′ic
dys·gno′si·a
dys·gram′ma·tism
dys·graph′i·a
dys·he′mo·poi·e′sis *pl.* -ses′
dys·he′mo·poi·et′ic
dys·hid′ri·a
dys′hi·dro′sis *pl.* -ses′
dys·in′su·lin·ism
dys·kar′y·o′sis
dys·kar′y·ot′ic
dys·ker′a·to′sis *pl.* -ses′
—— con·gen′i·ta
dys·ker′a·tot′ic
dys′ki·ne′si·a
dys′ki·net′ic

dys·la′li·a
dys·lex′i·a
dys·lex′ic
dys·lo′gi·a
dys′ma·tu′ri·ty
dys·me′li·a
dys·men′or·rhe′a
—— in′ter·men′stru·a′lis
dys·met′ri·a
dys·mim′i·a
dys·mne′si·a
dys·mor′phi·a
dys·mor′phic
dys·my′e·lin·o·gen′ic
dys·no′mi·a
dys′o·don·ti′a·sis
dys·on′to·gen′e·sis *pl.* -ses′
dys′on·to·ge·net′ic
dys·o′pi·a
dys′o·rex′i·a
dys·os′mi·a
dys·os′te·o·gen′e·sis *pl.* -ses′
dys′os·to′sis *pl.* -ses′
—— clei′do·cra′ni·a′lis
—— mul′ti·plex′
dys·par′a·thy′roid·ism
dys′pa·reu′ni·a
dys·pep′si·a
dys·pep′tic
dys·per′i·stal′sis *pl.* -ses′
dys·pha′gi·a
—— con·stric′ta
—— glo·bo′sa
—— lu·so′ri·a
—— spas′ti·ca
dys·phag′ic
dys·pha′si·a
dys·phe′mi·a
dys·phoi·te′sis *pl.* -ses′
dys·pho′ni·a
—— spas′ti·ca
dys·pho′ri·a
dys·pho′ric
dys·pho′ro·gen′ic
dys·phra′si·a
dys·phre′ni·a
dys·pi·tu′i·ta·rism
dys·pla′si·a
—— ep′i·phys′i·a′lis mul′ti·plex′
—— epiphysialis punc·ta′ta
—— epiphysialis punc·tic′u·lar′is
dys·plas′tic
dysp·ne′a

dysp·ne′al
dysp·ne′ic
dys′po·ne′sis
dys′po·net′ic
dys·prac′tic
dys·pra′gi·a
dys·prax′i·a
dys·pro′si·um
dys′ra·phism
dys·rhyth′mi·a
dys·rhyth′mic
dys·se′cre·to′sis
dys·so′cial
dys·som′ni·a
dys·sper′ma·tism
dys·sper′mi·a
dys·splen′ism
dys·sta′si·a
dys·stat′ic
dys·syn′chro·nous
dys·syn·er′gi·a
—— cer′e·bel·lar′is my′o·clon′i·ca
—— cerebellaris pro′gres·si′va
dys·syn′er·gy
dys·tax′i·a
dys·tec′ti·a
dys·tec′tic
dys′tha·na′si·a
dys·the′si·a
dys·thet′ic
dys·thy′mi·a
dys·thy′mic
dys·thy·roi′dal
dys·tith′i·a
dys·to′ci·a
dys·to′cic
dys·to′ni·a
—— mus′cu·lo′rum de·for′mans′
dys·ton′ic
dys·to′pi·a
dys·top′ic
dys·tro′phi·a
—— ad′i·po′so·gen′i·ta′is
—— brev′i·col′lis
—— me′di·a′na ca·nal′i·for′mis
—— my′o·ton′i·ca
—— per′i·os·ta′lis hy′per·plas′ti·ca fa·mil′i·ar′is
—— un′gui·um
dys·troph′ic
dys·tro′phy
dys·u′ri·a

E

Ea'gle
—— media
—— test
Eales disease
ear
ear'ache'
ear'drum'
Earle L fibrosarcoma
ear'wax'
Ea'ton
—— agent
—— virus
Ea'ton-Lam'bert syn-
  drome
Eb'ers pa·py'rus
E'ber·thel'la
—— ty·pho'sa
Eb'ner glands
e'bo·na'tion
é·bran·le·ment'
e·bri'e·tas
e·bri'e·ty
e'bri·ose'
e'bri·ous
Eb'stein'
—— anomaly
—— disease
e'bur
—— den'tis
eb'ur·nat'ed
e'bur·na'tion
Ec·bal'li·um
ec·bol'ic
ec·cen'tric also excentric
ec·cen'tro·chon'dro·os'te·
  o·dys'tro·phy
ec·cen'tro·chon'dro·
  pla'si·a
ec·cen'tro-os'te·o·
  chon'dro·dys·pla'si·a
ec·ceph'a·lo'sis pl. -ses'
ec'chon·dro'ma pl. -mas or
  -ma·ta
ec'chon·dro'sis pl. -ses'
—— phy'sa·liph'o·ra
ec·chon'dro·tome'
ec'chy·mo'ma pl. -mas or
  -ma·ta
ec'chy·mose'
ec'chy·mo'sis pl. -ses'
ec'chy·mot'ic
ec'crine
ec'cri·sis pl. -ses'
ec'cy·e'sis pl. -ses'

ec·dem'ic
ec'der·on'
ec'der·on'ic
ec'dy·sis pl. -ses'
ec'go·nine'
e·chid'nin
e·chi'no·coc·co'sis pl. -ses'
E·chi'no·coc'cus
—— gran'u·lo'sus
ech'i·no'sis pl. -ses'
E·chi'no·sto'ma
ech'o
ech'o·a·cou'si·a
ech'o·a'or·tog'ra·phy
ech'o·car'di·o·gram'
ech'o·car'di·og'ra·phy
ech'o·en·ceph'a·lo·gram'
ech'o·en·ceph'a·lo·graph'
ech'o·en·ceph'a·log'ra·phy
ech'o·gen'ic
ech'o·gram'
ech'o·graph'i·a
ech'o·ki·ne'sis pl. -ses'
ech'o·la'li·a
ech'o·lal'ic
ech'o·la'lus
e·cho'ma·tism
ech'o·mim'i·a
ech'o·mo'tism
ech·op'a·thy
ech·oph'o·ny
ech'o·phot'o·ny
ech'o·phra'si·a
ech'o·prax'i·a
ech'o·prax'is
ech'o·prax'y
ech'o·re'no·gram'
ech'o·son'o·gram'
ech'o·thi'o·phate'
ech'o·u'ter·o·gram'
ech'o·vi'rus
Eck'er
—— fissure
—— fluid
ec·la'bi·um
ec·lamp'si·a
—— grav'i·dar'um
—— nu'tans'
—— ro'tans'
ec·lamp'sism
ec·lamp'tic
ec·lamp'to·gen'ic
ec·lec'tic
ec·lec'ti·cism
ec'ly·sis pl. -ses'
ec·mne'si·a
e·coch'le·a'tion

e'co·ma'ni·a
E·con'o·mo disease
e·cos'tate'
e'cos·ta'tion
e·cos'ta·tism
ec'o·sys'tem
ec'phy·lac'tic
ec'phy·lax'is pl. -lax'es'
é·crase·ment'
é·cra·seur'
ec'ta·co'li·a
ec'tad'
ec'tal
ec·ta'si·a
—— ven·tric'u·li' par'a·dox'a
ec'ta·sis pl. -ses'
ec·tat'ic
ec·ten'tal
ect·eth'moid'
ec·thy'ma
—— gan'gre·no'sum
ec·thy're·o'sis pl. -ses'
ec'to·an'ti·gen
ec'to·blast'
ec'to·car'di·a
ec'to·cer'vi·cal
ec'to·cer'vix
ec'to·cho·roi'de·a
ec'to·ci·ne're·a
ec'to·ci·ne're·al
ec'to·co'lon
ec'to·con'dyle'
ec'to·cor'ne·a
ec'to·cu·ne'i·form'
ec'to·derm'
ec'to·der'mal
ec'to·der·mo'sis pl. -ses'
—— e·ro·si'va plu'ri·o'ri·fi'ci·
  a'lis
ec'to·en'tad'
ec'to·en'zyme'
ec·tog'e·nous
ec'to·hor'mone'
ec'to·men'inx pl. -me·
  nin'ges'
ec'to·mere'
ec'to·morph'
ec'to·mor'phic
ec'to·mor'phy
ec'to·pa'gi·a
ec·top'a·gus pl. -gi'
ec'to·par'a·site'
ec'to·par'a·sit'ic
ec'to·pec'to·ra'lis pl. -les'
ec'to·per'i·to·ne'al
ec'to·per'i·to·ni'tis
ec'to·phyte'

ec·to·phyt'ic
ec·to·pi·a
—— cor'dis
—— len'tis
—— pu·pil'lae'
—— re'nis
—— tes'tis
ec·top'ic
ec·to·pla·cen'ta
ec·to·pla·cen'tal
ec·to·plasm
ec·to·plas'mic
ec·to·plast'
ec·to·plas'tic
ec·to·pot'o·my
ec·to·pter'y·goid'
ec·to·py
ec·to·sarc'
ec·tos·to'sis pl. -ses'
ec'to·thrix'
ec·to·zo'on' pl. -zo'a
ec·tro·dac·tyl'i·a
ec·tro·dac'ty·lism
ec·tro·dac'ty·ly
ec·tro·gen'ic
ec·trog'e·ny
ec·tro·me'li·a
ec·tro·mel'ic
ec·trom'e·lus pl. -li'
ec·trom'e·ly
ec·tro'pi·on'
ec·tro'pi·on·i·za'tion
ec·tro'pi·on·ize', -ized', -iz'-
  ing
ec·tro'sis pl. -ses'
ec'tro·syn·dac'ty·ly
ec·trot'ic
ec·ty·lot'ic
ec'tyl·u·re'a
ec'ze·ma
—— er'y·the'ma·to'sum
—— fis'sum
—— her·pet'i·cum
—— hy'per·troph'i·cum
—— mad'i·dans'
—— mar'gi·na'tum
—— num'mu·lar'is
—— pap'u·lo'sum
—— pus'tu·lo'sum
—— ru'brum
—— seb'or·rhe'i·cum
—— so·lar'e'
—— squa·mo'sum
—— sy·co·ma·to'sum
—— sy·co'si·for'me'
—— ty·lot'i·cum
—— vac'ci·na'tum

—— ve·sic'u·lo'sum
ec·zem'a·ti·za'tion
ec·zem'a·to·gen'ic
ec·zem'a·toid'
ec·zem'a·to'sis pl. -ses'
ec·zem'a·tous
Ed'e·bohl' operation
Ed'el·mann sign
e·de'ma pl. -mas or -ma·ta
e·dem'a·tous
e·den'tate'
e·den'tu·lous
e'de·ol'o·gy
ed'e·tate'
e·det'ic
e·dis'yl·ate'
ed'ro·phon'i·um
ed'u·ca·ble
ef·fect'
ef·fec'tor
ef'fer·ent (centrifugal)
  ♦afferent
ef'fer·ves'cence
ef'fer·ves'cent
ef'flo·res'cence
ef'flu·ent (flowing out)
  ♦affluent
ef·flu'vi·um pl. -vi·a or -vi·
  ums
ef'fort
ef·fuse', -fused', -fus'ing
ef·fu'sion
e·ger'sis
e·ger'tic
e·ges'ta
egg
e'gi·lops'
e·glan'du·lar
e·glan'du·lose'
e·glan'du·lous
e'go
e'go·bron·choph'o·ny
e'go·cen'tric
e'go·cen·tric'i·ty
e'go·cen'trism
e'go-dys·to'ni·a
e'go-dys·ton'ic
e'go·ism
e'go·ist
e'go·is'tic
e'go·ma'ni·a
e·goph'o·ny
e'go-syn·to'ni·a
e'go-syn·ton'ic
e'go·tism
e'go·tist
e'go·tis'tic or e'go·tis'ti·cal

Eh'lers-Dan'los' syndrome
Eh'ren·rit'ter ganglion
Ehr'lich
—— hematoxylin
—— reagent
—— test
—— tumor
Ehr'mann test
ei·det'ic
ei'dop·tom'e·try
ei'ko·nom'e·ter
ei'loid'
Ei·me'ri·a
ein'stein'
ein·stein'i·um
Ei·se'ni·a
Ei'sen·men'ger
—— complex
—— syndrome
—— tetralogy
e·jac'u·late', -lat'ed, -lat'ing
e·jac'u·la'ti·o'
—— de·fi'ci·ens'
—— prae'cox'
—— re'tar·da'ta
e·jac'u·la'tion
e·jac'u·la·to'ry
e·jac'u·la'tor u·ri'nae'
e·jac'u·lum
e·ject'
e·jec'ta
e·jec'tion
e·jec'tor
e·lab'o·ra'tion
el'a·id'ic
e·la'i·din
e·lai·op'a·thy
e·las'mo·branch' poison-
  ing
e·las'tance
e·las'tase'
e·las'tic
e·las·tic'i·ty
e·las'tin
e·las'to·fi·bro'ma pl. -mas
  or -ma·ta
—— dor'si'
e·las'toid'
e·las·toi·do'sis pl. -ses'
e·las'to·ma pl. -mas or -ma·
  ta
e·las'to·mer
e·las'to·mer'ic
e·las·tom'e·ter
e·las'tose'
e·las'to·sis
—— se·ni'lis

el'bow
el'der
e·lec'tive
E·lec'tra complex
e·lec'tric *or* e·lec'tri·cal
e·lec'tri·fy', -fied', -fy'ing
e·lec'tri·za'tion
e·lec'tro·an'es·the'si·a
e·lec'tro·bi·o·log'ic *or* e·lec'tro·bi·o·log'i·cal
e·lec'tro·bi·ol'o·gy
e·lec'tro·car'di·o·gram'
e·lec'tro·car'di·o·graph'
e·lec'tro·car'di·o·graph'ic
e·lec'tro·car'di·og'ra·phy
e·lec'tro·car'di·o·scope'
e·lec'tro·ca·tal'y·sis *pl.* -ses'
e·lec'tro·cau'ter·y
e·lec'tro·chem'is·try
e·lec'tro·co·ag'u·la'tion
e·lec'tro·con'trac·til'i·ty
e·lec'tro·con·vul'sive
e·lec'tro·cor'ti·cal
e·lec'tro·cor'ti·co·gram'
e·lec'tro·cor'ti·cog'ra·phy
e·lec'tro·cute', -cut'ed, -cut'ing
e·lec'tro·cu'tion
e·lec'trode'
e·lec'tro·der'mal
e·lec'tro·der'ma·tome'
e·lec'tro·des'ic·ca'tion
e·lec'tro·di'ag·no'sis *pl.* -ses'
e·lec'tro·di·al'y·sis *pl.* -ses'
e·lec'tro·di·aph'a·ke
e·lec'tro·dy'na·mom'e·ter
e·lec'tro·en·ceph'a·lo·gram'
e·lec'tro·en·ceph'a·lo·graph'
e·lec'tro·en·ceph'a·lo·graph'ic
e·lec'tro·en·ceph'a·log'ra·phy
e·lec'tro·end'os·mo'sis *pl.* -ses'
e·lec'tro·ex·ci'sion
e·lec'tro·gram'
e'lec·trog'ra·phy
e·lec'tro·he·mos'ta·sis
e·lec'tro·ky'mo·graph'
e·lec'tro·ky·mog'ra·phy
e·lec'trol'y·sis
e·lec'tro·lyte'
e·lec'tro·lyt'ic

e·lec'tro·lyze', -lyzed', -lyz'ing
e·lec'tro·lyz'er
e·lec'tro·mas·sage'
e·lec'tro·my'o·gram'
e·lec'tro·my'o·graph'ic
e·lec'tro·my·og'ra·phy
e·lec'tron'
e·lec'tro·nar·co'sis *pl.* -ses'
e·lec'tro·neg'a·tive
e·lec'tro·neu·rog'ra·phy
e·lec'tron'ic
e·lec'tro·nys'tag·mog'ra·phy
e·lec'tro·oc'u·lo·gram'
e·lec'tro·os·mo'sis *pl.* -ses'
e·lec'tro·phil'ic
e·lec'tro·pho'bi·a
e·lec'tro·pho·re'sis
e·lec'tro·pho·ret'ic
e·lec'tro·pho'to·ther'a·py
e·lec'tro·phys'i·ol'o·gy
e·lec'tro·pos'i·tive
e·lec'tro·punc'ture
e·lec'tro·re·sec'tion
e·lec'tro·ret'i·no·gram'
e·lec'tro·scis'sion
e·lec'tro·scope'
e·lec'tro·shock'
e·lec'tro·stat'ic
e·lec'tro·sur'ger·y
e·lec'tro·sur'gi·cal
e·lec'tro·syn'the·sis *pl.* -ses'
e·lec'tro·tax'is
e·lec'tro·tha·na'si·a
e·lec'tro·ther'a·py
e·lec'tro·therm'
e·lec'tro·ther'mal
e·lec'tro·ther'mic
e·lec'tro·ther'my
e·lec'tro·tome'
e'lec·trot'o·my
e·lec'tro·ton'ic
e·lec'trot'o·nus
e·lec'tro·tro'pism
e·lec'tro·ver'sion
e·lec'tro·vert'
el'e·doi'sin
e·le'i·din
el'e·ment
el'e·men'tal
el'e·men'ta·ry
el'e·o'ma *pl.* -mas *or* -ma·ta
el'e·op'tene'
el'e·phan'ti·ac'
el'e·phan'ti·as'ic
el'e·phan·ti'a·sis *pl.* -ses'

—— neu·ro'ma·to'sa
—— nos'tras
el'e·phan'toid'
el'e·va'tor
El'ford membrane
e·lim'i·nant
e·lim'i·nate', -nat'ed, -nat'ing
e·lim'i·na'tion
e'lin·gua'tion
el'i·nin
e·lix'ir
El'kin operation
El'li·ot
—— operation
—— position
el·lip'soid'
el'lip·soi'dal
el·lip'tic *or* el·lip'ti·cal
el·lip'to·cyte'
el·lip'to·cy·to'sis *pl.* -ses'
el·lip'to·cy·tot'ic
El'lis curve
El'lis-van Crev'eld syndrome
Ells'worth-How'ard test
e·lon'gate', -gat'ed, -gat'ing
e'lon·ga'tion
El'schnig pearls
El Tor' cholera
el'u·ant *also* eluent
el'u·ate'
el'u·ent *var. of* eluant
e·lute', e·lut'ed, e·lut'ing
e·lu'tion
e·lu'tri·a'tion
e·ma'ci·ate', -at'ed, -at'ing
e·ma'ci·a'tion
e·mac'u·la'tion
em'a·nate', -nat'ed, -nat'ing
em'a·na'tion
e·man'ci·pate', -pat'ed, -pat'ing
e·man'ci·pa'tion
em'a·no·ther'a·py
e·man'si·o'
—— men'si·um
e·mas'cu·late', -lat'ed, -lat'ing
e·mas'cu·la'tion
em·bar'rass
em·bed', -bed'ded, -bed'ding, *also* imbed
em'bo·lec'to·my
em'bo·le'mi·a
em·bol'ic
em·bol'i·form'

em'bo·lism
em'bo·lo·la'li·a
em'bo·lo·phra'si·a
em'bo·loid'
em'bo·lus *pl.* -li'
em'bo·ly
em'bouche·ment'
em·bra'sure
em·bro·ca'tion
em'bry·ec'to·my
em'bry·o'
em'bry·o·car'di·a
em'bry·o·ci'dal
em'bry·oc·ton'ic
em'bry·oc'to·ny
em'bry·o·gen'e·sis
em'bry·o·ge·net'ic
em'bry·o·gen'ic
em'bry·og'e·ny
em'bry·oid'
em'bry·o·log'ic *or* em'bry·o·log'i·cal
em'bry·ol'o·gist
em'bry·ol'o·gy
em'bry·o'ma *pl.* -mas *or* -ma·ta
em'bry·o·mor'phous
em'bry·on'
em'bry·o·nal
em'bry·on'ic
em'bry·on'i·form'
em'bry·o·ni·za'tion
em'bry·o·noid'
em'bry·o·ny
em'bry·op'a·thy
em'bry·o·plas'tic
em'bry·o·to'ci·a
em'bry·o·tome'
em'bry·ot'o·my
em'bry·o·tox·ic'i·ty
em'bry·o·tox'on'
em'bry·o·troph'
em'bry·o·troph'ic
em'bry·ot'ro·phy
em'bry·ul'ci·a
em'bry·ul'cus
e·med'ul·late'
e·mer'gen·cy
e·mer'gent
em'e·sis *pl.* -ses'
e·met'ic
em'e·to·ca·thar'sis *pl.* -ses'
em'e·to·ca·thar'tic
em'e·to·ma'ni·a
em'e·to·pho'bi·a
e·mic'tion
e·mic'to·ry

em'i·grate', -grat'ed, -grat'-ing
em'i·gra'tion
em'i·nence
em'i·nen'ti·a
—— ar'cu·a'ta
—— car'pi' ra'di·a'lis
—— carpi ul·nar'is
—— cla'vae'
—— col·lat'er·a'lis
—— con'chae'
—— cru'ci·a'ta
—— cru'ci·for'mis
—— fa'ci·a'lis
—— fos'sae' tri·an'gu·lar'is
—— il'i·o·pec·tin'e·a
—— il'i·o·pu'bi·ca
—— in'ter·con'dy·lar'is
—— in'ter·con'dy·loi'de·a
—— me'di·a'lis
—— py·ram'i·da'lis
—— scaph'ae'
—— te'res'
em'i·o·cy·to'sis *pl.* -ses'
em'is·sar'i·um *pl.* -i·a
—— con'dy·loi'de·um
—— mas·toi'de·um
—— oc·cip'i·ta'le'
—— pa·ri'e·ta'le'
em'is·sar'y
e·mis'sion
em·men'a·gog'ic
em·men'a·gogue'
em·men'i·a
em·men'ic
em·men'i·op'a·thy
em'me·nol'o·gy
em'me·trope'
em'me·tro'pi·a
em'me·trop'ic
Em'mon·si·el'la cap'su·la'ta
em'o·din
e·mol'lient
e·mo'ti·o·met'a·bol'ic
e·mo'tion
e·mo'tion·al
e·mo'ti·o·vas'cu·lar
e·mo'tive
e'mo·tiv'i·ty
em·path'ic
em'pa·thize', -thized', -thi-z'ing
em'pa·thy
em·per'i·po·le'sis
em'phly·sis *pl.* -ses'
em·phrac'tic

em·phrax'is *pl.* -phrax'es'
em'phy·se'ma
em'phy·sem'a·tous
em·pir'ic *or* em·pir'i·cal
em·pir'i·cism
em·plas'tic
em·plas'trum *pl.* -tra
em·po·ri·at'ric
em'pros·thot'o·nos
emp'ty·sis
em'py·e'ma *pl.* -ma·ta *or* -mas
—— ne·ces'si·ta'tis
em'py·em'a·tous
em'py·e'mic
em'py·e'sis *pl.* -ses'
e·mul'gent
e·mul'si·fi·ca'tion
e·mul'si·fi'er
e·mul'si·fy', -fied', -fy'ing
e·mul'sin *(amygdalase)*
♦emulsion
e·mul'sion *(a suspension of small globules of one liquid in a second)*
♦emulsin
e·mul'sive
e·mul'soid'
e·munc'to·ry
em'yl·cam'ate'
e·nam'el
e·nam'e·lo·plas'ty
e·nam'e·lum
en·an'them
en'an·the'ma *pl.* -ma·ta
en'an·them'a·tous
e·nan'thic
en·an'ti·o·mer
en'ar·thri'tis
en'ar·thro'di·al
en'ar·thro'sis *pl.* -ses'
en bloc'
en·can'this *pl.* -thi·des'
en·cap'su·late', -lat'ed, -lat'-ing
en·cap'su·la'tion
en·cap'sule, -suled, -sul·ing
en·ce'li·al'gi·a
en·ce'li·i'tis
en·ceph'a·lal'gi·a
en·ceph'a·lat'ro·phy
en·ceph'a·laux'e
en·ceph'a·le'mi·a
en'ce·phal'ic
en·ceph'a·lit'ic
en·ceph'a·li'tis *pl.* -lit'i·des'
—— le·thar'gi·ca

—— per'i·ax'i·a'lis con·
cen'tri·ca
—— periaxialis dif·fu'sa
en·ceph'a·lo·cele' *(hernia
of brain)*
♦*encephalocoele*
en·ceph'a·lo·clas'tic
en·ceph'a·lo·coele' *(cranial cavity)*
♦*encephalocele*
en·ceph'a·lo·cys'to·cele'
en·ceph'a·lo·cys'to·me·
nin'go·cele'
en·ceph'a·lo'di·al'y·sis *pl.*
  -ses'
en·ceph'a·lo·dys·pla'si·a
en·ceph'a·lo·gram'
en·ceph'a·log'ra·phy
en·ceph'a·loid'
en·ceph'a·lo·lith'
en·ceph'a·lol'o·gy
en·ceph'a·lo'ma *pl.* -mas *or*
  -ma·ta
en·ceph'a·lo·ma·la'ci·a
en·ceph'a·lo·men'in·gi'tis
en·ceph'a·lo·me·nin'go·
  cele'
en·ceph'a·lo·men'i·gop'a·
  thy
en·ceph'a·lo·mere'
en·ceph'a·lo·mer'ic
en·ceph'a·lom'e·ter
en·ceph'a·lo·my'e·li'tis
en·ceph'a·lo·my'el·o·cele'
en·ceph'a·lo·my'e·lo·neu·
  rop'a·thy
en·ceph'a·lo·my'e·lon'ic
en·ceph'a·lo·my'e·lop'a·
  thy
en·ceph'a·lo·my'e·lo·ra·
  dic'u·li'tis
en·ceph'a·lo·my'e·lo·ra·
  dic'u·lop'a·thy
en·ceph'a·lo·my'e·lo'sis *pl.*
  -ses'
en·ceph'a·lo·my'o·car·
  di'tis
en·ceph'a·lon' *pl.* -la
en·ceph'a·lo·nar·co'sis *pl.*
  -ses'
en·ceph'a·lop'a·thy
en·ceph'a·lo·punc'ture
en·ceph'a·lo·py·o'sis *pl.*
  -ses'
en·ceph'a·lo·ra·chid'i·an
en·ceph'a·lo·ra·dic'u·li'tis
en·ceph'a·lor·rha'gi·a

en·ceph'a·lo·scle·ro'sis *pl.*
  -ses'
en·ceph'a·lo·scope'
en·ceph'a·los'co·py
en·ceph'a·lo·sep'sis *pl.* -ses'
en·ceph'a·lo'sis *pl.* -ses'
en·ceph'a·lo·spi'nal
en·ceph'a·lo·thlip'sis *pl.*
  -ses'
en·ceph'a·lo·tome'
en·ceph'a·lot'o·my
en·ceph'a·lo·tri·gem'i·nal
en·chon'dral
en'chon·dro'ma *pl.* -mas *or*
  -ma·ta
en·chon'dro·ma·to'sis *pl.*
  -ses'
en'chon·drom'a·tous
en'chon·dro·sar·co'ma *pl.*
  -mas *or* -ma·ta
en'chon·dro'sis *pl.* -ses'
en'chy·ma
en'clave'
en·clit'ic
en·cod'ing
en'col·pi'tis
en'cop·re'sis *pl.* -ses'
en·cra'ni·us
en·crust'
en·crus·ta'tion
en·crust'ed
en'cy·e'sis *pl.* -ses'
en·cy'o·py'e·li'tis
en·cyst'
en·cys·ta'tion
en·cyst'ment
end'a·del'phus
end'an·gi·i'tis
en'da·or'tic
end'a·or·ti'tis
en'dar·ter·ec'to·mize',
  -mized', -miz'ing
end'ar·ter·ec'to·my
end'ar·te'ri·al
end'ar·te'ri·ec'to·my
end'ar·te·ri'tis
—— de·for'mans'
—— ob·lit'er·ans'
en'dar·te'ri·um
en'dar·ter·op'a·thy
end·au'ral
end'brain'
en·deic'tic
en·de'mi·a
en·dem'ic
end'er·gon'ic
en·der'mic

en'der·mo'sis *pl.* -ses'
en'der·on'
en'der·on'ic
en'do·ab·dom'i·nal
en'do·an'eu·rys·mor'rha·
  phy
en'do·an'gi·i'tis
en'do·a·or·ti'tis
en'do·ap·pen'di·ci'tis
en'do·ar·te·ri'tis
en'do·bi·ot'ic
en'do·blast'
en'do·blas'tic
en'do·bron'chi·al
en'do·bron·chi'tis
en'do·car'di·al
en'do·car'di·op'a·thy
en'do·car·di'tis
—— len'ta
en'do·car'di·um *pl.* -di·a
en'do·ce'li·ac'
en'do·cer'vi·cal
en'do·cer'vi·ci'tis
en'do·cer'vix *pl.* -vi·ces'
en'do·chon'dral
en'do·chon·dro'ma *pl.* -mas
  or -ma·ta
en'do·cho'ri·on'
en'do·chrome'
en'do·co·li'tis
en'do·col·pi'tis
en'do·cra'ni·al
en'do·cra·ni'tis
en'do·cra'ni·um *pl.* -ni·a
en'do·crine
en'do·crin'ic
en'do·crin·ism
en'do·cri·nol'o·gist
en'do·cri·nol'o·gy
en'do·cri·no'path'ic
en'do·cri·nop'a·thy
en'do·cri·no'sis *pl.* -ses'
en'do·cri·nos'i·ty
en'do·cri·no'ther'a·py
en·doc'ri·nous
en'do·cyst'
en'do·cys·ti'tis
en'do·derm'
en'do·di·as'co·py
en'do·don'ti·a
en'do·don'tic
en'do·don'tics
en'do·don'tist
en'do·don·ti'tis
en'do·don'ti·um
en'do·don·tol'o·gy
en'do·en·ter·i'tis

en′do·en′zyme′
en′do·ep′i·der′mal
en′do·ep′i·the′li·al
en′do·e·soph′a·gi′tis
en·dog′a·mous
en·dog′a·my
en·do·gas′tric
en·do·gas·tri′tis
en·do·ge·net′ic
en·do·gen′ic
en·dog′e·nous
en·dog′e·ny
en·do·gna′thi·on′
en·do·la·ryn′ge·al
en·do·lar′ynx
En′do·li′max′
—— na′na
en′do·lymph′
en′do·lym′pha
en′do·lym·phan′gi·al
en′do·lym·phat′ic
en′do·lym′phic
en′do·ly′sin
en′do·mas′toi·di′tis
en′do·men′inx pl. -me·
   nin′ges′
en′do·me·trec′to·my
en′do·me′tri·al
en′do·me′tri·o′ma pl. -mas
   or -ma·ta
en′do·me′tri·o′sis pl. -ses′
en′do·me′tri·ot′ic
en′do·me·tri′tis
—— ex·fo′li·a·ti′va
en′do·me′tri·um
en·dom′e·try
en′do·mi·to′sis pl. -ses′
en′do·morph′
en′do·mor′phic
en′do·my′o·car·di′tis
en′do·mys′i·um pl. -i·a
en′do·neu·ri′tis
en′do·neu·ri′um pl. -ri·a
en′do·nu′cle·ar
en′do·par′a·site′
en′do·par′a·sit′ic
en′do·pel′vic
en′do·pep′ti·dase′
en′do·per′i·car′di·al
en′do·per′i·car·di′tis
en′do·per′i·my′o·car·di′tis
en′do·per′i·to·ne′al
en′do·per′i·to·ni′tis
en′do·phle·bi′tis
en·doph′thal·mi′tis
—— pha′co·an′a·phy·lac′ti·
ca

en′do·phyte′
en′do·phyt′ic
en′do·plasm
en′do·plas′mic
en′do·plast′
en′do·rhi·ni′tis
en·dor′phin
en′do·sal·pin′gi·o′sis pl.
   -ses′
en′do·sal′pin·gi′tis
en′do·sal′pinx pl. -sal·
   pin′ges′
en′do·scope′
en′do·scop′ic
en·dos′co·py
en′do·se′cre·to′ry
en′do·skel′e·ton
en′dos·mom′e·ter
en′dos·mose′
en′dos·mo′sic
en′dos·mo′sis pl. -ses′
en′dos·mot′ic
en′do·spore′
en·dos′te·al
end′os·te·i′tis
end·os′te·o′ma pl. -mas or
   -ma·ta
end·os′te·um pl. -te·a
end′os·ti′tis
end′os·to′ma pl. -mas or
   -ma·ta
end′os·to′sis pl. -ses′
en′do·ten·din′e·um
en′do·ten′on
en′do·the′li·al
en′do·the′li·al·i·za′tion
en′do·the′li·i′tis
en′do·the′li·o·an′gi·i′tis
en′do·the′li·o′blas·to′ma
   pl. -mas or -ma·ta
en′do·the′li·o·cho′ri·al
en′do·the′li·o·cyte′
en′do·the′li·o·cy·to′sis pl.
   -ses′
en′do·the′li·oid′
en′do·the′li·o′ma pl. -mas
   or -ma·ta
—— an′gi·o·ma·to′sum
—— cap′i·tis
en′do·the′li·o·ma·to′sis pl.
   -ses′
en′do·the′li·o′sar·co′ma pl.
   -mas or -ma·ta
en′do·the′li·o′sis pl. -ses′
en′do·the′li·um pl. -li·a
—— cam′er·ae′ an·te′ri·o′ris
   cor′ne·ae′

—— camerae anterioris i′ri·
   dis
—— camerae anterioris
   oc′u·li′
en′do·ther′mic
en′do·ther′my
en′do·tho·rac′ic
en′do·thrix′
en′do·tox·e′mi·a
en′do·tox′ic
en′do·tox′i·co′sis pl. -ses′
en′do·tox′in
en′do·tra′che·al
en′do·u·re′thral
en′do·u′ter·ine
en′do·vas′cu·li·tis
en′e·ma
en′er·gom′e·ter
en′er·gy
en′er·vate′ (to weaken),
   -vat′ed, -vat′ing
♦innervate
en′er·va′tion
en·gage′ment
en·gas′tri·us
En′gel·mann disease
En′gel-Reck′ling·hau′sen
   disease
en·globe′ment
en·gorge′, -gorged′, -gorg′-
   ing
en·gorge′ment
en′gram′
en·hem′a·to·spore′
en·large′ment
e′nol′
e′no·lase′
e′no·ma′ni·a
en′oph·thal′mos′
en·os′to·sis pl. -ses′
En′roth′ sign
en·sheathed′
en′si·form′
en·som′pha·lus pl. -li′
en′som·phal′ic
en′stro·phe
en′tad′
en′tal
ent′a·me·bi′a·sis pl. -ses′
Ent′a·moe′ba
—— buc·ca′lis
—— co′li′
—— gin′gi·va′lis
—— his′to·lyt′i·ca
—— na′na
en·ta′si·a
en′ta·sis pl. -ses′

en·tat'ic
en'ter·ad'e·ni'tis
en'ter·al
en'ter·al'gi·a
en'ter·al'gic
en'ter·ec'ta·sis *pl.* -ses'
en'ter·ec'to·my
en'ter·e·pip'lo·cele'
en·ter'ic
en·ter'i·coid'
en·ter·i'tis
—— cam'py·lo·bac'ter
—— ne·crot'i·cans'
en'ter·o·a·nas'to·mo'sis
   pl. -ses'
En'ter·o·bac·te'ri·a'ce·ae'
en'ter·o·bi'a·sis *pl.* -ses'
En'ter·o'bi·us
—— ver·mic'u·lar'is
en'ter·o·cele'
en'ter·o·cen·te'sis *pl.* -ses'
en'ter·o·cep'tive
en'ter·oc'ly·sis *pl.* -ses'
en'ter·o·coc'cus *pl.* -ci'
en'ter·o·coele'
en'ter·o·coe'lic
en'ter·o·co·lec'to·my
en'ter·o·co'lic
en'ter·o·co·li'tis
en'ter·o·co·los'to·my
en'ter·o·crin'in
en'ter·o'cu·ta'ne·ous
en'ter·o·cyst'
en'ter·o·cys'to·cele'
en'ter·o·cys·to'ma *pl.* -mas
   or -ma·ta
en'ter·o·cys'to·plas'ty
en'ter·o·en·ter'ic
en'ter·o·en'ter·os'to·my
en'ter·o·gas'tric
en'ter·o·gas·tri'tis
en'ter·o·gas'tro·cele'
en'ter·o·gas'trone'
en'ter·og'e·nous
en'ter·o·graph'
en'ter·og'ra·phy
en'ter·o·ki'nase'
en'ter·o·lith'
en'ter·o·li·thi'a·sis *pl.* -ses'
en'ter·ol'o·gist
en'ter·ol'y·sis *pl.* -ses'
en'ter·o·meg'a·ly
en'ter·o·me'ro·cele'
en'ter·o·my·co'sis *pl.* -ses'
en'ter·o·my·i'a·sis *pl.* -ses'
en'ter·on'
en'ter·o'pa·re'sis *pl.* -ses'

en'ter·o·path'o·gen'ic
en'ter·op'a·thy
en'ter·o·pex'y
en'ter·o·plas'tic
en'ter·o·plas'ty
en'ter·o·ple'gi·a
en'ter·o·proc'ti·a
en'ter·op·to'sis *pl.* -ses'
en'ter·op·tot'ic
en'ter·or·rha'gi·a
en'ter·or'rha·phy
en'ter·or·rhe'a
en'ter·or·rhex'is *pl.*
   -rhex'es'
en'ter·o·scope'
en'ter·o·sep'sis *pl.* -ses'
en'ter·o·spasm
en'ter·o·sta'sis *pl.* -ses'
en'ter·o·stax'is
en'ter·o·ste·no'sis *pl.* -ses'
en'ter·o·sto'mal
en'ter·os'to·my
en'ter·o·tome'
en'ter·ot'o·my
en'ter·o·tox·e'mi·a
en'ter·o·tox'in
en'ter·o·trop'ic
en'ter·o·vag'i·nal
en'ter·o·ves'i·cal
en'ter·o·vi'rus
en'ter·o·zo'ic
en'ter·o·zo'on' *pl.* -zo'a
en'the·sis *pl.* -ses'
en·thet'ic
en'ti·ty
en'to·blast'
en'to·cele'
en'to·cone'
en'to·co'nid
en'to·derm'
en'to·der'mal
en'tome'
en·to'mi·on' *pl.* -mi·a
en'to·mol'o·gist
en'to·mol'o·gy
en'to·mo·pho'bi·a
ent·op'tic
ent'op'to·scop'ic
ent'op'tos'co·py
en'to·zo'al
en'to·zo'on' *pl.* -zo'a
en·trap'ment
en·tro'pi·on'
en·tro'pi·on·ize', -ized', -iz'-
   ing
en'tro·py
en'ty·py

e·nu'cle·ate', -at'ed, -at'ing
e·nu'cle·a'tion
e·nu'cle·a'tor
en'u·re'sis *pl.* -ses'
en'u·ret'ic
en'zy·got'ic
en'zy·mat'ic
en'zyme'
en·zy'mic
en'zy·mol'o·gy
en'zy·mol'y·sis *pl.* -ses'
en·zy'mo·lyt'ic
en'zy·mop'a·thy
en'zy·mu'ri·a
e'on·ism
e'o·sin
e'o·sin'o·pe'ni·a
e'o·sin'o·pe'nic
e'o·sin'o·phil'
e'o·sin'o·phile'
e'o·sin'o·phil'i·a
e'o·sin'o·phil'ic
e'o·sin'o·tac'tic
e·pac'tal
ep'ar·sal'gi·a
ep'ar·te'ri·al
ep·ax'i·al
ep·en'dy·ma
ep·en'dy·mal
ep·en'dy·mi'tis
e·pen'dy·mo·blast'
ep·en'dy·mo·blas·to'ma *pl.*
   -mas *or* -ma·ta
ep·en'dy·mo·cyte'
ep·en'dy·mo'ma *pl.* -mas *or*
   -ma·ta
eph'apse'
e·phe'bic
e·phe'lis *pl.* -li·des'
e·phem'er·a
—— ma·lig'na
e·phem'er·al
eph'i·dro'sis *pl.* -ses'
—— cru·en'ta
—— tinc'ta
ep'i·an·dros'ter·one'
ep'i·blast'
ep'i·bleph'a·ron'
ep'i·bol'ic
e·pib'o·ly
ep'i·bran'chi·al
ep'i·bul'bar
ep'i·can'thal
ep'i·can'thic
ep'i·can'thus
ep'i·car'di·a
ep'i·car'di·al

ep'i·car'di·ec'to·my
ep'i·car'di·um pl. -di·a
ep'i·carp'
ep'i·chor'dal
ep'i·cho'ri·al
ep'i·cho'ri·on'
ep'i·co'mus
ep'i·con·dyl·al'gi·a
ep'i·con'dy·lar
ep'i·con'dyle'
ep'i·con·dyl'i·an
ep'i·con·dyl'ic
ep'i·con·dy·li'tis
ep'i·con'dy·lus pl. -li'
—— lat'e·ra'lis fem'o·ris
—— lateralis hu'mer·i'
—— me'di·a'lis fem'o·ris
—— medialis hu'mer·i'
ep'i·cor'a·coid'
ep'i·cos'tal
ep'i·cra'ni·al
ep'i·cra'ni·um
ep'i·cra'ni·us pl. -ni·i'
ep'i·cri'sis pl. -ses'
e·pic'ri·sis pl. -ses'
ep'i·crit'ic
ep'i·cys·ti'tis
ep'i·cys·tot'o·my
ep'i·cyte'
ep'i·dem'ic
ep'i·de·mic'i·ty
ep'i·de'mi·o·log'ic
ep'i·de'mi·ol'o·gist
ep'i·de'mi·ol'o·gy
ep'i·derm'
ep'i·der'mal
ep'i·der·mat'ic
ep'i·der'ma·to·plas'ty
ep'i·der'mic
ep'i·der·mic'u·la
ep'i·der'mi·dal·i·za'tion
ep'i·der'mi·do'sis
ep'i·der'mis
ep'i·der'mi'tis
ep'i·der'mi·za'tion
ep'i·der'mo·dys·pla'si·a
—— ver·ru'ci·for'mis
ep'i·der'moid'
ep'i·der'moid·o'ma pl. -mas
or -ma·ta
ep'i·der·mol'y·sis pl. -ses'
—— bul·lo'sa
—— bullosa dys·troph'i·ca
—— bullosa he·red'i·tar'i·a
le·ta'lis
—— bullosa sim'plex'

ep'i·der·mo'ma pl. -mas or
-ma·ta
ep'i·der·mo·my·co'sis
Ep'i·der·moph'y·ton'
—— floc·co'sum
—— in'gui·na'le'
ep'i·der·mo·phy·to'sis pl.
-ses'
ep'i·der·mo'sis
ep'i·did'y·mal
ep'i·did'y·mec'to·my
ep'i·did'y·mis pl. -mi·des'
ep'i·did'y·mi'tis
ep'i·did'y·mo·or·chi'tis
ep'i·did'y·mot'o·my
ep'i·did'y·mo·va·sec'to·my
ep'i·did'y·mo·vas·os'to·my
ep'i·du'ral
ep'i·es'tri·ol'
ep'i·fas'ci·al
ep'i·fol·lic'u·li'tis
ep'i·gas·tral'gi·a
ep'i·gas'tric
ep'i·gas'tri·o·cele'
ep'i·gas'tri·um pl. -tri·a
ep'i·gas'tri·us
—— par'a·sit'i·cus
ep'i·gas'tro·cele'
ep'i·gen'e·sis
ep'i·ge·net'ic
ep'i·glot'tal
ep'i·glot'tic
ep'i·glot'ti·dec'to·my
ep'i·glot'tis
ep'i·glot·ti'tis
ep'i·gua'nine'
ep'i·hy'al
ep'i·hy'oid'
ep'i·la·mel'lar
ep'i·la'tion
ep'i·lem'ma
ep'i·lep'si·a
—— ar'ith·met'i·ca
—— mi'tis
—— par'ti·a'lis con·tin'u·a
—— ver·tig'i·no'sa
ep'i·lep'sy
ep'i·lep'tic
ep'i·lep'ti·form'
ep'i·lep'to·gen'ic
ep'i·lep·tog'e·nous
ep'i·lep'toid'
ep'i·man·dib'u·lar
ep'i·mer
ep'i·mer'ic
ep'i·mor'phic
ep'i·my'o·car'di·um

ep'i·mys'i·al
ep'i·mys'i·um pl. -i·a
ep'i·neph'rine
ep'i·neph·ri·ne'mi·a
ep'i·ne·phri'tis
ep'i·neph'ros'
ep'i·neu'ral
ep'i·neu'ri·al
ep'i·neu'ri·um
ep'i·ot'ic
ep'i·pa·tel'lar
ep'i·per'i·car'di·al
ep'i·pha·ryn'ge·al
ep'i·phar'ynx pl. -pha·
ryn'ges'
ep'i·phe·nom'e·non' pl. -na
e·piph'o·ra
ep'i·phre'nal
ep'i·phren'ic
ep'i·phy·lax'is pl. -lax'es'
e·piph'y·se'al var. of epi-
physial
ep'i·phys'i·al also epiphyseal
ep'i·phys'i·o·de'sis pl. -ses'
ep'i·phys'i·oid'
ep'i·phys'i·o·lis'the·sis pl.
-ses'
ep'i·phy'i·ol'y·sis pl. -ses'
ep'i·phys'i·o·ne·cro'sis
pl. -ses'
e·piph'y·sis pl. -ses'
—— cer'e·bri'
e·piph'y·si'tis
ep'i·phyte'
ep'i·pi'al
ep'i·pleu'ral
e·pip'o·cele'
ep'i·plo·ec'to·my
e·pip'lo·en'ter·o·cele'
ep'i·plo'ic
e·pip'lom·phal'o·cele'
e·pip'lo·on' pl. -lo·a
e·pip'lo·pex'y
ep'i·plor'rha·phy
ep'i·pro'pi·dine'
ep'ip·ter'ic
ep'i·scle'ra pl. -ras or -rae'
ep'i·scle'ral
ep'i·scle·ri'tis
e·pis'i·o·cli'si·a
e·pis'i·o·el'y·tror'rha·phy
e·pis'i·o·per'i·ne'o·plas'ty
e·pis'i·o·per'i·ne·or'rha·
phy
e·pis'i·o·plas'ty
e·pis'i·or·rha'gi·a
e·pis'i·or'rha·phy

e·pis′i·o·ste·no′sis *pl.* -ses′
e·pis′i·ot′o·my
ep′i·sode′
ep′i·sod′ic
ep′i·some′
ep′i·spa′di·a
ep′i·spa′di·ac′
ep′i·spa′di·al
ep′i·spa′di·as
ep′i·spas′tic
ep′i·sphe′noid′
ep′i·spi′nal
e·pis′ta·sis *pl.* -ses′
ep′i·stat′ic
ep′i·stax′is
ep′i·ster′nal
ep′i·ster′num *pl.* -nums *or*
  -na
ep′i·stro′phe·us
ep′i·stroph′ic
ep′i·tar′sus
ep′i·ten·din′e·um
ep′i·ten′on
ep′i·tha·lam′ic
ep′i·thal′a·mus *pl.* -mi′
ep′i·tha·lax′i·a
ep′i·the′li·al
ep′i·the′li·al·i·za′tion
ep′i·the′li·al·ize′, -ized′, -iz′-
  ing
ep′i·the′li·i′tis
ep′i·the′li·o·cho′ri·al
ep′i·the′li·o·ge·net′ic
ep′i·the′li·oid′
ep′i·the′li·o′ma *pl.* -mas *or*
  -ma·ta
—— ad′e·noi′des′ cys′ti·cum
—— ba′so·cel′lu·lar′e′
—— cho′ri·o·ep′i·der·ma′le′
—— con·ta′gi·o′sum
ep′i·the′li·o·ma·to′sis
ep′i·the′li·om′a·tous
ep′i·the′li·o·my·o′sis *pl.*
  -ses′
ep′i·the·li′tis
ep′i·the′li·um *pl.* -li·a
—— an·te′ri·us cor′ne·ae′
—— cor′ne·ae′
—— duc′tus sem′i·cir′cu·
  lar′is
—— len′tis
ep′i·the′li·za′tion
ep′i·the′lize′, -lized′, -liz′ing
e·pith′e·sis *pl.* -ses′
ep′i·thi′a·zide′
ep′i·trich′i·al
ep′i·trich′i·um

ep′i·troch′le·a
ep′i·troch′le·ar
ep′i·troch′le·ar′is
ep′i·tu·ber′cu·lo′sis *pl.* -ses′
ep′i·tym·pan′ic
ep′i·tym′pa·num
ep′i·zo′ic
ep′i·zo′on′ *pl.* -zo′a
ep′i·zo·ot′ic
ep′o·nych′i·um
ep′o·nym
ep′o·nym′ic
e·pon′y·mous
ep′o·oph′o·ron′
Ep′som salt
Ep′stein′
—— pearls
—— syndrome
Ep′stein-Barr′ virus
e·pu′lis *pl.* -li·des′
ep′u·loid′
ep′u·lo·fi·bro′ma *pl.* -mas *or*
  -ma·ta
ep′u·lo′sis
e′qual
e·qua′tion
e·qua′tion·al
e·qua′tor
—— bul′bi′ oc′u·li′
—— len′tis
e′qua·to′ri·al
e′qui·ax′i·al
e′qui·dom′i·nant
e′qui·lat′er·al
e·quil′i·brate′, -brat′ed,
  -brat′ing
e·quil′i·bra′tion
e′qui·lib′ra·to′ry
e′qui·lib′ri·um *pl.* -ri·ums *or*
  -ri·a
e′qui·lin
e′quine′
eq′ui·no·ca′vus
eq′ui·no·val′gus
eq′ui·no·var′us
e·qui′nus
e′qui·po·ten′tial
e·quiv′a·lence
e·quiv′a·lent
e·ra′sion
Er′a·ty′rus
—— cus′pi·da′tus
Erb
—— palsy
—— paralysis
—— point

—— scapulohumeral juve-
nile muscular dystrophy
—— sign
—— spastic spinal paraple-
gia
—— syphilitic paralysis
Erb′-Char·cot′ disease
Erb′-Du·chenne′ paralysis
Er′ben sign
Erb′-Gold′flam′ symptom
complex
Erb′-Zim′mer·lin type
Erd′mann reagent
e·rect′
e·rec′tile
e·rec′tion
e·rec′tor
—— cli·to′ri·dis
—— pe′nis
—— pi′li′
—— spi′nae′
e·rep′sin
er′e·thism
er′e·this′mic
er′e·this′tic
er′e·thit′ic
erg
er·ga′si·a
er·ga′si·a·try
er·gas′tic
er·gas′to·plasm
er′go·ba′sine′
er′go·ba′si·nine′
er′go·cal·cif′er·ol′
er′go·gram′
er′go·graph′
er·gom′e·ter
er′go·met′rine′
er′go·met′ri·nine′
er′go·no′vine′
er′go·phore′
er′go·plasm
er′go·sine′
er·go′si·nine′
er′go·some′
er·gos′ta·nol′
er·gos′ter·ol′
er′go·stet′rine′
er′got
er·got′a·mine′
er′go·tam′i·nine′
er′go·ther′a·py
er′go·thi′o·ne′ine′
er′got·in
er′got′i·nine′
er′got·ism
er′got·ized′

Er'ich·sen disease
er'i·gens
er'i·om'e·ter
E·ris'ta·lis
e·rode', e·rod'ed, e·rod'ing
er'o·gen'ic
e·rog'e·nous (arousing sex-
    ual desire)
♦aerogenous
er'o·ma'ni·a
e'ros' (the sum of all
    self-preservative instincts)
♦erose
e·rose' (having an irregularly
    toothed edge)
♦eros
e·ro'si·o' in'ter·dig'
    i·ta'lis blas'to·my·ce'ti·ca
e·ro'sion
e·ro'sive
e·rot'ic
e·rot'i·ca
e·rot'i·cism
e·rot'i·co·ma'ni·a
er'o·tism
e·ro'to·gen'ic
e·ro'to·ma'ni·a
e·ro'to·ma'ni·ac'
e·ro'to·path'
er'o·to·path'ic
er'o·top'a·thy
e·ro'to·pho'bi·a
er'rhine'
e·ru'cic
e·ruc'tate', -tat·ed, -tat'ing
e'ruc·ta'tion
e·rup'tion
e·rup'tive
E·ryn'gi·um
er'y·sip'e·las
—— am'bu·lans'
—— bul·lo'sum
—— chron'i·cum
—— dif·fu'sum
—— glab'rum
—— med'i·ca·men·to'sum
—— mi'grans'
—— per'stans'
er'y·si·pel'a·tous
er'y·sip'e·loid''
Er'y·sip'e·lo·thrix'
—— in·sid'i·o'sa
e·rys'i·phake'
er'y·the'ma
—— ab ig'ne'
—— an'nu·lar'e' cen·trif'u·
gum

—— ar·thrit'i·cum ep'i·
dem'i·cum
—— bru·cel'lum
—— bul·lo'sum
—— ca·lo'ri·cum
—— chron'i·cum mi'grans'
—— chronicum migrans Af·
ze'li·us
—— cir'ci·na'tum
—— el'e·va'tum di·u'ti·num
—— en·dem'i·cum
—— ep'i·dem'i·cum
—— fig'u·ra'tum per'stans'
—— fu'gax'
—— gan'gre·no'sum
—— glu'te·a'le'
—— gy·ra'tum mi'grans'
—— hy'per·e'mi·cum
—— in·du'ra·ti'vum
—— in'du·ra'tum
—— in·fec'ti·o'sum
—— in'ter·tri'go
—— i'ris
—— mar'gi·na'tum
—— mi'grans'
—— mul'ti·for'me'
—— no·do'sum
—— nu'chae'
—— pal·mar'e' he·red'i·tar'i·
um
—— pap'u·la'tum
—— par'a·lyt'i·cum
—— per'ni·o'
—— per'stans'
—— punc·ta'tum
—— scar'la·ti'ni·for'me'
—— sim'plex'
—— simplex gy·ra'tum
—— so·lar'e'
—— tox'i·cum ne·o'na·
to'rum
—— trau·mat'i·cum
—— tu·ber'cu·la'tum
—— ur'ti·cans'
—— ven·e'na'tum
—— ve·sic'u·lo'sum
er'y·the'ma·toid'
er'y·the'ma·tous
er'y·the'moid'
er'y·ther·mal'gi·a
er'y·thral'gi·a
er'y·thras'ma
e·ryth're·de'ma
er'y·thre'mi·a
er'y·thre'mic
er'y·thre'moid'
er'y·thrite'

e·ryth'ri·tol'
e·ryth'ri·tyl
e·ryth'ro·blast'
e·ryth'ro·blas·te'mi·a
e·ryth'ro·blas'tic
e·ryth'ro·blas'to·ma pl.
    -mas or -ma·ta
e·ryth'ro·blas'to·pe'ni·a
e·ryth'ro·blas'to·sis pl. -ses'
—— fe·ta'lis
—— ne·o'na·to'rum
e·ryth'ro·blas·tot'ic
e·ryth'ro·chlo·ro'pi·a
e·ryth'ro·chlo·rop'si·a
e·ryth'ro·chlo·ro·py
e·ryth'ro·chro'mi·a
er'y·throc'la·sis
e·ryth'ro·clas'tic
e·ryth'ro·conte'
e·ryth'ro·cy'a·no'sis pl.
    -ses'
e·ryth'ro·cyte'
e·ryth'ro·cy·the'mi·a
e·ryth'ro·cyt'ic
e·ryth'ro·cy'to·blast'
e·ryth'ro·cy'tol'y·sin
e·ryth'ro·cy'tol'y·sis pl.
    -ses'
e·ryth'ro·cy·tom'e·ter
e·ryth'ro·cy·tom'e·try
e·ryth'ro·cy'to·op'so·nin
e·ryth'ro·cy'to·pe'ni·a
e·ryth'ro·cy'to·poi·e'sis pl.
    -ses'
e·ryth'ro·cy'to·poi·et'ic
e·ryth'ro·cy'tor·rhex'is
e·ryth'ro·cy·tos'chi·sis
e·ryth'ro·cy·to'sis pl. -ses'
—— meg'a·lo·splen'i·ca
e·ryth'ro·cy'to·trop'ic
e·ryth'ro·de·gen'er·a·tive
e·ryth'ro·der'ma
—— des·quam'a·ti'vum
—— ich'thy·o'si·for'me' con·
gen'i·tum
—— mac'u·lo'sa per'stans'
—— pso'ri·at'i·cum
e·ryth'ro·der'mi·a
—— des·quam'a·ti'va
e·ryth'ro·dex'trin
e·ryth'ro·don'ti·a
e·ryth'ro·gen
e·ryth'ro·gen'e·sis pl. -ses'
e·ryth'ro·gen'ic
e·ryth'ro·gone'
e·ryth'ro·go'ni·um
er'y·throid'

e·ryth'ro·ker'a·to·der'mi·a
er'y·throl'
e·ryth'ro·leu·ke'mi·a
e·ryth'ro·leu·ko·blas·to'sis
e·ryth'ro·leu·ko'sis *pl.* -ses'
e·ryth'ro·leu'ko·throm'bo·
  cy·the'mi·a
er'y·throl'y·sin
er'y·throl'y·sis *pl.* -ses'
e·ryth'ro·me·lal'gi·a
e·ryth'ro·me'li·a
er'y·throm'e·ter
e·ryth'ro·my'cin
e·ryth'ro·my'e·lo'sis *pl.*
  -ses'
er'y·thron'
e·ryth'ro·ne'o·cy·to'sis *pl.*
  -ses'
e·ryth'ro·pe'ni·a
e·ryth'ro·phage'
e·ryth'ro·pha'gi·a
e·ryth'ro·phag'o·cy·to'sis
  pl. -ses'
e·ryth'ro·phe·re'sis *pl.* -ses'
e·ryth'ro·phil'
er'yth·roph'i·lous
e·ryth'ro·phle'ine'
e·ryth'ro·pho'bi·a
e·ryth'ro·phore'
e·ryth'ro·phose'
er'y·thro'pi·a
e·ryth'ro·pla'si·a of Quey·
  rat'
e·ryth'ro·plas'tid
e·ryth'ro·poi·e'sis *pl.* -ses'
e·ryth'ro·poi·et'ic
e·ryth'ro·poi'e·tin
e·ryth'ro·pros'o·pal'gi·a
er'y·throp'si·a
er'y·throp'sin
e·ryth'ror·rhex'is
er'y·throse'
—— per'i·buc·ca'le pig'men·
  taire'
e·ryth'ro·sed'i·men·ta'tion
e·ryth'ro·sin
e·ryth'ro·sin'o·phil'
er'y·thro'sis *pl.* -ses'
e·ryth'ro·sta'sis *pl.* -ses'
e·ryth'ro·tox'in
er'y·throx'y·lon'
e·ryth'ru·lose'
er'y·thru'ri·a
Es'bach'
—— method
—— reagent
es·cape', -caped', -cap'ing

es'char'
es'cha·ro'sis
es'cha·rot'ic
Esch'e·rich'i·a
—— co'li'
es'chro·la'li·a
es·cor'cin
es'cu·le'tin
es'cu·lin
es·cutch'eon
es·er'a·mine'
es·er'i·dine'
es'er·ine'
Es'march' operation
e'so·eth'moi·di'tis
es'o·gas·tri'tis
e·soph'a·gal'gi·a
e·soph'a·ge'al
e·soph'a·gec·ta'si·a
e·soph'a·gec·ta'sis *pl.* -ses'
e·soph'a·gec'to·my
e·soph'a·gism
e·soph'a·gis'mus
e·soph'a·gi'tis
e·soph'a·go·bron'chi·al
e·soph'a·go·cele'
e·soph'a·go·du'o·de·nos'to·
  my
e·soph'a·go·dyn'i·a
e·soph'a·go·en'ter·os'to·
  my
e·soph'a·go·e·soph'a·
  gos'to·my
e·soph'a·go·gas·trec'to·my
e·soph'a·go·gas'tric
e·soph'a·go·gas'tro·plas'ty
e·soph'a·go·gas'tro·scope'
e·soph'a·go'gas·tros'co·py
e·soph'a·go·gas·tros'to·my
e·soph'a·go·gram'
e·soph'a·go·hi·a'tal
e·soph'a·go·je'ju·nos'to·
  my
e·soph'a·go·lar'yn·gec'to·
  my
e·soph'a·gom'e·ter
e·soph'a·go·my'co·sis *pl.*
  -ses'
e·soph'a·go·my'ot'o·my
e·soph'a·gop'a·thy
e·soph'a·go·pha·ryn'ge·al
e·soph'a·go·plas'ty
e·soph'a·gop'to·sis *pl.* -ses'
e·soph'a·go·sal'i·var'y
e·soph'a·go·scope'
e·soph'a·gos'co·py
e·soph'a·go·spasm

e·soph'a·go·ste·no'sis *pl.*
  -ses'
e·soph'a·gos'to·ma
e·soph'a·go·sto·mi'a·sis *pl.*
  -ses'
e·soph'a·gos'to·my
—— ex·ter'na
—— in·ter'na
e·soph'a·go·tome'
e·soph'a·got'o·my
e·soph'a·go·tra'che·al
e·soph'a·gus *pl.* -gi'
e·soph'o·gram'
es'o·pho'ri·a
es'o·pho'ric
es'o·tro'pi·a
es·pun'di·a
es'sence
es·sen'tial
Es'ser inlay graft
Es'sick cell band
es'ter
es'ter·ase'
es·ter'i·fi·ca'tion
es·ter'i·fy', -fied', -fy'ing
es·the'si·a
es·the'si·ol'o·gy
es·the'si·om'e·ter
es·the'si·o·neu'ro·blas·
  to'ma *pl.* -mas *or* -ma·ta
es·the'si·o·neu'ro·ep'i·
  the'li·o'ma *pl.* -mas *or* -ma·
  ta
es·the'si·o·neu·ro'ma *pl.*
  -mas *or* -ma·ta
es·the'si·o·phys'i·ol'o·gy
es·thet'ic
es'thi·om'e·ne
es'ti·val
es'ti·va'tion
es'ti·vo-au·tum'nal
Est'lan'der operation
es'to·late'
es'tra·di'ol'
es'tra·zi·nol'
es·tri'a·sis *pl.* -ses'
es'trin
es'tri·ol'
es'tro·gen
es'tro·gen'ic
es'trone'
es'trous
es'tru·al
es'tru·a'tion
es'y·late'
et'a·fed'rine'
é·tat'

—— la·cu·naire′
—— ma·me·lon·ne′
—— mar·bre′
eth′a·cry′nate′
eth′a·cry′nic
e·tham′bu·tol′
e·tham′i·van′
e·tham′syl·ate′
eth′a·nal′
eth′ane′
eth′a·no′ic
eth′a·nol′
eth′a·nol′a·mine′
eth′a·ver′ine
eth′chlor·vy′nol′
eth′ene′
eth′e·noid′
eth′e·none′
e′ther
e·the′re·al
e′ther·i·za′tion
eth′i·cal
eth′ics
eth′i·dene′
eth′i·nam′ate′
eth′ine′
e·thi′nyl *var. of* ethynyl
e·thi′on·a·mide′
e·thi′o·nine′
e·this′ter·one′
eth′mo·car·di′tis
eth′mo·ceph′a·lus *pl.* -li′
eth′mo·fron′tal
eth′moid′
eth·moi′dal
eth′moid·ec′to·my
eth′moid·i′tis
eth′moid·ot′o·my
eth′mo·lac′ri·mal
eth′mo·max·il′lar·y
eth′mo·na′sal
eth′mo·pal′a·tal
eth′mo·sphe′noid′
eth′mo·tur′bi·nal
eth′mo·vo′mer·ine
eth′nic
eth′no·graph′ic *or* eth′no·graph′i·cal
eth·nog′ra·phy
eth′no·log′ic *or* eth′no·log′i·cal
eth·nol′o·gy
eth′o·caine
eth′o·hep′ta·zine′
eth′o·hex′a·di′ol′
e·thol′o·gy
eth′o·nam′

eth′o·pro′pa·zine′
eth′o·sux′i·mide′
eth′o·to′in
eth′ox·a·zene′
eth′ox′y
eth′ox·zol′a·mide′
eth′y·benz·tro′pine′
eth′yl
eth′yl·al′de·hyde′
eth′yl·ate′
eth′yl·a′tion
eth′yl·ene′
eth′yl·ene·di·a·mine′
eth′yl·ene·di·a·mine·tet′ra·a·ce′tic
eth′yl·e′nic
eth′yl·e·phed′rine
eth′yl·es′tren·ol′
eth′yl·hy′dro·cu′pre·ine′
eth′yl·i·dene′
eth′yl·mor′phine′
eth′yl·stib′a·mine′
eth′yne′
e·thy′ner·one′
e·thy′no·di′ol′
e·thy′nyl *also* ethinyl
e·thy′nyl·es′tra·di′ol′
e′ti·o·cho·lan′o·lone′
e′ti·o·la′tion
e′ti·o·log′ic
e·ti·ol′o·gy
e′ti·o·path′o·gen′e·sis *pl.* -ses′
e′ti·o·por′phy·rin
e·trot′o·my
Eu′bac·ter′ri·a′les′
eu·bac·te′ri·um *pl.* -ri·a
eu′caine′
euc·at′ro·pine′
eu′chlor·hy′dri·a
eu·chol′i·a
eu·chro·mat′ic
eu·chro′ma·tin
eu·chro′ma·top′si·a
eu·chro′mo·some′
eu·es·the′si·a
eu·gen′ic
eu·gen′ics
eu′ge·nol′
eu·glob′u·lin
eu·gnath′ic
eu·gon′ic
eu·kar′y·ote′
eu·ker′a·tin
eu·ki·ne′si·a
eu·lam′i·nate′
Eu′len·burg′ disease

eu·mor′phic
Eu′my·ce′tes′
eu·noi′a
eu′nuch
eu′nuch·ism
eu′nuch·oid′
eu′nuch·oid·ism
eu·pho′ni·a
eu′pho·ret′ic
eu·pho′ri·a
eu·pho′ic
eu·pho′ri·ant
eu′ploid′
eu·ploid′y
eup·ne′a
eu·prac′tic
eu·prax′i·a
eu·pro·cin
eu·py′rene′
eu′ro·pis′o·ceph′a·lus *pl.* -li′
eu′ro·pro·ceph′a·lus *pl.* -li′
eu′ry·ce·phal′ic
eu′ry·ceph′a·lous
eu·ryc·ne′mic
eu·ryg·nath′ic
eu·ryg′na·thism
eu·ryg′na·thous
eu′ry·ther′mic
eu·sta′chi·an
eu·sta′chi·um
eu·sys′to·le
eu·tha·na′si·a
eu·thy′roid′
eu·thy′roid·ism
eu·top′ic
Eu′tri·at′o·ma
e·vac′u·ant
e·vac′u·ate′, -at′ed, -at′ing
e·vac′u·a′tion
e·vac′u·a′tor
e·vag′i·nate′, -nat′ed, -nat′ing
e·vag′i·na′tion
ev′a·nes′cent
Ev′ans blue
e′ven·tra′tion
Ev′ers·busch′ operation
e·ver′sion
e·vert′
e·ver′tor
ev′i·ra′tion
e·vis′cer·ate′, -at′ed, -at′ing
e·vis′cer·a′tion
ev′o·ca′tion
ev′o·ca′tor
e·voke′, e·voked′, e·vok′ing
ev′o·lu′tion

e·vul′si·o′
e·vul′sion
E′wald
—— node
—— tube
Ew′art sign
E wave
Ew′ing sarcome
ex·ac′er·bate′, -bat′ed, -bat′-
  ing
ex·ac′er·ba′tion
ex·al·ta′tion
ex·am′i·na′tion
ex·am′ine, -ined, -in·ing
ex·am′in·ee′
ex·an′them
—— su′bi·tum
ex′an·the′ma pl. -ma·ta or
  -mas
ex′an·the·mat′ic
ex·an·them′a·tous
ex′ca·va′ti·o′ pl. -va′ti·o′nes′
—— dis′ci′
—— pa·pil′lae′ ner′vi′ op′ti·
  ci′
—— rec′to·u′ter·i′na
—— rec′to·ves′i·ca′lis
—— ves′i·co·u′ter·i′na
ex′ca·va′tion
exca·va′tor
ex·cen′tric var. of eccentric
ex·cer′e·bra′tion
ex·cip′i·ent
ex·cise′, -cised′, -cis′ing
ex·ci′sion
ex·cit′a·ble
ex·cit′a·bil′i·ty
ex·ci′tant
ex·ci·ta′tion
ex·cit′a·to′ry
ex·cite′, -cit′ed, -cit′ing
ex·ci′tor
ex·clu′sion
ex·coch′le·a′tion
ex·con′ju·gant
ex·co′ri·ate′, -at′ed, -at′ing
ex·co′ri·a′tion
ex′cre·ment
ex′cre·men·ti′tious
ex·cres′cence
ex·cres′cent
ex·cre′ta
ex·crete′, -cret′ed, -cret′ing
ex·cre′tion
ex′cre·to′ry
ex·cur′sion
ex·cur′sive

ex′cur·va′tion
ex′cur′va·ture
ex·cy′clo·pho′ri·a
ex·cy′clo·tro′pi·a
ex′cys·ta′tion
ex·ec′u·tant
ex′e·dens
ex′el·cy·mo′sis pl. -ses′
ex·e′mi·a
ex′en·ce·pha′li·a
ex′en·ce·phal′ic
ex′en·ceph′a·lus pl. -li′
ex′en·ceph′a·ly
ex·en′ter·ate′, -at′ed, -at′ing
ex·en′ter·a′tion
ex·en′ter·i′tis
ex′er·cise′, -cised′, -cis′ing
ex·er′e·sis pl. -ses′
ex′er·gon′ic
ex′fe·ta′tion
ex·flag′e·la′tion
ex·fo′li·ate′, -at′ed, -at′ing
ex·fo′li·a′tion
ex·fo′li·a·tive
ex′ha·la′tion
ex·hale′, -haled′, -hal′ing
ex·haus′tion
ex·haus′tive
ex·hib′it
ex′hi·bi′tion
ex′hi·bi′tion·ism
ex′hi·bi′tion·ist
ex·hil′a·rate′, -rat′ed, -rat′-
  ing
ex·hil′a·ra′tion
ex′hu·ma′tion
ex·hume′, -humed′, -hum′-
  ing
ex′is·ten′tial
ex′is·ten′tial·ism
ex′i·tus
ex′o·bi·ol′o·gy
ex′o·car′di·a
ex′o·car′di·al
ex′o·cat′a·pho′ri·a
ex·oc·cip′i·tal
ex′o·cer′vix pl. -vi·ces′ or
  -vix·es
ex′o·cho′ri·on′ pl. -ri·a
ex′o·coe′lom
ex′o·coe·lom′ic
ex′o·crine
ex′o·cy·to′sis pl. -ses′
ex′o·don′ti·a
ex′o·don′tics
ex′o·don′tist
ex′o·en′zyme′

ex′o·er′gic
ex′o·e·ryth′ro·cyt′ic
ex·og′a·mous
ex·og′a·my
ex′o·gas′tru·la
ex′o·gas′tru·la′tion
ex′o·ge·net′ic
ex·o·gen′ic
ex·og′e·nous (derived from
  external causes)
♦axogenous
ex′o·me·tri′tis
ex·om′pha·los
ex′o·pep′ti·dase′
ex′o·pho′ri·a
ex′o·pho′ric
ex′oph·thal′mic
ex′oph·thal·mom′e·ter
ex′oph·thal·mom′e·try
ex′oph·thal′mos
ex′o·phyt′ic
ex′o·plasm
ex′os·mose′
ex′os·mo′sis
ex′os·mot′ic
ex·os′to·sec′to·my
ex·os′tosed′
ex·os′to·sis pl. -ses′
—— car′ti·la·gin′e·a
ex′os·tot′ic
ex′o·ther′mal
ex′o·ther′mic
ex′o·tox′ic
ex′o·tox′in
ex′o·tro′pi·a
ex′o·tro′pic
ex·pan′sile
ex·pan′sive
ex·pect′ant
ex·pec′to·rant
ex·pec′to·rate′, -rat′ed,
  -rat′ing
ex·pec′to·ra′tion
ex·pel′, -pelled′, -pel′ling
ex·pe′ri·en′tial
ex·per′i·ment
ex·per′i·men′tal
ex·per′i·men·ta′tion
ex′pert′
ex′pi·ra′tion
ex·pi′ra·to′ry
ex·pire′, -pired′, -pir′ing
ex′plant′
ex·plode′, -plod′ed, -plod′ing
ex′plo·ra′tion
ex·plo′ra·to′ry
ex·plor′er

ex·plo'sion
ex·plo'sive
ex·pose', -posed', -pos'ing
ex·po'sure
ex·press'
ex·pres'sion
ex'pres·siv'i·ty
ex·pul'sion
ex·pul'sive
ex·san'gui·nate', -nat'ed, -nat'ing
ex·san'gui·na'tion
ex·san'guine
ex·sect'
ex·sec'tion
ex·sic'cant
ex'sic·cate', -cat'ed, -cat'ing
ex'sic·ca'tion
ex'sic·ca·tive
ex'sic·ca·tor
ex·sorp'tion
ex'stro·phy
ex'suf·fla'tion
ex'suf·fla'tor
ex·ten'sion
ex·ten'sor
—— car'pi ra'di·a'lis ac'ces·so'ri·us
—— carpi radialis brev'i·or'
—— carpi radialis brev'is
—— carpi radialis in'ter·me'di·us
—— carpi radialis lon'gi·or'
—— carpi radialis lon'gus
—— carpi ul·nar'is
—— carpi ulnaris dig'i·ti' min'i·mi'
—— coc·cyg'e·us
—— com·mu'nis pol'li·cis et in'di·cis
—— dig'i·ti' an'nu·lar'is
—— digiti me'di·i'
—— digiti min'i·mi'
—— digiti quin'ti' pro'pri·us
—— dig'i·to'rum
—— digitorum brev'is
—— digitorum brevis ma'nus
—— digitorum com·mu'nis
—— digitorum lon'gus
—— hal'lu·cis brev'is
—— hallucis lon'gus
—— hallucis pro'pri·us
—— in'di·cis
—— indicis pro'pri·us
—— os'sis met'a·car'pi' pol'li·cis

—— ossis met'a·tar'si' hal'lu·cis
—— pol'li·cis brev'is
—— pollicis lon'gus
—— pri'mi' in'ter·no'di·i' lon'gus hal'lu·cis
—— primi internodii pol'li·cis
—— se·cun'di' in'ter·no'di·i' pol'li·cis
ex·te'ri·or·i·za'tion
ex'tern'
ex·ter'nad'
ex·ter'nal
ex·ter'nal·ize', -ized, -iz'ing
ex'ter·o·cep'tive
ex'ter·o·cep'tor
ex'ter·o·fec'tive
ex·tinc'tion
ex'tir·pate', -pat'ed, -pat'ing
ex'tir·pa'tion
Ex'ton
—— and Rose test
—— method
—— quantitative reagent
—— test
ex·tor'sion
ex'tra·ar·tic'u·lar
ex'tra·buc'cal
ex'tra·bul'bar
ex'tra·cap'su·lar
ex'tra·car'di·ac'
ex'tra·car'di·al
ex'tra·car'pal
ex'tra·cel'lu·lar
ex'tra·cer'e·bral
ex'tra·chro'mo·so'mal
ex'tra·cor'po·ral
ex'tra·cor·po're·al
ex'tra·cor·pus'cu·lar
ex'tra·cra'ni·al
ex·tract' v.
ex'tract' n.
ex·trac'tion
ex·trac'tive
ex·trac'tor
ex'tra·cys'tic
ex'tra·du'ral
ex'tra·em'bry·on'ic
ex'tra·ep'i·phys'e·al
ex'tra·e·ryth'ro·cyt'ic
ex'tra·e·soph'a·ge'al
ex'tra·fas'ci·al
ex'tra·gen'i·tal
ex'tra·gin'gi·val
ex'tra·he·pat'ic
ex'tra·lig'a·men'tous

ex'tra·mam'ma·ry
ex'tra·med'ul·lar'y
ex'tra·mu'ral
ex'tra·ne·ous
ex'tra·nu'cle·ar
ex'tra·oc'u·lar
ex'tra·o'ral
ex'tra·os'se·ous
ex'tra·pa·ren'chy·mal
ex'tra·pel'vic
ex'tra·per'i·car'di·al
ex'tra·per'i·ne·al (outside the perineum)
♦extraperitoneal
ex'tra·per'i·os'te·al
ex'tra·per'i·to·ne·al (outside the peritoneum)
♦extraperineal
ex'tra·pla·cen'tal
ex'tra·pleu'ral
ex·trap'o·late', -lat'ed, -lat'ing
ex·trap'o·la'tion
ex'tra·pros·tat'ic
ex'tra·psy'chic
ex'tra·pul'mo·nar'y
ex'tra·py·ram'i·dal
ex'tra·rec'tus
ex'tra·re'nal
ex'tra·sen'so·ry
ex'tra·sphinc·ter'ic
ex'tra·spi'nal
ex'tra·sys'to·le
ex'tra·tho·rac'ic
ex'tra·thy·roi'dal
ex'tra·tu'bal
ex'tra·u'ter·ine
ex'tra·vag'i·nal
ex·trav'a·sate', -sat'ed, -sat'ing
ex·trav'a·sa'tion
ex'tra·vas'cu·lar
ex'tra·ven·tric'u·lar
ec'tra·ver'sion
ex'tra·vis'u·al
ex·tre'mis
ex·trem'i·tas pl. -trem'i·ta'tes'
—— a·cro'mi·a'lis cla·vic'u·lae'
—— anterior li·e'nis
—— inferior
—— inferior li·e'nis
—— inferior re'nis
—— inferior tes'tis
—— posterior li·e'nis
—— ster·na'lis cla·vic'u·lae'

—— superior
—— superior li·e′nis
—— superior re′nis
—— superior tes′tis
—— tu·bar′i·a o·var′i·i′
—— u′ter·i′na o·var′i·i′
ex·trem′i·ty
ex·trin′sic
ex·tro·gas′tru·la′tion
ex·tro·ver′sion
ex·tro·vert′
ex·trude′, -trud′ed, -trud′ing
ex·tru′sion
ex·tu′bate′, -bat′ed, -bat′ing
ex′tu·ba′tion
ex·u′ber·ance
ex·u′ber·ant
ex′u·date′
ex′u·da′tion
ex·u′da·tive
ex·ude′, -ud′ed, -ud′ing
ex·u′vi·a′tion
eye
eye′ball′
eye′brow′
eye′cup′
eye′lash′
eye′lid′
eye′piece′
eye′point′
eye′spot′
eye′strain′
eye′tooth′
eye′wash′

F

fa·bel′la pl. -lae′
Fa′ber anemia
Fab fragment
fab′ri·ca′tion
Fa·bri′cus-Mol′ler test
Fa′bry disease
face
face′bow′
face′-lift′
fac′et
fa′cial
fa′ci·a′lis
fa′ci·es′ pl. fa′ci·es′
—— ab·dom′i·na′lis
—— anterior an′te·bra′chi·i′
—— anterior bra′chi·i′
—— anterior cor′ne·ae′
—— anterior cru′ris

—— anterior den′ti·um
prae′mo·lar′i·um et mo·lar′i·um
—— anterior fem′o·ris
—— anterior glan′du·lae′
su′pra·re·na′lis
—— anterior i′ri·dis
—— anterior lat′er·a′lis
hu′mer·i′
—— anterior len′tis
—— anterior max·il′lae′
—— anterior me′di·a′lis
hu′mer·i′
—— anterior pal′pe·brar′um
—— anterior pan·cre′a·tis
—— anterior par′tis pe·tro′sae′ os′sis tem′po·ra′lis
—— anterior pa·tel′lae′
—— anterior pros′ta·tae′
—— anterior py·ram′i·dis
os′sis tem′po·ra′lis
—— anterior ra′di·i′
—— anterior re′nis
—— anterior ul′nae′
—— an′ter·o·lat′er·a′lis
car′ti·lag′i·nis ar′y·te·noi′de·ae′
—— ar·tic′u·lar′es in·fe′ri·o′res at·lan′tis
—— articulares inferiores ver′te·brae′
—— articulares su·pe′ri·o′res ver′te·brae′
—— ar·tic′u·lar′is
—— articularis a·cro′mi·a′lis cla·vic′u·lae′
—— articularis a·cro′mi·i′
—— articularis anterior ax′is
—— articularis anterior cal·ca′ne·i′
—— articularis anterior ep′i·stro′phe·i′
—— articularis ar′y·tae·noi′de·a car′ti·lag′i·nis cri·coi′de·ae′
—— articularis ar′y·te·noi′de·a car′ti·lag′i·nis cri·coi′de·ae′
—— articularis cal·ca′ne·a anterior ta′li′
—— articularis calcanea me′di·a ta′li′
—— articularis calcanea posterior ta′li′
—— articularis cap′i·tis cos′tae′

—— articularis capitis fib′u·lae′
—— articularis ca·pit′u·li′ cos′tae′
—— articularis capituli fib′u·lae′
—— articularis car′pe·a ra′di·i′
—— articularis car′ti·lag′i·nis ar′y·tae·noi′de·ae′
—— articularis cartilaginis ar′y·te·noi′de·ae′
—— articularis cu·boi′de·a cal·ca′ne·i′
—— articularis fib′u·lar′is tib′i·ae′
—— articularis inferior tib′i·ae′
—— articularis mal′le·o·lar′is fib′u·lae′
—— articularis malleolaris tib′i·ae′
—— articularis me′di·a cal·ca′ne·i′
—— articularis na·vic′u·lar′is ta′li′
—— articularis os′sis tem′po·ra′lis
—— articularis os′si·um
—— articularis pa·tel′lae′
—— articularis posterior ax′is
—— articularis posterior cal·ca′ne·i′
—— articularis posterior ep′is·tro′phe·i′
—— articularis ster·na′lis cla·vic′u·lae′
—— articularis superior tib′i·ae′
—— articularis ta·lar′is anterior cal·ca′ne·i′
—— articularis talaris me′di·a cal·ca′ne·i′
—— articularis talaris posterior cal·ca′ne·i′
—— articularis thy′re·oi′de·a car′ti·lag′i·nis cri·coi′de·ae′
—— articularis thy·roi′de·a car′ti·lag′i·nis cri·coi′de·ae′
—— articularis tu·ber′cu·li′ cos′tae′
—— au·ric′u·lar′is
—— auricularis os′sis il′i·i′
—— auricularis ossis il′i·um
—— auricularis ossis sa′cri′
—— bo·vi′na

—— buc·ca′lis den′tis
—— cer′e·bra′lis
—— cerebralis a′lae′ mag′nae′
—— cerebralis alae ma·jo′ris
—— cerebralis os′sis fron·ta′lis
—— cerebralis ossis pa·ri′e·ta′lis
—— cerebralis par′tis squa·mo′sae′ os′sis tem′po·ra′lis
—— cerebralis squa′mae′ tem′po·ra′is
—— co′li·ca li·e′nis
—— con·tac′tus den′tis
—— con·vex′a cer′e·bri′
—— cos·ta′lis
—— costalis pul·mo′nis
—— costalis scap′u·lae′
—— di′a·phrag·mat′i·ca
—— diaphragmatica cor′dis
—— diaphragmatica hep′a·tis
—— diaphragmatica li·e′nis
—— diaphragmatica pul·mo′nis
—— dis·ta′lis den′tis
—— dor·sa′les′ dig′i·to′rum ma′nus
—— dorsales digitorum pe′-dis
—— dor·sa′lis an′ti·bra′chi·i′
—— dorsalis os′sis sa′cri′
—— dorsalis ra′di·i′
—— dorsalis scap′u·lae′
—— dorsalis ul′nae′
—— ex·ter′na os′sis fron·ta′lis
—— externa ossis pa·ri′e·ta′lis
—— fa′ci·a′lis den′tis
—— fib′u·lar′is cru′ris
—— fron·ta′lis
—— frontalis os′sis fron·ta′lis
—— gas′tri·ca
—— gastrica li·e′nis
—— glu′te·a os′sis il′i·i′
—— hip′po·crat′i·ca
—— inferior cer′e·bri′
—— inferior hem′is·phae′ri·i′ cer′e·bel′li′
—— inferior hem′is·phe′ri·i′ cer′e·bel′li′
—— inferior hemispherii cer′e·bri′

—— inferior hep′a·tis
—— inferior lin′guae′
—— inferior mes′en·ceph′a·li′
—— inferior pan·cre′a·tis
—— inferior par′tis pe·tro′sae′ os′sis tem′po·ra′lis
—— inferior py·ram′i·dis os′sis tem′po·ra′lis
—— in′fer·o·lat′er·a′lis pros·ta′tae′
—— in′fra·tem′po·ra′lis max·il′lae′
—— in′ter·lo·bar′es′ pul·mo′nis
—— in·ter′na os′sis fron·ta′lis
—— interna ossis pa·ri′e·ta′lis
—— in·tes′ti·na′lis
—— intestinalis u′ter·i′
—— la′bi·a′lis den′tis
—— lat′er·a′les′ dig′i·to′rum ma′nus
—— laterales digitorum pe′-dis
—— lat′er·a′lis
—— lateralis bra′chi·i′
—— lateralis cru′ris
—— lateralis den′ti·um in′ci·si·vo′rum et ca′ni·no′rum
—— lateralis fem′o·ris
—— lateralis fib′u·lae′
—— lateralis os′sis zy′go·mat′i·ci′
—— lateralis o·var′i·i′
—— lateralis ra′di·i′
—— lateralis tes′tis
—— lateralis tib′i·ae′
—— le′on·ti′na
—— lin·gua′lis
—— lingualis den′tis
—— lu·na′ta ac′e·tab′u·li′
—— ma·lar′is
—— malaris os′sis zy′go·mat′i·ci′
—— mal′le·o·lar′is
—— malleolaris lat′er·a′lis ta′li′
—— malleolaris me′di·a′lis ta′li′
—— mas′ti·ca·to′ri·a den′tis
—— max′il·lar′is
—— maxillaris a′lae′ ma·jo′ris
—— maxillaris lam′i·nae′

—— per′pen·dic′u·lar′is os′sis pal′a·ti′ni′
—— maxillaris par′tis per′pen·dic′u·lar′is os′sis pal′a·ti′ni′
—— me′di·a′les′ dig′i·to′rum ma′nus
—— mediales digitorum pe′-dis
—— me′di·a′lis
—— medialis bra′chi·i′
—— medialis car′ti·lag′i·nis ar′y·te·noi′de·ae′
—— medialis cer′e·bri′
—— medialis cru′ris
—— medialis den′ti·um in′ci·si·vo′rum et ca′ni·no′rum
—— medialis fem′o·ris
—— medialis fib′u·lae′
—— medialis hem′is·phe′ri·i′ cer′e·bri′
—— medialis o·var′i·i′
—— medialis pul·mo′nis
—— medialis tes′tis
—— medialis tib′i·ae′
—— medialis ul′nae′
—— me′di·as′ti·na′lis
—— mediastinalis pul·mo′nis
—— me′si·a′lis den′tis
—— my′o·path′i·ca
—— na·sa′lis lam′i·nae′ ho′ri·zon·ta′lis os′sis pal′a·ti′ni′
—— nasalis laminae per′pen·dic′u·lar′is os′sis pal′a·ti′ni′
—— nasalis max·il′lae′
—— nasalis par′tis ho′ri·zon·ta′lis os′sis pal′a·ti′ni′
—— nasalis partis per′pen·dic′u·lar′is os′sis pal′a·ti′ni′
—— oc′clu·sa′lis den′tis
—— or′bi·ta′lis a′lae′ mag′nae′
—— orbitalis alae ma·jo′ris
—— orbitalis max·il′lae′
—— orbitalis os′sis fron·ta′lis
—— orbitalis ossis zy′go·mat′i·ci′
—— os′se·a
—— (ossea) cra′ni·i′
—— pal′a·ti′na

—— palatina lam'i·nae' ho'ri·zon·ta'lis os'sis pal'a·ti'ni'
—— palatina par'tis ho'ri·zon·ta'lis os'sis pal·a·ti'ni'
—— pal·mar'es' dig'i·to'rum ma'nus
—— pa·ri'e·ta'lis
—— parietalis os'sis parie·talis
—— pat'el·lar'is
—— patellaris fem'o·ris
—— pel·vi'na
—— pelvina os'sis sa'cri'
—— plan·tar'es' dig'i·to'rum pe'dis
—— pop·lit'e·a
—— posterior an'te·bra'chi·i'
—— posterior bra'chi·i'
—— posterior car'ti·lag'i·nis ar'y·te·noi'de·ae'
—— posterior cor'ne·ae'
—— posterior cru'ris
—— posterior den'ti·um prae'mo·lar'i·um et mo·lar'i·um
—— posterior fem'o·ris
—— posterior fib'u·lae'
—— posterior glan'du·lae' su'pra·re·na'lis
—— posterior hep'a·tis
—— posterior hu'mer·i'
—— posterior i'ri·dis
—— posterior len'tis
—— posterior pal'pe·brar'um
—— posterior pan·cre'a·tis
—— posterior par'tis pe·tro'sae' os'sis tem'po·ra'lis
—— posterior pros'ta·tae'
—— posterior py·ram'i·dis os'sis tem'po·ra'lis
—— posterior ra'di·i'
—— posterior re'nis
—— posterior tib'i·ae'
—— posterior ul'nae'
—— pul'mo·na'lis cor'dis
—— ra'di·a'les' dig'i·to'rum ma'nus
—— re·na'lis glan'du·lae' su'pra·re·na'lis
—— renalis li·e'nis
—— sa'cro·pel·vi'na os'sis il'i·i'
—— sphe'no·max'il·lar'is
—— sphenomaxillaris a'lae' mag'nae'

—— ster'no·cos·ta'lis cor'dis
—— superior he'mis·phae'ri·i' cer'e·bel'li'
—— superior he'mis·phe'ri·i' cer'e·bel'li'
—— superior hep'a·tis
—— superior troch'le·ae' ta'li'
—— su'per·o·lat'er·a'lis cer'e·bri'
—— sym·phys'e·os' os'sis pu'bis
—— sym·phys'i·a'lis
—— tem'po·ra'lis a'lae' mag'nae'
—— temporalis alae ma·jo'ris
—— temporalis os'sis fron·ta'lis
—— temporalis ossis zy'go·mat'i·ci'
—— temporalis par'tis squa·mo'sae
—— temporalis squa'mae' tem'po·ra'lis
—— tib'i·a'lis cru'ris
—— ul·nar'es' dig'i·to'rum ma'nus
—— u're·thra'lis pe'nis
—— ves'i·ca'lis u'ter·i'
—— ves·tib'u·lar'is den'tis
—— vis'ce·ra'lis hep'a·tis
—— visceralis li·e'nis
—— vo·lar'es' dig'i·to'rum ma'nus
—— vo·lar'is
—— volaris an'ti·bra'chi·i'
—— volaris ra'di·i'
—— volaris ul'nae'
fa·cil'i·ta'tion
fa·cil'i·ty
fac'ing
fa·ci·o·bra'chi·al
fa·ci·o·cer'vi·cal
fa·ci·o·lin'gual
fa·ci·o·plas'ty
fa·ci·o·ple'gic
fa·ci·o·scap'u·lo·hu'mer·al
fa·ci·o'ste·no'sis pl. -ses'
F-ac'tin
fac·ti'tious
fac'tor
fac'ul·ta'tive
fac'ul·ty
faex
—— me·dic'i·na'lis

Fah'rae·us sedimentation test
Fahr'en·heit'
fail'ure
faint
Fair'ley pigment
fal'cate'
fal'cial
fal'ci·form'
fal·cip'a·rum ma·lar'i·a
fal'cu·la
fal'cu·lar
fal·lo'pi·an
Falls test
false
falx *pl.* fal'ces'
—— ap'o·neu·rot'i·ca
—— cer'e·bel'li'
—— cer'e·bri'
—— in'gui·na'lis
—— sep'ti'
fa'mes'
fa·mil'i·al
fam'i·ly
fam'ine
Fan·co'ni
—— anemia
—— syndrome
fang
Fan'ni·a
fan'ning
fan'ta·sy
fan'tri·done'
Fa'ra·beuf' triangle
far'ad'
far'a·day'
far'a·di·za'tion
Far'ber disease
far'cy
far'i·na'ceous
Far'ley, St. Clair', and Rei'sin·ger method
Far'mer and Abt method
Farre white line
far'-sight'ed
far-sight'ed·ness
fas'ci·a *pl.* -ae' *or* -as
—— an'te·bra'chi·i'
—— an'ti·bra'chi·i'
—— ax'il·lar'is
—— bra'chi·i'
—— buc'co·pha·ryn'ge·a
—— bul'bi' (Te·no'ni)
—— cer'vi·ca'lis
—— clav'i·pec'to·ra'lis
—— cli·to'ri·dis
—— col'li'

—— co'ra·co·cla·vic'u·lar'is
—— cre'mas·te'ri·ca
—— cri·bro'sa
—— cru'ris
—— den·ta'ta hip'po·cam'pi'
—— di'a·phrag'ma·tis pel'vis inferior
—— diaphragmatis pelvis superior
—— diaphragmitis u'ro·gen'i·ta'lis inferior
—— diaphragmatis urogeni·talis superior
—— dor·sa'lis ma'nus
—— dorsalis pe'dis
—— en'do·tho·ra'ci·ca
—— i·li'a·ca
—— il'i·o·pec·tin'e·a
—— in·fra·spi·na'ta
—— la'ta
—— lum'bo·dor·sa'lis
—— lu·na'ta
—— mas'se·ter'i·ca
—— nu'chae'
—— ob·tu·ra·to'ri·a
—— par'o·tid'e·a
—— par'o·tid'e·o·mas'se·ter'i·ca
—— pec·tin'e·a
—— pec'to·ra'lis
—— pel'vis
—— pelvis pa·ri'e·ta'lis
—— pelvis vis'ce·ra'lis
—— pe'nis
—— penis pro·fun'da
—— penis su'per·fi'ci·a'lis
—— per'i·ne'i' su'per·fi'ci·a'lis
—— pha·ryn'go·bas'i·lar'is
—— phren'i·co·pleu·ra'lis
—— prae·ver'te·bra'lis
—— pros'ta·tae'
—— sper·mat'i·ca ex·ter'na
—— spermatica in·ter'na
—— sub·per'i·to·ne·a'lis
—— sub·scap'u·lar'is
—— su'per·fi'ci·a'lis
—— superficialis per'i·ne'i'
—— su'pra·spi·na'ta
—— tem'po·ra'lis
—— tho'ra·co·lum·ba'lis
—— trans'ver·sa'lis
fas'ci·ae'
—— mus'cu·lar'es' bul'bi'
—— musculares oc'u·li'
—— or'bi·ta'les'
fas'ci·al

fas'ci·cle
fas·cic'u·lar
fas·cic'u·lat'ed
fas·cic'u·la'tion
fas·cic'u·li'
—— cor'po·ris res'ti·for'mis
—— cor'ti·co·tha·lam'i·ci'
—— in'ter·seg'men·ta'les'
—— lon'gi·tu'di·na'les' lig'a·men'ti' cru'ci·for'mis at·lan'tis
—— longitudinales pon'tis
—— ma·mil'lo·teg'men·ta'les'
—— pe·dun'cu·lo·mam'il·lar'es'
—— pro'pri·i' me·dul'lae' spi·na'lis
—— py·ram'i·da'les'
—— ru'bro·re·tic'u·lar'es'
—— thal'a·mo·cor'ti·ca'les'
—— trans·ver'si' ap'o·neu·ro'sis pal·mar'is
—— transversi aponeurosis plan·tar'is
fas·cic'u·li'tis
fas·cic'u·lus pl. -li'
—— anterior pro'pri·us (Flech'sig·i')
—— an'ter·o·lat'er·a'lis su'per·fi'ci·a'lis (Go·wer'si')
—— a'tri·o·ven·tric'u·lar'is
—— cer'e·bel'lo·spi·na'lis
—— cer'e·bro·spi·na'lis ante·rior
—— cerebrospinalis lat'er·a'lis
—— cu'ne·a'tus (Bur·da'chi')
—— cuneatus me·dul'lae' ob'lon·ga'tae'
—— cuneatus medullae spi·na'lis
—— dor'so·lat'er·a'lis
—— grac'i·lis me·dul'lae' ob'lon·ga'tae'
—— gracilis medullae spi·na'lis
—— in'ter·fas·cic'u·lar'is
—— lat'er·a'lis plex'us bra'chi·a'lis
—— lateralis pro'pri·us
—— lon'gi·tu'di·na'lis dor·sa'lis
—— longitudinalis dorsalis me·dul'lae' ob'lon·ga'tae'

—— longitudinalis dorsalis mes'en·ceph'a·li'
—— longitudinalis dorsalis pon'tis
—— longitudinalis inferior cer'e·bri'
—— longitudinalis me'di·a'lis
—— longitudinalis medialis me·dul'lae' ob'lon·ga'tae'
—— longitudinalis medialis mes'en·ceph'a·li'
—— longitudinalis medialis pon'tis
—— longitudinalis superior
—— ma·mil'lo·teg'men·ta'lis
—— ma·mil'lo·tha·lam'i·cus
—— me'di·a'lis plex'us bra'chi·a'lis
—— ob·li'quus pon'tis
—— of Türck
—— posterior plex'us bra'chi·a'lis
—— pro'pri·us
—— ret'ro·flex'us
—— sem'i·lu·nar'is
—— sep'to·mar'gi·na'lis
—— sol'i·tar'i·us
—— sub'cal·lo'sus
—— thal'a·mo·mam'il·lar'is
—— un'ci·na'tus
fas'ci·ec'to·my
fas'ci·i'tis
fas'ci·num
fas·ci·od'e'sis pl. -ses'
fas·ci·o'la pl. -lae'
—— ci·ne're·a
Fas·ci·o'la
—— gi·gan'ti·ca
—— he·pat'i·ca
fas·ci'o·lar
fas·ci·o·li'a·sis pl. -ses'
fas·ci·o·lop·si'a·sis
Fas·ci·o·lop'sis
—— bus'ki'
fas·ci·o·plas'ty
fas·ci·or'rha·phy
fas·ci·o·scap'u·lo·hu'mer·al
fas·ci·ot'o·my
fast
fas·tid'i·um
fas·tig'i·al
fas·tig'i·o·bul'bar
fas·tig'i·um
fat
fa'tal
fa·tal'i·ty

fat'i·ga·bil'i·ty
fat'i·ga·ble
fa·tigue', -tigued', -tigu'ing
fat'ty
fau'ces'
fau'cial
fau'na pl. -nas or -nae'
Faust method
fa·ve'o·late'
fa·ve'o·lus pl. -li'
fa'vi·des'
fa'vism
Fa'vre disease
fa'vus
Fa'zi·o-Londe' atrophy
fear
feb'ri·fa'cient
fe·brif'ic
feb'ri·fuge'
fe'brile
fe'cal
fe'ca·lith'
fe'ca·loid'
fe'ces'
Fech'ner law
fec'u·la pl. -lae'
fec'u·lent
fe'cund
fe'cun·date', -dat'ed, -dat'-
  ing
fe'cun·da'tion
fe·cun'di·ty
Fe'de-Ri'ga disease
fee'ble·mind'ed
fee'ble·mind'ed·ness
feed'back'
feed'ing
feel, felt, feel'ing
Feer disease
Feh'ling
—— reagent
—— test
Feil'-Klip'pel syndrome
fel
fel·la'ti·o'
fel'la·tor
fel'la·trice'
Fell'-O'Dwy'er method
fel'on
felt'work'
Fel'ty syndrome
fel'y·pres'sin
fe'male'
fem'i·nine
fem'i·ni·za'tion
fem'i·nize', -nized', -niz'ing
fem'o·ral

fem'o·ro·cele'
fem'o·ro·il'i·ac'
fem'o·ro·pop·lit'e·al
fem'o·ro·tib'i·al
fe'mur pl. fem'o·ra
fen·al'a·mide'
fen'a·mole'
fen·clo'nine'
fe·nes'tra pl. -trae'
—— coch'le·ae'
—— o·va'lis
—— ro·tun'da
—— ves·tib'u·li'
fe·nes'tral
fen'es·trat'ed
fen'es·tra'tion
fen·eth'yl·line'
fen·flu'ra·mine'
fen'i·mide'
fen·met'ra·mide'
fe'no·pro'fen
fen'ta·nyl
Fen'wick disease
fen·yr'i·pol'
Fé'ré·ol' node
Fer'gu·son operation
fer'ment n.
fer·ment' v.
fer'men·ta'tion
fer·men'ta·tive
fer'rat'ed
fer're·dox'in
fer'ric
fer'ri·heme'
fer'ri·he'mo·glo'bin
fer'ri·tin
fer'ro·cho'li·nate'
fer'ro·cy'a·nide'
fer'ro·he'mo·glo'bin
fer'ro·ther'a·py
fer'rous
fer·ru'gi·nous
fer'rule'
fer'rum
fer'tile
fer·til'i·ty
fer·til·i·za'tion
fer'til·ize', -ized', -iz'ing
fes'ter
fes'ti·nate', -nat'ed, -nat'ing
fes'ti·na'tion
fes·toon'
fe'tal
fe·ta'tion
fe'ti·cide'
fet'id
fet'ish

fet'ish·ism
fet'ish·ist
fe'to·am'ni·ot'ic
fe'to·glob'u·lin
fe·tom'e·try
fe'to·pro'tein'
fe'tor
—— ex o're'
—— he·pat'i·cus
fe·tox'y·late'
fe'tus
—— com·pres'sus
—— cy·lin'dri·cus
—— in fe'tu'
—— pap'y·ra'ce·us
Feul'gen reaction
fe'ver
fe'ver·ish
fi'at'
fi'ber·op'tic
fi'ber·scope'
fi'bra pl. -brae'
fi'brae'
—— ar'cu·a'tae' cer'e·bri'
—— arcuatae ex·ter'nae'
—— arcuatae externae dor·
sa'les'
—— arcuatae externae ven·
tra'les'
—— arcuatae in·ter'nae'
—— cer'e·bel'lo·ol'i·var'es'
—— cir'cu·lar'es' mus'cu·li'
cil'i·ar'is
—— cor'ti·co·nu'cle·ar'es'
—— cor'ti·co·pon·ti'nae'
—— cor'ti·co·re·tic'u·lar'es'
mes'en·ceph'a·li'
—— corticoreticulares pon'-
tis
—— cor'ti·co·spi·na'les'
—— in'ter·cru·ra'les'
—— len'tis
—— me·rid'i·o·na'les'
mus'cu·li' cil'i·ar'is
—— ob·li'quae' ven·tric'u·li'
—— per'i·ven·tric'u·lar'es'
—— pon'tis pro·fun'dae'
—— pontis su'per·fi'ci·a'les'
—— pontis trans·ver'sae'
—— py·ram'i·da'les' me·
dul'lae' ob'lon·ga'tae'
—— zon'u·lar'es'
fi'bri·form'
fi'bril
fi·bril'la pl. -lae'
fi'bril·lar
fi'bril·lar'y

fi′bril·late′, -lat′ed, -lat′ing
fi′bril·la′tion
fi′bril·la·to′ry
fi·bril′lo·gen′e·sis pl. -ses′
fi′brin
fi′brin·ase′
fi·bri·no·cel′lu·lar
fi·brin′o·gen
fi·brin·o·gen′ic
fi·brin·o·gen·o·pe′ni·a
fi′bri·nog′e·nous
fi·bri·no·hem′or·rhag′ic
fi′brin·oid′
fi·bri·no·ki′nase′
fi·bri·nol′y·sin
fi·bri·nol′y·sis pl. -ses′
fi′bri·no·lyt′ic
fi·bri·no·pe′ni·a
fi′brin·ous
fi′bro·ad′e·no′ma pl. -mas
  or -ma·ta
—— xan′tho·ma·to′des′
fi′bro·ad′e·no′sis pl. -ses′
fi′bro·ad′i·pose′
fi′bro·am′e·lo·blas·to′ma
  pl. -mas or -ma·ta
fi′bro·an′gi·o·li·po′ma
  pl. -mas or -ma·ta
fi′bro·an′gi·o′ma pl. -mas or
  -ma·ta
fi′bro·a·re′o·lar
fi′bro·blast′
fi′bro·blas′tic
fi′bro·blas·to′ma pl. -mas or
  -ma·ta
fi′bro·bron·chi′tis
fi′bro·cal·car′e·ous
fi′bro·cal·cif′ic
fi′bro·car′ci·no′ma pl. -mas
  or -ma·ta
fi′bro·car′ti·lage
fi′bro·car′ti·lag′i·nes′
  in′ter·ver′te·bra′les′
fi′bro·car′ti·lag′i·nous
fi′bro·car′ti·la′go′ pl. -lag′i·
  nes′
—— ba·sa′lis
—— na·vic′u·lar′is
fi′bro·ca′se·ous
fi′bro·cav′i·tar′y
fi′bro·cel′lu·lar
fi′bro·ce′men·to′ma
  pl. -mas or -ma·ta
fi′bro·chon·dri′tis
fi′bro·chon·dro′ma pl. -mas
  or -ma·ta

fi′bro·chon′dro·os′te·o′ma
  pl. -mas or -ma·ta
fi′bro·col·lag′e·nous
fi′bro·cyst′
fi′bro·cys′tic
fi′bro·cys·to′ma pl. -mas or
  -ma·ta
fi′bro·cyte′
fi′bro·cy′to·gen′e·sis pl.
  -ses′
fi′bro·dys·pla′si·a
fi′bro·e·las′tic
fi′bro·e′las·to′sis pl. -ses′
fi′bro·en′chon·dro′ma
  pl. -mas or -ma·ta
fi′bro·en·do·the′li·o′ma
  pl. -mas or -ma·ta
fi′bro·fat′ty
fi′bro·gen′e·sis pl. -ses′
fi′bro·gen′ic
fi·brog′li·a
fi′bro·gli·o′ma pl. -mas or
  -ma·ta
fi′bro·hem′or·rhag′ic
fi′bro·he′mo·tho′rax′
fi′broid′
fi′broid·ec′to·my
fi′bro·lam′i·nar
fi′bro·lei′o·my·o′ma
  pl. -mas or -ma·ta
fi′bro·li·po′ma pl. -mas or
  -ma·ta
fi′bro·li·pom′a·tous
fi′bro·lip′o·sar·co′ma
  pl. -mas or -ma·ta
fi′bro·lym′pho·an′gi·o′blas·
  to′ma pl. -mas or -ma·ta
fi·brol′y·sis pl. -ses′
fi·bro′ma pl. -mas or -ma·ta
—— du′rum
—— fun·goi′des′
—— li·po′ma·to′des′
—— mol′le′
—— mol·lus′cum
—— pen′du·lum
—— sim′plex′
fi·bro′ma·to·gen′ic
fi·bro′ma·toid′
fi·bro′ma·to′sis pl. -ses′
—— gin·gi′vae′
fi·brom′a·tous
fi′bro·mec′to·my
fi′bro·mem′bra·nous
fi′bro·mus′cu·lar
fi′bro·my·i′tis
fi′bro·my·o′ma pl. -mas or
  -ma·ta

fi′bro·my′o·mec′to·my
fi′bro·my′o·si′tis pl. -ses′
fi′bro·myx′o·li·po′ma
  pl. -mas or -ma·ta
fi′bro·myx·o′ma pl. -mas or
  -ma·ta
fi′bro·myx′o·sar·co′ma
  pl. -mas or -ma·ta
fi′bro·nec′tin
fi′bro·neu·ro′ma pl. -mas or
  -ma·ta
fi′bro·os′te·o·chon·dro′ma
  pl. -mas or -ma·ta
fi′bro·os′te·o′ma pl. -mas or
  -ma·ta
fi′bro·os′te·o·sar·co′ma pl.
  -mas or -ma·ta
fi′bro·pap′il·lo′ma pl. -mas
  or -ma·ta
fi′bro·pla′si·a
fi′bro·plas′tic
fi′bro·plate′
fi′bro·pu′ru·lent
fi′bro·sar·co′ma pl. -mas or
  -ma·ta
—— myx′o·ma·to′des′
—— phyl·lo′des′
fi′bro·sar·com′a·tous
fi′bro·scle·ro′sis pl. -ses′
fi′brose′
fi′bro·se′rous
fi·bro′sis pl. -ses′
fi′bro·sit′ic
fi′bro·si′tis
—— os·sif′i·cans′ pro′gres·
  si′va
fi′bro·tho′rax′
fi·brot′ic
fi′brous
fi′bro·vas′cu·lar
fi′bro·xan·tho′ma pl. -mas
  or -ma·ta
fi′bro·xan·thom′a·tous
fib′u·la pl. -lae′ or -las
fib′u·lar
fib′u·la′ris
fib′u·lo·cal·ca′ne·al
fib′u·lo·cal·ca′ne·us
fib′u·lo·tib′i·a′lis
Fied′ler
—— disease
—— myocarditis
field
fi·èv′re bou′ton·neuse′
fig′ure
fig′ure-ground′
fi′la

—— a·nas'to·mot'i·ca ner'vi'
a·cus'ti·ci'
—— cor'o·nar'i·a
—— lat'er·a'li·a pon'tis
—— ol'fac·to'ri·a
—— ra·dic'u·lar'i·a
—— radicularia ner·vo'rum
spi·na'li·um
fi·la'ceous
fil'a·ment
fil'a·men'ta·ry
fil'a·men·ta'tion
fil'a·men'tous
fil'a·men'tum
fi'lar
fi·lar'i·a pl. -ae'
fi·lar'i·al
fil'a·ri'a·sis pl. -ses'
fi·lar'i·ci'dal
fi·lar'i·cide'
fi·lar'i·form'
Fil'a·tov'
—— disease
—— spots
Fil'a·tov-Dukes' disease
fil'i·cin
fil'i·form'
fil'i·pin
Fi·lip'o·wicz' sign
fil'let
fill'ing
film
Fi'lo·ba·sid'i·el'la ne'o·
for'mans'
fil'o·po'di·um pl. -di·a
fil'ter
fil'tra·ble
fil'trate'
fil·tra'tion
fil'trum pl. -tra
—— ven·tric'u·li'
fi'lum pl. -la
—— du'rae' ma'tris spi·na'lis
—— lat'er·a'lis pon'tis
—— ter'mi·na'le'
fim'bri·a pl. -ae'
—— hip'po·cam'pi'
—— o·var'i·ca
fim'bri·ae' tu'bae' u'ter·
i'nae'
fim'bri·al
fim'bri·ate'
fim'bri·at'ed
fim'bri·ec'to·my
fim'bri·o·cele'
Find'lay operation
fin'ger

fin'ger·nail'
fin'ger·print'
fin'ger·print'ing
Fin'ney
—— operation
—— pyloroplasty
Fin'ney-von Ha'ber·er op-
eration
Fi·no·chet'ti stirrup
first'-aid' kit
first'-de·gree'
—— burn
—— heart block
Fish'berg' test
fis'sile
fis'sion
fis'sion·a·ble
fis·su'la pl. -lae'
—— an'te fe·nes'tram'
fis·su'ra pl. -rae'
—— an'ti·tra'go·hel'i·ci'na
—— cal'ca·ri'na
—— cer'e·bri' lat'er·a'lis
(Syl'vi·i')
—— cho·roi'de·a
—— col·lat'er·a'lis
—— hip'po·cam'pi'
—— ho'ri·zon·ta'lis cer'e·
bel'li'
—— horizontalis pul·mo'nis
dex'tri'
—— lig'a·men'ti' ter'e·tis
—— ligamenti ve·no'si'
—— lon'gi·tu'di·na'lis cer'e·
bri'
—— me'di·a'na anterior me·
dul'lae' ob'lon·ga'tae'
—— mediana anterior me-
dullae spi·na'lis
—— mediana posterior me-
dullae ob'lon·ga'tae'
—— ob·li'qua pul·mo'nis
—— or'bi·ta'lis inferior
—— orbitalis superior
—— pa·ri'e·to·oc·cip'i·ta'lis
—— pet'ro·oc·cip'i·ta'lis
—— pet'ro·squa·mo'sa
—— pet'ro·tym·pan'i·ca
—— pos'ter·o·lat'er·a'lis
cer'e·bel'li'
—— pri'ma
—— pter'y·goi'de·a
—— pter'y·go·max'il·lar'is
—— pter'y·go·pal'a·ti'na
—— se·cun'da
—— sphe'no·oc·cip'i·ta'lis
—— sphe'no·pe·tro'sa

—— ster'ni'
—— trans·ver'sa cer'e·bel'li'
—— transversa cer'e·bri'
—— tym'pa·no·mas·toi'de·a
—— tym'pa·no·squa·mo'sa
fis·su'rae' cer'e·bel'li'
fis'su·ral
fis'su·ra'tion
fis'sure
—— in a'no'
—— of Ro·lan'do
fis'tu·la pl. -las or -lae'
—— au'ris con·gen'i·ta
—— in a'no'
fis'tu·lar
fis'tu·late'
fis'tu·la'tion
fis'tu·lec'to·my
fis'tu·li·za'tion
fis'tu·lize', -lized', -liz'ing
fis'tu·lo·en'ter·os'to·my
fis'tu·lo·gram'
fis'tu·lot'o·my
fis'tu·lous
fit
Fitz·ger'ald-Gard'ner syndrome
Fitz-Hugh'–Cur'tis syn-
drome
fix'ate', -at'ed, -at'ing
fix·a'tion
fix'a·tive
flac'cid
flac·cid'i·ty
Flack node
flag'el·lant
fla·gel'lar
flag'el·late', -lat'ed,
-lat'ing
flag'el·la'tion
fla·gel'li·form'
flag'el·lo·ma'ni·a
flag'el·lo'sis pl. -ses'
fla·gel'lum pl. -la
Flagg resuscitation
flail
Fla·ja'ni disease
flange
flank
flap
flare
flask
Fla'tau' law
Fla'tau'-Schil'der disease
flat'foot'
flat'u·lence
flat'u·lent

fla'tus
—— vag'i·na'lis
fla·ve'do
fla'vin
fla'vine'
Fla'vi·vi'rus
Fla'vo·bac·te'ri·um
fla'vo·ki'nase'
fla'vo·noid'
fla'vo·nol'
fla'vo·pro'tein'
fla'vo·xan'thin
fla·vox'ate'
Flech'sig tract
fleck'fie'ber
fleck'milz'
Fleck test
Flei'scher-Kay'ser ring
flex
flex'i·bil'i·tas ce're·a
flex'i·bil'i·ty
flex'i·ble
flex'ile
flex·im'e·ter
flex'ion
Flex'ner
—— bacillus
—— report
Flex'ner-Job'ling carcino-
sarcoma
flex'or
—— ac'ces·so'ri·us
—— car'pi' ra'di·a'lis
—— carpi radialis brev'is
—— carpi ul·nar'is
—— carpi ulnaris brev'is
—— dig'i·ti' min'i·mi' brev'is
—— digiti quin'ti' brev'is
—— dig'i·to'rum ac'ces·so'ri·
us
—— digitorum brev'is
—— digitorum lon'gus
—— digitorum pro·fun'dus
—— digitorum sub·li'mis
—— digitorum su'per·fi'ci·
a'lis
—— hal'lu·cis brev'is
—— hallucis lon'gus
—— os'sis met'a·car'pi'
pol'li·cis
—— pol'li·cis brev'is
—— pollicis lon'gus
flex·u'ous
flex·u'ra pl. -rae'
—— co'li' dex'tra
—— coli si·nis'tra
—— du'o·de'ni' inferior

—— duodeni superior
—— du'o·de'no·je'ju·na'lis
—— per'i·ne·a'lis rec'ti'
—— sa·cra'lis rec'ti'
flex'ure
flick'er
Flindt spots
Flint murmur
float'ers
floc'cil·la'tion
floc'cu·lar
floc'cu·late', -lat'ed, -lat'ing
floc'cu·la'tion
floc'cu·lent
floc'cu·lo·nod'u·lar
floc'cu·lus pl. -li'
—— sec'on·dar'i·i'
flo'ra pl. -ras or -rae'
flor·an'ty·rone'
Flo'rence
—— flask
—— test
flo'res'
Flo'rey unit
flo'rid
flo'ri·form'
flow
flow'er bas'ket of
Boch'da·lek'
Flow'er index
flow'me'ter
flox·u'ri·dine'
flu·ban'i·late'
flu·cin'o·nide'
fluc'tu·ance
fluc'tu·ate', -at'ed, -at'ing
fluc'tu·a'tion
flu·cy'to·sine'
flu'do·rex'
flu'dro·cor'ti·sone'
flu'fen·am'ic
Fluh'mann test
flu'id
flu'id·ex'tract'
flu·id'i·ty
flu'id·ounce'
flu'i·dram'
fluke
flu'men pl. -mi·na
flu·meth'a·sone'
flu·met'ra·mide'
flu'mi·na
—— pi·lo'rum
flu·min'o·rex'
flu·nid'a·zole'
flu'o·cin'o·lone' a·cet'o·
nide'

flu'o·cor'to·lone'
flu'or'
—— al'bus
flu'or·chrome'
flu'o·res'ce·in
flu'o·res'cence
flu'o·res'cent
flu'o·res'cin
fluor'i·date', -dat'ed, -dat'-
ing
fluor'i·da'tion
flu'o·ride'
fluor'i·di·za'tion
fluor'i·dize', -dized', -diz'ing
flu'o·rine'
flu'o·ro·a·ce'tic
fluor'o·chrome'
flu'o·ro·graph'ic
flu'o·rog'ra·phy
flu'o·rom'e·ter
flu'o·ro·met'ric
flu'o·ro·meth'o·lone'
flu'o·ro·phos'phate'
flu'o·ro·pho'to·met'ric
flu'o·ro·pho·tom'e·try
flu'o·ro·roent'ge·nog'ra·
phy
flu'o·ro·sal'an
fluor'o·scope'
fluor'o·scop'ic
fluor·os'co·py
flu'o·ro'sis pl. -ses'
flu'o·ro·u'ra·cil
flu'ox·y·mes'ter·one'
flu·per'o·lone'
flu·phen'a·zine'
flu'pred·nis'o·lone'
flu'ran·dren'o·lide'
flu·raz'e·pam'
flu·ro·ges'tone'
flu'ro·thyl
flu·rox'ene'
Flu'ry strain
flush
flut'ter
flux
Fo'à-Kur'lov' cell
fo'cal
fo'cal·i·za'tion
fo'cal·ize', -ized', -iz'ing
fo'cus pl. -cus·es or -ci'
Foer'ster
—— cutaneous numeral test
—— operation
—— sign
Foer'ster-Pen'field' operation

fog'ging
fo'go sel·va'gem
foil
Foix
—— sign
—— syndrome
Foix'-A'la·jou'a·nine' syndrome
fo'late'
fold
Fo'ley Y'-plas'ty
fo'li·a'ceous
fo'li·a cer'e·bel'li
fo'li·ate'
fol'ic
fo·lie'
—— à deux
—— du doute
Fo'lin
—— and Sved'berg' method
—— and Wu method
—— and Young'burg' method
—— method
—— reagent
—— theory
Folin, Can'non, and Den'-is method
Fo'lin-Cio·cal'teu reagent
Fo'lin-Far'mer method
Fo'lin-Mc'Ell·roy' test
Fo'lin-Schaf'fer method
Fo'lin-Wu' test
fo'li·um *pl.* -li·a
—— ca·cu'mi·nis
—— cer'e·bel'li'
—— ver'mis
fol'li·cle
fol·lic'u·lar
fol·lic'u·li'
—— glan'du·lae' thy·roi'de·ae'
—— lin·gua'les'
—— lym·phat'i·ci' ag·gre·ga'ti' ap·pen'di·cis ver'mi·for'mis
—— lymphatici aggregati in'tes·ti'ni' ten'u·is
—— lymphatici gas'tri·ci'
—— lymphatici la·ryn'ge·i'
—— lymphatici li'e·na'les'
—— lymphatici rec'ti'
—— lymphatici sol'i·tar'i·i' co'li'
—— lymphatici solitarii in'tes·ti'ni' ten'u·is
—— o·oph'o·ri' pri·mar'i·i'

—— oophori ve·sic'u·lo'si'
—— o·var'i·ci' pri·mar'i·i'
—— ovarici ve·sic'u·lo'si'
fol·lic'u·lin
fol·lic'u·li'tis
—— ab·sce'dens et suf·fo'di·ens
—— ag'mi·na'ta
—— bar'bae'
—— de·cal'vans'
—— ke'loi·da'lis
—— sim'plex'
—— u·ler'y·the'ma·to'sa re·tic'u·la'ta
fol·lic'u·loid'
fol·lic'u·lo'ma *pl.* -mas *or* -ma·ta
fol·lic'u·lo'sis *pl.* -ses'
fol·lic'u·lus *pl.* -li'
—— lym·phat'i·cus
—— pi'li'
fo'men·ta'tion
fo'mes' *pl.* fom'i·tes'
fo'mite'
Fong lesion
Fon·se'ca disease
Fon'se·cae'a
Fon·tan'a
—— spaces
—— stain
fon'ta·nel' *or* fon'ta·nelle'
fon·tic'u·li' cra'ni·i'
fon·tic'u·lus *pl.* -li'
—— anterior
—— fron·ta'lis
—— mas·toi'de·us
—— oc·cip'i·ta'lis
—— posterior
—— sphe'noi·da'lis
foot
foot'-can'dle
for'age, -aged, -ag·ing
fo·ra'men *pl.* -mens *or* fo·ram'i·na
—— a'pi·cis den'tis
—— cae'cum lin'guae'
—— caecum me·dul'lae' ob·lon·ga'tae'
—— caecum os'sis fron·ta'lis
—— ca·rot'i·cum ex·ter'num
—— caroticum in·ter'num
—— ce'cum
—— cecum lin'guae'
—— cecum os'sis fron·ta'lis
—— cos'to·trans·ver·sar'i·um

—— di'a·phrag'ma·tis sel'lae'
—— ep'i·plo'i·cum
—— eth'moi·da'le' an·te'ri·us
—— ethmoidale pos·te'ri·us
—— fron·ta'le'
—— in'ci·si'vum
—— in'fra·or'bi·ta'le'
—— in'fra·pir'i·for'me'
—— in·nom'i·na'tum
—— in'ter·ven·tric'u·lar'e'
—— in'ter·ver'te·bra'le
—— is'chi·ad'i·cum ma'jus
—— ischiadicum mi'nus
—— jug'u·lar'e'
—— lac'er·um
—— mag'num
—— man·dib'u·lae'
—— man·dib'u·lar'e'
—— mas·toi'de·um
—— men·ta'le'
—— nu·tri'ci·um
—— ob'tu·ra'tum
—— oc·cip'i·ta'le' mag'num
—— of Boch'da·lek'
—— of Husch'ke
—— of Key
—— of Lusch'ka
—— of Ma·gen'die
—— of Mon·ro'
—— of Mor·ga'gni
—— of Ret'zi·us
—— of Scar'pa
—— of Sten'sen
—— of Ve·sa'li·us
—— of Wins'low'
—— op'ti·cum
—— o·va'le'
—— ovale cor'dis
—— ovale os'sis sphe'noi·da'lis
—— ovale pri'mum
—— pal'a·ti'num ma'jus
—— pa·ri'e·ta'le'
—— pri'mum
—— ro·tun'dum
—— rotundum os'sis sphe'noi·da'lis
—— se·cun'dum
—— sin'gu·lar'e'
—— sphe'no·pal'a·ti'num
—— spi·no'sum
—— sty'lo·mas·toi'de·um
—— su'pra·or'bi·ta'lis
—— su'pra·pir'i·for'me'
—— thy're·oi'de·um

—— thy·roi'de·um
—— trans'ver·sar'i·um
—— ve'nae' ca'vae'
—— ve·no'sum
—— ver'te·bra'le'
—— zy'go·mat'i·co·fa·ci·a'le'
—— zy'go·mat'i·co·or'bi·ta'le'
—— zy'go·mat'i·co·tem'po·ra'le'
fo·ra'mens
—— of Scar'pa
—— of Sten'sen
fo·ram'i·na
—— al've·o·lar'i·a max·il'lae'
—— eth'moi·da'li·a
—— in'ci·si'va
—— in'ter·ver'te·bra'li·a os'-sis sa'cri'
—— na·sa'li·a
—— ner·vo'sa lam'i·nae' spi·ra'lis
—— nervosa lim'bus lam'i·nae' spi·ra'lis
—— pal'a·ti'na mi·no'ra
—— pap'il·lar'i·a re'nis
—— sa·cra'li·a an·te'ri·o'ra
—— sacralia dor·sa'li·a
—— sacralia pel·vi'na
—— sacralia pos·te'ri·o'ra
—— ve·nar'um min'i·mar'um cor'dis
fo·ram'i·nal
fo·ram'i·not'o·my
fo'ra·min'u·late'
fo'ra·min'u·lum pl. -la
Forbes disease
force
for'ceps
Forch'hei'mer sign
for'ci·pate'
for·cip'i·tal
for'ci·pres'sure
fore'arm'
fore'brain
fore'con'scious
fore'fin'ger
fore'foot'
fore'gut'
fore'head'
for'eign
fore'kid'ney
Fo·rel'
—— bundle
—— decussation
fore'milk'
fo·ren'sic

fore'play'
fore'pleas'ure
fore'skin'
fore'stom'ach
fore'wa'ters
form
for·mal'de·hyde'
for'ma·lin
form·am'ide'
for'mate'
for·ma'ti·o' pl. -ma'ti·o'nes'
—— re·tic'u·lar'is
—— reticularis me·dul'lae'
ob'lon·ga'tae'
—— reticularis medullae
spi·na'lis
—— reticularis mes'en·ceph'a·li'
—— reticularis pe·dun'cu·li'
cer'e·bri'
—— reticularis pon'tis
for·ma'tion
for'ma·tive
for·mi·ca'tion
for'mol'
for'mu·la pl. -las or -lae'
for'mu·lar'y
for'myl
for'myl·am'ide'
for'myl·ase'
for'ni·cal
for'ni·cate', -cat'ed, -cat'ing
for'ni·ca'tion
for'nix pl. -ni·ces'
—— cer'e·bri'
—— con·junc·ti'vae' inferior
—— conjunctivae superior
—— pha·ryn'gis
—— sac'ci' lac'ri·ma'lis
—— va·gi'nae'
For'o·blique'
Fors'gren method
Forss'man antigens
Fort Bragg fever
Fo·shay' test (tularemia)
♦Fouchet test
fos'pi·rate'
fos'sa pl. -sae'
—— ac'e·tab'u·li'
—— ant·hel'i·cis
—— ax'il·lar'is
—— cae·ca'lis
—— ca·ni'na
—— ca·rot'i·ca
—— cer'e·bri' lat'er·a'lis
(Syl'vi·i')
—— con'dy·lar'is

—— con'dy·loi'de·a
—— cor'o·noi'de·a
—— cra'ni·i' anterior
—— cranii me'di·a
—— cranii posterior
—— cu'bi·ta'lis
—— di·gas'tri·ca
—— duc'tus ve·no'si'
—— ep'i·gas'tri·ca
—— glan'du·lae' lac'ri·ma'lis
—— hy·a·loi'de·a
—— hy'po·phys'e·os'
—— hy'po·phys'i·a'lis
—— i·li'a·ca
—— i·li'a·co·sub·fas'ci·a'lis
—— il'i·o·pec·tin'e·a
—— in'ci·si'va
—— in·cu'dis
—— in'fra·spi·na'ta
—— in'fra·tem'po·ra'lis
—— in'gui·na'lis lat'er·a'lis
—— inguinalis me'di·a'lis
—— in·nom'i·na'ta
—— in'ter·con'dy·lar'is
fem'or·is
—— in'ter·con'dy·loi'de·a
anterior tib'i·ae'
—— intercondyloidea fem'o·ris
—— intercondyloidea poste-rior tib'i·ae'
—— in'ter·pe·dun'cu·lar'is
—— is'chi·o·rec·ta'lis
—— jug'u·lar'is
—— jugularis os'sis tem'po·ra'lis
—— la'ter·a'lis cer'e·bri'
—— mal·le'o·li' lat'er·a'lis
—— man·dib'u·lar'is
—— na·vic'u·lar'is
u·re'thrae'
—— navicularis ves·tib'u·li'
va·gi'nae'
—— oc·cip'i·ta'lis
—— o'le·cra'ni'
—— o·va'lis
—— ovalis cor'dis
—— ovalis fas'ci·ae' la'tae'
—— ovalis fem'o·ris
—— pop·lit'e·a
—— prae'na·sa'lis
—— pter'y·goi'de·a
—— pter'y·go·pal'a·ti'na
—— ra·di·a'lis
—— ret'ro·man·dib'u·lar'is
—— rhom·boi'de·a
—— sac'ci' lac'ri·ma'lis

—— sag'it·ta'lis si·nis'tra hep'a·tis
—— sca·phoi'de·a
—— scar'pae' major
—— sem'i·lu·nar'is
—— sub·ar'cu·a'ta
—— sub·in'gui·na'lis
—— sub·scap'u·lar'is
—— su'pra·cla·vic'u·lar'is major
—— supraclavicularis minor
—— su'pra·spi·na'ta
—— su'pra·ton'sil·lar'is
—— su'pra·ves'i·ca'lis
—— tem'po·ra'lis
—— ton'sil·lar'is
—— tri·an'gu·lar'is au·ric'u·lae'
—— tro'chan·ter'i·ca
—— ve'nae' ca'vae'
—— venae um·bil'i·ca'lis
—— ve·si'cae' fel'le·ae'
—— ves·tib'u·li' va·gi'nae'
fos'sae' sag'it·ta'les' dex'-trae' hep'a·tis
fos·sette'
fos'su·la pl. -lae'
—— fe·nes'trae' coch'le·ae'
—— fenestrae ves·tib'u·li'
—— pe·tro'sa
—— post fe·nes'tram
fos'su·lae'
—— ton'sil·lar'es' ton·sil'lae' pal'a·ti'nae'
—— tonsillares tonsillae pha·ryn'ge·ae'ee
Fos'ter Ken'ne·dy syndrome
Fos'ter rule
Foth'er·gill disease
Fou·chet' reagent
Fou·chet' test (bilirubin)
♦Foshay test
fou·droy'ant
foul
four·chette'
fo've·a pl. -ae'
—— ar·tic'u·lar'is inferior at·lan'tis
—— articularis superior atlantis
—— cap'i·tis fem'o·ris
—— ca·pit'u·li' ra'di·i'
—— cen·tra'lis
—— cos·ta'lis inferior
—— costalis superior
—— costalis trans·ver·sa'lis

—— den'tis at·lan'tis
—— hem'i·el·lip'ti·ca
—— hem'i·sphe'ri·ca
—— inferior fos'sae' rhom·boi'de·ae'
—— in'gui·na'lis lat'er·a'lis
—— inguinalis me'di·a'lis
—— nu'chae'
—— ob·lon'ga car'ti·lag'i·nis ar'y·tae·noi'de·ae'
—— oblonga cartilaginis ar'y·te·noi'de·ae'
—— pal'a·ti'na
—— pter'y·goi'de·a man·dib'u·lae'
—— pterygoidea pro·ces'sus con'dy·loi'de·i'
—— sa'cro·coc·cyg'e·a
—— sub·lin·gua'lis
—— sub'man·dib'u·lar'is
—— sub·max'il·lar'is
—— superior fos'sae' rhom·boi'de·ae'
—— su'pra·ves'i·ca'lis per'i·to·nae'i'
—— tri·an'gu·lar'is car'ti·lag'i·nis
—— triangularis cartilaginis ar'y·te·noi'de·ae'
—— troch'le·ar'is
fo've·ae' ar·tic'u·lar'es' in·fe'ri·o'res' at·lan'tis
fo've·al
fo've·ate'
fo've·o'la pl. -lae' or -las
—— coc·cyg'e·a
—— pal'a·ti'na
fo've·o'lae'
—— gas'tri·cae'
—— gran'u·lar'es'
fo've·o'lar
fo've·o·late'
Fo'ville paralysis
Fow'ler
—— position
—— solution
fox'glove'
frac'tion·al
frac'tion·ate', -at'ed, -at'ing
frac'tion·a'tion
frac'ture, -tured, -tur·ing
Fraenk'el
—— glands
—— nodule
Fraentz'el murmur
frag'ile
fra·gil'i·tas

—— cri'ni·um
—— os'si·um
fra·gil'i·ty
frag'men·ta'tion
fraise
fram·be'si·a
Frame, Rus'sell, and Wil'-hel'mi method
Fran'ce·schet'ti syndrome
Fran'ci·sel'la
—— tu'la·ren'sis
Fran'cis test
Fran·çois' syndrome
frank
Frank
—— capillary toxicosis
—— operation
Frank'en·häu'ser ganglion
Franke method
Frank'fort horizontal plane
fra·ter'nal
frat'ri·cide'
Fraun'ho'fer lines
freck'le
Fre·det'-Ram'stedt operation
Free'man rule
freeze, froze, fro'zen, freez'-ing
Frei
—— disease
—— test
Frei'berg' disease
frem'i·tus
fre'nal
fre·nec'to·my
fre·net'ic var. of phrenetic
fre'no·plas'ty
fre·not'o·my
fren'u·lum pl. -la
—— cli·to'ri·dis
—— la'bi·i' in·fe'ri·o'ris
—— labii su·pe'ri·o'ris
—— la'bi·o'rum pu·den'di'
—— lin'guae'
—— of Gia'co·mi'ni
—— pre·pu'ti·i' pe'nis
—— val'vae' il'e·o·ce·ca'lis
—— val'vu·lae' co'li'
—— ve'li' med'ul·lar'is an·te'ri·o'ris
—— veli medullaris su·pe'ri·o'ris
fre'num pl. -nums or -na
Fren'zel maneuver
fren'zy

fre'quen·cy
Frer'ich theory
fre'tum
—— hal'ler·i'
freud'i·an
Freund adjuvant
Freund'lich adsorption
  equation
Frey syndrome
fri'a·ble
fric'tion
fric'tion·al
Frid'er·ich·sen
—— syndrome
—— test
Frie'de·mann and Grae's-
  er method
Frie'den·wald' nomogram
Fried'län'der
—— bacillus
—— cells
—— pneumonia
Fried'mann vasomotor
  symptom complex
Fried'man test
Fried'reich'
—— ataxia
—— disease
—— sign
Fried'rich-Bau'er opera-
  tion
Fried rule
fri·gid'i·ty
fringe
Frisch bacillus
Froh'de reagent
Froin syndrome
frole·ment'
Fro'ment sign
From'mel
—— disease
—— operation
frons
fron'tad'
fron'tal
fron·ta'lis
fron·tip'e·tal
fron'to·eth'moid'
fron'to·lac'ri·mal
fron'to·ma'lar
fron'to·max'il·lar'y
fron'to·men'tal
fron'to·na'sal
fron'to·oc·cip'i·tal
fron'to·pa·ri'e·tal
fron'to·pon'tine'
fron'to·pon'to·cer'e·bel'lar

fron'to·sphe'noid'
fron'to·tem'por·al
fron'to·tem'po·ra'le' pl.
  -ra'li·a
fron'to·zy'go·mat'ic
Fro'riep'
—— ganglion
—— induration
frost'bite'
frot·tage'
frot·teur'
fruc'to·fu·ran'o·san'
fruc'to·fu'ra·nose'
fruc'to·fu·ran'o·side'
fruc'to·ki'nase'
fruc'to·py'ra·nose'
fruc'to·san'
fruc'tose'
fruc'to·side'
fruc'to·su'ri·a
fru·giv'o·rous
fru'men·ta'ceous
fru·men'tum
frus'trate', -trat'ed, -trat'ing
frus·tra'tion
Fuchs
—— dystrophy
—— iridocyclitis
—— phenomenon
fuch'sin
fuch·sin'o·phil'
fu'cose'
fu·co'si·dase'
fu'co·si·do'sis pl. -ses'
Fuer'bring'er
—— law
—— sign
fu·ga'cious
fu'gi·tive
fugue
ful'gu·rant
ful'gu·rate', -rat'ed, -rat'ing
ful'gu·ra'tion
fu·lig'i·nous
Ful'ler Al'bright' syn-
  drome
Fuller operation
full'-thick'ness graft
ful'mi·nant
ful'mi·nat'ing
fu'ma·gil'lin
fu'ma·rase'
fu'ma·rate'
Fu·mar'i·a'ce·ae'
fu·mig'a·cin
fu'mi·gant
fu'mi·gate', -gat'ed, -gat'ing

fu'mi·ga'tion
fum'ing
func'ti·o'
—— lae'sa
func'tion
func'tion·al
fun'dal
fun'da·ment
fun'da·men'tal
fun·dec'to·my
fun'dic
fun'di·form'
fun'do·plas'ty
fun'do·pli·ca'tion
fun'do·scop'ic
fun·dos'co·py
fun'dus pl. -di'
—— fla'vi·mac'u·la'tus
—— fol·lic'u·li' pi'li'
—— me·a'tus a·cu'sti·ci'
  in·ter'ni'
—— oc'u·li'
—— u'ter·i'
—— ven·tric'u·li'
—— ve·si'cae' fel'le·ae'
—— vesicae u'ri·nar'i·ae'
fun'du·scope'
fun'du·scop'ic
fun·dus'co·py
fun'du·sec'to·my
fun'gal
fun'gate', -gat'ed, -gat'ing
fun·ge'mi·a
fun'gi·ci'dal
fun'gi·cide'
fun'gi·form'
fun'gi·sta'sis
fun'gi·stat'ic
fun'goid'
fun·gos'i·ty
fun'gous (of a fungus)
  ♦fungus
fun'gus (plant), pl. -gi' or
  -gus·es
  ♦fungous
fu'nic
fu'ni·cle
fu·nic'u·lar
fu·nic'u·li' me·dul'lae' spi·
  na'lis
fu·nic'u·li'tis
fu·nic'u·lus pl. -li'
—— anterior me·dul'lae' spi·
  na'lis
—— cu'ne·a'tus me·dul'lae'
  ob'lon·ga'tae'

—— grac'i·lis me·dul'lae'
ob'lon·ga'tae'
—— lat'er·a'lis me·dul'lae'
ob'lon·ga'tae'
—— lateralis medullae spi·
na'lis
—— posterior medullae spi·
nalis
—— sep'a·rans'
—— sper·mat'i·cus
—— um·bil'i·ca'lis
fu'ni·form'
fu'nis
fun'nel
fu'ra·zol'i·done'
fu'ra·zo'li·um
fur·az'o·sin
fur'ca pl. -cae'
—— or'bi·ta'lis
fur'cal
fur·ca'lis
fur'cate'
fur·cu·la pl. -lae'
fur'fu·ra'ceous
fu'ri·bund'
fu'ror'
—— am'a·to'ri·us
—— ep'i·lep'ti·cus
—— gen'i·ta'lis
fu'ro·sem'ide
fur'row
fur'sa·lan'
fu'run·cle
fu·run'cu·lar
fu·run'cu·loid'
fu·run'cu·lo'sis pl. -ses'
—— o'ri·en·ta'lis
fu·run'cu·lus pl. -li'
Fu·sar'i·um
fus'cin
fuse, fused, fus'ing
fu·seau' pl. -seaux'
fu'sel
fu'si·ble
fu'si·form'
fu'si·mo'tor
fu'sion
fu'so·bac·te'ri·um pl. -ri·a
Fu'so·bac·te'ri·um
—— fu'si·for'me'
—— plau'ti·vin·cen'ti'
fu'so·cel'lu·lar
fu'so·spi'ro·che'tal
fu'so·spi'ro·che·to'sis pl.
-ses'

G

G'-ac'tin
Gaert'ner tonometer
Gaff'ky·a
—— te·trag'e·na
gag, gagged, gag'ging
Gais'böck'
—— disease
—— syndrome
gait
ga·lac'ta·cra'si·a
ga·lac'ta·gog'in
ga·lac'ta·gogue'
ga·lac'tan'
ga·lac'tase'
gal'ac·te'mi·a
ga·lact'hi·dro'sis
ga·lac'tic
ga·lac'tin
gal'ac·tis'chi·a
ga·lac'to·blast'
ga·lac'to·bol'ic
ga·lac'to·cele'
ga·lac'to·fla'vin
ga·lac'toid'
ga·lac'to·lip'in
gal'ac·to'ma pl. -mas or
-ma·ta
gal'ac·ton'ic
ga·lac'to·pex'ic
ga·lac'to·pex'y
gal'ac·toph'a·gous (subsist-
ing on milk)
♦galactophygous
gal'ac·toph'ly·sis pl. -ses'
ga·lac'to·phore'
gal'ac·toph'o·ri'tis
gal'ac·toph'o·rous
gal'ac·toph'y·gous (arrest-
ing the secretion of milk)
♦galactophagous
ga·lac'to·poi·e'sis pl. -ses'
ga·lac'to·poi·et'ic
ga·lac'to·py'ra
ga·lac'to·py'ra·nose'
ga·lac'to·py·ret'ic
ga·lac'tor·rhe'a
gal'ac·to'sa·mine'
ga·lac'tose'
ga·lac'tos·e'mi·a
ga·lac'to·sid'ase'
ga·lac'to·side'
gal'ac·to'sis pl. -ses'
gal'ac·tos'ta·sis pl. -ses'
ga·lac'tos·u'ri·a

ga·lac'to·tox'i·con'
ga·lac'to·tox'in
ga·lac'to·tox'ism
gal'ac·tot'ro·phy
ga·lac'to·zy'mase'
gal'ac·tu'ri·a
ga·lac'tu·ron'ic
Gal'ant
—— reflex
—— response
ga'le·a pl. -as or -ae'
—— ap'o·neu·rot'i·ca
—— cap'i·tis
gal'e·ro'pi·a
gall
gal'la·mine' tri·eth·i'o·
dide'
gall'blad'der
Gal'lie-Le Me·su'ri·er operation
Gal'lie operation
gal'li·um
gal'lon
gall'stone'
Gal'ton
—— law
—— system
gal·van'ic
gal'va·nism
gal'va·ni·za'tion
gal'va·nize', -nized', -niz'ing
gal'va·no·cau'ter·y
gal'va·no·con'trac·til'i·ty
gal'va·nom'e·ter
gal'va·no·sur'ger·y
gal'va·no·ther'a·py
gal'va·no·ther'my
gal'va·not'ro·pism
gam·boge'
gam'e·tan'gi·um pl. -gi·a
gam'ete'
ga·met'ic
ga·me'to·cyte'
gam'e·to·gen'e·sis
gam'e·to·gen'ic
gam'e·tog'o·ny
gam·fex'ine'
gam'ic
gam'ma
—— globulin
Gam'mel syndrome
gam·mop'a·thy
Gam'na
—— disease
—— nodules
—— spleen
Gam'na-Fa'vre bodies

Gam'na-Gan'dy bodies
gam'o·sep'al·ous
Gam'per bowing reflex
Gam'storp' disease
Gan'dy-Gam'na
—— nodules
—— spleen
gan'gli·a
—— a·or'ti·co·re·na'li·a
—— car·di'a·ca
—— ce·li'a·ca
—— coe·li'a·ca
—— in'ter·me'di·a
—— lum·ba'li·a
—— pel·vi'na
—— phren'i·ca
—— plex'u·um au'to·nom'i·co'rum
—— plexuum sym·path'i·co'rum
—— re·na'li·a
—— sa·cra'li·a
—— tho'ra·ca'li·a
—— tho·ra'ci·ca
—— trun'ci' sym·path'i·ci'
gan'gli·al
gan'gli·ar
gan'gli·at'ed
gan'gli·ec'to·my
gan'gli·form'
gan'gli·i'tis
gan'gli·o·blast'
gan'gli·o·cyte'
gan'gli·o·cy·to'ma pl. -mas or -ma·ta
gan'gli·oid'
gan'gli·o'ma pl. -mas or -ma·ta
gan'gli·on pl. -gli·a or -gli·ons
—— car·di'a·cum (Wris'ber·gi')
—— cer'vi·ca'le' in·fe'ri·us
—— cervicale medium
—— cervicale su·pe'ri·us
—— cer'vi·co·tho·ra'ci·cum
—— cil'i·ar·e'
—— ge·nic'u·li'
—— ha·ben'u·lae'
—— im'par'
—— in·fe'ri·us
—— inferius ner'vi' glos'so·pha·ryn'ge·i'
—— inferius nervi va'gi'
—— jug'u·lar'e' ner'vi' va'gi'
—— mes'en·ter'i·cum in·fe'ri·us

—— mesentericum su·pe'ri·us
—— mol'le'
—— no·do'sum
—— o'ti·cum
—— pe·tro'sum
—— pter'y·go·pal'a·ti'num
—— re·na'le'
—— sphe'no·pa·lat'i·num
—— spi·na'le'
—— spi·ra'le' coch'le·ae'
—— splanch'ni·cum
—— stel·la'tum
—— sub'man·dib'u·lar'e'
—— sub·max'il·lar'e'
—— su·pe'ri·us
—— superius ner'vi' glos'so·pha·ryn'ge·i'
—— superius nervi va'gi'
—— ter'mi·na'le'
—— tri·gem'i·na'le'
—— tym·pan'i·cum
—— ver'te·bra'le'
—— ves·tib'u·lar'e'
gan'gli·o·nat'ed
gan'gli·on·ec'to·my
Gan'gli·o·ne'ma
gan'gli·o·neu·ro·blas·to'ma pl. -mas or -ma·ta
—— sim'plex'
—— sym·path'i·cum
gan'gli·o·neu·ro·cy·to'ma pl. -mas or -ma·ta
gan'gli·o·neu·ro'ma pl. -mas or -ma·ta
—— te·lan'gi·ec·ta'tum cys'ti·cum
gan'gli·on'ic
gan'gli·on·i'tis
gan'gli·o·ple'gic
gan'gli·o·side'
gan'gli·o·si·do'sis'
gan·go'sa
gan'gre·ne'
gan'gre·no'sis pl. -ses'
gan'gre·nous
gan'o·blast'
Gan'ser
—— commissure
—— syndrome
Gant operation
Gant'zer muscle
gap, gapped, gap'ping
Gard'ner syndrome
gar'gle, -gled, -gling
gar'goyl·ism
Gar'land triangle

Gar·ré'
—— disease
—— osteomyelitis
Gar'rod test
Gart'ner
—— cyst
—— duct
gas, gassed, gas'sing
gas'e·ous
gas·om'e·ter
gas'o·met'ric
gas·se'ri·an
gas'ter
Gas'ter·oph'i·lus
—— hem'or·rhoi·da'lis
—— in·tes'ti·na'lis
—— na·sa'lis
gas·tral'gi·a
gas·tral'go·ke·no'sis
gas·tras·the'ni·a
gas·tra·tro'phi·a
gas·trec'to·my
gas'tric
gas'trin
gas·trit'ic
gas·tri'tis
gas·tro·a·nas'to·mo'sis
gas'tro·cele' (hernia of the stomach)
◊gastrocoel
gas'tro·cne'mi·us pl. -mi·i'
gas'tro·coel' (archenteron)
◊gastrocele
gas'tro·col'ic
gas'tro·co·li'tis
gas'tro·co·los'to·my
gas'tro·co·lot'o·my
gas'tro·col·pot'o·my
gas'tro·cu·ta'ne·ous
gas'tro·did'y·mus pl. -mi'
gas'tro·dis·ci'a·sis pl. -ses'
Gas'tro·dis·coi'des'
—— hom'i·nis
gas'tro·disk'
gas'tro·du'o·de'nal
gas'tro·du'o·de·nec'to·my
gas'tro·du'o·de·ni'tis
gas'tro·du'o·de·nos'to·my
gas'tro·dyn'i·a
gas'tro·en·ter·al'gi·a
gas'tro·en·ter·ic
gas'tro·en·ter·it'ic
gas'tro·en·ter·i'tis
gas'tro·en·ter·o·a·nas'to·mo'sis
gas'tro·en·ter·ol'o·gist
gas'tro·en·ter·ol'o·gy

gas'tro•en'ter•op'a•thy
gas'tro•en'ter•op•to'sis
gas'tro•en'ter•os'to•my
gas'tro•en'ter•ot'o•my
gas'tro•ep'i•plo'ic
gas'tro•e•soph'a•ge'al
gas'tro•e•soph'a•gi'tis
gas'tro•e•soph'a•go•plas'ty
gas'tro•e•soph'a•gos'to•my
gas'tro•fi'ber•scope'
gas'tro•gas•tros'to•my
gas'tro•ga•vage'
gas'tro•gen'ic
gas'tro•graph'
gas'tro•he•pat'ic
gas'tro•hep'a•ti'tis pl. -tis•es
   or -tit'i•des'
gas'tro•hy'per•ton'ic
gas'tro•il'e•ac'
gas'tro•il'e•i'tis
gas'tro•il'e•os'to•my
gas'tro•in•tes'ti•nal
gas'tro•je•ju'nal
gas'tro•je'ju•ni'tis
gas'tro•je'ju•nos'to•my
gas'tro•la•vage'
gas'tro•li'e•nal
gas'tro•lith'
gas'tro•li•thi'a•sis pl. -ses'
gas•trol'o•gy
gas•trol'y•sis pl. -ses'
gas'tro•ma•la'ci•a
gas'tro•meg'a•ly
gas'tro•mes'en•ter'ic
gas'tro•my•co'sis pl. -ses'
gas'tro•my•ot'o•my
gas'tro•pan'cre•at'ic
gas'tro•pan'cre•a•ti'tis
gas'tro•pa•re'sis di'a•bet'i•
   co'rum
gas'tro•path'ic
gas•trop'a•thy
gas'tro•per'i•to•ni'tis
gas'tro•pex'y
gas'tro•phren'ic
gas'tro•phthis'is pl. -ses'
gas'tro•plas'ty
gas'tro•pli•ca'tion
gas•trop•to'sis
gas'tro•pul'mo•nar'y
gas'tro•py'lo•rec'to•my
gas'tro•py•lo'ric
gas'tro•ra•dic'u•li'tis
gas•tror•rha'gi•a
gas•tror'rha•phy
gas•tror•rhe'a
gas•tror•rhex'is

gas'tro•sal'i•var'y
gas•tros'chi•sis
gas'tro•scope'
gas'tro•scop'ic
gas•tros'co•py
gas•tro'sis pl. -ses'
gas'tro•spasm
gas'tro•splen'ic
gas'tro•stax'is
gas'tro•ste•no'sis pl. -ses'
gas•tros'to•ma pl. -mas or
   -ma•ta
gas•tros'to•my
gas'tro•suc'cor•rhe'a
gas'tro•tho'ra•cop'a•gus pl.
   -gi'
gas'tro•tome'
gas•trot'o•my
gas'tro•tox'ic
gas'tro•tox'in
gas'tro•tym'pa•ni'tes'
gas'tru•la pl. -las or -lae'
gas'tru•la'tion
Gau•cher'
—— cells
—— disease
—— lipid
gauge
Gault reflex
gaunt'let
gauss
Gaus•sel' sign
Gauss'i•an points
gauze
ga•vage'
gaze, gazed, gaz'ing
g'-com•po'nent
Gee'-Her'ter disease
Gee-Thay'sen disease
Ge'gen•baur' muscle
ge'gen•hal'ten
Gei'gel reflex
Gei'ger
—— counter
—— region
—— threshold
—— tube
Gei'ger-Mül'ler
—— counter
—— counting circuit
—— tube
gel
ge•las'mus
ge•las'tic
ge•lat'i•fi•ca'tion
gel'a•tin
ge•lat'i•nase'

ge•lat'i•nize', -nized', -niz'-
   ing
ge•lat'i•noid'
ge•lat'i•no•lyt'ic
ge•lat'i•no'sa
ge•lat'i•nous
ge•la'tion
gel'a•tose'
Gé'li•neau'-Red'lich syn-
   drome
Gé'li•neau' syndrome
Gel•lé' test
gel'ose'
ge•lo'sis pl. -ses'
gem'i•nate', -nat'ed, -nat'ing
gem'i•na'tion
gem'i•nous
ge•mis'to•cyte'
ge•mis'to•cyt'ic
gem'ma pl. -mae'
gem'mule'
gem•py'lid poisoning
ge'na pl. -nae'
ge•nal
gen'der
Gen'dre fixing fluid
gene
gen'er•al•i•za'tion
gen'er•al•ize', -ized', -iz'ing
ge•ner'ic
ge•ne'si•al
ge•nes'ic
ge•ne'si•ol'o•gy
gen'e•sis pl. -ses'
ge•net'ic
ge•net'i•cist
ge•net'ics
ge•net'o•troph'ic
gen'e•tous
ge'ni•al
gen'ic
ge•nic'u•lar
ge•nic'u•late
ge•nic'u•lo•cal'ca•rine'
ge•nic'u•lo•tem'po•ral
ge•nic'u•lum pl. -la
—— ca•na'lis fa'ci•a'lis
—— ner'vi' fa'ci•a'lis
ge'ni•o•glos'sus pl. -si'
ge'ni•o•hy'o•glos'sus pl. -si'
ge'ni•o•hy'oid'
ge•ni'on'
ge'ni•o•pha•ryn'ge•us
ge'ni•o•plas'ty
gen'i•tal
gen'i•ta'li•a
gen'i•tal'i•ty

gen′i·tal·oid′
gen′i·to·cru′ral
gen′i·to·fem′o·ral
gen′i·to·u′ri·nar′y
gen′i·to·ves′i·cal
gen′ius
—— ep′i·dem′i·cus
—— mor′bi′
gen′o·blast′
gen′o·cide′
gen′o·der′ma·to′sis *pl.* -ses′
ge′nome′
gen′o·pho′bi·a
gen′o·type′
gen′o·typ′ic *or* gen′o·typ′i·
cal
gen′ta·mi′cin
gen′tian
ge′nu *pl.* gen′u·a
—— cap′su·lae′ in·ter′nae′
—— cor′po·ris cal·lo′si′
—— fa′ci·a′lis
—— ner′vi′ fa′ci·a′lis
—— rad′i·cis ner′vi′ fa′ci·
a′lis
—— re′cur·va′tum
—— val′gum
—— var′um
gen′u·al
gen′u·cu′bi·tal
gen′u·fa′cial
gen′u·pec′to·ral
ge′nus *pl.* gen′er·a
gen′y·an′trum
gen′y·plas′ty
ge′o·med′i·cine
ge′o·pha′gi·a
ge·oph′a·gism
ge·oph′a·gist
ge·oph′a·gous
ge·oph′a·gy
Geor′gi-Sachs′ test
ge·ot′ri·cho′sis *pl.* -ses′
Ge·ot′ri·chum
Ger′agh·ty operation
ge·rat′ic
ger′a·tol′o·gy
Ger′dy tubercle
Ger′hardt′
—— disease
—— sign
ger′i·at′ric
ger′i·at′rics
ger′i·o·psy·cho′sis *pl.* -ses′
Ger′lach′
—— tubal tonsil
—— valve

Ger′li·er
—— disease
—— syndrome
germ
ger′mi·ci′dal
ger′mi·cide′
ger′mi·nal
ger′mi·nate′, -nat′ed, -nat′-
ing
ger′mi·na′tion
ger′mi·na·tive
ger′mi·no′ma *pl.* -mas *or*
-ma·ta
Ger′mis·ton fever
ger′o·co′mi·a
ger′o·com′i·cal
ge·roc′o·my
ger′o·der′ma
ger′o·don′ti·a
ger′o·don′tic
ger′o·ma·ras′mus
ger′o·mor′phism
ge·ron′tal
ge·ron′tic
ger′on·tol′o·gy
ge·ron′to·phil′i·a
ge·ron′to·pho′bi·a
ge·ron′to·ther′a·py
ger′on·tox′on′
Ge′ro′ta fascia
Gersh′-Ma·cal′lum meth-
od
Gerst′mann syndrome
Ge·sell′ developmental
schedule
ge·stalt′
ge·stalt′ism
ges′tate′, -tat′ed, -tat′ing
ges·ta′tion
ges·ta′tion·al
ges·to′sis *pl.* -ses′
Get′so·wa adenoma
Ghon
—— complex
—— tubercle
Gia′co·mi′ni
—— band
—— frenulum
Gian·nuz′zi
—— cells
—— crescent
gi′ant
gi′ant·ism
Gi·ar′di·a
—— lam′bli·a
gi′ar·di′a·sis *pl.* -ses′
Gib′bon-Lan′dis test

gib·bos′i·ty
gib′bous *(swollen, convex,
or protuberant)*
♦*gibbus*
Gibbs adsorption law
Gibbs′-Don′nan equilibri-
um
Gibbs′-Helm′holtz′ equa-
tion
gib′bus *(a hump)*
♦*gibbous*
Gi·bral′tar fever
Gib′son
—— bandage
—— rule
Giem′sa stain
Gier′ke
—— corpuscles
—— disease
—— respiratory bundle
Gif′ford
—— operation
—— reflex
—— sign
gi·gan′tism
gi·gan′to·blast′
gi·gan′to·chro′mo·blast′
gi·gan′to·cyte′
Gi′gli operation
Gil·bert′
—— disease
—— sign
—— syndrome
Gil′christ disease
Gil′e·ad balm
Gil′ford-Hutch′in·son disease
Gilles de la Tou·rette′
—— disease
—— syndrome
Gil′lies operation
Gim′ber·nat′ ligament
gin′gi·va *pl.* -vae′
gin′gi·val
gin′gi·vec′to·my
gin′gi·vi′tis
gin′gi·vo·ax′i·al
gin′gi·vo·buc′cal
gin′gi·vo·glos′sal
gin′gi·vo·la′bi·al
gin′gi·vo·plas′ty
gin′gi·vo·sis *pl.* -ses′
gin′gi·vo·sto′ma·ti′tis
gin′gly·moid′
gin′gly·mus *pl.* -mi′
Gi·ral′dès organ
gir′dle

Gir'dle·stone' operation
git'a·lin
Git'lin syndrome
gla·bel'la pl. -lae'
gla·bel'lar
gla'brate'
gla'brous
gla'cial
glad'i·o'lus pl. -li'
glair'in
glair'y
gland
—— of Vir'chow-
Troi'si·er
glan'ders
glands
—— of Sham'baugh'
—— of Zeis
glan'du·la pl. -lae'
—— bul'bo·u're·thra'lis
—— lac'ri·ma'lis
—— lacrimalis inferior
—— lacrimalis superior
—— lin·gua'lis anterior
—— mam·mar'i·a
—— mu·co'sa
—— par'a·thy·roi'de·a inferi-
or
—— parathyroidea superior
—— pa·ro'tis
—— parotis ac'ces·so'ri·a
—— pi·tu'i·tar'i·a
—— se'ro·mu·co'sa
—— se·ro'sa
—— sub'lin·gua'lis
—— sub'man·dib'u·lar'is
—— sub·max'il·lar'is
—— su'pra·re·na'lis
—— thy're·oi'de·a
—— thyreoidea ac'ces·
so'ri·a su'pra·hy·oi'de·a
—— thy·roi'de·a
—— tym·pan'i·ca
—— ves·tib'u·lar'is major
glan'du·lae'
—— ar'e·o·lar'es'
—— bron'chi·a'les'
—— buc·ca'les'
—— ce·ru'mi·no'sae'
—— cer'vi·ca'les' u'ter·i'
—— cil'i·ar'es'
—— cir'cum·a·na'les'
—— con·junc'ti·va'les'
—— cu'tis
—— du'o·de·na'les'
—— e'so·pha'ge·ae'
—— gas'tri·cae'

—— glom'i·for'mes'
—— in·tes'ti·na'les' in'tes·
ti'ni' cras'si'
—— intestinales intestini
ten'u·is
—— intestinales rec'ti'
—— la'bi·a'les'
—— lac'ri·ma'les' ac'ces·
so'ri·ae'
—— la·ryn'ge·ae'
—— laryngeae an·te'ri·o'res'
—— laryngeae me'di·ae'
—— laryngeae pos·te'ri·
o'res'
—— lin·gua'les'
—— mo·lar'es'
—— mu·co'sae' bil'i·o'sae'
—— mucosae tu'ni·cae'
con'junc·ti'vae'
—— mucosae u're·te'ris
—— na·sa'les'
—— ol'fac·to'ri·ae'
—— o'ris
—— pal'a·ti'nae'
—— pel'vis re·na'lis
—— pha·ryn'ge·ae'
—— prae·pu'ti·a'les'
—— pre·pu'ti·a'les'
—— pro'pri·ae'
—— py·lo'ri·cae'
—— se·ba'ce·ae'
—— sebaceae a·re'o·lae'
mam'mae'
—— sebaceae con·junc'ti·
va'les'
—— sebaceae la'bi·o'rum
pu·den'di'
—— si'ne' duc'ti·bus
—— su'do·rif'er·ae'
—— su'pra·re·na'les' ac'ces·
so'ri·ae'
—— tar·sa'les'
—— thy're·oi'de·ae' ac'ces·
so'ri·ae'
—— thy·roi'de·ae' ac'ces·
so'ri·ae'
—— tra'che·a'les'
—— tu·bar'i·ae'
—— u're·thra'les'
—— urethrales
u·re'thrae' mu'li·e'bris
—— u'ter·i'nae'
—— ves'i·ca'les'
—— ves·tib'u·lar'es' mi·
no'res'
glan'du·lar
glans pl. glan'des'

—— cli·to'ri·dis
—— pe'nis
Glanz'mann and Rin'i·ker
lym'pho·cy·toph'thi·sis
Gla·se'ri·an fissure
Glau'ber salt
glau·co'ma
glau·co'ma·tous
gleet
gleet'y
Glé·nard' disease
glen'o·hu'mer·al
gle'noid'
Gley
—— cells
—— glands
gli'a
gli'a·cyte'
gli'a·din
gli'al
gli'o·bac·te'ri·a
gli'o·blas·to'ma pl. -mas or
-ma·ta
—— i'so·mor'phe'
—— mul'ti·for'me'
gli'o·car'ci·no'ma pl. -mas
or -ma·ta
gli'o·coc'cus pl. -ci'
gli'o·fi'bro·sar·co'ma
pl. -mas or -ma·ta
gli·og'e·nous
gli'o·ma pl. -mas or -ma·ta
gli'o·ma·to'sis pl. -ses'
—— cer'e·bri'
gli·om'a·tous
gli'o·neu'ro·blas·to'ma
pl. -mas or -ma·ta
gli'o·neu·ro'ma pl. -mas or
-ma·ta
gli'o·sar·co'ma pl. -mas or
-ma·ta
gli·o'sis pl. -ses'
gli'o·some'
Glis'son
—— capsule
—— disease
glob'al
globe
glo'bin
glo'bose'
glob'u·lar
glob'ule'
glob'u·lin
α-globulin
β-globulin
γ-globulin
glob'u·li·ne'mi·a

glob'u·lin·u'ri·a
glo'bus *pl.* -bi'
—— hys·ter'i·cus
—— major ep'i·di·dym'i·dis
—— minor epididymidis
—— pal'li·dus
glo'man·gi·o'ma *pl.* -mas *or*
 -ma·ta
glom'er·a a·or'ti·ca
glom'er·ate
glo·mer'u·lar
glom'er·ule'
glo·mer'u·li'
—— ar·te'ri·o'si' coch'le·ae'
—— re'nis
glo·mer'u·li'tis
glo·mer'u·lo·ne·phri'tis
glo·mer'u·lop'a·thy
glo·mer'u·lo·scle·ro'sis *pl.*
 -ses'
glo·mer'u·lose'
glo·mer'u·lo·tro'pin
glo·mer'u·lus *pl.* -li'
glo'mic
glo'mus *pl.* glom'er·a
—— a·or'ti·cum
—— ca·rot'i·cum
—— cho'ri·oi'de·um
—— cho·roi'de·um
—— coc·cyg'e·um
—— jug'u·lar'e'
glon'o·in
glos'sa *pl.* -sae'
glos'sal
glos·sal'gi·a
glos·san'thrax'
glos·sec'to·my
Glos·si'na
glos·sit'ic
glos·si'tis
—— ar'e·a'ta ex·fo'li·a·ti'va
glos'so·cele'
glos'so·dy'na·mom'e·ter
glos'so·dyn'i·a
—— ex·fo'li·a·ti'va
glos'so·ep'i·glot'tic
glos'so·ep'i·glot·tid'e·an
glos'so·graph'
glos'so·hy'al
glos'so·hy'oid'
glos'so·kin'es·thet'ic
glos'so·la'bi·al
glos'so·la'bi·o·la·ryn'ge·al
glos'so·la'bi·o·pha·ryn'ge·
 al
glos'so·la'li·a
glos·sol'o·gy

glos'so·man'ti·a
glos'so·pal'a·tine'
glos'so·pal'a·ti'nus
glos'so·pal'a·to·la'bi·al
glos·sop'a·thy
glos'so·pha·ryn'ge·al
glos'so·pha·ryn'ge·o·
 la'bi·al
glos'so·pha·ryn'ge·us
glos'so·plas'ty
glos'so·ple'gi·a
glos'sop·to'sis *pl.* -ses'
glos'so·py·ro'sis
glos·sor'rha·phy
glos·sos'co·py
glos'so·spasm
glos·sot'o·my
glos'so·trich'i·a
glot'tal
glot'tic
glot·tid'e·an
glot'tis *pl.* -tis·es *or*
 -ti·des'
glu'ca·gon'
glu'ca·to'ni·a
glu·cep'tate'
glu'cide'
glu·cid'ic
glu'co·cor'ti·coid'
glu'co·he'mi·a
glu'co·ki'nase'
glu'co·ki·net'ic
glu'co·kin'in
glu·col'y·sis *pl.* -ses'
glu'co·nate'
glu'co·ne'o·gen'e·sis
glu·con'ic
glu'co·pro'tein
glu·co'sa·mine'
glu'cose'
glu·co'si·dase'
glu'co·side'
glu'co·sin
glu'co·sul'fone'
glu·cos·u'ri·a
glu·cu·ron'i·dase'
glu·cu'ro·nide'
glu'ta·mate'
glu·tam'ic
glu'ta·mine'
glu·tam·in'ic
glu·tam'yl
glu'ta·ral'de·hyde'
glu·tar'ic
glu'ta·thi'one'
glu'ta·thi'o·nu'ri·a

glu'te·al
glu'te·lin
glu'ten *(a mixture of pro-*
 teins found in cereal seeds)
 ♦glutin
glu'te·nin
glu'te·o·fas'ci·al
glu'te·o·fem'o·ral
glu'te·o·in'gui·nal
glu'te·o·tro'chan·ter'ic
glu·teth'i·mide'
glu'te·us *pl.* -te'i'
—— max'i·mus
—— me'di·us
—— min'i·mus
glu'tin *(a protein obtained*
 from gelatin)
 ♦gluten
glu'ti·nous
gly·bu'ride'
gly'case'
gly·ce'mi·a
glyc'er·al'de·hyde'
glyc'er·i·dase'
glyc'er·ide'
glyc'er·in
glyc'er·in·at'ed
glyc'er·ite'
glyc'er·o·gel'a·tin
glyc'er·ol'
glyc'er·o·phos'phate'
glyc'er·ose'
glyc'er·yl
gly'ci·nate'
gly'cine'
gly'ci·nin
gly'co·bi·ar'sol'
gly'co·ca'lyx
gly'co·cho'late'
gly'co·cy·am'i·nase'
gly'co·cy'a·mine'
gly'co·gen
gly'co·ge·nase'
gly'co·gen'e·sis *(process of*
 formation of glycogen)
 ♦glycogenosis
gly'co·ge·net'ic
gly'co·gen'ic
gly'co·ge·nol'y·sis *pl.* -ses'
gly'co·gen·o·lyt'ic
gly'co·gen·o'sis *(one of sev-*
 eral inborn errors in the me-
 tabolism of glycogen) pl.
 -ses'
 ♦glycogenesis
gly·cog'e·nous
gly'co·he'mi·a

gly′co·his·tech′i·a
gly′col′
gly′co·lip′id
gly′co·lyl
gly′col′y·sis *pl.* -ses′
gly′co·lyt′ic
gly′co·met′a·bol′ic
gly′co·me·tab′o·lism
gly′co·pe′ni·a
gly′co·pex′is
gly′co·phil′i·a
gly′co·pro′tein′
gly′co·pyr′ro·late′
gly′cor·rha′chi·a
gly′cor·rhe′a
gly·co′sa·mine′
gly′co·se′cre·to′ry
gly′co·se′mi·a
gly′co·si·al′i·a
gly′co·si′dal
gly′co·side′
gly′co·sid′ic
gly′co·sphin′go·lip′id
gly′co·sphin′go·side′
gly′co·stat′ic
gly′cos·u′ri·a
gly′cos·u′ric
gly′co·troph′ic
glyc′u·re′sis *pl.* -ses′
gly′cu·ron′ic
gly′cu·ron′i·dase′
gly·cu′ro·nide′
gly·cu′ro·nu′ri·a
gly′cyl
gly·hex′a·mide′
gly·oc′ta·mide′
gly·ox′al
gly·ox′a·lase′
gly·ox′yl′ic
gly·par′a·mide′
Gmel′in test
gna·thal′gi·a
gnath′ic
gna′thi·on′
gna·thi′tis
gnath′o·ceph′a·lus *pl.* -li′
gnath′o·dy′na·mom′e·ter
gnath′o·dyn′i·a
gnath′o·pal′a·tos′chi·sis *pl.*
  -ses′
gna′tho·plas′ty
gna·thos′chi·sis *pl.* -ses′
Gna·thos′to·ma
—— his′pi·dum
—— spi·nig′er·um
gna·thos′to·mi′a·sis
gno′si·a

gno′sis *pl.* -ses′
gnos′tic
gno′to·bi·ote′
gno′to·bi·ot′ic
gno′to·bi·ot′ics
go·det′
Godt′fred′sen syndrome
Goetsch test
Gof′man test
goi′ter
goi′tro·gen
goi′tro·gen′ic
goi′trous
Gold′ber′ger limb lead
Gold′blatt′
—— hypertension
—— kidney
Gol′den·har′ syndrome
Gold′flam′
—— disease
—— symptom complex
Gold′schei′der disease
Gold′stein′ reaction
Gold′stein-Schee′rer tests
Gold′thwait′ operation
Gol′gi
—— apparatus
—— body
—— bottle neuron
—— cells
—— complex
—— corpuscle
—— element
—— law
—— material
—— membranes
—— network
—— remnant
—— substance
—— tendon organ
Gol′gi-Maz·zo′ni corpus-
cle
Gol′gi-Rez·zon′i·co spirals
Goll
—— column
—— nucleus
—— tract
Goltz syndrome
Gom·bault′
—— degeneration
—— demyelination
—— neuritis
Gom·bault′-Phi·lippe′ triangle
go·mit′o·li′
gom·pho′sis *pl.* -ses′
gon′a·cra′ti·a

go′nad′
go·nad′al
go′na·dec′to·mize′, -mized′,
  -miz′ing
go′nad·ec′to·my
go·nad′o·blas·to′ma
  pl. -mas *or* -ma·ta
go·nad′o·cen′tric
go·nad′o·in·hib′i·to′ry
go·nad′o·ki·net′ic
go′na·dop′a·thy
go·nad′o·ther′a·py
go·nad′o·trop′ic
go·nad′o·tro′pin
gon′a·duct′
go·nag′ra
go·nal′gi·a
gon·an′gi·ec′to·my
gon·ar·thri′tis
gon·ar·thro′sis *pl.* -ses′
gon·ar·throt′o·my
go·nat′o·cele′
Gon′da reflex
Gon′gy·lo·ne′ma
—— pul′chrum
gon·gy·lo′ne·mi′a·sis *pl.*
  -ses′
go′ni·al
gon′ic
go·nid′i·al
go·nid′i·um *pl.* -i·a
go′ni·o·chei·los′chi·sis
go′ni·o·cra′ni·om′e·try
go′ni·om′e·ter
go′ni·on′
go′ni·o·punc′ture
go′ni·o·scope′
go′ni·os′co·py
go′ni·ot′o·my
go·ni′tis
gon′o·blast′
gon′o·blen′nor·rhe′a
gon′o·camp′sis
gon′o·cele′
gon′o·coc′cal
gon′o·coc·ce′mi·a
gon′o·coc′cic
gon′o·coc′cide′
gon′o·coc′cus *pl.* -ci′
gon′o·cyte′
gon′o·cy·to′ma *pl.* -mas *or*
  -ma·ta
go·nom′er·y
gon′or·rhe′a
gon′or·rhe′al
gon′y·camp′sis
gon′y·o·cele′

gon'y·on'cus
Gon·za'les blood group
Goo·dell' sign
Good'e·nough' test
Good'pas'ture
—— stain
—— syndrome
Good'sall rule
Good syndrome
Gop'a·lan' syndrome
Gor'di·a'ce·a
Gor'don
—— reflex
—— test
gor'get
Gor'lin syndrome
Gos·syp'i·um
Gott'lieb' cuticle
gouge
Gou'ger·ot'-Blum'
  disease
Gou'ger·ot'- Hou'wer-
  Sjö'gren syndrome
Gou·lard' extract
goun'dou'
gout
gout'y
Gow'er-Hen'ry reflex
Gow'ers
—— column
—— fasciculus
—— myopathy
—— phenomenon
—— sign
—— solution
—— syndrome
—— tract
graaf'i·an
grac'ile
gra·da'tim
Gra'de·ni'go
—— sign
—— syndrome
gra'di·ent
grad'u·ate
grad'u·at'ed
Grae'fe sign
Grae'ser method
Graff method
graft
Gra'ham
—— law
—— operation
Gra'ham-Cole' test
Gra'ham Steell' murmur
grain
grain'age

gram
Gram
—— iodine
—— stain
Gram'-Clau'di·us stain
gram'-neg'a·tive
gram'-pos'i·tive
gra'na
gra·na'tum
Gran·cher'
—— pneumonia
—— system
grand mal
Gran'dry-Mer'kel corpus-
  cle
Gran'ger line
gran'u·la
gran'u·lar
gra'nu·la'ti·o' pl. -la'ti·o'nes'
gran'u·la'tion
gran'u·la'ti·o'nes'
  a·rach'noi·de·a'les'
gran'ule'
gran'u·li·form'
gran'u·lo·blast'
gran'u·lo'blas·to'sis pl. -ses'
gran'u·lo·cyte'
gran'u·lo·cyt'ic
gran'u·lo·cy'to·pe'ni·a
gran'u·lo·cy'to·poi·e'sis
  pl. -ses'
gran'u·lo·cy'to·poi·et'ic
gran'u·lo'ma pl. -mas or
  -ma·ta
—— an'nu·lar'e'
—— con·ta'gi·o'sa
—— fa'ci·a'le'
—— faciale e'o·sin'o·phil'i·
cum
—— fis'su·ra'tum
—— fun·goi'des'
—— gen'i·to·in'gui·na'le'
—— in'gui·na'le'
—— pen'du·lum
—— py'o·gen'i·cum
—— tel·an'gi·ec'ti·cum
—— trop'i·cum
—— ve·ne're·um
gran'u·lo'ma·to'sis pl. -ses'
—— dis'ci·for'mis chron'i·ca
pro'gres·si'va
—— in·fan'ti·sep'ti·ca
gran'u·lom'a·tous
gran'u·lo·mere'
gran'u·lo·pe'ni·a
gran'u·lo·plasm
gran'u·lo·plas'tic

gran'u·lo·poi·e'sis pl. -ses'
gran'u·lo·poi·et'ic
gran'u·lo'sa
gran'u·lo'sis pl. -ses'
—— ru'bra na'si'
graph
graph'an·es·the'si·a
graph'es·the'si·a
graph'ic
graph'ite'
graph'o·mo'tor
graph'or·rhe'a
Gra'ser diverticulum
Gras·set'-Gaus·sel'
—— phenomenon
—— sign
Gras·set' law
Gra'tio·let' optic radiation
grat·tage'
grave
grav'el
Graves disease
grav'id
grav'i·da pl. -das or -dae'
gra·vid'ic
grav'id·ism
gra·vid'i·tas
—— ex·am'i·na'lis
—— ex'o·cho'ri·a'li·a
gra·vid'i·ty
grav'i·do·car'di·ac'
gra·vim'e·ter
grav'i·met'ric
gra·vim'e·try
grav'is ne'o·na·to'rum
  jaundice
grav'i·stat'ic
grav'i·tate', -tat'ed, -tat'ing
grav'i·ta'tion
grav'i·ta'tion·al
grav'i·ty
Gra'witz tumor
Gray stain
Green'berg' method
Green'field' disease
Greg'er·sen test
Greg'o·ry powder
Greig hypertelorism
grenz
Grey Tur'ner sign
Grie'sin'ger
—— disease
—— sign
Grif'fith method
grip
grippe
gris'e·o·ful'vin

gris'e·o·my'cin
Gri·solle' sign
Grit'ti-Stokes' amputation
Groc'co
—— sign
—— triangle
Groen'blad-Strand'berg' syndrome
Groe'nouw corneal dystrophy
groin
groove
gross
growth
Gru'ber
—— ligament
—— muscle
—— speculum
—— syndrome
—— test
Grüb'ler stain
gru'mose'
gru'mous
Grün'wald' stain
Gryn'feltt' triangle
gry'o·chrome'
gry·po'sis pl. -ses'
G'-stro·phan'thin
gua'co
guai'ac'
guai'a·col'
guai·fen'e·sin
Gua·ma fever
gua'na·cline'
gua'na·drel'
gua'nase'
guan·cy'dine'
guan·eth'i·dine'
gua'ni·dine'
gua'nine'
guan·i'so·quin
gua'no·clor'
guan·oc'tine'
gua'no·sine'
guan·ox'an'
guan·ox'y·fen'
gua·nyl'ic
Guar·nie'ri bodies
Gua·ro'a fever
gua'za
gu'ber·nac'u·lar
gu'ber·nac'u·lum pl. -la
—— den'tis
—— tes'tis
Gub'ler paralysis
Gud'den commissure
Gu'der·natsch' test

Gué·neau' de Mus·sy' point
Gué·rin'
—— fold
—— sinus
—— valve
Guil·lain'-Bar·ré'
—— disease
—— syndrome
Guil·lain' sign
guil'lo·tine'
Guld'berg-Waa'ge law
Gull
—— and Sut'ton disease
—— disease
gul'let
gum'ma pl. -mas or -ma·ta
gum'ma·tous
Gum'precht' shadows
Gun'ning test
Gün'ther disease
gur'ney
Gur'vich radiation
gus·ta'tion
gus'ta·to'ry
gus'to·lac'ri·mal
gut
Guth'rie test
Gut'stein' stain
gut'ta pl. -tae'
gut'ta-per'cha
gut'tate'
gut·ta'tim
gut'ter
gut'ti·form'
Gutt'mann sign
gut'tur·al
gut'tur·oph'o·ny
gut'tur·o·tet'a·ny
Gut'zeit' test
Gwath'mey method
gym'no·tho'rax' poisoning
gynaec-. See words spelled gynec-.
gynaeco-. See words spelled gyneco-.
gy·nan'der
gy·nan'dri·a
gy·nan'drism
gy·nan'dro·blas·to'ma pl. -mas or -ma·ta
gy·nan'droid'
gy·nan'dro·morph'
gy·nan'dro·mor'phic
gy·nan'dro·mor'phism
gy·nan'drous
gy·nan'dry

gyn'a·tre'si·a
gy·ne'cic
gyn'e·co·gen
gy'ne·co·gen'ic
gy'ne·cog'ra·phy
gy'ne·coid'
gy'ne·co·log'ic or gy'ne·co·log'i·cal
gy'ne·col'o·gist
gy'ne·col'o·gy
gy'ne·co·ma'ni·a
gy'ne·co·mas'ti·a
gy'ne·co·mas'ty
gy'ne·co·ma'zi·a
gy'ne·cop'a·thy
gy'ne·pho'bi·a
gy'ne·pho'ric
gy'no·gam'one'
gy'no·gen'e·sis
gy'no·plas'tic
gy'no·plas'ty
gy'ral
gy'rate'
gy·ra'tion
Gy·rau'lus
—— sai'go·nen'sis
gy·rec'to·my
gyr'en·ceph'a·late'
gyr'en·ce·phal'ic
gyr'en·ceph'a·lous
gy'ri'
—— An'dre·ae' Ret'zi·i'
—— an'nec·ten'tes'
—— brev'es' in'su·lae'
—— cer'e·bel'li'
—— cer'e·bri'
—— in'su·lae'
—— oc·cip'i·ta'les' lat'er·a'les'
—— occipitales su·pe'ri·o'res'
—— o·per'ti'
—— or'bi·ta'les'
—— pro·fun'di' cer'e·bri'
—— tem'po·ra'les' trans·ver'si'
—— tran·si·ti'vi' cer'e·bri'
gy'rose'
gy'ro·spasm
gy'rus pl. -ri'
—— am'bi·ens
—— an'gu·lar'is
—— cal·lo'sus
—— cen·tra'lis anterior
—— centralis posterior
—— cin'gu·li'
—— cu'ne·us

—— den·ta'tus
—— ep'i·cal·lo'sus
—— fas'ci·o·lar'is
—— for'ni·ca'tus
—— fron·ta'lis inferior
—— frontalis me'di·us
—— frontalis superior
—— fu'si·for'mis
—— hip'po·cam'pi'
—— in'fra·cal'ca·ri'nus
—— in'tra·lim'bi·cus
—— lim'bi·cus
—— lin·gua'lis
—— lon'gus in'su·lae'
—— mar'gi·na'lis
—— oc·cip'i·to·tem'po·ra'lis lat'er·a'lis
—— occipitotemporalis me'di·a'lis
—— of Bro'ca
—— ol'fac·to'ri·us
—— par'a·hip'po·cam·pa'lis
—— par'a·ter'mi·na'lis
—— post'cen·tra'lis
—— pre'cen·tra'lis
—— rec'tus
—— ro·lan'di·cus
—— sem'i·lu·nar'is
—— sub'cal·lo'sus
—— su'pra·cal·lo'sus
—— su'pra·mar'gi·na'lis
—— tem'po·ra'lis inferior
—— temporalis me'di·us
—— temporalis superior
—— un'ci·na'tus

H

Haab reflex
Haa'se rule
ha·be'na
ha·be'nar
ha·ben'u·la pl. -lae'
—— per'fo·ra'ta
ha·ben'u·lar
ha·ben'u·lo·pe·dun'cu·lar
hab'it
hab'i·tat'
ha·bit'u·al
ha·bit'u·a'tion
hab'i·tus
Ha'den-Haus'ser method
haem–. See words spelled hem–.

haema–. See words spelled hema–.
Hae'ma·dip'sa
Hae'ma·gog'us
haemat–. See words spelled hemat–.
haemato–. See words spelled hemato–.
haemo–. See words spelled hemo–.
Hae'nel
—— sign
—— variant
Hae'ser
—— coefficient
—— formula
Haff disease
Haff'kine vaccine
Hag'e·dorn' and Jen'sen method
Hagedorn needle
Ha'ge·man
—— factor
—— trait
Hag'ner bag
Hahn'e·mann·ism
Hai'din·ger brushes
Hai'ley-Hai'ley disease
Haines test
hair'ball'
Haj'ek operation
ha·la'tion
hal'a·zone'
Hal'ber·staedt'er bodies
hal·cin'o·nide'
Hal'dane'
—— chamber
—— scale
half'-life'
half'-val'ue
hal'ide'
hal'i·ste·re'sis pl. -ses'
hal'i·ste·ret'ic
hal'i·to'sis pl. -ses'
hal'i·tus
Hal'lé point
Hal'ler
—— habenula
—— isthmus
Hal'ler·mann-Streiff'-Fran·çois' syndrome
Hal'ler·vor'den-Spatz'
—— disease
—— syndrome
Hal'lion law
Hall muscle
Hal'lo·peau' disease

hal'lu·cal
hal·lu'ci·nate', -nat'ed, -nat'ing
hal·lu'ci·na'tion
hal·lu'ci·na·tive
hal·lu'ci·na·to'ry
hal·lu'ci·no·gen
hal·lu'ci·no·gen'e·sis
hal·lu'ci·no·gen'ic
hal·lu'ci·no'sis pl. -ses'
hal·lu'ci·not'ic
hal'lux pl. -lu·ces'
—— flex'us
—— rig'i·dus
—— val'gus
—— var'us
hal'ma·to·gen'e·sis pl. -ses'
ha'lo'
hal'o·gen
hal'o·gen·ate', -at'ed, -at'ing
hal'oid'
ha·lom'e·ter
hal'o·per'i·dol'
hal'o·pro·ges'ter·one'
hal'o·pro'gin
hal'o·thane'
hal'qui·nols'
Hal'stead tests
Hal'sted
—— herniorrhaphy
—— mastectomy
ha·mar'ti·a
ha·mar'to·blas·to'ma pl. -mas or -ma·ta
ham'ar·to'ma pl. -mas or -ma·ta
ham'ar·tom'a·tous
ha'mate'
ha·ma'tum pl. -ta
Ham'burg'er rule
Ham'il·ton sign
Ham'man
—— disease
—— sign
Ham'man-Rich' syndrome
Ham'mar·sten test
ham'mer
Ham'mer·schlag' method
ham'mer·toe'
Ham'mond disease
Hamp'ton
—— maneuver
—— technique
ham'string'
ham'u·lar
ham'u·late'
ham'u·lus pl. -li'

—— lac'ri·ma'lis
—— lam'i·nae' spi·ra'lis
—— os'sis ha·ma'ti'
—— pter'y·goi'de·us
ha·my'cin
hand
—— sign of Brun
hand'ed·ness
hand'i·cap'
Hand'ley method
Hand'-Schül'ler-Chris'tian disease
Han'ger test
hang'nail'
hang'o'ver
Han'ot
—— cirrhosis
—— disease
Han'sen
—— bacillus
—— disease
han'se·nid
H antigen
hap'a·lo·nych'i·a
haph'al·ge'si·a
hap'lo·dont'
hap'loid'
hap'lo·my·co'sis
hap·lo'pi·a
hap'lo·scope'
hap'ten
hap'te·pho'bi·a
hap'tic
hap'tics
hap'to·glo'bin
hap'to·phore'
Ha·ra'da syndrome
hard'en
Har'den-Young' ester
Har·de'ri·an gland
Har'ding-Pas'sey melano-ma
hard'ness
hard'-of-hear'ing
Har'dy-Wein'berg' equilibrium
hare'lip'
Hare syndrome
Har'kins method
Har'ley disease
Har'ring·ton operation
Har'ris
—— and Ben'e·dict standards
—— hematoxylin
Har'ri·son
—— groove

—— spot test
Har'row·er-Er'ick·son test
Hart'ley-Krause' operation
Hart'mann
—— fossa
—— pouch
—— solution
Hart'man·nel'la
—— cas'tel·lan'i·i'
—— hy'a·li'na
Hart'nup disease
harts'horn'
Hash'i·mo'to disease
hash'ish'
Has'kins test
Has'ner valve
Has'sall
—— body
—— corpuscle
Has'sall-Hen'le warts
Hau'dek' niche
haunch
Haus'ser method
haus'tra co'li'
haus·tra'tion
haus'trum *pl.* -tra
haut mal
Ha'ver·hill fever
Hav'er·hil'li·a mul'ti·for'mis
ha·ver'sian
Haxt'hau'sen disease
Hay'em
—— corpuscle
—— solution
Hay'em-Wi·dal' syndrome
Hay'garth' nodes
Haynes operation
head
Head
—— areas
—— zones
head'ache'
heal
health
health'y
hear, heard, hear'ing
heart
heart'beat'
heart'burn'
heat'stroke'
he'be·phre'ni·a
he'be·phren'ic
Heb'er·den
—— arthritis
—— disease

—— node
Heb'er·den-Ro'sen·bach' node
he·bet'ic
heb'e·tude'
heb'e·tu'di·nous
he·bos'te·ot'o·my
he·bot'o·my
Heb'ra pityriasis
Hecht'-Schla'er adaptom-eter
hec'to·gram'
hec'to·li'ter
Hed'blom' syndrome
he·do'ni·a
he'don·ism
heel
Heer'fordt' disease
Hef'ke-Tur'ner sign
Hegg'lin anomaly
Hei'den·hain'
—— cells
—— iron hematoxylin
—— pouch
Heim'-Krey'sig sign
Hei'ne·ke-Mik'u·licz operation
Hei'ne-Med'in disease
Hei'ner syndrome
Heinz bodies
Heinz'-Ehr'lich bodies
Heis'ter valve
Hek'toen' phenomenon
hel'coid'
hel·co'ma *pl.* -mas *or* -ma·ta
hel·co'sis
hel·cot'ic
Held
—— spaces
—— stria
hel'i·cal
he·lic'i·form'
hel'i·coid'
hel'i·co·pod'
hel'i·co·po'di·a
hel'i·co·tre'ma
he·li·en·ceph'a·li'tis
he·li·o·tax'is
he·li·o·trop'ic
he·li·o·tro'pin
he·li·ot'ro·pism
he'li·ox'
he'li·um
he'lix *pl.* hel'i·ces' *or* -lix·es
Hel'ke·si·mas'tix
—— fae·cic'o·la
hel'le·bore'

Hel'ler test
Hel'li·ge method
Hel'lin law
Hel'ly fixing fluid
Helm'holtz' theory
hel'minth'
hel·min'tha·gogue'
hel'min·them'e·sis
hel'min·thi'a·sis *pl.* -ses'
—— e·las'ti·ca
hel·min'thic
hel'minth·ism
hel·min'thoid'
hel'min·tho'ma *pl.* -mas or
 -ma·ta
hel·min'thous
He'lo·der'ma
—— hor'ri·dum
—— sus·pec'tum
he·lo'ma *pl.* -mas or -ma·ta
he·lot'o·my
Hel'weg'
—— bundle
—— tract
he·ma·cy·tom'e·ter
hem·a·den
hem'a·do·ste·no'sis *pl.* -ses'
he'ma·dro·mom'e·ter
hem'a·dy'na·mom'e·try
hem'a·fa'cient
he'mag·glu'ti·na'tion
he'mag·glu'ti·nin
he'mal
he·mal'um
hem'a·nal'y·sis *pl.* -ses'
he·man'gi·ec·ta'si·a
he·man'gi·ec·ta·sis *pl.* -ses'
he·man'gi·ec·tat'ic
he·man'gi·o·am'e·lo·blas·
 to'ma *pl.* -mas or -ma·ta
he·man'gi·o·blast'
he·man'gi·o·blas·to'ma *pl.*
 -mas or -ma·ta
he·man'gi·o·blas'to·ma·
 to'sis
he·man'gi·o·e·las'to·myx·
 o'ma *pl.* -mas or -ma·ta
he·man'gi·o·en'do·the'li·o·
 blas·to'ma *pl.* -mas or -ma·ta
he·man'gi·o·en'do·the'li·
 o'ma *pl.* -mas or -ma·ta
he·man'gi·o·en'do·the'li·o·
 sar·co'ma *pl.* -mas or -ma·ta
he·man'gi·o·li·po'ma
 pl. -mas or -ma·ta
he·man'gi·o'ma *pl.* -mas or
 -ma·ta

he·man'gi·o·ma·to'sis
 pl. -ses'
—— ret'i·nae'
he·man'gi·om'a·tous
he·man'gi·o·my'o·li·po'ma
 pl. -mas or -ma·ta
he·man'gi·o·per'i·cy·to'ma
 pl. -mas or -ma·ta
he·man'gi·o·sar·co'ma *pl.*
 -mas or -ma·ta
hem'a·poph'y·sis *pl.* -ses'
hem'ar·thro'sis *pl.* -ses'
he'ma·te'in
he'ma·tem'e·sis
he'ma·ther'mous
he'mat·hi·dro'sis
he·mat'ic
he'ma·tim'e·ter
he'ma·tim'e·try
hem'a·tin
hem'a·ti·ne'mi·a
hem'a·tin'ic
hem'a·ti·nu'ri·a
hem'a·tite'
hem'a·to·bil'i·a
hem'a·to·blast'
hem'a·to·cele'
hem'a·to·che'zi·a
hem'a·to·chro·ma·to'sis
 pl. -ses'
hem'a·to·chro'mi·a
hem'a·to·chy'lo·cele'
hem'a·to·chy·lu'ri·a
hem'a·to·col'pos
hem'a·to·crit'
hem'a·to·crys'tal·lin
hem'a·to·cyst'
hem'a·to·cyte'
hem'a·to·cy·tol'y·sis
 pl. -ses'
hem'a·to'cy·to'sis *pl.* -ses'
hem'a·to'cy·tu'ri·a
hem'a·to·dys·cra'si·a
hem'a·to·en'ce·phal'ic
hem'a·to·gen'
hem'a·to·gen'e·sis *pl.* -ses'
hem'a·to·gen'ic
hem'a·tog'e·nous
hem'a·to·glo'bin
hem'a·to·gone'
hem'a·to·hi·dro'sis
he'ma·toid'
he'ma·toi'din
he'ma·to·log'ic
he'ma·tol'o·gist
he'ma·tol'o·gy

hem'a·to·lymph·an'gi·
 o'ma *pl.* -mas or -ma·ta
hem'a·to·lymph·u'ri·a
he'ma·tol'y·sis *pl.* -ses'
he'ma·to·lyt'o·poi·et'ic
he'ma·to'ma *pl.* -mas or
 -ma·ta
he·ma·to·me'di·as·ti'num
he'ma·tom'e·ter
he'ma·to·me'tra
he'ma·tom'e·try
he'ma·to·mole'
he'ma·to·my·e'li·a
hem'a·to·my'e·li'tis
he'ma·ton'ic
hem'a·to·pa·thol'o·gy
hem'a·to·pe'ni·a
hem'a·to·per'i·car'di·um
hem'a·to·per'i·to·ne'um
hem'a·to·phage'
hem'a·to·pha'gi·a
hem'a·toph'a·gous
hem'a·to·phil'i·a
hem'a·to·plas'tic
hem'a·to·poi·e'sis *pl.* -ses'
hem'a·to·poi·et'ic
hem'a·to·por·phyr'i·a
hem'a·to·por'phy·rin
hem'a·to·por'phy·ri·
 ne'mi·a
hem'a·to·por'phy·ri·nu'ri·a
hem'a·to·pre·cip'i·tin
hem'a·tor·rha'chis
hem'a·tor·rhe'a
hem'a·to·sal'pinx'
hem'a·to·scope'
hem'a·tose'
he'ma·to'sis *pl.* -ses'
hem'a·to·spec'tro·scope'
hem'a·to·spec·tros'co·py
hem'a·to·sper'ma·to·cele'
hem'a·to·sper'mi·a
hem'a·to·stat'ic
hem'a·to·ther'a·py
hem'a·to·ther'mal
hem'a·to·ther'mous
hem'a·to·tho'rax'
hem'a·to·tox'ic
hem'a·to·tox·ic'i·ty
hem'a·to·tox'i·co'sis
hem'a·to·trop'ic
hem'a·to·tym'pa·num
he'ma·tox'y·lin
hem'a·tu'ri·a
hem'a·tu'ric
heme
hem'er·a·lo'pi·a

hem'i·a·blep'si·a
hem'i·a·car'di·us
hem'i·a·ceph'a·lus pl. -li'
hem'i·a·chro'ma·top'si·a
hem'i·a·geu'si·a
hem'i·al'bu·mose'
hem'i·al'bu·mo·su'ri·a
hem'i·al'gi·a
hem'i·am'bly·o'pi·a
hem'i·an'a·cu'si·a
hem'i·an'al·ge'si·a
hem'i·an'en·ceph'a·ly
hem'i·an·es·the'si·a
hem'i·an·o'pi·a
hem'i·a·no'pic
hem'i·an·op'si·a
hem'i·a·prax'i·a
hem'i·ar·thro'sis pl. -ses'
hem'i·a·tax'i·a
hem'i·ath'e·to'sis pl. -ses'
hem'i·at'ro·phy
hem'i·bal·lis'mus
he'mic
hem'i·car'di·a
hem'i·cel'lu·lose'
hem'i·cen'trum
hem'i·ce·pha'li·a
hem'i·ceph'a·lus pl. -li'
hem'i·ceph'a·ly
hem'i·cer'e·bral
hem'i·cer'e·brum pl. -brums
  or -bra
hem'i·cho·re'a
hem'i·chro'ma·top'si·a
hem'i·co·lec'to·my
hem'i·cra'ni·a
hem'i·cra'ni·ec'to·my
hem'i·cra'ni·o'sis
hem'i·cra'ni·ot'o·my
hem'i·cys·tec'to·my
hem'i·de·cor'ti·ca'tion
hem'i·di'a·phragm'
hem'i·dys'es·the'si·a
hem'i·dys'tro·phy
hem'i·el·lip'tic
hem'i·ep'i·lep'sy
hem'i·fa'cial
hem'i·gas·trec'to·my
hem'i·glos'sal
hem'i·glos·sec'to·my
hem'i·glos·si'tis
hem'i·gna'thi·a
hem'i·gnath'us
hem'i·hi·dro'sis pl. -ses'
hem'i·hyp'al·ge'si·a
hem'i·hy'per·es·the'si·a
hem'i·hy'per·hi·dro'sis

hem'i·hy'per·pla'si·a
hem'i·hy'per·to'ni·a
hem'i·hy·per'tro·phy
hem'i·hyp'es·the'si·a
hem'i·hy'po·to'ni·a
hem'i·lam'i·nec'to·my
hem'i·lar'yn·gec'to·my
hem'i·lar'ynx
hem'i·lat'er·al
hem'i·mac'ro·ceph'a·ly
hem'i·man·dib'u·lec'to·my
hem'i·man·dib'u·lo·glos·
  sec'to·my
hem'i·max'il·lec'to·my
hem'i·me'li·a
hem'i·me'lus pl. -li'
hem'i·me·tab'o·lous
he'min
hem'i·ne·phrec'to·my
hem'i·o'pi·a
hem'i·op'ic
he·mip'a·gus pl. -gi'
hem'i·pal'a·tec'to·my
hem'i·pa·ral'y·sis
hem'i·par'an·es·the'si·a
hem'i·par'a·ple'gi·a
hem'i·pa·re'sis pl. -ses'
hem'i·par'es·the'si·a
hem'i·pa·ret'ic
hem'i·par'kin·son·ism
hem'i·pel·vec'to·my
hem'i·ple'gi·a
—— cru'ci·a'ta
hem'i·ple'gic
hem'i·pros'ta·tec'to·my
hem'i·ra·chis'chi·sis pl.
  -ses'
hem'i·sco·to'sis pl. -ses'
hem'i·sect'
hem'i·sec'tion
hem'i·sep'tum pl. -tums or
  -ta
hem'i·so'mus
hem'i·spasm
hem'i·sphae'ri·a bul'bi'
  u·re'thrae'
hem'i·sphae'ri·um
—— cer'e·bel'li'
—— tel'en·ceph'a·li'
hem'i·sphere'
hem'i·spher·ec'to·my
hem'i·sphe'ric
hem'i·sphe'ri·um
—— cer'e·bel'li'
—— cer'e·bri'
hem'i·spo·ro'sis pl. -ses'
hem'i·sys'to·le

hem'i·ter'a·ta
hem'i·te·rat'ic
hem'i·tho'rax'
hem'i·thy'roi·dec'to·my
hem'i·ver'te·bra
hem'i·zy'gote'
hem'i·zy'gous
Hem'me·ler thrombop-
  athy
he'mo·al'ka·lim'e·ter
he'mo·bil'i·a
he'mo·bil'i·ru'bin
he'mo·blast'
he'mo·blas'tic
he'mo·blas·to'sis pl. -ses'
he'mo·ca·ther'e·sis
he'mo·cath'er·et'ic
he'mo·che'zi·a
he'mo·cho'le·cys·ti'tis
he'mo·cho'ri·al
he'mo·chro'ma·to'sis pl.
  -ses'
he'mo·chro'ma·tot'ic
he'mo·chrome'
he'mo·chro'mo·gen
he'mo·chro·mom'e·ter
he'mo·cid'al
he'mo·cla'si·a
he·moc'la·sis pl. -ses'
he'mo·clas'tic
he'mo·co·ag'u·la'tion
he'mo·co·ag'u·lin
he'mo·coe'lom
he'mo·con'cen·tra'tion
he'mo·co'ni·a
he'mo·co'ni·o'sis pl. -ses'
he'mo·crine
he'mo·crin'i·a
he'mo·cry·os'co·py
he'mo·cul'ture
he'mo·cy'a·nin
he'mo·cyte'
he'mo·cy'to·blast'
he'mo·cy'to·blas'tic
he'mo·cy'to·blas·to'ma
  pl. -mas or -ma·ta
he'mo·cy'to·gen'e·sis pl.
  -ses'
he'mo·cy'tol'y·sis pl. -ses'
he'mo·cy'to·lyt'ic
he'mo·cy'to'ma pl. -mas or
  -ma·ta
he'mo·cy·tom'e·ter
he'mo·cy·tom'e·try
he'mo·cy'to·poi·e'sis
  pl. -ses'

he′mo·di·al′y·sis *pl.* -ses′
he′mo·di′a·stase′
he′mo·di·lu′tion
he′mo·dy·nam′ic
he′mo·dy·nam′ics
he′mo·dy·na·mom′e·ter
he′mo·dy·na·mom′e·try
he′mo·en′do·the′li·al
he′mo·e·ryth′rin
he′mo·fil·tra′tion
he′mo′flag′el·late′
he′mo·fus′cin
he′mo·gen′e·sis *pl.* -ses′
he′mo·gen′ic
he·mog′e·nous
he′mo·glo′bin
he′mo·glo′bi·ne′mi·a
he′mo·glo′bi·nif′er·ous
he′mo·glo′bi·nom′e·ter
he′mo·glo′bi·nom′e·try
he′mo·glo′bi·nop′a·thy
he′mo·glo′bi·no·phil′ic
he′mo·glo′bi·nu′ri·a
he′mo·glo′bi·nu′ric
he′mo·gram′
he′mo·his′ti·o·blast′
he′mo·ki·ne′sis *pl.* -ses′
he′mo·ki·net′ic
he′mo·lymph′
he·mol′y·sate′
he·mol′y·sin
he·mol′y·sis *pl.* -ses′
he′mo·lyt′ic
he′mo·lyt′o·poi·et′ic
he′mo·ly·za′tion
he′mo·lyze′, -lyzed′, -lyz′ing
he′mo·ma·nom′e·ter
he′mo·me′di·as·ti′num
he·mom′e·ter
he·mom′e·try
he′mo·my′e·lo·gram′
he′mo·path′ic
he′mo·pa·thol′o·gy
he·mop′a·thy
he′mo·per·fu′sion
he′mo·per′i·car′di·um
he′mo·per′i·to·ne′um
he′mo·pex′in
he′mo·phage′
he′mo·pha′gi·a
he′mo·phag′ic
he·moph′a·gous
he′mo·phil′
he′mo·phil′i·a
he′mo·phil′i·ac′
he′mo·phil′ic
he′mo·phil′i·oid′

He·moph′i·lus
— ae·gyp′ti·us
— bron′chi·sep′ti·ca
— con·junc′ti·vi′ti·dis
— du·crey′i′
— gal′li·nar′um
— in′flu·en′zae′
— par′a·per·tus′sis
— per·tus′sis
— su′is
he′moph·thal′mi·a
he′moph·thal′mos
he·moph′thi·sis *pl.* -ses′
he′mo·plas′tic
he′mo·pleu′ra
he′mo·pneu′mo·tho′rax′
he′mo·poi·e′sis *pl.* -ses′
he′mo·poi·et′ic
he′mo·poi′e·tin
he′mo·por′phy·rin
he′mo·pre·cip′i·tin
he′mo·pro′tein′
he·mop′tic
he·mop′ty·sis *pl.* -ses′
hem′or·rhage
hem′or·rhag′ic
hem′or·rhag′in
hem′or·rhoid′
hem′or·rhoi′dal
hem′or·rhoi·dec′to·my
he′mo·sal′pinx
he′mo·sid′er·in
he′mo·sid′er·i·nu′ri·a
he′mo·sid′er·o′sis *pl.* -ses′
he′mo·sper′mi·a
he′mo·sta′si·a
he′mo·sta′sis *pl.* -ses′
he′mo·stat′
he′mo·stat′ic
he′mo·ther′a·py
he′mo·tho′rax′
he′mo·tox′ic
he′mo·tox·ic′i·ty
he′mo·tox′in
he′mo·troph′ic
he′mo·tym′pa·num
Hench and Al′drich test
Hen′der·son operation
Hen′le
— ampulla
— layer
— ligament
— loop
— muscle
— sheath
— spine
— warts

Hen′ne·berg′
— disease
— reflex
Hen′och-Schön′lein′ pur-
  pura
hen′pu·e
Hen·ri′ques-Sor′en·sen
  method
hen′ry *pl.* -rys *or* -ries
Hen′ry
— law
— melanoflocculation test
Hen′sen
— canal
— disk
— duct
— knot
— node
he′par′
— lo·ba′tum
— sul′fu·ris
hep′a·rin
hep′a·ri·ne′mi·a
hep′a·rin·ize′, -ized′, -iz′ing
hep′a·rin·oid′
hep′a·tal′gi·a
hep′a·tec′to·my
he·pat′ic
he·pat′i·co·du′o·de·nos′to·
  my
he·pat′i·co·en′ter·os′to·my
he·pat′i·co·gas·tros′to·my
he·pat′i·co·je′ju·nos′to·my
He·pat′i·co′la he·pat′i·ca
he·pat′i·co·li·thot′o·my
he·pat′i·co·pan′cre·at′ic
he·pat′i·co·pul′mo·nar′y
he·pat′i·co·re′nal
he·pat′i·cos′to·my
he·pat′i·cot′o·my
hep′a·ti′tis *pl.* -tis·es *or* -tit′i·
  des′
hep′a·ti·za′tion
hep′a·tized′
hep′a·to·bil′i·ar′y
hep′a·to′blas·to′ma *pl.* -mas
  or -ma·ta
hep′a·to·bron′chi·al
hep′a·to·cel′lu·lar
hep′a·to·chol·an′gi·o·du′o·
  de·nos′to·my
hep′a·to·chol·an′gi·o·
  en′ter·os′to·my
hep′a·to·chol·an′gi·o·gas·
  tros′to·my
hep′a·to·chol·an′gi·o·je′ju·
  nos′to·my

hep′a·to·chol′an·gi′tis
hep′a·to·cir·rho′sis pl. -ses′
hep′a·to·col′ic
hep′a·to·cu′pre·in
hep′a·to·cys′tic
hep′a·to·cyte′
hep′a·to·du′o·de′nal
hep′a·to·du′o·de·nos′to·my
hep′a·to·dyn′i·a
hep′a·to·dys′tro·phy
hep′a·to·en·ter′ic
hep′a·to·en′ter·os′to·my
hep′a·to·fla′vin
hep′a·to·gas′tric
hep′a·to·gen′ic
hep′a·tog′e·nous
hep′a·to·gram′
hep′a·toid′
hep′a·to·je·ju′nal
hep′a·to·jug′u·lar
hep′a·to·len·tic′u·lar
hep′a·to·li·e′nal
hep′a·to·li′e·nog′ra·phy
hep′a·to·lith′
hep′a·to·li·thec′to·my
hep′a·to·li·thi′a·sis pl. -ses′
hep′a·tol′o·gist
hep′a·tol′o·gy
hep′a·tol′y·sin
hep′a·to·lyt′ic
hep′a·to′ma pl. -mas or -ma·ta
hep′a·to·me·ga′li·a
hep′a·to·meg′a·ly
hep′a·tom·phal′o·cele′
hep′a·to·neph′ric
hep′a·to′ne·phri′tis
hep′a·to·pan′cre·at′ic
hep′a·top′a·thy
hep′a·to·pex′y
hep′a·to·pleu′ral
hep′a·top·to′sis
hep′a·to·pul′mo·nar′y
hep′a·to·re′nal
hep′a·tor′rha·phy
hep′a·tor·rhex′is pl. -es′
hep′a·to·scan′
hep′a·tos′co·py
hep′a·to′sis pl. -ses′
hep′a·to·sple′no·meg′a·ly
hep′a·to·sple·nop′a·thy
hep′a·tot′o·my
hep′a·to·tox′ic
hep′a·to·tox′in
hep′a·to·trop′ic
hep′a·to·u′ro·log′ic
hep′ta·bar′bi·tal′

hep′to·glo′bin
Herbst
—— bodies
—— corpuscles
he·red′i·tar′y
he·red′i·ty
her′e·do·fa·mil′i·al
Her′ing
—— canal
—— theory
Her′ing-Breu′er reflex
Her·man′sky-Pud′lak′ syndrome
her·maph′ro·dism
her·maph′ro·dite′
her·maph′ro·dit′ic
her·maph′ro·dit·ism
her·maph′ro·di·tis′mus
her·met′ic
her′ni·a pl. -as or -ae′
her′ni·al
her′ni·ate′, -at′ed, at′ing
her′ni·a′tion
her′ni·o·plas′ty
her′ni·or′rha·phy
her′ni·ot′o·my
her′o·in
her′o·in·ism
her′pan·gi′na
her′pes′
—— cir′ci·na′tus
—— des·qua′mans′
—— fa′ci·a′lis
—— fe·bri′lis
—— gen′i·ta′lis
—— ges·ta′ti·o′nis
—— hom′i·nis
—— i′ris
—— la′bi·a′lis
—— oph·thal′mi·cus
—— pro·gen′i·ta′lis
—— re·cur′rens
—— sim′i·ae′
—— sim′plex′
—— ton·su′rans′
—— tonsurans mac′u·lo′sus
—— zos′ter
—— zoster au·ric′u·lar′is
—— zoster oph·thal′mi·cus
—— zoster o′ti·cus her′pes·vi′rus
—— zos′ter var′i·cel·lo′sus
her·pet′ic
her·pet′i·form′
Her′rick anemia
Her′ring bodies
Hers disease

Her′ter-Fos′ter method
Her′ter infantilism
Hert′wig root sheath
hertz
Her′yng
—— benign ulcer
—— sign
Hesch′l gyri
Hes′sel·bach′
—— ligament
—— triangle
het′er·a·de′ni·a
het′er·a·den′ic
het′er·a′li·us
het′er·aux·e′sis
het′er·es·the′si·a
het′er·o·ag·glu′ti·nin
het′er·o·al′bu·mose′
het′er·o·al′bu·mo·su′ri·a
het′er·o·al·lele′
het′er·o·an′ti·bod′y
het′er·o·aux′in
het′er·o·blas′tic
het′er·o·cel′lu·lar
het′er·o·chro·mat′ic
het′er·o·chro′ma·tin
het′er·o·chro′mi·a
het′er·o·chro′mic
het′er·o·chro′mo·some′
het′er·o·chro′ni·a
het′er·o·chron′ic
het′er·och′ro·nous
het′er·o·e·rot′ic
het′er·o·er′o·tism
het′er·og′a·my
het′er·o·ge·ne′i·ty
het′er·o·ge′ne·ous
het′er·o·gen′e·sis
het′er·o·ge·net′ic
het′er·o·gen′ic
het′er·og′e·nous
het′er·og′o·ny
het′er·o·graft′
het′er·o·hem·ag·glu·ti′nin
het′er·o·he·mol′y·sin
het′er·o·in·tox′i·ca′tion
het′er·o·ker′a·to·plas′ty
het′er·o·ki·ne′si·a
het′er·o·ki·ne′sis pl. -ses′
het′er·o·la′li·a
het′er·o·lat′er·al
het′er·ol′o·gous
het′er·ol′o·gy
het′er·ol′y·sin
het′er·o·lyt′ic
het′er·o·mer′ic
het′er·om′er·ous

het′er·o·met′a·pla′si·a
het′er·o·met′ric
het′er·o·me·tro′pi·a
het′er·o·mor′phic
het′er·o·mor′phism
het′er·o·mor·pho·sis′ pl.
  -ses′
het′er·o·mor′phous
het′er·on′o·mous
het′er·o·os′te·o·plas′ty
het′er·op′a·gus pl. -gi′
het′er·o·path′ic
het′er·op′a·thy
het′er·o·pha′si·a
het′er·o·phil′
het′er·o·phil′ic
het′er·o·pho′ni·a
het′er·o·pho′ri·a
Het′er·oph′y·es′
het′er·o·pla′si·a
het′er·o·plas′tic
het′er·o·plas′ty
het′er·o·ploid′
het′er·o·ploi′dy
het′er·op′si·a
het′er·op′tics
het′er·o·sex′u·al
het′er·o·sex′u·al′i·ty
het′er·os′mi·a
het′er·o·sug·ges′ti·bil′i·ty
het′er·o·sug·ges′tion
het′er·o·tax′ic
het′er·o·tax′is pl. -tax′es′
het′er·o·to′ni·a
het′er·o·ton′ic
het′er·o·to′pi·a
het′er·o·top′ic
het′er·o·tox′in
het′er·o·trans′plant′
het′er·o·trans′plan·ta′tion
het′er·o·troph′
het′er·o·troph′ic
het′er·o·tro′pi·a
het′er·o·typ′ic or het′er·o·
  typ′i·cal
het′er·o·zy·go′sis pl. -ses′
het′er·o·zy′gote′
het′er·o·zy′gous
Heth′er·ing·ton stain
Heub′ner
—— disease
—— endarteritis
Heub′ner-Her′ter disease
heu·ris′tic
Heu′ser membrane
hex′a·chlo′ro·phene′
hex′a·chro′mic

hex′ad′
hex′a·dac′ty·lism
hex′a·dec′yl
hex′a·di·meth′rine′
hex′a·eth′yl tet′ra·
  phos′phate′
hex′a·flu′o·re′ni·um
hex·al′de·hyde′
hex′a·me·tho′ni·um
hex·ane′
hex′a·no′ic
hex′a·va′lent
hex′a·vi′ta·min
hex·ax′i·al
hex′es·trol′
hex′e·thal′
hex·et′i·dine′
hex′o·bar′bi·tal′
hex′o·bar′bi·tone′
hex′o·cy′cli·um
hex′o·ki′nase′
hex′one′
hex·os′a·mine′
hex′o·san′
hex′ose′
hex′yl
hex′yl·caine′
hex′yl·re·sor′ci·nol′
Hey amputation
hi·a′tal
hi·a′tus
—— ad′duc·to′ri·us
—— a·or′ti·cus
—— ca·na′lis fa·ci·a′lis
—— canalis ner′vi′ pe·tro′si′
ma·jo′ris
—— canalis nervi petrosi
mi·no′ris
—— e′so·phag′e·us
—— eth′moi·da′lis
—— max′il·lar′is
—— oe′so·phag′e·us
—— of Fal·lo′pi·us
—— of Schwal′be
—— pleu′ro·per′i·to′ne·a′lis
—— sa·cra′lis
—— sa·phe′nus
—— sem′i·lu·nar′is
—— ten·din′e·us
Hibbs operation
hi′ber·nate′, -nat′ed, -nat′-
ing
hi′ber·na′tion
hi′ber·no′ma pl. -mas or
  -ma·ta
hic′cup
Hicks

—— sign
—— version
hi·drad′e·ni′tis
—— ax′il·lar′is
—— sup′pu·ra·ti′va
hi·drad′e·noid′
hi·drad′e·no′ma pl. -mas or
-ma·ta
—— pap′il·lif′e·rum
hid′ro·cyst·ad′e·no′ma
  pl. -mas or -ma·ta
hid′ro·cys·to′ma pl. -mas or
  -ma·ta
hid′ro·poi·e′sis pl. -ses′
hid′ro·poi·et′ic
hid′ror·rhe′a
hi′dros·ad′e·ni′tis
hi·dros′che·sis pl. -ses′
hi′drose′
hi·dro′sis pl. -ses′
hi·drot′ic
hi′lar
Hill′-Flack′ sign
Hil′liard lupus
hill′ock
Hill sign
Hil′ton law
hi′lum pl. -la
hi′lus pl. -li′
—— glan′du·lae′ su′pra·re·
na′lis
—— li·e′nis
—— lym′pho·glan′du·lae′
—— no′di′ lym·phat′i·ci′
—— nu′cle·i′ den·ta′ti′
—— nuclei ol′i·var′is
—— o·var′i·i′
—— pul·mo′nis
—— re·na′lis
hind′gut′
Hines and Brown test
Hin′kle pill
Hin′ton test
hip
Hip′pe·la′tes′
—— fla′vi·pes′
—— pu′si·o′
Hip′pel-Lin′dau′ disease
hip′po·cam′pal
hip′po·cam′pus pl. -pi′
Hip′po·crat′ic oath
hip′po·lith′
hip′pu·ran′
hip′pu·rase′
hip·pu′ri·a
hip·pu′ric
hip·pu·ri·case′

hip′pus
hir′ci′ *sing.* -cus
hir·cis′mus
Hirsch′berg′
—— reflex
—— sign
—— test
Hirsch′feld′ nerve
Hirsch′sprung′ disease
hir′sute′
hir′sut·ism
Hirtz rale
hir′u·din
His′-Held′ spaces
His spaces
Hiss serum water
his·tam′i·nase′
his′ta·mine′
his′ta·min′ic
His′-Ta·wa′ra
—— node
—— system
his′ti·dase′
his′ti·dine′
his′ti·di·ne′mi·a
his′ti·di·nu′ri·a
his′ti·o·cyte′
his′ti·o·cyt′ic
his′ti·o·cy·to′ma *pl.* -mas *or*
 -ma·ta
his′ti·o′cy·to′ma·to′sis *pl.*
 -ses′
his′ti·o·cy′to·sar·co′ma *pl.*
 -mas *or* -ma·ta
his′ti·o·cy′to′sis *pl.* -ses′
his′ti·o·gen′ic
his′ti·o′ma *pl.* -mas *or*
 -ma·ta
his′ti·o·troph′ic
his′to·chem′i·cal
his′to·com·pat′i·ble
his′to·com·pat′i·bil′i·ty
his′to·cyte′
his′to·di·al′y·sis *pl.* -ses′
his′to·flu′o·res′cence
his′to·gen′e·sis
his′to·ge·net′ic
his′to·gram′
his′to·hem′a·tin
his′toid′
his′to·in′com·pat′i·bil′i·ty
his′to·in′com·pat′i·ble
his′to·ki·ne′sis
his′to·log′ic *or* his′to·log′i·
 cal
his·tol′o·gy
his·tol′y·sis

his′to·lyt′ic
his′to·ma *pl.* -mas *or* -ma·ta
his′to·mor·phol′o·gy
his′to·my·co′sis *pl.* -ses′
his′tone′
his′to·neu·rol′o·gy
his′to·nu′ri·a
his′to·path′o·log′ic
his′to·pa·thol′o·gy
his′to·phys′i·ol′o·gy
His′to·plas′ma
—— cap′su·la′tum
his′to·plas′min
his′to·plas·mo′ma *pl.* -mas
 or -ma·ta
his′to·plas·mo′sis *pl.* -ses′
his′to·ra′di·og′ra·phy
his′to·ry
his′to·spec·tros′co·py
his′to·ther′a·py
his′to·throm′bin
his′to·tome′
his·tot′o·my
his′to·tox′ic
his′to·troph′ic
his′to·zo′ic
his′to·zyme′
his·tri·on′ic
his′tri·o·nism
His′-Wer′ner disease
Hitch′cock′ reagent
Hit′zig center
hives
Hjär′re disease
hoarse
hoarse′ness
hoar′y
hob′ble, -bled, -bling
Hoch′sin′ger sign
Hodg′kin
—— disease
—— granuloma
—— lymphoreticuloma
—— sarcoma
Hodg′son disease
Hoehn′e sign
hof
Hof′bau′er cell
Hoff′fa disease
Hoff′mann
—— anodyne
—— atrophy
—— drops
—— duct
—— finger reflex
—— phenomenon
—— sign

—— syndrome
Hoff′mann-Werd′nig
—— disease
—— syndrome
Hof′meis′ter series
Hö′gyes treatment
Hoke operation
hol·an′dric
Hol′ger Niel′sen method
ho′lism
ho·lis′tic
Hol′la disease
Hol′lan·der test
Hol′len·horst′ bodies
Holmes
—— phenomenon
—— sign
Holm′gren-Gol′gi canals
Holm′gren test
hol′o·a·car′di·us
—— a·ceph′a·lus
—— a·cor′mus
—— a·mor′phus
hol′o·blas′tic
hol′o·ce·phal′ic
hol′o·crine
ho·loc′ri·nous
hol′o·di′as·tol′ic
hol′o·en′zyme′
hol′o·gas·tros′chi·sis *pl.*
 -ses′
hol′o·gram′
ho·log′ra·phy
hol′o·gyn′ic
hol′o·ra·chis′chi·sis *pl.* -ses′
hol′o·sys·tol′ic
hol′o·zo′ic
Hol′ter-Doyle′ method
hom′a·lo·ceph′a·lus *pl.* -li′
hom′a·lu′ri·a
Ho′mans sign
ho·mat′ro·pine′
hom·ax′i·al
ho′me·o·chrome′
ho′me·o·ki·ne′sis *pl.* -ses′
ho′me·o·mor′phous
ho′me·o·path′
ho′me·o·path′ic
ho′me·op′a·thist
ho′me·op′a·thy
ho′me·o·pla′si·a
ho′me·o·plas′tic
ho′me·o′sis *pl.* -ses′
ho′me·o·sta′sis *pl.* -ses′
ho′me·o·stat′ic
ho′me·o·ther′mal
ho′me·o·ther′mic

ho'me·ot'ic
ho'me·o·trans'plant'
ho'me·o·typ'ic
Home
—— gland
—— lobe
hom'i·ci'dal
hom'i·cide'
Ho'mo
—— sa'pi·ens
ho'mo·bi'o·tin
ho'mo·cen'tric or ho'mo·
   cen'tri·cal
ho'mo·clad'ic
ho'mo·cys'ti·ne'mi·a
ho'mo·cys'ti·nu'ri·a
ho'mo·e·rot'ic
ho'mo·er'o·tism
ho'mo·ga·met'ic
ho·mog'a·my
ho·mog'e·nate'
ho'mo·ge·ne'i·ty
ho'mo·ge'ne·ous
ho'mo·ge·net'ic
ho'mo·gen'ic
ho·mog'e·ni·za'tion
ho·mog'e·nize', -nized',
   -niz'ing
ho·mog'e·nous
ho'mo·gen·tis'ic
ho'mo·glan'du·lar
ho'mo·graft'
ho'mo·lat'er·al
ho'mo·log'ic
ho·mol'o·gous
ho'mo·logue'
ho·mol'o·gy
ho'mo·mor'phic
ho'mo·phil
ho'mo·phil'ic
ho'mo·plast'
ho'mo·plas'tic
ho'mo·plas'ty
ho'mo·sex'u·al
ho'mo·sex'u·al'i·ty
ho'mo·top'ic
ho'mo·trans'plant'
ho'mo·trans'plan·ta'tion
ho'mo·type'
ho'mo·typ'ic
ho'mo·zy'gote
ho'mo·zy'gous
ho·mun'cu·lus pl. -li'
hook
Hook'er method
hook'worm'

Hoo'ver sign
Hope murmur
Hopf disease
Hop'kins-Cole' reaction
Hop'mann polyp
Hop'pe-Gold'flam'
—— disease
—— symptom complex
ho'qui·zil
ho'ra
—— de·cu'bi·tus
—— som'ni'
hor·de'o·lum pl. -la
hor'i·zon'tal
hor'i·zon·ta'lis
hor'mi·on'
hor·mo'nal
hor'mone'
hor·mon'ic
hor·mo'no·poi·e'sis pl. -ses'
hor·mo'no·poi·et'ic
horn
Hor'ner
—— muscle
—— syndrome
horn'i·fi·ca'tion
horn'y
ho·rop'ter
hor'op·ter'ic
hor·rip'i·la'tion
Hors'ley
—— operation
—— sign
Hor·te'ga
—— cell
—— silver stain
Hor'ton
—— headache
—— syndrome
hos'pi·tal
hos'pi·tal·ism
hos'pi·tal·i·za'tion
hos'pi·tal·ize', -ized', -iz'ing
host
hos'tile
hos·til'i·ty
Hotch'kiss
—— method
—— operation
Hot'ten·tot'
—— apron
—— bustle
hot'ten·tot·ism
Hous·say'
—— animal
—— phenomenon
Hous'ton

—— muscle
—— valves
ho'ven
How'ard-Dol'man test
How'ard method
How'ell-Jol'ly bodies
How'ship lacunas
How'ship-Rom'berg'
—— sign
—— syndrome
Hu·chard'
—— disease
—— sign
Hud'dle·son test
Hud'son line
Hue'ter bandage
Hug'gins-Mil'ler-Jen'sen
   test
Hug'gins test
Hughes reflex
Hu·guier'
—— canal
—— disease
Huh'ner test
hum
hu'man
hu·man'o·scope'
hu·mec'tant
hu'mer·al
hu'mer·o·ra'di·al
hu'mer·o·scap'u·lar
hu'mer·o·ul'nar
hu'mer·us pl. -mer·i'
hu'mic
hu·mic'o·lin
hu'mid
hu·mid'i·fi·ca'tion
hu·mid'i·fi'er
hu·mid'i·ty
hu'min
hu'mor
—— a·quo'sus
—— vit're·us
hu'mor·al
hunch'back'
hun'ger
Hun'ner ulcer
Hunt
—— atrophy
—— neuralgia
—— tremor
Hun'ter
—— canal
—— glossitis
—— operation
—— syndrome
Hun'ter·i·an chancre

Hun'ter-Schre'ger bands
Hun'ting·ton chorea
Hup'pert test
Hur'ler syndrome
Hürth'le cells
Husch'ke
—— cartilage
—— foramen
—— papilla
—— teeth
Hutch'in·son
—— disease
—— freckle
—— prurigo
—— pupil
—— teeth
—— triad
Hutch'in·son-Boeck' disease
Hutch'in·son-Gil'ford syndrome
hutch'in·so'ni·an
Hutch'i·son type
hy'a·lin
hy'a·line
hy'a·lin·i·za'tion
hy'a·lin·ize', -ized', -iz'ing
hy'·li·no'sis pl. -ses'
hy'a·li·nu'ri·a
hy'a·li'tis
hy·al'o·gen
hy'a·loid'
hy'a·loid·i'tis
hy'a·lo·mere'
hy'a·lo·nyx'is
hy'a·lo·plasm
hy'a·lo·se'ro·si'tis
hy'a·lu'ro·nate'
hy'a·lu·ron'i·dase'
hy·ben'zate'
hy'brid
hy'brid·ism
hy'brid·i·ty
hy'brid·i·za'tion
hy·can'thone'
hy·dan'to·in
hy·dat'ic
hy·dat'id
—— of Mor·ga'gni
hy'da·tid'i·form'
hy'da·tid'o·cele'
hy·da·ti·do'sis pl. -ses'
hy·drac'id
hy·dra'er·o·per'i·to·ne'um
hy·dra·gogue'
hy·dral'a·zine'
hy·dram'ni·on'

hy·dram'ni·os'
hy·dran·en·ceph'a·ly
hy·drar·gyr'i·a
hy·drar'gyr·oph·thal'mi·a
hy·drar'gy·rum
hy·drar·thro'sis pl. -ses'
hy'drase'
hy'drate'
hy'drat'ed
hy·dra'tion
hy·drau'lics
hy·dra·zine'
hy·dre'mi·a
hy·dre'mic
hy'dren·ceph'a·lo·cele'
hy'dren·ceph'a·lo·me·nin'go·cele'
hy·drep'i·gas'tri·um
hy'dride'
hy·dri·od'ic
hy·dri'o·dide'
hy·dro'a
—— her·pet'i·for'me'
—— vac·cin'i·for'me'
hy'dro·ap·pen'dix pl. -dix·es or -di·ces'
hy·dro·bil'i·ru'bin
hy·dro·bleph'a·ron'
hy·dro·bro'mide'
hy·dro·cal'y·co'sis pl. -ses'
hy·dro·ca'lyx
hy·dro·car'bon
hy·dro·cele'
—— her'ni·a'lis
hy·dro·ce·lec'to·my
hy·dro·ce·phal'ic
hy·dro·ceph'a·lo·cele'
hy·dro·ceph'a·lus
hy·dro·ceph'a·ly
—— ex vac'u·o
hy·dro·chlo'ric
hy·dro·chlo'ride'
hy·dro·chlo·ro·thi'a·zide'
hy·dro·cho'le·cys'tis
hy·dro·chol'er·e'sis pl. -ses'
hy·dro·chol'er·et'ic
hy·dro·cho·les'ter·ol'
hy·dro·co'done'
hy·dro·col'pos
hy·dro·co'ni·on'
hy·dro·con'qui·nine'
hy·dro·cor'ta·mate'
hy·dro·cor'ti·sone'
hy·dro·cy·an'ic
hy·dro·cyst·ad'e·no'ma pl. -mas or -ma·ta
hy'dro·dip'si·a

hy'dro·dip'so·ma'ni·a
hy'dro·di'u·re'sis pl. -ses'
hy'dro·dy·nam'ic
hy'dro·dy·nam'ics
hy'dro·en·ceph'a·lo·cele'
hy'dro·er·got'i·nine'
hy'dro·flu'me·thi'a·zide'
hy'dro·flu·or'ic
hy'dro·gen
hy·drog'e·nase'
hy'dro·gen·at'ed
hy'dro·gen·a'tion
hy'dro·gen·ly'ase'
hy'dro·hem'a·to·ne·phro'sis
hy'dro·hep'a·to'sis pl. -ses'
hy'dro·ki·net'ic
hy'dro·ki·net'ics
hy'drol'
hyd'ro·la'bile
hy'dro·la·bil'i·ty
hy'dro·lase'
hy·drol'y·sate'
hy·drol'y·sis
hy'dro·lyt'ic
hy·drol'yze', -lyzed', -lyz'ing
hy·dro'ma
hy'dro·mas·sage'
hy'dro·men·in·gi'tis
hy'dro·me·nin'go·cele'
hy·drom'e·ter
hy'dro·me'tra
hy'dro·met'ric
hy'dro·me'tro·col'pos
hy·drom'e·try
hy'dro·mi'cro·ceph'a·ly
hy'dro·mor'phone'
hy'dro·my·e'li·a
hy'dro·my'e·lo·cele'
hy'dro·my'e·lo'me·nin'go·cele'
hy'dro·my·o'ma pl. -mas or -ma·ta
hy'dro·ne·phro'sis pl. -ses'
hy'dro·ne·phrot'ic
hy'dro·path'ic
hy'dro·pro'a·thy
hy'dro·pel'vis
hy'dro·pe'ni·a
hy'dro·pe'nic
hy'dro·per'i·car·di'tis
hy'dro·per'i·car·di·um
hy'dro·per'i·ne·phro'sis pl. -ses'
hy'dro·per'i·on'
hy'dro·per'i·to·ne'um
hy'dro·pex'ic

hy′dro·phag′o·cy·to′sis *pl.*
  -ses′
hy′dro·phil′
hy′dro·phil′i·a
hy′dro·phil′ic
hy·droph′i·lism
hy·droph′i·lous
hy′dro·pho′bi·a
hy′dro·pho′bic
hy′droph·thal′mos
hy·drop′ic
hy′dro·pleu′ra
hy′dro·pneu′ma·to′sis *pl.*
  -ses′
hy′dro·pneu′mo·per′i·
  car′di·um
hy′dro·pneu′mo·per′i·to·
  ne′um
hy′dro·pneu′mo·tho′rax′
hy′drops′
—— an′tri′
—— ar·tic′u·lo′rum
—— fe·ta′lis
—— grav′i·dar′um
hy′dro·py′o·ne·phro′sis *pl.*
  -ses′
hy′dro·quin′i·dine′
hy′dro·quin′ine′
hy′dro·quin′ol′
hy′dro·qui·none′
hy·dror′a·chis
hy′dro·ra·chi′tis
hy′dror·rhe′a
—— grav′i·dar′um
hy′dro·sal′pinx
hy′dro·sol′u·ble
hy′dro·sper′ma·to·cele′
hy′dro·sper′ma·to·cyst′
hy′dro·spi·rom′e·ter
hy′dro·stat′ic
hy′dro·sy·rin′go·my·e′li·a
hy′dro·ther′a·py
hy′dro·thi′o·nu′ri·a
hy′dro·tho·rac′ic
hy′dro·tho′rax′
hy′dro′tis
hy′dro·tym′pa·num
hy′dro·u′ri·a
hy′dro·u·re′ter
hy′dro·u·re′ter·o·ne·
  phro′sis *pl.* -ses′
hy′dro·u·re′ter·o′sis *pl.* -ses′
hy′drous
hy·drox′ide′
hy·drox′y·a·ce′tic
hy·drox′y·am·phet′a·mine
hy·drox′y·ap′a·tite′

hy·drox′y·ben′zene′
hy·drox′y·ben·zo′ic
hy·drox′y·chlo′ro·quine′
hy·drox′y·cor′ti·cos′ter·
  one′
hy·drox′y·di′one′
hy·drox′yl
hy·drox′yl·a·mine′
hy·drox′yl·ase′
hy·drox′y·pro·ges′ter·one′
hy·drox′y·pro′line′
hy·drox′y·quin′o·line′
hy·drox′y·stil·bam′i·dine′
hy·drox′y·u·re′a
hy·drox′y·zine′
hy·dru′ri·a
hy·dru′ric
hy′giene′
hy′gi·en′ic
hy′gien′ist
hy′gre·che′ma
hy′gric
hy′gro·ble·phar′ic
hy·gro′ma *pl.* -mas *or*
  -ma·ta
—— cys′ti·cum col′li′
hy·grom′a·tous
hy·grom′e·ter
hy′gro·met′ric *or* hy′gro·
  met′ri·cal
hy′lic
hy′men
hy′men·al
hy′men·ec′to·my
hy′men·i′tis
hy′me·no·le·pi′a·sis *pl.* -ses′
Hy′me·no·le·pid′i·dae′
—— dim′i·nu′ta
—— na′na
hy′me·nop′ter·ous
hy′men·or′rha·phy
hy′men·ot′o·my
hy′o·ep′i·glot′tic
hy′o·ep′i·glot·tid′e·an
hy′o·glos′sal
hy′o·glos′sus *pl.* -si′
hy′oid′
hy′o·man·dib′u·lar
hy′o·scine′
hy′o·scy′a·mine′
hy′o·scy′a·mus
hy′o·sta·pe′di·al
hy′o·thy′roid′
hyp′a·cu′si·a
hyp′a·cu′sis
hyp·al·bu′mi·ne′mi·a

hyp′al·bu·mi·no′sis
hyp′al·ge′si·a
hyp′al·ge′sic
hyp·al′gi·a
hyp·ar·te′ri·al
hyp·as·the′ni·a
hyp·ax′i·al
hyp·az′o·tu′ri·a
hy·pen′gy·o·pho′bi·a
hyp′e·o·sin′o·phil
hy′per·ab·duc′tion
hy′per·ac′id
hy′per·ac′id·am′i·nu′ri·a
hy′per·a·cid′i·ty
hy′per·ac′tive
hy′per·ac·tiv′i·ty
hy′per·a·cu′i·ty
hy′per·a·cu′si·a
hy′per·a·cu′sis
hy′per·a·cute′
hy′per·ad·e·no′sis *pl.* -ses′
hy′per·ad′i·po′sis *pl.* -ses′
hy′per·a·dre′nal·cor′ti·cal·
  ism
hy′per·a·dre′nal·ism
hy′per·a·dre′ni·a
hy′per·a·dre′no·cor′ti·cism
hy′per·af·fec′tive
hy′per·af′fec·tiv′i·ty
hy′per·al·bu′mi·ne′mi·a
hy′per·al·bu′mi·no′sis *pl.*
  -ses′
hy′per·al′do·ster·o·ne′mi·a
hy′per·al′do·ster′o·nism
hy′per·al′do·ster′o·nu′ri·a
hy′per·al·ge′si·a
hy′per·al·ge′sic
hy′per·al′i·men·ta′tion
hy′per·al′i·men·to′sis *pl.*
  -ses′
hy′per·al′ka·lin′i·ty
hy′per·am′i·no·ac′id·u′ri·a
hy′per·am′mo·ne′mi·a
hy′per·am·ne′si·a
hy′per·am′y·la·se′mi·a
hy′per·an·a·ki·ne′si·a
—— ven·tric′u·li′
hy′per·a·phi·a
hy′per·aph′ic
hy′per·az·o·te′mi·a
hy′per·az′o·tu′ri·a
hy′per·bar′ic
hy′per·bil′i·ru′bi·ne′mi·a
hy′per·blas·to′sis *pl.* -ses′
hy′per·brach′y·ceph′a·ly
hy′per·bu′li·a
hy′per·cal·ce′mi·a

hy'per·cal'ci·nu'ri·a
hy'per·cap'ni·a
hy'per·cap'nic
hy'per·car'bi·a
hy'per·car'o·te·ne'mi·a
hy'per·ca·thar'sis pl. -ses'
hy'per·ca·thar'tic
hy'per·ca·thex'is
hy'per·cel'lu·lar
hy'per·cel'lu·lar'i·ty
hy'per·ce'men·to'sis
 pl. -ses'
hy'per·chlo·re'mi·a
hy'per·chlo·re'mic
hy'per·chlor·hy'dri·a
hy'per·cho·les'ter·e'mi·a
hy'per·cho·les'ter·ol·e'mi·a
hy'per·cho·les'ter·o·le'mic
hy'per·cho'li·a
hy'per·chon'dro·pla'si·a
hy'per·chro·maf'fi·nism
hy'per·chro·ma'si·a
hy'per·chro·mat'ic
hy'per·chro·ma·tism
hy'per·chro'ma·to'sis pl.
 -ses'
hy'per·chro'mi·a
hy'per·chro'mic
hy'per·chy'li·a
hy'per·chy'lo·mi'cro·
 ne'mi·a
hy'per·co·ag'u·la·bil'i·ty
hy'per·cor'ti·cism
hy'per·cre'a·ti·ne'mi·a
hy'per·cri'nism
hy'per·cry'al·ge'si·a
hy'per·cry'es·the'si·a
hy'per·cu·pre'mi·a
hy'per·cu·pri·u'ri·a
hy'per·cy'a·not'ic
hy'per·cy·the'mi·a
hy'per·cy·to'sis pl. -ses'
hy'per·dac'ty·ly
hy'per·di·crot'ic
hy'per·di'cro·tism
hy'per·dip'si·a
hy'per·dis·ten'tion
hy'per·di'u·re'sis pl. -ses'
hy'per·dy·na'mi·a
hy'per·dy'nam·ic
hy'per·e·che'ma
hy'per·e·las'tic
hy'per·e·las'tic'i·ty
hy'per·em'e·sis pl. -ses'
 —— grav'i·dar'um
 —— lac·ten'ti·um
hy'per·e·met'ic

hy'per·e'mi·a
hy'per·e'mic
hy'per·en·dem'ic
hy'per·en·doc'rin·ism
hy'per·e·o·sin'o·phil'i·a
hy'per·ep'i·thy'mi·a
hy'per·e·qui·lib'ri·um
hy'per·er'gi·a
hy'per·er'gy
hy'per·es·o·pho'ri·a
hy'per·es·the'si·a
 —— un'gui·um
hy'per·es·thet'ic
hy'per·es·tro·ge·ne'mi·a
hy'per·es·tro·gen·ism
hy'per·ex·cit'a·bil'i·ty
hy'per·ex·o·pho'ri·a
hy'per·ex·ten'si·ble
hy'per·ex·ten'sion
hy'per·fer·re'mi·a
hy'per·flex'ion
hy'per·fo'cal
hy'per·gam'ma·glob'u·li·
 ne'mi·a
hy'per·gen'e·sis pl. -ses'
hy'per·ge·net'ic
hy'per·geu'si·a
hy'per·glob·u·li·ne'mi·a
hy'per·gly·ce'mi·a
hy'per·gly·ce'mic
hy'per·gly'ci·ne'mi·a
hy'per·gly'co·ge·nol'y·sis
 pl. -ses'
hy'per·gly'cor·rha'chi·a
hy'per·gly'co·su'ri·a
hy'per·gly·ox'a·la·tu'ri·a
hy'per·go'nad·ism
hy'per·go'ni·a
hy'per·he·do'ni·a
hy'per·he'don·ism
hy'per·he'mo·glo'bi·
 ne'mi·a
hy'per·he'mo·lyt'ic
hy'per·hep'a·ri·ne'mi·a
hy'per·hi·dro'sis pl. -ses'
hy'per·his'ta·mi·ne'mi·a
hy'per·hor·mon'al
hy'per·im·mune'
hy'per·im'mu·no·glob'u·li·
 ne'mi·a
hy'per·in·fla'tion
hy'per·in·o'se·mi·a
hy'per·in'su·lin·ism
hy'per·in'vo·lu'tion
hy'per·ir'ri·ta·bil'i·ty
hy'per·ka·le'mi·a
hy'per·ka·le'mic

hy'per·ker'a·tin·i·za'tion
hy'per·ker'a·to'sis pl. -ses'
 —— ex·cen'tri·ca
 —— fol·lic'u·lar'is par'a·fol·
lic'u·lar'is
 —— lac'u·nar'is pha·ryn'gis
 —— lin'guae'
 —— sub'un·gua'lis
hy'per·ker'a·tot'ic
hy'per·ke'to·ne'mi·a
hy'per·ke'to·nu'ri·a
hy'per·ki·ne'mi·a
hy'per·ki·ne'si·a
hy'per·ki·ne'sis
hy'per·ki·net'ic
hy'per·lac·ta'tion
hy'per·leu'ko·cy·to'sis pl.
 -ses'
hy'per·li·pe'mi·a
hy'per·li·pe'mic
hy'per·lip'i·de'mi·a
hy'per·lip'o·pro'tein·
 e'mi·a
hy'per·lith'ic
hy'per·li·thu'ri·a
hy'per·lu'cen·cy
hy'per·mag'ne·se'mi·a
hy'per·ma'ni·a
hy'per·man'ic
hy'per·mas'ti·a
hy'per·mel'a·no'sis pl. -ses'
hy'per·mel'a·not'ic
hy'per·men'or·rhe'a
hy'per·met'a·bol'ic
hy'per·me·tab'o·lism
hy'per·met'a·pla'si·a
hy'per·met'rope'
hy'per·me·tro'pi·a
hy'per·me·tro'pic
hy'per·mi'cro·so'ma
hy'per·mim'i·a
hy'per·min'er·al·o·cor'ti·
 coid·ism
hy'perm·ne'si·a
hy'perm·ne'sic
hy'per·mo·til'i·ty
hy'per·my'o·to'ni·a
hy'per·na·tre'mi·a
hy'per·na·tre'mic
hy'per·ne·phri'tis
hy'per·ne'phroid'
hy'per·ne·phro'ma pl. -mas
 or -ma·ta
hy'per·noi'a
hy'per·nor'mal
hy'per·nu·tri'tion
hy'per·on'to·morph'

hy′per·o·nych′i·a
hy′per·ope′
hy′per·o′pi·a
hy′per·op′ic
hy′per·o·rex′i·a
hy′per·os′mo·lar′i·ty
hy′per·os·mot′ic
hy′per·os·te·og′e·ny
hy′per·os·to′sis pl. -ses′
hy′per·os·tot′ic
hy′per·ox·a·lu′ri·a
hy′per·ox·e′mi·a
hy′per·ox′i·a
hy′per·ox′ic
hy′per·par′a·thy′roid·ism
hy′per·path′i·a
hy′per·pep·sin′i·a
hy′per·per′i·stal′sis pl. -ses′
hy′per·per′me·a·bil′i·ty
hy′per·pex′i·a
hy′per·pha′gi·a
hy′per·pha·lan′gi·a
hy′per·pha·lan′gism
hy′per·pha·lan′gy
hy′per·pho′ni·a
hy′per·pho′ri·a
hy′per·phos′pha·te′mi·a
hy′per·phos′pha·tu′ri·a
hy′per·phos′pho·re′mi·a
hy′per·phre′ni·a
hy′per·pig′men·ta′tion
hy′per·pi·tu′i·ta·rism
hy′per·pla′si·a
hy′per·plas′mi·a
hy′per·plas′tic
hy′per·plat′y·mer′ic
hy′per·pne′a
hy′per·po′lar·i·za′tion
hy′per·po·ro′sis pl. -ses′
hy′per·po′tas·se′mi·a
hy′per·pra′gi·a
hy′per·prag′ic
hy′per·prax′i·a
hy′per·pres′by·o′pi·a
hy′per·pro′li·ne′mi·a
hy′per·pro′tein·e′mi·a
hy′per·psy·cho′sis
hy′per·py·re′mi·a
hy′per·py·ret′ic
hy′per·py·rex′i·a
hy′per·re·ac′tive
hy′per·re·flex′i·a
hy′per·re·flex′ic
hy′per·ren′i·ne′mi·a
hy′per·res′o·nance
hy′per·sal′i·va′tion

hy′per·se·cre′tion
hy′per·se·cre′to·ry
hy′per·seg′men·ta′tion
hy′per·sen′si·tive
hy′per·sen′si·tiv′i·ty
hy′per·sen′si·ti·za′tion
hy′per·ser′o·to·ni·ne′mi·a
hy′per·som′ni·a
hy′per·sple·nism
hy′per·sthe′ni·a
hy′per·sthe′nic
hy′per·tel′o·rism
hy′per·ten·sin′o·gen
hy′per·ten′sion
hy′per·ten′sive
hy′per·ten′sor
hy′per·the·co′sis pl. -ses′
hy′per·the′li·a
hy′per·therm′al
hy′per·ther′mes·the′si·a
hy′per·ther′mi·a
hy′per·ther′mic
hy′per·ther′my
hy′per·thy′mi·a
hy′per·thy′mic
hy′per·thy′mism
hy′per·thy′mi·za′tion
hy′per·thy′roid′
hy′per·thy′roid·ism
hy′per·thy′roi·do′sis
hy′per·to′ni·a
hy′per·ton′ic
hy′per·to·nic′i·ty
hy′per·to′nus
hy′per·tri·cho′sis pl. -ses′
hy′per·tri·glyc′er·i·de′mi·a
hy′per·tro′phic
hy′per′tro·phy
hy′per·tro′pi·a
hy′per·u·re′sis pl. -ses′
hy′per·u′ri·ce′mi·a
hy′per·u′ri·ce′mic
hy′per·val′i·ne′mi·a
hy′per·vas′cu·lar
hy′per·veg′e·ta′tive
hy′per·ven′ti·la′tion
hy′per·vis·cos′i·ty
hy′per·vis′cous
hy′per·vi′ta·min·o′sis
  pl. -ses′
hy′per·vo·le′mi·a
hy′per·vo·le′mic
hyp′es·the′si·a
hyp′es·the′sic
hyp′es·thet′ic
hy′pha pl.
  -phae′

hy·phe′ma
hy·phe′mi·a
hyp′hi·dro′sis
hyp′na·gog′ic
hyp′na·gogue′
hyp·nal′gi·a
hyp′nic
hyp′no·a·nal′y·sis pl. -ses′
hyp′no·an′es·the′si·a
hyp′no·gen′e·sis
hyp′no·gen′ic
hyp′noid′
hyp′no·lep′sy
hyp′no·nar·co′sis pl. -ses′
hyp′no·pom′pic
hyp·no′sis pl. -ses′
hyp′no·ther′a·py
hyp·not′ic
hyp′no·tism
hyp′no·tist
hyp′no·tize′, -tized′, -tiz′ing
hyp′no·toid′
hy′po
hy′po·a·cid′i·ty
hy′po·ac′tive
hy′po·ac·tiv′i·ty
hy′po·a·cu′si·a
hy′po·a·cu′sis
hy′po·a·dren′a·li·ne′mi·a
hy′po·a·dre′nal·ism
hy′po·a·dre′ni·a
hy′po·a·dre′no·cor′ti·cism
hy′po·af·fec′tive
hy′po·af·fec·tiv′i·ty
hy′po·ag′na·thus
hy′po·al·bu′mi·ne′mi·a
hy′po·al′do·ster′o·nism
hy′po·al′i·men·ta′tion
hy′po·al′ka·line
hy′po·al′ler·gen′ic
hy′po·az′o·tu′ri·a
hy′po·bar′ic
hy′po·bar′ism
hy′po·ba·rop′a·thy
hy′po·be·ta·lip′o·pro′tein·
  e′mi·a
hy′po·bil′i·ru′bi·ne′mi·a
hy′po·blast′
hy′po·blas′tic
hy′po·bran′chi·al
hy′po·bro′mite′
hy′po·cal·ce′mi·a
hy′po·cal·cif′ic
hy′po·cal′ci·fi·ca′tion
hy′po·cal′ci·fy′, -fied′,
  -fy′ing
hy′po·cal·ci·u′ri·a

hy′po·cap′ni·a
hy′po·car′bi·a
hy′po·chlo·re′mi·a
hy′po·chlo·re′mic
hy′po·chlor·hy′dri·a
hy′po·chlo′rite′
hy′po·chlo′ri·za′tion
hy′po·chlo′rous
hy′po·chlor·u′ri·a
hy′po·cho·les′ter·o·le′mi·a
hy′po·chon′dri·a
hy′po·chon′dri·ac′
hy′po·chon·dri·a·cal
hy′po·chon′dri·al
hy′po·chon·dri′a·sis
pl. -ses′
hy′po·chon′dri·um pl. -dri·a
hy′po·chord′al
hy′po·chro·ma′si·a
hy′po·chro·mat′ic
hy′po·chro′ma·tism
hy′po·chro′mi·a
hy′po·chro′mic
hy′po·chy′li·a
hy′po·ci·ne′si·a
hy′po·coe′lom
hy′po·con′dy·lar
hy′po·cone′
hy′po·con′id
hy′po·con′ule′
hy′po·con′u·lid
hy′po·crine
hy′po·crin′i·a
hy′po·cri′nism
hy′po·cu·pre′mi·a
hy′po·cy·clo′sis pl. -ses′
hy′po·cys·tot′o·my
hy′po·cy·the′mi·a
hy′po·cy·to′sis pl. -ses′
hy′po·der·mat′o·my
hy′po·der·mi′a·sis pl. -ses′
hy′po·der′mic
hy′po·der′mis
hy′po·der·moc′ly·sis
pl. -ses′
hy′po·der′mo·li·thi′a·sis pl.
-ses′
hy′po·di′a·phrag·mat′ic
hy′po·dip′si·a
hy′po·don′ti·a
hy′po·dy·nam′ic
hy′po·ec·cris′i·a
hy′po·en·doc′rin·ism
hy′po·e·o·sin′o·phil′i·a
hy′po·er′gic
hy′po·er′gy
hy′po·es·o·pho′ri·a

hy′po·es·the′si·a
hy′po·es′trin·ism
hy′po·es·tro·ge·ne′mi·a
hy′po·ex′o·pho′ri·a
hy′po·fer·re′mi·a
hy′po·fer′rism
hy′po·fi′bri·no·ge·ne′mi·a
hy′po·func′tion
hy′po·func′tion·al
hy′po·ga·lac′ti·a
hy′po·gam′ma·glob′u·li·
ne′mi·a
hy′po·gas′tric
hy′po·gas′tri·um pl. -tri·a
hy′po·gas·trop′a·gus
hy′po·gas·tros′chi·sis pl.
-ses′
hy′po·gen′e·sis
hy′po·ge·net′ic
hy′po·gen′i·tal·ism
hy′po·geu′si·a
hy′po·glan′du·lar
hy′po·glos′sal
hy′po·glos′sus pl. -si′
hy′po·glot′tis
hy′po·gly·ce′mi·a
hy′po·gly·ce′mic
hy′po·gly′ce·mo′sis pl. -ses′
hy′po·gly′co·ge·nol′y·sis
pl. -ses′
hy′po·gly′cor·rha′chi·a
hy′po·go′nad·ism
hy′po·gran′u·lo·cy·to′sis
pl. -ses′
hy′po·hi·dro′sis pl. -ses′
hy′po·in′su·lin·ism
hy′po·ka·le′mi·a
hy′po·ka·le′mic
hy′po·ker′a·to′sis pl. -ses′
hy′po·ki·ne′si·a
hy′po·ki·ne′sis pl. -ses′
hy′po·ki·net′ic
hy′po·lar′ynx pl. -ynx·es or
-la·ryn′ges′
hy′po·lem′mal
hy′po·leu′ko·cyt′ic
hy′po·ley′dig·ism
hy′po·li·pe′mi·a
hy′po·li·pe′mic
hy′po·lip′o·pro′tein·e′mi·a
hy′po·li·po′sis pl. -ses′
hy′po·lo′gi·a
hy′po·lu·te′mi·a
hy′po·mag′ne·se′mi·a
hy′po·ma′ni·a
hy′po·man′ic
hy′po·mas′ti·a

hy′po·mel′a·nism
hy′po·mel′a·no′sis pl. -ses′
hy′po·mel′a·not′ic
hy′po·men·or·rhe′a
hy′po·mere′
hy′po·me·tab′o·lism
hy′po·me·tro′pi·a
hy′po·mi′cron′
hy′po·mi′cro·so′ma
hy′pom·ne′si·a
hy′po·morph′
hy′po·mo·til′i·ty
hy′po·myx′i·a
hy′po·na·tre′mi·a
hy′po·ni′trous
hy′po·nych′i·al
hy′po·nych′i·um
hy′po·or′chi·dism
hy′po·os·to′sis pl. -ses′
hy′po·o·var′i·an·ism
hy′po·pan′cre·a·tism
hy′po·par′a·thy′roid′
hy′po·par′a·thy′roid·ism
hy′po·per·fu′sion
hy′po·per′i·stal′sis pl. -ses′
hy′po·per′me·a·bil′i·ty
hy′po·pha·lan′gism
hy′po·phar′yn·gi′tis
hy′po·phar′yn·gos′co·py
hy′po·phar′ynx
hy′po·pho′ni·a
hy′po·pho′ri·a
hy′po·phos′pha·ta′si·a
hy′po·phos′pha·te′mi·a
hy′po·phos′pha·tu′ri·a
hy′po·phos′phite′
hy′po·phre′ni·a
hy′po·phren′ic
hy·poph′y·se′al
hy·poph′y·sec′to·mize′,
-mized′, -miz′ing
hy·poph′y·sec′to·my
hy·poph′y·se′o·por′tal
hy′po·phys′i·o·priv′ic
hy·poph′y·sis pl. -ses′
—— cer′e·bri′
hy·poph′y·si′tis
hy′po·pi·e′si·a
hy′po·pi·e′sis pl. -ses′
hy′po·pi·et′ic
hy′po·pig′men·ta′tion
hy′po·pin′e·al·ism
hy′po·pi·tu′i·ta·rism
hy′po·pla′si·a
—— cu′tis con·gen′i·ta
hy′po·plas′tic
hy′po·plas′ty

hy′po·pne′a
hy′po·po·ro′sis *pl.* -ses′
hy′po·po′si·a
hy′po·po′tas·se′mi·a
hy′po·prax′i·a
hy′po·pro·tein·e′mi·a
hy′po·pro·tein′ic
hy′po·pro·throm′bi·
  ne′mi·a
hy′po·psel′a·phe′si·a
hy′po·psy·cho′sis *pl.* -ses′
hy·po′py·on′
hy′po·re·ac′tive
hy′po·re·flex′i·a
hy′po·re·flex′ic
hy′po·ren′i·ne′mi·a
hy′po·sal′i·va′tion
hy′po·scle′ral
hy′po·se·cre′tion
hy′po·sen′si·tive
hy′po·sen′si·tiv′i·ty
hy′pos′mi·a
hy′po·so′mi·a
hy′po·som′ni·a
hy′po·spa′di·ac′
hy′po·spa′di·as
hy′po·sper′ma·to·gen′e·sis
  pl. -ses′
hy·pos′ta·sis *pl.* -ses′
hy′po·stat′ic
hy′po·sthe′ni·a
hy′po·sthe′ni·ant
hy′po·sthen′ic
hy·pos′the·nu′ri·a
hy′po·sto′mi·a
hy′po·sul′fite′
hy′po·syn·er′gi·a
hy′po·sys′to·le
hy′po·tax′i·a
hy′po·tax′is
hy′po·tel′o·rism
hy′po·ten′sion
hy′po·ten′sive
hy′po·ten′sor
hy′po·tha·lam′ic
hy′po·thal′a·mus
hy′po·the′nar
hy′po·ther′mal
hy′po·therm′es·the′si·a
hy′po·ther′mi·a
hy′po·ther′mic
hy′po·ther′my
hy·poth′e·sis *pl.* -ses′
hy′po·thy′mi·a
hy′po·thy′roid′
hy′po·thy′roid′ism
hy′po·thy·ro′sis

hy′po·to′ni·a
hy′po·ton′ic
hy′po·to·nic′i·ty
hy′po·tri·cho′sis
hy·pot′ro·phy
hy′po·tro′pi·a
hy′po·tym·pan′ic
hy′po·tym′pa·num
hy′po·u·re′mi·a
hy′po·var′i·a
hy′po·veg′e·ta′tive
hy′po·ve·nos′i·ty
hy′po·ven′ti·la′tion
hy′po·vi′ta·min·o′sis
  pl. -ses′
hy′po·vo·le′mi·a
hy′po·vo·le′mic
hy′po·vo·lu′mic
hy′pox·e′mi·a
hy′pox·e′mic
hy·pox′i·a
hy·pox′ic
hy′po·zinc·e′mi·a
hyp′sar·rhyth′mi·a
hyp′si·brach′y·ce·phal′ic
hyp′si·ce·phal′ic
hyp′si·ceph′a·ly
hyp′si·conch′
hyp′si·con′chous
hyp′si·sta·phyl′i·a
hyp′si·sta·phyl′ic
hyp′si·staph′y·line′
hyp′so·ceph′a·lous
hyp′so·ki·ne′sis *pl.* -ses′
Hyr′tl loop
hys′ter·al′gi·a
hys′ter·al′gic
hys′ter·a·tre′si·a
hys′ter·ec′to·my
hys′ter·e′sis *pl.* -ses′
hys′ter·eu·ryn′ter
hys·te′ri·a
hys·ter′ic *or* hys·ter′i·cal
hys·ter′i·cism
hys·ter′ics
hys·ter′i·form′
hys′ter·o·bu·bon′o·cele′
hys′ter·o·car′ci·no′ma *pl.*
  -mas *or* -ma·ta
hys′ter·o·cele′
hys′ter·o·clei′sis *pl.* -ses′
hys′ter·o·col·pec′to·my
hys′ter·o·cys′tic
hys′ter·o·cys′to·clei′sis *pl.*
  -ses′
hys′ter·o·cys′to·pex′y
hys′ter·o·dyn′i·a

hys′ter·o·ep′i·lep′sy
hys′ter·o·gen′ic
hys′ter·og′e·nous
hys′ter·o·gram′
hys′ter·og′ra·phy
hys′ter·oid′
hys′ter·oi′dal
hys′ter·o·lap′a·rot′o·my
hys′ter·o·lith′
hys′ter·o·li·thi′a·sis *pl.* -ses′
hys′ter·ol′o·gy
hys′ter·ol′y·sis *pl.* -ses′
hys′ter·o·ma′ni·a
hys′ter·om′e·ter
hys′ter·om′e·try
hys′ter·o·my·o′ma *pl.* -mas
  or -ma·ta
hys′ter·o·my′o·mec′to·my
hys′ter·o·my·ot′o·my
hys′ter·o·neu′ras·the′ni·a
hys′ter·o·o′o·pho·rec′to·
  my
hys′ter·o·path′ic
hys′ter·op′a·thy
hys′ter·o·pex′y
hys′ter·op·to′sis
hys′ter·or′rha·phy
hys′ter·or·rhex′is *pl.*
  -rhex′es′
hys′ter·o·sal′pin·gec′to·my
hys′ter·o·sal′pin·go·gram′
hys′ter·o·sal′pin·gog′ra·
  phy
hys′ter·o·sal′pin·go-o′o·
  pho·rec′to·my
hys′ter·o·sal′pin·gos′to·my
hys′ter·o·scope′
hys′ter·os′co·py
hys′ter·o·spasm
hys′ter·o·tome′
hys′ter·ot′o·my
hys′ter·o·tra′che·lec′to·my
hys′ter·o·tra′che·lo·plas′ty
hys′ter·o·tra′che·lor·rha·
  phy
hys′ter·o·tra′che·lot′o·my
hys′ter·o·trau·mat′ic
hys′ter·o·trau′ma·tism

I

i·at′ro·gen′e·sis
i·at′ro·gen′ic
i′bo·ga′ine′
i·bu′fe·nac′

i·bu′pro·fen
Ice′land
—— disease
—— moss
—— spar
ich′no·gram′
i′chor′
i′chor·e′mi·a
i′chor·oid′
i′chor·ous
i′chor·rhe′a
i′chor·rhe′mi·a
ich′tham·mol′
ich′thy·ism
ich′thy·oid′
ich′thy·oph′a·gous
ich′thy·o·sar′co·tox′ism
ich′thy·o·si·form′
ich′thy·o′sis pl. -ses′
—— con·gen′i·ta
—— fe·ta′lis
—— fol·lic′u·lar′is
—— hys′trix
—— le·tha′lis
—— sim′plex′
—— vul·gar′is
ich′thy·ot′ic
ich′thy·o·tox′in
ich′thy·o·tox′ism
ich′thy·o·tox·is′mus
ic′tal
ic·ter′ic
ic·ter·o·gen′ic
ic·ter·og′e·nous
ic·ter·o·hem′a·tu′ri·a
ic·ter·o·hem′a·tu′ric
ic·ter·o·he′mo·lyt′ic
ic·ter·o·hem′or·rhag′ic
ic·ter·o·hep′a·ti′tis pl. -tis·es
  or -tit′i·des′
ic′ter·oid′
ic′ter·us
—— grav′is
—— ne′o·na·to′rum
ic′tus
id
i·de′al·i·za′tion
i′de·a′tion
i′de·a′tion·al
i·dée′ fixe′
i·den′ti·cal
i·den′ti·fi·ca′tion
i·den′ti·ty
id′e·o·ge·net′ic
id′e·og′e·nous
id′e·o·glan′du·lar
id′e·o·ki·net′ic

id′e·ol′o·gy
id′e·o·met′a·bol′ic
id′e·o·me·tab′o·lism
id′e·o·mo′tor
id′e·o·mus′cu·lar
id′e·o·vas′cu·lar
id′i·o·blast′
id′i·o·chro′mo·some′
id′i·o·cra′si·a
id′i·oc′ra·sis pl. -ses′
id′i·oc′ra·sy
id′i·o·crat′ic
id′i·o·cy
id′i·o·gen′e·sis
id′i·o·glos′si·a
id′i·o·glot′tic
id′i·o·gram′
id′i·o·het′er·ol′y·sin
id′i·o·hyp′no·tism
id′i·ol′o·gism
id′i·o·me·tri′tis
id′i·o·mus′cu·lar
id′i·o·neu·ro′sis pl. -ses′
id′i·o·pa·thet′ic
id′i·o·path′ic
id′i·op′a·thy
id′i·o·phren′ic
id′i·o·plasm
id′i·o·re·flex′
id′i·o·ret′i·nal
id′i·o·some′
id′i·o·spasm
id′i·o·spas′tic
id′i·o·syn′cra·sy
id′i·o·syn·crat′ic
id′i·ot
—— sa·vant′
id′i·o·tope′
id′i·o·tox′in
id′i·o·trop′ic
id′i·o·ven·tric′u·lar
i′do·lo·ma′ni·a
i′dox·u′ri·dine′
ig′ni·punc′ture
ig·ni′tion
il′e·ac′ (pertaining to the ileum)
◆iliac
il′e·al
il′e·ec′to·my
il′e·i′tis pl. -it′i·des′
il′e·o·ap′pen·dic′u·lar
il′e·o·ce′cal
il′e·o·ce·cos′to·my
il′e·o·ce′cum
il′e·o·co′lic
il′e·o·co·li′tis

il′e·o·co·lon′ic
il′e·o·co·los′to·my
il′e·o·co·lot′o·my
il′e·o·cu·ta′ne·ous
il′e·o·cys′to·plas′ty
il′e·o·cys·tos′to·my
il′e·o·il′e·al
il′e·o·il′e·os′to·my
il′e·o·proc·tos′to·my
il′e·o·rec′tal
il′e·or′rha·phy
il′e·o·sig′moid′
il′e·o·sig′moid·os′to·my
il′e·os′to·my
il′e·ot′o·my
il′e·o·trans·verse′
il′e·o·trans′ver·sos′to·my
il′e·o·ves′i·cal
I·le′sha fever
il′e·tin
il′e·um (lower portion of the
  small intestine), pl. -e·a
◆ilium
il′e·us
il′i·ac′ (pertaining to the ilium)
◆ileac
i·li′a·cus pl. -ci′
il′i·a·del′phus
il′i·o·cap′su·lar′is
il′i·o·coc·cyg′e·al
il′i·o·coc·cyg′e·us
il′i·o′co·lot′o·my
il′i·o·cos′tal
il′i·o·cos·ta′lis
—— cer′vi·cis
—— dor′si′
—— lum·bo′rum
—— tho·ra′cis
il′i·o·cos·to·cer′vi·ca′lis
il′i·o·fem′o·ral
il′i·o·hy′po·gas′tric
il′i·o·in′gui·nal
il′i·o·lum′bar
il′i·op′a·gus
il′i·o·pec·tin′e·al
il′i·o·pel′vic
il′i·o·pso′as
il′i·o·pu′bic
il′i·o·sa′cral
il′i·o·tho′ra·cop′a·gus
il′i·o·tib′i·al
il′i·o·tro′chan·ter′ic
il′i·um (the flank), pl. -i·a
◆ileum
ill
il·laq′ue·ate′, -at′ed, -at′ing

il·laq'ue·a'tion
il'le·git'i·ma·cy
il'le·git'i·mate
il'li·ni'tion
il·lin'i·um
ill'ness
il·lu'mi·nance
il·lu'mi·nate', -nat'ed, -nat'-
  ing
il·lu'mi·na'tion
il·lu'mi·na'tor
il·lu'mi·nism
il·lu'sion
il·lu'sion·al
il·lu'so·ry
i'ma
im'age
i·mag'i·nar'y
i·mag'i·na'tion
i·ma'go pl. -goes or i·mag'i·
  nes'
im·bal'ance
im'be·cile
im'be·cil'i·ty
im·bed', -bed'ded, -bed'ding,
  var. of embed
im·bibe', -bibed', -bib'ing
im·bi·bi'tion
im·bri·cate', -cat'ed, -cat'ing
im·bri·ca'tion
im'i·daz'ole'
im'ide'
i·mid'o·line'
im'i·no·gly'ci·nu'ri·a
im'i·no·u·re'a
i·mip'ra·mine'
im'i·tate', -tat'ed, -tat'ing
im'i·ta'tion
im'i·ta'tive
im·ma·ture'
im'ma·tu'ri·ty
im·med'i·ca·ble
im·merse', -mersed', -mers'-
  ing
im·mer'sion
im·mis'ci·ble
im·mo·bil'i·ty
im·mo'bi·li·za'tion
im·mo'bi·lize', -lized', -liz'-
  ing
im·mor·tal'i·ty
im·mune'
im·mu'ni·ty
im'mu·ni·za'tion
im'mu·nize', -nized', -niz'ing
im'mu·no·as'say'
im'mu·no·bi·ol'o·gy

im'mu·no·blast'
im'mu·no·chem'is·try
im'mu·no·con·glu'ti·nin
im'mu·no·cyte'
im'mu·no·de·fi'cien·cy
im'mu·no·de·pres'sive
im'mu·no·di'ag·no'sis pl.
  -ses'
im'mu·no·dif·fu'sion
im'mu·no·e·lec'tro·pho·
  re'sis pl. -ses'
im'mu·no·e·lec'tro·pho·
  ret'ic
im'mu·no·flu'o·res'cence
im'mu·no·gen
im'mu·no·ge·net'ic
im'mu·no·gen'ic
im'mu·no·glob'u·lin
im'mu·no·glob'u·lin·op'a·
  thy
im'mu·no·he'ma·tol'o·gy
im'mu·no·he'mo·lyt'ic
im'mu·no·log'ic
im'mu·no·log'i·cal
im'mu·nol'o·gist
im'mu·nol'o·gy
im'mu·no·path'o·log'ic or
  im'mu·no·path'o·log'i·cal
im'mu·no·pa·thol'o·gy
im'mu·no·pho·re'sis pl.
  -ses'
im'mu·no·pro·lif'er·a·tive
im'mu·no·pro'tein'
im'mu·no·re·ac'tion
im'mu·no·sup·pres'sant
im'mu·no·sup·pres'sion
im'mu·no·sup·pres'sive
im'mu·no·ther'a·py
im'mu·no·tox'in
im'mu·no·trans·fu'sion
im·pact'ed
im·pac'tion
im·pal'pa·ble
im'par'
im·par'i·dig'i·tate'
im'passe'
im·pa'ten·cy
im·pa'tent
im·ped'ance
im·per'a·tive
im'per·cep'tion
im·per'fo·rate
im·per'me·a·ble
im·per'vi·ous
im'pe·tig'i·ni·za'tion
im'pe·tig'i·noid'
im'pe·tig'i·nous

im'pe·ti'go
—— cir'ci·na'ta
—— cir'cum·pi·lar'is
—— con·ta'gi·o'sa
—— fol·lic'u·lar'is
—— her·pet'i·for'mis
—— ne'o·na·to'rum
—— vul·gar'is
im·plant'
im'plan·ta'tion
im'po·tence
im'po·ten·cy
im'po·tent
im·po·ten'ti·a
—— co'e·un'di'
—— er'i·gen'di'
im·preg'nate', -nat'ed, -nat'-
  ing
im'preg·na'tion
im·pres'si·o' pl. im·pres'si·
  o'nes'
—— car·di'a·ca hep'a·tis
—— cardiaca pul·mo'nis
—— co'li·ca
—— du'o·de·na'lis hep'a·tis
—— e'so·pha'ge·a hep'a·tis
—— gas'tri·ca hep'a·tis
—— gastrica re'nis
—— he·pat'i·ca re'nis
—— lig'a·men'ti' cos'to·cla·
  vic'u·lar'is
—— mus'cu·lar'is re'nis
—— oe'so·pha'ge·a hep'a·tis
—— pe·tro'sa cer'e·bri'
—— re·na'lis hep'a·tis
—— su'pra·re·na'lis hep'a·tis
—— tri·gem'i·ni' os'sis
tem'po·ra'lis
im·pres'sion
im·pres'si·o'nes' dig'i·
  ta'tae'
im·print'
im·print'ing
im·pro'cre·ance
im·pro'cre·ant
im·pu'ber·al
im·pu'bic
im'pulse
im·pul'sion
im·pul'sive
im·pu'ta·bil'i·ty
im'vic
in'a·cid'i·ty
in·ac'tion
in·ac'ti·va'tion
in·ac'ti·vate', -vat'ed, -vat'-
  ing

in·ac'tive
in'ac·tiv'i·ty
in·ad'e·qua·cy
in·ad'e·quate
in·al'i·men'tal
in·an'i·mate
in·a'ni'tion
in·ap'pe·tence
in·ar'tic'u·late
in ar·tic'u·lo' mor'tis
in·as·sim'i·la·ble
in'born'
in'bred'
in'breed'ing
In'ca bone
in·car'cer·ate', -at'ed, -at'-
ing
in·car'cer·a'tion
in·car'i·al
in·car'nant
in'car·na'ti·o' un'guis
in·car'na·tive
in·case'ment
in·cep'tion
in·cep'tus
in'cest'
in'ci·dence
in'ci·dent
in'ci·den'tal
in·cin'er·ate', -at'ed, -at'ing
in·cin'er·a'tion
in·cip'i·ence
in·cip'i·en·cy
in·cip'i·ent
in·ci'sal
in·cise', -cised', -cis'ing
in·ci'sion
in·ci'sive
in'ci·si'vus
—— la'bi·i' in·fe'ri·o'ris
—— labii su·pe'ri·o'ris
in·ci'so·la'bi·al
in·ci'so·lin'gual
in·ci'so·prox'i·mal
in·ci'sor
in'ci·su'ra pl. -rae'
—— ac'e·tab'u·li'
—— an'gu·lar'is
—— anterior au'ris
—— ap'i·cis cor'dis
—— car·di'a·ca
—— cardiaca pul·mo'nis
si·nis'tri'
—— cardiaca ven·tric'u·li'
—— cer'e·bel'li' anterior
—— cerebelli posterior
—— cla·vic'u·lar'is

—— cos·ta'lis
—— eth'moi·da'lis
—— fib'u·lar'is
—— fron·ta'lis
—— in'ter·ar'y·tae·noi'de·a
—— in'ter·ar'y·te·noi'de·a
—— in'ter·lo·bar'is pul·
mo'nis
—— in'ter·trag'i·ca
—— is'chi·ad'i·ca major
—— ischiadica minor
—— jug'u·lar'is os'sis oc·
cip'i·ta'lis
—— jugularis ossis tem'po·
ra'lis
—— jugularis ster'ni'
—— lac'ri·ma'lis
—— lig'a·men'ti' te're·tis
—— man·dib'u·lae'
—— mas·toi'de·a
—— na·sa'lis
—— pan·cre'a·tis
—— pa·ri'e·ta'lis
—— pre'oc·cip'i·ta'lis
—— pter'y·goi'de·a
—— ra'di·a'lis
—— scap'u·lae'
—— sem'i·lu·nar'is
—— sphe'no·pal'a·ti'na
—— su'pra·or·bi·ta'lis
—— ten·to'ri·i'
—— ter'mi·na'lis au'ris
—— thy're·oi'de·a inferior
—— thyreoidea superior
—— thy·roi'de·a inferior
—— thyroidea superior
—— troch'le·ar'is
—— tym·pan'i·ca
—— ul·nar'is
—— um·bil'i·ca'lis
—— ver'te·bra'lis inferior
—— vertebralis superior
in'ci·su'rae'
—— car'ti·lag'i·nis me·a'tus
a·cu'sti·ci'
—— cartilaginis meatus
acustici ex·ter'ni' (San·to·
ri'ni)
—— cos·ta'les'
—— hel'i·cis
in·ci'su·ral
in·ci'sure
—— of Ri·vi'nus
—— of Schmidt'-Lan'ter·
mann
in·ci'tant
in'cli·na'ti·o' pl. -na'ti·o'nes'

in'cli·na'tion
in·cline', -clined', -clin'ing
in'cli·nom'e·ter
in·clu'sion
in'co·ag'u·la·bil'i·ty
in'co·ag'u·la·ble
in·co·her'ence
in·co·her'ent
in'com·pat'i·bil'i·ty
in'com·pat'i·ble
in·com'pe·tence
in·com'pe·ten·cy
in·com'pe·tent
in'com·plete'
in·con'gru·ence
in·con'gru·ent
in'con·gru'i·ty
in·con'stant
in·con'ti·nence
in·con'ti·nent
in·con'ti·nen'ti·a
—— al'vi'
—— pig·men'ti'
—— u·ri'nae'
—— vul'vae
in'co·or'di·nate
in'co·or'di·na'tion
in·cor'po·rate', -rat'ed, -rat'-
ing
in·cor'po·ra'tion
in'co·sta·pe'di·al
in'cre·ment
in'cre·men'tal
in·cre'to·ry
in·crust'
in'crus·ta'tion
in'cu·bate', -bat'ed, -bat'ing
in'cu·ba'tion
in'cu·ba'tor
in'cu·bus pl. -bi' or -bus·es
in'cu·dal
in'cu·dec'to·my
in'cu·do·mal'le·al
in'cu·do·sta·pe'di·al
in·cur'a·ble
in'cur·vate', -vat'ed, -vat'ing
in'cur·va'tion
in'cus pl. in·cu'des'
in·cy'clo·pho'ri·a
in·cy'co·tro'pi·a
in·dent'
in'den·ta'tion
in'dex' pl. -dex'es or -di·ces'
—— of Flow'er
In'dex' Med'i·cus
In'di·a ink
—— method

—— nucleus
in'di·can'
in'di·cant
in'di·ca·nu'ri·a
in'di·ca'ti·o'
—— cau·sa'lis
—— cu'ra·ti'va
—— symp'to·mat'i·ca
in'di·ca'tion
in'di·ca'tor
in'di·co·phose'
in di'es
in·dif'fer·ent
in·dig'e·nous
in'di·gest'i·ble
in'di·ges'tion
in·dig'i·ta'tion
in'di·go
in·dig'o·tin
in'di·go·u'ri·a
in'di·rect'
in'dis·posed'
in·dis·po·si'tion
in'di·vid'u·al·i·za'tion
in'di·vid'u·al·ize', -ized',
  -iz'ing
in'di·vid'u·a'tion
in'dol·ac'e·tu'ri·a
in'dole'
in'dole·a·ce'tic
in'do·lent
in'dole·pro'pi·on'ic
in'dole·py·ru'vic
in'do·log'e·nous
in'do·lu'ri·a
in'do·lyl·a·cryl'o·yl·
  gly'cine
in'do·lyl·a·cryl'o·yl·gly'ci·
  nu'ri·a
in'do·meth'a·cin
in'do·phe'nol'
in·dox'ole'
in·dox'yl
in·dox'yl·e'mi·a
in·dox'y·log'e·nous
in·dox'yl·sul'fate'
in·dox'yl·sul·fu'ric
in·dox'yl·u'ri·a
in'dri·line'
in·duce', -duced', -duc'ing
in·duc'tion
in·duc'to·py·rex'i·a
in'du·lin
in'du·rate', -rat'ed, -rat'ing
in'du·ra'tion
in'du·ra'tive
in·du'si·um pl. -si·a

—— gris'e·um
in'dwell'ing
in·e'bri·ant
in·e'bri·ate', -at'ed, -at'ing
in·e'bri·a'tion
in'e·bri'e·ty
in·ef'fi·ca'cious
in·ef'fi·ca·cy
in·e·las'tic
in·ert'
in·er'tia
in ex·tre'mis
in'fan·cy
in'fant
in·fan'ti·cide'
in'fan·tile'
in·fan'ti·lism
in'farct'
in·farc'tion
in·fect'
in·fec'tion
in·fec'tious
in·fec'tive
in'fe·cun'di·ty
in·fe'ri·or
in'fe·ro·lat'er·al
in'fe·ro·me'di·al
in'fe·ro·pa·ri'e·tal
in'fe·ro·pos·te'ri·or
in'fer·til'i·ty
in·fest'
in'fes·ta'tion
in·fes'tive
in·fib'u·la'tion
in'fil·trate', -trat'ed, -trat'ing
in'fil·tra'tion
in·firm'
in·fir'ma·ry
in·fir'mi·ty
in·flame', -flamed', -flam'ing
in·flam'ma·ble
in·flam·ma'tion
in·flam'ma·to'ry
in·flate', -flat'ed, -flat'ing
in·fla'tion
in·flec'tion
in·flo·res'cence
in·flu·en'za
in·flu·en'zal
in·fold'
in'foot'ed
in'fra·al·ve'o·lar
in'fra·au·ric'u·lar
in'fra·ax'il·lar'y
in'fra·bo'ny
in'fra·car'di·ac'
in'fra·cla·vic'u·lar

in'fra·cla·vic'u·lar'is
in'fra·cli'noid'
in'fra·clu'sion
in'fra·con'dy·lism
in'fra·cor'ti·cal
in'fra·cos'tal
in·frac'tion
in'fra·den·ta'le'
in'fra·di'a·phrag·mat'ic
in'fra·gle'noid'
in'fra·glot'tic
in'fra·gran'u·lar
in'fra·hy'oid'
in'fra·mam'ma·ry
in'fra·man·dib'u·lar
in'fra·mar'gin·al
in'fra·max'il·lar'y
in'fra·na'sal
in'fra·nu'cle·ar
in'fra·oc·clu'sion
in'fra·or'bi·tal
in'fra·pa·tel'lar
in'fra·phys'i·o·log'ic
in'fra·red'
in'fra·scap'u·lar
in'fra·son'ic
in'fra·spi·na'tus
in'fra·spi'nous
in'fra·ster'nal
in'fra·tem'po·ral
in'fra·tra'che·al
in'fra·troch'le·ar
in'fra·tur'bin·al
in'fra·um·bil'i·cal
in'fra·vag'i·nal
in'fra·ver'sion
in'fra·ves'i·cal
in'fra·zy'go·mat'ic
in·fric'tion
in'fun·dib'u·lar
in'fun·dib'u·lec'to·my
in'fun·dib'u·li·form'
in'fun·dib'u·lo'ma pl. -mas
  or -ma·ta
in'fun·dib'u·lo·pel'vic
in'fun·dib'u·lo·ven·tric'u·
  lar
in'fun·dib'u·lum pl. -la
  —— eth'moid·da'le'
  —— hy'po·thal'a·mi'
  —— tu'bae' u'te·ri'nae'
in·fu'sion
in·ges'ta
in·ges'tant
in·ges'tion
in·ges'tive
In·gras'si·a wings

in'gra·ves'cent
in·gre'di·ent
in'grow'ing
in'grown'
in'growth'
in'guen pl. -gui·na
in'gui·nal
in'gui·no·ab·dom'i·nal
in'gui·no·cru'ral
in'gui·no·dyn'i·a
in'gui·no·la'bi·al
in'gui·no·scro'tal
in·hal'ant
in'ha·la'tion
in'ha·la'tor
in·hale', -haled', -hal'ing
in·hal'er
in·her'ent
in·her'it
in·her'i·tance
in·hib'in
in·hib'it
in'hi·bi'tion
in·hib'i·tor
in·hib'i·to'ry
in'i·en·ceph'a·lus
in'i·en·ceph'a·ly
in'i·od'y·mus
in'i·on'
in'i·op'a·gus
i·ni'tial
i·ni'ti·a'tor
in·i'tis
in·ject'
in·ject'a·ble
in·jec'ti·o' pl. in·jec'ti·o'nes'
in·jec'tion
in'ju·ry
ink'blot'
in'lay'
in'let
in'ly'ing
in·nate'
in'ner·vate' (to supply with
   nerves), -vat'ed, -vat'ing
♦enervate
in'ner·va'tion
in'no·cent
in·noc'u·ous
in·nom'i·na'tal
in·nom'i·nate
in·nox'ious
in'o·blast'
in'oc·ci·pit'i·a
in'o·chon·dri'tis
in·oc'u·la·bil'i·ty
in·oc'u·la·ble

in·oc'u·late', -lat'ed, -lat'ing
in·oc'u·la'tion
in·oc'u·la'tor
in·oc'u·lum pl. -la
in'o·cyte'
in'o·gen
in·og'li·a
in'o·lith'
in·op'er·a·ble
in·or·gan'ic
in·os'cu·late', -lat'ed, -lat'-
   ing
in·os'cu·la'tion
in'o·se'mi·a
in'o·sine'
i·no'si·tol'
in'o·si·tu'ri·a
in'o·su'ri·a
i'no·trope'
in'o·trop'ic
in'pa'tient
in'quest'
in·ruc·ta'tion
in·sal'i·vate', -vat'ed, -vat'-
   ing
in·sal'i·va'tion
in'sa·lu'bri·ous
in'sa·lu'bri·ty
in·sane'
in·san'i·tar'y
in·san'i·ty
in·scrip'ti·o' pl. in·scrip'ti·
   o'nes'
in·scrip'tion
in'sect'
in·sec'ti·ci'dal
in·sec'ti·cide'
in·sec'ti·fuge'
in·sem'i·na'tion
in'se·nes'cence
in·sen'si·bil'i·ty
in·sen'si·ble
in·sert' v.
in·sert' n.
in·ser'tion
in·sid'i·ous
in'sight'
in·sip'id
in si'tu
in'so·la'tion
in·sol'u·bil'i·ty
in·sol'u·ble
in·som'ni·a
in·som'ni·ac'
in·sorp'tion
in·spec'tion
in·sper'sion

in'spi·ra'tion
in'spi·ra'tor
in'spi'ra·to'ry
in'spi·rom'e·ter
in·spis'sate', -sat'ed, -sat'ing
in'spis·sa'tion
in·spis'sa'tor
in·sta·bil'i·ty
in'step'
in'stil·la'tion
in'stil·la'tor
in'stinct
in·stinc'tive
in·stinc'tu·al
in'stru·ment
in'stru·men'tal
in'stru·men·ta'tion
in'suf·fi'cien·cy
in'suf·fi'cient
in'suf·fla'tion
in'suf·fla'tor
in'su·la pl. -lae'
in'su·lar
in'su·lin
in'su·li·nase'
in'su·li·ne'mi·a
in'su·lin·o'gen·e'sis pl. -ses'
in'su·lin·o'gen'ic
in'su·li·no'ma pl. -mas or
   -ma·ta
in'su·lo'ma pl. -mas or
   -ma·ta
in'sult'
in'sus·cep'ti·bil'i·ty
in'take'
in'te·gra'tion
in·teg'u·ment
in·teg'u·men'ta·ry
in·teg'u·men'tum
—— com·mu'ne'
in'tel·lect'
in'tel·lec'tu·al·i·za'tion
in'tel·lec'tu·al·ize', -ized',
   -iz'ing
in·tel'li·gence
in·tem'per·ance
in·tem'per·ate
in·tense'
in·ten'si·fi·ca'tion
in·ten'si·fy', -fied', -fy'ing
in·ten·sim'e·ter
in·ten'si·ty
in·ten'sive
in·ten'tion
in'ter·ac·ces'so·ry
in'ter·ac'i·nar
in'ter·ac'i·nous

in'ter·al·ve'o·lar
in'ter·an'nu·lar
in'ter·ar·tic'u·lar
in'ter·ar'y·te'noid'
in'ter·ar'y·te·noi'de·us
in'ter·a'tri·al
in'ter·ax'o·nal
in'ter·bod'y
in·ter'ca·lar'y
in·ter'ca·late' -lat'ed, -lat'-
   ing
in·ter'ca·la'tion
in'ter·can'a·lic'u·lar
in'ter·cap'il·lar'y
in'ter·ca·rot'id
in'ter·car'pal
in'ter·car'ti·lag'i·nous
in'ter·cav'er·nous
in'ter·cel'lu·lar
in'ter·cer'e·bral
in'ter·chon'dral
in'ter·cil'i·um
in'ter·cla·vic'u·lar
in'ter·cli'noid'
in'ter·co·lum'nar
in'ter·con'dy·lar
in'ter·con'dy·loid'
in'ter·cor'o·nar'y
in'ter·cos'tal
in'ter·cos'to·bra'chi·al
in'ter·cos'to·hu'mer·al
in'ter·cou'pler
in'ter·course'
in'ter·cri'co·thy·rot'o·my
in'ter·cris'tal
in'ter·cru'ral
in'ter·cur'rent
in'ter·cus·pa'tion
in'ter·cusp'ing
in'ter·den'tal
in'ter·den'ti·um
in'ter·dic'tion
in'ter·dig'it
in'ter·dig'i·tal
in'ter·dig'i·tate', -tat'ed,
   -tat'ing
in'ter·dig'i·ta'tion
in'ter·duc'tal
in'ter·face' (a surface forming the boundary between
   two phases)
   ◆interphase
in'ter·fa'cial
in'ter·fas·cic'u·lar
in'ter·fere', -fered', -fer'ing
in'ter·fer'ence
in'ter·fe·rom'e·ter

in'ter·fer'o·met'ric
in'ter·fe·rom'e·try
in'ter·fer'on'
in'ter·fer·on'o·gen
in'ter·fi'bril·lar
in'ter·fi'bril·lar'y
in'ter·fi'brous
in'ter·fil'a·men'tous
in'ter·fi'lar
in'ter·fol·lic'u·lar
in'ter·fo·ve'o·lar
in'ter·fur'ca pl. -cae'
in'ter·gem'mal
in'ter·glob'u·lar
in'ter·glu'te·al
in'ter·go'ni·al
in'ter·gran'u·lar
in'ter·gy'ral
in'ter·he'mal
in'ter·hem'i·cer'e·bral
in'ter·hem'i·sphe'ric
in'ter·ic'tal
in·te'ri·or
in'ter·ja'cent
in'ter·ki·ne'sis pl. -ses'
in'ter·la'bi·al
in'ter·la·mel'lar
in'ter·lam'i·nar
in'ter·lig'a·men'ta·ry
in'ter·lig'a·men'tous
in'ter·lo'bar
in'ter·lob'u·lar
in'ter·mal·le'o·lar
in'ter·mam'ma·ry
in'ter·mar'riage
in'ter·max·il'la pl. -lae' or
   -las
in'ter·max'il·lar'y
in'ter·me'di·ar'y
in'ter·me'di·ate
in'ter·me'di·o·lat'er·al
in'ter·me'di·o·me'di·al
in'ter·me'di·us
in'ter·mem'bra·nous
in'ter·me·nin'ge·al
in'ter·men'stru·al
in·ter'ment
in'ter·mes'o·blas'tic
in'ter·met'a·car'pal
in'ter·met'a·mer'ic
in'ter·met'a·tar'sal
in'ter·mi·tot'ic
in'ter·mit'tent
in'ter·mu'ral
in'ter·mus'cu·lar
in'tern'
in·ter'nal

in·ter'nal·i·za'tion
in'ter·nar'i·al
in'ter·na'sal
in'ter·na'tal
in'ter·neu'ral
in'ter·neu'ron'
in'ter·neu'ro·nal
in·tern'ist
in'ter·no'dal
in'ter·node'
in'tern·ship'
in'ter·nu'cle·ar
in'ter·nun'ci·al
in·ter'nus
in'ter·oc·clu'sal
in'ter·o·cep'tive
in'ter·o·cep'tor
in'ter·o·fec'tion
in'ter·o·fec'tive
in'ter·o·ges'tate'
in'ter·ol'i·var'y
in'ter·or'bi·tal
in'ter·os'se·al
in'ter·os'se·i' sing. -se·us
in'ter·os'se·ous
in'ter·pal'a·tine'
in'ter·pal'pe·bral
in'ter·pap'il·lar'y
in'ter·pa·ri'e·tal
in'ter·par'ox·ys'mal
in'ter·pe·dun'cu·lar
in'ter·pel'vi·o·ab·dom'i·nal
in'ter·pha·lan'ge·al
in'ter·phase' (a period in
   the life of a cell during
   which there is no mitotic division)
   ◆interface
in'ter·pha'sic
in'ter·pleu'ral
in·ter'po·late', -lat'ed, -lat'-
   ing
in·ter'po·la'tion
in·ter'pose', -posed', -pos'ing
in·ter'po·si'tion
in·ter'pre·ta'tion
in'ter·pris·mat'ic
in'ter·prox'i·mal
in'ter·prox'i·mate
in'ter·pu'pil·lar'y
in'ter·py·ram'i·dal
in'ter·ra'di·al
in'ter·ra·dic'u·lar
in'ter·re·tic'u·lar
in'ter·scap'u·lar
in'ter·scap'u·lo·tho·rac'ic

in′ter·sec′ti·o′ *pl.* -sec′ti·
o′nes′
in′ter·sec′tion
in′ter·sec′ti·o′nes′ ten·
din′e·ae′
in′ter·seg·men′tal
in′ter·sep′tal
in′ter·sep′tum *pl.* -tums *or*
-ta
in′ter·sex′
in′ter·sex′u·al
in′ter·sex′u·al′i·ty
in′ter·sig′moid′
in′ter·space′
in′ter·sphe′noid′
in′ter·spi′nal
in′ter·spi·na′les′ *sing.* -na′lis
in′ter·spi′nous
in·ter′stic·es *sing.* -stice
in′ter·sti′tial
in′ter·sti′ti·o′ma *pl.* -mas *or*
-ma·ta
in′ter·sti′ti·um
in′ter·sys·tol′ic
in′ter·tar′sal
in′ter·ter′ri·to′ri·al
in′ter·trans′ver·sa′les′
in′ter·trans·verse′
in′ter·tri·gem′i·nal
in′ter·trig′i·nous
in′ter·tri′go
in′ter·tro′chan·ter′ic
in′ter·tu′ber·al
in′ter·tu·ber′cu·lar
in′ter·tu′bu·lar
in′ter·u·re′ter·al
in′ter·u′re·ter′ic
in′ter·vag′i·nal
in′ter·val
in′ter·vas′cu·lar
in′ter·ve′nous *(between
veins)*
◆*intravenous*
in′ter·ven·tric′u·lar *(situat-
ed between ventricles)*
◆*intraventricular*
in′ter·ver′te·bral
in′ter·vil′lous
in·tes′ti·nal
in·tes′tine
in·tes·ti′num *pl.* -na
—— cae′cum
—— cras′sum
—— il′e·um
—— je·ju′num
—— rec′tum
—— ten′u·e′

—— tenue mes′en·ter′i·a′le′
in′ti·ma
in′ti·mal
in′ti·mi′tis
in′tine′
in′toe′ing
in·tol′er·ance
in·tor′sion
in·tort′
in·tort′er
in·tox′i·cant
in·tox′i·ca′tion
in′tra·ab·dom′i·nal
in′tra·ac′i·nar
in′tra·al·ve′o·lar
in′tra·ar·tic′u·lar
in′tra·a′tri·al
in′tra·au′ral
in′tra·au·ric′u·lar
in′tra·bron′chi·al
in′tra·bron·chi′o·lar
in′tra·buc′cal
in′tra·cal′y·ce′al
in′tra·can′a·lic′u·lar
in′tra·cap′su·lar
in′tra·car′di·ac′
in′tra·car′pal
in′tra·car′ti·lag′i·nous
in′tra·cav′er·nous
in′tra·cav′i·tar′y
in′tra·cel′lu·lar
in′tra·ce·phal′ic
in′tra·cer′e·bel′lar
in′tra·cer′e·bral
in′tra·cer′vi·cal
in′tra·cho′ri·on′ic
in′tra·cho·roi′dal
in′tra·cis·ter′nal
in′tra·col′ic
in′tra·cor′ne·al
in′tra·cor·po′re·al
in′tra·cor·pus′cu·lar
in′tra·cos′tal
in′tra·cra′ni·al
in·trac′ta·ble
in′tra·cu·ta′ne·ous
in′tra·cu·tic′u·lar
in′tra·cys′tic
in′tra·cy′to·plas′mic
in′tra·der′mal
in′tra·der′mic
in′tra·duc′tal
in′tra·du′ral
in′tra·em′bry·on′ic
in′tra·ep′i·der′mal
in′tra·ep′i·the′li·al
in′tra·e·ryth′ro·cyt′ic

in′tra·e·soph′a·ge′al
in′tra·fa′cial
in′tra·fas·cic′u·lar
in′tra·fi′lar
in′tra·fis′su·ral
in′tra·fis′tu·lar
in′tra·fol·lic′u·lar
in′tra·fu′sal
in′tra·gas′tric
in′tra·gem′mal
in′tra·gen′ic
in′tra·glan′du·lar
in′tra·glob′u·lar
in′tra·glu′te·al
in′tra·gy′ral
in′tra·he·pat′ic
in′tra·hy′oid′
in′tra·ic′tal
in′tra·in·tes′ti·nal
in′tra·jug′u·lar
in′tra·lam′i·nar
in′tra·la·ryn′ge·al
in′tra·le′sion·al
in′tra·leu′ko·cyt′ic
in′tra·lig′a·men′tous
in′tra·lo′bar
in′tra·lob′u·lar
in′tra·loc′u·lar
in′tra·lu′mi·nal
in′tra·mam′ma·ry
in′tra·mar′gin·al
in′tra·med′ul·lar′y
in′tra·mem′bra·nous
in′tra·me·nin′ge·al
in′tra·men′stru·al
in′tra·mu·co′sal
in′tra·mu′ral
in′tra·mus′cu·lar
in′tra·my′o·car′di·al
in′tra·my′o·me′tri·al
in′tra·nar′i·al
in′tra·na′sal
in′tra·na′tal
in′tra·neu′ral
in′tra·nu′cle·ar
in′tra·oc′u·lar
in′tra·op′er·a·tive
in′tra·op′tic
in′tra·o′ral
in′tra·or′bi·tal
in′tra·os′te·al
in′tra·pan′cre·at′ic
in′tra·pa·ren′chy·mal
in′tra·pa·ri′e·tal
in′tra·par′tum
in′tra·pel′vic
in′tra·per′i·car′di·al

in′tra·per′i·ne′al
in′tra·per′i·to·ne′al
in′tra·pha·lan′ge·al
in′tra·pi′al
in′tra·pla·cen′tal
in′tra·pleu′ral
in′tra·pros·tat′ic
in′tra·psy′chic
in′tra·pul′mo·nar′y
in′tra·py·ret′ic
in′tra·rec′tal
in′tra·re′nal
in′tra·ret′i·nal
in′tra·scap′u·lar
in′tra·scle′ral
in′tra·scro′tal
in′tra·seg·men′tal
in′tra·sel′lar
in′tra·se′rous
in′tra·spi′nal
in′tra·spi′nous
in′tra·sple′nic
in′tra·sti′tial
in′tra·stro′mal
in′tra·syn·o′vi·al
in′tra·tar′sal
in′tra·tes·tic′u·lar
in′tra·the′cal
in′tra·tho·rac′ic
in′tra·ton′sil·lar
in′tra·tra·bec′u·lar
in′tra·tra′che·al
in′tra·tro′chan·ter′ic
in′tra·tu′bal
in′tra·tu′bu·lar
in′tra·um·bil′i·cal
in′tra·u·re′ter·al
in′tra·u·re′thral
in′tra·u′ter·ine
in′tra·vag′i·nal
in·trav′a·sate′
in·trav′a·sa′tion
in′tra·vas′cu·lar
in′tra·ve·na′tion
in′tra·ve·nous *(within the veins)*
◆intravenous
in′tra·ven·tric′u·lar *(located within a ventricle)*
◆interventricular
in′tra·ver′te·bral
in′tra·ves′i·cal
in′tra·vi′tal
in·trin′sic
in·tro·flex′ion
in·troi′tal
in·troi′tus *pl.* in·troi′tus

in′tro·jec′tion
in′tro·mis′sion
in′tro·mit′tent
in′tro·spec′tion
in′tro·sus·cep′tion
in′tro·ver′sion
in′tro·vert′
in·trude′, -trud′ed, -trud′ing
in′tu·bate′ -bat′ed, -bat′ing
in′tu·ba′tion
in′tu·ba′tor
in·tu·i′tion
in·tu′i·tive
in′tu·mes′cence
in′tu·mes′cent
in·tu′mes·cen′ti·a *pl.* -ae′
—— cer′vi·ca′lis
—— lum·ba′lis
—— tym·pan′i·ca
in′tus·sus·cep′tion
in′tus·sus·cep′tum
in′tus·sus·cip′i·ens
in′u·lase′
in′u·lin
in·unc′tion
in u′ter·o′
in vac′u·o′
in·vade′, -vad′ed, -vad′ing
in·vad′er
in·vag′i·nate′, -nat′ed, -nat′-ing
in·vag′i·na′tion
in′va·lid
in′va·lid·ism
in·va′sin
in·va′sion
in·va′sive
in·verse′
in·ver′sion
in·ver′sive
in·ver′sus
in·vert′ *v.*
in′vert′ *n.*
in·ver′tase′
in·ver′te·bral
in·ver′te·brate′
in·vert′ed
in·ver′tor
in′ver·tose′
in·vest′
in·vest′ment
in·vet′er·ate
in′vi·ril′i·ty
in′vis·ca′tion
in vi′tro′
in vi′vo′
in′vo·lu′crum *pl.* -cra

in·vol′un·tar′y
in′vo·lute′
in′vo·lu′tion
in′vo·lu′tion·al
i′o·ben·zam′ic
i·o′da·mide′
I·o′da·moe′ba
—— bütsch′li·i′
—— wil·liam′si′
i′o·date′
i·od′ic
i′o·dide′
i′o·dim′e·try
i′o·dine′
i·od′i·nin
i′o·din·o·phil′
i′o·din′o·phil′i·a
i′o·din′o·phil′ic
i′o·dip′a·mide′
i′o·dism
i′o·dize′, -dized′, -diz′ing
i·o′do·chlor′hy·drox′y·quin
i·o′do·der′ma
i·o′do·form′
i·o′do·met′ric
i′o·dom′e·try
i·o′do·phe′nol′
i·o′do·phil′
i·o′do·phil′i·a
i·o′do·phthal′ein′
i′o·dop′sin
i·o′do·pyr′a·cet
i·o′do·ther′a·py
i·o′do·thy′ro·glob′u·lin
i′o·dox′yl
i′o·gly·cam′ic
i′on′
i·on′ic
i·o′ni·um
i′on·i·za′tion
i′on·ize′, -ized′, -iz′ing
i′on·om′e·ter
i·on′to·pho·re′sis *pl.* -ses′
i′o·phen′dy·late′
i′o·phen·ox′ic
i′o·pho′bi·a
i′o·py′dol′
i′o·py′done′
i′o·tha·lam′ic
i′o·thi′o·u′ra·cil
ip′e·cac′
ip′o·me′a
i·prin′dole′
i·pro′ni·a·zid
i·pro′nid′a·zole′
ip·sa′tion
ip′si·lat′er·al

i·ras′ci·bil′i·ty
i′ri·dal
i′ri·dal′gi·a
ir′id·aux·e′sis *pl.* -ses′
ir′i·dec′ta·sis
ir′i·dec′tome′
ir′i·dec′to·mize′, -mized′, -miz′ing
ir′i·dec′to·my
ir′i·dec·tro′pi·um
ir′i·de′mi·a
ir′i·den·clei′sis *pl.* -ses′
ir′i·den·tro′pi·um
ir′i·de·re′mi·a
i·rid′e·sis *pl.* -ses′
i·rid′i·al
i·rid′i·an
i·rid′ic
ir′i·di·za′tion
ir′i·do·a·vul′sion
ir′i·do·cap′su·li′tis
ir′i·do·cap′su·lot′o·my
i·rid′o·cele′
ir′i·do·cho′roi·di′tis
ir′i·do·col′o·bo′ma
ir′i·do·cor′ne·al
ir′i·do·cy·clec′to·my
ir′i·do·cy·cli′tis
ir′i·do·cy′clo·cho′roi·di′tis
ir′i·do·cys·tec′to·my
ir′i·dod′e·sis *pl.* -ses′
ir′i·do·di′ag·no′sis *pl.* -ses′
ir′i·do·di·al′y·sis *pl.* -ses′
ir′i·do·di·as′ta·sis *pl.* -ses′
ir′i·do·di′la′tor
ir′i·do·do·ne′sis *pl.* -ses′
ir′i·do·ker′a·ti′tis
ir′i·do·ki·ne′si·a
ir′i·do·ki·ne′sis *pl.* -ses′
ir′i·do·ki·net′ic
ir′i·dol′y·sis *pl.* -ses′
ir′i·do·ma·la′ci·a
ir′id·on·co′sis
ir′i·don′cus
ir′i·do·pa·ral′y·sis *pl.* -ses′
ir′i·do·pa·re′sis *pl.* -ses′
ir′i·dop′a·thy
ir′i·do·ple′gi·a
ir′i·dop·to′sis *pl.* -ses′
ir′i·do·pu′pil·lar′y
ir′i·do·rhex′is *pl.* -rhex′es′
ir′i·dos′chi·sis *pl.* -ses′
ir′i·do·scle·rot′o·my
ir′i·do·ste·re′sis *pl.* -ses′
ir′i·dot′a·sis *pl.* -ses′
ir′i·do·tome′
ir′i·dot′o·my

i′ris *pl.* i′ri·des′
—— bom·bé′
i·ri′tis
ir′i·to·ec′to·my
i·rit′o·my
i·rot′o·my
ir·ra′di·ate′, -at′ed, -at′ing
ir·ra′di·a′tion
ir·ra′tion·al
ir′re·duc′i·ble
ir·reg′u·lar′i·ty
ir·re′me·a·ble
ir′re·me′di·a·ble
ir′re·sus′ci·ta·ble
ir′re·ver′si·bil′i·ty
ir′re·ver′si·ble
ir′ri·gate′, -gat′ed, -gat′ing
ir′ri·ga′tion
ir′ri·ga′tor
ir′ri·ta·bil′i·ty
ir′ri·ta·ble
ir′ri·tant
ir′ri·ta′tion
ir′ri·ta′tive
I′saac′ granules
I·sam·bert′ disease
is′aux·e′sis *pl.* -ses′
is·che′mi·a
is·che′mic
is·che′sis
is′chi·ad′ic
is′chi·al
is′chi·al′gi·a
is′chi·al′gic
is′chi·at′ic
is′chi·a·ti′tis
is′chi·dro′sis *pl.* -ses′
is′chi·drot′ic
is′chi·ec′to·my
is′chi·o·a′nal
is′chi·o·bul′bar
is′chi·o·cap′su·lar
is′chi·o·cav′er·no′sus
is′chi·o·cav′er·nous
is′chi·o·cele′
is′chi·o·coc·cyg′e·al
is′chi·o·coc·cyg′e·us
is′chi·o·did′y·mus
is′chi·o·dyn′i·a
is′chi·o·fem′o·ral
is′chi·o·fem′o·ra′lis
is′chi·o·fib′u·lar
is′chi·om′e·lus
is′chi·o·my′e·li′tis
is′chi·o·neu·ral′gi·a
is′chi·o·ni′tis
is′chi·op′a·gus

—— tet′ra·pus
—— tri′pus
is′chi·op′a·gy
is′chi·o·pu′bic
is′chi·o·pu′bi·cus
is′chi·o·pu′bis
is′chi·o·rec′tal
is′chi·o·sa′cral
is′chi·o·vag′i·nal
is′chi·um *pl.* -chi·a
is′cho·gy′ri·a
is′cho·me′ni·a
is·chu′ri·a
Ish′i·ha′ra test
is′land
—— of Lan′ger·hans′
—— of Reil
is′let
i′so·a·dre′no·cor′ti·cism
i′so·ag·glu′ti·nin
i′so·ag·glu′ti·no·gen
i′so·am′yl
i′so·an·dros′ter·one′
i′so·an′ti·bod′ies
i′so·an′ti·bod′y
i′so·an′ti·gen
i′so·bar′
i′so·bar′ic
i′so·bor′nyl thi′o·cy′a·no·ac′e·tate′
i′so·bu′caine′
i′so·cel′lo·bi′ose′
i′so·cel′lu·lar
i′so·cho·les′ter·ol′
i′so·chro·mat′ic
i′so·chro·mat′o·phil′
i′so·chro′mo·some′
i·soch′ro·nal
i·soch′ro·nism
i·soch′ro·nous
i′so·com′ple·ment
i′so·co′ri·a
i′so·cor′tex′
i′so·cy′a·nide′
i′so·cy·tol′y·sin
i′so·dac′ty·lism
i′so·dac′ty·lous
i′so·dont′
i′so·dose′
i′so·dy·nam′ic
i′so·en′zyme′
i′so·eth′a·rine′
i′so·feb′ri·fu′gine′
i′so·flu′ro·phate′
i′so·gam′ete′
i·sog′a·mous
i·sog′a·my

i'so·gen'e·sis *pl.* -ses'
i'so·gen'ic
i·sog'e·nous
i·sog'na·thous
i'so·graft'
i'so·hem'ag·glu'ti·nin
i'so·he·mol'y·sin
i'so·he·mol'y·sis *pl.* -ses'
i'so·he'mo·lyt'ic
i'so·hy'dric
i'so·i·co'ni·a
i'so·i·con'ic
i'so·im'mu·ni·za'tion
i'so·i·on'ic
i'so·lac'tose'
i'so·late', -lat'ed, -lat'ing
i'so·lat'er·al
i'so·la'tion
i'so·la'tor
i'so·lec'i·thal
i'so·leu'cine'
i·sol'o·gous
i'so·ly'sin
i'so·mal'tose'
i'so·mer
i·som'er·ase'
i'so·mer'ic
i·som'er·ide'
i·som'er·ism
i·som'er·i·za'tion
i·som'er·ize', -ized', -iz'ing
i'so·meth'a·done'
i'so·me·thep'tene'
i'so·met'ric
i'so·me·tro'pi·a
i·som'e·try
i'so·morph'
i'so·mor'phic
i'so·mor'phism
i'so·mor'phous
i'so·ni'a·zid
i'so·nic'o·tin'ic
i'so·nip'e·caine'
i'so·ni'trile'
i'so·path'ic
i·sop'a·thy
i'so·pho'ri·a
i·so'pi·a
i'so·pre·cip'i·tin
i'so·pren'a·line'
i'so·prene'
i'so·pro'pa·mide'
i'so·pro'pa·nol'
i'so·pro'pyl
i'so·pro·te're·nol'
i·sop'ter

i'so·quin'o·line'
i'so·rau·wol'fine'
i'so·ri'bo·fla'vin
i'so·scope'
i'sos·mot'ic
i'so·sor'bide'
I·sos'po·ra
—— hom'i·nis
i'so·spo·ro'sis *pl.* -ses'
i'so·stere'
i'so·ster'ic
i·sos'ter·ism
i'sos·the·nu'ri·a
i'so·therm'
i'so·ther'mal
i'so·ther'mic
i'so·ton'ic
i'so·tope'
i'so·top'ic
i'so·trop'ic
i·sot'ro·py
i'so·va·ler'ic
i'so·va·le'ric·ac'i·de'mi·a
i'so·vol'u·met'ric
i'sox·su'prine'
isth·mec'to·my
isth'mic
isth'mus
—— a·or'tae'
—— car'ti·lag'i·nis au'ris
—— fau'ci·um
—— glan'du·lae' thy're·
oi'de·ae'
—— glandulae thy·roi'de·ae'
—— gy'ri' cin'gu·li'
—— gyri for'ni·ca'ti'
—— hip'po·cam'pi'
—— pros'ta·tae'
—— rhom'ben·ceph'a·li'
—— tu'bae' au'di·ti'vae'
—— tubae u'ter·i'nae'
—— u'ter·i'
i·su'ri·a
I·ta'qui fever
itch
i'ter
—— ad in'fun·dib'u·lum
—— chor'dae' an·te'ri·us
—— chordae pos·te'ri·us
—— den'ti·um
i'ter·al
it'er·a'tion
ith'y·lor·do'sis *pl.* -ses'
ith'y·o·ky·pho'sis *pl.* -ses'
I'to-Reen·stier'na
—— reaction
—— test

Ive'mark' syndrome
I'vy
—— method
—— test
I'wa·noff' cysts
Ix·o'des'
ix'o·di'a·sis
ix·od'ic
ix'y·o·my'e·li'tis

J

Ja·bou·lay'
Jac·coud'
—— arthritis
—— fever
—— sign
jack'screw'
Jack'son
—— membrane
—— re-evolution
—— sign
—— syndrome
—— veil
Jack'son-Bab'cock' opera-
tion
Jack·so'ni·an
—— convulsion
—— epilepsy
—— march
Ja'cob·sohn reflex
Ja'cob·son
—— cartilage
—— nerve
—— plexus
Ja'cob ulcer
Ja·cod'
—— syndrome
—— triad
Jac·quet' erythema
jac·ta'tion
jac'ti·ta'tion
Jad'as·sohn
—— disease
—— nevus
Jad'as·sohn-Lew'an·
dow'sky law
Jad'as·sohn-Ti·èche' ne-
vus
Jae'ger test
Jaf'fé
—— test
—— reaction
Jaf'fé-Lich'ten·stein'
—— disease

—— syndrome
Ja′kob-Creutz′feldt′
—— disease
—— syndrome
Ja·net′ disease
Jane′way′ lesions
jan′i·ceps′
—— a·sym′me·tros′
—— a·te′le·us
Jan′sen
—— operation
—— syndrome
Jan′sky
—— classification
—— groups
ja′nus
—— a·sym′me·tros′
Ja·nu′si·an
Jar′isch-Herx′hei′mer re-
action
Jat′ro·pha
jaun′dice
jaw
jaw′bone′
Ja·wor′ski
—— corpuscles
—— test
Jed′dah ulcer
Jegh′ers-Peutz′ syndrome
je·ju′nal
je′ju·nec′to·my
je′ju·ni′tis
je·ju′no·ce·cos′to·my
je·ju′no·co·los′to·my
je·ju′no·gas′tric
je·ju′no·il′e·i′tis
je·ju′no·il′e·os′to·my
je·ju′no·il′e·um
je·ju′no·je′ju·nos′to·my
je′ju·nor′rha·phy
je′ju·nos′to·my
je·ju·not′o·my
je·ju′num *pl.* -na
Jel′li·nek′ sign
jel′ly
—— of Whar′ton
Je′na Nom′i·na An′a·
tom′i·ca
Jen′dra·sic test
Jen′dras·sik maneuver
Jen·ne′ri·an
—— vaccination
—— vaccine
Jen′ner stain
Jen′sen
—— method
—— retinopathy

—— sarcoma
jerk
jerk′y
Jew′ett nail
Jez′ler-Ta·ka′ta test
jig′ger
Jir′gl reaction
Jo·bert′ fossa
Job syndrome
Jof′froy
—— reflex
—— sign
joint
Jol′ly
—— bodies
—— reaction
Jones
—— position
—— test
Jor′ge Lo′bo blastomyco-
sis
Jo′seph syndrome
joule
Joule equivalent
juc·cu′ya
Ju·det′ operation
ju′ga
—— al·ve′o·lar′i·a man·
dib′u·lae′
—— alveolaria max·il′lae′
—— cer′e·bra′li·a os′si·um
cra′ni·i′
ju′ga al′ve·o·lar′i·a max·
il′lae′
ju′gal
jug′u·lar
jug′u·la′tion
ju′gum *pl.* -ga
—— sphe′noi·da′le′
Jukes unit
jump′ers
jump′ing French′men of
Maine
junc′tion
junc′tion·al
junc·tu′ra *pl.* -rae′
—— car′ti·la·gin′e·a
—— fi·bro′sa
—— lum′bo·sa·cra′lis
—— os′si·um
—— sac′ro·coc·cyg′e·a
—— sy·no′vi·a′lis
junc·tu′rae′
—— cin′gu·li′ mem′bri′ in·
fe′ri·o′ris
—— cinguli membri su·pe′ri·
o′ris

—— co·lum′nae′ ver′te·
bra′lis, tho·ra′cis, et cra′ni·i′
—— mem′bri′ in·fe′ri·o′ris
lib′er·i′
—— membri su·pe′ri·o′ris
lib′er·i′
—— os′si·um
—— ten′di·num
—— zyg′a·poph′y·se·a′les′
Jung′i·an
Jüng′ling disease
Jung muscle
Ju′ni·us-Kuhnt′ disease
ju′ris·pru′dence
Jus′ter reflex
jus′to
—— major
—— minor
ju·van′ti·a
ju′ve·nile
jux′ta-ar·tic′u·lar
jux′ta·cor′ti·cal
jux′ta·e·piph′y·se′al
jux′ta·glo·mer′u·lar
jux′ta·pap′il·lar′y
jux′ta·pose′, -posed′, -pos′-
ing
jux′ta·po·si′tion
jux′ta·py·lo′ric
jux′ta·res′ti·form′

K

Ka′der operation
Ka′der-Senn′ operation
Kaes′-Bekh′ter·ev layer
Kaf′fir pox
Kahl′den tumor
Kah′ler disease
Kahn
—— method
—— test
Kai′ser·ling method
kak′er·ga′si·a
ka·la a·zar′
ka·la·fun′gin
ka·le′mi·a
ka·lim′e·ter
Kal′i·scher disease
ka′li·um
kal′i·u·re′sis
kal′i·u·ret′ic
kal′li·kre′in
kal′li·krein′o·gen

Kam′mer‑er‑Bat′tle incision
Kan′a·ga′wa phenomenon
kan′a·my′cin
Kan′a·vel
—— operation
—— sign
Kan′da·har′ sore
Kan·din′sky complex
Kan′ner syndrome
ka′o·lin
ka′o·li·no′sis pl. -ses′
Ka·po′si
—— disease
—— sarcoma
—— syndrome
—— varicelliform eruption
ka·ra′ya
Kar′men unit
Karr method
Kar′ta·gen′er syndrome
kar′y·en′chy·ma
kar′y·o·blast′
kar′y·o·chrome′
kar′y·oc′la·sis pl. -ses′
kar′y·o·clas′tic
kar′y·o·cyte′
kar′y·o·gam′ic
kar′y·og′a·my
kar′y·o·gen′
kar′y·o·gen′e·sis
kar′y·o·gen′ic
kar′y·o·ki·ne′sis pl. -ses′
kar′y·o′ki·net′ic
kar′y·o·lo′bic
kar′y·o·lymph′
kar′y·ol′y·sis
kar′y·o·meg′a·ly
kar′y·o·mere′
kar′y·om′e·try
kar′y·o·mi′cro·so′ma
kar′y·o·mi′tome′
kar′y·o·mi·to′sis pl. -ses′
kar′y·o′mi·tot′ic
kar′y·o·mor′phism
kar′y·on′
kar′y·o·phage′
kar′y·o·plasm
kar′y·o·plas′mic
kar′y·or·rhex′is pl. -rhex′es′
kar′y·o·some′
kar′y·os′ta·sis pl. -ses′
kar′y·o·the′ca
kar′y·o·type′
Kas′a·bach‑Mer′ritt syndrome
ka·sai′

Ka·shi′da thermic sign
Kash′in‑Beck′ disease
Kast syndrome
kat′a·did′y·mus
kat′a·ther·mom′e·ter
Kat′a·ya′ma
—— for′mo·sa′na
—— no·soph′o·ra
Katz′‑Wach′tel sign
Kauff′mann medium
Ka′wa·sa′ki disease
Kay′‑Gra′ham pasteurization test
Kay′ser‑Flei′scher ring
Ke·da′ni fever
Keen point
Kehr
—— operation
—— sign
Kehr′er reflex
Keith node
Keith′‑Wag′e·ner‑Bar′ker classification
Kell blood group system
Kel′ler
—— micromethod
—— operation
Kel′ling test
Kel′ly‑Pat′er·son syndrome
Kel′ly sign
ke′loid′
ke·loi′dal
ke·lo′ma pl. -mas or -ma·ta
Kel′vin scale
Kemp′ner rice diet
Ken′ne·dy syndrome
Ken′ny treatment
ken′o·tox′in
Kent mental test
Ker′an·del′ sign
ker′a·sin
ker′a·tal′gi·a
ker′a·tec·ta′si·a
ker′a·tec′to·my
ke·rat′ic
ker′a·tin
ker′a·tin·i·za′tion
ke·rat′i·no·cyte′
ker′a·tin·oid′
ke·rat′i·nous
ker′a·tit′ic
ker′a·ti′tis
—— ar′bo·res′cens
—— bul·lo′sa
—— dis′ci·for′mis
—— neu′ro·par′a·lyt′i·ca

—— pa·ren′chy·ma·to′sa
an′a·phy·lac′ti·ca
—— punc·ta′ta
—— punctata le·pro′sa
—— punctata pro·fun′da
—— pu′ru·len′ta
—— pus′tu·li·for′mis pro·fun′da
—— ro·sa′ce·a
—— sic′ca
ker′a·to·ac′an·tho′ma pl. -mas or -ma·ta
ker′a·to·cele′
ker′a·to·cen·te′sis pl. -ses′
ker′a·to·chro′ma·to′sis pl. -ses′
ker′a·to·con·junc′ti·vi′tis
—— sic′ca
ker′a·to·co′nus
ker′a·to·cyte′
ker′a·to·der′ma
—— blen′nor·rhag′i·cum
—— cli′mac·ter′i·cum
—— punc·ta′tum
ker′a·to·der′mat′o·cele′
ker′a·to·der′mi·a
ker′a·to′ec·ta′si·a
ker′a·to·gen′e·sis pl. -ses′
ker′a·to·glo′bus
ker′a·to·hel·co′sis
ker′a·to·he′mi·a
ker′a·to·hy′a·lin
ker′a·toid′
ker′a·to·i·ri′tis
ker′a·to·leu·ko′ma pl. -mas or -ma·ta
ker′a·tol′y·sis
ker′a·to·lyt′ic
ker′a·to′ma
—— sul·ca′tum plan·tar′um
ker′a·to·ma·la′ci·a
ker′a·tome′
ker′a·to·meg′a·ly
ker′a·tom′e·ter
ker′a·tom′e·try
ker′a·to·my′co′sis pl. -ses′
ker′a·ton′o·sus
ker′a·top′a·thy
ker′a·to·plas′tic
ker′a·to·plas′ty
ker′a·to·pros·the′sis
ker′a·tor·rhex′is pl. -rhex′es′
ker′a·to·scle·ri′tis
ker′a·to·scope′
ker′a·tos′co·py
ker′a·tose′

ker'a·to'sis *pl.* -ses'
—— blen'nor·rhag'i·ca
—— fol·lic'u·lar'is
—— ni'gri·cans'
—— pal·mar'is et plan·tar'is
—— pha·ryn'ge·us
—— pi·lar'is
—— punc·ta'ta
—— seb'or·rhe'i·ca
—— se·ni'lis
—— u'ni·ver·sa'lis con·gen'i·ta
ker'a·to·sul'fate'
ker'a·to·sul'fa·tu'ri·a
ker'a·tot'ic
ker'a·tot'o·my
Kerck'ring
—— folds
—— ossicle
ker'i·on' cel'si'
Ker'ley lines
ker·nic'ter·us
Ker'nig sign
Ker'no·han' syndrome
Ker'no·han-Wolt'man syndrome
ke'ta·mine'
ke'tip'ra·mine'
ke'to
ke'to·ac'i·do'sis *pl.* -ses'
ke'to·ac'i·du'ri·a
ke'to·a·dip'ic
ke'to·gen'e·sis
ke'to·gen'ic
ke'to·glu·tar'ic
ke'to·hy·drox'y·es'trin
ke'tol'
ke·tol'y·sis
ke'to·lyt'ic
ke'tone'
ke'to·ne'mi·a
ke'to·nu'ri·a
ke·to'sis *pl.* -ses'
ke'to·ste'roid'
ke'to·su'ri·a
ke·tot'ic
khel'lin
khel'li·nin
Kidd blood group system
kid'ney
Kien'böck'
—— atrophy
—— disease
Kies'sel·bach'
—— area
—— triangle
Kil'li·an operation

kil'o·cal'o·rie
kil'o·gram'
kil'o·li'ter
kil'o·me'ter
kil'o·nem'
kil'o·volt'
kil'o·watt'
Kim'mel·stiel-Wil'son disease
ki'nase'
kin'e·mat'o·graph'
ki·ne'mi·a
ki·ne'mic
kin'e·plas'tic
kin'e·plas'ty
kin'es·al'gi·a
kin'e·scope'
ki·ne'si·a
ki·ne'si·at'rics
ki·ne'sic
ki·ne'si·es·the'si·om'e·ter
kin'e·sim'e·ter
ki·ne'si·ol'o·gy
ki·ne'sis *pl.* -ses'
—— par'a·dox'a
ki·ne'si·ther'a·py
ki·ne'so·pho'bi·a
kin'es·the'si·a
kin'es·the'si·om'e·ter
kin'es·the'sis *pl.* -ses'
kin'es·thet'ic
ki·net'ic
ki·net'ics
ki·ne'tism
ki·net'o·car'di·o·gram'
ki·ne'to·chore'
ki·net'o·gen'ic
ki·net'o·graph'ic
ki·ne'to·nu'cle·us
ki·net'o·plasm
ki·ne'to·plast'
kin'e·to'sis *pl.* -ses'
ki·ne'to·ther'a·py
King operation
Kings'bur·y test
ki'nin
Kin'ney law
Kin'ni·er Wil'son sign
kin'o·cen'trum
Kin'youn stain
Kirch'ner diverticulum
Kirk'-Bent'ley method
Kir·mis'sion operation
Kirsch'ner traction
Kisch reflex
ki·ta'sa·my'cin
Kjel'dahl' method

Klatsch preparation
Klebs disease
Kleb'si·el'la
—— gran'u·lo'ma·tis
—— o·zae'nae'
—— pneu·mo'ni·ae'
—— rhi'no·scle·ro'ma·tis
Klebs'-Loef'fler bacillus
klee'blatt·schä'del deformity syndrome
Kleine'-Lev'in syndrome
Klein'ert flap
Klein muscle
Klem'per·er tuberculin
klep'to·lag'ni·a
klep'to·ma'ni·a
klep'to·pho'bi·a
Kline'fel'ter-Ref'fen·stein-Al'bright' syndrome
Kline'fel'ter syndrome
Kline test
Klip'pel disease
Klip'pel-Feil syndrome
Klip'pel-Tré'nau·nay'-We'ber syndrome
Klip'pel-Weil' sign
Klump'ke paralysis
knee
knee'cap'
Knies sign
knife *pl.* knives
knob
knock
knock'-knee'
Knoop theory
Knopf treatment
Knop test
knot
knuck'le
Ko'belt' cyst
Ko'bert test
Koch
—— law
—— phenomenon
Koch'er
—— maneuver
—— reflex
Koch'er-De·bré'-Sé·mé·laigne' syndrome
koch'er·i·za'tion
Koch'-Mc·Mee'kin method
Koch'-Weeks'
—— bacillus
—— conjunctivitis
Koeb'ner phenomenon

Koep'pe nodules
Koer'ber-Sa'lus-Elsch'nig syndrome
Köh'ler
—— disease
—— method
—— tarsal scaphoiditis
Köhl'mei'er-De·gos' disease
koi'lo·cy·to'sis
koi'lo·cy·tot'ic
koi'lo·nych'i·a
koi'lor·rhach'ic
koi'lo·ster'ni·a
koi'no·trop'ic
koi·not'ro·py
Kol'mer test
Kom'mer·ell diverticulum
Kon·do'lé·on operation
Kö'nig disease
ko'ni·o·cor'tex'
ko·phe'mi·a
Kop'lik spots
kop'ro·ste'a·rin
Korff fibers
Kor'ner-Shil'ling·ford method
ko'ro·cyte'
ko·ros'co·py
Ko·rot'kov'
—— method
—— sounds
—— test
Kor'sa·koff' syndrome
Kos'sel test
Koss koilocytotic atypia
Ko·zhev'ni·kov' epilepsy
Krab'be disease
Kraep'e·lin classification
Kraep'e·lin-Mo·rel' disease
Kra'mer-Tis'dall method
Kras'ke operation
kra·tom'e·ter
krau·ro'sis pl. -ses'
Krause
—— corpuscle
—— glands
—— membrane
Krause'-Wolfe' graft
Kraus fetal cells
kre'a·tin
kre·at'i·nine'
Krebs
—— cycle
—— tumor
Krebs'-Hen'se·leit' cycle

kre'o·tox'in
kre'o·tox'ism
Kretsch'mer type
Krey'sig sign
Krom'pech'er tumor
Krö'nig
—— fields
—— isthmus
Kru'ken·berg'
—— spindle
—— tumor
ku·bis'a·ga'ri
Kufs disease
Ku'gel artery
Ku'gel·berg-Wel'an·der syndrome
Kuhnt'-Ju'ni·us disease
Kult·schitz'sky
—— carcinoma
—— cells
—— hematoxylin
Kum'lin·ge disease
Küm'mell disease
Kun'drat' lymphosarcoma
Kun'kel test
Kupf'fer cells
Kur'lov'
—— bodies
—— cell
Kus·kok'wim disease
Küss'-Ghon' focus
Kuss'maul'
—— disease
—— respiration
—— sign
Kuss'maul-Mai'er disease
Kut'ter flap
Kveim
—— antigen
—— test
kwa'shi·or'kor'
Kwi·leck'i method
ky'a·nop'si·a
Kya·sa'nur forest disease
kyl·lo'sis
ky'mo·gram'
ky'mo·graph'
ky'mo·graph'ic
ky·mog'ra·phy
ky'phos'
ky'pho·sco'li·o'sis pl. -ses'
ky'pho·sco'li·ot'ic
ky·pho'sis pl. -ses'
ky·phot'ic
Kyrle disease
kyr'tor·rhach'ic

L

Lab'ar·raque' solution
la'bel
la'bi·a
—— ma·jo'ra
—— mi·no'ra
—— o'ris
—— pu·den'di'
la'bi·al
la'bi·al·ism
La'bi·a'tae'
la'bile
la·bil'i·ty
la'bi·o·al·ve'o·lar
la'bi·o·cer'vi·cal
la'bi·o·cho·re'a
la'bi·o'cli·na'tion
la'bi·o·den'tal
la'bi·o·gin'gi·val
la'bi·o·glos'so·la·ryn'ge·al
la'bi·o·glos'so·pha·ryn'ge·al
la'bi·o·in·ci'sal
la'bi·o·lin'gual
la'bi·o·men'tal
la'bi·o·my·co'sis pl. -ses'
la'bi·o·na'sal
la'bi·o·pal'a·tine'
la'bi·o·plas'ty
la'bi·o·scro'tal
la'bi·o·ver'sion
la'bi·um pl. -bi·a
—— an·te'ri·us os'ti·i' u'ter·i'
—— anterius por'ti·o'nis vag'i·na'lis u'ter·i'
—— anterius tu'bae' au'di·ti'vae'
—— ex·ter'num cris'tae' i·li'a·cae'
—— in·fe'ri·us o'ris
—— inferius val'vu·lae' co'li'
—— in·ter'num cris'tae' i·li'a·cae'
—— lat'er·a'le' lin'e·ae' as'per·ae' fem'o·ris
—— lep'o·ri'num
—— lim'bi' tym·pan'i·cum
—— limbi ves·tib'u·lar'e'
—— ma'jus
—— majus pu·den'di'
—— me'di·a'le' lin'e·ae' as'per·ae' fem'o·ris
—— mi'nus
—— minus pu·den'di'

—— pos·te'ri·us os'ti·i' u'ter·i'
—— posterius por'ti·o'nis vag'i·na'lis u'ter·i'
—— posterius tu'bae' au'di·ti'vae'
—— su·pe'ri·us o'ris
—— superius val'vu·lae' co'li'
—— tym·pan'i·cum
—— ves·tib'u·lar'e'
—— vo·ca'le'
la'bor
lab'o·ra·to'ry
La·borde' method
lab·ra'le
—— in·fe'ri·us
—— su·pe'ri·us
lab'ro·cyte'
la'brum
—— ac'e·tab'u·lar'e'
—— glen'oi·da'le'
—— glenoidale ar·tic'u·la'ti·o'nis cox'ae'
—— glenoidale articula-tionis hu'mer·i'
lab'y·rinth'
lab'y·rin·thec'to·my
lab'y·rin'thine'
lab'y·rin·thi'tis
lab'y·rin·thot'o·my
lab'y·rin'thus pl. -thi'
—— eth'moi·da'lis
—— mem'bra·na'ce·us
—— os'se·us
lac pl. lac'ta
—— fem'i·ni'num
—— sul·fu'ris
lac'case'
lac'er·ate', -at'ed, -at'ing
lac'er·a'tion
lac'er·o·con'dy·lar
la·cer'tus
—— fi·bro'sus
—— mus'cu·li' rec'ti' lat'er·a'lis
la·cin'i·ate'
lac'ri·ma pl. -mae'
lac'ri·mal (pertaining to tears)
♦lacrimale
lac'ri·ma'le' (a point in the skull)
♦lacrimal
lac'ri·ma'tion
lac'ri·ma'tor
lac'ri·ma·to'ry

lac'ri·mo·max'il·lar'y
lac'ri·mo·na'sal
lac'ri·mot'o·my
lac·tac'i·de'mi·a
lac·tac'i·du'ri·a
lac'ta·gogue'
lac'tal·bu'min
lac'tam'
lac·tam'ic
lac·tam'ide'
lac·tar'o·vi'o·lin
lac'tase'
lac'tate', -tat'ed, -tat'ing
lac·ta'tion
lac·ta'tion·al
lac'te·al
lac·tes'cence
lac'tic
lac·ti·ce'mi·a
lac·tif'er·ous
lac'ti·fuge'
lac'tig·e'nous
lac·tig'er·ous
lac'tin
lac·ti·su'gi·um
lac·tiv'o·rous
lac'to·ba·cil'lic
lac'to·ba·cil'lin
Lac'to·ba·cil'lus
—— ac'i·doph'i·lus
—— bi'fi·dus
—— bul·gar'i·cus
—— ca'se·i' factor
—— gas·troph'i·lus
—— lac'tis Dor'ner
—— of Bo'as-Op'pler
lac'to·cele'
lac'to·fla'vin
lac'to·gen
lac'to·gen'ic
lac'to·glob'u·lin
lac'tone'
lac·ton'ic
lac'to·phos'phate'
lac'to·pro'te·in
lac'tor·rhe'a
lac'tose'
lac'to·su'ri·a
lac'to·ther'a·py
lac'to·tox'in
lac'tu·car'i·um
lac'tu·lose'
la·cu'na pl. -nas or -nae'
—— mag'na
—— mus'cu·lo'rum
—— va·so'rum
—— ve·no'sa du'rae' ma'tris

la·cu'nae'
—— lat'er·a'les'
—— u're·thra'les'
la·cu'nar
la·cu'nas of Mor·ga'gni
la·cu'nule'
la'cus
—— lac'ri·ma'lis
Ladd'-Frank'lin theory
Lad'e·wig stain
Laehr'-Hen'ne·berg' hard palate reflex
Laen·nec'
—— cirrhosis
—— pearl
—— thrombus
La·fo'ra
—— bodies
—— disease
lag
la·ge'na pl. -nas or -nae'
la·ge'ni·form'
lag'oph·thal'mi·a
lag'oph·thal'·mic
lag'oph·thal'mos
La·grange' operation
la grippe'
Laid'law' stain
Laid'low' method
L-al'a·nine'
lal'i·o·pho'bi·a
lal·la'tion
lal'og·no'sis
la·lop'a·thy
lal'o·ple'gi·a
lal'or·rhe'a
lamb'da
lamb'da·cism
lamb'doid'
lam'bert
Lam'bl excrescences
Lam'bli·a
lam·bli'a·sis pl. -ses'
lame
la·mel'la pl. -las or -lae'
la·mel'lar
lam'i·na pl. -nas or -nae'
—— af·fix'a
—— a·lar'is
—— anterior va·gi'nae' mus'cu·li' rec'ti' ab·dom'i·nis
—— ar'cus ver'te·brae'
—— ba·sa'lis
—— basalis cho'ri·oi'de·ae'
—— basalis cho·roi'de·ae'
—— basalis cor'po·ris cil'i·ar'is

—— bas'i·lar'is
—— car'ti·lag'i·nis cri·coi'de·ae'
—— cartilaginis lat'er·a'lis tu'bae' au'di·ti'vae'
—— cartilaginis me'di·a'lis tu'bae' au'di·ti'vae'
—— cho'ri·o·cap'il·lar'is
—— cho'ri·oi'de·a ep'i·the'li·a'lis ven·tric'u·li' lat'er·a'lis
—— chorioidea epithelialis ventriculi quar'ti'
—— cho·roi'do·cap'il·lar'is
—— ci·ne're·a
—— cri·bro'sa
—— cribrosa os'sis eth'moi·da'lis
—— cribrosa scle'rae'
—— dex'tra car'ti·lag'i·nis thy·roi'de·ae'
—— du'ra
—— e·las'ti·ca
—— elastica anterior
—— elastica posterior
—— ep'i·scle·ra'lis
—— ep'i·the'li·a'lis
—— ex·ter'na os'si·um cra'ni·i'
—— fi'bro·car'ti·la·gin'e·a in'ter·pu'bi·ca
—— for'ni·cis
—— fus'ca scle'rae'
—— ho'ri·zon·ta'lis os'sis pal'a·ti'ni'
—— in·ter'na os'si·um cra'ni·i'
—— lat'er·a'lis pro·ces'sus pter'y·goi'de·i'
—— lim'i·tans' anterior cor'ne·ae'
—— limitans posterior corneae
—— me'di·a'lis pro·ces'sus pter'y·goi'de·i'
—— med'ul·lar'is lat'er·a'lis cor'po·ris stri·a'ti'
—— medullaris me'di·a'lis cor'po·ris stri·a'ti'
—— mem'bra·na'ce·a tu'·bae' au'di·ti'vae'
—— mo·di'o·li'
—— mus'cu·lar'is mu·co'sae'
—— muscularis mucosae co'li'
—— muscularis mucosae e·soph'a·gi'

—— muscularis mucosae in'tes·ti'ni' cras'si'
—— muscularis mucosae in·testini ten'u·is
—— muscularis mucosae oe·soph'a·gi'
—— muscularis mucosae rec'ti'
—— muscularis mucosae ven·tric'u·li'
—— or'bi·ta'lis
—— pap'y·ra'ce·a
—— pa·ri'e·ta'lis per'i·car'di·i'
—— parietalis tu'ni·cae' vag'i·na'lis pro'pri·ae' tes'tis
—— parietalis tunicae vaginalis tes'tis
—— per'pen·dic'u·lar'is os'·sis eth'moi·da'lis
—— perpendicularis ossis pal'a·ti'ni'
—— posterior va·gi'nae' mus'cu·li' rec'ti' ab·dom'i·nis
—— pre·tra'che·a'lis fas'ci·ae' cer'vi·ca'lis
—— pre·ver'te·bra'lis fas'ci·ae' cer'vi·ca'lis
—— pro·fun'da fas'ci·ae' tem'po·ra'lis
—— profunda mus'cu·li' lev'a·to'ris pal·pe'brae' su·pe'ri·o'ris
—— pro'pri·a mem·bra'nae' tym'pa·ni'
—— propria mu·co'sae'
—— qua'dri·gem'i·na
—— ros·tra'lis
—— sep'ti' pel·lu'ci·di'
—— si·nis'tra car'ti·lag'i·nis thy·roi'de·ae'
—— spi·ra'lis os'se·a
—— spiralis sec'un·dar'i·a
—— su'per·fi'ci·a'lis fas'ci·ae' cer'vi·ca'lis
—— superficialis fasciae tem'po·ra'lis
—— superficialis mus'cu·li' lev'a·to'ris pal·pe'brae' su·pe'ri·o'ris
—— su'pra·cho·ri·oi'de·a
—— su'pra·cho·roi'de·a
—— tec'ti'
—— ter'mi·na'lis
—— tra'gi'
—— vas'cu·lo'sa cho'ri·oi'de·ae'

—— vasculosa cho·roi'de·ae'
—— vasculosa tes'tis
—— vis'ce·ra'lis per'i·car'di·i'
—— visceralis tu'ni·cae'
vag'i·na'lis pro'pri·ae' tes'tis
—— visceralis tunicae vaginalis tes'tis
—— vit're·a
lam'i·nae'
—— al'bae' cer'e·bel'li'
—— car'ti·lag'i·nis thy·roi'de·ae'
—— me'di·as'ti·na'les'
—— med'ul·lar'es' cer'e·bel'li'
—— medullares thal'a·mi'
lam'i·na·gram'
lam'i·nag'ra·phy
lam'i·nar
lam'i·nate', -nat'ed, -nat'ing
lam'i·na'tion
lam'i·nec'to·my
lam'i·nog'ra·phy
lam'i·not'o·my
lam'pro·phon'ic
lam·proph'o·ny
La'mus me·gis'tus
la·nat'o·side'
Lan'cas'ter advancement
lance, lanced, lanc'ing
Lance'field' groups
Lan'ce·reaux'
—— diabetes
—— law
lan'cet
lan'ci·nate', -nat'ed, -nat'ing
Lan·ci'si
—— sign
—— striae
Lan'dau' position
Lan'dis-Gib'bon test
land'mark'
Lan'dolt'
—— broken C test
—— ring
Lan'dou·zy'
—— disease
—— purpura
—— sciatica
Lan'dou·zy'-Dé'je·rine' dystrophy
Lan'dou·zy'-Gras·set' law
Lan'dry-Guil·lain' Bar·ré' syndrome
Land'stei'ner classification

Land'ström muscle
Lane
—— disease
—— kink
—— operation
Lang'don Down anomaly
Lan'gen·beck' operation
Lan'gen·dorf' preparation
Lan'ger·han'si·an adenoma
Lan'ger lines
Lan'ge test
Lang'hans'
—— cell
—— layer
—— stria
lan'guor
Lan'ne·longue' operation
lan'o·lin
la·nos'ter·ol'
Lan'sing virus
Lan'ter·mann incisure
lan'tha·nic
la·nu'gi·nous
la·nu'go
la·pac'tic
lap'a·rec'to·my
lap'a·ro·cele'
lap'a·ro'co·lec'to·my
lap'a·ro'cys·tec'to·my
lap'a·ro'cys·tot'o·my
lap'a·ro·en'ter·os'to·my
lap'a·ro·en'ter·ot'o·my
lap'a·ro'gas·tros'co·py
lap'a·ro'gas·tros'to·my
lap'a·ro'gas·trot'o·my
lap'a·ro·hep'a·tot'o·my
lap'a·ro·hys'ter·ec'to·my
lap'a·ro·hys'ter·ot'o·my
lap'a·ro·il'e·ot'o·my
lap'a·ro·my·i'tis
lap'a·ro·my'o·mec'to·my
lap'a·ro'ne·phrec'to·my
lap'a·ror'rha·phy
lap'a·ro·sal'pin·gec'to·my
lap'a·ro'sal·pin·go-o·oph'o·rec'to·my
lap'a·ro'sal·pin·got'o·my
lap'a·ro·scope'
lap'a·ros'co·py
lap'a·ro'sple·nec'to·my
lap'a·ro'sple·not'o·my
lap'a·ro·tome'
lap'a·rot'o·my
lap'is
—— cal'a·mi·nar'is
—— im·pe'ri·a'lis

—— in'fer·na'lis
lap'sus pl. lap'sus
—— cal'a·mi'
—— lin'guae'
—— pal·pe'brae' su·pe'ri·o'ris
—— pi·lo'rum
—— un'gui·um
La Roque' sign
La'roy·enne' operation
Lar·rey' sign
Lar'sen-Jo·han'sson disease
lar'va pl. -vae'
—— mi'grans'
lar'val
lar'vate'
lar'vi·cide'
lar'yn·gal'gi·a
la·ryn'ge·al
lar'yn·gec'to·my
lar'yn·gem·phrax'is
lar'yn·gis'mal
lar'yn·gis'mus pl. -mi'
—— stri'du·lus
lar'yn·git'ic
lar'yn·gi'tis
—— sic'ca
la·ryn'go·cele'
la·ryn'go·cen·te'sis
la·ryn'go·fis'sure
la·ryn'go·gram'
la·ryn'go·graph'
lar'yn·gog'ra·phy
lar'yn·go·log'ic
lar'yn·gol'o·gy
lar'yn·gom'e·try
la·ryn'go·pa·ral'y·sis pl. -ses'
lar'yn·gop'a·thy
la·ryn'go·pha·ryn'ge·al
la·ryn'go·phar'yn·gec'to·my
la·ryn'go·pha·ryn'ge·us
la·ryn'go·phar'yn·gi'tis
la·ryn'go·phar'ynx
lar'yn·goph'o·ny
lar'yn·goph'thi·sis
la·ryn'go·plas'ty
la·ryn'go·ple'gi·a
la·ryn'go·pto'sis
la·ryn'gor·rha'gi·a
lar'yn·gor'rha·phy
la·ryn'gor·rhe'a
la·ryn'go·scle·ro'ma
la·ryn'go·scope'
la·ryn'go·scop'ic

lar'yn·gos'co·py
la·ryn'go·spasm
lar'yn·gos'ta·sis
la·ryn'go·stat'
lar'yn·go·ste·no'sis pl. -ses'
lar'yn·gos'to·my
la·ryn'go·stro'bo·scope'
la·ryn'go·tome'
lar'yn·got'o·my
la·ryn'go·tra'che·al
la·ryn'go·tra'che·i'tis
la·ryn'go·tra'che·o·bron·chi'tis
la·ryn'go·tra'che·os'co·py
la·ryn'go·tra'che·ot'o·my
la·ryn'go·ves·tib'u·li'tis
la·ryn'go·xe·ro'sis
lar'ynx pl. -ynx·es or la·ryn'ges'
La·sègue'
—— law
—— sign
la'ser
Lash'met and New'burgh' test
Las·kow'ski method
Las·saigne' test
Las'sa
—— fever
—— virus
las'si·tude'
la'ten·cy
la'tent
lat'er·ad'
lat'er·al
lat'er·al'is
lat'er·al'i·ty
lat'er·al·i·za'tion
lat'er·al·ize', -ized', -iz'ing
lat'er·o·ab·dom'i·nal
lat'er·o·duc'tion
lat'er·o·flex'ion
lat'er·o·mar'gin·al
lat'er·o·pul'sion
lat'er·o·tor'sion
lat'er·o·ver'sion
la'tex' pl. -ti·ces' or -tex'es
lath'y·rism
lath'y·ro·gen'ic
la·tis'si·mus
—— dor'si'
—— tho·ra'cis
Lat'ro·dec'tus
lat'tice (a network)
♦latus
la'tus (the flank)
♦lattice

laud'a·ble
lau'da·num
Laugh'len test
Lau'rence-Moon'-Bie'dl
  syndrome
Lauth violet
la·vage'
la·va'tion
La've·ran' bodies
la·veur'
Lav·ren'ti·ev phenomenon
law
—— of A'vo·ga'dro
—— of Bun'sen-Ros'coe
—— of Du·long' and Pe·tit'
—— of Lam'bert
—— of Wal·ler'i·an degeneration
Law projection
lax·a'tion
lax'a·tive
lax'a'tor
lax'i·ty
lay'er
—— of Hen'le
—— of Lang'hans'
Laz'a·row' method
L-do'pa
leach (to percolate away)
  ♦leech
lead
Lead'bet'ter procedure
Leake and Guy method
Le'ber disease
Le·cat' gulf
lech'o·py'ra
lec'i·thal
lec'ith·al·bu'min
lec'i·thin
lec'i·tho·blast'
lec'i·tho·pro'te·in
lec'i·tho·vi·tel'lin
lec'tin
Led'der·hose' disease
Led'er·er acute anemia
Le·duc' current
leech (parasitic annelid)
  ♦leach
Lee test
Lee'-White' method
Le Fort' operation
left'-hand'ed
leg
Le'gal
—— disease
—— test

Legg'-Cal·vé'-Per·thes'
  disease
Legg'-Per·thes' disease
Le'gion·el'la
—— mic·da'de·i'
—— pneu'mo·phil'i·a
le'gion·el·lo'sis pl. -ses'
Le'gion·naire' disease
le·gu'min
Lei'boff' and Kahn meth-
  od
Leich'ten·stern' phenom-
  enon
Leif'son method
Leigh syndrome
Lei'ner disease
lei'o·der'ma·tous
lei'o·der'mi·a
lei'o·dys·to'ni·a
lei'o·my'o·blas·to'ma pl.
  -mas or -ma·ta
lei'o·my'o·fi·bro'ma
  pl. -mas or -ma·ta
lei'o·my·o'ma pl. -mas or
  -ma·ta
lei'o·my'o·sar·co'ma
  pl. -mas or -ma·ta
lei·ot'ri·chous
Leish'man-Don'o·van
—— bodies
—— parasite
Leish·ma'ni·a
—— bra·sil'i·en'sis
—— don'o·va'ni'
—— in·fan'tum
—— pe·ru'vi·a'na
—— trop'i·ca
leish·ma'ni·al
leish'ma·ni·a·sis pl. -ses'
—— a·mer'i·ca'na
Leish'man stain
le'ma
Lem'bert suture
le'mic
lem'mo·blast'
lem'mo·blas·to'ma pl. -mas
  or -ma·ta
lem'mo·cyte'
lem'mo·cy·to'ma pl. -mas
  or -ma·ta
lem·nis'cal
lem·nis'cus pl. -ci'
—— a·cus'ti·cus
—— lat'er·a'lis
—— me'di·a'lis
—— op'ti·cus
—— sen'si·ti'vus

—— spi·na'lis
—— tri·gem'i·na'lis
le'mo·pa·ral'y·sis pl. -ses'
le'mo·ste·no'sis
  pl. -ses'
Lem'pert operation
Len'drum stain
Len'hartz' diet
len'i·ceps'
len'i·quin'sin
len'i·tive
Len'nox-Gas'taut' syn-
  drome
Len'nox syndrome
lens
—— crys'tal·li'na
len·tec'to·mize', -mized',
  -miz'ing
len·tec'to·my
len·ti·co'nus
len·tic'u·la
len·tic'u·lar
len·tic'u·late'
len·tic'u·lo·stri'ate'
len·tic'u·lo·tha·lam'ic
len'ti·form'
len·tig'i·nes' le·pro'sae'
len'ti·glo'bus
len·ti'go pl. -tig'i·nes'
—— ma·lig'na
lep'er
lep'i·do'ma pl. -mas or
  -ma·ta
Lep'i·dop'ter·a
lep'o·thrix'
lep'ra
lep're·chaun·ism
lep'rid
lep·ro'ma pl. -mas or -ma·ta
lep·rom'a·tous
lep'ro·stat'ic
lep'ro·sy
lep·rot'ic
lep'rous
lep·tan'dra
lep'ta·zol'
lep'to·ce·pha'li·a
lep'to·ceph'a·lus pl. -li'
lep'to·chro·mat'ic
lep'to·cyte'
lep'to·cyt'ic
lep'to·cy·to'sis pl. -ses'
lep'to·dac'ty·lous
lep'to·don'tous
lep'to·me·nin'ges'
lep'to·me·nin'gi·o'ma
  pl. -mas or -ma·ta

lep'to·men'in·gi'tis
lep'to·men'in·gop'a·thy
lep'to·me'ninx *pl.* -me·
  nin'ges'
lep'to·pel'lic
lep'to·pho'ni·a
lep'to·phon'ic
lep'to·pro·so'pi·a
lep'to·pro·sop'ic
lep'tor·rhine'
Lep'to·sphaer'i·a sen'e·
  gal·en'sis
lep'to·spi'ra *pl.* -ras *or* -rae'
Lep'to·spi'ra
—— au'tum·na'lis
—— ca·nic'o·la
—— grip'po·ty·pho'sa
—— heb·dom'a·dis
—— ic'ter·o·haem'or·rha'gi·
ae'
lep'to·spi·ro'sis *pl.* -ses'
—— ic'ter·o·hem'or·rhag'i·ca
lep'to·tri·cho'sis *pl.* -ses'
—— con'junc·ti'vae'
le·re'sis
Le·riche'
—— operation
—— syndrome
Lé·ri'
—— disease
—— sign
Ler'man-Means' scratch
Ler'mo·yez' syndrome
les'bi·an
les'bi·an·ism
Lesch'ke method
Lesch'-Ny'han' disease
le'sion
le'thal
le·thar'gic
leth'ar·gy
le'the
Let'o·noff' and Rein'hold'
  method
Let'ter·er-Si'we disease
leuc-. See words spelled
  leuk-.
leu'cine'
leu'ci·nu'ri·a
leuco-. See words spelled
  leuko-.
Leu'co·nos'toc'
leu'co·sin
leu'co·vor'in
leu'cyl
Leu·det' sign
leuk'a·ne'mi·a

leu·ke'mi·a
leu·ke'mic
leu·ke'mid
leu·ke'moid'
leu'kin
leu'ko·blast'
leu'ko·blas·to'sis *pl.* -ses'
leu'ko·ci'din
leu'ko·co'ri·a
leu'ko·cyte'
leu'ko·cy·the'mi·a
leu'ko·cyt'ic
leu'ko·cy'to·blast'
leu'ko·cy'to·gen'e·sis
  pl. -ses'
leu'ko·cy·tol'o·gy
leu'ko·cy·tol'y·sin
leu'ko·cy·tol'y·sis *pl.* -ses'
leu'ko·cy'to·lyt'ic
leu'ko·cy'to·ma *pl.* -mas *or*
  -ma·ta
leu'ko·cy·tom'e·ter
leu'ko·cy'to·pe'ni·a
leu'ko·cy'to·poi·e'sis
  pl. -ses'
leu'ko·cy'to·poi·et'ic
leu'ko·cy'to·sis *pl.* -ses'
leu'ko·cy·tot'ic
leu'ko·der'ma
—— ac'qui·si'tum cen·trif'u·
gum
—— col'li'
—— pso'ri·at'i·cum
—— punc·ta'tum
leu'ko·der'mic
leu'ko·dys'tro·phy
leu'ko·e·de'ma *pl.* -mas *or*
  -ma·ta
leu'ko·en·ceph'a·li'tis
leu'ko·en·ceph'a·lop'a·thy
leu'ko·en·ceph'a·ly
leu'ko·e·ryth'ro·blas'tic
leu'ko·e·ryth'ro·blas·to'sis
leu'ko·ker'a·to'sis *pl.* -ses'
leu'ko·ki·ne'sis *pl.* -ses'
leu'ko·ki·net'ic
leu'ko·lym'pho·sar·co'ma
  pl. -mas *or* -ma·ta
leu·kol'y·sis *pl.* -ses'
leu'ko·lyt'ic
leu·ko'ma *pl.* -mas *or* -ma·ta
leu·kom'a·tous
leu'ko·my·o'ma *pl.* -mas *or*
  -ma·ta
leu'ko·ne·cro'sis
leu'ko·nych'i·a
—— par'ti·a'lis

—— stri·a'ta
—— striata lon'gi·tu'di·na'lis
—— to·ta'lis
leu'ko·path'i·a
leu·kop'a·thy
leu'ko·pe·de'sis *pl.* -ses'
leu'ko·pe'ni·a
leu'ko·pe'nic
leu'ko·phe·re'sis *pl.* -ses'
leu'ko·phleg·ma'si·a
leu'ko·phyll
leu'ko·pla'ki·a
—— buc·ca'lis
—— o'ris
—— vul'vae'
leu'ko·pla'ki·al
leu'ko·pla'si·a
leu'ko·plas'tid
leu'ko·poi·e'sis *pl.* -ses'
leu'ko·poi·et'ic
leu·kop'sin
leu'kor·rha'gi·a
leu'kor·rhe'a
leu'kor·rhe'al
leu'ko·sar·co'ma *pl.* -mas *or*
  -ma·ta
leu'ko·sar·co'ma·to'sis *pl.*
  -ses'
leu'ko'sis *pl.* -ses'
leu'ko·tac'tic
leu'ko·tax'ine'
leu'ko·tax'is
leu'ko·throm'bo·pe'ni·a
leu'ko·tome'
leu'ko·tox'ic
leu'ko·tox'in
leu'ko·trich'i·a
leu·kot'ri·chous
leu'ko·u'ro·bil'in
leu'kous
Lev'a·di'ti
—— method
—— spirochete stain
lev'am·fet'a·mine'
lev'ar·te're·nol'
le·va'tor *pl.* lev'a·to'res'
—— an'gu·li' o'ris
—— anguli scap'u·lae'
—— a'ni'
—— cla·vic'u·lae'
—— ep'i·glot'ti·dis
—— glan'du·lae' thy·roi'de·
ae'
—— la'bi·i' su·pe'ri·o'ris
—— labii superioris
a·lae'que' na'si'

—— men′ti′
—— pa·la′ti′
—— pal·pe′brae′ su·pe′ri·
o′ris
—— pros′ta·tae′
—— scap′u·lae′
—— ve′li′ pal·a·ti′ni′
lev′a·to′res′ cos·tar′um
lev′el
le·vid′u·lin·ose′
lev′i·gate′, -gat′ed, -gat′ing
lev′i·ga′tion
Lé·vi′-Lo·rain′ disease
Le·vine′ clenched′-fist′
sign
Lev′in·son test
Lé·vi′ syndrome
lev′i·ta′tion
le′vo·car′di·a
le′vo·car′di·o·gram′
le′vo·do′pa
le′vo·duc′tion
le′vo·gram′
le′vo·gy′ral
le′vo·gy′rate′
le′vo·nor′de·frin
le′vo·pro·pox′y·phene′
le′vo·ro·ta′tion
le′vo·ro′ta·to′ry
le′vo·thy·rox′ine′
le′vo·ver′sion
lev′u·lin
lev′u·lo′san′
lev′u·lose′
lev′u·lo·se′mi·a
lev′u·lo·su′ri·a
lev′u·rid
Le′vy-Pal′mer method
Lé·vy′-Rous·sy′ syndrome
Le′vy test
Lew′is
—— blood group system
—— disease
Ley′den
—— ataxia
—— crystals
—— jar
Ley′den-Mö′bi·us dystro-
phy
Ley′dig
—— cell
—— pause
ley′dig·ar′che
Ley′dig-cell′ tumor
Lher·mitte′ sign
li·bid′i·nal
li·bid′i·nous

li·bi′do
Lib′man-Sacks′ endocar-
ditis
li′bra pl. -brae′
li′cense
li·cen′ti·ate
li′chen
—— chron′i·cus sim′plex′
—— cor′ne·us hy′per·
troph′i·cus
—— myx′e·de′ma·to′sus
—— nit′i·dus
—— ob·tu′sus cor′ne·us
—— pi·lar′is
—— pla′nus
—— ru′ber a·cu′mi·na′tus
—— ruber mo·nil′i·for′mis
—— scle·ro′sus et a·troph′i·
cus
—— scrof′u·lo′sus
—— spi′nu·lo′sus
—— stri·a′tus
—— trop′i·cus
—— ur′ti·ca′tus
li·chen′i·fi·ca′tion
li′chen·oid′
li′chen·ous
Licht′heim′
—— aphasia
—— syndrome
lid
lid′o·caine′
li′do·fla′zine′
Lie′ben test
Lie′ber·kühn′ glands
Lie′ber·mann-Bur′chard
reaction
Lie′ber·mann reaction
Lie′big test
li′en
—— ac′ces·so′ri·us
li·e′nal
li·en′cu·lus pl. -li′
li′e·ni′tis
li·e′no·cele′
li·e′nog′ra·phy
li·e′no·ma·la′ci·a
li·e′no·med′ul·lar′y
li·e′no·my′e·lo·ma·la′ci·a
li·e′no·pan′cre·at′ic
li′e·nop′a·thy
li·e′no·re′nal
li·e′no·tox′in
li′en·ter′ic
li′en·ter′y
li′e·nun′cu·lus pl. -li′
Liep′mann apraxia

Lie′se·gang′ phenomenon
lig′a·ment
—— of Coo′per
—— of Treitz
—— of Zinn
lig′a·men′ta
—— ac′ces·so′ri·a plan·
tar′i·a
—— accessoria vo·lar′i·a
—— a·lar′i·a ar·tic′u·la′ti·
o′nis at·lan′to·ax′i·a′lis
me′di·a′nae′
—— an′nu·lar′i·a dig′i·
to′rum ma′nus
—— annularia digitorum
pe′dis
—— annularia tra′che·a′li·a
—— an′nu·lar′i·a tra′che·a′li·a
—— au·ric′u·lar′i·a
—— ba′si·um os′si·um
met′a·car·pa′li·um dor·sa′li·a
—— basium ossium meta-
carpalium in′ter·os′se·a
—— basium ossium meta-
carpalium vo·lar′i·a
—— basium ossium met′a·
tar·sa′li·um dor·sa′li·a
—— basium ossium meta-
tarsalium in′ter·os′se·a
—— basium ossium meta-
tarsalium plan·tar′i·a
—— ca·pit′u·li′ fib′u·lae′
—— ca·pit′u·lo′rum os′si·um
met′a·car·pa′li·um trans·
ver′sa
—— capitulorum ossium
met′a·tar·sa′li·um trans·
ver′sa
—— car′po·met′a·car′-
pe·a dor·sa′li·a
—— carpometacarpea pal·
mar′i·a
—— carpometacarpea vo·
lar′i·a
—— cer′a·to·cri·coi′de·a
lat′er·a′li·a
—— ceratocricoidea pos·
te′ri·o·ra
—— cin′gu·li′ ex·trem′i·ta′tis
in·fe′ri·o′ris
—— cinguli extremitatis su·
pe′ri·o′ris
—— col·lat′er·a′li·a ar·tic′u·
la′ti·o′num dig′i·to′rum ma′-
nus
—— collateralia articulatio-
num digitorum pe′dis

—— collateralia articulatio-
num in'ter·pha·lan'ge·ar'um
ma'nus
—— collateralia articulatio-
num interphalangearum pe'-
dis
—— collateralia articulatio-
num met'a·car'po·pha·
lan'ge·ar'um
—— collateralia articulatio-
num met'a·tar'so·pha·lan'ge·
ar'um
—— co·lum'·nae' ver'te·
bra'lis et cra'ni·i'
—— cos'to·xi·phoi'de·a
—— cru'ci·a'ta dig'i·to'rum
ma'nus
—— cruciata digitorum pe'-
dis
—— cruciata ge'nu'
—— cruciata ge'nus
—— cu'ne·o·met'a·tar'se·a
in'ter·os'se·a
—— cu'ne·o·na·vic'u·lar'i·a
dor·sa'li·a
—— cuneonavicularia plan·
tar'i·a
—— ex'tra·cap'su·lar'i·a
—— fla'va
—— glen'o·hu'mer·a'li·a
—— in'ter·car'pe·a dor·
sa'li·a
—— intercarpea in'ter·
os'se·a
—— intercarpea pal·mar'i·a
—— intercarpea vo·lar'i·a
—— in'ter·cos·ta'li·a
—— intercostalia ex·ter'na
—— intercostalia in·ter'na
—— in'ter·cu'ne·i·for'mi·a
dor·sa'li·a
—— intercuneiformia in'ter·
os'se·a
—— intercuneiformia plan·
tar'i·a
—— in'ter·spi·na'li·a
—— in'ter·trans·ver·sar'i·a
—— in'tra·cap'su·lar'i·a
—— met'a·car'pe·a dor·
sa'li· a
—— metacarpea in'ter·
os'se·a
—— metacarpea pal·mar'i·a
—— met'a·tar'se·a dor·sa'li·a
—— metatarsea in'ter·
os'se·a
—— metatarsea plan·tar'i·a

—— os·sic'u·lo'rum au·di'tus
—— pal·mar'i·a ar·tic'u·la'ti·
o'num in'ter·pha·lan'ge·
ar'um ma'nus
—— palmaria articulatio-
num met'a·car'po·pha·
lan'ge·ar'um
—— plan·tar'i·a ar·tic'u·la'ti·
o'num in'ter·pha·lan'ge·
ar'um pe'dis
—— plantaria articulatio-
num met'a·tar'so·pha·lan'ge·
ar'um
—— py·lo'ri'
—— sac'ro·i·li'a·ca an·te'ri·
o'ra
—— sacroiliaca dor·sa'li·a
—— sacroiliaca in'ter·os'se·a
—— sacroiliaca ven·tra'li·a
—— ster'no·cos·ta'li·a ra'di·
a'ta
—— ster'no·per'i·car·di'a·ca
—— sus'pen·so'ri·a mam'-
mae'
—— tar'si' dor·sa'li·a
—— tarsi in'ter·os'se·a
—— tarsi plan·tar'i·a
—— tarsi pro·fun'da
—— tar'so·met'a·tar'se·a
dor·sa'li·a
—— tarsometatarsea in'ter·
os'se·a
—— tarsometatarsea plan·
tar'i·a
—— vag'i·na'li·a dig'i·to'rum
ma'nus
—— vaginalia digitorum
pe'dis
lig'a·men'tal
lig'a·men'to·pex'y
lig'a·men'tous
lig'a·men'tum pl. -ta
—— a·cro'mi·o·cla·vic'u·
lar'e'
—— an'nu·lar'e' ba'se·os'
sta·pe'dis
—— annulare ra'di·i'
—— a'no·coc'cyg'e·um
—— an'u·lar'e' ra'di·i'
—— anulare sta·pe'dis
—— a'pi·cis den'tis
—— ar'cu·a'tum lat'er·a'le'
—— arcuatum me'di·a'le'
—— arcuatum me'di·a'num
—— arcuatum pu'bis
—— ar·te'ri·o'sum
—— au·ric'u·lar'e' an·te'ri·us

—— auriculare pos·te'ri·us
—— auriculare su·pe'ri·us
—— bi'fur·ca'tum
—— cal·ca'ne·o·cu·boi'de·
um
—— calcaneocuboideum
plan·tar'e'
—— cal·ca'ne·o·fib'u·lar'e'
—— cal·ca'ne·o·na·vic'u·
lar'e'
—— calcaneonaviculare
dor·sa'le'
—— calcaneonaviculare
plan·tar'e'
—— cal·ca'ne·o·tib'i·a'le'
—— cap'i·tis cos'tae' in'tra·
ar·tic'u·lar'e'
—— capitis costae ra'di·
a'tum
—— capitis fem'o·ris
—— capitis fib'u·lae' an·
te'ri·us
—— capitis fibulae pos·te'ri·
us
—— ca·pit'u·li' cos'tae'
in'ter·ar·tic'u·lar'e'
—— capituli costae ra'di·
a'tum
—— car'pi' dor·sa'le'
—— carpi ra'di·a'tum
—— carpi trans·ver'sum
—— carpi vo·lar'e'
—— cau·da'le'
—— cer'a·to·cri·coi'de·um
an·te'ri·us
—— col·lat'er·a'le' car'pi'
ra'di·a'le'
—— collaterale carpi
ul·nar'e'
—— collaterale fib'u·lar'e'
—— collaterale ra'di·a'le'
—— collaterale tib'i·a'le'
—— collaterale ul·nar'e'
—— col'li' cos'tae'
—— co·noi'de·um
—— co'ra·co·a·cro'mi·a'le'
—— co'ra·co·cla·vic'u·lar'e'
—— co'ra·co·hu'mer·a'le'
—— co'ro·nar'i·um hep'a·tis
—— cos'to·cla·vic'u·lar'e'
—— cos'to·trans·ver'sar'i·
um
—— costotransversarium
an·te'ri·us
—— costotransversarium
lat'er·a'le'

—— costotransversarium pos·te′ri·us
—— costotransversarium su·pe′ri·us
—— cri′co·ar′y·tae′noi′de·um pos·te′ri·us
—— cri′co·ar′y·te·noi′de·um pos·te′ri·us
—— cri′co·pha·ryn′ge·um
—— cri′co·thy′re·oi′de·um
—— cri′co·thy·roi′de·um
—— cri′co·tra′che·a′le
—— cru′ci·a′tum an·te′ri·us
—— cruciatum at·lan′tis
—— cruciatum cru′ris
—— cruciatum pos·te′ri·us
—— cru′ci·for′me′ at·lan′tis
—— cu·boi′de·o·na·vic′u·lar′e′ dor·sa′le
—— cuboideonaviculare plan·tar′e′
—— cu′ne·o·cu·boi′de·um dor·sa′le
—— cuneocuboideum in′ter·os′se·um
—— cuneocuboideum plan·tar′e′
—— del·toi′de·um
—— den·tic′u·la′tum
—— du′o·de′no·re·na′le
—— ep′i·di·dym′i·dis in·fe′ri·us
—— epididymidis su·pe′ri·us
—— fal′ci·for′me′ hep′a·tis
—— fla′vum
—— fun′di·for′me′ pe′nis
—— gas′tro·co′li·cum
—— gas′tro·li′e·na′le
—— gas′tro·phren′i·cum
—— gen′i·to·in′gui·na′le
—— hep′a·to·co′li·cum
—— hep′a·to·du′o·de·na′le
—— hep′a·to·gas′tri·cum
—— hep′a·to·re·na′le
—— hy′o·ep′i·glot′ti·cum
—— hy′o·thy′re·oi′de·um lat′er·a′le
—— hyothyreoideum me′di·um
—— il′i·o·fem′o·ra′le
—— il′i·o·lum·ba′le
—— in·cu′dis pos·te′ri·us
—— incudis su·pe′ri·us
—— in′gui·na′le
—— in′ter·cla·vic′u·lar′e′
—— in′ter·fo′ve·o·lar′e′
—— in′ter·spi·na′le

—— in′ter·trans′ver·sar′i·um
—— is′chi·o·cap′su·lar′e′
—— is′chi·o·fem′o·ra′le
—— la·cin′i·a′tum
—— lac′u·nar′e′
—— lat′er·a′le
—— la′tum u′ter·i
—— li·e′no·re·na′le
—— lon′gi·tu′di·na′le an·te′ri·us
—— longitudinale pos·te′ri·us
—— mal′le·i′ an·te′ri·us
—— mallei lat′er·a′le
—— mallei su·pe′ri·us
—— mal·le′o·li′ lat′er·a′lis an·te′ri·us
—— malleoli lateralis pos·te′ri·us
—— me′di·a′le
—— me·nis′co·fem′o·ra′le an·te′ri·us
—— meniscofemorale pos·te′ri·us
—— met′a·car′pe·um trans·ver′sum pro·fun′dum
—— metacarpeum transver′sum su′per·fi′ci·a′le
—— met′a·tar′se·um trans·ver′sum pro·fun′dum
—— metatarseum transver′sum su′per·fi′ci·a′le
—— nu′chae
—— o·var′i·i′ pro′pri·um
—— pal′pe·bra′le lat′er·a′le
—— palpebrale me′di·a′le
—— pa·tel′lae′
—— pec′ti·na′tum an′gu·li′ i′ri·do·cor′ne·a′lis
—— pectinatum i′ri·dis
—— pec′tin′e·a′le
—— phren′i·co·co′li·cum
—— phren′i·co·li′e·na′le
—— pi′so·ha·ma′tum
—— pi′so·met′a·car′pe·um
—— plan·tar′e′ lon′gum
—— pop·lit′e·um ar′cu·a′tum
—— popliteum o·bli′quum
—— pter′y·go·spi·na′le
—— pter′y·go·spi·no′sum
—— pu′bi·cum su·pe′ri·us
—— pu′bo·cap′su·lar′e′
—— pu′bo·fem′o·ra′le
—— pu′bo·pros·tat′i·cum
—— puboprostaticum lat′er·a′le

—— puboprostaticum me′di·um
—— pu′bo·ves′i·ca′le
—— pubovesicale lat′er·a′le
—— pubovesicale me′di·um
—— pul′mo·na′le
—— pul·mo′nis
—— qua·dra′tum
—— ra′di·o·car′pe·um dor·sa′le
—— radiocarpeum pal·mar′e′
—— radiocarpeum vo·lar′e′
—— re·flex′um
—— sac′ro·coc·cyg′e·um an·te′ri·us
—— sacrococcygeum dor·sa′le pro·fun′dum
—— sacrococcygeum dorsale su′per·fi′ci·a′le
—— sacrococcygeum lat′er·a′le
—— sacrococcygeum pos·te′ri·us pro·fun′dum
—— sacrococcygeum posterius su′per·fi′ci·a′lis
—— sacrococcygeum ven·tra′le
—— sac′ro·i·li′a·cum pos·te′ri·us brev′e′
—— sacroiliacum posterius long′um
—— sac′ro·spi·na′le
—— sac′ro·spi·no′sum
—— sac′ro·tu·ber·a′le
—— sac′ro·tu·ber·o′sum
—— se·ro′sum
—— sphe′no·man·dib′u·lar′e′
—— spi·ra′le coch′le·ae
—— ster′no·cla·vic′u·lar′e′
—— sternoclaviculare an·te′ri·us
—— sternoclaviculare pos·te′ri·us
—— ster′no·cos·ta′le in′ter·ar·tic′u·lar′e′
—— sternocostale in′tra·ar·tic′u·lar′e′
—— sty′lo·hy·oi′de·um
—— sty′lo·man·dib′u·lar′e′
—— su′pra·spi·na′le
—— sus′pen·so′ri·um cli·to′ri·dis
—— suspensorium o·var′i·i′
—— suspensorium pe′nis
—— ta′lo·cal·ca′ne·um an·te′ri·us

—— talocalcaneum in·ter·os'se·um
—— talocalcaneum lat'er·a'le'
—— talocalcaneum me'di·a'le'
—— talocalcaneum pos·te'ri·us
—— ta'lo·fib'u·lar'e' an·te'ri·us
—— talofibulare pos·te'ri·us
—— ta'lo·na·vic'u·lar'e'
—— ta'lo·tib'i·a'le' an·te'ri·us
—— talotibiale pos·te'ri·us
—— tem'po·ro·man·dib'u·lar'e'
—— te'res' fem'o·ris
—— teres hep'a·tis
—— teres u'ter·i'
—— tes'tis
—— thy're·o·ep'i·glot'ti·cum
—— thy'ro·ep'i·glot'ti·cum
—— thy'ro·hy·oi'de·um
—— thyrohyoideum me'di·a'num
—— tib'i·o·fib'u·lar'e' an·te'ri·us
—— tibiofibulare pos·te'ri·us
—— tib'i·o·na·vic'u·lar'e'
—— trans·ver'sum ac'e·tab'u·li'
—— transversum at·lan'tis
—— transversum cru'ris
—— transversum gen'u'
—— transversum ge'nus
—— transversum pel'vis
—— transversum per'i·ne'i'
—— transversum scap'u·lae' in·fe'ri·us
—— transversum scapulae su·pe'ri·us
—— trap'e·zoi'de·um
—— tri·an'gu·lar'e' dex'trum
—— triangulare si·nis'trum
—— tu·ber'cu·li' cos'tae'
—— ul'no·car'pe·um pal·mar'e'
—— um·bil'i·ca'le' lat'er·a'le'
—— umbilicale me'di·a'le'
—— umbilicale me'di·a'num
—— umbilicale me'di·um
—— vag'i·na'le'
—— ve'nae' ca'vae' si·nis'trae'
—— ve·no'sum
—— ven·tric'u·lar'e'

—— ves·tib'u·lar'e'
—— vo·ca'le'
lig'and'
li'gase'
li'gate', -gat'ed, -gat'ing
li·ga'tion
lig'a·ture
Lig'et sign
light'-head'ed
Li·gnac'-de To'ni-Fan·co'ni syndrome
Li·gnac'-Fan·co'ni syn-drome
lig'ne·ous
lig'nin
lig'no·caine'
lig'num
Lil'i·en·thal' operation
limb
lim'bal
lim'ber·neck'
lim'bi'
—— pal'pe·bra'les' an·te'ri·o'res'
—— palpebrales pos·te'ri·o'res'
lim'bic
lim'bus pl. -bus·es or -bi'
—— al've·o·lar'is man·dib'u·lae'
—— alveolaris max·il'lae'
—— cor'ne·ae'
—— fos'sae' o·va'lis
—— lam'i·nae' spi·ra'lis os'se·ae'
—— mem·bra'nae' tym'pa·ni'
—— pal'pe·bra'lis anterior
—— palpebralis posterior
—— sphe'noi·da'lis
—— spi·ra'lis
li'men pl. lim'i·na
—— in'su·lae'
—— na'si'
lim'i·nal
lim'i·tans'
lim'i·troph'ic
Lim·na'tis
—— ni·lot'i·ca
li·moph'thi·sis
li·mo'sis
limp
lin'co·my'cin
linc'tus
lin'dane'
Lin'dau' disease
Lind'bergh' flask

Lin'der·strom-Lang'-Dus·pi'va method
Lin'der·strom-Lang'-En'gel method
Lin'der·strom-Lang'-Glick' method
Lin'der·strom-Lang'-Hol'ter method
Lin'der·strom-Lang'-Lanz' method
Lin'der·strom-Lang' method
Lin'der·strom-Lang'-Weil'-Hol'ter methods
line
—— of Gen·na'ri
lin'e·a pl. -ae'
—— al'ba
—— ar'cu·a'ta os'sis il'i·i'
—— arcuata ossis il'i·um
—— arcuata va·gi'nae' mus'cu·li' rec'ti' ab·dom'i·nis
—— as'per·a
—— ax'il·lar'is
—— ep'i·phy'si·a'lis
—— glu'tae·a anterior
—— glutaea inferior
—— glutaea posterior
—— glu'te·a anterior
—— glutea inferior
—— glutea posterior
—— in'ter·con'dy·lar'is
—— in'ter·con'dy·loi'de·a
—— in'ter·me'di·a
—— in'ter·tro'chan·ter'i·ca
—— mam'mil·lar'is
—— me'di·a'na anterior
—— mediana posterior
—— me'di·o·cla·vic'u·lar'is
—— men·sa'lis
—— mus'cu·li' so'le·i'
—— my'lo·hy·oi'de·a
—— ni'gra
—— nu'chae' inferior
—— nuchae superior
—— nuchae su·pre'ma
—— o·bli'qua car'ti·lag'i·nis thy·roi'de·ae'
—— obliqua man·dib'u·lae'
—— par'a·ster·na'lis
—— pec·tin'e·a
—— pop·lit'e·a
—— scap'u·lar'is
—— sem'i·cir'cu·lar'is (Doug'la·si')
—— sem'i·lu·nar'is
—— sin'u·o'sa a·na'lis

—— splen'dens
—— ster·na'lis
—— tem'po·ra'lis inferior os'sis pa·ri'e·ta'lis
—— temporalis ossis fron·ta'lis
—— temporalis superior ossis pa·ri'e·ta'lis
—— ter'mi·na'lis
—— trap'e·zoi'de·a
lin'e·ae'
—— al'bi·can'tes'
—— grav'i·dar'um
—— mus'cu·lar'es' scap'u·lae'
—— trans·ver'sae' os'sis sa'·cri'
lin'e·al
lin'e·ar
lines
—— of Bail·lar·ger'
—— of O'wen
—— of Ret'zi·us
—— of Sal'ter
—— of Schre'ger
lin'gua pl. -guae'
—— ni'gra
—— pli·ca'ta
lin'gual
lin·gua'le
lin·gua'lis
lin'gual·ly
Lin·gua'tu·la
—— ser·ra'ta
lin'gu·la pl. -lae'
—— cer'e·bel'li'
—— man·dib'u·lae'
—— pul·mo'nis si·nis'tri'
—— sphe'noi·da'lis
lin'gu·lar
lin'gu·lec'to·my
lin'guo·ax'i·al
lin'guo·cer'vi·cal
lin'guo·den'tal
lin'guo·dis'tal
lin'guo·gin'gi·val
lin'guo·in·ci'sal
lin'guo·me'si·al
lin'guo·oc·clu'sal
lin'guo·pap'il·li'tis
lin'guo·pul'pal
lin'guo·ver'sion
lin'i·ment
li'nin
li·ni'tis
—— plas'ti·ca
link'age

lin'tin
Linz'en·mei'er test
li·o'thy'ro·nine'
li'o·trix'
lip
lip'ac·i·de'mi·a
lip'ac·i·du'ri·a
li·par'o·cele'
lip'a·roid'
lip'a·ro·trich'i·a
lip'a·rous
li'pase'
lip'a·su'ri·a
li·pec'to·my
lip'e·de'ma pl. -mas or -ma·ta
li·pe'mi·a
—— ret'i·na'lis
lip'id
lip'i·dase'
lip'i·de'mi·a
li·pid'ic
lip'i·dol'y·sis pl. -ses'
lip'i·do'sis pl. -ses'
lip'i·du'ri·a
lip'o·ad'e·no'ma pl. -mas or -ma·ta
lip'o·ar·thri'tis
lip'o·blast'
lip'o·blas'tic
lip'o·blas·to'ma pl. -mas or -ma·ta
lip'o·blas·to'sis
lip'o·car'di·ac'
lip'o·cele'
lip'o·cere'
lip'o·chon·dro·dys'tro·phy
lip'o·chon·dro'ma pl. -mas or -ma·ta
lip'o·chrome'
lip'o·chro·me'mi·a
lip'o·cor'ti·coid'
lip'o·cyte'
lip'o·di·er'e·sis pl. -ses'
lip'o·dys·tro'phi·a
—— pro'gres·si'va
lip'o·dys'tro·phy
lip'o·fi·bro'ma pl. -mas or -ma·ta
lip'o·fi'bro·myx·o'ma pl. -mas or -ma·ta
lip'o·fi'bro·sar·co'ma pl. -mas or -ma·ta
lip'o·fus'cin
lip'o·gen'e·sis pl. -ses'
lip'o·gen'ic
li·pog'e·nous

lip'o·gran'u·lo'ma pl. -mas or -ma·ta
lip'o·gran'u·lo·ma·to'sis
lip'o·he'mar·thro'sis pl. -ses'
lip'oid'
li·poi'dal
lip'oi·de'mi·a
li·poi'dic
lip'oi·do'sis pl. -ses'
—— cor'ne·ae'
—— cu'tis et mu·co'sae'
li·pol'y·sis pl. -ses'
lip'o·lyt'ic
li·po'ma pl. -mas or -ma·ta
—— foe·ta'lo·cel'lu·lar'e'
li·pom'a·toid'
li·po'ma·to'sis pl. -ses'
li·pom'a·tous
lip'o·mel'a·not'ic
lip'o·me·nin'go·cele'
lip'o·met'a·bol'ic
lip'o·me·tab'o·lism
lip'o·my'e·lo·me·nin'go·cele'
lip'o·my'o·he·man'gi·o'ma pl. -mas or -ma·ta
lip'o·my'o·ma pl. -mas or -ma·ta
lip'o·my'o·sar·co'ma pl. -mas or -ma·ta
lip'o·myx·o'ma pl. -mas or -ma·ta
lip'o·myx'o·sar·co'ma pl. -mas or -ma·ta
lip'o·ne·phro'sis
Lip'o·nys'sus
—— ba·co'ti
lip'o·pe'ni·a
lip'o·pe'nic
lip'o·pep'tide'
lip'o·pex'i·a
lip'o·phage'
lip'o·pha'gi·a
lip'o·pha'gic
lip'o·pha'gy
lip'o·phil'
lip'o·phil'i·a
lip'o·phil'ic
lip'o·plas'tic
lip'o·pol'y·sac'cha·ride'
lip'o·pro'tein'
lip'o·rho'din
lip'o·sar·co'ma pl. -mas or -ma·ta
lip'o·sar·co'ma·tous
li·po'sis pl. -ses'

lip'o·sol'u·ble
li·pos'to·my
li'po·thy'mi·a
lip'o·tro'pi·a
lip'o·trop'ic
li·pox'i·dase'
lip'pa
lip'ping
lip'pi·tude'
Lip'schütz'
—— body
—— cell
li·pu'ri·a
li·pu'ric
liq·ue·fa'cient
liq'ue·fac'tion
liq'ue·fac'tive
liq'ue·fy', -fied', -fy'ing
li·ques'cent
liq'uid
li'quor'
—— am'ni·i'
—— amnii spu'ri·us
—— cer'e·bro·spi·na'lis
—— fol·lic'u·li'
—— per'i·car'di·i'
—— san'gui·nis
—— se'mi·nis
li·quo'res'
Lis'franc'
—— amputation
—— tubercle
lisp
Lis'sau'er
—— column
—— paralysis
lis'sive
lis'ter·el·lo'sis pl. -ses'
Lis·te'ri·a
—— mon'o·cy·tog'e·nes'
lis·te'ri·al
lis·te'ri·o'sis pl. -ses'
Lis'ting law
li'ter also litre
lith'a·gogue'
li·thec'to·my
li·the'mi·a
li·the'mic
lith'i·a
li·thi'a·sic
li·thi'a·sis pl. -ses'
lith'ic
lith'i·co'sis pl. -ses'
lith'i·um
lith'o·cho'lic
lith'o·clast'
lith'o·cys·tot'o·my

lith'o·di·al'y·sis
lith'o·gen'e·sis
lith'o·ge·net'ic
li·thog'e·nous
li·thog'e·ny
lith'oid'
lith'o·kel'y·phos'
lith'o·labe'
li·thol'a·pax'y
li·thol'y·sis
lith'o·lyte'
lith'o·ne·phri'tis
lith'o·ne·phrot'o·my
lith'o·pe'di·on'
lith'o·scope'
lith'o·tome'
li·thot'o·mist
li·thot'o·my
lith'o·trip'sy
lith'o·trip'tic
lith'o·trip'to·scope'
lith'o·trite'
lith'o·trit'ic
li·thot'ri·ty
lith'ous
lith'u·re'sis
li·thu'ri·a
lit'mus
li'tre var. of liter
Lit'ten sign
lit'ter
Lit'tle disease
Lit'tler operation
Litt'man ox'-gall' medium
Lit·tré' glands
lit·tri'tis
Litz'mann ob·liq'ui·ty
li·ve'do
—— re·tic'u·lar'is
liv'er
liv'id
li·vid'i·ty
Li·vi·e·ra'to sign
li'vor'
—— mor'tis
Liz'ars operation
Lju·bin'sky stain
lo'bar
lo'bate'
lo'bat'ed
lobe
lo·bec'to·my
lo·be'li·a
lo'be·line'
lo'bi'
—— cer'e·bri'

—— glan'du·lae' mam·mar'i·ae'
—— mam'mae'
—— re·na'les'
lo'bo·cyte'
lo'bo·po'di·um pl. -di·a
Lo'bo's disease
lo·bot'o·my
Lob'stein' disease
lob'u·lar
lob'u·lat'ed
lob'u·la'tion
lob'ule'
lob'u·li'
—— cor'ti·ca'les' re'nis
—— ep'i·di·dym'i·dis
—— glan'du·lae' mam·mar'i·ae'
—— glandulae thy're·oi'de·ae'
—— glandulae thy·roi'de·ae'
—— hep'a·tis
—— mam'mae'
—— pul·mo'num
—— tes'tis
—— thy'mi'
lob'u·lose'
lob'u·lus pl. -li'
—— au·ric'u·lae'
—— bi·ven'ter
—— cen·tra'lis
—— me'di·us me'di·a'nus
—— par'a·cen·tra'lis
—— pa·ri'e·ta'lis inferior
—— parietalis superior
—— qua·dran'gu·lar'is
—— sem'i·lu·nar'is inferior
—— semilunaris superior
—— sim'plex'
lo'bus pl. -bi'
—— anterior hy'po·phys'e·os'
—— cau·da'tus
—— fron·ta'lis
—— glan'du·lae' thy're·oi'de·ae'
—— glandulae thy·roi'de·ae'
—— hep'a·tis dex'ter
—— hepatis si·nis'ter
—— inferior pul·mo'nis
—— inferior pulmonis dex'·tri'
—— inferior pulmonis si·nis'tri'
—— me'di·us pros'ta·tae'
—— medius pul·mo'nis dex'·trae

—— medius pulmonis dex′-
tri′
—— oc·cip′i·ta′lis
—— ol′fac·to′ri·us
—— pa·ri′e·ta′lis
—— posterior hy′po·phy′se·
os′
—— pros′ta·tae′
—— py·ram′i·da′lis
—— qua·dra′tus
—— superior pul·mo′nis
—— superior pulmonis dex′-
tri′
—— superior pulmonis si·
nis′tri′
—— tem′po·ra′lis
—— thy′mi′
lo′cal
lo′cal·i·za′tion
lo′cal·ize′, -ized′, -iz′ing
lo′ca·tor
lo′chi·a
—— al′ba
—— cru·en′ta
—— ru′bra
—— se·ro′sa
lo′chi·al
lo′chi·o·col′pos′
lo′chi·o·cyte′
lo′chi·o·me′tra
lo′chi·o·me·tri′tis
lo′chi·or·rha′gi·a
lo′chi·or·rhe′a
lo′chi·os′che·sis
lo′cho·me·tri′tis
lo′cho·per′i·to·ni′tis
Locke′-Rin′ger solution
lock′jaw′
Lock′wood′ sign
lo′co·mo′tion
lo′co·mo′tive
lo′co·mo′tor
loc′u·lar
loc′u·late′
loc′u·lat′ed
loc′u·la′tion
loc′u·lus pl. -li′
lo′cum ten′ens
lo′cus pl. -ci′
—— cae·ru′le·us
—— ce·ru′le·us
—— mi·no′ris res′is·ten′ti·ae′
—— per′fo·ra′tus
Loeb decidual reaction
Loef′fler
—— disease
—— pneumonia

—— stain
—— syndrome
Loele method
Loe′wen·thal′ tract
Loe′wi sign
log′ag·no′si·a
log′a·graph′i·a
log′am·ne′si·a
log′a·pha′si·a
log′o·clo′ni·a
log′o·ko·pho′sis pl. -ses′
log′o·ma′ni·a
log′o·neu·ro′sis pl. -ses′
lo·gop′a·thy
log′o·pe′di·a
log′o·pe′dics
log′o·pha′si·a
log′o·ple′gi·a
log′or·rhe′a
log′o·spasm
Loh′mann reaction
loin
lo′mo·fun′gin
Londe atrophy
Long coefficient
lon·gev′i·ty
lon′gi·lin′e·al
lon′gi·ma′nous
lon′gi·ped′ate′
lon·gis′si·mus
lon′gi·tu′di·nal
lon′gi·tu′di·na′lis
lon′gi·typ′i·cal
lon′gus
—— cap′i·tis
—— cer′vi·cis
—— col′li′
Loo′ney and Dy′er meth-
od
loop (a bend in a cordlike
structure)
↓loupe
—— of Hen′le
Loo′ser zones
Lo·phoph′o·ra
lo·phoph′o·rine′
lo·phot′ri·chous
lo·quac′i·ty
Lo·rain′-Lé·vi′ syndrome
lo·raz′e·pam′
lor′do·sco′li·o′sis pl. -ses′
lor·do′sis pl. -ses′
lor·dot′ic
Lo′renz method
Lo·ri′ga disease
Lor·rain′ Smith stain
Los′sen operation

Lo′theis′sen operation
lo′ti·o′
lo′tion
Lou′is-Bar′ syndrome
loupe (a magnifying lens)
↓loop
loup′ing ill
louse pl. lice
lov′age
Lo′vén reflex
Love′set maneuver
Lo′vi·bond′ unit
Lö′wen·stein-Jen′sen me-
dium
Low′er tubercle
Lowe syndrome
Lowe′-Ter′ryMc·Clach′lan
syndrome
Low′ry-Lo′pez-Bes′sey
method
Low′sley operation
lox·os′ce·lism
loz′enge
L-phen′yl·al′a·nine′
L-sar′co·ly′sin
Lu′barsch′ crystals
Lu′barsch-Pick′ syndrome
lubb
lubb-dupp′
lu·can′thone′
Lu′cas-Cham′pion·nière′
disease
Lu′cas sign
lu′cen·cy
lu′cent
Lu′ci·a′ni triad
lu′cid
lu′cid′i·ty
lu·cif′u·gal
Lu·ci′o leprosy
Lück′en·schä′del
Lud′wig
—— angina
—— filtration theory
—— muscle
lu′es′
lu·et′ic
lu′e·tin
Lu′gol solution
lu′ic
Lu′kens test
lum·ba′go′
lum′bar
lum′bar·i·za′tion
lum′bo·co·los′to·my
lum′bo·co·lot′o·my
lum′bo·cos′tal

lum'bo·dor'sal
lum'bo·dyn'i·a
lum'bo·in'gui·nal
lum'bo·is'chi·al
lum'bo·sa'cral
lum'bo·ver'te·bral
lum'bri·cal
lum'bus *pl.* -bi'
lu'men *pl.* -mi·na *or* -mens
lu'mi·nal
lu'mi·nance
lu'mi·nes'cence
lu'mi·nif'er·ous
lu'mi·nos'i·ty
lu'mi·nous
lump
lump·ec'to·my
lu'na·cy
lu'nar
lu'nate'
lu'na·tic
lu'na·to·ma·la'ci·a
lung
lu'nu·la *pl.* -lae'
lu'nu·lae'
—— val'vu·lar'um sem'i·lu·nar'i·um a·or'tae'
—— valvularum semilunarium trun'ci' pul·mo'nis
lu'pi·form'
lu'pine
lu'pi·no'sis
lu'poid'
lu'pus
—— crus·to'sus
—— en·dem'i·cus
—— er'y·the'ma·to'sus
—— ex·ce'dens
—— hy'per·troph'i·cus
—— lym·phat'i·cus
—— mac'u·lo'sus
—— mil'i·ar'is dis·sem'i·na'tus fa'ci·e'i'
—— per'ni·o'
—— pernio of Bes'ni·er
—— se·ba'ce·us
—— ser·pig'i·no'sus
—— su'per·fi'ci·a'lis
—— tu'mi·dus
—— veg'e·tans'
—— ver'ru·co'sus
—— vul·gar'is
Lusch'ka
—— bursa
—— cartilage
—— foramen
—— glands

—— subpharyngeal cartilage
—— tonsil
—— tubercle
Lust phenomenon
lu'sus na·tu'rae'
lu'te·al
lu'te·in
lu'te·in·i·za'tion
lu'te·in·ize', -ized', -iz'ing
Lu'tem·bach'er
—— disease
—— syndrome
lu'te·no'ma *pl.* -mas *or* -ma·ta
lu'te·o·blas·to'ma *pl.* -mas *or* -ma·ta
lu'te·o'ma *pl.* -mas *or* -ma·ta
Lütt'ke test
lu'tu·trin
Lutz'o·my'i·a
Lutz'-Splen·do're-Al·mei'da disease
lux *pl.* lux *or* lux'es'
lux·a'ti·o'
—— cox'ae'
—— con·gen'i·ta
—— e·rec'ta
—— im'per·fec'ta
—— per·in'e·a'lis
lux·a'tion
lux·u'ri·ant
lux'us
Luys body lesion
ly'ase'
ly'cine'
ly'co·per'don·o'sis *pl.* -ses'
ly'di·my'cin
Ly'ell syndrome
ly'ing-in'
Lyme
—— arthritis
—— disease
lymph
lym'pha
lymph·ad'e·nec'to·my
lym'pha·de'ni·a
lymph·ad'e·ni'tis
lymph·ad'e·no·cele'
lymph·ad'e·no·cyst'
lymph·ad'e·noid'
lymph·ad'e·no'ma *pl.* -mas *or* -ma·ta
lymph·ad'e·no'ma·to'sis *pl.* -ses'
lymph·ad'e·nop'a·thy
lymph·ad'e·no'sis *pl.* -ses'

—— be·nig'na cu'tis
lymph·ad'e·not'o·my
lym'pha·gogue'
lym·phan'gi·ec·ta'si·a
lym·phan'gi·ec'ta·sis *pl.* -ses'
lym·phan'gi·ec·tat'ic
lym·phan'gi·ec'to·my
lym·phan'gi·o·en'do·the'li·al
lym·phan'gi·o·en'do·the'li·o'ma *pl.* -mas *or* -ma·ta
lym·phan'gi·o·fi·bro'ma *pl.* -mas *or* -ma·ta
lym·phan'gi·o·gram'
lym·phan'gi·og'ra·phy
lym·phan'gi·o'ma *pl.* -mas *or* -ma·ta
—— cir'cum·scrip'tum con·gen'i·ta'le'
—— tu'be·ro'sum mul'ti·plex'
lym·phan'gi·o·plas'ty
lym·phan'gi·o·sar·co'ma *pl.* -mas *or* -ma·ta
lym·phan'gi·ot'o·my
lym'phan·git'ic
lym'phan·gi'tis *pl.* -git'i·des'
lym'phat'ic
lym·phat'i·cos'to·my
lym'pha·tism
lym'pha·ti'tis *pl.* -tis·es *or* -tit'i·des'
lym'phec·ta'si·a
lymph'e·de'ma
lym'pho·blast'
lym'pho·blas'tic
lym'pho·blas·to'ma *pl.* -mas *or* -ma·ta
—— ma·lig'num
lym'pho·blas'to·ma·to'sis *pl.* -ses'
lym'pho·blas·to'sis *pl.* -ses'
lym'pho·cyte'
lym'pho·cyt'ic
lym'pho·cy·the'mi·a
lym'pho·cyt'ic
lym'pho·cy·to'ma *pl.* -mas *or* -ma·ta
—— cu'tis
lym'pho·cy'to·pe'ni·a
lym'pho·cy'to·poi·e'sis *pl.* -ses'
lym'pho·cy·to'sis *pl.* -ses'
lym'pho·der'mi·a
—— per·ni'ci·o'sa

lym'pho·ep'i·the'li·o'ma pl.
 -mas or -ma·ta
lym'pho·ep'i·the'li·o'ma·
 tous
lymph'o·gen'e·sis pl. -ses'
lym'pho·gen'ic
lym·phog'e·nous
lym'pho·glan'du·la pl. -lae
lym'pho·go'ni·a
lym'pho·gran'u·lo'ma
 pl. -mas or -ma·ta
—— in'gui·na'le'
—— ve·ne're·um
lym'pho·gran'u·lo'ma·
 to'sis pl. -ses'
—— cu'tis
—— of Schau'mann
lym'pho·his'ti·o·cyt'ic
lym'phoid'
lym'phoi·dec'to·my
lym·phoi'do·cyte'
lym'pho·ken'tric
lym'pho·kine'
lym·pho'ma pl. -mas or
 -ma·ta
lym·pho'ma·toid'
lym'pho·ma·to'sis pl. -ses'
lym'pho·ma·tous
lym'pho·mon'o·cyte'
lym'pho·mon'o·cy·to'sis pl.
 -ses'
lym'pho·no'dus pl. -di'
lym'pho·path'i·a ve·ne're·
 um
lym·phop'a·thy
lym'pho·pe'ni·a
lym'pho·poi·e'sis pl. -ses'
lym'pho·poi·et'ic
lym'pho·pro·lif'er·a·tive
lym'pho·re·tic'u·lar
lym'pho·re·tic'u·lo'ma
 pl. -mas or -ma·ta
lym'pho·re·tic'u·lo'sis pl.
 -ses'
lym'phor·rhage
lym'phor·rhe'a
lym'pho·sar·co'ma pl. -mas
 or -ma·ta
lym'pho·sar·co'ma·to'sis
 pl. -ses'
lym'phous
lyn·es'tre·nol'
ly'o·chrome'
ly'o·en'zyme'
Ly'on hypothesis
ly'o·phile'
ly'o·phil'ic

ly·oph'i·lized'
ly'o·sol'
ly'o·sorp'tion
ly'o·trop'ic
ly·pres'sin
ly'ra Da'vi·dis
ly'sate'
lyse, lysed, lys'ing
ly·ser'gic
ly'ser·gide'
Lys'holm'
—— grid
—— line
—— projection
ly'sin
ly'sine'
ly'sis pl. -ses'
ly'so·gen'e·sis pl. -ses'
ly'so·gen'ic
ly·sog'e·ny
ly'so·ki'nase'
ly'so·lec'i·thin
ly'so·so'mal
ly'so·some'
ly'so·zyme'
lys'sa
lys'sic
lys'soid'
lys'so·pho'bi·a
ly'syl
lyt'ic

M

Mac·al'lis·ter muscle
Mac·Cal'lum
—— patch
—— stain
Mac·chi·a·vel'lo stain
Mac·Cor'mac reflex
mac'er·ate', -at'ed, -at'ing
mac'er·a'tion
mac'er·a'tive
Mac·ew'en
—— osteotomy
—— sign
—— triangle
Ma·cha'do-Guer·rei'ro re-
 action
Mache unit
Mach number
Mach'o'ver test
Mac·Kee-Herr'mann-
 Ba'ker-Sulz'ber'ger
 method

Mack'en·rodt' ligament
Mac·ken'zie
—— amputation
—— disease
—— syndrome
Mac·Lean' test
Mac·leod' syndrome
Mac·Neal' stain
Mac'ra·can'tho·rhyn'chus
—— hi·ru'di·na'ce·us
mac·rad'e·nous
mac'ren·ce·phal'ic
mac'ren·ceph'a·lous
mac'ren·ceph'a·ly
mac'ro·am'y·lase'
mac'ro·am'y·la·se'mi·a
mac'ro·blast'
mac'ro·ble·phar'i·a
mac'ro·bra'chi·a
mac'ro·car'di·us
mac'ro·ce·pha'li·a
mac'ro·ce·phal'ic
mac'ro·ceph'a·lous
mac'ro·ceph'a·lus pl. -li'
mac'ro·ceph'a·ly
mac'ro·chei'li·a
mac'ro·chei'ri·a
mac'ro·cne'mi·a
mac'ro·co·nid'i·um pl. -i·a
mac'ro·cra'ni·a
mac'ro·cyst'
mac'ro·cyte'
mac'ro·cy·the'mi·a
mac'ro·cyt'ic
mac'ro·cy·to'sis pl. -ses'
mac'ro·dac·tyl'i·a
mac'ro·dac'ty·lism
mac'ro·dac'ty·ly
mac'ro·dont'
mac'ro·don'ti·a
mac'ro·fol·lic'u·lar
mac'ro·gam'ete'
mac'ro·ga·me'to·cyte'
mac'ro·gen'i·to·so'mi·a
ma·crog'li·a
mac'ro·glob'u·lin
mac'ro·glob'u·li·ne'mi·a
mac'ro·glos'si·a
mac'ro·gnath'i·a
mac'ro·gnath'ic
mac'ro·gy'ri·a
mac'ro·lym'pho·cyte'
mac'ro·mas'ti·a
mac'ro·me'li·a
mac'ro·mo·lec'u·lar
mac'ro·mol'e·cule'
mac'ro·mon'o·cyte'

mac'ro·my'e·lo·blast'
mac'ro·nod'u·lar
mac'ro·nor'mo·blast'
mac'ro·nor'mo·cyte'
mac'ro·nu'cle·us *pl.* -cle·i'
mac'ro·phage'
ma·croph'a·gy
mac'roph·thal'mos'
mac'ro·pla'si·a
mac'ro·po'di·a
mac'ro·pol'y·cyte'
mac'ro·pro·so'pi·a
ma·crop'si·a
mac'rop'sy
mac'ro·scop'ic
mac'ros·mat'ic
mac'ro·so'mi·a
mac'ro·spore'
mac'ro·spo'ric
mac'ro·sto'mi·a
ma·cro'ti·a
Ma·cruz' index
mac'u·la *pl.* -lae'
—— a·cu'sti·ca sac'cu·li'
—— acustica u·tric'u·li'
—— ad·hae'rens
—— ce·ru'le·a
—— com·mu'nis
—— cor'ne·ae'
—— cri·bro'sa inferior
—— cribrosa me'di·a
—— cribrosa superior
—— den'sa
—— fla'va
—— ger'mi·na·ti'va
—— lu'te·a
—— sac'cu·li'
—— u·tric'u·li'
mac'u·lae'
——·a·cu'sti·cae'
—— cri·bro'sae'
mac'u·lar
mac'ule'
mac'u·lo·an'es·thet'ic
mac'u·lo·cer'e·bral
mac'u·lo·pap'u·lar
mac'u·lo·pap'ule'
mac'u·lo've·sic'u·lar
mad'a·ro'sis *pl.* -ses'
mad'a·rot'ic
mad'a·rous
Mad'e·lung' deformity
mad'u·ro·my·co'sis *pl.* -ses'
ma'fe·nide'
Maf·fu'cci syndrome
mag'al·drate'
ma'gen·bla'se

Ma·gen'die
—— foramen
—— law
ma'gen·stras'se
ma·gen'ta
mag'is·tral
mag'ma
—— re·tic'u·lar'e'
Mag'nan sign
mag'ne·se'mi·a
mag'ne·si·a
mag'ne·si·um
mag'ne·tron'
mag'ni·fi·ca'tion
mag'ni·fy', -fied', -fy'ing
mag'num
Mag'nus-de Kleijn' reflex-
  es
Ma·haim' fibers
maid'en·head'
maim
main
—— en griffe
—— en lor·gnette'
Mais·sat' band
Ma·joc'chi disease
ma'jor
mal
—— de ca·de'ras
—— de Ca·yenne'
—— de co·ït'
—— de la ro'sa
—— del pin'to
—— del so'le
—— de Me·le'da
—— de mer
—— des bas·sines'
—— per'fo·rant'
ma'la
Mal'a·bar' itch
mal'ab·sorp'tion
ma·la'ci·a
—— cor'dis
mal'a·co'ma
mal'a·co·pla'ki·a
mal'a·die'
—— bleue
—— bron·zée'
—— de Cap'de·pont'
—— de Ni'co·las' et Fav·re'
—— de plon·geurs'
—— de Rog·er'
—— des jam·bes'
—— des tics
—— de tic con·vul·sif'
—— du doute
—— du som·meil'

mal'ad·just'ed
mal'ad·just'ment
mal'a·dy
ma·laise'
mal'a·lign'ment
ma'lar
ma·lar'i·a
ma·lar'i·al
ma·lar'i·ous
mal'ar·tic'u·la'tion
Mal'as·se'zi·a
—— fur'fur
mal'as·sim'i·la'tion
mal'ate'
mal'de·vel'op·ment
mal'di·ges'tion
male
ma'le·ate'
mal'e·rup'tion
mal·eth'a·mer
mal'for·ma'tion
mal·func'tion
Mal·gaigne' amputation
Mal'i·bu' disease
ma·lig'nan·cy
ma·lig'nant
ma·lin'ger
ma·lin'ger·er
Mall
—— formula
—— technique
mal'le·a·bil'i·ty
mal'le·able
mal'le·al
mal'le·ar
mal'le·a'tion
mal'le·o·in'cu·dal
mal·le'o·lar
mal·le'o·lus *pl.* -li'
—— lat'er·a'lis
—— me'di·a'lis
Mal'le·o·my'ces'
—— mal'le·i'
—— pseu'do·mal'le·i'
mal'le·o·my·rin'go·plas'ty
mal'le·ot'o·my
mal'le·us *pl.* -le·i'
Mal'lo·ry
—— bodies
—— stain
Mal'lo·ry-Weiss' syn-
  drome
Mal·loy'-Ev'e·lyn method
mal·nour'ish
mal·nu·tri'tion
mal'oc·clu'sion
mal·pigh'i·an

mal·posed'
mal'po·si'tion
mal'prac'tice
mal'pre·sen·ta'tion
mal'ro·ta'tion
malt'ase'
malt'ose'
malt'os·u'ri·a
mal'um
—— cox'ae'
—— coxae se·ni'lis
—— per'fo·rans' pe'dis
—— ve·ne're·um
mal·un'ion
ma·man'pi·an'
mam'e·lon'
ma·mil'la pl. -lae'
mam'il·lar'y
mam'il·lat'ed
mam'il·la'tion
ma·mil'li·form'
mam'il·li'tis
mam'ma pl. -mae'
—— a·ber'rans'
—— er·rat'i·ca
—— mas'cu·li'na
—— vi·ri'lis
mam'mae'
—— ac'ces·so'ri·ae' fem'i·
ni'nae' et mas·cu·li'nae'
—— accessoriae mu'li·
e'bres' et vi·ri'les'
mam'mal
mam·mal'gi·a
mam·ma'li·an
mam·ma·plas'ty
mam'ma·ry
mam·mec'to·my
mam'mi·form'
mam'mi'tis
mam'mo·gen
mam'mo·gen'e·sis pl. -ses'
mam'mo·gen'ic
mam'mo·gram'
mam·mog'ra·phy
mam'mo·pla'si·a
mam'mo·plas'ty
mam'mose'
mam·mot'o·my
mam'mo·tro'phin
mam'mo·trop'ic
mam'mo·tro'pin
man·cha'da
man·chette'
Man'cke-Som'mer test
Man'cke test
man'del·ate'

Man'del·baum' reaction
man·del'ic
man'di·ble
man·dib'u·la pl. -lae'
man·dib'u·lar
man·dib'u·lec'to·my
man·dib'u·lo·fa'cial
man·dib'u·lo·glos'sus
man·dib'u·lo·mar'gi·na'lis
Man'dl operation
man'drel
Man·dril'lus
man'drin
ma·neu'ver
man'ga·nese'
man·gan'ic
man'ga·nous
ma'ni·a
—— a po'tu
ma'ni·ac'
man'ic-de·pres'sive
man'i·kin
man'i·pha'lanx' pl. -pha·
lan'ges'
ma·nip'u·late', -lat'ed, -lat'-
ing
ma·nip'u·la'tion
Mann
—— palsy
—— sign
man'na
Mann'-Boll'man fistula
man'ner·ism
man'nite'
man'ni·tol'
Mann'-Wil'liam·son ulcer
ma·nom'e·ter
man'o·met'ric
ma·nom'e·try
man'tle
Man·toux' test
man'u·al
ma·nu'bri·al
ma·nu'bri·um pl. -bri·a
—— mal'le·i'
—— ster'ni'
ma'nus pl. ma'nus
—— ca'va
—— cur'ta
—— ex·ten'sa
—— flex'a
—— val'ga
—— var'a
ma·ran'tic
ma·ras'mic
ma·ras'mus
mar'ble·i·za'tion

Mar'burg' virus
marche à pe·tit' pas
Mar'chi·a·fa'va-Bi·gna'mi
syndrome
Mar'chi·a·fa'va disease
Mar'chi·a·fa'va-Mi·che'li
syndrome
Marck'wald' operation
Mar'cus Gunn phenom-
enon
Mar'é·chal' test
Mar'esch stain
Ma·rey'
—— law
—— reflex
Mar'fan' syndrome
mar'ga·ri·to'ma pl. -mas or
-ma·ta
mar'gin
mar'gin·al
mar'gin·a'tion
mar'gin·o·plas'ty
mar'go' pl. -gi·nes'
—— a·cu'tus cor'dis
—— anterior fib'u·lae'
—— anterior hep'a·tis
—— anterior li·e'nis
—— anterior pan·cre'a·tis
—— anterior pul·mo'nis
—— anterior ra'di·i'
—— anterior tes'tis
—— anterior tib'i·ae'
—— anterior ul'nae'
—— ax'il·lar'is scap'u·lae'
—— cil'i·ar'is
—— dex'ter cor'dis
—— dor·sa'lis ra'di·i'
—— dorsalis ul'nae'
—— fal'ci·for'mis fas'ci·ae'
la'tae'
—— falciformis hi·a'tus sa·
phe'ni'
—— fib'u·lar'is pe'dis
—— fron·ta'lis a'lae'
mag'nae'
—— frontalis alae ma·jo'ris
—— frontalis os'sis pa·ri'e·
ta'lis
—— in'ci·sa'lis
—— inferior cer'e·bri'
—— inferior hep'a·tis
—— inferior li·e'nis
—— inferior pan·cre'a·tis
—— inferior pul·mo'nis
—— in'fer·o·lat'er·a'lis cer'e·
bri'

—— in'fer·o·me'di·a'lis cer'e·bri'

—— in'fra·gle'noi·da'lis

—— in'fra·or'bi·ta'lis

—— in'ter·os'se·us fib'u·lae'

—— interosseus ra'di·i'

—— interosseus tib'i·ae'

—— interosseus ul'nae'

—— lac'ri·ma'lis max·il'lae'

—— lamb·doi'de·us

—— lat'er·a'lis an'te·bra'chi·i'

—— lateralis hu'mer·i'

—— lateralis lin'guae'

—— lateralis pe'dis

—— lateralis re'nis

—— lateralis scap'u·lae'

—— lateralis un'guis

—— li'ber o·var'i·i'

—— liber un'guis

—— lin'guae'

—— mas·toi'de·us

—— me'di·a'lis an'te·bra'chi·i'

—— medialis cer'e·bri'

—— medialis glan'du·lae' su'pra·re·na'lis

—— medialis hu'mer·i'

—— medialis pe'dis

—— medialis re'nis

—— medialis scap'u·lae'

—— medialis tib'i·ae'

—— mes'o·var'i·cus

—— na·sa'lis

—— na'si'

—— ob·tu'sus cor'dis

—— oc·cip'i·ta'lis os'sis pa·ri'e·ta'lis

—— occipitalis ossis tem'po·ra'lis

—— oc·cul'tus un'guis

—— pa·ri'e·ta'lis a'lae' ma·jo'ris

—— parietalis os'sis fron·ta'lis

—— parietalis ossis tem'po·ra'lis

—— pe'dis lat'er·a'lis

—— pedis me'di·a'lis

—— posterior fib'u·lae'

—— posterior li·e'nis

—— posterior pan·cre'a·tis

—— posterior par'tis pe·tro'sae'

—— posterior ra'di·i'

—— posterior tes'tis

—— posterior ul'nae'

—— pu'pil·lar'is i'ri·dis

—— ra'di·a'lis an'te·bra'chi·i'

—— sag'it·ta'lis

—— sphe'noi·da'lis

—— squa·mo'sus a'lae' mag'nae'

—— squamosus alae ma·jo'ris

—— squamosus os'sis pa·ri'e·ta'lis

—— superior cer'e·bri'

—— superior glan'du·lae' su'pra·re·na'lis

—— superior li·e'nis

—— superior pan·cre'a·tis

—— superior par'tis pe·tro'sae'

—— superior scap'u·lae'

—— su'per·o·me'di·a'lis cer'e·bri'

—— su'pra·or'bi·ta'lis

—— tib'i·a'lis pe'dis

—— ul·nar'is an'te·bra'chi·i'

—— u'ter·i'

—— ver'te·bra'lis scap'u·lae'

—— vo·lar'is ra'di·i'

—— volaris ul'nae'

—— zy'go·mat'i·cus a'lae' mag'nae'

—— zygomaticus alae ma·jo'ris

Ma·rie'

—— ataxia

—— disease

—— syndrome

Ma·rie'-Bam'ber'ger disease

Ma·rie'-Foix' sign

Ma·rie'-Strüm'pell

—— arthritis

—— disease

—— encephalitis

—— spondylitis

Ma·rie'-Tooth' disease

mar'i·hua'na *also* marijuana

mar'i·jua'na *var. of* marihuana

Ma·rin' A'mat syndrome

Ma'ri·nes'co hand

Ma'ri·nes'co-Sjö'gren-Gar'land syndrome

Ma·ri·otte' blind spot

Mar·jo·lin' ulcer

mark

mar'mo·ri·za'tion

Ma·ro·teaux'-La·my' syndrome

mar'row

Mar'shall Hall method

Mar'shall-Mar·chet'ti-Krantz' procedure

Mar'shall vein

Marsh test

mar·su'pi·al·i·za'tion

mar·su'pi·um *pl.* -pi·a

—— pa'tel·lar'is

Mar'ti·not'ti cells

mas'cu·line

mas'cu·lin'i·ty

mas'cu·lin·i·za'tion

mas'cu·lin·ize', -ized', -iz'ing

mas'cu·lin·o·vo·blas·to'ma *pl.* -mas *or* -ma·ta

ma'ser

mask

masked

mask'ing

mas'o·chism

mas'o·chist

mas'o·chis'tic

Ma'son incision

masque' bi·liaire'

mass

mas'sa *pl.* -sae'

—— in'ter·me'di·a

—— lat'er·a'lis at·lan'tis

mas·sage'

mas·se'ter

mas·se·ter'ic

mas'sive

Mas·son'

—— body

—— trichrome stain

mast'ad·e·ni'tis

mast'ad·e·no'ma *pl.* -mas *or* -ma·ta

mas·tal'gi·a

mas'ta·tro'phi·a

mas·tat'ro·phy

mas·taux'e'

mast·ec'chy·mo'sis *pl.* -ses'

mas·tec'to·my

Mas'ter two'-step' test

mast'hel·co'sis *pl.* -ses'

mas'tic

mas'ti·cate', -cat'ed, -cat'ing

mas'ti·ca'tion

mas'ti·ca·to·ry

mas·ti'tis

mas'to·car'ci·no'ma *pl.* -mas *or* -ma·ta

mas'to·chon·dro'ma pl.
  -mas or -ma·ta
mas'to·cyte'
mas'to·cy·to'ma pl. -mas or
  -ma·ta
mas'to·cy·to'sis pl. -ses'
mas'to·dyn'i·a
mas'toid'
mas'toid·al
mas'toid·al'gi·a
mas·toi'de·a
mas·toid·ec'to·my
mas·toi'de·um
mas'toid·i'tis
mas'toid·ot'o·my
mas·ton'cus
mas'to·oc·cip'i·tal
mas'to·pa·ri'e·tal
mas'to·path'i·a cys'ti·ca
mas·top'a·thy
mas'to·pex'y
mas'to·pla'si·a
mas'to·plas'ti·a
mas'to·plas'ty
mas·top·to'sis
mas'tor·rha'gi·a
mas'to·scir'rhus pl. -ri' or
  -rhus·es
mas·to'sis pl. -ses'
mas·tos'to·my
mas·tot'o·my
mas'tur·bate', -bat'ed, -bat'-
  ing
mas'tur·ba'tion
Mat'as operation
match
mate, mat'ed, mat'ing
ma·te'ri·a
  —— al'ba
  —— med'i·ca
ma·te'ri·al
ma·te'ri·es'
  —— mor'bi'
  —— pec'cans'
ma·ter'nal
ma·ter'ni·ty
mat'ri·lin'e·al
ma'trix pl. -tri·ces' or -trix·es
  —— un'guis
matt
mat'ter
mat'u·rate', -rat'ed, -rat'ing
mat'u·ra'tion
ma·ture', -tured', -tur'ing
ma·tur'i·ty
ma·tu'ti·nal
Mau·chart' ligament

Mau·noir' hydrocele
Mau'rer
  —— clefts
  —— dots
Mau'ri·ac' syndrome
Mau'ri·ceau' method
Mauth'ner sheath
max·il'la pl. -lae' or -las
max'il·lar'y
max'il·lec'to·my
max'il·li'tis
max·il'lo·den'tal
max·il'lo·fa'cial
max·il'lo·fron·ta'le'
max·il'lo·la'bi·al
max·il'lo·lac'ri·mal
max·il'lo·man·dib'u·lar
max·il'lo·pal'a·tine'
max·il'lo·pha·ryn'ge·al
max'il·lot'o·my
max·il'lo·tur'bi·nal
max'i·mal
max'i·mum pl. -ma
May'dl operation
May'er reflex
May'-Grün'wald' stain
May'-Heg'glin anomaly
Ma'yo operation
Ma'yo-Rob'son
  —— incision
  —— point
  —— position
ma'za
maz'ic
maz'in·dol'
ma'zo·dyn'i·a
ma'zo·pex'y
ma'zo·pla'si·a
Maz·zi'ni test
Maz·zo'ni corpuscle
Maz·zot'ti reaction
Mc·Ar'dle syndrome
Mc·Bur'ney
  —— operation
  —— point
  —— sign
Mc·Car'thy reflex
Mc·Ell·roy' test
Mc·Gill' operation
Mc'In·tosh' test
Mc·Lean' formula
Mc·Mur'ray sign
mean
mea'sles
mea'sly
me·a'tal
me·a·ti'tis

me'a·tor'rha·phy
me'a·tot'o·my
me·a'tus pl. me·a'tus or
  -tus·es
  —— a·cu'sti·cus ex·ter'nus
  —— acusticus externus
car'ti·la·gin'e·us
  —— acusticus in·ter'nus
  —— na'si' com·mu'nis
  —— nasi inferior
  —— nasi me'di·us
  —— nasi superior
  —— na'so·pha·ryn'ge·us
  —— u·re'thrae'
me·bev'er·ine'
me·bu'ta·mate'
mec'a·myl'a·mine'
me·chan'i·cal
mech'a·nism
mech'lor·eth'a·mine'
me'cism
Meck'el
  —— cartilage
  —— cavity
  —— diverticulum
  —— ganglion
  —— stalk
  —— syndrome
mec'li·zine'
mec'lo·qua'lone'
mec'o·nate'
me·co'ni·um
me·cys'ta·sis pl. -ses'
mec'y·stat'ic
me·daz'e·pam'
me'di·a
me'di·ad'
me'di·al
me'di·an
me'di·a'nus
me'di·as·ti'nal
me'di·as·ti·ni'tis
me'di·as·ti'no·per'i·car·
  di'tis
me'di·as·ti'nos'co·py
me'di·as·ti'not'o·my
me'di·as·ti'num pl. -na
  —— an·te'ri·us
  —— me'di·um
  —— pos·te'ri·us
  —— su·pe'ri·us
  —— tes'tis
me'di·ate', -at'ed, -at'ing
me'di·a'tion
me'di·a'tor
med'i·ca·ble
med'i·cal

me·dic′a·ment
med′i·ca·men·to′sus
med′i·cant
med′i·cate′, -cat′ed, -cat′ing
med′i·ca′tion
med′i·ca′tor
me′di·ce·phal′ic
me·dic′i·nal
med′i·cine
med′i·co·le′gal
med′i·co·sur′gi·cal
med′i·cus pl. -ci′
Med′in disease
me′di·o·car′pal
me′di·oc·cip′i·tal
me′di·o·cen′tric
me′di·o·dor′sal
me′di·o·fron′tal
me′di·o·lat′er·al
me′di·o·ne·cro′sis pl. -ses′
    a·or′tae′ id′i·o·path′i·ca
    cys′ti·ca
me′di·o·plan′tar′
me′di·o·su·pe′ri·or
me′di·o·tar′sal
Med′i·ter·ra′ne·an
    anemia
    fever
me′di·um pl. -di·a
me′di·us
med·pred′ni·sone′
med′ro·ges′tone′
me·drox′y·pro·ges′ter·one′
med′ry·sone′
me·dul′la pl. -las or -lae′
    glan′du·lae′ su′pra·re·
    na′lis
    no′di′ lym·phat′i·ci′
    ob′lon·ga′ta
    os′si·um
    ossium fla′va
    ossium ru′bra
    re′nis
    spi·na′lis
med′ul·lar′y
med′ul·lat′ed
med′ul·la′tion
med′ul·lec′to·my
med′ul·li·za′tion
me·dul′lo·a·dre′nal
me·dul′lo·ar·thri′tis
med′ul·lo·blast′
med′ul·lo·blas·to′ma
    pl. -mas or -ma·ta
me·dul′lo·en′ce·phal′ic
med′ul·lo·ep′i·the′li·o′ma
    pl. -mas or -ma·ta

med′ul·loid′
Mees lines
me·fen′o·rex′
me·fex′a·mide′
mef′ru·side′
meg′a·blad′der
meg′a·car′di·a
meg′a·ce′cum pl. -ca
meg′a·ce·phal′ic
meg′a·ceph′a·ly
meg′a·cho·led′o·chus pl.
    -chi′
meg′a·coc′cus pl. -ci′
meg′a·co′lon
meg′a·dont′
meg′a·du′o·de′num pl. -na
    or -nums
meg′a·kar′y·o·blast′
meg′a·kar′y·o·blas·to′ma
    pl. -mas or -ma·ta
meg′a·kar′y·o·cyte′
meg′a·kar′y·o·cyt′ic
meg′a·kar′y·o·cy′to·pe′ni·a
meg′a·kar′y·o·cy·to′sis
meg′a·kar′y·oph′thi·sis pl.
    -ses′
meg′a·lec′i·thal
meg′a·len·ceph′a·lon′ pl.
    -la
meg′a·len·ceph′a·ly
meg′a·ler′y·the′ma
me·gal′gi·a
meg′a·lo·blast′
    of Sa′bin
meg′a·lo·blas′tic
meg′a·lo·blas′toid′
meg′a·lo·car′di·a
meg′a·lo·ce·pha′li·a
meg′a·lo·ce·phal′ic
meg′a·lo·ceph′a·ly
meg′a·lo·chei′rous
meg′a·lo·cor′ne·a
meg′a·lo·cys′tis
meg′a·lo·cyte′
meg′a·lo·cyt′ic
meg′a·lo·cy·to′sis pl. -ses′
meg′a·lo·dac′ty·lous
meg′a·lo·dac′ty·ly
meg′a·lo·don′ti·a
meg′a·lo·gas′tri·a
meg′a·lo·glos′si·a
meg′a·lo·he·pat′i·a
meg′a·lo·kar′y·o·blast′
meg′a·lo·kar′y·o·cyte′
meg′a·lo·ma′ni·a
meg′a·lo·ma′ni·ac′
meg′a·lo·me′li·a

meg′a·lo·pe′nis
meg′a·loph·thal′mos
meg′a·lo′pi·a
meg′a·lo·po′di·a
meg′a·lop′si·a
meg′a·lo·splanch′nic
meg′a·lo·sple′ni·a
meg′a·lo·spore′
meg′a·lo·thy′mus pl. -mus·
    es or -mi′
meg′a·lo·u·re′ter
meg′a·nu′cle·us pl. -cle·i′
meg′a·pros′o·pous
meg′a·rec′tum
meg′a·sig′moid′
meg′a·spore′
meg′a·u·re′ter
meg′a·vi′ta·min
meg′a·volt′
me·ges′trol′
me·glu′mine′
    di′a·tri·zo′ate′
    i′o·dip′a·mide′
    i′o·tha·lam′ate′
meg′oph·thal′mos
me′grim
Mei·bo′mi·an
    cyst
    glands
mei·bo′mi·a·ni′tis
mei′bo·mi′tis
Meige disease
Meigs syndrome
Mei′ni·cke test
mei·o′sis (cell division),
    pl. -ses′
♦miosis
mei·ot′ic
Meiss′ner
    corpuscle
    plexus
me·lag′ra
me·lal′gi·a
mel′an·cho′li·a
    ag′i·ta′ta
    at·ton′i·ta
    sim′plex′
mel′an·cho′li·ac′
mel′an·chol′ic
mel′an·chol′y
mel′a·ne′mi·a
mel′a·nif′er·ous
mel′a·nin
mel′a·nism
mel′a·nis′tic
mel′a·ni·za′tion
mel′a·nize′, -nized′, -niz′ing

mel'a·no·am'e·lo·blas·
  to'ma pl. -mas or -ma·ta
mel'a·no·blast'
mel'a·no·blas·to'ma
  pl. -mas or -ma·ta
mel'a·no·car'ci·no'ma
  pl. -mas or -ma·ta
mel'a·no·cyte'
mel'a·no·cyt'ic
mel'a·no·cy·to'ma pl. -mas
  or -ma·ta
mel'a·no·cy·to'sis pl. -ses'
mel'a·no·der'ma
mel'a·no·der'ma·ti·tis
—— tox'i·ca
mel'a·no·der'mi·a
mel'a·no·der'mic
mel'a·no·ep'i·the'li·o'ma
  pl. -mas or -ma·ta
mel'a·no·floc'cu·la'tion
me·lan'o·gen
mel'a·no·gen'e·sis pl. -ses'
mel'a·no·gen'ic
mel'a·no·glos'si·a
mel'a·no:id'
mel'a·no·leu'ko·der'ma
  col'li'
mel'a·no'ma pl. -mas or
  -ma·ta
—— su'pra·re·na'le'
mel'a·no'ma·to'sis pl. -ses'
mel'a·no'ma·tous
mel'a·no·nych'i·a
mel'a·no·phage'
mel'a·no·phore'
mel'a·no·pla'ki·a
mel'a·nor·rhe'a
mel'a·no·sar·co'ma pl. -mas
  or -ma·ta
mel'a·no·sar·co'ma·to'sis
  pl. -ses'
mel'a·no'sis pl. -ses'
—— cir'cum·scrip'ta
pre·blas'to·ma·to'sa of
  Du·breuilh'
—— co'li'
—— i'ri·dis
mel'a·no·some'
mel'a·not'ic
mel'a·no·trich'i·a lin'guae'
mel'a·no·trop'ic
mel'a·nu'ri·a
mel'a·nu'ric
me·las'ma
me·le'na
mel'en·ges'trol'
me·le'nic

mel'e·tin
mel'i·lo·tox'in
mel'i·oi·do'sis pl. -ses'
me·li'tis
mel'i·tra'cen
mel'i·tu'ri·a
mel'i·tu'ric
Mel'kers·son-Ro'sen·thal'
  syndrome
mel'o·di·dy'mi·a
mel'o·did'y·mus
me·lom'e·lus
mel'o·rhe'os·to'sis pl. -ses'
me·los'chi·sis
me·lo'ti·a
me·lo'tus
mel'pha·lan'
Melt'zer-Ly'on test
Melt'zer method
mem'ber
mem·bra'na pl. -nae'
—— at·lan'to·oc·cip'i·ta'lis
anterior
—— atlantooccipitalis posterior
—— ba·sa'lis duc'tus sem'i·
cir'cu·lar'is
—— de·cid'u·a
—— de·cid'u·ae'
—— e·las'ti·ca la·ryn'gis
—— fi'bro·e·las'ti·ca la·
ryn'gis
—— fi·bro'sa cap'su·lae' ar·
tic'u·lar'is
—— gran'u·lo'sa
—— hy'a·loi'de·a
—— hy'o·thy're·oi'de·a
—— in'ter·cos·ta'lis ex·
ter'na
—— intercostalis in·ter'na
—— in'ter·os'se·a an'te·
bra'chi·i'
—— interossea cru'ris
—— mu·co'sa na'si'
—— ob'tu·ra·to'ri·a
—— obturatoria sta·pe'dis
—— per'i·ne'i'
—— pro'pri·a duc'tus sem'i·
cir'cu·lar'is
—— pu'pil·lar'is
—— pupillaris per·sis'tens
—— qua·dran'gu·lar'is
—— re·tic'u·lar'is
—— spi·ra'lis
—— sta·pe'dis
—— stat'o·co'ni·o'rum
mac'u·lar'um

—— ster'ni'
—— su'pra·pleu·ra'lis
—— sy·no'vi·a'lis
—— tec·to'ri·a
—— tectoria duc'tus
coch'le·ar'is
—— thy'ro·hy·oi'de·a
—— tym'pa·ni'
—— tympani sec'un·dar'i·a
—— ves·tib'u·lar'is
—— vit're·a
mem'brane'
mem'bra·nec'to·my
mem'bra·no'pro·lif'er·a·
tive
mem'bra·nous
mem'brum pl. -bra
—— in·fe'ri·us
—— mu'li·e'bre'
—— su·pe'ri·us
—— vi·ri'le'
mem'o·ry
men·ac'me
men'a·di'ol'
men'a·di'one'
men·al'gi·a
me·nar'chal
me·nar'che
Men'del
—— reaction
—— reflex
Men'de·lé'ev law
Mé'né·trier' disease
men'hi·dro'sis pl. -ses'
Mé·nière' syndrome
me·nin'ge·al
me·nin'ge·or'rha·phy
me·nin'gi·o·blas·to'ma
  pl. -mas or -ma·ta
me·nin'gi·o·fi'bro·blas·
to'ma pl. -mas or -ma·ta
me·nin'gi·o'ma pl. -mas or
  -ma·ta
me·nin'gi·o·ma·to'sis
me·nin'gi·o·sar·co'ma
  pl. -mas or -ma·ta
me·nin'gi·o·the'li·o'ma
  pl. -mas or -ma·ta
me·nin'gism
men'in·gis'mus
men'in·git'ic
men'in·gi'tis pl. -git'i·des'
—— cir'cum·scrip'ta spi·
na'lis
—— se·ro'sa cir'cum·scrip'ta
—— serosa spi·na'lis
me·nin'go·ar·te'ri·tis

me·nin'go·cele'
me·nin'go·ceph'a·li'tis
me·nin'go·cer'e·bral
me·nin'go·cer'e·bri'tis
me·nin'go·coc'cal
me·nin'go·coc·ce'mi·a
me·nin'go·coc'cic
me·nin'go·coc'cus pl. -ci'
me·nin'go·cor'ti·cal
me·nin'go·cyte'
me·nin'go·en·ceph'a·li'tis
me·nin'go·en·ceph'a·lo·cele'
me·nin'go·en·ceph'a·lo·my'e·li'tis
me·nin'go·en·ceph'a·lop'a·thy
me·nin'go·fi'bro·blas·to'ma pl. -mas or -ma·ta
me·nin'go·ma·la'ci·a
me·nin'go·my'e·li'tis
me·nin'go·my'e·lo·cele'
men'in·gop'a·thy
me·nin'go·ra·chid'i·an
me·nin'go·ra·dic'u·lar
me·nin'go·ra·dic'u·li'tis
me·nin'gor·rha'gi·a
me·nin'gor·rhe'a
men'or·rhe'al
men'in·go'sis
me·nin'go·the'li·al
me·nin'go·the'li·o'ma pl. -mas or -ma·ta
me·nin'go·the'li·om'a·tous
me·nin'go·the'li·um
me·nin'go·vas'cu·lar
men'in·gu'ri·a
me·ninx pl. me·nin'ges
—— prim'i·ti'va
men'is·cec'to·my
me·nis'ci' tac'tus
men'is·ci'tis
me·nis'co·cyte'
me·nis'co·cy·to'sis
me·nis'cus pl. -ci' or -cus·es
—— ar·tic'u·lar'is
—— lat'er·a'lis
—— me'di·a'lis
—— tac'tus
me·noc'tone'
men'o·me'tror·rha'gi·a
men'o·pau'sal
men'o·pause'
men'o·pau'sic
men'o·pla'ni·a
men'or·rha'gi·a
men'or·rhal'gi·a

men'or·rhe'a
me·nos'che·sis pl. -ses'
men'o·sta'si·a
me·nos'ta·sis pl. -ses'
men'o·stax'is
men'o·tro'pins
mens
—— sa'na in cor'po·re sa'no
men'ses'
men'stru·al
men'stru·ant
men'stru·ate', -at'ed, -at'ing
men'stru·a'tion
men'stru·ous
men'stru·um
men'su·al
men'su·ra'tion
men'tal
men·ta'lis
men·ta'tion
men'thol'
men'to·la'bi·al
men'thyl
men'ti·cide'
men'to·an·te'ri·or
men'to·hy'oid'
men'ton'
men'to·pa·ri'e·tal
men'to·pos·te'ri·or
men'tum pl. -ta
mep'a·crine'
mep'a·zine'
me·pen'zo·late'
me·per'i·dine'
me·phen'e·sin
meph'en·ox'a·lone'
me·phen'ter·mine'
me·phen'y·to'in
me·phit'ic
meph'o·bar'bi·tal'
me·piv'a·caine'
me·pred'ni·sone'
me·pro'ba·mate'
mep'ryl·caine'
me·pyr'a·mine'
me·pyr'a·pone'
meq'ui·dox'
me·ral'gi·a
—— par'es·thet'i·ca
mer·al'lu·ride'
mer·bro'min
mer·cap'tan'
mer·cap'tide'
mer·cap'tol'
mer·cap'to·mer'in
mer·cap'to·pu'rine'
mer·cap'tu·ric

Mer·cier' bar
mer·cu'ri·al
mer·cu'ri·al·ism
mer·cu'ric
mer·cu·ro·phyl'line'
mer·cu'rous
mer'cu·ry
mer'er·ga'si·a
mer'er·gas'tic
mer·eth·ox'yl·line'
me·rid'i·an
me·rid'i·a·ni' bul'bi' oc'u·li'
me·rid'i·a'nus pl. -ni'
me·rid'i·o·nal
mer'i·sis pl. -ses'
Mer'kel
—— disk
—— filtrum
mer'o·a·cra'ni·a
mer'o·blas'tic
mer'o·crine
me·roc'ri·nous
mer'o·di'a·stol'ic
mer'o·en·ceph'a·ly
mer'o·gen'e·sis pl. -ses'
mer'o·me'li·a
mer'o·mi'cro·so'mi·a
me·ro'pi·a
mer'o·ra·chis'chi·sis pl. -ses'
me·ros'mi·a
me·rot'o·my
mer'o·zo'ite'
mer'sal·yl
mer'y·cism
Merz'bach'er-Pel'i·zae'us disease
me'sad'
mes'a·me'boid'
mes·an'gi·al
mes·an'gi·um
mes·a'or·ti'tis
mes·ar·te·ri'tis
me·sat'i·ce·phal'ic
me·sat'i·pel'lic
me·sat'i·pel'vic
mes·ax'on'
mes'ca·line'
mes·ec'to·derm'
mes·en'ce·phal'ic
mes·en·ceph'a·li'tis
mes·en·ceph'a·lon'
mes·en·ceph'a·lot'o·my
me·sen'chy·ma
mes·en'chy·mal
mes'en·chyme'

mes·en·chy·mo′ma pl. -mas
    or -ma·ta
mes·en·ter·ec′to·my
mes·en·ter′ic
mes·en·ter′i·o·lum pl. -la
    —— pro·ces′sus ver′mi·
    for′mis
mes·en·ter′i·o·pex′y
mes·en·ter′i·or·rha·phy
mes·en·ter′i·pli·ca′tion
mes·en·ter·i′tis
mes·en·te′ri·um pl. -ri·a
    —— com·mu′ne′
    —— dor·sa′le′ com·nu·ne′
mes·en·ter·on′
mes·en·ter′y
mes·en·to·derm′
mes·en·tor′rha·phy
me′si·ad′
me′si·al
me′si·al·ly
me′si·o·buc′cal
me′si·o·buc′co·oc·clu′sal
me′si·o·cer′vi·cal
me′si·o·clu′sion
me′si·o·dis′tal
me′si·o·gin′gi·val
me′si·o·in·ci′sal
me′si·o·la′bi·al
me′si·o·lin′gual
me′si·o·lin′guo·in·ci′sal
me′si·o·lin′guo·oc·clu′sal
me′si·on′
me′si·o·oc·clu′sal
me′si·o·oc·clu′sion
me′si·o·pul′pal
me′si·o·ver′sion
mes·i′ris
mes·o·ap·pen′di·ci′tis
mes·o·ap·pen′dix pl. -dix·es
    or di·ces′
mes·o·bil′i·ru·bin′o·gen
mes·o·bil′i·vi·o′lin
mes·o·blast′
mes·o·blas·te′ma
mes·o·blas·tem′ic
mes·o·blas′tic
mes·o·bran′chi·al
mes·o·bron·chi′tis
mes·o·car′di·a pl. -ae′ or -as
mes·o·car′di·um
mes·o·car′pal
mes·o·ce′cal
mes·o·ce′cum
mes·o·ce·phal′ic
mes·o·co′lic
mes·o·co′lon

—— as·cen′dens
—— de·scen′dens
—— sig·moi′de·um
—— trans·ver′sum
mes·o·conch′
mes·o·cord′
mes·o·cor′ne·a
mes·o·cra′ni·al
mes·o·cyst′
mes·o·cy·to′ma pl. -mas or
    -ma·ta
mes·o·derm′
mes·o·der′mal
mes·o·di·a·stol′ic
mes·o·dont′
mes·o·du·o·de′nal
mes·o·du·o·de′num pl. -na
    or -nums
mes·o·ep′i·did′y·mis pl. -mi·
    des′
mes·o·e·soph′a·gus
mes·o·gas′ter
mes·o·gas′tric
mes·o·gas′tri·um pl. -tri·a
mes·o·gle′a
me·sog′li·a
mes·o·gli·o′ma pl. -mas or
    -ma·ta
mes·o·glu′te·al
mes·o·glu′te·us pl. -te·i′
mes·o·gnath′ic
me·sog′na·thous
mes·o·il′e·um pl. -e·a
mes·o·je·ju′num pl. -na
mes·o·mere′
mes·o·me′tri·um pl. -tri·a
mes·o·morph′
mes·o·mor′phic
mes·o·mor′phy
mes·o·na′sal
mes·o·neph′ric
mes·o·neph′roid′
mes·o·ne·phro′ma pl. -mas
    or -ma·ta
    —— o·var′i·i′
mes·o·neph′ros′
    pl. -neph′roi′
mes·o·pex′y
mes·o·phle·bi′tis
me·so′pi·a
me·so′pic
mes·o·por′phy·rin
mes·o·pul′mo·num
me·sor·chi·um pl. -chi·a
mes·o·rec′tum
mes·o·rid′a·zine′
mes·o·rop′ter

mes·or·rha·phy
mes·or·rhine′
mes·o·sal·pin′ge·al
mes·o·sal′pinx pl. -sal·
    pin′ges
mes·o·scap′u·la pl. -lae′ or
    -las
mes·o·sig′moid′
mes·o·some′
mes·o·ster′num pl. -nums
    or -na
mes·o·sys·tol′ic
mes·o·ten·din′e·um
mes·o·ten′don
mes·o·the′li·al
mes·o·the′li·o′ma pl. -mas
    or -ma·ta
mes·o·the′li·um pl. -li·a
mes·o·the′nar′
mes·o·tho·ri·um
mes·o·var′i·um pl. -i·a
mes′tra·nol′
mes′u·prine′
me·tab′a·sis pl. -ses′
met′a·bi·o′sis
met′a·bi·sul′fite′
met′a·bol′ic
me·tab′o·lim′e·ter
me·tab′o·lism
me·tab′o·lite′
me·tab′o·lize′, -lized′, -liz′-
    ing
met′a·bu·teth′a·mine′
met′a·bu·tox′y·caine′
met′a·car′pal
met′a·car·pec′to·my
met′a·car′po·pha·lan′ge·al
met′a·car′pus pl. -pi′
met′a·cen′tric
met′a·cer·car′i·a pl. -ae′
met′a·chro·ma′si·a
met′a·chro·mat′ic
met′a·coele′
met′a·cone′
met′a·co′nid′
met′a·cre′sol′
met′a·cy·e′sis pl. -ses′
met′ag·glu′ti·nin
met′a·glob′u·lin
met′a·gran′u·lo·cyte′
met′a·he′mo·glo′bin
met′a·loid′
met′a·mer′ic
me·tam′er·ism
met′a·mor′phic
met′a·mor·phop′si·a

met'a·mor'phose', -phosed', -phos'ing
met'a·mor'pho·sis pl. -ses'
met'a·my'e·lo·cyte'
met'a·neph'ric
met'a·neph'rine'
met'a·neph'ro·gen'ic
met'a·neph'ros'
 pl. -neph'roi'
met'a·phase'
me·taph'y·se'al
me·taph'y·sis pl. -ses'
me·taph'y·si'tis
met'a·pla'si·a
me·tap'la·sis
met'a·plasm
met'a·plas'tic
met'a·pneu·mon'ic
met'a·poph'y·sis
met'a·pro·ter'e·nol'
met'a·ram'i·nol'
met'ar·te'ri·ole'
met'a·ru'bri·cyte'
me·tas'ta·sec'to·my
me·tas'ta·sis pl. -ses'
me·tas'ta·size', -sized', -siz'-ing
met'a·stat'ic
met'a·tar'sal
met'a·tar·sal'gi·a
met'a·tar·sec'to·my
met'a·tar'so·pha·lan'ge·al
met'a·tar'sus pl. -si'
—— ad·duc'to·var'us
—— ad·duc'tus
—— pri'mus var'us
—— var'us
met'a·thal'a·mus
me·tath'e·sis pl. -ses'
met'a·thet'ic
met'a·throm'bin
me·tax'a·lone'
Metch'ni·koff' theory
me·te'cious
met'en·ceph'a·lon'
me'te·or·ism
me'ter also metre
met·es'trus
met'for'min
meth'a·cho'line'
meth'a·cy'cline'
meth'a·done'
meth'al·le·nes'tril
meth'al·thi'a·zide'
meth'am·phet'a·mine'
meth·an'dri·ol'
meth·an'dro·sten'o·lone'

meth'a·nol'
meth·an'the·line'
meth'a·pyr'i·lene'
meth'a·qua'lone'
meth·ar'bi·tal'
meth·a·zol'a·mide'
meth·dil'a·zine'
met'hem·al·bu'min
met'hem·al·bu'mi·ne'mi·a
met'heme'
met·he'mo·glo'bin
met·he'mo·glo'bi·ne'mi·a
met·he'mo·glo'bi·nu'ri·a
me·the'na·mine'
meth'ene'
meth·et'o·in
meth'i·cil'lin
meth·im'a·zole'
me·thi'o·dal'
me·thi'o·nine'
me·this'a·zone'
me·thix'ene'
meth'o·car'ba·mol'
meth'od
meth'od·ol'o·gy
meth'o·hex'i·tal'
meth'o·pho'line'
meth'o·trex'ate'
meth'o·tri·mep'ra·zine'
me·thox'a·mine'
me·thox'sa·len
me·thox'y·flu'rane'
me·thox'y·phen'a·mine'
meth'sco·pol'a·mine'
meth·sux'i·mide'
meth'y·clo·thi'a·zide'
meth'yl
—— an'thra·nil'ate'
—— meth·ac'ryl·ate'
meth'yl·a·cet'y·lene'
meth'yl·al'
meth'yl·am'ine'
meth'yl·am·phet'a·mine'
meth'yl·ate'
meth'yl·a'tion
meth'yl·at'ro·pine'
meth'yl·benz'e·tho'ni·um
meth'yl·cel'lu·lose'
meth'yl·do'pa
meth'yl·do'pate'
meth'yl·ene'
meth'yl·en·o'phil'
meth'yl·e·noph'i·lous
meth'yl·er'go·no'vine'
meth'yl·glu'ca·mine'
meth'yl·gly·ox'al'

meth'yl·ma·lon'ic·ac'i·du'ri·a
meth'yl·mer·cap'tan'
meth'yl·mor'phine'
meth'yl·par'a·fy'nol'
meth'yl·phen'i·date'
meth'yl·phe'no·bar'bi·tal'
meth'yl·phe'nol
meth'yl·pred·nis'o·lone'
meth'yl·pu'rine'
meth'yl·tes·tos'ter·one'
meth'yl·thi'o·u'ra·cil
meth'yl·xan'thine'
meth'y·pry'lon'
meth'y·ser'gide'
me·ti'a·pine'
met'o·clo·pram'ide'
me·to'la·zone'
me·top'ic
met'o·pim'a·zine'
me·to'pi·on'
met'o·qui·zine'
me·tral'gi·a
me·tra·to'ni·a
me·tra·tro'phi·a
me'tre var. of meter
me'trec·ta'si·a
me·trec'to·my
me·trec·to'pi·a
me'treu·ryn'ter
me'treu'ry·sis pl. -ses'
me'tri·a
met'ric
met'ri·o·ce·phal'ic
me·tri'tis
me'tro·cele'
me'tro·col'po·cele'
me'tro·cys·to'sis pl. -ses'
me'tro·cyte'
me'tro·dyn'i·a
me'tro·ec·ta'si·a
me'tro·en'do·me·tri'tis
me'tro·fi·bro'ma pl. -mas or -ma·ta
me'tro·lym'phan·gi'tis
me'tro·ma·la'ci·a
met'ro·ni'da·zole'
me·tro·pa·ral'y·sis pl. -ses'
me'tro·path'i·a hem·or·rhag'i·ca
me'tro·path'ic
me·trop'a·thy
me'tro·per'i·to·ne'al
me'tro·per'i·to·ni'tis
me'tro·phle·bi'tis
me'tro·plas'ty
met'o·pro'lol'

me'trop·to'sis *pl.* -ses'
me'tror·rha'gi·a
me'tror·rhe'a
me'tror·rhex'is
me'tro·sal'pin·gi'tis
me'tro·sal'pin·gog'ra·phy
me'tro·scope'
me'tro·stax'is
me'tro·ste·no'sis *pl.* -ses'
Mett method
me·tu're·dep'a
me·tyr'a·pone'
Meu'len·gracht'
—— diet
—— method
Mey'er
—— loop
—— operation
—— system
Mey'nert
—— bundle
—— commissure
Mey·net' nodes
Mi·an'a fever
mi·an'ser·in
Mi·bel'li disease
mi'ca
mi·ca'ceous
mi'ca·to'sis *pl.* -ses'
mi·celle'
Mi·chae'lis constant
Mi·chel'i syndrome
mi·cra·cous'tic
mi·cran'gi·um
mi'cren·ceph'a·lon'
mi'cren·ceph'a·lous
mi'cren·ceph'a·ly
mi'cro·ab'scess'
mi'cro·ad'e·nop'a·thy
mi'cro·aer'o·phil'ic
mi'cro·a·nal'y·sis *pl.* -ses'
mi'cro·a·nat'o·my
mi'cro·an'eu·rysm
mi'cro·an'gi·o·path'ic
mi'cro·an'gi·op'a·thy
mi'cro·ar·te'ri·o·gram'
mi'cro·ar·te'ri·o·graph'ic
mi'cro·ar·te'ri·og'ra·phy
mi'cro·bac·te'ri·um
mi'crobe'
mi·cro'bi·al
mi·cro'bi·an
mi·cro'bic
mi·cro'bi·ci'dal
mi·cro'bi·cide'
mi'cro·bi·o·log'ic
mi'cro·bi·ol'o·gist

mi'cro·bi·ol'o·gy
mi'cro·bi·ot'ic
mi'cro·blast'
mi'cro·ble·phar'i·a
mi'cro·bleph'a·rism
mi'cro·bleph'a·ron'
mi'cro·bod'y
mi'cro·bra'chi·a
mi'cro·bu·ret'
mi'cro·cal'cu·lus *pl.* -li'
mi'cro·cal'o·rie
mi'cro·car'di·a
mi'cro·cen'trum
mi'cro·ce·phal'ic
mi'cro·ceph'a·lous
mi'cro·ceph'a·lus *pl.* -li'
mi'cro·ceph'a·ly
mi'cro·chei'li·a
mi'cro·chei'ri·a
mi'cro·chem'i·cal
mi'cro·chem'is·try
mi'cro·cir'cu·la'tion
mi'cro·cir'cu·la·to'ry
mi'cro·coc'cus *pl.* -ci'
Mi'cro·coc'cus
—— al'bus
—— au're·us
—— cat'ar·rha'lis
—— cit're·us
—— ga·zog'e·nes'
—— gon'or·rhe'ae'
—— in'tra·cel'lu·lar'is
men'in·git'i·dis
—— lan'ce·o·la'tus
—— mel'i·ten'sis
—— men'in·git'i·dis
—— par'vu·lus
—— pneu·mo'ni·ae'
—— py·og'e·nes'
—— te·trag'e·nus
mi'cro·co'lon
mi'cro·col'o·ny
mi'cro·co·nid'i·um *pl.* -i·a
mi'cro·co'ri·a
mi'cro·cor'ne·a
mi'cro·cous'tic
mi'cro·cra'ni·a
mi'cro·crys'tal·line
mi'cro·cu'rie
mi'cro·cyst'
mi'cro·cys'tic
mi'cro·cy'tase'
mi'cro·cyte'
mi'cro·cy·the'mi·a
mi'cro·cyt'ic
mi'cro·cy·to'sis
mi'cro·dac·tyl'i·a

mi'cro·dac'ty·lous
mi'cro·dac'ty·ly
mi'cro·dis·sec'tion
mi'cro·dont'
mi'cro·don'ti·a
mi'cro·dont·ism
mi'cro·drep'a·no·cyt'ic
mi'cro·drep'a·no·cy·to'sis
mi'cro·e·lec'tro·pho·re'sis
  pl. -ses'
mi'cro·e·lec'tro·pho·
  ret'ic
mi'cro·em'bo·lus *pl.* -li'
mi'cro·en·ceph'a·ly
mi'cro·e·ryth'ro·cyte'
mi'cro·fi'bro·ad'e·no'ma
  pl. -mas *or* -ma·ta
mi'cro·fil'a·ment
mi'cro·fi·lar'i·a *pl.* -i·ae'
mi'cro·flo'ra
mi'cro·fol·lic'u·lar
mi'cro·frac'ture
mi'cro·gam'ete'
mi'cro·ga·me'to·cyte'
mi·crog'a·my
mi'cro·gas'tri·a
mi'cro·gen'e·sis
mi'cro·ge'ni·a
mi'cro·gen'i·tal·ism
mi·crog'li·a
mi·crog'li·al
mi·crog'li·o·cyte'
mi·crog'li·o'ma *pl.* -mas *or*
  -ma·ta
mi·crog'li·o·ma·to'sis *pl.*
  -ses'
mi'cro·glos'si·a
mi'cro·gna'thi·a
mi'cro·gnath'ic
mi·crog'na·thous
mi'cro·gram'
mi'cro·graph'
mi·crog'ra·phy
mi'cro·gy'ri·a
mi'cro·gy'rus
mi'cro·he·pat'i·a
mi'cro·hertz'
mi'crohm'
mi'cro·in·cin'er·a'tion
mi'cro·in'farct'
mi'cro·in·va'sion
mi'cro·ker'a·tome'
mi'cro·len'ti·a
mi'cro·leu'ko·blast'
mi'cro·li'ter
mi'cro·lith'

mi′cro·li·thi′a·sis
—— al′ve·o·lar′is pul·
  mo′num
mi′cro·ma·nom′e·ter
mi′cro·mas′ti·a
mi′cro·max·il′la *pl.* -lae′ *or*
  -las
mi′cro·ma′zi·a
mi′cro·me′li·a
mi·crom′e·ter
mi′cro·meth′od
mi·crom′e·try
mi′cro·mi′cron′
mi′cro·mil′li·gram′
mi′cro·my·e′li·a
mi′cro·my′e·lo·blast′
mi′cro·my′e·lo·lym′pho·
  cyte′
mi′cron′ *pl.* -crons′ *or* -cra
mi′cro·nee′dle
mi′cro·nod′u·lar
mi′cro·nod′u·la′tion
mi′cro·nu′cle·us *pl.* -cle·i′
mi′cro·nu′tri·ent
mi′cro·nych′i·a
mi′cro·or′chism
mi′cro·or·gan′ic
mi′cro·or′gan·ism
mi′cro·pap′u·lar
mi′cro·par′a·site′
mi′cro·pe′nis
mi′cro·phage′
mi′cro·pha′ki·a
mi′cro·phal′lus
mi′cro·phone′
mi′cro·pho′ni·a
mi′cro·pho′no·graph′
mi′croph·thal′mi·a
mi′croph·thal′mos′
mi′croph·thal′mus
mi′cro·phys′ics
mi·cro′pi·a
mi′cro·pi·pet′
mi′cro·pla′si·a
mi′cro·pleth′ys·mog′ra·
  phy
mi′cro·po′di·a
mi·crop′o·dy
mi′cro·po·lar′i·scope′
mi′cro·probe′
mi′cro·pro·so′pi·a
mi′cro·pro′so·pus
mi′cro·pros′o·py
mi′crop′si·a
mi·crop′tic
mi′cro·punc′ture
mi′cro·pus

mi′cro·pyle′
mi′cro·ra′di·og′ra·phy
mi′cror·chid′i·a
mi′cro·res′pi·rom′e·ter
mi′cror·rhi′ni·a
mi′cro·scel′ous
mi′cro·scope′
mi′cro·scop′ic *or* mi′cro·
  scop′i·cal
mi·cros′co·py
mi′cro·sec′ond
mi′cro·sec′tion
mi′cros·mat′ic
mi′cro·so′ma·tog·no′si·a
mi′cro·some′
mi′cro·so′mi·a
mi′cro·spec·trog′ra·phy
mi′cro·spec′tro·pho·tom′e·
  try
mi′cro·spec′tro·scope′
mi′cro·sphe′ro·cyte′
mi′cro·sphe′ro·cy·to′sis
mi′cro·sphyg′mi·a
mi′cro·splanch′nic
mi′cro·sple′ni·a
mi′cro·splen′ic
Mi′cro·spo·rid′i·a
mi′cro·spo·ro′sis *pl.* -ses′
Mi·cros′po·rum
—— au·dou′i·ni′
—— ca′nis
—— fur′fur
—— gyp′se·um
—— la·no′sum
—— mi′nu·tis′si·mus
mi′cro·steth′o·scope′
mi′cro·sto′mi·a
mi′cro·sur′ger·y
mi′cro·the′li·a
mi·cro′ti·a
mi′cro·tome′
mi·crot′o·my
mi′cro·to·pos′co·py
mi′cro·trans·fu′sion
mi′cro·trau′ma
mi′cro·u′nit
mi′cro·vas′cu·lar
mi′cro·vas′cu·la·ture
mi′cro·vil′lus *pl.* -li′
mi′cro·volt′
mi′cro·wave′
mi·crox′y·cyte′
mi′cro·zo′on′ *pl.* -zo′a
mi′cro·zo′o·sper′mi·a
mic′tion
mic′tu·rate′, -rat′ed, -rat′ing
mic′tu·ri′tion

mi′da·flur′
mid′ax·il′la
mid·ax′il·lar′y
mid′bod′y
mid′brain′
mid·car′pal
mid′cla·vic′u·lar
mid′ep·i·gas′tric
mid·fron′tal
midg′et
mid′gut′
mid′line′
mid·oc·cip′i·tal
mid′pain′
mid·pal′mar
mid′riff
mid·sag′it·tal
mid·sec′tion
mid·ster′nal
mid·tar′sal
mid·ven′tral
mid·ves′i·cal
mid′wife′
mid′wife′ry
Mie′scher
—— granuloma
—— tubes
mi′graine′
mi′grain′ous
mi′grant
mi′grate′, -grat′ed, -grat′ing
mi·gra′tion
mi′gra·to′ry
Mik′u·licz
—— cell
—— disease
—— operation
mil·am′me′ter
Mi·lan′-Mark′ley tech-
  nique
mil′dew′
Miles operation
mile′stones′
Mil′i·an
—— erythema
—— sign
mil′i·ar′i·a
—— crys′tal·li′na
—— pro·fun′da
—— pus′tu·lo′sa
mil′i·ar′y
mi·lieu′ *pl.* -lieux′ *or* -lieus′
—— ex·té·rieur′
—— in·té·rieur′
mil′i·per′tine′
mil′i·um *pl.* -i·a
milk

Mil'lar asthma
Mil'lard-Gub'ler syn-
  drome
mil'li·am'me'ter
mil'li·am'pere'
mil'li·bar'
mil'li·cu'rie
mil'li·e·quiv'a·lent
mil'li·gram'
mil'li·li'ter
mil'li·me'ter
mil'li·mi'cro·cu'rie
mil'li·mi'cro·gram'
mil'li·mi'cron'
mil'li·mi'cro·sec'ond
mil'li·mol'
mil'li·mo'lar
mil'li·os'mol'
mil'li·rad'
mil'li·sec'ond
mil'li·u'nit
mil'li·volt'
Mil'lon reagent
mil'phae'
mil·pho'sis
Mil'roy' disease
mim'bane'
mi·me'sis
mi·met'ic
mim·ma'tion
Min'a·ma'ta disease
mind
min'er·al
min'er·al·i·za'tion
min'er·al·o·cor'ti·coid'
min'im
min'i·mal
min'i·mum pl. -ma
——— cog'no·scib'i·le'
——— dis'cer·nib'i·le'
——— le·gib'i·le'
——— sep'a·rab'i·le'
——— vi·sib'i·le'
Min·kow'ski-Chauf·fard'
  syndrome
min'o·cy'cline'
mi'nor
Mi'nor
——— disease
——— tremor
Mi'not-Mur'phy diet
mi'o·car'di·a
mi'o·did'y·mus
mi'o·lec'i·thal
mi·o'sis (contraction of the
  pupil of the eye), pl. -ses'
  ♦meiosis

mi·ot'ic
mire
mir'ror
mir·ya'chit
mis'an·thrope'
mis·an·throp'ic
mis·an'thro·py
mis·car'riage
mis·car'ry, -ried, -ry·ing
mis'ce
mis·ce·ge·na'tion
mis'ci·ble
mi·sog'a·mist
mi·sog'a·my (aversion to
  marriage)
  ♦misogyny
mi·sog'y·nist
mi·sog'y·ny (hatred of wom-
  en)
  ♦misogamy
Mitch'ell disease
mite
mith'ra·my'cin
mith'ri·da'tism
mi'ti·ci'dal
mi'ti·cide'
mit'i·gate', -gat'ed, -gat'ing
mi'tis
mi'to·chon'dri·a sing. -dri·
  on
mi'to·chon'dri·al
mi'to·cro'min
mi'to·gen
mi'to·gen·e'sis pl. -ses'
mi'to·ge·net'ic
mi'to·gen'ic
mi'to·gil'lin
mi'to·mal'cin
mi'tome'
mi'to·my'cin
mi'to·plasm
mi·to'sis pl. -ses'
mi'to·some'
mi'to·tane'
mi·tot'ic
mi'tral
mi'tral·i·za'tion
Mit·su'da reaction
mit'tel·schmerz'
Mit'ten·dorf' dot
mix'o·sco'pi·a
mix'o·scop'ic
mix'ture
mne'mas·the'ni·a
mne'mic
mne·mo·der'mi·a
mne·mon'ic

mne·mon'ics
mo·bil'i·ty
mo·bi·li·za'tion
mo'bi·lize', -lized', -liz'ing
Mö'bi·us
——— disease
——— sign
——— syndrome
Mö'bi·us-Ley'den dystro-
  phy
mo'dal
mod'a·line'
mo·dal'i·ty
mode
mod'er·ate', -at'ed, -at'ing
mod'er·a'tor
mo·di'o·lus pl. -li'
mod'u·la'tion
mod'u·la'tor
Moel'ler
——— fluid
——— glossitis
Moel'ler-Bar'low disease
Mo·ë'na anomaly
mog'i·la'li·a
mog'i·pho'ni·a
Mohr salt
Mohs excision
moi'e·ty
mo'lar
mo·lar'i·form'
mold
mole
mo·lec'to·my
mo·lec'u·lar
mol'e·cule'
mo·li'men pl. -lim'i·na
mo·lin'a·zone'
mo·lin'done'
Mo'lisch test
Mol'ler test
Moll glands
mol·li'ti·es'
——— os'si·um
mol·lus'cum
——— con·ta'gi·o'sum
——— ep'i·the'li·a'le'
——— fi·bro'sum
——— se·ba'ce·um
Mo·lo'ney test
molt also moult
mo·lyb'date'
mo·lyb'de·no'sis
mo·lyb'de·num
mo·lyb'dic
mo·lyb'dous
mo'ment

mo·men'tum
mo'nad'
Mon'a·kow'
—— bundle
—— nucleus
—— striae
—— syndrome
Mo·nal'di drainage
mon·am'ide'
mon·am'ine'
mon·ar'thric
mon·ar·thri'tis
mon·ar'tic'u·lar
mon·as'ter
mon'ath·e·to'sis *pl.* -ses'
mon'a·tom'ic
Mön'cke·berg' arteriosclerosis
Mon·dor'
—— disease
—— syndrome
mo·nen'sin
mon·es'trous
Mon'ge disease
mon'gol·ism
mon'gol·oid'
mo·nil'e·thrix'
Mo·nil'i·a
mo·nil'i·al
Mo·nil'i·a'les'
mon'i·li·a'sis *pl.* -ses'
mo·nil'i·form'
Mo·nil'i·for'mis
mo·nil'i·id
mon'i·tor
Mo·niz' sign
Mon'ne·ret' pulse
mon'o·ar·tic'u·lar
mon'o·az'o
mon'o·ba'sic
mon'o·ben'zone'
mon'o·blast'
mon'o·blep'si·a
mon'o·blep'sis
mon'o·bra'chi·a
mon'o·bra'chi·us
mon'o·bro'mat'ed
mon'o·cel'lu·lar
mon'o·ceph'a·lus *pl.* -li'
mon'o·chord'
mon'o·cho·re'a
mon'o·cho'ri·on'ic
mon'o·chro'ic
mon'o·chro·ma'si·a
mon'o·chro'mat'
mon'o·chro·mat'ic
mon'o·chro'ma·tism

mon'o·chro·mat'o·phil'
mon'o·chro'mic
mon'o·clo'nal
mon'o·cra'ni·us
mon'o·crot'ic
mo·noc'u·lar
mo·noc'u·lus
mon'o·cy·e'sis *pl.* -ses'
mon'o·cys'tic
mon'o·cyte'
mon'o·cyt'ic
mon'o·cy·to'ma *pl.* -mas *or* -ma·ta
mon'o·cy·to·pe'ni·a
mon'o·cy·to'sis *pl.* -ses'
mon'o·dac'ty·lism
mon'o·dac'ty·ly
mon'o·der·mo'ma
mon'o·di·plo'pi·a
mon'o·eth'a·nol'a·mine'
mo·nog'a·my
mon'o·gas'tric
mon'o·ger'mi·nal
mon'o·graph'
mon'o·hy'brid
mon'o·hy'drate'
mon'o·hy'drat'ed
mon'o·hy'dric
mon'o·lay'er
mon'o·lep'sis *pl.* -ses'
mon'o·lob'u·lar
mon'o·loc'u·lar
mon'o·mel'ic
mon'o·mer
mon'o·mer'ic
mon'o·mo·lec'u·lar
mon'o·mo'ri·a
mon'o·mor'phic
mon'o·mor'phous
mon'o·neph'rous
mon'o·neu'ral
mon'o·neu·ri'tis
mon'o·nu'cle·ar
mon'o·nu'cle·ate'
mon'o·nu'cle·o'sis *pl.* -ses'
mon'o·nu'cle·o·tide'
mon'o·pa·re'sis *pl.* -ses'
mon'o·pha'gi·a
mon'o·pha'si·a
mon'o·pha'sic
mon'o·pho'bi·a
mon'o·phos'phate'
mon'o·ple'gi·a
—— fa'ci·a'lis
mon'o·ple'gic
mon'o·po'lar
mon'ops'

mo·nop'si·a
mon'o·pty'chi·al
mon'o·pus
mon·or'chid
mon·or'chid·ism
mon·or'chism
mon'o·sac'cha·ride'
mon'ose'
mon'o·so'di·um
mon'o·some'
mon'o·so'mic
mon'o·so'my
mon'o·spasm
mon'os·tot'ic
mon'o·stra'tal
mon'o·symp'to·mat'ic
mon'o·sy·nap'tic
mon'o·ther'mi·a
mon'o·treme'
mon'o·trich'ic
mo·not'ri·chous
mon'o·trop'ic
mon'o·typ'ic
mon'o·va'lent
mon·ox'ide'
mon'o·zy·got'ic
Mon·ro' foramen
mons *pl.* mon'tes'
—— pu'bis
—— ven'er·is
mon'ster
mon·stros'i·ty
mon'strum *pl.* -stra
Mon·teg'gi·a fracture
Mon'te·ne'gro test
Mont·gom'er·y
—— glands
—— tubercles
mon·tic'u·lus
Moon molars
Moore
—— lightning streaks
—— syndrome
Moor'en ulcer
Moo'ser
—— bodies
—— reaction
—— test
mo·ran'tel
Mo'rax-Ax'en·feld'
—— bacillus
—— conjunctivitis
Mo'rax·el'la
—— lac'u·na'ta
mor'bid
mor·bid'i·ty
mor·bif'ic

mor·bil'li'
mor·bil'li·form'
mor'bus *pl.* -bi'
—— an'gli·cus
—— ca·du'cus
—— cae·ru'le·us
—— car·di'a·cus
—— cas·tren'sis
—— coe·li'a·cus
—— cor'dis
—— cox'ae'
—— cu'cul·lar'is
—— di·vi'nus
—— gal'li·cus
—— hem'or·rhag'i·cus ne'o·na·to'rum
—— hun·gar'i·cus
—— mac'u·lo'sus ne'o·na·to'rum
—— maculosus Werl·hof'i·i'
—— mag'nus
—— major
—— med'i·co'rum
—— mi·ser'i·ae'
—— Pa·get'i' pa·pil'lae'
—— phlyc'te·noi'des'
—— pu'li·car'is
—— re'gi·us
—— sa'cer
—— sal'ta·to'ri·us
—— ve·sic'u·lar'is
—— vir·gin'e·us
—— vul'pis
mor'cel·la'tion
mor'dant
Mo·rel'
—— ear
—— syndrome
Mo·rel'-Krae'pe·lin disease
Mo·rel'-Moore' syndrome
Mor·ga'gni
—— caruncle
—— concha
—— disease
—— foramen
—— glands
—— hernia
—— sinuses
—— syndrome
—— ventricle
Mor·ga'gni-Ad'ams-Stokes' syndrome
Mor·ga'gni·an
—— cataract
—— cyst
—— globules

Mor·ga'gni-Stew'art-Mo·rel' syndrome
Mor'gan bacillus
morgue
mo'ri·a
mor'i·bund
Mor'i·son pouch
Mör'ner
—— reagent
—— test
Mo'ro
—— reflex
—— reaction
—— test
mo'ron'
mor'phe·a *(scleroderma)*
✦morphia
mor'phi·a *(morphine)*
✦morphea
mor'phine'
mor'phin·ism
mor'phi·no·ma'ni·a
mor'pho·gen'e·sis
mor'pho·ge·net'ic
mor'pho·gen'ic
mor·phog'e·ny
mor'pho·log'ic *or* mor'pho·log'i·cal
mor·phol'o·gist
mor·phol'o·gy
mor·phom'e·try
Mor'qui·o syndrome
Mor'ris method
mors
—— pu'ta·ti'va
—— su'bi·ta
mor'sal
mor'sus
—— stom'a·chi'
—— ven·tric'u·li'
mor'tal
mor·tal'i·ty
mor'tar
mor'ti·fi·ca'tion
mor'ti·fy', -fied', -fy'ing
Mor'ton
—— foot
—— metatarsalgia
—— syndrome
—— toe
mor'tu·ar'y
mor'u·la
Mor'van disease
mo·sa'ic
mo·sa'i·cism
Mosch'co·witz'
—— disease

—— operation
—— test
Mo'sen·thal' test
mos·qui'to *pl.* -toes *or* -tos
Moss groups
Moss'man fever
Mo·tais' operation
moth'er
mo'tile
mo·til'i·ty
mo'ti·va'tion
mo'to·neu'ron'
mo'tor
mo·tor'ic
mo·to'ri·us
Mott law
mot'tle, -tled, -tling
mouches' vo·lantes'
mou·lage'
moult *var. of* molt
mound
moun'tant
mouth
mouth'-to-mouth'
mouth'wash'
mouve·ment' de ma·nège'
move'a·ble
move'ment
Mu·cam'bo fever
mu·ci·car'mine
mu·cif'er·ous
mu·ci·gen
mu·cig'e·nous
mu·ci·lage
mu·ci·lag'i·nous
mu·ci·la'go' *pl.* -lag'i·nes'
mu'cin
mu·ci·no·blast'
mu·cin'o·gen
mu·ci·noid'
mu·ci·no'sis
mu·ci·nous
mu·ci·nu'ri·a
mu·cip'a·rous
mu·co·buc'cal
mu·co·cele'
mu·co·co·li'tis
mu·co·col'pos
mu·co·cu·ta'ne·ous
mu·co·derm'
mu·co·en·ter·i'tis
mu'coid'
mu·co·i'tin·sul·fu'ric
mu·co·lip'i·do'sis *pl.* -ses'
mu·co·lyt'ic
mu·co·mem'bra·nous
mu·co·per'i·os'te·al

mu'co·per'i·os'te·um *pl.*
-te·a
mu'co·pol'y·sac'cha·ride'
mu'co·pol'y·sac'cha·ri·
do'sis *pl.* -ses'
mu'co·pro'tein'
mu'co·pu'ru·lent
mu'co·pus
Mu'cor'
Mu'co·ra'les'
mu'cor·my·co'sis *pl.* -ses'
mu·co'sa
mu·co'sal
mu·co·sal'pinx *pl.* -sal·
pin'ges
mu'co·san·guin'e·ous
mu'co·se'rous
mu·co'sin
mu·co'sis *pl.* -ses'
mu·co·si'tis
mu·cos'i·ty
mu'co·stat'ic
mu'cous *(pertaining to mucus)*
♦*mucus*
mu'co·vis'ci·do'sis *pl.* -ses'
mu'cro·nate'
mu'cus *(the secretion of mucous membranes)*
♦*mucous*
Muehr'cke lines
Muel'ler maneuver
mu·guet'
mu·lat'to
mu'li·e'bri·a
mu'li·eb'ri·ty
Mül'ler
—— duct
—— fibers
—— fixing fluid
—— hillock
—— law
—— muscle
—— syndrome
—— test
—— tubercle
mül·le'ri·an
mult·an'gu·lar
mult·an'gu·lum *pl.* -la
—— ma'jus
—— mi'nus
mul'ti·ar·tic'u·lar
mul'ti·cap'su·lar
mul'ti·cel'lu·lar
mul'ti·cen'tric
mul'ti·cus'pid
mul'ti·cus'pi·date'

mul'ti·cys'tic
mul'ti·den'tate'
mul'ti·dig'i·tate'
mul'ti·fac'et·ed
mul'ti·fac·to'ri·al
mul'ti·fa·mil'i·al
mul'ti·fid
mul·tif'i·dus *pl.* -di'
mul'ti·flag'el·late'
mul'ti·fo'cal
mul'ti·form'
mul'ti·glan'du·lar
mul'ti·grav'i·da
mul'ti·gra·vid'i·ty
mul'ti·lo'bar
mul'ti·lobed'
mul'ti·lob'u·lar
mul'ti·loc'u·lar
mul'ti·loc'u·lat'ed
mul'ti·mam'mae'
mul'ti·nod'u·lar
mul'ti·nu'cle·ar
mul'ti·nu'cle·ate'
mul'ti·nu'cle·at'ed
mul·tip'a·ra
mul'ti·par'i·ty
mul·tip'a·rous
mul'ti·par'tite'
mul'ti·pen'nate'
mul'ti·pha'sic
mul'ti·ple
mul'ti·plex'
mul'ti·plic'i·ty
mul'ti·po'lar
mul'ti·va'lent
mum'mi·fi·ca'tion
mum'mi·fied'
mumps
Mun'chau'sen syndrome
Münch'mey'er disease
mu'ral
mu·ram'i·dase'
mu'ri·at'ic
mur'mur
Mur'phy
—— button
—— sign
Mur'phy-Sturm' lympho-
sarcoma
mur·ri'na
Mu'ru·tu'cu fever
Mus'ca
—— do·mes'ti·ca
—— vet'us·tis'si·ma
—— vi·ci'na
mus'cae' vol'i·tan'tes'
mus'ca·rine'

mus'ca·rin·ism
mus'cle
—— of Bell
—— of Gant'zer
—— of Geg'en·baur'
—— of Gru'ber
—— of Hall
—— of Hen'le
—— of Hor'ner
—— of Hous'ton
—— of Jung
—— of Klein
—— of Land'ström
—— of Lud'wig
—— of Ma·cal'lis·ter
—— of Mül'ler
—— of Raux
—— of Ri'o·lan'
—— of San'to·ri'ni
—— of Sap'pey
—— of Treitz
—— of Wood
mus'cu·lar
mus'cu·lar'is
—— mu·co'sae'
mus'cu·lar'i·ty
mus'cu·la'tion
mus'cu·la·ture
mus'cu·li'
—— ab·dom'i·nis
—— ar'rec·to'res' pi·lo'rum
—— bul'bi'
—— cap'i·tis
—— coc·cyg'e·i'
—— col'li'
—— dor'si'
—— ex·trem'i·ta'tis in·fe'ri·
o'ris
—— extremitatis su·pe'ri·
o'ris
—— in·ci·si'vi' la'bi·i' in·fe'ri·
o'ris
—— incisivi labii su·pe'ri·
o'ris
—— in'fra·hy·oi'de·i'
—— in'ter·cos·ta'les' ex·
ter'ni'
—— intercostales in·ter'ni'
—— intercostales in'ti·mi'
—— in'ter·os'se·i' dor·sa'les'
ma'nus
—— interossei dorsales pe'-
dis
—— interossei pal·mar'es'
—— interossei plan·tar'es'
—— interossei vo·lar'es'
—— in'ter·spi·na'les'

—— interspinales cer'vi·cis
—— interspinales lum·bo'rum
—— interspinales tho·ra'cis
—— in'ter·trans'ver·sar'i·i'
—— intertransversarii an·te'ri·o'res'
—— intertransversarii anteriores cer'vi·cis
—— intertransversarii lat'er·a'les'
—— intertransversarii lat·er·a·les lum·bo'rum
—— intertransversarii me'di·a'les'
—— intertransversarii mediales lum·bo'rum
—— intertransversarii pos·te'ri·o'res'
—— intertransversarii posteriores cer'vi·cis
—— intertransversarii tho·ra'cis
—— la·ryn'gis
—— lev'a·to'res' cos·tar'um
—— levatores costarum brev'es'
—— levatores costarum lon'gi'
—— lin'guae'
—— lum'bri·ca'les'
—— lumbricales ma'nus
—— lumbricales pe'dis
—— mem'bri' in·fe'ri·o'ris
—— membri su·pe'ri·o'ris
—— mul·tif'i·di'
—— oc'u·li'
—— os·sic'u·lo'rum au·di'tus
—— os'sis hy·oi'de·i'
—— pa·la'ti' et fau'ci·um
—— pap'il·lar'es'
—— papillares sep·ta'les'
—— pec'ti·na'ti'
—— per'i·ne'i'
—— ro'ta·to'res'
—— rotatores brev'es'
—— rotatores cer'vi·cis
—— rotatores lon'gi'
—— rotatores lum·bo'rum
—— rotatores tho·ra'cis
—— sub'cos·ta'les'
—— su'pra·hy·oi'de·i'
—— tho·ra'cis
mus·cu·lo·ap'o·neu·rot'ic
mus'cu·lo·cu·ta'ne·ous
mus'cu·lo·der'mic

mus'cu·lo·fas'ci·al
mus'cu·lo·fi'brous
mus'cu·lo·in·tes'ti·nal
mus'cu·lo·mem'bra·nous
mus'cu·lo·phren'ic
mus'cu·lo·skel'e·tal
mus'cu·lo·spi'ral
mus'cu·lo·ten'di·nous
mus'cu·lus *pl.* -li'
—— ab·duc'tor dig'i·ti' min'i·mi'
—— abductor digiti quin'ti'
—— abductor hal'lu·cis
—— abductor pol'li·cis brev'is
—— abductor pollicis lon'-gus
—— ad·duc'tor brev'is
—— adductor hal'lu·cis
—— adductor lon'gus
—— adductor mag'nus
—— adductor min'i·mus
—— adductor pol'li·cis
—— an·co'nae·us
—— an·co'ne·us
—— an'ti·trag'i·cus
—— ar·tic'u·lar'is
—— articularis cu'bi·ti'
—— articularis ge'nu'
—— articularis ge'nus
—— ar'y·ep'i·glot'ti·cus
—— ar'y·tae·noi'de·us ob·li'quus
—— arytaenoideus trans·ver'sus
—— ar'y·te·noi'de·us ob·li'quus
—— arytenoideus trans·ver'sus
—— au·ric'u·lar'is anterior
—— auricularis posterior
—— auricularis superior
—— bi'ceps' bra'chi·i'
—— biceps fem'o·ris
—— bi'pen·na'tus
—— bra'chi·a'lis
—— bra'chi·o·ra'di·a'lis
—— bron'cho·e'so·phag'e·us
—— bron'cho·oe'so·phag'e·us
—— buc'ci·na'tor
—— buc'co·pha·ryn'ge·us
—— bul'bo·cav'er·no'sus
—— bul'bo·spon'gi·o'sus
—— ca·ni'nus
—— cer'a·to·cri·coi'de·us
—— cer'a·to·pha·ryn'ge·us

—— chon'dro·glos'sus
—— chon'dro·pha·ryn'ge·us
—— cil'i·ar'is
—— coc·cyg'e·us
—— con·stric'tor pha·ryn'gis inferior
—— constrictor pharyngis me'di·us
—— constrictor pharyngis superior
—— co'ra·co·bra'chi·a'lis
—— cor'ru·ga'tor su'per·cil'i·i'
—— cre·mas'ter
—— cri'co·ar'y·tae·noi'de·us lat'er·a'lis
—— cricoarytaenoideus posterior
—— cri'co·ar'y·te·noi'de·us lat'er·a'lis
—— cricoarytenoideus posterior
—— cri'co·pha·ryn'ge·us
—— cri'co·thy're·oi'de·us
—— cri'co·thy·roi'de·us
—— cu·ta'ne·us
—— del·toi'de·us
—— de·pres'sor an'gu·li' o'ris
—— depressor la'bi·i' in·fe'ri·o'ris
—— depressor sep'ti' na'si'
—— depressor su'per·cil'i·i'
—— di·gas'tri·cus
—— dil'a·ta'tor pu·pil'lae'
—— di·la'tor pu·pil'lae'
—— ep'i·cra'ni·us
—— ep'i·troch'le·o·an·co'nae·us
—— e·rec'tor spi'nae'
—— ex·ten'sor car'pi' ra'di·a'lis brev'is
—— extensor carpi radialis lon'gus
—— extensor carpi ul·nar'is
—— extensor dig'i·ti' min'i·mi'
—— extensor digiti quin'ti' pro'pri·us
—— extensor dig'i·to'rum brev'is
—— extensor digitorum com·mu'nis
—— extensor digitorum lon'gus

—— extensor hal'lu·cis brev'is
—— extensor hallucis lon'-gus
—— extensor in'di·cis
—— extensor indicis pro'pri·us
—— extensor pol'li·cis brev'is
—— extensor pollicis lon'-gus
—— fib'u·lar'is brev'is
—— fibularis lon'gus
—— fibularis ter'ti·us
—— fix·a'tor ba'se·os' sta·pe'dis
—— flex'or ac'ces·so'ri·us
—— flexor car'pi' ra'di·a'lis
—— flexor carpi ul·nar'is
—— flexor dig'i·ti' min'i·mi' brev'is
—— flexor digiti quin'ti' brev'is
—— flexor dig'i·to'rum brev'is
—— flexor digitorum lon'-gus
—— flexor digitorum pro·fun'dus
—— flexor digitorum sub·li'mis
—— flexor digitorum su'per·fi'ci·a'lis
—— flexor hal'lu·cis brev'is
—— flexor hallucis lon'gus
—— flexor pol'li·cis brev'is
—— flexor pollicis lon'gus
—— fron·ta'lis
—— fu'si·for'mis
—— gas'troc·ne'mi·us
—— ge·mel'lus inferior
—— gemellus superior
—— ge'ni·o·glos'sus
—— ge'ni·o·hy·oi'de·us
—— glos'so·pal'a·ti'nus
—— glos'so·pha·ryn'ge·us
—— glu'tae·us max'i·mus
—— glutaeus me'di·us
—— glutaeus min'i·mus
—— glu'te·us max'i·mus
—— gluteus me'di·us
—— gluteus min'i·mus
—— grac'i·lis
—— hel'i·cis major
—— helicis minor
—— hy'o·glos'sus
—— i·li'a·cus

—— il'i·o·coc·cyg'e·us
—— il'i·o·cos·ta'lis
—— iliocostalis cer'vi·cis
—— iliocostalis dor'si'
—— iliocostalis lum·bo'rum
—— iliocostalis tho·ra'cis
—— il'i·o·pso'as
—— in'ci·su'rae' hel'i·cis
—— in'fra·spi·na'tus
—— is'chi·o·cav'er·no'sus
—— la·tis'si·mus dor'si'
—— le·va'tor an'gu·li' o'ris
—— levator a'ni'
—— levator glan'du·lae' thy're·oi'de·ae'
—— levator glandulae thy·roi'de·ae'
—— levator la'bi·i' su·pe'ri·o'ris
—— levator labii superioris a·lae'que' na'si'
—— levator pal·pe'brae' su·pe'ri·o'ris
—— levator pros'ta·tae'
—— levator scap'u·lae'
—— levator ve'li' pal'a·ti'ni'
—— lon·gis'si·mus
—— longissimus cap'i·tis
—— longissimus cer'vi·cis
—— longissimus dor'si'
—— longissimus tho·ra'cis
—— lon'gi·tu'di·na'lis inferior lin'guae'
—— longitudinalis superior lin'guae'
—— lon'gus cap'i·tis
—— longus col'li'
—— mas·se'ter
—— men·ta'lis
—— mul·tif'i·dus
—— my'lo·hy·oi'de·us
—— my'lo·pha·ryn'ge·us
—— na·sa'lis
—— ob·li'quus au·ric'u·lae'
—— obliquus cap'i·tis inferi·or
—— obliquus capitis superi·or
—— obliquus ex·ter'nus ab·dom'i·nis
—— obliquus inferior bul'bi'
—— obliquus inferior oc'u·li'
—— obliquus in·ter'nus ab·dom'i·nis
—— obliquus superior bul'-bi'

—— obliquus superior oc'u·li'
—— ob·tu·ra'tor ex·ter'nus
—— obturator in·ter'nus
—— ob·tu·ra·to'ri·us ex·ter'nus
—— obturatorius in·ter'nus
—— oc·cip'i·ta'lis
—— oc·cip'i·to·fron·ta'lis
—— o'mo·hy·oi'de·us
—— op·po'nens dig'i·ti' min'i·mi'
—— opponens digiti quin'ti' ma'nus
—— opponens digiti quinti pe'dis
—— opponens pol'li·cis
—— or·bic'u·lar'is
—— orbicularis oc'u·li'
—— orbicularis o'ris
—— or'bi·ta'lis
—— pal'a·to·glos'sus
—— pal'a·to·pha·ryn'ge·us
—— pal·mar'is brev'is
—— palmaris lon'gus
—— pap'il·lar'is anterior ven·tric'u·li' dex'tri'
—— papillaris anterior ven·triculi si·nis'tri'
—— papillaris posterior ventriculi dex'tri'
—— papillaris posterior ventriculi si·nis'tri'
—— pec·tin'e·us
—— pec'to·ra'lis major
—— pectoralis minor
—— per'o·nae'us brev'is
—— peronaeus lon'gus
—— peronaeus ter'ti·us
—— per'o·ne'us brev'is
—— peroneus lon'gus
—— peroneus ter'ti·us
—— pha·ryn'go·pal'a·ti'nus
—— pir'i·for'mis
—— plan·tar'is
—— pleu'ro·e'so·phag'e·us
—— pleu'ro·oe·so'phag'e·us
—— pop·lit'e·us
—— pro·ce'rus
—— pro·na'tor qua·dra'tus
—— pronator te'res'
—— pros·tat'i·cus
—— pso'as major
—— psoas minor
—— pter'y·goi'de·us ex·ter'nus
—— pterygoideus in·ter'nus

—— pterygoideus lat′er·a′lis
—— pterygoideus me′di·a′lis
—— pter′y·go·pha·ryn′ge·us
—— pu′bo·coc·cyg′e·us
—— pu′bo·pros·tat′i·cus
—— pu′bo·rec·ta′lis
—— pu′bo·vag′i·na′lis
—— pu′bo·ves′i·ca′lis
—— py·ram′i·da′lis
—— pyramidalis au·ric′u·lae′
—— qua·dra′tus fem′o·ris
—— quadratus la′bi·i′ in·fe′ri·o′ris
—— quadratus labii su·pe′ri·o′ris
—— quadratus lum·bo′rum
—— quadratus plan′tae′
—— qua′dri·ceps′ fem′o·ris
—— rec′to·coc·cyg′e·us
—— rec′to·u′re·thra′lis
—— rec′to·u′ter·i′nus
—— rec′to·ves′i·ca′lis
—— rec′tus ab·dom′i·nis
—— rectus cap′i·tis anterior
—— rectus capitis lat′er·a′lis
—— rectus capitis posterior major
—— rectus capitis posterior minor
—— rectus fem′o·ris
—— rectus inferior bul′bi′
—— rectus inferior oc′u·li′
—— rectus lat′er·a′lis bul′bi′
—— rectus lateralis oc′u·li′
—— rectus me′di·a′lis bul′bi′
—— rectus medialis oc′u·li′
—— rectus superior bul′bi′
—— rectus superior oc′u·li′
—— rhom·boi′de·us major
—— rhomboideus minor
—— ri·so′ri·us
—— sa′cro·coc·cyg′e·us anterior
—— sacrococcygeus dor·sa′lis
—— sacrococcygeus posterior
—— sacrococcygeus ven·tra′lis
—— sa′cro·spi·na′lis
—— sal·pin′go·pha·ryn′ge·us
—— sar·to′ri·us
—— sca·le′nus anterior
—— scalenus me′di·us
—— scalenus min′i·mus
—— scalenus posterior

—— sem′i·mem′bra·no′sus
—— sem′i·spi·na′lis
—— semispinalis cap′i·tis
—— semispinalis cer′vi·cis
—— semispinalis dor′si′
—— semispinalis tho·ra′cis
—— sem′i·ten′di·no′sus
—— ser·ra′tus anterior
—— serratus posterior inferior
—— serratus posterior superior
—— skel′e·ti′
—— so′le·us
—— sphinc′ter
—— sphincter am·pul′lae′
—— sphincter ampullae hep′a·to·pan′cre·at′i·cae′
—— sphincter a′ni′ ex·ter′nus
—— sphincter ani in·ter′nus
—— sphincter duc′tus cho·led′o·chi′
—— sphincter pu·pil′lae′
—— sphincter py·lo′ri′
—— sphincter u·re′thrae′
—— sphincter urethrae mem′bra·na′ce·ae′
—— spi·na′lis
—— spinalis cap′i·tis
—— spinalis cer′vi·cis
—— spinalis dor′si′
—— spinalis tho·ra′cis
—— sple′ni·us cap′i·tis
—— splenius cer′vi·cis
—— sta·pe′di·us
—— ster·na′lis
—— ster′no·clei′do·mas·toi′de·us
—— ster′no·hy·oi′de·us
—— ster′no·thy′re·oi′de·us
—— ster′no·thy·roi′de·us
—— sty′lo·glos′sus
—— sty′lo·hy·oi′de·us
—— sty′lo·pha·ryn′ge·us
—— sub·cla′vi·us
—— sub·scap′u·lar′is
—— su′pi·na′tor
—— su′pra·spi·na′tus
—— sus′pen·so′ri·us du′o·de′ni′
—— tar·sa′lis inferior
—— tarsalis superior
—— tem′po·ra′lis
—— tem′po·ro·pa·ri′e·ta′lis
—— ten′sor fas′ci·ae′ la′tae′
—— tensor tym′pa·ni′

—— tensor ve′li′ pal′a·ti′ni′
—— te′res′ major
—— teres minor
—— thy′re·o·ar′y·tae·noi′de·us
—— thy′re·o·ar′y·te·noi′de·us
—— thy′re·o·ep′i·glot′ti·cus
—— thy′re·o·hy·oi′de·us
—— thy′re·o·pha·ryn′ge·us
—— thy′ro·ar′y·te·noi′de·us
—— thy′ro·ep′i·glot′ti·cus
—— thy′ro·hy·oi′de·us
—— tib′i·a′lis anterior
—— tibialis posterior
—— tra·che·a′lis
—— trag′i·cus
—— trans·ver′so·spi·na′lis
—— trans·ver′sus ab·dom′i·nis
—— transversus au·ric′u·lae′
—— transversus lin′guae′
—— transversus men′ti′
—— transversus nu′chae′
—— transversus per′i·ne′i′ pro·fun′dus
—— transversus perinei su′per·fi′ci·a′lis
—— transversus tho·ra′cis
—— tra·pe′zi·us
—— tri·an′gu·lar′is
—— tri′ceps′ bra′chi·i′
—— triceps su′rae′
—— u′ni·pen·na′tus
—— u′vu·lae′
—— vas′tus in·ter·me′di·us
—— vastus lat′er·a′lis
—— vastus me′di·a′lis
—— ven·tric′u·lar′is
—— ver′ti·ca′lis lin′guae′
—— vis′ce·rum
—— vo·ca′lis
—— zy′go·mat′i·cus
—— zygomaticus major
—— zygomaticus minor
mus·si·ta′tion
mus′tard
mus′tine′
mu′ta·cism
mu′ta·gen
mu′ta·gen′e·sis
mu′ta·gen′ic
mu′tant
mu′tase′
mu·ta′tion
mu·ta′tion·al

mute
mu'ti·late', -lat'ed, -lat'ing
mu'ti·la'tion
mut'ism
mu'tu·al·ism
my·al'gi·a
my·al'gic
my'as·the'ni·a
—— grav'is
my'as·then'ic
my'a·to'ni·a *(absence of muscle tone)*
♦myotonia
—— con·gen'i·ta
my·at'ro·phy
my·ce'li·al
my·ce'li·oid'
my·ce'li·um *pl.* -li·a
my·ce'tes'
my·ce·the'mi·a
my·ce·tis'mus *pl.* -mi'
my·ce'to·gen'ic
my'ce·tog'e·nous
my'ce·to'ma
My'co·bac·te'ri·a'ce·ae'
my'co·bac·te'ri·um *pl.* -a
My'co·bac·te'ri·um
—— bo'vis
—— lep'rae'
—— par'a·tu·ber'cu·lo'sis
—— phle'i'
—— tu·ber'cu·lo'sis
—— tuberculosis var. mu'ris
—— ul'cer·ans'
my'co·ci'din
my'co·der'ma
my'coid'
my·col'o·gy
my'co·myr'in·gi'tis
My'co·plas'ma
—— ar·thrit'i·dis
—— my·coi'des'
—— pneu·mo'ni·ae'
—— pul·mo'nis
My'co·plas'ma·ta'ce·ae'
my'co·plas·mo'sis *pl.* -ses'
my'cose'
my·co'sis *pl.* -ses'
—— fun·goi'des'
—— fungoides d'em·blée'
my·cot'ic
—— o·ti'tis ex·ter'na
my'co·tox'i·co'sis *pl.* -ses'
myc·ter'ic
my·de'sis
my·dri'a·sis *pl.* -ses'
myd'ri·at'ic

my·ec'to·my
my·ec'to·py
my'el·ap'o·plex'y
my'el·at'ro·phy
my'e·le'mi·a
my'el·en·ce·phal'ic
my'el·en·ceph'a·li'tis
my'el·en·ceph'a·lon'
my·el'ic
my'e·lin
my'e·li·nat'ed
my'e·lin'ic
my'e·lin·i·za'tion
my'e·li·noc'la·sis
my'e·lin'o·gen'e·sis
my'e·li·nol'y·sis *pl.* -ses'
my'e·li·nop'a·thy
my'e·li·no'sis
my'e·lit'ic
my'e·li'tis
my'e·lo·blast'
my'e·lo·blas·te'mi·a
my'e·lo·blas'tic
my'e·lo·blas·to'ma *pl.* -mas *or* -ma·ta
my'e·lo·blas·to'sis
my'e·lo·cele'
my'e·lo·cys'to·cele'
my'e·lo·cys·tog'ra·phy
my'e·lo·cyte'
my'e·lo·cy·the'mi·a
my'e·lo·cyt'ic
my'e·lo·cy·to'ma *pl.* -mas *or* -ma·ta
my'e·lo·cy·to'sis *pl.* -ses'
my'e·lo·dys·pla'si·a
my'e·lo·en·ce·phal'ic
my'e·lo·en·ceph'a·li'tis
my'e·lo·fi·bro'sis *pl.* -ses'
my'e·lo·gen'e·sis
my'e·lo·gen'ic
my'e·log'e·nous
my'e·log'e·ny
my'e·lo·gone'
my'e·lo·gram'
my'e·log'ra·phy
my'e·loid'
my'e·lo·ken'tric
my'e·lo·li·po'ma *pl.* -mas *or* -ma·ta
my'e·lo·lym·phan'gi·o'ma
my'e·lo·lym'pho·cyte'
my'e·lol'y·sis *pl.* -ses'
my'e·lo'ma *pl.* -mas *or* -ma·ta
my'e·lo·ma·la'ci·a
my'e·lo·ma·to'sis *pl.* -ses'

my'e·lo·me·ni·a
my'e·lo·men·in·gi'tis
my'e·lo·me·nin'go·cele'
my'e·lo·mere'
my'e·lo·mon'o·cyte'
my'e·lo·mon'o·cyt'ic
my'e·lon'
my'e·lo·neu·ri'tis
my'e·lo·pa·ral'y·sis *pl.* -ses'
my'e·lo·path'ic
my'e·lop'a·thy
my'e·lop'e·tal
my'e·lo·phthi'sis *pl.* -ses'
my'e·lo·plast'
my'e·lo·plax'
my'e·lo·ple'gi·a
my'e·lo·poi·e'sis *pl.* -ses'
my'e·lo·pore'
my'e·lo·pro·lif'er·a·tive
my'e·lo·ra·dic'u·li'tis
my'e·lo·ra·dic'u·lo·dys· pla'si·a
my'e·lo·ra·dic'u·lop'a·thy
my'e·lor·rha'gi·a
my'e·lo·sar·co'ma *pl.* -mas *or* -ma·ta
my'e·los'chi·sis *pl.* -ses'
my'e·lo·scin'to·gram'
my'e·lo·scin·tog'ra·phy
my'e·lo·scle·ro'sis *pl.* -ses'
my'e·lo·scle·rot'ic
my'e·lo'sis *pl.* -ses'
my'e·lo·spon'gi·um *pl.* -gi·a
my'e·lot'o·my
my'e·lo·tox'ic
my'en·ter'ic
my·en'ter·on'
My'er·son reflex
my'es·the'si·a
my·i'a·sis *pl.* -ses'
my·i'o·des·op'si·a
my·i'tis
my·o·ar'chi·tec·ton'ic
my'o·blast'
my'o·blas'tic
my'o·blas·to'ma *pl.* -mas *or* -ma·ta
my'o·bra'di·a
my'o·car'di·al
my'o·car'di·op'a·thy
my'o·car·di'tis
my'o·car'di·um *pl.* -di·a
my'o·car·do'sis *pl.* -ses'
my'o·cele'
my'o·ce'li·al'gi·a
my'o·cep'tor
my'o·chor·di'tis

my′o·clo′ni·a
my′o·clon′ic
my′o·clo′nus
my′o·coele′
my′o·col·pi′tis
my′o·cyte′
my′o·cy·tol′y·sis
my′o·cy·to′ma *pl.* -mas *or*
  -ma·ta
my′o·dyn′i·a
my′o·dys·to′ni·a
my′o·dys·tro′phi·a
—— fe·ta′lis
my′o·dys′tro·phy
my′o·e·de′ma
my′o·e·las′tic
my′o·en′do·car·di′tis
my′o·ep′i·the′li·al
my′o·ep′i·the′li·o′ma
  pl. -mas *or* -ma·ta
my′o·ep′i·the′li·um
my′o·fas′ci·al
my′o·fas·ci′tis
my′o·fi′bril
my′o·fi·bro′ma *pl.* -mas *or*
  -ma·ta
my′o·fi′bro·sar·co′ma
  pl. -mas *or* -ma·ta
my′o·fi·bro′sis *pl.* -ses′
my′o·fi′bro·si′tis
my′o·fil′a·ment
my′o·ge·lo′sis *pl.* -ses′
my′o·gen
my′o·gen′ic
my·og′e·nous
my′o·glo′bin
my′o·glo′bi·nu′ri·a
my′o·glob′u·lin
my′o·gram′
my′o·graph′
my′o·graph′ic
my′o·hem′a·tin
my′o·he′mo·glo′bin
my′o·he′mo·glo′bi·nu′ri·a
my′oid′
my′o·ki′nase′
my′o·ki·ne′si·o·gram′
my′o·ki·ne′si·og′ra·phy
my′o·ky′mi·a
my′o·li·po′ma *pl.* -mas *or*
  -ma·ta
my′o·lo′gi·a
my·ol′y·sis
my·o′ma *pl.* -mas *or* -ma·ta
—— stri′o·cel′lu·lar′e′
—— tel·an′gi·ec′to·des′
my′o·ma·la′ci·a

—— cor′dis
my·o′ma·to′sis
my·om′a·tous
my′o·mec′to·my
my′o·mere′
my′o·me′tri·al
my′o·me·tri′tis
my′o·me′tri·um
my′o·ne·cro′sis
my′o·neu′ral
my′o·neu·ral′gi·a
my′o·pal′mus
my′o·pa·ral′y·sis *pl.* -ses′
my′o·pa·re′sis *pl.* -ses′
my′o·path′i·a
—— ra·chit′i·ca
my′o·path′ic
my·op′a·thy
my′ope′
my′o·per′i·car·di′tis
my′o·pha′gi·a
my·o′pi·a
my·op′ic
my′o·plasm
my′o·plas′tic
my′o·plas′ty
my′o·psy·chop′a·thy
my′o·psy·cho′sis *pl.* -ses′
my·or′rha·phy
my′o·sal′pin·gi′tis
my′o·sal′pinx′ *pl.* -sal·
  pin′ges′
my′o·san′
my′o·sar·co′ma *pl.* -mas *or*
  -ma·ta
my′o·schwan·no′ma
  pl. -mas *or* -ma·ta
my′o·scle·ro′sis *pl.* -ses′
my′o·sin
my′o·sin′o·gen
my′o·sit′ic
my′o·si′tis
—— os·sif′i·cans′
my′o·spasm
my′o·su′ture
my′o·syn′o·vi′tis
my′o·tac′tic *(pertaining to*
  muscular sense)
♦*myotatic*
my′ot′a·sis
my′o·tat′ic *(pertaining to*
  stretching of a muscle)
♦*myotactic*
my′o·ten′di·nous
my′o·ten′o·si′tis
my′o·te·not′o·my
my′o·tome′

my·ot′o·my
my′o·to′ni·a *(tonic muscle*
  spasm)
♦*myatonia*
—— ac′qui·si′ta
—— a·troph′i·ca
—— con·gen′i·ta
—— congenita in′ter·
  mit′tens
—— dys·troph′i·ca
my′o·ton′ic
my·ot′o·nus
my′o·tro′phic
my·ot′ro·phy
my′o·tube′
my·rin′ga
myr′in·gec′to·my
myr′in·gi′tis
—— bul·lo′sa
mŷ·rin′go·dec′to·my
my·rin′go·my·co′sis *pl.*
  -ses′
my·rin′go·plas′tic
my·rin′go·plas′ty
my·rin′go·sta·pe′di·o·pex′y
my·rin′go·tome′
myr′in·got′o·my
my′rinx′
my′so·pho′bi·a
myth′o·ma′ni·a
myth′o·pho′bi·a
myt′i·lo·tox′in
myt′i·lo·tox′ism
myx·ad′e·ni′tis
—— la′bi·a′lis
myx·ad′e·no′ma *pl.* -mas *or*
  -ma·ta
myx′an·gi′tis
myx′as·the′ni·a
myx′e·de′ma
—— cir′cum·scrip′tum
thy′ro·tox′i·cum
myx′e·de′ma·tous
myx′i·o′sis
myx′o·ad′e·no′ma *pl.* -mas
  or -ma·ta
myx′o·chon′dro·fi′bro·sar·
  co′ma *pl.* -mas *or* -ma·ta
myx′o·chon·dro′ma
  pl. -mas *or* -ma·ta
myx′o·chon′dro·sar·co′ma
  pl. -mas *or* -ma·ta
myx′o·cys·to′ma *pl.* -mas *or*
  -ma·ta
myx′o·cyte′
myx′o·en′do·the′li·o′ma *pl.*
  -mas *or* -ma·ta

myx'o·fi·bro'ma pl. -mas or
-ma·ta
myx'o·fi'bro·sar·co'ma
pl. -mas or -ma·ta
myx'o·gli·o'ma pl. -mas or
-ma·ta
myx'oid'
myx'o·li·po'ma pl. -mas or
-ma·ta
myx'o·lip'o·sar·co'ma
pl. -mas or -ma·ta
myx·o'ma pl. -mas or -ma·ta
—— cav'er·no'sum
—— fi·bro'sum
—— ge·lat'i·no'sum
—— lip'o·ma·to'des'
—— med'ul·lar'e'
—— sim'plex'
myx'o·ma·to'sis pl. -ses'
myx·om'a·tous
Myx'o·my·ce'tes'
myx'o·neu·ro'ma pl. -mas
or -ma·ta
myx'o·pap'il·lo'ma pl. -mas
or -ma·ta
myx'or·rhe'a
myx'o·sar·co'ma pl. -mas or
-ma·ta
myx'o·sar·com'a·tous
myx'o·spore'
myx'o·vi'rus
My'zo·my'ia

N

Na·bo'thi·an
—— cyst
—— glands
na'cre·ous
na·do'lol'
Nae'ge·le
—— obliquity
—— pelvis
Nae'ge·li
—— test
—— type leukemia
nae'paine'
na'fate'
naf·cil'lin
Naff'zi·ger
—— operation
—— syndrome
—— test
naf·ox'i·dine'
Na'ga sore

Na'gel test
Na·gle'ri·a fow'ler·i'
Na'gler reaction
nail
—— en ra·quette'
na'ked
nal'bu·phine'
nal'i·dix'ic
nal'mex·one'
nal'or·phine'
nal·ox'one'
nam·ox'y·rate'
nan'dro·lone'
na'nism
na'no·ceph'a·lus pl. -li'
na'no·cor'mi·a
na'no·cu'rie
na'no·gram'
na'noid'
na'no·me'li·a
na·nom'e·lus
na'no·me'ter
nan'oph·thal'mi·a
nan'oph·thal'mos
Na'no·phy·e'tus sal·
min'co·la
na'no·sec'ond
na'no·so'ma
na'no·so'mi·a
na'no·so'mus
nape
na'pex'
na·phaz'o·line'
naph'tha
naph'tha·lene'
naph'thyl
na'pi·form'
na·prox'en
Nar'ath operation
nar'cism
nar'cis·sism
nar'cis·sist
nar'cis·sis'tic
nar'co·a·nal'y·sis pl. -ses'
nar'co·hyp'ni·a
nar'co·hyp·no'sis pl. -ses'
nar'co·lep'sy
nar'co·lep'tic
nar·co'ma
nar·co'sis pl. -ses'
nar'co·spasm
nar'co·syn'the·sis pl. -ses'
nar'co·ther'a·py
nar·cot'ic
nar·cot'i·co-ir'ri·tant
nar'co·tize', -tized', -tiz'ing
nar'i·al

nar'is pl. -nar'es'
na'sal
na·sa'lis
nas'cent
na·si·o·al·ve'o·lar
na'si·on'
na·si'tis
Na'smyth membrane
na·so·al·ve'o·lar
na'so·an'tral
na·so·bas'i·lar
na·so·breg·mat'ic
na'so·cil'i·ar'y
na'so·fa'cial
na'so·fron'tal
na'so·gas'tric
na'so·gen'i·tal
na·so·la'bi·al
na·so·la·bi·a'lis
na'so·lac'ri·mal
na·so·lat'er·al
na·so·ma'lar
na'so·max'il·lar'y
na·so·me'di·al
na·so·me'di·an
na·so·men'tal
na·so·oc·cip'i·tal
na·so·o'ral
na·so·or'bit·al
na'so·pal'a·tine'
na·so·pal'pe·bral
na·so·pha·ryn'ge·al
na·so·phar'yn·gi'tis
na·so·pha·ryn'go·scope'
na·so·phar'yn·gos'co·py
na·so·phar'ynx pl. -pha·
ryn'ges'
na'so·scope'
na·so·sep'tal
na·so·spi·na'le'
na·so·tra'che·al
na·so·tur'bi·nal
na'sus pl. -si'
—— a·dun'cus
—— car'ti·la·gin'e·us
—— ex·ter'nus
—— in·cur'vus
—— os'se·us
—— si'mus
na'tal
na·tal'i·ty
na'tant
na'tes'
na·tre'mi·a
na'tri·um
na'tri·u·re'sis
na'tri·u·ret'ic

na'tron'
Nau'heim' bath
nau'se·a
nau'se·ant
nau'se·ate', -at'ed, -at'ing
nau'seous
na'vel
na·vic'u·la
na·vic'u·lar
na·vic'u·lar·thri'tis
na·vic'u·lo·cu'boid'
na·vic'u·lo·cu·ne'i·form'
near'sight'ed
near'sight'ed·ness
ne'ar·thro'sis pl. -ses'
neb'ra·my'cin
neb'u·la pl. -lae' or -las
neb'u·li·za'tion
neb'ulize', -lized', -liz'ing
neb'u·liz'er
Ne·ca'tor
—— a·mer'i·ca'nus
ne·ca'to·ri'a·sis
neck
nec'ro·bac'il·lo'sis pl. -ses'
Nec'ro·bac·te'ri·um
—— ne·croph'o·rum
nec'ro·bi·o'sis pl. -ses'
—— li·poi'di·ca
—— lipoidica di·a·bet'i·
co'rum
nec'ro·bi·ot'ic
nec'ro·cy·to'sis pl. -ses'
nec'ro·cy'to·tox'in
nec'ro·gen'ic
ne·crog'e·nous
ne·crol'y·sis pl. -ses'
nec'ro·ma'ni·a
nec'ro·pha'gi·a
nec'ro·pha'gic
ne·croph'a·gous
nec'ro·phile'
nec'ro·phil'i·a
nec'ro·phil'ic
ne·croph'i·lism
ne·croph'i·lous
ne·croph'i·ly
nec'ro·pho'bi·a
nec'rop'sy
ne·crose', -crosed', -cros'ing
nec'ro·sin
ne·cro'sis pl. -ses'
nec'ro·sper'mi·a
nec'ro·sper'mic
ne·crot'ic
nec'ro·tize', -tized', -tiz'ing

nec'ro·tox'in
nee'dle
Neel'sen
—— method
—— stain
ne'frens' pl. ne·fren'des'
neg'a·tive
neg'a·ti·vism
Ne·gish'i encephalitis
neg'li·gence
Neg'ri bodies
Neg'ri-Ja·cod' syndrome
Ne'gro
—— sign
Neill'-Moo'ser
—— bodies
—— reaction
Neis'ser
—— coccus
—— stain
Neis·se'ri·a
—— cat'ar·rha'lis
—— fla·ves'cens
—— gon'or·rhoe'ae'
—— in'tra·cel'lu·lar'is
—— men'in·git'i·dis
—— sic'ca
Né'la·ton'
—— fibers
—— line
—— tumor
Nel'son test
nem
nem'a·ti·za'tion
Nem'a·to'da
nem'a·tode'
nem'a·to·di'a·sis pl. -ses'
nem'a·toid'
nem'a·tol'o·gy
nem'a·to'sis pl. -ses'
nem'a·to·sper'mi·a
nem'ic
ne'o·an'ti·gen
ne'o·ar·thro'sis pl. -ses'
ne'o·blas'tic
ne'o·cer'e·bel'lar
ne'o·cer'e·bel'lum
ne'o·cor'tex'
ne'o·cyte'
ne'o·cy·to'sis pl. -ses'
ne·og'a·la
ne'o·gen'e·sis pl. -ses'
ne'o·ge·net'ic
ne'o·ki·net'ic
ne·ol'o·gism
ne'o·mem'brane'
ne'o·mor'phism

ne'o·my'cin
ne'o·na'tal
ne'o·nate'
ne'o·na'ti·cide'
ne'o·na'tus pl. -ti'
ne'o·pal'li·al
ne'o·pal'li·um
ne'o·pla'si·a
ne'o·plasm
ne'o·plas'tic
ne'o·plas'ty
ne'o·stig'mine'
ne'o·stri·a'tum
ne·ot'e·ny
Ne'o·tes·tu'di·na ro·sa'ti·i'
ne'o·vas'cu·lar
ne'o·vas·cu·lar·i·za'tion
ne'o·vas'cu·la·ture
neph'e·lom'e·ter
neph'e·lo·met'ric
neph'e·lom'e·try
ne·phral'gi·a
ne·phral'gic
neph'ra·to'ni·a
neph'rec·ta'si·a
ne·phrec'to·mize', -mized',
-miz'ing
ne·phrec'to·my
neph're·de'ma pl. -mas or
-ma·ta
neph'ric
ne·phrid'i·um pl. -i·a
ne·phrit'ic
ne·phri'tis pl. -phrit'i·des' or
-tis·es
neph'ri·to·gen'ic
neph'ro·ab·dom'i·nal
neph'ro·an'gi·o·scle·ro'sis
pl. -ses'
neph'ro·blas·to'ma pl. -mas
or -ma·ta
neph'ro·cal'ci·no'sis pl.
-ses'
neph'ro·cap·sec'to·my
neph'ro·cap'su·lec'to·my
neph'ro·cap'su·lot'o·my
neph'ro·car·ci·no'ma
pl. -mas or -ma·ta
neph'ro·car'di·ac'
neph'ro·cele'
neph'ro·co'lic
neph'ro·col'o·pex'y
neph'ro·co·lop·to'sis pl.
-ses'
neph'ro·cyst'an·as'to·
mo'sis pl. -ses'
neph'ro·cys·ti'tis

neph′ro·cys·to′sis *pl.* -ses′
neph′ro·dys′tro·phy
neph′ro·gas′tric
neph′ro·gen′e·sis *pl.* -ses′
neph′ro·gen′ic
ne·phrog′e·nous
neph′ro·gram′
neph′ro·graph′ic
ne·phrog′ra·phy
neph′ro·hy·dro′sis *pl.* -ses′
neph′ro·hy·per′tro·phy
neph′roid′
neph′ro·lith′
neph′ro·lith′ic
neph′ro·li·thi′a·sis *pl.* -ses′
neph′ro·li·thot′o·my
ne·phrol′o·gist
ne·phrol′o·gy
ne·phrol′y·sin
ne·phrol′y·sis *pl.* -ses′
neph′ro·lyt′ic
ne·phro·ma *pl.* -mas or
  -ma·ta
neph′ro·meg′a·ly
neph′ro·mere′
neph′ron′
neph′ro·path′ic
ne·phrop′a·thy
neph′ro·pex′y
neph′ro·poi′e·tin
neph′rop·to′si·a
neph′rop·to′sis *pl.* -ses′
neph′ro·py′e·li′tis
neph′ro·py′e·log′ra·phy
neph′ro·py′e·lo·li·thot′o·
  my
neph′ro·py′e·lo·plas′ty
neph′ror·rha′gi·a
ne·phror′rha·phy
neph′ros′ *pl.* neph′roi′
neph′ro·scle·ro′sis *pl.* -ses′
ne·phro′sis *pl.* -ses′
ne·phro·so·ne·phri′tis
neph′ro·so·nog′ra·phy
ne·phros′to·ma *pl.* neph′ro·
  sto′ma·ta
neph′ro·sto′mal
neph′ro·stome′
ne·phros′to·my
ne·phrot′ic
neph′ro·tome′
neph′ro·to′mo·gram′
neph′ro·to·mog′ra·phy
ne·phrot′o·my
neph′ro·tox′ic
neph′ro·tox·ic′i·ty
neph′ro·tox′in

neph′ro·trop′ic
neph′ro·tu·ber′cu·lo′sis
neph′ro·u·re′ter·al
neph′ro·u·re′ter·ec′to·my
Nernst equation
nerve
—— of Ar′nold
—— of Bell
—— of Co·tun′ni·us
—— of Cru′veil·hier′
—— of Cy′on′
—— of Eis′ler
—— of Ja′cob·son
—— of Lan·ci′si
—— of Scar′pa
—— of Vid′i·us
—— of Vieus·sens′
—— of Wris′berg′
ner′vi′
—— al′ve·o·lar′es′ su·pe′ri·
  o′res′
—— a′no·coc·cyg′e·i′
—— au·ric′u·lar′es′ an·te′ri·
  o′res′
—— car·di′a·ci′ tho·ra′·ci·ci′
—— ca·rot′i·ci′ ex·ter′·ni′
—— ca·rot′i·co·tym·pan′i·ci′
—— cav′er·no′si′ cli·to′ri·dis
—— cavernosi clitoridis mi·
no′res′
—— cavernosi pe′nis
—— cavernosi penis mi·
no′res′
—— cer′e·bra′les′
—— cer′vi·ca′les′
—— cil′i·ar′es′ brev′es′
—— ciliares lon′gi′
—— clu′ni·um in·fe′ri·o′res′
—— clunium me′di·i′
—— clunium su·pe′ri·o′res′
—— cra′ni·a′les′
—— dig′i·ta′les′ dor·sa′les′
hal′lu·cis lat′er·a′lis et dig′i·
ti′ se·cun′·di′ me′di·a′lis
—— digitales dorsales ner′·
vi′ ra′di·a′lis
—— digitales dorsales nervi
ul·nar′is
—— digitales dorsales pe′dis
—— digitales pal·mar′es′
com·mu′nes′ ner′vi′ me′di·
a′ni′
—— digitales palmares
communes nervi ul·nar′is
—— digitales palmares
pro′pri·i′ ner′vi′ me′di·a′ni′

—— digitales palmares pro·
prii nervi ul·nar′is
—— digitales plan·tar′es′
com·mu′nes′ ner′vi′ plan·
tar′is lat′er·a′lis
—— digitales plantares
communes nervi plantaris
me′di·a′lis
—— digitales plantares
pro′pri·i′ ner′vi′ plan·tar′is
lat′er·a′lis
—— digitales plantares pro·
prii nervi plantaris me′di·
a′lis
—— digitales vo·lar′es′ com·
mu′nes′ ner′vi′ me′di·a′ni′
—— digitales volares com·
munes nervi ul·nar′is
—— digitales volares
pro′pri·i′ ner′vi′ me′di·a′ni′
—— digitales volares proprii
nervi ul·nar′is
—— er′i·gen′tes′
—— haem′or·rhoi·da′les′ in·
fe′ri·o′res′
—— haemorrhoidales
me′di· i′
—— haemorrhoidales su·
pe′ri·o′res′
—— in′ter·cos·ta′les′
—— in′ter·cos′to·bra′chi·
a′les′
—— la′bi·a′les′ an·te′ri·o′res′
—— labiales pos·te′ri·o′res′
—— lum·ba′les′
—— ner·vo′rum
—— ol′fac·to′ri·i′
—— pal′a·ti′ni′
—— palatini mi·no′res′
—— per′i·ne·a′les′
—— per′i·ne′i′
—— phren′i·ci′ ac′ces·so′ri·i′
—— pter′y·go·pal′a·ti′ni′
—— rec·ta′les′ in·fe′ri·o′res′
—— sa·cra′les′
—— scro·ta′les′ an·te′·ri·
o′res′
—— scrotales pos·te′·ri·
o′res′
—— sphe′no·pal′a·ti′ni′
—— spi·na′les′
—— splanch′ni·ci′ lum·
ba′les′
—— splanchnici pel·vi′·ni′
—— splanchnici sa·cra′les′
—— sub·scap′u·lar′es′
—— su′pra·cla·vic′u·lar′es′

—— supraclaviculares in·ter·me'di·i'
—— supraclaviculares lat'er·a'les'
—— supraclaviculares me'di·a'les'
—— supraclaviculares me'di·i'
—— supraclaviculares pos·te'ri·o'res'
—— tem'po·ra'les' pro·fun'di'
—— ter'mi·na'les'
—— tho'ra·ca'les'
—— thoracales an·te'·ri·o'res'
—— thoracales pos·te'·ri·o'res'
—— tho·ra·ci·ci'
—— vag'i·na'les'
—— va·so'rum
—— ves'i·ca'les' in·fe'ri·o'res' plex'us pu·den'di'
—— vesicales inferiores sys·te'ma·tis sym·path'i·ci'
—— vesicales su·pe'ri·o'res' sys·te'ma·tis sym·path'i·ci'
ner'vous (pertaining to nerves)
♦nervus
ner'vous·ness
ner'vus (a nerve), pl. -vi'
♦nervous
—— ab·du'cens
—— ac'ces·so'ri·us
—— a·cus'ti·cus
—— al've·o·lar'is inferior
—— am'pul·lar'is anterior
—— ampullaris inferior
—— ampullaris lat'er·a'lis
—— ampullaris posterior
—— ampullaris superior
—— an'te·bra'chi·i' anterior
—— antebrachii posterior
—— ar·tic'u·lar'is
—— au·ric'u·lar'is mag'nus
—— auricularis posterior
—— au·ric'u·lo·tem'po·ra'lis
—— ax'il·lar'is
—— buc·ca'lis
—— buc'ci·na·to'ri·us
—— ca·na'lis pter'y·goi'de·i'
—— car·di'a·cus cer'vi·ca'lis inferior
—— cardiacus cervicalis me'di·us

—— cardiacus cervicalis superior
—— cardiacus inferior
—— cardiacus me'di·us
—— cardiacus superior
—— ca·rot'i·co·tym·pan'i·cus inferior
—— caroticotympanicus superior
—— ca·rot'i·cus in·ter'nus
—— cav'er·no'sus cli·to'ri·dis major
—— cavernosus pe'nis major
—— coc·cyg'e·us
—— coch'le·ae'
—— cu·ta'ne·us
—— cutaneus an'te·bra'·chi·i' lat'er·a'lis
—— cutaneus antebrachii me'di·a'lis
—— cutaneus antebrachii posterior
—— cutaneus an'ti·bra'chi·i' dor·sa'lis
—— cutaneus antibrachii lat'er·a'lis
—— cutaneus antibrachii me'di·a'lis
—— cutaneus bra'chi·i' lat'er·a'lis
—— cutaneus brachii lateralis inferior
—— cutaneus brachii lateralis superior
—— cutaneus brachii me'di·a'lis
—— cutaneus brachii posterior
—— cutaneus col'li'
—— cutaneus dor·sa'lis in'ter·me'di·us
—— cutaneus dorsalis lat'er·a'lis
—— cutaneus dorsalis me'di·a'lis
—— cutaneus fem'o·ris lat'er·a'lis
—— cutaneus femoris posterior
—— cutaneus su'rae' lat'er·a'lis
—— cutaneus surae me'di·a'lis
—— dor·sa'lis cli·to'ri·dis
—— dorsalis pe'nis
—— dorsalis scap'u·lae'

—— eth'moi·da'lis anterior
—— ethmoidalis posterior
—— fa'ci·a'lis
—— fem'o·ra'lis
—— fib'u·lar'is com·mu'nis
—— fibularis pro·fun'dus
—— fibularis su'per·fi'ci·a'lis
—— fron·ta'lis
—— fur·ca'lis
—— gen'i·to·fem'o·ra'lis
—— glos'so·pha·ryn'·ge·us
—— glu·tae'us inferior
—— glutaeus superior
—— glu·te'us inferior
—— gluteus superior
—— hy'po·gas'tri·cus (dex'ter et si·nis'ter)
—— hy'po·glos'sus
—— il'i·o·hy'po·gas'tri·cus
—— il'i·o·in'gui·na'lis
—— in'fra·or'bi·ta'lis
—— in'fra·troch'le·ar'is
—— in'ter·me'di·us
—— in'ter·os'se·us anterior
—— interosseus cru'ris
—— interosseus dor·sa'lis
—— interosseus posterior
—— interosseus vo·lar'is
—— is'chi·ad'i·cus
—— jug'u·lar'is
—— lac'ri·ma'lis
—— la·ryn'ge·us inferior
—— laryngeus re·cur'rens
—— laryngeus superior
—— lin·gua'lis
—— man·dib'u·lar'is
—— mas'se·ter'i·cus
—— mas'ti·ca·to'ri·us
—— max'il·lar'is
—— me·a'tus a·cus'ti·ci' ex·ter'ni'
—— meatus au'di'·to'ri·i' ex·ter'ni'
—— me'di·a'nus
—— me·nin'ge·us me'di·us
—— men·ta'lis
—— mus'cu·lo·cu·ta'ne·us
—— my'lo·hy·oi'de·us
—— na'so·cil'i·ar'is
—— na'so·pal'a·ti'nus
—— ob'tu·ra·to'ri·us
—— oc·cip'i·ta'lis major
—— occipitalis minor
—— occipitalis ter'ti·us
—— oc·ta'vus
—— oc'u·lo·mo·to'ri·us
—— ol'fac·to'ri·us

—— oph·thal'mi·cus
—— op'ti·cus
—— pal'a·ti'nus anterior
—— palatinus major
—— palatinus me'di·us
—— palatinus posterior
—— pec'to·ra'lis lat'er·a'lis
—— pectoralis me'di·a'lis
—— per'o·nae'us com·mu'nis
—— peronaeus pro·fun'dus
—— peronaeus su'per·fi'ci·a'lis
—— per'o·ne'us com·mu'nis
—— peroneus pro·fun'dus
—— peroneus su'per·fi'ci·a'lis
—— pe·tro'sus major
—— petrosus minor
—— petrosus pro·fun'dus
—— petrosus su'per·fi'ci·a'lis major
—— petrosus superficialis minor
—— phren'i·cus
—— plan·tar'is lat'er·a'lis
—— plantaris me'di·a'lis
—— pre'sa·cra'lis
—— pter'y·goi'de·us ex·ter'nus
—— pterygoideus in·ter'nus
—— pterygoideus lat'er·a'lis
—— pterygoideus me'di·a'lis
—— pu·den'dus
—— ra'di·a'lis
—— re·cur'rens
—— sac'cu·lar'is
—— sa·phe'nus
—— sper·mat'i·cus ex·ter'nus
—— spi·no'sus
—— splanch'ni·cus i'mus
—— splanchnicus major
—— splanchnicus minor
—— sta·pe'di·us
—— sub·cla'vi·us
—— sub'cos·ta'lis
—— sub'lin·gua'lis
—— sub'oc·cip'i·ta'lis
—— sub·scap'u·lar'is
—— su'pra·or'bi·ta'lis
—— su'pra·scap'u·lar'is
—— su'pra·troch'le·ar'is
—— su·ra'lis
—— tem'po·ra'lis pro·fun'dus anterior

—— temporalis profundus posterior
—— ten·so'ris tym'pa·ni'
—— tensoris ve'li' pal'a·ti'ni'
—— ten·to'ri·i'
—— tho'ra·ca'lis lon'gus
—— tho'ra·ci·cus lon'gus
—— tho'ra·co·dor·sa'lis
—— tib'i·a'lis
—— trans·ver'sus col'li'
—— tri·gem'i·nus
—— troch'le·ar'is
—— tym·pan'i·cus
—— ul·nar'is
—— u·tric'u·lar'is
—— u·tric'u·lo·am'pul·lar'is
—— va'gus
—— vas'cu·lar'is
—— ver'te·bra'lis
—— ves·tib'u·li'
—— ves·tib'u·lo·coch'le·ar'is
—— zy'go·mat'i·cus
ne·sid'i·ec'to·my
ne·sid'i·o·blast'
ne·sid'i·o·blas·to'ma pl. -mas or -ma·ta
ne·sid'i·o·blas·to'sis
ness'ler·ize', -ized', -iz'ing
Ness'ler reagent
nes'to·ther'a·py
nests of Gol'gi-Holm'gren
neth'a·lide'
net'work'
Neu'ber tubes
Neu'feld'
—— nail
Neu'hau'ser sign
Neu'mann
—— cells
—— method
—— operation
—— sheath
neu'ral
neu·ral'gi·a
neu·ral'gic
neu·ral'gi·form'
neur'a·min'ic
neur'a·min'i·dase'
neur'a·poph'y·sis pl. -ses'
neur'a·prax'i·a
neur'as·the'ni·a
neur'as·then'ic
neu·ra·tro'phi·a
neu·ra·troph'ic
neur·at'ro·phy
neur·ax'i·al
neur·ax'is

neur·ax'on'
neur'ec·ta'si·a
neu·rec'ta·sis pl. -ses'
neu·rec'to·my
neur'ec·to'pi·a
neu·rec'to·py
neur'en·ter'ic
neur·ep'i·the'li·um
neu·rer'gic
neur'ex·er'e·sis pl. -ses'
neu·ri'a·sis pl. -ses'
neu·ri·lem'ma
neu·ri·lem'mal
neu·ri·lem·mi'tis
neu·ri·lem·mo'ma pl. -mas or -ma·ta
neu·ri·lem·mo·sar·co'ma pl. -mas or -ma·ta
neu·ri·mo'tor
neu'rine'
neu·ri·no'ma pl. -mas or -ma·ta
neu·ri·no·ma·to'sis pl. -ses'
neu'rit'
neu·rit'ic
neu·ri'tis
neu·ro·a·nas'to·mo'sis pl. -ses'
neu·ro·a·nat'o·my
neu·ro·a·ne'mi·a
neu·ro·a·ne'mic
neu·ro·ar·throp'a·thy
neu·ro·as·the'ni·a
neu·ro·as'tro·cy·to'ma pl. -mas or -ma·ta
neu·ro·ax'on·al
neu·ro·bi·ol'o·gy
neu·ro·bi'o·tax'is
neu·ro·blast'
neu·ro·blas·to'ma pl. -mas or -ma·ta
—— sym'pa·thet'i·cum
—— sym·path'i·cum
neu·ro·blas'to·ma·to'sis
neu·ro·ca·nal'
neu·ro·car'di·ac'
neu·ro·cen'tral
neu·ro·cen'trum
neu·ro·cep'tor
neu·ro·chem'is·try
neu·ro·cho'ri·o·ret'i·ni'tis
neu·ro·cho'roi·di'tis
neu·ro·cir'cu·la·to'ry
neu·ro·clon'ic
neu·ro·coele'
neu·ro·cra'ni·al
neu·ro·cra'ni·um

neu′ro·crine′
neu′ro·cu·ta′ne·ous
neu′ro·cyte′
neu′ro·cy·tol′y·sin
neu′ro·cy·tol′y·sis
neu′ro·cy·to′ma *pl.* -mas *or*
  -ma·ta
neu·ro′de·a·tro′phi·a
neu′ro·de·gen′er·a·tive
neu′ro·den′drite′
neu′ro·den′dron′
neu′ro·der′ma·ti′tis
  —— cir′cum·scrip′ta
  —— dis·sem′i·na′ta
neu′ro·der′ma·to′sis *pl.*
  -ses′
neu′ro·der′ma·tro′phi·a
neu′ro·di·as′ta·sis *pl.* -ses′
neu′ro·dyn′i·a
neu′ro·en·ceph′a·lo·my′e·
  lop′a·thy
neu′ro·en′do·crine
neu′ro·en·ter′ic
neu′ro·ep′i·der′mal
neu′ro·ep′i·the′li·al
neu′ro·ep′i·the′li·o′ma *pl.*
  -mas *or* -ma·ta
neu′ro·ep′i·the′li·um
  pl. -li·a
neu′ro·fi′bril
neu′ro·fi′bril·lar
neu′ro·fi′bril·lar′y
neu′ro·fi·bro′ma *pl.* -mas *or*
  -ma·ta
  —— gan′gli·o·cel′lu·lar′e′
  —— gan′gli·o·nar′e′
neu′ro·fi·bro′ma·to′sis *pl.*
  -ses′
neu′ro·fi′bro·myx·o′ma
  pl. -mas *or* -ma·ta
neu′ro·fi′bro·sar·co′ma
  pl. -mas *or* -ma·ta
neu′ro·fil′a·ment
neu′ro·fix·a′tion
neu′ro·gan′gli·i′tis
neu′ro·gan′gli·o′ma my′e·
  lin′i·cum ve′rum
neu′ro·gan′gli·on *pl.* -gli·a
  or -gli·ons
neu′ro·gan′gli·on·i′tis
neu′ro·gas′tric
neu′ro·gen·e′sis *pl.* -ses′
neu′ro·ge·net′ic
neu′ro·gen′ic
neu·rog′e·nous
neu·rog′e·ny
neu·rog′li·a

neu·rog′li·o·cyte′
neu·rog′li·o·cy·to′ma
  pl. -mas *or* -ma·ta
neu·rog′li·o′ma *pl.* -mas *or*
  -ma·ta
neu·rog′li·o′sis *pl.* -ses′
neu′ro·gram′
neu′ro·his·tol′o·gy
neu′ro·hor·mo′nal
neu′ro·hu′mor
neu′ro·hu′mor·al
neu′ro·hy·poph′y·se′al
neu′ro·hy·poph′y·sec′to·
  my
neu′ro·hy·poph′y·sis *pl.*
  -ses′
neu′roid′
neu′ro·in·duc′tion
neu′ro·ker′a·tin
neu′ro·lab′y·rin·thi′tis
neu′ro·lath′y·rism
neu′ro·lem′ma
neu′ro·lep′rid
neu′ro·lep·tan·al·ge′si·a
neu′ro·lep·tan·es·the′si·a
neu′ro·lep·tan·es·thet′ic
neu′ro·lep′tic
neu′ro·lo′gi·a
neu′ro·log′ic *or* neu′ro·log′i·
  cal
neu·rol′o·gist
neu·rol′o·gy
neu′ro·lu′es′
neu′ro·lymph′
neu′ro·lym′pho·ma·to′sis
  pl. -ses′
  —— gal′li·nar′um
neu·rol′y·sin
neu·rol′y·sis *pl.* -ses′
neu′ro·lyt′ic
neu·ro′ma *pl.* -mas *or* -ma·ta
  —— cu′tis
  —— gan′gli·o·cel′lu·lar′e′
  —— gangliocellulare ma·
  lig′num
  —— tel·an′gi·ec·to′des′
  —— ve′rum
  —— verum gan′gli·o′sum
a′my·e·lin′i·cum
neu′ro·ma·la′ci·a
neu·rom′a·toid′
neu′ro·ma·to′sis *pl.* -ses′
neu·rom′a·tous
neu′ro·mech′a·nism
neu′ro·mere′
neu′ro·mi·me′sis
neu′ro·mi·met′ic

neu′ro·mo′tor
neu′ro·mus′cu·lar
neu′ro·my′al
neu′ro·my′as·the′ni·a
neu′ro·my′e·li′tis
  —— hy′per·al·bu′mi·not′i·ca
  —— op′ti·ca
neu′ro·my′ic
neu′ro·my′o·path′ic
neu′ro·my′o·si′tis
neu′ron′
neu′ro·nal
neu′ro·neph′ric
neu′ro·ne′vus *pl.* -vi′
neu′ro·ni′tis
neu′ro·nop′a·thy
neu·ro·no·pha′gi·a
neu′ro·oph·thal′mo·log′ic
neu′ro·op′tic
neu′ro·pa·ral′y·sis *pl.* -ses′
neu′ro·par′a·lyt′ic
neu′ro·path′
neu′ro·path′ic
neu′ro·path′o·gen′e·sis *pl.*
  -ses′
neu′ro·path′o·log′ic
neu′ro·pa·thol′o·gy
neu·rop′a·thy
neu′ro·phar′ma·col′o·gy
neu′ro·pho′ni·a
neu′ro·phre′ni·a
neu′ro·phys′ine′
neu′ro·phys′i·o·log′ic
neu′ro·phys′i·ol′o·gist
neu′ro·phys′i·ol′o·gy
neu′ro·pil
neu′ro·plasm
neu′ro·plas′ty
neu′ro·ple′gic
neu′ro·po′di·a *sing.* -di·um
neu′ro·pore′
neu′ro·po·ten′tial
neu′ro·psy′chi·at′ric
neu′ro·psy·chi′a·trist
neu′ro·psy·chi′a·try
neu′ro·psy′chic
neu′ro·psy′chol′o·gy
neu′ro·psy′cho·path′ic
neu′ro·psy′chop′a·thy
neu′ro·psy′cho′sis *pl.* -ses′
neu′ro·ra′di·o·log′ic
neu′ro·ra′di·ol′o·gy
neu′ro·rec′i·dive′
neu′ro·re·cur′rence
neu′ro·re·lapse′
neu′ro·ret′i·ni′tis
neu′ro·ret′i·nop′a·thy

neu'ro·roent'ge·nol'o·gy
neu·ror'rha·phy
neu·ror·rhex'is
neu'ro·sar·co'ma pl. -mas
   or -ma·ta
neu'ro·scle·ro'sis pl. -ses'
neu'ro·se·cre'tion
neu'ro·se·cre'to·ry
neu'ro·seg·men'tal
neu'ro·sen'so·ry
neu·ro'sis pl. -ses'
neu'ro·skel'e·tal
neu'ro·some'
neu'ro·spasm
neu'ro·spon'gi·o'ma
   pl. -mas or -ma·ta
neu'ro·spon'gi·um
Neu·ros'po·ra
neu'ro·ste'a·ric
neu'ro·sthe'ni·a
neu'ro·sthen'ic
neu'ro·sur'geon
neu'ro·sur'ger·y
neu'ro·sur'gi·cal
neu'ro·su'ture
neu'ro·syph'i·lis
neu'ro·ten'di·nal
neu'ro·ten'di·nous
—— organ of Gol'gi
—— xan·tho'ma·to'sis
neu'ro·ther'a·py
neu·rot'ic
neu·rot'i·ca
neu·rot'i·cism
neu·rot'i·gen'ic
neu'ro·ti·za'tion
neu'ro·tize', -tized', -tiz'ing
neu·rot·me'sis
neu·rot'o·gen'ic
neu'ro·tome'
neu·rot'o·my
neu'ro·ton'ic
neu'ro·tox'ic
neu'ro·tox·ic'i·ty
neu'ro·tox'in
neu'ro·trans·mit'ter
neu'ro·trau'ma
neu'ro·trip'sy
neu'ro·troph'ic (pertaining
   to neurotrophy)
♦neurotropic
neu·rot'ro·phy
neu'ro·trop'ic (pertaining to
   neurotropism)
♦neurotrophic
neu·rot'ro·pism
neu'ro·tu'bule'

neu'ro·var'i·co'sis pl. -ses'
neu'ro·vas'cu·lar
neu'ro·vir'u·lent
neu'ro·vi'rus
neu'ro·vis'cer·al
neu'ru·la pl. -las or -lae'
neu'ru·la'tion
Neus'ser granules
neu'tral
neu'tral·i·za'tion
neu'tral·ize', -ized', -iz'ing
neu·tri'no
neu'tro·clu'sion
neu'tro·cyte'
neu'tron'
neu'tro·pe'ni·a
neu'tro·phil'
neu'tro·phil'i·a
heu'tro·phil'ic
ne'vi·form'
ne'vo·car'ci·no'ma pl. -mas
   or -ma·ta
ne'void'
ne'vo·mel'a·no'ma pl. -mas
   or -ma·ta
ne'vose'
ne'vo·xan'tho·en'do·the'li·
   o'ma pl. -mas or -ma·ta
ne'vus pl. -vi'
—— ac'ne·i·for'mis u'ni·
   lat'er·a'lis
—— an'gi·o·li·po'ma·to'sus
—— a·rach·noi'de·us
—— a·ra'ne·us
—— com'e·do'ni·cus
—— ep'i·the'li·o'ma·
   to·cyl'in·dro'ma·to'sus
—— flam'me·us
—— fol·lic'u·lar'is
—— fus'co·cae·ru'li·us oph·
   thal'mo·max·il·lar'is of O'ta
—— li·po'ma·to'des'
—— lipomatodes su'per·fi'ci·
a'lis
—— li·po'ma·to'sus
—— lum'bo·in'gui·na'lis
—— pap'il·lar'is
—— pap'il·lo'ma·to'sus
—— pel·li'nus
—— pig'men·to'sus
—— pi·lo'sus
—— se·ba'ce·us
—— spi'lus
—— spon'gi·o'sus al'bus
—— u'ni·lat'er·a'lis
—— u'ni·us lat'er·is
—— vas·cu·lo'sus

—— ver'ru·co'sus
new'born'
New'cas'tle
—— disease
—— virus
new'ton
nex'us pl. nex'us or -us·es
ni'a·cin
ni'a·cin'a·mide'
ni·al'a·mide'
niche
nick'el
nick'ing
ni·clo'sa·mide'
Ni·co·las'-Fa'vre disease
nic'o·tin'a·mide'
nic'o·tin·ate'
nic'o·tine'
nic'o·tin'ic
nic'ti·tate', -tat'ed, -tat'ing
nic'ti·ta'tion
ni'dal
ni·da'tion
ni'dus pl. -di'
—— a'vis cer'e·bel'li'
Niel'sen method
ni·fed'i·pine'
ni·fu'ri·mide'
ni'fur·ox'ime'
nig'gle
night'mare'
ni'gral
ni'gri·cans'
ni·gri'ti·es'
ni'gro·sine'
ni'hil·ism
nik·eth'a·mide'
Ni·kol'sky sign
niph'a·blep'si·a
niph'o·typh·lo'sis
nip'ple
ni·rid'a·zole'
ni'sin
ni'so·bam'ate'
Nis'sl
—— bodies
—— stains
—— substance
ni'sus
—— for'ma·ti'vus
nit
Nit'a·buch'
—— membrane
—— stria
ni'ton'
ni'trate'
ni·tra'tion

ni·tra'ze·pam'
ni'tre
ni'tre'mi·a
ni'tric
ni'tride'
ni'tri·fi·ca'tion
ni'tri·fi'er
ni'tri·fy', -fied', -fy'ing
ni'trile'
ni'trite'
ni'tri·toid'
ni'tri·tu'ri·a
ni'tro·cel'lu·lose'
ni'tro·cy'cline'
ni'tro·dan'
ni'tro·fu·ran'to·in
ni'tro·fu'ra·zone'
ni'tro·gen
ni·trog'e·nous
ni'tro·glyc'er·in
ni'tro·mer'sol'
ni·trom'e·ter
ni'tron'
ni'tro·prus'side'
ni'tros·a'mine'
ni'trous
N·jo'ver·a
No'ble posture
No·car'di·a
  —— as'ter·oi'des'
  —— ma·du'rae'
no·car'di·al
no·car'di·o'sis *pl.* -ses'
no'ci·cep'tive
no'ci·cep'tor
no'ci·per·cep'tion
noc'tal·bu'mi·nu'ri·a
noc·tam'bu·la'tion
noc'ti·pho'bi·a
noc·tu'ri·a
noc·tur'nal
no'dal
node
  —— of Keith and Flack
  —— of Ran'vi·er'
  —— of Vir'chow-Troi'si·er'
no'di'
  —— lym·phat'i·ci'
  —— lymphatici ap'i·ca'les
  —— lymphatici ax'il·lar'es'
  —— lymphatici bron'cho·
pul'mo·na'les'
  —— lymphatici buc·ca'les'
  —— lymphatici ce·li'a·ci'
  —— lymphatici cen·tra'les'
  —— lymphatici cer'vi·ca'les'
pro·fun'di'

  —— lymphatici cervicales
su'per·fi'ci·a'les'
  —— lymphatici co'li·ci'
dex'tri'
  —— lymphatici colici
me'di· i'
  —— lymphatici colici
si·nis'tri'
  —— lymphatici cu'bi·ta'les'
  —— lymphatici ep'i·gas'tri·
ci'
  —— lymphatici gas'tri·ci'
dex'tri'
  —— lymphatici gastrici si·
nis'tri'
  —— lymphatici gas'tro·ep'i·
plo'i·ci' dex'tri'
  —— lymphatici gastroepi-
ploici si·nis'tri'
  —— lymphatici he·pat'i·ci'
  —— lymphatici il'e·o·co'li·ci'
  —— lymphatici i·li'a·ci'
com·mu'nes'
  —— lymphatici iliaci ex·
ter'ni'
  —— lymphatici iliaci in·
ter'ni'
  —— lymphatici in'gui·
na'les' pro·fun'di'
  —— lymphatici inguinales
su'per·fi'ci·a'les'
  —— lymphatici in'ter·cos·
ta'les'
  —— lymphatici lat'er·a'les'
  —— lymphatici lin·gua'les'
  —— lymphatici lum·ba'les'
  —— lymphatici man·dib'u·
lar'es'
  —— lymphatici me'di·as'ti·
na'les' an·te'ri·o'res'
  —— lymphatici mediastinales pos·te'ri·o'res'
  —— lymphatici mes'en·ter'i·
ci' in·fe'ri·or'es'
  —— lymphatici mesenterici
su·pe'ri·o'res'
  —— lymphatici oc·cip'i·
ta'les'
  —— lymphatici pan'cre·at'i·
co·li'e·na'les'
  —— lymphatici par·a·ster·
na'les'
  —— lymphatici pa·rot'i·de'i'
su'per·fi'ci·a'les' et pro·
fun'di'
  —— lymphatici pec'to·ra'les'
  —— lymphatici phren'i·ci'

  —— lymphatici pop·lit'e·i'
  —— lymphatici pul'mo·
na'les'
  —— lymphatici py·lo'ri·ci'
  —— lymphatici ret'ro·au·
ric'u·lar'es'
  —— lymphatici ret'ro·pha·
ryn'ge·i'
  —— lymphatici sa·cra'les'
  —— lymphatici sub'man·
dib'u·lar'es
  —— lymphatici sub'men·
ta'les'
  —— lymphatici sub·scap'u·
lar'es'
  —— lymphatici tra'che·
a'les'
  —— lymphatici tra'che·o·
bron'chi·a'les' in·fe'ri·o'res'
  —— lymphatici tracheo-
bronchiales su·pe'ri·o'res'
no'dose'
no·dos'i·ty
nod'u·lar
nod'u·lat'ed
nod'u·la'tion
nod'ule'
nod'u·li'
  —— ag'gre·ga'ti' pro·ces'sus
ver'mi·for'mis
  —— A·ran'ti·i'
  —— cu·ta'ne·i'
  —— lym·phat'i·ci' ag'gre·
ga'ti'
  —— lymphatici bron'chi·
a'les'
  —— lymphatici con·junc'ti·
va'les'
  —— lymphatici gas'tri·ci'
  —— lymphatici in'tes·ti'ni'
rec'ti'
  —— lymphatici la·ryn'ge·i'
  —— lymphatici li'e·na'les'
  —— lymphatici sol'i·tar'i·i'
  —— lymphatici tu·bar'i·i'
  —— lymphatici vag'i·na'les'
  —— lymphatici ves'i·ca'les'
thy'mi·ci' ac'ces·so'ri·i'
val'vu·lar'um sem'i·lu·
nar'i·um
nod'u·lus *pl.* -li'
  —— lym·phat'i·cus
no'dus *pl.* -di'
  —— a'tri·o·ven·tric'u·lar'is
  —— lym·phat'i·cus
  —— lymphaticus jug'u·lo·di·
gas'tri·cus

—— lymphaticus jug'u·lo·o'mo·hy·oi'de·us
—— lymphaticus tib'i·a'lis anterior
——— si'nu·a'tri·a'lis
no'e·gen'e·sis
no'e·mat'ic
no·e'sis
no·et'ic
no·gal'a·my'cin
no'ma
no'men·cla'ture
Nom'i·na An'a·tom'i·ca
nom'i·nal
nom'o·top'ic
no'na
non'ab·sorb'a·ble
non'ad·her'ent
non·a'que·ous
non·ar·tic'u·lar
non'com·mu'ni·cat'ing
non com'pos men'tis
non'con·duc'tor
non'con·ges'tive
non·gran'u·lar
no'ni·grav'i·da
non'i·on'ic
non·lip'id
non'lu·et'ic
non·med'ul·lat'ed
non·mo'tile
non·my'e·li·nat'ed
Non'ne disease
Non'ne-Mil'roy-Meige' syndrome
non-nu'cle·at'ed
non'o·paque'
non'os'te·o·gen'ic
non·ox'y·nol'
non·par'ous
non'pro·pri'e·tar'y
non'psy·chot'ic
non're·frac'tive
non·sep'tate'
non'spe·cif'ic
non·sur'gi·cal
non·trop'i·cal
non·un'ion
non·va'lent
non·vi'a·ble
non'yl
no'o·psy'che
nor'a·cy·meth'a·dol'
nor·a·dren'a·line
nor·bol'eth·one'
Nor'dau' disease
nor·dau·ism

nor'de·frin
nor'e·phed'rine
nor·ep'i·neph'rine'
nor'eth·an'dro·lone'
nor·eth'in·drone'
nor'e·thy'no·drel'
nor·flu'rane'
nor·ges'trel
norm
nor'ma pl. -mae'
—— anterior
—— bas'i·lar'is
—— fa'ci·a'lis
—— inferior
—— lat'er·a'lis
—— oc·cip'i·ta'lis
—— sag'it·ta'lis
—— superior
—— ven·tra'lis
—— ver'ti·ca'lis
nor'mal
nor'mal·cy
nor·mal'i·ty
nor'met'a·neph'rine'
nor'mo·blast'
nor'mo·blas'tic
nor'mo·blas·to'sis
nor'mo·cal·ce'mi·a
nor'mo·cal·ce'mic
nor'mo·chro·ma'si·a
nor'mo·chro·mat'ic
nor'mo·chro'mi·a
nor'mo·chro'mic
nor'mo·cyte'
nor'mo·cyt'ic
nor'mo·cy·to'sis
nor'mo·gly·ce'mic
nor'mo·ka·le'mic
nor'mo·re·flex'i·a
nor'mo·ten'sive
nor'mo·ther'mi·a
nor'mo·to'ni·a
nor'mo·ton'ic
nor'mo·to'pi·a
nor'mo·vo·le'mi·a
nor'mo·vo·le'mic
nor·mox'i·a
nor·mox'ic
Nor'walk' agent
nor·trip'ty·line'
nos'ca·pine'
nose
nose'bleed'
nos'o·co'mi·al
nos'o·gen'e·sis
nos'o·gen'ic
no·sog'e·ny

nos'o·log'ic or nos'o·log'i·cal
no·sol'o·gy
nos'o·ma·ni·a
no·som'e·try
nos'o·my·co'sis pl. -ses'
nos'o·phil'i·a
nos'o·pho'bi·a
nos'o·phyte'
nos'o·poi·et'ic
Nos'o·psyl'lus
—— fas'ci·a'tus
nos'o·tax'y
nos'tril
nos'trum
no·tal'gi·a
—— par'es·thet'i·ca
no'tan·ce·pha'li·a
no'tan·en'ce·pha'li·a
notch
—— of Ri·vi'nus
no'ten·ceph'a·lo·cele'
no'ten·ceph'a·lus pl. -li'
Noth'na'gel
—— disease
—— paralysis
—— syndrome
no'ti·fi'a·ble
no'to·chord'
no'to·gen'e·sis
no'vo·bi'o·cin
nox'ious
nu·bil'i·ty
nu'cha pl. -chae'
nu'chal
Nuck
—— canal
—— hydrocele
nu'cle·ar
nu'cle·ase'
nu'cle·at'ed
nu'cle·a'tion
nu'cle·i'
—— an·te'ri·o'res' thal'a·mi'
—— ar'cu·a'ti'
—— coch'le·ar'es' ven·tra'lis et dor·sa'lis
—— cor'po·ris ge·nic'u·la'ti' lat'er·a'lis
—— corporis mam'il·lar'is
—— corporis trap'e·zoi'de·i'
—— ha·ben'u·lae' me'di·a'lis et lat'er·a'lis
—— in'tra·lam'i·nar'es' thal'a·mi'
—— lat'er·a'les' thal'a·mi'
—— mo·to'ri·i' ner'vi' tri·gem'i·ni'

—— ner'vi' a·cus'ti·ci'
—— nervi coch'le·ar'is
—— nervi glos'so·pha·
ryn'ge·i'
—— nervi tri·gem'i·ni'
—— nervi va'gi'
—— nervi ves·tib'u·lar'is
—— nervi ves·tib'u·lo·
coch'le·ar'is
—— ner·vo'rum cer'e·bra'li·
um
—— nervorum cra'ni·a'li·um
—— o·ri'gi·nis
—— pon'tis
—— pul·po'si'
—— sys·te'ma·tis ner·vo'si'
cen·tra'lis
—— teg·men'ti'
—— ter'mi·na'les'
—— ter'mi·na·ti·o'nis
—— tu'ber·a'les'
—— ves·tib'u·lar'es'
nu'cle·ic
nu'cle·ide'
nu'cle·i·form'
nu'cle·in
nu'cle·in·ase'
nu'cle·in'ic
nu'cle·o·cap'sid
nu'cle·o·chy·le'ma
nu'cle·o·chyme'
nu'cle·o·cy'to·plas·mic
nu'cle·of'u·gal
nu'cle·o·his'tone'
nu'cle·o·hy'a·lo·plasm
nu'cle·oid'
nu'cle·o·lar
nu'cle·o·li·form'
nu'cle·o·lin
nu'cle·o·loid'
nu·cle·o'o·lus pl. -li'
nu'cle·on'
nu'cle·on'ics
nu'cle·op'e·tal
nu'cle·o·phil'ic
nu'cle·o·plasm
nu'cle·o·plas'mic
nu'cle·o·pro'te·in
nu'cle·o·re·tic'u·lum
nu'cle·o·si'dase'
nu'cle·o·side'
nu'cle·o'sis pl. -ses'
nu'cle·o·spin'dle
nu'cle·o·ti'dase'
nu'cle·o·tide'
nu'cle·o·tox'ic
nu'cle·o·tox'in

nu'cle·us pl. -cle·i'
—— ac'ces·so'ri·us
—— accessorius ner'vi'
oc'u·lo·mo·to'ri·i'
—— a'lae' ci·ne're·ae'
—— am·big'u·us
—— a·myg'da·lae'
—— an'gu·lar'is
—— anterior thal'a·mi'
—— an'ter·o·dor·sa'lis
thal'a·mi'
—— an'ter·o·me'di·a'lis
thal'a·mi'
—— an'ter·o·ven·tra'lis
thal'a·mi'
—— ba·sa'lis
—— cau·da'lis cen·tra'lis
—— cau·da'tus
—— cen'tra'lis thal'a·mi'
—— cen'tro·me'di·a'nus
—— centromedianus thal'a·
mi'
—— cen'trum me'di·a'num
—— coch'le·ar'is dor·sa'lis
—— cochlearis ven·tra'lis
—— col·lic'u·li' in·fe'ri·o'ris
—— con·ter'mi·na'lis
—— cor'po·ris ge·nic'u·la'ti'
lat'er·a'lis
—— corporis geniculati
me'di·a'lis
—— corporis mam'il·lar'is
—— cu'ne·a'tus
—— cuneatus ac'ces·so'ri·us
—— den·ta'tus cer'e·bel'li'
—— dor·sa'lis
—— dorsalis cor'po·ris
trap'e·zoi'de·i'
—— dorsalis ner'vi' glos'so·
pha·ryn'ge·i'
—— dorsalis nervi va'gi'
—— dor'so·lat'er·a'lis
—— dor'so·me'di·a'lis hy'po·
thal'a·mi'
—— em·bol'i·for'mis cer'e·
bel'li'
—— em'i·nen'ti·ae' te're·tis
—— fas·tig'i·i'
—— fu·nic'u·li' cu'ne·a'ti'
—— funiculi grac'i·lis
—— glo·bo'sus cer'e·bel'li'
—— grac'i·lis
—— ha·ben'u·lae'
—— hy'po·tha·lam'i·cus
—— inferior pon'tis
—— in'ter·ca·la'tus
—— in'ter·me'di·o·lat'er·a'lis

—— in'ter·me'di·o·me'di·a'lis
—— in'ter·pe·dun'cu·lar'is
—— in'ter·sti'ti·a'lis
—— lat'er·a'lis dor·sa'lis
thal'a·mi'
—— lateralis me·dul'lae'
ob'lon·ga'tae'
—— lateralis medullae spi·
na'lis
—— lateralis thal'a·mi'
—— lem·nis'ci' lat'er·a'lis
—— len'ti·for'mis
—— len'tis
—— mag'no·cel'lu·lar'is
—— me'di·a'lis cen·tra'lis
thal'a·mi'
—— medialis dor·sa'lis
—— medialis me·dul'lae'
spi·na'lis
—— medialis pon'tis
—— medialis thal'a·mi'
—— mo·to'ri·us ner'vi' tri·
gem'i·ni'
—— ner'vi' ab'du·cen'tis
—— nervi ac'ces·so'ri·i'
—— nervi fa·ci·a'lis
—— nervi hy'po·glos'si'
—— nervi oc'u·lo·mo·to'ri·i'
—— nervi troch'le·ar'is
—— of Bekh'ter·ev
—— of Bur'dach'
—— of Dark'sche·witsch
—— of Ed'in·ger-West'phal'
—— of Goll
—— of Mo·na'kow'
—— of Per'li·a
—— of Rol'ler
—— of Schwal'be
—— ol'i·var'is
—— olivaris ac'ces·so'ri·us
dor·sa'lis
—— olivaris accessorius
me'di·a'lis
—— olivaris inferior
—— olivaris superior
—— o·ri'gi·nis
—— par'a·ven·tric'u·lar'is
hy'po·thal'a·mi'
—— pig'men'to'sus pon'tis
—— posterior hy'po·thal'a·
mi'
—— posterior thal'a·mi'
—— pre·pos'i·tus
—— pre'tec·ta'lis
—— pro'pri·us
—— pul·po'sus

—— rad'i·cis de'scen·den'tis ner'vi' tri·gem'i·ni'
—— re·tic'u·lar'is thal'a·mi'
—— ru'ber
—— sal'i·va·to'ri·us inferior
—— salivatorius superior
—— sen·so'ri·us inferior ner'vi' tri·gem'i·ni'
—— sensorius prin·ci·pa'lis ner'vi' tri·gem'i·ni'
—— spi·na'lis ner'vi' ac'ces·so'ri·i'
—— sub'tha·lam'i·cus
—— superior pon'tis
—— su'pra·op'ti·cus hy'po·thal'a·mi'
—— sym·path'i·cus lat'er·a'lis
—— teg·men'ti'
—— ter'mi·na·ti·o'nis
—— thal'a·mi' lat'er·a'lis
—— tho·ra'ci·cus
—— trac'tus mes'en·ce·phal'i·ci' ner'vi' tri·gem'i·ni'
—— tractus sol'i·tar'i·i'
—— tractus spi·na'lis ner'vi' tri·gem'i·ni'
—— ven·tra'lis anterior
—— ventralis an'ter·o·lat'er·a'lis thal'a·mi'
—— ventralis cor'po·ris trap'e·zoi'de·i'
—— ventralis in'ter·me'di·us thal'a·mi'
—— ventralis lat'er·a'lis
—— ventralis pos'ter·o·lat'er·a'lis thal'a·mi'
—— ventralis pos'ter·o·me'di·a'lis thal'a·mi'
—— ventralis thal'a·mi'
—— ventralis thalami anterior
—— ventralis thalami in'ter·me'di·us
—— ventralis thalami posterior
—— ven'tro·me'di·a'lis hy'po·thal'a·mi'
—— ves·tib'u·lar'is inferior
—— vestibularis lat'er·a'lis
—— vestibularis me'di·a'lis
—— vestibularis superior
nu'clide'
Nu·el' space
Nuhn glands
nul·lip'a·ra
nul'li·par'i·ty

nul·lip'a·rous
numb
num'ber
numb'ness
nu'mer·al
nu'mer'i·cal
num'mi·form'
num'mu·lar
nurse, nursed, nurs'ing
nu·ta'tion
nu'tri·ent
nu'tri·lite'
nu'tri·ment
nu·tri'tion
nu·tri'tion·al
nu·tri'tion·ist
nu·tri'tious
nu'tri·tive
nu'tri·ture
nux' vom'i·ca
Ny·an'do fever
nyc·tal'gi·a
nyc'ta·lope'
nyc'ta·lo'pi·a
nyc'ta·pho·ni·a
nyc'ter·ine'
nyc'to·hem'er·al
nyc'to·phil'i·a
nyc'to·pho'bi·a
nyc'to·pho'ni·a
nyc'to·typh·lo'sis
Ny'lan'der
—— reagent
—— test
ny'li·drin
nymph
nym'pha pl. -phae'
nym·phec'to·my
nym·phi'tis
nym'pho·ca·run'cu·lar
nym'pho·hy'men·e'al
nym'pho·lep'sy
nym'pho·ma'ni·a
nym'pho·ma'ni·ac'
nym·phon'cus
nym·phot'o·my
nys·tag'mic
nys·tag'mi·form'
nys·tag'mo·graph'
nys·tag'mog'ra·phy
nys·tag'moid'
nys·tag'mus
—— re'trac·to'ri·us
nys·ta·tin
nys·tax'is
Nys'ten law

O

oat'-cell'
oath of Hip·poc'ra·tes'
ob'ce·ca'tion
ob·du'cent
ob·duc'tion
o·be'li·ac'
o·be'li·ad'
o·be'li·on' pl. -li·a
O'ber
—— operations
—— sign
O'ber·may'er test
O'ber·stei'ner-Red'lich area
o·bese'
o·be'si·tas
o·be'si·ty
o'bex'
ob'fus·ca'tion
ob·jec'tive
ob'late'
ob'li·gate
o·blig'a·to'ry
o·blique'
o·bliq'ui·ty
o·bli'quus
o·blit'er·ate', -at'ed, -at'ing
o·blit'er·a'tion
o·blit'er·a·tive
ob'lon·ga'tal
ob'mu·tes'cence
ob·nu'bi·la'tion
ob·ses'sion
ob·ses'sion·al
ob·ses'sive
ob·ses'sive-com·pul'sive
ob'so·les'cence
ob'so·les'cent
ob·stet'ric or ob·stet'ri·cal
ob·ste·tri'cian
ob·stet'rics
ob·sti·pa'tion
ob·struct'
ob·struct'ed
ob·struc'tion
ob·struc'tive
ob'stru·ent
ob·tund'
ob·tun·da'tion
ob·tun'dent
ob·tu·rate', -rat'ed, -rat'ing
ob·tu·ra'tion
ob·tu·ra'tor
—— ex·ter'nus

—— in·ter′nus
ob·tuse′
ob·tu′sion
oc·cip′i·tal
oc·cip′i·ta′lis
oc·cip′i·tal·ize′, -ized′, -iz′-
  ing
oc·cip′i·to·an·te′ri·or
oc·cip′i·to·ax′i·al
oc·cip′i·to·bas′i·lar
oc·cip′i·to·breg·mat′ic
oc·cip′i·to·cer′vi·cal
oc·cip′i·to·fa′cial
oc·cip′i·to·fron′tal
oc·cip′i·to·fron·ta′lis
oc·cip′i·to·mas′toid′
oc·cip′i·to·men′tal
oc·cip′i·to·pa·ri′e·tal
oc·cip′i·to·pon′tine′
oc·cip′i·to·pos·te′ri·or
oc·cip′i·to·scap′u·lar′is
oc·cip′i·to·tem′po·ral
oc·cip′i·to·tha·lam′ic
oc′ci·put
oc·clude′, -clud′ed, -clud′ing
oc·clud′er
oc·clu′sal
oc·clu′si·o′
—— pu·pil′lae′
oc·clu′sion
oc·clu′sive
oc·clu′so·cer′vi·cal
oc′clu·som′e·ter
oc·cult′
o·cel′lus pl. -li′
och·le′sis
och′lo·pho′bi·a
o·chrom′e·ter
o′chro·no′sis pl. -ses′
o′chro·not′ic
Ochs′ner
—— muscle
—— ring
—— treatment
oc′tad′
oc′ta·meth′yl py′ro·
  phos′phor·am′ide′
oc′ta·pep′tide′
oc·tar′i·us
oc′ta·va′lent
oc′to·drine′
oc′tose′
oc·u·lar
oc·u·len′tum
oc·u·li′ mar′ma·ry·go′des′
oc·u·list

oc′u·lo·au·ric′u·lo·ver′te·
  bral
oc′u·lo·car′di·ac′
oc′u·lo·ceph′a·lo·gy′ric
oc′u·lo·cer′e·bro·re′nal
oc′u·lo·cu·ta′ne·ous
oc′u·lo·den·to·dig′i·tal
oc′u·lo·fa′cial
oc′u·lo·glan′du·lar
oc′u·lo·gy′ral
oc′u·lo·gy·ra′tion
oc′u·lo·gy′ric
oc′u·lo·mo′tor
oc′u·lo·my·co′sis pl. -ses′
oc′u·lo·na′sal
oc′u·lo·pha·ryn′ge·al
oc′u·lo·pu′pil·lar′y
oc′u·lo·sen′so·ry
oc′u·lo·zy′go·mat′ic
oc′u·lus pl. -li′
—— cae·si·us
—— dex′ter
—— lac′ri·mans′
—— lep′o·ri′nus
—— pu′ru·len′tus
—— sim′plex′
—— sin′is·ter
—— u′ni·tas
—— u·ter′que′
o′dax·es′mus
o′don·tal′gi·a
o′don·tal′gic
o′don·tec′to·my
o′don·thy′a·lus
o·don′tic
o·don′ti·noid′
o·don′ti·tis
o·don′to·am′e·lo·sar·co′ma
  pl. -mas or -ma·ta
o·don′to·at·lan′tal
o·don′to·blast′
o·don′to·blas′tic
o·don′to·blas·to′ma
  pl. -mas or -ma·ta
o·don′to·cele′
o·don′to·cla′sis pl. -ses′
o·don′to·clast′
o·don′to·gen
o·don′to·gen′e·sis pl. -ses′
o·don′to·gen′ic
o′don·tog′e·ny
o·don′to·graph′ic
o′don·tog′ra·phy
o·don′toid′
o·don′to·lith′
o·don′to·li·thi′a·sis pl. -ses′
o′don·tol′o·gist

o′don·tol′o·gy
o′don·tol′y·sis
o′don·to′ma pl. -mas or
  -ma·ta
o·don′to·pho′bi·a
o·don′to·plas′ty
o·don′to·pri′sis
o′don·tos′co·py
o·don′to·sei′sis
o′don·to′sis pl. -ses′
o′don·tot′o·my
o′dor
o′do·ra′tism
o′dor·if′er·ous
o′dor·im′e·try
o′dor·ous
o·dyn′a·cou′sis
o·dyn′o·pha′gi·a
oed′i·pal
oed′i·pism
Oed′i·pus complex
Oer′tel treatment
oesophag–. See words
  spelled *esophag*-.
oesophago–. See words
  spelled *esophago*-.
O·ga′wa serotype
Og′ston-Luc′ operation
O·gu′chi disease
O·ha′ra disease
ohm
ohm′me·ter
o·id′i·o·my·co′sis pl. -ses′
oil
oil′y
oi′no·ma′ni·a
oint′ment
o′le·ag′i·nous
o′le·an′do·my′cin
o′le·ate′
o·lec′ra·nal
o′le·cra′nar·thri′tis
o′le·cra′nar·throc′a·ce
o′le·cra′nar·throp′a·thy
o·lec′ra·noid′
o·lec′ra·non′
o′le·fin
o′le·in
o′le·o·gran′u·lo′ma pl. -mas
  or -ma·ta
o′le·om′e·ter
o′le·o·res′in
o′le·o·vi′ta·min
o′le·um pl. o′le·a
—— suc′ci·ni′
ol·fac′tion
ol′fac·tom′e·ter

ol·fac'to·ry
ol'i·ge'mi·a
ol'i·ge'mic
ol'i·ger·ga'si·a
ol'i·go·am'ni·os'
ol'i·go·blast'
ol'i·go·car'di·a pl. -ae' or -as
ol'i·go·chro·ma'si·a
ol'i·go·chro·me'mi·a
ol'i·go·cys'tic
ol'i·go·cy·the'mi·a
ol'i·go·cy·the'mic
ol'i·go·dac·tyl'i·a
ol'i·go·dac'ty·ly
ol'i·go·den'dro·blas·to'ma
    pl. -mas or -ma·ta
ol'i·go·den'dro·cyte'
ol'i·go·den'dro·cy·to'ma
    pl. -mas or -ma·ta
ol'i·go·den·drog'li·a
ol'i·go·den·drog'li·al
ol'i·go·den'dro·gli·o'ma
    pl. -mas or -ma·ta
ol'i·go·den·drog'li·o·ma·
    to'sis pl. -ses'
ol'i·go·den·dro'ma pl. -mas
    or -ma·ta
ol'i·go·don'ti·a
ol'i·go·dy·nam'ic
ol'i·go·en·ceph'a·ly
ol'i·go·ga·lac'ti·a
ol'i·go·gen'ic
ol'i·go·gen'ics
ol'i·gog'li·a
ol'i·go·hy·dram'ni·os
ol'i·go·hy'dri·a
ol'i·go·hy·dru'ri·a
ol'i·go·hy'per·men·or·rhe'a
ol'i·go·hy'po·men·or·rhe'a
ol'i·go·lec'i·thal
ol'i·go·men·or·rhe'a
ol'i·go·nu'cle·o·tide'
ol'i·go·phos'pha·tu'ri·a
ol'i·go·phre'ni·a
ol'i·go·phren'ic
ol'i·gop·ne'a
ol'i·go·pty'a·lism
ol'i·go·py'rene'
ol'i·go·sac'cha·ride'
ol'i·go·si·al'i·a
ol'i·go·sper'mi·a
ol'i·go·trich'i·a
    —— con·gen'i·ta
ol'i·go·tro'phi·a
ol'i·go·troph'ic
ol'i·got'ro·phy
ol'i·go·zo'o·sper'mi·a

ol'i·gu·re'sis pl. -ses'
ol'i·gu'ri·a
ol'i·gu'ric
o·lis'thy
o·li'va
ol'i·var'y
ol'ive
Ol'i·ver sign
ol'i·vif'u·gal
ol'i·vip'e·tal
ol'i·vo·cer'e·bel'lar
ol'i·vo·pon'to·cer'e·bel'lar
ol'i·vo·spi'nal
Ol·lier' disease
ol'o·pho'ni·a
o'ma·ceph'a·lus pl. -li'
o·ma'gra
o·mal'gi·a
o'mar·thral'gi·a
o'mar·thri'tis
o'ma·si'tis
o·ma'sum
o·me'ga
o·men'tal
o'men·tec'to·my
o'men·ti'tis
o·men'to·fix·a'tion
o·men'to·pex'y
o'men·tor'rha·phy
o'men·tot'o·my
o·men'tum pl. -ta
    —— ma'jus
    —— mi'nus
o·men'tum·ec'to·my
o·mi'tis
om'ma·tid'i·um pl. -i·a
om·niv'o·rous
o'mo·cer'vi·ca'lis
o'mo·cla·vic'u·lar
o'mo·dyn'i·a
o'mo·hy'oid'
o'mo·pha'gi·a
o'mo·plat'a
o'mo·ster'num pl. -nums or
    -na
o'mo·ver'te·bral
om'pha·lec'to·my
om·phal'ic
om'pha·li'tis
om'pha·lo·cele'
om'pha·lo·cho'ri·on'
om'pha·lo·did'y·mus
om'pha·lo·gen'e·sis pl. -ses'
om'pha·lo·mes'en·ter'ic
om'pha·lop'a·gus
om'pha·lo'phle·bi'tis

om'pha·lo·prop·to'sis pl.
    -ses'
om'pha·lor·rha'gi·a
om'pha·los' pl. -li'
om'pha·lo·site'
om'pha·lot'o·my
o'nan·ism
On'cho·cer'ca
    —— cae·cu'ti·ens
    —— vol'vu·lus
on'cho·cer·ci'a·sis pl. -ses'
on'cho·cer·co'ma
on'co·cyte'
on'co·cy·to'ma pl. -mas or
    -ma·ta
on'co·gen'e·sis pl. -ses'
on'co·ge·net'ic
on'co·gen'ic
on'co·graph'
on·cog'ra·phy
on·col'o·gist
on·col'o·gy
on·col'y·sis
on'co·lyt'ic
on·co'ma pl. -mas or -ma·ta
On'co·me·la'ni·a
    —— for'mo·sa'na
    —— hu·pen'sis
    —— hy'dro·bi·op'sis
    —— no·soph'o·ra
on'co·sis pl. -ses'
on'co·sphere'
on'co·thlip'sis
on·cot'ic
on·cot'o·my
on'co·trop'ic
o·nei'ric
o·nei'rism
o·nei'ro·dyn'i·a
o'nei·rog'mus
o'nei·rol'o·gy
o'nei·ros'co·py
on·kin'o·cele'
on'o·mat'o·ma'ni·a
on'o·mat'o·pho'bi·a
on'o·mat'o·poi·e'sis pl. -ses'
on'o·mat'o·poi·et'ic
on'set'
on'to·gen'e·sis pl. -ses'
on'to·ge·net'ic
on·tog'e·ny
on'y·al'ai'
on'y·cha·tro'phi·a
on'y·chat'ro·phy
on'ych·aux'is pl. -aux'es·
on'y·chec'to·my
o·nych'i·a

—— cra·que·lé′
—— ma·lig′na
—— punc·ta′ta
—— sim′plex′
—— su′per·fi′ci·a′lis un′du·
   la′ta
on′y·chin
on′y·choc′la·sis
on′y·cho·dys′tro·phy
on′y·cho·gen′ic
on′y·cho·gry·po′sis pl. -ses′
on′y·cho·het′er·o·to′pi·a
on′y·choid′
on′y·chol′y·sis
on′y·cho′ma pl. -mas or
   -ma·ta
on′y·cho′ma·de′sis
on′y·cho′ma·la′ci·a
on′y·cho·my·co′sis pl. -ses′
on′y·cho·os′te·o·dys·
   pla′si·a
on′y·cho·pac′i·ty
on′y·cho·path′ic
on′y·chop′a·thy
on′y·cho·pha′gi·a
on′y·chop′to′sis
on′y·chor·rhex′is pl.
   -rhex′es′
on′y·cho′sis pl. -ses′
on′y·chot′il·lo·ma′ni·a
on′y·chot′o·my
on′y·chot′ro·phy
O′nyong′-nyong′ fever
on′yx
on′yx·i′tis
o′o·ceph′a·lus
o′o·cyte′
o′o·gen′e·sis pl. -ses′
o′o·go′ni·um pl. -ni·a
o′o·ki·ne′sis pl. -ses′
o′o·ki′nete′
o′o·ki·net′ic
o′o·lem′ma
o′o·pho·rec′to·my
o′o·pho·ri′tis
o·oph′o·ro·cys·tec′to·my
o·oph′o·ro·cys·to′sis pl.
   -ses′
o·oph′o·ro·cys·tos′to·my
o·oph′o·ro·hys′ter·ec′to·
   my
o·oph′o·ro′ma pl. -mas or
   -ma·ta
   —— fol·lic′u·lar·e′
o·oph′o·ro·ma·la′ci·a
o·oph′o·ron′
o·oph′o·rop′a·thy

o·oph′o·ro·pex′y
o·oph′o·ro·plas′ty
o·oph′o·ro·sal′pin·gec′to·
   my
o·oph′o·ro·sal′pin·gi′tis
o·oph′o·ros′to·my
o′o·phor′rha·phy
o′o·plasm
o′o·sperm′
o′o·tid
o·pac′i·fi·ca′tion
o·pac′i·fy′, -fied′, -fy′ing
o·pac′i·ty
o′pal·es′cence
o′pal·es′cent
o·paque′
op′er·a·ble
op′er·ant
op′er·ate′, -at′ed, -at′ing
op′er·a′tion
op′er·a′tion·al
op′er·a·tive
op′er·a′tor
o·per′cu·lar
o·per′cu·late
o·per′cu·lum pl. -la or -lums
   —— fron·ta′le′
   —— fron′to·pa·ri′e·ta′le′
   —— il′e·i′
   —— tem′po·ra′le′
op′er·on′
o·phi′a·sis
o′phid·ism
oph′ry·on′
oph′ry·o′sis pl. -ses′
oph′thal·ma′gra
oph′thal·mal′gi·a
oph′thal·mec′to·my
oph′thal·men·ceph′a·lon′
oph′thal′mi·a
   —— e·lec′tri·ca
   —— ne′o·na·to′rum
   —— ni·va′lis
   —— no·do′sa
oph·thal′mi·at′rics
oph·thal′mic
oph·thal′mit′ic
oph·thal·mi′tis
oph·thal′mo·blen′nor·
   rhe′a
oph·thal′mo·cele′
oph·thal′mo·co′pi·a
oph·thal′mo·di′as·tim′e·ter
oph·thal′mo·do·ne′sis pl.
   -ses′
oph·thal′mo·dy′na·mom′e·
   ter

oph·thal′mo·dy′na·mom′e·
   try
oph·thal′mo·dyn′i·a
oph·thal′mo·ei′ko·nom′e·
   ter
oph·thal′mo·ei′ko·nom′e·
   try
oph·thal′mo·graph′
oph′thal·mog′ra·phy
oph·thal′mo·gy′ric
oph·thal′mo·leu′ko·scope′
oph′thal′mo·lith′
oph·thal′mo·log′ic
oph′thal·mol′o·gist
oph′thal·mol′o·gy
oph·thal′mo·ma·la′ci·a
oph′thal·mom′e·ter
oph′thal·mom′e·try
oph·thal′mo·my·co′sis pl.
   -ses′
oph·thal′mo·my·i′a·sis
oph·thal′mo·my·i′tis
oph·thal′mo·my·o′si′tis
oph·thal′mo·my·ot′o·my
oph·thal′mo·neu·ri′tis
oph·thal′mo·neu′ro·my′e·
   li′tis
oph′thal·mop′a·thy
oph·thal′mo·pha·com′e·ter
oph·thal′mo·phle·bot′o·my
oph·thal′mo·pho′bi·a
oph′thal·moph′thi·sis
oph·thal′mo·phy′ma
oph·thal′mo·plas′tic
oph·thal′mo·plas′ty
oph·thal′mo·ple′gi·a
oph·thal′mo·ple′gic
oph·thal′mop·to′sis
oph·thal′mor·rha′gi·a
oph·thal′mor·rhe′a
oph·thal′mor·rhex′is pl.
   -rhex′es′
oph·thal′mos′
oph·thal′mo·scope′
oph·thal′mo·scop′ic
oph′thal·mos′co·py
oph·thal′mos·ta′sis pl. -ses′
oph·thal′mo·stat′
oph·thal′mo·sta·tom′e·ter
oph·thal′mo·ste·re′sis
oph·thal′mo·syn′chy·sis
oph′thal·mot′o·my
oph′thal·mo·to·nom′e·ter
oph′thal·mo·to·nom′e·try
oph·thal′mo·trope′
oph′thal′mo·tro·pom′e·ter
oph′thal′mo·tro·pom′e·try

oph·thal'mo·vas'cu·lar
oph·thal'mo·xe·ro'sis pl.
  -ses'
oph·thal'mus pl. -mi'
o'pi·ate
O'pie paradox
o'pi·oid'
o'pi·o·ma'ni·a
o'pi·o·ma'ni·ac'
o'pi·o·pha'gi·a
o'pi·oph'a·gism
o'pi·oph'a·gy
o'pi·o·phile'
o·pis'then
o·pis'the·nar'
o·pis'thi·on'
o·pis'tho·cra'ni·on'
o'pis·thog'na·thism
o·pis'tho·neph'ros'
o·pis'tho·po·rei'a
o·pis'thor·chi'a·sis pl. -ses'
Op'is·thor'chis
—— fe·lin'e·us
—— no·ver'ca
—— viv'er·ri'ni'
o'pis·thot'ic
o·pis'tho·ton'ic
op'is·thot'o·noid'
op'is·thot'o·nos
o'pi·um
op'o·ceph'a·lus pl. -li'
op'o·did'y·mus
o·pod'y·mus
Op'pen·heim'
—— disease
—— reflex
Op'pen·heim-Ur'bach' dis-
  ease
op'pi·la'tion
op'pi·la'tive
op·po'nens
—— dig'i·ti' min'i·mi'
—— digiti quin'ti'
—— pol'li·cis
op'si·al'gi·a
op'por·tun'ist
op·sig'e·nes'
op'sin
op·sin'o·gen
op·si·nog'e·nous
op'si·om'e·ter
op'si·o·no'sis pl. -ses'
op'si·u'ri·a
op'so·clo'ni·a
op'so·clo'nus
op'so·ma'ni·a
op'so·ma'ni·ac'

op'son'ic
op'so·nin
op'so·ni·za'tion
op'so·nize', -nized', -niz'ing
op'so·no·cy'to·pha'gic
op'so·nom'e·try
op'so·no·ther'a·py
op'tes·the'si·a
op'tic or op'ti·cal
op·ti'cian
op·ti'cian·ry
op'ti·co·chi'as·mat'ic
op'ti·co·chi·as'mic
op'ti·co·cil'i·ar'y
op'ti·coele'
op'ti·co·fa'cial
op'ti·co·ki·net'ic
op'ti·co·pu'pil·lar'y
op'tics
op'ti·mal
op'ti·mum
op'to·blast'
op'to·chi·as'mic
op'to·gram'
op'to·ki·net'ic
op'to·me'ninx
op·tom'e·ter
op·tom'e·trist
op·tom'e·try
op'to·my·om'e·ter
op'to·phone'
op'to·type'
o'ra
—— ser·ra'ta
o'rad'
o'ral (pertaining to the
  mouth)
♦aural
o·ra'le'
Or·be'li effect
or·bic'u·lar
or·bic'u·lar'e
or·bic'u·lar'is
—— oc'u·li'
—— o'ris
—— pal'pe·brar'um
or·bic'u·lus pl. -li'
—— cil'i·ar'is
or'bit
or'bi·ta pl. -tae'
or'bi·tal
or'bi·ta'le' pl. -ta'li·a
or'bi·ta'lis
or'bi·to·na'sal
or'bi·to·nom'e·ter
or'bi·to·nom'e·try
or'bi·to·sphe'noid'

or'bi·to·stat'
or'bi·to·tem'po·ral
or'bi·tot'o·my
or'ce·in
or'che·i'tis
or·ches'tro·ma'ni·a
or'chi·al'gi·a
or'chic
or'chi·cho·re'a
or'chi·dal'gi·a
or'chi·dec'to·my
or·chid'ic
or'chi·di'tis
or'chi·do·ce'li·o·plas'ty
or'chi·do·ep'i·did'y·mec'to·
  my
or'chi·don'cus
or'chi·do·pa'thy
or'chi·do·pex'y
or'chi·do·plas'ty
or'chi·dop·to'sis
or'chi·dor'rha·phy
or'chi·dot'o·my
or'chi·ec'to·my
or'chi·en·ceph'a·lo'ma
  pl. -mas or -ma·ta
or'chi·ep'i·did'y·mi'tis
or'chi·o·ca·tab'a·sis pl. -ses'
or'chi·o·cele'
or'chi·o·my'e·lo'ma pl.
  -mas or -ma·ta
or'chi·on'cus
or'chi·o·pa'thy
or'chi·o·pex'y
or'chi·o·plas'ty
or'chi·or'rha·phy
or'chi·o·scir'rhus pl. -rhi' or
  -rhus·es
or'chi·ot'o·my
or'chis
or'chit'ic
or·chi'tis
or·chit'o·my
or·chot'o·my
or'ci·nol'
or'der
or'der·ly
or'di·nate
o·rex'i·a
o·rex'is
orf
or'gan
—— of Cor'ti
—— of Gol'gi
—— of Ja'cob·son
or'ga·na
—— gen'i·ta'li·a fem'i·ni'na

—— genitalia mas'cu·li'na
—— genitalia mu'li·
e'bri·a
—— genitalia vi·ril'i·a
—— oc'u·li' ac'ces·so'ri·a
—— sen'su·um
—— u'ro·po·ët'i·ca
or'gan·elle'
or·gan'ic
or·gan'i·cism
or·gan'i·cist
or'gan·ism
or'ga·ni·za'tion
or'ga·nize', -nized', -niz'ing
or'ga·niz'er
or'ga·no·ax'i·al
or·gan'o·gel'
or'ga·no·gen'e·sis
or'ga·no·ge·net'ic
or'ga·nog'e·ny
or'ga·noid'
or'ga·nol'o·gy
or'ga·no·meg'a·ly
or·gan'o·mer·cu'ri·al
or·gan'o·me·tal'lic
or'ga·non' pl. -na
—— au·di'tus
—— gus'tus
—— ol·fac'tus
—— pa·ren'chy·ma·to'sum
—— spi·ra'le'
—— vi'sus
—— vom'er·o·na·sa'le'
or'ga·nop'a·thy
or'ga·no·pex'y
or'ga·nos'co·py
or·gan'o·sol'
or'ga·no·tax'is
or'ga·no·ther'a·py
or'ga·no·troph'ic (pertaining to the nutrition of organs)
♦organotropic
or'ga·no·trop'ic (pertaining
   to chemical affinity)
♦organotrophic
or'ga·not'ro·pism
or'ga·not'ro·py
organs of Zuck'er·kandl'
or'ga·nule'
or'ga·num pl. -na
—— gus'tus
—— ol·fac'tus
—— spi·ra'le'
—— ves·tib'u·lo·coch'le·ar'e'
—— vi'sus
—— vom'er·o·na·sa'le'

or'gasm
or·gas'mo·lep'sy
or'go·tein'
o'ri·en·ta'tion
or'i·fice
or'i·fi'cial
o'ri·fi'ci·um pl. -ci·a
—— ex·ter'num u'ter·i'
—— in·ter'num u'ter·i'
—— u·re'ter·is
—— u·re'thrae' in·ter'num
—— urethrae mu'li·e'bris
ex·ter'num
—— urethrae vi·ri'lis ex·
ter'num
—— va·gi'nae'
or'i·gin
Orms'by method
or'ni·thine'
or'ni·thi·ne'mi·a
Or'ni·thod'o·rus
or'ni·tho'sis pl. -ses'
or'ni·thyl
o'ro·an'tral
o'ro·di·ag·no'sis pl. -ses'
o'ro·fa'cial
o'ro·lin'gual
o'ro·max·il'·lar'y
o'ro·na'sal
o'ro·pha·ryn'ge·al
o'ro·phar'ynx pl. -pha·
ryn'ges'
o'ro·sin
o'ro·so·mu'coid'
o·rot'ic
O·roy'a fever
or·phen'a·drine'
or'rho·im·mu'ni·ty
or'rho·men'in·gi'tis
or'rho·re·ac'tion
or'rhos'
or'ris·root'
Or'ta·la'ni sign
or'ther·ga'si·a
or·the'sis pl. -ses'
or'tho
or'tho·ar·te'ri·ot'o·ny
or'tho·bo'ric
or'tho·car'di·ac'
or'tho·ce·phal'ic
or'tho·ceph'a·ly
or'tho·chlo'ro·phe'nol'
or'tho·cho·re'a
or'tho·chro·mat'ic
or'tho·chro'mi·a
or'tho·chro'mic
or'tho·cra'si·a

or'tho·cre'sol'
or'tho·cy'to·sis pl. -ses'
or'tho·dac'ty·lous
or'tho·den'tin
or'tho·di'a·gram'
or'tho·di'a·graph'
or'tho·di·ag'ra·phy
or'tho·dol'i·cho·ceph'a·
lous
or'tho·don'ti·a
or'tho·don'tic
or'tho·don'tics
or'tho·don'tist
or'tho·gen'e·sis
or'tho·ge·net'ic
or'tho·gen'ic
or'tho·gly·ce'mic
or'thog·nath'ic
or'thog'na·thism
or·thog'o·nal
or'tho·grade'
or'tho·hy·drox'y·ben·zo'ic
or'tho·mes'o·ceph'a·lous
or·thom'e·ter
or'tho·pae'dic var. of ortho-
pedic
or'tho·pae'dics var. of or-
thopedics
or'tho·pae'dist var. of
orthopedist
or'tho·pan'to·mo·gram'
or'tho·pe'dic also orthopae-
dic
or'tho·pe'dics also ortho-
paedics
or'tho·pe'dist also orthopae-
dist
or'tho·per·cus'sion
or'tho·phe·nan'thro·line'
or'tho·phen'yl·phe'nol'
or'tho·pho'ri·a
or'tho·phos·pho'ric
or'thop·ne'a
or'thop·ne'ic
or'tho·prax'is pl. -prax'es'
or'tho·prax'y
or'tho·psy·chi'a·try
Or·thop'ter·a
or·thop'tic
or·thop'tics
or·thop'to·scope'
or'tho·rhom'bic
or'tho·roent'gen·og'ra·phy
or'thor·rhach'ic
or'tho·scope'
or'tho·scop'ic
or·thos'co·py

or·tho'sis pl. -ses'
or'tho·stat'ic
or'tho·stat'ism
or'tho·ste're·o·scope'
or'tho·sym'pa·thet'ic
or'tho·tast'
or'tho·ter'i·on'
or'tho·ther'a·py
or·thot'ic
or·thot'ics
or'tho·tist
or'tho·ton'ic
or·thot'o·nos var. of ortho-
tonus
or·thot'o·nus also ortho-
tonos
or'tho·to'pi·a
or'tho·top'ic
or'tho·trop'ic
or·thot'ro·pism
or'tho·volt'age
o·ry'za·min
os (mouth), pl. o'ra
os (bone), pl. os'sa
— ac'e·tab'u·li'
— a·cro'mi·a'le'
— ar·tic'u·lar'e'
— bas'i·lar'e'
— ba'si·ot'i·cum
— breg·mat'i·cum
— brev'e'
— cal'cis
— cap'i·ta'tum
— cen·tra'le'
— cli·to'ri·dis
— coc'cy·gis
— cor'dis
— cos·ta'le'
— cox'ae'
— cu·boi'de·um
— cu'ne·i·for'me' in'ter·
me'di·um
— cuneiforme lat'er·a'le'
— cuneiforme me'di·a'le'
— cuneiforme pri'mum
— cuneiforme se·cun'dum
— cuneiforme ter'ti·um
— den·ta'le'
— en·to'mi·on'
— ep'i·pter'i·cum
— eth'moi·da'le'
— fal'ci·for'me'
— fron·ta'le'
— ha·ma'tum
— hy·oi'de·um
— il'i·um
— in'ci·si'vum

— in'ter·cu'ne·i·for'me'
— in'ter·fron·ta'le'
— in'ter·met'a·tar'se·um
— in'ter·pa·ri'e·ta'le'
— is'chi·i'
— ja·pon'i·cum
— lac'ri·ma'le'
— len·tic'u·lar'e'
— lon'gum
— lu·na'tum
— mag'num
— met'a·car·pa'le'
— mul·tan'gu·lum ma'jus
— multangulum mi'nus
— na·sa'le'
— na·vic'u·lar'e'
— naviculare ma'nus
— naviculare pe'dis
— no'vum
— oc·cip'i·ta'le'
— o'don·toi'de·um
— or·bic'u·lar'e'
— or'bi·ta'le'
— pal'a·ti'num
— pa·ri'e·ta'le
— pe'dis
— pe'nis
— per'o·ne'um
— pi'si·for'me'
— pla'num
— pneu·mat'i·cum
— pre·ba'si·oc·cip'i·ta'le'
— pu'bis
— pu'rum
— sa'crum
— sca·phoi'de·um
— sphe'noi·da'le'
— sty·loi'de·um
— suf·frag'i·nis
— su'pra·ster·na'le'
— tem'po·ra'le'
— tib'i·a'le' ex·ter'num
— tra·pe'zi·um
— trap'e·zoi'de·um
— tri·go'num
— tri·que'trum
— u'ter·i'
— uteri ex·ter'num
— uteri in·ter'num
— Ve·sa'li·i'
— zy'go·mat'i·cum
o'sa·mine'
o'sa·zone'
Os'borne' wave
os'che·a
os'che·al
os'che·i'tis

os'che·o·cele'
os'che·o·hy'dro·cele'
os'che·o·lith'
os'che·i·o'ma pl. -mas or -ma·
ta
os'che·o·plas'ty
Os'cil·lar'i·a ma·lar'i·ae'
os'cil·late', -lat'ed, -lat'ing
os'cil·la'tion
os'cil·la·tor
os'cil·la·to'ry
os'cil·lo·graph'
os'cil·lo·graph'ic
os'cil·log'ra·phy
os'cil·lom'e·ter
os'cil·lo·met'ric
os'cil·lom'e·try
os'cil·lop'si·a
os'cil·lo·scope'
Os'ci·nis
— pal'li·pes'
os'ci·tan·cy
os'ci·ta'tion
os'cu·la'tion
os'cu·lum
Os'er·et'sky test
Os'good-Has'kins test
Os'good-Schlat'ter disease
O'Shaugh'nes·sy opera-
tion
Os'ler
— disease
— nodes
Os'ler-Va·quez'
— disease
— nodes
os'mate'
os·mat'ic
os·me'sis
os'mes·the'si·a
os'mic
os'mics
os'mi·dro'sis pl. -ses'
os'mi·o·phil'ic
os'mi·um
os'mo·dys·pho'ri·a
os'mol'
os·mo'lal
os·mo'lal'i·ty
os·mo'lar
os·mo'lar'i·ty
os·mol'o·gy
os·mom'e·ter
os'mo·no·sol'o·gy
os'mo·phil'ic
os'mo·pho'bi·a
os'mo·phore'

os′mo·re·cep′tor
os′mo·reg′u·la·to′ry
os′mose′
os·mo′sis
os·mot′ic
os′phre·si·ol′o·gy
os′phre·si·om′e·ter
os·phre′sis
os′phy·o·my′e·li′tis
os′phy·ot′o·my
os′sa
—— car′pi·i
—— cra′ni·i′
—— dig′i·to′rum ma′nus
—— digitorum pe′dis
—— ex·trem′i·ta′tis in·fe′ri·o′ris
—— extremitatis su·pe′ri·o′ris
—— fa′ci·e′i′
—— in′ter·ca·lar′i·a
—— mem′bri′ in·fe′ri·o′ris
—— membri su·pe′ri·o′ris
—— met′a·car·pa′li·a
—— met′a·tar·sa′li·a
—— ses′a·moi′de·a
—— su′pra·ster·na′li·a
—— su′tu·rar′um
—— tar′si′
os′se·in
os′se·o·al·bu′min·oid′
os′se·o·car·ti·lag′i·nous
os′se·o·fi′brous
os′se·o·lig′a·men′tous
os′se·o·mu′coid′
os′se·ous
os′si·cle
—— of Ber·tin′
os·sic′u·la au·di′tus
os·sic′u·lar
os′si·cu·lec′to·my
os·sic′u·lo·plas′ty
os·sic′u·lot′o·my
os·sic′u·lum pl. -la
os·sif′er·ous
os·sif′ic
os·si·fi·ca′tion
os·sif′lu·ence
os·sif′lu·ent
os′si·form′
os′si·fy′, -fied′, -fy′ing
os·tal′gi·a
os·tal′gic
os′tal·gi′tis
os′te·al
os′te·al′gi·a
os′te·al′le·o′sis pl. -ses′

os′te·an′a·gen′e·sis pl. -ses′
os′tec′to·my
os′tec′to·py
os′te·ec′to·my
os′te·ec·to′pi·a
os′te·in
os′te·it′ic
os′te·i′tis
—— car·no′sa
—— con·den·sans′ il′i·i′
—— cys′ti·ca
—— de·for′mans′
—— fi·bro′sa cys′ti·ca
—— fibrosa cystica dis·sem′i·na′ta
—— fibrosa gen·er·al·i·sa′ta
—— fra·gil′i·tans′
—— fun·go′sa
—— pu′bis
—— tu·ber′cu·lo′sa mul′ti·plex′ cys·toi′des′
ost·em′bry·on′
os′tem·py·e′sis
os′te·o·a·cu′sis
os′te·o·an′a·gen′e·sis pl. -ses′
os′te·o·an·es·the′si·a
os′te·o·an′eu·rysm
os′te·o·ar·threc′to·my
os′te·o·ar·thri′tis
os′te·o·ar·throp′a·thy
os′te·o·ar·thro′sis pl. -ses′
os′te·o·ar·throt′o·my
os′te·o′ar·tic′u·lar
os′te·o·blast′
os′te·o·blas′tic
os′te·o·blas·to′ma pl. -mas or -ma·ta
os′te·o′ca·chec′tic
os′te·o′ca·chex′i·a
os′te·o·camp′
os′te·o·camp′si·a
os′te·o·car′ci·no′ma pl. -mas or -ma·ta
os′te·o·car′ti·lag′i·nous
os′te·o·cele′
os′te·o′ce·men′tum pl. -ta
os′te·o·chon′dral
os′te·o·chon·dri′tis
—— de·for′mans′ cox′ae′ ju′ve·ni′lis
—— deformans ju′ve·ni′lis
—— dis′se·cans′
os′te·o·chon′dro·dys·pla′si·a
os′te·o·chon′dro·dys·tro′phi·a de·for′mans′

os′te·o·chon′dro·dys·tro·phy
os′te·o·chon·dro′ma pl. -mas or -ma·ta
os′te·o·chon·dro′ma·to′sis
os′te·o·chon′dro·myx·o′ma pl. -mas or -ma·ta
os′te·o·chon′dro·myx′o·sar·co′ma pl. -mas or -ma·ta
os′te·o′chon·drop′a·thy
os′te·o·chon′dro·sar·co′ma pl. -mas or -ma·ta
os′te·o·chon·dro′sis pl. -ses′
—— de·for′mans′ ju′ve·ni′lis
—— deformans tib′i·ae′
—— dis′se·cans′
os′te·o·chon′drous
os′te·o·cla′si·a
os′te·oc·la′sis pl. -ses′
os′te·o·clast′
os′te·o·clas′tic
os′te·o·clas·to′ma pl. -mas or -ma·ta
os′te·o·cope′
os′te·o·cop′ic
os′te·o·cra′ni·um pl. -ni·ums or -ni·a
os′te·o·cys·to′ma pl. -mas or -ma·ta
os′te·o·cyte′
os′te·o·den′tin
os′te·o·der′ma·to·plas′tic
os′te·o·der′mi·a
os′te·o′des·mo′sis pl. -ses′
os′te·o·di·as′ta·sis pl. -ses′
os′te·o·dyn′i·a
os′te·o′dys·plas′ty
os′te·o′dys·tro′phi·a
—— de·for′mans′
—— fi·bro′sa
os′te·o·dys·tro′phy
os′te·o·e·piph′y·sis pl. -ses′
os′te·o·fi′bro·chon·dro′ma pl. -mas or -ma·ta
os′te·o·fi′bro·chon′dro·sar·co′ma pl. -mas or -ma·ta
os′te·o·fi′bro·li·po′ma pl. -mas or -ma·ta
os′te·o·fi′bro′ma pl. -mas or -ma·ta
os′te·o′fi·bro′ma·to′sis pl. -ses′
os′te·o·fi′bro·sar·co′ma pl. -mas or -ma·ta
os′te·o·fi′bro′sis pl. -ses′
os′te·o·gen

os'te·o·gen'e·sis
—— im'per·fec'ta
—— imperfecta con·gen'i·ta
—— imperfecta cys'ti·ca
—— imperfecta tar'da
os'te·o·ge·net'ic
os'te·o·gen'ic
os'te·og'e·nous
os'te·og'e·ny
os'te·o·hal'i·ste·re'sis pl. -ses'
os'te·o·hem'a·chro'ma·to'sis pl. -ses'
os'te·o·hy'per·troph'ic
os'te·oid'
os'te·o·in·duc'tive
os'te·o·lip'o·chon·dro'ma pl. -mas or -ma·ta
os'te·o'li·po'ma pl. -mas or -ma·ta
os'te·o·lith'
os'te·o·lo'gi·a
os'te·ol'o·gy
os'te·ol'y·sis
os'te·o·lyt'ic
os'te·o'ma pl. -mas or -ma·ta
—— cu'tis
—— du'rum
—— e·bur'ne·um
—— med'ul·lar'e'
—— spon'gi·o'sum
os'te·o·ma·la'ci·a
os'te·o·ma·la'ci·al
os'te·o·ma·la'cic
os'te·o·ma·to'sis
os'te·o·met'ric
os'te·om'e·try
os'te·o'mi·o'sis
os'te·o·mu'coid'
os'te·o·my'e·lit'ic
os'te·o·my'e·li'tis
os'te·o·my'e·log'ra·phy
os'te·o·myx'o·chon·dro'ma pl. -mas or -ma·ta
os'te·on'
os'te·o·ne·cro'sis
os'te·o·ne·phrop'a·thy
os'te·o·neu·ral'gi·a
os'te·o·path'
os'te·o·path'i·a
—— con·den'sans' dis·sem'i·na'ta
—— hy'per·os·tot'i·ca mul'ti·plex' in·fan'ti·lis
—— stri·a'ta
os'te·o·path'ic

os'te·op'a·thy
os'te·o·pe·cil'i·a
os'te·o·pe'di·on'
os'te·o·pe'ni·a
os'te·o·per'i·os'te·al
os'te·o·per'i·os·ti'tis
os'te·o·pe·tro'sis
—— gal'li·nar'um
—— gen'er·al·i·sa'ta
os'te·o·pe·trot'ic
os'te·o·phage'
os'te·o'phle·bi'tis
os'te·oph'o·ny
os'te·o·phy'ma pl. -mas or -ma·ta
os'te·o·phyte'
os'te·o·phyt'ic
os'te·o·phy·to'sis
os'te·o·plaque'
os'te·o·plast'
os'te·o·plas'tic
os'te·o·plas'ty
os'te·o·poi'ki·lo'sis pl. -ses'
os'te·o·po·ro'sis pl. -ses'
os'te·o·po·rot'ic
os'te·op·sath'y·ro'sis pl. -ses'
os'te·o·pul'mo·nar'y
os'te·o·ra'di·o·ne·cro'sis
os'te·or·rha'gi·a
os'te·or'rha·phy
os'te·o·sar·co'ma pl. -mas or -ma·ta
os'te·o·sar·co'ma·tous
os'te·o·scle·ro'sis pl. -ses'
—— frag'i·lis gen'er·al·i·sa'ta
os'te·o·scle·rot'ic
os'te·o'sis
—— cu'tis
os'te·o·spon'gi·o'ma pl. -mas or -ma·ta
os'te·o·stix'is
os'te·o·su'ture
os'te·o·syn'o·vi'tis
os'te·o·syn'the·sis pl. -ses'
os'te·o·ta'bes'
os'te·o·te·lan'gi·ec·ta'si·a
os'te·o·throm'bo·phle·bi'tis
os'te·o·throm·bo'sis pl. -ses'
os'te·o·tome'
os'te·o·to'mo·cla'si·a
os'te·ot'o·moc'la·sis pl. -ses'
os'te·ot'o·my
os'te·o·tribe'

os'te·o·trite'
os'te·ot'ro·phy
Os'ter·berg' test
os'ti·a
—— a'tri·o·ven·tric'u·lar'i·a dex'trum et si·nis'trum
—— ve·nar'um pul'mo·na'li·um
os'ti·al
os·ti'tis
os'ti·um pl. -ti·a
—— ab·dom'i·na'le' tu'bae' u'ter·i'nae'
—— a·or'tae'
—— ap·pen'di·cis ver'mi·for'mis
—— ar·te'ri·o'sum cor'dis
—— a'tri·o·ven·tric'u·lar'e'
—— atrioventriculare dex'trum
—— atrioventriculare si·nis'trum
—— il'e·o·ce·ca'le'
—— max'il·lar'e'
—— pha·ryn'ge·um tu'bae' au'di·ti'vae'
—— py·lo'ri·cum
—— trun'ci' pul'mo·na'lis
—— tym·pan'i·cum tu'bae' au'di·ti'vae'
—— u·re'ter·is
—— u·re'thrae' fem'i·ni'nae' ex·ter'num
—— urethrae in·ter'num
—— urethrae mas'cu·li·nae' ex·ter'num
—— u'ter·i'
—— u'ter·i'num tu'bae'
—— va·gi'nae'
—— ve'nae' ca'vae' in·fe'ri·o'ris
—— venae cavae su·pe'ri·o'ris
—— ve·no'sum cor'dis
os'to·my
os·to'sis
os'tre·o·tox'ism
o·tal'gi·a
o·tal'gic
o·tec'to·my
o'thel·co'sis pl. -ses'
ot·he'ma·to'ma pl. -mas or -ma·ta
ot·hem'or·rha'gi·a
ot·hem'or·rhe'a
o'tic
o'ti·co·din'i·a

o•tit′ic
o•ti′tis
—— ex•ter′na
—— in•ter′na
—— lab′y•rin′thi•ca
—— mas•toi′de•a
—— me′di•a
—— par′a•sit′i•ca
—— scle•rot′i•ca
o′to•blen′nor•rhe′a
o′to•ceph′a•lus pl. -li′
o′to•ceph′a•ly
o′to•cer′e•bri′tis
o′to•clei′sis
o′to•co′ni•a sing. -ni•um
o′to•cra′ni•al
o′to•cra′ni•um pl. -ums or
  -i•a
o′to•cyst′
o′to•dyn′i•a
o′to•en•ceph′a•li′tis
o′to•gan′gli•on pl. -gli•a or
  -gli•ons
o′to•gen′ic
o•tog′e•nous
o′to•hem′i•neur′as•the′ni•a
o′to•lar′yn•gol′o•gist
o′to•lar′yn•gol′o•gy
o′to•lith′
o′to•li•thi′a•sis pl. -ses′
o′to•log′ic or o′to•log′i•cal
o•tol′o•gist
o•tol′o•gy
o′to•mas′toid•i′tis
o′to•my′as•the′ni•a
o′to•my•co′sis pl. -ses′
o′to•neu•ral′gi•a
o′to•neur′as•the′ni•a
o•top′a•thy
o′to•pha•ryn′ge•al
o′to•plas′ty
o′to•pol′y•pus
o′to•py′or•rhe′a
o′to•py•o′sis
o′to•rhi′no•lar′yn•gol′o•gy
o′to•rhi•nol′o•gy
o′tor•rha′gi•a
o′tor•rhe′a
o′to•sal′pinx pl. -sal•pin′ges
o′to•scle•rec′to•my
o′to•scle•ro′sis pl. -ses′
o′to•scle•rot′ic
o′to•scope′
o′to•scop′ic
o•tos′co•py
o′to•spon′gi•o′sis pl. -ses′
o•tos′te•al

o•tos′te•on′
o•tot′o•my
o′to•tox′ic
o′to•tox•ic′i•ty
Ot′to
—— disease
—— pelvis
Ott precipitation test
oua•ba′in
ounce
out′flow′
out′growth′
out′let′
out′pa′tient
out′pouch′ing
out′put′
o′val
ov′al•bu′min
o•va′le′
o•val′o•cyte′
o•val′o•cy•to′sis pl. -ses′
o•var′i•al′gi•a
o•var′i•an
o•var′i•ec′to•my
o•var′i•o•cele′
o•var′i•o•cen•te′sis pl. -ses′
o•var′i•o•cy•e′sis pl. -ses′
o•var′i•o•dys•neu′ri•a
o•var′i•o•gen′ic
o•var′i•o•hys′ter•ec′to•my
o•var′i•o•pex′y
o•var′i•or•rhex′is pl.
  -rhex′es′
o•var′i•o•sal′pin•gec′to•my
o•var′i•o•ste•re′sis pl. -ses′
o•var′i•os′to•my
o•var′i•ot′o•my
o•var′i•o•tu′bal
o′va•ri′tis
o•var′i•um pl. -i•a
o′va•ry
o′va•tes•tic′u•lar
o′ver•a•chieve′, -chieved′,
  -chiev′ing
o′ver•a•chiev′er
o′ver•bite′
o′ver•clo′sure
o′ver•com′pen•sate′, -sat′-
  ed, -sat′ing
o′ver•com′pen•sa′tion
o′ver•de•ter′mi•na′tion
o′ver•flex′ion
o′ver•rid′ing
o•vert′
o′ver•toe′
o′ver•weight′
o′vi•cap′sule

o′vi•duct′
o′vi•duc′tal
o•vif′er•ous
o′vi•form′
o′vi•gen′e•sis pl. -ses′
o′vi•ge•net′ic
o•vig′e•nous
o′vi•germ′
o•vig′er•ous
o′vi•sac′
o′vo•cen′ter
o′vo•cyte′
o′vo•fla′vin
o′vo•gen′e•sis pl. -ses′
o′vo•glob′u•lin
o′vo•go′ni•um pl. -ni•a
o′void′
o′vo•mu′cin
o′vo•mu′coid′
o′vo•plasm
o′vo•tes•tic′u•lar
o′vo•tes′tis pl. -tes′
o′vo•vi•tel′lin
o′vu•lar
o′vu•late′, -lat′ed, -lat′ing
o′vu•la′tion
o′vu•la′tion•al
o′vu•la•to′ry
o′vule′
o′vu•log′e•nous
o′vu•lum pl. -la
o′vum pl. o′va
—— tu•ber′cu•lo′sum
O′wen lines
Ow′ren disease
ox′a•cil′lin
ox′a•late′, -lat′ed, -lat′ing
ox′a•le′mi•a
ox•al′ic
ox′a•lism
ox′a•lo′sis
ox′a•lo•suc•cin′ic
ox•al•u′ri•a
ox•al•u′ric
ox•am′i•dine′
ox•an′a•mide′
ox•an′dro•lone′
ox•a′ze•pam′
ox•eth′a•zaine′
ox′i•dant
ox′i•dase′
ox′i•date′, -dat′ed, -dat′ing
ox′i•da′tion
ox′i•da′tive
ox′ide′
ox′i•dize′, -dized′, -diz′ing
ox′i•do-re•duc′tase′

ox'ime'
ox·im'e·ter
ox·im'e·try
ox'o·ges'tone'
ox'o·lin'ic
ox'o·phen·ar'sine'
ox·pren'o·lol'
ox'tri·phyl'line'
ox'y·a·koi'a
ox'y·a'phi·a
ox'y·ben'zone'
ox'y·blep'si·a
ox'y·bu'ty·nin
ox'y·ce·phal'ic
ox'y·ceph'a·ly
ox'y·chlo'ride'
ox'y·chro'ma·tin
ox'y·ci·ne'si·a
ox'y·ci·ne'sis
ox'y·cor'ti·co·ste'roid'
ox'y·es·the'si·a
ox'y·gen
ox'y·gen·ase'
ox'y·gen·ate', -at'ed, -at'ing
ox'y·gen·a'tion
ox'y·gen·a'tor
ox'y·gen'ic
ox'y·geu'si·a
ox'y·hem'a·tin
ox'y·hem'a·to·por'phy·rin
ox'y·he'mo·glo'bin
ox'y·hy'per·gly·ce'mi·a
ox'y·la'li·a
ox'y·me·taz'o·line'
ox'y·meth'o·lone'
ox'y·mor'phone'
ox'y·ner'von'
ox'y·neu'rine'
ox'y·o'pi·a
ox'y·op'ter
ox'y·os'mi·a
ox'y·os·phre'si·a
ox'y·per'tine'
ox'y·phen·bu'ta·zone'
ox'y·phen·cy'cli·mine'
ox'y·phen'ic
ox'y·phen·i'sa·tin
ox'y·phe·no'ni·um
ox'y·phil'
ox'y·phil'i·a
ox'y·phil'ic
ox'y·pho'ni·a
ox'y·pro'line'
ox'y·pu'ri·nol'
ox'y·quin'o·line'
ox'y·rhine'
ox·yt'a·lan'

ox'y·tet'ra·cy'cline'
ox'y·to'ci·a
ox'y·to'cic
ox'y·to'cin
ox'y·u·ri'a·sis *pl.* -ses'
Ox'y·u'ris
o·ze'na
o'zone'
o'zon·ide'
o'zo·sto'mi·a

P

pab'u·lum
Pac'chi·o'ni·an bodies
pace'mak'er
pa·chom'e·ter
pach'y·ac'ri·a
pach'y·bleph'a·ron'
pach'y·bleph'a·ro'sis
pach'y·ce·pha'li·a
pach'y·ce·phal'ic
pach'y·ceph'a·lous
pach'y·ceph'a·ly
pach'y·chei'li·a
pach'y·chro·mat'ic
pach'y·dac·tyl'i·a
pach'y·dac'ty·ly
pach'y·der'ma
pach'y·der'ma·to·cele'
pach'y·der'ma·to'sis *pl.*
   -ses'
pach'y·der'ma·tous
pach'y·der'mi·a
—— la·ryn'gis
—— lym·phan'gi·ec·tat'i·ca
pach'y·der'mic
pach'y·glos'si·a
pach'y·gy'ri·a
pach'y·hem'a·tous
pach'y·hy·men'ic
pach'y·lep'to·men·in·gi'tis
pach'y·men·in·git'ic
pach'y·men·in·gi'tis
—— cer'vi·ca'lis hy'per·
troph'i·ca
—— ex·ter'na
—— in·ter'na hem'or·rha'gi·
ca
pach'y·men·in·gop'a·thy
pach'y·me'ninx
pach'y·mu·co'sa
pach'y·ne'ma
pa·chyn'sis *pl.* -ses'
pa·chyn'tic

pach'y·o·nych'i·a
—— con·gen'i·ta
pach'y·pel'vi·per'i·to·ni'tis
pach'y·per'i·os·to'sis
pach'y·per'i·to·ni'tis
pa·chyp'o·dous
pach'y·sal'pin·gi'tis
pach'y·sal·pin·go·o'va·
ri'tis
pach'y·tene'
pach'y·vag'i·ni'tis
pa·cin'i·an
pack
pack'er
pack'ing
pad, pad'ded, pad'ding
Padg'ett operation
paed–. See words spelled
   ped-.
paedo–. See words spelled
   pedo-.
Pa·get'
—— cancer
—— cells
—— disease
pag'et·oid'
pa'go·pha'gi·a
pa'go·plex'i·a
pain
pain'ful
pain'less
pal'a·tal
pal'ate
pa·lat'ic
pa·lat'i·form'
pal'a·tine'
pal'a·ti'tis
pal'a·to·glos'sal
pal'a·to·graph'
pal'a·to·max'il·lar'y
pal'a·to·my'o·graph'
pal'a·to·na'sal
pal'a·top'a·gus par'a·sit'i·
cus
pal'a·to·pha·ryn'ge·al
pal'a·to·plas'ty
pal'a·to·ple'gi·a
pal'a·to·prox'i·mal
pal'a·to·pter'y·goid'
pal'a·tor'rha·phy
pal'a·to·sal·pin'ge·us
pal'a·tos'chi·sis *pl.* -ses'
pa·la'tum *pl.* -ta
—— du'rum
—— fis'sum
—— mo'bi·le'
—— mol'le'

—— os′se·um
pa′le·en·ceph′a·lon′
pa′le·o·cer′e·bel′lum
pa′le·o·en·ceph′a·lon′
pa′le·o·ki·net′ic
pa′le·o·pal′li·um
pa′le·o·stri·a′tal
pa′le·o·stri·a′tum
pa′le·o·thal′a·mus
pal′i·ki·ne′si·a
pal′i·ki·ne′sis
pal′i·la′li·a
pal′in·dro′mi·a
pal′in·drom′ic
pal′in·gen′e·sis
pal′in·graph′i·a
pal′i·nop′si·a
pal′in·phra′si·a
pal′i·phra′si·a
pal·la′di·um
pall′an·es·the′si·a
pall′es·the′si·a
pal′li·ate′, -at′ed, -at′ing
pal′li·a′tion
pal′li·a·tive
pal′li·dal
pal′li·do·py·ram′i·dal
pal′li·do·re·tic′u·lar
pal′li·do·sub′tha·lam′ic
pal′li·dot′o·my
pal′li·dum
pal′li·um pl. -li·a or -li·ums
pal′lor
palm
pal′ma pl. -mae′
—— ma′nus
pal′mar
pal′mar·is pl. -mar′es′
pal′mate′
pal′ma·ture
pal′mi·tate′
pal′mi·tin
pal·mod′ic
pal′mo·men′tal
pal′mo·plan′tar
pal′mus pl. -mi′
pal′pa·ble
pal′pate′, -pat′ed, -pat′ing
pal·pa′tion
pal′pa·to·per·cus′sion
pal′pa·to′ry
pal′pe·bra pl. -brae′
pal′pe·bral
pal′pe·brate′, -brat′ed,
 -brat′ing
pal′pe·bra′tion
pal′pe·bri′tis

pal′pi·tate′, -tat′ed, -tat′ing
pal′pi·ta′tion
pal′sied
pal′sy
Pal′tauf′ dwarfism
pal′u·dal
pal′u·dism
pa·lus′tral
pam·pin′i·form′
pan′a·ce′a
pan·ag·glu′ti·nin
pan·an′gi·i′tis
pan′a·ris
pan·a·ri′ti·um pl. -ti·a
pan·ar′te·ri′tis
pan·ar·thri′tis
pan·at′ro·phy
pan′car·di′tis
Pan′coast′
—— operation
—— syndrome
—— tumor
pan′co·lec′to·my
pan·col′po·hys′ter·ec′to·
 my
pan′cre·as pl. pan·cre′a·ta
—— ac′ces·so′ri·um
—— of A·sel′li
pan′cre·a·tec′to·my
pan′cre·at′ic
pan·cre·at′i·co·du·o·de′nal
pan·cre·at′i·co·du·o·de·
 nec′to·my
pan·cre·at′i·co·du·o·de·
 nos′to·my
pan′cre·at′i·co·en′ter·os′to·
 my
pan′cre·at′i·co·gas·tros′to·
 my
pan′cre·at′i·co·je′ju·
 nos′to·my
pan′cre·at′i·co·li·thot′o·my
pan′cre·at′i·co·splen′ic
pan′cre·a·tin
pan′cre·a·tism
pan′cre·a·tit′ic
pan·cre·a·ti′tis pl. -tit′i·des′
pan·cre·a·to·du·o·de·
 nec′to·my
pan·cre·a·to·du·o·de·
 nos′to·my
pan′cre·a·to·en′ter·os′to·
 my
pan′cre·a·tog′e·nous
pan′cre·a·tog′ra·phy
pan′cre·a·to·li′pase′
pan′cre·at′o·lith′

pan′cre·a·to·li·thec′to·my
pan′cre·a·to·li·thot′o·my
pan′cre·a·tol′y·sis
pan′cre·at′o·lyt′ic
pan′cre·a·tot′o·my
pan′cre·ec′to·my
pan′cre·li′pase′
pan′cre·o·lith′
pan′cre·o·li·thot′o·my
pan′cre·ol′y·sis
pan′cre·o·lyt′ic
pan′cre·o·path′i·a
pan′cre·op′a·thy
pan′cre·o·zy′min
pan′cu·ro′ni·um
pan·cy′to·pe′ni·a
pan·de′mi·a
pan·dem′ic
Pan′dy
—— reagent
—— test
pan′e·lec′tro·scope′
pan′en·ceph′a·li′tis
pan·en′do·scope′
pan′en·dos′co·py
pan·es·the′si·a
Pa′neth cells
pang
pan·gen′e·sis
pan·glos′si·a
pan·hem′a·to·pe′ni·a
pan′hi·dro′sis
pan·hy′po·go′nad·ism
pan·hy′po·pi·tu′i·ta·rism
pan·hys′ter·ec′to·my
pan·hys′ter·o·o·oph′o·
 rec′to·my
pan·hys′ter·o·sal′pin·
 gec′to·my
pan·hys′ter·o·sal·pin′go-
 o·oph′o·rec′to·my
pan′ic
pan·im·mu′ni·ty
pan·my′e·lop′a·thy
pan·my′e·lo·phthi′sis pl.
 -ses′
pan·my′e·lo′sis pl. -ses′
pan·my′o·si′tis
pan·nic′u·li′tis
pan·nic′u·lus pl. -li′
—— ad′i·po′sus
—— car·no′sus
pan′nus pl. -ni′
—— ca·ra′te·us
—— car·no′sus
—— cras′sus
—— de·gen′er·a·ti′vus

—— he·pat'i·cus
—— sic'cus
—— ten'u·is
—— tra·cho'ma·to'sus
pan'o·pho'bi·a
pan'oph·thal'mi·a
pan·oph'thal·mi'tis
—— pu'ru·len'ta
pan'os·te·i'tis
pan'o·ti'tis
pan'phle·bi'tis
pan·pho'bi·a
pan'scle·ro'sis pl. -ses'
pan·si'nus·i'tis
pan'sys·tol'ic
pan'ta·mor'phic
pan'tan·en'ce·phal'ic
pan·tan'ky·lo·bleph'a·ron'
pan'ta·tro'phi·a
pan·tat'ro·phy
pan'the·nol'
pan·to'ic
pan'to·mime'
pan'to·mim'ic
pan'to·scop'ic
pan·tur'bi·nate'
Pa'num areas
pa'nus pl. -ni'
—— fau'ci·um
—— in'gui·na'lis
pan'u·ve·i'tis
pap
pa·pa'in
Pap·a·nic'o·la'ou
—— classes
—— stains
—— test
pa·pav'er·a·mine'
pa·pav'er·ine'
pa·pes'cent
Pa·pez' circuit
pa·pil'la pl. -lae'
—— den'tis
—— du'o·de'ni' major
—— duodeni minor
—— in'ci·si'va
—— lac'ri·ma'lis
—— mam'mae'
—— ner'vi' op'ti·ci'
—— of Mor'ga'gni
—— of San'to·ri'ni
—— of Va'ter
—— pa·rot'i·de'a
—— pi'li'
pa·pil'lae'
—— con'i·cae'
—— co'ri·i'

—— fi'li·for'mes'
—— fo'li·a'tae'
—— fun'gi·for'mes'
—— lac'ri·ma'les'
—— len·tic'u·lar'es'
—— lin·gua'les'
—— re·na'les'
—— val·la'tae'
pap'il·lar'y
pap'il·late'
pap'il·lec'to·my
pa·pil'le·de'ma
pap'il·lif'er·ous
pa·pil'li·form'
pap'il·li'tis
pa·pil'lo·car'ci·no'ma pl.
—— -mas or -ma·ta
pap'il·lo·cys·to'ma pl. -mas
or -ma·ta
pap'il·lo'ma pl. -mas or
-ma·ta
—— cho·roi'de·um
pap'il·lo·mac'u·lar
pap'il·lo·ma·to'sis pl. -ses'
pap'il·lom'a·tous
pap'il·lo·ret'i·ni'tis
pa·po'va·vi'rus
Pap'pen·hei'mer bodies
pap'pose'
Pap test
pap'u·la pl. -lae'
pap'u·lar
pap'u·la'tion
pap'ule'
pap'u·lif'er·ous
pap'u·lo·er'y·the'ma·tous
pap'u·lo·ne·crot'ic
pap'u·lo·pus'tu·lar
pap'u·lo'sis
—— a·troph'i·cans' ma·
lig'na
pap'u·lo·squa'mous
pap'u·lo·ve·sic'u·lar
pap'y·ra'ceous
par'a pl. -as or -ae'
par·a·an·al·ge'si·a
par·a·an·es·the'si·a
par·a·a·or'tic
par·a·ap·pen'di·ci'tis
par'a·ba'sal
par·ab·du'cent
par'a·bi·o'sis pl. -ses'
par'a·blep'si·a
par'a·blep'sis pl. -ses'
pa·rac'an·tho'ma pl. -mas
or -ma·ta
pa·rac'an·tho'sis pl. -ses'

par'a·ce'cal
par·a·cen·te'sis pl. -ses'
—— oc'u·li
par·a·cen'tral
par·a·ceph'a·lus pl. -li'
par·a·chlo'ro·phe'nol'
par·a·chol'er·a
par·a·chor'dal
par·a·chro'ma·tism
par·a·chro'ma·top'si·a
par·a·chro'ma·to'sis pl.
-ses'
par·a·coc·cid'i·oi'dal
Par'a·coc·cid'i·oi'des
—— bra·sil'i·en'sis
par'a·coc·cid'i·oi'do·my·
co'sis pl. -ses'
par·a·co·li'tis
par·a·col·pi'tis
par·a·col'pi·um
par·a·con'dy·lar
par'a·cone'
par·a·cor·po're·al
par·a·cu'si·a
—— a'cris
—— du'pli·ca'ta
—— lo·ca'lis
—— ob·tu'sa
—— Wil·lis'i·i'
par'a·cu'sis pl. -ses'
par·a·cy·e'sis pl. -ses'
par·a·cys'tic
par·a·cys·ti'tis
par·a·cyt'ic (lying among
cells)
♦parasitic
par'ad·e·ni'tis
par'a·den'tal
par·a·den·to'sis pl. -ses'
par·a·did'y·mal
par·a·did'y·mis pl. -di·dym'i·
des'
par·a·dox'i·a sex'u·a'lis
par·a·dox'ic or par·a·dox'i·
cal
par·a·du'o·de'nal
par·a·dys'en·ter'y
par·a·ep'i·lep'sy
par·a·e'qui·lib'ri·um
par·a·e·ryth'ro·blast'
par·a·e·soph'a·ge'al
par·a·fas·cic'u·lar
par'af·fin
par·af·fin·o'ma
par·a·floc'cu·lus pl. -li'
par·a·fol·lic'u·lar
par'a·form

par′a·gan′gli·o′ma *pl.* -mas
 or -ma·ta
par′a·gan′gli·on′ *pl.* -gli·a *or*
 -gli·ons′
—— ca·rot′i·cum
—— caroticum sar·co′ma
—— ca·rot′i·cus tumor
par′a·gan′gli·o·neu·ro′ma
 pl. -mas *or* -ma·ta
par′a·gan′gli·on′ic
par′a·gen′i·tal
par′a·gen′i·ta′lis
par′a·geu′si·a
par′a·geu′sic
par′a·geu′sis
par′ag·glu′ti·na′tion
par′a·glob′u·lin
par′a·glob′u·li·nu′ri·a
par′a·glos′si·a
par′a·gon′i·mi′a·sis *pl.* -ses′
Par′a·gon′i·mus
—— wes′ter·man′i′
par′a·gran′u·lo′ma
par′a·he′mo·phil′i·a
par′a·he·pat′ic
par′a·hep′a·ti′tis
par′a·hi·a′tal
par′a·hip′po·cam′pal
par′a·hyp·no′sis *pl.* -ses′
par′a·in′flu·en′za
par′a·ker′a·to′sis *pl.* -ses′
—— gon′or·rhe′i·ca
—— scu′tu·lar′is
—— var′i·e·ga′ta
par′a·ker′a·tot′ic
par′a·ki·ne′si·a
par′a·ki·ne′sis *pl.* -ses′
par′a·lac′tic
par′a·la′li·a
par′al·bu′min
par·al′de·hyde′
par′a·lep′sy
par′a·lex′i·a
par′a·lex′ic
par′al·ge′si·a
par′al·ge′sic
par′al·lax′
par′al·lel·ism
par′al·lel·om′e·ter
par′a·lo′gi·a
par′a·log′i·cal
pa·ral′o·gism
pa·ral′y·sis *pl.* -ses′
—— ag′i·tans′
par′a·lys′sa
par′a·lyt′ic
par′a·ly′zant

par′a·lyze′, -lyzed′, -lyz′ing
par′a·lyz′er
par′a·ma′ni·a
par′a·mas·ti′tis
par′a·mas′toid′
par′a·mas′toid·i′tis
Par′a·me′ci·um
par′a·me′di·al
par′a·me′di·an
par′a·med′ic
par′a·med′i·cal
par′a·me′ni·a
par′a·me·nis′cus *pl.* -ci′ *or*
 -cus·es
par′a·men′tal
par′a·me′si·al
pa·ram′e·ter
par′a·meth′a·di·one′
par′a·meth′a·sone′
par′a·me′tri·al
par′a·me′tric
par′a·me·trit′ic
par′a·me·tri′tis
par′a·me′tri·um *pl.* -tri·a
par′a·mim′i·a
par′a·mi′tome′
par′am·ne′si·a
par′am·ne′sis
par′a·mo′lar
par′a·mu′cin
par′a·mu·ta′tion
pa·ram′y·loi·do′sis
par′a·my·oc′lo·nus mul′ti·
 plex′
par′a·my′o·to′ni·a
par′a·myx′o·vi′rus
par′a·na′sal
par′a·ne′mic
par′a·neph′ric
par′a·ne·phri′tis
par′a·ne·phro′ma *pl.* -mas
 or -ma·ta
par′a·neph′ros′
 pl. -neph′roi′
par′a·neu′ral
par′a·ni′tro·sul′fa·thi′a·
 zole′
par′a·noi′a
par′a·noid′
par′a·noid·ism
par′a·no′mi·a
par′a·nu′cle·ar
par′a·nu′cle·us *pl.* -cle·i′
par′a·ny′line′
par′a·oc·cip′i·tal
par′a·o′ral
par′a·os′ti·al

par′a·pan′cre·at′ic
par′a·pa·re′sis *pl.* -ses′
par′a·pa·ret′ic
par′a·pa·tel′lar
par′a·per·tus′sis
par′a·pha·ryn′ge·al
par′a·pha′si·a
par′a·pha′sic
par′a·phe′mi·a
pa·ra′phi·a
par′a·phil′i·a
par′a·phil′i·ac′
par′a·phi·mo′sis *pl.* -ses′
—— oc′u·li′
par′a·pho′bi·a
par′a·pho′ni·a
—— pu′ber·um
—— pu′bes·cen′ti·um
pa·raph′o·ra
par′a·phra′si·a
—— ve·sa′na
par′a·phre′ni·a
par′a·phre·ni′tis
pa·raph′y·se′al
pa·raph′y·sis *pl.* -ses′
par′a·pin′e·al
par′a·pla′si·a
par′a·plasm
par′a·plas′tic
par′a·plas′tin
par′a·plec′tic
par′a·ple′gi·a
par′a·ple′gic
par′a·ple′gi·form′
par′a·pleu·ri′tis
par′a·pneu·mo′ni·a
par′a·poph′y·sis *pl.* -ses′
par·ap′o·plex′y
par′a·prax′i·a
par′a·proc·ti′tis
par′a·proc′ti·um *pl.* -ti·a
par′a·pros·ta·ti′tis
par′a·pro′te·in
par′a·pro′te·in·e′mi·a
par′a·pso·ri′a·sis *pl.* -ses′
—— en plaques′
—— gut·ta′ta
—— var′i·o′li·for′mis a·cu′ta
par′a·psy·chol′o·gy
par′a·pyk′no·mor′phous
par′a·rec′tal
par′a·rho′ta·cism
par′ar·rhyth′mi·a
par′ar·rhyth′mic
par′a·sa′cral
par′a·sag′it·tal
par′a·sal′pin·gi′tis

par′a·scap′u·lar
par′a·scar′la·ti′na
par′a·se·cre′tion
par′a·sel′lar
par′a·sep′tal
par′a·sex′u·al′i·ty
par′a·si′nus·oi′dal
par′a·site′
par′a·si·te′mi·a
par′a·sit′ic *(pertaining to a parasite)*
 ♦*paracytic*
par′a·sit′i·ci′dal
par′a·sit′i·cide′
par′a·sit·ism
par′a·sit·i·za′tion
par′a·si′to·gen′ic
par′a·si·tol′o·gist
par′a·si·tol′o·gy
par′a·si·to′sis *pl.* -ses′
par′a·si′to·trope′
par′a·si′to·trop′ic
par′a·si·tot′ro·pism
par′a·si·tot′ro·py
par′a·some′
par′a·spa′di·as
par′a·spasm
par′a·spas′mus
par′a·sple′nic
par′a·ster′nal
par′a·stri′ate′
par′a·sym′pa·thet′ic
par′a·sym·path′i·co·to′ni·a
par′a·sym′pa·tho·mi·met′ic
par′a·syn·ap′sis *pl.* -ses′
par′a·syn′o·vi′tis
par′a·syph′i·lis
par′a·syph′i·lit′ic
par′a·sys′to·le
par′a·sys·tol′ic
par′a·tax′i·a
par′a·tax′ic
par′a·tax′is
par′a·ten′on
par′a·ter′mi·nal
par′a·the′li·o′ma *pl.* -mas *or* -ma·ta
par′a·thy′mi·a
par′a·thy′roid′
par′a·thy′roid′al
par′a·thy′roi·dec′to·my
par′a·thy′roi′din
par′a·thy′roi·do′ma *pl.* -mas *or* -ma·ta
par′a·thy′ro·pri′val

par′a·thy′ro·tox′i·co′sis *pl.* -ses′
par′a·thy′ro·trop′ic
par′a·to′ni·a
par′a·ton′sil·lar
par′a·tra′che·al
par′a·tra·cho′ma
par′a·tri·cho′sis *pl.* -ses′
par′a·tri·gem′i·nal
par′a·trip′sis *pl.* -ses′
par′a·troph′ic
pa·rat′ro·phy
par′a·tu′bal
par′a·tu·ber′cu·lo′sis
par′a·typh·li′tis
par′a·ty′phoid′
par′a·um·bil′i·cal
par′a·u·re′ter·ic
par′a·u·re′ter·i′tis
par′a·u·re′thra *pl.* -thras *or* -thrae′
par′a·u·re′thral
par′a·u′ter·ine
par′a·vac·cin′i·a
par′a·vag′i·nal
par′a·vag′i·ni′tis
par′a·vas′cu·lar
par′a·ve′nous
par′a·ven·tric′u·lar
par′a·ver′te·bral
par′a·ves′i·cal
par′a·vi′ta·min·o′sis *pl.* -ses′
par′a·xan′thine′
par·ax′i·al
par·ax′on′
par′ec·ta′si·a
par·ec′ta·sis *pl.* -ses′
par′e·gor′ic
par′en·ceph′a·lon′ *pl.* -la
par′en·ceph′a·lous
pa·ren′chy·ma
pa·ren′chy·mal
par′en·chym′a·ti′tis
par′en·chym′a·tous
par′ent
pa·ren′ter·al
par′ep·i·did′y·mis
par′ep·i·gas′tric
pa·re′sis *pl.* -ses′
 — si′ne′ pa·re′si′
par′es·the′si·a
par′es·thet′ic
pa·ret′ic
pa·reu′ni·a
par·fo′cal
par′gy·line′

Par′ham band
par′i·es′ *pl.* pa·ri′e·tes′
 —— anterior
 —— anterior va·gi′nae′
 —— anterior ven·tric′u·li′
 —— ca·rot′i·ca ca′vi′ tym′pa·ni′
 —— ca·rot′i·cus ca′vi′ tym′pa·ni′
 —— ex·ter′nus duc′tus coch′le·ar′is
 —— inferior
 —— inferior or′bi·tae′
 —— jug′u·lar′is ca′vi′ tym′pan·i′
 —— lab′y·rin′thi·ca ca′vi′ tym′pa·ni′
 —— lab′y·rin′thi·cus ca′vi′ tym′pa·ni′
 —— lat′er·a′lis
 —— lateralis or′bi·tae′
 —— mas·toi′de·us ca′vi′ tym′pa·ni′
 — me′di·a′lis
 —— medialis or′bi·tae′
 —— mem′bra·na′ce·us ca′vi′ tym′pa·ni′
 —— membranaceus tra′che·ae′
 —— posterior
 —— posterior va·gi′nae′
 —— posterior ven·tric′u·li′
 —— superior
 —— superior or′bi·tae′
 —— teg′men·ta′lis ca′vi′ tym′pa·ni′
 —— tym·pan′i·cus duc′tus coch′le·ar′is
 —— ves·tib′u·lar′is duc′tus coch′le·ar′is
pa·ri′e·tal
pa·ri′e·to·fron′tal
pa·ri′e·to·mas′toid′
pa·ri′e·to·oc·cip′i·tal
pa·ri′e·to·pon′tine′
pa·ri′e·to·sphe′noid′
pa·ri′e·to·splanch′nic
pa·ri′e·to·squa·mo′sal
pa·ri′e·to·tem′po·ral
pa·ri′e·to·vis′cer·al
Pa·ri·naud′
 —— conjunctivitis
 —— syndrome
par′i·ty
Park aneurysm
Par′ker
 —— fluid

—— incision
—— method
Par′kin·son disease
par′kin·so′ni·an
par′kin·son·ism
par′oc·cip′i·tal
par′o·don′tal
par′o·don·ti′tis
par′o·don·ti′um *pl.* -ti·a
par′o·dyn′i·a
par′ol·fac′to·ry
par·ol′i·var′y
par′o·mo·my′cin
par′o·ni′ri·a
—— am′bu·lans′
par′o·nych′i·a
—— diph′the·rit′i·ca
par′o·nych′i·al
par′o·nych′i·um *pl.* -i·a
pa·ron′y·cho·my·co′sis *pl.*
  -ses′
pa·ron′y·cho′sis *pl.* -ses′
par′o·oph′o·ri′tis
par′o·oph′o·ron′
par′oph·thal′mi·a
par′oph·thal·mon′cus
par·op′si·a
par·op′sis
par·op′tic
par·or′chis
par·o·rex′i·a
par·os′mi·a
par·os·phre′sis
par·os·te·i′tis
par·os·ti′tis
par·os·to′sis
pa·rot′ic
pa·rot′id
pa·rot′i·de′an
pa·rot′i·dec′to·my
pa·rot′i·di′tis
pa·rot′i·do·scle·ro′sis *pl.*
  -ses′
par′o·tit′ic
par′o·ti′tis
par′ous
par′o·var′i·an
par′o·var′i·ot′o·my
par′o·va·ri′tis
par′o·var′i·um *pl.* -i·a
par·ox·ysm
par·ox·ys′mal
Par′rot
—— atrophy
—— disease
—— nodes
Par′ry disease

pars *pl.* par′tes′
—— ab·dom′i·na′lis
e·soph′a·gi′
—— abdominalis et pel·
vi′na sys·te′ma·tis au′to·
nom′i·ci′
—— abdominalis mus′cu·li′
pec′to·ra′lis ma·jo′ris
—— abdominalis oe·soph′a·
gi′
—— abdominalis sys·te′ma·
tis sym·path′i·ci′
—— abdominalis u·re′ter·is
—— a·lar′is mus′cu·li′ na·
sa′lis
—— al′ve·o·lar′is man·dib′u·
lae′
—— anterior com′mis·
su′rae′ an·te′ri·o′ris cer′e·bri′
—— anterior fa′ci·e′i′ di′a·
phrag·mat′i·cae′ hep′a·tis
—— anterior lob′u·li′ qua·
dran′gu·lar′is
—— anterior rhi′nen·ceph′a·
li′
—— an′u·lar′is va·gi′nae′ fi·
bro′sae′ dig′i·to′rum ma′nus
—— anularis vaginae fibrosae digitorum pe′dis
—— as·cen′dens du′o·de′ni′
—— ba·sa′lis
—— basalis ar·te′ri·ae′
pul′mo·na′lis dex′trae′
—— basalis arteriae pulmonalis si·nis′trae′
—— bas′i·lar′is os′sis oc·
cip′i·ta′lis
—— basilaris pon′tis
—— buc·ca′lis
—— buc′co·pha·ryn′ge·a
mus′cu·li′ con′stric·to′ris
pha·ryn′gis su·pe′ri·o′ris
—— cal·ca′ne·o·cu·boi′de·a
lig′a·men′ti′ bi·fur·ca′ti′
—— cal·ca′ne·o·na·vic′u·
lar′is lig′a·men′ti′ bi·fur·ca′ti′
—— car·di′a·ca ven·tric′u·li′
—— car′ti·la·gin′e·a
—— cartilaginea sep′ti′
na′si′
—— cartilaginea tu′bae′
au′di·ti′vae′
—— cav′er·no′sa u·re′thrae′
—— cen·tra′lis ven·tric′u·li′
lat′er·a′lis
—— ce·phal′i·ca et cer′vi·

ca′lis sy·ste′ma·tis au′to·
nom′i·ci′
—— cephalica et cervicalis
systematis sym·path′i·ci′
—— cer′a·to·pha·ryn′ge·a
mus′cu·li′ con′stric·to′ris
pha·ryn′gis me′di·i′
—— cer′vi·ca′lis e·soph′a·gi′
—— cervicalis me·dul′lae′
spi·na′lis
—— cervicalis oe·soph′a·gi′
—— chon′dro·pha·ryn′ge·a
mus′cu·li′ con′stric·to′ris
pha·ryn′gis me′di·i′
—— cil′i·ar′is ret′i·nae′
—— cla·vic′u·lar′is mus′cu·
li′ pec′to·ra′lis ma·jo′ris
—— coch′le·ar′is ner′vi′ oc·
ta′vi′
—— con′vo·lu′ta lob′u·li′
cor′ti·ca′lis re′nis
—— cos·ta′lis di′a·phrag′ma·
tis
—— cri′co·pha·ryn′ge·a
mus′cu·li′ con′stric·to′ris
pha·ryn′gis in·fe′ri·o′ris
—— cru′ci·for′mis va·gi′nae′
fi·bro′sae′ dig′i·to′rum ma′-
nus
—— cruciformis vaginae fibrosae digitorum pe′dis
—— cu′pu·lar′is re·ces′sus
ep′i·tym·pan′i·ci′
—— de·scen′dens du′o·de′ni′
—— dex′tra fa′ci·e′i′ di′a·
phrag·mat′i·cae′ hep′a·tis
—— dis·ta′lis
—— distalis lo′bi′ an·te′ri·
o′ris hy′po·phys′e·os′
—— dor·sa′lis pon′tis
—— fe·ta′lis pla·cen′tae′
—— flac′ci·da mem·bra′nae′
tym′pa·ni′
—— fron·ta′lis cap′su·lae′
in·ter′nae′
—— frontalis co·ro′nae′
ra′di·a′tae′
—— frontalis o·per′cu·li′
—— frontalis ra′di·a′ti·o′nis
cor′po·ris cal·lo′si′
—— glan′du·lar′is
—— glos′so·pha·ryn′ge·a
mus′cu·li′ con′stric·to′ris
pha·ryn′gis su·pe′ri·o′ris
—— gris′e·a hy′po·thal′a·mi′
—— hor′i·zon·ta′lis du′o·
de′ni′

—— horizontalis os'sis pal'a·ti'ni'

—— i·li·a·ca lin'e·ae' ter'mi·na'lis

—— inferior du'o·de'ni'

—— inferior fos'sae' rhom·boi'de·ae'

—— inferior gy'ri' fron·ta'lis me'di·i'

—— inferior par'tis ves·tib'u·lar'is ner'vi' oc·ta'vi'

—— in'fra·cla·vic'u·lar'is plex'us bra·chi·a'lis

—— in'fun·dib'u·lar'is

—— in'ter·car'ti·la·gin'e·a ri'mae' glot'ti·dis

—— in'ter·me'di·a

—— intermedia fos'sae' rhom·boi'de·ae'

—— intermedia lo'bi' an·te'ri·o'ris hy'po·phys'e·os'

—— in'ter·mem'bra·na'ce·a ri'mae' glot'ti·dis

—— i·rid'i·ca ret'i·nae'

—— la'bi·a'lis mus'cu·li' or·bic'u·lar'is o'ris

—— lac'ri·ma'lis mus'cu·li' or·bic'u·lar'is oc'u·li'

—— la·ryn'ge·a pha·ryn'gis

—— lat'er·a'lis

—— lateralis ar'cus pe'dis lon'gi·tu'di·na'lis

—— lateralis mus'cu·lo'rum in'ter·trans·ver·sar'i·o'rum pos·te'ri·o'rum cer'vi·cis

—— lateralis os'sis oc·cip'i·ta'lis

—— lateralis ossis sa'cri'

—— lum·ba'lis

—— lumbalis di'a·phrag'ma·tis

—— lumbalis me·dul'lae' spi·na'lis

—— mam'il·lar'is hy'po·thal'a·mi'

—— mar'gi·na'lis mus'cu·li' or·bic'u·lar'is o'ris

—— marginalis sul'ci' cin'gu·li'

—— mas·toi'de·a os'sis tem'po·ra'lis

—— me'di·a'lis ar'cus pe'dis lon'gi·tu'di·na'lis

—— medialis mus'cu·lo'rum in'ter·trans·ver·sar'i·o'rum pos·te'ri·o'rum cer'vi·cis

—— me'di·as'ti·na'lis fa·ci·e'i' me'di·a'lis pul·mo'nis

—— mem'bra·na'ce·a sep'ti' a'tri·o'rum

—— membranacea septi in'ter·ven·tric'u·lar'is cor'dis

—— membranacea septi na'si'

—— membranacea u·re'thrae' mas'cu·li'nae'

—— membranacea urethrae vi·ri'lis

—— mo'bi·lis sep'ti' na'si'

—— mus'cu·lar'is sep'ti' in'ter·ven·tric'u·lar'is cor'dis

—— my'lo·pha·ryn'ge·a mus'cu·li' con'stric·to'ris pha·ryn'gis su·pe'ri·o'ris

—— na·sa'lis os'sis fron·ta'lis

—— nasalis pha·ryn'gis

—— ner'vo·sa

—— neu·ra'lis

—— o·bli'qua mus'cu·li' cri'co·thy're·oi'de·i'

—— obliqua musculi cri'co·thy·roi'de·i'

—— oc·cip'i·ta'lis cap'su·lae' in·ter'nae'

—— occipitalis co·ro'nae' ra·di·a'tae'

—— occipitalis ra·di·a'ti·o'nis cor'po·ris cal·lo'si'

—— ol'fac·to'ri·a

—— o·per'cu·lar'is gy'ri' fron·ta'lis in·fe'ri·o'ris

—— op'ti·ca hy'po·thal'a·mi'

—— optica ret'i·nae'

—— o·ra'lis pha·ryn'gis

—— or'bi·ta'lis

—— orbitalis glan'du·lae' lac'ri·ma'lis

—— orbitalis gy'ri' fron·ta'lis in·fe'ri·o'ris

—— orbitalis mus'cu·li' or·bic'u·lar'is oc'u·li'

—— orbitalis os'sis fron·ta'lis

—— os'se·a

—— ossea sep'ti' na'si'

—— ossea tu'bae' au'di·ti'vae'

—— pal'pe·bra'lis

—— palpebralis glan'du·lae' lac'ri·ma'lis

—— palpebralis mus'cu·li' or·bic'u·lar'is oc'u·li'

—— par'a·sym·path'i·ca sy·ste'ma·tis ner·vo'si' au'to·nom'i·ci'

—— pa·ri'e·ta'lis co·ro'nae' ra·di·a'tae'

—— parietalis o·per'cu·li'

—— parietalis ra·di·a'ti·o'nis cor'po·ris cal·lo'si'

—— pel·vi'na u·re'ter·is

—— per'pen·dic'u·lar'is os'·sis pal·a·ti'ni'

—— pe·tro'sa os'sis tem'po·ra'lis

—— posterior com'mis·su'rae' an·te'ri·o'ris cer'e·bri'

—— posterior hep'a·tis

—— posterior lob'u·li' quad·ran'gu·lar'is

—— posterior rhi'nen·ceph'a·li'

—— pro·fun'da

—— profunda glan'du·lae' pa·rot'i·dis

—— profunda mus'cu·li' mas'se·te'ris

—— profunda musculi sphinc·te'ris a'ni' ex·ter'ni'

—— pros·tat'i·ca u·re'thrae' mas'cu·li'nae'

—— prostatica urethrae vi·ri'lis

—— pter'y·go·pha·ryn'ge·a mus'cu·li' con'stric·to'ris pha·ryn'gis su·pe'ri·o'ris

—— pu'bi·ca lin'e·ae' ter'mi·na'lis

—— py·lo'ri·ca ven·tric'u·li'

—— qua·dra'ta lo'bi' hep'a·tis si·nis'tri'

—— ra·di·a'ta lob'u·li' cor'ti·ca'lis re'nis

—— rec'ta mus'cu·li' cri'co·thy're·oi'de·i'

—— recta musculi cri'co·thy·roi'de·i'

—— ret'ro·len'ti·for'mis cap'su·lae' in·ter'nae'

—— sa·cra'lis lin'e·ae' ter'mi·na'lis

—— spon'gi·o'sa u·re'thrae' mas'cu·li'nae'

—— squa·mo'sa os'sis tem'po·ra'lis

—— ster·na'lis di·a·phrag'ma·tis

—— ster'no·cos·ta'lis

mus'cu·li' pec'to·ra'lis ma·
jo'ris
—— sub·cu·ta'ne·a mus'cu·
li' sphinc·te'ris a'ni' ex·
ter'ni'
—— sub·fron·ta'lis sul'ci'
cin'gu·li'
—— sub·len'ti·for'mis
cap'su·lae' in·ter'nae'
—— su'per·fi'ci·a'lis
—— superficialis glan'du·
lae' pa·rot'i·dis
—— superficialis mus'cu·li'
mas·se·te'ris
—— superficialis musculi
sphinc·te'ris a'ni' ex·ter'ni'
—— superior du'o·de'ni'
—— superior fa·ci·e'i' di'a·
phrag·mat'i·cae' hep'a·tis
—— superior fos'sae' rhom·
boi'de·ae'
—— superior gy'ri' fron·
ta'lis me'di·i'
—— superior par'tis ves·
tib'u·lar'is ner'vi' oc·ta'vi'
—— su'pra·cla·vic'u·lar'is
plex'us bra·chi·a'lis
—— su'pra·op'ti·ca
—— sym·path'i·ca sy·
ste'ma·tis ner·vo'si' au'to·
nom'i·ci'
—— tem'po·ra'lis co·ro'nae'
ra'di·a·tae'
—— temporalis o·per'cu·li'
—— temporalis ra'di·a'ti·
o'nis cor'po·ris cal·lo'si'
—— ten'sa mem·bra'nae'
tym'pa·ni'
—— tho'ra·ca'lis me·dul'lae'
spi·na'lis
—— thoracalis oe·soph'a·gi'
—— thoracalis sy·ste'ma·tis
sym·path'i·ci'
—— tho·ra'ci·ca
—— thoracica e·soph'a·gi'
—— thoracica me·dul'lae'
spi·na'lis
—— thoracica sy·ste'ma·tis
au'to·nom'i·ci'
—— thy'ro·pha·ryn'ge·a
mus'cu·li' con'stric·to'ris
pha·ryn'gis in·fe'ri·o'ris
—— tib'i·o·cal·ca'ne·a lig'a·
men'ti' me'di·a'lis
—— tib'i·o·na·vic'u·lar'is
lig'a·men'ti' me'di·a'lis

—— tib'i·o·ta·lar'is anterior
lig'a·men'ti' me'di·a'lis
—— tibiotalaris posterior
ligamenti medialis
—— trans·ver'sa mus'cu·li'
na·sa'lis
—— tri·an'gu·lar'is gy'ri'
fron·ta'lis in·fe'ri·o'ris
—— tu'be·ra'lis
—— tym·pan'i·ca os'sis
tem'po·ra'lis
—— u'ter·i'na pla·cen'tae'
—— uterina tu'bae' u'ter·
i'nae'
—— ven·tra'lis pon'tis
—— ver'te·bra'lis fa·ci·e'i'
me'di·a'lis pul·mo'nis
—— ves·tib'u·lar'is ner'vi'
oc·ta'vi'
par'tal
par'tes'
—— gen'i·ta'les' ex·ter'nae'
mu'li·e'bres'
—— genitales externae vi·
ri'les'
—— genitales fem'i·ni'nae'
ex·ter'nae'
—— genitales mas'cu·li'nae'
ex·ter'nae'
par'ti·cle
par·tic'u·late
par·ti'tion
par·tu'ri·ent
par·tu'ri·fa'cient
par·tu'ri·om'e·ter
par·tu·ri'tion
pa·ru'lis pl. -li·des'
par'um·bil'i·cal
par·u'ri·a
par'vi·cel'lu·lar
par'vi·loc'u·lar
par'vule
Pasch'en bodies
Pa·schu'tin degeneration
pas'sage
Pas'sa·vant'
—— bar
—— cushion
pas'sive
pas·sive-ag·gres'sive
pas·sive-de·pend'ent
pas'siv·ism
pas'siv·ist
paste
Pas·teur'
—— effect
—— treatment

pas'teur·el·lo'sis pl. -ses'
pas'teur·i·za'tion
pas'teur·ize', -ized', -iz'ing
pas'teur·iz'er
Pas'ti·a
—— lines
—— sign
patch
pa·tel'la pl. -lae'
—— bi·par'ta
—— cu'bi·ti'
pa·tel'la·pex'y
pa·tel'lar
pat'el·lec'to·my
pa·tel'lo·ad·duc'tor
pa·tel'lo·fem'o·ral
pat'en·cy
pat'ent
pa·ter'nal
pa·ter'ni·ty
Pat'er·son
—— bodies
—— syndrome
path
pa·the'ma
path'er·ga'si·a
path'er·gy
pa·thet'ic
path'o·clis'is
path'o·gen
path'o·gen'e·sis
path'o·gen'ic
path'o·ge·nic'i·ty
path'og·nom'ic
pa·thog'no·mon'ic
path'og·nos'tic
path'o·log'ic or path'o·log'i·
cal
pa·thol'o·gist
pa·thol'o·gy
path'o·ma'ni·a
path'o·met'ric
pa·thom'e·try
path'o·mi·me'sis pl. -ses'
path'o·mim'ic·ry
path'o·pho·re'sis
path'o·pho'ric
pa·thoph'o·rous
path'o·phys'i·o·log'ic
path'o·phys'i·ol'o·gy
path'o·psy·chol'o·gy
path'o·psy·cho'sis pl. -ses'
pa·tho'sis pl. -ses'
path'way'
pa'tient
pat'ri·lin'e·al
pat'ten

pat'tern
pat'tern·ing
pat'u·lin
pat'u·lous
Paul
—— operation
—— test
—— tube
Paul'-Bun·nell' test
Paul Bert effect
Paul·lin'i·a
Paul'-Mik'u·licz operation
paunch
pause
Pau·trier' microabscess
pave'ment·ing
Pav·lov'i·an
Pav'lov' pouch
pa'vor
—— di·ur'nus
—— noc·tur'nus
Pa'vy
—— disease
—— joint
—— solution
Paw'lik
—— folds
—— triangle
pearl
peau d'o·range'
pec'tase'
pec'ten (a comblike structure of the body),
pl. -ti·nes'
♦pectin
pec'te·no'sis
pec'tic
pec'tin (a substance in ripe
fruit)
♦pecten
pec'tin·ase'
pec'ti·nate'
pec'tin·e·al
pec'tin·e·us
pec·tin'i·form'
pec'tin·ose'
pec'to·ral
pec'to·ral'gi·a
pec'to·ra'lis pl. -les'
pec'to·ril'o·quy
pec'tus
—— car'i·na'tum
—— ex'ca·va'tum
ped'al
ped'a·tro'phi·a
pe·dat'ro·phy
ped'er·ast'

ped'er·as'ty
ped'i·al'gi·a
pe·di·at'ric
pe·di·a·tri'cian
pe·di·at'rics
pe·di·at'rist
pe·di·at'ry
ped'i·cel·late'
ped'i·cle
pe·dic'ter·us
pe·dic'u·lar
pe·dic'u·late'
pe·dic'u·la'tion
pe·dic'u·li·cide'
Pe·dic'u·loi'des'
—— ven'tri·co'sus
pe·dic'u·lo'sis pl. -ses'
—— cap'i·tis
—— cor'po·ris
—— pal'pe·brar'um
—— pu'bis
pe·dic'u·lous (lice-infested)
♦pediculus, Pediculus
pe·dic'u·lus (a stemlike
structure; pedicle)
♦pediculous, Pediculus
—— ar'cus ver'te·brae'
Pe·dic'u·lus (louse)
♦pediculous, pediculus
—— hu·ma'nus cap'i·tis
—— humanus cor'po·ris
pe·di'tis
pe'do·don'ti·a
pe'do·don'tics
pe'do·don'tist
pe'do·don·tol'o·gy
ped'o·dy'na·mom'e·ter
pe'do·gen'e·sis
pe·dol'o·gist
pe·dol'o·gy
pe·dom'e·ter
pe'do·no·sol'o·gy
pe·dop'a·thy
pe'do·phil'i·a
pe'do·psy·chi'a·trist
pe·dun'cle
pe·dun'cu·lar
pe·dun'cu·late
pe·dun'cu·lat'ed
pe·dun'cu·lot'o·my
pe·dun'cu·lus pl. -li'
—— cer'e·bel·lar'is inferior
—— cerebellaris me'di·us
—— cerebellaris superior
—— ce'e·bri'
—— cor'po·ris mam'il·lar'is
—— floc'cu·li'

—— thal'a·mi' inferior
peg
pe·lade'
pel'age
pel'a·gism
Pel crises
Pel'-Eb'stein'
—— disease
—— fever
—— syndrome
Pel'ger anomaly
pel'i·di'si
pel'i·o'sis
pel'i·ot'ic
Pel'i·zae'us-Merz'bach'er
disease
pel·lag'ra
—— si'ne' pellagra
pel·lag'rin
pel'la·gro'sis
pel'la·grous
Pel'le·gri'ni-Stie'da disease
pel'let
pel'li·cle
pel·lic'u·lar
pel·lic'u·lous
pel'lu·cid
pe·lo·he'mi·a
pe·lol'o·gy
pel'vi·ab·dom'i·nal
pel'vic
pel'vi·fem'o·ral
pel'vi·fix·a'tion
pel·vim'e·ter
pel·vim'e·try
pel'vi·o·li·thot'o·my
pel'vi·o·ne'o·cys·tos'to·my
pel'vi·o·per'i·to·ni'tis
pel'vi·o·plas'ty
pel'vi·o·ra'di·og'ra·phy
pel'vi·ot'o·my
pel'vi·per'i·to·ni'tis
pel'vi·rec'tal
pel'vis pl. -vis·es or -ves'
—— ae'qua·bil'i·ter jus'to'
major
—— aequabiliter justo mi-
nor
—— fis'sa
—— major
—— minor
—— na'na
—— re·na'lis
—— spi·no'sa
pel'vi·sa'cral
pel'vi·scope'

pel'vi·sec'tion
pel'vi·ver'te·bral
pel'vo·cal'i·ec'ta·sis *pl.* -ses'
pel'vo·cal'y·ce'al
pem'phi·goid'
pem'phi·gus *pl.* -gus·es
  or -gi'
—— a· cu'tus
—— chron'i·cus
—— con·ta'gi·o'sus
—— er'y·them'a·to'sus
—— fo'li·a'ce·us
—— ne'o·na·to'rum
—— trop'i·cus
—— veg'e·tans'
—— vul·gar'is
pem'pi·dine'
pen'du·lar
pen'du·lous
pen'e·trance
pen'e·trat'ing
pen'e·tra'tion
pen'i·cil'la·mine'
pen'i·cil'lase'
pen'i·cil'lic
pen'i·cil'li' li·e'nis
pen'i·cil'lin
pen'i·cil'li·nase'
pen'i·cil'li·o'sis *pl.* -ses'
Pen'i·cil'li·um
pen'i·cil·lo'ic
pen'i·cil'lus *pl.* -li'
pe'nile'
pe'nis *pl.* -nis·es *or* -nes'
pen'nate'
pen'ni·form'
pe'no·scro'tal
Pen'rose' drain
pen'ta·bam'ate'
pen'ta·ba'sic
pen'tad'
pen'ta·dac'tyl
pen'ta·e·ryth'ri·tol'
pen'ta·gas'trin
pen'ta·gen'ic
pen·tal'o·gy
—— of Fal·lot'
pen'tane'
Pen'ta·trich'o·mo'nas
pen·taz'o·cine
pent·dy'o·pent'
pen'tene'
pen·thi'e·nate'
pen'to·bar'bi·tal'
pen·to·lin'i·um
pen·to'sa·zone'
pen·to·su'ri·a

pen'to·thal'
pent·ox'ide'
pen'ty·lene·tet'ra·zol'
Pen'zoldt' test
pe'o·til'lo·ma'ni·a
Pep'per
—— syndrome
—— treatment
—— type
pep'sin
pep'tic
pep'ti·dase'
pep'tide'
pep'ti·do·lyt'ic
pep'tize', -tized', -tiz'ing
pep'to·gen'ic
pep·tog'e·nous
pep·tol'y·sis *pl.* -ses'
pep'tone'
pep'to·ne'mi·a
pep·ton'ic
pep'to·nize', -nized', -niz'ing
pep'to·nu'ri·a
per'a·cid'i·ty
per'a·cute'
per a'num
per·cent' *or* per cent
per·cent'age
per·cen'tile'
per'cept'
per·cep'tion
per·cep'tive
per·cep·tiv'i·ty
per'cep·to'ri·um *pl.* -ri·ums
  or -ri·a
per·cep'tu·al
per·chlo'rate'
per·cuss', -cussed', -cuss'ing
per·cus'si·ble
per·cus'sion
per·cus'sor
per·cu·ta'ne·ous
per'en·ceph'a·ly
per'fo·rans'
per'fo·rate', -rat'ed, -rat'ing
per'fo·ra'tion
per'fo·ra'tor
per'fo·ra·to'ri·um *pl.* -ri·a
per·form'ance
per'fri·ca'tion
per·fus'ate'
per·fuse', -fused', -fus'ing
per·fu'sion
per'i·ac'i·nar
per'i·ad'e·ni'tis
—— mu·co'sae' ne·crot'i·ca
re·cur'rens

per'i·ad'ven·ti'tial
per'i·a'li·e·ni'tis
per'i·a'nal
per'i·an·gi·i'tis
per'i·an'gi·o·cho·li'tis
per'i·an'gi·o'ma *pl.* -mas *or*
  -ma·ta
per'i·a·or'tic
per'i·a'or·ti'tis
per'i·a'pex' *pl.* -pex'es *or* -pi·
  ces'
per'i·ap'i·cal
per'i·ap·pen'di·ci'tis
per'i·ap'pen·dic'u·lar
per'i·aq'ue·duc'tal
per'i·a·re'o·lar
per'i·ar·te'ri·al
per'i·ar·te'ri·o'lar
per'i·ar'te·ri'tis
per'i·ar'thric
per'i·ar·thri'tis
—— cal·car'e·a
per'i·ar·tic'u·lar
per'i·a'tri·al
per'i·au·ric'u·lar
per'i·ax'i·al
per'i·ax'il·lar'y
per'i·bron'chi·al
per'i·bron'chi·o'lar
per'i·bron'chi·o·li'tis
per'i·bron·chi'tis
per'i·bul'bar
per'i·bur'sal
per'i·cal'y·ce'al
per'i·can'a·lic'u·lar
per'i·cap'il·lar'y
per'i·car'di·ac'
per'i·car'di·al
per'i·car'di·ec'to·my
per'i·car'di·o·cen·te'sis *pl.*
  -ses'
per'i·car'di·ol'y·sis *pl.* -ses'
per'i·car'di·o·me'di·as'ti·
  ni'tis
per'i·car'di·o·phren'ic
per'i·car'di·o·pleu'ral
per'i·car'di·or'rha·phy
per'i·car'di·os'to·my
per'i·car'di·ot'o·my
per'i·car·dit'ic
per'i·car·di'tis *pl.* -dit'i·des'
—— o·blit'er·ans'
per'i·car'di·um *pl.* -di·a
—— fi·bro'sum
—— se·ro'sum
per'i·ca'val
per'i·ce'cal

per'i·ce·ci'tis
per'i·cel'lu·lar
per'i·ce·men'tal
per'i·ce·men·ti'tis
per'i·ce·men·to·cla'si·a
per'i·ce·men'tum
per'i·cen'tral
per'i·cen'tric
per'i·cen·tri·o'lar
per'i·ce·phal'ic
per'i·chol'an·git'ic
per'i·chol'an·gi'tis
per'i·chol'e·cys'tic
per'i·chol'e·cys·ti'tis
per'i·chon'dri·al
per'i·chon·drit'ic
per'i·chon·dri'tis
per'i·chon'dri·um pl. -dri·a
per'i·chon·dro'ma pl. -mas
  or -ma·ta
per'i·chord'
per'i·chor'dal
per'i·cho'roid'
per'i·cho·roi'dal
per'i·coc·cyg'e·al
per'i·co'lic
per'i·co·li'tis
per'i·co·lon'ic
per'i·co·lon·i'tis
per'i·col·pi'tis
per'i·con'chal
per'i·con·chi'tis
per'i·cor'ne·al
per'i·cor'o·nal
per'i·cor'o·ni'tis
per'i·cos'tal
per'i·cox·i'tis
per'i·cra'ni·al
per'i·cra·ni'tis
per'i·cra'ni·um pl. -ni·a
per'i·cys'tic
per'i·cys·ti'tis
per'i·cys'ti·um pl. -ti·a
per'i·cyte'
per'i·cy'ti·al
per'i·cy·to'ma pl. -mas or
  -ma·ta
per'i·dec'to·my
per'i·den·drit'ic
per'i·derm'
per'i·der'mal
per'i·des·mi'tis
per'i·des'mi·um
per'i·did'y·mis pl. -mi·des'
per'i·did'y·mi'tis
per'i·di·ver·tic'u·li'tis
per'i·duc'tal

per'i·du'o·de·ni'tis
per'i·du'ral
per'i·en·ceph'a·li'tis
per'i·en·ceph'a·log'ra·phy
per'i·en·ceph'a·lo·men·in·
  gi'tis
per'i·en·ter'ic
per'i·en·ter·i'tis
per'i·e·pen'dy·mal
per'i·ep'i·did'y·mi'tis
per'i·ep'i·glot'tic
per'i·ep'i·the'li·o'ma pl.
  -mas or -ma·ta
per'i·e·soph'a·ge'al
per'i·e·soph'a·gi'tis
per'i·fas·cic'u·lar
per'i·fis'tu·lar
per'i·fol·lic'u·lar
per'i·fol·lic'u·li'tis
—— cap'i·tis ab·sce'dens et
  suf·fod'i·ens
per'i·for'ni·cal
per'i·fu·nic'u·lar
per'i·gan'gli·i'tis
per'i·gan'gli·on'ic
per'i·gas'tric
per'i·gas·tri'tis
per'i·gem'mal
per'i·gen'i·tal
per'i·glan'du·lar
per'i·glos·si'tis
per'i·glot'tic
per'i·glot'tis
per'i·he·pat'ic
per'i·hep'a·ti'tis
per'i·her'ni·al
per'i·hi'lar
per'i·je'ju·ni'tis
per'i·kar'y·on'
per'i·ke·rat'ic
per'i·ky'ma·ta sing. -ky'ma
per'i·lab'y·rinth'
per'i·lab'y·rin·thi'tis
per'i·la·ryn'ge·al
per'i·lar'yn·gi'tis
per'i·len·tic'u·lar
per'i·lig'a·men'tous
per'i·lo'bar
per'i·lymph'
per'i·lym'pha
per'i·lym·phan'ge·al
per'i·lym'phan·gi'tis
per'i·lym·phat'ic
per'i·mac'u·lar
per'i·mas·ti'tis
per'i·med'ul·lar'y
per'i·men'in·gi'tis

pe·rim'e·ter
per'i·met'ric
per'i·me·trit'ic
per'i·me·tri'tis
per'i·me'tri·um pl. -tri·a
per'i·me'tro·sal'pin·gi'tis
pe·rim'e·try
per'i·my'e·li'tis
per'i·my'o·car·di'tis
per'i·my'o·en'do·car·di'tis
per'i·my'o·si'tis
per'i·my'si·um pl. -si·a
—— ex·ter'num
—— in·ter'num
per'i·na'tal
per'i·ne'al (pertaining to the
  perineum)
♦peroneal
per'i·ne'o·cele'
per'i·ne'o·om'e·ter
per'i·ne'o·plas'ty
per'i·ne·or'rha·phy
per'i·ne'o·scro'tal
per'i·ne·ot'o·my
per'i·ne'o·vag'i·nal
per'i·ne'o·vag'i·no·rec'tal
per'i·ne'o·vul'var
per'i·neph'ri·al
per'i·neph'ric
per'i·ne·phrit'ic
per'i·ne·phri'tis
per'i·neph'ri·um pl. -ri·a
per'i·ne'um pl. -ne·a
per'i·neu'ral
per'i·neu'ri·al
per'i·neu·ri'tis
per'i·neu'ri·um pl. -ri·a
per'i·neu'ro·nal
per'i·nu'cle·ar
per'i·oc'u·lar
pe'ri·od
pe'ri·od'ic
pe·ri·o·dic'i·ty
per'i·o·don'tal
per'i·o·don'tic
per'i·o·don'tics
per'i·o·don'tist
per'i·o·don·ti'tis
per'i·o·don'ti·um pl. -ti·a
per'i·o·don·to·cla'si·a
per'i·o·don·to'sis pl. -ses'
per'i·om·phal'ic
per'i·o·nych'i·a
per'i·o·nych'i·um pl. -i·a
per'i·on'yx
per'i·o·oph'o·ri'tis

per′i·o·oph′or·o·sal′pin·
  gi′tis
per′i·o′o·the·ci′tis
per′i·oph·thal′mic
per′i·oph′thal·mi′tis
per′i·op·tom′e·try
per′i·o′ral
per′i·or′bit
per′i·or′bi·ta
per′i·or′bit·al
per′i·or′bi·ti′tis
per′i·or·chi′tis
per′i·or′ch·ium
per′i·os′te·al
per′i·os′te·i′tis
per′i·os′te·o′ma pl. -mas or
  -ma·ta
per′i·os′te·o·my′e·li′tis
per′i·os′te·o·phyte′
per′i·os′te·ot′o·my
per′i·os′te·ous
per′i·os′te·um pl. -te·a
—— al′ve·o·lar′e′
per′i·os·ti′tis
per′i·os·to′ma pl. -mas or
  -ma·ta
per′i·os·to′sis pl. -ses′
per′i·o′tic
per′i·o′va·ri′tis
per′i·o′vu·lar
per′i·pach′y·men·in·gi′tis
per′i·pan′cre·at′ic
per′i·pan′cre·a·ti′tis
per′i·pap′il·lar′y
per′i·pa·tel′lar
per′i·pe·dun′cu·lar
per′i·pha·ryn′ge·al
pe·riph′er·ad′
pe·riph′er·al
pe·riph′er·a·phose′ (an
  aphose)
◆peripherophose
pe·riph′er·o·phose′ (a
  phose)
◆peripheraphose
pe·riph′er·y
per′i·phle·bit′ic
per′i·phle·bi′tis
pe·riph′ra·sis pl. -ses′
per′i·pleu′ral
per′i·pleu·ri′tis
Pe·rip′lo·ca
pe·rip′lo·cin
per′i·pneu′mo·ni′tis
per′i·po·ri′tis
per′i·por′tal
per′i·proc′tal

per′i·proc′tic
per′i·proc·ti′tis
per′i·pros·tat′ic
per′i·pros′ta·ti′tis
per′i·py′e·li′tis
per′i·py·e′ma
per′i·py′le·phle·bi′tis
per′i·py·lo′ric
per′i·ra·dic′u·lar
per′i·rec′tal
per′i·rec·ti′tis
per′i·re′nal (around a kidney)
◆perirhinal
per′i·rhi′nal (around the
  nose)
◆perirenal
per′i·sal′pin·gi′tis
per′i·sal′pin·go-o′va·ri′tis
per′i·sal′pinx pl. -sal·pin′ges′
per′i·scop′ic
per′i·sig′moid·i′tis
per′i·sin′u·ous
per′i·si′nus·i′tis
per′i·si′nu·soi′dal
per′i·sper·ma·ti′tis
per′i·sple′nic
per′i·sple·ni′tis
—— car′ti·la·gin′e·a
per′i·spon·dyl′ic
per′i·spon′dy·li′tis
per′i·stal′sis pl. -ses′
per′i·stal′tic
per′i·staph′y·line′
per′i·sta′sis
per′i·stat′ic
per′i·stol′ic
pe·ris′to·ma pl. -ma·ta
per′i·stome′
per′i·sy·no′vi·al
per′i·sys·tol′ic
per′i·tec′to·my
per′i·ten·din′e·um pl. -e·a
per′i·ten′di·ni′tis
—— cal·car′e·a
per′i·ten′on
per′i·ten′o·ne′um
per′i·ten′o·ni′tis
per′i·the′li·al
per′i·the′li·o′ma pl. -mas or
  -ma·ta
per′i·the′li·um pl. -li·a
per′i·tho·rac′ic
per′i·thy′roid·i′tis
pe·rit′o·my
per′i·to·ne′al
per′i·to·ne′a·li·za′tion

per′i·to·ne′a·lize′, -lized′,
  -liz′ing
per′i·to·ne′o·cen·te′sis pl.
  -ses′
per′i·to·ne·op′a·thy
per′i·to·ne′o·per′i·car′di·al
per′i·to·ne′o·pex′y
per′i·to·ne′o·plas′ty
per′i·to·ne′o·scope′
per′i·to·ne·os′co·py
per′i·to·ne′o·tome′
per′i·to·ne·ot′o·my
per′i·to·ne′um pl. -ne′ums
  or -ne′a
—— pa·ri′e·ta′le′
—— vis′cer·a′le′
per′i·to·ni′tis
per′i·to·nize′, -nized′, -niz′-
  ing
per′i·ton′sil·lar
per′i·ton′sil·li′tis
per′i·tra′che·al
per′i·tra′che·i′tis
pe·rit′ri·chal
per′i·trich′i·al
pe·rit′ri·chous
per′i·typh′lic
per′i·typh·li′tis
per′i·um·bil′i·cal
per′i·un′gual
per′i·u·re′ter·al
per′i·u·re·ter′ic
per′i·u·re′ter·i′tis
per′i·u·re′thral
per′i·u·re·thri′tis
per′i·u′ter·ine
per′i·u′vu·lar
per′i·vag′i·nal
per′i·vag′i·ni′tis
per′i·vas′cu·lar
per′i·vas′cu·li′tis
per′i·ve′nous
per′i·ven·tric′u·lar
per′i·ver′te·bral
per′i·ves′i·cal
per′i·ve·sic′u·lar
per′i·ve·sic′u·li′tis
per′i·vis′cer·al
per′i·vis′cer·i′tis
per′i·vi·tel′line′
per′i·vul′var
per′i·xe·ni′tis
per·leche′
Per′li·a nucleus
Perls reaction
per·man′ga·nate′
per′man·gan′ic

per'me·a·bil'i·ty
per'me·a·ble
per'me·ase'
per'me·ate', -at'ed, -at'ing
per'me·a'tion
per·ni'cious
per·ni·o' *pl.* per·ni·o'nes'
per·o·bra'chi·us
per·o·ceph'a·lus
per·o·chi'rus
per·o·cor'mus
per·o·dac·tyl'i·a
per·o·dac'ty·lus *pl.* -li'
per·o·me'li·a
pe·rom'e·lus
pe·rom'e·ly
per·o·ne'al *(of the fibular side of the leg)*
♦perineal
per·o·ne'o·cal·ca'ne·us
—— ex·ter'nus
—— in·ter'nus
per·o·ne'o·cu·boi'de·us
per·o·ne'o·tib'i·a'lis
per·o·ne'us
—— ac'ces·so'ri·us
—— accessorius dig'i·ti' min'i·mi'
—— accessorius quar'tus
—— accessorius ter'ti·us
—— brev'is
—— lon'gus
—— ter'ti·us
pe·ro'ni·a
pe·ro·pla'si·a
pe·ro·pus
per·o'ral
per os
pe·ro·so'mus
pe·ro·splanch'ni·a
per·os'se·ous
per·ox'i·dase'
per·ox'ide'
per·ox'i·dize', -dized', -diz'ing
per·phen'a·zine'
per pri'mam
per rec'tum
Per·rin'-Fer·ra·ton' dis-ease
per·sev'er·a'tion
per·so'na *pl.* -nae'
per·son'i·fi·ca'tion
per'spi·ra'ti·o' in'sen·sib'i·lis
per'spi·ra'tion
per·spi'ra·to'ry

per·spire', -spired', -spir'ing
per·sua'sion
per·sul'fate'
per·sul'fide'
Per'thes'
—— disease
—— test
Per'tik diverticulum
per·tur·ba'tion
per·tus'sal
per·tus'sis
per·tus'soid'
per' va·gi'nam
per·ver'sion
per·vert' *v.*
per'vert *n.*
per'vi·gil'i·um
per'vi·ous
pes *pl.* pe'des'
—— an'se·ri'nus
—— ca'vus
—— con·tor'tus
—— gi'gas
—— pe·dun'cu·li'
—— pla'no·val'gus
—— pla'nus
pes'sa·ry
pest
pes'ti·cide'
pes'ti·lence
pes'tis *pl.* -tes'
pes'tle
pe·te'chi·a *pl.* -ae'
pe·te'chi·al
Pe'ters
—— embryo
—— method
Pe'ter·sen
—— bag
—— operation
pet'i·ole'
pe·ti'o·lus *pl.* -li'
—— ep'i·glot'ti·dis
pe·tit' mal'
Pe·tit' triangle
Pe'tri
—— dish
—— plate
pet'ri·fac'tion
pet'ro·bas'i·lar
pet'ro·la'tum
pet'ro·mas'toid'
pet'ro·oc·cip'i·tal
pet'ro·pha·ryn'ge·us *pl.* -ge·i'
pe·tro'sa *pl.* -sae'
pe·tro'sal

pet'ro·si'tis
pet'ro·sphe'noid'
pet'ro·squa·mo'sal
pet'ro·squa'mous
pet'ro·tym·pan'ic
pet'rous
Pet'te-Dö'ring
—— disease
—— panencephalitis
Pet'ten·kof'er test
Pet'ze·ta'ki disease
pex'is
Pey'er
—— glands
—— patches
pe·yo'te
Pey·ro·nie' disease
Pey·rot' thorax
Pfan'nen·stiel' incision
Pfeif'fer
—— bacillus
—— disease
Pflü'ger
—— laws
—— tube
phac'o·an'a·phy·lac'tic
phac'o·an'a·phy·lax'is
phac'o·cele'
phac'o·cyst'
phac'o·cys·tec'to·my
phac'o·cys·ti'tis
phac'o·er'y·sis
phac'oid'
pha·col'y·sis *pl.* -ses'
phac'o·lyt'ic
pha·co'ma *pl.* -mas *or* -ma·ta
pha'co·ma·to'sis *pl.* -sis'
—— of Bourne'ville
phac'o·met'a·cho·re'sis *pl.* -ses'
phac'o·met'e·ce'sis *pl.* -ses'
pha·com'e·ter
phac'o·pla·ne'sis *pl.* -ses'
phac'o·scle·ro'sis *pl.* -ses'
phac'o·scope'
pha·cos'co·py
phac'o·sco·tas'mus
phac'o·ther'a·py
phac'o·tox'ic
phage
phag'o·cyt'a·ble
phag'o·cy'tal
phag'o·cyte'
phag'o·cyt'ic
phag'o·cy·tize', -tized', -tiz'ing

phag'o·cy'to·blast'
phag'o·cy'to·lit'ic
phag'o·cy·tol'y·sis
phag'o·cy·tose', -tosed',
  -tos'ing
phag'o·cy·to'sis pl. -ses'
phag'o·dy'na·mom'e·ter
phag'o·kar'y·o'sis
pha·gol'y·sis pl. -ses'
phag'o·ma'ni·a
phag'o·some'
pha·ki'tis
pha·ko'ma pl. -mas or -ma·
  ta
phal'a·cro'sis
pha·lan'ge·al
phal'an·gec'to·my
pha·lan'ges'
—— dig'i·to'rum ma'nus
—— digitorum pe'dis
phal'an·gi'tis
pha·lan'gi·za'tion
pha·lan'go·pha·lan'ge·al
pha'lanx' pl. pha·lan'ges'
—— dis·ta'lis dig'i·to'rum
  ma'nus
—— distalis digitorum pe'-
  dis
—— me'di·a dig'i·to'rum
  ma'nus
—— media digitorum pe'dis
—— pri'ma dig'i·to'rum ma'-
  nus
—— prima digitorum pe'dis
—— prox'i·ma'lis dig'i·
  to'rum ma'nus
—— proximalis digitorum
  pe'dis
—— se·cun'da dig'i·to'rum
  ma'nus
—— secunda digitorum pe'-
  dis
—— ter'ti·a dig'i·to'rum
  ma'nus
—— tertia digitorum pe'dis
phal'lic
phal'li·form'
phal'lo·cryp'sis
phal'lo·dyn'i·a
phal'loid'
phal·lon'cus
phal'lo·plas'ty
phal·lot'o·my
phal'lus pl. -li' or -lus·es
phan'er·o·gen'ic
phan'er·o'sis pl. -ses'
phan'quone'

phan'tasm
phan·tas'ma·to·mo'ri·a
phan'tom
phar'ma·cal
phar'ma·ceu'tic or phar'ma·
  ceu'ti·cal
phar'ma·ceu'tics
phar'ma·cist
phar'ma·co·chem'is·try
phar'ma·co·dy·nam'ic
phar'ma·co·dy·nam'ics
phar'ma·co·ge·net'ics
phar'ma·co'ki·net'ic
phar'ma·co'ki·net'ics
phar'ma·co·log'ic or
  phar'ma·co·log'i·cal
phar'ma·col'o·gist
phar'ma·col'o·gy
phar'ma·co·ma'ni·a
phar'ma·co·pe'dics
phar'ma·co·pe'ia
phar'ma·co·pe'ial
phar'ma·co·pho'bi·a
phar'ma·co·phore'
phar'ma·co·psy·cho'sis pl.
  -ses'
phar'ma·co·ther'a·py
phar'ma·cy
phar'yn·gal'gi·a
pha·ryn'ge·al
phar'yn·gec·ta'si·a
phar'yn·gec'to·my
phar'yn·gem·phrax'is
pha·ryn'ge·us
phar'yn·gism
phar'yn·gis'mus
phar'yn·git'ic
phar'yn·gi'tis pl. -git'i·des'
—— sic'ca
pha·ryn'go·bran'chi·al
pha·ryn'go·cele'
pha·ryn'go·con·junc·ti'val
pha·ryn'go·con·junc'ti·
  vi'tis
pha·ryn'go·dyn'i·a
pha·ryn'go·ep'i·glot'tic
pha·ryn'go·ep'i·glot'ti·cus
  pl. -ci'
pha·ryn'go·e·soph'a·ge'al
pha·ryn'go·e·soph'a·gus
  pl. -gi'
pha·ryn'go·glos'sal
pha·ryn'go·glos'sus pl. -si'
pha·ryn'go·ker'a·to'sis pl.
  -ses'
pha·ryn'go·la·ryn'ge·al
pha·ryn'go·lar'yn·gi'tis

pha·ryn'go·lith'
phar'yn·gol'y·sis pl. -ses'
pha·ryn'go·max'il·lar'y
pha·ryn'go·my·co'sis pl.
  -ses'
pha·ryn'go·na'sal
pha·ryn'go·pal'a·tine'
pha·ryn'go·pa·ral'y·sis pl.
  -ses'
phar'yn·gop'a·thy
pha·ryn'go·pe·ris'to·le
pha·ryn'go·plas'ty
pha·ryn'go·ple'gi·a
pha·ryn'go·rhi·ni'tis
pha·ryn'go·rhi·nos'co·py
pha·ryn'gor·rha'gi·a
pha·ryn'gor·rhe'a
pha·ryn'go·sal'pin·gi'tis
pha·ryn'go·scle·ro·ma
pha·ryn'go·scope'
phar'yn·gos'co·py
pha·ryn'go·spasm
pha·ryn'go·spas·mod'ic
pha·ryn'go·ste·no'sis pl.
  -ses'
phar'yn·gos'to·ma pl. -mas
  or -ma·ta
pha·ryn'go·tome'
phar'yn·got'o·my
pha·ryn'go·ton·sil·li'tis
pha·ryn'go·tra'che·al
pha·ryn'go·tym·pan'ic
pha·ryn'go·xe·ro'sis pl.
  -ses'
phar'ynx pl. pha·ryn'ges'
phase
pha·se'o·lin
pha'sic
pha'sin
phen'a·caine'
phe·nac'e·mide'
phe·nac'e·tin
phen'a·gly'co·dol'
phe·naph'tha·zine'
phe'nate'
phen·az'o·cine'
phen'a·zone'
phen·az'o·pyr'i·dine'
phen·car'ba·mide'
phen·cy'cli·dine'
phene
phen'el·zine'
phen·eth'i·cil'lin
phe·net'i·din
phe·net'i·di·nu'ri·a
phen·for'min
phen'go·pho'bi·a

phe·nin'da·mine'
phen'in·di'one'
phen·ir'a·mine
phen·met'ra·zine'
phe'no·bar'bi·tal'
phe'no·bar'bi·tone'
phe'no·din
phe'nol'
phe'no·late'
phe·no'lic
phe'nol·phthal'ein'
phe'nol·phthal'in
phe'nol·tet'ra·chlo'ro·
  phthal'ein'
phe'nol·u'ri·a
phe·nom'e·non pl. -na
phe'no·pro'pa·zine'
phe'no·thi'a·zine'
phe'no·type'
phe'no·typ'ic
phe·nox'y
phe·nox'y·ben'za·mine'
phe·noz'y·gous
phen'pro·cou'mon'
phen·sux'i·mide'
phen'ter·mine'
phen·tol'a·mine'
phen'yl
phen'yl·a·ce'tyl·u·re'a
phen'yl·al'a·nine'
phen'yl·al'a·ni·ne'mi·a
phen'yl·bu'ta·zone'
phen'yl·car'bi·nol'
phen'yl·ene'
phen'yl·eph'rine'
phen'yl·hy'dra·zine'
phen'yl·hy'dra·zone'
phe·nyl'ic
phen'yl·ke'to·nu'ri·a
phen'yl·ke'to·nu'ric
phen'yl·mer·cu'ric
phen'yl·pro'pa·nol'a·mine'
phe'o·chrome'
phe'o·chro'mo·blast'
phe'o·chro'mo·blas·to'ma
  pl. -mas or -ma·ta
phe'o·chro'mo·cyte'
phe'o·chro'mo·cy·to'ma
  pl. -mas or -ma·ta
Phi'a·loph'o·ra
  —— jean·sel'me·i'
  —— ver'ru·co'sa
phi·mo'si·ec'to·my
phi·mo'sis pl. -ses'
phi·mot'ic
phle·bal'gi·a

phleb·an'gi·o'ma pl. -mas
  or -ma·ta
phleb'ar·te'ri·ec·ta'si·a
phleb'ec·ta'si·a
phle·bec'to·my
phleb'ec·to'pi·a
phleb'em·phrax'is
phleb'ex·er'e·sis
phleb'hep·a·ti'tis
phle·bis'mus
phle·bit'ic
phle·bi'tis
phleb'o·car'ci·no'ma pl.
  -mas or -ma·ta
phle·boc'ly·sis pl. -ses'
phleb'o·gram'
phleb'o·graph'
phle·bog'ra·phy
phleb'oid'
phleb'o·lith'
phleb'o·li·thi'a·sis pl. -ses'
phleb'o·lith'ic
phleb'o·ma·nom'e·ter
phleb'o·phle·bos'to·my
phleb'o·plas'ty
phleb'or·rha'gi·a
phle·bor'rha·phy
phleb'or·rhex'is pl. -rhex'es'
phleb'o·scle·ro'sis pl. -ses'
phle·bo'sis pl. -ses'
phle·bos'ta·sis pl. -ses'
phleb'o·ste·no'sis pl. -ses'
phleb'o·throm·bo'sis pl.
  -ses'
phleb'o·tome'
phle·bot'o·mist
phle·bot'o·mize', -mized',
  -miz'ing
phle·bot'o·my
phlegm
phleg·ma'si·a
  —— ad'e·no'sa
  —— al'ba do'lens
  —— cel'lu·lar'is
  —— ce·ru'le·a do'lens
  —— mem·bra'nae' mu·
  co'sae' gas'tro·pul'mo·na'lis
  —— my·o'i·ca
phleg·mat'ic
phleg'mon'
phleg'mo·na dif·fu'sa
phleg'mon·ous
phlo'em
phlo·gis'tic
phlog'o·gen'ic
phlo·gog'e·nous
phlo·go'sis pl. -ses'

phlo'ro·glu'cine'
phlo'ro·glu'ci·nol'
phlox'ine'
phlyc·te'na pl. -nae'
phlyc'te·nar
phlyc·ten'u·la pl. -lae'
phlyc·ten'u·lar
phlyc'te·nule'
phlyc·ten'u·lo'sis
pho'bi·a
pho'bic
pho'bo·dip'si·a
pho'bo·pho'bi·a
Pho·cas' disease
pho'co·me'li·a
pho'co·me'lic
pho·com'e·lus pl. -li'
pho·com'e·ly
pho'nal
phon'ar·te'ri·o·gram'
pho'nas·the'ni·a
pho'nate', -nat'ed, -nat'ing
pho·na'tion
pho'na·to'ry
pho·nen'do·scope'
pho·net'ic
pho·net'ics
phon'ic
pho'nism
pho'no·an'gi·og'ra·phy
pho'no·aus'cul·ta'tion
pho'no·car'di·o·gram'
pho'no·car'di·o·graph'
pho'no·car'di·o·graph'ic
pho'no·car'di·og'ra·phy
pho'no·gram'
pho·nol'o·gy
pho·nom'e·ter
pho·nom'e·try
pho'no·my·oc'lo·nus
pho'no·my·og'ra·phy
pho'no·pa'thy
pho'no·pho'bi·a
pho'no·pho·tog'ra·phy
pho·nop'si·a
pho'ri·a
Phor'i·dae'
phor'o·blast'
phor'o·cyte'
pho·rom'e·ter
pho'ro·op·tom'e·ter
phor'o·scope'
phor'o·tone'
phose
phos·gen'ic
phos'pha·gen
phos'pha·tase'

phos'phate'
phos'pha·te'mi·a
phos·phat'ic
phos'pha·tide'
phos'pha·tid'ic
phos'pha·ti·do'sis
phos'pha·tu'ri·a
phos'phene'
phos'phide'
phos'phite'
phos'pho·am'i·dase'
phos'pho·ar'gi·nine'
phos'pho·cre'a·tine'
phos'pho·di·es'ter·ase'
phos'pho·fruc'to·ki'nase'
phos'pho·ga·lac'tose'
phos'pho·glob'u·lin
phos'pho·glu'co·ki'nase'
phos'pho·glu'co·mu'tase'
phos'pho·glu·con'ic
phos'pho·glu'cose'
phos'pho·glyc'er·al'de·
  hyde'
phos'pho·gly·cer'ic
phos'pho·glyc'er·o·
  mu'tase'
phos'pho·i·no'si·tide'
phos'pho·ki'nase'
phos'pho·li'pase'
phos'pho·lip'id
phos'pho·lip'i·de'mi·a
phos'pho·lip'in
phos'pho·mon'o·es'ter·ase'
phos·pho·ne·cro'sis
phos·pho'ni·um
phos'pho·pe'ni·a
phos'pho·pro'tein'
phos'pho·resce', -resced',
  -resc'ing
phos'pho·res'cence
phos'pho·res'cent
phos'phor·hi·dro'sis pl.
  -ses'
phos·pho'ric
phos'pho·rism
phos'phor·ol'y·sis pl. -ses'
phos'pho·rus
phos'pho·ryl·ase'
phos'pho·ryl·a'tion
phos'pho·trans'fer·ase'
phos·vi'tin
pho·tal'gi·a
pho·tau'gi·o·pho'bi·a
pho'tes·the'si·a
pho'tes·the'sis
pho'tic
pho'tism

pho'to·ac·tin'ic
pho'to·al·ler'gic
pho'to·bac·te'ri·um pl. -ri·a
pho'to·ca·tal'y·sis pl. -ses'
pho'to·chem'i·cal
pho'to·chem'is·try
pho'to·chro·mat'ic
pho'to·chro'mo·gen
pho'to·chro'mo·gen'ic
pho'to·co·ag'u·la'tion
pho'to·col'or·im'e·ter
pho'to·con·duc'tive
pho'to·con'duc·tiv'i·ty
pho'to·con·junc'ti·vi'tis
pho'to·cu·ta'ne·ous
pho'to·der'ma·ti'tis
pho'to·der'ma·to'sis pl.
  -ses'
pho'to·dyn'i·a
pho'to·dys·pho'ri·a
pho'to·e·lec'tric
pho'to·e·lec'tron'
pho'to·flu'o·rog'ra·phy
pho'to·flu'o·ros'co·py
pho'to·gene'
pho'to·gen'e·sis pl. -ses'
pho'to·gen'ic
pho'to·gram'
pho'to·ki·net'ic
pho'to·ky'mo·graph'
pho'to·lu'mi·nes'cence
pho·tol'y·sis pl. -ses'
pho'to·lyte'
pho·tom'e·ter
pho'to·met'ric
pho·tom'e·try
pho'to·mi'cro·graph'
pho'to·mi·crog'ra·phy
pho'to·mi'cro·scope'
pho'to·mi·cros'co·py
pho'to·mul'ti·pli'er
pho'ton'
pho'to·par'es·the'si·a
pho'to·path'o·log'ic
pho·top'a·thy
pho'to·per·cep'tive
pho'to·phil'ic
pho'to·pho'bi·a
pho'to·pho'bic
pho'to·phore'
pho'toph·thal'mi·a
pho·to'pi·a
pho·to'pic
pho·top'si·a
pho·top'sin
pho'to·re·cep'tive
pho'to·re·cep'tors

pho'to·ret'i·ni'tis
pho'to·scan'
pho'to·sen'si·tive
pho'to·sen'si·tiv'i·ty
pho'to·sen'si·ti·za'tion
pho'to·syn'the·sis pl. -ses'
pho'to·syn·thet'ic
pho'to·tac'tic
pho'to·tax'is
pho'to·ther'a·py
pho'to·ton'ic
pho·tot'o·nus
pho'to·tox'ic
pho'to·tox·ic'i·ty
pho'to·troph'ic
pho·tot'ro·pism
pho·tu'ri·a
phre·nal'gi·a
phre·nec'to·my
phren'em·phrax'is pl.
  -phrax'es'
phre·net'ic also frenetic
phren'ic
phren'i·cec'to·my
phren'i·cla'si·a
phren'i·co·e·soph'a·ge'al
phren'i·co·ex·er'e·sis
phren'i·co·gas'tric
phren'i·co'neu·rec'to·my
phren'i·co·splen'ic
phren'i·cot'o·my
phren'i·co·trip'sy
phre·ni'tis
phren'o·car'di·a
phren'o·col'ic
phren'o·co'lo·pex'y
phren'o·dyn'i·a
phren'o·e·soph'a·ge'al
phren'o·gas'tric
phren'o·glot'tic
phren'o·he·pat'ic
phren'o·lep'si·a
phren'o·pa·ral'y·sis pl. -ses'
phren'o·ple'gi·a
phren'o·spasm
phren'o·splen'ic
phro·ne'ma
phryn'o·der'ma
phthal'yl·sul'fa·cet'a·mide'
phthal'yl·sul'fa·thi'a·zole'
phthin'oid'
phthi'o·col'
phthi·ri'a·sis pl. -ses'
Phthir'i·us
——— pu'bis
phthis'ic or phthis'i·cal
phthi'sis pl. -ses'

—— bul'bi'
—— cor'ne·ae'
phy'co·my·co'sis pl. -ses'
phy'go·ga·lac'tic
phy·lac'tic
phy·lax'is
phy·let'ic
phyl'lo·er'y·thrin
phyl'lo·por'phy·rin
phyl'lo·qui·none'
phy'lo·gen'e·sis pl. -ses'
phy'lo·ge·net'ic
phy·log'e·ny
phy'lum pl. -la
phy'ma pl. -mas or -ma·ta
phy'ma·toid'
phy'ma·to'sis pl. -ses'
phy·sal'i·form'
phy·sal'i·phore'
phy'sa·liph'o·rous
phys'a·lis
Phy'sa·lop'ter·a
—— cau·cas'i·ca
phys·co'ni·a
phys'if·at'rics
phys'i·at'rist
phys'ic (a cathartic)
 ◆physique
phys'i·cal
phy·si'cian
Phy'sick operation
phys'i·co·chem'i·cal
phys'i·co·gen'ic
phys'i·no'sis pl. -ses'
phys'i·o·chem'i·cal
phys'i·og'no·my
phys'i·og·no'sis pl. -ses'
phys'i·o·log'ic or phys'i·o·
 log'i·cal
phys'i·o·log'i·co·an'a·
 tom'ic
phys'i·ol'o·gist
phys'i·ol'o·gy
phys'i·o·path'o·log'ic
phys'i·o'pa·thol'o·gy
phys'i·o·ther'a·pist
phys'i·o·ther'a·py
phy·sique' (body)
 ◆physic
phy'so·hem'a·to·me'tra
phy'so·hy'dro·me'tra
phy'so·me'tra
phy'so·py'o·sal'pinx pl.
 -sal·pin'ges'
phy'so·stig·mine'
phy'to·be'zo·ar
phy'to·hem'ag·glu'ti·nin

phy'toid'
phy'to·na·di'one'
phy'to·par'a·site'
phy'to·pa·thol'o·gy
phy'to·pho'to·der'ma·ti'tis
phy'to·pre·cip'i·tin
phy·to'sis pl. -ses'
phy'to·ste'a·rin
phy·tos'ter·in
phy·tos'ter·ol'
phy·tos'ter·o·lin
phy'to·throm'bo·ki'nase'
phy'to·tox'in
pi'a
—— ma'ter
—— mater en·ceph'a·li'
—— mater spi·na'lis
pi'a-a·rach'noid'
pi'al
pi·an'
pi·as'tre·ne'mi·a
pi'ca
Pick
—— cell
—— disease
—— syndrome
Pick·wick'i·an syndrome
pi'co·cu'rie
pi'co·gram'
pi'co·pi'co·gram'
pi·cor'na·vi'rus
pi'co·sec'ond
pic·ram'ic
Pic·ras'ma
pic'rate'
pic'ric
pic'ro·car'mine
pic'ro·ni'gro·sin
pic'ro·pod'o·phyl'lin
pic'ro·tox'in
pie'bald'
pie'bald·ism
pi·e'dra
Pi·erre' Ro·bin' syndrome
pi'es·es·the'si·a
pi'e·sim'e·ter
pi'gion-toed'
pig'ment
pig'men·tar'y
pig'men·ta'tion
pig'ment'ed
pig'men·to·gen'e·sis
pig'men·to·phage'
pig'men'tum ni'grum
pi·i'tis
pi'lar
pi'la·ry

pi·las'ter
pi·las'tered
Pilcz reflex
piles
pi'le·us
pi'li'
—— an'nu·la'ti'
—— in'car·na'ti'
—— mul'ti·gem'i·ni'
—— tac'ti·les'
—— tor'ti'
pi'li·a'tion
pi'li·form'
pi'li·mic'tion
pill
pil'lar
pil'let
pi'lo·car'pine'
pi'lo·cys'tic
pi'lo·e·rec'tion
pi'lo·ma'tri·co'ma pl. -mas
 or -ma·ta
pi'lo·ma'trix·o'ma pl. -mas
 or -ma·ta
pi'lo·mo'tor
pi'lo·ni'dal
pi'lose'
pi'lo·se·ba'ceous
pi·lo'sis
pil'u·la pl. -lae'
pil'u·lar
pil'ule'
pi'lus pl. -li'
—— cu·nic'u·la'tus
—— in'car·na'tus
—— incarnatus re·cur'vus
pi·mel'ic
pim'e·li'tis
pim'e·lo'ma pl. -mas or -ma·
 ta
pim'e·lo·pte·ryg'i·um
pim'e·lor·rhe'a
pim'e·lor·thop'ne·a
pim'e·lu'ri·a
pi·min'o·dine'
pim'o·zide'
pim'ple
pin
pin'a·coid'
pin'a·cy'a·nol'
Pi·nard'
—— maneuver
—— sign
pin'cers
pin'e·al
pin'e·a·lec'to·my
pin'e·al·ism

pin'e·a·lo'ma pl. -mas or
  -ma·ta
Pi·nel' system
pin'e·o·blas·to'ma pl. -mas
  or -ma·ta
pin'e·o·cy·to'ma. -mas or
  -ma·ta
pin·guec'u·la pl. -lae'
pi'ni·form'
pink'eye'
pin'na pl. -nae' or -nas
pin'o·cyte'
pin'o·cy·to'sis pl. -ses'
pin'o·cy·tot'ic
pin'o·some'
pin·ox'e·pin
Pins sign
pint
pin'ta
pin'tid
pin'worm'
pi'o·ep'i·the'li·um pl. -li·a
pi'o·ne'mi·a
pi'or·thop'ne·a
Pi'o·trow'ski
—— reflex
—— sign
pi·pam'a·zine'
pi·pam'per·one'
pi·paz'e·thate'
pi·pen'zo·late'
pip'er·a·cet'a·zine'
pip'er·a·mide'
pi·per'a·zine'
pi·per'i·dine'
pip'er·i·do'late'
pip'er·ine'
pip'er·o·caine'
pip'er·ox'an'
pi·pet' also pipette
pi·pette' var. of pipet
pip'o·bro'man'
pip'o·sul'fan'
pip'ra·drol'
pip'ro·zol'in
piq'ui·zil
pir'i·form' also pyriform
pir'i·for'mis
Pi·ro'goff' amputation
Pir·quet' test
Pir'y fever
pi'si·form'
pit, pit'ted, pit'ting
pitch
pith'i·a·tism
pith'i·at'ric
Pi·tot' tube

Pi·tres' sections
pi·tu'i·cyte'
pi·tu'i·ta·rism
pi·tu'i·tar'i·um
—— an·te'ri·us
—— pos·te'ri·us
—— to'tum
pi·tu'i·tar'y
pi·tu'i·tec'to·my
pi·tu'i·tous
pi·tu'i·trism
pit'y·ri'a·sis pl. -ses'
—— cap'i·tis
—— cir'ci·na'ta
—— li'che·noi'des' chron'i·
ca
—— lichenoides et var'i·o'li·
for'mis a·cu'ta
—— lin'guae'
—— ni'gra
—— pi·lar'is
—— ro'se·a
—— ru'bra
—— rubra pi·lar'is
—— sim'plex'
—— ste'a·toi'des'
—— ver'si·col'or
pit'y·roid'
Pit'y·ro·spo'rum
—— or·bic'u·lar'e
—— o·va'le'
pix'el
pla·ce'bo
pla·cen'ta pl. -tas or -tae'
—— ac·cre'ta
—— cir·soi'de·a
—— dif·fu'sa
—— ex'tra·cho'ri·a'la
—— fen'es·tra'ta
—— foe·ta'lis
—— in·cre'ta
—— mem'bra·na·ce·a
—— nep'pi·for'mis
—— per·cre'ta
—— pre'vi·a
—— previa cen·tra'lis
—— previa mar'gi·na'lis
—— previa par'ti·a'lis
—— re·flex'a
—— ren'i·for'mis
—— spu'ri·a
—— suc'cen·tu'ri·a'ta
—— u'ter·i'na
pla·cen'tal
plac'en·ta'tion
plac'en·ti'tis pl. -tit'i·des'
plac'en·tog'ra·phy

pla·cen'toid'
plac'en·to'ma pl. -mas or
  -ma·ta
plac'en·to'sis pl. -ses'
Pla·ci'do disk
pla·co'dal
plac'ode'
pla·gi·o·ce·phal'ic
pla·gi·o·ceph'a·lism
pla·gi·o·ceph'a·lous
pla·gi·o·ceph'a·ly
plague
plane
pla'nar
plan'chet
pla·nim'e·ter
plan'ing
plank'ton
pla·no·cel'lu·lar
pla'no·con'cave'
pla'no·con'ic
pla'no·con'vex'
plan'o·cyte'
pla·no·val'gus
plan'ta pl. -tae'
plan'tar
plan·tar'is
plan·ta'tion
plan'ti·grade'
plan·u'la pl. -lae'
pla'num pl. -na
—— nu·cha'le'
—— oc·cip'i·ta'le'
—— or'bi·ta'le'
—— pop·lit'e·um
—— ster·na'le'
—— tem'po·ra'le'
plaque
—— jaune
plasm
plas'ma
plas'ma·blast'
plas'ma·cyte'
plas'ma·cyt'ic
plas'ma·cy'toid'
plas'ma·cy·to'ma pl. -mas
  or -ma·ta
plas'ma·cy·to'sis pl. -ses'
plas'ma·gel'
plas'ma·gene'
plas'mal
plas'ma·lem'ma
plas·mal'o·gen
plas'ma·pher'e·sis pl. -ses'
plas'ma·some'
plas'ma·ther'a·py
plas·mat'ic

plas·ma·tog′a·my
plas·ma·to′sis
plas′mic
plas′mid
plas′min
plas·min′o·gen
plas′mo·cyte′
plas′mo·cyt′ic
plas′mo·cy·to′ma pl. -mas
  or -ma·ta
plas·mo′di·al
plas·mo′di·blast′
plas·mod′ic
plas·mo′di·cide′
plas·mo′di·tro′pho·blast′
Plas·mo′di·um
—— fal·cip′a·rum
—— ma·lar′i·ae′
—— o·va′le′
—— vi′vax′
plas·mog′a·my
plas′mo·gen
plas·mol′y·sis pl. -ses′
plas′mo·lyt′ic
plas′mo·lyze′, -lyzed′, -lyz′-
  ing
plas·mo′ma pl. -mas or
  -ma·ta
plas′mon′
plas·mop′ty·sis pl. -ses′
plas′mor·rhex′is pl.
  -rhex′es′
plas·mos′chi·sis pl. -ses′
plas′mo·sin
plas′mo·some′
plas′mo·trop′ic
plas·mot′ro·pism
plas′te·in
plas′ter
—— of Par′is
plas′tic
plas·tic′i·ty
plas′ti·ciz′er
plas′tics
plas′tid
plas′ti·dule′
plas′tin
plas·to·dy·nam′i·a
plas·tog′a·my
plas′to·some′
plate
pla·teau′ pl. -teaus′ or
  -teaux′
plate′let
plat′y·ba′si·a
plat′y·ce′lous
plat′y·ce·phal′ic

plat′y·ceph′a·ly
plat′y·cne′mi·a
plat′y·cne′mic
plat′y·co·ri·a
plat′y·co·ri·a·sis
plat′y·cra′ni·a
plat′y·hi·er′ic
plat′y·mer′ic
plat′y·mor′phi·a
plat′y·mor′phic
plat′y·o′pi·a
plat′y·op′ic
plat′y·pel′lic
plat′y·pel′loid′
plat′yr·rhine′
pla·tys′ma pl. -ma·ta or
  -mas
—— my·oi′des′
pla·tys′mal
plat′ys·ten′ce·pha′li·a
plat′ys·ten·ceph′a·ly
pled′get
plei′o·trop′ic
plei·ot′ro·pism
ple·o·chro′ic
ple·och′ro·ism
ple′o·chro·mat′ic
ple·o·cy·to′sis pl. -ses′
ple′o·kar′y·o·cyte′
ple′o·mas′ti·a
ple′o·ma′zi·a
ple′o·mor′phic
ple′o·mor′phism
ple′o·mor′phous
ple′o·nasm
ple′o·nas′tic
ple′o·nec′tic
ple·o·nex′i·a
ple·o·nex′y
ple′on·os′te·o′sis
—— of Lé·ri′
ple′o·no′tus
ple·op′tics
ple·ro′sis
ple′si·o·mor′phism
ples′ses·the′si·a
ples′sor
ples′sus
pleth′o·ra
—— ap′o·cop′ti·ca
pleth′o·ric
ple·thys′mo·gram′
ple·thys′mo·graph′
ple·thys′mo·graph′ic
pleth′ys·mog′ra·phy
pleu′ra pl. -rae′
—— cos·ta′lis

—— di′a·phrag·mat′i·ca
—— me′di·as′ti·na′lis
—— pa·ri′e·ta′lis
—— per′i·car·di′a·ca
—— pul′mo·na′lis
pleu′ra·cen·te′sis pl. -ses′
pleu′ra·cot′o·my
pleu′ral
pleu·ral′gi·a
pleu·ral′gic
pleur·am′ni·on′
pleur′a·po·phys′i·al
pleur′a·poph′y·sis
pleu′ra·tome′
pleu·rec′to·my
pleu′ri·sy
pleu·rit′ic
pleu·ri′tis
pleu′ro·bron·chi′tis
pleu′ro·cele′
pleu′ro·cen·te′sis pl. -ses′
pleu′ro·cen′tral
pleu′ro·cen′trum
pleu′ro·chol′e·cys·ti′tis
pleu′ro·cu·ta′ne·ous
pleu′ro·dyn′i·a
pleu′ro·gen′ic
pleu·rog′e·nous
pleu·rog′ra·phy
pleu′ro·hep′a·ti′tis
pleu′ro·lith′
pleu·rol′y·sis pl. -ses′
pleu·ro′ma pl. -mas or
  -ma·ta
pleu′ro·me′lus
pleu′ro·per′i·car′di·al
pleu′ro·per′i·car·di′tis
pleu′ro·per′i·to·ne′al
pleu′ro·pneu·mo′ni·a
pleu′ro·pneu·mo·nol′y·sis
  pl. -ses′
pleu′ro·pros′o·pos′chi·sis
  pl. -ses′
pleu′ro·pul′mo·nar′y
pleu·ros′co·py
pleu′ro·so′ma
pleu′ro·so′ma·tos′chi·sis pl.
  -ses′
pleu′ro·so′mus
pleu′ro·spasm
pleu′ro·thot′o·nos
pleu′ro·tome′
pleu·rot′o·my
pleu′ro·ty′phoid′
pleu′ro·vis′cer·al
plex′al
plex′i·form′

plex·im′e·ter
plex′or
plex′us *pl.* plex′us *or* -us·es
—— a·or′ti·cus ab·dom′i·na′lis
—— aorticus tho′ra·ca′lis
—— aorticus tho·ra′ci·cus
—— ar·te′ri·ae′ cer′e·bri′ an·te′ri·o′ris
—— arteriae cerebri me′di·i′
—— arteriae cho′ri·oi′de·ae′
—— arteriae o·var′i·cae′
—— au·ric′u·lar′is posterior
—— au′to·nom′i·ci′
—— ax′il·lar′is
—— bas′il·lar′is
—— bra′chi·a′lis
—— car·di′a·cus
—— ca·rot′i·cus com·mu′nis
—— caroticus ex·ter′nus
—— caroticus in·ter′nus
—— cav′er·no′si′ con·char′um
—— cav′er·no′sus cli·to′ri·dis
—— cavernosus pe′nis
—— ce·li′a·cus
—— cer′vi·ca′lis
—— cho′ri·oi′de·us ven·tric′u·li′ lat′er·a′lis
—— chorioideus ventriculi quar′ti′
—— chorioideus ventriculi ter′ti·i′
—— cho·roi′de·us ven·tric′u·li′ lat′er·a′lis
—— choroideus ventriculi quar′ti′
—— choroideus ventriculi ter′ti·i′
—— coc·cyg′e·us
—— coe·li′a·cus
—— co·ro·nar′i·us cor′dis anterior
—— coronarius cordis posterior
—— def′e·ren′ti·a′lis
—— den·ta′lis inferior
—— dentalis superior
—— en·ter′i·cus
—— e′so·phag′e·us
—— fem′o·ra′lis
—— gan′gli·o′sus cil′i·ar′is
—— gas′tri·ci′
—— gas′tri·cus anterior
—— gastricus inferior
—— gastricus posterior

—— gastricus superior
—— haem′or·rhoi·da′lis me′di·us
—— haemorrhoidalis superior
—— haemorrhoidalis ve·no′sus
—— he·pat′i·cus
—— hy′po·gas′tri·cus
—— hypogastricus inferior
—— hypogastricus superior
—— i·li′a·ci′
—— i·li′a·cus
—— iliacus ex·ter′nus
—— in′gui·na′lis
—— in·ter·mes′en·ter′i·cus
—— jug′u·lar′is
—— li′e·na′lis
—— lin·gua′lis
—— lum·ba′lis
—— lum′bo·sa·cra′lis
—— lym·phat′i·cus
—— mam·mar′i·us
—— mammarius in·ter′nus
—— max′il·lar′is ex·ter′nus
—— maxillaris in·ter′nus
—— me·nin′ge·us
—— mes′en·ter′i·cus inferior
—— mesentericus superior
—— my′en·ter′i·cus
—— ner·vo′rum spi·na′li·um
—— oc·cip′i·ta′lis
—— oe·soph′a·ge·us anterior
—— oesophageus posterior
—— of Cru·veil·hier′
—— oph·thal′mi·cus
—— o·var′i·cus
—— pam·pin′i·for′mis
—— pan′cre·at′i·cus
—— pa·rot′i·de′us
—— pel′vi·nus
—— per′i·ar·ter′i·a′lis
—— pha·ryn′ge·us
—— pharyngeus as·cen′dens
—— pharyngeus ner′vi′ va′gi′
—— phren′i·cus
—— pop·lit′e·us
—— pros·tat′i·cus
—— pter′y·goi′de·us
—— pu·den·da′lis ve·no′sus
—— pu·den′dus ner·vo′sus
—— pul′mo·na′lis
—— pulmonalis anterior
—— pulmonalis posterior

—— rec·ta′lis inferior
—— rectalis me′di·us
—— rectalis superior
—— re·na′lis
—— sa·cra′lis
—— sacralis anterior
—— sacralis me′di·us
—— sper·mat′i·cus
—— sub·cla′vi·us
—— sub′mu·co′sus
—— sub·se·ro′sus
—— su′pra·re·na′lis
—— sym·path′i·ci′
—— tem′po·ra′lis su′per·fi′ci·a′lis
—— tes·tic′u·lar′is
—— thy′re·oi′de·us im′par′
—— thyreoideus inferior
—— thyreoideus superior
—— thy·roi′de·us im′par′
—— tym·pan′i·cus
—— u′re·ter′i·cus
—— u′ter·o·vag′i·na′lis
—— uterovaginalis ve·no′sus
—— vas′cu·lo′sus
—— ve·no′si′ ver′te·bra′les′ an·te′ri·o′res′
—— venosi vertebrales ex·ter′ni′ anterior et posterior
—— venosi vertebrales in·ter′ni′ anterior et posterior
—— venosi vertebrales pos·te′ri·o′res′
—— ve·no′sus
—— venosus ar′e·o·lar′is
—— venosus ca·na′lis hy′po·glos′si′
—— venosus ca·rot′i·cus in·ter′nus
—— venosus fo·ram′i·nis o·va′lis
—— venosus ma·mil′lae′
—— venosus pros·tat′i·cus
—— venosus rec·ta′lis
—— venosus sa·cra′lis
—— venosus sem′i·na′lis
—— venosus sub·oc·cip′i·ta′lis
—— venosus u′ter·i′nus
—— venosus vag′i·na′lis
—— venosus ves′i·ca′lis
—— ver′te·bra′lis
—— ves′i·ca′lis
pli′ca *pl.* -cae′
—— ar′y·ep′i·glot′ti·ca
—— ax′il·lar′is anterior

—— axillaris posterior
—— cae·ca'lis
—— ce·ca'lis vas'cu·lar'is
—— chor'dae' tym'pa·ni'
—— du'o·de·na'lis inferior
—— duodenalis superior
—— du'o·de'no·je'ju·na'lis
—— du'o·de'no·mes'o·col'i·ca
—— ep'i·gas'tri·ca
—— fim'bri·a'ta
—— gas'tro·pan'cre·at'i·ca
—— glos'so·ep'i·glot'ti·ca lat'er·a'lis
—— glossoepiglottica me'di·a'na
—— il'e·o·cae·ca'lis
—— il'e·o·ce·ca'lis
—— in'cu·dis
—— in'gui·na'lis
—— in'ter·u're·ter'i·ca
—— lac'ri·ma'lis
—— lon'gi·tu'di·na'lis du'o·de'ni'
—— mal'le·ar'is anterior mem·bra'nae' tym'pa·ni'
—— mallearis anterior tu'ni·cae' mu·co'sae' ca'vi' tym'pa·ni'
—— mallearis posterior mem·bra'nae' tym'pa·ni'
—— mallearis posterior tu'ni·cae' mu·co'sae' ca'vi' tym'pa·ni'
—— mal'le·o·lar'is anterior mem·bra'nae' tym'pa·ni'
—— malleolaris anterior tu'ni·cae' mu·co'sae' tym·pan'i·cae'
—— malleolaris posterior mem·bra'nae' tym'pa·ni'
—— malleolaris posterior tu'ni·cae' mu·co'sae' tym·pan'i·cae'
—— mu·co'sa
—— pal·pe'bro·na·sa'lis
—— par'a·du'o·de·na'lis
—— po·lon'i·ca
—— pu'bo·ves'i·ca'lis
—— rec'to·u'ter·i'na
—— sal·pin'go·pal'a·ti'na
—— sal·pin'go·pha·ryn'ge·a
—— sem'i·lu·nar'is
—— semilunaris con'junc·ti'vae'
—— se·ro'sa
—— spi·ra'lis

—— sta·pe'dis
—— sub'lin·gua'lis
—— sy'no·vi·a'lis
—— synovialis in'fra·pat'el·lar'is
—— synovialis pat'el·lar'is
—— tri·an'gu·lar'is
—— um·bil'i·ca'lis lat'er·a'lis
—— umbilicalis me'di·a
—— umbilicalis me'di·a'lis
—— umbilicalis me'di·a'na
—— u're·ter'i·ca
—— ve'nae' ca'vae' si·nis'trae'
—— ven·tric'u·lar'is
—— ves'i·ca'lis trans·ver'sa
—— ves·tib'u·lar'is
—— vo·ca'lis
pli'cae'
—— ad'i·po'sae' pleu'rae'
—— a·lar'es'
—— am'pul·lar'es' tu'bae' u'ter·i'nae'
—— cae·ca'lis'
—— ce·ca'les'
—— cil'i·ar'es'
—— cir'cu·lar'es'
—— gas'tri·cae'
—— gas'tro·pan'cre·at'i·cae'
—— i'ri·dis
—— isth'mi·cae' tu'bae' u'ter·i'nae'
—— pal'a·ti'nae' trans·ver'sae'
—— pal·ma'tae'
—— sem'i·lu·nar'es' co'li'
—— trans'ver·sa'les' rec'ti'
—— tu·bar'i·ae'
—— tu'ni·cae' mu·co'sae' ve·si'cae' fel'le·ae'
—— vil·lo'sae' ven·tric'u·li'
pli'cate', -cat'ed, -cat'ing
pli·ca'tion
pli·cot'o·my
plom·bage'
plug
plug'ger
plum'bic
plum'bism
plum'bum
Plum'mer
—— disease
—— sign
—— treatment
Plum'mer-Vin'son syn-drome
plu'ri·cy'to·pe'ni·a

plu'ri·fo'cal
plu'ri·glan'du·lar
plu'ri·grav'i·da
plu'ri·loc'u·lar
plu'ri·men'or·rhe'a
plu·rip'a·ra
plu'ri·par'i·ty
pne'o·graph'
pne·om'e·ter
pneu'mar·throg'ra·phy
pneu'mar·thro'sis
pneu·mat'ic
pneu'ma·ti·za'tion
pneu'ma·tize', -tized', -tiz'-ing
pneu'ma·to·car'di·a
pneu'ma·to·cele'
pneu'ma·to·dysp'ne·a
pneu'ma·to·gram'
pneu'ma·to·graph'
pneu'ma·tom'e·ter
pneu'ma·tom'e·try
pneu'ma·tor'ra·chis
pneu'ma·to'sis *pl.* -ses'
—— cys·toi'des' in·tes'ti·na'lis
pneu'ma·tu'ri·a
pneu·mec'to·my
pneu'mo·an'gi·og'ra·phy
pneu'mo·ar·thro·gram'
pneu'mo·ar·throg'ra·phy
pneu'mo·ba·cil'lus *pl.* -li'
pneu'mo·bul'bar
pneu'mo·car'di·og'ra·phy
pneu'mo·cele'
pneu'mo·cen·te'sis *pl.* -ses'
pneu'mo·ceph'a·lus
pneu'mo·cho'le·cys·ti'tis
pneu'mo·coc'cal
pneu'mo·coc·ce'mi·a
pneu'mo·coc'cic
pneu'mo·coc·ci'dal
pneu'mo·coc·co'sis *pl.* -ses'
pneu'mo·coc·co·su'ri·a
pneu'mo·coc'cus *pl.* -ci'
pneu'mo·co'lon
pneu'mo·co'ni·o'sis *pl.* -ses'
pneu'mo·cra'ni·um
pneu'mo·cys'tic
Pneu'mo·cys'tis
—— ca·ri'ni·i'
pneu'mo·cys'to·gram'
pneu'mo·cys'tog'ra·phy
pneu'mo·cys'to'sis *pl.* -ses'
pneu'mo·cyte'
pneu'mo·der'ma
pneu'mo·dy·nam'ics

pneu'mo·en·ceph'a·li'tis
pneu'mo·en·ceph'a·lo·cele'
pneu'mo·en·ceph'a·lo·gram'
pneu'mo·en·ceph'a·log'ra·phy
pneu'mo·en·ceph'a·lo·my'e·lo·gram'
pneu'mo·en·ceph'a·lo·my'e·log'ra·phy
pneu'mo·en·ter'ic
pneu'mo·en·ter·i'tis
pneu'mo·gas'tric
pneu'mo·gas·tros'co·py
pneu'mo·gram'
pneu'mo·graph'
pneu·mog'ra·phy
pneu·mo·he'mi·a
pneu·mo·he'mo·per'i·car'di·um
pneu·mo·he'mo·tho'rax'
pneu·mo·hy'dro·per'i·car'di·um
pneu·mo·hy'dro·tho'rax'
pneu·mo·hy'po·der'ma
pneu·mo·lip'i·do'sis
pneu·mo·lith'
pneu·mo·li·thi'a·sis pl. -ses'
pneu·mol'y·sis pl. -ses'
pneu'mo·ma·la'ci·a
pneu'mo·me'di·as·ti'num
pneu·mom'e·try
pneu'mo·my·co'sis pl. -ses'
pneu'mo·my'e·log'ra·phy
pneu'mo·nec'to·my
pneu·mo'ni·a
—— al'ba
pneu·mon'ic
pneu'mo·ni'tis
pneu'mo·no·cele'
pneu'mo·no·cen·te'sis pl. -ses'
pneu'mo·no·cir·rho'sis pl. -ses'
pneu·mon'o·cyte'
pneu·mo·nol'y·sis pl. -ses'
pneu'mo·no·mel'a·no'sis pl. -ses'
pneu'mo·no·my·co'sis pl. -ses'
pneu'mo·nop'a·thy
pneu·mo'no·pex'y
pneu·mo·nor'rha·phy
pneu·mo'no·sis pl. -ses'
pneu·mo·not'o·my
pneu'mo·per'i·car·di'tis
pneu'mo·per'i·car'di·um

pneu'mo·per'i·to·ne'um
pneu'mo·per'i·to·ne'um pl. -ums or -ne'a
pneu'mo·per'i·to·ni'tis
pneu'mo·pex'y
pneu'mo·pleu·ri'tis
pneu'mo·py'e·lo·gram'
pneu'mo·py'o·per'i·car'di·um
pneu'mo·ra'chis
pneu'mo·ra'di·og'ra·phy
pneu'mor·rha'gi·a
pneu'mo·tax'ic
pneu'mo·tax'is
pneu'mo·ther'a·py
pneu'mo·tho'rax' pl. -rax·es or -ra·ces'
pneu·mot'o·my
pneu'mo·tox'ic
pneu'mo·tox'in
pneu'mo·ty'phoid'
pneu'mo·ty'phus
pneu'mo·ven'tri·cle
pneu'mo·ven·tric'u·log'ra·phy
pneu'sis
pnig'ma
pni'go·pho'bi·a
pock
pocked
pock'et
pock'mark'
po·dag'ra
pod'a·gral
po·dag'ric
po·dal'gi·a
po·dal'ic
pod'ar·thri'tis
pod'e·de'ma
po·di'a·trist
po·di'a·try
pod'o·cyte'
pod'o·cyt'ic
pod'o·dyn'i·a
pod'o·phyl'lum pl. -li'
po·go'ni·on
poi'ki·lo·blast'
poi'ki·lo·cyte'
poi'ki·lo·cy·the'mi·a
poi'ki·lo·cy·to'sis pl. -ses'
poi'ki·lo·der'ma
—— a·troph'i·cans' vas'cu·lar·e'
—— con·gen'i·ta'le'
—— of Ci·vatte'
—— re·tic'u·lar·e' of Ci·vatte'

poi'ki·lo·der'ma·to·my'o·si'tis
poi'ki·lo·ther'mal
poi'ki·lo·ther'mic
poi'ki·lo·ther'mism
poi'ki·lo·ther'mous
poi'ki·lo·ther'my
poi'ki·lo·throm'bo·cyte'
poi'ki·lo·zo'o·sper'mi·a
point
points' dou·lou·reux'
poise
Poi·seuille' layer
poi'son
poi'son·ing
poi'son·ous
Po'land syndrome
po'lar
po·la·rim'e·ter
po·la·rim'e·try
po·lar'i·scope'
po·lar'i·stro·bom'e·ter
po·lar'i·ty
po·lar·i·za'tion
po'lar·ize', -ized', -iz'ing
po'lar·iz'er
po·lar'o·gram'
po·lar'o·graph'
po·lar'o·graph'ic
po·la·rog'ra·phy
pole
po'li·en·ceph'a·li'tis
po'li·o·dys·tro'phi·a
—— cer'e·bri' pro'gres·si'va in·fan'ti·lis
po'li·o·dys'tro·phy
po'li·o·en·ceph'a·li'tis
—— a·cu'ta
—— hem'or·rha'gi·ca
po'li·o·en·ceph'a·lo·me·nin'go·my'e·li'tis
po'li·o·en·ceph'a·lo·my'e·li'tis
po'li·o·en·ceph'a·lop'a·thy
po'li·o·my'el·en·ceph'a·li'tis
po'li·o·my'e·li'tis
po'li·o·my'e·lop'a·thy
po'li·o·my'o·si'tis
po'li·o·plasm
po'li·o'sis pl. -ses'
pol'i·o·thrix'
po'li·o·vi'rus
Pol'it·zer
—— cone
—— maneuver
—— test

pol′lit·zer·i·za′tion
pol′la·ki·u′ri·a
pol′len
pol′lex′ pl. -li·ces′
—— val′gus
—— var′us
pol′li·ci·za′tion
pol′li·cize′, -cized′, -ciz′ing
pol′li·no′sis pl. -ses′
pol·lu′tion
po′lo·cyte′
pol·toph′a·gy
po′lus pl. -li′
—— anterior bul′bi′ oc′u·li′
—— anterior len′tis
—— fron·ta′lis
—— oc·cip′i·ta′lis
—— posterior bul′bi′ oc′u·li′
—— posterior len′tis
—— tem′po·ra′lis
pol′y·ac′id
pol′y·ad′e·ni′tis
pol′y·ad′e·no′ma pl. -mas or -ma·ta
pol′y·ad′e·nop′a·thy
pol′y·ad′e·no′sis pl. -ses′
pol′y·ad′e·nous
pol′y·an′gi·i′tis
pol′y·ar′te·ri′tis
—— no·do′sa
pol′y·ar′thric
pol′y·ar·thri′tis
pol′y·ar·throp′a·thy
pol′y·ar·tic′u·lar
pol′y·ba′sic
pol′y·blast′
pol′y·ble·phar′i·a
pol′y·bleph′a·ron′
pol′y·bleph′a·ry
pol′y·car′bo·phil′
pol′y·cel′lu·lar
pol′y·cen′tric
pol′y·chei′ri·a
pol′y·che·mo·ther′a·py
pol′y·cho′li·a
pol′y·chon·dri′tis
pol′y·chro·ma′si·a
pol′y·chro·ma′ti·a
pol′y·chro·mat′ic
pol′y·chro·mat′o·cyte′
pol′y·chro′ma·to·phil
pol′y·chro′ma·to·phil′i·a
pol′y·chro′ma·to·phil′ic
pol′y·chro′ma·to′sis pl. -ses′
pol′y·chrome′
pol′y·chro′mi·a

pol′y·chro′mo·cy·to′sis pl. -ses′
pol′y·chy′li·a
pol′y·clo′nal
pol′y·clo′ni·a
pol′y·co′ri·a
pol′y·cy′clic
pol′y·cy·e′sis
pol′y·cys′tic
pol′y·cy·the′mi·a
—— hy′per·ton′i·ca
—— ru′bra ve′ra
—— ve′ra
pol′y·cys·to′ma pl. -mas or -ma·ta
pol′y·cyte′
pol′y·dac·tyl′i·a
pol′y·dac′ty·lism
pol′y·dac′ty·ly
pol′y·dip′si·a
pol′y·dys·pla′si·a
pol′y·dys·troph′ic
pol′y·dys·tro·phy
pol′y·e·lec′tro·lyte′
pol′y·em′bry·o·ny
pol′y·e′mi·a
pol′y·es·the′si·a
pol′y·es′trus
pol′y·eth′a·dene′
pol′y·eth′yl·ene′
pol′y·ga·lac′ti·a
po·lyg′a·mous
po·lyg′a·my
pol′y·gen′ic
pol′y·glan′du·lar
pol′y·glo·bu′li·a
pol′y·glob′u·lism
pol′y·gyr′i·a
pol′y·he′dral
pol′y·he′mi·a
pol′y·hi·dro′sis pl. -ses′
pol′y·hy′dric
pol′y·hy·drox′y
pol′y·hy·dru′ri·a
pol′y·i·dro′sis pl. -ses′
pol′y·in·fec′tion
pol′y·lep′tic
pol′y·lob′u·lar
pol′y·mas′ti·a
pol′y·ma′zi·a
pol′y·me′li·a
pol′y·me′lus pl. -li′
pol′y·me′ni·a
pol′y·men′or·rhe′a
pol′y·mer
pol′y·me′ri·a
pol′y·mer′ic

po·lym′er·i·za′tion
po·lym′er·ize′ -ized′, -iz′ing
pol′y·met′a·car′pi·a
pol′y·met′a·tar′si·a
pol′y·mi·cro′bi·al
pol′y·mi·cro′bic
pol′y·mi′cro·gy′ri·a
pol′y·morph′
pol′y·mor′phic
pol′y·mor′phism
pol′y·mor′pho·cel′lu·lar
pol′y·mor′pho·cyte′
pol′y·mor′pho·nu′cle·ar
pol′y·mor′phous
pol′y·my·al′gi·a
—— rheu·mat′i·ca
pol′y·my·oc′lo·nus
pol′y·my·op′a·thy
pol′y·my·o·si′tis
pol′y·myx′in
pol′y·ne′sic
pol′y·neu′ral
pol′y·neu·ral′gi·a
pol′y·neu′ric
pol′y·neu·rit′ic
pol′y·neu·ri′tis
pol′y·neu′ro·my′o·si′tis
pol′y·neu·rop′a·thy
pol′y·neu′ro·ra·dic′u·li′tis
pol′y·nu′cle·ar
pol′y·nu′cle·ate′
pol′y·nu′cle·o·ti′dase′
pol′y·nu′cle·o·tide′
pol′y·o·don′ti·a
pol′y·o′ma pl. -mas or -ma·ta
pol′y·o·nych′i·a
pol′y·o′pi·a
—— mon′oph·thal′mi·ca
pol′y·or′chi·dism
pol′y·or′chis
pol′y·o·rex′i·a
pol′y·or·rho·men·in·gi′tis
pol′y·os·tot′ic
pol′y·ov′u·la·to′ry
pol′yp
pol′y·pap′il·lo′ma pl. -mas or -ma·ta
pol′y·pa·re′sis pl. -ses′
pol′y·path′i·a
pol′y·pec′to·my
pol′y·pep′ti·dase′
pol′y·pep′tide′
pol′y·pep′ti·de·mi·a
pol′y·pep′ti·dor·rha′chi·a
pol′y·per′i·os·ti′tis hy′per·es·thet′i·ca

pol′y·pha′gi·a
pol′y·pha·lan′gism
pol′y·phar′ma·cy
pol′y·pha′sic
pol′y·pho′bi·a
pol′y·phy·let′ic
pol′y·phy′le·tism
pol′y·phy′o·dont′
pol′y·plas′tic
pol′y·ple′gi·a
pol′y·ploid′
pol′y·ploi′dy
pol′yp·ne′a
pol′y·po′di·a
pol′y·poid′
pol′y·poi·do′sis
po·lyp′o·rous
pol′y·po′sis *pl.* -ses′
  —— co′li′
  —— ven·tric′u·li′
pol′y·pous
pol′y·pty′chi·al
pol′y·pus *pl.* -pi′ *or* -pus·es
pol′y·ra·dic′u·li′tis
pol′y·ra·dic′u·lo·neu·ri′tis
pol′y·ra·dic′u·lo·neu·rop′a·
  thy
pol′y·ri′bo·some′
pol′yr·rhe′a
pol′y·sac′cha·ride′
pol′y·sce′li·a
po·lys′ce·lus
pol′y·scle·ro′sis *pl.* -ses′
pol′y·se·ro·si′tis
pol′y·si′nus·i′tis
pol′y·so′mi·a
pol′y·so′mic
pol′y·so′mus
pol′y·sor′bate′
pol′y·sper′mi·a
pol′y·sper′mism
pol′y·sper′my
pol′y·stich′i·a
pol′y·sto′ma·tous
pol′y·sty′rene′
pol′y·sus·pen′soid′
pol′y·syn·ap′tic
pol′y·syn·dac′ty·lism
pol′y·syn·dac′ty·ly
pol′y·syn′o·vi′tis
pol′y·the′li·a
pol′y·the′lism
pol′y·thi′a·zide′
po·lyt′o·cous
pol′y·trich′i·a
pol′y·tri·cho′sis
pol′y·tro′phi·a

po·lyt′ro·phy
pol′y·trop′ic
pol′y·u′ri·a
pol′y·u′ric
pol′y·va′lent
pol′y·vi′nyl·chlo′ride′
po·made′
pom′pho·ly·he′mi·a
pom′pho·lyx′
po′mum A·da′mi′
pon·ceau′
  —— de xy′li·dine′
Pon·cet′
  —— disease
  —— operation
Pon′fick shadow
po′no·graph′
pons *pl.* pon′tes′
  —— Va·ro′li·i′
Pon′ti·ac′ fever
pon′tic
pon·tic′u·lar
pon·tic′u·lus
pon′tile′
pon′tine′
pon′to·bul′bar
pon′to·cer′e·bel′lar
Pool′-Schles′in·ger sign
pop′les′
pop·lit′e·al
pop·lit′e·us *pl.* -e·i′
por′ad·e·ni′tis
por·ad′e·no·lym·phi′tis
por′cine′
pore
  —— of Kohn
por·en·ce·pha′li·a
por·en·ce·phal′ic
por·en·ceph′a·li′tis
por·en·ceph′a·lus *pl.* -li′
por·en·ceph′a·ly
po′ri·o·ma′ni·a
po′ri·on′ *pl.* -ri·a *or* -ri·ons′
po′ro·ceph′a·li′a·sis *pl.* -ses′
po′ro·ker′a·to′sis *pl.* -ses′
po·ro′ma *pl.* -ma·ta
po′ro·plas′tic
po·ro′sis *pl.* -ses′
po·ros′i·ty
po·rot′ic
po′rous
por′phin
por′pho·bi′lin
por′pho·bi·lin′o·gen
por·phyr′i·a
  —— cu·ta′ne·a tar′da
he·red′i·tar′i·a

  —— cutanea tarda symp′to·
mat′i·ca
  —— e·ryth′ro·poi·et′i·ca
  —— he′ma·to·poi·et′i·ca
  —— he·pat′i·ca
  —— var′i·e·ga′ta
por′phy·rin
por′phy·ri·ne′mi·a
por′phy·ri·nu′ri·a
por′phy·ri·za′tion
Por′ro operation
por′ta *pl.* -tae′
  —— hep′a·tis
  —— ves·tib′u·li′
por′ta·ca′val
por′tal
Por′ter sign
Por′ter-Sil′ber reaction
Por·tes′ operation
por′ti·o′ *pl.* por′ti·o′nes′
  —— major ner′vi′ tri·gem′i·
ni′
  —— minor nervi tri·gem′i·
ni′
  —— su′pra·vag′i·na′lis
cer′vi·cis
  —— vag′i·na′lis cer′vi·cis
  —— vaginalis u′ter·i′
por′to·ca′val
por′to·gram′
por·tog′ra·phy
por′to·ve′no·gram′
por·to·ve·nog′ra·phy
po′rus *pl.* -ri′
  —— a·cus′ti·cus ex·ter′nus
  —— acusticus in·ter′nus
  —— cro′ta·phit′i·co·buc′ci·
na·to′ri·us
  —— gus′ta·to′ri·us
  —— op′ti·cus
  —— su′do·rif′e·rus
po·si′tion
po·si′tion·al
pos′i·tive
pos′i·tron′
post′a·bor′tal
post·a′nal
post′an·es·thet′ic
post′ap·o·plec′tic
post·au′di·to′ry
post·ax′i·al
post·bra′chi·al
post·cap′il·lar′y
post·car′di·ac′
post′car·di·ot′o·my
post·ca′va
post·ca′val

post·cen'tral
post·ci'bal
post'cla·vic'u·lar
post·co'i·tal
post·con'dy·lar
post·con·i·za'tion
post·con·nu'bi·al
post·con·vul'sive
post·cor'di·al
post·cos'tal
post·cra'ni·al
post·cri'coid'
post·cu'bi·tal
post'di·a·stol'ic
post'di·crot'ic
post'di·ges'tive
post'diph·the·rit'ic
post·dor'mi·tal
post'em·bry·on'ic
post'en·ceph'a·lit'ic
post'ep·i·lep'tic
pos·te'ri·ad'
pos·te'ri·or
pos·ter·o·an·te'ri·or
pos·ter·o·ex·ter'nad'
pos·ter·o·ex·ter'nal
pos·ter·o·in·ter'nad'
pos·ter·o·in·ter'nal
pos·ter·o·lat'er·ad'
pos·ter·o·lat'er·al
pos·ter·o·mar'gi·nal
pos·ter·o·me'di·ad'
pos·ter·o·me'di·al
pos·ter·o·me'di·an
pos·ter·o·su·pe'ri·or
pos·ter·o·trans·verse'
post'e·soph'a·ge·al
post·fe'brile
post'gan·gli·on'ic
post'gas·trec'to·my
post·gle'noid'
post·grav'id
post'hem·i·ple'gic
post'hem·or·rhag'ic
post·he·pat'ic
post'hep'a·tit'ic
post'her·pet'ic
pos·thet'o·my
pos·thi'tis
pos'tho·lith'
post'hu·mous
post'hyp·not'ic
post·ic'tal
post'ic·ter'ic
pos·ti'cus
post'in·farc'tion
post'in·fec'tious

post'in·fec'tive
post'in·flu·en'zal
post·is'chi·al
post'ma·lar'i·al
post·mam'ma·ry
post'mas·tec'to·my
post·mas'toid'
post'ma·ture'
post'ma·tu'ri·ty
post'me·di·as'ti·nal
post'men·ar'che'
post·men·o·pau'sal
post·men'stru·al
post·mor'tal
post-mor'tem
post·nar'is
post'na'sal
post'na'tal
post'ne·crot'ic
post'neu·rit'ic
post·nod'u·lar
post·oc'u·lar
post·ol'i·var'y
post·op'er·a·tive
post·o'ral
post·or'bit·al
post·pal'a·tine'
post'pa·lu'dal
post'par·a·lyt'ic
post·par'tum
post'pha·ryn'ge·al
post'phle·bit'ic
post·pran'di·al
post'pros·tat'ic
post·pu'ber·al
post'pu·bes'cent
post'pyc·not'ic
post'py·ram'i·dal
post'ra·di·a'tion
post're·duc'tion
post're'nal
post'rhi'nal
post'ro·lan'dic
post'sphe'noid'
post'sphyg'mic
post'sple·nec'to·my
post'ste·not'ic
post'syn·ap'tic
post'syph·i·lit'ic
post'throm·bot'ic
post'trans·verse'
post'trau·mat'ic
post·tus'sive
post·ty'phoid'
pos'tu·late', -lat'ed, -lat'ing
pos'tur·al
pos'ture

post·vac'ci·nal
post·ves'i·cal
po'ta·ble
Po·tain'
—— disease
—— syndrome
pot·as·se'mi·a
po·tas'si·um
po'ten·cy
po'tent
po·ten'tial
po·ten'ti·ate', -at'ed, -at'ing
po·ten'ti·a'tion
po'tion
po'to·ma'ni·a
Pott
—— curvature
—— disease
—— fracture
—— gangrene
—— puffy tumor
Potts
—— anastomosis
—— operation
pouch
—— of Doug'las
—— of Mor'i·son
pound
Pou·part' ligament
po'vi·done-i'o·dine'
pow'der
pow'er
pox
pox·vi'rus
P pul'mo·na'le'
prac'tice, -ticed, -tic·ing
prac·ti'tion·er
Pra'der-Wil'li syndrome
prae'cox'
prae·pu'ti·um pl. -ti·a, var.
  of preputium
prae·vi'a var. of previa
prag'mat·ag·no'si·a
prag'mat·am·ne'si·a
Prague maneuver
pral'i·dox'ime'
pra·mox'ine'
pran'di·al
pran'di·al'i·ty
Praus'nitz-Küst'ner
—— reaction
—— test
prax'i·ol'o·gy
prax'is pl. -prax'es'
pra'ze·pam'
pra'zo·sin
pre·ag'o·nal

pre′al·bu′mi·nu′ric
pre·a′nal
pre′an·es·the′si·a
pre′an·es·thet′ic
pre′an·ti·sep′tic
pre·a·tax′ic
pre·au·ric′u·lar
pre·ax′i·al
pre·be·ta·lip′o·pro′tein
pre·be·ta·lip′o·pro′tein·
    e′mi·a
pre·can′cer·ous
pre·cap′il·lar′y
pre·car′ci·nom′a·tous
pre·car′di·ac′
pre·car′ti·lage
pre·ca′va
pre·cen′tral
pre·cer′vi·cal
pre·chor′dal
pre·cip′i·tant
pre·cip′i·tate′, -tat′ed, -tat′-
    ing
pre·cip′i·ta′tion
pre·cip′i·tin
pre·cip′i·tin′o·gen
pre·cip′i·tin·oid′
pre·cla·vic′u·lar
pre·clin′i·cal
pre·coc·cyg′e·al
pre·co′cious
pre·coc′i·ty
pre′cog·ni′tion
pre·co′i·tal
pre′col·lag′e·nous
pre·com′a·tose′
pre′com·mis′sur·al
pre′con·scious
pre′con·vul′sant
pre′con·vul′sive
pre·cor′di·al
pre·cor′di·um pl. -di·a
pre·cos′tal
pre·cri′coid′
pre·cu′ne·us pl. -ne·i′
pre·cur′sor
pre·den′tin
pre·di′a·be′tes′
pre·di·as′to·le
pre·di′a·stol′ic
pre·di·crot′ic
pre·di·gest′ed
pre·di·ges′tion
pre′dis·pose′, -posed′, -pos′-
    ing
pre′dis·po·si′tion
pred·nis′o·lone′

pred′ni·sone′
pred′ni·val
pre·dor′mi·tal
pre′dor·mi′tion
pre·dor′mi·tum
pre′e·clamp′si·a
pre′e·clamp′tic
pre·ep′i·glot′tic
pre′e·rup′tive
pre′fi·brot′ic
pre·fron′tal
pre′gan·gli·on′ic
pre·gen′i·tal
pre·gle′noid′
preg′nan·cy
preg′nane′
preg′nane·di·ol′
preg′nant
preg′nene′
preg·nen′o·lone′
pre·gran′u·lar
pre·hal′lux
pre′hem·i·ple′gic
pre′hen′sile
pre′hen′sion
pre′he·pat′ic
pre·ic′tal
pre′ic·ter′ic
pre′in·va′sive
Prei′ser disease
pre·lac′ri·mal
pre′leu·ke′mi·a
pre′leu·ke′mic
pre′lo·co·mo′tion
pre′lum
—— ab·dom′i·na′le′
pre′ma·lig′nant
pre·mam′mil·lar′y
pre′ma·ni′a·cal
pre·mar′i·tal
pre′ma·ture′
pre′ma·tur′i·ty
pre·max·il′la
pre·max′il·lar′y
pre·med′i·cant
pre·med′i·cate′, -cat′ed,
    -cat′ing
pre·med′i·cat′ed
pre·med·i·ca′tion
pre·men′o·paus′al
pre·men′stru·al
pre·mo′lar
pre·mon′i·to′ry
pre·mor′bid
pre·mor′tal
pre′mu·ni′tion
pre′my′e·lo·blast′

pre′my′e·lo·cyte′
pre′nar·co′sis pl. -ses′
pre·na′tal
pre′ne·o·plas′tic
pre·nod′u·lar
pre·nyl′a·mine′
pre′oc·cip′i·tal
pre·op′er·a·tive
pre·op′tic
prep, prepped, prep′ping
pre′par·a·lyt′ic
prep′a·ra′tion
pre′pa·ret′ic
pre·par′tal
pre·par′tum
pre·pa·tel′lar
pre·pat′ent
pre·pel′vic
pre′per·i·to·ne′al
pre·pol′lex′ pl. -li·ces′
pre·pon′der·ance
pre·po′tent
pre·pran′di·al
pre·psy·chot′ic
pre·pu′ber·al
pre·pu·bes′cent
pre·puce′
pre·pu·cot′o·my
pre·pu′tial
pre·pu·ti·um pl. -ti·a, also
    praeputium
—— cli·to′ri·dis
—— pe·nis
pre′py·lo′ric
pre·rec′tal
pre·re′nal
pre′re·pro·duc′tive
pre·ret′i·nal
pre·sa′cral
pres′by·a·cu′si·a
pres′by·at′rics
pres′by·car′di·a
pres′by·cu′sis pl. -ses′
pres′by·der′ma
pres′by·o·phre′ni·a
pres′by·o·phren′ic
pres′by·ope′
pres′by·o′pi·a
pres′by·op′ic
pres′by·o·sphac′e·lus
pres·by′ti·a
pres·byt′ic
pres′by·tism
pre′schiz·o·phren′ic
pre′scle·ro′sis pl. -ses′
pre′scle·rot′ic

pre·scribe', -scribed, -scrib'-
ing
pre·scrip'tion
pre·se'nile'
pre'se·nil'i·ty
pre·sent'
pres'en·ta'tion
pre·ser'va·tive
pre·spas'tic
pre·sphe'noid'
pre·sphyg'mic
pres'sor
pres'so·re·cep'tor
pres'so·sen'si·tive
pres'sure
pre·ster'num pl. -nums or
-na
pre·su·bic'u·lum
pre·sump'tive
pre·sup'pu·ra'tive
pre·syl'vi·an
pre'symp·to·mat'ic
pre·syn·ap'tic
pre·sys'to·le
pre·sys·tol'ic
pre·ter'mi·nal
pre'ter·nat'u·ral
pre'thy·roi'de·an
pre·tib'i·al
pre·tra'che·al
pre·tra'gal
pre·tu·ber'cu·lous
pre'u·re·thri'tis
prev'a·lence
pre·ven'tive
pre·ven·to'ri·um pl. -ri·a or
-ri·ums
pre·ven·tric'u·lus pl. -li'
pre·ver'te·bral
pre·ver'tig'i·nous
pre·ves'i·cal
pre'vi·a also praevia
Prey'er
—— reflex
—— test
pre'zone'
pre·zyg'a·poph'y·sis pl.
-ses'
pri'a·pism
Price'-Jones' curve
pril'o·caine'
pri'mal
pri'ma·quine'
pri'mar'y
pri'mate'
pri'mi·done'

pri'mi·grav'i·da pl. -das or
-dae
pri·mip'a·ra pl. -ras or -rae'
pri'mi·par'i·ty
pri·mip'a·rous
pri·mi'ti·ae'
prim'i·tive
pri·mor'di·al
pri·mor'di·um pl. -di·a
prin'ceps'
prin'ci·pal (foremost)
    ♦principle
prin'ci·ple (a chemical com-
    ponent; a rule)
    ♦principal
Prin'gle disease
Prinz'met'al angina
prism
pris'ma pl. -ma·ta
pris'ma·ta ad'a·man·ti'na
pris·mat'ic
pris'moid'
pris'mop·tom'e·ter
pris'mo·sphere'
pro'ac·cel'er·in
pro·ac'ti·va'tor
pro·ag·glu'ti·noid'
pro'al
pro·am'ni·on'
pro·at'las
pro'band'
pro'bang'
pro·bar'bi·tal'
probe, probed, prob'ing
pro·ben'e·cid
pro·bos'cis pl. -cis·es or
    -ci·des'
pro'cain·am'ide'
pro·caine'
pro·cal'lus
pro·car'ba·zine'
pro·cen'tri·ole'
pro'ce·phal'ic
pro·ce'rus pl. -ri' or -rus·es
proc'ess
pro·ces'sus pl. pro·ces'sus
—— ac'ces·so'ri·us verte-
brar'um lum·ba'li·um
—— a·lar'is os'sis eth'moi·
da'lis
—— al've·o·lar'is max·il·lae'
—— anterior mal'le·i'
—— ar·tic'u·lar'es' in·fe'ri·
o'res' ver'te·brae'
—— articulares su·pe'ri·
o'res' ver'te·brae'
—— ar·tic'u·lar'is inferior

—— articularis superior
—— articularis superior os'-
sis sa'cri'
—— articularis superior
zyg'a·poph'y·sis
—— cau·da'tus hep'a·tis
—— cil'i·ar'es'
—— cli·noi'de·us anterior
—— clinoideus me'di·us
—— clinoideus posterior
—— coch'le·ar'i·for'mis
—— con'dy·lar'is
—— con'dy·loi'de·us man·
dib'u·lae'
—— co'ra·coi'de·us
—— co'ro·noi'de·us man·
dib'u·lae'
—— coronoideus ul'nae'
—— cos·tar'i·us ver'te·brae'
—— eth'moi·da'lis
—— fal'ci·for'mis lig'a·
men'ti' sa'cro·tu·be·ro'si'
—— fron·ta'lis max·il'lae'
—— frontalis os'sis zy'go·
mat'i·ci'
—— fron'to·sphe'noi·da'lis
os'sis zy'go·mat'i·ci'
—— grac'i·lis
—— in'tra·jug'u·lar'is os'sis
oc·cip'i·ta'lis
—— intrajugularis ossis
tem'po·ra'lis
—— jug·u·lar'is os'sis oc·
cip'i·ta'lis
—— lac'ri·ma'lis
—— lat'er·a'lis mal'le·i'
—— lateralis ta'li'
—— lateralis tu'ber·is cal·
ca'ne·i'
—— len·tic'u·lar'is in·cu'dis
—— mam'il·lar'is
—— mar'gi·na'lis os'sis
zy'go·mat'i·ci'
—— mas·toi'de·us
—— max·il'lar'is con'chae'
na·sa'lis in·fe'ri·o'ris
—— me'di·a'lis tu'ber·is cal·
ca'ne·i'
—— mus·cu·lar'is car'ti·lag'i·
nis ar'y·tae·noi'de·i'
—— muscularis cartilaginis
ar'y·te·noi'de·i'
—— or'bi·ta'lis os'sis pal'a·
ti'ni'
—— pal'a·ti'nus max·il'lae'
—— pap'il·lar'is hep'a·tis

—— par'a·mas·toi'de·us os'-
sis oc·cip'i·ta'lis
—— posterior sphe'noi·da'lis
—— posterior ta'li'
—— pter'y·goi'de·us os'sis
sphe'noi·da'lis
—— pter'y·go·spi·no'sus
—— py·ram'i·da'lis os'sis
pal'a·ti'ni'
—— ret'ro·man·dib'u·lar'is
glan'du·lae' pa·rot'i·dis
—— sphe'noi·da'lis os'sis
pal'a·ti'ni'
—— sphenoidalis sep'ti'
car'ti·la·gin'e·i'
—— spi·no'sus
—— sty·loi'de·us os'sis
met'a·car·pa'lis III
—— styloideus ossis ra'di·i'
—— styloideus ossis tem'po·
ra'lis
—— styloideus ul'nae'
—— su'pra·con'dy·lar'is
—— su'pra·con'dy·loi'de·us
—— tem'po·ra'lis os'sis
zy'go·mat'i·ci'
—— trans·ver'sus
—— troch'le·ar'is cal·ca'ne·i'
—— un'ci·na'tus os'sis
eth'moi·da'lis
—— uncinatus pan·cre'a·tis
—— vag'i·na'lis os'sis
sphe'noi·da'lis
—— vaginalis per'i·to·nae'i'
—— vaginalis per'i·to·ne'i'
—— ver'mi·for'mis
—— vo·ca'lis
—— xi·phoi'de·us
—— zy'go·mat'i·cus max·
il'lae'
—— zygomaticus os'sis
fron·ta'lis
—— zygomaticus ossis
tem'po·ra'lis
pro·chei'li·a
pro·chei'lon'
pro'chlor·per'a·zine'
pro·chon'dral
pro·chor'dal
pro·cho·re'sis
Pro·chow'nick method
pro'ci·den'ti·a
pro'clo·nol'
pro'co·ag'u·lant
pro'con·ver'tin
pro'cre·ate', -at'ed, -at'ing
pro'cre·a'tion

pro'cre·a'tive
proc·tal'gi·a
—— fu'gax'
proc'ta·tre'si·a
proc'tec·ta'si·a
proc'tec'to·my
proc·ten'cli·sis pl. -ses'
proc'teu·ryn'ter
proc·ti'tis
proc'to·cele'
proc·toc'ly·sis pl. -ses'
proc'to·co·lec'to·my
proc'to·co·li'tis
proc'to·co·lon·os'co·py
proc'to·col'po·plas'ty
proc'to·cys'to·plas'ty
proc'to·cys·tot'o·my
proc'to·de'um pl. -de'a or
-ums
proc'to·dyn'i·a
proc'to·log'ic
proc·tol'o·gist
proc·tol'o·gy
proc'to·pa·ral'y·sis pl. -ses'
proc'to·pex'y
proc'to·plas'ty
proc'to·ple'gi·a
proc'top·to'sis pl. -ses'
proc'tor·rha'gi·a
proc'tor·rha·phy
proc'tor·rhe'a
proc'to·scope'
proc·tos'co·py
proc'to·sig'moid'
proc'to·sig'moi·dec'to·my
proc'to·sig'moi·di'tis
proc'to·sig'moi·dos'co·py
proc'to·spasm
proc·tos'ta·sis pl. -ses'
proc'to·ste·no'sis pl. -ses'
proc·tos'to·my
proc'to·tome'
proc·tot'o·my
pro·cum'bent
pro·cur'sive
pro'cur·va'tion
pro'cy'cli·dine'
pro·dig'i·o'sin
pro·dil'i·dine'
pro'dro·ma pl. -mas or
-ma·ta
prod'ro·mal
pro'drome'
pro·drom'ic
prod'ro·mous
prod'uct
pro·duc'tive

pro'en·ceph'a·lus pl. -li'
pro·en'zyme'
pro'e·ryth'ro·blast'
pro'e·ryth'ro·cyte'
pro·es'tro·gen
pro·es'trus
Proetz treatment
pro·fen'a·mine'
pro·fer'ment
pro·fes'sion·al
Pro·fi·chet' syndrome
pro'file'
pro·fla'vine
pro·flu'vi·um pl. -vi·a or
-vi·ums
—— al'vi'
—— lac'tis
pro·fun'dus
pro·gas'ter
pro·gen'i·tor
prog'e·ny
pro·ge'ri·a
pro'ges·ta'tion·al
pro·ges'ter·one'
pro·ges'tin
pro·ges'to·gen
prog·nath'ic
prog'na·thism
prog'na·thous
prog·nose', -nosed', -nos'ing
prog·no'sis pl. -ses'
prog·nos'tic
prog·nos'ti·cate', -cat'ed,
-cat'ing
pro'go·no'ma pl. -mas or
-ma·ta
pro·gran'u·lo·cyte'
pro·grav'id
pro·gress' v.
prog'ress n.
pro·gres'sion
pro·gres'sive
pro·gua'nil
pro·in'su·lin
pro·jec'tile
pro·jec'tion
pro·jec'tive
pro·kar'y·o·cyte'
pro·ki'nase'
pro·la'bi·um pl. -bi·a
pro·lac'tin
pro·lam'in
pro'lan'
pro·lapse', -lapsed', -laps'ing
pro·lap'sus
—— a'ni'
—— u'ter·i'

pro'late'
pro·lep'sis *pl.* -ses'
pro·lep'tic
pro·leu'ko·cyte'
pro·lif'er·ate', -at'ed, -at'ing
pro·lif'er·a'tion
pro·lif'er·a·tive
pro·lif'er·ous
pro·lif'ic
pro·lig'er·ous
pro·lin·ase'
pro'line'
pro·li·ne'mi·a
pro·lin'tane'
pro·lym'pho·cyte'
pro'ma·zine'
pro·meg'a·kar'y·o·cyte'
pro·meg'a·lo·blast'
pro·meg'a·lo·kar'y·o·cyte'
pro·meth'a·zine'
pro·meth'es·trol'
pro·me'thi·um
prom'i·nence
prom'i·nen'ti·a *pl.* -ae'
—— ca·na'lis fa'ci·a'lis
—— canalis sem'i·cir'cu·lar'is lat'er·a'lis
—— la·ryn'ge·a
—— mal'le·ar'is
—— mal'le·o·lar'is
—— spi·ra'lis
—— sty·loi'de·a
pro·mon'o·cyte'
prom'on·to'ri·um *pl.* -ri·a
—— ca'vi' tym'pa·ni'
—— os'sis sa'cri'
prom'on·to'ry
pro·mot'er
pro·my'e·lo·cyte'
pro'nate', -nat'ed, -nat'ing
pro·na'tion
pro·na'tor
—— ra'di·i' te'res'
prone
pro·neph'ric
pro·neph'ros' *pl.* -neph'roi'
pro·neth'al·ol'
pro·nor'mo·blast'
pro·nor'mo·cyte'
pro·nounced'
pro·nu'cle·us *pl.* -cle·i'
pro·o'tic
prop'a·gate', -gat'ed, -gat'-ing
prop'a·ga'tion
pro·pan'i·did
pro'pa·no'ic

pro·pan'the·line'
pro·par'a·caine'
pro'pa·tyl
pro·pen'zo·late'
pro·pep'to·nu'ri·a
pro·per'din
pro'per·i·to·ne'al
pro'phase'
pro·phen'py·rid'a·mine'
pro'phy·lac'tic
pro'phy·lax'is *pl.* -es'
pro·pi·o·lac'tone'
pro·pi·o'ma·zine'
pro·pi·on'ic
pro·plas'ma·cyte'
pro·pox'y·caine'
pro·pox'y·phene'
pro·pran'o·lol'
pro·pri'e·tar'y
pro·pri'o·cep'tion
pro·pri'o·cep'tive
pro·pri'o·cep'tor
pro'pri·us
prop·tom'e·ter
prop·to'sis *pl.* -ses'
prop·tot'ic
pro·pul'sion
pro·pul'sive
pro'pyl
pro'pyl·ene'
pro'pyl·hex'e·drine'
pro'pyl·i'o·done'
pro'pyl·par'a·ben
pro'pyl·thi'o·u'ra·cil
pro re na'ta
pro·ren'nin
pro·ru'bri·cyte'
pro'scil·lar'i·din
pro'se·cre'tin
pro·sect'
pro·sec'tor
pros'en·ce·phal'ic
pros'en·ceph'a·lon'
pros'o·dem'ic
pros'op·ag·no'si·a
pro·sop'a·gus
pros'o·pal'gi·a
pros'o·pal'gic
pro·sop'ic
pros'o·pla'si·a
pros'o·plas'tic
pros'o·po·a·nos'chi·sis *pl.* -ses'
pros'o·po·di·ple'gi·a
pros'o·po·dyn'i·a
pros'o·po·neu·ral'gi·a
pros'o·pop'a·gus *pl.* -gi'

pros'o·po·ple'gi·a
pros'o·po·ple'gic
pros'o·pos'chi·sis *pl.* -ses'
pros'o·po·spasm
pros'o·po·ster'no·did'y·mus
pros'o·po·ster'no·dym'i·a
pros'o·po·tho'ra·cop'a·gus *pl.* -gi'
pro·spec'tive
pros·ta·glan'din
pros·ta·ta
pros·tate' *(gland)*
♦prostrate
pros·ta·tec'to·my
pros·tat'ic
pros·tat'i·co·ves'i·cal
pros·ta·tism
pros·ta·tit'ic
pros·ta·ti'tis
pros·ta·to·cys·ti'tis
pros·ta·to·cys·tot'o·my
pros·ta·to·dyn'i·a
pros·ta·tog'ra·phy
pros·tat'o·lith'
pros·ta·to·li·thot'o·my
pros·ta·to·meg'a·ly
pros·ta·to·my'o·mec'to·my
pros·ta·tor·rhe'a
pros·ta·tot'o·my
pros·ta·to·tox'in
pros·ta·to·ve·sic'u·lec'to·my
pros·ta·to·ve·sic'u·li'tis
pros·the'sis *pl.* -ses'
pros·thet'ic
pros·thet'ics
pros·the·tist
pros·thi·on'
pros·tho·don'ti·a
pros·tho·don'tics
pros·tho·don'tist
pros·tig'mine'
pros'trate' *(to bow down),* -trat'ed, -trat'ing
♦prostate
pros·tra'tion
pro·tag'o·nist
pro'tal
pro·tal'bu·mose'
pro'ta·mine'
pro·ta·nom'a·ly
pro·ta·no'pi·a
pro·ta·nop'ic
pro'te·an *(changing form)*
♦protein
pro'te·ase'

pro·tec'tive
pro·te'ic
pro·te'id
pro·te'i·form'
pro'tein' *(substance)*
♦*protean*
pro'tei·na'ceous
pro'tei·nase'
pro'tei·ne'mi·a
pro'tein'ic
pro'tein·o'sis *pl.* -ses'
pro'tei·nu'ri·a
pro'tei·nu'ric
pro'te·ol'y·sis *pl.* -ses'
pro'te·o·lyt'ic
pro'te·o·met'a·bol'ic
pro'te·o·me·tab'o·lism
pro'te·o·pep'sis *pl.* -ses'
pro'te·o·pep'tic
pro'te·ose'
pro'te·o·su'ri·a
pro'te·u'ri·a
Pro'te·us
—— mi·rab'i·lis
—— mor·gan'i·i'
—— rett'ger·i'
—— vul·gar'is
pro·throm'bin
pro·throm'bin·ase'
pro·throm'bi·ne'mi·a
pro·throm'bi·no·gen'ic
pro·throm'bi·no·pe'ni·a
pro·throm'bo·gen'ic
pro·thy'mi·a
pro'ti·des'
pro'tis·tol'o·gist
pro'tis·tol'o·gy
pro'ti·um
pro'to·al'bu·mose'
pro'to·blast'
pro'to·blas'tic
pro'to·chlo'ride'
pro'to·col'
pro'to·cone'
pro'to·co'nid
pro'to·cop'ro·por·phyr'i·a
  he·red'i·tar'i·a
pro'to·di·a·stol'ic
pro'to·e·las'tose'
pro'to·fi'bril
pro'to·gas'ter
pro'to·glob'u·lose'
pro'to·tok'y·lol'
pro'to·leu'ko·cyte'
pro'tol'y·sis *pl.* -ses'
pro'tom'e·ter
pro'ton'

pro'to·neu'ron'
pro'to·path'ic
pro'to·phyte'
pro'to·pla'sis
pro'to·plasm
pro'to·plas·mat'ic
pro'to·plas'mic
pro'to·plast'
pro'to·por·phyr'i·a
pro'to·por'phy·rin
pro'to·por'phy·ri·nu'ri·a
pro'to·pro'te·ose'
pro'top'sis
pro'to·spasm
pro'to·sul'fate'
pro'to·syph'i·lis
pro'to·troph'ic
pro'tot'ro·py
pro'to·type'
pro'to·ver'a·trine'
pro'to·ver'te·bra
pro'to·ver'te·bral
Pro'to·zo'a
pro'to·zo'al
pro'to·zo'an
pro'to·zo'on' *pl.* -zo'a
pro'to·zo'o·phage'
pro·tract'
pro·trac'tor
pro·trip'ty·line'
pro·trude', -trud'ed, -trud'-
  ing
pro·tru'si·o' ac'e·tab'u·li'
pro·tru'sion
pro·tru'sive
pro·tryp'sin
pro·tu'ber·ance
pro·tu·be·ran'ti·a
—— men·ta'lis
—— oc·cip'i·ta'lis ex·ter'na
—— occipitalis in·ter'na
Proust'-Licht'heim' ma-
  neuver
pro·ven'tri·cule'
pro'ven·tric'u·lus *pl.* -li'
pro·voc'a·tive
Pro'wa·zek bodies
Prow'er factor
prox'a·zole'
prox'i·mad'
prox'i·mal
prox'i·ma'lis
prox'i·mate
prox'i·mo·a·tax'i·a
prox'i·mo·buc'cal
prox'i·mo·la'bi·al
prox'i·mo·lin'gual

pro'zone'
pru·rig'i·nous
pru·ri'go'
—— aes'ti·va'lis
—— ag'ri·a
—— der'mo·graph'i·ca
—— fer'ox'
—— mi'tis
—— nod'u·lar'is
—— sim'plex'
pru·rit'ic
pru·ri'tus
—— a'ni'
—— hi'e·ma'lis
—— se·ni'lis
—— vul'vae'
Prus'sak'
—— fibers
—— pouch
Prus'sian blue
prus'si·ate'
prus'sic
Pryce method
psa'lis
psal·te'ri·um *pl.* -ri·a
psam·mo'ma *pl.* -mas *or*
  -ma·ta
psam·mom'a·tous
psam'mo·sar·co'ma
  pl. -mas *or* -ma·ta
psam'mous
psel'a·phe'si·a
psel'lism
pseu·da·cous'ma
pseu·da·graph'i·a
pseu·dal·bu'mi·nu'ri·a
pseu·dam·ne'si·a
pseu·dan·gi'na
pseu·dan'ky·lo'sis *pl.* -ses'
pseu·daph'i·a
pseu·dar·thri'tis
pseu·dar·thro'sis *pl.* -ses'
pseu·des·the'si·a
pseu·do·ab'scess'
pseu·do·ac'an·tho'sis
  nig'ri·cans'
pseu·do·a·ceph'a·lus *pl.* -li'
pseu·do·ac'ro·meg'a·ly
pseu·do·ac'ti·no'my·co'sis
  pl. -ses'
pseu·do·ag·glu'ti·na'tion
pseu·do·a·graph'i·a
pseu·do·al·bu'mi·nu'ri·a
pseu·do·al·lele'
pseu·do·al·lel'ism
pseu·do·al·ve'o·lar
pseu·do·a·ne'mi·a

pseu'do·an'eu·rysm
pseu'do·an·gi'na
pseu'do·an·gi·o'ma
pseu'do·an'o·rex'i·a
pseu'do·a·pha'ki·a
pseu'do·ap'o·plex'y
pseu'do·ap·pen'di·ci'tis
pseu'do·ar·thri'tis
pseu'do·ar·thro'sis pl. -ses'
pseu'do·a·tax'i·a
pseu'do·ath'er·o'ma
pseu'do·ath'e·to'sis
pseu'do·at'ro·pho·der'ma
  col'li'
pseu'do·ba·cil'lus pl. -li'
pseu'do·blep'si·a
pseu'do·bul'bar
pseu'do·car'ti·lage
pseu'do·car'ti·lag'i·nous
pseu'do·cast'
pseu'do·cele' also pseudo-
  coele
pseu'do·ceph'a·lo·cele'
pseu'do·chan'cre
pseu'do·cho'le·cys·ti'tis
pseu'do·cho·les'te·a·to'ma
  pl. -mas or -ma·ta
pseu'do·cho'lin·es'ter·ase'
pseu'do·cho·re'a
pseu'do·chro'mes·the'si·a
pseu'do·chro'mi·a
pseu'do·chro'mo·some'
pseu'do·chy'lous
pseu'do·cir·rho'sis pl. -ses'
pseu'do·co'arc·ta'tion
pseu'do·coele' var. of pseu-
  docele
pseu'do·col'loid'
pseu'do·col'o·bo'ma pl.
  -mas or ma·ta
pseu'do·cox·al'gi·a
pseu'do·cri'sis pl. -ses'
pseu'do·croup'
pseu'do·cy·e'sis pl. -ses'
pseu'do·cyl'in·droid'
pseu'do·cyst'
pseu'do·de·men'ti·a
pseu'do·di'a·stol'ic
pseu'do·diph·the'ri·a
pseu'do·di'ver·tic'u·lum
pseu'do·dys'en·ter'y
pseu'do·e·de'ma
pseu'do·en'do·me·tri'tis
pseu'do·e'o·sin'o·phil'
pseu'do·e·phed'rine
pseu'do·ep'i·lep'sy
pseu'do·es·the'si·a

pseu'do·ex·fo'li·a'tion
pseu'do·ex'o·pho'ri·a
pseu'do·ex'oph·thal'mos
pseu'do·fluc'tu·a'tion
pseu'do·fol·lic'u·lar
pseu'do·frac'ture
pseu'do·gan'gli·on
pseu'do·geu'si·a
pseu'do·gli·o'ma
pseu'do·glob'u·lin
pseu'do·gon'or·rhe'a
pseu'do·gout'
pseu'do·gyn'e·co·mas'ti·a
pseu'do·hal·lu'ci·na'tion
pseu'do·he'mo·phil'i·a
pseu'do·her·maph'ro·dite'
pseu'do·her·maph'ro·dit'ic
pseu'do·her·maph'ro·dit·
  ism
pseu'do·her·maph'ro·di·
  tis'mus
—— fem'i·ni'nus
—— mas'cu·li'nus
pseu'do·hy'dro·ceph'a·ly
pseu'do·hy'dro·ne·phro'sis
  pl. -ses'
pseu'do·hy'per·troph'ic
pseu'do·hy'per·tro'phy
pseu'do·hy'po·na·tre'mi·a
pseu'do·hy'po·par·a·
  thy'roid·ism
pseu'do·in·farc'tion
pseu'do·i'so·chro·mat'ic
pseu'do·jaun'dice
pseu'do·ke'loid'
pseu'do·ker'a·tin
pseu'do·ker'a·to'sis pl. -ses'
pseu'do·leu·ke'mi·a
pseu'do·li·po'ma pl. -mas or
  -ma·ta
pseu'do·li·thi'a·sis pl. -ses'
pseu'do·lo'gi·a fan·tas'ti·
  ca
pseu'do·mam'ma
pseu'do·ma'ni·a
pseu'do·mel'a·no'sis pl.
  -ses'
pseu'do·mem'brane'
pseu'do·mem'bra·nous
pseu'do·men·in·gi'tis
pseu'do·men'stru·a'tion
pseu'do·met·he'mo·glo'bin
pseu'do·mi'cro·ceph'a·ly
Pseu·dom'o·na·da'ce·ae'
Pseu·dom'o·nas
—— ae·ru·gi·no'sa
—— pseu'do·mal'le·i'

—— py'o·cy·a'ne·a
pseu'do·mu'cin
pseu'do·mu'cin·ous
pseu'do·my'as·then'ic
pseu'do·myx·o'ma pl. -mas
  or -ma·ta
—— per'i·to·ne'i'
pseu'do·myx·om'a·tous
pseu'do·nar'co·tism
pseu'do·ne'o·plasm
pseu'do·ne'o·plas'tic
pseu'do·neu·ri'tis
pseu'do·neu·ro'ma pl. -mas
  or -ma·ta
pseu'do·nu·cle'o·lus pl. -li'
pseu'do·nys·tag'mus
pseu'do·oph·thal'mo·
  ple'gi·a
pseu'do·os'te·o·ma·la'ci·a
pseu'do·pap'il·le·de'ma
pseu'do·pa·ral'y·sis pl. -ses'
pseu'do·par'a·ple'gi·a
pseu'do·par'a·site'
pseu'do·pa·re'sis pl. -ses'
pseu'do·pe'lade'
pseu'do·pep'tone'
pseu'do·per'i·car'di·al
pseu'do·per'i·to·ni'tis
pseu'do·pha'ki·a
pseu'do·pho'tes·the'si·a
pseu'do·ple'gi·a
pseu'do·pneu·mo'ni·a
pseu'do·po'di·o·spore'
pseu'do·po'di·um pl. -di·a
pseu'do·pol'y·po'sis pl. -ses'
pseu'do·por'en·ceph'a·ly
pseu'do·preg'nan·cy
pseu'do·pseu'do·hy'po·
  par'a·thy'roid·ism
pseu·dop'si·a
pseu'do·psy'cho·path'ic
pseu'do·pte·ryg'i·um
  pl. -i·ums or -i·a
pseu'do·pto'sis pl. -ses'
pseu'do·re·ac'tion
pseu'do·ret'i·ni'tis
—— pig'men·to'sa
pseu'do·ru·bel'la
pseu'do·sar·co'ma pl. -mas
  or -ma·ta
pseu'do·scar·la'ti·na
pseu'do·scle·re'ma
pseu'do·scle·ro'sis pl. -ses'
—— of West'phal' and
  Strüm'pell
pseu'do·se'rous
pseu'do·sto'ma

pseu'do·stra·bis'mus
pseu'do·struc'ture
pseu'do·tet'a·nus
pseu'do·tho'rax' pl. -rax'es
  or -ra·ces'
pseu·do·tin·ni'tus
pseu'do·tol'er·ance
pseu'do·trich'i·no'sis pl.
  -ses'
pseu'do·trun'cus ar·te'ri·
  o'sus
pseu'do·tu·ber'cu·lo'sis
pseu'do·tu·ber'cu·lous
pseu'do·tu'mor
  —— cer'e·bri'
pseu'do·tym'pa·ni'tes'
pseu'do·tym'pa·ny
pseu'do·ty'phoid'
pseu'do·u·re'mi·a
pseu'do·vac'u·ole'
pseu'do·vag'i·nal
pseu'do·ven'tri·cle
pseu'do·vom'it·ing
pseu'do·xan·tho'ma
  e·las'ti·cum
psi'lo·cin
psi'lo·cyb'in
psi·lo'sis pl. -ses'
psit'ta·co'sis pl. -ses'
pso'as pl. -ai' or -ae'
pso·i'tis
pso'mo·pha'gi·a
pso·mo·phag'ic
pso·moph'a·gy
pso'ra·len
pso·ri'a·si·form'
pso·ri'a·sis pl. -ses'
  —— buc·ca'lis
  —— cir'ci·na'ta
  —— dif·fu'sa
  —— dis·coi'de·a
  —— fol·lic'u·lar'is
  —— gut·ta'ta
  —— gy·ra'ta
  —— in·vet'er·a'ta
  —— num'mu·lar'is
  —— or·bic'u·lar'is
  —— pal·mar'is
  —— punc·ta'ta
  —— ru'pi·oi'des'
  —— u'ni·ver·sa'lis
pso·ri'at'ic
psor'oph·thal'mi·a
psy'chal'gi·a
psy'chal'gic
psy'cha·li·a
psych'as·the·ni·a

psych'as·then'ic
psych'a·tax'i·a
psy'che
psy'che·del'ic
psy·chi·at'ric
psy·chi·at'rics
psy·chi'a·trist
psy·chi'a·try
psy'chic
psy'chics
psy·chi·no'sis pl. -ses'
psy'cho·an·al·ge'si·a
psy'cho·a·nal'y·sis pl. -ses'
psy'cho·an'a·lyst
psy'cho·an·a·lyt'ic
psy'cho·au'di·to·ry
psy'cho·bi·o·log'ic or
  psy'cho·bi·o·log'i·cal
psy'cho·bi·ol'o·gist
psy'cho·bi·lo'o·gy
psy'cho·cor'ti·cal
psy'cho·cu·ta'ne·ous
psy'cho·del'ic
psy'cho·di·ag·no'sis pl. -ses'
psy'cho·di·ag·nos'tics
psy'cho·dom'e·ter
psy'cho·dom'e·try
psy'cho·dra'ma
psy'cho·dy·nam'ic
psy'cho·dy·nam'ics
psy'cho·gal·van'ic
psy'cho·gal'va·nom'e·ter
psy'cho·gen'ic
psy'cho·gen'e·sis
psy'cho·ge·net'ic
psy'chog·no'sis pl. -ses'
psy'chog·nos'tic
psy'cho·gram'
psy'cho·ki·ne'si·a
psy'cho·ki·ne'sis pl. -ses'
psy'cho·lag'ny
psy'cho·lep'sy
psy'cho·lep'tic
psy'cho·log'ic or psy'cho·
  log'i·cal
psy·chol'o·gist
psy·chol'o·gy
psy'cho·me·tri'cian
psy'cho·met'ric
psy'cho·met'rics
psy·chom'e·try
psy'cho·mo'tor
psy'cho·neu'ro·log'ic or
  psy'cho·neu'ro·log'i·cal
psy'cho·neu·ro'sis pl. -ses'
psy'cho·neu·rot'ic
psy'cho·pa·re'sis pl. -ses'

psy'cho·path'
psy'cho·path'i·a
  —— chi·rur'gi·ca'lis
  —— sex'u·a'lis
psy'cho·path'ic
psy'cho·pa·thol'o·gist
psy'cho·pa·thol'o·gy
psy'chop'a·thy
psy'cho·phar'ma·col'o·gy
psy'cho·phys'i·cal
psy'cho·phys'ics
psy'cho·phys'i·o·log'ic
psy'cho·phys'i·ol'o·gy
psy'cho·ple'gi·a
psy'cho·ple'gic
psy'cho·rhyth'mi·a
psy'chor·rha'gi·a
psy'chor·rhex'is pl.
  -rhex'es'
psy'cho·sen·so'ri·al
psy'cho·sen'so·ry
psy'cho·sex'u·al
psy'cho·sine'
psy·cho'sis (mental disor-
  der), pl. -ses'
  ♦sycosis
psy'cho·so'cial
psy'cho·so·mat'ic
psy'cho·sur'ger·y
psy'cho·ther'a·peu'tic
psy'cho·ther'a·pist
psy'cho·ther'a·py
psy·chot'ic
psy·chot'o·gen'ic
psy·chot'o·mi·met'ic
psy'cho·trop'ic
psy·chral'gi·a
psy'chro·es·the'si·a
psy'chro·phil'ic
psy'chro·phore'
psy'chro·ther'a·py
ptar'mic
ptar'mus
ptel'e·or·rhine'
pter'i·dine'
pter'i·do·phyte'
pter'in
pter'i·on'
pter'o·yl·glu·tam'ic
pte·ryg'i·al
pte·ryg'i·um pl. -i·ums or
  -i·a
  —— col'li'
pter'y·goid'
pter'y·go·man·dib'u·lar
pter'y·go·max'il·lar'y
pter'y·go·pal'a·tine'

pter′y·go·pha·ryn′ge·us
pter′y·go·spi′nous
pto′maine′
ptosed
pto′sis *pl.* -ses′
—— i′ri·dis
—— sym′pa·thet′i·ca
ptot′ic
pty·al′a·gogue′
pty′a·lec′ta·sis *pl.* -ses′
pty′a·lin
pty′a·lism
pty′a·lith′
pty′a·lo·cele′
pty′a·lo·gen′ic
pty′a·log′ra·phy
pty′a·lo·li·thi′a·sis *pl.* -ses′
pty′a·lor·rhe′a
pty′a·lose′
pty·oc′ri·nous
pu′ber·tal
pu′ber·tas
—— ple′na
—— prae′cox′
—— pre′cox′
pu′ber·ty
pu′bes′
pu·bes′cence
pu·bes′cent
pu·be·trot′o·my
pu′bic
pu′bi·ot′o·my
pu′bis
pu′bo·ad·duc′tor
pu′bo·cap′su·lar
pu′bo·cav′er·no′sus
pu′bo·coc·cyg′e·al
pu′bo·coc·cyg′e·us
pu′bo·fem′o·ral
pu′bo·per′i·to·ne·a′lis
pu′bo·pros·tat′ic
pu′bo·rec′tal
pu′bo·rec·ta′lis
pu′bo·scro′tal
pu′bo·tib′i·al
pu′bo·trans′ver·sa′lis
pu′bo·tu′ber·ous
pu′bo·ves′i·cal
pu′bo·ves′i·ca′lis
pu′den·dag′ra
pu·den′dal
pu·den′dum *pl.* -da
—— fem′i·ni′num
—— mu′li·e′bre′
pu′dic
pu′er·ile
pu·er′per·a *pl.* -ae′

pu·er′per·al
pu·er′per·al·ism
pu·er′per·ant
pu′er·pe′ri·um *pl.* -ri·a
Pu′lex′
—— ir′ri·tans′
pu′li·cide′
pul′lu·late′, -lat′ed, -lat′ing
pul′lu·la′tion
pul′mo *pl.* pul·mo′nes′
pul′mo·car′di·ac′
pul′mo·gas′tric
pul′mo·he·pat′ic
pul′mo·nal
pul′mo·nar′y
pul′mo·nec′to·my
pul·mon′ic
pul′mo·ni′tis
pul′mo·nol′o·gist
pul′mo·nol′o·gy
pul′mo′tor
pul′mo·vas′cu·lar
pulp
pul′pa
—— co′ro·na′le′
—— den′tis
—— li·e′nis
—— ra·dic′u·lar′is
pulp′al
pulp′ar
pul·pa′tion
pul·pec′to·my
pul′pe·fac′tion
pul·pi′tis *pl.* -pit′i·des′
pul′po·ax′i·al
pul′po·buc′co·ax′i·al
pul′po·dis′tal
pul′po·don′tics
pul′po·la′bi·al
pul′po·lin′gual
pul′po·lin′guo·ax′i·al
pul′po·me′si·al
pul·pot′o·my
pulp′stone′
pulp′y
pul′sate′, -sat′ed, -sat′ing
pul′sa·tile
pul·sa′tion
pul·sa′tor
pulse, pulsed, puls′ing
pulse′less
pul′sion
pul′sus
—— al′ter·nans′
—— bi·gem′i·nus
—— bis·fer′i·ens
—— ce′ler

—— celer et al′tus
—— deb′i·lis
—— du′plex′
—— du′rus
—— ir·reg′u·lar′is per·pet′u·us
—— par′a·dox′us
—— par′vus
—— parvus et tar′dus
—— tardus
pul·ta′ceous
pul′ver·i·za′tion
pul′ver·ize′, -ized′, -iz′ing
pul·ver′u·lent
pul·vi′nar
—— thal′a·mi′
pul′vis
—— an′ti·mo′ni·a′lis
pu′mex′
pum′ice
pump
punch
punc′ta
—— do′lo·ro′sa
—— lac′ri·ma′li·a
—— vas′cu·lo′sa
punc′tate′
punc′tat·ed
punc·tic′u·lum
punc′ti·form′
punc′tum *pl.* -ta
—— ce′cum
—— lac′ri·ma′le′
—— prox′i·mum
—— re·mo′tum
punc·tu′ra
—— ex·plo′ra·to′ri·a
punc′ture, -tured, -tur·ing
Pun′ta To′ro fever
pu′pa *pl.* -pae′ or -pas
pu′pal (*of a pupa*)
   ◆*pupil*
pu′pil (*a part of the eye*)
   ◆*pupal*
pu·pil′la *pl.* -lae′
pu′pil·lar′y
pu·pil·la·to′ni·a
pu·pil′lo·con·stric′tor
pu·pil′lo·di·la′tor
pu·pil·lom′e·ter
pu·pil·lom′e·try
pu·pil′lo·ple′gi·a
pu·pil′lo·sta·tom′e·ter
pu·pil·lo·to′ni·a
pu′pil·lo·ton′ic
pure
pur·ga′tion

pur′ga·tive
purge, purged, purg′ing
pu′ric
pu′ri·fy′, -fied′, -fy′ing
pu′ri·form′
pu′rine′
pu′ri·ne′mi·a
pu′ri·ne′mic
pu′ri·ty
Pur·kin′je
—— cells
—— fibers
Pur·kin′je-San·son′
images
pu′ro·hep′a·ti′tis pl. -tis·es
or -tit′i·des′
pu′ro·mu′cous
pu′ro·my′cin
pur′pu·ra
—— an′nu·lar′is te·lan′gi·ec·
to′des′
—— ful′mi·nans′
—— hem′or·rhag′i·ca
—— hy′per·glob′u·li·ne′mi·
ca
—— ne·crot′i·ca
—— rheu·mat′i·ca
—— se·ni′lis
—— sim′plex′
—— ur′ti·cans′
pur·pu′ric
pur′pu·rin
pur′pu·ri·nur′i·a
purr
pu′ru·lence
pu′ru·len·cy
pu′ru·lent
pu′ru·loid′
pus
pus′tu·lant
pus′tu·lar
pus′tu·la′tion
pus′tule′
pus′tu·li·form′
pus′tu·lo·der′ma
pus′tu·lo′sis pl. -ses′
—— pal·mar′is et plan·tar′is
pu·ta′men
Put′nam-Da′na syndrome
Put′nam sclerosis
pu′tre·fac′tion
pu′tre·fac′tive
pu′tre·fy′, -fied′, -fy′ing
pu·tres′cence
pu·tres′cent
pu·tres′cine′
pu′trid

pu′tro·maine′
Pu′us·sepp′
—— operation
—— reflex
py′ar·thro′sis pl. -ses′
py·ec′chy·sis pl. -ses′
py′e·lec·ta′si·a
py′e·lec′ta·sis pl. -ses′
py′e·lit′ic
py′e·li′tis
—— cys′ti·ca
py′e·lo·cal′i·ec′ta·sis pl.
-ses′
py′e·lo·cys·ti′tis
py′e·lo·cys′to·sto·mo′sis pl.
-ses′
py′e·lo·gen′ic
py′e·lo·gram′
py′e·log′ra·phy
py′e·lo·il′e·o′cu·ta′ne·ous
py′e·lo·li·thot′o·my
py′e·lom′e·try
py′e·lo·ne·phri′tis
py′e·lo′ne·phro′sis
py′e·lop′a·thy
py′e·lo′phle·bi′tis
py′e·lo·plas′ty
py′e·lo·pli·ca′tion
py′e·los′to·my
py′e·lot′o·my
py′e·lo·tu′bu·lar
py′e·lo·u·re′ter·al
py′e·lo·u·re′ter·ec′ta·sis pl.
-ses′
py′e·lo·u·re·ter′ic
py′e·lo·u·re·ter·og′ra·phy
py′e·lo·u·re′ter·ol′y·sis pl.
-ses′
py′e·lo·ve′nous
py·em′e·sis
py·e′mi·a
py·e′mic
py′en·ceph′a·lus
py·gal′gi·a
pyg·ma′li·on·ism
pyg′my
py′go·a·mor′phus
py′go·did′y·mus
py·gom′e·lus pl. -li′
py·gop′a·gus
py′ic
py′in
pyk·ne′mi·a
pyk′nic
pyk′no·cyte′
pyk′no·cy·to′ma pl. -mas or
-ma·ta

pyk′no·cy·to′sis
pyk′no·dys′os·to′sis pl.
-ses′
pyk·nom′e·ter
pyk′no·mor′phous
pyk′no·phra′si·a
pyk·no′sis
pyk·not′ic
py′le·phleb′ec·ta′si·a
py′le·phle·bec′ta·sis pl.
-ses′
py′le·phle·bi′tis
py′le·throm′bo·phle·bi′tis
py′le·throm·bo′sis pl. -ses′
py′lic
py′lon′
py′lo·ral′gi·a
py′lo·rec′to·my
py·lo′ric
py·lo′ri·ste·no′sis
py·lo′ri′tis
py·lo′ro·col′ic
py·lo′ro·di·o′sis pl. -ses′
py·lo′ro·du′o·de′nal
py·lo′ro·du′o·de·ni′tis
py·lo′ro·gas·trec′to·my
py·lo′ro·my·ot′o·my
py·lo′ro·plas′ty
py·lor′op·to′si·a
py·lor′op·to′sis
py′lo·ros′co·py
py′lo·ro·spasm
py·lo′ro·ste·no′sis
py′lo·ros′to·my
py′lo·rot′o·my
py·lo′rus pl. -ri′ or -rus·es
py′o·ar·thro′sis pl. -ses′
py′o·blen′nor·rhe′a
py′o·ca′lix pl. -li·ces′
py′o·cele′
py′o·ce′li·a
py′o·ceph′a·lus
py′o·che′zi·a
py′o·coc′cus pl. -ci′
py′o·col′po·cele′
py′o·col′pos′
py′o·cul′ture
py′o·cy′a·nase′
py′o·cy·an′ic
py′o·cy·a·nin
py′o·cy·a·no′sis pl. -ses′
py′o·cyst′
py′o·cys′tis
py′o·cyte′
py′o·der′ma
—— fa′ci·a′le′
—— gan′gre·no′sum

py′o·der′ma·ti′tis
py′o·der′ma·to′sis *pl.* -ses′
py′o·der′ma·tous
py′o·fe′ci·a
py′o·gen
py·og′e·nes′
py′o·gen′e·sis
py′o·ge·net′ic
py′o·gen′ic
py·og′e·nous
py′o·he′mi·a
py′o·he′mo·tho′rax′
py′oid′
py′o·lab′y·rin·thi′tis
py′o·me′tra
py′o·me·tri′tis
py′o·me′tri·um
py′o·my′o·si′tis
py′o·ne·phri′tis
py′o·neph′ro·li·thi′a·sis *pl.*
  -ses′
py′o·ne·phro′sis *pl.* -ses′
py′o·ne·phrot′ic
py′o·nych′i·a
py′o·o·var′i·um
py′o·per′i·car·di′tis
py′o·per′i·car′di·um
py′o·per′i·to·ne′um
py′o·per′i·to·ni′tis
py′o·pha′gi·a
py′oph·thal′mi·a
py′oph·thal·mi′tis
py′o·phy·lac′tic
py′o·phy′so·me′tra
py′o·pla′ni·a
py′o·pneu′mo·cyst′
py′o·pneu′mo·hep′a·ti′tis
  pl. -tis·es *or* -tit′i·des′
py′o·pneu′mo·per′i·car·
  di′tis
py′o·pneu′mo·per′i·car′di·
  um
py′o·pneu′mo·per′i·to·
  ne′um
py′o·pneu′mo·per′i·to·
  ni′tis
py′o·pneu′mo·tho′rax′
py′o·poi·e′sis *pl.* -ses′
py′o·poi·et′ic
py·op′ty·sis *pl.* -ses′
py′o·py·e·lec′ta·sis *pl.* -ses′
py′or·rhe′a
—— al′ve·o·lar′is
py′or·rhe′al
py′o·sal′pin·gi′tis
py′o·sal·pin′go-o′o·pho·
  ri′tis

py′o·sal′pinx *pl.* -sal·pin′ges′
py′o·scle·ro′sis *pl.* -ses′
py′o·sep′ti·ce′mi·a
py′o·sper′mi·a
py′o·stat′ic
py′o·sto′ma·ti′tis
py′o·ther′a·py
py′o·tho′rax′ *pl.* -rax′es *or*
  -ra·ces′
py′o·tox′i·ne′mi·a
py′o·um·bil′i·cus *pl.* -ci′ *or*
  -cus·es
py′o·u′ra·chus
py′o·u·re′ter
py′o·ve·sic′u·lo′sis *pl.* -ses′
pyr′a·mid
py·ram′i·dal
py·ram′i·da′le
py·ram′i·da′lis
—— na′si′
py·ram′i·des′ re·na′les′
pyr′a·mi·dot′o·my
pyr′a·mis *pl.* py·ram′i·des′
—— me·dul′lae′ ob′lon·
  ga′tae′
—— ver′mis
—— ves·tib′u·li′
py·ran′tel
pyr′a·zin′a·mide′
py·rec′tic
py′re·ne′mi·a
Py·re′no·chae′ta rom′er·oi′
py·ret′ic
py·ret′o·gen
pyr′e·to·gen′e·sis
pyr′e·to·ge·net′ic
pyr′e·to·gen′ic
pyr′e·tog′e·nous
pyr′e·tol′o·gy
pyr′e·tol′y·sis *pl.* -ses′
pyr′e·to·ther′a·py
pyr′e·to·ty·pho′sis *pl.* -ses′
py·rex′i·a
py·rex′i·al
pyr′i·dine′
pyr′i·do·stig′mine′
pyr′i·dox′al
pyr′i·dox′a·mine′
pyr′e·dox′ine′
pyr′i·form′ *var. of* piriform
py·ril′a·mine′
pyr′i·meth′a·mine′
pyr·rim′i·dine′
pyr·in′o·line′
pyr′i·thi′a·mine′
py′ro·cat′e·chin
py′ro·cat′e·chol′

py′ro·gal′lol′
py′ro·gen
py′ro·ge·net′ic
py′ro·gen′ic
py′ro·glob′u·lin
py′ro·glob′u·li·ne′mi·a
py′ro·glos′si·a
py′ro·lag′ni·a
py·rol′y·sis *pl.* -ses′
py′ro·lyt′ic
py′ro·ma′ni·a
py′ro·ma′ni·ac′
py′rone′
py′ro·nine′
py′ro·nin′o·phil′ic
py′ro·pho′bi·a
py′ro·phos′pha·tase′
py′ro·phos′phate′
py′ro·phos′pho·ki′nase′
py′ro·phos·pho′ric
py′ro·phos′pho·trans′fer·
  ase′
py′ro·punc′ture
py′ro·scope′
py·ro′sis
py·rot′ic
py′ro·tox′in
py′ro·va·ler′one′
py·rox′a·mine′
py·rox′y·lin
pyr·ro·bu′ta·mine′
pyr·ro·caine′
pyr′role′
pyr′rol′i·phene′
pyr′rol·ni′trin
pyr·ro·lo·por·phyr′i·a
py·ru′vic
pyr·vin′i·um pam′o·ate′
py·u′ri·a
py·u′ric

Q

quack
quack′er·y
quad′ran′gle
qua·dran′gu·lar
quad′rant
quad′ran·ta·no′pi·a
quad·ran′tic
qua·dra′tus *pl.* -ti′
—— fem′o·ris
—— la·bi·i′ in·fe′ri·o′ris
—— labii su·pe′ri·o′ris

—— lum·bo′rum
—— men′ti′
quad′ri·ceps′
—— fem′o·ris
—— su′rae′
quad′ri·cus′pid
quad′ri·gem′i·na
quad′ri·gem′i·nal
quad′ri·lat′er·al
qua·drip′a·ra
quad′ri·pa·re′sis *pl.* -ses′
quad′ri·par′i·ty
qua·drip′a·rous
quad′ri·ple′gi·a
quad′ri·va′lence
quad′ri·va′lent
quad·ru′ple
quad·ru′plet
Quain degeneration
qual′i·ta′tive
qual′i·ty
quan′tal
quan·tim′e·ter
quan′ti·ta′tive
quan′ti·ty
quan′tum *pl.* -ta
—— lib′et
—— plac′et
—— suf′fi·cit
—— vis
quar′an·tine′, -tined′, -tin′-
    ing
quart
quar′ter
quar′tile′
quar·tip′a·ra
quar·tip′a·rous
quar′ti·ster′nal
qua′ter in di′e
qua′ter·nar′y
qua′zo·dine′
que·bra′chine′
Queck′en·stedt′
—— sign
—— test
Qué·nu′ operation
que′nu·tho′ra·co·plas′ty
quer′ce·tin
Quer·vain′ disease
Quey·rat′ erythroplasia
quick
quick′en·ing
Quick test
qui·es′cence
qui·es′cent
quin′a·crine′
quin′al·bar′bi·tone′

quin·al′dine′
quin·az′o·sin
quin′bo·lone′
Quin′cke
—— disease
—— edema
—— pulse
quin·dec′a·mine′
quin·do′ni·um
quin·es′trol′
quin·eth′a·zone′
quin·ges′ta·nol′
quin·ges′trone′
quin′i·dine′
qui′nine′
qui′nin·ism
quin·i′no·der′ma
quin′ism
Quin′lan test
quin′oid′
quin′o·line′
qui·none
Quin·quaud′
—— disease
—— phenomenon
quin′que·tu·ber′cu·lar
quin′sy
quin′tan
quin·ter′e·nol′
quin·tip′a·ra
quin·tip′a·rous
quin′ti·ster′nal
quin·tu′plet
quip′a·zine′
quo·tid′i·an
quo′tient

R

rab′id
ra′bies′
ra′bi·form′
race
ra′ce·mase′
ra·ce′mic
ra′ce·mi·za′tion
rac′e·mose′
rac′e·phed′rine
ra′ce·phen′i·col′
ra′chi·al′gi·a
ra′chi·an′al·ge′si·a
ra′chi·an·es·the′si·a
ra′chi·cen·te′sis *pl.* -ses′
ra·chid′i·al
ra·chid′i·an

ra·chil′y·sis *pl.* -ses′
ra·chi·o·camp′sis *pl.* -ses′
ra·chi·o·cen·te′sis *pl.* -ses′
ra·chi·o·dyn′i·a
ra′chi·o·ky·pho′sis *pl.* -ses′
ra·chi·om′e·ter
ra′chi·o·my′e·li′tis
ra′chi·op′a·thy
ra′chi·o·ple′gi·a
ra′chi·o·sco′li·o′sis *pl.* -ses′
ra′chi·o·tome′
ra·chi·ot′o·my
ra·chip′a·gus *pl.* -gi′
ra′chi·re·sis′tance
ra′chis *pl.* -chis·es or rach′i·
    des′
ra′chi·sag′ra
ra·chis′chi·sis *pl.* -ses′
ra·chit′ic
ra·chi′tis
ra·chi·tism
rach′i·to·gen′ic
rach′i·tome′
ra·chit′o·my
ra′cial
ra′dar·ky′mo·gram′
ra′dar·ky·mog′ra·phy
ra·dec′to·my
ra′di·ad′
ra′di·al
ra′di·a′lis
ra′di·an
ra′di·ant
ra′di·ate′, -at′ed, -at′ing
ra′di·a′ti·o′ *pl.* -o′nes′
—— a·cus′ti·ca
—— cor′po·ris cal·lo′si′
—— corporis stri·a′ti′
—— oc·cip′i·to·tha·lam′i·ca
—— op′ti·ca
ra′di·a′tion
rad′i·cal *(basic, extreme)*
♦*radicle*
ra′di·ces′
—— cra′ni·a′les′ ner′vi′
ac′ces·so′ri·i′
—— spi·na′les′ ner′vi′
ac′ces·so′ri·i′
—— sym·path′i·cae′ gan′
gli· i′ cil′i·ar′is
—— vis′cer·a′les′ ve′nae′
ca′vae′ in·fe′ri·o′ris
rad′i·cle *(a small root)*
♦*radical*
rad′i·cot′o·my
ra·dic′u·lal′gi·a
ra·dic′u·lar

ra·dic′u·lec′to·my
ra·dic′u·li′tis
ra·dic′u·lo·gan′gli·o·ni′tis
ra·dic′u·lo·med′ul·lar′y
ra·dic′u·lo·me·nin′go·my′e·
  li′tis
ra·dic′u·lo·my′e·lop′a·thy
ra·dic′u·lo·neu·ri′tis
ra·dic′u·lo·neu′rop′a·thy
ra·dic′u·lop′a·thy
ra·dic′u·lo·sac·cog′ra·phy
ra′di·i′
—— len′tis
ra·di·o·ac·tin′i·um
ra′di·o·ac′tive
ra′di·o·ac·tiv′i·ty
ra′di·o′al·ler′go·sor′bent
ra′di·o·ar·te′ri·o·gram′
ra′di·obe′
ra′di·o·bi·cip′i·tal
ra′di·o·bi′o·log′i·cal
ra′di·o·bi·ol′o·gist
ra′di·o·bi·ol′o·gy
ra′di·o·car′ci·no·gen′e·sis
  pl. -ses′
ra·di·o·car′pal
ra′di·o·car′pus *pl.* -pi′
ra′di·o·chem′is·try
ra′di·o·cys·ti′tis
ra′di·ode′
ra′di·o·der′ma·ti′tis
ra′di·o·di′ag·no′sis *pl.* -ses′
ra′di·o·di′ag·nos′tic
ra′di·o·dig′i·tal
ra′di·o·don′ti·a
ra′di·o·don′tics
ra′di·o·don′tist
ra′di·o·el′e·ment
ra′di·o′en·ceph′a·lo·gram′
ra′di·o′en·ceph′a·log′ra·
  phy
ra′di·o·gen′ic
ra′di·o·gold′
ra′di·o·gram′
ra′di·o·graph′
ra′di·og′ra·pher
ra′di·o·graph′ic
ra′di·og′ra·phy
ra′di·o·hu′mer·al
ra′di·o′im·mu′ni·ty
ra′di·o·im′mu·no·as′say
ra′di·o·im′mu·no·e·lec′tro·
  pho·re′sis
ra′di·o·i′o·dine′
ra′di·o·i′ron
ra′di·o·i′so·tope′
ra′di·o·ky·mog′ra·phy

ra′di·o·log′ic
ra′di·o·log′i·cal
ra′di·ol′o·gist
ra′di·ol′o·gy
ra′di·o·lu′cen·cy
ra′di·o·lu′cent
ra′di·o·lu′mi·nes′cence
ra′di·ol′y·sis *pl.* -ses′
ra′di·om′e·ter
ra′di·o·met′ric
ra′di·o·mi·crom′e·ter
ra′di·o·mi·met′ic
ra′di·o·ne·cro′sis
ra′di·o·neu·ri′tis
ra′di·o·ni′tro·gen
ra′di·o·nu′clide′
ra′di·o·pac′i·ty
ra′di·o·paque′
ra′di·o·pa·thol′o·gy
ra′di·o·pel·vim′e·try
ra′di·o·phar′ma·ceu′ti·cal
ra′di·o·phos′pho·rus
ra′di·o·po·ten′ti·a′tion
ra′di·o·prax′is
ra′di·o·pul′mo·nog′ra·phy
ra′di·o·re·sist′ance
ra′di·o′re·sis′tant
ra′di·o′re·spon′sive
ra′di·os′co·py
ra′di·o·sen′si·tive
ra′di·o·sen′si·tiv′i·ty
ra′di·o·ster′e·os′co·py
ra′di·o·sur′ger·y
ra′di·o·ther′a·peu′tic
ra′di·o·ther′a·peu′tics
ra′di·o·ther′a·pist
ra′di·o·ther′a·py
ra′di·o·ther′my
ra′di·o·tox·e′mi·a
ra′di·o·trans·par′ent
ra′di·o·trop′ic
ra′di·o·tro′pism
ra′di·o·ul′nar
ra′di·um
ra′di·us *pl.* -di·i′ *or* -di·us·es
—— fix′us
ra′dix *pl.* -di·ces′ *or* -dix·es
—— anterior ner·vo′rum
spi·na′li·um
—— a·or′tae′
—— ar′cus ver′te·brae′
—— brev′is gan′gli·i′cil′i·
ar′is
—— clin′i·ca
—— coch′le·ar′is ner′vi′
a·cus′ti·ci′
—— den′tis

—— de·scen′dens ner′vi′ tri·
gem′i·ni′
—— dor·sa′lis ner·vo′rum
spi·na′li·um
—— fa′ci·a′lis
—— inferior an′sae′ cer′vi·
ca′lis
—— inferior coch′le·ar′is
—— inferior ner′vi′ ves·
tib′u·lo·coch′le·ar′is
—— lat′er·a′lis ner′vi′ me′di·
a′ni′
—— lateralis trac′tus op′ti·
ci′
—— lin′guae′
—— lon′ga gan′gli·i′ cil′i·
ar′is
—— me′di·a′lis ner′vi′ me′di·
a′ni′
—— medialis trac′tus op′ti·
ci′
—— mes′en·ter′i·i′
—— mo·to′ri·a ner′vi′ tri·
gem′i·ni′
—— na′si′
—— ner′vi′ fa′ci·a′lis
—— oc′u·lo·mo·to′ri·a
gan′gli·i′ cil′i·ar′is
—— pe′nis
—— pi′li′
—— posterior ner′vi′ spi·
na′lis
—— pul·mo′nis
—— sen·so′ri·a ner′vi′ tri·
gem′i·ni′
—— superior an′sae′ cer′vi·
ca′lis
—— superior ner′vi′ ves·
tib′u·lo·coch′le·ar′is
—— superior ves′tib′u·lar′is
—— sym·path′i·ca gan′gli·i′
sub·max′il·lar′is
—— un′guis
—— ven′tra′lis ner·vo′rum
spi·na′li·um
ra′don′
Ra·do·vi′ci reflex
Rae′der syndrome
raf′fi·nase′
raf′fi·nose′
rag′weed′
Rai′ney corpuscle
rale
ra′mal
ra′mi′
—— ad pon′tem ar·te′ri·ae′
bas′i·lar′is

—— al've·o·lar'es' su·pe'ri·o'res' an·te'ri·o'res' ner'vi in'fra·or'bi·ta'lis

—— alveolares superiores pos·te'ri·o'res' ner'vi in'fra·or'bi·ta'lis

—— alveolares superiores posteriores nervi max'il·lar'is

—— a·nas'to·mot'i·ci' ner'vi' au·ric'u·lo·tem'po·ra'lis cum ner'vo' fa'ci·a'li'

—— an·te'ri·o'res' ar·te'ri·o'rum in'ter·cos·ta'li·um

—— anteriores ner·vo'rum cer'vi·ca'li·um

—— anteriores nervorum lum·ba'li·um

—— anteriores nervorum tho'ra·ca'li·um

—— ar·te'ri·o'si' in'ter·lob'u·lar'es' hep'a·tis

—— ar·tic'u·lar'es' ar·te'ri·ae' ge'nus de'scen·den'tis

—— articulares arteriae ge'nu su·pre'mae'

—— au·ric'u·lar'es' an·te'ri·o'res' ar·te'ri·ae' tem'po·ra'lis su·per·fi'ci·a'lis

—— bron'chi·a'les' an·te'ri·o'res' ner'vi' va'gi'

—— bronchiales a·or'tae' tho·ra·ci·cae'

—— bronchiales ar·te'ri·ae' mam·mar'i·ae' in·ter'nae'

—— bronchiales arteriae tho'ra·ci·cae' in·ter'nae'

—— bronchiales bron·cho'rum

—— bronchiales hyp'ar·te'ri·a'les'

—— bronchiales ner'vi' va'gi'

—— bronchiales pos·te'ri·o'res' ner'vi' va'gi'

—— bronchiales seg'men·to'rum

—— buc·ca'les' ner'vi' fa'ci·a'lis

—— cal·ca'ne·i' ar·te'ri·ae' tib'i·a'lis pos·te'ri·o'ris

—— calcanei lat'er·a'les' ar·te'ri·ae' per'o·nae·ae'

—— calcanei laterales ner'·vi' su·ra'lis

—— calcanei me'di·a'les' ar·te'ri·ae tib'i·a'lis pos·te'ri·o'ris

—— calcanei mediales ner'·vi' tib'i·a'lis

—— calcanei ra·mo'rum mal'le·o·lar'i·um lat'er·a'li·um ar·te'ri·ae' fib'u·lar'is

—— calcanei ramorum malleolarium lateralium arteriae per'o·ne·ae'

—— cap'su·lar'es' ar·te'ri·ae' re'nis

—— car·di'a·ci' cer'vi·ca'les' in·fe'ri·o'res' ner'vi' va'gi'

—— cardiaci cervicales su·pe'ri·o'res' ner'vi' va'gi'

—— cardiaci in·fe'ri·o'res' ner'vi' rec'ur·ren'tis

—— cardiaci su·pe'ri·o'res' ner'vi' va'gi'

—— cardiaci tho·ra'ci·ci ner'vi' va'gi'

—— ca·rot'i·co·tym·pan'i·ci' ar·te'ri·ae' ca·rot'i·dis in·ter'nae'

—— ce·li'a·ci' ner'vi' va'gi'

—— cen·tra'les' ar·te'ri·ae' cer'e·bri' an·te'ri·o'ris

—— centrales arteriae cere·bri me'di·ae'

—— centrales arteriae cere·bri pos·te'ri·o'ris

—— cho·roi'de·i' pos·te'ri·o'res' ar·te'ri·ae' cer'e·bri' pos·te'ri·o'ris

—— coe'li·a·ci' ner'vi' va'gi'

—— com·mu'ni·can'tes'

—— communicantes gan'gli·i' sub'man·dib'u·lar'is cum ner'vo' lin·gua'li'

—— communicantes ganglii sub·max'il·lar'is cum ner'vo' lin·gua'li'

—— communicantes ner'vi' au·ric'u·lo·tem'po·ra'lis cum ner'vo' fa'ci·a'li'

—— communicantes nervi lin·gua'lis cum ner'vo' hy'po·glos'so'

—— communicantes ner·vo'rum spi·na'li·um

—— cor'ti·ca'les' ar·te'ri·ae' cer'e·bri' an·te'ri·o'ris

—— corticales arteriae cere·bri me'di·ae'

—— corticales arteriae cere·bri pos·te'ri·o'ris

—— cu·ta'ne·i' an·te'ri·o'res' ner'vi' fem'o·ra'lis

—— cutanei anteriores (pec'to·ra'les' et ab·dom'i·na'les') ra·mo'rum an·te'ri·o'rum ar·te'ri·ar'um in'ter·cos·ta'li·um

—— cutanei ar·te'ri·ae' man·mar'i·ae' in·ter'nae'

—— cutanei cru'ris me'di·a'les' ner'vi' sa·phe'ni'

—— cutanei lat'er·a'les' pec'to·ra'les' et ab·dom'i·na'les' ra·mo'rum an·te'ri·o'rum ar·te'ri·ar'um in'ter·cos·ta'li·um

—— den·ta'les' ar·te'ri·ae' al've·o·lar'is in·fe'ri·o'ris

—— dentales arteriae alveo·laris su·pe'ri·o'ris pos·te'ri·o'ris

—— dentales ar·te'ri·ar'um al've·o·lar'i·um su·pe'ri·o'rum an·te'ri·o'rum

—— dentales in·fe'ri·o'res' plex'us den·ta'lis in·fe'ri·o'ris

—— dentales su·pe'ri·o'res' plex'us den·ta'lis su·pe'ri·o'ris

—— dor·sa'les' ar·te'ri·ae' in'ter·cos·ta'lis su·pre'mae'

—— dorsales ar·te'ri·ar'um in'ter·cos·ta'li·um pos·te'ri·o'rum (III-XI)

—— dorsales lin'guae' ar·te'ri·ae' lin·gua'lis

—— dorsales ner·vo'rum cer'vi·ca'li·um

—— dorsales nervorum lum·ba'li·um

—— dorsales nervorum sa·cra'li·um

—— dorsales nervorum tho'ra·ci·co'rum

—— du'o·de·na'les' ar·te'ri·ae' pan'cre·at'i·co·du'o·de·na'lis su·pe'ri·o'ris

—— duodenales arteriae su'pra·du'o·de·na'les su·pe'ri·o'res'

—— ep'i·plo'i·ci' ar·te'ri·ae' gas'tro·ep'i·plo'i·cae' dex'·trae'

—— epiploici arteriae gas·troepiploicae si·nis'trae'

—— e·soph'a·ge'i' a·or'tae' tho·ra·ci·cae'

—— esophagei ar·te′ri·ae′ gas′tri·cae′ si·nis′trae′

—— esophagei arteriae thy·roi′de·ae′ in·fe′ri·o′ris

—— esophagei ner′vi′ la·ryn′ge·i′ rec′ur·ren′tis

—— fron·ta′les′ ar·te′ri·ae′ cer′e·bri′ an·te′ri·o′ris

—— frontales arteriae cere·bri me′di·ae′

—— gas′tri·ci′ an·te′ri·o′res′ ner′vi′ va′gi′

—— gastrici ner′vi′ va′gi′

—— gastrici pos·te′ri·o′res′ ner′vi′ va′gi′

—— gin′gi·va′les′ in·fe′ri·o′res′ plex′us den·ta′lis in·fe′ri·o′ris

—— gingivales su·pe′ri·o′res′ plex′us den·ta′lis su·pe′ri·o′ris

—— glan′du·lar′es′ ar·te′ri·ae fa′ci·a′lis

—— glandulares arteriae max′il·lar′is ex·ter′nae′

—— glandulares arteriae thy′re·oi′de·ae′ in·fe′ri·o′ris

—— glandulares arteriae thyreoideae su·pe′ri·o′ris

—— glandulares arteriae thy·roi′de·ae′ in·fe′ri·o′ris

—— glandulares gan′gli·i′ sub′man·dib′u·lar′is

—— he·pat′i·ci′ ner′vi′ va′gi′

—— in·fe′ri·o′res′ ner′vi′ cu·ta′ne·i′ col′li′

—— inferiores nervi trans·ver′si′ col′li′

—— in′gui·na′les′ ar·te′ri·ae′ fem′o·ra′lis

—— in′ter·cos·ta′les′ an·te′ri·o′res′ ar·te′ri·ae′ tho·ra′ci·cae′ in·ter′nae′

—— intercostales ar·te′ri·ae′ mam·mar′i·ae′ in·ter′nae′

—— in′ter·gan′gli·o·nar′es′

—— isth′mi′ fau′ci·um ner′·vi′ lin·gua′lis

—— la·bi·a′les′ an·te′ri·o′res′ ar·te′ri·ae′ fem′o·ra′lis

—— labiales in·fe′ri·o′res′ ner′vi′ men·ta′lis

—— labiales pos·te′ri·o′res′ ar·te′ri·ae′ pu′den′dae′ in·ter′nae′

—— labiales su·pe′ri·o′res′ ner′vi′ in′fra·or′bi·ta′lis

—— la·ryn′go·pha·ryn′ge·i′ gan′gli·i′ cer′vi·cal′is su·pe′ri·us

—— laryngopharyngei ner′·vi′ sym·path′i·ci′

—— li′e·na′les′ ar·te′ri·ae′ li′e·na′lis

—— lienales ner′vi′ va′gi′

—— lin·gua′les′ ner′vi′ glos′so·pha·ryn′ge·i′

—— linguales nervi hy′po·glos′si′

—— linguales nervi lin·gua′lis

—— mal′le·o·lar′es′ lat′er·a′les′ ar·te′ri·ae′ fib′u·lar′is

—— malleolares laterales arteriae per′o·ne′ae′

—— malleolares me′di·a′les′ ar·te′ri·ae′ tib′i·a′lis pos·te′ri·o′ris

—— mam·mar′i·i′ ar·te′ri·ae′ mam·mar′i·ae′ in·ter′nae′

—— mammarii arteriae tho·ra′ci·cae′ in·ter′nae′

—— mammarii ar·te′riar′um in′ter·cos·ta′li·um pos·te′ri·o′ri·um (III–XI)

—— mammarii ex·ter′ni′ ar·te′ri·ae′ tho′ra·ca′lis lat′er·a′lis

—— mammarii lat′er·a′les′ ar·te′ri·ae′ tho·ra′ci·cae′ lat′er·a′lis

—— mammarii laterales ner·vo′rum in′ter·cos·ta′li·um

—— mammarii laterales nervorum tho·ra′ci·co′rum

—— mammarii laterales ra·mo′rum cu·ta′ne·o′rum lat′er·a′li·um ra·mo′rum an·te′ri·o′rum ar·te′ri·ar′um in′ter·cos·ta′li·um

—— mammarii me′di·a′les′ ar·te′ri·ar′um in′ter·cos·ta′li·um

—— mammarii mediales ner·vo′rum in′ter·cos·ta′li·um

—— mammarii mediales nervorum tho·ra′ci·co′rum

—— mas·toi′de·i′ ar·te′ri·ae′ au·ric′u·lar′is pos·te′ri·o′ris

—— mastoidei arteriae sty′lo·mas·toi′de·ae′

—— me′di·as′ti·na′les′ a·or′tae′ tho′ra·ca′lis

—— mediastinales aortae tho·ra′ci·cae′

—— mediastinales aortae thoracicae in·ter′nae′

—— men·ta′les′ ner′vi′ men·ta′lis

—— mus′cu·lar′es′ ar·te′ri·ae′ cer′vi·ca′lis as·cen·den′tis

—— musculares arteriae fem′o·ra′lis

—— musculares arteriae ge′nu su·pre′mae′

—— musculares arteriae oc·cip′i·ta′lis

—— musculares arteriae oph·thal′mi·cae′

—— musculares arteriae ra′di·a′lis

—— musculares arteriae ul·nar′is

—— musculares ner′vi′ ax′il·lar′is

—— musculares nervi fem′o·ra′lis

—— musculares nervi fib′u·lar′is pro·fun′dus

—— musculares nervi fibu·laris su′per·fi′ci·a′lis

—— musculares nervi il′i·o·hy′po·gas′tri·ci

—— musculares nervi il′i·o·in′gui·na′lis

—— musculares nervi is·chi·ad′i·ci′

—— musculares nervi me′di·a′ni′

—— musculares nervi mus′cu·lo·cu·ta′ne·i′

—— musculares nervi ob·tu·ra·to′ri·i′

—— musculares nervi per′o·nae′i′ com·mu′nis

—— musculares nervi pero·naei pro·fun′di′

—— musculares nervi pero·naei su′per·fi′ci·a′lis

—— musculares nervi per′o·ne′i′ pro·fun′di′

—— musculares nervi pero·nei su′per·fi′ci·a′lis

—— musculares nervi ra′di·a′lis

—— musculares nervi tib′i·a′lis

—— sub·scap'u·lar·es ar·te'ri·ae' ax'il·lar'is

—— su·pe'ri·o'res' ner'vi' cu·ta'ne·i' col'li'

—— superiores nervi trans·ver'si' col'li'

—— su'pra·re·na'les' su·pe'ri·o'res' ar·te'ri·ae' phren'i·cae' in·fe'ri·o'ris

—— tem'po·ra'les' ar·te'ri·ae' cer·e·bri' me'di·ae'

—— temporales arteriae cerebri pos·te'ri·o'ris

—— temporales ner'vi' fa·ci·a'lis

—— temporales su'per·fi'ci·a'les' ner'vi' au·ric'u·lo·tem'po·ra'lis

—— thy'mi·ci' ar·te'ri·ae' tho·ra·ci·cae' in·ter'nae'

—— ton'sil·lar'es' ner'vi' glos'so·pha·ryn'ge·i'

—— tra·che·a'les' ar·te'ri·ae' thy·roi'de·ae' in·fe'ri·o'ris

—— tracheales ner'vi' la·ryn'ge·i' rec'ur·ren'tis

—— tracheales nervi rec'ur·ren'tis

—— tra·che·a'lis ar·te'ri·ae' thy're·oi'de·ae' in·fe'ri·o'ris

—— u're·ter'i·ci' ar·te'ri·ae' duc'tus def'e·ren'tis

—— ureterici arteriae o·var'i·cae'

—— ureterici arteriae re·na'lis

—— ureterici arteriae tes·tic'u·lar'is

—— ven·tra'les' ner·vo'rum cer'vi·ca'li·um

—— ventrales nervorum lum·ba'li·um

—— ventrales nervorum sa·cra'li·um

—— ventrales nervorum tho·ra·ci·co'rum

—— ves·tib'u·lar'es' ar·te'ri·ae' au'di·ti'vae' in'ter'nae'

—— vestibulares arteriae lab'y·rin'thi'

—— vis'cer·a'les' a·or'tae' ab·dom'i·na'lis

—— viscerales aortae tho·ra·ca'lis

—— viscerales ar·te'ri·ae' hy'po·gas'tri·cae'

—— zy'go·mat'i·ci' ner'vi' fa·ci·a'lis

ram'i·fi·ca'tion

ram'i·fy', -fied', -fy'ing

ram'i·sec'tion

ram'i·sec'to·my

ra'mose'

Ram'say Hunt syndrome

Rams'den eyepiece

Ram'stedt operation

ram'u·lus pl. -li'

ra'mus pl. -mi'

—— ac'e·tab'u·lar'is ar·te'ri·ae' cir'cum·flex'ae' fem'o·ris me'di·a'lis

—— acetabularis arteriae ob'tu·ra·to'ri·ae'

—— ac'e·tab'u·li' ar·te'ri·ae' cir'cum·flex'ae' fem'o·ris me'di·a'lis

—— a·cro'mi·a'lis ar·te'ri·ae' su'pra·scap'u·lar'is

—— acromialis arteriae tho'ra·co·a·cro'mi·a'lis

—— acromialis arteriae trans·ver'sae' scap'u·lae'

—— al've·o·lar'is superior me'di·us ner'vi' in'fra·or'bi·ta'lis

—— a·nas'to·mot'i·cus

—— anastomoticus ar·te'ri·ae' me·nin'ge·ae' me'di·ae' cum ar·te'ri·a lac'ri·ma'li'

—— anastomoticus gan'gli·i' o'ti·ci' cum chor'da tym'pa·ni'

—— anastomoticus ganglii otici cum ner'vo' au·ric'u·lo·tem'po·ra'li'

—— anastomoticus ganglii otici cum nervo spi·no'so'

—— anastomoticus ner'vi' fa'ci·a'lis cum ner'vo' glos'so·pha·ryn'ge·o'

—— anastomoticus nervi facialis cum plex'u tym·pan'i·co'

—— anastomoticus nervi glos'so·pha·ryn'ge·i cum ra'mo' au·ric'u·lar'i' ner'vi' va'gi'

—— anastomoticus nervi lac'ri·ma'lis cum ner'vo' zy'go·mat'i·co'

—— anastomoticus nervi la·ryn'ge·i' su·pe'ri·o'ris cum

ner'vo' la·ryn'ge·o' in·fe'ri·o're'

—— anastomoticus nervi lin·gua'lis cum ner'vo' hy'po·glos'so'

—— anastomoticus nervi me'di·a'ni' cum ner'vo' ul·nar'i'

—— anastomoticus nervi va'gi' cum ner'vo' glos'so·pha·ryn'ge·o'

—— anastomoticus per'o·nae'us

—— anastomoticus ul·nar'is ra'mi' su'per·fi'ci·a'lis ner'vi' ra'di·a'lis

—— anterior ar·te'ri·ae' ob'tu·ra·to'ri·ae'

—— anterior arteriae rec'ur·ren'tis ul·nar'is

—— anterior arteriae re·na'lis

—— anterior arteriae thy're·oi'de·ae' su·pe'ri·o'ris

—— anterior arteriae thy·roi'de·ae' su·pe·ri·o'ris

—— anterior as·cen'dens ar·te'ri·ae' pul'mo·na'lis dex'-trae'

—— anterior ascendens arteriae pulmonalis si·nis'trae'

—— anterior ascendens fis·su'rae' cer'e·bri' lat'er·a'lis

—— anterior de·scen'dens ar·te'ri·ae' pul'mo·na'lis dex'trae'

—— anterior descendens arteriae pulmonalis si·nis'trae'

—— anterior duc'tus he·pat'i·ci' dex'tri'

—— anterior ho'ri·zon·ta'lis fis·su'rae' cer'e·bri' lat'er·a'lis

—— anterior ner'vi' au·ric'u·lar'is mag'ni'

—— anterior nervi cu·ta'ne·i' an'te·bra'chi·i' me'di·a'lis

—— anterior nervi la·ryn'ge·i' in·fe'ri·o'ris

—— anterior nervi ob'tu·ra·to'ri·i'

—— anterior nervi spi·na'lis

—— anterior ra'mi' cu·ta'ne·i' lat'er·a'lis ner·vo'rum tho·ra·ca'li·um

—— anterior rami cutanei

lateralis rami an·te′ri·o′ris
ar·te′ri·ae′ in·ter·cos·ta′lis
—— anterior sul′ci′ lat′er·
a′lis cer′e·bri′
—— anterior ve′nae′
pul′mo·na′lis su·pe′ri·o′ris
dex′trae′
—— anterior venae pulmo-
nalis superioris si·nis′trae′
—— ap′i·ca′lis ar·te′ri·ae′
pul′mo·na′lis dex′trae′
—— apicalis arteriae pulmonalis si·nis′trae′
—— apicalis lo′bi′ in·fe′ri·
o′ris ar·te′ri·ae′ pul′mo·na′lis
dex′trae′
—— apicalis lobi inferioris
arteriae pulmonalis si·
nis′trae′
—— apicalis ve′nae′ pul′mo·
na′lis in·fe′ri·o′ris dex′trae′
—— apicalis venae pulmo-
nalis inferioris si·nis′trae′
—— apicalis venae pulmo-
nalis su·pe′ri·o′ris dex′trae′
—— ap′i·co·pos·te′ri·or ve′-
nae′ pul′mo·na′lis su·pe′ri·
o′ris si·nis′trae′
—— as·cen′dens ar·te′ri·ae′
cir′cum·flex′ae′ fem′o·ris
lat′er·a′lis
—— ascendens arteriae circumflexae femoris me′di·
a′lis
—— ascendens arteriae circumflexae il′i·i′ pro·fun′dae′
—— ascendens arteriae
trans·ver′sae′ col′li
—— ascendens sul′ci′ lat′er·
a′lis cer′e·bri′
—— au·ric′u·lar′is ar·te′ri·ae′
au·ric′u·lar·is pos·te′ri·o′ris
—— auricularis arteriae oc·
cip′i·ta′lis
—— auricularis ner′vi′ va′gi′
—— ba·sa′lis an·te′ri·or ar·
te′ri·ae′ pul′mo·na′lis dex′-
trae′
—— basalis anterior arteriae pulmonalis si·nis′trae′
—— basalis anterior ve′nae′
pul′mo·na′lis in·fe′ri·o′ris
dex′trae′
—— basalis anterior venae
pulmonalis inferioris si·
nis′trae′
—— basalis lat′er·a′lis ar·

te′ri·ae′ pul′mo·na′lis dex′-
trae′
—— basalis lateralis arteriae
pulmonalis si·nis′trae′
—— basalis me′di·a′lis ar·
te′ri·ae′ pul′mo·na′lis dex′-
trae′
—— basalis medialis arteriae pulmonalis si·nis′trae′
—— basalis posterior arteriae pulmonalis dex′trae′
—— basalis posterior arteriae pulmonalis si·nis′trae′
—— bron′chi·a′lis ep′ar·te′ri·
a′lis
—— car·di′a·cus
—— cardiacus ar·te′ri·ae′
pul′mo·na′lis dex′trae
—— ca·rot′i·co·tym·pan′i·
cus ar·te′ri·ae′ ca·rot′is in·
ter′nae′
—— ca·rot′i·cus
—— car′pe·us dor·sa′lis ar·
te′ri·ae′ ra′di·a′lis
—— carpeus dorsalis arteriae ul·nar′is
—— carpeus pal·mar′is ar·
te′ri·ae′ ra′di·a′lis
—— carpeus palmaris arte-
riae ul·nar′is
—— carpeus vo·lar′is ar·
te′ri·ae′ ra′di·a′lis
—— carpeus volaris arteriae
ul·nar′is
—— cho·roi′de·us ar·te′ri·ae′
cer′e·bri′ pos·te′ri·o′ris
—— cir′cum·flex′us ar·te′ri·
ae′ co′ro·nar′i·ae′ cor′dis si·
nis′trae′
—— circumflexus arteriae
coronariae si·nis′trae′
—— circumflexus fib′u·lae′
ar·te′ri·ae′ tib′i·a′lis pos·te′ri·
o′ris
—— cla·vic′u·lar′is ar·te′ri·
ae′ tho′ra·co·a·cro′mi·a′lis
—— coch′le·ae′ ar·te′ri·ae′
au′di·ti′vae′ in·ter′nae′
—— coch′le·ar′is ar·te′ri·ae′
lab′y·rin′thi′
—— col·lat′er·a′lis ar·te′ri·
ar′um in·ter·cos·ta′li·um pos·
te′ri·o′rum (III–XI)
—— col′li′ ner′vi′ fa·ci·a′lis
—— com·mu′ni·cans′
—— communicans ar·te′ri·
ae′ fib′u·lar′is

—— communicans arteriae
per′o·nae′ae′
—— communicans arteriae
per′o·ne′ae′
—— communicans fib′u·
lar′is ner′vi′ fib′u·lar′is com·
mu′nis
—— communicans gan′gli·i′
cil′i·ar′is cum ner′vo′ na′so·
cil′i·ar′i′
—— communicans ganglii
o′ti·ci′ cum chor′da tym′pa·
ni′
—— communicans ganglii
otici cum ner′vi′ au·ric′u·lo·
tem′po·ra′li′
—— communicans ganglii
otici cum ra′mo′ me·
nin′ge·o′ ner′ve′ man·dib′u·
lar′is
—— communicans ner′vi′
fa′ci·a′lis cum ner′vo′
glos′so·pha·ryn′ge·o′
—— communicans nervi fa-
cialis cum plex′u tym·pan′i·
co′
—— communicans nervi
glos′so·pha·ryn′ge·i′ cum
ra′mo′ au·ric′u·lar′i′ ner′vi′
va′gi′
—— communicans nervi
lac′ri·ma′lis cum ner′vo′
zy′go·mat′i·co′
—— communicans nervi la·
ryn′ge·i′ rec·ur·ren′tis cum
ra′mo′ la·ryn′ge·o′ in·ter′no′
—— communicans nervi la-
ryngei su·pe′ri·o′ris cum
ner′vo′ laryn′ge·o′ in·fe′ri·
o′re′
—— communicans nervi lin·
gua′lis cum chor′da tym′pa·
ni′
—— communicans nervi
lingualis cum ner′vo′ hy′po·
glos′so′
—— communicans nervi
me′di·a′ni′ cum ner′vo′ ul·
nar′i′
—— communicans nervi
na′so·cil′i·ar′is cum
gan′gli·o′ cil′i·ar′i′
—— communicans nervi
spi·na′lis
—— communicans nervi
va′gi′ cum ner′vo′ glos′so·
pha·ryn′ge·o′

—— communicans per'o·ne·us ner'vi' per·o·ne'i' com·mu'nis

—— communicans ul·nar'is ner'vi' ra'di·a'lis

—— cos·ta'lis lat'er·a'lis ar·te'ri·ae' mam·mar'i·ae' in·ter'nae'

—— costalis lateralis arteriae tho·ra'ci·cae' in·ter'nae'

—— cri·co·thy're·oi'de·us ar·te'ri·ae' thy're·oi'de·ae' su·pe'ri·o'ris

—— cri·co·thy·roi'de·us ar·te'ri·ae' thy·roi'de·ae' su·pe'ri·o'ris

—— cu·ta'ne·us an·te'ri·or ner'vi' il'i·o·hy'po·gas'tri·ci'

—— cutaneus anterior (pec'to·ra'lis et ab·dom'i·na'lis) ner'vi' in'ter·cos·ta'lis

—— cutaneus anterior (pectoralis et abdominalis) nervi tho·ra'ci·ci'

—— cutaneus lat'er·a'lis ar·te'ri·ar'um in'ter·cos·ta'li·um pos·te'ri·o'rum (III–XI)

—— cutaneus lateralis ner'·vi' il'i·o·hy'po·gas'tri·ci'

—— cutaneus lateralis (pec'to·ra'lis et ab·dom'i·na'lis) ner'vi' tho·ra'ci·ci'

—— cutaneus lateralis (pectoralis et abdominalis) ner·vo'rum in'ter·cos·ta'li·um

—— cutaneus lateralis ra'mi' dor·sa'lis ar·te'ri·ar'um in'ter·cos·ta'li·um pos·te'ri·o'rum (III–XI)

—— cutaneus lateralis ra·mo'rum dor·sa'li·um ner·vo'rum tho·ra'ci·co'rum

—— cutaneus lateralis ra·morum pos·te'ri·o'rum ar·te'ri·ar'um in'ter·cos·ta'li·um

—— cutaneus lateralis ra·morum posteriorum ner·vo'rum tho'ra·ca'li·um

—— cutaneus me'di·a'lis ra'mi' dor·sa'lis ar·te'ri·ar'um in'ter·cos·ta'li·um pos·te'ri·o'rum (III–XI)

—— cutaneus medialis ra·mo'rum dor·sa'li·um ner·vo'rum tho·ra'ci·co'rum

—— cutaneus medialis ra·

mo'rum pos·te'ri·o'rum ar·te'ri·o'rum in'ter·cos·ta'li·um

—— cutaneus medialis ra·morum posteriorum ner·vo'rum tho'ra·ca'li·um

—— cutaneus ner'vi' ob'tu·ra·to'ri·i'

—— cutaneus pal·mar'is ner'vi' ul·nar'is

—— del·toi'de·us ar·te'ri·ae' pro·fun'dae' bra'chi·i'

—— deltoideus arteriae tho'ra·co·a·cro'mi·a'lis

—— de·scen'dens anterior ar·te'ri·ae' co'ro·nar'i·ae' cor'dis si·nis'trae'

—— descendens ar·te'ri·ae' cir'cum·flex'ae' fem'o·ris lat'er·a'lis

—— descendens arteriae oc·cip'i·ta'lis

—— descendens arteriae trans·ver'sae col'li'

—— descendens cer'vi·cis

—— descendens hy'po·glos'si'

—— descendens ner'vi' hy'po·glos'si'

—— descendens posterior ar·te'ri·ae' cor'o·nar'i·ae' cordis dex'trae'

—— dex'ter ar·te'ri·ae' he·pat'i·cae' pro'pri·ae'

—— dexter arteriae pul'mo·na'lis

—— dexter ve'nae' por'tae'

—— di·gas'tri·cus ner'vi' fa'ci·a'lis

—— dor·sa'lis ar·te'ri·ae' sub'cos·ta'lis

—— dorsalis ar·te'ri·ar'um in'ter·cos·ta'li·um pos·te'ri·o'rum (III–XI)

—— dorsalis arteriarum lum·ba'li·um

—— dorsalis ma'nus ner'vi' ul·nar'is

—— dorsalis ner'vi' coc·cyg'e·i'

—— dorsalis nervi ul·nar'is

—— dorsalis ner·vo'rum spi·na'li·um

—— dorsalis ve·nar'um in'ter·cos·ta'li·um

—— dorsalis venarum intercostalium pos·te'ri·o'rum (IV–XI)

—— ex·ter'nus ner'vi' ac'ces·so'ri·i'

—— externus nervi la·ryn'ge·i' su·pe'ri·o'ris

—— fem'o·ra'lis ner'vi' gen'i·to·fem'o·ra'lis

—— fib'u·lar'is ar·te'ri·ae' tib'i·a'lis pos·te'ri·o'ris

—— fron·ta'lis ar·te'ri·ae' me·nin'ge·ae' me'di·ae'

—— frontalis arteriae tem'po·ra'lis su'per·fi'ci·a'lis

—— frontalis ner'vi' fron·ta'lis

—— gen'i·ta'lis ner'vi' gen'i·to·fem'o·ra'lis

—— hy·oi'de·us ar·te'ri·ae' lin·gua'lis

—— hyoideus arteriae thy're·oi'de·ae' su·pe'ri·o'ris

—— i·li'a·cus ar·te'ri·ae' il'i·o·lum·ba'lis

—— inferior ar·te'ri·ae' glu'tae·ae' su·pe'ri·o'ris

—— inferior arteriae glu'te·ae' su·pe'ri·o'ris

—— inferior ner'vi' oc'u·lo·mo·to'ri·i'

—— inferior os'sis is'chi·i'

—— inferior ossis pu'bis

—— in'fra·hy·oi'de·us ar·te'ri·ae' thy·roi'de·ae' su·pe'ri·o'ris

—— in'fra·pat'el·lar'is ner'vi' sa·phe'ni'

—— in·ter'nus ner'vi' ac'ces·so'ri·i'

—— internus nervi la·ryn'ge·i' su·pe'ri·o'ris

—— in'ter·ven·tric'u·lar'is anterior ar·te'ri·ae' co'ro·nar'i·ae' si·nis'trae'

—— interventricularis posterior arteriae coronariae dex'trae'

—— lat'er·a'lis ar·te'ri·ae' pul'mo·na'lis dex'trae'

—— lateralis duc'tus he·pat'i·ci' si·nis'tri'

—— lateralis ner'vi' su'pra·or'bi·ta'lis

—— lateralis ra'mi' pos·te'ri·o'ris ner·vo'rum cer'vi·ca'li·um

—— lateralis rami posterioris nervorum lum·ba'li·um

—— lateralis rami posteri-

oris nervorum sa·cra'li·um
et ner'vi' coc·cyg'e·i'
—— lateralis ra·mo'rum
dor·sa'li·um ner·vo'rum
cer·vi·ca'li·um
—— lateralis ramorum dorsalium nervorum lum·ba'li·um
—— lateralis ramorum dorsalium nervorum sa·cra'li·um et ner'vi' coc·cyg'e·i'
—— lin·gua'lis ner'vi' fa·ci·a'lis
—— lin'gu·lar'is ar·te'ri·ae' pul'mo·na'lis si·nis'trae'
—— lingularis inferior arteriae pulmonalis sinistrae
—— lingularis superior arteriae pulmonalis sinistrae
—— lingularis ve'nae' pul'mo·na'lis su·pe'ri·o'ris si·nis'trae'
—— lo'bi' me'di·i' ar·te'ri·ae' pul'mo·na'lis dex'trae'
—— lobi medii ve'nae' pul'mo·na'lis su·pe'ri·o'ris dex'trae'
—— lum·ba'lis ar·te'ri·ae' il'i·o·lum·ba'lis
—— man·dib'u·lae'
—— mar'gi·na'lis man·dib'u·lae' ner'vi' fa·ci·a'lis
—— mas·toi'de·us ar·te'ri·ae' oc·cip'i·ta'lis
—— me'di·a'lis ar·te'ri·ae' pul'mo·na'lis dex'trae'
—— medialis duc'tus he·pat'i·ci' si·nis'tri'
—— medialis ner'vi' su'pra·or'bi·ta'lis
—— medialis ra'mi' pos·te'ri·o'ris ner·vo'rum cer'vi·ca'li·um
—— medialis rami posterioris nervorum lum·ba'li·um
—— medialis rami posterioris nervorum sa·cra'li·um et ner'vi' coc·cyg'e·i'
—— medialis ra·mo'rum dor·sa'li·um ner·vo'rum cer'vi·ca'li·um
—— medialis ramorum dorsalium nervorum lum·ba'li·um
—— medialis ramorum dor-

salium nervorum sa·cra'li·um et ner'vi' coc·cyg'e·i'
—— mem·bra'nae' tym'pa·ni' ner'vi' au·ric'u·lo·tem'po·ra'lis
—— membrane tympani nervi me·a'tus au'di·to'ri·i' ex·ter'nae'
—— me·nin'ge·us ac'ces·so'ri·us ar·te'ri·ae' max·il'lae'
—— meningeus ar·te'ri·ae' oc·cip'i·ta'lis
—— meningeus arteriae ver'te·bra'lis
—— meningeus me'di·us ner'vi' max'il·lar'is
—— meningeus ner'vi' man·dib'u·lar'is
—— meningeus nervi spi·na'lis
—— meningeus nervi va·gi'
—— meningeus ner·vo'rum spi·na'li·um
—— mus'cu·lar'is
—— mus'cu·li' sty'lo·pha·ryn'ge·i' ner'vi' glos'so·pha·ryn'ge·i'
—— my'lo·hy·oi'de·us ar·te'ri·ae' al've·o·lar'is in·fe'ri·o'ris
—— mylohyoideus arteriae max'il·lar'is in·ter'nae'
—— na·sa'lis ex·ter'nus ner'vi' eth'moi·da'lis an·te'ri·o'ris
—— ob'tu·ra·to'ri·us ar·te'ri·ae' ep'i·gas'tri·cae' in·fe'ri·o'ris
—— oc·cip'i·ta'lis ar·te'ri·ae' au·ric'u·lar'is pos·te'ri·o'ris
—— occipitalis ner'vi' au·ric'u·lar'is pos·te'ri·o'ris
—— os'sis is'chi·i'
—— o·var'i·cus ar·te'ri·ae' u'ter·i'nae'
—— o·var'i·i' ar·te'ri·ae' u'ter·i'nae'
—— pal·mar'is ner'vi' me'di·a'ni'
—— palmaris nervi ul·nar'is
—— palmaris pro·fun'dus ar·te'ri·ae' ul·nar'is
—— palmaris su'per·fi·ci·a'lis ar·te'ri·ae' ra'di·a'lis
—— pal'pe·bra'lis inferior ner'vi' in'fra·troch'le·ar'is

—— palpebralis ner'vi' in'fra·troch'le·ar'is
—— palpebralis superior nervi infratrochlearis
—— pa·ri·e·ta'lis ar·te'ri·ae' me·nin'ge·ae' me'di·ae'
—— parietalis arteriae tem'po·ra'lis su'per·fi·ci·a'lis
—— pa·ri'e·to·oc·cip'i·ta'lis ar·te'ri·ae'cer'e·bri' pos·te'ri·o'ris
—— per'fo·rans' ar·te'ri·ae' fib'u·lar'is
—— perforans arteriae per·o'nae·ae'
—— perforans arteriae per·o'ne'ae'
—— per'i·car·di'a·cus ner'vi' phren'i·ci'
—— pe·tro'sus ar·te'ri·ae' me·nin'ge·ae' me'de·ae'
—— petrosus su'per·fi·ci·a'lis ar·te'ri·ae' me·nin'ge·ae' me'di·ae'
—— pha·ryn'ge·us gan'gli·i' pter'·go·pal·a·ti'ni'
—— plan·tar'is pro·fun'dus ar·te'ri·ae' dor·sa'lis ped'is
—— posterior ar·te'ri·ae' ob'tu·ra·to'ri·ae'
—— posterior arteriae pul'mo·na'lis si·nis'trae'
—— posterior arteriae rec'ur·ren'tis ul·nar'is
—— posterior arteriae re·na'lis
—— posterior arteriae thy're·oi'de·ae' su·pe'ri·o'ris
—— posterior arteriae thy·roi'de·ae' su·pe'ri·o'ris
—— posterior as·cen'dens' ar·te'ri·ae' pul'mo·na'lis dex'trae'
—— posterior de·scen'dens' ar·te'ri·ae' pul'mo·na'lis dex'trae'
—— posterior duc'tus he·pat'i·ci' dex'tri'
—— posterior fis·su'rae' cer'e·bri' lat'er·a'lis
—— posterior ner'vi' au·ric'u·lar'is mag'ni'
—— posterior nervi coc·cyg'e·i'
—— posterior nervi la·ryn'ge·i' in·fe'ri·o'ris

—— posterior nervi ob'tu·ra·to'ri·i'

—— posterior nervi spi·na'lis

—— posterior ra'mi' cu·ta'ne·i' lat'er·a'lis ner'vi' in'ter·cos·ta'lis

—— posterior rami cutanei lateralis (pec'to·ra'les' et ab·dom'i·na'les') ra·mo'rum an·te'ri·o'rum ar·te'ri·ar'um in'ter·cos·ta'li·um

—— posterior sul'ci' lat'er·a'lis cer'e·bri'

—— posterior ve'nae' pul'mo·na'lis su·pe'ri·o'ris dex'trae'

—— pro·fun'dus ar·te'ri·ae' cer'vi·ca'lis as·cen·den'tis

—— profundus arteriae cir·cum·flex'ae' fem'o·ris me'di·a'lis

—— profundus arteriae glu·te·ae' su·pe'ri·o'ris

—— profundus arteriae plan·tar'is me'di·a'lis

—— profundus arteriae trans·ver'sae' col'li'

—— profundus ner'vi' plan·tar'is lat'er·a'lis

—— profundus nervi ra'di·a'lis

—— profundus nervi ul·nar'is

—— profundus ra'mi' vo·lar'is ma'nus ner'vi' ul·nar'is

—— pu'bi·cus ar·te'ri·ae' ep'i·gas'tri·cae' in·fe'ri·o'ris

—— pubicus arteriae ob'tu·ra·to'ri·ae'

—— re·na'lis ner'vi' splanch'ni·ci' mi·no'ris

—— sa·phe'nus ar·te'ri·ae' ge'nus de·scen'dens

—— saphenus arteriae ge'nu su·pre'mae'

—— si·nis'ter ar·te'ri·ae' he·pat'i·cae' pro'pri·ae'

—— sinister arteriae pul'mo·na'lis

—— sinister ve'nae' por'tae'

—— si'nus ca·rot'i·ci' ner'vi' glos'so·pha·ryn'ge·i'

—— spi·na'lis ar·te'ri·ae' il'i·o·lum·ba'lis

—— spinalis arteriae sub'cos·ta'lis

—— spinalis ar·te'ri·ar'um lum·ba'li·um

—— spinalis ra'mi' dor·sa'lis ar·te'ri·ar'um in'ter·cos·ta'li·um pos·te'ri·o'rum (III–XI)

—— spinalis rami pos·te'ri·o'ris ar·te'ri·ae' in'ter·cos·ta'lis

—— spinalis ve·nar'um in'ter·cos·ta'li·um

—— spinalis venarum inter·costalium pos·te'ri·o'rum (IV–XI)

—— sta·pe'di·us ar·te'ri·ae' sty'lo·mas·toi'de·ae'

—— ster'no·clei'do·mas·toi'de·us ar·te'ri·ae' thy're·oi'de·ae' su·pe'ri·o'ris

—— sternocleidomastoideus arteriae thy·roi'de·ae' su·pe'ri·o'ris

—— sty'lo·hy·oi'de·us ner'vi' fa'ci·a'lis

—— sty'lo·pha·ryn'ge·us ner'vi' glos'so·pha·ryn'ge·i'

—— sub·ap'i·ca'lis ar·te'ri·ae' pul'mo·na'lis dex'trae'

—— subapicalis arteriae pulmonalis si·nis'trae'

—— sub·su·pe'ri·or ar·te'ri·ae' pul'mo·na'lis dex'trae'

—— subsuperior arteriae pulmonalis si·nis'trae'

—— su'per·fi'ci·a'lis ar·te'ri·ae' cir'cum·flex'ae' fem'o·ris me'di·a'lis

—— superficialis arteriae glu·te·ae' su·pe'ri·o'ris

—— superficialis arteriae plan·tar'is me'di·a'lis

—— superficialis arteriae trans·ver'sae' col'li

—— superficialis ner'vi' plan·tar'is lat'er·a'lis

—— superficialis nervi ra'di·a'lis

—— superficialis nervi ul·nar'is

—— superficialis ra'mi' vo·lar'is ma'nus ner'vi' ul·nar'is

—— superior ar·te'ri·ae' glu·te·ae' su·pe'ri·o'ris

—— superior lo'bi' in·fe'ri·o'ris ar·te'ri·ae' pul'mo·na'lis dex'trae'

—— superior lobi inferioris

arteriae pulmonalis si·nis'trae'

—— superior ner'vi' oc'u·lo·mo·to'ri·i'

—— superior os'sis is'chi·i'

—— superior ossis pu'bis

—— superior ve'nae' pul'mo·na'lis in·fe'ri·o'ris dex'trae'

—— superior venae pulmonalis inferioris si·nis'trae'

—— su'pra·hy·oi'de·us ar·te'ri·ae' lin·gua'lis

—— sym·path'i·cus ad gan'gli·on' cil'i·ar'e'

—— sympathicus ad ganglion sub·man·dib'u·lar'e'

—— ten·to'ri·i' ner'vi' oph·thal·mi·ci'

—— thy're·o·hy·oi'de·us ner'vi' hy'po·glos'si'

—— thy'ro·hy·oi'de·us an'·sae' cer'vi·ca'lis

—— ton'sil·lar'is ar·te'ri·ae' fa'ci·a'lis

—— tonsillaris arteriae max'il·lar'is ex·ter'nae'

—— trans·ver'sus ar·te'ri·ae' cir'cum·flex'ae' fem'o·ris lat'er·a'lis

—— transversus arteriae circumflexae femoris me'di·a'lis

—— tu'bae' plex'us tym·pan'i·ci'

—— tu·bar'i·us ar·te'ri·ae' u'ter·i'nae'

—— tubarius plex'us tym·pan'i·ci'

—— ul·nar'is ner'vi' cu·ta'ne·i' an'te·bra·chi·i' me'di·a'lis

—— ven·tra'lis ner·vo'rum spi·na'li·um

—— vo·lar'is ma'nus ner'vi' ul·nar'is

—— volaris ner'vi' cu·ta'·ne·i' an'ti·bra·chi·i' me'di·a'lis

—— volaris pro·fun'dus ar·te'ri·ae' ul·nar'is

—— volaris su'per·fi'ci·a'lis ar·te'ri·ae' ra·di·a'lis

—— zy'go·mat'i·co·fa'ci·a'lis ner'vi' zy'go·mat'i·ci'

—— zy'go·mat'i·co·tem'po·ra'lis ner'vi' zy'go·mat'i·ci'

ran'cid
range, ranged, rang'ing
ra·ni·my'cin
ra'nine'
Ran'ke
—— hypothesis
—— theory
Ran'kin operation
ran'u·la
ran'u·lar
Ran·vier' node
Ra·oult' law
rape, raped, rap'ing
ra·pha'ni·a
raph'a·nin
ra'phe'
—— inferior cor'po·ris cal·lo'si'
—— me·dul'lae' ob'long·ga'tae'
—— pa·la'ti'
—— palati du'ri'
—— pal'pe·bra'lis lat'er·a'lis
—— pe'nis
—— per'i·ne'i'
—— pha·ryn'gis
—— pon'tis
—— post'ob·lon·ga'ta
—— pter'y·go·man·dib'u·lar'is
—— scro'ti'
—— superior cor'po·ris cal·lo'si'
rap·port'
rap'tus pl. -ti'
—— haem'or·rha'gi·cus
—— ma·ni'a·cus
—— mel'an·chol'i·cus
—— ner·vo'rum
rar'e·fac'tion
rar'e·fy', -fied', -fy'ing
ra'ri·tas
rash
ra'sion
Ras'mus'sen aneurysm
ras'pa·to'ry
RAST test
rate, rat'ed, rat'ing
Rath'ke
—— duct
—— pouch
ra'ti·o'
ra'tion
ra'tion·al
ra'tio·nale'
ra'tion·al·i·za'tion
ra'tion·al·ize', -ized', -iz'ing

rat'tle, -tled, -tling
rat'tle-snake'
Rau'ber cell
rau·ce'do
rau·wol'fi·a
rau·wol'fine'
Ra·va·ton'
—— amputation
—— method
ray
Ray mania
Ray·mond'-Ces·tan' syndrome
Ray·mond' syndrome
Ray·naud'
—— disease
—— phenomenon
rays of Sa·gnac'
re'ac·quired'
re·ac'tant
re·ac'tion
re·ac'ti·vate', -vat'ed, -vat'ing
re·ac'ti·va'tion
re·ac'tive
re'ac·tiv'i·ty
re·ac'tor
re·a'gent
re·a'gin
re'a·gin'ic
ream'er
re·am'i·na'tion
re·am'pu·ta'tion
re·an'i·mate', -mat'ed, -mat'ing
re'at·tach'ment
Ré·au·mur' scale
re'bound' n.
re·bound' v.
re·breath'ing
re·cal'ci·fi·ca'tion
re·cal'ci·fy', -fied', -fy'ing
re·cal'ci·trant
re'call'
re'ca·pit'u·la'tion
re'cep·tac'u·lum pl. -la
—— chy'li'
re·cep'tive
re·cep'tor
re'cess'
—— of Tröltsch
re·ces'sion
re·ces'sive
re·ces'sus pl. re·ces'sus
—— anterior fos'sae' in'ter·pe·dun'cu·lar'is
—— coch'le·ar'is ves·tib'u·li'

—— cos'to·di·a·phrag·mat'i·cus pleu'rae'
—— cos'to·me'di·as'ti·na'lis pleu'rae'
—— du'o·de·na'lis inferior
—— duodenalis superior
—— du'o·de·no·je'ju·na'lis
—— el·lip'ti·cus ves·tib'u·li'
—— ep'i·tym·pan'i·cus
—— hep'a·to·re·na'lis
—— il'e·o·cae·ca'lis inferior
—— ileocaecalis superior
—— il'e·o·ce·ca'lis inferior
—— ileocecalis superior
—— inferior o'men·ta'lis
—— in'fun·dib'u·li'
—— in'ter·sig·moi'de·us
—— lat'er·a'lis fos'sae'
rhom·boi'de·ae'
—— lateralis ven·tric'u·li quar'ti'
—— li'e·na'lis
—— mem·bra'nae' tym'pa·ni' anterior
—— membranae tympani posterior
—— membranae tympani superior
—— op'ti·cus
—— par'a·co'li·ci'
—— par'a·du'o·de·na'lis
—— pha·ryn'ge·us
—— phren'i·co·he·pat'i·ci'
—— pin'e·a'lis
—— pir'i·for'mis
—— pleu·ra'les'
—— posterior fos'sae' in'ter·pe·dun'cu·lar'is
—— ret'ro·cae·ca'lis
—— ret'ro·ce·ca'lis
—— ret'ro·du'o·de·na'lis
—— sac'ci·for'mis ar·tic'u·la'ti·o'nis cu'bi·ti'
—— sacciformis articulationis ra'di·o·ul·nar'is dis·ta'lis
—— sphae'ri·cus
—— sphe'no·eth'moi·da'lis
—— sphe'ri·cus ves·tib'u·li'
—— sub'he·pat'i·ci'
—— sub·phren'i·ci'
—— sub·pop·lit'e·us
—— superior o'men·ta'lis
—— su'pra·pin'e·a'lis
—— tri·an'gu·lar'is
re·cid'i·va'tion
re·cid'i·vism

re·cid'i·vist
rec'i·div'i·ty
rec'i·pe
re·cip'i·ent
re·cip'i·o·mo'tor
re·cip'ro·cal
re·cip'ro·ca'tion
rec'i·proc'i·ty
Reck'ling·hau'sen disease
rec'li·na'ti·o'
rec'li·na'tion
Re·clus' disease
re'coil' n.
re·coil' v.
re·com'bi·nant
re·com'bi·na'tion
re·com'po·si'tion
re'com·pres'sion
re'con·stit'u·ent
re'con·sti·tu'tion
re'con·struc'tion
re'con·struc'tive
re·con'tour'
rec'ord n.
re·cord' v.
re·cov'er·y
rec're·ment
rec're·men'tal
rec're·men·ti'tial
rec're·men·ti'tious
re'cru·des'cence
re'cru·des'cent
re·cruit'ment
rec'tal
rec·tal'gi·a
rec·tec'to·my
rec'ti·fi·ca'tion
rec'ti·fy', -fied', -fy'ing
rec·ti·lin'e·ar
rec·ti'tis
rec'to·ab·dom'i·nal
rec'to·a'nal
rec'to·cele'
rec·toc'ly·sis pl. -ses'
rec'to·coc·cyg'e·al
rec'to·coc·cyg'e·us pl. -e·i'
rec'to·co·li'tis
rec'to·co·lon'ic
rec'to·cu·ta'ne·ous
rec'to·cys·tot'o·my
rec'to·fis'tu·la
rec'to·gen'i·tal
rec'to·la'bi·al
rec'to·per'i·ne'al
rec'to·per'i·ne·or·rha·phy
rec'to·pex'y
rec'to·plas'ty

rec'to·rec·tos'to·my
rec'tor'rha·py
rec'to·scope'
rec'tos'co·py
rec'to·sig'moid'
rec'to·sig'moi·dec'to·my
rec'to·sig'moi·dos'co·py
rec'to·ste·no'sis pl. -ses'
rec'to·tome'
rec'tos'to·my
rec'tot'o·my
rec'to·u·re'thral
rec'to·u're·thra'lis
rec'to·u'ter·ine
rec'to·vag'i·nal
rec'to·vag'i·no·ab·dom'i·
  nal
rec'to·ves'i·cal
rec'to·ves'i·ca'lis
rec'to·ves·tib'u·lar
rec'to·vul'var
rec'tum pl. -tums or -ta
rec'tus
—— ab·dom'i·nis
—— ac'ces·so'ri·us
re·cum'ben·cy
re·cum'bent
re·cu'per·ate', -at'ed, -at'ing
re·cu'per·a'tion
re·cu'per·a·tive
re·cur', -curred', -cur'ring
re·cur'rence
re·cur'rent
re'cur·va'tion
re·dif'fer·en'ti·a'tion
re·din'te·gra'tion
red'out'
re'dox'
re·dresse'ment
re·duce', -duced', -duc'ing
re·duc'i·ble
re·duc'tant
re·duc'tase'
re·duc'tion
re·dun'dan·cy
re·dun'dant
re·du'pli·cate', -cat'ed, -cat'-
  ing
re·du'pli·ca'tion
re·du'vi·id
Red'u·vi'i·dae'
Re·du'vi·us
—— per'so·na'tus
Reed'-Stern'berg' cell
re·ed'u·ca'tion
reef
reef'ing

Reen·stier'na
—— reaction
—— test
re·en'try
re·ep'i·the'li·al·i·za'tion
re·ep'i·the'li·al·ize', -ized',
  -iz'ing
Rees and Eck'er fluid
re·ev'o·lu'tion
re'ex·cise', -cised', -cis'ing
re'ex·ci·ta'tion
re'ex·pand'
re·fect'
re·fec'tion
re·fer', -ferred', -fer'ring
re·fine', -fined', -fin'ing
re·flect'
re·flec'tance
re·flect'ed
re·flec'tion
re·flec'tor
re'flex'
re·flex'i·o'
—— pal'pe·brar'um
re·flex'o·gen'ic
re·flex'o·graph'
re'flex·om'e·ter
re'flux'
re·fract'
re·frac'ta do'si'
re·frac'tile
re·frac'tion
re·frac'tion·ist
re·frac'tive
re'frac·tiv'i·ty
re'frac·tom'e·ter
re'frac·tom'e·try
re·frac'tor
re·frac'to·ry
re·frac'ture, -tured, -tur·ing
re·fran'gi·bil'i·ty
re·fran'gi·ble
re·fresh'
re·frig'er·ant
re·frig'er·a'tion
re·frin'gent
Ref'sum
—— disease
—— syndrome
re·fu'sion
re·gain'er
Re·gaud'
—— fixing fluid
—— stain
re'gel
re·gen'er·a·ble
re·gen'er·ate', -at'ed, -at'ing

re·gen'er·a'tion
re·gen'er·a·tive
reg'i·men
re'gi·o' pl. re'gi·o·nes'
—— ab·dom'i·na'lis lat'er·a'lis
—— a·cro'mi·a'lis
—— a·na'lis
—— an'te·bra'chi·i' anterior
—— antebrachii posterior
—— an'ti·bra'chi·i' dor·sa'lis
—— antibrachii ra'di·a'lis
—— antibrachii ul·nar'is
—— antibrachii vo·lar'is
—— au·ric'u·lar'is
—— ax'il·lar'is
—— bra'chi·i' anterior
—— brachii lat'er·a'lis
—— brachii me'di·a'lis
—— brachii posterior
—— buc·ca'lis
—— cal·ca'ne·a
—— cla·vic'u·lar'is
—— col'li' anterior
—— colli lat'er·a'lis
—— colli posterior
—— cos·ta'lis lat'er·a'lis
—— cox'ae'
—— cru'ris anterior
—— cruris lat'er·a'lis
—— cruris me'di·a'lis
—— cruris posterior
—— cu'bi·ti' anterior
—— cubiti lat'er·a'lis
—— cubiti me'di·a'lis
—— cubiti posterior
—— del·toi'de·a
—— dor·sa'lis ma'nus
—— dorsalis pe'dis
—— ep'i·gas'tri·ca
—— fem'o·ris anterior
—— femoris lat'er·a'lis
—— femoris me'di·a'lis
—— femoris posterior
—— fron·ta'lis
—— ge'nu anterior
—— genu posterior
—— ge'nus anterior
—— genus posterior
—— glu'tae·a
—— glu'te·a
—— hy·oi'de·a
—— hy'po·chon·dri'a·ca
—— hypochondriaca (dex'-tra et si·nis'tra)
—— hy'po·gas'tri·ca
—— in'fra·cla·vic'u·lar'is

—— in'fra·mam·ma'lis
—— in'fra·or·bi·ta'lis
—— in'fra·scap'u·lar'is
—— in'fra·tem'po·ra'lis
—— in'gui·na'lis
—— inguinalis (dex'tra et si·nis'tra)
—— in'ter·scap'u·lar'is
—— la·bi·a'lis inferior
—— labialis superior
—— la·ryn'ge·a
—— lat'er·a'lis ab·dom'i·nis (dex'tra et si·nis'tra)
—— lum·ba'lis
—— mal'le·o·lar'is lat'er·a'lis
—— malleolaris me'di·a'lis
—— mam·ma'lis
—— mam·mar'i·a
—— ma·stoi'de·a
—— me'di·a'na dor'si'
—— men·ta'lis
—— mes·o·gas'tri·ca
—— na·sa'lis
—— nu'chae'
—— oc·cip'i·ta'lis
—— o'le·cra'ni'
—— ol'fac·to'ri·a
—— olfactoria tu'ni·cae' mu·co'sae' na'si'
—— o·ra'lis
—— or·bi·ta'lis
—— pal'pe·bra'lis inferior
—— palpebralis superior
—— pa·ri·e·ta'lis
—— par'o·tid'e·o·mas'se·ter'i·ca
—— pat'el·lar'is
—— pec'to·ris anterior
—— pectoris lat'er·a'lis
—— per'i·ne·a'lis
—— plan·tar'is pe'dis
—— pu'bi·ca
—— pu'den·da'lis
—— re·spi'ra·to'ri·a
—— ret'ro·mal'le·o·lar'is lat'er·a'lis
—— retromalleolaris me'di·a'lis
—— sa·cra'lis
—— scap'u·lar'is
—— ster·na'lis
—— ster'no·clei'do·mas·toi'de·a
—— sub·hy·oi'de·a
—— sub·max'il·lar'is
—— sub·men·ta'lis
—— su'pra·or·bi·ta'lis

—— su'pra·scap'u·lar'is
—— su'pra·ster·na'lis
—— su·ra'lis
—— tem'po·ra'lis
—— thy're·oi'de·a
—— tro·chan·ter'i·ca
—— um·bil'i·ca'lis
—— u'ro·gen'i·ta'lis
—— ver'te·bra'lis
—— vo·lar'is ma'nus
—— zy'go·mat'i·ca
re'gion
re'gion·al
re'gi·o'nes'
—— ab·dom'i·nis
—— cap'i·tis
—— col'li'
—— cor'po·ris
—— corporis hu·ma'ni'
—— dig'i·ta'les' ma'nus
—— digitales pe'dis
—— dor·sa'les' dig'i·to'rum
—— dorsales digitorum pe'-dis
—— dor'si'
—— ex·trem'i·ta'tis in·fe'ri·o'ris
—— extremitatis su·pe'ri·o'ris
—— fa'ci·e'i'
—— mem'bri' in·fe'ri·o'ris
—— membri su·pe'ri·o'ris
—— pec'to·ris
—— plan·tar'es' dig'i·to'rum pe'dis
—— un·guic'u·lar'es' ma'nus
—— unguiculares pe'dis
—— vo·lar'es' dig'i·to'rum
reg'is·ter
reg'is·trant
reg'is·trar'
reg'u·lar
reg'is·tra'tion
reg'is·try
re·gress'
re·gres'sion
re·gres'sive
reg'u·lar
reg'u·late', -lat'ed, -lat'ing
reg'u·la'tion
reg'u·la'tive
reg'u·la'tor
re·gur'gi·tant
re·gur'gi·tate', -tat'ed, -tat'-ing
re·gur'gi·ta'tion

re′ha·bil′i·tate′, -tat′ed, -tat′ing
re′ha·bil′i·ta′tion
re′ha·la′tion
Reh′fuss
—— method
—— tube
Rehn operation
Rei′chel duct
Rei′chert
—— cartilage
—— membrane
Reich′mann disease
Reich′stein′ substance
Reil′ly bodies
re·im′plan·ta′tion
re′in·fec′tion
re′in·force′, -forced′, -forc′-
ing
re′in·force′ment
re′in·fu′sion
re·in′ner·va′tion
re′in·oc′u·late′, -lat′ed, -lat′-
ing
re′in·oc′u·la′tion
re·in′te·gra′tion
re′in·tu·ba′tion
re′in·ver′sion
Reiss′ner membrane
Rei′ter syndrome
re·jec′tion
re·ju′ve·nes′cence
re·lapse′, -lapsed′, -laps′ing
re·late′, -lat′ed, -lat′ing
re·la′tion
re·la′tion·al
rel′a·tive
re·lax′
re·lax′ant
re·lax·a′tion
re·lax′in
re·lease′
re·lief′
re·lieve′, -lieved′, -liev′ing
Re′mak′
—— band
—— fibers
—— ganglion
—— reflex
re·me′di·al
rem′e·dy
re·min′er·al·i·za′tion
re·mis′sion
re·mit′tence
re·mit′tent
rem′nant
re·mote′

ren pl. re′nes′
—— mo′bi·lis
—— un′gui·for′mis
re′nal
—— os·te·i′tis fi·bro′sa
gen′er·al′i·sa′ta
Ren·du′-Os′ler-Web′er disease
Ren·du′ tremor
ren′i·cap′sule
re·nic′u·lus pl. -li′
ren′i·form′
re′nin
re′ni·punc′ture
re′no·cor′ti·cal
re′no·cu·ta′ne·ous
re′no·gram′
re·nog′ra·phy
re′no·in·tes′ti·nal
Ré·non′-De·lille′ syn-
drome
re·nop′a·thy
re′no·pri′val
re′no·tro′phic
re′no·vas′cu·lar
Ren′shaw′ cell
re′o·vi′rus
re·ox′i·da′tion
re·pair′
re·par′a·tive
re·pa′ten·cy
re·pel′lent
re·pel′ler
re·per′co·la′tion
re′per·cus′sion
re′per·cus′sive
re·pe·ta′tur
re·place′ment
re′plan·ta′tion
re·plete′
re·ple′tion
rep′li·cate′, -cat′ed, -cat′ing
rep′li·ca′tion
re·po′lar·i·za′tion
re·port′
re′po·si′tion
re·pos′i·tor
re·pos′i·to′ry
re·pres′sion
re·pres′sor
re′pro·duce′, -duced′, -duc′-
ing
re′pro·duc′tion
re′pro·duc′tive
re·pul′sion
res·az′u·rin
res·cin′na·mine′

re·sect′
re·sec′tion
re·sec′to·scope′
re·ser′pine′
re·serve′, -served′, -serv′ing
res′er·voir′
res′i·dent
re·sid′u·al
res′i·due′
re·sid′u·um pl. -u·a
re·sil′ience
re·sil′ien·cy
re·sil′ient
res′in
res′in·oid′
res′in·ous
re·sis′tance
res′o·lu′tion
re·solve′, -solved′, -solv′ing
re·sol′vent
res′o·nance
res′o·nant
res′o·na′tor
re·sorb′
re·sorb′ent
re·sor′cin
re·sor′cin·ol′
re·sor′cin·ol·phthal′ein′
re·sorp′tion
re·sorp′tive
res′pi·ra·ble
res′pi·ra′tion
res′pi·ra′tor
res′pi·ra·to′ry
re·spire′, -spired′, -spir′ing
res′pi·rom′e·ter
res′pi·rom′e·try
re·sponse′
re·spon′si·bil′i·ty
rest
Res′tan fever
rest′bite′
re·ste·no′sis pl. -ses′
res′ti·bra′chi·um
res′ti·form′
res·ti·tu′ti·o′ ad in′te·grum
res·ti·tu′tion
res′to·ra′tion
re·stor′a·tive
re·store′, -stored′, -stor′ing
re·straint′
re·sul′tant
re·su′pi·nate′, -nat′ed, -nat′-
ing
re·su′pi·na′tion
re·sus′ci·tate′, -tat′ed, -tat′-
ing

re·sus′ci·ta′tion
re·sus′ci·ta′tor
re·su′ture, -tured, -tur·ing
re·tain′er
re·tar′date′
re′tar·da′tion
re·tard′ed
re·tard′er
retch
re′te′ *pl.* re′ti·a
—— a·cro′mi·a′le′
—— ar·te′ri·o′sum
—— ar·tic′u·lar′e′ cu′bi·ti′
—— articulare gen′u
—— articulare ge′nus
—— cal·ca′ne·um
—— ca·na′lis hy′po·glos′si′
—— car′pi′ dor·sa′le′
—— cu·ta′ne·um
—— dor·sa′le′ pe′dis
—— fo·ra′mi·nis o·va′lis
—— mal′le·o·lar′e′ lat′er·a′le′
—— malleolare me′di·a′le′
—— mi·ra′bi·le′
—— mu·co′sum
—— o′le·cra′ni′
—— o·var′i·i′
—— pa·tel′lae′
—— sub·pap′il·lar′e′
—— tes′tis
—— vas′cu·lo′sum
—— ve·no′sum
—— venosum dor·sa′le′ ma′-
nus
—— venosum dorsale pe′dis
—— venosum plan·tar′e′
re·ten′tion
re′te·the′li·o′ma *pl.* -mas *or*
 -ma·ta
re′ti·a
—— ve·no′sa ver′te·brar′um
re′ti·al
re·tic′u·lar
re·tic′u·late
re·tic′u·lat′ed
re·tic′u·la′tion
re·tic′u·lin
re·tic′u·li′tis
re·tic′u·lo·bul′bar
re·tic′u·lo·cyte′
re·tic′u·lo·cyt′ic
re·tic′u·lo·cy′to·pe′ni·a
re·tic′u·lo·cy·to′sis *pl.* -ses′
re·tic′u·lo·en′do·the′li·al
re·tic′u·lo·en′do·the·li·
 o′ma *pl.* -mas *or* -ma·ta

re·tic′u·lo·en′do·the′li·o′sis
 pl. -ses′
re·tic′u·lo·en′do·the′li·um
re·tic′u·lo·his′ti·o′cy·to′ma
 pl. -mas *or* -ma·ta
re·tic′u·loid′
re·tic′u·lo′ma *pl.* -mas *or*
 -ma·ta
re·tic′u·lo·pe′ni·a
re·tic′u·lo·sar·co′ma
 pl. -mas *or* -ma·ta
re·tic′u·lose′
re·tic′u·lo′sis *pl.* -ses′
re·tic′u·lo·spi′nal
re·tic′u·lo·the′li·a
re·tic′u·lo·the·li·o′ma
 pl. -mas *or* -ma·ta
re·tic′u·lo·the′li·um
re·tic′u·lum *pl.* -la
ret′i·form′
ret′i·na
ret′i·nac′u·la
—— cu′tis
—— un′guis
ret′i·nac′u·lum *pl.* -la
—— cau·da′le′
—— ex′ten·so′rum ma′nus
—— flex·o′rum ma′nus
—— lig′a·men′ti′ ar′cu·a′ti′
—— mus′cu·lo′rum ex′ten·
so′rum pe′dis in·fe′ri·us
—— musculorum extenso-
rum pedis su·pe′ri·us
—— musculorum fib′u·lar′i·
um in·fe′ri·us
—— musculorum fibularium
su·pe′ri·us
—— musculorum flex·o′rum
pe′dis
—— musculorum per′o·nae·
o′rum in·fe′ri·us
—— musculorum pero-
naeorum su·pe′ri·us
—— musculorum per′o·ne·
o′rum in·fe′ri·us
—— musculorum peroneo-
rum su·pe′ri·us
—— pa·tel′lae′ lat′er·a′le′
—— patellae me′di·a′le′
ret′i·nal
ret′i·nene′
ret′i·ni′tis
—— cir′ci·na′ta
—— cir′cum·pap′il·lar′is
—— dis′ci·for′mis
—— ex·u·da·ti′va
—— ne·phrit′i·ca

—— pig′men·to′sa
—— pro·lif′er·ans
—— punc·ta′ta al·bes′cens
—— se·ro′sa
—— sim′plex′
ret′i·no·blas·to′ma *pl.* -mas
 or -ma·ta
ret′i·no·cho′roid′
ret′i·no·cho′roid·i′tis
—— jux′ta·pap′il·lar′is
ret′i·no·cy·to′ma *pl.* -mas *or*
 -ma·ta
ret′i·no·di·al′y·sis *pl.* -ses′
ret′i·no′ic
ret′i·noid′
ret′i·nol′
ret′i·no·ma·la′ci·a
ret′i·no·pap′il·li′tis
ret′i·nop′a·thy
ret′i·no·pex′y
ret′i·nos′chi·sis *pl.* -ses′
ret′i·no·scope′
ret′i·nos′co·py
ret′i·no′sis *pl.* -ses′
ret′o·the′li·al
re′to·the′li·o′ma *pl.* -mas *or*
 -ma·ta
re′to·the′li·o·sar·co′ma
 pl. -mas *or* -ma·ta
ret′o·the′li·um
re·tract′
re·trac′tile
re′trac·til′i·ty
re·trac′tion
re·trac′tor
ret′ro·ac′tion
ret′ro·an′ter·o·grade′
ret′ro·au·ric′u·lar
ret′ro·bron′chi·al
ret′ro·buc′cal
ret′ro·bul′bar
ret′ro·cal·ca′ne·al
ret′ro·cal·ca′ne·o·bur·si′tis
ret′ro·car′di·ac′
ret′ro·ca′val
ret′ro·ce′cal
ret′ro·cele′
ret′ro·cer′vi·cal
ret′ro·ces′sion
ret′ro·chei′li·a
ret′ro·cla·vic′u·lar
ret′ro·co′lic *(behind the co-*
 lon)
♦retrocollic
ret′ro·col′lic *(pertaining to*
 the back of the neck)
♦retrocolic

ret′ro·col′lis
ret′ro·con′dy·lism
ret′ro·cru′ral
ret′ro·de·vi·a′tion
ret′ro·dis·place′ment
ret′ro·du′o·de′nal
ret′ro·e·soph′a·ge′al
ret′ro·flex′
ret′ro·flexed′
ret′ro·flex′ion
ret′ro·gas·se′ri·an
ret′ro·gnath′ism
ret′ro·grade′
re·trog′ra·phy
ret′ro·gres′sion
ret′ro·gres′sive
ret′ro·in′gui·nal
ret′ro·jec′tion
ret′ro·len′tal
ret′ro·len·tic′u·lar
ret′ro·lin′gual
ret′ro·ma′lar
ret′ro·mam′ma·ry
ret′ro·man·dib′u·lar
ret′ro·mas′toid′
ret′ro·max′il·lar′y
ret′ro·mes′en·ter′ic
ret′ro·mor′pho·sis pl. -ses′
ret′ro·na′sal
ret′ro·oc′u·lar
ret′ro·or′bi·tal
ret′ro·pa·rot′id
ret′ro·per′i·to·ne′al
ret′ro·per′i·to·ne′um pl.
 -ne′ums or -ne′a
ret′ro·per′i·to·ni′tis
ret′ro·pha·ryn′ge·al
ret′ro·phar′yn·gi′tis
ret′ro·phar′ynx
ret′ro·pla·cen′tal
ret′ro·pla′si·a
ret′ro·posed′
ret′ro·po·si′tion
ret′ro·pros·tat′ic
ret′ro·pu′bic
ret′ro·pul′sion
ret′ro·py·ram′i·dal
ret′ro·stal′sis pl. -ses′
ret′ro·ster′nal
ret′ro·tar′sal
ret′ro·ten′di·nous
ret′ro·thy′roid′
ret′ro·ton′sil·lar
ret′ro·tra′che·al
ret′ro·u′ter·ine
ret′ro·ver′si·o·flex′ion
ret′ro·ver′sion

ret′ro·vert′ed
ret′ro·ves′i·cal
re·trude′, -trud′ed, -trud′ing
re·tru′sion
Ret′zi·us
—— lines
—— striae
—— veins
re·un′ion
re·vac′ci·nate′, -nat′ed,
 -nat′ing
re·vac′ci·na′tion
re·vas′cu·lar·i·za′tion
re·vel′lent
re·ver′ber·ate′, -at′ed, -at′-
 ing
re·ver′ber·a′tion
Re·ver·din′ graft
re·ver′sal
re·verse′, -versed′, -vers′ing
re·vers′i·ble
re·ver′sion
Re·vil·liod′ sign
re·vi′tal·i·za′tion
re·vive′, -vived′, -viv′ing
re·viv′i·fi·ca′tion
rev′o·lute′
re·vul′sant
re·vul′sion
re·vul′sive
Reye syndrome
rhab′do·cyte′
rhab′doid′
rhab′do·my′o·blast′ic
rhab′do·my′o·blas·to′ma
 pl. -mas or -ma·ta
rhab′do·my·ol′y·sis pl. -ses′
rhab′do·my·o′ma pl. -mas
 or -ma·ta
—— u′ter·i′
rhab′do·my′o·sar·co′ma pl.
 -mas or -ma·ta
rha·co′ma pl. -mas or -ma·ta
rha′cous
rhag′a·des′
rha·ga′di·a
rha·gad′i·form′
rhag′i·o·crine
rhe
rhe′bo·sce′li·a
rhe′bo·sce′lic
rheg′ma
rhe′o·log′ic
rhe·ol′o·gy
rhe′o·nome′
rhe′o·stat′
rhe′os·to′sis

rhe′o·ta·chyg′ra·phy
rhe′o·tax′is pl. -tax′es′
rheum
rheu·mat′ic
rheu·ma·tism
rheu·ma·tis′mal
rheu·ma·toid′
rheu′ma·to·log′ic
rheu′ma·tol′o·gist
rheu′ma·tol′o·gy
rhex′is pl. -rhex′es′
Rh
—— factor
—— genes
rhi′nal
rhi·nal′gi·a
rhi′ne·de′ma pl. -mas or
 -ma·ta
rhi·nel′cos′
rhi′nen·ce·pha′li·a
rhin′en·ce·phal′ic
rhin′en·ceph′a·lon′ pl. -la
rhi′nen·chy′sis pl. -ses′
rhi′nes·the′si·a
rhi′neu·ryn′ter
rhin·he′ma·to′ma
rhin′i·on′
rhi′nism
rhi·ni′tis
—— sic′ca
rhi′no·an·tri′tis
rhi′no·by′on′
rhi′no·can·thec′to·my
rhi′no·ce·pha′li·a
rhi′no·ceph′a·lus pl. -li′
rhi′no·ceph′a·ly
rhi′no·chei′lo·plas′ty
rhi′no·clei′sis pl. -ses′
rhi′no·coele′
rhi′no·dac′ry·o·lith′
rhi′no·der′ma
rhi′no·dym′i·a
rhi·nod′y·mus
rhi′no·dyn′i·a
rhi·nog′e·nous
rhi′no·ky·pho′sis
rhi′no·la′li·a
—— a·per′ta
—— clau′sa
rhi′no·lar′yn·gi′tis
rhi′no·lar′yn·gol′o·gy
rhi′no·lith′
rhi′no·li·thi′a·sis pl. -ses′
rhi′no·log′ic
rhi·nol′o·gist
rhi·nol′o·gy
rhi′no·ma·nom′e·ter

rhi·nom'e·ter
rhi'no·mi·o'sis *pl.* -ses'
rhi'nom·mec'to·my
rhi'no·my·co'sis *pl.* -ses'
rhi'no·ne·cro'sis
rhi·nop'a·thy
rhi'no·pha·ryn'ge·al
rhi'no·phar'yn·gi'tis
—— mu'ti·lans'
rhi'no·pha·ryn'go·cele'
rhi'no·pha·ryn'go·lith'
rhi'no·phar'ynx *pl.* -pha·
  ryn'ges'
rhi'no·pho'ni·a
rhi'no·phy'ma
rhi'no·plas'tic
rhi'no·plas'ty
rhi'no·pneu'mo·ni'tis
rhi'no·pol'yp
rhi'no·pol'y·pus *pl.* -pi' *or*
  -pus·es
rhi·nop'si·a
rhi'nor·rha'gi·a
rhi'nor'rha·phy
rhi'nor·rhe'a
rhi'no·sal'pin·gi'tis
rhi·nos'chi·sis
rhi'no·scle·ro'ma *pl.* -ma·ta
rhi'no·scope'
rhi'no·scop'ic
rhi·nos'co·py
rhi'no·si'nu·si'tis
rhi'no·spo·rid'i·o'sis *pl.*
  -ses'
Rhi'no·spo·rid'i·um
—— see'ber·i'
rhi'no·ste·no'sis *pl.* -ses'
rhi'no·thrix'
rhi·not'o·my
rhi'no·tra'che·i'tis
rhi'no·vi'rus
Rhi'pi·ceph'a·lus
—— san·guin'e·us
rhi'zo·don'tro·py
rhi'zoid'
rhi'zome'
rhi'zo·mel'ic
rhi'zo·mor'phoid'
Rhi'zo·mu'cor'
rhi'zo·neure'
rhi'zo·nych'i·a
rhi'zo·nych'i·um
Rhi'zo·pus
—— ni'gri·cans'
rhi·zot'o·my
Rh-neg'a·tive
rho'da·mine'

Rho'din fixative
rho'do·phy·lac'tic
rho'do·phy·lax'is
rho·dop'sin
rhom'ben·ce·phal'ic
rhom'ben·ceph'a·lon'
  pl. -la
rhom'bic
rhom'bo·coele'
rhom'boid'
rhom·boi'de·us *pl.* -de·i'
—— oc·cip'i·ta'lis
rhom'bo·mere'
rhon'chal
rhon'chi·al
rhon'chus *pl.* -chi'
rho'phe·o·cy·to'sis *pl.* -ses'
Rh-pos'i·tive
rhythm
rhyth'mic
rhyth·mic'i·ty
rhyt'i·dec'tom·y
rhyt'i·do·plas'ty
rhyt'i·do'sis *pl.* -ses'
rib
ri·bam'in·ol'
rib'bon
ri'bo·des'ose'
ri'bo·fla'vin
ri'bo·nu'cle·ase'
ri'bo·nu·cle'ic
ri'bo·nu'cle·o·pro'tein'
ri'bo·nu'cle·o·side'
ri'bo·nu'cle·o·tide'
ri'bo·prine'
ri'bose'
ri'bo·side'
ri'bo·some'
Rich'ter hernia
ric'in·ism
rick'ets
rick·ett'si·a *pl.* -ae' *or* -as
Rick·ett'si·a
—— ak'a·mu'shi
—— ak'a·ri'
—— aus·tra'lis
—— bur·net'i·i'
—— co·no'ri·i'
—— di'a·po'ri·ca
—— me·loph'a·gi'
—— moo'ser·i'
—— or'i·en·ta'lis
—— pe·dic'u·li'
—— pro'wa·zek'i·i'
—— psit'ta·ci'
—— quin·ta'na
—— rick·ett'si·i'

—— ru'mi·nan'ti·um
—— si·be'ri·ca
—— tsu'tsu·ga·mu'shi
—— wol·hyn'i·ca
Rick·ett'si·a'ce·ae'
rick·ett'si·al
rick·ett'si·al·pox'
rick·ett'si·o'sis *pl.* -ses'
Ri·cord'
—— chancre
—— method
Rid'doch
—— mass reflex
—— syndrome
ri·deau'
ridge, ridged, ridg'ing
ridge'ling
Rie'del
—— disease
—— lobe
—— struma
Rie'der cell
Rie'gel test
Riehl melanosis
Ries'-Clark' operation
Ries'man
—— myocardosis
—— sign
Rieux hernia
rif'am·pin
rif'a·my'cin
Rift Val'ley fever
Ri'ga
—— aphthae
—— disease
Ri'ga-Fe'de disease
right'-eyed'
right'-foot'ed
right'-hand'ed
rig'id
ri·gid'i·tas
—— ar·tic'u·lo'rum
—— cad'a·ver'i·ca
ri·gid'i·ty
rig'or
—— mor'tis
Ri'ley-Day' syndrome
rim, rimmed, rim'ming
ri'ma *pl.* -mae'
—— cor'ne·a'lis
—— glot'ti·dis
—— o'ris
—— pal'pe·brar'um
—— pu·den'di'
—— ves·tib'u·li'
—— vul'vae'
ri·man'ta·dine'

ri'mose'
rim'u·la
ring
Ring'er
—— injection
—— lactate
—— solution
ring'worm'
Rin'ne test
ri'no·lite'
Ri·o·lan'
—— arc
—— muscle
—— ossicles
Ris'ley prism
ri·so'ri·us
ris'to·ce'tin
ri'sus
—— ca·ni'nus
—— sar·don'i·cus
Rit'gen maneuver
Rit'ter disease
Rit'ter-Val'li law
rit'u·al
ri'val·ry
Ri·val'ta test
Ri·vi'nus
—— ducts
—— gland
—— notch
ri'vus pl. -vi'
—— lac'ri·ma'lis
riz'i·form'
Rob'ert pelvis
Rob'erts
—— reagent
—— test
Rob'in·son disease
Rob'in·son-Kep'ler-Pow'er test
Rob'i·son ester
rob'o·rant
Ro·chelle' salt
Ro'cho·li·mae'a quin·ta'na
Ro'ci·o'
Rock'ley sign
Rock'y Moun'tain fever
rod
Rod'man incision
rods of Cor'ti
Roe'der·er
—— ecchymoses
—— obliquity
roent'gen
roent'gen·o·der'ma
roent'gen·o·gram'
roent'gen·o·graph'

roent'gen·o·graph'ic
roent'ge·nog'ra·phy
roent'gen·o·ky'mo·gram
roent'gen·o·ky·mog'ra·phy
roent'gen·o·log'ic
roent'ge·nol'o·gist
roent'ge·nol'o·gy
roent'gen·o·lu'cent
roent'gen·o·scope'
roent'ge·nos'co·py
roent'gen·o·ther'a·py
roe'theln
ro·flu'rane'
Ro·ger'
—— disease
—— murmur
Rohr stria
Ro'ki·tan'sky-Asch'off' si-nuses
Ro'ki·tan'sky disease
ro·lan'dic
Ro·lan'do
—— area
—— fibers
—— fissure
—— substance
ro·let'a·mide'
ro'li·cy'prine'
ro'li·tet'ra·cy'cline'
roll
roll'er
Rol'ler nucleus
Rolle'ston rule
Rol'let
—— cell
—— stroma
Rol·lett' disease
Rol·lier' method
ro'lo·dine'
Ro·ma'na sign
ro·man'o·scope'
Ro'ma·nov'sky stains
Rom'berg'
—— disease
—— sign
rom'berg·ism
Ro·mieu' reaction
ron·geur'
Rön'ne nasal step
roof
root
Ror'schach' test
ro·sa'ce·a
ro·sa'ce·i·form'
ro·sa'li·a
Rose

—— operations
—— position
—— tamponade
rose ben'gal
ro'se·in
ro·sel'la
Ro'sen·bach'
—— disease
—— law
—— sign
—— test
Ro'sen·muel'ler
—— fossa
—— gland
—— organ
Ro'sen·thal' canal
ro·se'o·la
—— cho·ler'i·ca
—— in·fan'tum
—— scar·la·ti'ni·forme'
—— syph'i·lit'i·ca
—— ty·pho'sa
—— vac·cin'i·a
ro·se'o·lous
Ro'ser sign
ro·sette'
Rose'-Waa'ler test
Ross'bach' disease
Ross bodies
Ros·so·li'mo reflex
Ros·tan' asthma
ros'trad'
ros'tral
ros'trum pl. -tra
—— cor'po·ris cal·lo'si'
—— sphe'noi·da'le'
rot, rot'ted, rot'ting
ro·tam'e·ter
ro'ta·ry
ro'tate', -tat'ed, -tat'ing
ro·ta'tion
ro'ta'tor
ro'ta·to'res'
—— spi'nae'
ro'ta·to'ri·a
ro'ta·to'ry
Ro'ta·vi'rus
Rotch sign
röteln
ro'texed'
ro·tex'ion
Roth
—— disease
—— spots
—— symptom complex
Roth'-Bern'hardt' disease
Rot'ter test

rot'u·la
rot'u·lad'
rot'u·lar
rough'age
Roug·non'-Heb'er·den dis-
ease
rou·leau' *pl.* -leaux'
round'worm'
Rous sarcoma
Rous·sy'-De·je·rine' syn-
drome
Rous·sy'-Lé·vy' disease
Roux
—— gastroenterostomy
—— operation
—— serum
Roux en Y
—— bypass
—— gastroenterostomy
—— loop
Roux'-Y'
—— anastomosis
—— bypass
—— drainage
—— gastrojejunostomy
Rown'tree-Ger'agh·ty test
rub
ru'be·fa'cient
ru'be·fac'tion
ru·bel'la
ru·bel'li·form'
ru·be'o·la
ru'be·o'sis
—— i'ri·dis
—— iridis di'a·bet'i·ca
ru'ber
ru·bes'cence
ru·bes'cent
ru·bid'i·um
ru·big'i·nous
ru'bi·jer'vine'
ru'bin
Ru'bin·stein-Tay'bi syn-
drome
Rub'in test
Rub'ner
—— laws
—— test
ru'bor
ru'bri·blast'
ru'bric
ru'bri·cyte'
ru'bri·u'ri·a
ru'bro·bul'bar
ru'bro·ol'i·var'y
ru'bro·re·tic'u·lar
ru'bro·spi'nal

ru'bro·sta'sis *pl.* -ses'
ru'bro·tha·lam'ic
ru'brum scar'la·ti'num
ruc·ta'tion
ruc'tus
—— hys·ter'i·cus
ru'di·ment
ru'di·men'ta·ry
ru'di·men'tum *pl.* -ta
—— pro·ces'sus vag'i·na'lis
Ruf·fi'ni
—— cell
—— corpuscle
—— end organ
ru'fous
ru'ga *pl.* -gae'
—— vag'i·na'les'
ru'gal
ru'gi·tus
ru'gose'
ru·gos'i·ty
rule
ru'men *pl.* -mi·na *or* -mens
ru·men·i'tis
ru'me·not'o·my
ru'mi·nant
ru'mi·nate', -nat'ed, -nat'ing
ru'mi·na'tion
ru'mi·na'tive
Rum'mo disease
rump
Rum'pel-Leede'
—— phenomenon
—— sign
—— test
run, ran, run, run'ning
Ru·otte' operation
ru'pi·a
ru'pi·al
ru'po·pho'bi·a
rup'ture, -tured, -tur·ing
rush
Rus'sell
—— bodies
—— dwarfism
—— syndrome
rust
Rust
—— disease
—— phenomenon
rut, rut'ted, rut'ting
ru'ta·my'cin
ruth'er·ford
ru'tin
ru'tin·ose'
rye
Rytz test

S

Sa'bin vaccine
Sab'ou·raud agar
sab'u·lous
sa·bur'ra
sac
sac·cade'
sac·cad'ic
sac'cate'
sac'cha·rase'
sac'cha·rate'
sac'cha·rat'ed
sac'char·eph'i·dro'sis *pl.*
-ses'
sac·char'ic
sac'cha·ride'
sac·char'i·fi·ca'tion
sac·char'i·fy', -fied', -fy'ing
sac'cha·rim'e·ter
sac'cha·rim'e·try
sac'cha·rin (*a calorie-free
sweetener*)
♦*saccharine*
sac'cha·rine (*pertaining to
sugar*)
♦*saccharin*
sac'cha·ro·bi'ose'
sac'cha·ro·ga·lac'tor·rhe'a
sac'cha·ro·lyt'ic
sac'cha·ro·met'a·bol'ic
sac'cha·ro·me·tab'o·lism
Sac'cha·ro·my'ces'
—— hom'i·nis
sac'cha·ro·my·ce'tic
sac'cha·ro·my·co'sis *pl.*
-ses'
sac'cha·ror·rhe'a
sac'cha·rose'
sac'cha·ro·su'ri·a
sac'ci·form'
sac'cu·lar
sac'cu·lat'ed
sac'cu·la'tion
sac'cule'
sac'cu·li'
—— al've·o·lar'es'
sac'cu·lo·coch'le·ar
sac'cu·lus *pl.* -li'
—— la·ryn'gis
sac'cus *pl.* -ci'
—— con'junc·ti'vae'
—— en'do·lym·phat'i·cus
—— lac'ri·ma'lis
—— om'pha·lo·en·ter'i·cus
—— vag'i·na'lis

Sachs disease
Sachs'-Geor'gi test
sa·crad'
sa·cral
sa·cral'gi·a
sa·cral·i·za'tion
sa·cral·ize', -ized', -iz'ing
sa·crec'to·my
sa·cro·an·te'ri·or
sa·cro·coc·cyg'e·al
sa·cro·coc·cyg'e·us pl. -e·i'
—— dor·sa'lis
—— ven·tra'lis
sa·cro·coc'cyx pl. -cy·ges' or
-cyx·es
sa·cro·cox·al'gi·a
sa·cro·cox·i'tis
sa·cro·dyn'i·a
sa·cro·gen'i·tal
sa·cro·il'i·ac'
sa·cro·il'i·i'tis
sa·cro·lis·the'sis
sa·cro·lum·ba'lis
sa·cro·lum'bar
sa·cro·per'i·ne'al
sa·cro·pos·te'ri·or
sa·cro·prom'on·to'ry
sa·cro·pu'bic
sa·cro·sci·at'ic
sa·cro·spi·na'lis
sa·cro·spi'nous
sa·cro·trans·verse'
sa·cro·tu'ber·ous
sa·cro·u'ter·ine
sa·cro·ver'te·bral
sa'crum pl. -cra
sac'to·sal'pinx pl. -sal·
pin'ges'
sad'dle
sad'dle·back'
sa'dism
sa'dist
sa·dis'tic
sa·do·mas'o·chism
sa·do·mas'o·chis'tic
sa'fu
sag'it·tal
sag'it·ta'lis
Sag·nac' rays
Sah'li
—— method
—— test
Sak'el method
sal
—— am·mo'ni·ac'
sal·eth'a·mide'
sal'i·cin

sal'i·cyl
sal'i·cyl·am'ide'
sal'i·cyl·an'i·lide'
sa·lic'yl·ase'
sa·lic'y·late'
sal'i·cyl·a'zo·sul'fa·pyr'i·
dine'
sal'i·cy·le'mi·a
sal'i·cyl'ic
sal'i·cyl·ism
sal'i·cyl·u'ric
sa·lic'y·lyl
sal'i·fi'a·ble
sal'i·fy', -fied', -fy'ing
sa·lim'e·ter
sa'line'
sa·li'va
sal'i·vant
sal'i·var'y
sal'i·vate', -vat'ed, -vat'ing
sal'i·va'tion
sal'i·va'tor
sal'i·va·to'ry
sal'i·vo·li·thi'a·sis pl. -ses'
sa·li'vous
Salk vaccine
Sal'mo·nel'la
—— a·bor'ti·vo·e·qui'na
—— aer'try·cke
—— chol'e·rae·su'is
—— en'ter·it'i·dis
—— hirsch·fel'di·i'
—— o·ra'ni·en·burg'
—— par'a·ty'phi'
—— par'a·ty·pho'sa
—— schott·mül'ler·i'
—— su'i·pes'ti·fer
—— ty'phi'
—— ty'phi·mu'ri·um
—— ty·pho'sa
Sal'mo·nel'le·ae'
sal'mo·nel·lo'sis pl. -ses'
sal'ol'
sal·pin'ge·al
sal'pin·gec'to·my
sal'pin·gem·phrax'is
sal·pin'gi·an
sal·pin'gi·on'
sal·pin'git·ic
sal·pin·gi'tis
sal·pin·go·cath'e·ter·ism
sal·pin'go·cele'
sal·pin'go·cy·e'sis pl. -ses'
sal·pin'go·gram'
sal·pin·gog'ra·phy
sal·pin'go·li·thi'a·sis pl.
-ses'

sal'pin·gol'y·sis
sal·pin'go-o'o·pho·rec'to·
my
sal·pin'go-o'o·pho·ri'tis
sal·pin'go-o·oph'o·ro·cele'
sal·pin'go-o'o·the·cec'to·
my
sal·pin'go-o'o·the·ci'tis
sal·pin'go-o'o'o·the·co·
cele'
sal·pin'go·o·var'i·ec'to·my
sal·pin'go·o·var'i·ot'o·my
sal·pin'go·o'va·ri'tis
sal·pin'go·pal'a·tine'
sal·pin'go·per'i·to·ni'tis
sal·pin'go·pex'y
sal·pin'go·pha·ryn'ge·al
sal·pin'go·pha·ryn'ge·us
sal·pin'go·plas'ty
sal'pin·gor'rha·phy
sal·pin'go·sal'pin·gos'to·
my
sal·pin'go·scope'
sal·pin'gos'co·py
sal·pin'go·sten·o'cho'ri·a
sal·pin'go·sto·mat'o·my
sal·pin'go·sto·mat'o·
plas'ty
sal·pin'gos'to·my
sal·pin'go·the'cal
sal·pin'got'o·my
sal'pinx pl. sal·pin'ges'
salt
sal·ta'tion
sal'ta·to'ric
sal'ta·to'ry
Sal'ter lines
salt·pe'ter
sa·lu'bri·ous
sa·lu'bri·ty
sal'u·re'sis
sal'u·ret'ic
sal'u·tar'y
sal'vage, -vaged, -vag·ing
salve
Salz'mann dystrophy
sam'ple, -pled, -pling
Samp'son cysts
San'a·rel'li virus
san'a·to'ri·um pl. -ri·ums or
-ri·a
san'a·to'ry
San'der disease
San'ders sign
sane
San'ger Brown ataxia
san·guic'o·lous

san·guif′er·ous
san′gui·fi·ca′tion
san′gui·nar′i·a
san′gui·nar′y
san′guine
san·guin′e·ous
san′guin′o·lent
san′gui·no′poi·et′ic
san′gui·no·pu′ru·lent
san′gui·no·se′rous
san′gui·nous
san′guis
san′gui·suc′tion
sa′ni·es′
sa′ni·ous
san′i·ta′ri·um pl. -ri·ums or -ri·a
san′i·tar′y
san′i·ta′tion
san′i·tize′, -tized′, -tiz′ing
san′i·ty
San Joa·quin′ Val′ley fever
San′som sign
san′to·nin
san′to·nism
San′to·ri′ni
— cartilages
— muscle
— tubercle
sap
sa·phe′na
saph′e·nec′to·my
sa·phe′no·fem′o·ral
sa·phe′nous
sap′id
sap′o·gen′in
sap′o·na′ceous
sap′o·nat′ed
sa·pon′i·form′
Sap·pey′ muscle
sap′phism
sa·pre′mi·a
sap′ro·phy·to′sis
sa·ral′a·sin
sar′a·pus
sar·ci′tis
sar′co·ad·e·no′ma pl. -mas or -ma·ta
sar′co·blast′
sar′co·car′ci·no′ma pl. -mas or -ma·ta
sar′co·cele′
Sar′co·cys′tis
— lin′de·man′ni′
sar′code′

sar′co·en′do·the′li·o′ma pl. -mas or -ma·ta
sar′co·gen′ic
sar′co·hy′dro·cele′
sar′coid′
sar′coid·o′sis pl. -ses′
sar′co·lac′tic
sar′co·lem′ma
sar′co·lem′mal
sar′co·lem′mic
sar′co·lem′mous
sar′co·leu·ke′mi·a
sar·col′y·sis pl. -ses′
sar′co·lyte′
sar′co·lyt′ic
sar′co·ma pl. -mas or -ma·ta
— bot′ry·oi′des′
— cap′i·tis
— col′li u′ter·i′ hy·drop′i·cum pap′il·lar′e′
— cu·ta′ne·um te·lan′gi·ec·tat′i·cum mul′ti·plex′
— myx′o·ma·to′des′
— phyl·loi′des′
sar′co·ma·gen′e·sis pl. -ses′
sar′co·ma·gen′ic
sar′co·ma·toid′
sar·co′ma·to′sis pl. -ses′
sar·co′ma·tous
sar′co·mere′
sar′co·mes′o·the′li·o′ma pl. -mas or -ma·ta
sar′co·my′ces′
Sar′co·phag′i·dae′
sar′co·plasm
sar′co·plas′mic
sar′co·plast′
sar′co·poi·e′sis
sar′co·poi·et′ic
sar′co·sine′
sar′co·si·ne′mi·a
sar·co′sis
sar′co·spo·rid′i·o′sis pl. -ses′
sar′cos·to′sis
sar′co·style′
sar·cot′ic
sar′co·tu′bule′
sar′cous
sar·don′ic
sa·rin′
sar·men′to·cy′ma·rin
sar′men·tog′e·nin
sar′men·tose′
sar′sa·sap′o·gen′in
sar′sa·sap′o·nin
sar·to′ri·us pl. -ri·i′

sat′el·lite′
sat′el·li·to′sis pl. -ses′
sa·ti′e·ty
Sat′ter·thwaite′ method
sat′u·rate′, -rat′ed, -rat′ing
sat′u·ra′tion
sat′ur·nine′
sat′urn·ism
sat′y·ri′a·sis pl. -ses′
sat′y·ro·ma′ni·a
sau′cer
sau′cer·i·za′tion
sau′cer·ize′, -ized′, -iz′ing
Saund′by test
Saun′ders disease
Sau·vi·neau′ ophthalmoplegia
sav′in
Sa·vi′no test
saw
scab, scabbed, scab′bing
sca·bet′ic
sca′bi·cide′
sca′bies′
— crus·to′sa
— pap′u·li·for′mis
— pap′u·lo′sa
— pus′tu·lo′sa
sca′bi·et′ic
sca′bi·o·pho′bi·a
sca′bi·ous
sca·bri′ti·es′
— un′gui·um syph′i·lit′i·ca
sca′la pl. -lae′
— me′di·a
— tym′pa·ni′
— ves·tib′u·li′
sca·lar′i·form′
scald
scale
sca·lene′
sca′le·nec′to·my
sca′le·not′o·my
sca·le′nus pl. -ni′
— an·ti′cus syndrome
— min′i·mus
— pleu·ra′lis
scal′er
scal′ing
scall
scalp
scal′pel
scal′y
scan, scanned, scan′ning
scan·so′ri·us
Scan·zo′ni maneuver
sca′pha

scaph'o·ce·phal'ic
scaph'o·ceph'a·lism
scaph'o·ceph'a·lous
scaph'o·ceph'a·ly
scaph'oid'
scaph'oid·i'tis
scap'u·la pl. -lae' or -las
— a·la'ta
scap'u·lal'gi·a
scap'u·lar
scap'u·lec'to·my
scap'u·lo'an·te'ri·or
scap'u·lo'cla·vic'u·lar
scap'u·lo·cla·vic'u·lar'is
scap'u·lo·cos'tal
scap'u·lo·dyn'i·a
scap'u·lo·hu'mer·al
scap'u·lo·per'i·os'te·al
scap'u·lo·pex'y
scap'u·lo'pos·te'ri·or
sca'pus pl. -pi'
— pi'li'
scar, scarred, scar'ring
scar'a·bi'a·sis pl. -ses'
scar'i·fi·ca'tion
scar'i·fi·ca'tor
scar'i·fi'er
scar'i·fy', -fied', -fy'ing
scar'la·ti'na
scar'la·ti'nal
scar'la·ti·nel'la
scar'la·ti'ni·form'
scar'la·ti'noid'
scar'la·ti'nous
scar'let
Scar'pa
— fascia
— foramen
— ganglion
— triangle
scat'a·cra'ti·a
sca·te'mi·a
scat'o·lo'gi·a
scat'o·log'ic or scat'o·log'i·cal
sca·tol'o·gy
sca·to'ma (fecal matter in the colon)
♦scotoma
sca·toph'a·gous
sca·toph'a·gy
scat'o·phil'i·a
scat'o·pho'bi·a
sca·tos'co·py
scat'ter
scel'o·tyr'be
Scha'fer method

Schäf'fer reflex
Scham'berg' disease
Schanz syndrome
Schar'lach' R stain
Schat'ski ring
Schau'dinn fixing fluid
Schau'mann bodies
Schau'ta-Wert'heim' operation
Sche'de
— method
— operation
Scheie syndrome
sched'ule, -uled, -ul·ing
sche'ma pl. -ma·ta
sche·mat'ic
sche·mat'o·gram'
sche·mat'o·graph'
sche'mo·graph'
Schenck disease
Scher'er test
sche·ro'ma
Scheu'er·mann disease
Schick test
Schiff reagent
Schil'der disease
Schil'ler test
Schil'ling
— classification
— test
— type leukemia
Schim'mel·busch' disease
schin'dy·le'sis pl. -ses'
Schiøtz tonometer
Schir'mer test
schis'ta·sis
schis'ten·ceph'a·ly
schis'to·ce'li·a
schis'to·ce·phal'ic
schis'to·ceph'a·lus pl. -li'
schis'to·cor'mi·a
schis'to·cor'mus
schis'to·cys'tis
schis'to·cyte'
schis'to·cy·to'sis
schis'to·glos'si·a
schis'tom'e·lus
schis'tom'e·ter
schis'to·pro·so'pi·a
schis'to·pros'o·pus
schis'to·pros'o·py
schis·tor'rha·chis
schis'to·sis pl. -ses'
Schis'to·so'ma
— hae'ma·to'bi·um
— ja·pon'i·cum
— man·so'ni'

schis'to·so'mal
schis'to·some'
schis'to·so·mi'a·sis pl. -ses'
schis'to·so'mi·cid'al
schis'to·so'mi·cide'
schis'to·so'mus
schis'to·ster'ni·a
schis'to·tho'rax' pl. -rax'es or -ra·ces'
schis'to·tra'che·lus
schiz·am'ni·on'
schiz·ax'on'
schiz'en·ce·phal'ic
schiz'en·ceph'a·ly
schiz'o·af·fec'tive
schiz'o·ble·phar'i·a
schiz'o·cyte'
schiz'o·cy·to'sis
schiz'o·gen'e·sis pl. -ses'
schi·zog'e·nous
schiz'o·gon'ic
schi·zog'o·ny
schiz'o·gy'ri·a
schiz'oid'
schiz'oid'ism
schiz'o·ki·ne'sis pl. -ses'
schiz'o·ma'ni·a
Schiz'o·my·ce'tes'
schiz'ont'
schi·zon'ti·cide'
schiz'o·nych'i·a
schiz'o·pha'si·a
schiz'o·phre'ni·a
schiz'o·phre'nic
schiz'o·the'mi·a
schiz'o·tho'rax' pl. -rax'es or -ra·ces'
schiz'o·thy'mi·a
schiz'o·thy'mic
schiz'o·try·pan'o·so·mi'a·sis pl. -ses'
Schla'er test
Schlat'ter disease
Schlemm canal
Schle'sin·ger
— sign
— test
Schlof'fer
— operation
— tumor
Schlös'ser treatment
Schmidt
— fibrinoplastin
— syndrome
— test
Schmin'cke tumor
Schmitz bacillus

Schmorl
—— grooves
—— nodules
Schmutz pyorrhea
Schna'bel atrophy
Schnei'der
—— index
—— stain
Schnei·de·ri·an membrane
Schoen'bein' test
Schoen'hei'mer and Sper'-
ry method
Scholz disease
Schön'lein'
—— disease
—— purpura
Schott'mül'ler disease
Schre'ger lines
Schrid'de disease
Schroe'der method
Schüff'ner dots
Schül'ler-Chris'tian syn-
drome
Schül'ler method
Schultz
—— method
—— syndrome
—— test
Schultz'-Charl'ton
—— test
Schultz'-Dale' test
Schult'ze
—— method
—— paresthesia
—— placenta
Schumm test
Schwa'bach' test
Schwal'be
—— nucleus
—— sheath
Schwann cell
schwan·no·gli·o'ma
pl. -mas or -ma·ta
schwan·no'ma pl. -mas or
-ma·ta
schwan·no·sar·co'ma
pl. -mas or -ma·ta
Schwann sheath
Schwartz test
Schweig'ger-Sei'del
sheath
Schwei'zer-Fo'ley
Y-plasty
Schwen'in·ger method
sci·at'ic
sci·at'i·ca
sci'ence

sci'en·tif'ic
sci'en·tist
sci'e·ro'pi·a
scil'la
scil'lism
scil'lo·ceph'a·lus pl. -li'
scil'lo·ceph'a·ly
scin'ti·gram'
scin'til·late', -lat'ed, -lat'ing
scin'til·la'tion
scin'ti·pho·tog'ra·phy
scin'ti·scan'
scin'ti·scan'ner
scir'rhoid'
scir·rho'ma pl. -mas or -ma·
ta
scir'rhoph·thal'mi·a
scir'rhous (hard)
♦scirrhus
scir'rhus (a carcinoma),
pl. -rhi' or -rhus·es
♦scirrhous
scissile
scis'sors
scis·su'ra pl. -rae'
scis'sure
scle'ra pl. -ras or -rae'
scler·ac'ne
scler'ad·e·ni'tis
scle'ral
scle'ra·ti'tis
scle'ra·tog'e·nous
scler'ec·ta'si·a
scle·rec'to·ir'i·dec'to·my
scle·rec'tome'
scle·rec'to·my
scler'e·de'ma
—— ad'ul·to'rum
—— ne'o·na·to'rum
scle·re'ma
—— ad'i·po'sum
—— cu'tis
—— e·dem'a·to'sum
—— ne'o·na·to'rum
scle'ren·ce·pha'li·a
scle'ren·ceph'a·ly
scle·ren'chy·ma pl. -mas or
scle'ren·chym'a·ta
scle'ren·chym'a·tous
scle·ri'a·sis pl. -ses'
scle·rit'ic
scle·ri'tis
scle'ro·ad'i·pose'
scle'ro·a·troph'ic
scle'ro·blas·te'ma pl. -mas
or -ma·ta
scle'ro·blas·tem'ic

scle'ro·cho'roi·di'tis
scle'ro·con'junc'ti'val
scle'ro·con·junc'ti·vi'tis
scle'ro·cor'ne·a
scle'ro·cor'ne·al
scle'ro·dac·tyl'i·a
scle'ro·dac'ty·ly
scle'ro·der'ma
scle'ro·der'ma·ti'tis
scle'ro·der'ma·tous
scle'ro·des'mi·a
scle'ro·gen'ic
scle·rog'e·nous
scle'ro·gum'ma·tous
scle'ro·gy'ri·a
scle'roid'
scle'ro·i·ri'tis
scle'ro·ker'a·ti'tis
scle·ro'ma pl. -mas or
-ma·ta
scle'ro·ma·la'ci·a
—— per'fo·rans'
scle'ro·me'ninx pl. -me·
nin'ges'
scle'ro·mere'
scle·rom'e·ter
scle'ro·myx'e·de'ma
scle'ro·nych'i·a
scle'ro·nyx'is
scle'ro·o'o·pho·ri'tis
scle'roph·thal'mi·a
scle'ro·plas'ty
scle'ro·pro'tein'
scle·ro'sal
scle'ro·sant
scle'ro·sar·co'ma pl. -mas
or -ma·ta
scle·rose', -rosed', -ros'ing
scle·ro'sis pl. -ses'
—— co'ri·i'
—— der'ma·tis
—— os'si·um
scle'ro·skel'e·ton
scle'ro·ste·no'sis pl. -ses'
—— cu·ta'ne·a
scle·ros'to·my
scle'ro·ther'a·py
scle·rot'ic
scle·rot'i·ca
scle·rot'i·cec'to·my
scle·rot'i·co·nyx'is
scle·rot'i·co·punc'ture
scle·rot'i·cot'o·my
scle·rot'i·dec'to·my
scle'ro·ti'tis
scle·ro'ti·um pl. -ti·a
scle'ro·tome'

scle'ro•tom'ic
scle•rot'o•my
scle'rous
sco•lec'i•form'
scol'e•coid'
sco'lex' *pl.* scol'i•ces', sco•
  le'ces', or sco'lex•es
sco'li•o•lor•do'sis *pl.* -ses'
sco'li•o•ra•chit'ic
sco'li•o'si•om'e•try
sco'li•o'sis *pl.* -ses'
sco'li•o•som'e•ter
sco'li•o•som'e•try
sco'li•ot'ic
sco'li•o•tone'
scom'broid'ism
scom'broid' poisoning
scom'bro•tox'ic
scoop
sco'po•la
sco•pol'a•mine'
sco•po•phil'i•a
sco•po•phil'ic
sco•po•pho'bi•a
Scop'u•lar'i•op'sis
  —— brev'i•cau'le'
scor•bu'tic
scor•bu'tus
scor'di•ne'ma
score, scored, scor'ing
scor'e•te'mi•a
scor'ing
scot'o•chro'mo•gen
scot'o•din'i•a
scot'o•gram'
sco•to'ma (*an area of de-
  pressed vision in the visual
  field),* pl. -mas or -ma•ta
  ♦*scatoma*
sco•to'ma•graph'
sco•tom'a•tous
sco•tom'e•ter
scot'o•phil'i•a
scot'o•pho'bi•a
sco•to'pi•a
sco•top'ic
sco•top'sin
sco•tos'co•py
scrap'er
screen
scro•bic'u•late'
scro•bic'u•lus *pl.* -li'
  —— cor'dis
scrof'u•la
scrof'u•lo•der'ma
scrof'u•lous
scro'tal

scro•tec'to•my
scro•ti'tis
scro'to•cele'
scro'to•plas'ty
scro'tum *pl.* -ta *or* -tums
scru'ple
scur'vy
scu'tate'
scute
scu•tel'lum *pl.* -la
scu'tu•lar
scu'tu•late'
scu'tu•lum *pl.* -la
scu'tum *pl.* -ta
  —— tym•pan'i•cum
scyb'a•lous
scyb'a•lum *pl.* -la
scy'phi•form'
Sea'bright-Ban'tam syn-
  drome
seam
sea'sick'
sea'sick'ness
seat
seat'worm'
se•ba'ce•o•fol•lic'u•lar
se•ba'ceous
se•bac'ic
se•bif'er•ous
se•bip'a•rous
seb'o•lith'
seb'or•rha'gi•a
seb'or•rhe'a
  —— cap'i•tis
  —— con'ges•ti'va
  —— cor'po•ris
  —— fur'fu•ra'ce•a
  —— ich'thy•o'sis
  —— na'si'
  —— ni'gri•cans'
  —— o'le•o'sa
  —— sic'ca
seb'or•rhe'al
seb'or•rhe'ic
seb'or•rhe'id
se'bum
  —— cu•ta'ne•um
  —— pal'pe•bra'le'
  —— prae•pu'ti•a'le'
Seck'el syndrome
se•clu'sion
sec'o•bar'bi•tal'
sec'o•dont'
sec'on•dar'y
se•cre'ta
se•cre'ta•gogue'
se•crete', -cret'ed, -cret'ing

se•cre'tin
se•cre'tin•ase'
se•cre'tion
se•cre'to•in•hib'i•tor
se•cre'to•in•hib'i•to'ry
se•cre'to•mo'tor
se•cre'tor
se•cre'to•ry
sec'tile'
sec'ti•o' *pl.* sec'ti•o'nes'
sec'tion
sec'tion•al
sec'ti•o'nes'
  —— cer'e•bel'li'
  —— cor'po•rum qua'dri•
  gem'i•no'rum
  —— hy'po•thal'a•mi'
  —— isth'mi'
  —— me•dul'lae' ob'lon•
  ga'tae'
  —— medullae spi•na'lis
  —— mes'en•ceph'a•li'
  —— pe•dun'cu•li' cer'e•bri'
  —— pon'tis
  —— tel'en•ceph'a•li'
  —— thal'a•men•ceph'a•li
sec'tor
sec•to'ri•al
se•cun'di•grav'i•da
se•cun•di•na *pl.* -nae'
sec'un•dines'
sec'un•dip'a•ra
sec'un•di•par'i•ty
sec'un•dip'a•rous
se•cun'dum ar'tem
se•date', -dat'ed, -dat'ing
se•da'tion
sed'a•tive
sed'en•tar'y
sed'i•ment
sed'i•men'ta•ry
sed'i•men•ta'tion
sed'i•men•tom'e•ter
seed
See'lig•muel'ler
  —— neuralgia
  —— sign
seg'ment *n.*
seg•ment' *v.*
seg•men'ta
  —— bron'cho•pul'mo•na'li•a
  —— re•na'li•a
seg•men'tal
seg'men•tar'y
seg'men•ta'tion
seg'men•tec'to•my
seg•men'tum *pl.* -ta

—— an·te'ri·us in·fe'ri·us re·na'lis
—— anterius lo'bi' hep'a·tis dex'tri'
—— anterius lobi su·pe'ri·o'ris pul·mo'nis dex'tri'
—— anterius lobi superioris pulmonis si·nis'tri'
—— anterius su·pe'ri·us re·na'lis
—— ap'i·ca'le' lo'bi' in·fe'ri·o'ris pul·mo'nis dex'tri'
—— apicale lobi inferioris pulmonis si·nis'tri'
—— apicale lobi su·pe'ri·o'ris pul·mo'nis dex'tri'
—— ap'i·co·pos·te'ri·us lo'bi' su·pe'ri·o'ris pul·mo'nis si·nis'tri'
—— ba·sa'le' an·te'ri·us lo'bi' in·fe'ri·o'ris pul·mo'nis dex'tri'
—— basale anterius lobi inferioris pulmonis si·nis'tri'
—— basale lat'er·a'le' lo'bi' in·fe'ri·o'ris pul·mo'nis dex'-tri'
—— basale laterale lobi inferioris pulmonis si·nis'tri'
—— basale me·di·a'le' lo'bi' in·fe'ri·o'ris pul·mo'nis dex'-tri'
—— basale mediale lobi inferioris pulmonis si·nis'tri'
—— basale pos·te'ri·us lo'bi' in·fe'ri·o'ris pul·mo'nis dex'-tri'
—— basale posterius lobi inferioris pulmonis si·nis'tri'
—— car·di'a·cum lo'bi' in·fe'ri·o'ris pul·mo'nis dex'tri'
—— cardiacum lobi inferioris pulmonis si·nis'tri'
—— in·fe'ri·us re·na'lis
—— lat'er·a'le' lo'bi' hep'a·tis si·nis'tri'
—— laterale lobi me·di·i' pul·mo'nis dex'tri'
—— lin'gu·lar'e' in·fe'ri·us lo'bi su·pe'ri·o'ris pul·mo'nis si·nis'tri'
—— linguare su·pe'ri·us lo'bi' su·pe'ri·o'ris pul·mo'nis si·nis'tri'
—— me·di·a'le' lo'bi' hep'a·tis si·nis'tri'

—— mediale lobi me'di·i' pul·mo'nis dex'tri'
—— pos·te'ri·us lo'bi' hep'a·tis dex'tri'
—— posterius lobi su·pe'ri·o'ris pul·mo'nis dex'tri'
—— posterius re·na'lis
—— sub·ap'i·ca'le' lo'bi' in·fe'ri·o'ris pul·mo'nis dex'tri'
—— subapicale lobi inferioris pulmonis si·nis'tri'
—— sub'su·pe'ri·us lo'bi in·fe'ri·o'ris pul·mo'nis dex'tri'
—— subsuperius lobi inferioris pulmonis si·nis'tri'
—— su·pe'ri·us lo'bi' in·fe'ri·o'ris pul·mo'nis dex'tri'
—— superius lobi inferioris pulmonis si·nis'tri'
—— superius re·na'lis
seg're·gate', -gat'ed, -gat'ing
seg're·ga'tion
seg're·ga'tion·al
seg're·ga'tor
Séguin' sign
sei'es·the'si·a
sei'zure
se·lec'tion
se·lec'tor
se·le'ne' pl. -nai'
se·le'nic
sel'e·nif'er·ous
se·le'ni·ous
sel'e·nite'
se·le'ni·um
sel'e·no'sis
self
self'-dif'fer·en'ti·a'tion
self'-di·ges'tion
self'-fer'men·ta'tion
self'-hyp·no'sis pl. -ses'
self'-in·fec'tion
self'-in·oc'u·la'tion
self'-lim'it·ed
self'-mu'ti·la'tion
self'-sus·pen'sion
Sel'i·wa'noff' test
sel'la (a saddle), pl. -lae'
  ♦cella
—— tur'ci·ca
sel'lar
Sel'ter disease
Semb operation
se'mei·og'ra·phy
se'mei·o·log'ic
se'mei·ol'o·gy
se'mei·ot'ics

se'men pl. sem'i·na or -mens
sem'i·a·ceph'a·lus pl. -li'
sem'i·ca·nal'
sem'i·ca·na'lis pl. -les'
—— mus'cu·li' ten·so'ris tym'pa·ni'
—— tu'bae' au'di·ti'vae'
sem'i·car'ti·lag'i·nous
sem'i·cir'cu·lar
sem'i·co'ma
sem'i·com'a·tose'
sem'i·con'scious
sem'i·cris'ta pl. -tae'
—— in'ci·si'va
sem'i·de'cus·sa'tion
sem'i·flex'ion
sem'i·len'te
sem'i·le'thal
sem'i·lu'nar
sem'i·lux·a'tion
sem'i·mem'bra·no'sus pl. -si'
sem'i·mem'bra·nous
sem'i·nal
sem'i·nar·co'sis pl. -ses'
sem'i·na'tion
sem'i·nif'er·ous
sem'i·no'ma pl. -mas or -ma·ta
sem'i·nor'mal
se'mi·nu'ri·a
sem'i·pen'ni·form'
sem'i·per'me·a·ble
sem'i·pla·cen'ta
sem'i·ple'gi·a
sem'i·pro·na'tion
sem'i·prone'
sem'i·re·cum'bent
se'mis
sem'i·sid'e·ra'ti·o'
sem'i·som'nus
sem'i·so'por
sem'i·spec'u·lum pl. -la or -lums
sem'i·spi·na'lis
sem'i·sul'cus
sem'i·su'pi·na'tion
sem'i·syn·thet'ic
sem'i·ten'di·no'sus pl. -si'
sem'i·ten'di·nous
Se'mon
—— law
—— symptom
Sen'e·ar-Ush'er syndrome
se·nec'ti·tude'
Sen'ek·jie medium
se·nes'cence

se·nes'cent
se'nile'
se'nil·ism
se·nil'i·ty
se'ni·um
—— prae'cox'
—— pre'cox'
Sen method
sen'na
sen'no·side'
se·no'pi·a
sen·sa'tion
sen·sa'tion·al
sense, sensed, sens'ing
sen'si·bil'i·ty
sen·si·bil·iz'er
sen·sib'i·lus pro'pri·us nucleus
sen'si·ble
sen'sim'e·ter
sen'si·tive
sen'si·tiv'i·ty
sen'si·ti·za'tion
sen'si·tize', -tized', -tiz'ing
sen'si·tiz'er
sen'so·mo'tor
sen'sor
sen·so'ri·al
sen·so'ri·glan'du·lar
sen·so'ri·mo'tor
sen·so'ri·neu'ral
sen·so'ri·um pl. -ri·ums or
-ri·a
sen'so·ri·va'so·mo'tor
sen'so·ry
sen'su·al
sen'su·al·ism
sen'sus
sen'ti·ent
sen'ti·ment
sep'a·ra'tor
sep'sis pl. -ses'
—— a·gran'u·lo·cyt'i·ca
sep'ta
—— in'ter·al've·o·lar'i·a
man·dib'u·lae'
—— interalveolaria max·
il'lae'
—— in'ter·ra·dic'u·lar'i·a
man·dib'u·lae'
—— interradicularia max·
il'lae'
sep'tal
sep'tate'
sep·ta'tion
sep·tec'to·my
sep·te'mi·a

sep'tic
sep'ti·ce'mi·a
sep'ti·ce'mic
sep'ti·co·phle·bi'tis
sep'ti·co'py·e'mi·a
sep'tile'
sep'ti·me·tri'tis
sep'to·mar'gi·nal
sep'tom'e·ter
sep'to·na'sal
sep'to·plas'ty
sep'to·tome'
sep·tot'o·my
sep'tu·la tes'tis
sep'tu·lum pl. -la
sep'tum pl. -tums or -ta
—— a'tri·o'rum
—— a'tri·o·ven·tric'u·lar'e'
—— bul'bae' u·re'thrae'
—— ca·na'lis mus'cu·lo·tu·
bar'i·i'
—— car'ti·la·gin'e·um na'si'
—— cer'vi·ca'le' in'ter·
me'di·um
—— cor'po·rum cav'er·no·
so'rum
—— corporum
cavernosorum cli·tor'i·dis
—— cru·ra'le'
—— fem'o·ra'le'
—— femorale (Clo·quet'i')
—— glan'dis pe'nis
—— in'ter·a'tri·a'le'
—— in'ter·mus'cu·lar'e' an·
te'ri·us cru'ris
—— intermusculare anteri-
us fib'u·lar'e'
—— intermusculare bra'-
chi·i' lat'er·a'le'
—— intermusculare brachii
me'di·a'le'
—— intermusculare fem'o·
ris lat'er·a'le'
—— intermusculare femoris
me'di·a'le'
—— intermusculare hu'-
mer·i' lat'er·a'le'
—— intermusculare humeri
me'di·a'le'
—— intermusculare pos·
te'ri·us cru'ris
—— intermusculare posterius fib'u·lar'e'
—— in'ter·ven·tric'u·lar'e'
—— interventriculare pri'-
mum
—— lin'guae'

—— lu'ci·dum
—— mem'bra·na'ce·um
na'si'
—— membranaceum ven·
tric'u·lo'rum
—— mo'bi·le' na'si'
—— mus'cu·lar'e' ven·tric'u·
lo'rum
—— na'si'
—— nasi os'se·um
—— or'bi·ta'le'
—— pel·lu'ci·dum
—— pe'nis
—— pri'mum
—— rec'to·vag'i·na'le'
—— rec'to·ves'i·ca'le'
—— scro'ti'
—— se·cun'dum
—— si'nu·um fron·ta'li·um
—— sinuum sphe'noi·da'li·
um
—— spu'ri·um
—— trans·ver'sum
—— ven·tric'u·lo'rum
sep·tup'let
se·quel'a pl. -ae'
se'quence
se·quen'tial
se·ques'ter
se·ques'tral
se·ques'trant
se·ques·tra'tion
se·ques·trec'to·my
se·ques·trot'o·my
se·ques'trum pl. -trums or
-tra
ser'al·bu'min
se'ra·phe·re'sis
se·rem'pi·on'
Ser'gent sign
se'ri·al
se'ries' pl. se'ries'
ser'i·flux'
ser'ine'
ser'i·scis'sion
se'ro·al·bu'min·ous
se'ro·al·bu'min·u'ri·a
se'ro·an'a·phy·lax'is pl.
-lax'es'
se'ro·che
se'ro·chrome'
se'ro·co·li'tis
se'ro·con·ver'sion
se'ro·cul'ture
se'ro·cys'tic
se'ro·der'ma·ti'tis
se'ro·der'ma·to'sis pl. -ses'

se'ro·der·mi'tis
se'ro·di'ag·no'sis *pl.* -ses'
se'ro·di·ag·nos'tic
se'ro·en'ter·i'tis
se'ro·ep'i·de'mi·o·log'ic
se'ro·ep'i·de'mi·ol'o·gy
se'ro·fi'brin·ous
se'ro·fi'brous
se'ro·floc'cu·la'tion
se'ro·flu'id
se'ro·gas'tri·a
se'ro·gen'e·sis
se'ro·glob'u·lin
se'ro·gly'coid'
se'ro·hem'or·rhag'ic
se'ro·hep'a·ti'tis *pl.* -tis·es
  or -tit'i·des'
se'ro·im·mu'ni·ty
se'ro·lem'ma
se'ro·li'pase'
se'ro·log'ic *or* se'ro·log'i·cal
se·rol'o·gist
se·rol'o·gy
se·rol'y·sin
se'ro·ma *pl.* -mas *or* -ma·ta
se'ro·mem'bra·nous
se'ro·mu'ci·nous
se'ro·mu'cous
se'ro·mus'cu·lar
se'ro·neg'a·tive
se'ro·per'i·to·ne'um
se'ro·plas'tic
se'ro·pos'i·tive
se'ro·prog·no'sis *pl.* -ses'
se'ro·pu'ru·lent
se'ro·pus
se'ro·re·ac'tion
se'ro·re·sis'tance
se·ro'sa *pl.* -sas *or* -sae'
se·ro'sal
se·ro'sa·mu'cin
se'ro·san·guin'e·ous
se'ro·se'rous
se'ro·si'tis
se'ro·sy·no'vi·al
se'ro·syn'o·vi'tis
se'ro·ther'a·py
se'ro·to'nin
se'ro·tox'in
se'ro·type'
se'rous
ser·pig'i·nous
ser'ra
ser'rate', -rat'ed, -rat'ing
Ser·ra'ti·a
  —— mar·ces'cens
ser·ra'tion

ser·ra'tus
  —— mag'nus
Ser'res angle
ser'ru·late'
Ser·to'li cells
se'rum *pl.* -rums *or* -ra
se'rum·al
se'rum-fast'
ser'vo·mech'a·nism
ses'a·moid'
ses'a·moi·di'tis
ses·qui·ho'ra
ses'qui·sul'fide'
ses'sile'
set, set, set'ting
se'ta *pl.* -tae'
se·ta'ceous
se'ton
17-hy·drox'y·cor'ti·cos'ter·
  one'
17-hy·drox'y-11-de·hy'dro·
  cor'ti·cos'ter·one'
Se'ver disease
sex
sex'i·dig'i·tal
sex'i·dig'i·tate'
sex'-lim'ited
sex'-linked'
sex'o·log'ic
sex·ol'o·gy
sex·tup'let
sex'u·al
sex'u·al'i·ty
sex'u·al·ize', -ized', -iz'ing
shad'ow
Shaf'fer method
shaft
sha·green'
Shar'pey fibers
sheath
  —— of Hen'le
  —— of Neu'mann
  —— of Schweig'ger-Sei'del
sheathe, sheathed, sheath'-
  ing
shed, shed, shed'ding
shelf
shell'shock'
Shep'herd fracture
Sher'man-Mun·sell' unit
Sher'ren triangle
Shev'sky test
Shib'ley sign
shield
shift
Shi'ga bacillus
Shi·gel'la

  —— al'ka·les'cens
  —— am·big'u·a
  —— dys'en·ter'i·ae'
  —— schmitz'i·i'
shig'el·lo'sis *pl.* -ses'
shi·kim'ic
shin
shin'bone'
shin'gles
shiv'er
shock
Shock and Has'tings
  method
Shope papilloma
Shorr trichrome stain
shot'ty
shoul'der
Shrap'nell membrane
shriv'el
shud'der
Shu'ni fever
shunt
Schwartz'man phenom-
  enon
Shy'-Dra'ger syndrome
si·al'a·den
si'al·ad'e·ni'tis
si'al·ad'e·nog'ra·phy
si'al·a·gog'ic
si·al'a·gogue'
si'al·an'gi·og'ra·phy
si'al·a·po'ri·a
si'al·ec·ta'si·a
si'a·lem'e·sis *pl.* -ses'
si·al'ic
si·al'ine'
si'a·li·thot'o·my
si'a·li'tis
si'a·lo·ad'e·nec'to·my
si'a·lo·ad'e·ni'tis
si'a·lo·ad'e·not'o·my
si'a·lo·aer'o·pha'gi·a
si'a·lo·an'gi·ec'ta·sis *pl.*
  -ses'
si'a·lo·an'gi·og'ra·phy
si'a·lo·an·gi'tis
si'a·lo·cele'
si'a·lo·do·chi'tis
si'a·lo·do·chi'um *pl.* -chi·a
si'a·lo·do·cho·li·thi'a·sis
si'a·lo·do·cho·plas'ty
si'a·lo·gas'trone'
si'a·log'e·nous
si·al'o·gram'
si·a·log'ra·phy
si·a'loid
si·al'o·lith'

si′a·lo·li·thi′a·sis
si′a·lo·li·thot′o·my
si′a·lo′ma *pl.* -mas *or* -ma·ta
si′a·lo·mu′cin
si′a·lon′
si′a·lor·rhe′a
si′a·los′che·sis
si′a·lo·se·mei·ol′o·gy
si′a·lo′sis
si′a·lo·ste·no′sis *pl.* -ses′
si′a·lo·syr′inx *pl.* -sy·rin′ges′ *or* -inx·es
si′a·lot′ic
Si′a·mese′ twins
Si′a water test
sib
sib′i·lant
sib′i·la′tion
sib′i·lis′mus
—— au′ri·um
sib′i·lus
sib′ling
sib′ship′
Sib′son fascia
Si·card′ syndrome
sic′cant
sic′ca·tive
sic·cha′si·a
sic′cus
sick
sick′le-cell′
sick′le-form′
sick·le′mi·a
sick·le′mic
sick′ling
sick′ness
side
sid′er·a′tion
sid′er·i·nu′ri·a
Sid′er·o·bac′ter
sid′er·o·blast′
sid′er·o·cyte′
sid′er·o·cy·to′sis *pl.* -ses′
sid′er·o·der′ma
sid′er·o·fi·bro′sis *pl.* -ses′
sid′er·o·pe′ni·a
sid′er·o·pe′nic
sid′e·ro·phage′
sid′er·o·phil′
sid′er·o·phil′i·a
sid′er·oph′i·lin
sid′er·oph′i·lous
sid′er·o·phyl′lin
sid′er·o·sil′i·co′sis *pl.* -ses′
sid′er·o′sis
—— bul′bi′
sid′er·ot′ic

Sie′gert sign
sigh
sight
sig′ma
sig′ma·tism *(lisping)*
♦stigmatism
sig′moid′
sig′moi·dec′to·my
sig′moi·di′tis
sig·moi′do·pex′y
sig·moi′do·proc·tos′to·my
sig·moi′do·rec·tos′to·my
sig·moid′o·scope′
sig′moi·dos′co·py
sig·moi′do·sig′moi·dos′to·my
sig′moi·dos′to·my
sig′moi·dot′o·my
sig·moi′do·ves′i·cal
sign
sig′na
sig′na·ture
signe
—— de jour·nal′
—— de peau′ d′o·range′
sig′num *pl.* -na
sil·lan′drone′
si′lent
sil′i·ca
sil′i·cate′
sil′i·ca·to′sis *pl.* -ses′
si·lic′ic
si·li′cious
si·li′ci·um
sil′i·co·an′thra·co′sis *pl.* -ses′
sil′i·co·flu′o·ride′
sil′i·con′ *(element)*
♦silicone
sil′i·cone′ *(polymer)*
♦silicon
sil′i·co·sid′er·o′sis *pl.* -ses′
sil′i·co′sis *pl.* -ses′
sil′i·cot′ic
sil′i·co·tu·ber′cu·lo′sis
si·lique′
sil′i·quose′
sil′ver
Sil·ves′ter method
si·meth′i·cone′
si·mil′i·a si·mil′i·bus cu·ran′tur
si·mil′i·mum
Sim′monds disease
Sim′mons citrate agar
Si′mon
—— foci

—— operation
—— position
—— septic factor
sim′ple
Simp′son syndrome
sim′tra·zene′
si′mul
sim′u·late′, -lat′ed, -lat′ing
sim′u·la′tion
sim′u·la′tor
si′nal
si·na′pis
sin′a·pism
sin·cip′i·tal
sin·cip′ut *pl.* -puts *or* sin·cip′i·ta
Sind′bis fever
sin′ew
sin′gul·ta′tion
sin·gul′tus *pl.* -ti′
sin·is′ter
sin′is·trad′
sin′is·tral
sin′is·tral′i·ty
sin′is·tra′tion
sin′is·trau′ral
si·nis′tro·car′di·a
sin′is·tro·cer′e·bral
sin′is·troc′u·lar
sin′is·tro·gy·ra′tion
sin′is·tro·gy′ric
sin′is·tro·man′u·al
sin′is·trop′e·dal
sin′is·trorse′
sin′is·tro·tor′sion
sin′is·trous
si′no·a′tri·al
si′no·au·ric′u·lar
si′no·bron·chi′tis
si′no·ca·rot′id
si′no·gram′
si·nog′ra·phy
si′no·spi′ral
si′no·vag′i·nal
si′no·ven·tric′u·lar
sin′u·ous
si′nus *pl.* -nus·es *or* si′nus
—— a′lae′ par′vae′
—— a·na′lis
—— a·or′tae′
—— aortae (Val·sal′vae′)
—— ca·rot′i·cus
—— cav′er·no′sus
—— cir′cu·lar′is
—— co·ro·nar′i·us
—— cos′to·me·di·as′ti·na′lis pleu′rae′

—— du'rae' ma'tris
—— ep'i·di·dym'i·dis
—— eth'moi·da'lis
—— fron·ta'lis
—— in'ter·cav'er·no'si'
—— in'ter·cav'er·no'sus anterior
—— intercavernosus posterior
—— lac·tif'er·i'
—— li·e'nis
—— max'il·lar'is
—— o·bli'quus per'i·car'di·i'
—— oc·cip'i·ta'lis
—— of Mor·ga'gni
—— of Val·sal'va
—— par'a·na·sa'les'
—— pe·tro'sus interior
—— petrosus superior
—— phren'i·co·cos·ta'lis
pleu'rae'
—— pleu'rae'
—— poc'u·lar'is
—— posterior ca'vi' tym'pa·ni'
—— pros·tat'i·cus
—— rec·ta'les'
—— rec'tus
—— re·na'lis
—— sag'it·ta'lis inferior
—— sagittalis superior
—— sig·moi'de·us
—— sphe'noi·da'lis
—— sphe'no·pa·ri'e·ta'lis
—— tar'si'
—— ton'sil·lar'is
—— trans·ver'sus du'rae' ma'tris
—— transversus per'i·car'di·i'
—— trun'ci' pul'mo·na'lis
—— tym'pa·ni'
—— un'guis
—— u'ro·gen'i·ta'lis
—— ve·nar'um ca·var'um
—— ve·no'sus
—— venosus scle'rae'
—— ver'te·bra'les' lon'gi·tu'di·na'les'
si'nus·al
si'nus·i'tis
si'nus·oid'
si'nus·oi'dal
si'nus·oi'dal·i·za'tion
si'nus·ot'o·my
si'phon
si'phon·age

Sip'py
—— diet
—— powder
si·ren·oid'
si·ri'a·sis pl. -ses'
Sis'to sign
Sis·tru'rus
site
si·tol'o·gy (dietetics)
♦cytology
si'to·ma'ni·a
si'to·pho'bi·a
si'to·ther'a·py
si'to·tox'in
si'to·tox'ism
sit'u·a'tion
sit'u·a'tion·al
si'tus pl. si'tus
—— in·ver'sus
—— inversus vis'cer·um
—— mu·ta'tus
—— per·ver'sus
—— trans·ver'sus
sitz bath
Sjö'gren syndrome
ske·lal'gi·a
ske'las·the'ni·a
skel'e·tal
skel'e·ti·za'tion
skel'e·tog'e·nous
skel'e·ton
—— ex·trem'i·ta'tis in·fe'ri·o'ris lib'er·ae'
—— extremitatis su·pe'ri·o'ris lib'er·ae'
—— mem'bri' in·fe'ri·o'ris lib'er·i
—— membri su·pe'ri·o'ris lib'er·i'
Skene
—— duct
—— glands
skene'o·scope'
ske·ni'tis
ske'o·cy·to'sis pl. -ses'
skew
skew'foot'
ski'a·gram'
ski·ag'ra·phy
ski·am'e·try
ski'a·po·res'co·py
ski'a·scope'
ski·as'co·py
skin
skin'ny
Sklow'sky symptom
skull

slake, slaked, slak'ing
slant
sleep, slept, sleep'ing
sleep'less·ness
sleep'walk'er
sleep'walk'ing
slide
sling
slip, slipped, slip'ping
slit
slit' lamp' test
slope, sloped, slop'ing
slough
Slu'der
—— method
—— syndrome
sludge
sluice'way'
slum'ber
slur, slurred, slur'ring
slur'ry
small'pox'
smear
smeg'ma
—— cli·tor'i·dis
—— em'bry·o'num
—— prae·pu'ti·i'
smeg·mat'ic
smeg'mo·lith'
Smel'lie method
Smith
—— phenomenon
—— test
smudg'ing
smut
snap, snapped, snap'ping
snare, snared, snar'ing
sneeze, sneezed, sneez'ing
Snel'len
—— chart
—— reflex
—— test
snore, snored, snor'ing
snuff'box'
sob, sobbed, sob'bing
so'ci·a
—— pa·rot'i·dis
—— pa·ro'tis
so'cial
so'cial·i·za'tion
so'ci·o·log'i·cal
so'ci·ol'o·gy
so'ci·o·med'i·cal
so'ci·o·path'
so'ci·o·path'ic
sock'et
so'da

Sö'der·bergh' pressure reflex
so'di·um
—— an·az'o·lene'
—— an'ti·mo'nyl·glu'co·
nate'
—— au'ro·thi'o·mal'ate'
—— eth'a·sul'fate'
—— eth'yl·mer·cu'ri·thi'o·
sal'i·cy·late'
—— flu'o·ro·ac'e·tate'
—— flu'o·sil'i·cate'
—— fu'si·date'
—— hy·drox'y·di'one' suc'ci·
nate'
—— in'di·go·tin'di·sul'fo·
nate'
—— i·o'do·hip'pur·ate'
—— i·o'do·meth'a·mate'
—— i'o·tha·lam'ate'
—— ip'o·date'
—— me·thi'o·dal'
—— mor'rhu·ate'
—— ni'tro·fer'ri·cy'a·nide'
—— ric'i·nate'
—— ric'in·o'le·ate'
—— stib'o·glu'co·nate'
—— su'per·ox'ide'
—— tet'ra·bo'rate'
—— tung'state'
so'do'ku
sod'o·mist
sod'o·mite'
sod'o·my
Soem'mer·ing
—— foramen
—— ganglion
—— spot
sol
so'la·na'ceous
so·lap'sone'
so'lar
so'lar·i·za'tion
so'lar·ize', -ized', -iz'ing
sol·a'tion
sole
so'le·no·nych'i·a
sole'plate'
So'ler·a reaction
so'le·us pl. -le·i' or -le·us·es
—— ac'ces·so'ri·us
sol'id
so·lid'i·fi·ca'tion
so·lid'i·fy', -fied', -fy'ing
sol'ip·sism
sol'i·tar'y
—— cells of Mey'nert

sol'-lu'nar
Sol'o·mon rule
Sol·pu'gi·da
sol'u·bil'i·ty
sol'u·bi·li·za'tion
sol'u·bi·lize', -lized', -liz'ing
sol'u·ble
so'lum tym'pa·ni'
so'lute'
so·lu'ti·o'
so·lu'tion
sol'vate'
sol·va'tion
sol'vent
so'ma pl. -ma·ta or -mas
so'mal
so'mas·the'ni·a
so'mat·es·the'si·a
so'mat·es·thet'ic
so·mat'ic
so·mat'i·co·splanch'nic
so·mat'i·co·vis'cer·al
so'ma·tist
so'ma·ti·za'tion
so'ma·tize', -tized', -tiz'ing
so·mat'o·cep'tor
so·mat'o·chrome
so·mat'o·derm'
so·ma·to·did'y·mus
so·ma·to·dym'i·a
so·mat'o·ge·net'ic
so·ma·to·gen'ic
so·ma·tog'e·ny
so'ma·to·log'ic
so'ma·tol'o·gy
so'ma·tome'
so·ma·to·meg'a·ly
so·ma·to·met'ric
so·ma·tom'e·try
so·ma·top'a·gus
so·ma·to·path'ic
so·ma·to·phre'ni·a
so'ma·to·plasm
so·ma·to·pleu'ral
so·ma·to·pleure'
so·ma·to·psy'chic
so·ma·to·psy'cho·sis pl.
  -ses'
so·ma·to·sen'so·ry
so·ma·to·splanch'no·
  pleu'ric
so·ma·to·ther'a·py
so·ma·to·to'ni·a
so·ma·to·ton'ic
so·ma·to·top'ag·no'si·a
so·ma·to·top'ic
so·ma·to·trid'y·mus

so'ma·to·tro'phin
so'ma·to·trop'ic
so'ma·to·tro'pin
so'ma·to·type'
so'mes·the'si·a
so'mes·thet'ic
som·nam'bu·lance
som·nam'bu·la'tion
som·nam'bu·la'tor
som·nam'bu·lism
som·nam'bu·lisme' pro·vo·
  qué'
som·nam'bu·list
som'ni·al
som'ni·fa'cient
som·nif'er·ous
som·nif'ic
som·nil'o·quence
som·nil'o·quism
som·nil'o·quist
som·nil'o·quy
som·nip'a·thist
som·nip'a·thy
som·no·cin'e·mat'o·graph'
som'no·lence
som'no·lent
som·no·len'ti·a
som·no·les'cent
som'no·lism
som'nus
So'mo·gyi
—— method
—— unit
sone
son'i·ca'tion
son'i·tus
Son'ne dysentery
son·o·en·ceph'a·lo·gram'
son'o·gram'
so·nog'ra·phy
so·nom'e·ter
so·no'rous
so'nus
soph'o·ma'ni·a
soph'o·rine'
so'por
so'po·rate', -rat'ed, -rat'ing
so'po·rif'er·ous
so'po·rif'ic
so'po·rose'
sor'be·fa'cient
sor'bent
sor'bic
sor'bi·tan'
sor'bite'
sor'bi·tol'
sor'bose'

sor'des' *pl.* sor'des'
sore
so·ro'ri·a'tion
sor'rel
so'ta·lol'
so·ter'e·nol'
souf'fle
sound
Souques sign
soy'bean'
space
—— of Burns
—— of Dis'se
—— of Ret'zi·us
—— of Te·non'
spaces
—— of Lit·tré'
—— of Vir'chow-Rob'in
Spal'ding sign
spal·la'tion
spare, spared, spar'ing
spar·go'sis *pl.* -ses'
spar'so·my'cin
spar'te·ine'
spasm
spas·mod'ic
spas'mo·gen
spas·mol'o·gy
spas·mo·lyg'mus
spas·mol'y·sis *pl.* -ses'
spas'mo·lyt'ic
spas'mo·phil'i·a
spas'mo·phil'ic
spas'mus
—— bron'chi·a'lis
—— glot'ti·dis
—— mus'cu·lar'is
—— nic'ti·tans'
—— nu'tans'
—— oc'u·li'
spas'tic
spas·tic'i·ty
spa'ti·a
—— an'gu·li' i'ri·dis
—— anguli i'ri·do·cor'ne·
a'lis
—— in'ter·cos·ta'li·a
—— in'ter·glob'u·lar'i·a
—— in'ter·os'se·a met'a·
car'pi'
—— interossea met'a·tar'si'
—— in'ter·vag'i·na'li·a
—— zon'u·lar'i·a
spa'tial
spa'tic
spa'ti·um *pl.* -ti·a
—— ep'i·scle·ra'le'

—— in'ter·cos·ta'le'
—— per'i·cho'ri·oi'de·a'le'
—— per'i·cho·roi'de·a'le'
—— per'i·lym·phat'i·cum
—— per'i·ne'i' pro·fun'dum
—— perinei su'per·fi'ci·a'le'
—— ret'ro·per'i·to·ne·a'le'
—— ret'ro·pu'bi·cum
spat'u·la
spat'u·late'
spe'cial·ist
spe'cial·i·za'tion
spe'cial·ty
spe'cies' *pl.* spe'cies'
spe·cif'ic
spec'i·fic'i·ty
spec'i·men
spec'ta·cles
spec'ti·no·my'cin
spec'tral
spec'tro·col'o·rim'e·ter
spec'tro·flu'o·rom'e·ter
spec'tro·gram'
spec'tro·graph'
spec·trom'e·ter
spec·trom'e·try
spec'tro·mi'cro·scope'
spec'tro·pho·tom'e·ter
spec'tro·pho'to·met'ric
spec'tro·pho·tom'e·try
spec'tro·po'la·rim'e·ter
spec'tro·scope'
spec'tro·scop'ic
spec·tros'co·py
spec'trum *pl.* -tra *or* -trums
spec'u·lum *pl.* -la *or* -lums
speech
Spee curve
Spen'cer-Par'ker vaccine
Speng'ler fragments
Spens syndrome
sperm *pl.* sperm *or* sperms
sper'ma·cra'si·a
sper'ma·ta·cra'si·a
sper·mat'ic
sper'ma·ti·ci'dal
sper·mat'i·cide'
sper'ma·tid
sper'ma·tism
sper·mat'o·cele'
sper'ma·to·ce·lec'to·my
sper'ma·to·ci'dal
sper'ma·to·cide'
sper'ma·to·cyst'
sper'ma·to·cys·tec'to·my
sper'ma·to·cys'tic
sper'ma·to·cys·ti'tis

sper'ma·to·cys·tot'o·my
sper·mat'o·cyte'
sper'ma·to·cy'to·gen'e·sis
sper'ma·to·cy'to'ma
    pl. -mas *or* -ma·ta
sper'ma·to·gen'e·sis
sper'ma·to·gen'ic
sper'ma·tog'e·nous
sper'ma·to·go'ni·um *pl.*
    -ni·a
sper'ma·toid'
sper'ma·tol'y·sin
sper'ma·tol'y·sis *pl.* -ses'
sper'ma·to·lyt'ic
sper'ma·to·mere'
sper'ma·to·me'rite'
sper'ma·top'a·thy
sper·mat'o·phore'
sper'ma·tor·rhe'a
—— dor'mi·en'tum
sper'ma·tos'che·sis
sper'ma·to·tox'in
sper'ma·tox'in
sper'ma·to·zo'i·cide'
sper'ma·to·zo'id
sper'ma·to·zo'on' *pl.* -zo'a
sper'ma·to·zo'al
sper'ma·tu'ri·a
sper·mec'to·my
sper'mi·cide'
sper'mine'
sper'mi·o·gen'e·sis
sper'mo·cy'to'ma *pl.* -mas
    or -ma·ta
sper'mo·lith'
sper'mo·lo'ro·pex'y
sper'mo·neu·ral'gi·a
sper'mo·tox'ic
sper'mo·tox'in
Sper'ry method
sphac'e·late', -lat'ed, -lat'ing
sphac'e·la'tion
sphac'e·lism
sphac'e·lo·der'ma
sphac'e·loid
sphac'e·lous
sphac'e·lus
spha'gi·as'mus
spha·gi'tis
sphe'ni·on'
sphe'no·bas'i·lar
sphe'no·ceph'a·lus *pl.* -li'
sphe'no·ceph'a·ly
sphe'no·eth'moid'
sphe'no·fron'tal
sphe'noid'
sphe·noi'dal

sphe'noid·i'tis
sphe'noi·dos'to·my
sphe'noid·ot'o·my
sphe'no·ma'lar
sphe'no·man·dib'u·lar
sphe'no·max'il·lar'y
sphe'no·oc·cip'i·tal
sphe'no·pal'a·tine'
sphe'no·pa·ri'e·tal
sphe'no·pe·tro'sal
sphe·no'sis
sphe'no·squa·mo'sal
sphe'no·tem'po·ral
sphe·not'ic
sphe'no·tre'si·a
sphe'no·tribe'
sphe'no·trip'sy
sphe'no·tur'bi·nal
sphe'no·vo'mer·ine
sphe'no·zy'go·mat'ic
sphere
sphe'res·the'si·a
spher'ic or sper'i·cal
sphe'ro·ceph'a·lus pl. -li'
sphe'ro·cyl'in·der
sphe'ro·cyte'
sphe'ro·cyt'ic
sphe'ro·cy·to'sis pl. -ses'
sphe'roid'
sphe·roi'dal
sphe·ro'ma pl. -mas or -ma·ta
sphe·rom'e·ter
spher'ule'
sphinc'ter
—— am·pul'lae'
—— a'ni' ex·ter'nus
—— ani in·ter'nus
—— duc'tus cho'led'o·chi'
—— of Boy'den
—— of Od'di
—— pan'cre·at'i·cus
—— u·re'thrae'
—— urethrae mem'bra·na'ce·ae'
—— ve·si'cae'
sphinc'ter·al
sphinc·ter'ic
sphinc'ter·al'gi·a
sphinc'ter·ec'to·my
sphinc'ter·is'mus
sphinc'ter·i'tis
sphinc'ter·ol'y·sis pl. -ses'
sphinc'ter·o·plas'ty
sphinc'ter·ot'o·my
sphin'go·lip'id
sphin'go·lip'i·do'sis pl. -ses'

sphin'go·li'po·dys'tro·phy
sphin'go·my'e·lin
sphin'go·my'e·li·no'sis
sphin'go·sine'
sphyg'mic or sphyg'mi·cal
sphyg'mo·bo·lom'e·ter
sphyg'mo·bo·lom'e·try
sphyg'mo·chron'o·graph'
sphyg'mo·chro·nog'ra·phy
sphyg·mod'ic
sphyg'mo·dy'na·mom'e·ter
sphyg'mo·gram'
sphyg'mo·graph'
sphyg'mo·graph'ic
sphyg·mog'ra·phy
sphyg'moid'
sphyg'mo·ma·nom'e·ter
sphyg'mo·ma·nom'e·try
sphyg·mom'e·ter
sphyg'mo·os'cil·lom'e·ter
sphyg'mo·pal·pa'tion
sphyg'mo·phone'
sphyg'mo·scope'
sphyg·mos'co·py
sphyg'mo·sys'to·le
sphyg'mo·tech'ny
sphyg'mo·to'no·graph'
sphyg'mo·to·nom'e·ter
sphyg'mus pl. -mi'
sphynx'-neck'
sphy·rec'to·my
sphy·rot'o·my
spi'ca pl. -cae' or -cas
spic'u·la pl. -lae'
spic'u·lar
spic'u·late'
spic'ule'
spi'der
Spie'gler
—— test
—— tumor
Spi·ge'li·an
—— hernia
—— lobe
spike
spi·lo'ma pl. -mas or -ma·ta
spi'lo·pla'ni·a
spi'lus pl. -li'
spi'na pl. -nae'
—— an'gu·lar'is
—— bi'fi·da
—— bifida oc·cul'ta
—— fron·ta'lis
—— hel'i·cis
—— i·li'a·ca anterior inferi·or

—— iliaca anterior superior
—— iliaca posterior inferior
—— iliaca posterior superi·or
—— is'chi·ad'i·ca
—— men·ta'lis
—— na·sa'lis anterior max·il'lae'
—— nasalis os'sis fron·ta'lis
—— nasalis posterior os'sis pal·a·ti'ni'
—— os'sis sphe'noi·da'lis
—— scap'u·lae'
—— su'pra·me·a'tum
—— troch'le·ar'is
—— tym·pan'i·ca major
—— tympanica minor
—— ven·to'sa
spi'nae' pal'a·ti'nae'
spi·nal
spi·nal'gi·a
spi·na'lis
spin'dle
spine
spi·nif'u·gal
spi·nip'e·tal
spi'no·bul'bar
spi'no·cel'lu·lar
spi'no·cer'e·bel'lar
spi'no·cor'ti·cal
spi'no·gle'noid'
spi'no·ol'i·var'y
spi·no'sal
spi·no'sus
spi'no·tec'tal
spi'no·tha·lam'ic
spi'no·trans'ver·sar'i·us
spi'nous
spin'ther·ism
spi'nu·lose'
spi'ny
spip'er·one'
spi·rad'e·ni'tis sup'pu·ra·ti'va
spi·rad'e·no'ma pl. -mas or -ma·ta
spi'ral
spi'ra·my'cin
spi'reme'
spi·ril'lar
spi·ril'lar'y
spi·ril'le·mi·a
spi·ril'li·ci'dal
spi·ril·lo'sis pl. -ses'
spi·ril'lum pl. -la
spir'i·tus
—— fru·men'ti'

Spi'ro·chae'ta
—— ic'ter·og'e·nes'
—— ic'ter·o·haem'or·rhag'i·ae'
—— mor'sus mu'ris
—— o'ber·mei'er·i'
—— pal'li·da
spi'ro·che'tal
spi'ro·chete'
spi'ro·che·te'mi·a
spi'ro·che·ti·cide'
spi'ro·che·tol'y·sis
   pl. -ses'
spi'ro·che·to'sis pl. -ses'
spi'ro·che·tot'ic
spi'ro·gram'
spi'ro·graph'
spi·rog'ra·phy
spi·rom'e·ter
spi'ro·met'ric
spi·rom'e·try
spi'ro·no·lac'tone'
spi'ro·scope'
spi·rox'a·sone'
spis'sat'ed
spis'si·tude'
splanch'nap·o·phys'e·al
splanch'na·poph'y·sis pl.
   -ses'
splanch'nec·to'pi·a
splanch'nem·phrax'is
splanch'nes·the'si·a
splanch'nic
splanch'ni·cec'to·my
splanch'ni·cot'o·my
splanch'no·blast'
splanch'no·cele' (a hernial
   protrusion)
‡splanchnocoele
splanch'no·coele' (part of
   the coelom)
‡splanchnocele
splanch'no·cra'ni·um pl.
   -ni·ums or -ni·a
splanch'no·di·as'ta·sis
splanch·nog'ra·phy
splanch'no·lith'
splanch'no·li·thi'a·sis pl.
   -ses'
splanch'no·lo'gi·a
splanch·nol'o·gy
splanch'no·meg'a·ly
splanch·no·mi'cri·a
splanch'no·nop'a·thy
splanch'no·pleu'ral
splanch'no·pleure'
splanch'nop·to'si·a

splanch'nop·to'sis pl. -ses'
splanch'no·scle·ro'sis pl.
   -ses'
splanch·nos'co·py
splanch'no·skel'e·ton
splanch'no·so·mat'ic
splanch·not'o·my
splanch'no·tribe'
splay'foot'
spleen
splen'ad·e·no'ma pl. -mas
   or -ma·ta
sple·nal'gi·a
sple·nat'ro·phy
sple·nec'ta·sis
sple·nec'to·mize', -mized',
   -miz'ing
sple·nec'to·my
splen'ec·to'pi·a
sple·nec'to·py
sple·ne'mi·a
sple·net'ic
sple'ni·al
splen'ic
splen'i·co·pan'cre·at'ic
sple·nic'ter·us
splen'i·form'
sple·ni'tis
sple'ni·um pl. -ni·a
   —— cor'po·ris cal·lo'si'
sple'ni·us pl. -ni·i'
   —— cer'vi·cis ac'ces·so'ri·us
splen'i·za'tion
sple'no·cele'
sple'no·clei'sis
sple'no·cyte'
sple'no·dyn'i·a
sple·nog'e·nous
sple'no·gram'
sple'no·gran'u·lo'ma·to'sis
   sid'er·ot'i·ca
sple·nog'ra·phy
sple'no·hep'a·to·meg'a·ly
sple'noid'
sple'no·ker'a·to'sis pl. -ses'
sple'no·lap'a·rot'o·my
sple'no·lym·phat'ic
sple·nol'y·sis
sple·no'ma pl. -mas or -ma·ta
sple'no·ma·la'ci·a
sple'no·me·ga'li·a
sple'no·meg'a·ly
sple'no·my'e·log'e·nous
sple'no·neph'ric
sple'no·neph'rop·to'sis
sple'no·pan'cre·at'ic

sple·nop'a·thy
sple'no·pex'y
splen'o·phren'ic
sple'no·pneu·mo'ni·a
sple'no·por·tog'ra·phy
sple'nop·to'sis pl. -ses'
sple·no·re'nal
sple'nor·rha'gi·a
sple·nor'rha·phy
sple·no'sis
sple·not'o·my
sple'no·tox'in
sple'no·ty'phoid'
splen'u·lus pl. -li'
sple·nun'cu·lus pl. -li'
splice, spliced, splic'ing
splint
splin'ter
splint'ing
split'-thick'ness
split'ting
spo'di·o·my'e·li'tis
spon'dy·lal'gi·a
spon'dyl·ar·thri'tis
spon'dyl·ar·throc'a·ce'
spon'dyl·ex'ar·thro'sis pl.
   -ses'
spon'dy·lit'ic
spon'dy·li'tis
   —— an'ky·lo·poi·et'i·ca
spon'dy·li·ze'ma
spon'dy·lo·ar·thri'tis
spon'dy·loc'a·ce'
spon'dy·lod'e·sis
spon'dy·lo·di·dym'i·a
spon'dy·lod'y·mus
spon'dy·lo·dyn'i·a
spon'dy·lo·lis·the'sis
spon'dy·lo·lis·thet'ic
spon'dy·lol'y·sis
spon'dy·lo'ma·la'ci·a
spon'dy·lop'a·thy
spon'dy·lo·py·o'sis pl. -ses'
spon'dy·lo'sis pl. -ses'
spon'dy·lo·syn·de'sis pl.
   -ses'
spon'dy·lot'o·my
spon'dy·lous
spon'dy·lus pl. -li'
sponge
spon'gi·a
spon'gi·form'
spon'gi·i'tis
spon'gi·o·blast'
spon'gi·o·blas·to'ma
   pl. -mas or -ma·ta
   —— mul'ti·for'me'

—— po·lar′e′
—— prim′i·ti′vum
—— u′ni·po·lar′e′
spon′gi·o·cyte′
spon′gi·o·cy·to′ma pl. -mas
 or -ma·ta
spon′gi·o·form′
spon′gi·oid′
spon′gi·o·neu′ro·blas·
 to′ma pl. -mas or -ma·ta
spon′gi·o·plasm
spon′gi·ose′
spon′gi·o′sis
spon′gi·o·si′tis
spon′gi·ot′ic
spon′gy
spon·ta′ne·ous
spoon
spo·rad′ic
spo·ran′gi·o·phore′
spo·ran′gi·o·spore′
spo·ran′gi·um pl. -gi·a
spore
spo′ri·ci·dal
spo′ri·cide′
spo′ro·ag·glu′ti·na′tion
spo′ro·cyst′
spo′ro·gen′e·sis
spo′ro·gen′ic
spo·rog′e·nous
spo·rog′o·ny
spo′ront′
spo′ro·phyte
Spo′ro·thrix′ schenk′i·i′
spo·rot′ri·chin
spo′ro·tri·cho′sis pl. -ses′
spo′ro·zo′an
spo′ro·zo′ite′
spo′ro·zo′on′ pl. -zo′a
spor·u·late′, -lat′ed, -lat′ing
spor·u·la′tion
spot, spot′ted, spot′ting
sprain
spray
Spren′gel deformity
sprue
spud
spur
spu′ri·ous
spu′tum pl. -ta or -tums
squa·lene′
squa′ma pl. -mae′
—— fron·ta′lis
—— oc·cip′i·ta′lis
—— tem′po·ra′lis
squa′ma·ti·za′tion
squa′mo·ba′sal

squa′mo·cel′lu·lar
squa′mo·fron′tal
squa′mo·mas′toid′
squa′mo·oc·cip′i·tal
squa′mo·pa·ri′e·tal
squa′mo·pe·tro′sal
squa·mo′sa pl. -sae′
squa·mo′sal
squa′mo·sphe′noid′
squa′mo·tem′po·ral
squa′mo·tym·pan′ic
squa′mous
squa′mo·zy′go·mat′ic
squeeze
squint
stab, stabbed, stab′bing
sta′bile (immobile)
 ♦stable
sta′bi·lize′, -lized′, -liz′ing
sta′bi·li′zer
sta′ble (immutable)
 ♦stabile
stac·ca′to
sta′di·um pl. -di·a
—— ac′mes′
—— am·phib′o·les′
—— an·ni′hi·la′ti·o′nis
—— aug·men′ti′
—— ca·lo′ris
—— con·ta′gi·i′
—— con′va·les·cen′ti·ae′
—— dec′re·men′ti′
—— de′crus·ta′ti·o·nis
—— des′qua·ma′ti·o·nis
—— e·rup′ti·o′nis
—— ex′sic·ca′ti·o′nis
—— flo·ri′ti·o′nis
—— frig′o·ris
—— in′cre·men′ti′
—— in′cu·ba′ti·o′nis
—— ma·ni′a·ca′le′
—— ner·vo′sum
—— pro′dro·mo′rum
—— su·do′ris
—— sup′pu·ra′ti·o′nis
—— ul′ti·mum
Staeh′li pigment line
stage
stag′nate′, -nat′ed, -nat′ing
stag·na′tion
Stahl ear
stain
stalk
sta′men pl. -mens or -mi·na
stam′i·na
stam′mer
stan′dard

stan′dard·i·za′tion
stan′dard·ize′, -ized′, -iz′ing
stand′still′
stan′nate′
stan′nic
stan′nous
stan′o·lone′
stan′o·zo′lol′
sta·pe·dec′to·my
sta·pe′di·al
sta·pe′di·o·te·not′o·my
sta·pe′di·o·ves·tib′u·lar
sta·pe′di·us pl. -di·i′
sta′pes′ pl. sta′pes′ or
 sta·pe′des′
staph′i·sa′gri·a
staph′y·le
staph′y·lec′to·my
staph′yl·e·de′ma
staph′yl·he′ma·to′ma
staph′y·line′
staph′y·li′no·pha·ryn′ge·us
staph′y·li′nus
—— ex·ter′nus
—— in·ter′nus
—— me′di·us
sta·phyl′i·on′
staph′y·li′tis
staph′y·lo·coc′cal
staph′y·lo·coc·ce′mi·a
staph′y·lo·coc′cic
staph′y·lo·coc·co′sis
staph′y·lo·coc′cus pl. -ci′
Staph′y·lo·coc′cus
—— al′bus
—— au′re·us
—— cit′re·us
—— ep′i·der′mi·dis
—— py·og′e·nes′
staph′y·lo·co′sis pl. -ses′
staph′y·lo·der′ma
staph′y·lo·der′ma·ti′tis
staph′y·lo·di·al′y·sis
staph′y·lo·ki′nase′
staph′y·lol′y·sin
staph′y·lo′ma pl. -mas or
 -ma·ta
—— cor′ne·ae′
—— u′ve·a′le′
staph′y·lom′a·tous
staph′y·lon′cus
staph′y·lo·pha·ryn′ge·us
staph′y·lo·phar′yn·
 gor′rha·phy
staph′y·lo·plas′ty
staph′y·lop·to′sis
staph′y·lor′rha·phy

staph'y·los'chi·sis *pl.* -ses'
staph'y·lot'o·my
staph'y·lo·tox'in
starch
start'er
star'tle, -tled, -tling
star·va'tion
starve, starved, starv'ing
sta'sis *pl.* -ses'
state
stat'ic
stat'ics
stat'im
sta'tion
sta'tion·ar'y
sta·tis'ti·cal
sta·tis'tic
stat'o·co'ni·a *sing.* -ni·um
stat'o·cyst'
stat'o·ki·net'ic
stat'o·lith'
sta'to·lon'
sta·tom'e·ter
stat'ur·al
stat'ure
sta'tus
—— an'gi·no'sus
—— ar·thrit'i·cus
—— asth·mat'i·cus
—— con'vul·si'vus
—— cri·bro'sus
—— dys·my'e·li·ni·sa'tus of
Vogt
—— dys·raph'i·cus
—— ep'i·lep'ti·cus
—— fi·bro'sus
—— lym·phat'i·cus
—— mar'mo·ra'tus
—— mi·grai'nus
—— par'a·thy're·o·pri'vus
—— prae'sens
—— rap'tus
—— spon'gi·o'sus
—— thy'mi·co·lym·phat'i·
cus
—— thy'mi·cus
—— ver'ru·co'sus
—— ver·tig'i·no'sus
sta'tu·vo'lence
sta'tu·vo'lent
Staub'-Trau'gott effect
stau'ri·on'
staves'a'cre
stax'is
steal
ste·ap'sin
ste'a·ral'de·hyde'

ste'a·rate'
ste·ar'ic
ste·ar'i·form'
ste'a·rin
ste'a·ro·der'mi·a
ste'ar·rhe'a
—— fla·ves'cens
—— ni'gri·cans'
—— sim'plex
ste'a·ti'tis
ste'a·to·cryp·to'sis *pl.* -ses'
ste'a·to·cys·to'ma mul'ti·
plex'
ste'a·tog'e·nous
ste'a·tol'y·sis *pl.* -ses'
ste'a·to·lyt'ic
ste'a·to'ma *pl.* -mas *or*
-ma·ta
ste'a·to'ma·to'sis
ste'a·tom'er·y
ste'a·to'ne·cro'sis
ste'a·to·pyg'i·a
ste'a·tor·rhe'a
ste'a·to'sis *pl.* -ses'
Steen'bock' unit
Steell murmur
stef'fi·my'cin
ste'ge
steg·no'sis *pl.* -ses'
steg·not'ic
Stei'nach' method
Stein'brock'er class
Steind'ler operation
Stei'nert disease
Stei'ner tumor
Stein'-Lev'en·thal' syn-
drome
Stein test
stel'la *pl.* -lae'
—— len'tis hy'a·loi'de·a
—— lentis i·rid'i·ca
stel'lar
stel'late'
stel·lec'to·my
stel'lu·la *pl.* -lae'
stel'lu·lae'
—— vas'cu·lo'sae' wins·
low'i·i'
—— ver·hey'en·i·i'
Stell'wag'
—— operation
—— sign
stem
Sten'ger test
ste'ni·on' *pl.* -ni·a
sten'o·car'di·a
sten'o·ceph'a·lous

sten'o·ceph'a·ly
sten'o·cho'ri·a
sten'o·co·ri'a·sis
sten'o·crot'a·phy
sten'o·dont'
sten'o·mer'ic
Ste·no'ni·an duct
sten'o·pe'ic
ste·no'sal
ste·nose', -nosed', -nos'ing
ste·no'sis *pl.* -ses'
sten'os'to·my
sten'o·ther'mal
sten'o·tho'rax'
ste·not'ic
Sten'sen
—— duct
—— foramen
stent
ste·pha'ni·al
ste·phan'ic
ste·pha'ni·on'
ster'co·bi'lin
ster'co·bi·lin'o·gen
ster'co·lith'
ster'co·por'phy·rin
ster'co·ra'ceous
ster'co·ral
ster'co·rar'y
ster'co·ro'ma *pl.* -mas *or*
-ma·ta
ster'co·rous
ster'cus
stere
ster'e·o·ag·no'sis *pl.* -ses'
ster'e·o·an'es·the'si·a
ster'e·o·ar·throl'y·sis *pl.*
-ses'
ster'e·o·blas'tu·la *pl.* -las *or*
-lae'
ster'e·o·cam·pim'e·ter
ster'e·o·chem'i·cal
ster'e·o·chem'is·try
ster'e·o·cil'i·a *sing.* i·um
ster'e·o·en·ceph'a·lo·tome'
ster'e·o·en·ceph'a·lot'o·my
ster'e·o'fluor·os'co·py
ster'e·og·no'sis
ster'e·og·nos'tic
ster'e·o·gram'
ster'e·o·graph'
ster'e·og'ra·phy
ster'e·o·i'so·mer
ster'e·o·i·som'er·ism
ster'e·o·mon'o·scope'
ster'e·o-oph·thal'mo·
scope'

ster'e·o·phan'to·scope
ster'e·o·pho'ro·scope'
ster'e·o·plasm
ster'e·op'sis
ster'e·op'ter
ster'e·o·ra'di·og'ra·phy
ster'e·o·roent'gen·og'ra·
  phy
ster'e·o·scope'
ster'e·o·scop'ic
ster'e·os'co·py
ster'e·o·stro'bo·scope'
ster'e·o·tac'tic
ster'e·o·tax'i·a
ster'e·o·tax'ic
ster'e·o·tax'is pl. -tax'es'
ster'e·o·tax'y
ster'e·o·trop'ic
ster'e·ot'ro·pism
ster'e·o·ty'py
ste'ric
ste'rid
ster·rig'ma pl. -ma·ta or -mas
ster'ig·mat'ic
Ste·rig'ma·to·cys'tis
—— cin'na·mo·mi'nus
ster'ile
ste·ril'i·ty
ster'il·i·za'tion
ster'il·ize', -ized', -iz'ing
ster'il·iz'er
ster'nal
ster·nal'gi·a
ster·na'lis
ster'ne·bra pl. -brae'
Stern'heim'er-Mal'bin
  cells
ster'no·chon'dro·scap'u·
  lar'is
ster'no·cla·vic'u·lar
ster'no·cla·vic'u·lar'is
ster'no·clei'dal
ster'no·clei'do·mas'toid'
ster'no·cos'tal
ster'no·cos·ta'lis
ster'no·dym'i·a
ster'nod'y·mus
ster'no·dyn'i·a
ster'no·hy'oid'
ster'no·hy·oi'de·us az'y·
  gos'
ster'no·mas'toid'
ster'no·pa'gi·a
ster'no·pa'gus
ster'nop'a·gy
ster'no·per'i·car'di·al
ster'no·scap'u·lar

ster·nos'chi·sis pl. -ses'
ster'no·thy'roid'
ster·not'o·my
ster'no·tra'che·al
ster'no·ver'te·bral
ster'num pl. -nums or -na
ster'nu·ta'ti·o'
—— con'vul·si'va
ster'nu·ta'tion
ster'nu·ta'tor
ster·nu'ta·to'ry
ste'roid'
ste·roi'do·gen'e·sis pl. -ses'
ste·roi'do·gen'ic
ste'rol'
ste'rone'
ster'tor
steth·al'gi·a
steth·ar'te·ri'tis
steth'o·gram'
ste·thog'ra·phy
steth'o·my'o·si'tis
steth'o·phone'
steth'o·scope'
steth'o·scop'ic
ste·thos'co·py
Ste'vens-John'son syn-
  drome
Stew'art-Holmes' phe-
  nomenon
sthe'ni·a
sthen'ic
sthe·nom'e·ter
sthen'o·plas'tic
stib'a·mine'
stib'i·ac'ne
stib'i·al·ism
stib'ine'
stib'i·um
sti·bo'ni·um
stib'o·phen'
stich'o·chrome'
Stick'er disease
Stie'da fracture
sti'fle, -fled, -fling
stig'ma pl. stig·ma'ta or
  -mas
stig·mas'ter·ol'
stig·ma'ta
—— ni'gra
—— of Ben'e·ke
—— ven·tric'u·li'
stig·mat'ic
stig'ma·tism (an eye condi-
  tion)
♦sigmatism
stig'ma·ti·za'tion

stig'ma·tom'e·ter
stig·mat'o·scope'
stig'ma·tos'co·py
stig'ma·tose'
stil·baz'i·um
stil'bene'
stil·bes'trol'
Still
—— disease
—— murmur
still'birth'
still'born'
Stil'ler
—— disease
—— sign
stil'li·cid'i·um
—— lac'ri·mar'um
—— u·ri'nae'
Stil'ling
—— canal
—— raphe
—— test
Stim'son method
stim'u·lant
stim'u·late', -lat'ed, -lat'ing
stim'u·la'tion
stim'u·la'tor
stim'u·lin
stim'u·lus pl. -li'
sting
stip'ple, -pled, -pling
stir'rup
stitch
sto·chas'tic
stock
stock'i·net'
Stock retinal atrophy
Stof'fel operation
stoi'chi·o·met'ric
stoi'chi·om'e·try
Stokes
—— expectorant
—— law
—— operation
Stokes'-Ad'ams syndrome
Stok'vis disease
Stoltz operation
sto'ma pl. -ma·ta or -mas
sto·mac'a·ce'
sto'ma·ceph'a·lus
stom'ach
sto·mach'ic
sto'mal
sto'ma·tal'gi·a
sto·mat'ic
sto'ma·ti'tis
—— ven'e·na'ta

sto'ma·toc'a·ce'
sto'ma·to·cyte'
sto'ma·to·dyn'i·a
sto'ma·to·dy·so'di·a
sto'ma·to·gas'tric
sto'ma·to·glos·si'tis
sto'ma·to·log'ic
sto'ma·tol'o·gy
sto'ma·to·ma·la'ci·a
sto'ma·to·me'ni·a
sto'ma·to·mi·a
sto·mat'o·my
sto'ma·to·my·co'sis *pl.* -ses'
sto'ma·to·ne·cro'sis
sto'ma·to·no'ma
sto'ma·top'a·thy
sto'ma·to·plas'tic
sto'ma·to·plas'ty
sto'ma·tor·rha'gi·a
sto'ma·tos'chi·sis
sto'ma·to·scope'
sto'ma·to'sis *pl.* -ses'
sto'ma·tot'o·my
sto·men'or·rha'gi·a
sto'mi·on'
sto'mo·de'um *pl.* -de'a *or*
  -de'ums
sto·mos'chi·sis *pl.* -ses'
stone
Stone operation
Stook'ey reflex
stool
stop'page
storm
stra·bis'mal
stra·bis'mic
stra'bis·mom'e·ter
stra'bis·mom'e·try
stra·bis'mus
stra·bom'e·ter
stra·bom'e·try
strab'o·tome'
stra·bot'o·my
strag'u·lum *pl.* -la
strain
strait
stra·mo'ni·um
stran'gle, -gled, -gling
stran'gu·lat'ed
stran'gu·la'tion
stran'gu·ry
strap, strapped, strap'ping
strat'i·fi·ca'tion
strat'i·fied'
stra'ti·graph'ic
stra·tig'ra·phy
stra'tum *pl.* -ta

—— al'bum pro·fun'dum
cor'po·rum qua'dri·gem'i·
no'rum
—— ba·sa'le'
—— basale ep'i·der'mi·dis
—— cer'e·bra'le' ret'i·nae'
—— ci·ne're·um
—— cinereum cer'e·bel'li'
—— cir'cu·lar'e' mem·
bra'nae' tym'pa·ni'
—— circulare tu'ni·cae'
mus'cu·lar'is col'li'
—— circulare tunicae mus-
cularis in'tes·ti'ni' ten'u·is
—— circulare tunicae mus-
cularis rec'ti'
—— circulare tunicae mus-
cularis tu'bae' u'ter·i'nae'
—— circulare tunicae mus-
cularis u·re'thrae' mu'li·
e'bris
—— circulare tunicae mus-
cularis ven·tric'u·li'
—— com·pac'tum
—— cor'ne·um
—— corneum un'guis
—— cu·ta'ne·um mem·
bra'nae' tym'pa·ni'
—— cy·lin'dri·cum
—— dis·junc'tum
—— ex·ter'num tu'ni·cae'
mus'cu·lar'is duc'tus def'e·
ren'tis
—— externum tunicae mus-
cularis u·re'ter·is
—— externum tunicae mus-
cularis ve·si'cae' u'ri·nar'i·
ae'
—— fi·bro'sum cap'su·lae'
ar·tic'u·lar'is
—— gan'gli·o·nar'e' ner'vi'
op'ti·ci'
—— ganglionare ret'i·nae'
—— gan'gli·o'sum cer'e·
bel'li'
—— ger'mi·na·ti'vum
—— germinativum (Mal·
pi'ghi·i'
—— germinativum un'guis
—— gran'u·lo'sum
—— granulosum cer'e·bel'li'
—— granulosum ep'i·der·mi·
dis
—— granulosum fol·lic'u·li'
o·var'i·ci' ve·sic'u·lo'si
—— granulosum o·var'i·i'

—— gris'e·um col'lic'u·li' su·
pe'ri·o'ris
—— in'ter·me'di·um
—— in·ter'num tu'ni·cae'
mus'cu·lar'is duc'tus def'er·
en'tis
—— internum tunicae mus-
cularis u·re'ter·is
—— internum tunicae mus-
cularis ve·si'cae' u'ri·nar'i·
ae'
—— in'ter·ol'i·var'e' lem·
nis'ci'
—— lem·nis'ci'
—— lon'gi·tu'di·na'le' tu'ni·
cae' mus'cu·lar'is co'li'
—— longitudinale tunicae
muscularis in·tes·ti'ni' ten'u·
is
—— longitudinale tunicae
muscularis rec'ti'
—— longitudinale tunicae
muscularis tu'bae' u'ter·
i'nae'
—— longitudinale tunicae
muscularis u·re'thrae mu'li·
e'bris
—— longitudinale tunicae
muscularis ven·tric'u·li'
—— lu'ci·dum
—— mal·pi'ghi·i'
—— medium tu'ni·cae'
mus'cu·lar'is duc'tus def'er·
en'tis
—— medium tunicae mus-
cularis u·re'ter·is
—— medium tunicae mus-
cularis ve·si'cae' u'ri·nar'i·
ae'
—— mo·lec'u·lar'e' cer'e·
bel'li'
—— mu·co'sum
—— mucosum mem·
bra'nae' tym'pa·ni'
—— neu'ro·ep'i·the'li·a'le'
ret'i·nae'
—— nu·cle·ar'e' me·dul'lae'
ob'lon·ga'tae'
—— pap'il·lar'e' co'ri·i'
—— pig·men'ti' bul'bi' oc'u·
li'
—— pigmenti cor'po·ris cil'i·
ar'is
—— pigmenti i'ri·dis
—— pigmenti ret'i·nae'
—— ra'di·a'tum mem·
bra'nae' tym'pa·ni'

—— re·tic′u·lar′e′
—— spi·no′sum ep′i·der′mi·dis
—— spon′gi·o′sum
—— sub′mu·co′sum
—— sub′se·ro′sum
—— su′pra·vas′cu·lar′e′
—— sy·no′vi·a′le′ cap′su·lae′ ar·tic′u·lar′is
—— vas′cu·lar′e′
—— zo·na′le′ cor′po·rum qua′dri·gem′i·no′rum
—— zonale thal′a·mi′
Straus reaction
Strauss
—— phenomenon
—— syndrome
—— test
streak
stream
strem′ma
strep
streph′o·po′di·a
streph′o·sym·bo′li·a
strep′i·tus pl. -ti′
—— au′ri·um
—— u′ter·i′
—— u′ter·i′nus
strep′o·gen′in
strep′ti·ce′mi·a
strep′ti·dine′
strep′to·an·gi′na
strep′to·bac′il·lar′y
strep′to·ba·cil′lus pl. -li′
Strep′to·ba·cil′lus
—— mo·nil′i·for′mis
strep′to·bac·te′ri·a sing. -ri· um
strep′to·bac′ter·in
strep′to·bi·o′sa·mine′
strep′to·coc′cal
Strep′to·coc′ce·ae′
strep′to·coc·ce′mi·a
strep′to·coc′cic
strep′to·coc′cus pl. -ci′
Strep′to·coc′cus
—— an·he′mo·lyt′i·cus
—— ep′i·dem′i·cus
—— fe·ca′lis
—— lac′tis
—— MG
—— py·og′e·nes′
strep′to·co·ly′sin
strep′to·dor′nase′
strep′to·he·mol′y·sin
strep′to·ki′nase′
strep′to·ly′sin

Strep′to·my′ces′
—— so·ma′li·en′sis
strep′to·my′cin
strep′to·my·co′sis pl. -ses′
strep′to·nic′o·zid
strep′to·ni′grin
strep′to·sep′ti·ce′mi·a
strep′to·tri·cho′sis pl. -ses′
stress
stretch′er
stri′a pl. -ae′
—— dis·ten′sa
—— in′ter·me′di·a tri·go′ni′ ol′fac·to′ri·i′
—— Lan·ci′si·i′
—— lon′gi·tu′di·na′lis lat′er· a′lis cor′po·ris cal·lo′si′
—— longitudinalis me′di· a′lis cor′po·ris cal·lo′si′
—— mal′le·ar′is
—— mal′le·o·lar′is
—— me′di·a′lis tri·go′ni′ ol′fac·to′ri·i′
—— med′ul·lar′is thal′a·mi′
—— of Gen·na′ri
—— of Lang′hans′
—— of Ni′ta·buch′
—— of Rohr
—— ol′fac·to′ri·a
—— olfactoria lat′er·a′lis
—— sem′i·cir′cu·lar′is
—— ter′mi·na′lis
—— vas′cu·lar′is duc′tus coch′le·ar′is
—— vascularis of Husch′ke
stri′ae′
—— a·cus′ti·cae′
—— al′bi·can′tes′ grav′i· dar′um
—— a·tro′phi·cae′
—— cer′e·bel·lar′is
—— cu′tis dis·ten′sae′
—— grav′i·dar′um
—— med′ul·lar′es′ fos′sae′ rhom·boi′de·ae′
—— medullares ven·tric′u·li′ quar′ti′
—— of Bail·lar·ger′
—— of Held
—— of Mon′a·kov′
—— of Pic′co·lo·mi′ni
—— of Ret′zi·us
—— trans·ver′sae′ cor′po·ris cal′lo·si′
stri·a′tal
stri′ate′
stri′at′ed

stri·a′tion
stri·a′tum pl. -ta
stric′ture
stri′dor
—— den′ti·um
—— ser·rat′i·cus
strid′u·lous
strin′gent
stri′o·cel′lu·lar
stri′o·cer′e·bel′lar
stri′o·mus′cu·lar
stri′o·ni′gral
stri′o·tha·lam′ic
strip, stripped, strip′ping
stripe
—— of Gen·na′ri
stripes of Bail·lar·ger′
strip′per
strob′ic
stro·bi′la pl. -lae′
strob′i·la′tion
strob′ile
strob′i·loid′
strob′i·lus pl. -li′
stro′bo·scope′
stro′bo·scop′ic
Stro′ga·nov′ method
stroke
stro′ma pl. -ma·ta
—— glan′du·lae′ thy′re· oi′de·ae′
—— glandulae thy·roi′de·ae′
—— i′ri·dis
—— o·var′i·i′
—— vit′re·um
stro′mal
stro·mat′ic
stro·ma·tin
stro′ma·tog′e·nous
stro′ma·tol′y·sis
stro′ma·to′sis
Stron′gy·loi′des′
—— in·tes′ti·na′lis
—— ster′co·ra′lis
stron′gy·loi·di·a′sis pl. -ses′
stron′gy·lo′sis pl. -ses′
stron′ti·a
stron′ti·um
stro·phan′thi·din
stro·phan′thin
stroph′o·ceph′a·lus pl. -li′
stroph′o·ceph′a·ly
stroph′u·lus pl. -li′
—— pru′ri·gi·no′sus
struc′tur·al
struc′ture
stru′ma pl. -mae′

—— ab'er·ra'ta
—— ci·bar'i·a
—— con·gen'i·ta
—— lin·gua'lis
—— lym'pho·ma·to'sa
—— ma·lig'na
—— med'i·ca·men·to'sa
—— o·var'i·i'
—— ovarii lu·te'i·no·cel'lu·
lar'e'
—— post·bran'chi·a'lis
stru·mec'to·my
Stru'mi·a stain
stru'mi·form'
stru'mi·pri'val
stru·mi·pri'vic
stru'mi·pri'vous
stru·mi'tis
stru'mous
Strüm'pell
—— sign
—— reflex
strych'nine'
stump
stunt
stu'pe·fa'cient
stu'pe·fac'tion
stu'pe·fy', -fied', -fy'ing
stu'por
—— mel'an·chol'i·cus
—— vig'i·lans'
stu'por·ous
Sturge'-Web'er disease
Sturm'dorf' operation
stut'ter
stut'ter·er
sty pl. sties, also stye
sty·co'sis
stye pl. styes, var. of sty
sty'let
sty'li·form'
sty'lo·glos'sus pl. -si'
sty'lo·hy'oid'
sty'loid'
sty'lo·man·dib'u·lar
sty'lo·mas'toid'
sty'lo·pha·ryn'ge·us
sty'lus pl. -lus·es or -li'
sty'ma·to'sis
styp'sis
styp'tic
sty'ra·mate'
sty'rene'
sty'rol'
sub'ab·dom'i·nal
sub·ac'e·tate'
sub'a·cro'mi·al

sub'a·cute'
sub·al'i·men·ta'tion
sub·an'co·ne'us
sub'a·or'tic
sub·ap'i·cal
sub·ap'o·neu·rot'ic
sub·a'que·ous
sub'a·rach'noid'
sub·ar'cu·ate'
sub'a·re'o·lar
sub·as·trag'a·lar
sub·as·trin'gent
sub·au·di'tion
sub·au'ral
sub'au·ric'u·lar
sub·ax'i·al
sub·ax'il·lar'y
sub·ba'sal
sub·bra'chi·al
sub·brach'y·ce·phal'ic
sub'cal·car'e·ous
sub·cal'ca·rine'
sub·cap'su·lar
sub·car'bon·ate'
sub·car'di·nal
sub·car'ti·lag'i·nous
sub·chlo'ride'
sub·chon'dral
sub·chor'dal
sub·cho'ri·al
sub·cho'ri·on'ic
sub'cho·roi'dal
sub·chron'ic
sub'class'
sub·cla'vi·an
sub·cla·vic'u·lar
sub·cla'vi·us pl. -vi·i'
sub·clin'i·cal
sub·con'junc·ti'val
sub·con'scious
sub·con·tin'u·ous
sub·cor'a·coid'
sub·cor'ne·al
sub·cor'tex'
sub·cor'ti·cal
sub·cos'tal
sub·cra'ni·al
sub·crep'i·tant
sub·crep'i·ta'tion
sub·cru're·us
sub·cul'ture
sub·cu·ta'ne·ous
sub·cu·tic'u·lar
sub·cu'tis
sub·de·lir'i·um
sub·del'toid'
sub·den'tal

sub·der'mal
sub·der'mic
sub·di'a·phrag·mat'ic
sub·dor'sal
sub·duct'
sub·duc'tion
sub·du'ral
sub·en'do·car'di·al
sub·en'do·the'li·al
sub·en'do·the'li·um
sub'e·pen'dy·mal
sub'e·pen'dy·mo'ma
   pl. -mas *or* -ma·ta
sub·ep'i·der'mal
sub·ep'i·glot'tic
sub·ep'i·the'li·al
sub·fas'ci·al
sub·ga'le·al
sub·gal'late'
sub·ger'mi·nal
sub·gin'gi·val
sub·gle'noid'
sub·glos'sal
sub·glos·si'tis
sub·gran'u·lar
sub·gron·da'tion
sub·he·pat'ic
sub·hu'mer·al
sub·hy'a·loid' *(under the*
   hyaloid membrane)
◊subhyoid
sub·hy'oid' *(under the hyoid*
   bone)
◊subhyaloid
su·bic'u·lar
su·bic'u·lum pl. -la
—— prom'on·to'ri·i'
sub·in·ci'sion
sub·in·fec'tion
sub·in'gui·nal
sub·in'ti·mal
sub·in'vo·lu'tion
sub·i'o·dide'
sub·ja'cent
sub·jec'tive
sub·ju'gal
sub·la'ti·o'
—— ret'i·nae'
sub·la'tion
sub·le'thal
sub'li·mate', -mat·ed, -mat'-
   ing
sub'li·ma'tion
sub·lime', -limed', -lim'ing
sub·lim'i·nal
sub·li'mis
sub·lin'gual

sub·lin·gui′tis
sub·lob′u·lar
sub·lux′
sub·lux·at′ed
sub·lux·a′tion
sub·mal′le·o·lar
sub·mam′ma·ry
sub·man·dib′u·lar
sub·max′il·lar′y
sub·me′di·al
sub·men′tal
sub·mi′cron′
sub·mi′cro·scop′ic
sub·mor′phous
sub·mu·co′sa *pl.* -sae′ *or* -sas
sub′mu·co′sal
sub′nar·cot′ic
sub·na′sal
sub·na·sa′le′
sub·ni′trate′
sub·nor′mal
sub·nor·mal′i·ty
sub·no′to·chord′al
sub·nu′cle·us *pl.* -cle·i′
sub′oc·cip′i·tal
sub′o·per′cu·lum
sub·op′ti·mal
sub·op′ti·mum *pl.* -ma
sub·or′bit·al
sub·or′der
sub·or′di·na′tion
sub·ox′ide′
sub·pap′il·lar′y
sub·pap′u·lar
sub·par′a·lyt′ic
sub′pa·ri′e·tal
sub′pa·tel′lar
sub·pec′to·ral
sub·per′i·car′di·al
sub·per′i·os′te·al
sub·per′i·to·ne′al
sub·pha·ryn′ge·al
sub·phren′ic
sub′phy′lum *pl.* -la
sub′pla·cen′ta
sub′pla·cen′tal
sub·pleu′ral
sub·pu′bic
sub·scap′u·lar
sub·scap′u·lar′is
sub·scle′ral
sub′scle·rot′ic
sub·scrip′tion
sub·sen·sa′tion
sub·se′rous
sub·sib′i·lant

sub·side′, -sid′ed, -sid′ing
sub·si′dence
sub·sig′moid′
sub·sist′ence
sub·spe′cies
sub·spi′nous
sub·stage′
sub·stance
sub·stan′ti·a *pl.* -ae
—— ad′a·man·ti′na den′tis
—— al′ba
—— alba me·dul′lae′ spi·na′lis
—— com·pac′ta
—— cor′ti·ca′lis
—— corticalis cer′e·bel′li′
—— corticalis cer′e·bri′
—— corticalis glan′du·lae′ su′pra·re·na′lis
—— corticalis len′tis
—— corticalis lym′pho·glan′du·lae′
—— corticalis os′sis
—— corticalis re′nis
—— e·bur′ne·a
—— fer′ru·gin′e·a
—— ge·lat′i·no′sa
—— gelatinosa cen·tra′lis
—— gelatinosa Ro·lan′di′
—— glan′du·lar·is pros′ta·tae′
—— gli·o′sa
—— gris′e·a
—— grisea cen·tra′lis me·dul′lae′ spi·na′lis
—— grisea centralis mes′en·ceph·a·li′
—— grisea me·dul′lae′ spi·na′lis
—— in′ter·me′di·a cen·tra′lis me·dul′lae′ spi·na′lis
—— intermedia lat′er·a′lis me·dul′lae′ spi·na′lis
—— len′tis
—— med·ul′lar·is glan′du·lae′ su′pra·re·na′lis
—— medullaris lym′pho·glan′du·lae′
—— medullaris re′nis
—— mus′cu·lar·is pros′ta·tae′
—— ni′gra
—— os′se·a den′tis
—— per′fo·ra′ta anterior
—— perforata posterior
—— pro′pri·a cor′ne·ae′
—— propria scle′rae′

—— re·tic′u·lar′is
—— reticularis al′ba (Ar·nol′di′)
—— reticularis alba me·dul′lae′ ob′lon·ga′tae′
—— reticularis gris′e·a me·dul′lae′ ob′lon·ga′tae′
—— spon′gi·o′sa
sub′stan·tive
sub·ster′nal
sub·ster′no·mas′toid′
sub·stit′u·ent
sub′sti·tute′, -tut′ed, -tut′ing
sub′sti·tu′tion
sub′sti·tu′tive
sub′strate′
sub′struc·ture
sub·sul′fate′
sub·sul′to·ry
sub·sul′tus
—— clo′nus
—— ten′di·num
sub·syn·ap′tic
sub·ta′lar
sub·tar′sal
sub·tem′po·ral
sub·te′ni·al
sub·ten·to′ri·al
sub·ter′mi·nal
sub·ter′tian
sub′te·tan′ic
sub′tha·lam′ic
sub·thal′a·mus *pl.* -mi′
sub·thresh′old′
sub·thy′roid·ism
sub·ti·lin
sub·to′tal
sub′tra·pe′zi·al
sub·trig′o·nal
sub′tro·chan·ter′ic
sub·trop′i·cal
sub·um·bil′i·cal
sub·un′gual
sub·u′re·thral
sub·vag′i·nal
sub·val′vu·lar
sub·ver′te·bral
sub·vir′ile
sub·vi′ta·min·o′sis
sub·vo·lu′tion
sub·vo′mer·ine′
sub·wak′ing
suc′cen·tu′ri·ate
suc·cif′er·ous
suc′ci·nate′
suc·cin′ic
suc′cor·rhe′a

suc'cus *(a secretion)*, pl. -ci'
♦*succuss*
—— en·ter'i·cus
—— gas'tri·cus
—— in·tes'ti·na'lis
—— pan'cre·at'i·cus
—— pro·stat'i·cus
suc·cuss' *(to shake)*
♦*succus*
suc·cus'sion
suck'le, -led, -ling
Suc·quet'-Hoy'er canal
su'crase'
su'crate'
su'crose'
su'cro·se'mi·a
su'cro·su'ri·a
suc'tion
suc·to'ri·al
su·da'men pl. -dam'i·na
Su·dan'
—— stain
su·dan'o·phil'
su·dan'o·phil'i·a
su·dan'o·phil'ic
su·da'tion
Su'deck' atrophy
su'do·mo'tor
su'do·re'sis
su'do·rif'er·ous
su'do·rif'ic
su'do·rip'a·rous
suf'fo·cate', -cat·ed, -cat'ing
suf'fo·ca'tion
suf·fuse', -fused', -fus'ing
suf·fu'sion
sug'ar
sug·gest'i·bil'i·ty
sug·gest'i·ble
sug·ges'tion
sug'gil·la'tion
su'i·ci'dal
su'i·cide'
Su'ker sign
sul·a'ze·pam'
sul'cal
sul'cate'
sul'ci
—— ar·te'ri·o'si'
—— cer'e·bel'li'
—— cer'e·bri'
—— cu'tis
—— oc·cip'i·ta'les' lat'er·a'les'
—— occipitales su·pe'ri·o'res'
—— or'bi·ta'les'

—— pal'a·ti'ni' max·il'lae'
—— par'a·co'li·ci'
—— par'a·gle'noi·da'les'
—— tem'po·ra'les' trans·ver'si'
—— ve·no'si'
sul'ci·form'
sul'cus pl. -ci'
—— am'pul·lar'is
—— ant·hel'i·cis trans·ver'sus
—— ar·te'ri·ae' oc·cip'i·ta'lis
—— arteriae sub·cla'vi·ae'
—— arteriae tem'po·ra'lis me'di·ae'
—— arteriae ver'te·bra'lis
—— au·ric'u·lae' posterior
—— bas'i·lar'is pon'tis
—— bi·cip'i·ta'lis lat'er·a'lis
—— bicipitalis me'di·a'lis
—— brev'is
—— cal·ca'ne·i'
—— cal'ca·ri'nus
—— can'a·lic'u·li' mas·toi'de·i'
—— ca·rot'i·cus
—— car'pi'
—— cen·tra'lis
—— centralis in'su·lae'
—— centralis (Ro·lan'di')
—— chi·as'ma·tis
—— cin'gu·li'
—— cir'cu·lar'is in'su·lae'
—— circularis (Rei'li')
—— col·lat'er·a'lis
—— co'ro·nar'i·us
—— cor'po·ris cal·lo'si'
—— cos'tae'
—— cru'ris hel'i·cis
—— eth'moi·da'lis
—— fron·ta'lis inferior
—— frontalis superior
—— glu·tae'us
—— glu·te'us
—— ham'u·li' pter'y·goi'de·i'
—— hip'po·cam'pi'
—— ho'ri·zon·ta'lis cer'e·bel'li'
—— hy'po·tha·lam'i·cus
—— hypothalamicus (Mon'ro·i')
—— in'fra·or'bi·ta'lis
—— in'fra·pal'pe·bra'lis
—— in'ter·me'di·us anterior me·dul'lae' spi·na'lis
—— intermedius posterior me·dul'lae' spi·na'lis

—— in'ter·pa·ri'e·ta'lis
—— in'ter·tu·ber'cu·lar'is
—— in'ter·ven·tric'u·lar'is anterior
—— interventricularis posterior
—— in'tra·pa·ri'e·ta'lis
—— lac'ri·ma'lis max·il'lae'
—— lacrimalis os'sis lac'ri·ma'lis
—— lat'er·a'lis anterior me·dul'lae' ob'lon·ga'tae'
—— lateralis anterior me·dul'lae' spi·na'lis
—— lateralis cer'e·bri'
—— lateralis mes'en·ceph'a·li'
—— lateralis posterior me·dul'lae' ob'lon·ga'tae'
—— lateralis posterior me·dul'lae' spi·na'lis
—— lim'i·tans'
—— limitans ven·tric'u·li' quar'ti'
—— limitans ven·tric'u·lo'rum cer'e·bri'
—— lon'gi·tu'di·na'lis anterior cor'dis
—— longitudinalis posterior
—— lu·na'tus
—— mal'le·o·lar'is
—— ma'tri·cis un'guis
—— me'di·a'lis cru'ris cer'e·bri'
—— me'di·a'nus lin'guae'
—— medianus posterior me·dul'lae' ob'lon·ga'tae'
—— medianus posterior me·dul'lae' spi·na'lis
—— medianus ven·tric'u·li' quar'ti'
—— men'to·la'bi·a'lis
—— mus'cu·li' flex·o'ris hal'lu·cis lon'gi' cal·ca'ne·i'
—— musculi flexoris hallucis longi ta'li'
—— musculi per'o·nae'i' lon'gi' cal·ca'ne·i'
—— musculi peronaei longi os'sis cu·boi'de·i'
—— my'lo·hy·oi'de·us
—— na'so·la'bi·a'lis
—— ner'vi' oc'u·lo·mo·to'ri·i'
—— nervi pe·tro'si' ma·jo'ris
—— nervi petrose mi·no'ris

—— nervi petrosi su′per·
fi′ci·a′lis ma·jo′ris
—— nervi petrosi superficialis mi·no′ris
—— nervi ra′di·a′lis
—— nervi spi·na′lis
—— nervi ul·nar′is
—— ob′tu·ra·to′ri·us
—— oc·cip′i·ta′lis trans·
ver′sus
—— oc·cip′i·to·tem′po·ra′lis
—— of Mon·ro′
—— ol′fac·to′ri·us ca′vi′
na′si′
—— olfactorius lo′bi′ fron·
ta′lis
—— or′bi·ta′lis
—— pal′a·ti′nus major max·
il′lae′
—— palatinus major os′sis
pal′a·ti′ni′
—— pal′a·to·vag′i·na′lis
—— pa·ri′e·to·oc·cip′i·ta′lis
—— par′ol·fac·to′ri·us anterior
—— parolfactorius posterior
—— pe·tro′sus inferior os′sis
oc·cip′i·ta′lis
—— petrosus inferior os′sis
tem′po·ra′lis
—— petrosus superior os′sis
tem′po·ra′lis
—— post′cen·tra′lis
—— prae′cen·tra′lis
—— pre′cen·tra′lis
—— pri·mar′i·us
—— prom′on·to′ri·i′
—— pter′y·go·pal′a·ti′nus
os′sis pal′a·ti′ni′
—— pul′mo·na′lis
—— rhi·na′lis
—— sag′it·ta′lis os′sis fron·
ta′lis
—— sagittalis ossis oc·cip′i·
ta′lis
—— sagittalis ossis pa·ri′e·
ta′lis
—— scle′rae′
—— sig·moi′de·us
—— si′nus pe·tro′si′ in·fe′ri·
o′ris os′sis oc·cip′i·ta′lis
—— sinus petrosi inferioris
ossis tem′po·ra′lis
—— sinus petrosi su·pe′ri·
o′ris os′sis tem′po·ra′lis
—— sinus sag′it·ta′lis su·
pe′ri·o′ris os′sis fron·ta′lis

—— sinus sagittalis superioris ossis oc·cip′i·ta′lis
—— sinus sagittalis superioris ossis pa·ri′e·ta′lis
—— sinus sig·moi′de·i′
—— sinus sigmoidei os′sis
oc·cip′i·ta′lis
—— sinus sigmoidei ossis
pa·ri′e·ta′lis
—— sinus sigmoidei ossis
tem′po·ra′lis
—— sinus trans·ver′si′
—— spi·ra′lis
—— spiralis ex·ter′nus
—— spiralis in·ter′nus
—— sub·cla′vi·ae′
—— sub·cla′vi·us pul·mo′nis
—— sub′pa·ri′e·ta′lis
—— su′pra·pa·ri′e·ta′lis
—— ta′li′
—— tem′po·ra′lis inferior
—— temporalis me′di·us
—— temporalis superior
—— ten′di·nis mus′cu·li′
fib′u·lar′is lon′gi′ cal·ca′ne·i′
—— tendinis musculi flex·
o′ris hal′lu·cis lon′gi′ cal·
ca′ne·i′
—— tendinis musculi flex-
oris hallucis longi ta′li′
—— tendinis musculi per′o·
ne′i′ lon′gi′ cal·ca′ne·i′
—— tendinis musculi pero-
nei longi os′sis cu·boi′de·i′
—— ter′mi·na′lis a′tri·i′
dex′tri′
—— terminalis lin′guae′
—— trans·ver′sus os′sis oc·
cip′i·ta′lis
—— transversus ossis pa·
ri′e·ta′lis
—— tu′bae′ au′di·ti′vae′
—— tym·pan′i·cus
—— ve′nae′ ca′vae′
—— venae sub·cla′vi·ae′
—— venae um·bil′i·ca′lis
—— vo′mer·o·vag′i·na′lis
sul′fa
sul′fa·ben′za·mide′
sul′fa·cet′a·mide′
sulf·ac′id
sul′fa·di′a·zine′
sul′fa·di′meth·ox′ine′
sul′fa·di′me·tine′
sul′fa·dox′ine′
sul′fa·eth′i·dole′
sul′fa·gua′ni·dine′

sul′fa·lene′
sul′fa·mer′a·zine′
sul′fa·me′ter
sul′fa·meth′a·zine′
sul′fa·meth′i·zole′
sul′fa·meth·ox′a·zole′
sul′fa·me·thox′y·py·rid′a·
zine
sul′fa·mon′o·meth·ox′ine′
sul′fa·mox′ole′
sul′fan′i·late′
sul′fa·pyr′i·dine′
sul′fa·sal′a·zine′
sul′fa·som′i·zole′
sul′fa·tase′
sul′fate′
sul′fat′ide′
sul′faz′a·met′
sulf·he′mo·glo′bin
sulf·he′mo·glo′bi·ne′mi·a
sulf·hy′drate′
sulf·hy′dryl
sul′fide′
sul′fin·pyr′a·zone
sul′fi·som′i·dine′
sul′fi·sox′a·zole′
sul′fite′
sulf′met·he′mo·glo′bin
sul′fo·bro′mo·phthal′e·in
sul′fo·cy′a·nate′
sul′fo·mu′cin
sul′fon′a·mide′
sul′fone′
sul′fon′ic
sul′fo·nyl
sul′fo·nyl·u′re·a
sul′fo·phen′yl·ate′
sul′fo·sal′i·cyl′ic
sulf·ox′ide′
sul′fur *also* sulphur
sul′fu·rat′ed
sul′fu′ric
sul′in·dac′
Sul′ko·witch test
sul′lage
Sul′li·van test
sul′pha·fu′ra·zole′
sul′phur *var. of* sulfur
sul·thi′ame′
su′mac′
sum·ma′tion
Sum′ner
—— method
—— sign
sump
sun′burn′
sun′spots′

sun'stroke'
su'per·ab·duc'tion
su'per·ac'id
su'per·a·cid'i·ty
su'per·a·cute'
su'per·al·bu'mi·no'sis pl.
  -ses'
su'per·al'i·men·ta'tion
su'per·al'ka·lin'i·ty
su'per·au·ra'le'
su'per·cer'e·bel'lar
su'per·cil'i·ar'y
su'per·cil'i·um pl. -i·a
su'per·di·crot'ic
su'per·dis·ten'tion
su'per·duct'
su'per·duc'tion
su'per·e'go
su'per·e·vac'u·a'tion
su'per·ex·ci·ta'tion
su'per·ex·ten'sion
su'per·fe'cun·da'tion
su'per·fe·ta'tion
su'per·fi'cial
su'per·fi'ci·a'lis
su'per·fi'ci·es' pl. su'per·
  fi'ci·es'
su'per·flex'ion
su'per·im'preg·na'tion
su'per·in·duce', -duced',
  -duc'ing
su'per·in·fec'tion
su'per·in'vo·lu'tion
su·pe'ri·or
su'per·lac·ta'tion
su'per·le'thal
su'per·max·il'la
su'per·me'di·al
su'per·na'tant
su'per·nate'
su'per·nor'mal
su'per·nu'mer·ar'y
su'per·nu·tri'tion
su'per·o·in·fe'ri·or
su'per·o·lat'er·al
su'per·o·me'di·al
su'per·phos'phate'
su'per·pig'men·ta'tion
su'per·salt'
su'per·sat'u·rate', -rat'ed,
  -rat'ing
su'per·scrip'tion
su'per·se·cre'tion
su'per·sen'si·tive
su'per·sen'si·ti·za'tion
su'per·son'ic
su'per·struc'ture

su'per·ten'sion
su'per·ve·nos'i·ty
su'per·ven'tion
su'per·ver'sion
su'pi·nate', -nat'ed, -nat'ing
su'pi·na'tion
su'pi·na'tor
su·pine'
sup'ple·men'tal
sup'ple·men'ta·ry
sup·port'
sup·port'ive
sup·pos'i·to·ry
sup·press'
sup·pres'sant
sup·pres'sion
sup·pres'sive
sup·pres'sor
sup'pu·rant
sup'pu·rate', -rat'ed, -rat'ing
sup'pu·ra'tion
sup'pu·ra'tive
su'pra·a·or'tic
su'pra·ar·tic'u·lar
su'pra·au·ric'u·lar
su'pra·buc'cal
su'pra·cal·lo'sal
su'pra·car'di·nal
su'pra·cer'vi·cal
su'pra·chi'as·mat'ic
su'pra·cho'roid'
su'pra·cho·roi'dal
su'pra·cla·vic'u·lar
su'pra·cla·vic'u·lar'is
su'pra·cli'noid'
su'pra·clu'sion
su'pra·con'dy·lar
su'pra·con'dy·loid'
su'pra·cos'tal
su'pra·cos·ta'lis pl. -les'
su'pra·cra'ni·al
su'pra·di'a·phrag·mat'ic
su'pra·ep'i·con'dy·lar
su'pra·ep'i·troch'le·ar
su'pra·gin'gi·val
su'pra·gle'noid'
su'pra·glot'tic
su'pra·gran'u·lar
su'pra·he·pat'ic
su'pra·hy'oid'
su'pra·in·gui·nal
su'pra·le·va'tor
su'pra·lim'i·nal
su'pra·lum'bar
su'pra·mal·le'o·lar
su'pra·mam'mil·lar'y
su'pra·man·dib'u·lar

su'pra·mar'gin·al
su'pra·mas'toid'
su'pra·max'il·lar'y
su'pra·me·a'tal
su'pra·nu'cle·ar
su'pra·oc·cip'i·tal
su'pra·oc·clu'sion
su'pra·oc'u·lar
su'pra·or'bit·al
su'pra·pa·tel'lar
su'pra·pel'vic
su'pra·pin'e·al
su'pra·pleu'ral
su'pra·pon'tine'
su'pra·pu'bic
su'pra·re'nal
su'pra·re'nal·ec'to·my
su'pra·re·na'lis ab'er·ra'ta
su'pra·re'nal·ism
su'pra·re'nal·op'a·thy
su'pra·scap'u·la
su'pra·scap'u·lar
su'pra·scle'ral
su'pra·sel'lar
su'pra·sep'tal
su'pra·spi'nal
su'pra·spi·na'tus
su'pra·spi'nous
su'pra·sple'ni·al
su'pra·ster'nal
su'pra·ste'rol'
su'pra·tem'po·ral
su'pra·ten·to'ri·al
su'pra·ton'sil·lar
su'pra·tri·gem'i·nal
su'pra·troch'le·ar
su'pra·tym·pan'ic
su'pra·um·bil'i·cal
su'pra·vag'i·nal
su'pra·val'vu·lar
su'pra·ven·tric'u·lar
su'pra·ver'gence
su'pra·ves'i·cal
su'pra·vi'tal
su'ra pl. -rae'
su'ral
sur·al'i·men·ta'tion
sur'a·min
sur'di·tas
  —— ver·ba'lis
sur'di·ty
sur·ex'ci·ta'tion
sur'face
sur·fac'tant
sur'geon
sur'ger·y
sur'gi·cal

sur′ro·gate′
sur′sum·duc′tion
sur′sum·ver′gence
sur′sum·ver′gent
sur′sum·ver′sion
sus·cep′ti·bil′i·ty
sus·cep′ti·ble
sus′ci·tate′, -tat′ed, -tat′ing
sus′ci·ta′tion
sus·pend′ed
sus·pen′sion
sus·pen′soid′
sus·pen·so′ri·um pl. -ri·a
—— hep′a·tis
—— tes′tis
—— ve·si′cae′
sus·pen′so·ry
sus′ten·tac′u·lar
sus′ten·tac′u·lum pl. -la
—— ta′li′
su·sur′rus
—— au′ri·um
Sut′ton disease
su·tu′ra pl. -rae′
—— co·ro·na′lis
—— den·ta′ta
—— eth·moi′de·o·max′il·lar′is
—— eth·moi′do·max′il·lar′is
—— fron·ta′lis
—— fron′to·eth′moi·da′lis
—— fron′to·lac′ri·ma′lis
—— fron′to·max′il·lar′is
—— fron′to·na·sa′lis
—— fron′to·zy′go·mat′i·ca
—— har·mo′ni·a
—— in′ci·si′va
—— in′fra·or′bi·ta′lis
—— in′ter·max′il·lar′is
—— in′ter·na·sa′lis
—— lac′ri·mo·con·cha′lis
—— lac′ri·mo·max′il·lar′is
—— lamb·doi′de·a
—— lim·bo′sa
—— me·top′i·ca
—— na′so·fron·ta′lis
—— na′so·max′il·lar′is
—— no′tha
—— oc·cip′i·to·mas′toi′de·a
—— pal′a·ti′na me′di·a′na
—— palatina trans·ver′sa
—— pal′a·to·eth′moi·da′lis
—— pal′a·to·max′il·lar′is
—— pa·ri′e·to·mas·toi′de·a
—— pla′na
—— sag′it·ta′lis
—— ser·ra′ta

—— sphe′no·eth′moi·da′lis
—— sphe′no·fron·ta′lis
—— sphe′no·max′il·lar′is
—— sphe′no·or′bi·ta′lis
—— sphe′no·pa·ri′e·ta′lis
—— sphe′nosqua·mo′sa
—— sphe′no·zy′go·mat′i·ca
—— squa′mo·mas·toi′de·a
—— squa·mo′sa
—— squamosa cra′ni·i′
—— tem′po·ro·zy′go·mat′i·ca
—— ve′ra
—— zy′go·mat′i·co·fron·ta′lis
—— zy′go·mat′i·co·max′il·lar′is
—— zy′go·mat′i·co·tem′po·ra′lis
su·tu′rae′ cra′ni·i′
su′tur·al
su′ture, -tured, -tur·ing
Sved′berg′ unit
swab, swabbed, swab′bing
swage, swaged, swag′ing
swal′low
swathe, swathed, swath′ing
sway′back′
sweat
Swe′di·aur′ disease
Sweet syndrome
swell′ing
Swift disease
swine′herd′ disease
swing
sy·co′ma pl. -mas or -ma·ta
sy·co′si·form′
sy·co′sis (hair-follicle inflammation) pl. -ses′
◆psychosis
—— bar′bae′
—— cap′il·li′ti·i′
—— con·ta′gi·o′sa
—— fram·boe′si·for′mis
—— men·tag′ra
—— pal′pe·brae′ mar′gi·na′lis
—— par′a·sit′i·ca
—— staph′y·log′e·nes′
—— vul·gar′is
Syd′en·ham chorea
syl′la·bus pl. -bi′ or -bus·es
syl·lep′sis pl. -ses′
syl·vat′ic
Syl′vi·an
—— angle
—— aqueduct

—— fissure
—— ossicle
—— point
—— valve
sym·bal′lo·phone′
sym′bi·o·gen′ic
sym′bi·on′
sym′bi·ont′
sym′bi·o′sis pl. -ses′
sym′bi·ot′ic
sym·bleph′a·ron′
sym·bleph′a·ro′sis
sym′bol
sym·bo′li·a
sym·bol′ic
sym′bol·ism
sym′bol·i·za′tion
Syme amputation
sym′e·tine′
sym′me·lus pl. -li′
sym·met′ric or sym·met′ri·cal
sym′me·try
sym′pa·thec′to·my
sym′pa·thec′to·mize′, -mized, -miz′ing
sym′pa·thet′ic
sym·pa·thet′i·co·to′ni·a
sym·pa·thet′i·co·ton′ic
sym′pa·thet′o·blast′
sym·path′i·cec′to·my
sym·path′i·co·blast′
sym·path′i·co·blas·to′ma pl. -mas or -ma·ta
sym·path′i·co·cy·to′ma pl. -mas or -ma·ta
sym·path′i·co·go′ni·o′ma pl. -mas or -ma·ta
sym·path′i·co·neu·ri′tis
sym·path′i·cop′a·thy
sym·path′i·co·to′ni·a
sym·path′i·co·trop′ic
sym·path′i·cus
sym′pa·thin
sym·path′o·blast′
sym′pa·tho·blas·to′ma pl. -mas or -ma·ta
sym′pa·tho·go′ni·a
sym′pa·tho·go′ni·o′ma pl. -mas or -ma·ta
sym′pa·tho·lyt′ic
sym′pa·tho·ma pl. -mas or -ma·ta
sym′pa·tho·mi·met′ic
sym′pa·thy
sym·pex′is
sym′pha·lan′gi·a

sym·phal'an·gism
sym'phy·o·ceph'a·lus
sym'phy·se'al
sym·phys'i·al
sym·phys'ic
sym·phy'i·ec'to·my
sym·phys'i·ol'y·sis
sym·phys'i·on'
sym'phys·i·or'rha·phy
sym'phys'i·o·tome'
sym·phys'i·ot'o·my
sym'phy·sis *pl.* -ses'
—— car'ti·lag'i·no'sa
—— lig'a·men·to'sa
—— man·dib'u·lae'
—— os'si·um pu'bis
—— pu'bi·ca
—— pu'bis
—— sa'cro·coc·cyg'e·a
sym'phy·so·dac·tyl'i·a
sym'phys·dac'ty·ly
sym'plasm
sym·po'di·a
symp'tom
symp'to·mat'ic
symp'to·mat'o·log'ic
symp'to·ma·tol'o·gy
symp·to'sis
sym'pus
—— a'pus
—— di'pus
—— mon'o·pus
sym·sep'a·lous
syn'a·del'phus
syn·al'gi·a
syn·al'gic
syn·an'throse'
syn'apse' *pl.* sy·nap'ses'
syn·ap'sis *pl.* -ses'
syn·ap'tase'
syn·ap'tic
syn·ap'to·some'
syn'ar·thro'di·a
syn'ar·thro'di·al
syn'ar'thro·phy'sis *pl.* -ses'
syn'ar·thro'sis *pl.* -ses'
syn·can'thus
syn·car'y·on' *var. of* synkar-
yon
syn·chei'li·a
syn·che'sis *var. of* synchysis
syn'chon·dro'ses'
—— cra'ni·i'
—— ster·na'les'
syn'chon·dro'si·al
syn'chon·dro'sis *pl.* -ses'
—— ar'y·cor·nic'u·la'ta

—— ep'i·phys'e·os'
—— in'ter·sphe'noi·da'lis
—— in'tra·oc·cip'i·ta'lis anterior
—— intraoccipitalis posteri-
or
—— ma·nu'bri·o·ster·na'lis
—— pet'ro·oc·cip'i·ta'lis
—— sphe'no·oc·cip'i·ta'lis
—— sphe'no·pe·tro'sa
—— ster·na'lis
—— xiph'o·ster·na'lis
syn'chon·drot'o·my
syn'chro·nism
syn'chro·nous
syn'chro·ny
syn'chy·sis *also* synchesis
—— scin'til·lans'
syn'ci·ne'sis *pl.* -ses'
syn'clit'ic
syn'cli·tism
syn'clon'ic
syn'clo·nus *pl.* -ni'
—— bal·lis'mus
—— tre'mens
syn'co·pal
syn'co·pe
—— an'gi·no'sa
syn·cop'ic
syn·cy'tial
syn·cy'ti·o'ma *pl.* -mas *or*
-ma·ta
syn·cy'ti·o·tox'in
syn·cy'ti·o·tro'pho·blast'
syn·cy'ti·um *pl.* -ti·a
syn·dac'tyl
syn·dac'tyl'i·a
syn·dac'ty·lus
syn·dac'ty·ly
syn·dec'to·my
syn'de·sis
syn'des·mec'to·my
syn'des·mec'to·pi·a
syn'des·mi'tis
syn'des'mo·cho'ri·al
syn'des'mo·di·as'ta·sis
syn'des'mo·lo'gi·a
syn'des·mol'o·gy
syn'des·mo'ma *pl.* -mas *or*
-ma·ta
syn·des'mo·pex'y
syn'des·mor'rha·phy
syn'des·mo'sis *pl.* -ses'
—— tib'i·o·fib'u·lar'is
—— tym'pa·no·sta·pe'di·a
syn'des·mot'o·my
syn'drome'

syn·drom'ic
syn·ech'i·a *pl.* -ae
—— vul'vae'
syn·ech'i·al
syn·ech'o·tome'
syn'e·chot'o·my
syn'en·ceph'a·lo·cele'
syn'en·ceph'a·ly
syn·er'e·sis *pl.* -ses'
syn·er·get'ic
syn·er'gi·a
syn'er·gism
syn'er·gist
syn'er·gis'tic
syn'er·gy
syn'es·the'si·a
syn·es·the'si·al'gi·a
syn·gam'ic
syn'ga·mous
syn'ga·my
syn·ge·ne'ic
syn·ge·ne'si·o·plas'tic
syn·ge·ne'si·o·plas'ty
syn·ge·ne'si·ous
syn·i·dro'sis *pl.* -ses'
syn·i·ze'sis
—— pu·pil'lae'
syn·kar'y·on' *also* syncar-
yon
syn'ki·ne'si·a
syn'ki·ne'sis *pl.* -ses'
syn'ki·net'ic
syn·oph'rys
syn'oph·thal'mi·a
syn'oph·thal'mus *pl.* -mi'
syn·op'si·a
syn·or'chi·dism
syn·os'te·o·phyte'
syn·os·tosed'
syn'os·to'sis *pl.* -ses'
syn·os·tot'ic
syn·o'ti·a
syn·o'tus
syn'o·vec'to·my
syn·o'vi·a
syn·o'vi·al
syn·o'vi·al·o'ma *pl.* -mas *or*
-ma·ta
syn·o'vi·o·en'do·the'li·
o'ma *pl.* -mas *or* -ma·ta
syn·o'vi·o'ma *pl.* -mas *or*
-ma·ta
syn'o·vip'a·rous
syn·o'vi·tis
—— hy'per·plas'ti·ca
syn·tac'tic *or* syn·tac'ti·cal
syn'ta·sis

syn'thase'
syn'the·sis pl. -ses'
syn'the·size', -sized', -siz'ing
syn·the'tase'
syn·thet'ic
syn·tho'rax'
syn·ton'ic
syn'tro·nin
syn'tro·phus pl. -phi'
syn'tro·py
syph'i·lid
syph'i·lis
—— d'em·blée'
—— he·red'i·tar'i·a
—— in·son'ti·um
—— tech'ni·ca
syph'i·lit'ic
syph'i·lo·derm'
syph'i·lo·der'ma
syph'i·lo·der'ma·tous
syph'i·lo·gen'e·sis
syph'i·loid'
syph'i·lo'ma pl. -mas or
-ma·ta
syph'i·lo·nych'i·a
—— ex·ul'cer·ans'
—— sic'ca
syph'i·lop'a·thy
syph'i·lo·pho'bi·a
syph'i·lo·phy'ma pl. -mas or
-ma·ta
syph'i·lo'psy·cho'sis pl.
-ses'
syph'i·lous
sy·rig'mo·pho'ni·a
sy·rig'mus
sy·ringe'
syr'in·gec'to·my
syr'in·gi'tis
syr'in·go·bul'bi·a
syr'in·go·car'ci·no'ma
pl. -mas or -ma·ta
sy·rin'go·cele' also syringo-
coele
sy·rin'go·coele' var. of sy-
ringocele
sy·rin'go·coe'li·a
sy·rin'go·cyst'ad·e·no'ma
pl. -mas or -ma·ta
sy·rin'go·cys·to'ma pl. -mas
or -ma·ta
sy·rin'go·en'ce·pha'li·a
sy·rin'goid'
syr'in·go'ma pl. -mas or
-ma·ta
sy·rin'go·me·nin'go·cele'
sy·rin'go·my·e'li·a

sy·rin'go·my'e·li'tis
sy·rin'go·my'e·lo·cele'
sy·rin'go·my'e·lus
sy·rin'go·tome'
syr'in·got'o·my
syr'inx pl. sy·rin'ges' or -inx·
es
syr'o·sing'o·pine'
syr'up
sys'sar·co'sis pl. -ses'
sys'sar·cot'ic
sys·so'mic
sys·so'mus
sys'tem
sys·te'ma
—— di'ges·to'ri·um
—— lym·phat'i·cum
—— ner·vo'rum cen·tra'le'
—— nervorum per'i·pher'i·
cum
—— ner·vo'sum
—— nervosum au'to·nom'i·
cum
—— nervosum cen·tra'le'
—— nervosum per'i·pher'i·
cum
—— nervosum sym·path'i·
cum
—— re·spi'ra·to'ri·um
—— u'ro·gen'i·ta'le'
sys'tem·at'ic
sys'tem·a·tize', -tized', -tiz'-
ing
sys'tem'ic
sys'tem·oid'
sys'to·le
sys·tol'ic
sys·trem'ma pl. -ma·ta or
-mas
sy·zyg'i·al
syz'y·gy
Sza'bo sign
Szent'-Györ'gyi test

T

Taarn'hoj operation
tab'a·co'sis
ta·ba'cum
tab'a·gism
tab'a·nid
ta'bar·di'llo
ta·ba·tiére' a·na·to·mique'
ta·bel'la pl. -lae'
ta'bes'

—— cox·ar'i·a
—— do'lo·ro'sa
—— dor·sa'lis
—— er·got'i·ca
—— mes'en·ter'i·ca
ta·bes'cence
ta·bes'cent
ta·bet'ic
ta·bet'i·form'
tab'ic
tab'id
tab'la·ture'
ta'ble
ta'ble·spoon'
tab'let
ta'bo·pa·ral'y·sis pl. -ses'
ta'bo·pa·re'sis pl. -ses'
tab'u·la pl. -lae'
tab'u·lar
tache
—— bleu·âtre'
—— cé·ré·brale'
—— mé·nin·gé·ale'
—— mo·trice'
—— noire
—— spi·nale
taches
—— blanches
—— du ca·fé' au lait
—— ro·sées' len·ti·cu·laires'
ta·chet'ic
ta·chis'to·scope'
ta·chis'to·scop'ic
tach'o·gram'
ta·chog'ra·phy
tach'y·al'i·men·ta'tion
tach'y·ar·rhyth'mi·a
tach'y·aux·e'sis pl. -ses'
tach'y·car'di·a
—— stru·mo'sa ex'oph·
thal'mi·ca
tach'y·car'di·ac'
tach'y·car'dic
tach'y·graph'
ta·chyg'ra·phy
ta·chym'e·ter
tach'y·pha'gi·a
tach'y·pha'si·a
tach'y·phe'mi·a
tach'y·phra'si·a
tach'y·phy·lax'is pl. -lax'es'
tach'y·pne'a
tach'y·rhyth'mi·a
ta·chys'ter·ol'
tach'y·sys'to·le
tac'tile
tae'di·um vi'tae'

tae'ni·a *(worm), pl.* -as
tae'ni·a *(band), pl.* -ae', *var. of* tenia
—— fim'bri·ae'
Tae'ni·a
—— e·chi'no·coc'cus
—— na'na
—— sag'i·na'ta
—— so'li·um
tae'ni·a·cide' *also* teniacide
tae'ni·a·fuge' *also* teniafuge
tae·ni'a·sis *also* teniasis
tae'ni·form' *also* teniform
tae'ni·oid' *also* tenioid
tae·ni'o·la *var. of* teniola
tag
tail
Ta·ka'ta-A'ra test
ta·lal'gi·a
ta'lar
tal'bu·tal'
talc
talc·o'sis *pl.* -ses'
tal'cum
tal'i·pes'
—— ar'cu·a'tus
—— cal·ca'ne·o·ca'vus
—— cal·ca'ne·o·val'gus
—— cal·ca'ne·us
—— ca'vus
—— e·qui'no·ca'vus
—— e·qui'no·val'gus
—— e·qui'no·var'us
—— e·qui'nus
—— per·ca'vus
—— pla'nus
—— spas·mod'i·ca
—— val'gus
—— var'us
tal'i·pom'a·nus
Tall'quist method
Tal'ma operation
ta·lo·cal·ca'ne·al
ta·lo·cru'ral
ta·lo·fib'u·lar
ta·lo·mal·le'o·lar
tal'on
ta·lo·na·vic'u·lar
tal'o·nid
tal'ose'
ta'lus *pl.* -li'
ta'ma
Tamm'-Hors'fall' protein
tam'pon'
tam'pon·ade'
tam'pon·age'
tam'pon·ing

tam·pon'ment
tan'dem
tan'gent
Tan'gi·er disease
tan'nase'
tan'nate'
tan'nic
tan'nin
Tan·ret'reagent
tan'ta·lum
tan'trum
tap, tapped, tap'ping
ta·pei'no·ceph'a·ly
ta·pe'tal
ta·pe'to·ret'i·nal
ta·pe'tum *pl.* -ta
—— al·ve'o·li'
—— lu'ci·dum
tape'worm'
Ta·pi'a syndrome
tap'i·no·ce·phal'ic
tap'i·no·ceph'a·ly
ta·pote'ment
Tar·dieu'ecchymoses
tar'dive
tare
tar'get
Tar·nier' sign
tars·ad'e·ni'tis
tar'sal
tar·sal'gi·a
tar·sa'lis
tar·sec'to·my
tar·si'tis
tar'so·chei'lo·plas'ty
tar'so·ma·la'ci·a
tar'so·met'a·tar'sal
tar'so·pha·lan'ge·al
tar'so·phy'ma *pl.* -mas *or* -ma·ta
tar'so·pla'si·a
tar'so·plas'ty
tar'sop·to'si·a
tar'sop·to'sis *pl.* -ses'
tar·sor'rha·phy
tar'so·tar'sal
tar'so·tib'i·al
tar·sot'o·my
tar'sus *pl.* -si'
—— inferior pal'pe·brae'
—— superior palpebrae
tar'tar
tar·tar'ic
tar'trate'
Tash'kent' ulcer
taste', tast'ed, tast'ing
tat·too'ing

Tau'ber test
tau'rine'
tau'ro·cho·lan'o·poi·e'sis
  pl. -ses'
tau'ro·cho'late'
tau'ro·cho'lic
tau'ro·dont'
Taus'sig-Bing' complex
Taus'sig-Bla'lock' operation
tau'to·me'ni·al
tau·tom'er·al
tau'to·mer'ic
tau·tom'er·ism
Ta·wa'ra node
tax'is *pl.* tax'es'
tax·o'di·um
tax'on' *pl.* tax'a
tax'o·nom'ic
tax·on'o·my
Tay choroiditis
Tay'-Sachs' disease
tear, teared, tear'ing
tease, teased, teas'ing
tea'spoon'
teat
tech·ne'ti·um
tech'nic
tech·ni'cian
tech'nics
tech·nique'
tech·nol'o·gist
tech·nol'o·gy
tec'lo·zan'
tec'tal
tec'to·bul'bar
tec'to·ceph'a·ly
tec'to·cer'e·bel'lar
tec·to'ri·al
tec·to'ri·um
tec'to·ru'bral
tec'to·spi'nal
tec'tum *pl.* -ta
—— mes'en·ceph'a·li'
teethe, teethed, teeth'ing
Tee'van law
teg'men *pl.* -mi·na
—— mas·toi'de·um
—— tym'pa·ni'
—— ven·tric'u·li' quar'ti'
teg·men'tal
teg·men'tum *pl.* -ta
—— rhom'ben·ceph'a·li'
teg'u·ment
teg·u·men'ta·ry
Teich'mann
—— crystals

—— test
tek′no·cyte′
te′la pl. -lae′
—— ad′i·po′sa
—— cho′ri·oi′de·a ven·tric′u·li′ quar′ti′
—— chorioidea ventriculi ter′ti·i′
—— cho·roi′de·a ven·tric′u·li′ quar′ti′
—— choroidea ventriculi ter′ti·i′
—— sub′cu·ta′ne·a
—— sub′mu·co′sa
—— submucosa co′li′
—— submucosa e·soph′a·gi′
—— submucosa in′tes·ti′ni′ rec′ti′
—— submucosa intestini ten′u·is
—— submucosa oe·soph′a·gi′
—— submucosa pha·ryn′gis
—— submucosa rec′ti′
—— submucosa tra′che·ae′ et bron·cho′rum
—— submucosa tu′bae′ u′ter·i′nae′
—— submucosa ven·tric′u·li′
—— submucosa ves′i·cae′ u′ri·nar′i·ae′
—— sub′se·ro′sa
—— subserosa co′li′
—— subserosa hep′a·tis
—— subserosa in′tes·ti′ni′ ten′u·is
—— subserosa per′i·to·nae′i′
—— subserosa per′i·to·ne′i′ pa·ri′e·ta′lis
—— subserosa peritonei vis′ce·ra′lis
—— subserosa tu′bae′ u′ter·i′nae′
—— subserosa u′ter·i′
—— subserosa ven·tric′u·li′
—— subserosa ves′i·cae′ fel′le·ae′
—— subserosa vesicae u′ri·nar′i·ae′
tel·al′gi·a
tel·an′gi·ec·ta′si·a
tel·an′gi·ec′ta·sis pl. -ses′
—— fa′ci·e′i′
—— lym·phat′i·ca
tel·an′gi·ec·tat′ic
tel·an′gi·ec·to′des′

tel·an′gi·o′ma pl. -mas or -ma·ta
tel·an′gi·on
tel·an′gi·o′sis pl. -ses′
tel′an·gi′tis
te′lar
tel·au′gic
tel′e·an′gi·ec·ta′sis pl. -ses′
tel′e·car′di·o·gram′
tel′e·car′di·o·phone′
tel′e·cep′tor
tel′e·ci·ne′sis pl. -ses′
tel′e·flu′or·os′co·py
tel′e·ki·ne′sis pl. -ses′
tel′e·lec′tro·car′di·o·gram′
te·lem′e·try
tel′en·ce·phal′ic
tel′en·ceph′a·lon′
tel′e·neu′rite′
tel′e·neu′ron′
tel′er·gy
tel′e·roent′gen·o·gram′
tel′e·roent′ge·nog′ra·phy
tel′es·the′si·a
tel′e·ther′a·py
tel′o·coele′
tel′o·lem′ma
tel′o·mer
tel′o·mere′
te·lom′er·i·za′tion
te·lom′er·ize′, -ized′, -iz′ing
tel′o·phase′
tel′o·syn·ap′sis
tem′per
tem′per·a·ment
tem′per·ance
tem′per·ate
tem′per·a·ture
tem′plate′
tem′ple
tem′po·ra
tem′po·ral
tem′po·ra′lis
—— su′per·fi′ci·a′lis
tem′po·ro·au·ric′u·lar
tem′po·ro·fa′cial
tem′po·ro·fron′tal
tem′po·ro·hy′oid′
tem′po·ro·ma′lar
tem′po·ro·man·dib′u·lar
tem′po·ro·max′il·lar′y
tem′po·ro·oc·cip′i·tal
tem′po·ro·pa·ri′e·tal
tem′po·ro·pon′tine′
tem′po·ro·spa′tial
tem′po·ro·sphe′noid′
tem′po·ro·zy′go·mat′ic

tem′u·lence
tem′u·len′ti·a
te·na′cious
te·nac′i·ty
te·nac′u·lum pl. -la or -lums
ten·al′gi·a
—— crep′i·tans′
ten′der
ten′di·ni′tis
ten′di·no·plas′ty
ten′di·nous
ten′do pl. -di·nes′
—— A·chil′lis
—— cal·ca′ne·us
—— con′junc·ti′vus
—— cri′co·e·soph′a·ge′us
ten·dol′y·sis
ten′do·mu′cin
ten′don
—— of Zinn
—— organ of Gol′gi
ten′don·i′tis
ten′do·plas′ty
ten′do·syn·o·vi′tis
ten′do·vag′i·nal
ten′do·vag′i·ni′tis
—— crep′i·tans′
—— gran′u·lo′sa
—— ste·no′sans′
te·neb′ric
te·nec′to·my
te·nes′mic
te·nes′mus
te′ni·a pl. -ae′, also taenia
—— cho·roi′de·a
—— for′ni·cis
—— li′be·ra
—— mes′o·co′li·ca
—— o′men·ta′lis
—— pon′tis
—— te′lae′
—— te·lar′um
—— thal′a·mi′
—— ven·tric′u·li′ quar′ti′
te′ni·a·cide′ var. of taeniacide
te′ni·ae′
—— a·cus′ti·cae′
—— co′li′
te′ni·a·fuge′ var. of taeniafuge
te′ni·al
te·ni′a·sis var. of taeniasis
te′ni·form′ var. of taeniform
te′ni·oid′ var. of taenioid
te·ni′o·la also taeniola
—— ci·ne′re·a

ten'o·de'sis *pl.* -ses'
ten'o·dyn'i·a
ten'o·fi'bril
te·nol'y·sis
te·nom'e·ter
ten'o·my·ot'o·my
Te·non' capsule
ten'o·nec'to·my
ten'o·ni'tis
te·non'to·my'o·plas'ty
te·non'to·my·ot'o·my
te·non'to·the·ci'tis
—— pro·lif'er·a cal·car'e·a
ten'o·phyte'
ten'o·plas'tic
ten'o·plas'ty
ten'o·re·cep'tor
te·nor'rha·phy
ten'os·to'sis *pl.* -ses'
ten'o·su'ture
ten'o·syn'o·vec'to·my
ten'o·syn·o'vi·al
ten'o·syn·o'vi·o'ma *pl.* -mas
  or -ma·ta
ten'o·syn'o·vi'tis
—— crep'i·tans'
ten'o·tome'
te·not'o·mize', -mized',
  -miz'ing
te·not'o·my
ten'o·vag'i·ni'tis
ten'sion
ten'si·ty
ten'sive
ten'sor
—— cap'su·lar'is ar·tic'u·
  la'ti·o'nis met'a·car'po·pha·
  lan'ge·i' dig'i·ti'
—— fas'ci·ae' la'tae' reflex
—— lam'i·nae' pos·te'ri·o'ris
  va·gi'nae' mus'cu·lae' rec'ti·
  ab·dom'i·nis
—— lig'a·men'ti' an'nu·lar'is
—— pa·la'ti' muscle
—— ve'li' pal·a·ti'ni' muscle
tent
ten'ta·tive
ten·tig'i·nous
ten·ti'go
—— ve·ne're·a
ten·to'ri·al
ten·to'ri·um *pl.* -ri·a
—— cer'e·bel'li'
ten'u·ate', -at'ed, -at'ing
ten'u·ous
teph'ro·my'e·li'tis
tep'id

ter'a·mor'phous
ter'as *pl.* ter'a·ta
ter·at'ic
ter'a·tism
ter'a·to·blas·to'ma *pl.* -mas
  or -ma·ta
ter'a·to·car'ci·no'ma
  pl. -mas *or* -ma·ta
ter'a·to·gen'e·sis *pl.* -ses'
ter'a·to·gen'ic
ter'a·tog'e·nous
ter'a·tog'e·ny
ter'a·toid'
ter'a·to·log'ic
ter'a·tol'o·gy
ter'a·to'ma *pl.* -mas *or*
  -ma·ta
ter'a·to'sis *pl.* -ses'
ter'a·to·sper'mi·a
ter·bu'ta·line'
te're'
ter'e·bene'
ter'e·bin'thism
ter'e·bra·che'sis *pl.* -ses'
ter'e·brat'ing
ter'e·bra'tion
te'res' *pl.* ter'e·es'
ter'gal
ter in di'e
term
ter'mi·nad'
ter'mi·nal
ter'mi·nal·i·za'tion
ter'mi·na'ti·o' *pl.* -na'ti·
  o'nes'
ter'mi·na'tion
ter'mi·na'ti·o'nes' ner·
  vo'rum li'ber·ae'
ter'mi·ni'
—— ad mem'bra spec·
  tan'tes'
—— gen'e·ra'les'
—— on'to·ge·net'i·ci'
—— si'tum et di·rec'ti·
  o'nem par'ti·um cor'po·ris
  in·di·can'tes'
ter'mi·nol'o·gy
ter'mi·nus *pl.* -ni'
ter'na·ry
ter'o·di'line'
ter·ox'a·lene'
ter'pe·nism
ter'pin
ter'ra *pl.* -rae'
—— al'ba
—— sig·il·la'ta
Ter'ry

—— method
—— stain
ter'ti·ar·ism
ter'ti·ar'y
ter'ti·grav'i·da
ter·tip'a·ra
tes'sel·lat'ed
test
tes·ta'ceous
tes·tal'gi·a
tes'ti·cle
tes·tic'u·lar
tes'tis *pl.* -tes'
tes·ti'tis
tes'toid'
tes'to·lac'tone'
tes·tos'ter·one'
tet'a·nal
te·ta'ni·a
te·tan'ic
te·tan'i·form'
tet'a·nig'e·ous
tet'a·nil'la
tet'a·nin
tet'a·nism
tet'a·ni·za'tion
tet'a·nize', -nized', -niz'ing
tet'a·node'
tet'a·noid'
tet'a·no·ly'sin
tet'a·no·ly'sis *pl.* -ses'
tet'a·nus
—— in·fan'tum
—— ne'o·na·to'rum
tet'a·ny
te·tar'ta·no'pi·a
te·tar'to·cone'
te·tar'to·co'nid
tet'ra·ba'sic
tet'ra·bra·chi·us
tet'ra·caine'
tet'ra·chei'rus
tet'ra·chlo'ro·eth'yl·ene'
tet'ra·cy'cline'
tet'rad'
tet'ra·dac'tyl
tet'ra·eth'yl·am·mo'ni·um
tet'ra·gen'ic
te·trag'e·nous
tet'ra·hy'dric
tet'ra·hy'dro·zo'line'
te·tral'o·gy
—— of Fal'lot'
tet'ra·mas'ti·a
tet'ra·mas'ti·gote'
tet'ra·ma'zi·a
te·tram'e·lus

tet'ra·mer
te·tram'er·ous
tet'ra·ni'trol'
tet'ra·pa·re'sis
tet'ra·pep'tide'
Tet'ra·pet'a·lo·ne'ma per'-
stans'
tet'ra·ple'gi·a
tet'ra·ploid'
tet'ra·sac'cha·ride'
tet'ra·so'mic
tet'ra·so'my
tet·ras'ter
tet'ra·tom'ic
tet'ra·vac'cine'
tet'ra·va'lent
tet'ro·do·tox'i·ca'tion
tet'ro·nal
tet'ro·qui·none'
tet'rose'
te·tryd'a·mine'
tex'is
tex'ti·form'
tex'to·blas'tic
tex'tur·al
tex'ture
tex'tus pl. tex'tus
thal'a·mec'to·my
thal'a·men·ceph'a·lon'
tha·lam'ic
thal'a·mo·coele'
thal'a·mo·cor'ti·cal
thal'a·mo·ge·nic'u·late
thal'a·mo·len·tic'u·lar
thal'a·mo·mam'mil·lar·y
thal'a·mo·pa·ri'e·tal
thal'a·mo·teg·men'tal
thal'a·mot'o·my
thal'a·mus pl. -mi'
thal'as·se'mi·a
tha·lid'o·mide'
thal'li·um
tha·mu'ri·a
than'a·to'gno·mon'ic
than'a·toid'
than'a·top'sy
thau·mat'ro·py
the·ba'ic
the·ba'ine'
the·be·si'an
the'ca pl. -cae'
——— ex·ter'na
——— fol·lic'u·li'
——— in·ter'na
the'cal
the·ci'tis
the'co·dont'

the·co'ma pl. -mas or -ma·ta
the'co·ma·to'sis
the'co·steg·no'sis
Thei'ler virus
the'ine'
the'in·ism
the·lal'gi·a
the·lar'che
the·las'is
thel'a·zi'a·sis
the·le·plas'ty
the·ler'e·thism
the·li·o'ma pl. -mas or
-ma·ta
the·li'tis
the·li'um pl. -li·a
the·lon'cus pl. -ci'
the·lor·rha'gi·a
the'lo·thism
thel'y·gen'ic
the'nad'
the'nal
the'nar'
then'yl·di'a·mine'
then'yl·pyr'a·mine'
the'o·bro'mine'
the'o·phyl'line'
the'o·ret'i·cal
the'o·ry
ther'a·peu'sis pl. -ses'
ther'a·peu'tic
ther'a·peu'tics
thre'a·peu'tist
ther'a·pi'a ster'i·li'sans'
mag'na
ther'a·pist
ther'a·py
the'ri·o'ma pl. -mas or
-ma·ta
therm
ther'mal
therm·al·ge'si·a
ther·mal'gi·a
therm·an·al·ge'si·a
therm·an·es·the'si·a
ther'ma·to·log'ic
ther'ma·tol'o·gy
therm'es·the'si·a
therm·es·the'si·om'e·ter
therm·hy'per·es·the'si·a
therm·hyp'es·the'si·a
ther'mic
ther'mis·tor
ther'mo·an'al·ge'si·a
ther'mo·an'es·the'si·a
ther'mo·cau'ter·y
ther'mo·chem'is·try

ther'mo·co·ag'u·la'tion
ther'mo·di·lu'tion
ther'mo·ex'ci·to'ry
ther'mo·gen'e·sis
ther'mo·gen'ic
ther'mo·gen'ics
ther·mog'e·nous
ther'mo·gram'
ther'mo·graph'
ther'mo·graph'ic
ther·mog'ra·phy
ther'mo·hy'per·al·ge'si·a
ther'mo·hy'per·es·the'si·a
ther'mo·hyp'es·the'si·a
ther'mo·in·hib'i·to'ry
ther'mo·ker'a·to·plas'ty
ther'mo·la'bile
ther·mol'y·sis
ther'mo·lyt'ic
ther'mo·mas·sage'
ther'mo·mas·tog'ra·phy
ther·mom'e·ter
ther'mo·met'ric
ther·mom'e·try
ther'mo·neu·ro'sis
ther'mo·phile'
ther'mo·phil'ic
ther'mo·ple'gi·a
ther'mo·pol'yp·ne'a
ther'mo·scope'
ther'mo·sta'sis
ther'mo·stro'muhr' of
Rein
ther'mo·sys·tal'tic
ther'mo·sys'tal·tism
ther'mo·tac'tic
ther'mo·tax'ic
ther'mo·tax'is
ther'mo·ther'a·py
ther'mo·to·nom'e·ter
the·sau'ris·mo'sis pl. -ses'
the'sis pl. -ses'
thi'a·ben'da·zole'
thi·am'i·nase'
thi'a·mine'
thi·am'i·prine'
thi·am'phen'i·col'
thi·am'y·lal'
thi·az'e·sim
thi'a·zine'
Thie'mann disease
Thiersch graft
thi·eth'yl·per'a·zine'
thigh
thigh'bone'
thig·man'es·the'si·a
thig'mes·the'si·a

thig'mo·tax'is *pl.* -tax'es'
thig'mo·trop'ic
thig·mot'ro·pism
thi·mer'o·sal'
thi'o·al'de·hyde'
thi'o·bar'bit'u·rate'
thi'o·car'bam·ide'
thi'o·cy'a·nate'
thi'o·cy·an'ic
thi'o·gua'nine'
thi'ol'
thi'o·pen'tal'
thi'o·pen'tone'
thi'o·pro'pa·zate'
thi'o·rid'a·zine'
thi'o·sul'fate'
thi'o·tep'a
thi'o·thix'ene'
thi'o·u'ra·cil
thi'o·u·re'a
thi·phen'a·mil
thi'ram'
third'-de·gree'
——— burn
——— heart block
thirst
Thi'ry fistula
thlip'sen·ceph'a·lus *pl.* -li'
Tho'ma ampulla
Thom'as
——— method
——— sign
——— test
Thom'as-La'vol·lay' meth-
  od
Tho'minx' aer'o·phil'a
Thom'sen disease
thon·zyl'a·mine'
tho'ra·cec'to·my
tho'ra·cen·te'sis *pl.* -ses'
tho·rac'ic
tho·rac'i·co·hu'mer·al
tho·rac'i·co·lum'bar
tho'ra·co'ab·dom'i·nal
tho'ra·co'a·cro'mi·al
tho'ra·co'bron·chot'o·my
tho'ra·co·ce'li·ot'o·my
tho'ra·co·ce·los'chi·sis *pl.*
  -ses'
tho'ra·co·cen·te'sis *pl.* -ses'
tho'ra·co·cyl·lo'sis *pl.* -ses'
tho'ra·co·cyr·to'sis
tho'ra·co·did'y·mus
tho'ra·co·dyn'i·a
tho'ra·co·gas·tro·did'y·
  mus

tho'ra·co·gas·tros'chi·sis
  pl. -ses'
tho'ra·co·lap'a·rot'o·my
tho'ra·co·lum'bar
tho'ra·col'y·sis *pl.* -ses'
tho'ra·com'e·try
tho'ra·cop'a·gus *pl.* -gus·es
  or -gi'
——— par'a·sit'i·cus
——— tri·bra'chi·us
——— tri'pus
tho'ra·co·par'a·ceph'a·lus
  pl. -li'
——— pseu'do·a·cor'mus
tho'ra·co·plas'ty
tho'ra·cos'chi·sis *pl.* -ses'
tho·ra'co·scope'
tho'ra·cos'co·py
tho'ra·cos'to·my
tho'ra·cot'o·my
tho'rax' *pl.* -rax'es *or* -ra·ces'
Thorn test
tho'ron'
tho·zal'i·none'
thread
thre'o·nine'
thre'ose'
thresh'old'
thrill
thrix an'nu·la'ta
throat
throb, throbbed, throb'bing
Throck'mor'ton reflex
throe
throm'bal·lo'sis
throm'bas·the'ni·a
throm·bec'to·my
throm'bin
throm·bin'o·gen
throm'bo·an'gi·i'tis
——— cu·ta'ne·o·in·tes'ti·na'lis
  dis·sem'i·na'ta
——— o·blit'er·ans'
throm'bo·ar'ter·i'tis
throm'bo·as·the'ni·a
throm'bo·blast'
throm'bo·cav'er·no·si'tis
throm·boc'la·sis
throm'bo·clas'tic
throm'bo·cyst'
throm'bo·cyte'
throm'bo·cy·the'mi·a
throm'bo·cyt'ic
throm'bo·cy'to·crit
throm'bo·cy·tol'y·sin
throm'bo·cy·tol'y·sis
throm'bo·cy'to·lyt'ic

throm'bo·cy'to·path'i·a
throm'bo·cy'to·path'ic
throm'bo·cy·top'a·thy
throm'bo·cy'to·pe'ni·a
throm'bo·cy'to·pe'nic
throm'bo·cy'to·pher'e·sis
throm'bo·cy'to·poi·e'sis *pl.*
  -ses'
throm'bo·cy'to·poi·et'ic
throm'bo·cy·to'sis *pl.* -ses'
throm'bo·em'bo·lec'to·my
throm'bo·em'bo·lism
throm'bo·em'bo·li·za'tion
throm'bo·em'bo·lus *pl.* -li'
throm'bo·en·dar'ter·ec'to·
  my
throm'bo·en·do·car·di'tis
throm'bo·gen
throm'bo·gen'e·sis *pl.* -ses'
throm'bo·gen'ic
throm'boid'
throm'bo·ki'nase'
throm'bo·ki·ne'sis *pl.* -ses'
throm'bo·lym'phan·gi'tis
throm·bol'y·sis *pl.* -ses'
throm'bo·lyt'ic
throm'bo·path'i·a
throm·bop'a·thy
throm'bo·pe'ni·a
throm'bo·pe'nic
throm'bo·phil'i·a
throm'bo·phle·bi'tis
throm'bo·plas'tic
throm'bo·plas'tid
throm'bo·plas'tin
throm'bo·plas·tin'o·gen
throm'bo·poi·e'sis
throm'bo·poi·et'ic
throm·bose', -bosed',
  -bos'ing
throm·bo'sis *pl.* -ses'
throm·bo·sta'sis *pl.* -ses'
throm'bo·sthe'nin
throm·bot'ic
throm'bo·zym'
throm'bus *pl.* -bi'
——— ne'o·na·to'rum
——— vul'vae'
throt'tle, -tled, -tling
thrush
thryp'sis
thumb
thy·mec'to·mize', -mized',
  -miz'ing
thy·mec'to·my
thy'mer·ga'si·a
thy'mer·ga'sic

thy′mic
thy′mi·co′lym·phat′ic
thy′mi·dine′
thy′mine′
thy′mi·on′
thy·mi′tis
thy′mo·cyte′
thy′mo·ke′sis
thy′mo·ki·net′ic
thy′mol′
thy·mol′y·sis
thy′mo·lyt′ic
thy·mo′ma *pl.* -mas *or*
-ma·ta
thy′mo·me·tas′ta·sis *pl.*
-ses′
thy′mo·no′ic
thy′mo·nu·cle′ic
thy′mo·path′ic
thy′mo·pa·thy
thy′mo·pha·ryn′ge·al
thy′mo·priv′ic
thy·mop′ri·vous
thy′mo·tox′ic
thy′mo·tox′in
thy′mus *pl.* -mus·es *or* -mi′
thy′mus·ec′to·my
thy′ro·ad′e·ni′tis
thy′ro·ar′y·te′noid′
thy′ro·cal′ci·to′nin
thy′ro·car′di·ac′
thy′ro·car·di′tis
thy′ro·cele′
thy′ro·cer′vi·cal
thy′ro·chon·drot′o·my
thy′ro·cri·cot′o·my
thy′ro·ep′i·glot′tic
thy′ro·gen′ic
thy·rog′e·nous
thy′ro·glob′u·lin
thy′ro·glos′sal
thy′ro·hy′al
thy′ro·hy′oid′
thy′roid′
thy′roid′al
thy·roi′de·a
thy′roi·dec′to·mize′,
-mized′, -miz′ing
thy′roi·dec′to·my
thy′roid·ism
thy′roid·i′tis
thy′roid·i·za′tion
thy′roi·dot′o·my
thy′roi·do·tox′in
thy·ro·me·dan′
thy′ro·meg′a·ly
thy′ro·mi·met′ic

thy·ron′cus
thy′ro·nyl
thy′ro·par′a·thy′roi·dec′to·
my
thy′ro·pe′ni·a
thy′ro·pha·ryn′ge·al
thy′ro·pha·ryn′ge·us
thy′ro·pri′val
thy′ro·pro′tein′
thy′rop·to′sis
thy·ro′sis *pl.* -ses′
thy′ro·ther′a·py
thy′ro·tome′
thy·rot′o·my
thy′ro·tox·e′mi·a
thy′ro·tox′ic
thy′ro·tox′i·co′sis *pl.* -ses′
thy′ro·tox′in
thy·rox′i·ne′mi·a
thy′ro·trop′ic
thy·rot′ro·pin
thy·rot′ro·pism
thy·rox′ine′
tib′i·a *pl.* -ae′ *or* -as
tib′i·ad′
tib′i·al
tib′i·al′gi·a
tib′i·a′lis
—— se·cun′dus
tib′i·o·fem′o·ral
tib′i·o·fib′u·lar
tib′i·o′na·vic′u·lar
tib′i·o·scaph′oid′
tib′i·o·tar′sal
ti′bro·fan′
tic *(spasm)*
♦*tick*
—— con·vul·sif′
—— de sa·laam′
—— dou·lou·reux′
—— of Gilles de la Tou·
rette′
—— ro·ta·toire′
ti′car·cil′lin
tick *(insect)*
♦*tic*
tic′po·lon′ga
tic·tol′o·gy
tid′al
tide
Tie′de·mann
—— gland
—— nerve
Tiet′ze
—— disease
—— syndrome
ti·ges′tol′

ti·gog′e·nin
ti·grol′y·sis
Til·laux′ disease
tim′bre
tinc·to′ri·al
tinc·tu′ra
tinc′ture
tine
tin′e·a
—— am′i·an·ta′ce·a
—— bar′bae′
—— cap′i·tis
—— cir′ci·na′ta
—— cor′po·ris
—— cru′ris
—— de·cal′vans′
—— fa′ci·a′le′
—— fa′ci·e′i′
—— fa·vo′sa
—— gla·bro′sa
—— im′bri·ca′ta
—— ni′gra
—— no·do′sa
—— ton′su·rans′
—— un′gui·um
—— ver′si·co′lor
Ti·nel′ sign
Tine test
tin′gle, -gled, -gling
tin·ni′tus
—— au′ri·um
—— cra′ni·i′
ti·queur′
tire, tired, tir′ing
tis′sue
tis′su·lar
ti′ter *also* titre
tit′il·la′tion
ti′trate′, -trat′ed, -trat′ing
ti·tra′tion
ti′tre *var. of* titer
ti·trim′e·ter
ti′tri·met′ric
ti·trim′e·try
tit′u·ba′tion
To′bey-Ay′er test
to′bra·my′cin
to′co·graph′
to·cog′ra·phy
to·col′o·gy
to·com′e·ter
to·com′e·try
to·coph′er·ol′
to·coph′er·so′lan′
to′cus
Todd paralysis
toe

toe'nail'
to'ga•vi'rus
Toi•son' solution
to'ko•dy'na•mom'e•ter
to•la'za•mide'
to•laz'o•line'
tol•bu'ta•mide'
tol'er•ance
tol'er•ant
tol'er•ate', -at'ed, -at'ing
tol'er•a'tion
Tol'lens test
tol'me•tin
tol•naf'tate'
to•lo'ni•um
tol•pyr'ra•mide'
tol'u•ene'
to•lu'i•dine'
tol'u•yl•ene'
tol'yl
to'ma•tine'
Tomes
—— fibers
—— granular layer
—— process
Tom'ma•sel'li syndrome
to'mo•gram'
to'mo•graph'ic
to•mog'ra•phy
ton'al
tone
tongue
tongue'-tie'
ton'ic
ton'ic-clo'nic
to•nic'i•ty
To'ni-Fan•co'ni syndrome
to'no•fi'bril
to'no•gram'
to'no•graph'
to•nog'ra•phy
to•nom'e•ter
to•nom'e•try
to'no•plast'
to'no•scope'
ton'sil
ton•sil'la pl. -lae'
—— cer'e•bel'li'
—— lin•gua'lis
—— pal'a•ti'na
—— pha•ryn'ge•a
—— tu•bar'i•a
ton'sil•lar
ton'sil•lec'tome'
ton'sil•lec'to•my
ton'sil•lit'ic
ton'sil•li'tis

ton•sil'lo•lith'
ton'sil•lo•phar'yn•gi'tis
ton•sil'lo•tome'
ton'sil•lot'o•my
ton'sil•lo•ty'phoid'
ton'sil•sec'tor
ton'sure
to'nus
tooth pl. teeth
tooth'ache'
toothed
Tooth muscular atrophy
top•ag•no'sis
to•pal'gi•a
to•pec'to•my
top•es•the'si•a
Töp'fer
—— reagent
—— test
to•pha'ceous
to'phus pl. -phi'
top'ic or top'i•cal
To•pi•nard' angle
top•o•al'gi•a
top•o•an•es•the'si•a
to'po•gen'e•sis
top•og•no'sis
top•og•nos'tic
top•o•graph'ic
to•pog'ra•phy
to•pol'o•gy
top•o•nar•co'sis pl. -ses'
top•o•neu•ro'sis pl. -ses'
tor'cu•lar He•roph'i•li'
To'rek' operation
to'ric
Tor'kild•sen procedure
tor'mi•na
—— al'vi'
tor'mi•nal
Torn'waldt'
—— bursitis
—— disease
tor•pes'cence
tor'pid
tor•pid'i•ty
tor'por
—— in•tes'ti•no'rum
torque
tor•sade' de pointes'
tor•si•oc•clu'sion
tor'si•om'e•ter
tor'sion
tor'sive
tor'si•ver'sion
tor'so pl. -sos, -si', or -soes
tor'soc•clu'sion

tort
tor'ti•col'lar
tor'ti•col'lis
—— spas'ti•ca
tor•tu•os'i•ty
tor'tu•ous
tor•u•lo'ma pl. -mas or
-ma•ta
Tor'u•lop'sis ne'o•
for'mans'
tor'u•lo'sis
tor'u•lus pl. -li'
to'rus pl. -ri'
—— gen'i•ta'lis
—— lev'a•to'ri•us
—— oc•cip'i•ta'lis
—— pal'a•ti'nus
—— pu'bi•cus
—— tu•bar'i•us
—— u're•ter'i•cus
—— u'ter•i'nus
to'tal
To'ti operation
to•tip'o•tent
to'ti•po•ten'tial
touch
tour de mai'tre
Tou•rette' disease
tour'ni•quet
Tou'ton cells
Town'send operation
tox•al'bu•min
tox•e'mi•a
tox•e'mic
tox•en'zyme'
tox'ic
tox'i•cant
tox'i•ce'mi•a
tox'i•cide'
tox•ic'i•ty
tox'i•co•der'ma•ti'tis
tox'i•co•gen'ic
tox'i•coid'
tox'i•co•log'ic or tox'i•co•
log'i•cal
tox'i•col'o•gist
tox'i•col'o•gy
tox'i•co•ma'ni•a
tox'i•co•ma'ni•ac'
tox'i•co•path'ic
tox'i•co•pho'bi•a
tox'i•co'sis pl. -ses'
tox'i•der'ma•to'sis pl. -ses'
tox'i•der•mi'tis
tox•if'er•ous
tox'i•gen'ic
tox'i•ge•nic'i•ty

tox·ig′e·nous
tox′ig·nom′ic
tox′in
tox′i·ne′mi·a
tox′in·fec′tion
tox′i·no′sis *pl.* -ses′
tox′i·phre′ni·a
tox·is′ter·ol′
tox′i·ther′a·py
tox′i·tu·ber′cu·lide′
tox′o·ca·ri′a·sis
tox′oid′
tox′o·no′sis *pl.* -ses′
tox′o·phil′
Tox′o·plas′ma
—— gon′di·i′
tox′o·plas·mat′ic
tox′o·plas′min
tox′o·plas·mo′sis *pl.* -ses′
Toyn′bee
—— corpuscle
—— ligament
tra·bec′u·la *pl.* -lae′
—— sep′to·mar′gi·na′lis
tra·bec′u·lae′
—— car′ne·ae′
—— cor′dis
—— cor′po·ris spon′gi·o′si′
—— cor′po·rum cav′er·no·so′rum
—— li·e′nis
tra·bec′u·lar
tra·bec′u·late′
tra·bec′u·la′tion
tra·bec′u·lec′to·my
tra·bec′u·lot′o·my
tra·bec′u·lo·plas′ty
trabs *pl.* tra′bes′
trace
trac′er
tra′che·a *pl.* -ae′ *or* -as
tra′che·a·ec′ta·sy
tra′che·al
tra′che·al′gi·a
tra′che·i′tis
trach′e·lec′to·my
trach′e·le′ma·to′ma
pl. -mas *or* -ma·ta
trach′e·lis′mus
trach′e·li′tis
trach′e·lo′cyl·lo′sis
trach′e·lo·dyn′i·a
trach′e·lo·ky·pho′sis
trach′e·lo·mas′toid′
trach′e·lo·par′a·si′tus
trach′e·lo·pex′i·a
trach′e·lo·plas′ty

trach′e·lor′rha·phy
trach′e·lor·rhec′tes′
trach′e·los′chi·sis *pl.* -ses′
trach′e·lo·syr′in·gor′rha·phy
trach′e·lot′o·my
tra′che·o·blen′nor·rhe′a
tra′che·o·bron′chi·al
tra′che·o·bron·chi′tis
tra′che·o·bron·chos′co·py
tra′che·o·cele′
tra′che·o·e·soph′a·ge′al
tra′che·o·fis′sure
tra′che·o·gen′ic
tra′che·o·la·ryn′ge·al
tra′che·o·lar′yn·got′o·my
tra′che·o·ma·la′ci·a
tra′che·o·path′i·a os′te·o·plas′ti·ca
tra′che·o′pha·ryn′ge·al
tra′che·oph′o·ny
tra′che·o·plas′ty
tra′che·o·py·o′sis
tra′che·or·rha′gi·a
tra′che·or′rha·phy
tra′che·os′chi·sis *pl.* -ses′
tra′che·o·scop′ic
tra′che·os′co·py
tra′che·o·ste·no′sis *pl.* -ses′
tra′che·os′to·ma *pl.* -ma·ta
or -mas
tra′che·os′to·my
tra′che·o·tome′
tra′che·ot′o·mist
tra′che·ot′o·mize′, -mized′, -miz′ing
tra′che·ot′o·my
tra·chi′tis
tra·cho′ma
tra·cho′ma·tous
tra′chy·chro·mat′ic
tra′chy·chro·mat′ic
tra′chy·o·nych′i·a
tra′chy·pho′ni·a
trac′ing
tract
—— of Al′len
—— of Schütz
trac′tion
trac′tor
trac·tot′o·my
trac′tus *pl.* trac′tus
—— cen·tra′lis thy′mi′
—— cer′e·bel′lo·ru·bra′lis
—— cer′e·bel′lo·tha·lam′i·cus

—— cor′ti·co·hy′po·tha·lam′i·ci′
—— cor′ti·co′pon·ti′ni′
—— cor′ti·co′pon·ti′nus
—— corticopontinus mes′en·ce·phal′i·cus
—— corticopontinus pon′tis
—— cor′ti·co′spi·na′lis anterior
—— corticospinalis lat′er·a′lis
—— dor′so·lat·er·a′lis
—— fron′to·pon·ti′nus
—— gen′i·ta′lis
—— il′i·o·tib′i·a′lis
—— iliotibialis (Mais′si·a′ti′)
—— mes′en·ce·phal′i·cus ner′vi′ tri·gem′i·ni′
—— ner·vo′si′ as·so·ci·a′ti·o′nis
—— nervosi com·mis′su·ra′les′
—— nervosi pro·jec′ti·o′nis
—— oc·cip′i·to·pon·ti′nus
—— ol′fac·to′ri·us
—— o·li′vo·cer′e·bel·lar′is
—— op′ti·cus
—— pa·ri′e·to′pon·ti′nus
—— py·ram′i·da′les′
—— py·ram′i·da′lis anterior
—— pyramidalis lat′er·a′lis
—— pyramidalis me·dul′lae′ ob′lon·ga′tae′
—— pyramidalis mes′en·ce·phal′i·cus
—— pyramidalis pon′tis
—— re·tic′u·lo·spi·na′lis
—— ru′bro·spi·na′lis
—— sol′i·tar′i·us
—— spi·na′lis ner′vi′ tri·gem′i·ni′
—— spi′no·cer′e·bel·lar′is anterior
—— spinocerebellaris posterior
—— spi′no·tec·ta′lis
—— spi′no·tha·lam′i·cus anterior
—— spinothalamicus lat′er·a′lis
—— spi·ra′lis fo·ram′i·no′sus
—— su′pra·op′ti·co·hy′po·phys′i·a′lis
—— sys·te′ma·tis ner·vo′si′ cen·tra′lis
—— tec′to·spi·na′lis

—— teg′men·ta′lis cen·
tra′lis
—— tem′po·ro′pon·ti′nus
—— ves·tib′u·lo′spi·na′lis
Tra′cy method
trade′mark′
tra′gal
Tra′gi·a
trag′o·mas·chal′i·a
trag′o·pho′ni·a
tra·goph′o·ny
trag′o·po′di·a
tra′gus *pl.* -gi′
train′a·ble
trait
tram′a·dol′
trance
tran′quil·ize′, -ized′, -iz′ing
tran′quil·iz′er
trans·ab·dom′i·nal
trans·am′i·nase′
trans·an′i·ma′tion
trans′a·or′tic
trans·a′tri·al
trans·au′di·ent
trans·ax′o·nal
trans·cav′i·tar′y
trans·cer′vi·cal
trans·con′dy·lar
trans·cor′ti·cal
trans·cor′tin
tran·scrip′tion
trans′cu·ta′ne·ous
trans·der′mal
trans·duc′er
trans·duc′tion
trans·du′o·de′nal
tran·sect′
tran·sec′tion
trans·fer′, -ferred′, -fer′ring
trans′fer·ase′
trans·fer·ence
trans·fer′rin
trans·fix′
trans·fix′ion
trans′fo·rate′, -rat′ed, -rat′-
ing
trans′fo·ra′tion
trans′fo·ra′tor
trans′for·ma′tion
trans·fuse′, -fused′, -fus′ing
trans·fu′sion
trans′he·pat′ic
tran′sient
trans·il′i·ac′
trans·il·lu′mi·na′tion
tran·si′tion·al

tran′si·to′ry
trans′lo·ca′tion
trans·lu′cent
trans·max′il·lar′y
trans′mi·gra′tion
trans·mis′si·bil′i·ty
trans·mis′si·ble
trans·mis′sion
trans·mit′tance
trans·mit′ter
trans·mu′ral
trans·mu·ta′tion
trans·oc′u·lar
tran′so·nance
trans·or′bi·tal
trans·pal′a·tal
trans·par′ent
trans·per′i·to·ne′al
tran·spi·ra′tion
trans·pla·cen′tal
trans·plant′ *n.*
trans·plant′ *v.*
trans′plan·ta′tion
trans·pleu′ral
trans·pose′, -posed′, -pos′ing
trans·po·si′tion
trans·py·lo′ric
trans·ra′di·ant
trans·sa′cral
trans·sec′tion
trans·sex′u·al
trans·sex′u·a·lism
trans·ten·to′ri·al
trans′tho·rac′ic
trans′tym·pan′ic
tran′su·date′
tran′su·da′tion
tran·sude′, -sud′ed, -sud′ing
trans′u·re′thral
trans′vag′i·nal
trans′ver·sa′lis
trans·verse′
trans·ver·sec′to·my
trans·ver·sot′o·my
trans·ver′sus
—— nu′chae′
trans·ves′i·cal
trans·ves′tism
trans·ves·tite′
tran′yl·cy′pro·mine′
tra·pe′zi·al
tra·pe′zi·o·met′a·car′pal
tra·pe′zi·um *pl.* -zi·ums or
-zi·a
tra·pe′zi·us
trap′e·zoid′
Trapp formula

Trau′be
—— membrane
—— sign
—— space
—— waves
trau′ma *pl.* -ma·ta *or* -mas
trau·mat′ic
trau′ma·tism
trau′ma·tize′, -tized′, -tiz′-
ing
trau′ma·top′a·thy
trau′ma·top·ne′a
trau′ma·to′sis *pl.* -ses′
Traut′mann triangle
tra·vail′
treat
treat′ment
Treitz
—— fossa
—— hernia
—— muscle
tre′ma
tre·mat′ic
Trem′a·to′da
trem′a·tode′
trem′a·to·di′a·sis *pl.* -ses′
trem′ble, -bled, -bling
trem·el′loid′
trem·el·lose′
trem·e·tol′
trem′o·la·bile′
trem′o·lo
trem′or
—— ar′tu·um
—— cap′i·tis
—— cor′dis
—— me·tal′li·cus
—— po′ta·to′rum
—— sat′ur·ni′nus
—— ten′di·num
trem′u·lous
Tren·del′en·burg′ test
tre·pan′, -panned′, -pan′ning
trep′a·na′tion
trep′a·nize′, -nized′, -niz′ing
tre·phine′, -phined′, -phin′-
ing
trep′i·dant
tre′pi·da′ti·o′
—— cor′dis
trep′i·da′tion
trep′o·ne′ma *pl.* -ma·ta *or*
-mas
Trep′o·ne′ma
—— a·mer′i·ca′num
—— ca·ra′te·um
—— cu·nic′u·li′

—— her're·jo'ni'
—— pal'li·dum
—— per·ten'u·e'
—— pic'tor'
—— pin'tae'
trep'o·ne'mal
trep'o·ne'ma·to'sis *pl.* -ses'
trep'o·ne·mi'a·sis *pl.* -ses'
trep'o·ne'mi·ci'dal
trep'o·ne'min
tre·pop'ne·a
trep'pe
Tre·sil'i·an sign
tri·ac'e·tate'
tri·ac'e·tin
tri·ac'e·tyl·o'le·an'do·my'cin
tri'ad'
—— of Whip'ple
tri·age'
tri·am·cin'o·lone'
tri·am'py·zine'
tri·am'ter·ene'
tri'an·gle
—— of Ca·lot'
—— of Gom·bault'-Phi·lippe'
tri·an'gu·lar
tri·an'gu·lar'is
Tri·at'o·ma
tri·a'tri·al
tri·ax'i·al
tri·bra'chi·us
tri·bro'mo·eth'a·nol'
tri·bro'mo·meth'ane'
tri·brom'sa·lan'
tri'ceps'
—— ex·ten'sor cu'bi·ti'
tri·cet'a·mide'
trich'es·the'si·a
tri·chi'a·sis
Trich'i·nel'la
—— spi·ra'lis
trich'i·nel·lo'sis *pl.* -ses'
trich'i·ni'a·sis *pl.* -ses'
trich'i·no'sis *pl.* -ses'
trich'i·nous
tri·chi'tis
tri'chlor·meth'ane'
tri'chlor·me·thi'a·zide'
tri·chlo'ro·ac'e·tal'de·hyde'
tri·chlo'ro·a·ce'tic
tri·chlo'ro·bu'tyl
tri·chlo'ro·eth'yl·ene'
tri·chlo'ro·meth'ane'
trich'o·an'es·the'si·a

trich'o·be'zo·ar
trich'o·car'di·a
trich'o·ceph'a·li'a·sis *pl.* -ses'
trich'o·cla'si·a
tri·choc'la·sis
trich'o·cryp·to'sis *pl.* -ses'
trich'o·cyst'
trich'o·ep'i·the'li·o'ma *pl.* -mas or -ma·ta
—— pap'u·lo'sum mul'ti·plex'
trich'o·es·the'si·a
trich'o·glos'si·a
trich'o·hy'a·lin
trich'oid'
trich'o·lith'
trich'o·lo'gi·a
tri·chol'o·gy
tri·cho'ma
trich'o·ma·de'sis
trich'o·ma'ni·a
tri·cho'ma·tose'
trich'o·ma·to'sis
trich'ome'
trich'o·mo'na·ci'dal
trich'o·mo'na·cide'
trich'o·mo'nad'
tri·chom'o·nal
Trich'o·mo'nas
—— hom'i·nis
—— vag'i·na'lis
—— vag'i·ni'tis
trich'o·mo·ni'a·sis *pl.* -ses'
trich'o·mo'ni·cide'
Trich'o·my'ce·tes'
trich'o·my·co'sis *pl.* -ses'
—— ax'il·lar'is
—— bar'bae'
—— cap'il·li·ti'i'
—— cir'ci·na'ta
—— fa·vo'sa
—— fla'va ni'gra
—— no·do'sa
—— pal'mel·li'na
—— pus'tu·lo'sa
—— ru'bra
tri'chon'
trich'o·no·car'di·o'sis
trich'o·no·do'sis
trich'o·no'sis *pl.* -ses'
trich'o·path'ic
trich'o·path'o·pho'bi·a
tri·chop'a·thy
trich'o·pha'gi·a
tri·choph'a·gy
trich'o·phyte'

trich'o·phy'tid
trich'o·phy'tin
trich'o·phy'to·be'zo·ar
trich'o·phy'ton' *pl.* -ta or -tons'
trich'o·phy·to'sis *pl.* -ses'
trich'o·pti·lo'sis
trich'or·rhe'a
trich'or·rhex'is
—— no·do'sa
trich'o·sid'er·in
tri·cho'sis *pl.* -ses'
Trich'o·spo'ron'
trich'o·spo·ro'sis *pl.* -ses'
trich'o·sta'sis spi'nu·lo'sa
trich'o·stron'gy·li'a·sis
trich'o·the'cin
tri·chot'o·my
tri'chro·ism
tri'chro·mat'
tri'chro·mat'ic
tri'chro·ma·top'si·a
tri'chro'mic
trich'ter·brust'
trich'u·ri'a·sis *pl.* -ses'
Trich·u'ris
—— trich'i·u'ra
tri·cip'i·tal
tri'clo·bi·son'i·um
tri'clo·car'ban'
tri'clo·fen'ol'
tric'lo·fos'
tri'corn'
tri·cor'nute'
tri·crot'ic
tri'cro·tism
tri·cus'pid
tri·cy'cla·mol'
tri·dac'tyl
tri'dent'
tri·den'tate'
tri·der'mic
tri·der'mo'ma *pl.* -mas or -ma·ta
tri·di·hex·eth'yl
tri'en·ceph'a·lus *pl.* -li'
tri·eth'a·nol'a·mine'
tri·eth'yl·ene·mel'a·mine'
tri·fa'cial
tri'fid
tri·flu'mi·date'
tri·flu'o·per'a·zine'
tri'flu·per'i·dol'
tri·flu·pro'ma·zine'
tri·fo'cal
tri·fur'cate', -cat'ed, -cat'ing
tri·fur·ca'tion

tri·gem'i·nal
tri·gem'i·no'tha·lam'ic
tri·gem'i·nus
  pl. -ni'
tri·gem'i·ny
tri·gen'ic
tri·glyc'er·ide'
tri·go'na fi·bro'sa cor'dis
trig'o·nal
tri'gone'
—— of Lieu·taud'
Trig'o·nel'la
tri'go·nid
tri'go·ni'tis
trig'o·no·ceph'a·lus *pl.* -li'
trig'o·no·ceph'a·ly
tri·go'no·tome'
tri·go'num *pl.* -nums *or* -na
—— a·cus'ti·ci'
—— ca·rot'i·cum
—— col·lat'er·a'le'
—— del·toi'de·o·pec'to·ra'le'
—— fem'o·ra'le'
—— fi·bro'sum cor'dis (dex'-
trum et si·nis'trum)
—— ha·ben'u·lae'
—— in'gui·na'le'
—— in'ter·pe·dun'cu·lar'e'
—— lem·nis'ci'
—— lum·ba'le'
—— lumbale (Pet'i·ti')
—— ner'vi' hy'po·glos'si'
—— nervi va'gi'
—— ol'fac·to'ri·um
—— o'mo·cla·vic'u·lar'e'
—— sub'man·dib'u·lar'e'
—— u'ro·gen'i·ta'le'
—— ve·si'cae'
—— vesicae (Lieu·tau'di')
tri'hex·y·phen'i·dyl
tri·hy'brid
tri'hy·drox'y·ben·zo'ic
tri'hy·drox'y·pro'pane'
tri·i'o·do·meth'ane'
tri·i'o·do·thy'ro·nine'
tri·ke'to·pu'rine'
tri'labe'
tri·lam'i·nar
tri·lat'er·al
tri·lo'bate'
tri·lo·bec'to·my
tri·loc'u·lar
tril'o·gy of Fal'lot
tri'mal·le'o·lar
tri·man'u·al
tri·mep'ra·zine'
tri·mes'ter

tri·meth'a·phan' cam'syl·
ate'
tri·meth'i·din'i·um meth'o·
sul'fate'
tri·meth'o·benz'a·mide'
tri·meth'o·prim
tri·meth'yl·a·mine'
tri·meth'yl·ene'
tri·meth'yl·gly'cine'
tri·meth'yl·xan'thine'
tri·met'o·zine'
tri·mip'ra·mine'
tri'mix'
tri·mor'phic
tri·mor'phism
tri·mox'a·mine'
tri·neu'ral
tri·ni'tro·glyc'er·in
tri·ni'tro·phe'nol'
tri·no'mi·al
tri·nu'cle·ate'
tri'o·lism
tri·or'chid
tri·or'chi·dism
tri·o'tus
tri·ox'sa·len
tri·ox'y·meth'yl·ene'
tri·ox'y·pu'rine'
tri·pal'mi·tin
trip'a·ra
tri·par'tite'
tri·pel·en'na·mine'
tri·pep'tide'
tri·pha·lan'gism
tri'pha·lan'gy
tri·pha'sic
tri·phos'pho·pyr'i·dine'
tri'ple
tri·ple'gi·a
trip'let
trip'lex'
trip'lo·blas'tic
trip'loid'
trip'loi·dy
trip'lo·ko·ri·a
trip·lo'pi·a
tri'pod'
tri·prol'i·dine'
trip'sis
tri·que'trum *pl.* -tra
tri·ra'di·ate
tri·sac'cha·ride'
tri'sect'
tris'mus
tri·so'mic
tri·so'mus
tri·so·my

tri·ste'a·rin
tris'ti·chi'a·sis
tris'ti·ma'ni·a
tris'tis
trit'a·no'pi·a
tri·ti'ceous
trit'o·cone'
trit'o·co'nid
trit'u·ra·ble
trit'u·rate', -rat'ed, -rat'ing
trit'u·ra'tion
tri·va'lence
tri·va'lent
tri'valve'
tri·val'vu·lar
tro'car' *also* trochar
tro·chan'ter
tro'chan·ter'ic
tro·chan'tin
tro·chan·tin'i·an
tro'char' *var. of* trocar
tro'che
tro'chin
tro'chis·ca'tion
tro·chis'cus *pl.* -ci'
troch'le·a *pl.* -ae'
—— fib'u·lar'is
—— hu'mer·i'
—— mus'cu·lar'is
—— mus'cu·li' ob·li'qui'
oc'u·li' su·pe'ri·o'ris
—— musculi obliqui superioris
—— per'o·ne·a'lis
—— pha·lan'gis
—— ta'li
troch'i·ter
troch'le·ar
troch'le·ar'is
troch'o·car'di·a
troch'o·ceph'a·lus
tro'cho·ceph'a·ly
tro'choid
Trog'lo·tre'ma
—— sal·min'co·la
Troi·sier'
—— sign
—— syndrome
trol'a·mine'
tro'le·an·do·my'cin
trol·ni'trate'
Tröltsch
—— corpuscles
—— recesses
Trom·bic'u·la
—— al'fred·du'ge·si'
—— ir'ri·tans'

trom·bic'u·lo'sis pl. -ses'
tro·meth'a·mine'
Trom'mer test
Tröm'ner sign
trom'o·ma'ni·a
tro'pa·co'caine'
tro'phe·de'ma
tro·phe'si·al
tro·phe'sic
troph'e·sy
troph'ic
tro·phic'i·ty
troph'ism
troph'o·blast'
troph'o·blas'tic
tro·ph'o·blas·to'ma pl. -mas
  or -ma·ta
troph'o·chrome'
troph'o·chro·mid'i·a
troph'o·cyte'
troph'o·derm'
troph'o·der'mal
troph'o·der'ma·to·neu·
  ro'sis pl. -ses'
troph'o·dy·nam'ics
tro·phol'o·gy
troph'o·neu·ro'sis pl. -ses'
troph'o·neu·rot'ic
troph'o·no'sis pl. -ses'
troph'o·nu'cle·us pl. -cle·i'
tro·phop'a·thy
troph'o·spon'gi·a
troph'o·spon'gi·um
troph'o·tax'is pl. -tax'es'
troph'o·ther'a·py
troph'o·trop'ic
tro·phot'ro·pism
troph'o·zo'ite'
tro'pi·a
trop'ic
trop'i·cal
tro·pic'a·mide'
tro'pin
tro'pism
tro'po·chrome'
tro'po·col'la·gen
tro·pom'e·ter
tro'po·pause'
tro'po·sphere'
Trous·seau'
—— disease
—— mark
—— sign
trox'i·done'
troy
Tru·e'ta shunt
trun'cal

trun'cate', -cat'ed, -cat'ing
trun'ci'
—— in·tes'ti·na'les'
—— lum·ba'les'
—— lumbales (dex'ter et si·
  nis'ter)
—— plex'us bra'chi·a'lis
trun'co·co'nal
trun'cus pl. -ci'
—— ar·te'ri·o'sus
—— bra'chi·o·ce·phal'i·cus
—— bron'cho·me·di·as'ti·
  na'lis
—— bronchomediastinalis
dex'ter
—— ce·li'a·cus
—— cor'po·ris cal·lo'si'
—— cos'to·cer'vi·ca'lis
—— fas·cic'u·li' a'tri·o·ven·
  tric'u·lar'is
—— inferior plex'us bra'chi·
a'lis
—— in·tes'ti·na'lis
—— jug'u·lar'is
—— lin'guo·fa'ci·a'lis
—— lum'bo·sa·cra'lis
—— me'di·us plex'us
bra'chi·a'lis
—— pul'mo·na'lis
—— sub·cla'vi·us
—— superior plex'us
bra'chi·a'lis
—— sym·path'i·cus
—— thy're·o·cer'vi·ca'lis
—— thy'ro·cer'vi·ca'lis
—— trans·ver'sus
—— va·ga'lis anterior
—— vagalis posterior
trunk
truss
tryp'an
try·pan'o·ci'dal
try·pan'o·cide'
Try·pan'o·so'ma
—— bru'ce·i'
—— cru'zi'
—— eq'ui·per'dum
—— ev'an·si'
—— gam'bi·en'se'
—— hip'pi·cum
—— lew'i·si'
—— rho·de·si·en'se'
—— vi'vax'
try·pan'o·so'mal
Try·pan'o·so·mat'i·dae'
try·pan'o·some'

try·pan'o·so·mi'a·sis
  pl. -ses'
try·pan'o·som'ic
try·pan'o·so'mi·cid'al
try·pan'o·so·mide'
tryp·ar'sa·mide'
tryp'sin
tryp·sin'o·gen
tryp'ta·mine'
tryp'tase'
tryp'tic
tryp'to·lyt'ic
tryp'to·phan'
tryp'to·pha·nase'
tryp'to·pha·ne'mi·a
tryp'to·phan·u'ri·a
tryp'to·phyl
tset'se
Tsu'chi·ya reagent
tsu'tsu·ga·mu'shi
tu'a·mi'no·hep'tane'
tu'ba pl. -bae'
—— au'di·ti'va
—— auditiva (Eu·sta'chi·i')
—— u'ter·i'na
—— uterina (Fal·lop'pi·i')
tub'al
tube
tu·bec'to·my
tu'ber pl. -bers or -ber·a
—— cal·ca'ne·i'
—— ci·ne're·um
—— fron·ta'le'
—— is'chi·ad'i·cum
—— max·il'lae
—— max·il·lar'e'
—— o'men·ta'le' hep'a·tis
—— omentale pan·cre'a·tis
—— pa·ri'e·ta'le'
—— ver'mis
tu'be·ral
tu·ber·cle
tu·ber'cu·la co·ro'nae'
  den'tis
tu·ber'cu·lar
tu·ber'cu·lat'ed
tu·ber'cu·la'tion
tu·ber'cu·lid
tu·ber'cu·lig'e·nous
tu·ber'cu·lin
tu·ber'cu·lin·i·za'tion
tu'ber·cu·li'tis
tu·ber'cu·li·za'tion
tu·ber'cu·lo·cele'
tu·ber'cu·lo·cid'al
tu·ber'cu·lo·ci'din
tu·ber'cu·lo·fi'broid'

tu·ber′cu·lo′fi·bro′sis pl.
-ses′
tu·ber′cu·loid′
tu·ber′cu·lo′ma pl. -mas or
-ma·ta
—— en plaque
tu·ber′cu·lo·pro′tein′
tu·ber′cu·lo·lose′
tu·ber′cu·lo·sil′i·co′sis
tu·ber′cu·lo′sis
—— cu′tis
—— cutis in·du′ra·ti′va
—— cutis o′ri·fi′ci·a′lis
—— li′che·noi′des′
—— lu·po′sa
—— ver′ru·co′sa
tu·ber′cu·lo·stat′ic
tu·ber′cu·lo·ste′ar·ic
tu·ber′cu·lous
tu·ber′cu·lum pl. -la
—— a·cus′ti·cum
—— ad′duc·to′ri·um
—— an·te′ri·us at·lan′tis
—— anterius thal′a·mi′
—— anterius ver′te·brar′um
cer′vi·ca′li·um
—— ar·tic′u·lar′e′ os′sis
tem′po·ra′lis
—— au·ric′u·lae′
—— auriculae (Dar′wi·ni′)
—— ca·rot′i·cum ver′te·
brae′ cer′vi·ca′lis VI
—— cau·da′tum
—— ci·ne′re·um
—— co·noi′de·um
—— cor·nic′u·la′tum
—— corniculatum (San′to·
ri′ni′)
—— co·ro′nae′ den′tis
—— cos′tae′
—— cu′ne·i·for′me′
—— cuneiforme (Wris·
ber′gi′)
—— ep′i·glot′ti·cum
—— gen′i·ta′le′
—— im′par′
—— in′fra·gle′noi·da′le′
—— in′ter·con′dy·lar′e′
lat′er·a′le′
—— intercondylare me′di·
a′le′
—— in′ter·con′dy·loi′de·um
lat′er·a′le′
—— intercondyloideum
me′di·a′le′
—— in′ter·ve·no′sum

—— intervenosum (Low′e·
ri′)
—— jug′u·lar′e′ os′sis oc·
cip′i·ta′lis
—— la′bi·i′ su·pe′ri·o′ris
—— lat′er·a′le′ pro·ces′sus
pos·te′ri·o′ris ta′li′
—— lin·gua′le′ lat′er·a′le′
—— linguale me′di·a′le′
—— ma′jus hu′mer·i′
—— mar′gi·na′le′ os′sis
zy′go·mat′i·ci′
—— me′di·a′le′ pro·ces′sus
pos·te′ri·o′ris ta′li′
—— men·ta′le′ man·dib′u·
lae′
—— mi′nus hu′mer·i′
—— mus′cu·li′ sca·le′ni′ an·
te′ri·o′ris
—— nu′cle·i′ cu′ne·a′ti′
—— nuclei grac′i·lis
—— ob·tu·ra·to′ri·um an·
te′ri·us
—— obturatorium pos·te′ri·
us
—— of San′to·ri′ni
—— os′sis mul·tan′gu·li′ ma·
jo′ris
—— ossis na·vic′u·lar′is
—— ossis sca·phoi′de·i′
—— ossis tra·pe′zi·i′
—— pha·ryn′ge·um
—— pos·te′ri·us at·lan′tis
—— posterius ver′te·
brar′um cer′vi·ca′li·um
—— pu′bi·cum os′sis pu′bis
—— sca·le′ni′ (Lis·fran′ci′)
—— sel′lae′ tur′ci·cae′
—— su′pra·gle′noi·da′le′
—— su′pra·tra′gi·cum
—— thy′re·oi′de·um in·fe′ri·
us
—— thyreoideum su·pe′ri·us
—— thy′roi′de·um in·fe′ri·us
—— thyroideum su·pe′ri·us
tu·ber·o·hy′po·phys′e·al
tu·ber·o′sis
tu·ber·os′i·tas′ pl. -os′i·
ta′tes′
—— co·ra·coi′de·a cla·vic′u·
lae′
—— cos′tae′ II
—— cos·ta′lis cla·vic′u·lae′
—— del·toi′de·a
—— glu′tae·a
—— glu′te·a
—— i·li′a·ca

—— in′fra·gle′noi·da′lis
—— mas′se·ter′i·ca
—— mus′cu·li′ ser·ra′ti′ an·
te′ri·o′ris
—— os′sis cu·boi′de·i′
—— ossis met′a·tar·sa′lis I
—— ossis metatarsalis V
—— ossis na·vic′u·lar′is
—— pha·lan′gis dis·ta′lis
—— pter′y·goi′de·a
—— ra′di·i′
—— sa·cra′lis
—— su′pra·gle′noi·da′lis
—— tib′i·ae′
—— ul′nae′
—— un·guic′u·lar′is
tu·ber·os′i·ty
tu·bo·ab·dom′i·nal
tu·bo·ad·nex′o·pex′y
tu·bo·cu·ra′re
tu·bo·cu·ra′rine′
tu·bo·lig′a·men′ta·ry
tu·bo·lig′a·men′tous
tu·bo·o·var′i·an
tu·bo·o·var′i·ot′o·my
tu·bo·per′i·to·ne′al
tu·bo·plas′ty
tu·bo·tym′pa·nal
tu·bo·tym·pan′ic
tu·bo·u′ter·ine
tu·bo·vag′i·nal
tu·bu·lar
tu′bule′
tu′bu·li′
—— lac·tif′er·i′
—— re·na′les′
—— renales con·tor′ti′
—— renales rec′ti′
—— sem′i·nif′er·i′ con·tor′ti′
—— seminiferi rec′ti′
tu′bu·lin
tu′bu·li·za′tion
tu′bu·lize′, -lized′, -liz′ing
tu′bu·lo·ac′i·nar
tu′bu·lo·ac′i·nous
tu′bu·lo·al·ve′o·lar
tu′bu·lo·cyst′
tu′bu·lo·in′ter·sti′tial
tu′bu·lo·rac′e·mose′
tu′bu·lus pl. -li′
tu′bus pl. -bi′
—— di·ges′to′ri·us
—— med·ul·lar′is
—— ver′te·bra′lis
Tuf·fier′ ligament
tu′la·re′mi·a
tu·me·fa′cient

tu‧me‧fac′tion
tu′me‧fy′, -fied′, -fy′ing
tu‧men′ti‧a
tu‧mes′cence
tu‧mes′cent
tu′mid
tu‧mid′i‧ty
tu′mor
tu′mor‧af′fin
tu′mor‧al
tu′mor‧i‧cid′al
tu′mo‧ri‧gen′ic
tu′mor‧let
tu′mor‧ous
tu‧mul′tus
—— cor′dis
—— ser‧mo′nis
Tun′ga
—— pen′e‧trans′
tun‧gi′a‧sis *pl.* -ses′
tu′nic
tu′ni‧ca *pl.* -cae′
—— ad′ven‧ti′ti‧a
—— adventitia duc′tus def′e‧ren′tis
—— adventitia e‧soph′a‧gi′
—— adventitia oe‧soph′a‧gi′
—— adventitia tu′bae′ u′ter‧i′nae′
—— adventitia u‧re′ter‧is
—— adventitia ve‧si′cae′ sem′i‧na′lis
—— adventitia ve‧sic′u‧lae′ sem′i‧na′lis
—— al′bu‧gin′e‧a
—— albuginea cor′po‧ris spon′gi‧o′si′
—— albuginea cor′po‧rum cav′er‧no‧so′rum
—— albuginea li‧e′nis
—— albuginea oc′u‧li′
—— albuginea o‧var′i‧i′
—— albuginea pe′nis
—— albuginea tes′tis
—— con′junc‧ti′va
—— conjunctiva bul′bi′
—— conjunctiva pal′pe‧brar′um
—— dar′tos′
—— de‧cid′u‧a
—— e‧las′ti‧ca
—— ex‧ter′na
—— externa the′cae′ fol‧lic′u‧li′
—— externa va‧so′rum
—— fi‧bro′sa
—— fibrosa bul′bi′

—— fibrosa hep′a‧tis
—— fibrosa li‧e′nis
—— fibrosa oc′u‧li′
—— fibrosa re′nis
—— in‧ter′na
—— interna bul′bi′
—— interna the′cae′ fol‧lic′u‧li′
—— in′ti‧ma
—— me′di‧a
—— mu‧co′sa
—— mucosa ca′vi′ tym′pa‧ni′
—— mucosa co′li′
—— mucosa duc′tus def′e‧ren′tis
—— mucosa e‧soph′a‧gi′
—— mucosa in′tes‧ti′ni′ cras′si′
—— mucosa intestini rec′ti′
—— mucosa intestini ten′u‧is
—— mucosa la‧ryn′gis
—— mucosa lin′guae′
—— mucosa na′si′
—— mucosa oe‧soph′a‧gi′
—— mucosa o′ris
—— mucosa pha‧ryn′gis
—— mucosa rec′ti′
—— mucosa tra′che‧ae′ et bron‧cho′rum
—— mucosa tu′bae′ au′di‧ti′vae′
—— mucosa tubae u′ter‧i′nae′
—— mucosa tym‧pan′i‧ca
—— mucosa u‧re′ter‧is
—— mucosa u‧re′thrae′ fem′i‧ni′nae′
—— mucosa urethrae mu′li‧e′bris
—— mucosa u′ter‧i′
—— mucosa va‧gi′nae′
—— mucosa ven‧tric′u‧li′
—— mucosa ve‧si′cae′ fel′le‧ae′
—— mucosa vesicae u′ri‧nar′i‧ae′
—— mucosa ve‧sic′u‧lae′ sem′i‧na′lis
—— mus′cu‧lar′is
—— muscularis bron‧cho′rum
—— muscularis cer′vi‧cis u′ter‧i′
—— muscularis co′li′

—— muscularis duc′tus def′e‧ren′tis
—— muscularis e‧soph′a‧gi′
—— muscularis in′tes‧ti′ni′ cras′si′
—— muscularis intestini rec′ti′
—— muscularis intestini ten′u‧is
—— muscularis oe‧soph′a‧gi′
—— muscularis pha‧ryn′gis
—— muscularis rec′ti′
—— muscularis tra′che‧ae′ et bron‧cho′rum
—— muscularis tu′bae′ u′ter‧i′nae′
—— muscularis u‧re′ter‧is
—— muscularis u‧re′thrae′ fem′i‧ni′nae′
—— muscularis urethrae mu′li‧e′bris
—— muscularis u′ter‧i′
—— muscularis va‧gi′nae′
—— muscularis ven‧tric′u‧li′
—— muscularis ve‧si′cae′ fel′le‧ae′
—— muscularis vesicae u′ri‧nar′i‧ae′
—— muscularis ve‧sic′u‧lae′ sem′i‧na′lis
—— pro′pri‧a co′ri‧i′
—— propria mu‧co′sa
—— propria tu′bu‧li′ sem′i‧nif′er‧i′
—— se‧ro′sa
—— serosa co′li′
—— serosa hep′a‧tis
—— serosa in′tes‧ti′ni′ cras′si′
—— serosa intestini ten′u‧is
—— serosa li‧e′nis
—— serosa per′i‧to‧nae′i′
—— serosa per′i‧to‧ne′i′ pa‧ri′e‧ta′lis
—— serosa peritonei vis′cer‧a′lis
—— serosa tu′bae′ u′ter‧i′nae′
—— serosa u′tre‧i′
—— serosa ven‧tric′u‧li′
—— serosa ve‧si′cae′ fel′le‧ae′
—— serosa vesicae u′ri‧nar′i‧ae′
—— sub′mu‧co′sa

—— submucosa u·re'thrae'
mu'li·e'bris
—— tes'tis
—— u've·a
—— vag'i·na'lis com·mu'nis
—— vaginalis pro'pri·a tes'-
tis
—— vaginalis tes'tis
—— vas'cu·lo'sa bul'bi'
—— vasculosa len'tis
—— vasculosa oc'u·li'
—— vasculosa tes'tis
tu'ni·cae'
—— fu·nic'u·li' sper·mat'i·ci'
—— funiculi spermatici et
tes'tis
tun'nel
—— of Cor'ti'
tu'ran·ose'
tur'bid
tur'bi·dim'e·ter
tur'bi·di·met'ric
tur'bi·dim'e·try
tur·bid'i·ty
tur'bi·nal
tur'bi·nate'
tur'bi·nat'ed
tur'bi·nec'to·my
tur'bi·no·tome'
tur'bi·not'o·my
Türck
—— bundle
—— column
—— trachoma
tur·ges'cence
tur·ges'cent
tur'gid
tur'gor
Türk
—— cell
—— leukocyte
Tur'ling·ton balsam
tur'mer·ic
turn
Tur'ner syndrome
tur'pen·tine'
tur'ri·ceph'a·ly
tusk
tus'sal
tus·se'do
tus·sic'u·la
tus·sic'u·lar
tus·sic'u·la'tion
Tus'si·la'go
tus'sis
—— con'vul·si'va
tus'sive

tu·ta'men *pl.* -tam'i·na
Tut'hill method
Tut'tle operation
twang
tweez'ers
twig
twin
twinge, twinged, twing'ing
Twi'ning
—— kink
—— line
twin'ing
twitch
ty·bam'ate'
tyl'i·on' *pl.* -i·a
ty·lo'ma *pl.* -mas *or* -ma·ta
ty·lo'sis *pl.* -ses'
—— pal·mar'is et plan·tar'is
ty·lot'ic
ty·lox'a·pol'
tym'pa·nal
tym'pa·nec'to·my
tym·pan'i·a
tym·pan'ic
tym·pan'i·on
tym'pa·nism
tym'pa·ni'tes' *(abdominal
distention)*
♦tympanitis
tym'pa·nit'ic
tym'pa·ni'tis *(inflammation
of the tympanum)*
♦tympanites
tym'pa·no'eu·sta'chi·an
tym'pa·no'man·dib'u·lar
tym'pa·no·mas'toid'
tym'pa·no·mas'toi·di'tis
tym'pa·no·plas'ty
tym'pa·no·scle·ro'sis *pl.*
-ses'
tym'pa·no'sis *pl.* -ses'
tym'pa·no'squa·mo'sal
tym'pa·no'squa'mous
tym'pa·no·sta·pe'di·al
tym'pa·no·sym'pa·thec'to·
my
tym'pa·no·tem'po·ral
tym'pa·not'o·my
tym'pa·nous
tym'pa·num *pl.* -na *or*
-nums
tym'pa·ny
Tyn'dall
—— effect
—— phenomenon
tyn'dal·li·za'tion
type, typed, typ'ing

typh'lec·ta'si·a
typh'lec'to·my
typh'len'ter·i'tis
typh'li'tis
typh'lo·cele'
typh'lo·co·li'tis
typh'lo·dic'li·di'tis
typh'lo·em'py·e'ma
typh'lo·en'ter·i'tis
typh'loid'
typh'lo·lex'i·a
typh'lo·li·thi'a·sis
typh'lo·meg'a·ly
typh'lo·pex'y
typh'lo·pto'sis
typh'lo'sis
typh'lo·sole'
typh'lo·spasm
typh'lo·ste·no'sis *pl.* -ses'
typh·los'to·my
typh'lo·u·re'ter·os'to·my
ty'pho·bac'il·lo'sis of
Lan'dou·zy'
ty'pho·bac'ter·in
ty'phoid'
ty'phoid'al
ty'pho·ma·lar'i·al
ty'pho·ma'ni·a
ty'pho·pneu·mo'ni·a
ty'phous
ty'phus
—— ex·an·thé·ma·tique'
typ'i·cal
ty'po·scope'
ty'pus de·gen'er·a·ti'vus
am'ste·lo'da·men'sis
ty'ra·mine'
Ty'rode' solution
ty'roid'
ty·ros'a·mine'
tyr'o·sin·ase'
ty'ro·sine'
ty·ro·si·ne'mi·a
ty'ro·si·no'sis
ty'ro·si·nu'ri·a
ty·ro·thri'cin
Ty'son glands
Tyz'zer disease
Tzanck test

U

u'ber·ous
u'ber·ty
u·biq'ui·none'

ud'der
Uf'fel·mann test
Uhl anomaly
ul'cer
ul'cer·ate', -at'ed, -at'ing
ul'cer·a'tion
ul'cer·a·tive
ul'cer·o·gen'ic
ul'cer·o·gran'u·lo'ma pl.
  -mas or -ma·ta
ul'cer·o·mem'bra·nous
ul'cer·ous
ul'cus pl. -ce·ra
—— can·cro'sum
—— cru'ris
—— ex'e·dens
—— in'du·ra'tus
—— mol'le'
—— ro'dens
—— ser'pens
—— tu·ber'cu·lo'sum
—— ve·ne're·um
—— ven·tric'u·li'
—— vul'vae' a·cu'tum
u·lec'to·my
u·le·gy'ri·a
u·ler'y·the'ma
—— cen·trif'u·gum
—— oph'ry·og'e·nes'
—— sy·co'si·for'me'
u·let'ic
u·li'tis
Ull'rich-Tur'ner syndrome
ul'na pl. -nae' or -nas
ul'nad'
ul'nar
ul·nar'is
ul'no·car'pe·us
ul'no·ra'di·al
u·loc'a·ce
u'lo·der'ma·ti'tis
u'lo·glos·si'tis
u'loid'
u·lon'cus
u·lor·rha'gi·a
u·lor·rhe'a
u·lo'sis
U'lo·so'ni·a par'vi·cor'nis
u·lot'ic
u·lot'o·my
Ul'rich test
ul'ti·mate
ul'ti·mum mo'ri·ens
ul'tra·brach'y·ce·phal'ic
ul'tra·brach'y·cra'ni·al
ul'tra·cen·trif'u·gal
ul'tra·cen·tri'fuge'

ul'tra·dol'i·cho·cra'ni·al
ul'tra·fil'ter
ul'tra·fil·tra'tion
ul'tra·len'te
ul'tra·mi'cro·scope'
ul'tra·mi'cro·scop'ic or
  ul'tra·mi'cro·scop'i·cal
ul'tra·mi·cros'co·py
ul'tra·mi'cro·tome'
ul'tra·phag'o·cy·to'sis pl.
  -ses'
ul'tra·red'
ul'tra·son'ic
ul'tra·son'o·gram'
ul'tra·so·nog'ra·phy
ul'tra·son'o·scope'
ul'tra·sound'
ul'tra·struc'ture
ul'tra·vi'o·let
ul'tra·vi'rus
um·bel'li·fer
um'bel·lif'er·ous
um'ber
Um'ber test
um·bi·lec'to·my
um·bil'i·cal
um·bil'i·cate
um·bil'i·cat'ed
um·bil'i·ca'tion
um·bil'i·cus pl. -ci' or
  -cus·es
um'bo' pl. um·bo'nes' or
  -bos'
—— mem·bra'nae' tym'pa·
  ni'
um'bo·nate'
um·bras'co·py
un·bal'ance, -anced,
  -anc·ing
un'cal
un'ci·a pl. -ae'
un'ci·form'
un'ci·na·ri'a·sis pl. -ses'
un'ci·nate'
un'ci·pi'si·for'mis
un·com'pen·sat'ed
un·con·di'tioned
un·con'ju·gat'ed
un·con'scious
un·con'scious·ness
un·co·ver'te·bral
unc'tion
unc'tu·ous
un'cus pl. -ci'
—— gy'ri' hip'po·cam'pi'
un'der·a·chieve', -chieved',
  -chiev'ing

un'der·a·chiev'er
un'der·weight
Un'der·wood' disease
un'de·scend'ed
un·dif'fer·en'ti·at'ed
un·dine'
un'din·ism
un·do'ing
un·du·la'tion
un·du·la·to'ry
un·e'qual
un'gual
un'guent
un·guen'tum
un'guis pl. -gues'
—— in·car'na·tus
un·health'y
u'ni·ar·tic'u·lar
u'ni·ax'i·al
u'ni·cam'er·al
u'ni·cel'lu·lar
u'ni·cen'tral
u'ni·cen'tric
u'ni·ceps'
u'ni·cep'tor
u'ni·cor'nous
u'ni·cus'pid
u'ni·cus'pi·date'
u'ni·fo'cal
u'ni·glan'du·lar
u'ni·grav'i·da
u'ni·lat'er·al
u'ni·lo'bar
u'ni·loc'u·lar
un'in·cised'
un'in·hib'it·ed
u'ni·nu'cle·ar
u'ni·oc'u·lar
un'ion
u'ni·ov'u·lar
u·nip'ar·a
u'ni·par'i·ens
u·nip'a·rous
u'ni·po'lar
u'ni·po'ten·cy
u·nip'o·tent
u'ni·po·ten'tial
u'ni·sex'u·al
u'nit
u'ni·tar'y
u'ni·va'lent
u'ni·ver'sal
un·load'ing
un·mod'i·fied'
un·my'e·li·nat'ed
Un'na
—— bodies

—— boot
Un'na-Thost' syndrome
un·or'ga·nized'
un·rest'
un·sat'u·rat'ed
un·sex'
un·spec'i·fied'
un·sta'ble
un·stri'at'ed
Un'ver·richt
—— disease
—— myoclonus
un·well'
up'per
up'take'
u'ra·chal
u'ra·chus
u'ra·cil
u'ra·cra'si·a
u'ra·cra'ti·a
u'ra·gogue'
u'ra·nal
u'ra·nal'y·sis pl. -ses'
u'ra·nin
u·ran'i·nite'
u'ra·nis'co·plas'ty
u'ra·nis·cor'rha·phy
u'ra·nis'cus
u'ra·nism
u·ra'ni·um
u'ra·no·col'o·bo'ma pl.
  -mas or -ma·ta
u'ra·no·plas'tic
u'ra·no·plas'ty
u'ra·no·ple'gi·a
u'ra·nor'rha·phy
u'ra·nos'chi·sis pl. -ses'
u·ran'o·schism
u'ra·no·schis'ma
u'ra·no·staph'y·lo·plas'ty
u'ra·no·staph'y·lor'rha·
  phy
u'ra·nyl
u'ra·ro'ma
u'rase'
u'ra·sin
u'rate'
u'ra·te'mi·a
u'ra·tu'ri·a
u·re'a
u're·am'e·ter
u're·am'e·try
U·re'a·plas'ma u·re'a·lyt'i·
  cum
u're·ase'
u·rec'chy·sis
u're·de'ma

u're·dep'a
u're·he·pat'ic
u're·ide'
u·re'mi·a
u·re'mic
u're·o·tel'ic
u're·o·tel'ism
u·re'si·es·the'si·a
u·re'si·es·the'sis
u·re'sis
u·re'tal
u·re'ter
u·re'ter·al
u·re'ter·ec'ta·sis pl. -ses'
u·re'ter·ec'to·my
u're·ter'ic
u·re'ter·i'tis
  —— cys'ti·ca
u·re'ter·o·cele'
u·re'ter·o·ce·lec'to·my
u·re'ter·o·cer'vi·cal
u·re'ter·o·co·los'to·my
u·re'ter·o'cu·ta'ne·os'to·
  my
u·re'ter·o·cys'ta·nas'to·
  mo'sis pl. -ses'
u·re'ter·o·cys'tic
u·re'ter·o·cys'to·scope'
u·re'ter·o·cys·tos'to·my
u·re'ter·o·di·al'y·sis pl. -ses'
u·re'ter·o·en·ter'ic
u·re'ter·o·en'ter·os'to·my
u·re'ter·o·gram'
u·re'ter·og'ra·phy
u·re'ter·o·hem'i·ne·
  phrec'to·my
u·re'ter·o·hy'dro·ne·
  phro'sis pl. -ses'
u·re'ter·o·il'e·al
u·re'ter·o·il'e·os'to·my
u·re'ter·o·in·tes'ti·nal
u·re'ter·o·lith'
u·re'ter·o·li·thi'a·sis pl. -ses'
u·re'ter·o·li·thot'o·my
u·re'ter·ol'y·sis pl. -ses'
u·re'ter·o·me·a'tot·o'my
u·re'ter·o·meg'a·ly
u·re'ter·o·ne'o·cys·tos'to·
  my
u·re'ter·o·ne'o·py'e·los'to·
  my
u·re'ter·o·ne·phrec'to·my
u·re'ter·o·pel'vic
u·re'ter·o·pel'vi·o·plas'ty
u·re'ter·o·phleg'ma
u·re'ter·o·plas'ty
u·re'ter·o·proc·tos'to·my

u·re'ter·o·py'e·li'tis
u·re'ter·o·py'e·log'ra·phy
u·re'ter·o·py'e·lo·ne·os'to·
  my
u·re'ter·o·py'e·lo·ne·
  phri'tis
u·re'ter·o·py'e·lo·ne·
  phros'to·my
u·re'ter·o·py'e·lo·plas'ty
u·re'ter·o·py'e·los'to·my
u·re'ter·o·rec'tal
u·re'ter·or·rha'gi·a
u·re'ter·or'rha·phy
u·re'ter·o·sig'moi·dos'to·
  my
u·re'ter·o'ste·no'sis pl. -ses'
u're·ter·os'to·ma pl. -mas or
  -ma·ta
u·re'ter·os'to·my
u·re'ter·o·the'cal
u·re'ter·ot'o·my
u·re'ter·o·u·re'ter·al
u·re'ter·o·u·re'ter·os'to·my
u·re'ter·o·u'ter·ine'
u·re'ter·o·vag'i·nal
u·re'ter·o·ves'i·cal
u·re'ter·o·ves'i·co·plas'ty
u·re'ter·o·ves'i·cos'to·my
u're·than'
u·re'thra pl. -thras or -thrae'
  —— fem'i·ni'na
  —— mas'cu·li'na
  —— mu'li·e·bris
  —— vi·ri'lis
u·re'thral
u're·threc'to·my
u're·thrism
u're·thri'tis
  —— cys'ti·ca
  —— o'ri·fi'ci·i' ex·ter'ni'
  —— ve·ne're·a
u·re'thro·blen'nor·rhe'a
u·re'thro·bul'bar
u·re'thro·cele'
u·re'thro·cu·ta'ne·ous
u·re'thro·cys·ti'tis
u·re'thro·cys'to·cele'
u·re'thro·dyn'i·a
u·re'thro·gram'
u·re'thro·graph'
u're·throg'ra·phy
u·re'throm'e·ter
u·re'thro·per'i·ne'al
u·re'thro·phy'ma
u·re'thro·plas'ty
u·re'thro·pros·tat'ic
u·re'thro·rec'tal

u·re′thror·rha′gi·a
u·re′thror′rha·phy
u·re′thror·rhe′a
—— ex li·bid′i·ne′
u·re′thro·scope′
u·re′thro·scop′ic
u·re′thros′co·py
u·re′thro·spasm
u·re′thro·stax′is
u·re·thro·ste·no′sis pl. -ses′
u·re·thros′to·my
u·re′thro·tome′
u·re′throt′o·my
u·re′thro·tri′go·ni′tis
u·re′thro·vag′i·nal
u·re′thro·ves′i·cal
u·re′thro·ves′i·co·vag′i·nal
u·ret′ic
ur′gen·cy
ur′hi·dro′sis pl. -ses′
u′ric
u′ric·ac·i·de′mi·a
u′ric·ac·i·du′ri·a
u′ri·case′
u′ri·ce′mi·a
u′ri·col′y·sis
u′ri·co·lyt′ic
u′ri·co·su′ri·a
u′ri·co·su′ric
u′ri·co·tel′ic
u′ri·co·tel′ism
u′ri·dine′
u′ri·dro′sis pl. -ses′
u′ri·dyl
u′ri·dyl′ic
u·ri′na
—— chy′li′
—— ju′men·to′sa
—— po′tus
—— san′gui·nis
u′ri·nal
u′ri·nal′y·sis pl. -ses′
u′ri·nar′y
u′ri·nate′, -nat′ed, -nat′ing
u′ri·na′tion
u′ri·na·tive
u′rine
u′ri·nif′er·ous
u′ri·nif′ic
u′ri·nip′a·rous
u′ri·no·cry·os′co·py
u′ri·no·gen′i·tal
u′ri·nog′e·nous
u′ri·nol′o·gy
u′ri·no′ma pl. -mas or
 -ma·ta
u′ri·nom′e·ter

u′ri·nom′e·try
u′ri·no·scop′ic
u′ri·nos′co·py
u′ri·nous
u′ri′tis
u′ro·ac′i·dim′e·ter
u′ro·am·mo′ni·ac′
u′ro·an′the·lone′
u′ro·az′o·tom′e·ter
u′ro·ben·zo′ic
u′ro·bi′lin
u′ro·bi·li·ne′mi·a
u′ro·bi·li·nic′ter·us
u′ro·bi·lin′o·gen
u′ro·bi·lin′o·ge·nu′ri·a
u′ro·bi·li·noi′din
u′ro·bi·li·nu′ri·a
u′ro·can′ic
u·roch′e·ras
u′ro·che′zi·a
u′ro·chlo·ral′ic
u′ro·chrome′
u′ro·chro′mo·gen
u′ro·clep′si·a
u′ro·cris′i·a
u′ro·cri′sis pl. -ses′
u′ro·cy′a·nin
u′ro·cy·an′o·gen
u′ro·cy′a·nose′
u′ro·cy′a·no′sis
u′ro·cys′tis
u′ro·cys·ti′tis
u′ro·de′um
u′ro·dy·nam′ics
u′ro·dyn′i·a
u′ro·e·de′ma
u′ro·en′ter·one′
u′ro·er′y·thrin
u′ro·fla′vin
u′ro·fus′cin
u′ro·fus′co·hem′a·tin
u′ro·gas′trone′
u′ro·gen′i·tal
u·rog′e·nous
u′ro·glau′cin
u′ro·gram′
u·rog′ra·phy
u′ro·gra·vim′·ter
u′ro·hem′a·tin
u′ro·hem′a·to·ne·phro′sis
u′ro·hem′a·to·por′phy·rin
u′ro·hy′per·ten′sin
u′ro·ki′nase′
u′ro·ki·net′ic
u′ro·ky·mog′ra·phy
u′ro·leu·kin′ic
u′ro·lith′

u′ro·li·thi′a·sis
u′ro·lith′ic
u′ro·li·thot′o·my
u′ro·log′ic or u′ro·log′i·cal
u·rol′o·gist
u·rol′o·gy
u′ro·lu′te·in
u′ro·man′cy
u′ro·man′ti·a
u′ro·mel′a·nin
u′ro·ne·phro′sis
u·ron′ic
u′ro·nol′o·gy
u′ron·on·com′e·try
u′ro·nos′co·py
u·rop′a·thy
u′ro·pe′ni·a
u′ro·pep′sin
u′ro·phe′in
u′ro·pla′ni·a
u′ro·poi·e′sis
u′ro·por′phy·rin
u′ro·psam′mus
u′ro·rec′tal
u′ro·ro′se·in
u′ror·rha′gi·a
u′ror·rhe′a
u′ror·rho′din
u′ror·rho·din′o·gen
u′ro·ru′bin
u′ro·ru·bin′o·gen
u·ros′che·sis
u′ro·scop′ic
u·ros′co·py
u′ro·sem′i·ol′o·gy
u′ro·sep′sis
u′ro·sep′tic
u′ro·spec′trin
u′ro·ste′a·lith′
u′ro·the′li·al
u′ro·the′li·um
u′ro·tox′i·a
u′ro·tox′ic
u′ro·tox·ic′i·ty
u′ro·tox′in
u′ro·tox′y
u′ro·xan′thin
ur′ti·cant
ur′ti·car′i·a
—— bul·lo′sa
—— fac·ti′ti·a
—— hem·or·rhag′i·ca
—— med′i·ca·men·to′sa
—— pap′u·lo′sa
—— pig′men·to′sa
—— so·lar′is
ur′ti·car′i·al

ur'ti·car'i·o·gen'ic
ur'ti·cate'
ur'ti·ca'tion
us'ne·in
us'nic
us'tion
U·su'tu fever
u'ta
u'ter·al'gi·a
u'ter·ine
u'ter·i'tis
u'ter·o·ab·dom'i·nal
u'ter·o·ad·nex'al
u'ter·o·cer'vi·cal
u'ter·o·col'ic
u'ter·o·dyn'i·a
u'ter·o·en·ter'ic
u'ter·o·fix·a'tion
u'ter·o·ges·ta'tion
u'ter·og'ra·phy
u'ter·o·in·tes'ti·nal
u'ter·o·lith'
u'ter·om'e·ter
u'ter·o-o·var'i·an
u'ter·o·pa·ri'e·tal
u'ter·o·pel'vic
u'ter·o·pex'i·a
u'ter·o·pex'y
u'ter·o·pla·cen'tal
u'ter·o·plas'ty
u'ter·o·rec'tal
u'ter·o·sa'cral
u'ter·o·sal'pin·gog'ra·phy
u'ter·o·scope'
u'ter·ot'o·my
u'ter·o·ton'ic
u'ter·o·trac'tor
u'ter·o·trop'ic
u'ter·o·tu'bal
u'ter·o·vag'i·nal
u'ter·o·ven'tral
u'ter·o·ves'i·cal
u'ter·us pl. u'ter·i'
—— a·col'lis
—— ar'cu·a'tus
—— bi·cor'nis
—— bi·loc'u·lar'is
—— di·del'phys
—— du'plex'
—— mas'cu·li'nus
—— par'vi·col'lis
—— sep'tus
—— u'ni·cor'nis
u'tri·cle
u·tric'u·lar
u·tric'u·li'tis
u·tric'u·lo·sac'cu·lar

u·tric'u·lus pl. -li'
—— mas'cu·li'nus
—— pros·tat'i·cus
u'va-ur'si'
u've·a
u've·al
u've·it'ic
u've·i'tis
u've·o·en·ceph'a·li'tis
u've·o·lab'y·rin·thi'tis
u've·o·men'in·gi'tis
u've·o·me·nin'go·en·
ceph'a·li'tis
u've·o·neur'ax·i'tis
u've·o·pa·rot'id
u've·o·par'o·ti'tis
u've·o·scle·ri'tis
u'vi·form'
u'vu·la pl. -las or -lae'
—— cer'e·bel'li'
—— fis'sa
—— pal'a·ti'na
—— ver'mis
—— ve·si'cae'
u'vu·lap·to'sis
u'vu·lar
u'vu·la·tome' var. of uvulo-
tome
u'vu·lec'to·my
u'vu·li'tis
u'vu·lo·nod'u·lar
u'vu·lop·to'sis
u'vu·lo·tome' also uvula-
tome
u'vu·lot'o·my

V

vac'cin
vac'ci·na·ble
vac'ci·nal
vac'ci·nate', -nat'ed, -nat'-
ing
vac'ci·na'tion
vac·cine'
vac·cin'i·a
—— gan'gre·no'sa
—— ne·cro'sum
vac·cin'i·al
vac·cin'i·form'
vac'ci·noid'
vac'u·o·late'
vac'u·o·lat'ed
vac'u·o·la'tion
vac'u·ole'

vac'u·ol·i·za'tion
vac'u·ome'
vac'u·um pl. -u·ums or -u·a
va'gal
va·gi'na pl. -nas or -nae'
—— bul'bi'
—— ca·rot'i·ca fas'ci·ae'
cer'vi·ca'lis
—— den'tis
—— ex·ter'na ner'vi' op'ti·ci'
—— fi·bro'sa ten'di·nis
—— in·ter'na ner'vi' op'ti·ci'
—— mas'cu·li'na
—— mu·co'sa in·ter·tu·
ber'cu·lar'is
—— mus'cu·li' rec'ti' ab·
dom'i·nis
—— pro·ces'sus sty·loi'de·i'
—— sy·no'vi·a'lis com·
mu'nis mus'cu·lo'rum flex·
o'rum
—— synovialis in·ter·tu·
ber'cu·lar'is
—— synovialis mus'cu·li'
ob·li'qui' su·pe'ri·o'ris
—— synovialis mus'cu·
lo'rum fib'u·lar'i·um com·
mu'nis
—— synovialis musculorum
per'o·ne·o'rum com·mu'nis
—— synovialis ten'di·nis
—— synovialis tendinis
mus'cu·li' flex·o'ris car'pi'
ra'di·a'lis
—— synovialis tendinis
musculi flexoris hal'lu·cis
lon'gi'
—— synovialis tendinis
musculi tib'i·a'lis pos·te'ri·
o'ris
—— ten'di·nis mus'cu·li'
ex'ten·so'ris car'pi' ul·nar'is
—— tendinis musculi exten-
soris dig'i·ti' min'i·mi'
—— tendinis musculi exten-
soris hal'lu·cis lon'gi'
—— tendinis musculi exten-
soris pol'li·cis lon'gi'
—— tendinis musculi fib'u·
lar'is lon'gi'
—— tendinis musculi flex·
o'ris hal'lu·cis lon'gi'
—— tendinis musculi flex-
oris pol'li·cis lon'gi'
—— tendinis musculi per'o·
nae'i' lon'gi'

—— tendinis musculi per'o·
ne'i' lon'gi'
—— tendinis musculi tib'i·
a'lis an·te'ri·o'ris
—— tendinis musculi tibialis pos·te'ri·o'ris
—— ten'di·num mus'cu·li'
ex·ten·so'ris dig'i·to'rum pe'-
dis lon'gi'
—— tendinum musculi flex·
o'ris dig'i·to'rum pe'dis
lon'gi'
—— tendinum mus'cu·
lo'rum ab'duc·to'ris lon'gi'
et ex·ten·so'ris brev'is pol'li·
cis
—— tendinum musculorum
ex·ten·so'ris dig'i·to'rum et
ex·ten·so'ris in'di·cis
—— tendinum musculorum
ex·ten·so'rum car'pi' ra'di·
a'li·um
—— tendinum musculorum
flex·o'rum com·mu'ni·um
—— tendinum musculorum
per'o·nae·o'rum com·mu'nis
—— va·so'rum
va·gi'nae'
—— fi·bro'sae' dig'i·to'rum
ma'nus
—— fibrosae digitorum pe'-
dis
—— mu·co'sae' dig'i·to'rum
ma'nus
—— mucosae digitorum pe'-
dis
—— ner'vi' op'ti·ci'
—— sy·no'vi·a'les' dig'i·
to'rum ma'nus
—— synoviales digitorum
pe'dis
—— synoviales ten'di·num
dig'i·to'rum ma'nus
—— synoviales tendinum
digitorum pe'dis
—— ten'di·num dig'i·ta'les'
ma'nus
—— tendinum digitales pe'-
dis
vag'i·nal
vag'i·na·li'tis
va·gi'na·pex'y
vag'i·nate'
vag'i·nec'to·my
vag'i·nis'mus
vag'i·ni'tis
vag'i·no'ab·dom'i·nal

vag'i·no·cele'
vag'i·no'cu·ta'ne·ous
vag'i·no·dyn'i·a
vag'i·no·fix·a'tion
vag'i·no·la'bi·al
vag'i·no·my·co'sis *pl.* -ses'
vag'i·nop'a·thy
vag'i·no·per'i·ne'al
vag'i·no·per'i·ne·ot'o·my
vag'i·no·per'i·to·ne'al
va·gi'no·pex'y
vag'i·no·plas'ty
vag'i·no·scope'
vag'i·nos'co·py
vag'i·not'o·my
vag'i·no·vul'var
va·gi'tus
—— u'ter·i'nus
—— vag'i·na'lis
va·go·ac·ces'so·ry
va·go·gram'
va·go·hy'po·glos'sal
va·gol'y·sis
va·go·lyt'ic
va·go·pres'sor
va·got'o·mized'
va·got'o·my
va·go·to'ni·a
va·go·ton'ic
va·got'o·nin
va·go·trop'ic
va·go·va'gal
va'grant
va'gus *pl.* -gi'
va'gus·stoff'
va'lence
va'len·cy
va'lent
Va·len·tin'
—— corpuscles
—— ganglion
va·le'ric
val'e·tham'ate'
val'e·tu'di·nar'i·an
val'e·tu'di·nar'i·an·ism
val'gus
val'ine'
val'late'
val·lec'u·la *pl.* -lae'
—— cer'e·bel'li'
—— ep'i·glot'ti·ca
—— lin'guae'
—— un'guis
val·lec'u·lar
Val·leix' points
Val·let' mass
val'lum *pl.* -la *or* -lums

—— un'guis
val·noc'ta·mide'
val·pro'ate'
Val·sal'va
—— maneuver
—— sinus
—— test
Val·su·a'ni disease
val'va *pl.* -vae'
—— a·or'tae'
—— a'tri·o·ven·tric'u·lar'is
dex'tra
—— atrioventricularis si·
nis'tra
—— il'e·o·ce·ca'lis
—— mi·tra'lis
—— tri·cus'pi·da'lis
—— trun'ci' pul'mo·na'lis
valve
val'vo·tome'
val·vot'o·my
val'vu·la *pl.* -lae'
—— bi·cus'pi·da'lis
—— co'li'
—— fo·ram'i·nis o·va'lis
—— fos'sae' na·vic'u·lar'is
—— lym·phat'i·ca
—— pro·ces'sus ver'mi·
for'mis
—— py·lo'ri'
—— sem'i·lu·nar'is anterior
ar·te'ri·ae' pul'mo·na'lis
—— semilunaris anterior
trun'ci' pul'mo·na'lis
—— semilunaris dex'tra
a·or'tae'
—— semilunaris dextra ar·
te'ri·ae' pul'mo·na'lis
—— semilunaris dextra val'-
vae' a·or'tae'
—— semilunaris dextra valvae trun'ci' pul'mo·na'lis
—— semilunaris posterior
a·or'tae'
—— semilunaris posterior
val'vae' a·or'tae'
—— semilunaris si·nis'tra
a·or'tae'
—— semilunaris sinistra ar·
te'ri·ae' pul'mo·na'lis
—— semilunaris sinistra
val'vae' a·or'tae'
—— semilunaris sinistra
valvae trun'ci' pul'mo·na'lis
—— si'nus co'ro·nar'i·i'
—— sinus coronarii (The·
be'si·i')

—— spi·ra'lis (Heis'ter·i')
—— tri·cus'pi·da'lis
—— ve'nae' ca'vae' in·fe'ri·o'ris
—— venae cavae inferioris (Eu·sta'chi·i')
—— ve·no'sa
val'vu·lae'
—— a·na'les'
—— con'ni·ven'tes'
—— sem'i·lu·nar'es' a·or'tae'
—— semilunares ar·te'ri·ae' pul'mo·na'lis
val'vu·lar
val'vu·lec'to·my
val'vu·li'tis
val'vu·lo·plas'ty
val'vu·lo·tome'
val'vu·lot'o·my
van'co·my'cin
van Deen test
van den Bergh
—— disease
—— test
van der Hoeve syndrome
van Ge·huch'ten cell
Van Gie'son stain
van Han'se·mann cells
va·nil'lin
Van Slyke
—— apparatus
—— method
va'por
va·po'res' u'ter·i'ni'
va'por·ize', -ized', -iz'ing
va'por·iz'er
Va·quez' disease
var'i·a·bil'i·ty
var'i·a·ble
var'i·ance
var'i·ant
var'i·a'tion
var'i·ca'tion
var'i·ce'al
var'i·cec'to·my
var'i·cel'la
—— gan'gre·no'sa
—— in·oc'u·la'ta
var'i·cel·la'tion
var'i·cel'li·form'
var'i·cel'loid'
var·ic'i·form'
var'i·co·bleph'a·ron'
var'i·co·cele'
var'i·co·ce·lec'to·my
var'i·cog'ra·phy

var'i·coid'
var'i·com'pha·lus *pl.* -li'
var'i·co·phle·bi'tis
var'i·cose'
var'i·co'sis *pl.* -ses'
var'i·cos'i·ty
var'i·cot'o·my
va·ric'u·la *pl.* -las *or* -lae'
var'i·e·gate'
va·ri'e·ty
var'i·form'
va·ri'o·la
—— ve'ra
va·ri'o·lar
var'i·o·late', -lat'ed, -lat'ing
var'i·o·la'tion
var'i·ol'ic
var'i·ol'i·form'
var'i·o·li·za'tion
var'i·o·loid'
va·ri'o·lous
va·ri'o·lo·vac·cine'
va·ri'o·lo·vac·cin'i·a
var'ix *pl.* -i·ces'
—— lym·phat'i·cus
var'us
vas *pl.* va'sa
—— af'fer·ens ar·te'ri·ae' in'ter·lob'u·lar'is
—— afferens glo·mer'u·li' re·na'lis
—— a·nas'to·mot'i·cum
—— cap'il·lar'e'
—— col·lat'er·a'le'
—— def'er·ens
—— ef'fer·ens ar·te'ri·ae' in'ter·lob'u·lar'is
—— efferens glo·mer'u·li' re·na'lis
—— lym·phat'i·cum
—— prom'i·nens
—— spi·ra'le'
va'sa
—— ab'er·ran'ti·a hep'a·tis
—— af'fe·ren'ti·a lym'pho·glan'du·lae'
—— afferentia no'di' lym·phat'i·ci'
—— au'ris in·ter'nae'
—— brev'is
—— ef'fe·ren'ti·a lym'pho·glan'du·lae'
—— efferentia no'di' lym·phat'i·ci'
—— lym·phat'i·ca
—— lymphatica pro·fun'da

—— lymphatica su'per·fi'ci·a'li·a
—— prae'vi·a
—— san·guin'e·a ret'i·nae'
—— va·so'rum
va'sal
vas'cu·lar
vas'cu·lar'i·ty
vas'cu·lar·i·za'tion
vas'cu·lar·ize', -ized', -iz'ing
vas'cu·la·ture
vas'cu·li'tis
vas'cu·lo·gen·e'sis
vas'cu·lo'lym·phat'ic
vas'cu·lum *pl.* -la
vas·ec'to·mize', -mized', -miz'ing
vas·ec'to·my
vas'i·cine'
vas'i·fac'tion
vas·i'tis
vas'o·ac'tive
va'so·con·stric'tion
va'so·con·stric'tive
va'so·con·stric'tor
vas'o·den'tin
vas'o·de·pres'sion
va'so·de·pres'sor
va'so·dil'a·ta'tion
va'so·di·la'tion
va'so·di·la'tive
va'so·di·la'tor
va'so·ep'i·did'y·mos'to·my
va'so·for·ma'tion
va'so·for'ma·tive
va'so·gen'ic
va·sog'ra·phy
va'so·hy'per·ton'ic
va'so·hy'po·ton'ic
va'so·in·hib'i·tor
va'so·in·hib'i·to'ry
va'so·li·ga'tion
va'so·mo'tion
va'so·mo'tor
vas'o·mo·to'ri·al
va'so·mo·tric'i·ty
vas'o·neu·rop'a·thy
va'so·neu·ro'sis *pl.* -ses'
va'so·or'chid·os'to·my
va'so·pa·ral'y·sis *pl.* -ses'
va'so·pa·re'sis *pl.* -ses'
va'so·pres'sin
va'so·pres'sor
va'so·punc'ture
va'so·re·lax·a'tion
vas·or'rha·phy
vas·os'cil·la'tor

va′so•sec′tion
va′so•spasm
va′so•spas′tic
va′so•stim′u•lant
vas•os′to•my
vas•ot′o•my
va′so•ton′ic
va′so•to′nin
va′so•tribe′
va′so•troph′ic
va′so•va′gal
va′so•vas•os′to•my
va′so•ve•sic′u•lec′to•my
vas′o•ve•sic′u•li′tis
vas′tus pl. -ti′
Va′ter ampulla
Va′ter-Pa•ci′ni corpuscle
vault
Veau operation
vec′tion
vec′tis
vec′tor
vec•to′ri•al
vec′tor•car′di•o•gram′
vec′tor•car′di•o•graph′
vec′tor•car′di•og′ra•phy
Ved′der sign
veg′an′
veg′e•tar′i•an
veg′e•ta′tion
veg′e•ta′tive
ve′hi•cle
veil
Veil′lo•nel′la
—— al′ca•les′cens
—— dis•coi′des′
—— or•bic′u•lus
—— par′vu•la
—— ren′i•for′mis
Veil•lon′ tube
vein
—— of Lab•bé′
—— of Tro•lard′
ve•la′men pl. -lam′i•na
—— vul′vae′
vel′a•men′tous
vel′a•men′tum pl. -ta
ve′lar
vel′li•cate′, -cat′ed, -cat′ing
vel′li•ca′tion
vel′lus
ve•loc′i•ty
Vel•peau′ deformity
ve′lum pl. -la
—— in′ter•pos′i•tum rhom′ben•ceph′a•li′
—— med•ul•lar′e′ an•te′ri•us

—— medulllare in•fe′ri•us
—— medullare pos•te′ri•us
—— medullare su•pe′ri•us
—— pa•la′ti′
—— pal′a•ti′num
—— pen′du•lum pa•la′ti′
—— ter′mi•na′le′
ve′na pl. -nae′
—— a•nas′to•mot′i•ca inferior
—— anastomotica superior
—— an′gu•lar′is
—— ap′pen•dic′u•lar′is
—— aq′ue•duc′tus coch′le•ae′
—— aqueductus ves•tib′u•li′
—— au•ric′u•lar′is posterior
—— ax′il•lar′is
—— az′y•gos′
—— ba•sa′lis
—— basalis com•mu′nis
—— basalis inferior
—— basalis (Ro′sen•tha′li′)
—— basalis superior
—— ba•sil′i•ca
—— bron′chi•a′les′ an•te′ri•o′res′
—— bul′bi′ pe′nis
—— bulbi ves•tib′u•li′
—— can•a•lic′u•li′ coch′le•ae′
—— ca•na′lis pter′y•goi′de•i′
—— canalis pterygoidei (Vi′di•i′)
—— ca′va
—— cava inferior
—— cava superior
—— cen•tra′lis glan′du•lae′ sup′pra•re•na′lis
—— centralis ret′i•nae′
—— ce•phal′i•ca
—— cephalica ac′ces•so′ri•a
—— cer′e•bri′ anterior
—— cerebri mag′na
—— cerebri magna (Ga•le′ni′)
—— cerebri me′di•a
—— cerebri media pro•fun′da
—— cerebri media su•per•fi′ci•a′lis
—— cer′vi•ca′lis pro•fun′da
—— cho′ri•oi′de•a
—— cho•roi′de•a
—— cir′cum•flex′a il′i•i′ pro•fun′da
—— circumflexa ilii su′per•fi′ci•a′lis

—— col′i•ca dex′tra
—— colica me′di•a
—— colica si•nis′tra
—— com′i•tans′
—— comitans ner′vi′ hy′po•glos′si′
—— cor′dis mag′na
—— cordis me′di•a
—— cordis par′va
—— co•ro•nar′i•a ven•tric′u•li′
—— cu•ta′ne•a
—— cys′ti•ca
—— di•plo′i•ca fron•ta′lis
—— diploica oc•cip′i•ta′lis
—— diploica tem′po•ra′lis anterior
—— diploica temporalis posterior
—— dor•sa′lis cli•to′ri•dis
—— dorsalis clitoridis pro•fun′da
—— dorsalis pe′nis
—— dorsalis penis pro•fun′da
—— em′is•sar′i•a
—— emissaria con′dy•lar′is
—— emissaria mas•toi′de•a
—— emissaria oc•cip′i•ta′lis
—— emissaria pa•ri′e•ta′lis
—— ep′i•gas′tri•ca inferior
—— epigastrica su′per•fi′ci•a′lis
—— epigastrica superior
—— eth′moi•da′lis
—— ethmoidalis anterior
—— ethmoidalis posterior
—— fa′ci•a′lis
—— facialis anterior
—— facialis com•mu′nis
—— fascialis posterior
—— fa′ci•e′i′ pro•fun′da
—— fem′o•ra′lis
—— fem′o•ro•pop•lit′e•a
—— Ga•le′ni′
—— gas′tri•ca dex′tra
—— gastrica si•nis′tra
—— gas′tro•ep′i•plo′i•ca dex′tra
—— gastroepiploica si•nis′tra
—— haem′or•rhoi•da′lis me′di•a
—— haemorrhoidalis superior
—— hem′i•az′y•gos′

—— hemiazygos ac′ces·so′ri·a
—— hy′po·gas′tri·ca
—— il′e·o·col′i·ca
—— i·li′a·ca com·mu′nis
—— iliaca ex·ter′na
—— iliaca in·ter′na
—— il′e·o·lum·ba′lis
—— in′ter·cos·ta′lis superior dex′tra
—— intercostalis superior si·nis′tra
—— intercostalis su·pre′ma
—— in′ter·ver′te·bra′lis
—— jug′u·lar′is anterior
—— jugularis ex·ter′na
—— jugularis in·ter′na
—— la′bi·a′lis inferior
—— labialis superior
—— lac′ri·ma′lis
—— la·ryn′ge·a inferior
—— laryngea superior
—— li′e·na′lis
—— lin·gua′lis
—— lum·ba′lis as·cen′dens
—— mam·mar′i·a in·ter′na
—— me′di·a′na an·te·bra′chi·i′
—— mediana an′ti·bra′chi·i′
—— mediana ba·sil′i·ca
—— mediana ce·phal′i·ca
—— mediana col′li′
—— mediana cu′bi·ti′
—— mes′en·ter′i·ca inferior
—— mesenterica superior
—— na′so·fron·ta′lis
—— ob·li′qua a′tri·i′ si·nis′tri′
—— obliqua atrii sinistri (Mar·shal′li′)
—— oc·cip′i·ta′lis
—— oph·thal′mi·ca inferior
—— ophthalmica superior
—— oph·thal′mo·me·nin′ge· a
—— o·var′i·ca
—— ovarica dex′tra
—— ovarica si·nis′tra
—— pal′a·ti′na
—— palatina ex·ter′na
—— phren′i·ca inferior
—— pop·lit′e·a
—— por′tae′
—— posterior ven·tric′u·li′ si·nis′tri′
—— pre′py·lo′ri·ca
—— pro·fun′da fem′o·ris

—— profunda lin′guae′
—— pu·den′da in·ter′na
—— pul′mo·na′lis inferior dex′tra
—— pulmonalis inferior si·nis′tra
—— pulmonalis superior dex′tra
—— pulmonalis superior si·nis′tra
—— rec·ta′lis me′di·a
—— rectalis superior
—— ret′ro·man·dib′u·lar′is
—— sa·cra′lis me′di·a
—— sacralis me′di·a′na
—— sa·phe′na ac′ces·so′ri·a
—— saphena mag′na
—— saphena par′va
—— scap′u·lar′is dor·sa′lis
—— sep′ti′ pel·lu′ci·di′
—— sper·mat′i·ca
—— spi·ra′lis mo·di′o·li′
—— ster′no·clei′do·mas·toi′de·a
—— stri·a′ta
—— sty′lo·mas·toi′de·a
—— sub·cla′vi·a
—— sub′cos·ta′lis
—— sub′lin·gua′lis
—— sub′men·ta′lis
—— su′pra·or′bi·ta′lis
—— su′pra·re·na′lis dex′tra
—— suprarenalis si·nis′tra
—— su′pra·scap′u·lar′is
—— tem′po·ra′lis me′di·a
—— ter′mi·na′lis
—— tes·tic′u·lar′is
—— testicularis dex′tra
—— testicularis si·nis′tra
—— thal′a·mo·stri·a′ta
—— tho′ra·ca′lis lat′er·a′lis
—— tho·rac′i·ca in·ter′na
—— thoracica lat′er·a′lis
—— tho′ra·co·a·cro′mi·a′lis
—— thy′re·oi′de·a i′ma
—— thyreoidea superior
—— thy·roi′de·a inferior
—— thyroidea superior
—— trans·ver′sa fa′ci·e′i′
—— transversa scap′u·lae′
—— um·bil′i·ca′lis
—— umbilicalis si·nis′tra
—— ver′te·bra′lis
—— vertebralis ac′ces·so′ri·a
—— vertebralis anterior
ve′na·ca′vo·gram′

ve′nae′
—— a·non′y·mae′ dex′tra et si·nis′tra
—— ar′ci·for′mes′ re′nis
—— ar·cu·a′tae′ re′nis
—— ar·tic′u·lar′es′ man·dib′u·lae′
—— articulares tem′po·ro·man·dib′u·lar′es′
—— au′di·ti′vae′ in·ter′nae′
—— au·ric′u·lar′es′ an·te′ri·o′res′
—— ba′si·ver′te·bra′les′
—— bra′chi·a′les′
—— bra′chi·o·ce·phal′i·cae′ dex′tra et si·nis′tra
—— bron′chi·a′les′
—— bronchiales pos·te′ri·o′res′
—— cav′er·no′sae′ pe′nis
—— cen·tra′les′ hep′a·tis
—— cer′e·bel′li′ in·fe′ri·o′res′
—— cerebelli su·pe′ri·o′res′
—— cer′e·bri′
—— cerebri in·fe′ri·o′res′
—— cerebri in·ter′nae′
—— cerebri su·pe′ri·o′res′
—— cho·roi′de·ae′ oc′u·li′
—— cil′i·ar′es′
—— ciliares an·te′ri·o′res′
—— ciliares pos·te′ri·o′res′
—— cir′cum·flex′ae′ fem′o·ris lat′er·a′les′
—— circumflexae femoris me′di·a′les′
—— col′i·cae′ dex′trae′
—— com′i·tan′tes′
—— con·junc′ti·va′les′
—— conjunctivales an·te′ri·o′res′
—— conjunctivales pos·te′ri·o′res′
—— cor′dis
—— cordis an·te′ri·o′res′
—— cordis min′i·mae′
—— cos′to·ax′il·lar′es′
—— dig′i·ta′les′ com·mu′nes′ pe′dis
—— digitales dor·sa′les′ pe′dis
—— digitales pal·mar′es′
—— digitales pe′dis dor·sa′les′
—— digitales plan·tar′es′
—— digitales vo·lar′es′ com·mu′nes′

—— digitales volares pro′pri·ae′
—— di·plo′i·cae′
—— dor·sa′les′ cli·to′ri·dis su′per·fi′ci·a′les′
—— dorsales lin′guae′
—— dorsales pe′nis sub′cu·ta′ne·ae′
—— dorsales penis su′per·fi′ci·a′les′
—— du′o·de·na′les′
—— em′is·sar′i·ae′
—— ep′i·gas′tri·cae′ su·pe′ri·o′res′
—— ep′i·scle·ra′les′
—— e′so·phag′e·ae′
—— eth′moi·da′les′
—— fib′u·lar′es′
—— fron·ta′les′
—— gas′tri·cae′ brev′es′
—— ge′nus
—— glu′tae·ae′ in·fe′ri·o′res′
—— glutaeae su·pe′ri·o′res′
—— glu′te·ae′ in·fe′ri·o′res′
—— gluteae su·pe′ri·o′res′
—— haem′or·rhoi·da′les′ in·fe′ri·o′res′
—— he·pat′i·cae′
—— hepaticae dex′trae′
—— hepaticae me′di·ae′
—— hepaticae si·nis′trae′
—— in′ter·cap′i·ta′les′
—— in′ter·ca·pit′u·lar′es ma′nus
—— intercapitulares pe′dis
—— in′ter·cos·ta′les′
—— intercostales an·te′ri·o′res′
—— intercostales pos·te′ri·o′res′ (IV–XI)
—— in′ter·lo·bar′es′ re′nis
—— in′ter·lob′u·lar′es hep′a·tis
—— interlobulares re′nis
—— in′ter·ver′te·bra′les′
—— in·tes′ti·na′les′
—— je′ju·na′les′ et il′e·i′
—— la′bi·a′les′ an·te′ri·o′res′
—— labiales in·fe′ri·o′res′
—— labiales pos·te′ri·o′res′
—— lab′y·rin′thi′
—— lum·ba′les′
—— lumbales (I et II)
—— lumbales (III et IV)
—— mas′se·ter′i·cae′
—— max′il·lar′es′
—— me′di·as′ti·na′les′

—— mediastinales an·te′ri·o′res′
—— me·nin′ge·ae′
—— meningeae me′di·ae′
—— met′a·car′pe·ae′ dor·sa′les′
—— metacarpeae pal·mar′es′
—— metacarpeae vo·lar′es′
—— met′a·tar′se·ae′ dor·sa′les′ pe′dis
—— metatarseae plan·tar′es′
—— mus′cu·lar′es′
—— mus′cu·lo·phren′i·cae′
—— na·sa′les′ ex·ter′nae′
—— ob·tu′ra·to′ri·ae′
—— oe′so·phag′e·ae′
—— pal′pe·bra′les′
—— palpebrales in·fe′ri·o′res′
—— palpebrales su·pe′ri·o′res′
—— pan′cre·at′i·cae′
—— pan′cre·at′i·co·du′o·de·na′les′
—— par′a·um·bil′i·ca′les′
—— pa·rot′i·de′ae′
—— parotideae an·te′ri·o′res′
—— parotideae pos·te′ri·o′res′
—— par′um·bil′i·ca′les′ (Sappey′i′)
—— pec′to·ra′les′
—— per′fo·ran′tes′
—— per′i·car·di′a·cae′
—— per′i·car·di′a·co·phren′i·cae′
—— per′o·nae′ae′
—— per′o·ne′ae′
—— pha·ryn′ge·ae′
—— phren′i·cae′ in·fe′ri·o′res′
—— phrenicae su·pe′ri·o′res′
—— pop·lit′e·ae′
—— pro·fun′dae′ cli·to′ri·dis
—— profundae fem′o·ris
—— profundae pe′nis
—— pu·den′dae′ ex·ter′nae′
—— pul′mo·na′les′
—— pulmonales dex′trae′
—— pulmonales si·nis′trae′
—— ra′di·a′les′
—— rec·ta′les′ in·fe′ri·o′res′
—— rectales me′di·ae′
—— re·na′les′

—— re′nis
—— sa·cra′les′ lat′er·a′les
—— scro·ta′les an·te′ri·o′res′
—— scrotales pos·te′ri·o′res′
—— sig·moi′de·ae′
—— spi·na′les′
—— spinales ex·ter′nae′ an·te′ri·o′res′
—— spinales externae pos·te′ri·o′res′
—— spinales in·ter′nae′
—— stel·la′tae′
—— sub′cu·ta′ne·ae′ ab·dom′i·nis
—— su′pra·re·na′les′
—— su′pra·troch′le·ar′es′
—— tem′po·ra′les′ pro·fun′dae′
—— temporales su′per·fi′ci·a′les′
—— The·be′si·i′
—— tho·ra′ci·cae′ in·ter′nae′
—— tho′ra·co·ep′i·gas′tri·cae′
—— thy′mi·cae′
—— thy′re·oi′de·ae′ in·fe′ri·o′res′
—— thyreoideae su·pe′ri·o′res′
—— thy·roi′de·ae′ me′di·ae′
—— tib′i·a′les′ an·te′ri·o′res′
—— tibiales pos·te′ri·o′res′
—— tra′che·a′les′
—— trans·ver′sae′ col′li′
—— tym·pan′i·cae′
—— ul·nar′es′
—— u′ter·i′nae′
—— ves′i·ca′les
—— ves·tib′u·lar′es′
—— vor′ti·co′sae′
ve·na′tion
ve·nec′to·my
ve·ne′re·al
ve·ne′re·ol′o·gist
ve·ne′re·ol′o·gy
ven′er·y
ven′e·sec′tion *also* venisection
ven′e·su′ture *also* veni-suture
ven′i·punc′ture
ven′i·sec′tion *var. of* vene-section
ven′i·su′ture *var. of* venesuture
ve′no·a′tri·al
ve·noc′ly·sis *pl.* -ses′

ve′no·fi·bro′sis
ve′no·gram′
ve·nog′ra·phy
ven′om
ven′o·mo·sal′i·var′y
ve′no·mo′tor
ven′om·ous
ve′no·per′i·to·ne·os′to·my
ve′no·pres′sor
ve′no·scle·ro′sis *pl.* -ses′
ve′nose′
ve′no·si′nal
ve·nos′i·ty
ve·nos′ta·sis
ve′no·throm·bot′ic
ve·not′o·my
ve′nous
ve′no·ve·nos′to·my
vent
ven′ter
—— anterior mus′cu·li′ di·gas′tri·ci′
—— fron·ta′lis mus′cu·li′ oc·cip′i·to·fron·ta′lis
—— inferior mus′cu·li′ o′mo·hy·oi′de·i′
—— mus′cu·li′
—— oc·cip′i·ta′lis mus′cu·li′ oc·cip′i·to·fron·ta′lis
—— posterior mus′cu·li′ di·gas′tri·ci′
—— superior mus′cu·li′ o′mo·hy·oi′de·i′
ven′ti·late′, -lat′ed, -lat′ing
ven′ti·la′tion
ven′ti·lom′e·ter
ven′trad′
ven′tral
ven·tra′lis
ven′tri·cle
—— of A·ran′ti·us
—— of Mor·ga′gni
ven·tric′u·lar
ven·tric′u·li′tis
ven·tric′u·lo·a′tri·al
ven·tric′u·lo·a′tri·os′to·my
ven·tric′u·lo·cis′ter·nos′to·my
ven·tric′u·lo·cor·dec′to·my
ven·tric′u·lo·gram′
ven·tric′u·lo·log′ra·phy
ven·tric′u·lo·jug′u·lar
ven·tric′u·lo·mas′toi·dos′to·my
ven·tric′u·lom′e·try
ven·tric′u·lo·per′i·to·ne′al
ven·tric′u·lo·pleu′ral

ven·tric′u·lo·punc′ture
ven·tric′u·lo·scope′
ven·tric′u·los′co·py
ven·tric′u·los′to·my
ven·tric′u·lo·sub′a·rach′noid′
ven·tric′u·lo·ve′nous
ven·tric′u·lus *pl.* -li′
—— cer′e·bri′
—— cor′dis
—— dex′ter
—— la·ryn′gis
—— laryngis (Mor·ga′gni·i′)
—— lat′er·a′lis
—— me′di·us
—— op′ti·cus
—— quar′tus
—— si·nis′ter
—— ter′mi·na′lis
—— ter′ti·us
ven′tri·cum′bent
ven′tri·duc′tion
ven′tri·lat′er·al
ven′tri·me′sal
ven′tro·cys′tor·rha·phy
ven′tro·fix·a′tion
ven′tro·hys′ter·o·pex′y
ven′tro·lat′er·al
ven′tro·me′di·al
ven′tro·me′di·an
ven′tro·pos·te′ri·or
ven′trop·to′sis *pl.* -ses′
ven·tros′co·py
ven′trose′
ven′tro·sus·pen′sion
ven·trot′o·my
ven′tro·ves′i·co·fix·a′tion
ven·u′la *pl.* -lae′
—— mac′u·lar′is inferior
—— mascularis superior
—— me′di·a′lis ret′i·nae′
—— na·sa′lis ret′i·nae′ inferior
—— nasalis retinae superior
—— tem′po·ra′lis ret′i·nae′ inferior
—— temporalis retinae superior
ven′u·lae′
—— rec′tae′
—— stel·la′tae′
ven′u·lar
ven′ule′
ve′nus
ve·ra′pa·mil
ve·rat′ri·dine′

ver′a·trine′
ver′bal
ver′do·per·ox′i·dase′
ver′gence
Ver′hoeff′ stain
ver′mi·ci′dal
ver′mi·cide′
ver·mic′u·lar
ver·mic′u·late
ver·mic′u·la′tion
ver′mi·cule′
ver·mic′u·lose′
ver·mic′u·lous
ver·mic′u·lus *pl.* li′
ver′mi·form′
ver′mi·fu′gal
ver′mi·fuge′
ver′mi·lin′gual
ver·mil′ion
ver·mil′ion·ec′to·my
ver′min
ver′mi·na′tion
ver′min·ous
ver′mis *pl.* -mes′
ver′nal
Ver·net′ syndrome
Ver·neuil′
—— bursitis
—— disease
—— neuroma
ver′ni·er
ver′nix ca′se·o′sa
Ver′o·cay′ bodies
ver·ru′ca *pl.* -cae′
—— a·cu′mi·na′ta
—— dig′i·ta′ta
—— fi′li·for′mis
—— nec′ro·gen′i·ca
—— pe′ru·a′na
—— pe·ru′vi·a′na
—— pla′na ju′ve·ni′lis
—— plan·tar′is
—— se·ni′lis
—— vul·gar′is
ver·ru′ci·form′
ver·ru′coid′
ver·ru′cose′
ver·ru′cous
ver′si·col′or
ver′sion
ver′te·bra *pl.* -brae′ *or* -bras
—— den·ta′ta
—— mag′na
—— pla′na
—— prom′i·nens
ver′te·brae′
—— cer′vi·ca′les′

—— coc·cyg'e·ae'
—— lum·ba'les'
—— sa·cra'les'
—— tho'ra·ca'les'
—— tho'ra·ci·cae'
ver'te·bral
ver'te·brar·te'ri·al
Ver'te·bra'ta
ver'te·brate
ver'te·brec'to·my
ver'te·bro'ar·te'ri·al
ver'te·bro·chon'dral
ver'te·bro·cos'tal
ver'te·bro·fem'o·ral
ver'te·bro·il'i·ac'
ver'te·bro·sa'cral
ver'te·bro·ster'nal
ver'tex' pl. -tex'es or -ti·ces'
—— cor'ne·ae'
—— ve·si'cae'
ver'ti·cal
ver'ti·ca'lis
ver'ti·cil
ver'ti·cil'late'
ver·tig'i·nous
ver'ti·go pl. -goes or
  ver·tig'i·nes'
—— par'a·ly'sant
—— te·neb'ri·co'sa
ver·tig'ra·phy
ver'u·mon'ta·ni'tis
ver'u·mon'ta'num
Ve·sa'li·us
—— foramen
—— ligament
ve·sa'ni·a
ve·sa'nic
ve·si'ca pl. -cae'
—— bi·par'ta
—— du'plex'
—— fel'le·a
—— um·bil'i·ca'lis
—— u'ri·nar'i·a
ves'i·cal (pertaining to a
  bladder)
♦vesicle
ves'i·cant
ves'i·cate', -cat'ed, -cat'ing
ves'i·ca'tion
ves'i·ca·to'ry
ves'i·cle (a small bladder;
  bulla)
♦vesical
ves'i·co·ab·dom'i·nal
ves'i·co·cele'
ves'i·co·cer'vi·cal
ves'i·co·en·ter'ic

ves'i·co·fix·a'tion
ves'i·co·in·tes'ti·nal
ves'i·co·pros·tat'ic
ves'i·co·pu'bic
ves'i·co·pu·den'dal
ves'i·co·pus'tu·lar
ves'i·co·pus'tule'
ves'i·co·rec'tal
ves'i·co·re'nal
ves'i·co·sig'moid'
ves'i·co·spi'nal
ves'i·cos'to·my
ves'i·cot'o·my
ves'i·co·um·bil'i·cal
ves'i·co·u·re'ter·al
ves'i·co·u·re'thral
ves'i·co·u'ter·ine
ves'i·co·u'ter·o·vag'i·nal
ves'i·co·vag'i·nal
ve·sic'u·la pl. -lae'
—— fel'le·a
—— oph·thal'mi·ca
—— op'ti·ca in·ver'sa
—— pros·tat'i·ca
—— sem'i·na'lis
ve·sic'u·lar
ve·sic'u·late'
ve·sic'u·la'tion
ve·sic'u·lec'to·my
ve·sic'u·li'tis
ve·sic'u·lo'bron'chi·al
ve·sic'u·lo·cav'ern·ous
ve·sic'u·lo'gram'
ve·sic'u·log'ra·phy
ve·sic'u·lo·pap'u·lar
ve·sic'u·lo·pus'tu·lar
ve·sic'u·lot'o·my
ves'sel
ves·tib'u·lar
ves'ti·bule'
ves·tib'u·li'tis
ves·tib'u·lo·cer'e·bel'lar
ves·tib'u·lo·coch'le·ar
ves·tib'u·lo·oc'u·lar
ves·tib'u·lo·plas'ty
ves·tib'u·lo·spi'nal
ves·tib'u·lot'o·my
ves·tib'u·lum pl. -la
—— au'ris in·ter'nae'
—— bur'sae' o'men·ta'lis
—— lab'y·rin'thi' os'se·i'
—— la·ryn'gis
—— na'si'
—— o'ris
—— va·gi'nae'
ves'tige
ves·tig'i·al

ves·tig'i·um pl. -i·a
—— pro·ces'sus vag'i·na'lis
vi'a·bil'i·ty
vi'a·ble
vi'al
vi'bes·ate'
vi'bex' pl. -bi·ces'
vi'bra·tile
vi'brate', -brat'ed, -brat'ing
vi·bra'tion
vi'bra'tor
vi'bra·to'ry
vib'ri·o'
Vib'ri·o'
—— chol'er·ae'
—— com'ma
—— fe'tus
vib'ri·o'sis pl. -ses'
vi'bro·mas·sage'
vi·car'i·ous
vice
vi'cious
Vicq d'A·zyr'
—— fasciculus
—— foramen
vi'da·ra·bine'
vid'e·og·no'sis
vid'i·an
Vieus·sens' ansa
vig'il
vig'il·am'bu·lism
vig'i·lance
Vil·la·ret' syndrome
vil'li'
—— in·tes'ti·na'les'
—— pleu·ra'les'
—— sy·no'vi·a'les'
vil·lik'i·nin
vil·li'tis
vil·lo'ma pl. -mas or -ma·ta
vil·lo·si'tis
vil'lous (pertaining to a vil-
  lus)
♦villus
vil'lus (any minute projection arising from a mucous
  membrane), pl. -li'
♦villous
vil·lus·ec'to·my
vin·bar'bi·tal'
vin·blas'tine'
vin'ca·leu'ko·blas'tine'
Vin'cent
—— angina
—— disease
—— gingivitis
—— infection

—— stomatitis
vin·cris'tine'
vin·cu·la
—— lin'gu·lae' cer'e·bel'li'
—— ten'di·num dig'i·to'rum
ma'nus
—— tendinum digitorum
pe'dis
vin'cu·lum *pl.* -la
—— brev'e'
—— lon'gum
—— ten'di·num
Vine'berg' operation
vin·gly'ci·nate'
vin·leu'ro·sine'
Vin'son syndrome
vi'nyl
vi'o·la'ceous
vi'o·la·quer'ci·trin
vi'o·la'tion
vi'o·my'cin
vi·os'ter·ol'
vi'ral
Vir'chow'
—— angle
—— cell
—— crystals
—— line
—— node
Vir'chow-Rob'in spaces
vi·re'mi·a
vir'gin
vir'gin·al
vir·gin'i·ty
vir·gin'i·um
vir'i·dans'
vi·rid'o·ful'vin
vir'ile
vir'i·les'cence
vir'i·les'cent
vi·ril'i·a
vir'i·lism
vi·ril'i·ty
vir'i·li·za'tion
vir'i·lize', -ized', -liz'ing
vi'ri·on'
vi·rip'o·tent
vi'ro·cyte'
vi·rol'o·gist
vi·rol'o·gy
vir'tu·al
vi'ru·cid'al
vir'u·lence
vir'u·lent
vi'rus
vis *pl.* vi'res'
—— a fron'te'

—— a ter'go
—— con'ser·va'trix
—— for'ma·ti'va
—— in·er'ti·ae'
—— in si'tu'
—— med'i·ca'trix na·tu'rae'
—— vi'tae'
vis·am'min
vis'cer·al
vis'cer·a lar'va mi'grans'
vis'cer·al'gi·a
vis'cer·o·car'di·ac'
vis'cer·o·cep'tor
vis'cer·o·in·hib'i·to'ry
vis'cer·o·meg'a·ly
vis'cer·o·mo'tor
vis'cer·o·pa·ri'e·tal
vis'cer·o·per'i·to·ne'al
vis'cer·o·pleu'ral
vis'cer·op·to'sis *pl.* -ses'
vis'cer·o·sen'so·ry
vis'cer·o·skel'e·tal
vis'cer·o·tome'
vis'cer·ot'o·my
vis'cer·o·to'ni·a
vis'cer·o·ton'ic
vis'cer·o·troph'ic
vis'cer·o·trop'ic
vis'cid
vis·cid'i·ty
vis·co·e·las·tic'i·ty
vis·cos'i·ty
vis'cous *(glutinous)*
  ♦viscus
vis'cus *(any of the organs
enclosed in the cranium,
thorax, abdomen, or pelvis),
pl.* -cer·a
  ♦viscous
vis'i·bil'i·ty
vis'i·ble
vi'sion
vis'u·al
vis'u·al·i·za'tion
vis'u·al·ize', -ized', -iz'ing
vis·u·o·au'di·to'ry
vis'u·og'no·sis
vis'u·o·mo'tor
vis'u·o·psy'chic
vis'u·o·sen'so·ry
vi'sus
—— ac'ris
—— brev'i·or'
—— col'o·ra'tus
—— de·bil'i·tas
—— de·col'o·ra'tus
—— dim'i·di·a'tus

—— di·ur'nus
—— du'pli·ca'tus
—— heb'e·tu'do'
—— ju've·num
—— lu'ci·dus
—— mus·car'um
—— se·ni'lis
—— vi'tae'
vi'tal
vi'tal·ism
vi·tal'i·ty
vi'tal·ize', -ized', -iz'ing
vi'ta·mer
vi'ta·min
vit'el·lar'y
vi·tel'li·cle
vi·tel'lin *(a protein found in
egg yolk)*
  ♦vitelline
vi·tel'line' *(pertaining to the
vitellus)*
  ♦vitellin
vi·tel'lo·lu'te·in
vi·tel'lo·mes'en·ter'ic
vi·tel'lo·ru'bin
vi·tel'lus *pl.* -li'
—— o'vi'
vi'ti·a'tion
vit'i·lig'i·nes'
vit'i·lig'i·nous
vit'i·li'go'
—— cap'i·tis
—— i'ri·dis
vit're·o·den'tin
vit're·ous
vit're·um
vit'ric
vi·tri'na
—— au'di·to'ri·a
—— au'ris
—— oc'u·lar'is
vit'ri·ol
vit'ri·ol'ic
vit'rum
viv'i·dif·fu'sion
viv'i·fi·ca'tion
vi·vip'a·rous
vo'cal
vo·ca'lis
Vo'ges-Pros'kau'er
—— reaction
—— test
Vogt
—— disease
—— point
—— syndrome
voice, voiced, voic'ing

void
Voille•mier' point
vo'la
—— ma'nus
vo'lar
vo•la'ris
vol'a•tile
vol'a•til•ize', -ized', -iz'ing
vol'a•til•i•za'tion
vol•az'o•cine'
vo•le'mic
Vol'hard' test
vo•li'tion
vo•li'tion•al
Volk'mann
—— canals
—— contracture
vol'ley
Voll'mer patch test
volt
volt'age
Vol'to•li'ni disease
vol'ume
vol'u•met'ric
vol'un•tar'y
vol'vu•lo'sis
vol'vu•lus
vo'mer
vo'mer•ine'
vom'er•o•na'sal
vom'i•cose'
vom'it
vom'i•tive
vóm'i•to' ne'gro'
vom'i•to'ry
vom'i•tu•ri'tion
vom'i•tus
—— cru•en'tes'
—— ma•ri'nus
—— mat'u•ti'nus
—— ni'ger
von Ec'o•no'mo disease
von Gier'ke disease
von Grae'fe sign
von Hip'pel-Lin'dau' disease
von Jaksch anemia
von Kós'sa stain
von Pir•quet' test
von Reck'ling•hau'sen
—— disease
—— hemofuscin
von Wil'le•brand' disease
Voor'hees bag
vo•ra'cious
Vo'ro•noff' operation
vor'tex' pl. -ti•ces'

—— coc•cyg'e•us
—— cor'dis
—— len'tis
vor•ti•ces' pi•lo'rum
Vos'si•us ring
vox
vo•yeur'
vo•yeur'ism
Vro'lik disease
vu'e•rom'e•ter
vul'can•ize', -ized', -iz'ing
vul•ga'ris
vul'ner•a•bil'i•ty
vul'ner•a•ble
vul'nus pl. -ner•a
Vul'pi•an
—— atrophy
—— effect
—— reaction
vul•sel'lum pl. -la
vul'va
—— con•ni'vens
—— hi'ans'
vul'vae' a•cu'tum ul'cus
vul'val
vul'var
vul•vec'to•my
vul•vis'mus
vul•vi'tis
vul'vo•rec'tal
vul'vo•u'ter•ine
vul'vo•vag'i•nal
vul'vo•vag'i•ni'tis

W

Wa'chen•stein-Zak' method
Wag'ner
—— corpuscles
—— operation
Wag'ner-Jau'regg' treatment
Wag'staffe' fracture
Wahl sign
waist
waist'line'
wake'ful•ness
Wal'den•ström'
—— disease
—— syndrome
Wal'dey'er
—— fossae
—— glands
—— ring

Wal'len•berg' syndrome
Wal•le'ri•an
—— degeneration
—— law
wall'eye'
Wal'thard' inclusions
Wal'ther
—— ganglion
—— ligament
Wal'ton operation
Wan'gen•steen'
—— apparatus
—— tube
Wang test
War'burg' apparatus
ward
Ward triangle
war'fa•rin
War'ner hand
War'ren
—— incision
—— operation
wart
War'ten•berg'
—— disease
—— sign
War'thin
—— sign
—— tumor
Was'ser•mann
—— antibody
—— test
Was'ser•mann-fast'
waste, wast'ed, wast'ing
wa'ter
Wa'ter•house-Fri'der•ich•sen syndrome
wa'ters
wa'ter•shed'
Wat'son-Schwartz' test
watt
watt'age
watt'me'ter
wave
wave'length'
wax
wean
web, webbed, web'bing
Web'er
—— disease
—— glands
—— law
—— organ
—— paralysis
—— syndrome
—— test
Web'er-Chris'tian disease

Web'er-Di·mi'tri-Ka'li·scher syndrome
Web'ster
—— operation
—— test
Wechs'ler-Belle'vue' intelligence scale
We·den'sky
—— facilitation
—— inhibition
weep'ing
We'ge·ner granulomatosis
Weg'ner disease
Weich'sel·baum' coccus
Wei'del reaction
Wei'gert
—— law
—— method
—— stain
weight
Weil
—— disease
—— test
Weil'-Fe'lix
—— reaction
—— test
Weir operation
Weis'bach' angle
Weiss sign
Welch bacillus
Wells facies
Wells'-Sten'ger test
wen
Wen'cke·bach' phenomenon
Werd'nig-Hoff'mann atrophy
Werl'hof' disease
Wer'ne·kinck' commissure
Wer'ner
—— disease
—— syndrome
Wer'ner-His' disease
Wer'ni·cke
—— aphasia
—— syndrome
Wer'ni·cke-Mann' paralysis
Wert'heim' operation
Wert'heim-Schau'ta operation
Werth tumor
Wes'sels·bron' fever
Wes'ter·gren method
West'phal'
—— disease

—— maneuver
—— nucleus
—— sign
West'phal-Pilcz' reflex
West'phal-Strüm'pell pseudosclerosis
West syndrome
Wet'zel grid
Weyl test
Whar'ton
—— duct
—— jelly
wheal
Wheel'house' operation
wheeze, wheezed, wheez'ing
whey
whip'lash'
Whip'ple
—— disease
—— operation
whirl'pool'
whis'per
White
—— method
—— operation
White'head' operation
white'pox'
Whit'field' ointment
whit'low'
Whit'man operation
Whit'more' bacillus
whooping cough
Whytt
—— disease
—— reflex
Wick'ham striae
Wi·dal'
—— syndrome
—— test
Wig'and maneuver
Wild'bolz' reaction
Wil'der·muth ear
Wilks
—— disease
—— syndrome
Wil'liam·son sign
Wil'lis
—— circle
—— nerve
—— paracusis
Wilms tumor
Wil'son
—— disease
—— sign
Wil'son-Mik'i·ty syndrome
Win'ckel disease

wind'age
win'dow
wind'pipe'
Win'i·war'ter operation
Wins'low
—— foramen
—— pancreas
—— stars
Win'ter·bot'tom sign
Win'ter·nitz sound
Win'trich sign
Win'trobe'-Lands'berg' method
Win'trobe' method
wire
Wir'sung canal
Wis'kott-Al'drich syndrome
with·draw'al
Wit'zel operation
wit'zel·sucht'
Wohl'ge·muth' test
Wolff
—— law
—— method
Wolff'-Eis'ner test
wolff'i·an
Wolff'-Park'in·son-White' syndrome
Wöl'fler operation
Wol'fring glands
Wol·hyn'i·an fever
Wol'las·ton doublet
Wol'man disease
womb
Wong method
Wood
—— light
—— muscle
Wool'ner tip
wool'sort'ers disease
worm
wound
W-plasty
Wre'den
—— operation
—— sign
Wre'den-Stone' operation
Wright
—— stain
—— syndrome
wrin'kle
Wris'berg'
—— cartilage
—— ganglion
—— nerve
wrist

wrist'drop'
wry'neck'
Wu'cher atrophy
Wu'cher·er'i·a
—— ban·crof'ti'
—— ma·lay'i'
wu'cher·e·ri'a·sis pl. -ses'
Wun'der·lich curve
Wundt tetanus
Wy'lie operation

X

xan'thate'
xan'the·las'ma pl. -mas or
  -ma·ta
xan'the·las'ma·to'sis
xan·the'mi·a
xan'thene' (non-nitrogenous
  compound)
♦xanthine
xan'thic
xan'thine' (nitrogenous
  compound)
♦xanthene
xan'thi·nol' ni'a·cin'ate'
xan'thi·nu'ri·a
xan'thi·nu'ric
xan'thi·u'ri·a
xan'tho·chro·mat'ic
xan'tho·chro'mi·a
xan'tho·chro'mic
xan·thoch'ro·ous
xan'tho·cy'·no'pi·a
xan'tho·cy'a·nop'si·a
xan'tho·cyte'
xan'tho·der'ma
xan'tho·don'tous
xan'tho·fi·bro'ma the'co·
  cel'lu·lar'e'
xan'tho·gran'u·lo'ma
  pl. -mas or -ma·ta
xan'tho·gran'u·lo'ma·
  to'sis
xan'tho·gran'u·lom'a·tous
xan'tho·ky·an'o·py
xan·tho'ma pl. -mas or
  -ma·ta
—— di'a·bet'i·co'rum
—— dis·sem'i·na'tum
—— pal'pe·brar'um
—— tu'ber·o'sum
—— tuberosum mul'ti·plex'
xan·tho'ma·to'sis pl. -ses'
xan·thom'a·tous

xan'thone'
xan'tho·phane'
xan'tho·phore'
xan'tho·phose'
xan'tho·phyll
xan'tho·pi·a
xan'tho·pro·te'ic
xan'tho·pro'te·in
xan·thop'si·a
xan·thop'sin
xan·thop'ter·in
xan'tho·rham'nin
xan'thor·rhe'a
xan'tho·sar·co'ma pl. -mas
  or -ma·ta
xan'tho·sine'
xan'tho'sis pl. -ses'
—— fun'di' di'a·bet'i·ca
xan'tho·tox'in
xan'thous
xan'thu·re'nic
xan·thu'ri·a
xan·thy'drol'
xan·thyl'ic
xan'to·ru'bin
xen'o·graft'
xe·nol'o·gy
xen'o·me'ni·a
xe'non'
xen'o·pho'bi·a
xen'o·plas'tic
xen'o·plas'ty
Xen'op·syl'la
—— che·o'pis
xe·ran'sis
xe·ran'tic
xe'ro·der'ma
—— pig'men·to'sum
xe'ro·der'mos·te·o'sis
xe·ro'ma pl. -mas or -ma·ta
xe·ro·mam·mog'ra·phy
xe'ro·me'ni·a
xe'ro·myc·te'ri·a
xe'roph·thal'mi·a
xe'ro·ra'di·og'ra·phy
xe·ro'sis pl. -ses'
—— con'junc·ti'vae'
—— in·fan'ti·lis
xe'ro·sto'mi·a
xe'ro·tes'
xe·rot'ic
xe'ro·trip'sis
xiph'i·ster'nal
xiph'i·ster'num
xiph'o·cos'tal
xi·phod'y·mus
xiph'o·dyn'i·a

xiph'oid'
xiph'oid·i'tis
xi·phop'a·gus
x'-ray' or X'-ray'
xy·lam'i·dine'
xy'lene'
xy'le·nol'
xy'lo·me·taz'o·line'
xy'lose'
xy'lo·su'ri·a
xy'lyl
xy'ro·spasm
xys'ma
xys'ter

Y

yawn
yaws
yeast
Yer·sin'i·a
—— pes'tis
—— pseu'do·tu·ber'cu·lo'sis
yer·sin'i·o'sis
yo·him'bine'
yolk
York'-Yendt' syndrome
Yo·shi'da tumor
Young
—— method
—— operation
y'per·ite'
yp·sil'i·form'
Yu'ge syndrome
Y·von' test

Z

Zang space
Zeis glands
Zel'ler test
Zen'ker
—— degeneration
—— diverticulum
—— fixative
Zie'hen-Op'pen·heim' dis-
  ease
Zieth'-Neel'sen
—— method
—— stain
Ziems'sen point
Zieve syndrome
Zi'ka fever

Zim′mer·lin type
Zim′mer·mann reaction
zinc
Zinn
—— annulus
—— artery
—— ligament
zir·co′ni·um
zo′la·mine′
zo′ler·tine′
Zol′lin·ger-El′li·son syndrome
zo′na pl. -nae′
—— ar′cu·a′ta
—— car′ti·la·gin′e·a
—— cil′i·ar′is
—— co′lum·nar′is rec′ti′
—— cu·ta′ne·a rec′ti′
—— den·tic′u·la′ta
—— fas·cic′u·la′ta
—— glo·mer′u·lo′sa
—— hem′or·rhoi·da′lis
—— in·cer′ta
—— in′ter·me′di·a rec′ti′
—— oph·thal′mi·ca
—— or·bic′u·lar′is
—— pec′ti·na′ta
—— pel·lu′ci·da
—— per′fo·ra′ta
—— re·tic′u·lar′is
—— spon′gi·o′sa
—— tec′ta
zo′nal
zo′na·ry
zo′nes·the′si·a
zo·nif′u·gal
zo·nip′e·tal
zo′nu·la pl. -lae′
—— ad·hae′rens
—— cil′i·ar′is

—— ciliaris (Zin′ni·i′)
—— oc·clu′dens
zo′nu·lar
zo′nule′
—— of Zinn
zo′nu·li′tis
zo′nu·lol′y·sis
zo′nu·lot′o·my
zo′nu·ly′sis
zo′o·der′mic
zo′o·e·ras′ti·a
zo′o·gle′a pl. -as or -ae′
zo·og′o·ny
zo′o·graft′
zo′o·lag′ni·a
zo·ol′o·gist
zo·ol′o·gy
zo′o·no′sis pl. -ses′
zo′o·not′ic
zo′o·par′a·site′
zo′o·par′a·sit′ic
zo·oph′i·lism
zo′o·pho′bi·a
zo′o·plas′tic
zo′o·plas′ty
zo′o·sperm′
zo′o·sper′mi·a
zo′o·spore′
zo·os′ter·ol′
zo′o·tox′in
zos′ter
—— au·ric′u·lar′is
—— bra′chi·a′lis
—— fa′ci·a′lis
—— fem′o·ra′lis
—— oph·thal′mi·cus
zos·ter′i·form′
zos′ter·oid′
Z′-plas′ty
Zuck′er·kan′dl

—— bodies
—— convolution
zyg′a·poph′y·se′al
zyg′a·poph′y·sis pl. -ses′
zyg′i·on′ pl. -i·a or -i·ons′
zy′go·dac′ty·ly
zy·go′ma pl. -ma·ta or -mas
zy′go·mat′ic
zy′go·mat′i·co·fa′cial
zy′go·mat′i·co·fron′tal
zy′go·mat′i·co·max′il·lar′y
zy′go·mat′i·co·or′bit·al
zy′go·mat′i·co·tem′po·ral
zy′go·mat′i·cus
zy′go·max′il·lar′e′
zy′go·my′co′sis pl. -ses′
zy·gos′i·ty
zy′go·spore′
zy′gote′
zy′go·tene′
zy·got′ic
zy′mase′
zyme
zy′mic
zy′mo·gen
zy′mo·gen′ic
zy·mog′e·nous
zy′moid′
zy′mo·log′ic
zy·mol′o·gy
zy·mol′y·sis
zy′mo·lyte′
zy′mo·lyt′ic
zy·mom′e·ter
zy′mo·phore′
zy′mo·pho′ric
zy′mo·plas′tic
zy′mo·pro′tein′
zy·mo′sis pl. -ses′
zy·mos′ter·ol′
zy·ot′ic

SURGICAL APPENDIX

The following list contains the names of surgical instruments, incisions, positions, dressings, suture materials, prostheses, and the like. The list cannot, of course, be exhaustive, because of the constant development of new techniques and implements, but the most commonly encountered names will be found here.

Abbe condenser
Abbott-Rawson tube
Abbott tube
Abelson
—— adenotome
—— cannula
Aberdeen tube
Abraham cannula
Abrams biopsy punch
Ace bandage
ACMI
—— antroscope
—— catheter
—— forceps
—— hysteroscope
—— irrigating valve
—— laparoscope
—— nasopharyngoscope
—— proctosigmoidoscope
Acmistat catheter
Acutrol suture
Adair forceps
Adams
—— adapter
—— aspirator
—— position
—— saw
—— screw compressor
Adams-Gilson adapter
Adaptic dressing
Adler punch forceps
Adson
—— bur
—— cannula
—— chisel
—— clip
—— drill
—— elevator
—— forceps
—— hook
—— knife
—— needle
—— retractor
—— rongeur
—— scissors
—— tube
Adson-Brown forceps
Aebli scissors

Aeroplast dressing
Aesculap approximator
Ahlquist-Durham clip
Ahmed device
Air-Lon
—— decannulation plub
—— trachea tube
Alabama University forceps
Albarran bridge
Albee
—— fracture table
—— saw
Albert
—— bronchoscope
—— position
—— suture
Alcock
—— bladder syringe
—— catheter
Alcon cryophake
Alden retractor
Alexander
—— chisel
—— gouge
—— incision
Alexander-Farabeuf periosteotome
Allen
—— applicator
—— clamp
—— forceps
—— stethoscope
—— trocar
Allingham speculum
Allis forceps
Allis-Ochsner forceps
Allport
—— bur
—— retractor
—— searcher
Allport-Babcock searcher
Alm retractor
Alvis curette
Alyea clamp
American umbilical scissors
Ames shunt

Amoils
—— cryoextractor
—— retractor
Amsler needle
Ancap silk suture
Andrew applicator
Andrews
—— chisel
—— retractor
Andrews-Hartmann forceps
Andrews-Pynchon tube
Angell James
—— dissector
—— forceps
Anger camera
Anthony
—— compressor
—— suction tube
Anthony-Fisher balloon
Appolito suture
Arbuckle probe
Argyle catheter
Argyll-Robertson suture
Arlt
—— lens scoop
—— suture
Aronson retractor
Arruga
—— forceps
—— implant
—— lens expressor
—— trephine
Artmann chisel
Asch straightener
ASR scalpel
Atlee clamp
Aufranc
—— awl
—— retractor
Aufricht
—— rasp
—— retractor
Aufricht-Lipsett rasp
Ault clamp
Austin
—— curette
—— knife

Berry clamp
Bertrandi suture
Best
—— clamp
—— forceps
Bethune
—— shears
—— tourniquet
Bevan
—— forceps
—— incision
Beyer rongeur forceps
Bier anesthesia
Bigelow clamp
Billroth
—— forceps
—— tube
Birnberg bow
Birtcher coagulator
Bishop chisel
Bishop-Harman
—— cannula
—— forceps
—— irrigator
Bjork drill
Bjork-Shiley valve
Black clamp
Blair
—— chisel
—— elevator
—— retractor
Blair-Brown
—— needle
—— retractor
Blake forceps
Blakemore tube
Blakesley
—— forceps
—— retractor
Blalock clamp
Blalock-Niedner clamp
Blanchard
—— clamp
—— cryptotome
—— forceps
Bloodwell forceps
Blount retractor
Boari button
Bodenheimer anoscope
Boehm
—— anoscope
—— proctoscope
—— sigmoidoscope
Boettcher
—— forceps
—— hook
—— scissors

Böhler
—— clamp
—— pin
Bohlman pin
Bonaccolto forceps
Bonney
—— forceps
—— needle
Bonn forceps
Bonta knife
Borsch bandage
Botvin forceps
Boucheron speculum
Bovie cautery
Bowen chisel
Bowman
—— needle
—— probe
Boyce position
Boyes clamp
Boyes-Goodfellow hook
Boynton needle holder
Boys-Allis forceps
Bozeman
—— catheter
—— forceps
—— position
—— suture
Bozeman-Wertheim needle holder
Braasch
—— catheter
—— cystoscope
—— forceps
Braastad retractor
Bracken forceps
Brackin incision
Bradford forceps
Bradshaw-O'Neill clamp
Braun
—— cranioclast
—— forceps
—— scissors
Braun-Jardine-Delee hook
Brawley retractor
Breck pin
Breisky-Navratil speculum
Breitman adenotome
Briggs transilluminator
Brighton balloon
Brinkerhoff
—— anoscope
—— speculum
Brittain chisel
Brock
—— clamp

—— incision
—— punch
Brockenbrough needle
Brodny
—— cannula
—— clamp
Bronner clamp
Brook scissors
Brophy
—— bistoury
—— forceps
—— knife
—— periosteotome
—— needle
—— tenaculum
Brophy-Deschamps needle
Brown
—— chisel
—— cotton applicator
—— dermatome
—— forceps
—— hook
—— retractor
—— snare
Brown-Adson forceps
Brown-Buerger cystoscope
Broyles
—— aspirator
—— bronchoscope
—— forceps
—— laryngoscope
—— nasopharyngoscope
Bruening
—— bronchoscope
—— cannula
—— chisel
—— forceps
—— otoscope
—— snare
—— speculum
Brun curette
Brunetti chisel
Brunner
—— chisel
—— dissector
—— forceps
Bruns chisel
Buck
—— applicator
—— curette
Buckstein insufflator
Bucy
—— knife
—— retractor
Bucy-Frazier

—— cannula
—— suction tube
Buerger bougie
Bugbee electrode
Buie
—— clamp
—— electrode
—— forceps
—— irrigator
—— position
—— probe
—— scissors
—— sigmoidoscope
—— suction tube
Buie-Hirschman
—— anoscope
—— speculum
Buie-Smith
—— retractor
—— speculum
Bumpus forceps
Bunge spoon
Bunnell
—— drill
—— needle
—— probe
—— stripper
—— suture
Bunts Catheter
Burch
—— caliper
—— pick
Burch-Greenwood tucker
Burdick cautery
Burford
—— retractor
—— spreader
Burford-Finochietto
—— retractor
—— spreader
Burnham
—— forceps
—— scissors
Burns chisel
Burwell bur
Buxton clamp
Byford retractor

Cairns hemostasis forceps
Calhoun-Merz needle
Calhoun needle
Calibri forceps
Callender clip
Caltagirone chisel
Calve cannula

Campbell
—— catheter
—— elevator
—— forceps
—— retractor
—— rongeur
Cannon endarterectomy
 loop
Cantfield tonsil knife
Cantor tube
Caparosa
—— bur
—— wire crimper
Caplan angular scissors
Cardillo retractor
Cargile suture
Carlens
—— catheter
—— mediastinoscope
—— sponge forceps
Carmack curette
Carmalt
—— clamp
—— forceps
Carman rectal tube
Carmody
—— aspirator
—— drill
—— forceps
—— suction-pressure pump
Carmody-Brophy forceps
Carrel clamp
Carter
—— clamp
—— sphere introducer
Casselberry cannula
Cassidy-Brophy forceps
Castallo retractor
Castroviejo
—— caliper
—— clamp
—— dilator
—— forceps
—— keratome
—— knife
—— punch
—— retractor
—— scissors
—— snare
—— spatula
—— trephine
Castroviejo-Arruga for-
 ceps
Castroviejo-Kalt needle
 holder
Cault punch
Cavanaugh bur

Celestin
—— prosthesis
—— tube
Chaffin
—— drain tube
—— suction catheter
Chaffin-Pratt suction unit
Chandler
—— elevator
—— forceps
Chaoul apparatus
Charnel
—— clamp
—— forceps
Charnley-Mueller pros-
 thesis
Chelsea-Eaton speculum
Cherney incision
Cherry
—— probe
—— retractor
—— scissors
—— traction tongs
Cherry-Kerrison forceps
Chevalier Jackson
—— bronchoscope
—— gastroscope
Chiene incision
Chilcott venoclysis can-
 nula
Child-Phillips needle
Chulmsky button
Cicherelli rongeur forceps
Cinelli chisel
Cinelli-McIndoe chisel
Clagett cannula
Claiborne clamp
Clawicz chisel
Clerf-Arrowsmith pin
 closer
Cloward chisel
Clute incision
Coakley
—— cannula
—— curette
—— forceps
—— trocar
Cobb
—— elevator
—— gouge
—— osteotome
Codman
—— clamp
—— drill
—— incision
Coffey incision
Cohen forceps

Cole retractor
Coles-Malis coagulator
Colibri
—— eye speculum
—— forceps
Coller hemostatic forceps
Collier needle holder
Collin forceps
Collings knife electrode
Collins
—— clamp
—— dynamometer
—— forceps
Collison drill
Collyer pelvimeter
Colt cannula
Colver
—— forceps
—— hook
—— knife
Comedo extractor
Compere
—— chisel
—— gouge
—— osteotome
Conco feltfoam padding
Cone
—— cannula
—— curette
—— forceps
—— needle
—— punch
Cone-Bucy cannula
Connell suture
Conrad-Crosby biopsy
needle
Constantine catheter
Controlflate catheter
Converse
—— chisel
—— osteotome
Cook eye speculum
Cooley
—— clamp
—— dilator
—— forceps
—— retractor
—— scissors
—— suction tube
Cooley-Pontius blade
Cooper
—— bougie
—— cannula
—— cryoprobe
Cope
—— biopsy needle
—— clamp

Cope-DeMartel clamp
Copper "7" device
Corbett
—— forceps
—— foreign body spud
Cordes punch forceps
Corrigan cautery
Corwin hemostat
Coryllos
—— raspatory
—— retractor
Coryllos-Bethune rib
shears
Cottle
—— caliper
—— chisel
—— clamp
—— elevator
—— forceps
—— hook
—— knife
—— mallet
—— rasp
—— retractor
—— saw
—— scissors
—— speculum
—— suction tube
—— tenaculum
Cottle-Jansen rongeur
forceps
Cottle-Kazanjian forceps
Cottle-Mackenty elevator
Cottle-Neivert retractor
Cottle-Walsham septum
straightener
Coude tip catheter
Councill
—— catheter
—— stone extractor
Councilman chisel
Cournand arterial needle
Cournand-Grino needle
Courvoisier incision
Coxeter catheter
Crabtree dissector
Crafoord
—— clamp
—— forceps
—— scissors
Craig
—— forceps
—— scissors
Crane
—— chisel
—— mallet
Crawford aorta retractor

Crawford-Cooley tunnel-
er
Creevy bladder evacuator
Crenshaw forceps
Crile
—— clamp
—— forceps
—— hook
—— knife
—— retractor
Crile-Crutchfield clamp
Crile-Murray needle hold-
er
Crile-Wood needle holder
Cruickshank clamp
Crutchfield
—— clamp
—— drill
—— traction tongs
Crutchfield-Raney trac-
tion tongs
Cummings catheter
Cunningham clamp
Curdy sclerotome
Curry needle
Curtis forceps
Cushing
—— bur
—— clip
—— drill
—— elevator
—— forceps
—— retractor
—— suture
—— spatula
Czerney-Lembert suture
Czerny suture

Dacron graft
Daems clamp
Dalkon Shield device
Dandy
—— forceps
—— hook
—— scissors
Daniel clamp
Daniels tonsillectome
Davidson
—— clamp
—— retractor
David speculum
Daviel lens scoop
Davis
—— bronchoscope
—— clamp

—— eye spud
—— forceps
—— gag
—— knife needle
—— needle
—— retractor
—— sound
—— spatula
—— splint
—— stone dislodger
Davis-Crowe mouth gag
Davol
—— catheter
—— suction tube
Day attic cannula
Dean
—— cotton applicator
—— forceps
—— knife
—— periosteotome
—— scissors
—— trocar
Deaver
—— incision
—— retractor
—— scissors
—— T-drain
DeBakey
—— clamp
—— forceps
—— graft
—— needle holder
—— prosthesis
—— scissors
—— tunneler
DeBakey-Bahnson clamp
DeBakey-Cooley
—— forceps
—— retractor
Decker culdoscope
DeCourcy clamp
Dedo laryngoscope
Dees suturing needle
Defourmental forceps
Deknatel suture
DeLee
—— catheter
—— forceps
—— retractor
DeLee-Breisky pelvimeter
DeLee-Perce perforator
DeMartel
—— forceps
—— scissors
DeMartel-Wolfson clamp
Denhardt-Dingman
mouth gag

Denis-Browne splint
Dennis
—— clamp
—— forceps
Depage position
DePuy
—— awl
—— bolt
—— curette
—— drill
—— pin
—— prosthesis
—— rongeur
—— splint
Derf needle holder
Derlacki
—— chisel
—— curette
—— knife
—— punch
Dermalene suture
Dermalon suture
Derra clamp
D'Errico
—— bur
—— chisel
—— forceps
—— retractor
—— trephine
D'Errico-Adson retractor
Desault bandage
Deschamps
—— compressor
—— ligature carrier
Deschamps-Navratil liga-
ture needle
Desjardin
—— forceps
—— probe
—— scoop
Desmarres
—— forceps
—— retractor
—— scarifier
Detakats-McKenzie for-
ceps
DeVilbiss
—— compressor
—— forceps
—— irrigator
—— rongeur
—— speculum
DeVilbiss-Stacey specu-
lum
Devonshire catheter
deWecker scissors
Deyerle

—— drill
—— pin
Dieffenbach
—— clamp
—— forceps
Diethrich clamp
Dieulafoy aspirator
Dimitry-Bell erysiphake
Dingman
—— abrader
—— clamp
—— elevator
—— forceps
—— mouth gag
—— needle
—— osteotome
—— ribbon retractor
Dingman-Denhardt
mouth gag
Dingman-Senn retractor
Dix eye spud
Dixon blade
Dixon-Thomas-Smith
clamp
Dobbie-Trout clamp
Docktor
—— forceps
—— needle
Dogliotti-Guglielmini
clamp
Donald clamp
Dormia
—— stone basket
—— stone dislodger
Dorsey
—— cannula
—— punch
Dos Santos aortography
needle
Dougherty irrigator
Dourmashkin bougie
Dow Corning cannula
Downes cautery
Downing
—— clamp
—— knife
Doyen
—— bur
—— clamp
—— elevator
—— forceps
—— retractor
—— scissors
—— screw
Drake aneurysm clip
Duane "U" clip
Dudley hook

Dudley-Smith speculum
Dufourmental rongeur
Dührssen incision
Duke
—— cannula
—— trocar
Duncan position
Dunhill hemostat
Duplay forceps
Dupuis cannula
Dupuytren
—— enterotome
—— suture
Duval-Crile forceps
Duvergier suture
Dynatech cryo-ophthal-
mic unit

Earle
—— clamp
—— probe
Eastman
—— clamp
—— retractor
Eber suture forceps
Edebohls
—— clamp
—— incision
Eder-Chamberlin gastro-
scope
Eder gastroscope
Eder-Hufford gastroscope
Eder-Palmer gastroscope
Edinburgh retractor
Edslab cholangiography
catheter
Edwards
—— arterial graft
—— catheter
—— clamp
—— intracardiac patch
Eicher
—— chisel
—— prosthesis
Elastoplast bandage
Ellik
—— bladder evacuator
—— sound
Elliot position
Elliott
—— forceps
—— trephine
Ellis needle holder
Ellsner gastroscope
Elsberg

—— cannula
—— incision
Elschnig
—— forceps
—— knife
—— spatula
Elschnig-O'Brien forceps
Emerson
—— bronchoscope
—— stripper
Emmet suture
Emmett
—— scissors
—— tenaculum hook
Emmett-Foley catheter
Engel plaster saw
Epstein hemilaminectomy
blade
Equisetene suture
Erhardt
—— clamp
—— forceps
Erich
—— biopsy forceps
—— nasal splint
Erlenmeyer flask
Esmarch
—— bandage
—— probe
—— scissors
—— tourniquet
Essrig forceps
Ethicon
—— clip
—— suture
Ethiflex suture
Ethilon suture
Evans forceps
Eves snare
Ewald evacuator

Falk clamp
Fansler
—— anoscope
—— proctoscope
—— speculum
Farabeuf elevator
Farabeuf-Lambotte clamp
Farrington forceps
Farrior
—— forceps
—— speculum
Farris forceps
Faulkner
—— chisel

—— curette
—— trocar
Faulkner-Browne chisel
Favaloro
—— retractor
Fehland clamp
Feilchenfeld forceps
Fell sucker tip
Feltfoam padding
Fenger probe
Fenton bolt
Ferguson
—— forceps
—— scissors
—— scoop
Ferguson-Moon retractor
Fergusson incision
Ferris
—— dilator
—— scoop
Ferris-Smith
—— forceps
Ferris-Smith-Halle bur
Ferris-Smith-Kerrison
—— forceps
—— rongeur
Ferris-Smith-Sewall re-
tractor
Fillauer splint
Filtzer
—— graft corkscrew
—— rasp
Finnoff transilluminator
Finochietto
—— clamp
—— forceps
—— needle holder
—— rib spreader
Fisch
—— dura hook
—— elevator
—— knife
—— neurotome
—— raspatory
—— scissors
Fischl blade holder
Fisher
—— cannula
—— knife
—— spud
Fitzgerald forceps
Flaxedil suture
Fleming conization in-
strument
Fletcher tonsil knife
Fletcher-Van Doren for-
ceps

Flexitone suture
Flexon suture
Flexsteel retractor
Foerster forceps
Fogarty
—— catheter
—— clamp
—— probe
Foley
—— catheter
—— forceps
Foley-Alcock catheter
Fomon
—— chisel
—— elevator
—— knife
—— periosteotome
—— rasp
—— retractor
—— scissors
Foregger
—— bronchoscope
—— laryngoscope
Foroblique
—— cystourethroscope
—— telescope
Forrester
—— brace
—— clamp
Foss
—— clamp
—— forceps
—— retractor
Fowler
—— incision
—— position
Fowler-Weir incision
Fox
—— curette
—— eye conformer
—— eye shield
—— irrigator
Frackelton needle
Fraenkel forceps
Frahur clamp
Francis
—— forceps
—— knife spud
Frankfeldt
—— forceps
—— needle
—— sigmoidoscope
—— snare
Franklin-Silverman biopsy needle
Franz retractor
Frater retractor

Frazier
—— cannula
—— elevator
—— hook
—— retractor
—— suction tube
Frazier-Adson clamp
Frazier-Paparella suction tube
Frazier-Sachs clamp
Freeman clamp
Freer
—— chisel
—— elevator
—— hook
—— knife
Freimuth curette
Fremont-Smith manometer
French
—— catheter
—— eye needle holder
—— retractor
Freyer drain
Frey-Freer bur
Fricke bandage
Friedman-Otis bougie
Friedrich-Petz clamp
Friend catheter
Frigitronic cryoextractor
Fritsch catheter
Fuchs forceps
Fulpit forceps
Fulton rongeur
Furniss
—— catheter
—— clamp
—— incision
Furniss-Clute clamp
Furniss-McClure-Hinton clamp

Gabriel proctoscope
Gaillard-Arlt suture
Gallie needle
Galt trephine
Gandhi knife
Gant clamp
Garceau catheter
Gardner needle
Garland clamp
Garrett dilator
Garrigue speculum
Gatch bed
Gatellier incision

Gavin-Miller clamp
Gaylor biopsy forceps
Geiger-Downes cautery
Gelfilm
Gelfoam
Gellhorn
—— forceps
—— punch
Gelpi
—— forceps
—— retractor
Gély suture
Genga bandage
Gerald forceps
Geuder needle
Gibney bandage
Gibson-Balfour retractor
Gibson irrigator
Giertz-Shoemaker shears
Gifford
—— applicator
—— curette
—— forceps
—— retractor
Gilbert catheter
Gilgi saw
Giliberty prosthesis
Gill
—— forceps
—— knife
Gilles-Dingman hook
Gilles hook
Gillies needle holder
Gilson mixing adaptor
Glassman
—— clamp
—— forceps
Glassman-Allis forceps
Glenner
—— forceps
—— retractor
Glover
—— clamp
—— forceps
Gluck rib shears
Goelet retractor
Goldbacher
—— anoscope
—— needle
—— proctoscope
—— speculum
Goldblatt clamp
Goldstein
—— cannula
—— retractor
Gomco
—— clamp

—— drainage pump
Gonnin-Amsler marker
Goodell dilator
Goodfellow cannula
Goodhill forceps
Good rasp
Goodwin clamp
Goodyear knife
Gordon
—— forceps
—— stethoscope
Gorman-Rupp K-thermia unit
Gosset retractor
Gottschalk
—— aspirator
—— transverse saw
Gould suture
Gouley catheter
Gradle electrode
Graefe
—— cystotome
—— forceps
—— knife
—— knife needle
—— strabismus hook
Graham blunt hook
Graham-Kerrison punch
Grantham needle
Grant needle holder
Graves speculum
Gray
—— clamp
—— forceps
—— resectoscope
Green
—— caliper
—— clamp
—— curette
—— dissector
—— forceps
—— hook
—— knife
—— resectoscope
—— retractor
Greenwood forceps
Greiling tube
Grieshaber
—— needle holder
—— retractor
—— trephine
Gruber
—— bougie
—— speculum
Gruenwald
—— forceps
—— rongeur

Gruenwald-Bryant forceps
Gruppe forceps
Gudebrod suture
Guedel
—— airway
—— laryngoscope blade
Guild-Pratt speculum
Guilford-Schuknecht scissors
Gundelach punch
Gunderson forceps
Gunning splint
Gusberg
—— curette
—— punch
Gussenbauer
—— clamp
—— suture
Gutglass forceps
Guttmann
—— retractor
—— speculum
Guy gouge
Guyon
—— bougie
—— clamp
Guyon-Pean clamp
Guyton-Park speculum
Gynecoil device
Gynefold pessary

Hagedorn needle
Hagenbarth forceps
Hagner catheter
Hahn cannula
Hajek
—— chisel
—— retractor
Hajek-Ballenger
—— dissector
—— elevator
Hajek-Koffler forceps
Hajek-Skillern punch
Hakim valve
Hall
—— drill
—— mastoid bur
Halle
—— bur
—— chisel
—— curette
Halle-Tieck speculum
Halogen
—— ophthalmoscope

—— otoscope
Halsey needle
Halsted
—— forceps
—— hemostat
—— incision
—— suture
Hamby retractor
Hamilton bandage
Hamm electrode
Hammond retractor blade
Hamrick elevator
Handley incision
Hank-Bradley dilator
Hank dilator
Hannon curette
Hardy
—— bivalve speculum
—— dissector
—— enucleator
—— implant fork
Harken
—— clamp
—— forceps
—— rib spreader
Harmon incision
Harrington
—— clamp forceps
—— erysiphake
—— retractor
Harrington-Mayo forceps
Harrington-Mixter
—— clamp
—— forceps
Harrington-Pemberton retractor
Harris
—— flush tube
—— forceps
—— suture
Harrison
—— knife
—— speculum
—— scissors
—— teflon mesh
Harrison-Shea curette
Hartman
—— ear forceps
—— speculum
Hartmann
—— catheter
—— forceps
—— punch
—— rongeur
—— tuning fork
Hartmann-Citelli punch
Harvard manometer

Haseltine clamp
Haslinger
—— esophagoscope
—— retractor
Hatch catheter
Haverfield cannula
Haverfield-Scoville retractor
Hayes clamp
Haynes cannula
Heaney
—— curette
—— forceps
—— needle holder
—— retractor
Heaney-Ballentine forceps
Heaney-Kanter forceps
Heaney-Rezek forceps
Heaney-Simon retractor
Heath
—— curette
—— dilator
—— forceps
—— scissors
Hedblom
—— elevator
—— rib retractor
Heerman incision
Hegar
—— dilator
—— needle holder
Hegar-Baumgartner needle holder
Heidbrink-Lombard airway
Heitz-Boyer clamp
Heliodorus bandage
Hemovac
—— drain
—— suction tube
Henderson chisel
Hendren
—— clamp
—— forceps
Hendrickson lithotrite
Henke punch forceps
Henner retractor
Hennig spreader
Henrotin forceps
Henry incision
Henson-Dormia basket
Henton
—— needle
—— suture hook
Hercules plaster shears
Herff clamp

Herman-Taylor gastroscope
Herrick clamp
Hess-Barraquer forceps
Hesseltine umbiliclip
Hess forceps
Hess-Horwitz forceps
Heymann-Paparella scissors
Hibbs
—— chisel
—— clamp
—— curette
—— forceps
—— gouge
—— osteotome
—— retractor
—— spinal fusion gouge
Higgins
—— catheter
—— incision
Hill-Ferguson retractor
Hillis
—— lid retractor
—— perforator
Hilsinger knife
Hinckle-James speculum
Hinderer forceps
Hippocrates bandage
Hirschman
—— anoscope
—— clamp
—— forceps
—— proctoscope
Hirschman-Martin proctoscope
Hirschowitz fiberscope
Hirst-Emmett forceps
Hodgen splint
Hoen
—— cannula
—— elevator
Hoffman punch forceps
Hoke osteotome
Holinger
—— applicator
—— aspirating tube
—— bronchoscope
—— cannula
—— laryngoscope
—— needle
Holinger-Jackson bronchoscope
Holmes
—— gouge
—— nasopharyngoscope
Holth sclerectomy punch

Hood and Kirklin incision
Hood dermatome
Hope resuscitator
Hopkins
—— clamp
—— forceps
Hopp laryngoscope blade
Horgan center blade
Horsley
—— dura separator
—— forceps
Hosford eye spud
Hotz curette
Hough-Sanders hoe
House
—— alligator forceps
—— chisel
—— crura hook
—— curette
—— elevator
—— excavator
—— forceps
—— hook
—— knife
—— needle
—— perforating bur
—— separator
—— shunt tube
—— speculum
—— tapping hammer
—— wire prosthesis
House-Barbara needle
House-Bellucci scissors
House-Dieter nipper
House-Metzenbaum scissors
House-Paparella curette
House-Radpour irrigator
House-Rosen needle
House-Urban
—— beam splitter
—— bipolar electrode
—— camera
—— retractor
—— rotary dissector
House-Wullstein forceps
Houtz curette
Howell stethoscope
Hoxworth clip
Hryntschak catheter
Hubbard
—— electrode
—— nylok bolt
Hudgins cannula
Hudson
—— brace
—— bur

—— clamp
—— forceps
—— rongeur
Huey scissors
Huffman-Graves speculum
Huffman vaginoscope
Hufnagel clamp
Hume clamp
Hunt
—— clamp
—— forceps
—— needle
Hunter curette
Hurd
—— dissector
—— forceps
—— retractor
Hurst bougie
Hurwitz
—— clamp
—— trocar
Hutchins biopsy needle
Hyfrecator coagulator

IBC
—— catheter
—— electrode
Iglesias resectoscope
Illinois sternal needle
Immergut suction tube
Ingals
—— cannula
—— speculum
Ingersoll curette
Ingraham-Fowler clip
Iowa
—— cotton applicator
—— forceps
Irvine scissors
Israel retractor
Itard catheter
Iverson dermabrader
Ives anoscope

Jaboulay button
Jackson
—— aspirating tube
—— bistoury
—— bronchoscope
—— clamp
—— dilator
—— esophagoscope

—— filiform bougie
—— forceps
—— hemostat
—— incision
—— retractor
—— scissors
—— tenaculum
—— tracheal tube
Jacob forceps
Jacobs clamp
Jacobson
—— clamp
—— forceps
—— retractor
—— scissors
—— spatula
—— suture pusher
Jaeger keratome
Jaeger-Whiteley catheter
Jahnke-Cook-Seeley
  clamp
Jako laryngoscope
Jameson
—— caliper
—— forceps
—— hook
Jansen
—— retractor
—— rongeur forceps
Jansen-Middleton forceps
Jansen-Newhart probe
Jansen-Struycken forceps
Jarcho
—— cannula
—— forceps
Jarvis clamp
Javid
—— bypass tube
—— clamp
Jelm catheter
Jennings mouth gag
Jesberg
—— aspirating tube
—— bronchoscope
—— clamp
—— esophagoscope
—— forceps
Jewett
—— nail
—— screw
—— urethral sound
Jobert suture
Johns Hopkins
—— clamp
—— needle holder
—— retractor
—— stone basket

—— tube
Johnston clamp
Jolly uterine dilator
Jones
—— clamp
—— curette
—— dilator
—— forceps
—— scissors
—— splint
Jordan Day bur
Jorgenson scissors
Joseph
—— chisel
—— clamp
—— knife
—— periosteotome
—— rasp
—— saw
—— scissors
Joseph-Maltz saw
Judd-Allis forceps
Judd-DeMartel forceps
Judd forceps
Juers-Derlacki speculum
  holder
Juers-Lempert forceps
Juevenelle clamp
Julian
—— forceps
—— needle holder
Julian-Fildes clamp
Jutte tube

Kahler forceps
Kahn cannula
Kahn-Graves speculum
Kal-Dermic suture
Kalt
—— needle
—— suture
Kammerer incision
Kanavel
—— cannula
—— splint
Kane clamp
Kantor
—— clamp
—— forceps
Kantrowicz clamp
Kaplan needle
Kapp-Beck clamp
Kapp clamp
Karras needle
Katsch chisel

Katzin-Barraquer forceps
Katzin scissors
Kaufman
—— forceps
—— syringe
Kazanjian forceps
Kearns dilator
Keeley vein stripper
Kehr incision
Keith needle
Keitzer urethrotome
Kelling gastroscope
Kelly
—— dilator
—— forceps
—— gauze packer
—— needle
—— retractor
—— scissors
Kelly-Gray curette
Kelly-Sims retractor
Kelsey clamp
Kennedy forceps
Kerlix dressing
Kernan-Jackson broncho-
scope
Kern forceps
Kerrison
—— punch
—— rongeur forceps
Kevorkian-Younge
—— curette
—— forceps
Keyes
—— chisel
—— punch
Kezerian chisel
K-Gar clamp
Khodadad
—— clip
—— forceps
Kidde
—— insufflator
—— tourniquet
Kielland forceps
Killian
—— cannula
—— chisel
—— elevator
—— knife
—— speculum
Killian-Eicken cannula
Killian-Reinhard chisel
Kilner sharp hook
Kimball catheter
Kindt clamp
King

—— brace
—— needle
—— retractor
Kinsella-Buie clamp
Kirby forceps
Kirmission raspatory
Kirschner
—— apparatus
—— wire
Kistner probe
Kiwisch bandage
KleenSpec
—— laryngoscope
—— sigmoidoscope
—— speculum
Klemme retractor
Knapp
—— knife
—— lens scoop
—— needle
—— retractor
—— scissors
—— spatula
—— speculum
Knight
—— forceps
—— scissors
Knowles
—— pin
—— scissors
Kocher
—— clamp
—— dissector
—— forceps
—— incision
—— retractor
—— sound
Kocher-Crotti retractor
Koffler forceps
Koffler-Lillie forceps
Kogan endospeculum
Kollmann dilator
Kopetzky bur
Kos cannula
Kramer speculum
Krasky retractor
Krause
—— cannula
—— forceps
—— snare
Kreischer chisel
Kreuscher scissors
Kron
—— dilator
—— probe
Kronfeld electrode
Kryostik

K. S. Wing device
Kuhlman
—— brace
—— cast cutter
Kuhnt forceps
Kulvin-Kalt forceps
Kuntscher
—— nail
—— pin
Kurten stripper
Kurze
—— forceps
—— microscope
—— scissors
Küstner incision

Ladd
—— caliper
—— clamp
LaForce
—— knife spud
—— tonsillectome
LaForce-Grieshaber ade-
notome
LaGrange scissors
Lahey
—— clamp
—— forceps
—— ligature carrier
—— retractor
—— tenaculum
—— Y-drain
Lahey-Pean forceps
Lambert forceps
Lambert-Lowman clamp
Lambotte
—— chisel
—— clamp
—— osteotome
Lambotte-Henderson os-
teotome
Lamm incision
Lamont elevator
Lancaster
—— eye speculum
—— knife
Lane
—— catheter
—— clamp
—— forceps
—— mouth gag
—— needle
Langenbeck
—— elevator
—— incision

—— saw
Lapides needle holder
Lardennois button
Larry
—— director
—— probe
Lash-Loeffler implant
Lathbury applicator
Latrobe retractor
Laufe-Barton-Kielland
  forceps
Laufe forceps
Laufe-Piper forceps
Leader-Kollmann dilator
Lebsche
—— chisel
—— forceps
—— knife
—— rongeur
—— shears
LeDentu suture
LeDran suture
Lees clamp
LeFort
—— bougie
—— catheter
—— sound
—— suture
Lehman
—— catheter
—— syringe
Lejeune applicator
Leksell
—— approximator
—— rongeur
—— rongeur forceps
—— sternal spreader
Lem-Bay clamp
Lembert suture
Lempert
—— curette
—— curved knife
—— elevator
—— incision
—— knife
—— perforator
—— retractor
—— rongeur forceps
Lempert-Clover speculum
Lempka stripper
Lennarson suction tube
Leriche forceps
Lespinasse suture
Levant stone dislodger
Levin tube
Lewin
—— clamp

—— dissector
—— perforating forceps
—— splint
Lewis
—— cystometer
—— laryngeal tube
—— lens scoop
—— rasp
—— snare
—— stone forceps
Lewy
—— laryngoscope
—— suspension apparatus
Leyla retractor
Lichtwicz needle
Lieberman
—— abrader
—— proctoscope
—— sigmoidoscope
Lilienthal incision
Lilienthal-Sauerbruch rib
  spreader
Lillehei-Warden catheter
Lillie
—— cannula
—— forceps
—— hook
—— retractor
—— rongeur
—— scissors
—— speculum
Lillie-Killian forceps
Lilly clamp
Lindeman
—— cannula
—— needle
Lindeman-Silverstein
  tube
Lindley
—— artery scissors
—— needle holder
Lindner spatula
Linnartz clamp
Linton
—— clamp
—— tube
Lister
—— dressing
—— forceps
—— scissors
Lister-Burch speculum
Liston
—— forceps
—— knife
Liston-Stille forceps
Littauer
—— forceps

—— scissors
Littauer-Liston forceps
Littre suture
Litwak scissors
Litwin scissors
Livingston bar
Lloyd catheter
Lockwood
—— clamp
—— forceps
Loffler suture
Longdwel needle
Longmire-Storm clamp
Lonquet incision
Love
—— nasal splint
—— retractor
Love-Adson elevator
Love-Gruenwald forceps
Love-Kerrison forceps
Lovelace forceps
Lowe-Breck knife
Lowman clamp
Lowsley
—— forceps
—— prostatic tractor
Lucae
—— forceps
—— mallet
Luc ethmoid forceps
Luck fasciatome
Luedde exophthalmome-
  ter
Luer
—— curette
—— forceps
—— tube
Luer-Korte scoop
Luer-Whiting forceps
Luikart-Kielland forceps
Luikart-McLane forceps
Luikart-Simpson forceps
Lukens
—— aspirator
—— cannula
—— catgut suture
—— retractor
Lundsgaard blade
Lundsgaard-Burch sclero-
  tome
Luongo
—— cannula
—— curette
—— elevator
—— needle
Lusskin drill
Lutz forceps

Lyman-Smith brace
Lynch
—— forceps
—— spatula
—— suspension apparatus

MacAusland chisel
MacDonald clamp
MacIntosh blade
MacKay retractor
Mackenrodt incision
MacKenty
—— elevator
—— scissors
Mackler tube
Maclay scissors
Magielski
—— cautery
—— chisel
—— curette
—— elevator
—— forceps
—— needle
Magill
—— endotracheal tube
—— forceps
Magovern valve
Mahoney dilator
Maier dressing forceps
Maingot hemostat
Maisonneuve bandage
Malecot
—— catheter
—— drain
Maliniac retractor
Malis coagulator
Maloney bougie
Maltz
—— knife
—— rasp
—— saw
Maltz-Anderson rasp
Maltz-Lipsett rasp
Mandler filter
Marin bur
Markham-Meyerding retractor
Marlex
—— graft
—— mesh
—— suture
Martel clamp
Martin
—— bandage
—— clamp

—— forceps
—— pelvimeter
—— retractor
—— speculum
—— wire cutter
Mason incision
Masson
—— needle holder
—— stripper
Masson-Judd retractor
Mathew speculum
Matson elevator
Matzenauer speculum
Maumenee forceps
Maumenee-Park speculum
Maunsell suture
Mayfield
—— clip
—— curette
—— forceps
Mayo
—— cannula
—— carrier
—— clamp
—— forceps
—— hook
—— knife
—— linen suture
—— needle
—— probe
—— retractor
—— scissors
—— scoop
—— vein stripper
Mayo-Blake forceps
Mayo-Collins retractor
Mayo-Guyon clamp
Mayo-Harrington scissors
Mayo-Hegar needle holder
Mayo-Lovelace
—— clamp
—— retractor
Mayo-Myers stripper
Mayo-Noble scissors
Mayo-Ochsner forceps
Mayo-Robson
—— forceps
—— incision
—— position
—— scoop
Mayo-Russian forceps
Mayo-Sims scissors
McArthur incision
McBurney incision
McCarthy

—— cystoscope
—— electrode
—— electrotome
—— fiber optic telescope
—— forceps
—— fulgurating electrode
—— panendoscope
—— resectoscope
McCarthy-Alcock forceps
McCaskey
—— catheter
—— curette
McCleery-Miller clamp
McClure scissors
McCrea infant sound
McCullough forceps
McDermott clip
McFadden clip
McGee forceps
McGivney ligator
McGraw elastic ligature
McGuire scissors
McHenry forceps
McHugh
—— knife
—— speculum
McIntosh suture holder
McIver catheter
McIvor mouth gag
McKenzie
—— bur
—— clip
—— drill
McLane-Tucker forceps
McLaughlin incision
McLean
—— clamp
—— scissors
—— suture
McNealy-Glassman-Babcock forceps
McNealy-Glassman-Mixter
—— clamp
—— forceps
McPherson
—— forceps
—— needle holder
—— scissors
—— spatula
—— speculum
McPherson-Castroviejo scissors
McPherson-Pierse forceps
McPherson-Vannas scissors
McPherson-Wheeler knife

McPherson-Ziegler knife
McQuigg clamp
McReynolds knife
Measuroll suture
Medrafil suture wire
Meigs curette
Mellinger eye speculum
Meltzer punch
Menghini needle
Mercier catheter
Mercurio position
Mersilene
—— strip ligatures
—— suture
Merz forceps
Metras catheter
Metzenbaum
—— chisel
—— forceps
—— knife
—— scissors
Metzenbaum-Lipsett scissors
Meyerding
—— chisel
—— curette
—— gouge
—— mallet
—— osteotome
—— retractor
Meyer incision
Meyhoeffer curette
Michel
—— clamp
—— clip
—— forceps
Michele trephine
Michelson bronchoscope
Microspore surgical tape
Mikulicz
—— clamp
—— drain
Miles clamp
Miller
—— laryngoscope blade
—— scissors
—— speculum
Miller-Abbott tube
Millin
—— forceps
—— suction tube
Millin-Bacon
—— retractor
—— spreader
Mills forceps
Mitchell knife
Mixter

—— clamp
—— dilator
—— forceps
—— needle
—— tube
Mobin-Uddin
—— filter
—— umbrella
Moersch
—— bronchoscope
—— forceps
Mohr clamp
Moncrieff
—— cannula
—— irrigator
Montague
—— abrader
—— proctoscope
—— sigmoidoscope
Moore
—— chisel
—— drill
—— nail
—— pin
—— reamer
—— scoop
—— spoon
—— tracheostomy tube
Moorehead clamp
Morch tracheostomy tube
Moreno clamp
Morison incision
Morris drain
Morse scissors
Mosher
—— speculum
—— tube
Moynihan
—— clamp
—— forceps
—— probe
—— scoop
Moynihan-Navratil forceps
Mueller
—— bur
—— cautery
—— clamp
—— curette
—— eye cautery
—— forceps
—— needle
—— saw
Mueller-Balfour retractor
Mueller-Frazier tube
Mueller-LaForce adenotome

Mueller-Merz forceps
Mueller-Pool tube
Mueller-Pynchon tube
Mueller-Yankauer tube
Muer anoscope
Muir clamp
Muldoon dilator
Mules sphere implant
Muller clamp
Murdock-Weiner speculum
Murphy
—— button
—— chisel
—— dilator
—— needle
—— plaster cast knife
—— retractor
Museholdt forceps
Myers
—— forceps
—— punch
—— stripper
Myerson
—— forceps
—— saw
—— trocar
Myles
—— curette
—— speculum

Nabotoff stripper
Nachlas tube
Neal
—— cannula
—— catheter
Neivert
—— chisel
—— hook
—— needle holder
—— retractor
Nelaton catheter
Nelson
—— forceps
—— scissors
Nesbit
—— cystoscope
—— resectoscope
Nettleship-Wilder dilator
New
—— forceps
—— hook
—— needle
—— scissors
New-Lambotte osteotome

Newman proctoscope
New Margulies Spiral device
New Orleans stripper
Nichols
—— clamp
—— speculum
Nicola
—— clamp
—— raspatory
Niedner clamp
Nobis aortic occluder
Nolan-Budd curette
Norman bolt
Northbent scissors
Norwood snare
Nourse bladder syringe
Novak curette
Noyes forceps
Noyes-Shambaugh scissors
Nugent
—— forceps
—— hook
Nugent-Gradle scissors
Nunez clamp
Nussbaum clamp
Nylok bolt

O'Beirne tube
Oberhill retractor
O'Brien forceps
Ochsner
—— clamp
—— forceps
—— scissors
—— trocar
—— tube
Ochsner-Dixon forceps
Ockerblad clamp
O'Connor
—— clamp
—— hook
Oertli silk suture
Oldberg
—— dissector
—— retractor
—— rongeur
Olivecrona
—— clip
—— forceps
—— scissors
Ollier incision
Olsen-Hegar needle holder

O'Neill clamp
Orandi knife
Orr incision
O'Shaughnessy forceps
O'Sullivan-O'Connor
—— retractor
—— speculum
Ota ring
Otis
—— anoscope
—— bougie
—— sound
—— urethrotome
Ottenheimer dilator
Overholt
—— elevator
—— needle
Overholt-Jackson bronchoscope
Overstreet forceps
Owens
—— catheter
—— suture
Oyloiden suture

Padgett dermatome
Pagenstecher suture
Pajot hook
Palfyn suture
Palmer dilator
Pang forceps
Panzer scissors
Paparella
—— curette
—— elevator
—— fenestrometer
—— knife
—— needle
—— pick
—— retractor
—— scissors
—— tube
Paquelin cautery
Paré sutrue
Parham-Martin
—— band
—— clamp
Parker
—— clamp
—— incision
—— retractor
Park-Guyton speculum
Park speculum
Partipilo clamp
Paton needle holder

Patterson
—— forceps
—— trocar
Paufique
—— knife
—— trephine
Payr clamp
Péan
—— clamp
—— forceps
—— incision
—— position
Pearman implant
Pearsall silk suture
Pederson speculum
Pemberton clamp
Penfield
—— clip
—— dissector
Pennington
—— clamp
—— forceps
—— speculum
Penrose drain
Percy forceps
Pereya cannula
Perma-hand silk suture
Perritt forceps
Perthes incision
Peterson forceps
Petit suture
Petz clamp
Pezzer
—— catheter
—— drain
Pfannenstiel incision
Phaneuf forceps
Pharmaseal
—— catheter
—— drain
Phemister incision
Phiefer-Young retractor
Phillips
—— bougie
—— clamp
Picot speculum
Pierce
—— dissector
—— forceps
—— retractor
—— syringe
Pilcher catheter
Piper forceps
Pischel electrode
Pitkin
—— needle
—— syringe

Pleur-evac suction tube
Pley forceps
Plummer
—— bougie
—— dilator
Polley-Bickel trephine
Polydek sutrue
Poppen
—— clamp
—— coagulator
—— rongeur
Poppen-Blalock clamp
Porter forceps
Portex tube
Porto-vac suction tube
Posey safety belt
Potain
—— aspirator
—— trocar
Potts
—— clamp
—— forceps
—— rib shears
—— scissors
—— tenaculum
Potts-Niedner clamp
Potts-Satinsky clamp
Potts-Smith
—— clamp
—— forceps
—— scissors
Poufasse forceps
Pratt
—— anoscope
—— curette
—— dilator
—— director
—— hook
—— probe
—— speculum
Pratt-Smith forceps
Prentiss forceps
Preshaw clamp
Price-Thomas clamp
Prince
—— cautery
—— clamp
—— forceps
—— scissors
Pringle clamp
Pritchard syringe
Proctor retractor
Proetz syringe
Providence forceps
Pruitt
—— anoscope
—— proctoscope

Pudenz shunt
Purcell retractor
Putti rasp
Pynchon
—— applicator
—— tube

Quervain forceps
Quevedo forceps
Quincke-Babcock needle
Quisling hammer

Ralks
—— clamp
—— drill
Ramdohr suture
Ramstedt dilator
Randall
—— curette
—— forceps
Randolph cannula
Raney
—— clip
—— curette
—— forceps
—— Gigli saw guide
Rankin
—— clamp
—— forceps
—— retractor
Ranzewski clamp
Ratliff-Blake forceps
Ravich
—— bougie
—— cystoscope
Ravitch spreader
Ray
—— curette
—— forceps
Reaves punch
Recamier curette
Reese
—— dermatone
—— forceps
Reich-Nechtow
—— clamp
—— curette
—— dilator
—— forceps
Reiner curette
Reisinger forceps
Reverdin needle
Reynolds

—— clamp
—— traction tongs
Rezek forceps
Rheinstaedter curette
Rhinelander clamp
Ribble bandage
Richards
—— clamp
—— curette
Richardson-Eastman retractor
Richardson retractor
Richet bandage
Richter
—— forceps
—— suture
Ridlon plaster knife
Riecker bronchoscope
Riedel needle
Rienhoff clamp
Rienhoff-Finochietto rib spreader
Rigal suture
Rigby retractor
Riley needle
Ringenberg electrode
Risdon incision
Rish chisel
Ritchie tenaculum
Ritisch suture
Ritter
—— coagulator
Robb
—— forceps
—— needle
—— syringe
Robertazzi airway
Roberts
—— applicator
—— chisel
—— forceps
Robertson knife
Robinson
—— catheter
—— retractor
—— stone dislodger
Robinson-Jackson saw
Robinson-Smith graft tamper
Rochester
—— awl
—— clamp
—— elevator
—— forceps
—— needle
—— retractor
—— syringe

Rochester-Carmalt forceps
Rochester-Ewald forceps
Rochester-Ferguson
—— retractor
—— scissors
Rochester-Mixter forceps
Rochester-Péan forceps
Rochester-Rankin forceps
Rochester-Russian forceps
Rockey clamp
Rocky-Davis incision
Rodman incision
Rodriguez-Alvarez catheter
Roeder
—— clamp
—— forceps
Rogers dissector
Rolf
—— forceps
—— lance
Rollet incision
Rollett irrigator
Rommel-Hildreth cautery
Roosevelt clamp
Roper cannula
Rosen
—— explorer
—— fenestrater
—— incision
—— knife
—— probe
—— suction tube
Rosenmueller curette
Rosenthal speculum
Rose position
Roser mouth gag
Ross
—— catheter
—— retractor
Rosser hook
Roux retractor
Rowland
—— forceps
—— osteotome
Royce perforator
Rubin
—— clamp
—— needle
—— osteotome
Rubin-Holth punch
Rubovits clamp
Rumel
—— clamp
—— forceps

—— tourniquet
Rusch catheter
Ruschelit
—— bougie
—— catheter
Rush
—— clamp
—— extractor
—— mallet
—— reamer
Ruskin
—— forceps
—— needle
Russell forceps
Russian forceps
Ryerson tenotome
Ryle tube

Saafeld comedo extractor
Sachs
—— bur
—— retractor
—— spatula
—— suction tube
Saenger suture
Saf-T-Coil device
Saklad airway
Salibi clamp
Sanders
—— forceps
—— incision
Sandt forceps
Sani-dril suture
Santulli clamp
Sarnoff clamp
Sarot
—— clamp
—— forceps
—— needle holder
Satinsky
—— clamp
—— forceps
—— scissors
Satterlee saw
Sauer
—— debrider
—— speculum
Sauerbruch
—— retractor
—— rib shears
—— rongeur
Saunders-Paparella
—— hook
—— needle
—— rasp

Sauvage prosthesis
Sawtell
—— applicator
—— forceps
Sawyer retractor
Sayre apparatus
"S" cannula
Schamberg comedo extractor
Scheie
—— cautery
—— knife
Scherback-Porges speculum
Schindler gastroscope
Schlesinger punch forceps
Schmeden punch
Schmidt clamp
Schnidt forceps
Schobinger incision
Schoenberg forceps
Schroeder
—— forceps
—— scissors
Schrotters catheter
Schubert forceps
Schuknecht
—— chisel
—— gouge
—— knife
—— prosthesis
—— retractor
—— spatula
—— speculum
Schutz
—— clamp
—— clip
—— forceps
Schwartz
—— clip
—— forceps
Scott
—— cannula
—— suction tube
Scoville
—— curette
—— forceps
—— needle
—— retractor
Scoville-Greenwood forceps
Scoville-Lewis clip
Scudder
—— clamp
—— forceps
Scultetus position

Sedillot elevator
Segond forceps
Seiler
—— knife
—— scissors
Seldinger needle
Seletz cannula
Seletz-Gelpi retractor
Sellors clamp
Selman
—— clamp
—— forceps
—— traction clip
Selverstone
—— clamp
—— rongeur
Semb
—— forceps
—— retractor
—— rongeur
Semken forceps
Senn-Dingman retractor
Senning bulldog clamp
Senn retractor
Serature clip
Seutin bandage
Sewall
—— chisel
—— elevator
—— forceps
Sexton knife
Shaaf forceps
Shallcross forceps
Shambaugh
—— adenotome
—— elevator
—— hook
—— irrigator
—— needle
—— retractor
Shambaugh-Derlacki
—— chisel
—— elevator
Shambaugh-Lempert
knife
Shea
—— drill
—— hook
—— speculum holder
—— suction irrigator
Shearer
—— forceps
—— rongeur
Sheehan chisel
Sheehan-Gillies
—— needle holder
—— scissors

Sheehy
—— forceps
—— knife
—— tube
Sheehy-House prosthesis
Sheldon retractor
Sheldon-Swann needle
Shirodkar needle
Shoemaker
—— aortic clamp
—— shears
Shortbent scissors
Shrady saw
Shurly retractor
Siegel pneumatic oto-
scope
Silastic
—— adhesive
—— block
—— catheter
—— cuff
—— drain
—— implant
—— prosthesis
—— shunt
—— sponge
—— tube
Silverman needle
Simon
—— dermatome
—— incision
—— position
—— speculum
—— suture
Simplex screw compres-
sor
Simpson
—— forceps
—— sound
Sims
—— anoscope
—— curette
—— plug
—— position
—— probe
—— retractor
—— scissors
—— speculum
—— suture
Singleton incision
Sippy dilator
Sistrunk
—— retractor
—— scissors
Skeele curette
Skene
—— catheter

—— curette
—— forceps
Slaughter saw
Sloan
—— incision
—— retractor
Sluder guillotine
Sluder-Jansen mouth gag
Sluder-Sauer guillotine
Smart
—— forceps
—— scissors
Smead-Jones closure
Smellie perforator
Smillie knife
Smith
—— clamp
—— clip
—— electrode
—— expressor
—— forceps
—— knife
—— retractor
—— speculum
Smith-Green knife
Smith-Peterson
—— chisel
—— curette
—— forceps
—— nail
—— osteotome
—— pin
—— plate
—— prosthesis
—— reamer
—— rongeur
Smithwick
—— clamp
—— clip
—— forceps
—— hook
SMR speculum
Snellen suture
Snitman retractor
Solow sigmoidoscope
Somerset bur
Somers forceps
Sonnenschein speculum
Southey trocar
Southwick clamp
Souttar
—— cautery
—— tube
Spence-Adson forceps
Spence forceps
Spencer
—— probe

—— scissors
Spero meibomian forceps
Spica cast
Spratt curette
Spurling-Kerrison
—— forceps
—— rongeur
Spurling rongeur
Stallard suture
Stanmore prosthesis
Stanton clamp
Starlinger dilator
Stedman suction pump
Steele dilator
Steinmann pin
Stein perforator
Stepita clamp
Steri-drape
Steri-strip skin closure
Stern position
Stevens
—— forceps
—— tenotomy hook
—— tenotomy scissors
Stevenson
—— clamp
—— forceps
—— retractor
—— scissors
Stewart
—— hook
—— incision
Stille
—— clamp
—— chisel
—— drill
—— forceps
—— gouge
—— osteotome
—— rongeur
Stille-French needle holder
Stille-Giertz rib shears
Stille-Leksell rongeur
Stille-Liston forceps
Stille-Luer
—— forceps
—— rongeur
Stitt catheter
Stockman clamp
Stone
—— clamp
—— forceps
Stone-Holcombe clamp
Stookey rongeur
Storz-Beck snare
Storz-Iglesias resecto-

scope
Straight tenaculum
Stratte clamp
Strauss clamp
Strelinger clamp
Struempel forceps
Strully
—— curette
—— hook
—— scissors
Stryker
—— dermatome
—— saw
—— screw
Stubbs curette
Sugar clip
Sundt-Kees clip
Supramid suture
Surgaloy suture
Surgicel gauze
Surgiclip clip
Surgilon suture
Surgilope Sp suture
Surgi-Med clamp
Sutton needle
Swan clamp
Swan-Ganz catheter
Swanson prosthesis
Sweet
—— forceps
—— retractor
—— scissors
Sylva irrigator
Sztehlo clamp

Takahashi
—— forceps
—— punch
Tantalum mesh
Tarnier
—— basiotribe
—— forceps
Tatum clamp
Tatum-T
Tauber
—— catheter
—— spatula
Taylor
—— aspirator
—— blade
—— brace
—— curette
—— retractor
—— scissors
—— suture

Teflon
—— graft
—— mesh
Tenax lead
Tenner cannula
Teufel brace
Tevdek suture
Theden bandage
Theis retractor
Theobald probe
Thermistor probe
Thermo-flex suture
Thomas
—— cryoextractor
—— curette
—— splint
Thomas-Warren incision
Thompson
—— catheter
—— clamp
—— drape
—— resectoscope
—— syringe
Thoms
—— forceps
—— pelvimeter
Thoms-Gaylor forceps
Thorek
—— aspirator
—— scissors
Thorek-Feldman scissors
Thorek-Mixter forceps
Thornwald perforator
Thorpe
—— caliper
—— curette
—— forceps
—— scissors
Thorpe-Castroviejo scissors
Thorpe-Westcott scissors
Tiemann catheter
Tiemann-Coude catheter
Timberlake
—— evacuator
—— obturator
—— resectoscope
Tischler
—— forceps
—— punch
Titnius pigtail probe
Titus needle
Tobold-Fauvel forceps
Todd
—— bur hole button
—— gouge
Toennis scissors

Tomac catheter
Tooke knife
Toomey syringe
Torkildsen shunt
Totco clip
Touhy catheter
Tower retractor
Toynbee speculum
Trace stripper
Trattner catheter
Trendelenburg-Crafoord clamp
Trenedenburg position
Trousseau bougie
Trousseau-Jackson dilator
Troutman
—— chisel
—— forceps
Troutman-Barraquer needle holder
Trusler clamp
T-tube
Tubbs dilator
Tucker
—— bronchoscope
—— tube
Tucker-McLane forceps
Tudor-Edwards costotome
Tuffier
—— retractor
—— rib spreader
Tuffier-Raney retractor
Tuohy needle
Turek spreader
Turell
—— forceps
—— proctoscope
—— sigmoidoscope
Turkel
—— punch
—— trephine
Turner-Babcock forceps
Turner-Doyen retractor
Turner-Warwick
—— forceps
—— scissors
Tuttle
—— proctoscope
—— sigmoidoscope
Tycron suture
Tydings
—— forceps
—— snare
Tyrell hook

Uebe applicator
Ulrich
—— forceps
—— retractor
Undine dropper
Universal
—— cystoscope
—— forceps
—— saw
Unna comedo extractor
Urbantschitsch bougie
Usher Marlex mesh

Vacutome knife
Valentine
—— position
—— tube
Van Alyea
—— cannula
—— trocar
Van Buren
—— forceps
—— sound
Vanderbilt
—— clamp
—— forceps
Van Doren forceps
Vannas scissors
Van Struycken forceps
Vasconcelos-Baretto clamp
Veenema-Gusberg punch
Veenema retractor
Veirs erysiphake
Velcro tourniquet
Velpeau
—— bandage
—— sling
Verbrugge clamp
Verhoeff
—— forceps
—— scissors
—— suture
Vernon-David
—— proctoscope
—— sigmoidoscope
—— speculum
Vesien scissors
Viatrode electrode
Vicryl suture
Vi-drape surgical film
Vienna speculum
Villard button
Vim-Silverman needle
Vinke tong

Virchow
—— chisel
—— knife
Virden catheter
Viro-Tec suture
Virtus forceps
Visscher incision
Vitallium
—— mesh
—— nail
—— plate
—— screw
Vogel curette
Volkmann
—— curette
—— rake
—— retractor
von Graefe
—— cystotome
—— forceps
—— knife
von Petz
—— clamp
—— clip
von Saal pin

Wachsberger bur
Wachtenfeldt
—— clip
—— forceps
Wadsworth-Todd cautery
Wagner punch
Walcher position
Waldeau forceps
Waldmann scissors
Wales
—— bougie
—— dilator
Walker
—— curette
—— dissector
—— retractor
Walsham straightener
Walsh curette
Walter
—— forceps
—— spud
Walter-Deaver retractor
Walther
—— catheter
—— dilator
—— forceps
—— sound
Walther-Crenshaw clamp
Wangensteen

—— awl
—— carrier
—— clamp
—— dissector
—— dressing
—— forceps
—— needle
—— trocar
Wappler
—— cautery
—— cystoscope
—— electrode
Ward French needle
Warren incision
Warthen clamp
Waterman bronchoscope
Watson-Williams needle
Watts clamp
Weavenit graft
Weaver clamp
Webb
—— bolt
—— stripper
Weber
—— catheter
—— knife
Weber-Fergusson incision
Webril
Webster retractor
Weck clamp
Weder-Solenberger retractor
Weeks
—— needle
—— speculum
Weinberg
—— retractor
—— spreader
Weingartner
—— forceps
—— rongeur
Weisenbach forceps
Weitlaner retractor
Welch-Allyn
—— anoscope
—— forceps
—— hook
—— laryngoscope
—— probe
—— proctoscope
—— sigmoidoscope
—— speculum
—— transilluminator
Wellaminski perforator
Wells
—— clamp
—— pick

Wertheim
—— clamp
—— forceps
Wertheim-Cullen
—— clamp
—— forceps
Wertheim-Navratil needle
Westcott scissors
Wheeler
—— cyclodialysis spatula
—— cystome
—— knife
—— sphere implant
Whipple incision
Whistler bougie
Whitacre needle
White forceps
White-Lillie forceps
White-Oslay forceps
Whiting curette
Whitver clamp
Wiener hook
Wiener-Pierce
—— rasp
—— trocar
Wigmore plaster saw
Wilde
—— forceps
—— incision
—— punch
Wildgen-Reck metal locator
Wilkerson bur
Willett
—— clamp
—— forceps
Williams
—— craniotome
—— forceps
—— probe
—— speculum
Williamson needle
Wilmer
—— chisel
—— retractor
—— scissors
Wilson
—— awl
—— spreader
—— stripper
Wiltberger spreader
Winer catheter
Wis-Foregger laryngoscope
Wishard catheter
Wolf catheter
Wolfenden position

Wölfler suture
Wolf-Schindler gastroscope
Wolfson
—— clamp
—— retractor
Woodruff catheter
Woodson spoon
Woodward forceps
Worth chisel
Wullstein
—— bur
—— curette
—— forceps
—— knife
—— scissors
Wylie dilator
Wysler suture

Yamanda knife
Yankauer
—— bronchoscope
—— catheter
—— curette
—— esophagoscope
—— forceps
—— laryngoscope
—— needle
—— punch
—— speculum
—— suction tube
Yankauer-Little forceps
Yasargil
—— clamp
—— clip
—— dissector
—— forceps
—— knife
—— operating microscope
—— raspatory
—— retractor
—— scissors
—— scoop
Yazujian bur
Yellen clamp
Yeomans
—— forceps
—— proctoscope
—— punch
Young
—— clamp
—— dilator
—— enucleator
—— forceps
—— retractor

YSI thermistor probe

Zachary-Cope-Demartel
  clamp
Zavod catheter
Zeiss operating micro-
  scope
Ziegler
  —— cautery

—— dilator
—— forceps
—— knife
—— needle
—— probe
Ziegler-Furniss clamp
Zimaloy
  —— prosthesis
  —— staple
Zimmer
  —— bolt

—— clamp
—— drill
—— pin
—— sling
Zipper ring
Zipser clamp
Zoellner needle
Z-plasty incision
Zuelzer awl
Zutt clamp
Zytor suture

TRADE NAMES OF DRUGS

This list, although not comprehensive, contains the names of many of the most commonly used drugs.

Abbokinase
Acetophen
Acetyl-Sal
Achromycin
Achrostatin
Acidogen
Acidoride
Acidulin
Aci-Jel
Aclor
Acon
Acorto
Acriflex
Actamer
Actase
ACTHAR
Actidil
Actifed
Actospar
Acylanid
Adanon
Adapin
Adenex
Adrenalin
Adrestat
Adriamycin
Adroyd
Adsorbocarpine
Aerolone
Aeroseb
Aerosporin
Afaxin
A-Fil
Afrin
Airbron
Akineton
Akrinol
Albalon
Albamycin
Alboline
Albumisol
Albumotope
Alcaine
Alcopar
Aldactazide
Aldactone
Aldoclor
Aldomet
Alevaire
Alflorone
Alkagel
Alkeran
Alkets
Allbee
Allerest
Almora
Alpen

Alphadrol
Alphosyl-hc
Altacite
Al-U-Creme
Aludrine
Aludrox
Alupent
Alurate
Alu-Tab
Ambenyl
Ambodryl
Ambomycin
Ambutonium
Amchlor
Amcill
Amid-Sal
Amikin
Aminophyllin
Amipaque
Amitril
Amnestrogen
Amoebicon
Amoxil
Amphedrine
Amphex
Amphojel
Ampicin
Amylgestin
Amytal
Anacobin
Anadrol
Anafranil
Anahist
Analexin
Ananase
Anapolon
Anaprox
Anavar
Anayodin
Ancef
Ancobon
Androdiol
Android
Androlin
Andronate
Andrusol
Anectine
Anestacon
Angio-Conray
Anhydron
Anspor
Antabuse
Antepar
Anthra-Derm
Antilirium
Antiminth

Antivert
Antrenyl
Antrocol
Antuitrin
Anturane
Anusol
Apamide
Apodol
Apresazide
Apresoline
AquaMephyton
Aquamox
Aquasol
Aquatensen
Aralen
Aramine
Arcofac
Ar-Ex
Arfonad
Argyrol
Aristocort
Aristoderm
Aristospan
Arlidin
Artane
Arthropan
Asbron
Ascorbin
Ascoril
Ascriptin
Asendin
Asterol
Atabrine
Atarax
Athrombin-K
Ativan
Atromid-S
Auralgan
Aureomycin
Avazyme
Aveeno
Aventyl
Avertin
Avlosulfon
Azene
Azochloramid
Azodyne
Azo Gantanol
Azo Gantrisin
Azo-Mandelamine
Azotrex
Azulfidine

Baciguent
Bacimycin

Bactrim
Banthine
Barbidonna
Barosperse
Basaljel
Beclovent
Beconase
Becotin
Belladenal
Bellafoline
Bellergal
Beminal
Benadryl
Benasept
Benemid
Benoquin
Benoxaprofen
Benoxyl
Bentyl
Benylin
Benzapas
Benzedrine
Berocca
Berubigen
Betadine
Betalin
Betapar
Betapen-VK
Bewon
Bicillin
BiCNU
Bilopaque
Bilron
Biogastrone
Biopar
Blenoxane
Bleph-10
Bonamine
Bonine
Borofax
Bradosol
Brethine
Bretylol
Brevicon
Brevital
Bricanyl
Bristamycin
Bromsulphalein
Bronchovent
Brondecon
Bronkephrine
Bronkodyl
Bronkolixir
Bronkosol
Buro-Sol
Buta-Barb
Butazolidin

Butibel
Butisol
Butyn

Cafergot
Calcidrine
Calciferol
Calcimar
Caldesene
Calurin
Camalox
Camoquin
Candeptin
Cantharone
Cantil
Capastat
Caprocin
Carbased
Carbocaine
Carbrital
Cardiazol
Cardilate
Cardiografin
Cardioquin
Cardrase
Caroid
Cartrax
Catapres
Catarase
Cathomycin
Ceclor
Cedilanid
Ceepryn
Cefadyl
Cefol
Celbenin
Celestone
Cellothyl
Cenolate
Centrax
Centrum
Cepacol
Cephulac
Cetamide
Cetazine
Cevalin
Cevex
Ce-Vi-Sol
Chel-Iron
Chemipen
Cheracol
Chinosol
Chloraseptic
Chlorazene
Chloresium
Chloromycetin
Chloroprednisone
Chloroptic
Chlor-Trimeton
Chlor-Tripolon
Cholebrine
Choledyl

Cholografin
Choloxin
Chronulac
Chymar
Cinchophen
Cinobac
Citanest
Cleocin
Clinoril
Clistin
Clomid
Clonopin
Clopane
Cloxapen
Cobroxin
Cogentin
Colace
ColBENEMID
Coldecon
Cologel
Colprone
Coly-Mycin
Combipres
Compazine
Comycin
Conar
Conray
Constiban
Contac
Contratuss
Co-Pyronil
Coramine
Cordran
Corgard
Coricidin
Corivin
Cor-Tar-Quin
Cort-Dome
Cortef
Cortenema
Cortisporin
Cortogen
Cortone
Cortril
Cortrophin
Cortrosyn
Cosmegen
Cotazym
Coumadin
Covicone
Creamalin
Cruex
Crysticillin
Crystodigin
Cuprex
Cuprimine
Cyclapen
Cyclocort
Cyclogyl
Cyclopal
Cyclopar
Cyclospasmol
Cylert
Cystospaz

Cytadren
Cytellin
Cytomel
Cytosar
Cytoxan

Dactil
Dainite
Dalacin
Dalmane
Danalone
Danocrine
Dantrium
Daranide
Daraprim
Darbid
Darcil
Darenthin
Daricon
Darvocet-N
Darvon
Datril
Deaner
Debrisan
Debrox
Decaderm
Decadron
Deca-Durabolin
Decapryn
Decholin
Declomycin
Deconamine
Decortin
Degest
Dehydrocholin
Delalutin
Delatestryl
Delestrogen
Delfen
Delta-Cortef
Deltalin
Deltasone
Demazin
Demerol
Demi-Regroton
Demulen
Denyl
Depakene
Depen
Depo-Estradiol
Depo-Medrol
Depo-Provera
Depo-Testosterone
Desenex
Desferal
Desoxyn
Desquam-X
Desyphed
Dexamyl
Dexasone
Dexedrine
DEXTROSTIX

DiaBeta
Diabinese
Diafen
Diamox
Diamthazole
Dianabol
Dibenzyline
Dicarbosil
Dicodid
Dicumarol
Dicurin
Didrex
Digifortis
Digiglusin
Digitaline Nativelle
Digitora
Dilantin
Dilaudid
Dilin
Dimacol
Dimelor
Dimetane
Dimetapp
Dionosil
Di-Paralene
Diprosone
Disipal
Disophrol
Diucardin
Diulo
Diupres
Diuril
Diutensen
Doca
Dolonil
Dolophine
Domeboro
Donnacin
Donnagel
Donnamine
Donnatal
Dopar
Dopram
Doraxamin
Dorbane
Doriden
Dormethan
Dormin
Dorsacaine
Dramamine
Drisdol
Drixoral
Drolban
Droxolan
Dulcolax
Duphalac
Duphaston
Durabolin
Duracillin
Duricef
Dyazide
Dyclone
Dymelor
Dynapen

Dyrenium

Ecofrol
Ecolid
Ecotrin
Edecrin
Efedron
Efudex
Elavil
Eldopaque
Eldoquin
Elixophyllin
Elspar
Emetrol
Emko
Emprazil
E-Mycin
Enarax
Endep
Endotussin-NN
Enduron
Enduronyl
Enfamil
Enovid
Entero-Vioform
Enzactin
Enzeon
Ephedrol
Epifrin
Epinal
Epitrate
Eppy
Eprolin
Epsilan
Equagesic
Equanil
Equanitrate
Equinex
Ergomar
Ergostat
Ergotrate Maleate
Erypar
Erythrocin
Esidrix
Esimil
Eskabarb
Eskalith
Eskatrol
Estinyl
Estrace
Estradurin
Estrovis
Ethamide
Ethaquin
Ethiodol
Ethrane
Ethril
Eticylol
Etrafon
Eurax
Euthroid
Eutonyl

Eutron
ExNa
Exorbin

Fastin
Fedahist
Fedrazil
Femogen
Fenicol
Feosol
Fergon
Fer-in-Sol
Fero-Grad
Ferralyn
Ferrolip
Ferronord
Ferro-Sequels
Festal
Festalan
Fibrindex
Filibon
Fiogesic
Fiorinal
Firon
Flagyl
Flaxedil
Fleet
Flexeril
Floraquin
Florinal
Florinef
Florone
Floropryl
Fluor-I-Strip
Fluoromar
Fluoroplex
Fluothane
Follutein
Folvite
Forhistal
Fortespan
Fostex
Foxalin
FreAmine
Frenquel
Fugillin
Ful-Glo
Fulvicin
Fungacetin
Fungizone
Furacin
Furadantin
Furoxone

Gamophen
Gantanol
Gantrisin
Garamycin
Gardenal
Gaviscon

Gelusil
Gemonil
Gentran
Geocillin
Geopen
Geriplex
Gesterol
Gevrabon
Glaucon
Glucola
Glucosol
Gly-Oxide
Glysennid
Grifulvin
Grisactin
Gris-PEG
Gynergen

Haldol
Haldrone
Halotestin
Halotex
Harmonyl
Hedulin
Hemo-Vite
Heptuna
Herplex
Hetrazan
Hexa-Betalin
Hexadrol
Hexalet
Hexavibex
Hibitane
Hippuran
Hipputope
Hiprex
Hispril
Histabid
Histadyl
Histalet
Histalog
Holocaine
Hormonin
Humatin
Humorsol
Hybephen
Hycodan
Hycomine
Hydeltra
Hydeltrasol
Hydergine
Hydrazide
Hydrocortone
HydroDiuril
Hydromox
Hydropres
Hydrozide
Hygroton
Hykinone
Hypaque
Hyperstat
Hyskon

Hytakerol
Hytone

Iberet
Iberol
Iletin
Ilidar
Ilopan
Ilosone
Ilotycin
Imavate
Imferon
Imodium
Imuran
Inapsine
Inderal
Inderide
Indocid
Indocin
Indoklon
Inflamase
Inhiston
Innovar
Insulin
Intal
Intropin
Inversine
Iodotope
Ionamin
Ionosol
Ismelin
Isobarb
Isoclor
Isocrin
Isodine
Isofedrol
Iso-Iodeikon
Isomil
Isopaque
Isopto Atropine
Isopto Carbachol
Isopto Carpine
Isopto Cetamide
Isopto Eserine
Isopto Frin
Isopto Homatropine
Isopto Hyoscine
Isordil
Isosorb
Isuprel
Ivadantin

Kafocin
Kantrex
Kaochlor
Kaon
Kappadione
Karidium
Kay Ciel
Kayexalate

Keflex
Keflin
Kefzol
Kemadrin
Kenacort
Kenalog
Ketaject
Ketalar
Ketamine
Ketochol
K-Lor
Klorvess
Klotrix
K-Lyte
Kolantyl
Konakion
Kondremul
Konsyl
Koromex
Kwell

Lacril
Lanacillin
Lanoxin
Largactil
Largon
Larodopa
Larotid
Lasan
Lasix
Laxa-Tab
Ledercillin
Lederplex
Lenetran
Leritine
Leucovorin
Leukeran
Levo-Dromoran
Levopa
Levophed
Levoprome
Levsin
Levsinex
Levucal
Librax
Libritabs
Librium
Lidex
Lidone
Limbitrol
Linocin
Lioresal
Lipo Gantrisin
Lipo-Lutin
Liposyn
Liquaemin
Liquamar
Liquiprin
Listica
Lithane
Lithonate
Lobeline

Locorten
Loestrin
Lomotil
Loniten
Lopressor
Lorfan
Loridine
Lotrimin
Lotusate
Loxitane
Ludiomil
Lufyllin
Luminal
Lutocylol
Lutrexin
Lynoral
Lyophrin
Lysodren
Lyteca

Maalox
Macrodantin
Macrodex
Madribon
Magnacort
Malogen
Mandelamine
Mandol
Mannitol
Manvene
Maolate
Marax
Marcaine
Marezine
Marplan
Matulane
Maxibolin
Maxidex
Mebaral
Mecholyl
Medihaler-Epi
Medihaler-Iso
Medrol
Megace
Megimide
Melfiat
Mellaril
Menomune
Menrium
Mepergan
Mephyton
Meprane
Meprospan
Mequin
Mercresin
Mercuhydrin
Mercurochrome
Mercurophyllin
Mersalyn
Merthiolate
Mesantoin
Mestinon

Metahydrin
Metamine
Metamucil
Metandren
Metaprel
Metaspas
Metatensin
Methergine
Methosarb
Meticortelone
Meticorten
Meti-Derm
Metopirone
Metrazol
Metubine
Metycaine
Micatin
Micofur
Microcort
Micronor
Midicel
Midrin
Milontin
Miltown
Miltrate
Minipress
Minizide
Minocin
Mintezol
Miochol
Miostat
Miradon
Mithracin
Moban
Modane
Moderil
Modicon
Mol-Iron
Monistat
Motrin
Mucilose
Mucogel
Mucomyst
Mudrane
Multifuge
Muracil
Mustargen
Mutamycin
Myadec
My-B-Den
Mycelex
Mycifradin
Myciguent
Mycil
Mycolog
Mycostatin
Mydriacyl
Mylanta
Mylaxen
Myleran
Mylicon
Myochrysine
Myroflex
Mysoline

Mysteclin
Mytelase

Nafcil
Naldecon
Nalfon
Naprosyn
Naproxen
Naqua
Naquival
Narcan
Nardil
Narspan
Natabec
Natafort
Natcyn
Natulan
Naturetin
Nauseatol
Navane
Nebcin
Nefrolan
NegGram
Nembutal
Neobiotic
Neo-Calglucon
Neocin
Neo-Cortef
NeoDECADRON
Neo-Delta-Cortef
Neo-Hombreol
Neo-Hydeltrasol
Neolin
Neo-Medrol
Neo-Mercazole
Neosporin
Neo-Synalar
Neo-Synephrine
Neotrizine
Neptazane
Nesacaine
Nethamine
Neutra-Phos
Niac
Nicalex
Nicobid
Niconyl
Nico-Span
Nicozide
Nilcol
Nilstat
Nipride
Nisentil
Nitro-Bid
Nitroglyn
Nitrol
Nitrong
Nitrospan
Nitrostat
Noctec
Nolamine
Noludar

Norflex
Norgesic
Norinyl
Norisodrine
Norlestrin
Norlutate
Norlutin
Norpramin
Noscatuss
Novafed
Novahistine
Novocain
Novocain-Suprarenin
Nubain
Nujol
Nupercainal
Nupercaine
Nutracort
Nydrazid
Nyloxin
Nytol

Obetrol
Octyl
Ogen
Omnipen
Oncovin
Ophthaine
Ophthetic
Orabilex
Oragrafin
Oratrol
Oretic
Oreticyl
Oreton
Organidin
Orinase
Ornade
Ortho-Novum
Orthoxine
Os-Cal
Osmitrol
Otobiotic
Otocort
Otrivin
Ouabain
Ovcon
Ovocylin
Ovol
Ovral
Ovrette
Ovulen
Oxsoralen
Oxycel
Oxylone

Pabalate
Pabanol
Pagitane
Palaflor

Palfium
Paludrine
Pamelor
Pamine
Pancrease
Panmycin
Panoxyl
Panparnit
Panthoderm
Pantholin
Pantopaque
Pantopon
Panwarfin
Papase
Paracort
Paradione
Paraflex
Parafon
Parasal
Parazine
Parlodel
Parnate
Parsidol
Paskalium
Pathibamate
Pathilon
Pathocil
Pavabid
Paveril
Pavulon
Pedameth
Pedi-Dent
Pediamycin
Peganone
Penapar
Penasoid
Penbritin
Pendiomid
Pensyn
Pentazine
Penthrane
Pentids
Pentothal
Pentritol
Pen-Vee-K
Peptavlon
Perandren
Percocet
Percodan
Percogesic
Percorten
Perdiem
Pergonal
Peri-Colace
Periactin
Peritrate
Permapen
Permitil
Pernaemon
Persa-gel
Persantine
Pertofrane
Pfi-Lithium
Pfizerpen

Phanodorn
Phazyme
Phe-Mer-Nite
Phenaphen
Phenazine
Phenazo
Phenbutazone
Phenergan
Phenolor
Phenoxene
Phenurone
pHisoDerm
pHisoHex
pHos-pHaid
Phosphaljel
Phospholine
Phrenilin
Phyllocontin
Pipanol
Pitocin
Pitressin
Pituitrin
Placidyl
Plaquenil
Plasmochin
Platinol
Plegine
Plexonal
Polaramine
Polybrene
Polycillin
Polycycline
Polymagma
Polymox
Polysorb
Poly-Vi-Sol
Pondimin
Ponstel
Pontocaine
Povan
Prantal
Pred Mild
Pregnyl
Preludin
Premarin
Presamine
Pre-Sate
Principen
Priodax
Priscoline
Privine
Pro-Banthine
Probec-T
Progesic
Progynon
Proketazine
Prolax
Prolixin
Proloid
Proloprim
Promaquid
Pronestyl
Propaderm
Propadrine

Propion
Prostaphlin
Prostin
Protopam
Proventil
Provera
Purodigin
Pyopen
Pyra-Maleate
Pyribenzamine
Pyrictal
Pyridium
Pyronil

Quaalude
Quadnite
Quadrinal
Quarzan
Quelicin
Quertine
Questran
Quibron
Quide
Quilene
Quinaglute
Quinamm
Quinidex
Quinolor
Quotane

Radio-Cholografin
Raubaserp
Raudixin
Rauren
Raurine
Rau-Sed
Rautensin
Rauwiloid
Rauzide
Rectacort
Redisol
Regitine
Reglan
Regroton
Regutol
Rela
Renese
Renografin
Renoquid
Renovist
Repoise
Resercen
Reserpoid
Reticulogen
Retin-A
Rheomacrodex
Rhindecon
Rhinex
RhoGAM
Rifadin

Rimactane
Riopan
Ritalin
Robalate
Robaxin
Robaxisal
Robicillin
Robimycin
Robinul
Robitussin
RoeriBeC
Romilar
Roniacol
Rovamycine
Rubramin
Rynatan
Rynatuss

Salazopyrin
Sal-Ethyl
Salophen
Saluron
Salutensin
Sandril
Sanorex
Sansert
Santyl
Seconal
Sedamyl
Segontin
Selacryn
Selsun
Senokot
Septra
Ser-Ap-Es
Serax
Serenium
Serentil
Seromycin
Serpasil
Serpate
Serpoid
Sethotope
Sidonna
Silain
Silvadene
Sinaxar
Sinemet
Sinequan
Singoserp
Sinografin
Sintrom
Sinubid
Sinulin
Sinutab
SK-Ampicillin
Skelaxin
Skiodan
Slo-phyllin
Slow-K
Softran
Solfoton
Solganal

Solu-Cortef
Solu-Medrol
Soma
Sombulex
Somophyllin
Soneryl
Sonilyn
Sopor
Sopronol
Sorbitrate
Sordinol
Sotradecol
Sparine
Stadol
Staphcillin
Statobex
Statomin
Stelazine
Stemetil
Sterane
Stilphostrol
Stoxil
Stresscaps
Stresstabs
Striatran
Sublimaze
Sucaryl
Sucostrin
Sudafed
Suladyne
Sulfose
Sulla
Sumycin
Supen
Surbex
Surfacaine
Surfak
Surital
Surmontil
Sus-Phrine
Symmetrel
Synacthen
Synalar
Synalgos
Syncillin
Syncurine
Synemol
Synkayvite
Synophylate
Synthroid
Syntocinon
Sytobex

Tacaryl
Tace
Tagamet
Taka-Diastase
Talwin
Tandearil
Tao
Tapazole
Taractan
Tarbonis

Tarcortin
Tavist
T-Caps
Tedral
Tegopen
Tegretol
Teldrin
Telepaque
Temaril
Temposil
Tempra
Tenormin
Tensilon
Tenuate
Tepanil
Terfonyl
Terra-Cortril
Terramycin
Terrastatin
Tersaseptic
Teslac
Tessalon
Testrone
Tetracaps
Tetracyn
Tetrastatin
Tetrex
Tham
Theelin
Theobid
Theo-Dur
Theoglycinate
Theokin
Theolair
Theolixir
Theophyl
Thera-Combex
Theragran
Theruhistin
Thioguanine
Thiomerin
Thiosulfil
Thiotepa
Thorazine
Thrombolysin
Thyrar
Thyrolar
Thytropar
Ticar
Tigan
Timolol
Timoptic
Tinactin
Tindal
Titralac
Tocosamine
Tofranil
Tolectin
Toleron
Tolinase
Tolseram
Topicort
Topsyn
Torantil

Torecan
Totacillin
Tral
Trancopal
Transderm
Tranxene
Trasylol
Travase
Travert
Trecator
Trest
Triaminic
Triaminicin
Triavil
Triclos
Tricofuron
Tridesilon
Tridione
TriHEMIC
Trilafon
Trilisate
Trimeton
Trimox
Trinsicon
Trionamide
Trisem
Trisogel
Trisoralen
Trobicin
Trocinate
Tronothane
Trophenium
Trophite
Tuinal
Turbinaire
Tussagesic
Tuss-Ornade
Tybatran
Tylenol
Tylox

Ulo
Ultandren
Unicap
Unipen
Unipres
Unitensen
Ureaphil
Urecholine
Urex
Urised
Urispas
Urobiotic
Uroscreen
Uticillin VK
Uticort
Uval

Vagisec Plus
Vagitrol
Valadol
Valisone

Valium	Ventolin	Vlem-Dome	Xylocaine
Valmid	Ventolin	Vonedrine	
Valpin 50	Veracillin	Vontrol	
Vancenase	Veriloid	Voranil	
Vanceril	Vermizine	VOXIN-PG	Yodoxin
Vancocin	Versapen	Vytone	Yomesan
Vanobid	Verstran		
Vanoxide-HC	Vesprin		
Vanquin	Viadril		
Vaponefrin	Vibazine	Wigraine	Zactane
Varidase	Vibramycin	Wingel	Zactirin
Vasocon	Vicon	Winstrol	Zarontin
Vasodilan	Vi-Daylin	Wyamine	Zaroxolyn
Vasoxyl	Vinactane	Wycillin	Zephiran
V-Cillin	Vinblastine	Wydase	Zetar
Vectrin	Vincristine	Wygesic	Zincofax
Veetids	Vioform		Zolyse
Velacycline	Viokase		Zomax
Velban	Vistaril		Zorane
Velosef	Vivactil	Xeroform	Zyloprim

SOUND-SPELLING CORRESPONDENCES

The following table is designed to aid the user in locating in the list words whose pronunciation is known but whose spelling presents difficulties. Such difficulties are caused by the fact that so many speech sounds can be spelled in more than one way, since the standard alphabet has twenty-six characters to represent the forty or more sounds used in the English language. If you are unable to find a word when you look it up, check this table and try another combination of letters that represent the same sound.

Sound	Spelling	In these sample words
a (as in pat)	ai	plaid
	al	half-life
	au	laugh
a (as in mane)	ai	pain, ailurophobia, ainhum
	ao	gaol
	au	gauge
	ay	pay
	e	suede, bouquet
	ea	break, great
	ei	vein
	eig	feign
	eigh	eight, neighbor
	ey	fey
a (as in care)	ae	aerial, aerobic
	ai	air
	ay	prayer
	e	there, where
	ea	pear
	ei	Eire
a (as in father)	ah	ah
	al	balm, calm
	e	sergeant
	ea	heart
b (as in bib)	bb	blubber, cabbage
	bh	bhang
	pb	cupboard, raspberry
ch (as in church)	c	cello
	Cz	Czech, Czerny
	tch	latch, patch, stitch
	ti	question
	tu	denture
d (as in deed)	bd	bdellium, bdelygmia
	dd	ladder
	ed	mailed
	dh	dhobie

345

Sound	Spelling	In these sample words
e (as in pet)	a	any
	ae	aesthetic, haematolysis
	ai	said
	ay	says
	ea	thread
	ei	heifer
	eo	leopard
	ie	friendly
	oe	roentgen, oestrus
	u	burial
e (as in be)	ae	Caesar, haemoglobin
	ay	quay
	ea	each, beach
	ee	beet
	ei	conceit
	eo	people
	ey	key
	i	piano, hemicardia
	ie	siege
	oe	phoenix, amoeba
	y	ichthyosis, tracheotomy
f (as in fife)	ff	stiff
	gh	enough
	lf	half
	ph	photo, phosphate, aphtha, esophagus, graph, sphincter
g (as in gag)	gg	bragged
	gh	ghost
	gu	guest
	gue	epilogue
h (as in hat)	wh	who
	g	Gila monster
	j	Jerez
i (as in pit)	a	village, climate
	e	enough
	ee	been
	ia	carriage
	ie	sieve
	o	women
	u	busy
	ui	built
	y	cyst, erythremia, dystrophy, onychia, pharynx, myxoma
i (as in pie)	ai	aisle, aichmophobia, guaiac
	ay	aye, bayou
	ei	height, eidetic, meiosis, leiomyoma
	ey	eye
	ie	lie

Sound	Spelling	In these sample words
i (as in pie)	igh	sigh, right
	is	island, islet
	uy	buy
	y	sky, myograph, chymotrypsin, achylia
	ye	rye
i (as in pier)	e	here
	ea	ear
	ee	beer
	ei	weird
j (as in jar)	d	gradual
	dg	lodging
	di	soldier
	dj	adjective
	g	register, geraniol, argyria
	ge	vengeance
	gg	exaggerate
k (as in kick)	c	call, ecstasy, cachexia, eczema
	cc	account, saccular, eccrine
	cch	ecchymosis, saccharin
	ch	chaos, schedule, cochlea, ichthyosis, chyle, acholia, schizophrenia, diaschistic
	ck	crack
	cqu	lacquer
	cu	biscuit
	lk	talk
	q	Aqaba
	qu	quay
	que	plaque, torque
kw (as in quick)	ch	choir
	cqu	acquire
l (as in lid)	ll	tall, llama
	lh	Lhasa
m (as in mum)	chm	drachm
	gm	paradigm, phlegm
	lm	balm
	mb	plumb
	mm	hammer
	mn	solemn
n (as in no)	cn	cnemis, gastrocnemium
	gn	gnat, gnathic, gnosis
	kn	knife
	mn	mnemasthenia, mnemonic, panmnesia
	nn	canny, cachinnation, inn
	pn	pneumonia, pnigma

Sound	Spelling	In these sample words
ng (as in thing)	n	congress, anchor, ink, uncle
	ngue	tongue
o (as in pot)	a	waffle, watch, water, what
	ho	honest
	ou	trough
o (as in no)	au	hautboy, mauve
	eau	beau, bureau
	eo	yeoman
	ew	sew
	oa	foal, foam
	oe	Joe
	oh	oh
	oo	brooch
	ou	shoulder
	ough	borough, dough
	ow	low, row
	owe	owe, Marlowe
o (as in paw or for)	a	all, water
	al	talk
	ah	Utah
	ar	warm
	as	Arkansas
	au	caught, gaunt, aulophobia
	aw	awful, awe
	oa	broad, oar
	ough	bought
oi (as in noise)	oy	boy
ou (as in out)	au	sauerkraut
	aue	sauerbraten
	hou	hour
	ough	bough
	ow	scowl, sow
oo (as in took)	o	woman, wolf
	ou	should
	u	cushion, full
oo (as in boot)	eu	leukemia, maneuver, rheumatic
	ew	shrew
	ieu	lieutenant
	o	do, move, two
	oe	canoe
	ou	group, soup
	ough	through
	u	rude
	ue	blue, flue
	ui	bruise, fruit
p (as in pop)	pp	happy, stipple

Sound	Spelling	In these sample words
r (as in roar)	rh	rhabdocyte, rhegma, rhythm
	rr	cherry
	rrh	cirrhosis, hemorrhoid, scirrhous
	wr	write
s (as in say)	c	ancylostomiasis, cellar, cyst, decidua, lecithin
	ce	sauce
	ps	psalm, pseudocyst, iliopsoas
	sc	scene, sciatic, abscess, ascites, monoscelous, dehiscence
	sch	schism
	ss	pass, byssinosis
	sth	isthmus, isthmic
sh (as in ship)	ce	oceanic
	ch	chandelier, chancre
	ci	special, deficient
	psh	pshaw
	s	sugar
	sc	conscience
	sch	schist, schistosis
	se	nauseous
	si	pension
	ss	tissue, mission
	ti	election, nation
t (as in tie)	ct	ctenoids
	ed	stopped
	ght	caught
	phth	phthisis, phthisiology
	pt	ptosis, ptyalism, pterygium
	th	Thomas
	tt	letter
	tw	two
th (as in think)	chth	chthonophagy
	phth	phthalic, phthiocol
u (as in cut)	o	son, income
	oe	does
	oo	blood
	ou	couple, trouble
yoo (as in use)	eau	beautiful
	eu	feud, eugenic, euphoria
	eue	queue
	ew	pew
	ieu	adieu
	iew	view
	u	ulotomy, unipennate
	ue	cue
	ui	suit
	you	you
	yu	yule

Sound	Spelling	In these sample words
u (as in fur)	ear	earn, learn
	er	herd, fern, term
	eur	restaurateur
	ir	bird, first
	or	work, word
	our	journey, journal, scourge
	yr	myrtle
	yrrh	myrrh
v (as in valve)	f	of
	ph	Stephen
w (as in with)	o	one
	ou	ouabain
	u	guanase, guanine, guaiacol
y (as in yes)	i	onion
	j	hallelujah
z (as in zebra)	cz	czar
	s	rise, hers
	ss	dessert
	x	xylophone, xiphoid, xanthocyte, ilioxiphopagus
	zz	fuzz
zh	ge	garage, mirage
	s	pleasure, vision

Note: The letter *x* spells six sounds in English: ks, as in box, exit; gz, as in exact, exist; sh, as in anxious; gzh, as in luxurious, luxury; ksh (a variant of gzh), also as in luxurious, luxury; and z, as in anxiety, Xerox.

ABBREVIATIONS

In accordance with the style preferred by the American Medical Association, no periods are used in the following list of abbreviations.

A

A absolute; acetum; area of heart shadow; mass number
A absorbance
A₂ aortic second sound
Å angstrom unit
a accommodation; anterior; aqua; arteria
a absorptivity
AA achievement age; Alcoholics Anonymous
abd abdomen
abort abortion
AC air conduction; alternating current; anodic closure; axiocervical
Ac acetyl
ac, a-c alternating current
ACE adrenocortical extract
ACG apex cardiogram
acG accelerator globulin (factor V)
AcPase acid phosphatase
ACTH adrenocorticotropic hormone
AD right ear (*auris dextra*)
Ad anisotropic disk
ADC anodic duration contraction; axiodistocervical
ADH antidiuretic hormone
A disk anisotropic disk
ADP adenosine diphosphate
ADPase adenosine diphosphatase
AGA accelerated growth area
A/G ratio albumin-globulin ratio
ah hypermetropic astigmatism
AHF antihemophilic factor (factor VIII)
AHG antihemophilic globulin (factor VIII)
AI aortic insufficiency
AJ ankle jerk
AK above knee
alb albumin
AM amperemeter
am ametropia; meter-angle; myopic astigmatism

AMA against medical advice
AMI acute myocardial infarction
AML acute myoblastic leukemia
AMP adenosine monophosphate
amp amperage; ampere; ampule
AMpase adenosine monophosphatase
An anisometropia; anodal; anode
anat anatomic; anatomical; anatomy
ANS anterior nasal spine; autonomic nervous system
A-P anteroposterior
A+P auscultation and percussion
APC aspirin, phenacetin, and caffeine
APC virus adenovirus
A-P&Lat anteroposterior and lateral
APF animal protein factor (vitamin B₁₂)
AQ achievement quotient
AQRS mean manifest electrical axis of the QRS complex
AR alarm reaction
ARD acute respiratory disease
AS left ear (*auris sinistra*)
ASCVD arteriosclerotic cardiovascular disease
ASLO antistreptolysin-O
Ast astigmatism
AT mean manifest magnitude of repolarization of the myocardium
ATCC American Type Culture Collection
atm atmosphere
ATN acute tubular necrosis
ATP adenosine triphosphate
ATPase adenosine triphosphatase
ATS equine antitetanus serum
at vol atomic volume
at wt atomic weight
AV arteriovenous;

atrioventricular; auriculoventricular
Av avoirdupois weight
aV augmented unipolar limb lead
ax axis
Az azote
AZT Aschheim-Zondek test

B

B bacillus; boils at; buccal
BBB bundle branch block
BBT basal body temperature
BE barium enema
bev billion electron volts
BFP biologic false positive reaction
BM bowel movement
BMR basal metabolic rate
BNA Basle Nomina Anatomica
BP blood pressure; British Pharmacopoeia
bp boiling point
BR British or Birmingham Revision
BS blood sugar; breath sounds
BSA body surface area
BSR blood sedimentation rate
BTU British thermal unit
BUN blood urea nitrogen

C

C canine of second dentition; cathode; Celsius; centigrade; chest; closure; contraction; cylinder
c centum; deciduous canine
CA chronological age
Ca cancer
Cal large calorie
cal small calorie
CAR conditioned avoidance response
CBC complete blood count
CBG corticosteroid-binding globulin

CBS chronic brain syndrome
CC chief complaint
cc cubic centimeter
Ccr creatinine clearance
CCU coronary care unit
cd candela
CDC Center for Disease Control
CER conditioned escape response
CFT complement-fixation test
cg centigram
CHD congenital heart disease; coronary heart disease
CHINA chronic infectious neuropathic agent
CI color index
Ci curie
CID cytomegalic inclusion disease
cl centiliter
CLSH corpus luteum stimulating hormone
cm centimeter
cmm cubic millimeter
CMR cerebral metabolic rate
CNS central nervous system
CoA coenzyme A
COPD chronic obstructive pulmonary disease
CP chemically pure
CPD cephalopelvic disproportion
cpm cycles per minute
cps cycles per second
CR conditioned reflex; conditioned response
CRM cross-reacting material
CRS Chinese restaurant syndrome
CS conditioned stimulus
CSF cerebrospinal fluid
CSM cerebrospinal meningitis
CSR corrected sedimentation rate
CST convulsive shock therapy
CTR cardiothoracic ratio
cu ft cubic foot
cu in cubic inch
cu m cubic meter
CV cardiovascular
CVA cardiovascular accident; costovertebral angle
CVD cardiovascular disease
cwt hundredweight
Cx cervix

Cyl cylinder; cylindrical lens

D

D, d dead; deciduous; density; dexter; died; diopter; distal; dorsal; dose; duration; give (*da*); let it be given (*detur*)
D de
d dextrorotatory
DA developmental age
D&C dilatation and curettage
dB decibel
dc, d-c direct current
dg decigram
DIP distal interphalangeal
DJD degenerative joint disease
dl deciliter
dm decimeter
DOA dead on arrival
DOE dyspnea on exertion
DQ developmental quotient
dr dram
DT delirium tremens
DTR deep tendon reflex
dx diagnosis

E

E einstein; electromotive force
e electron
EA educational age
ECG electrocardiogram
ECS electroconvulsive shock
ECT electroconvulsive therapy
ED effective dose; erythema dose
ED50 median effective dose
EDR effective direct radiation; electrodermal response
EEG electroencephalogram; electroencephalograph; electroencephalography
EHBF estimated hepatic blood flow
EKG electrocardiogram
EKY electrokymogram
EMC encephalomyocarditis
EMF electromotive force; erythrocyte maturation factor

EMG electromyogram
ENT ear, nose, and throat
EOM extraocular movement
ERBF effective renal blood flow
ERG electroretinogram
ERPF effective renal plasma flow
ERV expiratory reserve volume
EQ educational quotient
ESP extrasensory perception
ESR erythrocyte sedimentation rate
EST electroshock therapy
eV electron volt

F

F Fahrenheit; fellow; fluorine; formula
FB foreign body
fb finger-breadth
FBS fasting blood sugar
FD focal distance
FFA free fatty acids
FFT flicker fusion threshold
FH family history
fl fluid
fl dr fluid dram
fl oz fluid ounce
fp foot-pound
FRC functional residual capacity
FRF follicle-stimulating hormone releasing factor
FSF fibrin stabilizing factor
FSH follicle-stimulating hormone
ft foot
FUO fever of undetermined origin
fx fracture

G

G gonidial (colony)
g gram
G, g gauge; gravitational constant
G, Ĝ, g, ĝ ventricular gradient
gal gallon
GBS gallbladder series
GI gastrointestinal
gl gland; glands (*glandula; glandulae*)

GOT glutamic-oxaloacetic trans-aminase
GP general paresis; general practitioner
GPT glutamic-py-ruvic transaminase
GTH gonadotropic hormone
GU genitourinary
GYN gynecology

H

H henry; horizontal; hour
H+ hydrogen ion
h height; hundred; Planck constant
HAA hepatitis-associated antigen
hb hemoglobin
HCG human chori-onic gonadotropin
HCT hematocrit
HEENT head, eye, ear, nose, and throat
HF Hageman factor (factor XII)
hg hyperglycemic factor (hectogram)
hgb hemoglobin
HGF hyperglycemic factor (hyper-glycemic-glyco-genolytic factor)
hl hectoliter
hm hectometer
HOP high-pressure oxygen
Hp haptoglobin
hpf high-power field
HSV herpes simplex virus
HVD hypertensive vascular disease
Hz hertz

I

IB inclusion body
IC inspiratory capacity
ICT insulin coma therapy
ICU intensive care unit
I&D incision and drainage
ID intradermal
Ig immunoglobulin
IH infectious hepa-titis
IHSS idiopathic hy-pertrophic subaortic stenosis
IM intramuscular
in inch
IOP intraocular pressure
IP interphalangeal

IPPB intermittent positive pressure breathing
IQ intelligence quo-tient
IS intercostal space
IST insulin shock therapy
IU immunizing unit; international unit
IUD intrauterine contraceptive de-vice
IV, iv intravenous
IVCD intraventricu-lar conduction delay
IVP intravenous pyelogram

J

J joule
JNA Jena Nomina Anatomica

K

kc kilocycle
kcal kilocalorie
kCi kilocurie
kcps kilocycle per second
keV kiloelectron volt
kg kilogram
Kg-cal kilogram-calorie
kHz kilohertz
km kilometer
kMc kilomegacycle
kMcps kilomegacy-cles per second
KUB kidney, ureter, and bladder
kV kilovolt
kW kilowatt
kW-hr kilowatt hour

L

L Latin
l left; lethal
L&A light and ac-commodation
lab laboratory
LATS long-acting thyroid stimulator
LD lethal dose
LE lupus erythemato-sus
LLL left lower lobe
LLQ left lower quadrant
LMP last menstrual period
LNMP last normal menstrual period
LP lumbar puncture
lpf low-power field
LPN licensed prac-tical nurse

LS lumbosacral
LUL left upper lobe
LUQ left upper quadrant
LVH left ventricular hypertrophy
lymphs lymphocytes

M

M Micrococcus; muscle
m meter
MA mental age
mA milliampere
MBC maximum breathing capacity
Mc megacycle
mcg microgram
MCH mean corpus-cular hemoglobin
mch millicurie hour
MCHC mean cor-puscular hemoglobin concentration
MCi megacurie
mCi millicurie
MCV mean corpus-cular volume
MD Doctor of Medi-cine (*Medicinae Doctor*)
MED minimal effec-tive dose; minimum erythema dose
mEq milliequivalent
mg milligram
mHg millimeters of mercury
MHz megahertz
ml milliliter
MLD minimum lethal dose
MM mucous mem-branes
mm millimeter
mono monocyte
MP metacarpopha-langeal (wrist); metatarsophalan-geal (ankle)
mp melting point
MRD minimum re-acting dose
mrd millirutherford
MS mitral stenosis; multiple sclerosis
msec millisecond
MSL midsternal line
myelo myelocyte

N

N normal
NA Nomina Ana-tomica
NAD no appreciable disease
nc nanocurie
NG nasogastric
ng nanogram
nl nanoliter
nm nanometer

NPO nothing by mouth
NSR normal sinus rhythm
NTP normal temperature and pressure

O

O occiput; oculus (eye); oxygen
O₂cap oxygen capacity
O₂sat oxygen saturation
OB obstetrics
OD right eye (*oculus dexter*)
OFC occipitofrontal circumference
OPD outpatient department
OR operating room
OS left eye (*oculus sinister*)

P

P position; premolar; pulse; pupil
P radiant flux
P₂ pulmonic second heart sound
PA posteroanterior projection
P&A percussion and auscultation
PBI protein-bound iodine
PCG phonocardiogram
pCi picocurie
PD doctor of pharmacy; interpupillary distance
pd prism diopter; pupillary distance
PE physical examination
PEG pneumoencephalogram; pneumoencephalography
pg picogram
PH past history; Pharmacopeia
pH hydrogen ion concentration
ph phenyl
PI present illness; protamine insulin
PIP proximal interphalangeal
PKU phenylketonuria
PMB polymorphonuclear basophil leukocytes
PME polymorphonuclear eosinophil leukocytes
PMI point of maximal impulse

PMN polymorphonuclear neutrophil leukocytes
PP near point (*punctum proximum*)
PPD purified protein derivative
ppg picopicogram
Pr presbyopia; prism
psi pounds per square inch
PT physical therapy
PTT partial thromboplastin time
PVC premature ventricular contraction
PZI protamine zinc insulin

Q

Q electric quantity
qt quart

R

R electrical resistance; regression coefficient; respiration; right
r roentgen
RBC, rbc red blood cell; red blood count
rd rutherford
Rh Rhesus blood factor
RHD relative hepatic dullness
RLL right lower lobe
RM respiratory movement
RN registered nurse
R/O rule out
RPF renal plasma flow
rpm revolutions per minute
RQ respiratory quotient
RUL right upper lobe
RV residual volume
RVH right ventricular hypertrophy

S

S spherical; spherical lens
s left (*sinister*); half (*semis*)
SA sinoatrial
sat saturated
sc subcutaneously
SCAT sheep cell agglutination test
SD skin dose; standard deviation

SE standard error
SED skin erythema dose
sed rate erythrocyte sedimentation rate
SFW slow-filling wave
SGOT serum glutamic oxaloacetic transaminase
SGPT serum glutamic pyruvic transaminase
SH serum hepatitis; social history
SI soluble insulin
SIADH syndrome of inappropriate antidiuretic hormone
sp gr specific gravity
SQ subcutaneous
SR review of systems; sedimentation rate
Staph Staphylococcus
STD skin test dose
STREP Streptococcus
STS serologic test for syphilis
sym symmetrical

T

T temperature; thoracic
t temporal
tab tablet
T&A tonsillectomy and adenoidectomy
TAT Thematic Apperception Test; toxin-antitoxin
TB tuberculosis
tbsp tablespoon
TGA thyroglobin antibodies
TLC tender loving care; total lung capacity
TPR temperature, pulse, and respiration
tr tincture
TS test solution
TSH thyroid-stimulating hormone
tsp teaspoon
TU toxic unit
tus a cough (*tussis*)

U

U unit
UGI upper gastrointestinal
UP uteropelvic
USP United States Pharmacopeia
URI upper respiratory infection
UV uterovesical

V

V vision; visual acuity; volt
VC vital capacity
VCG vectorcardiogram
VD venereal disease
VDH valvular disease of the heart
VDRL Venereal Disease Research Laboratories

VF vocal fremitus
vf field of vision
VPB ventricular premature beat
VR vocal resonance

W

W watt
WBC, wbc white blood cell; white blood count
WD well developed

WN well nourished
wt weight

X Y Z

X Kienböck unit of x-ray dosage

yd yard

Z contraction (*Zuckung*)
z atomic number

MEDICAL SIGNS AND SYMBOLS

$\bar{a}\bar{a}$, $\bar{a}$a	of each	‴	line (1/12 inch), trivalent
A, Å	angstrom unit	μ	micron
C′	complement	$\mu\mu$	micromicron
E₀	electroaffinity	mμ	millimicron, micromillimeter
F₁	first filial generation	σ	¹⁄₁₀₀₀ of a second
F₂	second filial generation	π	3.1416—ratio of circumference of a circle to its diameter
L₊	limes death		
L₀	limes zero	®	registered trademark status
Q₀₂	oxygen consumption	mg %	milligrams per cent
m-	meta-	vol. %	volume per cent
o-	ortho-	μg	microgram
p-	para-	gr.	grain
℞	(*L. recipe*). Take	□, ♂	male
S.	(*L. signa*). Write	○, ♀	female
c̄, c	(*L. cum*). With	*	birth
s̄s̄, ss	(*L. semis*). One half	†	death
m̶, M̶	(*L. misce*). Mix	∞	infinity
O.	(*L. octarius*). Pint	:	ratio
C.	(*L. congius*). Gallon	: :	equality between ratios
C	Centigrade (Celsius)	—	negative, levorotatory
F	Fahrenheit	+	positive, dextrorotatory
°	degree	±	either positive or negative, not definite, racemic
♏, ♍	minim		
℈	scruple	÷	divided by
℈ i	one scruple	×	multiplied by
℈ ss′	half a scruple	=	equal to
ʒ	dram (apothecaries')	>	greater than
ʒi	one dram	<	less than
fʒ	fluid dram	√	root, square root
℥	ounce (troy)	∛	square root
℥i	one ounce	∜	cube root
℥ss	half an ounce	⇌	denotes a reversible reaction
℥iss	an ounce and a half	#	number
℥ij	two ounces	∧	value considered as a vector in electrocardiography
f℥	fluid ounce		
′	foot, minute, univalent	w/v	weight in volume
″	inch, second, bivalent		

COMMON LATIN AND GREEK TERMS
USED IN PRESCRIPTION WRITING

Latin or Greek word or phrase	Abbreviation	English meaning
ad	ad	to, up to
ad libitum	ad lib.	freely
alternis horis	alternis horis	every other hour
ana	āā, āa	of each
ante	ante	before
ante cibum	a.c.	before meals
aqua	aq.	water
aqua destillata	aq. dest.	distilled water
bis	bis	twice
bis in die	b.i.d.	twice a day
capsula	caps.	capsule
charta	chart.	paper
collyrium	collyr.	eyewash
cum	c̄, c	with
dentur tales doses	d.t.d.	give of such doses
divide	divid.	divide (thou)
elixir	elix.	elixir
enema	enem.	enema
et	et	and
fac, fiat, fiant	ft.	make
fiant chartulae vi	ft. chart. vi	let 6 powders be made
fiat pulvis	ft. pulv.	make a powder
fluidextractum	fldxt.	fluid extract
gutta, guttae	gtt.	drop, drops
hora	h., H.	an hour
hora somni	H.S., hor. som.	just before sleep
in die	in d.	in a day
infusum	inf.	an infusion
injectio	inj.	an injection
inter	inter	between
linimentum	lin.	liniment
liquor	liquor, liq.	a solution
lotio	lot.	lotion
minimum	m., min.	a minim
misce	M.	mix (thou)
mistura	mist.	mixture
nocte, noctis	noct., noctis	at night
non	non	not
non repetatur	non rep.	do not repeat
numero, numerus	no.	number
oculo dextro	O.D.	in the right eye
oculo laevus	O.L.	in the left eye
omni hora	omn. hor.	every hour
omni nocte	omn. noct.	every night
pilula(e)	pil.	pill(s)
post cibum, cibos	p.c.	after meals
pro re nata	p.r.n.	as occasion arises
pulvis, pulveres, pulveratus	pulv.	powder, powders, powdered
quantum sufficiat	q.s.	a sufficient quantity

Latin or Greek word or phrase	Abbreviation	English meaning
quaque hora	qq. hor., q.h.	every hour
quaque secunda hora	qq. 2 hor., q. 2h	every two hours
quater in die	q.i.d.	four times a day
secundum artem	s.a., S.A.	according to art
semi, semis	sem., ss, s̄s̄	a half
signa	sig., s.	write, label
sine	sine	without
solutio	sol.	a solution
spiritus	sp.	spirit
suppositorium	suppos.	a suppository
syrupus	syr.	syrup
tabella	tabel.	a lozenge
talis, tales	talis, tales	such, like this
ter die	t.d.	three times a day
ter in die	t.i.d.	three times a day
tinctura	tinct., tr.	a tincture
unguentum	ung.	an ointment
ut dictum	ut dict.	as directed

TABLE OF THE ELEMENTS

Name	Symbol	Atomic weight*	Atomic number	Name	Symbol	Atomic weight*	Atomic number
Actinium	Ac	(227)	89	Erbium	Er	167.26	68
Aluminum	Al	26.9815	13	Europium	Eu	151.96	63
Americium	Am	(243)	95	Fermium	Fm	(257)	100
Antimony	Sb	121.75	51	Fluorine	F	18.9984	9
Argon	Ar	39.948	18	Francium	Fr	(223)	87
Arsenic	As	74.9216	33	Gadolinium	Gd	157.25	64
Astatine	At	(210)	85	Gallium	Ga	69.72	31
Barium	Ba	137.34	56	Germanium	Ge	72.59	32
Berkelium	Bk	(247)	97	Gold	Au	196.967	79
Beryllium	Be	9.0122	4	Hafnium	Hf	178.49	72
Bismuth	Bi	208.980	83	Helium	He	4.0026	2
Boron	B	10.811	5	Holmium	Ho	164.930	67
Bromine	Br	79.909	35	Hydrogen	H	1.00797	1
Cadmium	Cd	112.40	48	Indium	In	114.82	49
Calcium	Ca	40.08	20	Iodine	I	126.9044	53
Californium	Cf	(251)	98	Iridium	Ir	192.2	77
Carbon	C	12.01115	6	Iron	Fe	55.847	26
Cerium	Ce	140.12	58	Krypton	Kr	83.80	36
Cesium	Cs	132.905	55	Lanthanum	La	138.91	57
Chlorine	Cl	35.453	17	Lawrencium	Lr	(256)	103
Chromium	Cr	51.996	24	Lead	Pb	207.19	82
Cobalt	Co	58.9332	27	Lithium	Li	6.939	3
Copper	Cu	63.546	29	Lutetium	Lu	174.97	71
Curium	Cm	(247)	96	Magnesium	Mg	24.312	12
Dysprosium	Dy	162.50	66	Manganese	Mn	54.9380	25
Einsteinium	Es	(254)	99	Mendelevium	Md	(258)	101
Element 104			104	Mercury	Hg	200.59	80

* A number in parentheses indicates the mass number of the most stable isotope.

TABLE OF THE ELEMENTS (cont.)

Name	Symbol	Atomic weight*	Atomic number	Name	Symbol	Atomic weight*	Atomic number
Molybdenum	Mo	95.94	42	Samarium	Sm	150.35	62
Neodymium	Nd	144.24	60	Scandium	Sc	44.956	21
Neon	Ne	20.183	10	Selenium	Se	78.96	34
Neptunium	Np	(237)	93	Silicon	Si	28.086	14
Nickel	Ni	58.71	28	Silver	Ag	107.870	47
Niobium	Nb	92.906	41	Sodium	Na	22.9898	11
Nitrogen	N	14.0067	7	Strontium	Sr	87.62	38
Nobelium	No	(255)	102	Sulfur	S	32.064	16
Osmium	Os	190.2	76	Tantalum	Ta	180.948	73
Oxygen	O	15.9994	8	Technetium	Tc	(97)	43
Palladium	Pd	106.4	46	Tellurium	Te	127.60	52
Phosphorus	P	30.9738	15	Terbium	Tb	158.924	65
Platinum	Pt	195.09	78	Thallium	Tl	204.37	81
Plutonium	Pu	(244)	94	Thorium	Th	(232)	90
Polonium	Po	(209)	84	Thulium	Tm	168.934	69
Potassium	K	39.102	19	Tin	Sn	118.69	50
Praseodymium	Pr	140.907	59	Titanium	Ti	47.90	22
Promethium	Pm	(145)	61	Tungsten	W	183.85	74
Protactinium	Pa	(231)	91	Uranium	U	(238)	92
Radium	Ra	(226)	88	Vanadium	V	50.942	23
Radon	Rn	(222)	86	Xenon	Xe	131.30	54
Rhenium	Re	186.2	75	Ytterbium	Yb	173.04	70
Rhodium	Rh	102.905	45	Yttrium	Y	88.905	39
Rubidium	Rb	85.47	37	Zinc	Zn	65.37	30
Ruthenium	Ru	101.07	44	Zirconium	Zr	91.22	40

* A number in parentheses indicates the mass number of the most stable isotope.

TABLES OF WEIGHTS AND MEASURES

Metric Weights

		Grams*		Grains		Av. ounces
Milligram	=	0.001	=	0.01543		
Centigram	=	0.01	=	0.15432		
Decigram	=	0.1	=	1.54324		
Gram	=	1	=	15.43236	=	.03527
Decagram	=	10	=		=	.3527
Hectogram	=	100	=		=	3.52739
Kilogram	=	1000	=		=	35.2739

* 1 gram = 1 cubic centimeter of distilled water at 4°C

Metric Linear Measure

		Meter		U.S. Inches		Feet		Yards		Miles
Millimeter	=	.001	=	.03937	=	.00328				
Centimeter	=	.01	=	.3937	=	.03280				
Decimeter	=	.1	=	3.937	=	.32808	=	.10936		
Meter	=	1	=	39.37	=	3.2808	=	1.0936		
Decameter	=	10	=		=	32.808	=	10.936		
Hectometer	=	100	=		=	328.08	=	109.36	=	.062137
Kilometer	=	1000	=		=	3280.8	=	1093.6	=	.62137

TABLES OF WEIGHTS AND MEASURES

Troy Weights

Pound *		Ounces		Pennyweights		Grains
1	=	12	=	240	=	5760
		1	=	20	=	480
				1	=	24

* 1 pound = 22.816 cubic inches of distilled water at 62°F

Apothecaries' Weights

Pound *		Ounces		Drams		Scruples		Grains
1	=	12	=	96	=	288	=	5760
		1	=	8	=	24	=	480
				1	=	3	=	60
						1	=	20

* 1 pound = 1 pound troy

Avoirdupois Weights

Pound *		Ounces		Drams		Grains
1	=	16	=	256	=	7000
		1	=	16	=	437.5
				1	=	27.34375

* 1 pound = 1.2153 pounds troy

U.S. Apothecaries' Measures

Gallon		Quarts		Pints		Fluid ounces		Fluid drams		Minims
1	=	4	=	8	=	128	=	1024	=	61,440
		1	=	2	=	32	=	256	=	15,360
				1	=	16	=	128	=	7680
						1	=	8	=	480
								1	=	60

Imperial Apothecaries' Measures

Gallon		Quarts		Pints		Fluid ounces		Fluid drams		Minims
1	=	4	=	8	=	160	=	1280	=	76,800
		1	=	2	=	40	=	320	=	19,200
				1	=	20	=	160	=	9600
						1	=	8	=	480
								1	=	60

The minim, fluid dram, and fluid ounce of the U.S. apothecaries' measures are slightly larger than the corresponding denominations of the Imperial (British) measures; the pint, quart, and gallon, on the other hand, are smaller.

	U.S.		Imp.	Imp.		U.S.
Minim, fluid dram, fluid ounce	1	=	1.0406	1	=	0.9609
Pint, quart, gallon	1	=	0.8325	1	=	1.2011

CONVERSION TABLES

Metric Equivalents of Apothecaries' Weights

Grains	Grams	Grains	Grams	Grains	Grams	Grains	Grams
1/50	0.00130	18	1.166	50	3.240	82	5.314
1/32	0.00202	19	1.231	51	3.305	83	5.378
1/20	0.00324	20	1.296	52	3.370	84	5.443
1/18	0.00360	21	1.361	53	3.434	85	5.508
1/16	0.00405	22	1.426	54	3.499	86	5.573
1/15	0.00432	23	1.490	55	3.564	87	5.638
1/12	0.00540	24	1.555	56	3.629	88	5.702
1/10	0.00648	25	1.620	57	3.694	89	5.767
1/8	0.00810	26	1.685	58	3.758	90	5.832
1/6	0.01080	27	1.749	59	3.823	91	5.897
1/5	0.01296	28	1.814	60	3.888	92	5.962
1/4	0.01620	29	1.879	61	3.953	93	6.026
1/3	0.02160	30	1.944	62	4.018	94	6.091
1/2	0.03240	31	2.009	63	4.082	95	6.156
3/4	0.04860	32	2.074	64	4.147	96	6.221
1	0.0648	33	2.138	65	4.212	97	6.286
2	0.1296	34	2.203	66	4.277	98	6.350
3	0.1944	35	2.268	67	4.342	99	6.415
4	0.2592	36	2.333	68	4.406	100	6.480
5	0.3240	37	2.398	69	4.471	120	7.776
6	0.3888	38	2.462	70	4.536	180	11.664
7	0.4536	39	2.527	71	4.601	200	12.960
8	0.5184	40	2.592	72	4.666	240	15.552
9	0.5832	41	2.657	73	4.730	300	19.440
10	0.6480	42	2.722	74	4.795	360	23.328
11	0.7128	43	2.786	75	4.860	400	25.920
12	0.7776	44	2.851	76	4.925	500	32.399
13	0.8424	45	2.916	77	4.990	600	38.879
14	0.9072	46	2.981	78	5.054	700	45.359
15	0.9720	47	3.046	79	5.119	800	51.839
16	1.037	48	3.110	80	5.184	900	58.319
17	1.102	49	3.175	81	5.249	1000	64.799

Equivalents of Metric in Apothecaries' Weights

Grams	Grains	Grams	Grains	Grams	Grains	Grams	Grains
0.01	0.1543	0.7	10.803	13	200.621	27	416.674
0.02	0.3086	0.8	12.346	14	216.054	28	432.106
0.03	0.4630	0.9	13.889	15	231.486	29	447.538
0.04	0.6173	1	15.432	16	246.918	30	462.971
0.05	0.7716	2	30.865	17	262.350	35	540.133
0.06	0.9259	3	46.297	18	277.782	40	617.294
0.07	1.0803	4	61.730	19	293.215	45	694.456
0.08	1.2346	5	77.162	20	308.647	50	771.618
0.09	1.3889	6	92.594	21	324.080	55	848.780
0.1	1.543	7	108.027	22	339.512	60	925.941
0.2	3.086	8	123.459	23	354.944	70	1080.265
0.3	4.630	9	138.892	24	370.377	80	1234.589
0.4	6.173	10	154.324	25	385.809	90	1388.912
0.5	7.716	11	169.756	26	401.241	100	1543.236
0.6	9.259	12	185.189				

CONVERSION TABLES

Equivalents of Metric in U.S. Apothecaries' Measures

Cubic centimeters	Minims	Cubic centimeters	Fluid drams
0.01	0.16	5	1.35
0.02	0.32	6	1.62
0.03	0.49	7	1.89
0.04	0.65	8	2.17
0.05	0.81	9	2.43
0.06	0.97	10	2.71
0.07	1.14	25	6.76
0.08	1.30		**Fluid ounces**
0.09	1.46		
0.1	1.62	30	1.01
0.2	3.25	50	1.69
0.3	4.87	75	2.54
0.4	6.49	100	3.38
0.5	8.12	200	6.76
0.6	9.74	300	10.15
0.7	11.36	400	13.53
0.8	12.99	500	16.91
0.9	14.61	600	20.29
1	16.23	700	23.67
2	32.47	800	27.05
3	48.70	900	30.43
4	64.94	1000	33.82

Metric Equivalents of U.S. Apothecaries' Measures

Minims	Cubic centimeters	Fluid ounces	Cubic centimeters
1	0.06	1	29.57
2	0.12	2	59.15
3	0.19	3	88.72
4	0.25	4	118.29
5	0.31	5	147.87
6	0.37	6	177.44
7	0.43	7	207.01
8	0.49	8	236.58
9	0.55	9	266.16
10	0.62	10	295.73
11	0.68	11	325.30
12	0.74	12	354.88
13	0.80	13	384.45
14	0.86	14	414.02
15	0.92	15	443.59
16	0.99	16	473.17
17	1.05	17	502.74
18	1.11	18	532.31
19	1.17	19	561.89
20	1.23	20	591.46
25	1.54	21	621.03
30	1.85	22	650.60
35	2.16	23	680.18
40	2.46	24	709.75
45	2.77	25	739.32
50	3.08	26	768.90
55	3.39	27	798.47
		28	828.04

Fluid drams	Cubic centimeters	Fluid ounces	Cubic centimeters
		29	857.61
		30	887.19
		31	916.76
1	3.70	32	946.33
2	7.39	48	1419.49
3	11.09	56	1656.08
4	14.79	64	1892.66
5	18.48	72	2129.25
6	22.18	80	2365.83
7	25.88	96	2839.00
		112	3312.16
		128	3785.32

Metric Equivalents of Avoirdupois Weights

Av. Ounces	Grams	Av. Pounds	Grams
1/16	1.772	1	453.59
1/8	3.544	2	907.18
1/4	7.088	2.2	1000
1/2	14.175	3	1360.78
1	28.350	4	1814.37
2	56.699	5	2267.96
3	85.049	6	2721.55
4	113.398	7	3175.15
5	141.748	8	3628.74
6	170.097	9	4082.33
7	198.447	10	4535.92
8	226.796		
9	255.146		
10	283.495		
11	311.845		
12	340.194		
13	368.544		
14	396.893		
15	425.243		

TEMPERATURE CONVERSION TABLE

This table permits one to convert from Celsius degrees to Fahrenheit degrees or from Fahrenheit degrees to Celsius degrees. The conversion is accomplished by first locating in a column printed in boldface type the number that is to be converted. If the number to be converted is in Fahrenheit degrees, one may find its equivalent in Celsius degrees by reading to the left. If the number to be converted is in Celsius degrees, one may find its equivalent in Fahrenheit degrees by reading to the right. Celsius degrees are identical to Centigrade degrees.

The approved international symbolic abbreviation for Celsius degrees is °C, whereas for Fahrenheit degrees it is °F. The relation between Fahrenheit degrees and Celsius degrees may be expressed by

$$°C = 5/9 \ °F - 32$$
or
$$°F = 9/5°C + 32$$

| | To convert | | | To convert | | | To convert | |
To °C	←°F or °C→	To °F	To °C	←°F or °C→	To °F	To °C	←°F or °C→	To °F
−28.89	−20	−4	−12.22	10	50	4.44	40	104
−28.33	−19	−2.2	−11.67	11	51.8	5	41	105.8
−27.78	−18	−0.4	−11.11	12	53.6	5.56	42	107.6
−27.22	−17	1.4	−10.56	13	55.4	6.11	43	109.4
−26.67	−16	3.2	−10	14	57.2	6.67	44	111.2
−26.11	−15	5	−9.44	15	59	7.22	45	113
−25.56	−14	6.8	−8.89	16	60.8	7.78	46	114.8
−25	−13	8.6	−8.33	17	62.6	8.33	47	116.6
−24.44	−12	10.4	−7.78	18	64.4	8.89	48	118.4
−23.89	−11	12.2	−7.22	19	66.2	9.44	49	120.2
−23.33	−10	14	−6.67	20	68	10	50	122
−22.78	−9	15.8	−6.11	21	69.8	10.56	51	123.8
−22.22	−8	17.6	−5.56	22	71.6	11.11	52	125.6
−21.67	−7	19.4	−5	23	73.4	11.67	53	127.4
−21.11	−6	21.2	−4.44	24	75.2	12.22	54	129.2
−20.56	−5	23	−3.89	25	77	12.78	55	131
−20	−4	24.8	−3.33	26	78.8	13.33	56	132.8
−19.44	−3	26.6	−2.78	27	80.6	13.89	57	134.6
−18.89	−2	28.4	−2.22	28	82.4	14.44	58	136.4
−18.33	−1	30.2	−1.67	29	84.2	15	59	138.2
−17.78	0	32	−1.11	30	86	15.56	60	140
−17.22	1	33.8	−0.56	31	87.8	16.11	61	141.8
−16.67	2	35.6	0	32	89.6	16.67	62	143.6
−16.11	3	37.4	.56	33	91.4	17.22	63	145.4
−15.56	4	39.2	1.11	34	93.2	17.78	64	147.2
−15	5	41	1.67	35	95	18.33	65	149
−14.44	6	42.8	2.22	36	96.8	18.89	66	150.8
−13.89	7	44.6	2.78	37	98.6	19.44	67	152.6
−13.33	8	46.4	3.33	38	100.4	20	68	154.4
−12.78	9	48.2	3.89	39	102.2	20.56	69	156.2

To °C	To convert ←°F or °C→	To °F	To °C	To convert ←°F or °C→	To °F	To °C	To convert ←°F or °C→	To °F
21.11	70	158	48.89	120	248	76.67	170	338
21.67	71	159.8	49.44	121	249.8	77.22	171	339.8
22.22	72	161.6	50	122	251.6	77.78	172	341.6
22.78	73	163.4	50.56	123	253.4	78.33	173	343.4
23.33	74	165.2	51.11	124	255.2	78.89	174	345.2
23.89	75	167	51.67	125	257	79.44	175	347
24.44	76	168.8	52.22	126	258.8	80	176	348.8
25	77	170.6	52.78	127	260.6	80.56	177	350.6
25.56	78	172.4	53.33	128	262.4	81.11	178	352.4
26.11	79	174.2	53.89	129	264.2	81.67	179	354.2
26.67	80	176	54.44	130	266	82.22	180	356
27.22	81	177.8	55	131	267.8	82.78	181	357.8
27.78	82	179.6	55.56	132	269.6	83.33	182	359.6
28.33	83	181.4	56.11	133	271.4	83.89	183	361.4
28.89	84	183.2	56.67	134	273.2	84.44	184	363.2
29.44	85	185	57.22	135	275	85	185	365
30	86	186.8	57.78	136	276.8	85.56	186	366.8
30.56	87	188.6	58.33	137	278.6	86.11	187	368.6
31.11	88	190.4	58.89	138	280.4	86.67	188	370.4
31.67	89	192.2	59.44	139	282.2	87.22	189	372.2
32.22	90	194	60	140	284	87.78	190	374
32.78	91	195.8	60.56	141	285.8	88.33	191	375.8
33.33	92	197.6	61.11	142	287.6	88.89	192	377.6
33.89	93	199.4	61.67	143	289.4	89.44	193	379.4
34.44	94	201.2	62.22	144	291.2	90	194	381.2
35	95	203	62.78	145	293	90.56	195	383
35.56	96	204.8	63.33	146	294.8	91.11	196	384.8
36.11	97	206.6	63.89	147	296.6	91.67	197	386.6
36.67	98	208.4	64.44	148	298.4	92.22	198	388.4
37.22	99	210.2	65	149	300.2	92.78	199	390.2
37.78	100	212	65.56	150	302	93.33	200	392
38.33	101	213.8	66.11	151	303.8	93.89	201	393.8
38.89	102	215.6	66.67	152	305.6	94.44	202	395.6
39.44	103	217.4	67.22	153	307.4	95	203	397.4
40	104	219.2	67.78	154	309.2	95.56	204	399.2
40.56	105	221	68.33	155	311	96.11	205	401
41.11	106	222.8	68.89	156	312.8	96.67	206	402.8
41.67	107	224.6	69.44	157	314.6	97.22	207	404.6
42.22	108	226.4	70	158	316.4	97.78	208	406.4
42.78	109	228.2	70.56	159	318.2	98.33	209	408.2
43.33	110	230	71.11	160	320	98.89	210	410
43.89	111	231.8	71.67	161	321.8	99.44	211	411.8
44.44	112	233.6	72.22	162	323.6	100	212	413.6
45	113	235.4	72.78	163	325.4	100.56	213	415.4
45.56	114	237.2	73.33	164	327.2	101.11	214	417.2
46.11	115	239	73.89	165	329	101.67	215	419
46.67	116	240.8	74.44	166	330.8	102.22	216	420.8
47.22	117	242.6	75	167	332.6	102.78	217	422.6
47.78	118	244.4	75.56	168	334.4	103.33	218	424.4
48.33	119	246.2	76.11	169	336.2	103.89	219	426.2

	To convert			To convert			To convert	
To °C	←°F or °C→	To °F	To °C	←°F or °C→	To °F	To °C	←°F or °C→	To °F
104.44	220	428	131.11	268	514.4	157.22	315	599
105	221	429.8	131.67	269	516.2	157.78	316	600.8
105.56	222	431.6	132.22	270	518	158.33	317	602.6
106.11	223	433.4	132.78	271	519.8	158.89	318	604.4
106.67	224	435.2	133.33	272	521.6	159.44	319	606.2
107.22	225	437	133.89	273	523.4	160	320	608
107.78	226	438.8	134.44	274	525.2	160.56	321	609.8
108.33	227	440.6	135	275	527	161.11	322	611.6
108.89	228	442.4	135.56	276	528.8	161.67	323	613.4
109.44	229	444.2	136.11	277	530.6	162.22	324	615.2
110	230	446	136.67	278	532.4	162.78	325	617
110.56	231	447.8	137.22	279	534.2	163.33	326	618.8
111.11	232	449.6	137.78	280	536	163.89	327	620.6
111.67	233	451.4	138.33	281	537.8	164.44	328	622.4
112.22	234	453.2	138.89	282	539.6	165	329	624.2
112.78	235	455	139.44	283	541.4	165.56	330	626
113.33	236	456.8	140	284	543.2	166.11	331	627.8
113.89	237	458.6	140.56	285	545	166.67	332	629.6
114.44	238	460.4	141.11	286	546.8	167.22	333	631.4
115	239	462.2	141.67	287	548.6	167.78	334	633.2
115.56	240	464	142.22	288	550.4	168.33	335	635
116.11	241	465.8	142.78	289	552.2	168.89	336	636.8
116.67	242	467.6	143.33	290	554	169.44	337	638.6
117.22	243	469.4	143.89	291	555.8	170	338	640.4
117.78	244	471.2	144.44	292	557.6	170.56	339	642.2
118.33	245	473	145	293	559.4	171.11	340	644
118.89	246	474.8	145.56	294	561.2	171.67	341	645.8
119.44	247	476.6	146.11	295	563	172.22	342	647.6
120	248	478.4	146.67	296	564.8	172.78	343	649.4
120.56	249	480.2	147.22	297	566.6	173.33	344	651.2
121.11	250	482	147.78	298	568.4	173.89	345	653
121.67	251	483.8	148.33	299	570.2	174.44	346	654.8
122.22	252	485.6	148.89	300	572	175	347	656.6
122.78	253	487.4	149.44	301	573.8	175.56	348	658.4
123.33	254	489.2	150	302	575.6	176.11	349	660.2
123.89	255	491	150.56	303	577.4	176.67	350	662
124.44	256	492.8	151.11	304	579.2	177.22	351	663.8
125	257	494.6	151.67	305	581	177.78	352	665.6
125.56	258	496.4	152.22	306	582.8	178.33	353	667.4
126.11	259	498.2	152.78	307	584.6	178.89	354	669.2
126.67	260	500	153.33	308	586.4	179.44	355	671
127.22	261	501.8	153.89	309	588.2	180	356	672.8
127.78	262	503.6	154.44	310	590	180.56	357	674.6
128.33	263	505.4	155	311	591.8	181.11	358	676.4
128.89	264	507.2	155.56	312	593.6	181.67	359	678.2
129.44	265	509	156.11	313	595.4	182.22	360	680
130	266	510.8	156.67	314	597.2			
130.56	267	512.6						